THE ARMY AND ECONOMIC
MOBILIZATION

THE HONORABLE ROBERT P. PATTERSON, *Assistant Secretary of War until 19 December 1940, when he became Under Secretary. (Photograph taken in 1944.)*

UNITED STATES ARMY IN WORLD WAR II

The War Department

THE ARMY AND ECONOMIC MOBILIZATION

by

R. Elberton Smith

MILITARY INSTRVCTION

CENTER OF MILITARY HISTORY
UNITED STATES ARMY
WASHINGTON, D.C., 1985

Library of Congress Catalog Card Number: 58–60001

First Printed 1959—CMH Pub 1-7

. . .   to Those Who Served

The U.S. Army Center of Military History

The Center of Military History prepares and publishes histories as required by the U.S. Army. It coordinates Army historical matters, including historical properties, and supervises the Army museum system. It also maintains liaison with public and private agencies and individuals to stimulate interest and study in the field of military history. The Center is located at 20 Massachusetts Avenue, N.W., Washington, D.C. 20314–0200.

Foreword

In World War II the War Department, whose primary and traditional mission was to mobilize, train, and equip military forces and direct them in combat, found itself drawn into the center of the gigantic effort to mobilize America's industries for war. It became one of the principal agencies of the Government in administering as well as planning the nation's economic mobilization. This book, by an economist, tells how the War Department operated in performing these tasks.

The experience had a lasting effect on the mission, organization, and outlook of both the Army and the Air Force. Their present functions and structure cannot be understood without reference to it. This volume is therefore of vital interest to every officer.

Furnishing, as Dr. Smith's approach to his subject does, a comprehensive view of the impact of war on the national economy, his book should prove invaluable to staff planners in all agencies of the Government, to industrial leaders, to the civilian scholar, and to the thoughtful citizen.

The Army and Economic Mobilization is a complement, in the area of domestic economy, to the two-volume work, *Global Logistics and Strategy,* in the area of international economy. It is the capstone to others in the U.S. ARMY IN WORLD WAR II that deal with the procurement and distribution of supplies in their organizational and operative aspects. The relations with labor into which the War Department was drawn are set forth in a forthcoming volume, *The Army and Industrial Manpower.* A separate volume, *Buying Air Power,* is being devoted to the special problems of procurement by and for the Army Air Forces.

Washington, D. C.   R. W. STEPHENS
10 October 1957   Maj. Gen. U. S. A.
                                                                      Chief of Military History

The Author

R. Elberton Smith is a graduate of the College of Wooster and received his M.A. and Ph.D. degrees in economics at the University of Chicago. He has taught economics at the University of Denver, Northwestern University, the University of Maryland, and Indiana University. At present, he is an economist for the International Cooperation Administration at the United States Operations Mission in Tokyo, Japan.

After a number of years in teaching and business, Mr. Smith entered government service early in World War II as an economist for the War Production Board in Washington, D.C. In September 1942 he was commissioned in the United States Naval Reserve and assigned for a year in the Office of Procurement and Material in the Navy Department. Subsequently he served for two years as industrial relations officer in the Navy Yard at Long Beach, California. In 1950 he joined the staff of the Office, Chief of Military History, U.S. Army.

In addition to writing the present volume, Mr. Smith is also author of the book *Customs Valuation in the United States—A Study in Tariff Administration,* as well as articles and reviews for professional journals.

Preface

The subject matter of the present volume derives its importance from a number of basic considerations. The achievements of the United States in the production of munitions and supplies for World War II provided this country, and to a large extent its allies, with a decisive superiority in military power. Moreover, in the process of establishing and attaining its war production objectives, the United States reshaped the structure of its economy and ushered in an era of supertechnology which marked the beginning of a new epoch in history.

Now, some twelve years after the war, military procurement programs still represent a substantial portion of the nation's economic activity. Also, to judge from contemporary news items, the complexities, problems, and misunderstandings associated with military procurement are no less confusing to the general public today than they were during the period of rearmament in the early 1940's. Although both the nature of the procurement process and the character of military end items have increased in complexity since World War II, most of the current issues and administrative problems have their origins or their counterparts in the last great war.

These and other considerations all reinforce the basic purpose of the present volume, which is to provide the reader with a fund of knowledge that will enable him to understand the complex tasks associated with Army procurement and economic mobilization in World War II. To achieve this purpose the author has attempted to select and describe as clearly as possible the major areas of the subject matter—beginning with prewar planning and the determination of military requirements, and running in logical sequence all the way to the settlement and liquidation of the World War II procurement effort. To the extent that the stated objective has been realized it is believed that the reader upon completion of the volume will feel at home in any discussion of basic problems of procurement and economic mobilization.

The term "history" includes potentially "everything that existed or happened" during a specified period of time in the past. Manifestly, nothing purporting to be a "complete" history of so large a subject as the one in hand will ever be written. The present study aims not at exhaustiveness but at maximum illumination of the subject matter. It attempts, therefore, to deal systematically with the broad substantive issues of procurement and economic mobilization faced by the War Department in World War II, and the basic policies and procedures developed to meet these issues. This approach, rather than the narration of numerous incidents or illustrations in the form of procurement "case histories," is believed to offer a maximum of significance and usefulness in a single volume devoted to the subject. Although the individual segments of each area are treated in broad chronological fashion, the larger areas as well as the volume as a whole are portrayed in topical, rather than chronological, sequence.

Until some time after World War II the Army consisted of ground forces, air forces, service forces, and their multitudinous headquarters and field establishments, all operating under one administration known as the "War Department." For simplicity, and in keeping with the parallel usage of the term "Navy," the word "Army" in the present volume is used synonymously with "War Department." In view of the predominant size and importance of the War Department as a procuring agency, and because of its special responsibilities for the planning of nationwide economic mobilization, the experience of the Army in these areas reflects to a large extent the experience of the nation as a whole.

In planning and executing his assignment the author has necessarily had in mind many different classes of reader. So far as possible he has attempted to assume the mantle of all his potential readers in the quest for what was most significant and relevant. Nevertheless, he is well aware that the painful pressures of time and space, as well as other limitations, have resulted in many important omissions and other shortcomings. To help redress these imbalances and to exploit more fully the government's great wealth of experience in all areas of procurement and economic mobilization in World War II, the reader is urged to consult other studies in this field—in particular, the numerous technical service volumes in the U.S. ARMY IN WORLD WAR II series.

The present volume has been made possible by the efforts, ideas, and specific suggestions of many individuals. For a period of a year the author enjoyed the research assistance of Dr. Marvin Bernstein, who unearthed and synthesized basic materials for a large part of the study in the areas of production and material controls, facilities, and renegotiation. Dr. Albert A. Blum and Miss Ann Kann-macher provided valuable research and general assistance to the author at successive stages of the project. Mr. Israel Wice, Chief of the General Reference Branch, OCMH, and numbers of his staff—especially Naomi Allen, Hannah Zeidlik, and Valerie Stubbs—were perennially helpful in supplying specific information. Mrs. Eva Gediman and her staff in the Legal Reference Unit of the Army Library contributed indispensable services in checking statutes, codes, and other legal references. Mrs. Hazel Ward and her associates in the Departmental Records Branch, AGO, Alexandria, furnished skillful guidance through the labyrinthine collection of records and files of the Army Service Forces and the Office of the Under Secretary of War.

During most of the author's assignment it was his good fortune to occupy a quiet and spacious office in the Industrial College of the Armed Forces at Ft.

McNair, Washington, D.C. This made possible continuous and unlimited access to the unique collection of materials in the college's Library, carefully accumulated and vigilantly preserved over the years by the indefatigable efforts of the librarian, Miss Clara Widger. For this collection, as well as for her initiative in supplying important specific materials for this study, both the author and the users of this volume are permanently indebted to Miss Widger. Other members of the library staff, especially Ruth Heisey and Myron Smith, were unfailingly helpful.

Colleagues both within and outside the Army's Office of Military History kept the author supplied with ideas and encouragement for the present volume. Special mention should be made of Drs. Richard Leighton (Chief), Robert Coakley, and Jonathan Grossman, the author's colleagues in the Logistics Section, OCMH; Drs. Benjamin Williams, Louis Hunter, and Marlin Reichley, and Mr. Clarence Niklason, of the Industrial College of the Armed Forces; Dr. Harry Thomson, Chief, Historical Section, Office of the Chief of Ordnance; Dr. Alfred Goldberg, Chief, Air University Historical Liaison Office; Professor I. B. Holley, Department of History, Duke University; and Mr. Stephen S. Fishe, formerly of the Bureau of Aeronautics, now with the Office of Naval Material, Department of the Navy.

All students of the United States' World War II experience in procurement and economic mobilization are deeply indebted to Dr. Harry B. Yoshpe, now historian of the Army Transportation Corps, for his accurate, cogent, and voluminous monographic writings in this field when it was pioneer territory. The author wishes to pay special tribute to Dr. Yoshpe for thus laying the foundation for much of the present volume, as well as for his specific helpfulness and criticism at various intervals in the course of this study.

Col. Joseph Bent, Jr., of the Industrial College of the Armed Forces, and Col. Ridgway Smith, of the Office of Military History, read the entire preliminary manuscript and made numerous suggestions. Others who read and made helpful comments on chapters or sections of varying length include David Novick, Gustav Seidler, Norman Parkin, William Coulson, Frank Fox, Reynold Bennett, Hans Klagsbrunn, Melvin Copeland, Mark Massel, James Oates, Jr., Cols. Elmer E. Barnes, George S. Foster, Vincent J. Esposito, George O'Connor, Seneca Foote, and Lt. Col. Simon Frank. To Joseph Logan and Theodore Whiting of the Army Comptroller's Office fell the thankless but highly important task of reviewing the manuscript for the accuracy of statistical and tabular data. Mrs. Norma Sherris located and selected the photographs.

The author's greatest debt is to the Army's Chief Historian, Dr. Kent Roberts Greenfield, who prepared a critique that brought together and evaluated a wide variety of ideas, suggestions, and criticisms. Dr. Greenfield's perennial good nature, understanding, and sympathy were a dependable source of encouragement to the author during his protracted efforts to complete the project.

In the final stages of the tortuous journey from idea to finished volume, Dr. Stetson Conn, the Army's Deputy Chief Historian, reviewed the entire revised manuscript and made numerous helpful suggestions. Mr. Joseph Friedman, Editor in Chief of the World War II series, lent his wise counsel and personal assistance to the author on many occasions. Mr. David Jaffé, senior editor assigned to the volume, guided the book through the editorial process and substantially improved its readability. Mrs. Virginia Bosse, eagle-eyed copy editor, rescued the author from many a typographical error and erroneous citation; and Mrs. Helen Whittington, coming to her task late in the game, gathered up the loose ends and put the volume to bed.

Two other specific acknowledgments are essential: first, to Mr. Glen A. Lloyd, the Army's pricing director in World War II, who took the time from a busy schedule to return to Washington for the volume's panel review; and second, to Mrs. Mary Eva Oldfather, who typed most of the original manuscript and supplied the author with first-hand knowledge of many developments in the Asistant Secretary of War's Office dating back to its establishment shortly after World War I.

Finally, the author wishes to thank the many others who provided assistance directly or indirectly but whose names have been omitted either through inadvertence or for lack of space.

Bloomington, Indiana   R. ELBERTON SMITH
7 December 1957

Contents

PART ONE

Introduction

PART TWO

Prewar Plans and Wartime Organization

PART THREE

Determination of Army Requirements

PART FOUR
Army Purchasing Problems and Policies

PART SIX

Production and Material Controls

PART SEVEN
Contract Termination and Settlement

PART EIGHT
Epilogue

Tables

Charts

Illustrations

All illustrations are from U.S. Department of Defense files with the exception of the one appearing on pages 638–39, which is from the National Archives.

Charts

Illustrations

PART ONE

INTRODUCTION

CHAPTER I

The Task and the Achievement

The outstanding characteristics of World War II were its magnitude and its highly technological nature. The victory of the United Nations in that war was attributable basically to their ability to wage technological warfare on a scale far surpassing that of the Axis Powers, and indeed that of any other military coalition in all history. This capacity for technological warfare on a global scale required an abundance of superior weapons in the hands of highly trained troops. But behind the lines of battle it required the capacity to develop, manufacture, and deliver a torrent of equipment and supplies sufficient to overwhelm the enemy. It was predominantly the United States that demonstrated this capacity and furnished the economic and industrial power which proved to be the decisive factor in the winning of the war.

The United States was fortunate in having a superior combination of total resources—materials, manpower, productive equipment, widely diffused skills, and technical know-how—long before the outbreak of World War II. Contrary to popular feeling, however, superiority in economic resources carried no automatic guarantee of victory in war. As the United States learned to its peril, there was a wide and dangerous gulf between "economic potential" and the capacity to deliver specific munitions in the quality, quantity, and time needed to win a major war. When America belatedly undertook rearmament after the British armies were swept into the sea at Dunkerque and France surrendered to Adolf Hitler at Compiègne, there was grave doubt that the U.S. industrial effort could bear sufficient fruit in the limited time available to forestall a German invasion of the Western Hemisphere. And in the dark weeks and months after Pearl Harbor, despite a year and a half of intensive preparation in the United States, the outcome of the battle of production was still far from clear.

The task of harnessing a nation's economic potential for war has come to be known as "economic mobilization." Its basic purpose is to insure the procurement of finished munitions—the sum total of equipment, supplies, and services required by the armed forces—while at the same time supplying the essential needs of the civilian economy. The demands of modern technological warfare, when suddenly thrust upon a nation lacking the specific equipment for war, are so novel, so complex, and of such magnitude that their fulfillment requires a nationwide industrial and social revolution. Such a revolution does not automatically "occur" when a nation goes to war. It must be planned, directed, and carried out in a manner which will accomplish its objectives with a minimum of hardship and dislocation. A faulty program of economic mobilization might easily bog down in a welter of confusion and disorder,

TABLE 1—BUDGET EXPENDITURES OF U.S. GOVERNMENT, 1 JULY 1940–31 AUGUST 1945

[Billions of Dollars]

Agency and Category	Total	Calendar Year					
		1940 a	1941	1942	1943	1944	1945 a
U.S. Government—Total	$336. 7	$5. 3	$20. 2	$57. 8	$90. 2	$97. 2	$66. 0
Non-Defense Activities	32. 3	3. 4	6. 0	5. 4	5. 0	6. 3	6. 2
National Defense and Related Activities—Total	304. 4	1. 9	14. 2	52. 4	85. 2	90. 9	59. 8
War Department	167. 4	0. 9	7. 3	29. 5	46. 5	49. 2	34. 0
Navy Department	92. 7	0. 9	4. 2	14. 0	24. 6	29. 6	19. 4
Other Federal Agencies	44. 3	0. 1	2. 7	8. 9	14. 1	12. 1	6. 4

a Figures for 1940 include only period 1 July through 31 December; for 1945 only 1 January through 31 August.

Source: U.S. Treasury Department, Treasury Bulletin, Feb 52, Tables 6 and 6B, pp. 5, 9.

fail to accomplish its wartime mission, or make impossible the reconversion and restoration of the economy at the end of the war.

The experience of the United States in developing and utilizing its industrial capacity for World War II may well go down in history as the classic example of economic mobilization. Despite all the confusion, error, and uncertainty that characterized the two-and-a-half-year period from mid-1940 through 1942, the broad pattern of economic mobilization for the war as a whole represented an orderly and systematic process, which ran the full cycle of planning, build-up, full-scale war production, and demobilization. This pattern was possible because of a happy conjuncture of idle resources and the gift of a lengthy period of "borrowed time" furnished by the insular position of the United States and the heroic resistance of its subsequent allies. Moreover, the global character of World War II, with its far-flung navies, immense land armies, and massive airpower—for the most part all built from scratch—gave rise to total military requirements which for sheer bulk and quantity of matériel were without parallel in the history of warfare. Military requirements for World War II constituted a heavy drain upon economic resources all across the board, creating some of the most stubborn and characteristic administrative problems of the war.

The starting point in understanding the nature and complexity of economic mobilization for World War II is a knowledge of the magnitude of the war program and the kinds and quantities of munitions required to fight the war.[1] Actual dollar expenditures of the U.S. Government during the war period totaled some $337 billion, of which $304 billion was devoted to national defense (Table 1). These amounts, as reported by the Treasury Department, include prewar expenditures of $16 billion during the eighteen months of the defense period, but

---

[1] From the standpoint of economic mobilization in the United States, World War II is generally viewed as beginning in mid-1940 and ending on 31 August 1945.

omit substantial postwar expenditures associated with the final liquidation of the war effort.[2]

The broad pattern of U.S. production for World War II, and its progress throughout the defense and war years, is revealed by War Production Board estimates for the war program as a whole (*Tables 2 and 3*). The WPB statistics portray the gradual beginning of rearmament in the last half of 1940; the rising tempo of defense production in 1941; the greatest absolute increase for the whole war period in 1942; the reaching of peak production—virtually determining the outcome of the war—by the end of 1943; and the sustained high level of production throughout 1944 until August 1945 when the collapse of enemy resistance signaled the end of the World War II production effort.

The role of the War Department (the Army and its Air Forces) as the largest of the war agencies is clearly indicated by the expenditure of $167 billion out of the $304 billion total for the entire period. (*See Table 1.*) Whether measured in terms of actual expenditures or by the WPB estimates of physical production, the War Department share represents approximately 55 to 58 percent of the total for all agencies.[3]

It should be observed at the outset that no statistical tables—however carefully devised—can hope to provide an accurate measure of the total "cost" of World War II, even if such cost is limited by definition to money expenditures. Broad problems of classification and allocation of expenditures, both within and between the "war" and "non-war" categories [4]—to say nothing of continuing postwar disbursements for veterans' benefits and interest on the public debt—make impossible any precise measure of the "true" money cost of the war. At a more fundamental level of analysis, the impact of the war upon the national real income, and the permanent influence of the war upon the structure and future growth of the national economy, render any accurate dollar or other statistical measure of the costs of the war a will-of-the-wisp. Finally, the ultimate "real" or human costs of the war are largely a matter for individual reflection and conjecture.

A broad panoramic view of the Army's procurement objectives and achievements in World War II is represented by the quantities of major specific items of equipment and supplies delivered to War Department

---

[2] Statistics of Federal expenditures, especially for particular categories, do not always provide a reliable measure of either the rate or the quantity of war production. In World War II billions of dollars in payments of many varieties—loans, progress payments, partial payments, advance payments, and others—were made to contractors in advance of delivery, production, or even incurrence of costs, in order to supply the needs of manufacturers for both fixed and working capital; thousands of procurement contracts were terminated in mid-stream, and settlement charges bore no specific relationship to current output; prices for identical items under different contracts were often divergent at a given time and were constantly changing over periods of time; contract renegotiation reclaimed contractor's earnings on an over-all basis, thus distorting the significance of budget expenditures for procurement as a whole, and of unit prices for individual items. Nevertheless, the pattern of total war expenditures of the Federal Government from 1940 to 1945 is remarkably similar to estimated physical production.

[3] (1) 55 percent, if measured by the 167.4–to–304.4 ratio of Table 1; (2) 57 percent, when measured by 179.9–to–315.8 "total war program" ratio in Table 2; (3) 58 percent, by the 107.9–to–184.5 "munitions" ratio of Table 2.

[4] Thus, the Army in World War II referred to all its procurement deliveries, including subsistence, as "munitions"; the War Production Board classified subsistence as "non-munitions."

TABLE 2—U.S. WAR PROGRAM FOR WORLD WAR II: BY PROCURING AGENCY, 1 JULY 1940–31 AUGUST 1945

[Estimated Magnitude in Billions of Dollars [a]]

Agency	Total	Calendar Year					
		1940 [b]	1941	1942	1943	1944	1945 [b]
War Program—Total	$315.8	$3.6	$17.8	$57.4	$86.2	$93.4	$57.4
War Department	$179.9	$1.7	$9.7	$33.6	$49.0	$52.5	$33.4
Navy Department	83.9	0.8	4.0	12.7	22.0	27.0	17.4
Maritime Comm. and War Shipping Adm	21.2	0.1	0.6	3.1	6.5	7.2	3.7
Overseas Purchases and Treasury Procured "Lend Lease"	30.8	1.0	3.5	8.0	8.7	6.7	2.9
Munitions—Total	$184.5	$2.1	$8.6	$30.5	$52.4	$57.7	$33.2
War Department	$107.9	$0.9	$4.8	$18.7	$30.9	$33.1	$19.5
Navy Department	54.8	0.5	2.3	7.9	15.5	18.1	10.5
Maritime Comm. and War Shipping Adm	15.8	0.1	0.5	2.5	5.1	5.3	2.3
Overseas Purchases and Treasury Procured "Lend Lease"	6.0	0.6	1.0	1.4	0.9	1.2	0.9
War Construction, Government Financed—Total	$31.4	$0.8	$4.9	$12.7	$8.5	$2.9	$1.6
War Department	$13.4	$0.4	$2.7	$6.5	$2.5	$0.7	$0.6
Navy Department	6.3	0.1	0.8	2.4	1.7	0.8	0.5
Maritime Comm. and War Shipping Adm	0.5	([c])	0.1	0.3	0.1	([c])	([c])
Overseas Purchases and Treasury Procured "Lend Lease"	11.2	0.3	1.3	3.5	4.2	1.4	0.5
Non-Munitions—Total	$99.9	$0.7	$4.3	$14.2	$25.3	$32.8	$22.6
War Department	$58.6	$0.4	$2.2	$8.4	$15.6	$18.7	$13.3
Navy Department	22.8	0.2	0.9	2.4	4.8	8.1	6.4
Maritime Comm. and War Shipping Adm	4.9	0.0	0.0	0.3	1.3	1.9	1.4
Overseas Purchases and Treasury Procured "Lend Lease"	13.6	0.1	1.2	3.1	3.6	4.1	1.5

[a] Figures contained herein were compiled by the War Production Board to show the pattern and progress of the war program for World War II. In general, figures for major categories represent the following:

Munitions: Physical quantities of production for each year multiplied by standard unit-cost weights of mid-1945. The figures, therefore, do not represent expenditures, or the value of output at current prices.

War Construction: Estimated cost of federally financed construction and equipment put in place during indicated periods.

Non-Munitions: Estimated expenditures for services, food, and other items.

War Program Total: Numerical sum of three major categories; shown as an index of general trends and to facilitate statistical calculation and comparison.

[b] Figures for 1940 include only period 1 July through 31 December; for 1945 only 1 January through 31 August.

[c] Less than .05 billions.

Source: Civilian Production Administration (WPB), The Production Statement, 1 May 47. Figures in "Total" column computed and all figures rounded by OCMH.

TABLE 3—U.S. WAR PROGRAM FOR WORLD WAR II: BY MAJOR CATEGORIES, 1 JULY 1940–
31 AUGUST 1945

[Estimated Magnitude in Billions of Dollars[a]]

Category	Total	Calendar Year					
		1940 [b]	1941	1942	1943	1944	1945 [b]
Total War Program	$315.8	$3.6	$17.8	$57.4	$86.2	$93.4	$57.4
Munitions—Total	$184.5	$2.1	8.6	30.5	52.4	57.7	33.2
Aircraft	44.8	0.4	1.8	5.8	12.5	16.0	8.3
Ships	41.2	0.4	1.9	7.0	12.5	13.4	6.0
Guns and Fire Control Equipment	9.9	0.1	0.4	1.8	3.2	2.9	1.5
Ammunition	18.1	0.1	0.4	2.7	4.9	5.8	4.2
Combat and Motor Vehicles	20.3	0.2	1.3	4.8	5.9	5.0	3.1
Communication and Electronic Equipment	10.7	(c)	0.2	1.5	3.1	3.7	2.2
Other Equipment and Supplies	39.5	0.9	2.6	6.9	10.3	10.9	7.9
War Construction, Government Financed—Total	31.4	0.8	4.9	12.7	8.5	2.9	1.6
Industrial Buildings	8.2	0.1	1.3	3.5	2.0	0.7	0.6
Industrial Machinery and Equipment	7.9	0.1	0.8	2.9	2.7	1.0	0.4
Non-Industrial Military Construction	10.7	0.3	1.8	5.1	2.4	0.7	0.4
Housing and Community Facilities	2.5	0.1	0.5	0.7	0.8	0.3	0.1
Other Construction	2.1	0.2	0.5	0.5	0.6	0.2	0.1
Non-Munitions—Total	99.9	0.7	4.3	14.2	25.3	32.8	22.6
Military Pay, Subsistence and Travel	60.5	0.4	1.9	6.3	14.7	21.1	16.1
Civilian Pay, Federal War Agencies	10.6	0.1	0.4	1.5	2.8	3.5	2.3
Purchases of Agric. Products for Export	5.8	0.0	0.3	1.2	1.8	1.7	0.8
Overseas Purchases and Construction	3.3	0.1	0.3	1.4	1.1	0.3	0.1
Transp. and Other Contractual Services	12.1	0.1	0.6	2.2	2.9	3.9	2.4
Other	7.6	(c)	0.8	1.6	2.0	2.3	0.9

[a] Figures contained herein were compiled by the War Production Board to show the pattern and progress of the war program for World War II. In general, figures for major categories represent the following:

Munitions: Physical quantities of production for each year multiplied by standard unit-cost weights of mid-1945. The figures, therefore, do not represent expenditures, or the value of output at current prices.

War Construction: Estimated cost of federally financed construction and equipment put in place during indicated periods.

Non-Munitions: Estimated expenditures for services, food, and other items.

War Program Total: Numerical sum of three major categories; shown as an index of general trends and to facilitate statistical calculation and comparison.

[b] Figures for 1940 include only period 1 July through 31 December; for 1945 only 1 January through 31 August.

[c] Less than .05 billions.

Source: Civilian Production Administration (WPB), The Production Statement, 1 May 47. Figures in "Total" column computed and all figures rounded by OCMH.

procuring agencies throughout the war (*Tables 4 through 11*).[5] A complete listing would contain thousands of additional items, although these in general would be smaller and less important. A careful scrutiny of the listed items and quantities suggests many things to the imagination: the highly mechanized, technological, yet diversified nature of Army activities and operations in World War II; the extensive planning, research, and development which necessarily had to precede, as well as accompany, the war production effort; the complex engineering and production problems which had to be solved by American industry before the completed items could become available to the Army; and the tremendous logistical problems involved in transporting, distributing, and servicing the vast quantities of equipment and supplies in all parts of the world. Because of the nature and diversity of military procurement all important sectors of the economy were involved, and military requirements absorbed a major share of the productive capacity of most industries. In both their quantitative and qualitative implications, the statistics of military procurement reveal the great lengths to which the Army went to increase the fighting power and effectiveness of its troops and to enhance the health, comfort, and chances of survival of the individual soldier.

The essence of economic mobilization for World War II was the development of a complex array of governmental agencies, activities, and controls for launching and managing the nation's war production program. Most of these governmental operations were made necessary by two fundamental difficulties of war production—both arising out of the nature of military requirements: (1.) the great technical and engineering difficulty of mass-producing novel, complex military items designed to meet the most exacting specifications; (2) the general shortage of resources—reflecting the great magnitude of military requirements—which complicated and frustrated production in almost all sectors of the economy. Both types of difficulty were aggravated by, and indeed owed much of their existence to, the compelling necessity for meeting the goals of war production in the shortest possible period of time. The time element greatly intensified the shocks and dislocations of all-out conversion to war production and magnified the task of devising and applying control measures at all stages of the war effort.

An appreciation of the physical characteristics and complexity of military items is prerequisite to an adequate understanding of the difficulties of war production. Consider, for a moment, a few of the technical problems in producing ammunition which had to be met before the Army could meet its requirements for World War II. First of all it was necessary to devise a type of propellant powder, for each of dozens of types of projectile, which would be powerful enough to hurl the projectile long distances with great penetrating force. The powder had to be uniform, with almost completely unvarying performance characteristics permitting close-to-perfect ballistic accuracy. It had to be chemically stable so that it would not deteriorate, even when stored for long periods in damp climates or

---

[5] Because of differences in the availability of data Tables 4–11 contain differences in the length of the period covered. For detailed explanation, as well as for dollar value summaries of War Department procurement, see UNITED STATES ARMY IN WORLD WAR II, Statistics, Procurement, 9 April 1952 draft, prepared by Richard H. Crawford and Lindsley F. Cook under the direction of Theodore E. Whiting.

TABLE 4—ORDNANCE DEPARTMENT: PROCUREMENT DELIVERIES OF SELECTED MAJOR ITEMS, 1 JULY 1940–31 DECEMBER 1945[a]

Item	Quantity	Item	Quantity
Tank-Automotive Items		*Tank-Automotive Items*—Continued	
Tanks—Total	[b] 88,410	Heavy–Heavy Trucks—Total	[b] 153,686
Light (7 types)	28,919	3½-Ton, 4x2 (2 types)	2,000
Medium (9 types)	57,027	4-Ton, 6x6 (4 types)	29,194
Heavy (5 types)	2,464	4-ton- 4x4 (2 types)	7,317
		4-5-Ton, 4x4 tractor	21,974
Motor Carriages for Self-propelled Weapons—Total	[b] 46,706	5-Ton, 4x2 (7 types)	20,567
Antiaircraft guns (10 types)	19,784	5–6-Ton, 4x4 (3 types)	8,179
Antitank guns (7 types)	17,944	5–6-Ton, 4x2 (3 types)	3,600
Medium field artillery (6 types)	6,969	6-Ton, 6x6 (5 types)	21,084
Heavy field artillery (5 types)	727	7½-Ton, 6x6, prime mover	2,067
Mortar carriers (3 types)	1,282	10-Ton, 6x6, heavy wrecker (2 types)	5,765
		10-Ton, 6x4 (3 types)	18,088
Other Combat Vehicles—Total	[b] 113,967	12-Ton, 6x4, tractor, M20, for trailer tank	5,871
Armored cars, wheeled (6 types)	16,438	20-Ton, 6x4, tractor	2,143
Cargo carriers—full-track (3 types)	15,889	Tractors, medium, for 50-passenger semi-trailer bus	1,492
Carriers, half-track (8 types)	39,328	Other (28 types)	4,345
Scout cars, wheeled	21,963		
Tank recovery vehicles (2 types)	241	Semi-Trailers—Total	[b] 59,731
Universal carriers—full-track	19,611	Bus, 50-passenger	1,231
Special purpose tank, on M4 series chassis	497	2½–4-Ton (4 types)	4,350
		5-Ton, 2-wheel, stake and platform	8,107
Light Trucks—Total	[b] 988,167	6-Ton, 2-wheel (13 types)	13,085
¼-Ton, 4x4, command (jeep)	634,569	7-Ton, 2-wheel, cargo	7,752
¼-Ton, 4x4, amphibian	12,774	10-Ton, 2-wheel (3 types)	18,989
½-Ton, 4x4 (12 types)	82,454	11–20-Ton (5 types)	1,965
½-Ton, 4x2 (8 types)	9,415	22½-Ton, 4-wheel, low bed	2,201
¾-Ton, 4x4 (6 types)	248,634	40–45-Ton (3 types)	1,408
Other (8 types)	321	Other (11 types)	643
Medium Trucks—Total	[b] 428,196	Trailers—Total	[b] 499,494
1½-Ton, 6x6, cargo	43,224	¼-Ton, 2-wheel, cargo	143,371
1½-Ton, 4x4 (12 types)	167,373	¾-Ton, 2-wheel (3 types)	4,931
1½-Ton, 4x2 (23 types)	217,012	Truck, bomb lift, M1	20,310
Ambulances (3 types)	587	1-Ton, 2-wheel, cargo	259,064
		1-Ton, 2-wheel, tank (250-gallon, water)	19,946
Light–Heavy Trucks—Total	[b] 812,262	Armored, M8	5,270
1½–3-Ton, 4x4 (2 types)	2,719	Bomb, M5	16,212
1½–3-Ton, 4x2 (2 types)	3,420	M20, for carriage, multiple caliber .50, M1, M55	6,471
2½-Ton, 6x6 (11 types)	676,433	Truck, bomb lift, M22	4,037
2½-Ton, 6x4 (2 types)	117,759	4 to 5–6-Ton (5 types)	3,771
2½-Ton, 4x4 (3 types)	1,279		
2½-Ton, 4x2 (14 types)	10,602		
Buses, 32- and 37-passenger, 4x2 integral	50		

See footnotes at end of table.

TABLE 4—Continued

Item	Quantity	Item	Quantity
Tank-Automotive Items—Continued		*Weapons and Equipment*—Continued	
6-Ton, full track	2,088	Gun, 155mm, M2 (M1 & M1A1) on carriage M1	1,882
8–12-Ton (3 types)	2,067	Howitzer, 155mm, M1 on carriage M1, M1A1 & M1A2	4,035
20–22-Ton (3 types)	1,164	Gun, 4.5-inch, M1 on carriage M1, M1A1 & M1A2	426
45-Ton, 12-wheel, M9	6,143		
Other (23 types)	4,649		
		Light Field and Antitank Weapons: Total for Types Listed	d 54,532
Tractors, Except Truck-tractors— Total	b 34,295	Howitzer, 105mm:	
Light, M2 series, D2 and D4 types	1,456	M2A1 (M2) on carriage M1, M1A1, M2, M2A1 & M2A2	8,536
Medium, M1 (winterized) D6 & diesel 45-hp types	4,941	M3 on carriage M3, M3A1, M3A2 & M3A3	2,580
Heavy, M1	2,915	Gun, 3-inch, antitank, M5 on carriage M1, M1A1 & M6	2,500
High speed, 7-ton, M2	8,519	Rifle, 75mm, M20 (T21, T21E4 & T25)	1,238
High speed, 13-ton, M5 series	5,880	Howitzer, 75mm, M1 & M1A1 on carriage, pack, M1 & M8	4,939
High speed, 18-ton, M4 series	5,811	Gun, 75mm, antitank, M1, M1A1 & Mark III on carriage M1, M1A1, M1A2, M1A3 & M2	16,037
High speed, 38-ton, M6	1,235	Gun, 37mm, antitank, M3A1 (M3) on carriage M4A1 (M4)	18,702
Cranes	2,667		
Other (3 types)	871		
		Tank Guns and Howitzers—Total for Types Listed	d 116,097
Other Vehicles—Total	b 224,272	Howitzer, 105mm, M4	5,135
Bicycles (3 types)	72,105	Gun, 90mm, M3	2,329
Motor scooters (2 types)	5,835	Gun, 76mm, M1, M1A1 & M1A2	12,445
Motorcycles (7 types)	101,385	Gun, 75mm, M2, M3 & M6 (M5 & T13E1)	46,651
Cars, passenger (5 types)	c 41,722	Howitzer, 75mm, M3 for landing vehicle, tracked	2,302
Other (4 types)	3,225	Gun, 37mm, M5 & M6	47,235
Vehicular Machine Gun Mounts— Total	b 332,579		
Truck mount, ring, supports complete	149,883	Guns and Howitzers for Self-propelled Weapons—Total for Types Listed	d 27,080
Pedestal truck mounts	98,655	Howitzer, 8-inch, M1 & M2 for motor carriage T89	48
Dash mount, M48, for .30 caliber	49,392	Gun, 155mm, M1 & M2 for motor carriage M40	394
Ring mount, M49 series	14,645		
Twin mount, for .50 caliber	2,160		
Multiple mount, for .50 caliber	17,844		
Weapons and Equipment			
Heavy Field Artillery Weapons— Total for Types Listed	d 7,803		
Howitzer, 240mm, M1 on carriage M1	315		
Gun, 8-inch, M1 on carriage M2	139		
Howitzer, 8-inch, M2 (M1) on carriage M1	1,006		

See footnotes at end of table.

TABLE 4—Continued

Item	Quantity	Item	Quantity
Weapons and Equipment—Continued		*Weapons and Equipment*—Continued	
Howitzer, 155mm, M1 for motor carriage M41 (T64E1)_____	143	Mortar:	
Howitzer, 105mm, for motor carriage M7, M36 & T19_____	5,195	155mm, T25, on mount T16E2_____	244
Gun, 90mm, M3 for motor carriage M36 (T71)_____	2,324	81mm, M1 & T27 on mount M1, M4 & T21_____	31,104
Gun, 3-inch, for motor carriage M10_____	6,824	60mm, M2 on mount, M2 & M5 and mortar T18E6_____	73,706
Gun, 76mm, for motor carriage T70_____	2,507	Small Arms	
Gun, 75mm, for half-track chassis_____	2,041	Machine Guns—Total_____	2,679,819
Howitzer, 75mm, for motor carriage T30_	392	Aircraft_____	1,634,756
Howitzer, 75mm, for motor carriage M8_	2,077	Antiaircraft_____	79,698
Gun, 57mm, antitank_____	962	Ground_____	965,365
Gun, 37mm, antitank, M6_____	4,173	Rifles—Total_____	6,552,290
		Garand, .30 cal_____	4,014,731
Aircraft Guns—Total for Types Listed_____	d 156,587	Springfield, .30 cal_____	1,318,951
Gun, 75mm, M4, M5, AN–M5 & AN–M5A1 on mounts M6&M9_____	2,098	Lee Enfield, .303 cal_____	1,030,228
Gun, 37mm, automatic, AN–M9, M10 (AN–M4 & M4E3)_____	19,826	Browning, automatic, .30 cal_____	188,380
Gun, 20mm, automatic, M1, M3 (Hispano-Suiza) & AN–M2_____	134,663	Carbines, .30 cal_____	6,117,827
		Submachine guns, .45 cal_____	2,008,267
Antiaircraft Guns—Total for Types Listed_____	d 49,775	Automatic pistol, .45 cal_____	1,877,069
Gun, 120mm, M1 on mount M1_____	550	Revolver, .38 cal_____	889,203
Gun, 90mm, M1, M1A1 & M2 on mount, M1, M1A1, M2, M3 and T2E1_____	7,831	Shotgun, 12-gauge, riot and sporting_____	429,074
Gun, 40mm, automatic:		Miscellaneous Weapons and Equipment_____	(d)
M1 on carriage M1, M1A1, M2 & M2A1_____	23,897	Armor, Flyer's Protective:	
M1 on mount, M3 (antisubmarine) & M5 (airborne)_____	10,219	Vests, M1, T46, and M2_____	434,700
Gun, 37mm:		Aprons, M3, T55, M4, and T56_____	351,958
Self-propelled, M1A2 & T28E1_____	3,180	Groin, M5 and T57_____	109,901
Automatic, M1A2 on carriage M3 & M3A1_____	4,098	Bayonet, M1905 and M1_____	4,490,000
		Bayonet scabbard, M7, for bayonet, M1__	2,113,000
Rocket Launchers and Mortars_____	(d)	Bayonet knife, M4, with scabbard, knife, M8A1 (includes trench knife, M3, with scabbard, M8)_____	4,851,000
Rocket Launcher:		Belt links, metallic (thousands):	
4.5-inch, aircraft, 3-tube, M10, M14 & M15 (T57)_____	158,500	.50 cal., aircraft, M2_____	9,414,000
2.36-inch, antitank, M1, M1A1, M9 & M9A1 (bazooka)_____	476,628	.30 cal., aircraft, M1_____	3,512,000
		.60 cal., aircraft_____	11,000
		Compass, M2_____	44,415
		Helmet, M1, body assembly_____	22,756,000
		Helmets, flyer's:	
		M3_____	213,543
		M4A2 (M4)_____	86,136
		M5_____	93,495

See footnotes at end of table.

TABLE 4—Continued

Item	Quantity	Item	Quantity
Weapons and Equipment—Continued		*Ammunition*—Continued	
Pyrotechnic:		155mm gun, M1, M1A1, M2 & M1917–18:	
Aircraft pistol (air-to-ground signal)___	342, 611	Shell, HE, M101, MK3 & MK3A1____	6, 234
Pistol, M2_____	45, 043	155mm howitzer, M1: Shell, HE, M107__	14, 072
Discharger, M5_____	24, 065	155mm howitzer, M1917–18: Shell, HE,	
Hand projector, M9_____	287, 422	M102, MK1 & MK1A1_____	4, 080
Watches:		4.5-inch gun: Shell, HE, M65_____	1, 969
Pocket, 15 or more jewels_____	46, 578		
Stop, Type A and Type B_____	52, 001	Ammunition for Light Field, Tank,	
Wrist, 7 or more jewels_____	974, 311	and Antitank Weapons (Thousand	
		Rounds)	([d])
Anti-aircraft Fire Control Equip-		105mm howitzer, M2, M2A1 & M4: Shell,	
ment (non-component items only)		HE, M1 & AT, M67_____	76, 505
Directors, M5 and M5A1, for 57mm and		105mm howitzer, M3: Shell, HE, M1 &	
40mm guns_____	30, 950	AT, M67_____	7, 408
Cable systems, M8_____	30, 652	90mm gun: Shell, HE, M71 for anti-	
Generating units, M5, for 37mm and		motor torpedo boat, antitank and	
40mm guns_____	41, 534	T15E2 guns_____	5, 410
Observation instrument, battery com-		3-inch gun: Shell, HE, M42A1 (M42) &	
mander, M1_____	3, 498	Mark III (Navy)_____	7, 639
Height finder, optical, M1A2 (M1, M2)__	2, 067	3-inch gun: Shot, HV, AP–T, M93 &	
		projectile, APC–T, M62A1 (M62)	
Miscellaneous Fire Control Equip-		and AP, M79_____	5, 718
ment (noncomponent items only)		76mm gun: Shell, HE, M42A1 (M42)____	6, 952
Aiming circle, M1_____	26, 330	76mm gun: Shot, AP–T, M93 (T4E17)	
Binoculars:		& projectile APC–T, M62A1 (M62)	
6x30, degree reticle, M5 (M6 and M12)_	90, 580	& AP, M79_____	5, 641
6x30, mil reticle, M13A1 (M13, M3,		75mm gun: Shell, HE, M48_____	25, 968
M8, and M9)_____	466, 208	75mm gun: Projectile, APC, M16A1	
7x50, mil reticle, M16 and M17_____	149, 294	(M61) & AP, M72_____	18, 097
7x50, (M7) (M2) M14, M15, and		75mm howitzer: Shell, HE, M41A1 &	
MK21 with rubber eyeguards and		M48 and AT, M66_____	23, 567
polaroid, without reticle_____	74, 983	57mm gun: Cartridge, APC–T, M86 &	
Board, plotting, M10_____	13, 673	AP–T, M70_____	10, 626
Gunner's quadrant, M1_____	106, 658	37mm gun: Shell, HE, M63 & M63	
Telescope, M65 (M1915A1 and 1917		(T32)_____	17, 222
series)_____	6, 390	37mm gun: Shot, APC, M51B1 (M51) &	
Telescope, observation, M4, M48, and		AP, M74_____	53, 976
M49_____	23, 660	37mm gun: Canister, M2 & M2 (T32)___	6, 895
Telescope, rifle sight, M73B1_____	36, 204		
Telescope, rifle sight, M82_____	12, 694	Ammunition for Aircraft Guns	
		(Thousand Rounds)	([d])
Ammunition		20mm gun (Hispano-Suiza):	
Ammunition for Heavy Field Artil-		Cartridge, HE–I, M97 (T23) and MK1_	139, 533
lery Weapons (Thousand Rounds)	([d])	Cartridge, AP–T, M95 (T9E5) and	
8-inch howitzer, M1 & M2: Shell, HE,		M75_____	112, 238
M106 & M1A1_____	2, 531	Cartridge, ball_____	122, 122

See footnotes at end of table.

TABLE 4—Continued

Item	Quantity	Item	Quantity
Ammunition—Continued		*Ammunition*—Continued	
		Aircraft Bombs (Thousands)	
Ammunition for Rocket Launchers and Mortars (Thousand Rounds)	(ᵈ)	General purpose and demolition:	
2.36-in. launcher: Rocket, HE, AT, M6, M6A1, 2, 3 & 4	12,996	500-pound: M43, AN–M43, AN–M64 & AN–M64A1	7,309
81mm mortar: Shell, HE, light, M43A1 & heavy, M56	32,245	250-pound: AN–M57, AN–M57A1 & Mk IV	2,455
60mm mortar: Shell, HE, M49, M49A1 & M49A2	49,274	100-pound: M30, AN–M30 & AN–M30A1	4,053
		Fragmentation:	
Ammunition for Small Arms (Thousand Rounds)	(ᵈ)	100-pound, cluster: AN–M1, AN–M1A1&2, and M2	4,607
.50-caliber cartridge: all types	10,042,259	23-pound: M72 & M72A1, with parachute	4,356
.45-caliber cartridge: all types	4,072,000		
.303-caliber cartridge, ball	1,068,000		
.30-caliber cartridge: all types	25,065,834		

ᵃ Data represent the numbers of listed items accepted by the procuring agency during the period indicated.   Includes items subsequently distributed to other U.S. agencies and through lend-lease procedures to foreign governments.   See source for additional information as to technical content.

ᵇ Includes stocks at depots and with troops 1 July 1939 plus deliveries from 1 July 1939 through 31 December 1945.

ᶜ Includes 23,689 vehicles from frozen commercial stocks.

ᵈ Deliveries from July 1940 through August 1945.

Source: U.S. Army in World War II, Statistics, Procurement, 9 April 1952 draft, prepared by Richard H. Crawford and Lindsley F. Cook under the direction of Theodore E. Whiting.

TABLE 5—QUARTERMASTER CORPS: PROCUREMENT DELIVERIES OF SELECTED MAJOR ITEMS, 1 JULY 1940–31 AUGUST 1945 [a]

Item	Quantity	Item	Quantity
Clothing		*Clothing*—Continued	
Footwear (Thousand Pairs)—Total for Types Listed	128, 315	Jacket, field:	
		M1943	17, 445
Boots, service, combat & boots, jumper, parachutist	28, 104	Olive drab	23, 667
Overshoes, arctic, M1945	10, 193	Wool, olive drab	10, 160
Shoes, Russian (War Aid)	14, 679	Jacket, herringbone twill	80, 527
Shoes, service, all types, men	75, 339	Overcoat, wool, olive drab, roll collar	16, 178
		Headgear (Thousands)—Total for Types Listed	139, 123
Socks (Thousand Pairs)—Total for Types Listed	519, 122	Cap:	
Cotton, tan	140, 163	Field, cotton, olive drab, with visor	10, 196
Wool, cushion sole	90, 075	Garrison, cotton, khaki, for enlisted men	27, 475
Wook, ski and arctic	19, 583	Garrison, wool, olive drab	28, 248
Wool, heavy and light	269, 301	Herringbone twill	28, 325
		Wool, knit, M1941 and cap, winter	18, 229
Drawers (Thousand Pairs)—Total for Types Listed	259, 784	Hood, jacket, field, M1943	10, 220
Cotton, shorts	186, 499	Hood, wool, olive drab, special	16, 430
Cotton, special	18, 517		
Wool and arctic	54, 768	Rainwear (Thousands)—Total for Types Listed	38, 328
		Poncho, light & medium weight, olive drab	5, 503
Undershirts (Thousands)—Total for Types Listed	212, 531	Poncho, synthetic resin-coated	3, 764
Cotton, summer, sleeveless	155, 043	Raincoat, for enlisted men, all types	29, 061
Wool	57, 488		
		Gloves (Thousand Pairs)—Total for Types Listed	90, 811
Shirts (Thousands)—Total for Types Listed	139, 069	Cotton, special	25, 527
Cotton, khaki	72, 869	Leather, heavy	23, 476
Flannel, olive drab, coat style, special	64, 310	Wool, olive drab, plain & with leather palm	41, 808
Knit, olive drab	1, 890		
		Miscellaneous Men's Wear (Thousands)	
Trousers (Thousand Pairs)—Total for Types Listed	229, 373	Belt, waist, web, M1937	36, 585
Cotton, khaki	71, 125	Handkerchief, cotton	209, 685
Field, cotton, olive drab	10, 170	Leggings, canvas, dismounted, M1938, pairs	56, 986
Herringbone twill	89, 787	Necktie, cotton, mohair, olive drab, khaki, black	64, 743
Wool, olive drab	58, 291	Suit, working, 1-piece, herringbone twill	27, 535
Coats & Jackets (Thousands)—Total for Types Listed	165, 531	Sweater, high neck	14, 818
Coat, wool, serge, olive drab	17, 554		

See footnotes at end of table.

TABLE 5—Continued

Item	Quantity	Item	Quantity
Clothing—Continued		*Equipage*—Continued	
Women's Wear (Thousands)		Knife, M1926	35, 298
Cap, summer, for WAC	438	Necklace, identification tag, with extension	27, 398
Coat, utility, for WAC	236	sion	27, 398
Dress, WAC, summer, beige	286	Pillow, feather, and pillow, cotton	11, 198
Jacket, WAC, winter	796	Pillow case	23, 071
Panties, winter, women's, pairs	1, 024	Pin, tent, 16-inch	b 106, 466
Shoes, service, women's, pairs	1, 295	Pocket, cartridge, and pocket, magazine,	
Skirt, summer, for WAC	1, 138	.30-cal., M1 carbine-rifle	17, 370
Skirt, winter, for WAC	844	Pouch, first-aid packet, M1942	25, 623
Stockings, rayon, women's, pairs	4, 833	Razor, safety, with 5 blades	16, 295
Waist, cotton, women's	816	Sheet, cotton, bed	24, 905
Waist, tropical worsted, khaki, women's	492	Spoon, M1926	36, 428
Waist, wool, women's	2, 566	Straps, carrying, general purpose; bag,	
		canvas field	11, 068
Equipage (*Thousands*)		Suspenders, belt, M1936, pairs, 2	8, 916
Bag, barrack	35, 921	Tag, identification	84, 949
Bag, canvas, field, olive drab, M1936	11, 263	Tent, shelter half	25, 132
Bag, duffel	13, 739	Towel, bath, olive drab and white	74, 519
Bag, food, waterproof, jungle and cold			
climate	9, 893	*General Supplies* (*Thousands*)	
Bag, sleeping, wool	8, 676	Bowl, general use	b 7, 563
Bar, insect, field, and bar, sandfly	11, 508	Broom, corn	c 10, 319
Bar, mosquito	9, 372	Calcium hypochlorite, tube	b 159, 109
Bedstead, wood, double-deck, and cot,		Calcium hypochlorite, 3¾ or 5-pound can	11, 649
folding steel	7, 000	Can, water, 5-gallon	b 6, 644
Belt, cartridge, .30-cal., dismounted,		Candle, type I and II	c 30, 851
M1923	10, 126	Compound, germicidal rinse, 3.3-ounce	
Belt, pistol or revolver, M1936	14, 411	package	c 49, 010
Blanket, wool, olive drab, M1934	53, 144	Detergent, mobile laundry, pounds	c 10, 088
Brush, shaving	15, 603	Drum, inflammable liquid, steel, 5-gallon	c 22, 443
Brush, tooth	18, 415	Drum, inflammable liquid, steel, 55-gal-	
Can, meat, all types	29, 307	lon	c 6, 255
Canteen, all types	27, 842	Fork, table	b 7, 173
Case, water repellant, for sleeping bag	9, 498	Fuel, ration-heating, 5-man meal	94, 335
Cot, folding, canvas	12, 527	Fuel, ration-heating, individual	94, 393
Cover, canteen, dismounted, M1910	24, 010	Insecticide, freon, aerosol, 1-pound dis-	
Cover, mattress	27, 964	penser	32, 439
Cover, waterproof, rifle-carbine	11, 731	Insecticide, powder, louse, bulk, pounds	10, 935
Cup, canteen, all types	30, 296	Insecticide, powder, louse, 2-ounce can	60, 091
Fork, M1926	34, 635	Insecticide, spray DDT, residual effect,	
Glasses, sun, with case	13, 473	gallons	5, 558
Goggles, M1938, M1942, M1943, M1944	7, 871	Knife, table, grill	b 6, 608
Haversack, M1928	7, 194	Larvicide, DDT powder, dissolving,	
Headnet, mosquito, M1942 and 1944	13, 500	pounds	12, 342

See footnotes at end of table.

TABLE 5—Continued

Item	Quantity	Item	Quantity
General Supplies—Continued		*Food—Continued*	
Lime, chlorinated, 20-pound export can, pounds	ᵇ 58,079	Fish and seafood	ᶜ 157
Plate, dinner, enamelware and china	ᵇ 6,129	Grapefruit	ᶜ 304
Repellent, insect, 2-ounce bottle	ᵇ 237,371	Lamb and mutton	ᶜ 285
Soap, grit, cake, pounds	ᶜ 27,587	Lard	ᶜ 339
Soap, ordinary issue, pounds	ᶜ 622,196	Lard, substitute	ᶜ 131
Soap, powdered, high and low titer, pounds	34,375	Lemons	ᶜ 152
		Lettuce	ᶜ 357
Soap, powder, hand scouring, mechanics, pounds	ᶜ 4,865	Melons, all kinds	ᶜ 160
		Oleomargarine	ᵉ 18
Soap, toilet, soft, hard or seawater	111,897	Onions, dry	ᵇ 381
Spoon, table, medium	ᵇ 6,014	Oranges	ᶜ 1,057
Stove, cooking, gasoline, M41 and M42, 1-burner	1,249	Pork, fresh	ᶜ 1,092
		Potatoes, Irish	ᵇ 4,384
Tablet, water-purification, individual, bottle of 100	ᶜ 49,506	Poultry, all kinds	ᵇ 964
		Sausage, all kinds	ᶜ 677
Trisodium phosphate, technical, pounds	ᶜ 17,020	Tomatoes	ᵇ 231
		Veal	ᶜ 242
Service Equipment (Single Units)	(ᶜ)		
Bath unit, mobile, field	488	*Food, Non-perishable Subsistence (Million Pounds)*	
Chamber, fumigation, methyl bromide	801	Apples, canned	ᵇ 133
Conveyor, gravity, roller, 10-foot section	131,837	Bacon, canned	ᵇ 338
Conveyor, gravity, wheel, 10-foot section	98,319	Beans, dry, white, Navy	ᶜ 353
Crane, warehouse, 6,000-pound mobile	1,259	Beans, string, canned	ᵇ 629
Crane, warehouse, 10,000-pound mobile	1,573	Beef, corned, canned	ᵇ 276
Laundry, mobile, 2-wheel, trailer type	1,251	Butter, stabilized, canned	ᵇ 119
Semi-trailer, 2-wheel, 10-ton refrigerator	940	Catsup, tomato	ᵇ 255
Tractor, gas, heavy duty	5,719	Coffee, green	ᵇ 1,397
Tractor, gas and electric, light duty	11,242	Corn, canned	ᵇ 706
Tractor, warehouse	80,717	Eggs, whole, dried	ᵇ 147
Truck, fork lift (6 types, 1 to 7½ ton capacity)	22,823	Flour, wheat, white	ᵇ 5,760
		Fruit cocktail, canned	ᵇ 342
		Hash, corned beef, canned	ᵇ 301
		Hash, meat and vegetable, canned	ᵇ 207
Food, Perishable Subsistence (Million Pounds)		Jam, all kinds	ᶜ 240
Apples	ᶜ 552	Juice, citrus, all kinds	ᵇ 936
Bacon, smoked, and ham, smoked	ᶜ 923	Juice, pineapple	ᵇ 368
Beef	ᶜ 3,076	Juice, tomato	ᵇ 648
Butter	ᵇ 857	Luncheon meat, canned	ᵇ 273
Cabbage	ᵇ 469	Milk, dry, powdered, skim	ᵇ 203
Carrots	ᶜ 279	Milk, dry, powdered, whole	ᵇ 175
Celery	ᶜ 247	Milk, evaporated	ᵇ 2,708
Cheese	ᵇ 361	Peaches, canned	ᵇ 743
Eggs	ᵇ 1,234	Peanut butter	ᶜ 116

See footnotes at end of table.

TABLE 5—Continued

Item	Quantity	Item	Quantity
Food—Continued		*Food*—Continued	
Peas, green, canned	[b] 845	Rice	[b] 607
Pears, canned	[b] 299	Salmon, canned	[b] 163
Pickles, assorted	[c] 111	Sauerkraut	[b] 206
Pineapple, canned	[b] 744	Sausages, pork and vienna, canned	[b] 512
Potatoes, white, dehydrated	[b] 265	Stew, meat and vegetable, canned	[b] 467
Prunes, evaporated	[b] 102	Sugar, granulated	[b] 2,129
Raisins	[b] 146	Tomatoes, canned	[b] 939

[a] Data represent the numbers of listed items accepted by the procuring agency during the period indicated. Includes items subsequently distributed to other U.S. agencies and through lend-lease procedures to foreign governments. See source for additional information as to technical content.

[b] Deliveries from 1 January 1942 through 31 December 1945.

[c] Deliveries from 1 January 1943 through 31 December 1945.

Source: U.S. Army in World War II, Statistics, Procurement, 9 April 1952 draft, prepared by Richard H. Crawford and Lindsley F. Cook under the direction of Theodore E. Whiting.

TABLE 6—SIGNAL CORPS: PROCUREMENT DELIVERIES OF SELECTED MAJOR ITEMS, 1 JANUARY 1940–31 DECEMBER 1945[a]

Item	Quantity	Item	Quantity
Ground Radio Communication Equipment		Radio remote control sets: RC–261, for use with SCR–608, –609, –610, –619 & –628	47,906
(Short Range: Up to 25 Miles)		Morale receiver; R–100–URR, 3 bands, AM	85,212
Portable radio sets:			
SCR–194, Early set for ground troops	11,427	**Air Radio Communication Equipment**	
SCR–195, Early set for ground & airborne units	9,253	Components for SCR–274–N, airborne command set:	
SCR–300, "Walkie Talkie" for ground troops	88,040	BC–453–A, Receiver	157,583
SCR–511, Lightweight guidon mounted cavalry set	24,384	BC–454, Receiver	161,875
		BC–455, Receiver	145,848
SCR–536, "Handie Talkie" for ground troops	206,753	BC–457, Transmitter	145,926
SCR–694, Voice-code set for tactical troops	23,732	BC–458, Transmitter	137,960
		BC–459, Transmitter	63,434
Vehicular radio sets:		BC–696, Transmitter	40,620
AN–VRC–3, Tank radio to talk with SCR–300	8,667	Airborne set, AN–ARC–3; 8 pushbutton channels	7,349
SCR–178, Early set for field artillery	3,137	Airborne set, SCR–522; for 24-volt battery use	198,398
SCR–284, CW and voice, command set	63,972	Airborne set, SCR–287; long range liaison	102,508
SCR–510, For armored force units	45,857	Modification of "Handie Talkie" for gliders; SCR–585	6,530
SCR–608, For ground troops	11,878		
SCR–610, Liaison set for artillery	108,780	**Wire Communication Equipment**	
		Intercommunication equipment:	
(Medium Range; 25 to 100 Miles)		BC–606, Interphone control box for various SCR's	[b] 608,746
Portable radio sets:			
SCR–177, For ground & ground-to-air use	4,627	RC–36, Aircraft interphone	[b] 113,845
SCR–593, Receiver for signals of SCR–543	55,371	RC–99, Interphone for tanks and other vehicles	28,280
Vehicular radio sets:		Telephone equipment:	
SCR–193, Voice-code set	18,931	BD–71, Portable field switchboard	42,382
SCR–245, CW voice set for air or ground units	11,513	C–114, Loading coil to extend field wire range	391,243
SCR–506, Tank-combat car voice-code set	17,272	EE–8, Portable field telephone, in leather case	1,363,061
SCR–538, For mechanized and armored units	40,097	SB–18–GT, Light emergency field switchboard	15,611
SCR–543, Voice command set for coast artillery	13,439	Teletype equipment:	
		EE–97, Teletype, used without commercial current	22,604
(Long Range, 100 Miles and over)		EE–98, Teletype, used with commercial current	4,860
Mobile radio sets; SCR–299, –399 & –499, for higher tactical command headquarters (Corps & Divisions)	14,706		

See footnotes at end of table.

TABLE 6—Continued

Item	Quantity	Item	Quantity
Teletype equipment—Continued		Operational Radio	
TC–18, Repeater, terminal set, long teletype lines	5, 252	Fighter control equipment:	
		SCR–573, Truck mounted transmitter	1, 663
TT–6–FG, Teletypewriter, M15, weather keyboard	7, 631	SCR–574, Truck mounted receiver	1, 649
		SCR–575, Truck mounted direction finder	1, 283
TT–8–FG, Teletypewriter, M19, weather keyboard	9, 185	Mine detection equipment:	
		AN–PRS–1, Non-metallic mine detector	29, 601
Other Communication Equipment		SCR–625, Metallic mine detector, portable	116, 000
Visual equipment:			
AP–50, 10 panels, cased, air support recognition	373, 698	Navigational Radar Equipment	(ᶜ)
M–238, Set, 3 colored flags, signals between tanks	357, 280	Altimeter:	
		AN–APN–1, Effective to 4,000 feet	35, 397
Pigeon equipment: PG–46–A, Loft, 60 or more pigeons	1, 050	SCR–518 and –718, Effective to 40,000 feet	11, 338
		Airborne equipment:	
Operational Radar, Airborne		AN–APN–2, Interrogator for paratroop beacons	13, 093
Range finding radar:		AN–APN–4- Long range receiver, navigation aid	42, 780
AN–APG–13, Range finder for B–25 bomber nose gun	1, 529		
AN–APS–13, Tail warning radar for fighters	33, 378	Navigational Radio Equipment	(ᶜ)
Air interception radar; SCR–720	5, 107	Airborne receiver:	
Search & bombing radar:		AN–ARN–5, For ground glide path transmission	44, 047
AN–APQ–7, "Eagle", bombing through overcast	963	RC–103, For alignment of approach	55, 869
AN–APQ–13, "Mickey", bombing through overcast	5, 865	RC–193, For vertical beams from marker beacons	91, 448
AN–APS–15, "Mickey", similar to AN–APQ–13	3, 205	Emergency transmitter:	
SCR–717, Airborne surface vessel detector	3, 820	SCR–578, For survivors at sea, "Gibson Girl"	117, 809
Radar Identification, Friend or Foe (IFF)		Countermeasures Radar and Radio	(ᶜ)
Airborne equipment:		Radar:	
SCR–535, Transponder, Mark II, IFF	27, 510	AN–APQ–2 and –9, Airborne barrage jammer	22, 860
SCR–695, Transponder, Mark III, IFF	156, 435	AN–APT–1 and –2, Airborne jammer, low power	13, 561
Operational Radar, Ground		Radio:	
Proximity fuse; AN–CPQ–1	889, 101	AN–ART–3, –7 and –11, Barrage jammers against tanks, radios and high frequencies	1, 300
Anti-aircraft control:			
SCR–268, Gun laying and searchlight control	2, 984	AN–CRT–2, Parachute dropped transmitters, set of 6, to disrupt enemy radio	6, 410
SCR–584, Mobile, microwave fire control set	1, 610		

See footnotes at end of table.

TABLE 6—Continued

Item	Quantity	Item	Quantity
Photographic Equipment		Wire—Continued	
Camera: PH–104, with accessories and case	4,182	W–130, Light weight assault, twisted pair (Miles)	950,458
Projector:		W–143, Two conductor, parallel, 7-strand (Miles)	179,548
PH–131, –398 and –402, 16mm movie, with accessories	16,195	W–1–T2, Single conductor (Miles)	1,422,557
PH–222, 2 x 2-inch slide	14,258		
Meteorological Equipment		Test, Tool and Maintenance Equipment	
Radiosonde:		Test set; I–56, For all radio servicing	38,308
AN–AMQ–1, To transmit weather data from air	333,279	Frequency meter; SCR–211, To adjust radio sets	142,311
BC–1253, To transmit weather data from balloons	126,112	Tool set; TE–33, With knife and pliers, in case	978,085
Wire and Equipment		Other Supplies and Equipment	
Reel:		Climbers for linemen: LC–5, –6 and –7	275,344
DR–4, For 2,000 feet, twisted pair, field wire	2,670,626	Poles, 25 to 45 foot, wooden, for wire lines	485,798
DR–5, For one mile of W–110 Wire	2,032,175		
DR–15, For spiral 4-way cable	839,971	International Aid Equipment	
Wire:		Russian-type field telephones: EE–8A	334,976
W–110–B, Twisted pair, 7–strand (Miles)	3,456,452	Radio sets 19 and 48, British	117,247

ᵃ Data represent the numbers of listed items accepted by the procuring agency during the period indicated. Includes items subsequently distributed to other U.S. agencies and through lend-lease procedures to foreign governments. See source for additional information as to technical content.

ᵇ Deliveries from January 1942 through December 1945.

ᶜ Deliveries from January 1940 through March 1945, Army Air Forces procured thereafter.

Source: U.S. Army in World War II, Statistics, Procurement, 9 April 1952 draft, prepared by Richard H. Crawford and Lindsley F. Cook under the direction of Theodore E. Whiting.

TABLE 7—MEDICAL DEPARTMENT: PROCUREMENT DELIVERIES OF SELECTED MAJOR ITEMS, 1 JANUARY 1940–31 DECEMBER 1945 [a]

Item	Quantity	Item	Quantity
Drugs, Chemicals and Biologicals		Plasma, normal, human, dried, 500cc	
Acetone, 1-pound bottle	447,917	bottle	3,114,892
Acid, acetylsalicylic, 1,000-tablet bottle	1,790,937	Plasma, normal, human dried, 250cc	
Alcohol, ethyl, USP, 1-quart bottle	1,381,503	bottle	3,060,594
Alcohol, ethyl, denatured, 1-quart bottle	544,540	Powder, developing, X-ray, 5-pound	
Ammonia, aromatic, 10-ampule package	2,606,665	package	579,591
Atabrine, 100-tablet bottle	24,111,625	Powder, fixing, X-ray, 5-pound package	923,971
Atabrine, 1,000-tablet bottle	1,521,871	Procaine hydrochloride, 20-cartridge box	2,822,718
Atropine, sulfate, 20-tablet (1/150 grain		Quinine dihydrochloride, 12-ampule box	490,539
hypo) bottle	2,868,314	Quinine sulfate, 1,000-tablet bottle	747,411
Bal ointment, two ¾-ounce tubes	2,308,444	Soap, soft, 1-pound jar	1,491,999
Benzedrine inhaler	4,680,000	Sodium bicarbonate, 1-pound box	1,412,492
Burn injury set, boric acid ointment	2,469,148	Sulfadiazine, 8-tablet package	28,880,871
Cholera vaccine, 20cc vial	2,045,455	Sulfanilamide, crystalline, 5-gram, 5-en-	
Cresole, saponated solution, 1-quart		velope box	4,587,694
bottle	1,073,008	Sulfanilamide, crystalline, 5-gram, 12-en-	
Dextrose, 1-pound bottle	513,453	velope box	10,237,422
Digitalis, 1 USP XII unit, 100-tablet		Sulfathiazole, 1,000-tablet bottle	1,239,181
bottle	642,261	Tincture opium, camphorated, 1-pint	
Ephedrine sulfate, 12-ampule box	537,989	bottle	878,350
Foot powder, ¼-pound can	28,794,919	Typhus vaccine, 20cc vial	8,860,010
Formaldehyde solution, 1-quart bottle	327,367	Vitamins, multivitamin, 100-tablet bottle	3,637,639
Gas gangrene antitoxin, trivalent, vial	888,220	Whiskey, 1-quart bottle	16,17,117
Glycerin, 1-pound bottle	580,160	**Surgical Instruments**	
Hydrogen peroxide, 3%, 1-pound bottle	2,722,904	Clamp, pylorus, 8-inch	111,928
Influenza virus vaccine, types A & B, 30-		Forceps, dressing, 5½-inch, straight	402,885
dose bottle	500,754	Forceps, hemostatic, 6¼-inch, curved,	
Iodine, ¼-pound bottle	725,798	Rochester-Pean	1,898,686
Iodine and potassium iodide powder,		Forceps, hysterectomy, 8½-inch, curved,	
10-tube carton	6,371,927	Pean	378,548
Iodine swab, 1½cc, box of 6	12,669,046	Forceps, towel, 5¼-inch, Backhaus	441,335
Mapharsen, 0.06-gram, 10-ampule box	1,401,781	Scissors, bandage	1,017,635
Mercuric ointment, ammoniated, 1-ounce		Scissors, dissecting, curved, 5½-inch	120,390
tube	5,965,158	Scissors, straight, 6¾-inch	107,868
Mercurous chloride ointment, 1-ounce		**Surgical Appliances**	
tube	8,585,277	Gloves, medium, size 7, pair	1,720,212
Mercury, ¼-pound bottle	715,615	Sphygmomanometer, aneroid	51,971
Morphine sulfate, 20-tablet (⅛-grain)		Splint, litter bar	375,244
tube	3,205,522	Splint, Thomas, arm, hinged	525,528
Morphine tartrate, 1-tube carton	9,358,665	Splint, Army, leg, half-ring	597,613
Motion sickness preventive, 6-tablet box	6,713,470	Suture, catgut, chromic, size 00, 1-suture	2,170,205
Oil, cod liver, 1-pint bottle	633,530	Suture, silk, dermal, medium, 1-suture	2,432,944
Penicillin sodium, 100,000 oxford unit		Syringe, Luer, 2cc (hypodermic)	3,293,717
vial	19,875,485	Syringe, Luer, hypodermic needle, 23-	
Pentothal sodium, 1-gram, 25-ampule box	380,524	gage, ¾-inch canula, dozen	1,560,059
Plague vaccine, 20cc vial	1,069,071		

See footnotes at end of table.

Table 7—Continued

Item	Quantity	Item	Quantity
Surgical Dressings		Denture, base material, acrylic, pink, 10 units	324, 259
Bandage, elastic, all-cotton, 3-inch x 5½ yards, 12s	356, 432	Engine, handpiece, angles, Doriot	102, 478
Bandage, gauze, roller, 2-inch x 6 yards, 12s	9, 710, 041	Engine, handpiece, straight, Doriot	44, 544
		Explorer, No. 23	209, 804
Bandage, gauze, roller, 3-inch x 10 yards, 12s	6, 623, 269	Forceps, tooth extracting:	
Gauze, plain, 36-inch, 5 yards	4, 378, 257	Number 18 R	40, 759
Gauze, plain, sterilized, 36-inch, 1 yard	12, 942, 897	Number 18 L	37, 955
Plaster, adhesive, surgical, 3-inch x 5 yards	24, 512, 357	Number 150 A	50, 007
		Number 151 A	54, 741
Hospital Equipment and Supplies		Gold solder, 18k, dwt	349, 929
Bag, hot water	3, 242, 017	Gold wire, 14-gage, half-round, 4dwt	244, 769
Bed, hospital	49, 471	Impression compound, 12 units	201, 495
Sterilizer, instrument, non-pressure type	1, 809	Lathe, dental	4, 285
Sterilizer, instrument, on stand, electric	1, 779	Mandrel, Morgan-Maxfield, angle handpiece, 6	339, 640
Thermometer, clinical	11, 380, 151	Pliers, Number 104	47, 175
		Unit, operating, dental	7, 343
Laboratory Equipment and Supplies			
Bottle, narrow mouth, 5-gallon, green	193, 745	**Field Equipment and Supplies**	
Clock, interval-timer	12, 463	Bandage, gauze, compressed, white, 3-inch x 6 yards, 72 to the box	1, 805, 168
Microscope, monocular	20, 367		
Microscope, dark field apparatus	3, 947	Bandage, gauze, compressed, field brown, 3-inch x 6 yards, 72 to the box	628, 113
Microscope, dissecting, low power, stereoscopic	299	Bandage, plaster of paris, 6-inch x 5 yards, 12 to the carton	2, 316, 062
		Bandage, triangular, olive drab, 12 to the package	67, 104
X-ray Equipment and Supplies		Chest, field, plain	152, 968
Apron, radiopaque	19, 395	Dressing, first-aid, large, field brown	4, 908, 664
Cassette, 10-inch x 12-inch	40, 262	Eye-dressing set	2, 041, 917
Gloves, radiopaque, pair	18, 742	Kit, first-aid, motor vehicle, 24-unit, complete	343, 799
Holder, film development, 8 x 10-inch	56, 789		
Holder, film development, 10 x 12-inch	60, 203	Litter, straight, aluminum	594, 695
Holder, film development, 14 x 17-inch	82, 360	Oxygen therapy apparatus, closed circuit	5, 049
		Packet, first-aid, field brown dressing	14, 388, 557
Dental Equipment and Supplies		Sponge, surgical, 4 x 4-inch, 100 to the box	39, 496
Alloy, amalgam, 1-ounce	1, 316, 934	Sterilizer, instrument, 18-inch	21, 639
Bur:		Stove, 2-burner, gasoline	18, 122
No. 6 angle, handpiece, 6	891, 322	X-ray field unit:	
No. 35 angle, handpiece, 6	1, 128, 633	Generator	3, 456
No. 39 angle, handpiece, 6	771, 844	Machine X-ray, 110–220 volts, 1/60c	4, 197
No. 557 angle, handpiece, 6	1, 043, 765	Darkroom tent	1, 605
No. 560 angle, handpiece, 6	864, 751	Shockproof cable	1, 616
No. 700 angle, handpiece, 6	743, 071		
No. 35 straight, handpiece, 6	367, 461		

ᵃ Data represent the numbers of listed items accepted by the procuring agency during the period indicated. Includes items subsequently distributed to other U.S. agencies and through lend-lease procedures to foreign governments. See source for additional information as to technical content.

Source: U.S. Army in World War II, Statistics, Procurement, 9 April 1952 draft, prepared by Richard H. Crawford and Lindsley F. Cook under the direction of Theodore E. Whiting.

TABLE 8—CORPS OF ENGINEERS: PROCUREMENT DELIVERIES OF SELECTED MAJOR ITEMS
1 JANUARY 1942–31 DECEMBER 1945 [a]

Item	Quantity	Item	Quantity
Boats and Bridging		Cranes and shovels—Continued	
Boats:		Rubber tired, ¾-cubic yard, 8- to 12-	
Assault, M2	37, 613	ton, Class XI	1, 134
Landing, pneumatic, rubber, 10-man	5, 768	Rubber tired, ¾-cubic yard, 14- to 18-	
Reconnaissance, pneumatic, canvas,		ton, Class XII	1, 303
2-man	28, 123	Drill, pneumatic, portable:	
Storm, plywood	5, 040	Rock, 45-pound class	1, 770
Utility, gasoline powered, 18-foot	1, 989	Rotary type, woodboring, 2-inch ca-	
Bridges, fixed, steel:		pacity	10, 402
Panel, Bailey type, M2, widened road-		Grader, road:	
way	1, 788	Diesel engine drive, 12-foot moldboard	6, 806
Box girder, H–10 & –20	776	Towed, leaning wheel, 12-foot mold-	
Highway, semi-permanent, 90-foot,		board	1, 642
truss span	176	Mixer, concrete, gasoline engine drive,	
Floats, pneumatic:		14-cubic foot	1, 831
13-ton, M-3, with carrying case	13, 905	Roller, road:	
18-ton, M-1, with carrying case	20, 910	Gasoline engine drive, 3-wheel, 10-ton	2, 046
Motors, outboard; 22hp and 50–55hp	18, 261	Gasoline engine drive, tandem, 2-axle,	
Ponton, steel, 25-ton	3, 682	5- to 8-ton	1, 411
Saddle, steel, treadway, M–1, 18-ton	13, 385	Towed type, sheepsfoot, 2 drum-in-line	1, 798
Trailers, 2-wheel, utility, pole type,		Saws:	
2½-ton	10, 662	Chain, portable, pneumatic, 24-inch	
Trestle, steel:		blade	9, 495
10-ton	1, 687	Chain, portable, gasoline engine drive,	
25-ton	4, 429	36-inch	11, 371
		Circular, woodworking, portable, 12-	
Tractors, Crawler Type		inch blade	10, 854
Diesel engine driven:		Scrapers, road:	
91–140 drawbar horsepower	10, 035	Motorized, cable operated, 12-cubic	
61–90 drawbar horsepower	25, 700	yard	1, 056
46–60 drawbar horsepower	17, 442	Towed type, cable operated, 8-cubic	
36–45 drawbar horsepower	24, 853	yard	4, 890
		Towed type, cable operated, 12-cubic	
Construction Equipment		yard	2, 234
Bulldozer, for mounting on M–4, A–1,		Sprayer, paint, pneumatic, with com-	
A–2 & A–3 tanks	1, 400	pressor, gasoline engine driven,	
Compressor, air, gasoline engine, truck		wheelbarrow type	4, 821
mounted	7, 054	Trailers, full, low bed, 8-ton	5, 363
Cranes and shovels:			
Crawler mounted; ½-cubic yard, 5- to		**Other Equipment**	
6-ton, Class II	3, 958	Air conditioner, self-contained, 70,000	
Crawler mounted; ¾-cubic yard, 7- to		Btu, 5hp motor	2, 042
10-ton, Class III	4, 279	Alidade, miniature, telescopic, Type B	2, 457
Rubber tired, ⅜-cubic yard, 4- to 8-ton,			
Class X	2, 032		

See footnotes at end of table.

TABLE 8—Continued

Item	Quantity	Item	Quantity
Generator sets, portable, gasoline engine drive:		Nets, camouflage, cotton twine, ungarnished—Continued	
3kw, 120 volt, 1 phase, 60 cycle, AC__	14,516	22 feet x 22 feet_____	163,650
5kw, 110 volt, 1 phase, 60 cycle, AC___	12,814	29 feet x 29 feet_____	138,043
Generator sets, portable, diesel engine drive:		36 feet x 44 feet_____	295,419
15kw, 127–220 volt, 3 phase, 60 cycle, AC_____	4,474	45 feet x 45 feet_____	76,517
		Pumps, centrifugal, gasoline engine driven:	
30kw, 127–220 volt, 3 phase, 60 cycle, AC_____	5,743	2-in. discharge, 55-gallons-per-min at 50-ft. head_____	26,683
50kw, 127–220 volt, 3 phase, 60 cycle, AC_____	2,391	2-in. discharge, 166-gal-per min at 25-ft head_____	2,794
100kw, 127–220 volt, 3 phase, 60 cycle, AC_____	1,370	4-in. discharge, 175-gal-per-min at 1,453-ft head_____	4,318
(Operated at 50 cycle, develops 230–400 volts)		4-in. discharge, 200-gal-per-min at 350-ft head_____	1,051
Mats, airplane, landing:		4-in. discharge, 480-gal-per-min at 300-ft head_____	921
Aluminum alloy, pierced plank (Thousand square feet)__	17,819	4-in. discharge, 500-gal-per-min at 20-foot head_____	735
Steel, pierced plank (Thousand square feet)__	702,398	Rail, railroad, 75-pounds-per-yard (feet)__	2,966,000
Welded wire fabric type (Thousand square feet)__	123,131	Refrigeration unit, gasoline engine driven, 12,000 Btu-per-hour capacity_____	6,659
Nets, camouflage, cotton shrimp, impregnated:		Searchlight, portable, 60-inch_____	6,962
29 feet x 29 feet_____	239,988	Tank, storage, canvas, water, 3,000 gallon_	48,587
36 feet x 44 feet_____	299,228	Transit, engineer, night illumination:	
Nets, camouflage, cotton twine, ungarnished:		20-second reading, with accessories and tripod_____	3,636
14 feet x 29 feet_____	114,340	1-minute reading, with accessories and tripod_____	5,851
15 feet x 15 feet_____	291,042		
17 feet x 35 feet_____	49,965		

ᵃ Data represent the numbers of listed items accepted by the procuring agency during the period indicated. Includes items subsequently distributed to other U.S. agencies and through lend-lease procedures to foreign governments. See source for additional information as to technical content.

Source: U.S. Army in World War II, Statistics, Procurement, 9 April 1952 draft, prepared by Richard H. Crawford and Lindsley F. Cook under the direction of Theodore E. Whiting.

TABLE 9—TRANSPORTATION CORPS: PROCUREMENT DELIVERIES OF SELECTED MAJOR ITEMS, 1 JANUARY 1942–31 DECEMBER 1945 [a]

Item	Quantity	Item	Quantity
Railway Cars		**Railway Locomotives**	
By type—Total	95,290	By type—Total	7,570
Ammunition cars	68	Diesel-battery	20
Box cars and brake vans (7 types)	42,426	Diesel-electric (12 types)	966
Caboose cars (2 types)	192	Diesel-mechanical (5 types)	8
Dump cars	1,050	Electric (3 types)	14
Fire control cars	29	Gas-mechanical (10 types)	276
Flat cars (7 types)	17,054	Steam (17 types)	6,286
Gondola cars (7 types)	26,141	By gauge—Total	7,570
Hospital cars (2 types)	249	Standard gauge (56.5-inch)	3,816
Kitchen cars	32	30-inch gauge	2
Machinery cars	35	36-inch gauge	113
Machine shop cars	10	42-inch gauge	186
Refrigerator cars	670	60-inch gauge	2,451
Store box cars	29	66-inch gauge	356
Tank cars (4 types)	7,236	750-mm gauge (29.25-inch)	16
		Meter gauge (39.37-inch)	630
Other types	69		
By gauge—Total	95,290	**Other Equipment**	
Standard gauge (56.5-inch)	63,045	Marine tugs (24 types)	1,409
36-inch gauge	395	Marine tractors (7 types)	2,387
42-inch gauge	3,392	Marine barges, non-self-propelled (35	
48-inch gauge	8	types)	5,839
60-inch gauge	11,597	Gantry portal cranes (10 types)	501
66-inch gauge	3,170	Derricks, stiff leg (4 types)	685
60-cm gauge (23.4-inch)	700		
750-mm gauge (29.25-inch)	100		
Meter gauge (39.37-inch)	12,883		

[a] Data represent the numbers of listed items accepted by the procuring agency during the period indicated. Includes items subsequently distributed to other U.S. agencies and through lend-lease procedures to foreign governments. See source for additional information as to technical content.

Source: U.S. Army in World War II, Statistics, Procurement, 9 April 1952 draft, prepared by Richard H. Crawford and Lindsley F. Cook under the direction of Theodore E. Whiting.

TABLE 10—CHEMICAL WARFARE SERVICE: PROCUREMENT DELIVERIES OF SELECTED MAJOR ITEMS, 1 JANUARY 1940–31 DECEMBER 1945[a]

Item	Quantity	Item	Quantity
Chemical Agents (Thousand Pounds)		Bombs—Continued	
CG (Phosgene)	40, 414	Clusters, incendiary bomb, 100-pound:	
CL (Chlorine)	369, 320	M6 (34 4-pound M50 bombs)	274, 940
CNB (Tear gas solution, weak)	5, 282	M8 (34 4-pound M54 bombs)	452, 053
CNS (Tear gas solution, strong)	3, 309	M12 (14 6-pound M69 bombs)	248, 221
FM (Smoke, titanium tetrachloride)	4, 227	British, box type (30 4-pound M50	
FS (Smoke, sulfur trioxide solution)	47, 923	bombs)	1, 042, 778
H (Mustard)	174, 610	Protective Material	
HC (Smoke mixture, hexachlorethane)	17, 322	Agent, decontaminating M4 (3 & 4⅓ gal.	
L (Lewisite)	40, 123	size) (gallons)	4, 846, 819
WP (Smoke and incendiary, white phosphorous)	160, 883	Apparatus, decontaminating, 1½-quart, M2	1, 908, 432
Ammunition (Rounds)		Apron, impermeable	1, 217, 098
Canisters, smoke:		Curtains, gas proof, M1 and anti-gas	1, 001, 765
HC, M1, for 105mm shell, M84	13, 796, 930	Eyeshield, M1	71, 928, 752
Colored, M2, for 105mm shell	2, 330, 007	Impregnite, shoe, M1, 8-ounce	70, 156, 767
HC, M1 & M2, for 155mm shell, M115 & M116	3, 331, 129	Kit, ointment protective, M5, 4-tube	26, 641, 088
Colored, M3 & M4, for 155mm shell	687, 666	Masks, gas:	
Grenades:		Animal types, dog and horse	40, 568
Hand, smoke (WP), M15	5, 828, 739	Non-combatant types	8, 311, 995
Incendiary, AN–M14	7, 621, 958	Military types:	
Smoke, colored, M16 & M18	4, 903, 502	Service, heavyweight	10, 473, 621
Smoke, white (HC), AN–M8	3, 378, 836	Service, lightweight	13, 036, 409
Napalm, Type A & B packaging (Pounds)	21, 453, 690	Ointment, protective, M4, 2.3-ounce	58, 319, 717
Shells, 4.2-inch chemical mortar:		Paint, liquid vesicant detector, M5, 4-ounce	7, 801, 968
Gas, non-persistent, CG, M2	497, 402	Paper, liquid vesicant detector, M6, 25-sheet	1, 131, 271
Gas, persistent, H, M2	540, 746	Pot, smoke, floating (HC) M4 series	2, 349, 950
High explosive, M3	6, 456, 250	Pot, smoke, (HC), M1 & M5	6, 120, 902
Smoke, FS, M2	355, 496	Respirator, dust, M1	6, 826, 819
Smoke, WP, M2	3, 119, 968	Sack, gas resistant, M1	8, 598, 945
Bombs (Number of Bombs or Bomb Clusters)		Service Equipment	
Bombs, Incendiary:		Kit, gas mask, waterproofing	10, 661, 678
100-pound, M47A1 & A-2 (including NP & NP special)	3, 514, 823	Kit, repair, gas mask, company, M2	1, 236, 512
500-pound, M76, PT1	277, 890	Weapons	
Clusters, aimable, incendiary bomb, 500-pound:		Flamethrower, portable, M1A1	14, 253
		Flamethrower, portable, M2–2	24, 601
M17 & M17A1 (110, 4-pound M50 bombs)	1, 103, 424	Flamethrower, mechanized, M3–4–3, & M3–E5R2	2, 134
Clusters, incendiary bomb, 500-pound:		Mine, land, chemical	1, 905, 667
M7 (128, 4-pound M50 bombs)	249, 833	Mortar, 4.2-inch, chemical, M1A1 & M2	8, 184
M13 (60 6-pound M69 bombs)	155, 956	Mortar, 4.2-inch, chemical, recoilless, M4	124

[a] Data represent the numbers of listed items accepted by the procuring agency during the period indicated. Includes items subsequently distributed to other U.S. agencies and through lend-lease procedures to foreign governments. See source for additional information as to technical content.

Source: U.S. Army in World War II, Statistics, Procurement, 9 April 1952 draft, prepared by Richard H. Crawford and Lindsley F. Cook under the direction of Theodore E. Whiting.

TABLE 11—ARMY AIR FORCES: PROCUREMENT DELIVERIES OF AIRPLANES, JANUARY 1940–DECEMBER 1945 [a]

Item	Quantity	Item	Quantity
Airplanes—Total, all Types	231, 099	Reconnaissance—Total	1, 117
Very heavy bombers—Total	3, 899	F-2 (version of C-45)	55
		F-4 & F-5, (version of P-38)	500
B-19 (Delivered in 1941)	1	F-6 (version of P-51)	299
B-29, Superfortress	3, 898	Other models	263
Heavy bombers—Total	31, 000	Transports—Total	22, 885
B-17, Flying Fortress	12, 692	C-43, Traveller	352
B-24, Liberator	18, 190	C-45, Expeditor	1, 771
B-32, Dominator	118	C-46, Commando	3, 180
		C-47, Skytrain	10, 368
Medium bombers—Total	16, 070	C-54, Skymaster	1, 162
		C-60, Lodestar	620
B-25, Mitchell	9, 816	C-61, Fowarder	1, 009
B-26, Marauder	5, 157	C-64, Norseman	756
Other models	1, 097	C-69, Constellation	15
		C-78 (AT-17 type), Bobcat	3, 206
Light bombers—Total	18, 113	C-87, Liberator Express	291
		Other models	155
A-20, Havoc	7, 385		
A-24, Dauntless	615	Trainers—Total	55, 712
A-25, Helldiver	900		
A-26, Invader	2, 450	AT-6, Texan	15, 094
A-28 & A-29, Hudson	2, 189	AT-7, AT-10 & AT-11, Navigator	
A-30, Baltimore	1, 575	(AT-7)	5, 775
A-31 & A-35, Vengence	1, 931	AT-8 & AT-17, Bobcat	2, 153
A-36 (P-51 type), Mustang	500	BT-13 & BT-15, Valiant	11, 537
Other models	568	PT-13, PT-17 & PT-27, Kaydet	7, 539
		PT-19, PT-23 & PT-26, Cornell	7,·802
Fighters—Total	68, 712	Other models	5, 812
P-38. Lightning	9, 536	Communications—Total	13, 591
P-39, Airacobra	9, 588		
P-40, Warhawk	13, 738	L-1, Vigilant	324
P-47, Thunderbolt	15, 683	L-2, Grasshopper type	1, 940
P-51, Mustang	14, 686	L-3, Grasshopper type	1, 439
P-59, Airacomet (jet propelled)	66	L-4 & L-14, Grasshopper type	5, 611
P-61, Black Widow	702	L-5, Sentinel	3, 590
P-63, Kingcobra	3, 292	R-4 & R-5 (helicopter)	161
P-70, night fighter type of A-20	60	R-6 (helicopter)	224
P-80, Shooting Star (jet propelled)	243	Other models	302
Other models	1, 118		

[a] Data represent factory acceptances or receipt of legal title by resident factory representative of procuring agency.   Includes all airplanes procured by the AAF regardless of subsequent distribution to Army, Navy, recipients of Lend-Lease, or others.   These airplane deliveries represent approximately 83% of all Army Air Forces procurement.

Source: U.S. Army in World War II, Statistics, Procurement, 9 April 1952 draft, prepared by Richard H. Crawford and Lindsley F. Cook under the direction of Theodore E. Whiting.

other unfavorable conditions. It had to be smokeless and, if possible, flashless. These and many other exacting technical requirements had to be met, most of them under the opposing pressures of urgency and tremendous safety hazards, while the nation was building an entire new powder industry from the ground up.

But the technical requirements for powder were inseparable from those of all the other ammunition components and from the controlling weapon itself. The designing, forging, and machining of projectiles for artillery—among the most exacting and troublesome production problems of World War II—were related, among other things, to the quality and character of powder. Not to be confused with propellant powder were the high explosives used to provide the lethal bursting charge in projectiles. The nature of high explosives likewise depended upon the total combination of components for each type of ammunition, and the safety hazards surrounding the production of high explosives were the greatest of any on the entire war production front. Perhaps the most complex of all ammunition components were the marvelously intricate and sensitive fuzes, which individually or as a class had to perform some of the most difficult and versatile assignments of the war. Some fuzes had to serve many different calibers of ammunition and had to permit a wide variety of settings. Others, despite their sensitivity, had to be capable of delayed detonation even after the successive shocks to their carrying projectile of launching, impact, and penetration through heavy armor plate. Still others had to be able to detonate upon attaining a certain proximity to an aerial target or, failing to attain such proximity, before reaching the ground in order to avoid casualties to friendly ground

personnel. The problems of inventing, developing, and then mass-producing such complex, sensitive, yet sturdy instruments were legion, requiring the finest efforts of pure and applied science, engineering, and industrial organization.

Even so prosaic an item as the .30-caliber cartridge case presented seemingly insoluble production problems in the face of material shortages in World War II. The pressures generated in small arms cartridges upon firing are extremely high—much higher per square inch than in the case of artillery. Years of experience and research had indicated brass as the only satisfactory material for cartridge cases. It possessed sufficient elasticity to expand under pressure and to contract instantly after the pressure was released. The expansion was necessary to provide a tight seal (obturation) to prevent the escape of gas backward into the breech. The instantaneous contraction thereafter was necessary to permit prompt ejection of the empty case from the chamber. When the copper shortage in World War II posed an across-the-board threat to ammunition supply, it became imperative to develop a substitute material—with steel the only practicable possibility—for the manufacture of cartridge cases. After many failures and months of around-the-clock efforts, scientists, engineers, production workers, and administrators finally succeeded in adapting steel to the purpose. Fortunately, the increased availability of copper made unnecessary the widespread substitution of steel cases, as these had not become fully satisfactory at the time of peak demand.[6]

---

[6] See Constance McLaughlin Green, Harry C. Thomson, and Peter C. Roots, *The Ordnance Department: Planning Munitions for War,* UNITED STATES ARMY IN WORLD WAR II (Washington: 1955), especially Chapter XVIII, from which this illustration was taken.

The exacting performance characteristics required of military items led to production problems of unprecedented difficulty in almost all categories of equipment. The Army's .50-caliber aircraft machine gun (M3), developed by Ordnance for the Air Forces, was capable of firing at a rate of 1,200 rounds per minute. (Let the reader try to visualize the discharge of 20 rounds per second from a single weapon!) Apart from the difficulties of producing a weapon which could achieve and stand up under such rates of fire, the resulting ammunition requirements became astronomical. In order to operate its machine guns the Army procured some thirteen billion metallic belt links, each of which had to meet exact specifications to prevent jamming of the guns. The 2½-ton Army truck—the workhorse of the Army—could climb a 65-degree hill fully loaded from a standing start and had such stability that it could proceed across the face of the same hill without toppling. It could speed smoothly along the highway at forty-five miles per hour or mow its way through a grove of 2½-inch trees without a tremor. Such a truck was manifestly of a different species from any commercial truck ever produced. The necessity for all-wheel drives in Army trucks gave rise to heavy demands for new and complex components—constant velocity joints, transfer cases, bogie rear axles, and the like—never before manufactured in quantity and requiring the building of a whole new industry. So great was the Army's procurement of automotive vehicles that by the end of the war it would have been literally possible to load and move its entire eight million troops on motor vehicles at one time.[7]

In addition to the high performance specifications required of military items, another factor dictated the necessity for extremely close manufacturing tolerances, calling for numerous machining and other operations which complicated production. This was the need for the interchangeability of parts and the complete uniformity in other respects of all units of a given type of equipment. One or two illustrations, from the perspective of the production engineer, will help to explain apparently unwarranted production delays in the case of items widely supposed to be easy of manufacture. The familiar Springfield rifle, model 1903—of which nearly a million and a half were produced for World War II—was made up of ninety-three different parts. Production of these parts, each of which had to be machined to perfection, required 103 different dies, 463 different jigs and fixtures, 506 different special cutting tools, 1,320 working gages, and 1,339 different inspection gages.[8]

The development, and preparation for mass production, of the successor to the Springfield—the more complex gas-operated, semiautomatic Garand (M1) rifle—was a most difficult undertaking. Prior to the setting up of production lines, an experienced engineering firm consulted by the Springfield Armory estimated that 20,000 hours of engineering study would be necessary to plan large-scale production and 200,000 hours of engineering and design time would be required to prepare the neces-

---

[7] Harry C. Thomson and Lida Mayo, The Ordnance Department: Procurement and Supply of Munitions, a volume in preparation for the series

UNITED STATES ARMY IN WORLD WAR II, Ch. IX, MS, OCMH.

[8] Maj Gen William H. Tschappat, CofOrd, Ordnance Procurement on M-Day, 15 Dec 37, AIC Lectures, 14:483. Lectures given at the Army Industrial College during the period 1924–41 have been bound into volumes and are on file in the library of the reconstituted Industrial College of the Armed Forces located at Fort Lesley J. McNair, Washington, D. C.

sary tool equipment.[9] Early in 1939, several years after the standardization of the M1, its production required some 1,100 separate machining operations, although new methods then in process of adoption promised to reduce this number by half.[10]

This complexity was increased manyfold for larger items of equipment. An antiaircraft gun carriage required 1,800 separate drawings; an Army tank, 2,300; and the number of drawings—including those containing specification changes—required for the production of heavy bomber planes ran into the thousands.[11] But such widespread complications were not peculiar to the manufacture of large or complex items of equipment procured by the Ordnance Department, the Signal Corps, and the Air Forces. Because of universal material shortages and higher priority for competitive items, the Quartermaster Corps and other technical services of the Army experienced production difficulties out of all proportion to the basic complexity of the items procured. A full appreciation of the technical difficulties of war production could be gained only by a detailed study of the history of each item.[12]

---

[9] Maj James L. Hatcher, Ordnance Production Difficulties and Their Solution, 20 Feb 39, AIC Lectures, 15:866 1/2.

[10] The number of separate machining operations for the major components of the M1 at this time was as follows: receiver, 104; bolt, 48; follower, 17; hammer, 13; trigger, 10; catch, 14; base, 13; gas cylinder, 34; guard, 26; housing, 37; operating rod assembly and handle, 42; slide, follower, 10. *Ibid.*, 15:868 1/2.

[11] (1) War Department Procurement Planning (Army Extension Course, Special Text 98, 1941 ed.), par. 112, ICAF Library. (2) Irving Brinton Holley, Jr., Buying Airpower, a volume in preparation for the series UNITED STATES ARMY IN WORLD WAR II, MS, OCMH.

[12] These difficulties include, among others, the whole array of problems associated with the inspection of military procurement—a function which at

---

In the face of the problems indicated thus far, as well as the administrative tasks to be described in the remainder of this volume, the production record of the United States for World War II—the fruits of its economic mobilization effort—represented a magnificent achievement. The costs of this achievement were great; how great, can never be measured or comprehended. But the basic nature of the task and its achievement is well summarized in these words written at the close of the war:

To turn potential into actual production capacity was a titanic and complicated task. It demanded policy decisions of extraordinary difficulty, and then the translation of policy into the infinite detail of execution. It touched every aspect of the complex social and economic mechanism of the Nation. It required the transfer of scientific genius from the research of peace to the development of new weapons of war. It enlisted the services, not merely of those in the prime of life, but of young and old, of women as well as men, and of even the partially crippled as well as those sound of limb. It even reached into our penal institutions, where valuable contributions were made to war supply. It entailed teaching those without mechanical experience and skill how to build tanks, airplanes, and the many other instruments of war. It compelled millions of people to move from communities in which they had long been settled to places which were crowded and uncomfortable. It asked business men to limit profits and workers to forego wage advances. In short, it involved a mass migration and a social and economic revolution of vast dimensions, much of it accomplished voluntarily under government direction, in order that our forces and those of our allies might have the superiority in weapons which is essential to victory in modern war.

---

its peak in World War II required more than thirty thousand War Department civilian personnel. The reader interested in pursuing further the whole subject of munitions manufacture will find a wealth of material in the various volumes on the technical services appearing in the series UNITED STATES ARMY IN WORLD WAR II.

As a result of this immense effort the goal of President Roosevelt, to make America the "arsenal of democracy," was fulfilled. American weapons were employed on every battlefield. American raw materials and American machinery increased the output of the factories of our allies. The headstart of the Axis was overcome, and it collapsed in defeat under our crushing material superiority.[13]

[13] Troyer S. Anderson, Munitions for the Army—A Five Year Report on the Procurement of Munitions by the War Department Under the Direction of the Under Secretary of War (9 April 1946), pp. 2–3, OCMH.

PART TWO

PREWAR PLANS AND
WARTIME ORGANIZATION

CHAPTER II

Background of Interwar Planning

Economic Mobilization in World War I

The experience of the United States in World War I was rich in object lessons for those responsible for the nation's security in future emergencies. Economic mobilization for that war was largely a story of hasty improvisation to meet unforeseen crises and fill the void left by inadequate planning and preparation. When war was declared on 6 April 1917, reserve supplies in most categories of military equipment were practically nonexistent and the Army had no clear knowledge of the character and magnitude of its wartime needs. No definite military plan was available to show the intended size and composition of the Army or the rate of its mobilization. Standardization of equipment and detailed specifications were badly lacking so that prospective manufacturers could not be informed precisely what it was that the Army wished to buy. The Army entered the war with a collection of independent supply arms and services, each with separate statutory powers to determine its requirements and to conduct procurement operations. As a result, there was only a vague knowledge of the war load to be placed upon industry, little semblance of a balanced program of requirements, and much overlapping of procurement responsibility.[1]

At the level of actual procurement operations, the various supply arms and services engaged in a competitive scramble for the products of industry, basic plant capacity, and contributory resources. This competition, augmented by the independent procurement activities of the Navy, resulted in skyrocketing prices, greatly increased procurement costs, and inordinate profits for manufacturers, middlemen, and speculators. Of even graver significance, the un-coordinated placement of contracts and scheduling of deliveries created heavy overconcentration of the war load in particular plants and areas, congestion of transportation and port facilities, and the near pa-

---

[1] For various accounts and interpretations of economic mobilization for World War I, see the following: (1) Grosvenor B. Clarkson, *Industrial America in the World War* (New York: Houghton Mifflin Company, 1923); (2) Bernard M. Baruch, *American Industry in the War* (New York: Prentice-Hall Inc., 1941); (3) William Crozier, *Ordnance and the World War* (New York: C. Scribner's Sons, 1920); (4) Thomas Goddard Frothingham, *The American Reinforcement in the World War* (Garden City, N. Y.: Doubleday, Page & Company, 1927); (5) William Franklin Willoughby, *Government Organization in War Time and After* (New York: D. Appleton & Company, 1919); (6) Harold J. Tobin and Percy W. Bidwell, *Mobilizing Civilian America* (New York: Council on Foreign Relations, 1940); (7) War Department Procurement Planning, Ch. I; (8) Lectures by Col Frank A. Scott, First Chairman, War Industries Board (1936), eleven lectures, 1925–35 (hereafter cited as Scott Lectures), ICAF Library; (9) Maj James C. Longino *et al.*, A Study of World War Procurement and Industrial Mobilization (1 June 1939), MS, ICAF Library.

ralysis of the war effort. The prevailing atmosphere is suggested by the following quotations:

Manufacturers, under a cross-fire of conflicting demands, attempted to please too many procuring agencies, at home and abroad, and became hopelessly overloaded. Promises were given which were impossible of fulfillment. Some of the prime contractors sublet the major portion of their contracts. In reality they became a secondary line of governmental procuring agencies, extending the confusion.[2]

Freight piled up at ocean terminals until freight trains had to be unloaded in fields ten to thirty miles inland.[3]

The situation got progressively worse. Finally, Senator Chamberlain of Oregon made a speech in New York in which he said the War Department supply program had fallen down. President Wilson replied angrily to that and in tactful words said Chamberlain was a liar. Senator Chamberlain made one of the most effective speeches ever heard in any Congress at a joint session of the Senate and the House of Representatives, not oratorical, mostly consisting of the reading of letters from mothers about the kinds of things going on in these camps due to the lack of all kinds of supply. It became so dramatic just in a conversational tone that you could hear people sob in the gallery. There was absolute silence when he was through with his speech. If he had cared to bring up a bill establishing a ministry of munitions in this country, it would have passed by acclamation.[4]

Much of the Army's lack of preparedness could be traced directly to niggardly appro-

priations over the years and to ill-conceived legislation which prevented effective planning and co-ordination of Army activities. For example, the National Defense Act of 1916 was passed on the eve of war for the purpose of facilitating American military preparedness. Yet it contained a provision forbidding more than half the officers of the small General Staff from being located in Washington at any one time. Thus the General Staff, which was the principal hope for directing a systematic and co-ordinated program of requirements determination, was precluded by law from mobilizing itself in time of emergency.[5]

But the military procuring agencies were not alone in their lack of preparedness. The government as a whole was unprepared for war. There were no long-range plans, carefully developed in peacetime, for the direction and co-ordination of the national productive effort in time of emergency. Hence, when the emergency arrived, the nation went through a lengthy trial-and-error process during which a pattern of wartime organization was eventually developed. The statute creating a Council of National Defense was not enacted until August 1916, and the council's executive arm—the Advisory Commission—did not hold its first meeting until the following December. One week before war was declared, the council, on recommendation of the Advisory Commission, voted to create a purchasing board to co-ordinate procurement, establish priorities, and facilitate the supply of materials and manufacturing facilities. The resulting General Munitions Board possessed only vague powers and operated chiefly through

---

[2] Maj Scott B. Ritchie, The Allocation System, 18 Feb 38, AIC Lectures, 14:812.

[3] War Department Procurement Planning, par. 5. In order to obtain unified co-ordination of transportation facilities, the government took over the operation of the railroads, effective 1 January 1918. This was followed on 1 August 1918 by government operation of telegraph, telephone, and cable facilities. James H. Bogman, Economic Planning and National Defense (Washington: Government Printing Office, 1933), p. 8.

[4] Brig Gen Hugh S. Johnson, Feasible Peacetime Approaches to Industrial Mobilization, 2 Feb 40, AIC Lectures, 16:392.

[5] See Clarkson, Industrial America in the World War, pp. 30–31. Congress feared that officers would be located in Washington for personal and social reasons rather than for the good of the service.

a proliferation of new committees, many of which duplicated the established committees of the Advisory Commission. Recognizing the need for an agency with centralized power and responsibility the council voted on 8 July 1917 to replace the General Munitions Board with the War Industries Board. The governing body of the War Industries Board was a seven-man group in contrast to the twenty-two members, representing various agencies and interests, of the General Munitions Board. But the new War Industries Board chairman lacked final authority and the board as a whole had no greater statutory power than its predecessor. For several months, after the breakdown of the first chairman and the resignation of the second, the War Industries Board was without a leader. Finally, on 4 March 1918, President Woodrow Wilson offered to Bernard M. Baruch the chairmanship of the board, with the power of ultimate decision in all matters except price control. Mr. Baruch accepted and two months later the Overman Act supplied the statutory basis for a wide concentration of power in the board. Thereafter, with steadily increasing powers and accumulating experience, the War Industries Board became an effective instrument of central mobilization control.[6]

In addition to their organizational difficulties the central mobilization control agencies were faced with seriously inadequate means for the discharge of their tasks. Prior to World War I relatively little systematic effort had been made by the government to accumulate detailed information on the existence, location, and capacity of the nation's industrial establishments:

A need . . . apparent from the first that became more vital every day and that was the cause of great delay and confusion is embodied in the word STATISTICS. A hundred times a day information was necessary that no one could produce quickly. Such questions as: How many looms are there in the United States that can produce heavy duck? How many spindles can make the necessary yarn? Perhaps the trade association had to be requested to procure the answer. Perhaps there was no trade association. . . .[7]

Only toward the end of the war did the United States—under the broad direction of the War Industries Board—succeed in establishing the information, organizations, policies, and procedures necessary to an orderly pattern of economic mobilization. The unexpected announcement of the armistice in November 1918 saw American troops in France largely equipped and supported by the Allies.[8]

It is understandable, therefore, that a widely held impression of America's performance in World War I is the one conveyed by the comments of England's wartime premier, David Lloyd George:

It is one of the inexplicable paradoxes of history, that the greatest machine-producing nation on earth failed to turn out the mecha-

---

[6] Clarkson, *Industrial America in the World War,* and Baruch, *American Industry in the War,* both contain a wealth of information on the World War I economic mobilization process.

[7] Brig Gen Seth Williams, The Quartermaster, U.S. Marine Corps, Thoughts on Industrial Mobilization Based on My Experience With the War Industries Board During 1917–1918, 25 Mar 38, AIC Lectures, 14: 919. The dearth of industrial statistics has been cited many times as typical of the difficulties faced by administrators in World War I. For example, Maj Ritchie, AIC Lectures, 14: 812½.

[8] See testimony of SW Henry L. Stimson, April 1941, Special S. Com. Investigating the National Defense Program, 77th Cong., 1st Sess., Hearings on S. Res. 71, *Investigation of the National Defense Program,* 1:11–14. These hearings, which extended from 1 March 1941 through 11 June 1948, will hereafter be cited as Truman Committee, *Hearings.* The successive chairmen of this Committee were Harry S. Truman, James M. Mead, and Owen Brewster.

nism of war after 18 months of sweating and toiling and hustling. . . . There were no braver or more fearless men in any Army, but the organization at home and behind the lines was not worthy of the reputation which American business men have deservedly won for smartness, promptitude and efficiency.[9]

In similar vein was the statement of General John J. Pershing concerning the dire shortage of tanks in the European theater in World War I:

It seems strange that, with American genius for manufacturing from iron and steel, we should find ourselves after a year and a half of war almost completely without those mechanical contrivances which had exercised such a great influence on the western front in reducing infantry losses.[10]

In spite of these shortcomings, when viewed in a larger perspective, America's industrial performance for World War I was ultimately successful. By virtue of improvisation, sacrifice, and the national will to victory, the industrial effort of the United States by the end of the war had reached prodigious proportions and was a decisive factor in attaining victory when it came. The capitulation of the Central Powers in World War I, like that of Japan in World War II, was far ahead of schedule in the Allied timetable. The formal inter-Allied decision had been to prepare for a major military effort in 1919 and 1920.[11] By the end of 1918 the United States was ready to pour out a torrent of supplies and equipment which would soon overwhelm the enemy. The following statement by the first chairman of the War Industries Board indicates the situation at the time of the armistice:

The big production, of course, was coming in 1919. . . . The guns that we produced in the winter of 1918, and would have been issued in 1919, fought for us even though they never fired a powder charge other than for experimentation and test. The Germans knew, probably almost as accurately as we ourselves did, the number of guns we had in preparation, and knew they had to meet not only the three thousand guns we had over there at that time, but also the three thousand additional guns coming over the next year.[12]

Similar testimony was given by Bernard Baruch:

When fighting ceased, war production in the United States was reaching its peak. Every unit of the vast machinery was keyed up to high speed. There is no doubt but that knowledge of this fact contributed materially to Germany's sudden realization of the hopelessness of her position.[13]

The classic tribute to America's industrial mobilization achievement in World War I is the eloquently exaggerated but frequently cited statement of the German Chief of Staff, Field Marshal Paul von Hindenburg:

Her brilliant, if pitiless, war industry had entered the service of patriotism and had not failed it. Under the compulsion of military necessity a ruthless autocracy was at work and rightly, even in this land at the portals of which the Statue of Liberty flashes its blinding light across the seas. *They understood war.*[14]

---

[9] *War Memoirs of David Lloyd George* (London: Odhams Press, Ltd., 1942), II, 1831, 1833.

[10] Commission Appointed Under the Authority of Public Resolution No. 98, 71st Cong., 2d Sess., Hearings on H. J. Res. 251, *War Policies Commission* (hereafter cited as *War Policies Commission Hearings, 1931*), p. 305.

[11] War Department Procurement Planning, par. 18.

[12] AIC Lecture, Col Scott, 10 Dec 25, title: Artillery Procurement in 1917, p. 10, in Scott Lectures.

[13] Ltr, Bernard Baruch, Chmn War Industries Board, to Hon. Woodrow Wilson, President of the United States, 24 Dec 19, reproduced in Baruch, *American Industry in the War*, pp. 6–7.

[14] (1) Baruch, *American Industry in the War*, p. 377. (2) Clarkson, *Industrial America in the World War*, Title Page.

Whatever the successes and failures of America's industrial performance in World War I, it was clear that many of the problems on the production front which arose to plague the Army and the nation as a whole were inherent in the nature of sudden, large-scale economic mobilization. The number one lesson brought home for the first time by World War I was the importance of the matériel side of modern war and the inevitable time lag between the mobilization of troops and the mobilization of their all-important supporting equipment and supplies. No longer could the United States rely upon the affirmation of William Jennings Bryan that in a national crisis "a million men would spring to arms overnight." The fighting of a major war under twentieth century conditions required elaborate plans for the industrial mobilization of the entire nation and, when war actually arrived, the subjection of the entire economy to a regime of extensive controls. More than this it required an indispensable period of time, reckoned not in hours or months but in years, before the nation's economic potential could be successfully harnessed and converted to producing munitions on the scale required.

Planning Responsibility Under the National Defense Act

The Office of the Assistant Secretary of War

With these lessons fresh in mind Congress took steps to provide for a similar emergency in the future. On 4 June 1920, the National Defense Act of 1920 was approved, and industrial preparedness was made the responsibility of the Assistant Secretary of War. Under the terms of the new act, the Assistant Secretary was made responsible not only for War Department procurement to meet its own needs in peace and war, but for peacetime industrial mobilization planning for the entire nation:

. . . the Assistant Secretary of War . . . shall be charged with supervision of the procurement of all military supplies and other business of the War Department pertaining thereto and the assurance of adequate provision for the mobilization of matériel and industrial organizations essential to wartime needs.[15]

Discharge of these two responsibilities became the principal occupation of the Assistant Secretary of War for the next twenty years. In the year after the passage of the National Defense Act of 1920, the Assistant Secretary utilized the War Department General Staff in carrying out his planning responsibilities. In the fall of 1921, after a change of administration and the clarification of certain jurisdictional problems, the Office of the Assistant Secretary of War (OASW) was reorganized.[16] At that time

---

[15] 41 *Stat.* 764, 4 Jun 20, National Defense Act of 1920, Sec. 5a. The 1920 act was passed in the form of a comprehensive series of amendments to the National Defense Act of 1916; for all practical purposes the 1920 legislation was an entirely new act. The circumstances surrounding the adoption of Section 5a have been recounted by Maj. Gen. Charles McK. Saltzman, in Reminiscences of the Battle of Washington, 26 Nov 35, AIC Lectures, 12:173.

[16] OASW Memo Order 1, 25 Oct 21. The jurisdictional problems referred to grew out of an apparent overlapping of the responsibilities of the Assistant Secretary and those of the General Staff. The resolution of this conflict was made by a board of officers headed by Maj. Gen. James G. Harbord, then the Deputy Chief of Staff. The decision of the Harbord Board was formally incorporated in War Department general orders and Army regulations. (1) WD GO 41, 16 Aug 21. (2) AR 10–15, 25 Nov 21. See also Ray S. Cline, *Washington Command Post: The Operations Division*, UNITED STATES ARMY IN WORLD WAR II (Washington: 1951), pp. 20–21.

the Procurement Division, OASW, was created to handle all the procurement and economic mobilization activities assigned by
statute to the Assistant Secretary. The
Procurement Division consisted of two
branches—a Current Procurement Branch
responsible for supervision of all peacetime
procurement operations of the War Department's several supply arms and services, and
a Planning Branch to handle all planning
activities. The Planning Branch became the
principal arm of the Assistant Secretary in
carrying out his mandate under the National
Defense Act.[17]

The Planning Branch began its life with
a nucleus of four officers whose initial assignment was "to start something to enable
the Assistant Secretary to carry out the provisions of Section 5a of the National Defense
Act." [18] During its twenty years of existence
it grew to a large organization and became
the focal point of the nation's peacetime
efforts to prepare for the effective harnessing of national resources in time of war. The
creation of the Army and Navy Munitions
Board (ANMB), the Army Industrial College (AIC), and the planning sections of the
supply arms and services, the formulation of
the basic pattern of procurement planning,
and the development of the Industrial Mobilization Plan (IMP) all resulted from the

efforts of the Planning Branch, OASW. In
time of war the Planning Branch was to be
merged with Current Procurement for the
execution of the manifold tasks of a wartime armament program. The life of the
Planning Branch came to an end on 14
February 1942 with its replacement by the
Resources Branch, Office of the Under
Secretary of War (OUSW).[19] Less than
one month later the bulk of the Office of the
Under Secretary of War, including the
former Planning Branch, was absorbed by
the Army's newly created Army Service
Forces (ASF) under Lt. Gen. Brehon B.
Somervell.[20]

The Army and Navy Munitions Board

During the early 1920's, largely through
the efforts of OASW, two other organizations were created to assist in preparing the
nation for eventual economic mobilization.
These were the Army and Navy Munitions
Board and the Army Industrial College.
The establishment of ANMB recognized the
clear need for joint planning by the Army
and Navy, who would become the principal, as well as rival, claimants upon the

---

[17] The War Department's planning activities between World War I and II have been described in
considerable detail in the following monographs:
(1) Harold W. Thatcher, Planning for Industrial
Mobilization, 1920–1940 (QMC Historical Study,
August 1943); (2) Thomas M. Pitkin and Herbert
R. Rifkind, Procurement Planning in the Quartermaster Corps, 1920–1940 (QMC Historical
Study 1, March 1943); (3) Army Industrial College R56, Plans for Industrial Mobilization, 1920–
1939 (November 1945). This valuable study, prepared by Dr. Harry B. Yoshpe and filed in ICAF
Library, is reproduced as Exhibit 2675 in Truman
Committee, *Hearings*, 42:25985–26035.

[18] Gen Saltzman, AIC Lectures, 12: 177½.

[19] The Assistant Secretary of War had become the
Under Secretary of War on 16 December 1940.

[20] M. Mildred Mohler, Administrative Log of the
Production Division, Headquarters, ASF, and Its
Antecedent Agencies, 1939–1945 (1946), p. 22,
OCMH. Excellent summaries of the organization
and work of the Planning Branch during its heyday
are to be found in the AIC lectures by the successive
directors. For example, see: (1) Col Charles T.
Harris, Jr., The Planning Branch and Its Problems,
6 Dec 37, AIC Lectures, 14: 339; (2) Col Harry
K. Rutherford, The Planning Branch, OASW, 6 Jan
40, AIC Lectures, 16: 292.

The Army Service Forces was originally designated as the Services of Supply. On 12 March 1943,
by War Department General Order 14, the Services
of Supply was redesignated as the ASF. In the interest of simplicity the ASF designation is used
throughout the text of the current volume.

economy in time of war. Although the National Defense Act of 1920 had given the Assistant Secretary of War the responsibility for nationwide economic mobilization planning, it soon became evident that effective and authoritative planning would require the active participation of the Navy. In order to provide a balanced military program to meet an emergency, the armed services would have to adopt co-ordinated strategic plans and make them the basis of joint plans for mobilizing the nation's resources. Particularly important was the determination of combined military requirements, the translation of military priorities into industrial priorities, and the equitable apportionment of industrial capacity between the Army and Navy. Other areas calling for co-ordination were the assignment of procurement responsibility for common items required by the two services, the compilation of raw material requirements, provision for obtaining and stockpiling strategic materials, and broad issues of joint organization and operation to meet emergency and wartime conditions.

The ANMB was originally established in October 1922 at the suggestion of OASW and consisted of the Assistant Secretaries of the War and Navy Departments.[21] The work of the board was to be done by committees formed of officers on duty in the two departments. Because of lack of interest on the part of the Navy, as well as the absence of co-ordinated strategic plans, the ANMB made little headway during the 1920's and, by the end of a decade, could show relatively little in the way of accomplishment.[22] The

apparent indifference of the Navy to industrial mobilization planning reflected a fundamental difference in the situation of the two services. The Navy, as the nation's "first line of defense," was to be kept in a state of readiness in peacetime. This envisaged a relatively smaller expansion of the Navy and therefore a less difficult procurement problem upon the nation's entry into war.[23] Nevertheless, by the end of 1929 a joint strategic plan had been adopted by the two services, and in 1931 the ANMB was reorganized to carry out its various missions more effectively. At that time an Executive Committee, consisting of two officers each from the Army and Navy, was created to guide the policies and activities of the organization, subject to the approval of the two Assistant Secretaries.[24]

After its reorganization the prestige and effectiveness of the ANMB steadily increased. It assumed sponsorship of the Industrial Mobilization Plan during the 1930's and was designated therein to act as the transitional agency to provide central mobilization control from the beginning of an emergency until a civilian "superagency" for this purpose could be developed. It established lists of strategic and critical materials, made basic studies of raw material

---

[21] (1) WD GO 51, 7 Oct 22. (2) JB 346, Ser. 181, 27 Jun 22, and reference therein to prior proposal of ASW.

[22] Comdr Paul Hendren, USN, Navy Secy ANMB, Organization and Functions of the Army and Navy Munitions Board, 15 Jan 38, AIC Lectures, 14:701½.

[23] See: (1) Robert H. Connery, *The Navy and the Industrial Mobilization in World War II* (Princeton: Princeton University Press, 1951), pp. 44–45; (2) Col Rutherford, AIC Lectures, 16:293½; (3) Capt Ralph T. Hanson, USN, Inspector of Naval Material, The Navy Inspection System, 11 Jan 38, AIC Lectures, 14:614½.

[24] In 1935 the Executive Committee was expanded to six members. The Army members were the executive assistant to ASW; director of the Planning Branch, OASW; and a representative of the Supply Division (G–4) of the General Staff. Members of the Executive Committee were usually graduates of the Army Industrial College. See Col Francis H. Miles, Jr., Comdt AIC, Orientation Talk, 15 Sep 39, AIC Lectures, 16:5½.

requirements in time of war, and eventually succeeded in obtaining modest appropriations for importation and stockpiling. In the field of procurement planning it conducted surveys of major industrial establishments and apportioned the productive capacity of firms and industries sought by both the services.[25]

Although the Navy became increasingly active in the ANMB during the late 1930's, the major force behind the board throughout most of its existence was the Planning Branch of the Office of the Assistant Secretary of War. With no full-time personnel available for ANMB until the eve of World War II, Army officers from the Planning Branch doubled as the "Army half" of ANMB, and the structure of ANMB as well as of the Planning Branch was modeled along the lines of the War Resources Administration proposed in the Industrial Mobilization Plan. Since the Assistant Secretary of War had been made responsible for nationwide industrial mobilization planning without a corresponding grant of power to compel the collaboration of other interested agencies, it was necessary for him to rely upon persuasion. The ANMB was his solution to the problem of achieving the joint action of the Army and Navy essential to a realistic and successful program.

In retrospect it would appear that the National Defense Act of 1920 was seriously deficient in assigning to the Assistant Secretary of War the planning responsibilities for the entire nation, without commensurate powers and without so much as mention of

the Navy and other important agencies. But the sponsors of Section 5a had been convinced of two things: first, that a statutory basis was indispensable to effective, long-range planning and the receipt of necessary appropriations in peacetime; and second, that any proposed legislation on this subject would not stand a chance of passage unless it was vaguely worded and innocuously presented. Section 5a had been quietly inserted when the National Defense Act of 1916 was up for revision by Congress two years after the end of World War I.[26] The following remarks indicate the slimness of the statutory basis for industrial mobilization planning and the necessity for close Army-Navy co-operation:

. . . somebody has to make that national plan and the Assistant Secretary of War is the only man or agency that has a legal mandate to do it. But it is a logical conclusion that no such plan would be acceptable to the President and the Congress unless it were acceptable to other Government departments, to industry and to labor; in other words to the American people. Both the Army and the Navy have come to realize this and, in consequence, . . . they must make their industrial mobilization plans in collaboration.[27]

On 5 July 1939 President Franklin D. Roosevelt placed the ANMB directly under the Executive Office of the President, giving the Assistant Secretary of War direct access to the Chief Executive at a time when the incumbent Secretary was lukewarm toward extensive rearmament. This action, together with the Strategic War Materials Act of 1939 and other legislation, conferred upon ANMB additional prestige and statutory recognition which it had not formerly

---

[25] See: (1) Comdr Hendren, USN, AIC Lectures, 14:700; (2) Lt Col Charles Hines, Secy ANMB, Organization and Functions of the Army and Navy Munitions Board, 29 Mar 39, AIC Lectures, 15: 1057; (3) Comdr L. B. Scott, USN, Navy Secy ANMB, The Army and Navy Munitions Board, 8 Jan 40, AIC Lectures, 16:328.

[26] Gen Salzman, AIC Lectures, 12:176½–77½.
[27] Lt Col Francis H. Miles, Jr., Orientation Talk, 15 Sep 38, AIC Lectures, 15:4.

possessed. With the arrival of the national emergency and the adoption of the Munitions Program of 30 June 1940, the activities and importance of the ANMB were greatly increased. Although it fulfilled only in part the emergency and wartime role cast for it under the Industrial Mobilization Plan, the ANMB made substantial contributions to the rearmament program. It launched and directed the original priorities system for World War II, apportioned basic industrial capacity between the Army and Navy, cleared foreign contracts for munitions production in the United States, had an important role in breaking the machine tools bottleneck, compiled military requirements for numerous raw materials, and performed a wide array of other services. At the peak of its activity it consisted of a network of divisions, sections, and committees, many of which were staffed with full-time officers and civilian personnel. Shortly after Pearl Harbor the ANMB was reconstituted under the leadership of Ferdinand Eberstadt, who became its first civilian chairman. But after the creation of the Army Service Forces under General Somervell and Eberstadt's appointment in September 1942 as vice chairman of the War Production Board, the importance of ANMB declined and its duties for the remainder of the war were mainly of a routine nature.[28]

---

[28] (1) The history and accomplishments of ANMB from its origin to the end of 1941 are concisely summarized in the Eberstadt Report, accompanying Ltr, Eberstadt to Hon. Robert P. Patterson, Under Secy War, and Hon. James V. Forrestal, Under Secy Navy, 26 Nov 41. A photostatic copy of the report (34 pages) and its seven appendixes is on file in OCMH. (2) For an account of the post-Pearl Harbor attempts to revive ANMB, see Connery, *The Navy and the Industrial Mobilization,* Chapter VIII.

The Army Industrial College

The Army Industrial College was established in 1924 under the direct supervision of the Assistant Secretary of War. Its basic purpose was to provide instruction and the opportunity for research in broad problems of procurement and industrial mobilization for officers in the armed forces who would be called to important posts in a wartime procurement administration. As the first institution of its kind anywhere in the world, the Industrial College provided a unique opportunity for full-time study and investigation of the basic industrial, economic, political, administrative, and other aspects of the total task of harnessing national resources in modern war. Beginning with a small faculty of Army officers in the Planning Branch, OASW, and a small student body composed solely of Army officers, the Industrial College by the end of the 1930's had developed into a genuine interservice school where selected officers of the Army, Navy, and Marine Corps were assigned for a full year's study. The curriculum of the college consisted of lectures, individual and group research, seminars, and extensive problem assignments calling for written solutions. The subject matter of the courses exhibited a wide range and varied from year to year. The principal fields forming a common nucleus throughout the prewar years were the history of industrial mobilization, principles of industrial organization and operation, basic economic concepts, government and governmental controls, military requirements, national resources, major industries of the United States, foreign economies and economic warfare, and current and proposed measures in the actual procurement and industrial mobilization plans of the armed forces.[29]

An important element in the instruction was the large body of lectures given by outstanding leaders in military affairs, government, business, and such fields as labor, public relations, social psychology, and international relations. Military personnel currently engaged in every important aspect of procurement and industrial mobilization planning told successive classes of students the detailed story of the War Department's problems and planning activities. General Staff officers responsible for strategic planning and the broad determination of military requirements furnished an insight into the nature of military operations which would have to be furthered by procurement. The lectures by civilian leaders brought a wealth of direct, comprehensive, and often "inside" knowledge in the many fields which constituted the broad framework within which all industrial mobilization planning would have to be made.[30] Most of these lectures for the entire interwar period were reproduced and bound in permanent volumes, thus providing successive classes of students as well as other readers with a rich heritage of information.

In addition to conducting its regular curriculum, the Industrial College advised and collaborated with the ANMB and the Planning Branch, OASW, in the development of the Industrial Mobilization Plan. The principal annexes to the 1939 edition of IMP were said to have been based heavily upon research and draft proposals prepared by AIC faculty and students.[31] Also, in 1938 the AIC undertook the preparation of textbooks in procurement and industrial mobilization for the education of Reserve officers throughout the country under the Army extension courses distributed by The Adjutant General. By 1941 impressive texts in procurement planning and industrial mobilization had been developed and reproduced for distribution.[32] These textbooks reflected nearly two decades of experience and indicated the great amount of planning which had been done by the War Department. Unfortunately, because of their late appearance and the disruption of the extension program with the outbreak of war in 1941, the texts received relatively little use for their intended purpose.

By 30 June 1940, when large-scale rearmament was undertaken by the United States, the Army Industrial College had trained over eight hundred Regular officers in the Army, Navy, and Marine Corps. Most of the Army graduates were promptly assigned to procurement responsibilities in

[29] Maj Joseph M. Scammell, History of the Industrial College of the Armed Forces (1946), Ch. III, MS, ICAF Library.

[30] The following were among the nonmilitary lecturers during the academic year 1938–39: John M. Hancock (industrial mobilization), William S. Knudsen (automotive industry), William S. Culbertson (foreign trade), Jan Masaryk (political democracy), Mordecai Ezekiel (fiscal policy and price controls), John P. Frey and William M. Leiserson (labor), Leo M. Cherne (wartime controls), and Lothrop Stoddard (world affairs). Bernard Baruch, head of the War Industries Board in World War I, was a frequent lecturer throughout the planning period.

[31] Comdr Scott, AIC Lectures, 16:331.
[32] (1) War Department Procurement Planning. (2) Industrial Mobilization (Army Extension Course, Special Text 20, 1941 ed.), copy in ICAF Library. Shorter AEC texts on industrial mobilization planning had been developed as early as 1934 by the Planning Branch, OASW. See Industrial Mobilization (Army Extension Course, Special Text 229, 1934 and 1936 eds.), copies in ICAF Library. The AEC texts were used in training Reserve officers for assignment to procurement planning districts. See Maj Hugh C. Minton, Ex Asst Pittsburgh Ord District, The Operation of a Procurement District, 8 Jan 38, AIC Lectures, 14:553.

OASW and the various supply arms and services.[33] Shortly after the beginning of the emergency the training program was stepped up to include Reserves as well as Regulars, and by 30 June 1941 an additional 234 students had graduated. Two weeks after Pearl Harbor the college was closed down, ostensibly for the duration of the war. Early in 1944 it was reactivated to meet the heavy demand for training in contract termination and settlement procedures. After V–J Day, it returned to peacetime status and embarked upon an expanded program of instruction and research, with special emphasis on the economic mobilization experience of World War II.[34]

The Supply Arms and Services

The actual purchasing, storage, and distribution of supplies for the Army in peace and war were conducted by the several procuring arms of the War Department. These organizations had been created by statute at various dates in the nation's history to meet the changing and specialized needs of the Army. Known as supply branches throughout the 1920's, the procuring arms were redesignated in 1931 as "supply arms and services," a nomenclature retained until after Pearl Harbor.[35] On the eve of World War II there were eight supply arms and services: the Air Corps, Chemical Warfare Service, Coast Artillery Corps, Corps of Engineers, Medical Department, Ordnance Department, Quartermaster Corps, and Signal Corps. Each of these consisted of a headquarters organization in Washington and a wide array of field offices and other establishments throughout the United States. The chiefs of the supply arms and services reported to the Chief of Staff in military matters, which included the determination of military requirements, and to the Assistant Secretary of War in procurement matters. The actual placing and administration of the Army's procurement contracts for World War II was accomplished by contracting officers of the supply arms and services, for the most part in field establishments outside of Washington.

In carrying out his procurement responsibilities, the Assistant Secretary of War established broad policies to be executed by the supply arms and services. Since these agencies would be the principal users of plans for emergency procurement, the Assistant Secretary relied heavily upon them for detailed planning. A procurement planning section was established in May 1921 in each of the supply arms and from these were eventually issued the thousands of specific procurement plans which guided the placement of contracts at the beginning of World War II.

---

[33] By the end of 1939 there were 110 AIC graduates among procurement officers in the field for the Army Ordnance Department alone. See Maj Gen Charles M. Wesson, CofOrd, Ordnance Department Procurement, 15 Jan 40, AIC Lectures, 16:338a.

[34] In 1946 the college was redesignated as The Industrial College of the Armed Forces. Two years later, in keeping with the reorganization of the National Military Establishment, the college was reconstituted as a joint educational institution operating under the direction of the Joint Chiefs of Staff and was formally accorded status "on the highest level of the educational field in the National Military Establishment." Pamphlet, The Industrial College of the Armed Forces, 1924–1949 (Twenty-Fifth Anniversary, 25 February 1949), pp. 18, 21, ICAF Library.

[35] For a brief period (9 April 1942 to 15 May 1943) the procuring arms were known simply as supply services. Thereafter they were known as technical services. The short term "supply arms" will be understood hereinafter to refer to the longer "supply arms and services."

Basic Conception of the Planning
Responsibility

The planning responsibility of the Assistant Secretary of War under the National Defense Act of 1920 embraced two closely interrelated planning missions. These soon came to be distinguished as (1) procurement planning, and (2) industrial mobilization planning. Procurement planning was focused upon arrangements for the purchase and production of specific munitions required by the Army in time of war. Industrial mobilization planning was concerned with broad governmental policies designed to facilitate the transition of the economy from peace to war and to support the entire war production effort. No hard and fast line of demarcation could be drawn between the two classes of activity. In general, they coincided or overlapped in areas where special action would be needed to prevent shortages of resources from interfering with the prompt execution of procurement contracts.

For a number of reasons procurement planning was given priority of attention in the first decade of the planning period. First of all it was evident that the initial step in getting industry launched on an emergency rearmament program would be the rapid placement of procurement contracts. This could not be done without a solid foundation of procurement planning. Moreover, the Army's procurement planning activities were concerned predominantly with measures for supplying its own needs and could be undertaken immediately without the need for consultation or collaboration with other agencies. Industrial mobilization planning, on the other hand, extended to the needs of the entire economy. While the Assistant Secretary of War had the basic authority to carry out his procurement responsibilities, his statutory responsibility for industrial mobilization planning was not accompanied by any specific grant of power. Hence, in this area he would have to rely in large measure upon the more time-consuming processes of persuasion and exhortation.

Finally, it became apparent that realistic industrial mobilization planning could not proceed very far in the absence of well-developed procurement plans. The primary occasion for broad industrial or economic mobilization would be the impact of large-scale procurement in time of emergency. The major economic problems which would arise and the methods for dealing with them would depend primarily upon the character and magnitude of military requirements and the manner in which procurement contracts would be placed and administered. The supporting mobilization of raw materials, labor, power, fuel, transportation, and other resources, as well as the associated development of economic controls, would be a derivative function whose difficulties would be minimized if procurement planning was done thoroughly and well. For all these reasons, and especially since War Department requirements would represent the bulk of a national war production program, the Planning Branch devoted its initial efforts to the fundamental task of procurement planning. As a result, War Department procurement planning was well developed by the late 1920's, whereas industrial mobilization planning on a significant scale did not begin until 1930.[36]

---

[36] It should be noted that by the mid-1930's the term *"industrial* mobilization" was seen to be inadequately descriptive of the total process of harnessing the nation's resources in time of emergency or war. This process would involve the broad direction of the entire economy (for example, controls over prices, profits, exports, imports, and the like) rather than merely the industrial sector thereof. In

1938 the director of the Planning Branch, OASW, proposed the name Economic Mobilization Plan in lieu of Industrial Mobilization Plan. But the term "industrial mobilization" had become so firmly established in the written, as well as oral, usage of the military, the press, and the public that its retention was considered desirable. See: (1) War Department Procurement Planning, par. 87; (2) Thatcher, Planning for Industrial Mobilization, 1920–1940, p. 58. Since World War II "economic mobilization" has become widely accepted and the old terminology has practically disappeared.

CHAPTER III

War Department Procurement Planning

The Preparation of Specific Procurement Plans

In their procurement planning activities throughout the 1920's and 1930's, the successive Assistant Secretaries attempted as thorough a program as available funds and personnel would allow. Early in the program the procurement planning function was seen to possess two major objectives: (1) the development of specific and detailed plans for the procurement of all important items for which the War Department had procurement responsibility; (2) the formulation of general policies, procedures, and organizational plans for the effective conduct of a wartime procurement program. The specific procurement plans were developed by the several supply arms of the Army within the framework of the general procurement policies laid down by the Planning Branch. These in turn were meshed with the broad plans for nationwide industrial mobilization. All plans were, so far as possible, kept up to date and responsive to current estimates of military requirements based on the latest staff plans for troop mobilization. Finally, it was taken for granted that the actual procurement of munitions in time of war, as in peacetime, would be accomplished by the established military procuring agencies.

The task of devising realistic plans for producing vast quantities of specific muni-tions was conceived as requiring a "cradle-to-the-grave" type of planning which would—for all important items—anticipate and prepare for every step in the procurement process. Because of statutory limitations on the allowable number of planning personnel and in order to reduce to manageable proportions the burden of procurement planning upon industry as well as the government, the War Department confined its detailed planning activities to items known to present the most difficult procurement problems. In the mid-1930's the supply arms were instructed to classify all their procurement requirements into three groups:

Section I–Those items which present difficult procurement problems and require intensive formal plans.

Section II–Those items which present only minor procurement problems within the branch, and for which only informal planning is necessary.

Section III–Those items which present no procurement problems, and for which no plans are necessary.[1]

---

[1] OASW Planning Br Cir 2, the basic directive for procurement planning. The first edition of Circular 2, issued on 20 July 1933, did not contain this classification. The 10 June 1938 edition refers to the three groups as "classes," but the term "section" was used throughout most of the planning period (undoubtedly to prevent confusion with the four official "classes" of Army supply as defined by Army Regulations). See also: (1) War Department Procurement Planning, par. 138; (2) Pitkin and Rifkind, Procurement Planning in

For all Section I items formal, detailed plans had to be prepared by the supply arms, written abstracts filed with OASW, and plans kept current. Specific plans were required for Section II items, but only the dates of their completion were to be transmitted to OASW. No specific plans were required for Section III items, which consisted mainly of commercial-type items considered to be readily available.

The total number of potential items of procurement, for which the War Department was responsible, was enormous. In World War I the Army's "shopping list" had contained some 700,000 different items; this large number included not only military-type end items but specialized parts and components, as well as regular commercial items.[2] At the end of 1940 the Signal Corps Supply Catalog alone listed some 50,000 items;[3] at this time, however, only 7,400 items for the War Department as a whole were recognized for procurement planning purposes. These 7,400 items, which with their major components made up Sections I, II, and II, represented important items of supply to be issued to troops, and the General Staff required them to be kept under surveillance for procurement planning purposes. The most important group, Sec-

tion I, contained some 1,200 items, 578 of which pertained to Ordnance.[4] Many Section I items, especially for Ordnance and Chemical Warfare Service, consisted of complex components and subassemblies to be separately procured and assembled into a single end item. The following figures indicate the relationship of Section I to the total procurement planning list at the end of 1937:[5]

Supply Arm	Procurement Planning List	Section I
Total Items	7,268	1,143
Air Corps	682	107
Chemical Warfare Service	64	86
Corps of Engineers	119	58
Medical Department	3,196	21
Ordnance Department	663	575
Quartermaster Corps	1,854	262
Signal Corps	690	34

The completion of formal procurement plans was the culmination of a lengthy process consisting of many separate steps, varying in number with the type of item concerned.[6] The principal stages in the development of procurement plans were:

1. determination of the types of end items required in an emergency;

QMC, p. 62; (3) Quartermaster Corps Procurement Planning Guide, 1935 (hereafter this Guide and others prepared under the direction of The Quartermaster General are cited as QMC Planning Guide, followed by the edition date), I, 2. A complete listing and classification of all Quartermaster items from 1932 to 1939 may be found in the several editions (1932, 1935, 1939) of the QMC Planning Guide. Volume I of the 1939 edition is an excellent source of information on procurement planning procedures. All editions filed in ICAF Library.

[2] War Department Procurement Planning, par. 136.

[3] AIC Short Course 1, January–April 1941, Problem 13, p. A3–2, ICAF Library.

[4] (1) Lt Col Edward E. MacMorland, Organization and Duties of the Planning Branch, 14 Sep 40, AIC Lectures, 17:211. (2) AIC Short Course 1, January–April 1941, Problem 13, p. 10.

[5] Lt Col Oscar J. Gatchell, Chf Procurement Plans Div OASW, Procurement Planning, 29 Jan 38, AIC Lectures, 14:763.

[6] In 1938 the Ordnance Department listed thirty-three steps in the entire cycle from item development through approval of a formal procurement plan. A number of these steps in turn comprised several subordinate parts, and it was said that "the whole cycle requires years for its completion." Lt Col Edward E. MacMorland, Chf Procurement Plans Div, Planning Br OASW, Procurement Planning, 10 Dec 38, AIC Lectures, 15:590.

2. computation of quantitative requirements by time periods beginning with M Day;

3. apportionment of the total procurement load for each item among the various manufacturing and procurement districts throughout the United States;

4. selection and allocation of specific manufacturing facilities for their productive tasks;

5. preparation of these facilities for their wartime responsibilities;

6. consolidation, approval, and revision of plans.

The following pages provide a brief summary of the nature of each of these stages and an indication of War Department achievements thereunder during the two decades of the interwar period.

Determination of Required Types

The determination of the types and specifications of military equipment and supplies was a complex process involving the joint action of many arms and agencies of the War Department. In general, specific military supplies and items of equipment had their genesis in a statement of desired military characteristics, followed by a successful development program, the official adoption and "standardization" of each item, and the preparation of accurate, detailed specifications for manufacture. The using arms (Infantry, Coast Artillery Corps, Field Artillery, Armored Force, Air Corps, and others) normally originated requests for development on the basis of desired performance characteristics. It was then up to the appropriate supply arm (Quartermaster, Ordnance, Chemical Warfare, and the like) to

undertake the necessary development through the point of engineering tests.[7]

The original authorization of development programs, as well as eventual approval of items as "standard," was made by the General Staff; final specifications for manufacture required the approval of the Assistant Secretary of War. In view of the mutually determining and all-pervasive interrelationships of military tactics, strategy, research, development, and industrial mass production, it was obviously essential for all these factors to be considered more or less simultaneously. Hence, the entire process of conception, development, standardization, and eventual procurement of munitions was a joint affair escaping precise definition in terms of organizational and jurisdictional boundaries. The General Staff was the principal supervisory agency in the determination of types, but liaison committees between the using and supply arms provided the bulk of day-to-day co-ordination of activities. The role of OASW was to insure that final specifications would be available in time and be of such nature as to permit the rapid placement of contracts and the utilization of mass-production techniques.

Inasmuch as the advance preparation of adequate specifications was crucial to industrial preparedness, responsibility for this work was placed in a separate division—the Standards Division, Planning Branch, OASW. The Standards Division was a policy-making, supervisory, and reviewing

---

[7] Several of the supply arms were also using arms. For example, the combat engineers, a part of the Corps of Engineers, were the recipients of equipment which the corps had procured; Ordnance personnel used trucks procured by Ordnance; Signal Corps personnel erected communications facilities with matériel procured by the corps. See the various volumes on the technical services in the series UNITED STATES ARMY IN WORLD WAR II.

organization. It was charged with the clearance of item-types for procurement feasibility, clearance of individual specifications submitted by the supply arm, and co-ordination of War Department activities on standardization and specifications with other federal agencies and with national engineering and technical societies. In its review of individual specifications, the division paid particular attention to the possibility of simplifying production processes, maximizing the use of regular commercial specifications, reducing or eliminating the use of strategic materials, and minimizing the need for specification changes after the commencement of actual production.[8]

The achievement of complete preparedness in the field of specifications was an ideal impossible of fulfillment. The using and supply arms inevitably tended to delay submission of final specifications as long as improvements in design were possible; preparation of individual specifications was a costly process requiring highly qualified personnel, and appropriations for this purpose were perennially inadequate; moreover, until large-scale production was actually undertaken, plans at the level of the drafting table were necessarily subject to change. In order to deal with this fluid

situation, OASW required monthly progress reports from all supply services on the status of their specifications and brought pressure to bear to insure the existence of at least minimum specifications, subject to later revision, of all adopted types. Although the Army's specifications were reportedly only about 75-percent complete toward the end of the planning period, this represented a major improvement over conditions on the eve of World War I.[9]

Computation of Requirements

The determination of types of equipment and supplies, as described above, represented the qualitative aspect of Army matériel requirements. Equally essential for War Department procurement planning was the determination of the quantitative requirements, by time periods, of the various items of munitions whose actual procurement would be undertaken beginning with M Day, the day on which a general mobilization would be announced. A knowledge of quantitative requirements was prerequisite to the determination of the planned procurement load to be placed upon industry, the apportionment of this load among the several procurement districts, and the advance selection and allocation of specific firms which would undertake actual production in time of war. Furthermore, the various activities involved in the larger area of nationwide industrial mobilization—the provision of adequate supplies of raw materials, power, fuel, transportation, and the like, and the establishment of systems of program control, priorities, and allocation of

[8] (1) Lt Col John Mather, Functions of the Standards Division, Planning Branch, OASW, 17 Feb 36, AIC Lectures, 12:386. (2) Col John Mather, Chf Standards Div, Planning Br OASW, Standards Division, 16 Feb 38, AIC Lectures, 14:795. (3) Lt Col William C. Young, Chf Standards Div OASW, The Functions and Duties of the Standards Division, 8 Dec 38, AIC Lectures, 15:496. (4) OASW, Notes on Industrial Mobilization, No. 3, 15 Jan 24, Changes in Specification During Production. (5) *Ibid.*, No. 13 (Revised), October 1930, Procurement Planning, Pt. II, Specifications, and reference therein to AR 850-25. Notes on Industrial Mobilization, Nos. 1 through 13, including No. 13 (Revised), have been bound together and are on file at ICAF Library.

[9] (1) Louis Johnson, ASW, A Battle-Axe to Bottlenecks, 1 Dec 38, AIC Lectures, 15:392–93. (2) Col Young, chart "Status of Specifications, October 1, 1938," AIC Lectures, 15:505.

production among the military, industrial, and civilian-consumption sectors of the economy—all depended for their planning and execution upon a knowledge of military requirements.

In view of its implications for the basic character and strength of the Army, the determination of total *supply* requirements was the responsibility of the General Staff. The actual computation of requirements was done by the several supply arms and services, under broad Staff directives.[10] *Procurement* requirements, on the other hand, were determined under the supervision of the Assistant Secretary of War and were defined as supply requirements minus stocks or reserves on hand; for procurement planning purposes they were time phased to meet the planned expansion of the Army after M Day.[11] Intimately related to the phasing of requirements in time was the question of relative priority of the various component portions of the supply program. Such "military" priorities within the Army were determined by the General Staff; as between the Army and Navy they were determined by the Joint Army and Navy Board, commonly called the Joint Board, and were translated into industrial priorities by the ANMB.[12]

The role of the Assistant Secretary of War with respect to requirements was one of broad supervision and co-ordination to insure "procurability." In this connection two major difficulties of requirements determination, which became the subject of much controversy after the beginning of large-scale procurement for World War II, were clearly recognized during the planning period between the two world wars. These issues were (1) the problem of obtaining reasonable stability or firmness in wartime requirements estimates, and (2) the task of appraising and resolving "feasibility" limitations upon stated requirements.[13]

Long before World War II, planning personnel in OASW were aware of the unsettling effects upon procurement of frequent changes in programed requirements. By the end of the planning period it had become established doctrine in OASW to attempt to hold changes in requirements to a desirable minimum while recognizing that there was no simple or permanent solution to the problem. On the one hand, OASW was to take measures to reduce frequent changes in requirements:

Changes imposed by unforeseen developments in strategy, tactics, technique, organization, Theaters of Operation, or of designs, requirements, and specifications, play havoc with orderly procurement and are to be avoided. The properly placed representatives of the Assistant Secretary of War can inform and influence the General Staff on these matters, and, if more forceful measures become necessary, appeal can be made to the Secretary of War.

---

[10] The general methods used by the Army in determining requirements are elaborated below in Part Three.

[11] See Fig. 23, "War Department Mobilization Requirements," and Figs. 22–A and 22–B, in War Department Procurement Planning.

[12] The Joint Board was composed of the Army Chief of Staff and the Chief of Naval Operations and their principal assistants for strategic planning. The Joint Board was created in 1903 and in most of its functions was supplanted by the Joint Chiefs of Staff early in 1942. Mark Skinner Watson, *Chief of Staff: Prewar Plans and Preparations,* UNITED STATES ARMY IN WORLD WAR II (Washington: 1950), p. 79.

---

[13] The term "feasibility," as applied to requirement programs in World War II, generally referred to limitations of nationwide productive capacity upon total requirement programs or major sectors thereof, rather than the effects of specific bottlenecks upon particular items or minor segments of the total program.

Continuous changes in requirements preclude the establishment of a definite and orderly procurement program. Furthermore, once industry has been committed to a production program any major change therein is sure to cause serious difficulties and delays in the receipt, by the combat forces, of necessary supplies and equipment.[14]

On the other hand, in view of the desirability and inevitability of many changes, an important objective of procurement planning was to prepare organizations and personnel to absorb essential changes with a minimum of dislocation:

Requirements are dynamic at best, and properly so. Desirable changes must be made from time to time as impelled by new designs, new weapons, foreign developments, the probable location and nature of the war. . . . many unforeseen situations will arise which will require the modification of prepared plans to meet actualities. The anticipation of a coming need for modification and the ready solution of the problem presented at the proper time will make the greatest demand on those responsible for procurement. . . . The best preparation appears to be a thorough knowledge of past procurement efforts in war to insure that past mistakes will not be repeated and a complete understanding of the industrial and economic organization of the United States so that maximum advantage may be taken of existing facilities and national resources.[15]

The problem of broad feasibility limitations upon the total procurement effort was encountered in procurement planning as early as 1928. At this time a revised General Mobilization Plan, based on the ability to assemble manpower, was announced by the General Staff. The plan proposed to mobilize three field armies, or about 1,600,000 men, within the first sixty days and one field army every thirty days thereafter until

mobilization objectives were attained.[16] It called for a procurement objective considered impossible of attainment by the supply arms, and a successor plan in 1933 reduced the planned rate of mobilization to 1,000,000 men in the first sixty days.[17] Subsequent studies indicated that even this rate of mobilization would place insuperable demands upon available manufacturing capacity. Anticipated shortages of Quartermaster equipment were so great that it was proposed, as late as 1936, to require Army enrollees in the event of a general mobilization to bring articles of clothing and equipment with them from their homes:

One is compelled to the conclusion . . . that the mobilization regulations should be more mandatory in requiring enrollees to bring with them articles of clothing and equipment from their homes. . . . And they should be recompensed if required to use their own equipment, which is not provided in the existing Mobilization Regulations.[18]

The comments of the ANMB on the 1933 mobilization plan are also revealing:

The Army Mobilization Plan of 1933 was apparently worked out with little or no reference to the possibility of equipping the troops mobilized and trained under it. The result was that when the supply possibilities were investigated, it was found that a war reserve costing more than two billion dollars would be necessary to provide the needed equipment before

---

[14] War Department Procurement Planning, par. 140.

[15] Ibid.

[16] Pitkin and Rifkind, Procurement Planning in QMC, p. 22. Mobilization objectives varied with the kind of war effort envisaged. The General Mobilization Plan of 1926 contemplated as many as 6 to 6.5 million men. The maximum defensive effort envisaged by the 1933 plan required 4 million men. Col Gatchell, AIC Lectures, 14:757.

[17] Pitkin and Rifkind, Procurement Planning in QMC, p. 22, citing Maj Douglas C. Cordiner, Requirements and Statistics, 2 Jan 34, AIC Lectures, 10:45.

[18] Memo, Chf War Procurement Br OQMG, 23 Nov 36, quoted in Pitkin and Rifkind, Procurement Planning in QMC, p. 23.

new production, under the most favorable circumstances, could meet the requirements. . . . When the above facts came to light, the 1933 Mobilization Plan was withdrawn.[19]

The basic difficulty of the 1933 General Mobilization Plan and its predecessors, from the standpoint of supply, was that they imposed the heaviest procurement loads in the earliest months of the mobilization period before industry could adequately convert to production of munitions. In order to eliminate the resulting gaps between time-phased requirements and feasible production schedules, the General Staff developed the concept of "protective mobilization" to replace the earlier "general mobilization" planning. The Protective Mobilization Plan (PMP) was announced in a directive by the Chief of Staff on 16 December 1936 and by 1939 had become well developed.[20] The various versions of PMP contemplated immediate mobilization of a small and well-equipped defensive force (essentially the existing Regular Army and National Guard), with rates of augmentation lower than those contemplated under the earlier general mobilization plans. Broad estimates of supply requirements under PMP became available in the spring of 1939, at which time OASW ordered procurement planning throughout the War Department to be stepped up from the earlier three-year cycle to a one-year basis, with the intention of completing essential

procurement plans by 30 June 1940.[21] Thereafter, matériel requirements were based on successive revisions of the PMP and were greatly augmented by the decision to undertake large-scale rearmament in the summer of 1940.[22]

Apportionment of the Procurement Load

The translation of mobilization requirements into specific procurement plans required the geographical "apportionment" of the anticipated wartime load. For purposes of peacetime planning, as well as to provide the necessary decentralization of procurement in time of war, the War Department had divided the United States into a number of procurement districts. The number and boundaries of these districts varied from one supply arm to another; in general, they were determined by the supply arms, subject to approval by the Assistant Secretary of War, in accordance with the procurement characteristics of each supply arm and the geographical distribution of manufacturing facilities. Many of the districts were inactive, except for planning purposes, until the launching of the huge rearmament program in 1940.[23]

---

[19] Annual Report of the Executive Committee of the Army and Navy Munitions Board, 1 Nov 37.

[20] (1) Maj Robert W. Hasbrouck, GSC, The Protective Mobilization Plan, 2 Jan 40, AIC Lectures, 16:269. (2) Col MacMorland, AIC Lectures, 15: 586½. (3) For an excellent description of the Protective Mobilization Plan as it stood at the beginning of 1939, see Col John H. Hester, GSC, The Protective Mobilization Plan, 16 Jan 39, AIC Lectures, 15:764, with charts, tables, maps, and diagrams.

[21] Pitkin and Rifkind, Procurement Planning in QMC, p. 24.

[22] See below, Part Three.

[23] The districting problem was much more complicated than indicated above. Originally the OASW thought it necessary to establish War Department procurement districts to provide supervision over the districts of the several supply arms. Hence, from 1923 to 1933 there were fourteen War Department districts roughly coinciding with those of the Ordnance Department. On 9 March 1933 these were reduced to four broad War Department procurement zones. The zone system was discontinued on 8 November 1938, leaving only the districts of the individual supply arms. Thereafter control over activities in the field was left to the chiefs of the several supply arms, subject to general

It was the duty of each procurement district to seek out and survey industrial capacity for the manufacture of items for which the cognizant supply arm was responsible. Reports of preliminary surveys, showing the productive capacity for each item in each district, were transmitted to the Washington headquarters of the respective arms. These reports formed the basis of a tentative apportionment, among the several districts, of the total procurement load called for by existing estimates of requirements. In developing these apportionment plans the supply arms were instructed to distribute the load throughout the United States in such a manner as to prevent the overloading of particular areas, to assure the availability of raw materials, power, fuel, and other contributory resources, to reduce the need for new construction, transportation, and migration of labor, and to prevent other undesirable consequences of large-scale procurement. Also, strategic considerations called for the wide dispersion of the load in order to minimize enemy interference with production through sabotage, air attack, or actual capture of territory.[24]

After the tentative apportionment of the load, each district conducted a detailed survey of the plant and equipment of individual firms to determine the specific facilities necessary for and capable of producing the district load. Reports of available capacity were transmitted to service headquarters for consolidation and adjustment of the apportionment until the load was best suited to military and industrial needs. Because of the magnitude and complexity of the task,

as well as continual changes in the underlying conditions, apportionments frequently had to be modified.[25]

Allocation of Industrial Facilities

A central ingredient of procurement planning during the interwar period was the selection and "allocation" of existing manufacturing establishments for the production of specific items of procurement in time of war. The allocation system was designed to earmark and prepare specific plants for particular tasks so that a minimum of time would be lost in getting emergency production under way. In addition to saving time, the careful advance selection of qualified facilities would lead to greater output, lower prices, improved quality of production, and a more even distribution of the procurement load. All these objectives had been seriously impaired during World War I as a result of ruinous interservice competition for particular facilities and frantic placement of contracts without adequate consideration of the many factors involved.[26]

An allocation was formally defined as the assignment, to a particular procuring arm or agency, of productive capacity in a facil-

---

policies of OASW. For further information, see Pitkin and Rifkind, Procurement Planning in QMC, pp. 43–58.

[24] War Department Procurement Planning, par. 146.

[25] *Ibid.* For additional information and insight into the nature of the apportionment, consult: (1) Lt Col Ray M. Hare, Chf Facilities Div OASW, The Allocation of Industrial Capacity for Emergency Procurement, 3 Oct 40, AIC Lectures, 17: 355; (2) QMC Planning Guide, 1935, I, 1–33; (3) *Ibid.*, 1939, I, 1–34; (4) OASW, Notes on Industrial Mobilization, No. 13 (Revised), October 1930, Procurement Planning, Pt. IV, Apportionment.

[26] (1) Maj Ritchie, AIC Lectures, 14: 809. (2) AIC R56, Plans for Industrial Mobilization, 1920–1939, Allocation of Facilities, pp. 22–26. (3) OASW Planning Br Cir 1, 1939, sub: Allocation of Industrial Facilities. (4) War Department Procurement Planning, The Allocation System, pars. 158ff.

ity for purposes of procurement planning and emergency procurement. The assigning authority was either the Planning Branch, OASW, or (in the case of possible Navy interest in a facility) the Army and Navy Munitions Board. Both allocation and the subsequent assignment of tentative schedules of production were made with the agreement and cooperation of the firms involved. Request for allocation originated with the procurement districts after apportionment of the procurement load. Each district of each arm would decide, on the basis of available data from plant surveys, which of the facilities within the district were to be selected for the production of each item. Possible conflicts among the different supply arms in the same area were ironed out by the several district chiefs, with appeal to the Planning Branch, OASW. Allocation requests were sent by the districts to the Planning Branch, via the chief of the supply arm. In the absence of conflict these were typically granted, and the supply arm receiving the allocation had first call on the facilities in question.[27]

Early in the development of the allocation system it was found that two or more supply arms often had an interest in the same establishment and that joint allocations were necessary. Increasing experience with the system indicated that unconditional allocations, of either the joint or single-service variety, were too inflexible and wasteful of capacity in the case of many large, complex establishments capable of producing a wide variety of components and military end products. In order to achieve the desired results, the planners designated many of these large multi-purpose plants as "reserved facilities." Reserved facilities were of two classes: ANMB facilities, in which both the Army and Navy had an interest; and OASW facilities, which were to serve two or more supply arms of the Army. All reserved facilities were allocated by the appropriate authority on the basis of "capacity credits," which meant that a certain percentage of total plant capacity would be allocated to each of several procuring agencies. This arrangement permitted greater utilization of capacity in the face of rapidly changing requirements and would make possible central co-ordination of wartime production involving common bottlenecks and other interrelated production problems. Many facilities in the steel, aeronautical, machine tool, medical, and radio industries were classified as reserved facilities.[28]

An important feature of the allocation system was the measurement and recording of the total planned production load to be placed in time of war upon individual facilities as well as upon industry as a whole. During the early stages of the program the measurement of load was based on a firm's "normal" capacity, assuming a single-shift, eight-hour day. In 1936 the system was converted to a basis of wartime "potential" capacity.[29] Under this method a firm's potential capacity was rated at 250 points, or $2\frac{1}{2}$ times normal peacetime capacity of 100 points.[30] Each supply arm was required to

---

[27] Allocation conferred the right to contact and survey a facility and to place schedules of production within the capacity credit authorized. Other procuring arms could make surveys and place schedules if they received the permission of the arm possessing the allocation. War Department Procurement Planning, par. 187.

[28] Maj Ritchie, AIC Lectures, 14:809, and pp. 8, 12, 16, 20–23 therein.

[29] See Pitkin and Rifkind, Procurement Planning in QMC, pp. 71–72.

[30] It was assumed that under wartime conditions most plants would be operating on a three-shift basis of eight hours per shift. The first two shifts were each rated at 100 points of capacity, the third shift at 50 points.

report the planned procurement load, under currently estimated requirements, to be placed upon each of its allocated facilities. Load reports were made by item as well as by plant. This meant that a plant with several departments each capable of producing a separate item was rated as having a potential capacity of 250 points for each item, as well as 250 points for the plant as a whole. For example, a particular plant might have three departments—automotive, aircraft engine, and drop-forging—representing respectively 50, 25, and 25 percent of total plant capacity. If half the drop-forging department were slated for conversion to armor-plate production for Ordnance, this would indicate an item load of 125 points and a plant load of 31 points. If at the same time three fourths of the aircraft engine department were scheduled for the production of engines for the Air Corps, this would account for an item load of 187 points and a plant load of 47 points. The combined plant loads for the two allocations would be 78 points, leaving 172 of the total 250 points for civilian needs or additional military requirements.[31]

The measurement and recording of the planned procurement load served several purposes. First of all it was used to prevent overloading individual facilities. From the beginning of the program it was established policy, except in special circumstances, to confine plant loads to 200 points, leaving a reserve of 50 points or 50 percent of normal capacity. This policy was designed to leave productive capacity for civilian and industrial needs in time of war, to maintain an emergency reserve from which additional military requirements might be met, and to minimize conversion and reconversion problems faced by individual firms. At the same time it would force a spreading of the load to other plants, broadening the total procurement base and affording a more equitable distribution of war contracts. In addition to indicating the plant-by-plant distribution of the load, recording load figures by broad procurement zones made it possible to spot geographical overloads and to take measures to improve the geographical distribution. Finally, excessive load factors for particular items suggested the extent to which new construction and plant expansion would have to be undertaken to supplement the existing structure of American industry.[32]

In general, allocations were confined to Section I items, that is, those which required formal procurement plans because of anticipated procurement difficulties resulting from their novelty, complexity, and other reasons. They were also made for items for which combined Army and Navy requirements exceeded 50 percent of an industry's normal capacity or which contained substantial amounts of strategic or critical materials. On the other hand, a number of industry and product groups were not normally subject to allocation. The former included "nonindustrial" enterprises, such as

---

[31] For practical purposes loads were rated at the nearest multiple of 5 points; thus the above figures of 78 and 172 points would be recorded as 80 and 170. Plant capacity and load were measured in terms most appropriate to each firm. Among the different criteria were machine tools, labor, floor space, organization, man-hours, physical output, and value added by manufacture. War Department Procurement Planning, pars. 150, 153.

[32] Load records by item, plant, and geographical area were maintained by the Allocation Division of the Planning Branch, OASW. They were periodically published in the form of the Directory of Load by the Allocations Division and later by the ANMB, The Directory of Load was often referred to as the "watchdog" or "policeman" and served a valuable purpose in promoting a balanced distribution of the planned procurement load. See AIC R56, Plans for Industrial Mobilization, 1920–1939, p. 25.

TABLE 12—NUMBER OF MANUFACTURING FACILITIES ALLOCATED OR RESERVED
SUMMARY FOR SPECIFIED YEARS, 1923–1941

Military Arm or Agency	1923	1924	1926	1928	1935	1936	1938	1941
Total	5,450	13,872	20,455	15,142	12,624	10,728	9,515	12,949
Reserved Facilities—total	—	—	—	—	597	370	536	835
ANMB	—	—	—	—	355	272	423	(a)
OASW	—	—	—	—	242	98	113	(a)
Joint Allocations	62	217	460	271	185	205	154	(a)
Single Allocations—total	5,388	13,655	19,995	14,871	11,842	10,153	8,825	12,114
Navy	—	—	17	171	367	395	397	2,083
Army	5,388	13,655	19,978	14,700	11,475	9,758	8,428	10,031
Quartermaster	2,463	9,110	13,665	9,232	7,805	6,604	5,772	4,549
Ordnance	1,082	1,328	1,375	1,140	874	858	793	2,498
Air Corps	400	590	700	623	470	422	404	868
Engineers	82	993	2,134	1,738	854	721	443	499
Chemical Warfare	199	284	330	304	372	278	243	337
Signal Corps	290	426	522	467	506	350	348	676
Medical Corps	872	924	1,252	1,196	594	525	425	604

a Not available.

Source: 1941 data: ANMB, Geographical Directory of Industrial Facilities, 15 Jan 42.   1923–38 data: AIC Lectures, 14–829, Ex. "D".

transportation, public utilities, warehouses, research laboratories, jobbers, distributors, and similar groups. Among the product groups eventually listed as not subject to allocation were food, fuel, furniture, and basic raw materials. Government facilities and industrial facilities outside the continental limits of the United States were not allocated.[33]

From its inception in 1922 until its discontinuance in 1942, the allocated-facilities program was kept flexible to permit desirable changes in specific allocations as well as in general policies and procedures. At the beginning of the program the various supply

arms and services rushed to stake out claims for facilities and the total number of allocations grew rapidly, rising from nearly 5,500 in 1923 to over 20,000 in 1926. (Table 12) More facilities were allocated than could be surveyed and utilized, and individual services frequently received an allocation of a giant corporation with all its plants and subsidiaries operating in many different states. Shortly thereafter efforts were made to reduce the number of allocations to the minimum consistent with safe planning. Single-service allocations were confined to plants and divisions operating directly under a main office, and many large plants and firms were given reserved-facility status. Likewise, the geographical distribution of the national load, which had been badly

[33] OASW Planning Br Cir 1, 1939, Sec. III, p. 2, and Sec. IV, pp. 1–2.

TABLE 13—DISTRIBUTION OF ALLOCATIONS AND PLANNED PROCUREMENT LOAD: BY ARMY SUPPLY ARMS AND SERVICES, 1 JANUARY 1938

Supply Arm or Service	Allocations		Planned Procurement Load		Average Load per Allocation
	Number	Percent	Value in Millions	Percent	Approximate Value in Thousands
Army Total	9,224	100	$6,576	100	$700
Quartermaster Corps	5,901	64	1,848	28	300
Ordnance	1,024	11	2,990	46	3,000
Air Corps	517	6	732	11	1,500
Engineers	555	6	657	10	1,200
Chemical Warfare	288	3	135	2	470
Signal Corps	376	4	150	2	400
Medical Corps	563	6	65	1	120

Source: AIC Lectures, 14–835, Ex. "F".

skewed under the initial allocations, was substantially improved.[34] Greater latitude was allowed the services, especially in the case of Quartermaster Corps (QMC), to utilize small firms.[35]

The progress of the allocated-facilities program throughout most of the planning period may be inferred from allocation statistics. (*See Table 12.*) The Navy was late in coming into the program and its interests

were confined mainly to large plants, especially those in the ANMB reserved-facilities category. The Quartermaster Corps accounted for by far the greater number of Army allocations, although the Ordnance Department claimed the largest dollar value of allocated productive capacity. This is borne out by a comparison of the number and dollar value of allocations, and of the average load per allocation, for each of the Army's supply arms. (*Table 13*) Despite efforts to distribute the procurement load widely throughout the United States, the geographical distribution of allocations as late as 1938 still exhibited heavy concentrations in the northeastern part of the United States. (*Table 14*)

The more than ten thousand plants kept under allocation throughout most of the planning period represented the bulk, as well as "the cream," of American productive capacity. Planning personnel were well aware that a prolonged war effort would require the participation of many tens of

[34] Procuring services initially tended to request allocations from plants which had supplied them in World War I, resulting in an undesirable concentration of the load. Maj Ritchie, AIC Lectures, 14:809, p. 7 therein.

[35] Many small firms which had been allocated in 1923 had gone out of business by the time they could be surveyed. Hence, in 1925 OASW ruled that allocations should be limited to firms capitalized at $100,000 or more, that is, firms receiving an "A" rating in *Thomas' Register of American Manufacturers* (New York: Thomas Publishing Company). This was reduced to $50,000 in 1934 and exceptions were made even to this figure. (1) Pitkin and Rifkind, Procurement Planning in QMC, pp. 65–68. (2) Maj Ritchie, AIC Lectures, 14:809, p. 9 therein.

TABLE 14—GEOGRAPHICAL DISTRIBUTION OF PLANNED PROCUREMENT LOAD, DATA AS OF 18 FEBRUARY 1938

[Percentage Distribution of Allocations and Load by Supply Arms and Zones]

Agency	War Department Procurement Planning Zones							
	[a] Zone I (Northeast)		[b] Zone II (Central)		[c] Zone III (Southern)		[d] Zone IV (Western)	
	Allocations	Load	Allocations	Load	Allocations	Load	Allocations	Load
	Percent							
NAVY	59	([e])	25	([e])	8	([e])	8	([e])
ARMY	46	39	36	50	10	8	8	3
Quartermaster	49	40	31	46	13	12	7	2
Ordnance	40	36	46	55	7	9	7	—
Air Corps	40	34	55	49	—	—	5	17
Engineers	40	47	44	40	5	9	11	4
Signal Corps	48	59	31	35	1	1	20	5
Medical Corps	51	51	38	49	4	—	7	—
Chemical Warfare	34	25	47	66	6	9	13	—
1929 Industrial Output (Est.)	36		46		11		7	

[a] Zone I—All New England, N. Y., N. J., Del., eastern Pa., eastern Md.
[b] Zone II—Western Pa. and western Md., W. Va., Ohio, Ky., Ind., Mich., Ill., Wis., Minn., Iowa, Mo., N. & S. Dak., Nebr., Kans., Colo.
[c] Zone III—Va., N. C., S. C., Ga., Fla., Ala., Miss., Tenn., Ark., La., Tex., Okla., N. Mex.
[d] Zone IV—Ariz., Nev., Utah, Wyo., Mont., Idaho, Wash., Oreg., Calif.
[e] Not available.

Source: Adapted from AIC Lectures, 14:834, Ex. "E".

thousands of smaller firms. But they also knew that in time of sudden emergency it would be a sheer physical impossibility to place and administer direct procurement contracts with each of the quarter of a million firms comprising all of American industry. In the view of the Planning Branch the most effective role which most small plants could fill under emergency conditions would be as subcontractors and suppliers of vital materials, parts, and components to firms operating under prime contracts with the government. Many small plants in wartime would continue to supply the same firms with which they maintained subcontracting and vendor relationships in peacetime. But all plants would be faced with readjustments of varying severity in the event of all-out war.

Although the allocation plans developed in peacetime were of necessity specific, they were not intended to be used without modification in time of emergency. In view of the many inevitable changes in requirements, technology, and commitments of the allocated facilities themselves—to mention only a few factors—it was understood that the plans would rarely be utilized in the form in which they stood at any particular time. Moreover, as it became evident in the late stages of the planning period that a prolonged period of limited emergency would precede actual war, even the extent to which the principle of allocation itself would be invoked remained an open question:

> The extent to which allocations are to be applied will depend upon the nature of the emergency and other circumstances which cannot now be determined. . . . During the period of strained relations information would undoubtedly be available upon which reasonable decisions could be made as to what items should be placed in allocation and what facilities should tool up for their production. Let us remember that the system is flexible—not fixed—moving—not static— responsive to changing conditions. If it is not kept up-to-date and fully in accord with the times it will lose of course much of its value.[36]

Preparation of Facilities for War Production

The preparation of individual facilities for their wartime responsibilities was attempted in various ways, the most common being the development and adoption of an "accepted schedule of production." After the receipt of a specific allocation, procurement planning districts conducted a detailed survey of the firm's plant, equipment, management, labor force, peacetime production characteristics, and other relevant factors. In co-operation with management, the district executive and his staff prepared a proposed emergency production schedule indicating the monthly deliveries, up to twenty-four months after the initiation of production, of each item of procurement for which the firm's capacity would be utilized. Acceptance of this schedule did not commit either the firm or the government to a spe-

cific contract but indicated the firm's willingness and ability in an emergency to produce the desired items in the quantities and time period specified.[37]

The amount of planning which went into the preparation of each accepted schedule of production varied with the complexity of the item, the willingness of the firm to make the necessary production studies, the availability of qualified district planning personnel, and other factors. A number of important items, especially of ordnance matériel, were the subject of intensive study and pilot production at government arsenals. Since they would be able to supply only a small fraction of wartime requirements, the arsenals prepared specific manufacturing plans to be turned over to private firms at the time of large-scale procurement. Manufacturing plans prepared by Ordnance were of two classes: (1) Descriptions of Manufacture, containing a detailed description of the process of manufacture; and (2) Preliminary Manufacturing Data, providing lists of operations, a bill of material, and a summary of machine tool requirements. The information in Preliminary Manufacturing Data was used primarily to permit more accurate surveys of plant capacity and the determination of the suitability of particular plants for producing specific items. The more complete Descriptions of Manufacture enabled firms to prepare specific production studies applicable to their own plants. Thus, the Description of Manufacture prepared in 1938 by the Frankford Arsenal for turning out the 3-inch antiair-

---

[36] Maj Ritchie, AIC Lectures, 14:824½–25.

[37] OASW Form 102, copy reproduced in War Department Procurement Planning as Figure 32. In view of the lack of appropriations, uncertainty as to eventual wartime requirements, and many other considerations, any attempt to place binding contracts long in advance of an emergency would have been pointless as well as without legal sanction.

craft shell by the "upsetter" method contained the following: (1) general data on the arsenal's shop practice and experience; (2) general drawings of the product and its component parts; (3) shop layout; (4) list of machines required; (5) list of operations, showing tools, number of operators, rate of output, and required jigs, fixtures, and gages; (6) drawings of tools, jigs, fixtures, and gages; (7) bill of material per shell and per 100,000 shells; (8) inspection procedures for contractor and government.[38] By 30 June 1939 the Ordnance Department had prepared some 260 manufacturing plans, consisting of Descriptions of Manufacture for 122 items and Preliminary Manufacturing Data for 139 items.[39]

An essential step in preparing allocated facilities to meet their accepted schedules was the development of production studies showing in detail the manner in which firms proposed to adapt their organization and equipment to meet the specified objectives. Production studies drew heavily from manufacturing plans, supplied by the arsenals when such plans were available, but were potentially more detailed and their scope broader. Unfortunately, very few firms in peacetime had the personnel, the funds, or sufficient interest in planning for wartime production to make adequate studies and prepare the necessary detailed plans. Accordingly, production studies ranged from detailed factory plans to "mere lists of re-

quirements."[40] Nevertheless, a number of firms prepared at their own expenses remarkably detailed factory plans showing the entire manufacturing process, including planned sources of supply for materials, parts, components, tools, power, labor, and other needs. Still, it was considered by some observers that the general lack of adequate production studies even as late as 1939 posed a substantial threat to the realism of accepted schedules of production and, hence, to the ability of the Army to supply its troops in time of emergency.[41] This condition was partly alleviated early in 1939 with the passage by Congress of a statute permitting the War Department to purchase, out of its regular appropriations, production studies from private firms. For the fiscal year ending 30 June 1940, the War Department had entered into contracts with ninety facilities to supply production studies for ninety-seven items at a cost of some $498,000.[42]

Whatever the status of production studies and accepted schedules of production, it was recognized by Army procurement planning personnel that these were essentially paper plans. Although planning of this kind was indispensable to the education and preparation of American industry for rapid conversion to war production, the heart of the conversion process would be the actual task of tooling up and eliminating the many thousands of production "bugs" certain to appear in the transition from paper plans to actual mass production. For many years

---

[38] Col MacMorland, AIC Lectures, 15:591. At this time emergency requirements for the 3-inch antiaircraft shell were estimated at 648,000 per month.

[39] Annual Report of the Chief of Ordnance, 1938. For the general background and evolution of manufacturing plans, see the annual reports of the Chief of Ordnance from 1931 through 1938. All filed in OHF.

[40] Col MacMorland, AIC Lectures, 15: 591. It was estimated that certain production studies for aircraft firms would cost from $15,000 to $20,000, a considerable outlay during the 1930's.

[41] AIC R56, Plans for Industrial Mobilization, 1920–1939, pp. 28–29.

[42] (1) Annual Report of the Secretary of War to the President, 1940 (Washington: Government Printing Office, 1940), p. 6. (2) Chapter 88, Public Law 44, 26 Apr 39, 76th Cong., 1st Sess.

TABLE 15—FIRST EDUCATIONAL ORDERS PROGRAM, FISCAL YEAR 1939

Item	Quantity	Contract Amount	Contractor
Total	—	$2,000,000	
Mask, gas	4,000	192,516	Goodyear Tire & Rubber
Searchlight 60″	3	205,400	General Electric
Rifle M1 (Semi-automatic)	500	1,384,500	Winchester Arms
Forging, 75-mm. shell	25,000	20,250	American Forge
Machining, 75-mm. shell	10,000	83,880	S. A. Woods Machine
Recoil Mechanism 3″ A. A. Gun	5	110,981	R. Hoe
OASW, Reserve	—	2,473	—

Source: ICAF, RP No. 28, VI–A, Jan 47, p. 15.

the various Assistant Secretaries of War had sought to reduce the time involved in this transition by requesting appropriations and authority to place small-scale "educational orders" for selected items with qualified firms to enable them to resolve their tooling-up problems well in advance of a national crisis. But the War Department's requests were regularly turned down, partly through apathy, partly for reasons of economy, and partly because of vocal opposition by pacifist groups who objected to any kind of preparation for war.

Proposals for educational orders antedated World War I. The Naval Consulting Board, in connection with nationwide surveys in 1916 and early 1917, recommended educational orders as a measure of industrial preparedness, but Congress failed to provide the necessary funds. The delays in getting production under way after America's entry into the war were notorious. By the end of the decade following World War I most of the experience and know-how in the field of munitions production, painfully accumulated by the time of the armistice, had become dissipated. In December 1927 an educational orders bill was introduced in the House of Representatives. When it came

to a vote fifteen months later, it was overwhelmingly defeated. Similar bills introduced in 1929, 1931, and 1933 suffered the same fate. Finally, with the growing threat of war in Europe, Congress passed the first Educational Orders Act, approved 16 June 1938.[43] This act authorized the expenditure of $2,000,000 in each of the five fiscal years beginning with 1939. All educational orders under the act were to be placed with firms deemed by the Secretary of War to be competent to manufacture the particular item in time of war. The selection of items and firms was to be made by the Secretary solely on the basis of the best interests of the United States and the promotion of national defense.

To obtain the maximum benefits from available funds the War Department appointed a board of officers to appraise requirements, select items for orders, and recommend specific objectives to be achieved. Out of fifty-six critical items proposed by the supply arms, the board selected six for inclusion in the first year's program. (*Table 15*)

[43](1) 52 *Stat.* 707. (2) Industrial College of the Armed Forces R85, Plant Surveys and Educational Orders (January 1947), pp. 1–3, ICAF Library.

The review of the Army's requirements of critical items in connection with the first educational orders program revealed that at least 50 additional items were so difficult of manufacture as to warrant educational orders with some 250 plants. Accordingly, after the Munich crisis and the dismemberment of Czechoslovakia, Acting Secretary of War Louis A. Johnson recommended the appropriation of an additional $32,500,000 for this purpose. The President supported this recommendation and Congress authorized funds substantially as requested, permitting an acceleration of the program so that the bulk of the funds would be available by fiscal year 1941.[44]

The trend of world events and America's adoption of a huge rearmament program in the summer of 1940 relegated the educational orders program into the background. By 1941 many of the educational orders had been translated into quantity production orders under the rearmament program; others had been completed; and still others were lost in the administrative maze of the multi-billion-dollar contract-placement activities shortly before and after Pearl Harbor. But despite its late beginning the program provided nearly three hundred key firms with actual experience in tooling up for war production. Although educational orders were confined to facilities previously or newly allocated, they were placed after competitive bidding with those firms deemed to be most qualified. Contractors were requested to review the designs for each item, recommend appropriate changes in order to facilitate quantity production, obtain the necessary machine tools, devise jigs, dies, fixtures, and other manufacturing aids, and for all manufacturing aids to prepare complete sets of

drawings to be made available to the government for subsequent distribution to other contractors. Production methods were to be actually tested, but only enough items were to be manufactured to assure acceptability of the methods adopted. Title to all tools, equipment, and other manufacturing aids obtained under the contract was to be vested in the government. Personnel and matériel requirements, as well as unit costs under quantity production and other data, were to be estimated and reported. The educational orders program was invaluable not only in training industry but in educating and preparing Army procurement personnel at many levels in the task which they were soon to face on a large scale.[45]

The final and most effective means of preparing industry for war production was, of course, the placement of actual quantity production orders. But opportunities in this direction, until the end of the 1930's, were negligible. Of the slim appropriations available for current procurement throughout the planning period, the predominant share necessarily had to go to government arsenals in order to help keep alive the art of munitions making. The remainder, chiefly expended through contracts placed by competitive bidding, could not be directed to allocated facilities and, in any case, could not serve the purpose of educating large numbers of firms. In the fall of 1938 the influx of foreign orders and the gradual stepping up of current procurement provided

---

[44] (1) 53 *Stat.* 560, 3 Apr 39. (2) H. Doc. 105, 76th Cong., 1st Sess., 12 Jan 39.

[45] For further information on the educational orders program, see: (1) Col. Harry K. Rutherford, "Educational Orders," *Army Ordnance,* XX (November–December 1939), 2–6; (2) AIC R56, Plans for Industrial Mobilization, 1920–1939, pp. 28–37, and references cited therein; (3) ICAF R85, Plant Surveys and Educational Orders; (4) Annual reports of the Assistant Secretary of War, 1938–41, in annual reports of the Secretary of War to the President.

solid education and training for many firms. But it was only after the replacement of the era of planning by the gigantic rearmament program of 1940 that industry on a wide scale received the actual experience in munitions production which was to bring the nation to a relatively high degree of industrial preparedness by the time of Pearl Harbor.[46]

Consolidation, Approval, and Revision of Plans

The final stage in preparing formal procurement plans was the consolidation of all accepted schedules of production and other relevant information into a master plan for each Section I item of procurement. This was done by the planning office in the headquarters of each supply arm for all items for which it was responsible. The master plans varied in scope and detail in accordance with the importance and complexity of the item under consideration, the magnitude of requirements, and the stage of development reached by interwar planning activities as a whole. An indication of the contents of formal plans in the early 1930's appears in this digest of minimum information required by OASW: [47]

1. Statement showing status of specifications, with War Department index number for each specification.

2. Statement of basis for computation of requirements in sufficient detail to permit checking of branch computations.

3. Table of monthly requirements for the number of months prescribed in the current general mobilization plan.

4. Table of apportionment of the load to procurement districts.

5. Table of accepted schedules of production for all facilities in each district.

6. Statement of estimated time lag between initial production and delivery to troops.

7. Statement of additional facilities required, and whether from new construction or conversion of existing facilities.

8. Branch plans for inspection and acceptance of item, including plan for procurement of inspection gages.

9. Estimated unit cost of finished item and table of total monthly cost of procurement program for the number of months prescribed.

10. Charts indicating the following:
    a. Cumulative requirements curve;
    b. Cumulative expected production and delivery curve;
    c. Stock on hand;
    d. Stock authorized.

11. Statement of following:
    a. Weight of article;
    b. Number of articles per container or package;
    c. Weight, size, and cubical content of standard loaded container;
    d. Number and weight of loaded containers per standard railroad box car.

12. Summary of problems associated with procurement of the item, and steps to be taken to increase production in case of indicated deficits.

---

[46] See below, pages 132–33.

[47] (1) Check List–Specific Procurement Plans for Finished Articles, in OASW, Notes on Industrial Mobilization, No. 13 (Revised), October 1930, Procurement Planning, pp. 21–23. (2) For comparison of planning details required at various dates in the prewar planning period, see the excellent presentation in QMC Planning Guide, 1932; *Ibid.*, 1935, Vol. I; *Ibid.*, 1939, Vol. I. See also various editions of OASW Planning Br Cir 2 (for example, editions of 9 Nov 34, 20 Oct 36, 10 Jun 38).

Special consideration in the consolidated plans was given to the question of contributory items essential to production of the item in question. These included not only machine tools, gages, and other special equipment but important raw and semi-finished materials, components, fuel, power, and labor. Although accepted schedules of production were necessarily based on the assumption that contributory items would be made available to military contractors in time of national shortage, the availability of such items was not left to chance. Contributory requirements as indicated in individual procurement plans were consolidated into Army-wide estimates by personnel in the Commodities Division or other appropriate office of the Planning Branch, and these estimates were used in the larger program of nationwide industrial mobilization planning.[48]

All procurement plans for Section I items had to be approved by OASW and were revised at least once every three years until 1939, when the procurement planning cycle was speeded up and placed on an annual basis. For approval purposes the supply arms were required to file with the Planning Branch, OASW, abstracts of each plan containing the minimum information for formal plans as listed above. By 1934 Ordnance Department procurement planning had yielded substantial fruit in the form of completed plans submitted for OASW approval. In that year Ordnance submitted plans for fuzes, small arms ammunition, cannon, artillery carriages, artillery cartridge cases, armor plate, recoil mechanisms, loading plants, cannon forgings, artillery projectile forgings, small arms, bombs, adapter boost-

ers, and high explosives.[49] In 1936, in order to simplify administration, Ordnance divided its formal procurement plans into nine major groups: small arms and equipment, small arms ammunition, cannon, artillery carriages and equipment, fire control, automotive, inspection gages, artillery ammunition components, and loading.[50] By mid-1937 some 739 plans for major items within the above categories had been completed and were on file with OASW.[51] During the same period the Quartermaster Corps listed some 370 Section I items for which formal plans were kept on file with OASW and periodically revised.[52]

On the basis of the information received, the Planning Branch, OASW, was able to raise significant questions regarding the status of specifications, the realism of accepted schedules of production, the degree of balance achieved by each of the supply arms in developing its programs, and the adequacy of proposed steps for removing anticipated deficits as revealed by the plans. Collectively, the plans gave the Assistant Secretary a summary picture of the status of procurement planning for the War Department as a whole and furnished a valuable check upon General Staff plans for troop mobilization.

---

[48] See below, Chapter IV.

[49] Memo, Capt David N. Hauseman, OCofOrd, for Dir Planning Br OASW, 15 Oct 35, sub: Plans Submitted, OO 381/13955.

[50] Memo, Lt Col Charles A. Walker, Jr., OCofOrd, for Dir Planning Br OASW, 14 Nov 36, sub: Program on Procurement Plans, Planning Br OASW 400.12/208.15.

[51] Memo, Capt Hauseman, OCofOrd, for Dir Planning Br OASW, 16 Aug 37, sub: Program for Procurement Planning, Planning Br OASW 400.12/208.15. For a sample of Ordnance prewar planning, see the bound copy of the study, Procurement Plan for Fire Control Instruments Under the War Department Mobilization Plan, 1933, approved 4 November 1936, ICAF Library.

[52] QMC Planning Guide, 1935, I, Sec. I, 1–12.

The specific procurement plans developed by the Army during the interwar period proved to be invaluable when the crisis arrived in 1940 and the United States was suddenly compelled to launch a rearmament program of unprecedented size. On this occasion, in contrast to the confusion of World War I, the Army knew what it wanted to buy and where to obtain it. With this knowledge it was able to place contracts and get production rolling in a minimum of time. Without such knowledge and planning, the inevitable confusion attending large-scale industrial mobilization would have been magnified manyfold. These comments by a spokesman for the machine tool industry are representative of the testimony of those who were close to procurement operations at the beginning of World War II:

The army and navy knew *what* they wanted when the present emergency began. That, in the opinion of expert military men, is the outstanding difference between 1917 and today. The thousands of plants surveyed are now starting to make the products allocated to them under the plan. From the list of 20,000 plants have come many of the 30,000 manufacturers with direct defense contracts. Precious time has been saved . . . . Altogether, the efforts quietly exerted by the army and navy during the years when war seemed remote have paid dividends.[53]

General Planning for Wartime Procurement

The preparation of specific plans for the procurement of individual items of munitions, as just described, represented the core of War Department procurement planning. At the same time it was necessary for planning personnel to anticipate and provide for

---

[53] Burnham Finney (Editor, *American Machinist*), *Arsenal of Democracy* (New York: Whittlesey House, 1941), pp. 23–24.

a wide array of general problems which would inevitably arise under the changed conditions of wartime procurement. These problems included the need for removing numerous legislative and administrative barriers to efficient, large-scale procurement; obtaining many positive powers previously nonexistent; developing new contract forms, terms, and procedures which would effectively deal with difficult issues in wartime pricing and other contractual matters; reaching decisions as to when, how, and to what extent to replace competitive bidding with direct contract negotiation; planning for the heavy expansion and adaptation of organizations and personnel to meet new responsibilities; and devising procedures for the control and supervision of procurement in order to assure timely deliveries, balance among programs, and responsiveness of procurement to changing requirements. Although many of these issues ramified into the larger area of nationwide industrial mobilization planning, they arose primarily out of procurement, that is, the basic task of contract placement and administration. Limitations of time and space do not permit an extensive review of these planning efforts. The following paragraphs contain only a brief summary of problems and developments in two major areas of general procurement planning—legislation and contractual instruments.

Legislation

Few persons outside the specialized field of federal procurement law can appreciate the number, variety, and consequences of laws and regulations which have accumulated over the years to complicate the peacetime tasks of government procurement personnel. On the eve of World War II

War Department procurement procedures bore little resemblance to the direct, efficient, and relatively simple purchasing practices of private enterprise. Like barnacles on an ocean-going vessel, a superfetation of statutes, court decisions, administrative regulations, decisions of the Comptroller General, opinions of the Attorney General, and rulings of the Judge Advocate General had developed to slow down or prohibit the Army's effective purchase and procurement of the matériel which it would need in time of war.

Many of the basic statutes responsible for this condition were designed to protect the public purse; others were designed to favor special interests at the expense of the public purse; still others represented legislation enacted to meet specific problems which had long since disappeared. In any case, whatever the purposes or merits of the laws and regulations in question, they posed an impossible barrier to winning a war which depended upon prompt and efficient military procurement. During World War I many of these barriers to streamlined procurement had been relaxed, but only after costly delays; by the mid-1930's they were back approximately to their status in 1917.[54]

Moreover, in the period since World War I, Congress had enacted a whole new crop of special-purpose statutes further complicating government procurement. For example, under the terms of the Buy-American Act of 1933, purchases had to be made at higher prices and for slower deliveries from domestic firms in preference to procurement from foreign sources. In the case of strategic materials, a special provision of the Buy-American Act gave domestic producers up

to a year to develop and produce—without giving bond for delivery—the needed materials in preference to spot purchases from foreign suppliers.[55] These conditions in the face of a totally inadequate domestic supply made impossible the development of an adequate stockpile of desperately needed strategic materials before America's entry into World War II.

Laws designed to protect or improve the status of labor also interfered with efficient procurement. The Copeland Anti-Kickback Act of 1934, the Bacon-Davis Act of 1935 pertaining to construction contracts, and the Walsh-Healey Act of 1936 concerning the letting of public contracts all imposed time-consuming procedural and enforcement requirements upon the procuring agencies and their contractors which could not be tolerated in time of war.[56] Severally or individually these acts complicated the entire process of contract placement and administration—from the solicitation, obtaining, and evaluation of competitive bids through the award of contracts, the supervision of work done, and the final settlement of contracts. In time of peace many firms preferred to forego all government business rather than segregate their work forces,

[54] Maj Clarence C. Fenn, Legal Div Planning Br OASW, sub: Legal Division, 12 Dec 38, AIC Lectures, 15:595½–606.

[55] See below, page 603.

[56] For example, the Anti-Kickback Act was passed for the eminently desirable purpose of preventing the sale of jobs under government construction contracts. But it was hardly recognizable after receiving administrative treatment at the hands of the numerous departments, offices, and agencies involved. Government contractors on construction projects were debarred from making any payroll deductions whatsoever, including hospitalization, group insurance, and payments for services rendered. Then the Attorney General, by a reinterpretation of the term "public works," extended the provisions of the act to all contracts for the procurement of supplies involving governmental partial payments. The Department of Labor disagreed and the Army was in the middle. Cited from Gen Wesson, AIC Lectures, 16:386.

establish separate bookkeeping arrangements, and submit to other "red tape" required in order to participate in government contracts. In time of war, however, the output of these firms would be desperately needed regardless of their predilections, and the urgency of the war effort would not permit the continuation af the time-consuming procedures.[57]

Procedural requirements were not the only objectional features of these laws. Some of their substantive provisions were clearly undesirable in time of war or large-scale procurement. For example, the Walsh-Healey Act prohibited the employment, by government suppliers, of female labor under eighteen years of age. In the highly rural and seasonal food-canning industry, which was of vital importance to Army Quartermaster procurement, a significant portion of the regular labor supply consisted of able-bodied girls of sixteen and seventeen. Their employment in regular commercial production was permitted by the Fair Labor Standards Act, but unless the Walsh-Healey prohibition was relaxed they would not be available to government suppliers even in time of war when drastic manpower shortages would make their services indispensable. Many other industries would be similarly affected.[58]

Numerous other statutes and regulations, both federal and state, stood between the Army and efficient wartime procurement. *Revised Statute* 3648 prohibited advance payments to government contractors, but in time of war hundreds of millions of dollars in such payments would be needed to enable contractors to convert quickly to war production. The eight-hour law of 19 June 1912 carried an outright prohibition of the employment of mechanics and laborers, under government contracts or subcontracts, in excess of eight hours per day. This would clearly play havoc with emergency production. Even more devastating was the series of laws and regulations requiring formal advertising and the placement of government contracts with low bidders. In time of emergency the procuring agencies would need the power to negotiate contracts directly and to pay prices which would cover the costs of each producer. Federal laws and regulations governing the assignment of claims, the amendment of contracts, accountability for government property, patent rights and royalties, the delegation of powers, and countless other features of both governmental and private economic activity would have to be relaxed, modified, or otherwise adapted to wartime conditions. A galaxy of state laws and regulations which had a direct or indirect bearing upon military procurement would also have to be dealt with. These included sales and income tax laws and laws governing employment, the transfer of real estate, the licensing and weight limits of trucks, the transportation of explosives, the price and distribution of milk, and so on ad infinitum.

The task of keeping the entire wartime legislative picture under surveillance fell to the Legal Division of the Planning Branch, OASW. This task went beyond the development of a program for the removal of existing legislative and administrative barriers to procurement. It included the preparation of drafts of new legislation, designed to confer positive new powers upon the procuring agencies and the central mobilization control agencies to be established under the

---

[57] For an elaboration of provisions and administrative requirements of the above-mentioned laws, see Harry B. Yoshpe, Labor Problems in Quartermaster Procurement, 1939–1944 (QMC Historical Study 11, April 1945).

[58] *Ibid.*, especially p. 26, n. 51.

Industrial Mobilization Plan. Among these were the powers in the industrial field matching those of selective service in the field of manpower—requisitioning supplies, commandeering industrial plants, and adopting priorities and price controls.

Some of the results of the legislative planning activities of the War Department during the interwar period appeared in the legislative appendix to the Industrial Mobilization Plan; others were introduced and debated in Congress during this period; still others were kept within the files of the War Department to be presented upon the arrival of an emergency. A substantial portion of the program consisted of plans to negotiate the desired changes with federal department heads and others who possessed the statutory power to waive legal requirements in time of war. The fruits of these activities were to be seen in the crisis of 1940, when Congress promptly conferred the extensive new powers requested by the procuring agencies, along with freedom from many existing statutory barriers to rapid procurement. Shortly after Pearl Harbor all remaining statutory barriers to full-scale war production were swept away.[59]

Contractual Instruments

A second major area of general procurement planning involved the development of suitable contractual instruments for the efficient conduct of large-scale procurement. Experience in World War I indicated many opportunities for improvement in this area.

First of all, in 1917 each of the six existing supply branches had devised or adapted its own contracts, with the result that War Department contracts had been let on some four hundred different forms. The multiplicity of forms and terms had led to confusion and difficulties of administration, variations in policy between the different procuring agencies, and uncertainties of interpretation by the Attorney General and the courts. Secondly, the use of fixed-price contracts had been hampered by the lack of provision for price escalation or variation to meet unpredictable changes in the costs of materials and labor. This had resulted in the extensive use of the inefficient cost-plus-a-percentage-of-cost (CPPC) type of contract. A third major difficulty was the absence of termination clauses in contracts, giving rise to numerous legal and other difficulties in the settlement of contracts when mass terminations took place after the armistice. Finally, the widespread signing of contracts by deputies of regular contracting officers, followed by a ruling of the Comptroller of the Treasury that contracts so signed were nonenforceable against the United States, resulted in great confusion. Of some twenty-seven thousand War Department contracts in existence at the time of the armistice, four thousand were said to have been "proxy signed." A special act of Congress was required to permit payment of the contractors.[60]

In 1922 a permanent War Contract Board was appointed within the War Department to make a continuous study of all phases of contracting and to devise suitable terms and forms. The board was composed of officers in the Planning Branch, OASW, and the several supply arms and services and

[59] For additional material on prewar legislative planning, see: (1) Maj Clarence C. Fenn, Legal Division–Planning Branch, 21 Feb 38, AIC Lectures, 14:848; (2) Maj Fenn, AIC Lectures, 15:594; (3) Gen Wesson, AIC Lectures, 16:381, especially pp. 385ff.; (4) Lt Col Robert H. Young, Patents in Relation to Procurement of Munitions and Matériel, 20 Nov 37, AIC Lectures, 14:278.

[60] OASW Planning Br Rpt, General Procurement Planning Conference, 1–2 December 1938, Incl 5, p. 41, ICAF Library.

was assisted by a special committee from the office of the Judge Advocate General. By the end of 1938 many of the contractual problems of the kind experienced in World War I had been resolved by the adoption of suitable measures. Four basic contract forms had been designed to meet most contractual situations; [61] termination clauses had been developed; the "proxy-signing" difficulty overcome; and a number of the problems which would be encountered in the administration of price-adjustment clauses had been revealed.[62]

A brief view of the nature and purposes of the several contract forms developed during the planning period affords a basis for comparison with those which were actually used in World War II. The War Department planned to use fixed-price contracts to the largest practicable extent, for the reason that this would place responsibility squarely on the contractor for holding costs to a minimum. It was recognized that contractors would exert a greater effort to keep costs low when their own money was at stake; also, the use of fixed-price contracts would keep administrative costs to a minimum, making unnecessary the employment of an army of government auditors at contractors' plants throughout the nation.

Nevertheless, the planners knew that the use of some kind of cost-reimbursing contract would be essential for novel and complex projects or items which could not be fairly priced in advance of contract performance. Two forms were developed to fill this need: the "evaluated-fee" contract for construction projects and the "adjusted-compensation" contract for the production of supply items such as planes, tanks, motors, and ammunition. The evaluated-fee contract was similar to the cost-plus-a-fixed-fee (CPFF) construction contract of World War II, except that the fee was variable, depending on the quality of the contractor's actual performance. The maximum fee was a percentage of estimated cost almost identical with the scale adopted for World War II; the minimum fee was about 60 percent of the maximum. (*See Table 27*, page 284.) Within this range the actual fee would be determined, upon completion of the project, by the chief of the technical service concerned. The planners anticipated that most large construction projects would be covered by the evaluated-fee contract:

The fixed price Contract for *Construction* will be used in contracting for small projects when the scope of the work is known, specifications prepared, and where there is small possibility of substantial changes in the cost of labor or material; and where under ordinary peace-time conditions bids would be invited. For the larger construction projects the use of the Evaluated Fee Construction Contract is contemplated.[63]

The adjusted-compensation contract was designed for projects of the type covered by the big Ordnance and Air Forces CPFF contracts of World War II. Under this form the contractor's basic fee was to be set at 6 percent of his investment with the added incentive of sharing in the savings or losses when actual costs were less than, or in excess of, the advance estimates. The contractor's investment was considered to include both fixed and working capital allocated to the

---

[61] These were (1) contract for supplies (fixed-price); (2) contract for construction (fixed-price); (3) evaluated-fee construction contract, with subcontract form; (4) adjusted-compensation contract.

[62] OASW Planning Br Rpt, General Procurement Planning Conference, 1–2 December 1938, Incl 5.

[63] Capt Charles E. Cheever, JAGD, Planning Br OASW, Emergency Legislation—War-time Contracts, 11 Jan 36, AIC Lectures, 12:337.

contract over the life of the contract. The proposed incentive addition to, or subtraction from, the contractor's basic fee was equal to 25 percent of the savings or losses, as indicated above, subject to a maximum addition of 100 percent of the basic fee, or a maximum subtraction equal to 50 percent of the fee. If the contractor completed his contract ahead of schedule, the effective rate of return on his investment would automatically increase, since his facilities could then be used for further contracts.

These forms and the rationale behind their use were well developed by 1935. The basic philosophy behind the adjusted-compensation contract, and the Army's prewar pricing policy in general, was that the contractor's reward should bear a definite relation to his property investment. Spokesmen for the planners defended this view against critics who felt that the contract lacked "sufficient incentive":

Why is the additional compensation for reducing actual costs below the estimated cost limited to the amount of the basic fee? The limitation on the additional compensation was to avoid a repetition of the World War experience with certain of the cost plus contracts, for example, the Liberty engine contracts, where the estimates of cost were almost double the actual costs, resulting in very large profits to the contractors as compared with their actual investments involved.[64]

As indicated hereinafter, the principle of gearing contractor rewards to the size of invested capital fell by the wayside in procurement pricing for World War II.

The twenty years of procurement planning by the War Department provided a far greater degree of industrial and military preparedness than had existed a generation earlier when the nation was suddenly drawn into World War I. Procurement planning was vital not merely as a prerequisite to broad industrial mobilization planning. Military procurement in time of war represents the very heart of the entire economic mobilization process. Without a solid foundation in procurement planning, emergency production for war could not get started. A detailed study of the planning efforts of the interwar period would uncover many inadequacies, blind alleys, and other shortcomings. Nevertheless, even a cursory review conveys some idea of the magnitude of the task involved and reveals an impressive number of achievements.

---

[64] *Ibid.*, 12:338. Captain Cheever's lecture includes illustrative figures showing in detail how estimated costs and return on fixed and working capital were to be determined.

CHAPTER IV

Industrial Mobilization Planning

Development of the Industrial Mobilization Plan

Industrial mobilization planning, as the term had come to be used by the end of the 1920's, concerned all activities which would be necessary to insure the success and minimize the burdens of a wartime procurement program. More specifically, it was designed to insure the availability of all contributory resources—raw materials, labor, power, fuel, transportation, and the like—for the large-scale production of munitions, while at the same time maintaining the nation's industrial establishment and supplying essential civilian needs. Planning of this nature envisaged widespread controls over the entire economy—controls which would vitally affect all segments of the population and raise important and delicate questions of national policy in many different areas.

In discharging his industrial mobilization planning responsibilities under the National Defense Act, the Assistant Secretary of War suffered under a number of limitations. He could not assure the preparation of adequate procurement plans by the Navy and other agencies external to the War Department, and it was not until the early 1930's that estimates of the Navy's wartime needs began to become available as a basis for industrial mobilization planning. Moreover, in time of emergency or war the actual execution of the broad plans for industrial mobilization—in contrast to the specific procurement plans—would not be the responsibility of the War Department. Throughout most of the planning period it was taken for granted that general controls over the entire economy would be exercised by one or more specially created wartime superagencies operating under civilian administrators appointed by the President. The Assistant Secretary was thus obligated to make industrial mobilization plans for someone else to carry out in time of war. The many doubts as to the nature and number of wartime superagencies, and the extent to which they would adopt the plans prepared by OASW, threw a cloud of uncertainty over the whole planning operation.

Another difficulty faced by OASW throughout much of the planning period was the prevailing climate of public indifference or actual hostility toward measures of any kind which could be described as "preparation for war." The failure of World War I to create a lasting peace, widespread discussion of the costs and causes of the war, assignment of war guilt to "munitions makers and militarists," and faith in disarmament as the only guarantee of peace were among the many conditions which characterized the aftermath of that war. Coupled with these influences were the seeming remoteness of American involvement in any future war and the general preoccupation with peacetime pursuits in the two decades of alternate high prosperity and serious depression. On the one hand it was difficult to arouse any considerable public interest in planning for a hypothetical future war; yet without such interest the appropriations and staff necessary for a thorough planning job were not forthcoming. On the other hand—especially in the early and middle 1930's—it was virtually impossible to conduct any public discussion of even minimum plans for military preparedness without generating accusations of "militarism" "war mongering," and the like. A significant section of the general public was suspicious of "war" plans, a "War" Department, and other instrumentalities with similar nomenclature which failed to distinguish between aggressive intention and defensive preparation. Yet widespread public understanding and support would be indispensable to eventual adoption and success of any plans for nationwide industrial mobilization.[1]

Nevertheless, in the decade after World War I a number of accomplishments were registered in various areas of industrial mobilization planning. By 1926 an elaborate study of the nation's power industry had been made and preliminary plans adopted for control and distribution in wartime of the electric power supply.[2] In 1927 similar accomplishment in the field of transportation was recorded.[3] But these and similar planning efforts pertained only to certain

functions of industrial mobilization. Equally important, as continually emphasized by Bernard Baruch and other expositors of World War I experience, was the need for proper *organizational* planning. This required the development of clear-cut plans for the emergency creation of central mobilization control agencies adequate to the task of effectively marshaling all the nation's resources in time of war.

By 1929 OASW felt that the time was ripe for intensified efforts in this area. In mid-1931 the Assistant Secretary of War reported:

Approximately two years ago it was appreciated that procurement planning in the Army had progressed to the point . . . where attention should be turned to the broader aspects of developing a system under which the President could efficiently control and direct American industry in a grave emergency.

With this in view, my office initiated a series of studies, conferences, and negotiations which finally resulted in the formulation of a fundamental proposal for national industrial mobilization in emergency.[4]

The result of these efforts was the Industrial Mobilization Plan of 1930, the first of four major planning documents of this name developed during the 1930's. The several industrial mobilization plans (often collectively referred to as the Industrial Mobilization Plan) were essentially the broad recommendations of the Army and Navy as to the functions and organizations essential to effective mobilization of the nation's re-

[1] Thatcher, Planning for Industrial Mobilization, 1920–1940, especially pp. 187ff. An informative résumé of the issues and influences underlying industrial mobilization planning in the interwar period may be found in Connery, *The Navy and the Industrial Mobilization,* Chapter III.

[2] OASW, Notes on Industrial Mobilization, No. 9, June 1926, Relation of Power to Procurement Planning.

[3] *Ibid.,* No. 12, July 1927, Relation of Transportation to Procurement Planning.

[4] Annual Report of the Assistant Secretary of War, Hon. Frederick H. Payne, in Annual *Report of the Secretary of War to the President, 1931* (Washington: Government Printing Office, 1931), p. 25. See also the informative 14-page summary by Maj Dwight D. Eisenhower, Brief History of Planning for Procurement and Industrial Mobilization Since the World War, 2 Oct 31, AIC Lectures, 8:15.

sources for war production. The four editions of IMP appeared in 1930, 1933, 1936, and 1939.[5]

The first edition of IMP was purely a War Department plan, prepared by the Planning Branch, OASW, although it was accepted shortly thereafter by the Navy. Meanwhile, in the summer of 1930, the 71st Congress created a temporary War Policies Commission to conduct hearings and study "policies to be pursued in the event of war." The basic purpose of the joint resolution creating the commission was "to promote peace and to equalize the burdens and to minimize the profits of war." [6] The hearings and recommendations of the commission were focused mainly on problems of price and profit control in time of war, but they brought public attention to the War Department's plans for industrial mobilization and stimulated closer co-operation of the Navy in joint planning. As a result, the Army and Navy Munitions Board was reorganized and work was begun on a revision of the 1930 plan. The 1933 edition of IMP, which represented substantial improvement over the earlier version, was in part a response to the hearings and findings of the War Policies Commission and reflected the increased activity of the ANMB.[7]

In 1934 the Senate appointed a special committee to investigate the munitions industry.[8] This committee, popularly known as the Nye Committee, held extensive hearings over a two-year period on military procurement practices, the extent of profit-making in the munitions industry, the influence of profits upon governmental and diplomatic activities, the desirability of government monopoly in the manufacture of munitions, and many related issues. During this investigation the Industrial Mobilization Plan was subjected to analysis and criticism, but the Assistant Secretary of War felt that the plan had successfully withstood the test.[9]

The findings of the Nye Committee had little effect upon the Industrial Mobilization Plan, although the ensuing 1936 edition took "into consideration" proposed legislation recommended by the committee.[10] The 1936 edition represented merely a slight modification of the 1933 plan. A number of significant changes were made by the 1939 revision, the most important concerning the organizational aspects of wartime industrial mobilization.

All four published editions of IMP were brief, highly concentrated documents approximately twenty pages in length, amplified by additional material in the several appendixes. In general, each edition was divided into two parts, one devoted to a summary of procurement planning activities, the other to proposals for broad industrial mobilization in time of war. The latter part was in turn subdivided into two sections, the first of which described briefly the control measures to be adopted in time of

---

[5] The first edition of IMP (copy available in original form in ICAF Library) is often referred to as the 1931 edition because it was first published in that year. It appears in full in *War Policies Commission Hearings, 1931,* pages 395–470. The other three editions, sponsored by the ANMB, were published by the Government Printing Office. (Hereafter all versions will be cited as *IMP,* followed by the edition date.)

[6] H. J. Res. 251, 71st Cong., 2d Sess., 27 Jun 30.

[7] *IMP, 1933,* Foreword, p. *v.*

[8] S. Res. 206, 73d Cong., 2d Sess., 12 Apr 34.

[9] (1) Annual *Report of the Secretary of War to the President, 1936* (Washington: Government Printing Office, 1936), p. 19. (2) Thatcher, Planning for Industrial Mobilization, 1920–1940, p. 213. (3) The Nye Committee's treatment of IMP and the planning activities of the War Department was, on the whole, friendly. See S. Rpt. 944, Pt. 4, 74th Cong., 2d Sess., 1 Jun 36, pp. 7–11.

[10] *IMP, 1936,* Foreword, p. *v.*

war. These included priorities, price controls, control of foreign trade, commandeering of plant facilities as a reserve measure, and the use of specially created government corporations to carry on such activities as trading in raw materials and the like. The second section described the proposed governmental organization in time of war, listing the names and functions of the several superagencies to be established. The appendixes, in turn, described in greater detail the organization and functions of each of the superagencies and included a final section on needed legislation.[11]

Despite the epithets frequently hurled at the Industrial Mobilization Plan as a "fascist blueprint for war," an "unblinking Frankenstein monster," and similar terms, those who took the trouble to look at the plan found it a mild document setting forth in a systematic and rational manner the basic requirements for effective utilization of the nation's productive resources in time of war. The plan was recommendatory only, and its application in whole or in part in time of emergency would be a matter for the President to decide.[12]

Another fundamental misconception was that the published summaries of IMP represented the Industrial Mobilization Plan in its entirety. Thus, even as late as 1946 IMP was characterized as follows:

The plan, however, scarcely merited the build-up it had been given; it was a document dealing only in generalities with the problem of governmental organization for war and it was formulated for conditions unlike those which actually arose.[13]

As indicated in the following pages the Industrial Mobilization Plan consisted not only of the published summaries and their appendixes or annexes, but of a great variety of unpublished annexes, unit mobilization plans, functional plans, studies, recommendations, and other data dealing with policies and methods as well as with governmental organization for harnessing the nation's economic resources. The comprehensive nature of IMP was recognized by students of the subject long before World War II:

Considering this document as the product of 20 years of discussion . . . an uninformed person might get the impression that nothing much had been accomplished . . . .
The thin document issued in 1939 . . . no more comprehends our entire plan for industrial mobilization than does the document drafted in Philadelphia in 1787 comprehend the entire scheme of federal government.[14]

Nevertheless, only a handful of people outside the Army and Navy ever took the time to become familiar with any but the

---

[11] The above description applies most closely to the 1933 and 1936 editions, which were quite similar in both format and substance. The 1939 edition omitted the appendixes but included similar material in the more elaborate "annexes", which were separately published and given only limited circulation. The following eight annexes eventually made their appearance, all in mimeographed form and containing, with supplementary materials, approximately the number of pages indicated: War Trade, 100; War Finance, 70; Facilities, 50; Labor, 90; Commodities, 50; Power and Fuel, 25; Transportation, 80; Price Control, 75. Copies of the annexes are in ICAF Library.

[12] This was evident in all editions but was made explicit in the foreword to the 1939 plan and was implicit throughout the body of the plan. "This plan does not propose the modification of any of our constitutional processes. Indeed the prime purpose of procurement planning and of the Industrial

Mobilization Plan is the preservation of these processes for the people of the United States." *IMP, 1939,* Foreword, p. *iv.*

[13] U.S. Bureau of the Budget, Committee of Records of War Administration, *The United States at War* (Washington: Government Printing Office, 1946), p. 23.

[14] Tobin and Bidwell, *Mobilizing Civilian America,* p. 55.

superficial aspects of the Industrial Mobilization Plan, and opinions thereof continued to be based on hearsay or, at most, on the published summaries. In testimony at one of the final hearings of the Senate's Special Committee Investigating the National Defense Program, commonly known as the Truman Committee, former Assistant Secretary of War Louis Johnson was still attempting to dispel the conception of IMP held even by those who had been active in the economic mobilization program for World War II:

> Therefore, with all kindness, I say, this sentence is unfair. . . . This statement should be made in justice to the men who signed this report and to the men who worked out the details of the 1939 program. Your first witness did not reveal that the detail annexes of the report are three to four feet thick.[15]

The summary nature of the published editions of the Industrial Mobilization Plan reflected two basic considerations—the desire to avoid needless controversy over details which were even less spectacular than the published material, and the necessity for preserving flexibility in plans subject to countless, day-to-day changes inevitable in an undertaking so wide in scope. The more important organizational and functional proposals contained in the several versions of the plans are summarized in the following sections.

The Role of Superagencies Under IMP

In the decade before the appearance of the Industrial Mobilization Plan, there had been some variation of opinion within the Army on the need for central mobilization control agencies in future emergencies. This need was taken for granted in the early 1920's when the experience of World War I was fresh in mind. Since most of the key civilians who had created and directed the superagencies in that war were still in the prime of life, it was assumed that they would be available for similar activity in the foreseeable future. Hence, the Army planners at this time felt it was unnecessary or even gratuitous to make detailed plans for wartime superagencies. In the latter half of the 1920's, the incumbent director of the Planning Branch was opposed to the creation of superagencies unless and until events in the actual course of war compelled such action. It was his belief that the Army's detailed procurement plans, including the allocation of industrial facilities, made unnecessary any outside supervisory control over industrial mobilization. This view was changed in 1929 with the appointment of Brig. Gen. George Van Horn Moseley as Executive to the Assistant Secretary of War. General Moseley was a vigorous exponent of thorough industrial mobilization planning and believed it was the duty of the Assistant Secretary to prepare in detail the operational and organizational plans of the needed superagencies. This position was supported by Bernard Baruch and other reviewers of early drafts of the Industrial Mobilization Plan. Accordingly, a major element of the several versions of IMP was the provision for central mobilization control agencies to guide and direct a nation-wide war production effort.[16]

The superagency features of IMP rested upon three basic premises: (1) The agencies would be temporary, created only in an

---

[15] Truman Committee, *Hearings,* 23 Oct 47, 42:25664.

[16] This paragraph is based on the account in Maj Eisenhower, AIC Lectures, 8:19ff. See also Thatcher, Planning for Industrial Mobilization, 1920–1940, Chs. I–V.

emergency and disbanded at the end of the war. (2) They would be created by the President under the terms of existing and supplementary legislation and would be subject to his control. (3) They would be directed, and for the most part staffed, by civilians.[17]

Many reasons were cited to support the use of temporary wartime agencies rather than the established departments of the government. The following statement made by Chief of Staff Douglas MacArthur before the War Policies Commission in 1931 summarizes the major considerations:

It is evident that the existing Cabinet departments are not adaptable to the performance of these duties.

(a) Their functions are specifically defined by law and custom and are not directly related to any of the activities which must be undertaken by the central industrial control in war. In general, they are overburdened by their normal peace-time functions.

(b) Several of the more important departments exist to serve particular classes, both in peace and war. It would be unfair to expect them to exercise emergency restrictive control over the people that they were created to serve.

(c) The changes required in our institutions to make use of the Cabinet departments as control organizations in war would be immensely greater than those necessary if a temporary organization is created especially for the emergency.

(d) The controls and functions under discussion are not and should not be exercised in peace. The emergency organization would automatically terminate after the war. If these controls were exercised by a Cabinet department, they might be continued after the end of the war, to the great detriment of the country.

(e) The greatest objection to the use of Cabinet departments for war control is the difficulty of collecting all the scattered agencies and authorities into a focus and directing them toward the accomplishment of a definite purpose.[18]

In elaborating upon the desirability of temporary war agencies, the War Trade Annex of the 1939 IMP made the following observation:

Confusion or lack of cooperation might result from a condition where one peacetime agency attempts to direct the activities of branches or departments of another equally powerful peacetime agency. War trade measures are often harsh and cause resentment in foreign relations when applied. . . . Individuals stationed in foreign countries and assigned the duty of applying harsh War Trade measures will undoubtedly become "persona non grata" before the war ends. . . . For this reason it is desirable that in the early stages of the transition period the peacetime foreign representatives of the Departments of State, Commerce, and Agriculture be relieved of responsibilities connected with the execution of war trade measures.[19]

The number of proposed superagencies and their position in the wartime governmental hierarchy varied from one edition of IMP to another. The 1930 version provided four separate superagencies to direct the following: war industries, war labor, selective service, and public relations. The directors of these agencies, together with the secretaries of the War and Navy Departments and their military chiefs of staff, would compose a wartime Advisory Council to the President. Broad decisions of wartime policy would be made by the President and his council, to be executed by the council members through their respective organizations.

---

[17] (1) *IMP, 1930* (original paging), pp. 10, 34 ff., 170. (2) *IMP, 1933,* p. 13. (3) *IMP, 1936,* pp. 13–14. (4) *IMP, 1939,* pp. 2–5.

[18] *War Policies Commission Hearings, 1931,* p. 369. Several of these points were later criticized by those who favored the use of the existing departments of the government. See Thatcher, Planning for Industrial Mobilization, 1920–1940, pp. 289–90.

[19] *IMP, 1939,* War Trade Annex, pp. 5–5½.

The 1933 edition specifically added a fifth superagency, a War Trade Administration (foreign trade), and suggested other possibilities, such as food, fuel, and transportation. A Price Control Committee and a Capital Issues Committee were shown under the heading of "independent boards and commissions." Several "national service corporations," a category which had appeared in the 1930 plan, were included as supplemental to the basic superagencies. This general arrangement, under which all the superagencies would have independent and co-ordinate status, with representatives on an Advisory Council to the President, persisted until the appearance of the 1939 edition of IMP.

Despite the co-ordinate status assigned to the several superagencies under the first three editions of IMP, the War Industries Administration had been recognized from the outset as the largest and most important agency of the new wartime organization. This agency, comparable to the powerful War Industries Board of World War I, would have the basic responsibility for harnessing the nation's resources to meet all production requirements in time of war. It would have numerous powers and functions, an elaborate organization, and wide contacts with industry, the armed forces, and other governmental agencies.[20] In the 1933 edition of IMP this superagency was described as follows:

The War Industries Administration is the industrial pivot about which war-time control turns. It is the most powerful arm of the President for converting the industries into war uses. It is the meeting point of the war machine and industry. It will clear requirements for the Government war agencies, industry, and the civilian population, allocate to the trade the output of commodities re-

quired immediately or in the future, assign priority of production and delivery to war materials, curtail nonessential production, conserve wasteful production by various restrictions, and collaborate with other governmental agencies in controlling prices.[21]

In the 1936 plan, the name of this proposed superagency was changed to War Resources Administration. Its nature and functions as described above were elaborated. Also, in recognition of the probability of a transition period of indeterminate length between peace and war, the 1936 plan gave this agency a special place in the superagency hierarchy:

When a war emergency is imminent, the establishment of the War Resources Administration should be effected by the President based upon the wartime powers of the Government and existing supporting legislation.

Other administrations provided later in this plan will require definite legislative authority for their establishment. The War Resources Administration is initially in effect a transition organization to bridge over economic control from peace to war. Pending the establishment of other superagencies, it would, insofar as it is able, perform the duties prescribed for all superagencies. Legislative authority does not now exist for some of the control measures set forth to be exercised, but the plan provides drafts for the necessary legislation.

The War Resources Administration is the pivot about which the wartime industrial control turns.[22]

By 1939, with war clouds looming on the horizon, the ANMB planners had concluded that the existing scheme for independent superagencies was altogether too loose to provide the degree of co-ordination needed in time of war. Also, it was incompatible with the successful functioning of a War Resources Administration in the discharge of its broad responsibilities. Accord-

---

[20] IMP, 1930, p. 45, and Charts 4 and 5.

[21] IMP, 1933, p. 17.
[22] IMP, 1936, p. 17.

ingly, the 1939 plan called for the establishment of the War Resources Administration
as the key superagency with supervisory
power over all other superagencies whose
principal functions were directly related to
economic mobilization:

All economic functions which must be
exercised in time of war are interrelated and
interdependent. It is therefore highly important that one emergency agency be created
to coordinate the performance of these functions and that other agencies be set up only
as the necessity arises to supplement the work
of the key agency.

It is considered highly desirable that the
key superagency for wartime industrial co-
ordination should be the War Resources Administration. In order that . . . planned
measures may anticipate the problems which
will inevitably arise to disrupt our national
war economy, the War Resources Administration in skeleton form should be set up as early
as practicable when an emergency is
envisioned.[23]

In keeping with this prescription, four
principal superagencies—War Finance,
War Trade, War Labor, and the Price Control Authority—were shown as subordinate
to the War Resources Administration in
the 1939 plan. The other two superagencies—Selective Service and Public Relations—would be independent, reporting
directly to the President. These agencies
would be less directly concerned than the
War Resources Administration with the administration of wartime industrial effort and
would deal with important matters outside
the scope of industrial mobilization. The
War Resources administrator, who would
report directly to the President, would be
assisted by an Advisory Council composed
of the heads of all superagencies, including
Selective Service and Public Relations. This
arrangement would relieve an overburdened

wartime President of the responsibility for
the regular co-ordination of economic mobilization matters:

While it has long been recognized that such
direction in time of war is a function of the
President, acting under the authority accorded him by the Constitution and by the
Congress, it is obvious that the magnitude
and emergency nature of the task require the
services of an adequate organizational set-up
to which this responsibility may be delegated.
It is contemplated that such a set-up will be
manned by qualified civilians chosen by the
President.[24]

A further important organizational proposal of the 1939 plan was the transitional
role to be played by the Army and Navy
Munitions Board. Foreseeing the possibility
of a delay in creation of the War Resources
Administration upon the arrival of an emergency, the planners proposed that the
ANMB guide and co-ordinate the industrial
mobilization effort until the establishment
of the key superagency. The relevant personnel and records of the ANMB would
then become available for assimilation into
the new agency. Regardless of the period
of time required to set up the War Resources
Administration, the ANMB would perform
the important function of transmitting to
the personnel of the newly created superagency the accumulated knowledge and
preparations of years of peacetime planning.

The 1939 plan devoted more attention
than its predecessors to the role of existing
federal agencies and departments in time of
war. By 1939 many new governmental
agencies had been created and the general
functions of the federal government had
been greatly expanded. The 1939 version
of IMP proposed that existing agencies, in
addition to performing their normal func-

---

[23] *IMP, 1939,* p. 6.

[24] *IMP, 1939,* p. 4.

tions, be utilized to "administer any assigned war missions for which they are naturally adapted." At various points the plan mentioned the prospective wartime contributions of existing agencies, specifically referring to the Departments of State, Commerce, Treasury, and Agriculture, as well as the Federal Reserve Board, the Federal Loan Agency, the U.S. Maritime Commission, the Reconstruction Finance Corporation, the Securities and Exchange Commission, and the Export-Import Bank.[25]

In one of its provisions the 1939 plan was unfortunate. This was the statement that "positions of responsibility" in the War Resources Administration should be filled by "patriotic business leaders of the Nation." This provision was designed to insure the recruitment of able men, well-known to the public, who would themselves be familiar with the resources and industries they would be directing in time of war. But the implication—which was easily and frequently drawn—that the management of the entire wartime economy would be "turned over to business interests" did not rest well with many important groups.

For various reasons, to be indicated later, the foregoing plan of organization was not, as such, adopted, either at the beginning of the national emergency in 1940 or at any other time. But the creation of the War Production Board shortly after Pearl Harbor did reflect, in many respects, the conception of the War Resources Administration set forth in the Industrial Mobilization Plan. Most of the plan's other features, both organizational and functional, were utilized in the course of the emergency, as well as after

Pearl Harbor, but without specific attribution to or necessarily resulting from the Industrial Mobilization Plan itself.

The Concept of M Day

Throughout its history prior to World War II, the United States had never subscribed to a large standing Army or large reserves of military equipment. In the event of a serious emergency the nation's defensive strength would depend upon the rapid mobilization of troops and munitions, relying heavily upon selective service and new production. The basic responsibility of military planning in peacetime was therefore conceived to be the preparation of plans to meet a *major* emergency. This would require the expansion of the Army, in the shortest possible period of time, from its peacetime skeleton status to a force of several million men. Accordingly, the bulk of military planning during the interwar period centered upon plans for a *general* mobilization.[26]

Plans for the rapid, large-scale mobilization of troops required the most careful and elaborate attention to problems of timing. Without a detailed time schedule—carefully planned in advance and providing comprehensive operations in support of a balanced program of troop induction, training, organization, movement, and progressive supply—the sudden mobilization of hundreds

---

[25] *IMP, 1939*, pp. 5, 8, 9, 10, and 11. The annexes went into greater detail; thus the Labor Annex referred to nine separate divisions and offices of the Department of Labor.

[26] (1) Testimony of Gen Douglas MacArthur, *War Policies Commission Hearings, 1931*, pp. 356ff. (2) Lt Col Marvin A. Kreidberg and 1st Lt Merton G. Henry, History of Military Mobilization in the United States Army, 1775–1945 (Department of the Army Pamphlet 20–212, June 1955), especially Chs. XII–XIII. In addition to general mobilization plans, the General Staff also prepared, in collaboration with the Navy, strategic concentration or "color" plans to meet specific types of attack.

of thousands or millions of men would result in complete chaos.[27]

The concept of M Day (Mobilization Day) was the device adopted by the General Staff in the early 1920's to permit the construction of such a time schedule. In the absence of foreknowledge of the specific calendar date in the future upon which a general mobilization would be ordered, the Staff resorted to simple algebra. The beginning date of such a mobilization was considered to be a hypothetical date in the future, which might or might not ever occur. This hypothetical date was labeled as "M Day," and related points in the schedule were identified as "M plus" or, where appropriate, "M minus" days or months.[28] For planning purposes all the manifold operations of troop induction, training, organization, and movement, the supply and distribution of matériel, and the underlying procurement and industrial mobilization efforts required for Army supply were to be co-ordinated in a master time schedule with M Day as the common denominator in time. Some such nomenclature, and the underlying concept which it represented, was indispensable to the advance planning of time-phased mobilization of troops and all their supporting equipment, facilities, and supplies.

The M-Day concept was loosely applied to procurement planning as early as 1925:

M-Day for the supply branches is the day on which they receive adequate funds to operate; M-Day for the combatant arms is the day they receive orders to mobilize. These two days should be brought as close together as possible.[29]

This statement reflected the hope of the Assistant Secretary that in a future emergency the mobilization of matériel would begin at least as soon as troop mobilization. In World War I this had not been the case; even the appropriations indispensable to wartime procurement had not become available to the Army until three months after the declaration of war.[30]

With the elaboration of planning in the late 1920's and early 1930's, the concept of M Day was utilized in many ways—often in an idealized and oversimplified fashion—especially in the field of procurement planning. Estimated supply requirements for an emergency, and in turn procurement requirements, were time phased with M Day as the point of origin. Required war reserves, to be sought in peacetime through special appropriations, were determined on the basis of estimated production deficits at various periods after M Day. Accepted schedules of production placed with allocated facilities were to be implemented by actual contracts, and to go into operation, on M Day. The announcement of M Day would be the signal for the activation of the procurement districts, the merger of the planning and current procurement organizations and activities throughout the War

[27] The extremely complex nature of the process of mass mobilization of troops and the kind of planning undertaken to support such mobilization are described in Kreidberg and Henry, History of Military Mobilization. For excellent short statements, see the following papers: (1) Col Hester, AIC Lectures, 15:764; (2) Maj Hasbrouck, AIC Lectures, 16:267.

[28] The nomenclature of M-Day chronology varied from time to time, making use of days, months, or even "mobilization periods" defined in terms of attained objectives rather than in fixed time units. Kreidberg and Henry, History of Military Mobilization, Chs. XII–XIII.

[29] Col Dwight F. Davis, ASW, . . . Principles of Industrial Preparedness, in OASW, Notes on Industrial Mobilization, No. 8, 20 May 25, p. 5.

[30] War Department Procurement Planning, par. 219.

Department, and the adoption of wartime procurement procedures and policies. Finally, M Day would call for the passage of emergency legislation and the launching of the many organizations and activities contemplated by the Industrial Mobilization Plan.[31]

The spectacular possibilities of the M-Day concept lent themselves to wide excesses of the popular imagination, especially during the 1930's when a substantial body of left-wing and pacifist opinion was opposed to any kind of preparation—at least by the United States—for war. The Industrial Mobilization Plan was violently attacked shortly after the publication of its first edition by the War Policies Commission.[32] By 1938 M Day had been widely publicized as the date marking the adoption of a complete "military dictatorship," an "iron-heeled Fascism," whose basic purpose was to "save capitalism" and the opportunities for war and postwar profits. M Day would bring the sudden end of all individual liberties, the "crushing of every democratic principle," and the denial of the right of workers to strike, to quit their jobs, to choose their occupations, and demand higher wages.[33] Two years later, when the emergency was at hand, other writers sought to reassure the public of America's state of preparedness by dramatically portraying the government's readiness to impose complete wartime controls over all facets of individual and public activity in a matter of hours after the arrival of M Day.[34] One result of these interpretations, apart from their effects upon public enthusiasm for the Industrial Mobilization Plan, was to make it appear that the substance and validity of all the Army's twenty years of planning were inextricably bound to the M-Day concept. This led to the facile inference, in a number of accounts of the subject, that inasmuch as M Day was never actually invoked the twenty years of interwar planning were worthless and therefore wasted.

Despite the wide use of the M-Day concept in the War Department's planning activities, the validity and usefulness of most of the plans did not depend upon the invocation of M Day at any particular date in the future. M Day represented a major methodological tool, but not the substance of the prewar plans. Most of the procurement and industrial mobilization plans concerned matters of function and policy which would have to be dealt with in any major

---

[31] *Ibid., passim*, especially pars. 65, 66, 72, 86, 91, 114, 122–26, 133, 158, 170, 183, 194, 218, 220, and Figs. 22–A to 27.

[32] For example: (1) Seymour Waldman, "Seven Per Cent: Hearings of the War Policies Commission," *World Tomorrow,* XIV (July 1931), 216–18; (2) Seymour Waldman, *Death and Profits: A Study of the War Policies Commission* (New York: Brewer, Warren, and Putnam, 1932).

[33] These sentiments are variously expressed in the following samples: (1) Rose M. Stein, *M-Day, the First Day of War* (New York: Harcourt, Brace and Company, Inc., 1936); (2) Harold E. Fey, "M-Day Marches On," *Christian Century,* LV (January 12, 1938), 43; (3) American League Against War and Fascism (Cleveland Chapter), Resolution on Industrial Mobilization Plan Presented at the Annual

Conference, February 28, 1937; (4) National Council for the Prevention of War, Pamphlet, Industrial Mobilization Plan as of October 1, 1936; (5) Frank B. Blumenfield, pamphlet, *A Blueprint for Fascism* (New York, February 1937). All cited in Thatcher, Planning for Industrial Mobilization, 1920–1940, pp. 213–14, 254–60.

[34] Donald M. Keyhoe, *M-Day—What Your Government Plans for You* (New York: E. P. Dutton & Co., 1940). See also: (1) "Be Ready for M-Day," *New Republic,* Vol. 100 (October 4, 1939), 229–30; (2) Leo M. Cherne, "M-Day and the Business Man," *Harper's Magazine,* Vol. 181 (July 1940), 113–35; (3) Harold J. Tobin and Percy W. Bidwell, "M-Day and the Press: Review of Mobilizing Civilian America," *Publisher's Weekly,* Vol. 137 (June 22, 1940), 2330.

war, whether this war came suddenly or after a prolonged period of transition from a peacetime situation. The M-Day aspect of the prewar plans represented the War Department's response to its gravest planning responsibility—preparation to meet a major emergency suddenly thrust upon the nation with little or no warning and requiring immediate action to get war production rolling. If actual events turned out to be more favorable, the substantive plans could be adapted to a modified time schedule or otherwise adjusted to meet existing conditions.

An examination of the Industrial Mobilization Plan in its context of general prewar planning indicates that the M-Day concept was much more important to procurement planning than to broad industrial mobilization planning. The several versions of IMP made practically no reference to M Day. Only the 1930 edition explicitly used the term in the body of the plan, and then only incidentally.[35] The activities discussed in the various editions of IMP were envisaged as taking place "in time of war," "in time of emergency," "when" or "after" a state of war or emergency was declared, and the like. Early in its development the Industrial Mobilization Plan recognized that the most urgent requirement in the event of sudden involvement in war would be the immediate placement of procurement contracts to start production going:

Provisions for procuring equipment must be detailed and exact and essential production must begin immediately upon the outbreak of war.[36]

Industrial mobilization, on the other hand, was seen as a gradual process:

The measures adopted must be such as to minimize damaging effects of sudden changes in industrial activity and to maintain an approximate equilibrium throughout the Nation. No radical changes in normal economic relationships between individuals and between an individual and the Government should be instituted. The methods and customs of peace must be employed as far as practicable, otherwise confusion and chaos will result. The attempt should be to guide and influence the operation of natural forces rather than to oppose them by arbitrary and unfair regulations.[37]

By the mid-1930's it had become clear that industrial mobilization planning should explicitly deal with the period of transition from normal peacetime operations to the full-fledged establishment of a war economy. At first this transition period was thought of as the period from the outbreak of war to the time when the wartime superagencies could be brought to the stage of full operation.[38] Later it was seen that the transition period would probably begin before the nation's actual involvement in war, thus overlapping in both directions a formal declaration of war. The 1936 edition of IMP provided for the Army and Navy Munitions Board to exercise, so far as possible, co-ordination of the industrial mobilization effort during this period of transition. The transition was defined as the period of time beginning "when a war emergency is imminent" and lasting until the "War Resources Administration is functioning."[39]

---

[35] IMP, 1930, pp. 21, 23. One or two of the annexes to the 1939 edition explicitly referred to M Day as a possible date for the initiation of certain controls.

[36] IMP, 1933, p. 1.

[37] Ibid., p. 10.

[38] Kreidberg and Henry, History of Military Mobilization, pp. 524–25, citing Memo, Com To Develop Organization for Transition Phase for Ex Com ANMB, 19 Jul 34.

[39] IMP, 1936, p. 6.

Under the 1939 version of IMP, the key War Resources Administration was to be established in skeleton form and begin operations "as early as practicable when an emergency is envisioned." Thus, the basic organizational program was not tied to the announcement of M-Day. Extensive provision for the transition problem was made in the several annexes to the 1939 edition. Six of the eight annexes recognized at least three distinct stages for which various degrees of economic control would be necessary.[40] Because of the different conditions and circumstances affecting their respective areas, the several annexes did not—and could not—exhibit uniformity in their delineation of the various stages of the transition. It was evident from the context of the annexes as well as other data in support of the prewar plans as a whole that any division of an anticipated transition period into hard and fast stages would be highly artificial. The major effort in dealing with the transition period was therefore the identification of the problems to be faced and the various danger signals indicating when appropriate controls should be applied.

The increased recognition given to the transitional aspects of economic mobilization in the latter part of the planning period was a reflection of the gradual deterioration in international relations, the rearmament of hostile nations with avowed aggressive intentions, and the abandonment by such nations of the honorable procedure of a formal declaration of war prior to military action. With the outbreak of war in

Europe in September 1939 it was evident that the United States could not much longer afford to remain in its chronic state of military unpreparedness. The fall of France at the end of May 1940 brought the crisis which resulted in the adoption of the Army's huge, across-the-board Munitions Program of 30 June 1940. In many respects this date was the equivalent of the M Day for which the Army had long planned. In other respects, however, it clearly was not. In the face of a tremendous reservoir of idle manpower and industrial capacity and a procurement program still well below the major effort contemplated in the M-Day plans, strict adherence to planned facility allocations and other proposed M-Day procedures was deemed unnecessary. The formal invocation of M Day, as well as the formal adoption of the Industrial Mobilization Plan, was considered by President Roosevelt to be politically and otherwise undesirable at the time. Moreover, the important but delicate task of passing a selective service law had not yet officially come before Congress, and this body would not reconvene until the fall. Until such an act was passed, the Army could not execute its M-Day plans for troop mobilization, and certainly there would be little point in announcing two M Days, one for matériel, the other for manpower mobilization. In view of these and other circumstances M Day was not invoked at the beginning of the emergency in the summer of 1940.

The Selective Service Act was passed in the fall of 1940 and large-scale troop mobilization began almost immediately. As the defense period lengthened and the goals of troop mobilization and defense production were successively raised, it became increasingly evident that the M-Day concept, as such, was no longer relevant. In his testi-

[40] These were the Price Control, Labor, Transportation, Finance, Power and Fuel, and War Trade Annexes. Several of the annexes did not appear until after the beginning of the defense period, when many of the problems of transition were already present.

mony before a Senate committee in the spring of 1941, a high-ranking Army officer responsible for troop mobilization made the following observation:

It is impossible to compare the rate of mobilization actually achieved with that which was provided in the protective mobilization plan. As has been pointed out, M-Day—the day set in the plan on which mobilization is to begin—has never been announced. This day has been reached and passed but no one can say when it actually occurred. As a matter of fact M-Day has no significance other than as a basis for the computation of time in mobilization planning.[41]

Although little was heard thereafter of the possibility of a future announcement of M Day, the idea did not altogether die out until after Pearl Harbor. Because of the frequent association of this concept with the Industrial Mobilization Plan as a whole, there were many who felt that to abandon the M-Day concept in its entirety would be to abandon all hope of getting the kind of unified direction of the national economy which was provided for in the Industrial Mobilization Plan. Pearl Harbor came and went without any formal invocation of M Day, but America's entry into the war left no doubt that M Day had, in substance, been reached and passed.

Functional Aspects of Industrial Mobilization Planning

The structural or organizational aspects of the Industrial Mobilization Plan, culminating in the proposal for a key superagency to guide a major industrial effort, represented the endeavor to fulfill two major planning objectives: (1) to provide in ad-

vance an appropriate pattern of governmental agencies needed to carry out the many functional activities required in time of emergency; and (2) to insure that a nationwide industrial mobilization program would be given unified direction and control. On the functional side, industrial mobilization planning attempted to anticipate the major problems which would arise in the process of harnessing national resources and to provide techniques, procedures, and policies for minimizing and resolving these problems.

Supply and Control of Materials

Shortages of contributory materials in the World War I production program had brought home to the War Department the necessity for advance planning to meet the requirements of a future emergency. As early as 4 December 1920 this type of planning was begun, with a request by the General Staff upon the various supply branches to prepare, in order of their importance, a list of raw materials not produced in the United States in sufficient quantities to meet the needs of the country in time of war.[42] As a result, the so-called Harbord List of forty-two strategic items was prepared, and studies were made looking to a consolidated estimate of War Department requirements. Shortly thereafter, the newly organized Planning Branch, OASW, took over the task of determining the nation's material requirements for emergency procurement and the steps which would be necessary to their fulfillment. During the next twenty years a substantial foundation was laid for coping

---

[41] Testimony of Brig Gen Harry L. Twaddle, Chf Opns and Training Div (G–3) WDGS, 22 Apr 41, Truman Committee, *Hearings,* 1:194.

[42] Lt Col Harold D. Rogers, Chf Commodities Div, Planning Br OASW, The Commodities Division, 13 Dec 38, AIC Lectures, 15:617.

with material problems which arose in World War II.

The War Department's material planning activities were assigned to the Commodities Division of the Planning Branch. The basic responsibility of the Commodities Division was to identify the various materials essential to war production, to compute requirements, to estimate the availability of supplies, and to prepare plans to meet deficits. By 1930 the organization and procedures for the discharge of this responsibility had become well established.[43]

For administrative purposes essential materials were divided into two broad groups. The first of these consisted of "strategic" materials whose principal source of supply lay outside the United States. Included in this strategic material list, which comprised twenty-six items in October 1930, were manganese, chromium, nickel, tungsten, other metals, rubber, coffee, hides, wool, fibers, and a number of medical and other items. Each of the strategic materials was assigned for study and recommendations to the procurement branch having the largest total requirements (direct and indirect). The branch was responsible for computing total Army requirements, as well as estimating civilian and Navy needs (if the latter were not obtainable from the Navy). Requirements were estimated for twenty-four months after the beginning of an emergency, based on procurement needs under the existing general mobilization plan, and arranged in order of relative essentiality to indicate a basis for apportionment in the event of shortage. The responsible branch was also required to estimate the available supply and to make studies of foreign and domestic sources, quantities and locations of normal stocks, shipping lanes, and other factors. All this information, together with recommended plans to meet deficits—including proposals for conservation, substitution, and material controls in time of emergency—was to be submitted to OASW as a formal "procurement plan." These plans were to be revised annually.[44]

The efforts of the Commodities Division, OASW, and later the ANMB, to plan for an adequate supply of strategic materials were more successful in providing knowledge of what ought to be done than in obtaining the necessary action. Repeated proposals for legislative authority and funds to import and stockpile strategic materials were regularly turned down by Congress, partly out of apathy and economy-mindedness and partly because of the chronic resistance of domestic producers.[45]

The second broad group of essential materials comprised a larger list (fifty-two item classes in October 1930) of semiprocessed and manufactured "commodities." The commodity list was a heterogeneous group of items representing all major domestic industries whose products would be essential to the operation of a wartime economy. Most of these items were basic materials which would be physically incorporated into end products needed by the armed services. Among these were building materials, chemicals, dyes, textiles, basic foodstuffs, leather, optical glass, paints and pigments, paper and pulp, iron and steel, and wood products.

[43] OASW, Notes on Industrial Mobilization, No. 13 (Revised), Oct 30, Procurement Planning, pp. 26–30.

[44] Procurement plans for strategic raw materials were, in general, to follow a detailed outline supplied by the Commodities Division, OASW. A copy of this outline appears in OASW, Notes on Industrial Mobilization, No. 13 (Revised), October 1930, Procurement Planning, pp. 29–30.

[45] See below, Chapter XXVI, and references cited therein.

Also on the commodity list were important items of equipment, materials, and supplies not to be incorporated in end products but nonetheless essential to manufacturing processes or military operations. In this category were abrasives, alcohol, coal and coke, hardware and hand tools, machine tools, petroleum products, railway equipment, vehicles, and refractories.[46]

The organization and procedures for dealing with the commodity group differed considerably from those used for strategic materials. Each of the fifty-two items or item groups on the commodity list was handled by an individual "commodity committee," which operated as a unit of OASW and was responsible to the Assistant Secretary of War. Each committee was composed of a chairman selected from the procurement branch having the major interest in the commodity (for example, Ordnance for iron and steel), representatives of the other branches with requirements for the commodity, and a technical adviser from OASW. The commodity committees had the basic mission of obtaining and consolidating estimates of requirements, planning the assurance of adequate supply in time of emergency, maintaining contacts with the industry concerned, and keeping abreast of all relevant developments therein.

The OASW commodity committees were thus the counterpart of the commodity sections of the War Industries Board in World War I. The commodity sections, which had been described by Bernard Baruch as "the background of the whole structure," were the focal point of demand and supply for the basic material resources of the nation. Their essential purpose was to provide the

mechanism whereby the indirect material requirements of the procuring agencies, which were organized along end-product lines in accordance with their procurement mission, could be translated into terms appropriate to the organization of American industry in the field of raw material supply. It was only through some such organization that the so-called functional activities of industrial mobilization—conservation, distribution, price-fixing, and the like—could be developed and executed with any degree of effectiveness and co-ordination.[47]

The length and composition of the strategic material and commodity lists varied from time to time with the stage of procurement planning, developments in manufacturing technology, changes in military requirements, and the availability of supply. In making studies and developing plans for materials on both lists, the Army developed an extensive array of contacts with other governmental agencies, trade associations, manufacturers, engineering institutes, scientific societies, and other sources of industrial and technical information.[48]

These relationships were expanded in the 1930's as the ANMB took over the task of sponsoring the Industrial Mobilization Plan and co-ordinating the efforts of the Army and Navy. The Commodities Division, ANMB, was organized along lines parallel to the Commodities Division in the Planning Branch, OASW. Since ANMB had no full-time personnel (other than an executive secretary) until the end of the planning period, the Commodities Division,

---

[46] OASW, Notes on Industrial Mobilization, No. 13 (Revised), October 1930, Procurement Planning, p. 26.

[47] (1) Baruch, *American Industry in the War,* Bk. One, Pt. II, Ch. 1. (2) Clarkson, *Industrial America in the World War,* Ch. XVII. (3) Donald M. Nelson, *Arsenal of Democracy* (New York: Harcourt, Brace and Company, 1946), p. 90.

[48] Some 260 organizations and agencies are listed in the Commodities Annex, *IMP, 1939.*

OASW, did most of the basic work and became the office of record for ANMB in the area of material planning.[49] Beginning in 1936 the ANMB commodity committees (which consisted of the Army chairman of the corresponding OASW committee and his opposite number in the Navy) assumed the task of reviewing and approving the strategic material and commodity plans prepared within OASW and the Navy. These plans then became the basic supporting data underlying the commodities annex of the Industrial Mobilization Plan.

An important responsibility of the Commodities Division, OASW, was the preparation of broad plans for the emergency control of materials which would insure the distribution of scarce items to their most important uses. Because of wide variation in the conditions under which essential materials were customarily produced and distributed in the United States, the planners felt that different methods of control would have to be devised to fit different materials. Also, they did not attempt to work out control systems in elaborate detail; this could only be done during the transition period and later when the magnitude of wartime requirements, the structure of governmental control agencies, and other relevant conditions would take definite form. Hence, the planning efforts were directed primarily to the development of fundamental principles and basic methods of material control which could be translated into detailed procedures in time of emergency.[50]

The general concept of priority as the basis for all systems of material control was stated in the Industrial Mobilization Plan:

Priority can be applied in a number of forms, no one of which may be considered as a panacea for all the problems which may arise in war. All the various methods of applying priority may be required to meet varying conditions; they must be coordinated to assure a united, effective program.[51]

The plan went on to summarize three broad methods of applying priority:

(a) *Classification ratings.*—Priority classification of orders, items, facilities, or industries may be established to determine the order in which resources are to be used. Such ratings were found most useful during the World War in promulgating broad priority policies, capable of ready interpretation by all concerned, and avoided a tremendous load on the commodity divisions of the War Industries Board that would have been incurred in the assignment of individual priorities. There is every reason to believe that such an automatic priority classification would prove equally advantageous in any future national emegency.

(b) *Allocations.*—Allocations assign the productive capacity of individual plants, or parts thereof, to specific agencies in cases where serious procurement difficulties are anticipated or develop. This measure establishes priority for sources of supply among requiring agencies.

(c) *Licenses, embargoes, permits, and warrants.*—These are mechanisms of priority which may be set up to establish precedence in the utilization of resources in war. By such means, resources, especially materials in foreign and domestic trade, may be made to flow in such a manner as to insure their most advantageous use.[52]

In developing the supporting plans within each of these categories the Commodities Division, OASW, laid the foundation for

---

[49] Col Rogers, AIC Lectures, 15:615½.

[50] (1) OASW Planning Br, War Department Procurement Planning (October 1936) (draft copy intended to supersede Industrial Mobilization (Army Extension Course, Special Text 229, 1934)), Control and Distribution Measures, p. 46, ICAF Library. (2) Col Rogers, AIC Lectures, 15:621,

621½. (3) Col Rogers, Strategic and Critical Materials, 19 Feb 38, AIC Lectures, 14:840½, 841.
[51] *IMP, 1939*, p. 3.
[52] *Ibid.,* pp. 3–4.

the three familiar types of material control system used in World War II—the priorities system, allocations of mill capacity, and the Controlled Materials Plan (CMP).

Priorities—Plans for the use of simple priorities in the form of various preference rating classes were based largely on the experience of the War Industries Board in World War I. These ratings would indicate to industry the relative urgency of procurement contracts in accordance with military priorities for end items established by the Joint Board. At the beginning of an emergency these military priorities would be translated into industrial priorities and administered by the Army and Navy Munitions Board, acting with the voluntary compliance of industry until specific enabling legislation was passed.[53]

Two basic principles for the application of the priorities system were stated by the planners. First, the preference rating granted to finished items should automatically establish priority for the supply of contributory materials.[54] Unless this was done the priorities system would not be a system for material control but would only confer a preferred claim upon plant facilities for end products, a claim already provided by the facility-allocation system and contract-placement procedures. Secondly, the priorities system was not considered to be an adequate instrument for the distribution of materials under conditions of seriously short supply. It was to be used as a general system of material control at the beginning of an emergency, together with measures for conservation, increased importation, and augmented domestic production, until detailed

control procedures could be put into effect for specific commodities.[55]

The priorities system actually adopted at the beginning of the defense period made use of preference rating classes as envisaged above. But a ruling of the Advisory Commission to the Council of National Defense (NDAC), and later the Office of Production Management (OPM), prohibited the automatic extension of preference ratings to essential materials, however necessary these might be to the production of high-priority end items of procurement. This seriously limited the use of priorities as an instrument for the distribution of materials. By the time the automatic extension feature was generally permitted, material shortages had grown to the point where effective distribution could not be accomplished by an open-ended priorities system.

Allocations of Mill Capacity—In one area it was felt particularly essential that detailed plans should be developed in peacetime for the control of materials beyond the level of simple priorities. This was the important case of basic iron and steel production. Discussion of a plan for the allocation of steel mill capacity had begun as early as 1923, and the first "steel plan"—developed by the Army in collaboration with the American Iron and Steel Institute—appeared in 1927. In 1936 a revised and much more comprehensive Steel Mobilization Plan was completed. This version, sponsored by the Army and Navy Munitions Board, is the document customarily referred to as the Steel Plan.[56]

---

[53] Memo, Capt Wallace E. Niles, Production Div Planning Br OASW, 27 Dec 37, sub: Equitable Application of National Resources in War, p. 8, OCMH.

[54] Col Rogers, AIC Lectures, 15:521.

[55] *Ibid.*

[56] The original steel plan of 1927 was prepared by Maj. Raphael R. Nix, Planning Branch, OASW. The 1936 revision was prepared by Maj. (later Brig. Gen.) Hugh C. Minton, who was for a number of years the Executive Officer for the Pittsburgh Ordnance District. The 1936 edition was a printed and bound volume running to approximately 180 pages; only 100 individually numbered copies were

The Steel Plan was a plant-allocation system comparable in many respects to the facility-allocation system for end products under the War Department's procurement planning program. Some three hundred or more steel-producing plants throughout the country, representing virtually the entire steel-making capacity of the nation, were listed in the plan. The basic purpose of the plan was to insure an adequate and timely supply of steel to fabricators engaged in production for the wartime procurement agencies. The plan was also designed to present to OASW, the ANMB, and the appropriate superagency "a well-defined picture of the war requirements for steel, the productive capacity of the steel industry, the placement of the war load, and the percent of the placed war load to the capacity of individual companies and plants." [57] More specific objectives were to eliminate competition for steel-producing facilities among the wartime procuring agencies and their contractors; to reduce unnecessary cross-hauling; to uncover shortages of specific types of capacity; and to afford an equitable distribution of the war load throughout the steel industry. In furtherance of these ends the first year's emergency steel requirements of the three major wartime procurement agencies—Army,[58] Navy, and Emergency Fleet (Maritime)—were estimated and matched against available capacity. Re-

quirements and capacity data were broken down into considerable detail. The requirements classifications included nine principal classes of steel and numerous subdivisions thereof (forms, shapes, chemical composition, and so forth); the various supply arms of the Army and bureaus of the Navy; and the geographical districts of the procuring agencies.[59]

These requirements were then allocated to firms with available capacity of the desired type. Allocations were made in the form of annual capacity credits stated in terms of actual tonnage. Thus, each procurement district of each supply arm of the Army, each bureau of the Navy, and the agency for the Emergency Fleet was granted specific capacity in individual steel-producing plants substantially equal to its annual tonnage requirements. Apportionment of this capacity among fabricators of munitions within each procurement district would be made by agreement between the procuring agencies and their contractors under the broad direction of the Iron and Steel Commodity Committee, ANMB, and eventually by the iron and steel section of the War Resources Administration or its equivalent.

Total steel requirements of the three procuring agencies for a single year of war, estimated as indicated above, amounted to 13.5 million tons under the 1936 plan. This compared with equivalent shipments in 1918 of 9.9 million tons. Total capacity credits allocated under the plan amounted to 12 mil-

---

printed. A further revision, in the form of a summary of data in the current records of the ANMB, was made in 1940. See photostatic summary, The Steel Mobilization Plan, Revision of 1940, prepared by Maj. Ward E. Becker, Planning Branch, OASW, by direction of ANMB, 1 July 1940, copy in ICAF Library.

[57] Steel Mobilization Plan (1936), p. 1, ICAF Library.

[58] The Army's requirements (which omitted new plant and building construction) were for the maximum year of a two-year emergency.

[59] The naval districts were sixteen in number and included Pearl Harbor, Panama Canal Zone, and Cavite, Philippine Islands. The War Department's fourteen procurement districts were identical with those established by Ordnance; adjustments were made for supply arms using fewer districts. The Emergency Fleet procurement districts in the 1936 plan conformed to those of the War Department; in the 1940 revision they conformed to the continental naval districts.

lion tons or approximately 19 percent of the total existing capacity of the industry.[60]

The Steel Mobilization Plan did not purport to forecast total iron and steel requirements for the duration of any war. Rather, its basic mission was to provide the mechanism for an orderly transition from peace to war. It provided both a functional plan and the organizational structure and procedures for a progressive adjustment to actual conditions as they arose.[61] But as in the case of other aspects of the Industrial Mobilization Plan, the Steel Plan was not adopted by the central mobilization control agency during the defense period when it was badly needed. Even the application of priorities to steel was delayed beyond the period when priorities could successfully achieve their purpose. When it became evident to OPM in the summer of 1941 that priorities were an inadequate instrument for the effective distribution of steel, allocations were adopted on a piecemeal basis with little, if any, resemblance to the systematic procedures contemplated by the Steel Plan.[62]

---

[60] Steel Mobilization Plan (1936), pp. 4, 11, 178. Figures refer to short tons. It is interesting to note that the second Gano Dunn report on iron and steel, made in mid-1941, estimated total defense requirements for iron and steel at 12.4 million tons for 1941 and 13.8 million tons for 1952. See: (1) Civilian Production Administration (formerly War Production Board), *Wartime Production Achievements and the Reconversion Outlook: Report of the Chairman, War Production Board,* (Washington: Government Printing Office, 1945), p. 43; (2) Civilian Production Administration, *Industrial Mobilization for War,* I, *Program and Administration* (Washington: Government Printing Office, 1947) (hereafter cited as *Industrial Mobilization for War*), 137. This is the official history of the War Production Board.

[61] These were amplified in The Steel Mobilization Plan, Revision of 1940.

[62] See Chapter XXIV, Material Controls in Transition, especially pages 551–53.

Rationing Proposals—The foundations of the Controlled Materials Plan adopted at the end of 1942 are to be found in proposals developed during the 1930's by the Commodities Division, OASW, in conjunction with ANMB, for rationing scarce materials in time of war. As indicated above, the application of a simple priorities or preference rating system, with automatic extension of the indicated rating to essential materials, was recommended as an initial control system at the beginning of an emergency. During the transition to an all-out M Day, specific plans for a tighter control system would be developed for individual commodities:

Generally speaking such a plan should be based on a ration method using permits or commodity credits for the use of raw materials and the licensing of dealers.[63]

The nature of such a rationing system, as well as its essential similarity to the later Controlled Materials Plan, is indicated by the following description:

b. Methods after M-Day. It is proposed when strict control is necessary at the beginning of war to issue warrants from the Commodities Division of the highest control agency then in existence which will state the amount of a given commodity set aside for each department (Army and Navy) issuing "commodity credits" from existing stocks and make this amount immediately available to the supply arm or service (or Bureau) for use in its manufacturing problems. This does not assign a definite amount of a strategic raw material for a given project, but places at the disposal of the Chief of the Supply Arm or Service, as nearly as possible, his first three months requirement. The Chief of the Supply Arm or Service in turn issues subwarrants against his allotment to each manufacturer interested, each warrant listing the location and amount of the commodity under consideration. This method affords the desired flexibility to the Chief of the Supply Arm or

---

[63] Col Rogers, AIC Lectures, 15:621½.

Service, permitting him to shift stocks where-
ever needed; avoids competition and pro-
motes efficiency.[64]

This allotment procedure, making use of
the principle of decentralized operations
through the individual supply arms and
services and their respective procurement
districts, would be continued beyond the
first three-month period:

Subsequent commodity credits will be
cleared and readjustments of requirements
made based on needs of the procurement program. The district representatives must be
constantly informed regarding their own programs and are responsible for keeping their
supply arms and services conversant with their
needs. The supply arms and services will keep
the War Department Commodity Committees
informed as to their needs through their representatives on these committees and submit
requests of commodity clearance accordingly.
In a similar manner the War Department
representative on the Army and Navy Munitions Board submits combined requisitions to
this joint board. The Army and Navy Munitions Board will either issue the credit or
request clearances for credits from the Commodities Division of the War Resources
Administration.[65]

The central feature of the plan was summed
up as a system of "Apportioning controlled
materials to the various supply arms and
services, in accordance with established
priorities, by credits or warrants approved
by a higher authority." [66]

These proposals for a rationing type of
system for the controlled distribution of
scarce materials were relegated to temporary oblivion with the failure to adopt
the Industrial Mobilization Plan early in the
defense period. In the year after Pearl Harbor, when existing systems for the distribution of materials had broken down, the

growing demand for a closed system of material control resulted in the eventual adoption of the Controlled Materials Plan. This
plan, sponsored primarily by the military
agencies under the leadership of Ferdinand
Eberstadt, was far more complex than anything which could have been envisaged during the planning period. Nevertheless, its
main features represented the conceptual
framework developed by the OASW planners during the 1930's.

Price Control

Plans for emergency and wartime price
control formed an important part of the
several industrial mobilization plans. Responsibility for this area of planning fell
to the Contributory Division, Planning
Branch, OASW. Studies of the behavior
of prices during World War I led to the
inescapable conclusion that adequate and
timely control of prices would be essential
to the success of procurement and economic
mobilization in any future war. In the
eighteen months before America's entry
into World War I the "all commodity" price
index, under the stimulus of heavy European purchases, rose from 104 to 156. Many
individual commodities showed a much
more exaggerated price rise.[67]

Active price control to curb the rising tide
of inflation did not begin until the passage

---

[64] *Ibid.*, 14:841.
[65] *Ibid.*, 15:622.
[66] *Ibid.*, 14:841.

[67] For example, the price index for metals had
risen to 247 and by July 1917 reached a peak of
333. See Baruch, *American Industry in the War*,
p. 74; also, *IMP, 1939*, Price Control Annex, App.
A. By March 1917, prices of basic pig iron and
steel plate at Pittsburgh had risen some 800 percent
above pre-1914 quotations. See page 19 of draft,
Price Control Appendix to Industrial Mobilization
Plan, 1933, attached to Memo, Lt Col Earl Mc-
Farland, Ex OASW, for Col Alvin C. Voris, Dir
Planning Br OASW, 18 Jun 32, USW Planning
Br (ASF) file.

of the Food and Fuel Conservation Act on 10 August 1917, which provided the statutory basis for government price fixing in loosely defined areas of the economy. But American industry was skeptical of any "unnatural" interference with the law of supply and demand, and Congress failed to provide the President or any other agency with blanket authority to develop an integrated and balanced array of price controls.[68] Under the circumstances price control measures were improvised by a variety of federal agencies—including the Food and Fuel Administration, the Price Fixing Committee (established by Executive order in March 1918), the War Industries Board, the War Trade Board, the Federal Trade Commission, and the War and Navy Departments. Heavy reliance was placed on reaching voluntary price agreements with individual industries. This was aided by the power of the War Industries Board to control the distribution of materials, transportation, and other essentials of industrial operation. These powers proved to be highly persuasive, and despite its belated, piecemeal, and improvised nature, price control in World War I succeeded eventually in bringing a substantial degree of stability to the prices of basic commodities as well as to many consumer goods. In so doing it demonstrated the possibilities of price control in promoting an orderly procurement program, reducing the dollar costs of the war, curbing war profiteering, and promoting a more equitable distribution of the costs of the war.[69]

Beginning with the 1933 edition, the Industrial Mobilization Plan contained a separate price control appendix or annex describing the history, objectives, and methods of price control, together with recommended legislation and a wartime price control organization. The following distillation of the Price Control Annex of the 1939 IMP represents the thinking of industrial mobilization planners on the eve of the emergency leading to World War II:

1. Price control should be exercised immediately upon indication of significant price increases under an emergency procurement program. Delay would permit runaway markets, the development of an unbalanced general price structure, the disruption of orderly contractual arangements for military procurement, and the creation of hardship in the civilian sector of the economy.

2. Both general price ceilings and individual or piecemeal price controls would probably be necessary. Advance commitment to either method to the exclusion of the other would preclude flexibility in guiding the economy through the several stages of the transition from peace to all-out war. After their establishment, price ceilings would have to be kept responsive to the changing circumstances of a war economy.

3. Prices of military-type items with no prior price or production history should be exempt from formal price control. The desired results in this area could best be achieved by negotiation in the placement and administration of individual procurement contracts.

4. General price ceilings for commercial products should be established on a "bulk

[68] Baruch, *American Industry in the War*, p. 75.
[69] A wealth of information on the price behavior of specific commodities, as well as on general price control problems in World War I, with recommendations for future emergencies, may be found in Baruch, *American Industry in the War, passim*, especially Bk. One, Pt. II, and Bk. Two. See also

Bernard M. Baruch, "Priorities—the Synchronizing Force," *Harvard Business Review*, XIX (Spring 1941), 261–70.

line" basis to cover the marginal costs, including a reasonable profit, of the indispensable volume of output required. The tailoring of prices to the costs of individual firms was considered administratively impossible and productive of all the evils of "cost plus" pricing.

5. The control of wages and other "factor prices" was assumed as part of a general price control program.

6. Five possible stages were envisaged, for purposes of price control, in the transition from a purely peacetime situation to all-out war. Recommended actions, or possible alternative actions, were indicated for each stage.

7. An interim Price Control Council during the transition period would give way to a permanent wartime Price Control Authority. The Price Control Authority would be one of the civilian superagencies subject to broad supervision by the key superagency, the War Resources Administration. The functions of the Price Control Authority would be quasi-judicial, with enforcement left to other wartime and permanent agencies of the government.

Although the Industrial Mobilization Plan was not formally adopted, many of the foregoing elements of price control as proposed by the prewar planners were utilized in the World War II economic mobilization program.[70]

*Other Problems
in Industrial Mobilization*

Limitations of space preclude more than brief mention of the prewar plans in other functional areas of industrial mobilization.

The Contributory Division, OASW, had the responsibility for surveying the problems and formulating proposals to meet emergency requirements in the areas of labor, power and fuel, transportation, finance, and international trade. Continuous study during the interwar period resulted in the accumulation of much basic knowledge in the indicated areas and the development of systematic plans for meeting an emergency.

In the field of electric power, for example, a comprehensive and continuous survey of the nation's generating and distributing facilities had been maintained since the early 1920's. Responsibility for the electric power survey was placed upon the Corps of Engineers, which provided an annual report to OASW of available power in each War Department procurement district. Attempts were made to estimate power requirements for the military program by procurement districts, but the results were never considered satisfactory. For a time each supply branch was required to submit annual reports to OASW showing the direct power requirements for each accepted schedule of production in excess of $500,000 for one calendar year. These reports, which included anticipated war production from new facilities and government arsenals as well as existing private establishments, indicated the name and location of the facility, class of material to be manufactured, the peak electrical load, the kilowatt hours for the maximum month's production, and the expected source of electrical power.[71]

The major barrier to reliable estimates of wartime power requirements lay in the area of cumulative indirect requirements below the finished product level. The manufacture

---

[70] For a discussion of price control as it affected military procurement in World War II, see below, Chapter XVII.

[71] OASW, Notes on Industrial Mobilization, No. 9, June 1926, Relation of Power to Procurement Planning, pp. 6, 15.

of contributory raw materials, components, parts, and supplies below the prime contractor level required power in varying and unascertainable amounts at each level. Efforts were made to compute indirect requirements by the development and application of interindustry power factors, based on peacetime dollar-value or physical-output ratios, but these were considered unreliable in view of changes in interindustry alignments in time of war and for other reasons.[72] Hence, reliance was placed on the larger efforts of OASW to distribute the total procurement load equitably throughout the country and on the basic ability of the power industry to meet wartime requirements. Close relationships between the Army Engineers' power survey organization and key personnel in the industry, as well as with regional and local sectors thereof, were utilized to prepare the industry to meet the increased demands of war production.

Three principal measures were envisaged to cope with wartime power shortages: (1) redistribution of power to areas of power shortage; (2) partial reallocation of the procurement load; (3) provision of additional power-generating facilities. All of these, together with priorities and limitation orders upon nonessential power consumption, would be applied under the direction of a wartime power control administrator in the Power and Fuel Division of the proposed War Resources Administration.[73] In view of unused generating capacity, constantly increasing efficiency in distribution, other

conditions in the power industry, and plans for both normal and emergency expansion, it was believed by the Army as well as spokesmen for the industry that no nationwide power shortage would arise in time of war and that local shortages could be met by the methods indicated.[74]

In the field of transportation the capacities and characteristics of the five basic types—railroad, highway, waterway, airway, and pipeline—were studied and plans made for their efficient utilization in time of war. In view of the impossibility of calculating dependable wartime transportation requirements, planning activities were devoted mainly to the objectives and methods of wartime control. The broad objectives of control were to give preference to the movement of war traffic in accordance with its relative importance, to assure the effective use of all forms of transportation, to curtail nonwar traffic, as required, without unduly restricting essential civilian needs, and to maintain a high degree of mechanical effectiveness for all transportation facilities. Collateral objectives included the avoidance of unnecessary crosshauling and congestion of transportation facilities, the augmentation of transportation facilities where necessary, and so on. The basic rationale underlying the planning activities and proposals was to rely upon the voluntary co-operation of the various carriers and to make no greater use of government controls than was actually necessary. Govern-

---

[72] (1) *Ibid.,* pp. 9–14. (2) Maj Gen Edward M. Markham, CofEngrs, Power in War, 20 Apr 36, AIC Lectures, 12:520. (3) Col Warren T. Hannum, CE, AIC Lectures, 12:523.

[73] (1) Gen Markham, AIC Lectures, 12:520–21. (2) Maj William H. Sadler, The Contributory Division, OASW, 17 Feb 38, AIC Lectures, 14:807½. (3) *IMP, 1939,* Power and Fuel Annex.

[74] (1) AIC R56, Plans for Industrial Mobilization, 1920–1939, pp. 48–49. (2) Brig Gen Charles Keller, USA (Ret.), The Supply of Power to Meet a War Demand, 27 Apr 36, AIC Lectures, 12:535ff. (3) For a concise summary of how the power industry met wartime requirements, see CPA, *Wartime Production Achievements and the Reconversion Outlook,* pp. 39–43; also, Nelson, *Arsenal of Democracy,* pp. 365–66.

ment possession and operation of transportation systems, as in the case of the railroads in World War I, was considered unnecessary except as a last resort. Major attention was devoted to railroads as the key transportation agency.[75] Close collaboration between the military agencies and the Association of American Railroads resulted in the formulation of a wide array of plans for adapting practices in the railroad industry to emergency conditions. Relationships were also established with national trucking and motor bus associations, associations of marine, lake, and inland waterway carriers, with the American Petroleum Institute representing the pipelines, and the Air Transport Association of America. Studies were made of the numerous governmental agencies, including those within the armed services, for dealing with transportation problems in peace and war. Existing legislation affecting transportation, including antitrust laws, was reviewed and recommendations made to facilitate wartime operations and control. All wartime controls in the field of transportation were to be directed and co-ordinated by the chief of the Transportation Division in the proposed War Resources Administration, as indicated in the Industrial Mobilization Plan.[76]

Analogous planning was done in the fields of foreign trade, labor, finance, and construction, each of which was discussed in an appropriate annex to the Industrial Mobilization Plan. Some of the annexes were slim documents written in very general terms. But behind all of the annexes and all the published summaries of IMP was an abundance of supporting detail and information in the files of the relevant divisions of the Planning Branch, OASW, and the Army and Navy Munitions Board. All this material, together with informed and trained personnel from ANMB and OASW, would be assimilated at the outset of an emergency into the appropriate offices of the War Resources Administration and other super-agencies. This would make possible the utilization of the fruits of twenty years of industrial mobilization planning and provide an intimate working relationship between the military procuring agencies and the central mobilization control agencies. Out of this close relationship and familiarity with the nature of the problems to be faced—so the planners hoped—would emerge an integrated program of industrial mobilization which would keep to a minimum the inevitable dislocations of the nation's economy.

[75] In 1937 the railroads hauled 363 billion ton-miles, or 64 percent of all commercial freight traffic handled by the five types of transportation. *IMP, 1939,* Transportation Annex, p. 47. This annex was one of the better developed annexes to the 1939 IMP.

[76] *IMP, 1939,* Transportation Annex.

CHAPTER V

Organization for War

The Evolution of Central Mobilization Control Agencies

The transition period granted to the United States for converting its economy from peace to war was not a thirty-day, three-month, or even a twelve-month period. A full year and a half elapsed between the fall of France in June 1940 and the Japanese attack upon Pearl Harbor. A large-scale military procurement program was begun at the end of June 1940, but the nation did not embark upon an all-out war production program until after 7 December 1941.[1]

The Industrial Mobilization Plan had been devised to afford an orderly transition from peace to war, but it was not officially adopted at the beginning of the defense period or, indeed, at any other time. Nevertheless, many functional as well as organizational elements of the plan were utilized— some at the outset of the defense period and others at later dates both before and after Pearl Harbor. But what was regarded by some authorities as the keystone of the Industrial Mobilization Plan—the proposal to establish, at the very beginning of an emergency, unified organizational control over the economic mobilization program— was rejected. Both the reasons for and the consequences of this decision have been the subject of much speculation and debate.[2]

The decision to select an alternative organizational structure instead of the one proposed by IMP was made by President Roosevelt in a milieu of complex and delicate political circumstances. The factors which led to this decision are too numerous for more than a brief summary of the subject. Fundamentally, the President believed that the nation as a whole was not ready for the degree of economic control implied by the formal adoption of the plan. In particular, he had serious misgivings as to the desirability of creating, in time of peace, the kind of powerful superagency represented by the War Resources Administration. Such an agency, he felt, would interfere with his

[1] This eighteen-month period of preparation is usually referred to as the "defense period," in contrast to the "planning period" which preceded it and the "war period" which followed Pearl Harbor. From the standpoint of economic mobilization, World War II included both the defense and war periods.

[2] For example: (1) Truman Committee, *Hearings*, 21–24 Oct 47, 42:25573–789 and Exhibits 2672–83; (2) AIC R56, Plans for Industrial Mobilization, 1920–1939, especially pp. 66–85; (3) Connery, *The Navy and the Industrial Mobilization*, Ch. III; (4) Albert A. Blum, The Birth and Death of the M-Day Plan (draft copy for inclusion in Twentieth Century Fund, Study of Civil-Military Relations [circa 1955], OCMH; (5) CPA, *Industrial Mobilization for War*, Pt. I, Chs. 1 and 2; (6) U.S. Bureau of the Budget, *The United States at War*, Chs. 1–5, *passim*; (7) Nelson, *Arsenal of Democracy*, Ch. 5, especially pp. 87–92; (8) Eliot Janeway, *The Struggle for Survival* (New Haven: Yale University Press, 1951), Chs. I–V, especially Ch. III.

own close supervision of the rearmament program at a time when important political considerations, both domestic and international, required that all aspects of national policy be closely controlled by the Presidency.

The circumstance which precipitated the President's decision was the controversy arising out of the report of the War Resources Board, created early in August 1939. Two years previously Mr. Louis Johnson—a vigorous exponent of industrial preparedness—had been appointed Assistant Secretary of War. Shortly thereafter, Johnson took steps to obtain a wider public understanding and acceptance of the Industrial Mobilization Plan. In a letter to Bernard Baruch on 5 October 1937, he proposed the appointment of a board of distinguished citizens to review and pass upon the War Department's plans for mobilizing industry in time of emergency:

Plans for such magnitude and importance should be analyzed by a disinterested group of citizens who can not only pass upon the merits of the plans but whose review will carry sufficient prestige to be convincing to the country at large.[3]

No definite action was taken at the time but Johnson proceeded energetically to spread the gospel of industrial mobilization:

. . . I have visited industrial plants, Government arsenals, air fields, and airplane factories from coast to coast, and I have presented the problems of industrial mobilization and war-time procurement planning in 77 speeches to widely disparate groups—industrial, patriotic, military and social—in practically every section of the country. This

activity has required over 50,000 miles of travel. . . . As a result of this effort, I believe the purposes and objectives of industrial mobilization, as well as the necessity for cooperation between labor, capital, and industry . . . are more widely and more clearly understood.[4]

In the summer of 1939, shortly after completion of the 1939 edition of IMP and with tension in Europe reaching the breaking point, Johnson again approached the President with the proposal for such a board. The President agreed and suggested Mr. Edward R. Stettinius, Jr., chairman of the United States Steel Corporation, to head the board. Stettinius was a relatively young but well-known liberal businessman, whose father had held important posts in the World War I administration. Stettinius accepted the chairmanship of the new board and, together with the cochairmen of the ANMB, selected five additional members.[5] The formation of this board, designated as the War Resources Board, was announced to the press on 9 August 1939. The name of the board reflected Assistant Secretary Johnson's hope that it would not only perform the functions indicated in his letter to Baruch, but that it would be transformed into the nucleus of the War Resources Administration contemplated by the Industrial Mobilization Plan. The press release jointly sponsored by Johnson and Assistant Secretary of the Navy Charles Edison went so

---

[3] Ltr, Johnson to Baruch, 5 Oct 37, cited in Thatcher, Planning for Industrial Mobilization, 1920–1940, pp. 296–97. Johnson also broached the matter to President Roosevelt at this time. Blum, The Birth and Death of the M-Day Plan, p. 17.

[4] Annual Report of the Assistant Secretary of War, in Annual *Report of the Secretary of War to the President, 1938* (Washington: Government Printing Office, 1938), pp. 19–20.

[5] These were Karl T. Compton, President, Massachusetts Institute of Technology; Walter S. Gifford, President, American Telephone and Telegraph Company; Harold G. Moulton, President, The Brookings Institution; John L. Pratt, Director and former Vice President, General Motors Corporation; and Brig. Gen. Robert E. Wood, President, Sears, Roebuck and Company.

far as to state that in an emergency the War Resources Board "would become an executive agency of the Government with broad powers similar to those of the old War Industries Board" and "would report directly to the President as a War Resources Administration." [6]

In the political atmosphere of 1939, with its heritage of years of antiwar sentiment, strife between labor and industry, and controversy over the New Deal in all its aspects, the composition of the board and even its appointment were widely criticized. Pacifists, isolationists, and many others who opposed rearmament looked upon the board as a step toward war. Many New Dealers and heads of existing governmental agencies saw in the imminent creation of a War Resources Administration a threat both to the principles of the New Deal and to the status of established agencies. Anti-New Deal businessmen deplored the possibility of further interference by government in industry. The board was criticized as a "tool of Wall Street" heavily loaded with Morgan-DuPont men. The omission of representatives of labor and agriculture, especially unfortunate in view of the statement that the board might become the War Resources Administration, was looked upon as an indication that big business was about to displace the New Deal, take over the economy, and destroy the gains for which labor had fought so desperately during the past ten years. Other criticisms centered on the chairman's lack of experience in economic mobilization matters and noted the conspicuous absence of Bernard Baruch, the acknowledged authority in the field. [7]

In addition to criticisms of the War Resources Board there were other factors of long standing which influenced the President in his decision not to use the superagency proposed in the Industrial Mobilization Plan. As far back as 1931, Mr. Walter S. Gifford—who became a member of the War Resources Board in 1939—had recommended the revival, under existing statutes, of the Advisory Commission to the Council of National Defense as a peacetime planning agency for co-ordinating national resources, to be called upon in time of an emergency. [8] Shortly after his re-election in 1936, President Roosevelt discussed the problem of emergency management of the national economy with Louis Brownlow, chairman of the President's Committee on Administrative Management. At this time he suggested that Brownlow investigate the possibility of statutes remaining in effect from the World War I period which might serve the purpose. Brownlow learned that the Council of National Defense was technically still in existence and that the President had the power to appoint an Advisory Commission to the council. This information apparently made an impression on the President, for he later referred to it on several occasions. After the passage of the Reorganization Act of 1939, plans were made for the establishment of an Office for Emergency Management in the Executive Office of the President. On 29 August 1939,

[6] AIC R56, Plans for Industrial Mobilization, 1920–1939, p. 67.

[7] This last criticism was met by the appointment of Baruch's long-time associate, John M. Hancock, to board membership on 6 September 1939. For general criticisms of the board and its report, see sources cited in note 2, above.

[8] War Policies Commission Hearings, 1931, pp. 776–87, especially p. 781. Mr. Gifford had been the executive director of the old Council of National Defense from its inception in 1916. The council itself consisted of the Secretaries of the War, Navy, Interior, Agriculture, Commerce, and Labor Departments.

the day before his first and only meeting with the War Resources Board, Roosevelt discussed with Brownlow the possibilities of such an agency. On this occasion the President indicated misgivings over the concept of an all-powerful War Resources Administration which would stand between him and the public in the administration of important areas of national policy. Accordingly, he sketched out a proposal to reactivate the Council of National Defense and confine the activities of the "Stettinius Board" to the mobilization of industrial supplies, one of six contemplated subdivisions of the council's activities.[9]

On the following day the President met with the War Resources Board and indicated his views on governmental organization for economic mobilization. Again he sketched an outline of an advisory body of some six or seven members, reporting to him as co-ordinator. In view of "uncertainty over the dividing line" between the Council of National Defense and the War Resources Board, he requested that the functions of the board be described in detail before additional funds were granted for continuing its work. The meeting lasted only fifteen minutes, and at the Cabinet meeting two days later the President indicated his intention to revive the Council of National Defense if an emergency required.[10] This was on 1 September 1939, the day Germany invaded Poland. On 6 September the War Resources Board submitted to the President, in accordance with his earlier request, a memorandum describing its proposed functions. Included in these was the establishment of

a "nucleus of an adequate War Resources Administration, through which the President may, in an emergency, coordinate his war control over the industrial, material and economic resources of the nation." [11]

This memorandum did not alter the President's position. On 8 September 1939, five days after France and England had declared war against Germany, he proclaimed a limited national emergency and signed the order providing for the Office for Emergency Management (OEM) in the Executive Office of the President. At the 11 September Cabinet meeting he referred to "a very comprehensive blueprint prepared by the Stettinius committee, from which it appeared that this committee was prepared to take over all of the functions of the Government." He stated that "he had no intention of permitting this and that he would not approve this blueprint." [12] At the same time he reaffirmed his intention to utilize the Council of National Defense. Hence, when he received the final report of the War Resources Board some six weeks later, the President took no action on it and declined to make the report public. Thereafter the War Resources Board remained in a state of suspended animation until it became clear that its service would no longer be required.

The final report of the War Resources Board was a compromise to meet the President's objections and still retain the core of the organizational structure developed over the years in the Industrial Mobilization Plan. The report abandoned the key superagency role of the War Resources Administration while still retaining its basic structural and functional characteristics for

[9] See Blum, The Birth and Death of the M-Day Plan, pp. 33–37.

[10] The Secret Diary of Harold L. Ickes, II, The Inside Struggle, 1936–1939 (New York: Simon and Schuster, Inc., 1954), 710.

[11] Min, WRB Mtg, 6 Sep 39, and Memo, same date, cited in Blum, The Birth and Death of the M-Day Plan, p. 39.

[12] The Secret Diary of Harold L. Ickes, II, 720.

mobilizing the nation's material resources. Six other superagencies proposed for operation independent of a War Resources Administration were Selective Service, Public Relations, War Labor, War Finance, a Price Control Board, and if necessary a Food Administration. All of the proposed machinery would, as repeatedly emphasized in IMP, be under civilian control and subject to the authority of the President. But the report in its compromise form apparently had no more appeal to the President than the original position of the board; he had already committed himself to the concept of an advisory commission.[13]

An additional factor militating against the adoption of IMP at this time was the schism existing within the War Department itself. Secretary of War Harry H. Woodring was lukewarm toward rearmament on a large scale and took exception to the energetic activities in this direction on the part of the Assistant Secretary. Although he could not overrule Mr. Johnson in the discharge of the economic mobilization responsibilities conferred upon the Assistant Secretary by the National Defense Act, Mr. Woodring openly expressed disaproval of his nominal subordinate. At a Cabinet meeting on 26 September 1939 he criticized Mr. Johnson's promotion of the War Resources Board during his absence. When President Roosevelt, at a press conference after the meeting, indicated that the War Resources Board would file its report and then disband, Mr. Woodring stated to the press that the "War Department is not setting up any permanent war boards or war machinery and I hope never will." [14]

These developments in the fall of 1939—after war had been declared in Europe and while Congress was in the process of abandoning "neutrality"—made unlikely the formal adoption of IMP at any time in the future. When the crisis arrived in the spring of 1940 and the formulation of a huge military procurement program was under way, the actual establishment of a central mobilization control agency became imperative. A number of prominent individuals suggested the recall of the War Resources Board and the adoption of the Industrial Mobilization Plan. This was vigorously opposed by members of the White House staff, who objected that IMP was not geared to changes which had taken place since World War I and that it neglected the problem of civilian supply. Some of the objections were made in innocence of any but the most superficial knowledge of IMP and mobilization planning in its entirety:

They also told the President that the needs of the military were arrived at under IMP by the "most elementary rule-of-thumb" methods by Army officers "after a half-a-day lecture on statistics." In fact, the White House advisors stated that many of the war plans are "nothing more profound than student exercises, worked up in a few hours or days as a problem in a brief Army Industrial College course." [15]

At this time President Roosevelt again indicated his feeling that adoption of the Industrial Mobilization Plan would remove him from active control of the mobilization effort:

He told members of the Department of Commerce Business Advisory Council on May 23 that he would not set up a War Resources

---

[13] The report of the War Resources Board, kept secret until the end of World War II, is reproduced in full in Truman Committee, *Hearings*, 42: 25957–71.

[14] Press Conference, 26 Sep 39, cited in Blum,

The Birth and Death of the M-Day Plan, p. 42, and Janeway, *The Struggle for Survival*, p. 69.

[15] Blum, The Birth and Death of the M-Day Plan, p. 48.

Board or a War Industries Board and turn over the war effort to "complete outsiders who don't know anything about running government. It would be unconstitutional; the final responsibility is mine and I can't delegate it." [16]

In view of these circumstances and with such problems as the third-term decision and a controversial selective service bill looming upon the horizon, the President acted under existing law and revived the Advisory Commission to the Council of National Defense on 29 May 1940.[17]

It is probable that a War Resources Administration, or an equivalent organizational structure under a happier name, could have been created by Executive order under existing law. But many of the powers long contemplated as essential to a War Resources Administration under large-scale mobilization (for example, material and price controls) did require new legislation. This, of course, was equally true for NDAC and its successors. Nevertheless, the opportunity of reviving NDAC without additional legislation and presumably with a minimum of controversy formed an important element in the President's decision.[18]

The Advisory Commission was composed

of seven independent commissioners each representing a particular segment of the economy.[19] The commission had no chairman or other head, reporting to the President either directly or through its executive secretary via the Office for Emergency Management. With the ramification of the effects of the procurement program during the remainder of 1940, the problems of managing the defense economy became more and more complex. By the end of the year it was clear that the organizational form and powers of NDAC were unequal to the task. On 20 December 1940, the President announced plans to establish an Office of Production Management, and these were brought into effect by Executive order on 7 January 1941.[20]

The Office of Production Management immediately took over the functions formerly discharged by the NDAC commissioners for production, materials, and employment. On 11 April 1941, the President established the Office of Price Administration and Civilian Supply (OPACS), which became responsible for the duties previously exercised by the commissioners for price stabilization and consumer protection. In the following month, on 5 May 1941, the Office of Agricultural Defense Relations was created by Executive order, thereby relieving the commissioner for farm products of

---

[16] *Ibid.*, pp. 48–49.

[17] General Services Administration, *Federal Records of World War II* (Washington: Government Printing Office, 1950) I, 127.

[18] (1) CPA, *Industrial Mobilization for War*, p. 18. (2) U.S. Bureau of the Budget, *The United States at War*, pp. 23–24.

The subsequent development of the central mobilization control agencies for World War II has been recounted elsewhere and needs only a brief summary in the present discussion. See the following principal sources and references cited therein: (1) CPA, *Industrial Mobilization for War;* (2) U.S. Bureau of the Budget, *The United States at War;* (3) Herman Miles Somers, *Presidential Agency: OWMR, The Office of War Mobilization and Reconversion* (Cambridge: Harvard University Press, 1950) (hereafter cited as *OWMR*); (4) Nelson, *Arsenal of Democracy.*

---

[19] The seven commissioners and their respective spheres of interest were William S. Knudsen (industrial production), E. R. Stettinius, Jr. (industrial materials), Sidney Hillman (employment), Leon Henderson (price stabilization), Chester C. Davis (farm products), Ralph Budd (transportation), and Harriet Elliott (consumer protection). Donald M. Nelson was later appointed as Coordinator of National Defense Purchases, with status equivalent to that of a commissioner. The actual Council of National Defense was a nonoperative body. CPA, *Industrial Mobilization for War*, pp. 22–23.

[20] Executive Order 8629, 7 Jan. 41.

his responsibilities. On 21 October 1941, the principal remaining duties of NDAC— the review and certification of tax amortization applications—were ordered discontinued by a resolution of Congress, and the Advisory Commission held its last meeting on the following day.[21]

The policy-making powers of the Office of Production Management resided in its council, consisting of the director general (William S. Knudsen), the associate director (Sidney Hillman), and the Secretaries of the War and Navy Departments. In this respect it was an improvement over the NDAC, since it formally provided for a closer, high-level relationship between the control agency and the agencies for military procurement. But like NDAC, OPM lacked a head with final authority and looked to the President for decision on major policies and internal disagreements. The three major operating divisions of OPM—Purchases, Production, and Priorities—were "functional" divisions, each of which dealt independently with all product sectors of American industry. Thus, no industry had a central point of contact with OPM, and individual firms had to deal separately, under time-consuming procedures and often conflicting orders, with each of the functional divisions.[22] Not until mid-1941 were industry advisory committees and unified commodity committees—whose creation at the very beginning of an emergency was contemplated by the Industrial Mobilization Plan—established in OPM to permit an integrated approach to industry.

Nor did the structure of the Office of Production Management provide a satisfactory basis for dealing with the military procurement agencies. The Industrial Mobilization Plan had contemplated that the various echelons of ANMB would be to a large extent merged and integrated with the central control agency. Instead of fostering such an intimate relationship, OPM like its predecessor resisted proposals for War and Navy Department representation on its Priorities Board and elsewhere, preferring to deal at arm's length with the military agencies. This made impossible OPM participation in the formulation of programs and policies which by their nature had to emanate from the military agencies. Hence, urgent military programs, such as elaborate plans for locating and constructing complex high explosives and munitions plants, often had to be reviewed by OPM at short notice with little prior knowledge on which to base approval.

The conditions described above led to new proposals to adopt the War Resources Administration. Early in April 1941 the OPM Production Planning Board recommended a type of organization for OPM more closely aproaching the proposals of IMP.[23] This suggestion was repeated on 8 May 1941 with more specific recommenda-

---

[21] Civilian Production Administration, *Minutes of the Advisory Commision to the Council of National Defense, June 12, 1940, to October 22, 1941* (Washington: Government Printing Office, 1946) (hereafter cited as *NDAC Minutes*), pp. *iii–iv*. The NDAC commissioner for transportation continued to function as a part of the Office for Emergency Management until the establishment, on 18 December 1941, of the Office of Defense Transportation.

[22] (1) CPA, *Industrial Mobilization for War*, pp. 98, 101–02. (2) Nelson, *Arsenal of Democracy*, p. 144.

[23] CPA, *Industrial Mobilization for War*, p. 101. The OPM Production Planning Board was a broadly representative body for formulating long-range policies for OPM. It was composed of 2 representatives of labor, 3 from industry, 2 from the armed services, and 2 others. Its initial members were George W. Meany, AFL; James B. Carey, CIO; Samuel R. Fuller, Jr. (chairman), President, American Bemberg Corporation; William E. Levis, Owens-Illinois Glass Company; John L. Pratt, Gen-

tions concerning the establishment of industry "war service committees" and OPM commodity sections. Meanwhile, a bill was pending in the Senate which would replace OPM with a War Resources Administration.[24] On 27 May 1941 the President's declaration of an unlimited national emergency provided an additional basis for the formal adoption of the Industrial Mobilization Plan.

Although the proposals concerning the commodity sections and industry advisory committees were adopted in the June reorganization of OPM, no steps were taken to replace OPM as a whole with the War Resources Administration of IMP. Major problems in the field of priorities, allocations, and related matters were coming to a head, and their resolution was attempted by the establishment, on 28 August 1941, of the Supply Priorities and Allocations Board (SPAB). This was a more widely representative and powerful body than the OPM Priorities Board, which it replaced. Presided over by the Vice President and composed of representatives of the military agencies, civilian supply, foreign requirements, and other claimants on the nation's productive resources, SPAB made broad allocations of basic materials and attempted to assemble long-range estimates of requirements. It put increased pressure behind conversion of industry, curtailment of nonessential production, and expansion of the nation's capacity for producing basic materials. But SPAB was destined to be short-lived. It was a policy-making body only, without staff or organization, and relied

upon other agencies, chiefly OPM, to make the studies which it needed and to execute its decisions. Moreover, there were a number of internal contradictions in the OPM–SPAB lines of authority. Shortly after Pearl Harbor the entire structure was replaced by the War Production Board, which in many respects resembled the War Resources Administration proposed by the Industrial Mobilization Plan.

War Department Reorganization for World War II

Concurrently with the development of the superagencies for central mobilization control, the War Department underwent continuous expansion and reorganization. With the adoption of the Munitions Program of 30 June 1940, procurement districts, corps areas, arsenals, depots, and other field establishments both within and outside the continental limits of the United States were activated, expanded, or newly established. The Washington headquarters of the supply arms and services, the Office of the Assistant Secretary of War, the General Staff, and all other War Department offices and agencies began an extended period of expansion. This process culminated in a gigantic organization eventually containing nearly two million civilian workers, the largest of all U.S. governmental agencies and greater in size than the entire federal government at any time in all its previous peacetime history.[25]

---

eral Motors; Admiral William H. Standley, Navy; Maj. Gen. James H. Burns, Army; Harry L. Hopkins, representative of the President; and Robert E. Doherty, President, Carnegie Institute of Technology.

[24] *Ibid.*, pp. 102, 107.

[25] Civilian employment by the War Department reached the peak figure of 1,881,495 in the month of June 1945. Nearly 734,000 of these (mostly natives of foreign countries) were engaged in overseas theaters. Theodore E. Whiting *et al.*, Statistics, a volume in preparation for the series UNITED STATES ARMY IN WORLD WAR II, Civilian Personnel, 16 Jan 53 draft, Table CP–1, MS, OCMH.

*The Defense Period: Hegemony of the
Under Secretary of War*

On 11 July 1940, in order to facilitate
the launching of the Munitions Program
and to provide more effective supervision
of the procurement activities of the supply
arms and services, the Assistant Secretary of
War reorganized his office. The Current
Procurement Branch, OASW, which had
supervised the War Department's peacetime
contract placement and administration activities, was divided into two branches—
Purchases and Contracts (P&C) and
Production.[26]

The Purchases and Contracts Branch,
eventually composed of some eleven sections, had the basic mission of expediting the
placement of orders under the procurement
program. It reviewed and formulated purchase policy, established basic contract
forms and placement procedures, supervised
the assignment of claims and the making of
advance payments to contractors, administered the tax amortization program, established basic auditing policies of the War
Department, handled legal and legislative
matters for OASW, and co-ordinated generally the purchasing activities of the various
supply arms and services. In March 1941,
the Defense Aid Section was created to
supervise placement of all contracts for lend-
lease procurement assigned to the War Department. By the beginning of 1942, the
various sections of the Purchases and Contracts Branch had been consolidated into six
major divisions—Legal, Progress, Construction Contracts, Advance Payments, Defense
Aid, and Control.[27]

The newly created Production Branch,
OASW, had the mission of expediting the
production and delivery of munitions after
contracts had been placed. It established
and administered procedures for analyzing
the progress of production and construction
programs, discovering choke points and unbalanced production, expediting the flow of
materials, eliminating other bottlenecks,
and speeding the delivery of finished munitions. As a part of these activities the Production Branch was responsible for assembling requirements information, surveying
industrial capacity, executing priority policy,
and establishing and supervising plant protection procedures and agencies. The
branch at first consisted of four divisions—
Aircraft, Ordnance, Miscellaneous, and
Construction. Subsequently four new divisions—Labor, Priorities, Plant Protection,
and Steel—were added.[28]

The fortunes of the major peacetime
branch of OASW—the Planning Branch—
were curiously mixed during the defense
period. The various unit mobilization plans
of the War Department, as part of the Industrial Mobilization Plan, had contemplated the merger of the planning and
operating agencies of the War Department
as soon as IMP was put into effect. But the
failure to adopt the superagency features of
IMP at the beginning of the defense period
threw these plans off balance. The Assistant
Secretary of War, as well as officers in the
Planning Branch, still hoped for the future
invocation of IMP, if not of M Day, and
preferred to keep the planning organizations
and many of their functions intact.

The Munitions Program, great as it was
in terms of previous procurement magni-

---

[26] OASW Office Order, 11 Jul 40.

[27] Mohler, Administrative Log of the Production
Division, Headquarters, ASF, and Its Antecedent
Agencies, 1939–1945, pp. 5–8. By this time a num-

ber of functions had been transferred out of the
P&C Branch.

[28] *Ibid.,* pp. 8–13.

tudes, was roughly only half the size of the maximum effort contemplated by IMP. In the face of an abundance of idle plant capacity inherited from ten years of depression, strict observance of facility allocations was considered to be economically undesirable and politically unwise. Informal competitive bidding among allocated facilities as well as other qualified firms would secure the most advantageous terms to the government for the majority of contracts. Nevertheless, it was considered highly desirable to keep facility records and allocation plans up to date, both for current use and to provide for possible strict allocation at a later time. All this work, as well as many other planning activities, had been carried on by the Planning Branch and it was thought that these activities would be disrupted by a premature merger of planning with current procurement.[29]

As a result, the Planning Branch occupied a compromise position throughout the defense period. On the one hand, it continued its peacetime-type activities on an accelerated basis—revising and enlarging its records of available productive facilities, supervising the revision and augmentation of the procurement plans of the supply arms and services, bringing up to date its studies of strategic and critical materials, and continuing its role as the "Army half" of the Army and Navy Munitions Board. But these and other activities necessarily brought it into areas of current procurement and production occupied by the P&C and Production Branches. Thus, the Planning Branch

maintained a Legal Division, a Priorities Division, a Construction Division, a Defense Aid Division, and other offices identical in name and similar in many functions to counterparts in the P&C and Production Branches. A *modus vivendi* was gradually worked out, with the Planning Branch concentrating its efforts in fields not adequately covered by the operating branches—especially in the broader aspects of economic mobilization and longer-range planning. In this capacity the Planning Branch was deeply involved in launching and developing the priorities system, coping with the shortage of machine tools, computing raw material requirements, presenting the Army's views on economic mobilization matters to the NDAC and its successor agencies, and in many other activities of an operating as well as a planning nature.

Notwithstanding these adaptations to the circumstances, failure to provide an effective integration of the procurement planning and the operating agencies of the War Department at the outset of the defense period was the source of considerable confusion and frustration. This was evident not only within OASW but in the headquarters and field offices of several of the supply arms and services, most notably in the case of the Quartermaster Corps. Procurement planning in the QMC had envisaged a changeover in time of emergency from centralized depot procurement to decentralized purchasing, with each military corps area as nearly self-sufficient as possible. In the launching of the Munitions Program, the central depots simply expanded their current procurement operations and resisted any major organizational changes. This resulted in considerable friction between the planning and current procurement organizations in the QMC field establishments:

[29] (1) AIC R56, Plans for Industrial Mobilization, 1920–1939, pp. 76ff. (2) Pitkin and Rifkind, Procurement Planning in QMC, pp. 119–28. (3) Brig Gen Harry K. Rutherford, Dir Planning Br OASW, The Organization and Functions of OASW, 12 Sep 40, AIC Lectures, 17:168.

SECRETARY OF WAR HENRY L. STIMSON *(1940-45)*.

The unhappy relationship between the two field organizations was long a thorn in the side of the Quartermaster body. Its intended mission unrealized and its current efforts unappreciated, the procurement planning organization rapidly disintegrated. Much reduced in strength and effectiveness, it was ordered discontinued in the fall of 1942, and its remaining personnel absorbed in the current procurement depots.[30]

The Ordnance Department, on the other hand, was not confronted with this problem. Its peacetime procurement was relatively small and its emergency program followed very closely the pattern established by procurement planning. These basic differences partly account for the wide divergences of opinion on the issue of whether

and to what extent the results of the Army's peacetime planning efforts were actually utilized for World War II.

Effective 12 December 1940, Congress passed new legislation transferring to the Secretary of War all the statutory duties assigned to the Assistant Secretary by the National Defense Act of 1920. The new law also permitted the appointment of an Under Secretary of War and the complete delegation by the Secretary—to any of his staff members—of his procurement and industrial mobilization responsibilities. Assistant Secretary Robert P. Patterson, who had joined the War Department shortly after Secretary Henry L. Stimson in the summer of 1940, was promoted to the Under Secretariat, and the Office of the Under Secretary of War completely replaced the Office of the Assistant Secretary of War. The new legislation, by removing the statutory authority formerly conferred upon the Assistant Secretary, insured a unified civilian command in the War Department, preventing the possibility of a recurrence of the kind of schism which had existed in 1939.

The responsibilities of the Office of the Under Secretary of War (OUSW) and its predecessor, OASW, during the defense period were of a magnitude and importance seldom visited upon a single organization or agency. Relatively few persons in the United States as a whole knew or understood the nation's utter lack of military preparedness to defend itself against a major aggressor, or that it would require some two years before this deficiency could be substantially overcome. Under Secretary Patterson, like Louis Johnson before him, was keenly aware of this situation and, from the time of his appointment to the end of the war, devoted his efforts with singleness of purpose to filling the Army's needs for munitions and the asso-

---

[30] AIC R56, Plans for Industrial Mobilization, 1920–1939, p. 79.

ciated tasks of mobilizing the nation's productive resources.

The dominant mood prevalent in OUSW during the defense period was the sense of urgency, coupled with the frustration inevitably flowing from the difficulties of getting rapid action when the nation was still at peace. Urgency required that many things be done which could not be done without a revolution in national psychology, statutory requirements, administrative regulations, organizational prerogatives, and countless other elements in the institutional fabric of government as well as of the community at large. Above all was the huge question mark, with its many ramifications, which pervaded the entire rearmament effort: Would war actually come to the United States, and if so, would our preparations be enough and in time? Or would all the elaborate efforts of economic mobilization—the conversion of industry, the creation of a vast empire of industrial plant and equipment, the erection and expansion of military posts, camps, stations, and other field establishments throughout the nation, all requiring the expenditure of billions of dollars and vast changes in the way of life of millions of people—turn out to be unnecessary, or at best a form of insurance against the advent of a war which never came?

The burden of decision as to the proper course of national policy in the midst of this uncertainty fell upon the Congress of the United States and—more than any other single individual—upon the President. But the task of formulating the vast program of action to be taken fell chiefly to the military agencies, the senior and largest of which was the War Department. Among the War Department's many responsibilities, none were greater than those resting upon the Under Secretary and his office. Mr. Patterson was determined that whether war came or not the responsibilities of his office would be met.

The relationship which developed between the War Department—as represented by OUSW—and the Advisory Commission to the Council of National Defense was considerably different from that envisaged by the Industrial Mobilization Plan and from the corresponding relationship achieved by the end of World War. I. At the beginning of that war the department's serious lack of a distinguishable military program and supporting plans for procurement placed it in roughly the same position as the embryonic central mobilization control agencies. All offices of the government were feeling their way on a trial-and-error basis toward a positive and integrated war munitions program. This experimental period came to an end with the revitalization of the War Industries Board under the leadership of Bernard Baruch. Thereafter the Army and Navy leaned heavily upon the board and looked to it as their guide and advocate.

When the crisis of 1940 arrived the military procuring agencies were in a position much different from that of their predecessors a generation before. Twenty years of planning had given them far more specific ideas of what they needed and of the vigorous measures which would be necessary to supply these needs. The NDAC, on the other hand, came suddenly and without preparation to a bewildering task which had to be discovered and defined in the midst of day-to-day decisions and operations of the first magnitude. In addition to this handicap, NDAC's seven independent advisory commissioners lacked the organization and clear-cut authority to adopt many of the policies essential to rapid mobilization. Moreover, the vaguely defined charters of the individual commissioners carried at least some implication that they represented the interest of special groups rather than a unified effort to rearm the nation as quickly as possible.

These and many other considerations produced a kind of administrative vacuum in the area of central mobilization control for which the military agencies, who for years had looked to the establishment of a powerful War Resources Administration, were unprepared. Anxious to get on with their procurement programs, which required the immediate placement of contracts with the most capable firms, the launching of vast new construction projects, the expansion and conversion of existing industrial establishments, and the application of production control measures, the services chafed over what they thought were unnecessary delays and reviewing procedures. As a result the Army and Navy moved in to fill the vacuum left by the absence of decisive action on various issues and went ahead with specific programs without waiting for the formal approval which NDAC often felt should have been obtained in advance of action.

In several areas in particular, the Under Secretary of War and many of his staff often felt that NDAC and its successor, OPM, were too cautious and overly concerned with considerations secondary in importance to preparation for the war which seemed imminent. These areas were the approval of new plant facilities, the administration of the tax amortization program, the application of adequate priority controls, and the curtailment of regular commercial production. For their part, authorities in NDAC and OPM felt that the Under Secretary of War was indifferent to civilian

needs, to the dangers of sudden dislocations of industry, and to the permanent effects of a hastily adopted economic mobilization program upon the national economy and social structure. These attitudes on both sides were far from universally or permanently held but they tended to establish a pattern which persisted on into the war, when—with the aid of the nation's ubiquitous and eager press—they occasionally broke out into open controversy. A number of the major disputes over the economic mobilization program for World War II can be traced to foundations established during the defense period.[31]

A factor in the development of OUSW which had an important bearing on War Department policies and activities during the defense period was the change in character of its key personnel. Throughout the planning period OASW had been manned and operated almost exclusively by Army officers. Years of military tradition and practice had provided the greatest opportunities for advancement in command and General Staff positions, resulting in the relegation of procurement duty to secondary status if not to that of poor relation. Even for officers specializing in matters of procurement and supply, assignment to OASW—especially at middle and low echelons—was often regarded as a period of alienation from the supply arm or service in which they were permanently commissioned and to which they looked for long-run advancement.

---

[31] For the further exploration of this subject as well as the general history of OUSW, the reader is referred to Troyer S. Anderson, Introduction to the History of the Under Secretary of War's Office (1947), copy in OCMH. This manuscript provides a highly readable and informative account of the evolution of OUSW from its antecedents in World War I, and of the problems of economic mobilization during the defense period.

Hence, it was not the custom of the various supply arms to send their best men for duty with OASW. Furthermore, relations between OASW and the General Staff were marked by a certain atmosphere of aloofness. This resulted partly from the failure of the General Staff to obtain full control of procurement in the early 1920's and partly from the minor frictions accumulating out of conflicts of authority and interest in areas, such as requirements and specifications, where the acitvities of the two offices met.

For all these reasons the officers in OASW, including those of superior ability in key positions, did not possess the rank which was clearly called for in an office having policy-making powers and authority over all the supply arms and services, the procurement districts, and other field establishments. The highest ranking officer in OASW, the executive officer, was still only a colonel several months after the launching of the defense program. In a body as "rank conscious" as the Army this was a serious handicap in dealing with other agencies both within and outside the War Department. Apart from general matters of prestige and authority in day-to-day operations, this factor made it difficult to get and retain the most capable officers in OASW.

In order to offset this disadvantage and to obtain personnel who could adjust rapidly to the unusual problems faced by his office, Mr. Patterson built up a personal staff of key civilians who became largely responsible for the formulation of policies in OASW throughout the defense period. Most of these were lawyers, trained at Harvard and with professional practice in the New York area. Since many of the major problems connected with the launching of the defense program were legal in nature—involving complex issues in contractual

policy, negotiations with the nation's leading corporations, the exploitation of existing statutes to the advantage of the rearmament program, recommendation of new legislation, and testifying before Congress—the services of the group of legally trained advisers came to be indispensable. Although a few of them were recalled to active duty as Reserve officers, they constituted a closely knit team with a definite civilian orientation. This important and often decisive influence of civilians in the Under Secretary's office, as well as elsewhere in the War Department, was usually overlooked in the course of various interagency conflicts which took place from time to time throughout World War II. Differences in viewpoint between civilians in the War Department and civilians in other agencies were typically labeled as "military-versus-civilian" controversies, when more often they merely reflected understandable divergences of interest between different agencies responsible for the accomplishment of distinctive missions.[32]

The basic foundation for the great outpouring of Army munitions during World War II was laid during the period of OUSW hegemony as the War Department policy-making and co-ordinating body in the field of procurement and economic mobilization. Actual deliveries of finished munitions during the defense period were small in comparison with the astronomical quantities reached at the peak of the war. But they were large by peacetime standards and were of critical importance to the lend-lease program in its initial stages, as well as to the rehabilitation and expansion of the U.S. Army. The most significant element of

[32] The above discussion of OUSW personnel has been based on Anderson, Introduction to the History of the Under Secretary of War's Office, Chapter VI, especially pages 57–63.

progress during the defense period was not
the increase in procurement deliveries but
the creation of productive facilities essential
to the output of munitions. This rate of
facilities expansion greatly overshadowed
the rate of actual production prior to Pearl
Harbor, which accounted only for some 4
to 5 percent of total production for the entire war. Some $3 billion, or nearly one
third, of all War Department sponsored facilities for World War II had been authorized by the end of 1941. According to one
estimate, some three fourths of these were
in at least partial operation by the end of
1942.[33] Closely related to the preparation
of facilities was the entire array of developments in the field of contract placement, the
tooling up of industry, and other steps in the
total field of economic mobilization—factors not susceptible of statistical measurement but vital to the eventual outcome of
the war.

*The War Period: Regime
of the Army Service Forces*

The role of OUSW as the active director
of the War Department's procurement and
production program came to an end with
the basic reorganization of the War Department on 9 March 1942.[34] At this time the
War Department organization in the United
States was divided into three main parts:
the Army Ground Forces (AGF), the Army
Air Forces (AAF), and the Army Service
Forces (ASF). The Army Service Forces,
under the command of Lieutenant General
Brehon B. Somervell, was made responsible

for all Army procurement and economic
mobilization (except for items peculiar to
the Air Forces) as well as many other activities, subject only to general supervision by
the Under Secretary of War and the Chief
of Staff.

The Army Service Forces embraced three
broad echelons of War Department offices
and agencies: (1) ASF headquarters, which
included a wide array of functional staff
divisions; (2) headquarters and field establishments of the several technical services;
(3) the nine geographical service commands throughout the United States.
(*Chart 1*) Collectively, the ASF organization comprised the vast bulk of War Department activities and civilian personnel within
the United States. On 30 June 1943, when
the number of War Department civilians
within the continental United States reached
its peak, the ASF accounted for over a million civilian employees, or some 75 percent
of the War Department total in the
country: [35]

Location	Number of Employees
Total War Department	1, 545, 457
Total Within United States	1, 375, 457
Total Army Service Forces	1, 022, 074
Headquarters, Army Service Forces	32, 778
Technical Services	635, 714
Service Commands	352, 075
U.S. Military Academy and Command and General Staff School	1, 507

Headquarters, ASF, absorbed all but a
handful of the office and staff formerly attached to OUSW. It also absorbed large
portions of the War Department General
Staff. These included most of G–4 (Supply
Division), portions of G–1 and G–3 (the
Personnel, and Organization and Training

---

[33] Anderson, Munitions for the Army—A Five
Year Report on the Procurement of Munitions by
the War Department Under the Direction of the
Under Secretary of War, p. 22.

[34] (1) Executive Order 9082, 28 Feb 42, effective
9 Mar 42. (2) WD Cir 59, 2 Mar 42.

[35] Whiting *et al.*, Statistics, Civilian Personnel, 16
Jan 53 draft, Table CP–4.

CHART 1—ORGANIZATION OF THE ARMY SERVICE FORCES: 15 AUGUST 1944

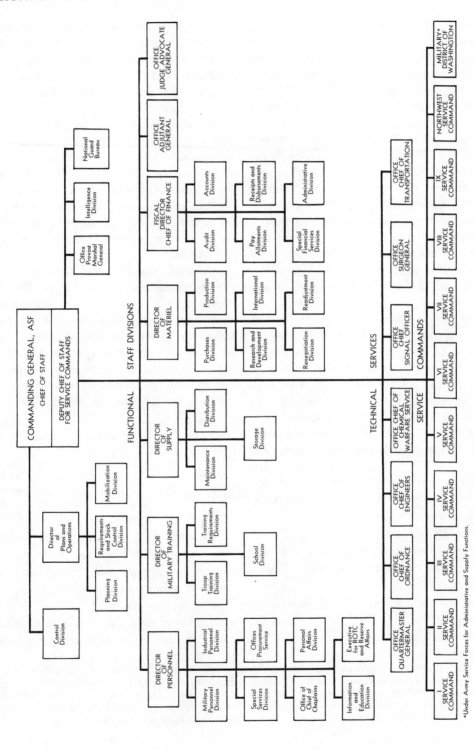

*Under Army Service Forces for Administrative and Supply Functions.

Divisions, respectively), and minor functions of G–2 (Intelligence Division). In addition, ASF headquarters took over bodily a large number of administrative offices formerly reporting to the Chief of Staff. These included the offices of The Adjutant General, Judge Advocate General, The Inspector General, Provost Marshal General, Chief of Finance, and Chief of Chaplains. Many new offices were soon created within ASF to meet the rising demands of war in all of the functional areas concerned. Throughout the war, the Army's coordinating machinery for procurement and economic mobilization—lodged primarily in the Office of the Director of Materiel—constituted the hard core of ASF headquarters.

The second echelon of ASF consisted of the seven technical services and their multitudinous field establishments—procurement district and field offices, arsenals and proving grounds, powder, high explosives, and loading plants, ammunition and storage depots, ports of embarkation, market centers, and many other varieties. The technical services were the renamed "supply arms and services" of the 1930's, which in turn had replaced the "supply branches" of the 1920's. The seven technical services were the Ordnance Department, Quartermaster Corps, Signal Corps, Corps of Engineers, Medical Department, Chemical Warfare Service, and the newly established Transportation Corps.[36]

The technical services were the operating agencies of the War Department in all its supply activities. They were responsible for the design and development of equipment, detailed computation of requirements, the placing and administration of procurement contracts, and the inspection, receipt, storage, and distribution of finished munitions. Each technical service specialized in major categories of equipment, supplies, and services assigned to it by statute or administrative order. All of the technical services procured equipment for lend-lease, the Navy, and other users in addition to the combat and service arms of the U.S. Army. They also had service or combat functions to perform in overseas theaters of military operations.

Although the technical services varied greatly in size and scope of operations, all were gigantic organizations, with headquarters in Washington and field establishments throughout the United States. Some idea of their size is conveyed by the following figures indicating the peak number of civilians (in addition to all military personnel) employed by each in World War II: [37]

Technical Service	Employees
Ordnance	259,484
Engineers	174,906
Quartermaster	138,711
Transportation	91,533
Signal	61,628
Medical	33,632
Chemical	29,058

The third ASF echelon referred to above was composed of the nine former corps areas—the nine geographical districts for military administration throughout the United States—renamed in June 1942 as service commands. The service commands, each headed by a commanding general,

---

[36] The procurement activities of the former Coast Artillery Corps were transferred to Ordnance, and the Air Corps had become the Army Air Forces—one of the three major components of the reorganized War Department.

[37] Whiting et al., Statistics, Civilian Personnel, 16 Jan 53 draft, Table CP–4. The figures shown are for various dates. Engineer figure includes civilians in civil functions (for example, rivers and harbors) as well as in military functions.

were responsible for a variety of administrative and "housekeeping" functions for the Army within their respective geographical areas. They had administrative and supply responsibilities in the operation of AGF posts, camps, and stations but no control over troops in training therein. Although field installations of the AAF and the technical services were exempt from service command jurisdiction, minor functions—such as supervision of army exchanges, repair and maintenance, laundry operations, and disbursing—were performed for these installations by the service commands. On the whole, the procurement and related activities performed by the service commands were of a local and minor nature and of relatively small importance to the present study.[38]

---

[38] John D. Millett, *The Organization and Role of the Army Service Forces,* UNITED STATES ARMY IN WORLD WAR II (Washington: 1954).

The ASF organization brought together under one command all the scattered functions of the War Department concerned with services and matériel. It greatly reduced the number of officers reporting to the Chief of Staff, thereby enabling General Marshall to give his full attention to problems of strategy and national policy requiring decisions at the highest level. Under the vigorous leadership of General Somervell the Army Service Forces made an outstanding contribution to the war effort and to the program of economic demobilization at the war's end. The life of the ASF came to an end, on 30 June 1946, as a prelude to the authorization of a separate U.S. Air Force and the creation of a unified National Military Establishment.

The reader is also referred to the other volumes in the UNITED STATES ARMY IN WORLD WAR II series covering the activities of the various technical services.

PART THREE

DETERMINATION OF ARMY
REQUIREMENTS

CHAPTER VI

Army Requirement Programs: World War I to Pearl Harbor

Nature and Implications of Army Requirements

The starting point for all military procurement is the determination of military requirements—the kinds and quantities of end items required to carry out the military mission. Until some decision is reached as to what and how much is to be procured in a definite time period, no procurement operations can take place. Likewise, in the absence of knowledge of the types and quantities of end items needed, requirements for productive facilities, materials, manpower, and other contributory resources cannot be estimated, requests for appropriations cannot effectively be made, and even procurement planning cannot be projected much beyond the level of broad generalities.

Paradoxically, although it is the starting point for procurement activity, the formulation of military requirements is, of all aspects of industrial mobilization and procurement, the most difficult of satisfactory achievement. For World War II in particular, two decades of disarmament, grave divisions in political opinion prior to Pearl Harbor, the eventual magnitude and scope of Army operations, their dispersion to all parts of the world, their technological complexity, the rapidity of change in the kinds and uses

of needed equipment, and the heavy Allied claims upon the United States as the "arsenal of democracy," all made the task of accurately estimating requirements well-nigh impossible. The domestic political difficulties which hindered the formulation of national objectives previous to 7 December 1941 gave way thereafter to broad problems of determining Allied strategy and its supporting logistical arrangements on a global basis.

To the many political and methodological problems involved in computing requirements for World War II were added numerous practical barriers of an administrative nature. These included shortages of experienced personnel, the necessity for developing new organizations and procedures, the pressure of cruel deadlines in an atmosphere of urgency, and many other elements—all contributing to the difficulty of the underlying task. It is not surprising, therefore, that the armed services were sometimes slow in computing firm, long-range estimates of requirements and that these were subject to a substantial margin of error and the necessity for constant revision.

The importance of timely and accurate determination of its requirements for World War II extended far beyond the procurement operations of the Army itself. Since the Army in that war was the greatest single claimant upon the nation's productive resources the industrial mobilization plans of the entire nation depended heavily upon the nature and magnitude of Army requirements. Thus the central economic mobilization control agencies had a vital interest and stake in the designation of Army needs. But beyond the Army, and beyond the technical problems of industrial mobilization and war production, was the ultimate interest of the nation as a whole in the adoption of procurement objectives which were at once adequate to assure victory and sufficiently controlled to keep wasteful procurement to a minimum. The magnitude of Army requirements for World War II was such that overstatement could easily nullify economies of both materials and money painfully obtained by conservation, substitution, close pricing, contract renegotiation, and other measures. On the other hand, understatement would not only jeopardize the nation's security but would also be economically costly by resulting in piecemeal procurement and other inefficient production arrangements.

A detailed exposition of the Army's activities in planning its requirements for the World War II period, its achievements and its shortcomings, would require many volumes. The present condensation (Part Three) attempts only a broad portrayal of the evolution of requirement programs, the methods by which the Army computed its requirements, and some of the major issues in the area of requirements determination which arose throughout the planning cycle.[1]

[1] The best source of primary information on Army requirements and their relation to procurement in World War II is the interim history, The Determination of Army Supply Requirements, prepared in 1945 by Lt. Col. Simon M. Frank, QMC, of the

Army Attrition and Gradual Rehabilitation: 1920 to 1939

During the two decades between World War I and II, Army requirements problems rested upon two related but distinguishable questions: (1) What should be the peacetime strength and equipment of the Army?

Requirements and Stock Control Division, ASF. The documentary collection (159 documents) in support of this monograph is unusually rich in pertinent materials. The Frank monograph, a copy of which may be found in OCMH, is hereafter cited as Frank, Requirements; specific documents in the collection are cited by number as Frank, Doc. (no.). For a broad chronological treatment of the influence of strategy and logistics upon Army requirements, see the two volumes by Richard M. Leighton and Robert W. Coakley, *Global Logistics and Strategy, 1940–1943*, UNITED STATES ARMY IN WORLD WAR II (Washington: 1955), and Global Logistics and Strategy, 1943–1945, in preparation for the series UNITED STATES ARMY IN WORLD WAR II, MS, OCMH. On this subject, see also Logistics in World War II, Final Report of the Army Service Forces, A Report to the Under Secretary of War and the Chief of Staff by the Director of the Service, Supply, and Procurement Division of the War Department General Staff (1947), especially Chapter 4, in OCMH. A wealth of illustrative detail concerning specific items as well as general trends in Army requirements throughout the war period may be found in the chapters on requirements in the annual reports of the Army Service Forces for fiscal years 1942 through 1945. Copies of the reports are filed in the Pentagon Army Library. Two other useful references are Richard U. Sherman, Jr., The Formulation of Military Requirements for Munitions and Raw Materials (Ph.D. thesis, Harvard, March 1953); and George A. Lincoln (professor at U.S. Military Academy), "Economic Problems of Military Mobilization—Planning Military Requirements," *American Economic Review,* XLII (May 1952), 438–52.

The complex task of determining the Army's indirect requirements for raw materials is discussed in Chapter XXV, "The Controlled Materials Plan." Throughout the present volume the term "matériel" is used to refer collectively to the complex array of end items procured by the Army. "Material" is used to refer to raw materials and components entering completed end items.

(2) What plans should be made regarding the size and equipment of the Army to be mobilized in case of war? The answers to these questions were furnished by the interaction of a complex set of factors and influences, many of which were outside the jurisdiction and scope of War Department activity.

At the end of World War I the United States had approximately 3.5 million men under arms, together with huge surpluses of war matériel belatedly accumulated before the sudden cessation of hostilities. With painful memories of poorly planned mobilization fresh in mind, Congress in 1920 adopted the statutory expression of U.S. peacetime military policy. The National Defense Act of that year provided the basis for definite answers to the two questions stated above: (1) it defined in considerable detail the organization, composition, and size of the peacetime Army; and (2) it made specific provision for advance planning of the mobilization process to be used in the event of war.[2] It is of interest to examine the record during the interwar years in the light of the policy expressed in this act.

The National Defense Act specified, in Section 2, the size of the peacetime Army as "not to exceed" 280,000 men. This figure, plus some 425,000 men contemplated under the National Guard, would give the United States nearly three quarters of a million trained soldiers as an Initial Protective Force (IPF) in case of emergency.[3] Such a force was regarded by military planners as the minimum needed for initial defense and for providing a balanced nucleus from which Army expansion would be evenly and rapidly made in the event of war.

The size of the Army contemplated by the National Defense Act was never realized in the two decades following its enactment. Lack of funds, together with specific limitations upon the Army's size by successive appropriation acts, confined the Army's actual strength throughout most of the interwar period to a fraction of the 1920 objective.[4] The desire of a war-weary nation to "return to normalcy," the heritage of a war debt of unprecedented size, the lack of any apparent urgency, and faith in disarmament as the only sure pathway to peace were among the factors contributing to Army deterioration. As early as mid-1923, the enlisted strength of the Army had fallen to less than 120,000 and not until a dozen years later did it exceed 130,000. For the bulk of the period, Army strength hovered around 40 percent of the target expressed in 1920. The National Guard fared little better, becoming stabilized at around 190,000 men in the early 1930's. (*Table 16*)

The effects upon the Army of its attrition in manpower could not be adequately measured by the simple ratio expressed by

---

[2] 41 *Stat.* 759, 4 Jun 20.

[3] The National Defense Act of 1916 (39 *Stat.* 166, 3 June 1916) provided for the creation of a National Guard with a strength of eight hundred enlisted men per member of Congress.

[4] An analysis of strength limitations in the eighteen regular appropriation acts from 1923 to 1940 reveals a number of methods used by Congress to limit the size of the Army. From fiscal year 1923 through fiscal year 1927, the appropriation Pay of the Army flatly prohibited any excess over 125,000 enlisted men. From 1928 to 1935 there was no limit on numbers but guns were provided for an average strength of only 118,750. The 1936 and 1938 appropriations authorized an average of 165,000; 1939 and 1940, an average "not to exceed 165,000." The 1937 appropriation interestingly provided for an enlisted strength of "not less than an average of 165,000." All such numerical limitations were eliminated by the Supplemental Appropriation Act of 1940 and successive acts throughout World War II. See *Military Laws of the United States, 1939* (8th ed.; Washington: Government Printing Office, 1940), pp. 28, 32.

TABLE 16—STRENGTH OF ARMY AND NATIONAL GUARD, 1920–1945

[Actual Strength as of 30 June for Each Year]

Year	U.S. Army [a]			National Guard		
	Officers	Men	Total	Officers	Men	Total
1920	18,999	184,848	203,847	2,073	54,017	56,090
1921	16,501	213,341	229,842	5,843	107,787	113,630
1922	15,667	132,106	147,773	8,744	150,914	159,658
1923	14,021	118,348	132,369	9,675	150,924	160,598
1924	13,784	128,233	142,007	10,996	166,432	177,428
1925	14,594	121,762	136,356	11,595	165,930	177,525
1926	14,143	119,973	134,116	11,435	163,534	174,969
1927	14,020	119,929	133,949	12,192	168,950	181,142
1928	14,019	121,185	135,204	12,428	168,793	181,221
1929	14,047	124,216	138,263	12,535	164,453	176,988
1930	14,151	124,301	138,452	12,930	169,785	182,715
1931	14,159	125,467	139,626	13,249	174,137	187,386
1932	14,111	119,913	134,024	13,550	173,863	187,413
1933	13,896	121,788	135,684	13,569	172,356	185,925
1934	13,761	123,823	137,584	13,507	171,284	184,791
1935	13,471	125,098	138,569	13,571	172,344	185,915
1936	13,512	153,212	166,724	13,721	175,452	189,173
1937	13,740	164,993	178,733	14,110	178,051	192,161
1938	13,975	170,151	184,126	14,443	182,745	197,188
1939	14,486	174,079	188,565	14,666	184,825	199,491
1940	18,326	249,441	267,767	14,775	226,837	241,612
1941	99,536	1,341,462	1,460,998	(b)	(b)	(b)
1942	206,422	2,867,762	3,074,184	(b)	(b)	(b)
1943	579,576	6,413,526	6,993,102	(b)	(b)	(b)
1944	776,980	7,215,888	7,992,868	(b)	(b)	(b)
1945	891,663	7,374,710	8,266,373	(b)	(b)	(b)

[a] U.S. Army figures include personnel in AAF and its predecessors, Philippine Scouts, Army Nurse Corps, WAC, and miscellaneous components on active duty.

[b] Assimilated into U.S. Army.

Source: Records of Statistics Branch, Program Review and Analysis Division, Office of the Comptroller of the Army, Office, Chief of Staff.

a 60-percent reduction from the National Defense Act objective. This curtailment meant the virtual abandonment of the major peacetime function of the Army—the progressive training of both individuals and organizations as specialized and co-operating units in military activity. The balance in the size and composition of the several combat arms—the Infantry, Cavalry, Field Artillery, Coast Artillery Corps, combat engineers, and others—as well as of individual battalions, regiments, divisions, and larger organizational units, was drastically upset. The necessity for preserving essential overhead activities, vital to the existence of the Army as a national unit, threw the burden of reduction heavily upon functional units at lower echelons. The end results were cogently expressed by General Mac-Arthur in his annual report as Chief of Staff in 1932:

After all these essential needs have been satisfied there is left in the United States for organization into tactical units approximately 3,000 officers and 55,000 men. Due to the requirements of civilian training, and because of the distribution of existing housing facilities, these units are scattered in small posts and detachments throughout the length and breadth of continental United States. . . . in this situation combined training by the various arms and services of the Regular Army is limited to small concentrations. Many garrisons are at such reduced strength as to constitute little more than service detachments for local maintenance and for civilian training camps. . . . it has become extremely difficult, and in some cases almost impossible, for even the smallest units to follow a progressive training program.[5]

This attrition in the size and quality of the Army was accompanied by an even more serious deterioration in the Army's stock of effective equipment. Several factors combined to intensify the matériel deterioration. The existence of huge surpluses of equipment at the end of World War I proved to be an embarrassment for the next decade and a half. Much of this surplus stock was already obsolescent at the war's end, and the rapid, world-wide technological advance of the 1920's rendered it still less usable. Yet it was manifestly out of the question in the early postwar years for the Army to ask for any appreciable funds for new equipment. Without relaxing its attempts to develop improved weapons and other equipment for future procurement, the War Department adopted the policy of continuing to issue old types until existing stocks were exhausted.[6]

By the beginning of the 1930's most of the Army's equipment, apart from quantitative considerations, was antiquated or depreciated to the point of being worn out. Unfortunately for prospects of replacement, the arrival of the prolonged economic depression resulted in substantial cuts in the War Department budget—already heavily deficient in its provision for equipment. From a figure of $345 million for fiscal year 1931, War Department military expenditures were cut over the next three years to a new postwar low of $243 million for fiscal year 1934. In the face of such retrenchment, the Army chose the alternative of further sacrificing its position in matériel:

So far as possible every reduction has been absorbed by continuing in service obsolete and inefficient equipment, and where absolutely necessary, by suspending technical research and development work. There has resulted also a serious shortage in ammunition both for target practice and for reserve stocks.

The risks involved in such a policy are clearly recognized, yet in view of the necessities of the situation, it has been followed as a lesser evil than that of permitting deterioration either in strength or efficiency of the human organization maintained as the backbone of our land defense establishment.[7]

Long before retrenchment had reached its maximum in 1933–34, the various Secre-

---

[5] Annual *Report of the Secretary of War to the President, 1932* (Washington: Government Printing Office, 1932), p. 59. Of total Army strength as of 30 June 1932, 1,915 officers and some 36,000 men were stationed in overseas garrisons. Another 7,000 officers and nearly 30,000 men were required in departmental and corps area overhead, the supply arms and services, river and harbor development, and miscellaneous activities.

[6] Ltr, TAG to TQMG, 15 Sep 22, sub: Annual Survey of Adopted Types of Equipment, AG 400.114 (9–14–22) (Misc.) D, cited in Erna Risch, *The Quartermaster Corps: Organization, Supply, and Services,* UNITED STATES ARMY IN WORLD WAR II (Washington: 1953) (hereafter cited as *QMC Supply*), I, 52.

[7] Annual Report of the Chief of Staff, in Annual *Report of the Secretary of War to the President, 1933* (Washington: Government Printing Office, 1933), p. 19.

taries of War, Chiefs of Staff, and other War Department spokesmen had repeatedly called to the attention of Congress the seriousness of the Army's position with respect to equipment.[8] The following statements near the end of the years of attrition summarize the entire period:

This deficit has not occurred suddenly but . . . is the cumulative result of years of failure to provide adequately for procurement and replacement.[9]
Ten years of relative stagnation . . . cannot, under any circumstances, be overcome instantaneously.[10]
Concerning such matters, the War Department function is advisory only and in this capacity it frequently, between 1922 and 1935, expressed its conviction that in conditions then prevailing resided grave potentialities for disaster. During the past 5 years, the Department has insistently urged upon appropriate congressional committees the stark seriousness of this situation.[11]

Thus, in the early 1930's the Army was seriously deficient in almost all items of equipment required to fight a modern war. Specifically, it lacked motorized equipment essential to rapid transportation of troops: the Army still moved almost entirely on foot. Its mechanized combat equipment was limited principally to tanks, and these (with the exception of a handful of test units) were the obsolete World War I stocks with a maximum speed of four to five miles per hour and highly vulnerable armor. Its field artillery consisted largely of 75-mm. units lacking both mobility and flexibility of fire power: the lateral traverse was limited to 6 degrees, as compared with 90 degrees for later models, and the guns could not be towed at even moderate speeds. The infantry rifle was still the Springfield 1903 bolt-action model: as of 30 June 1934 the Army possessed only eighty semiautomatic rifles.[12] Ammunition reserves were inadequate for any emergency; in mid-1935 General MacArthur hopefully proposed as a concrete objective the gradual accumulation of a thirty-day operating supply of ammunition in the essential calibers for the small peacetime Army called for by the National Defense Act. Such items as antiaircraft guns, aircraft cannon, and aircraft detection equipment had only recently been developed and improved models of these items were needed in large quantities. Only in airplane development was the Army's equipment situation deemed reasonably satisfactory, but vastly greater numbers of the new planes would be needed in wartime.[13]

In order to remedy its manifest weakness in matériel and to remove its peacetime procurement program from a hand-to-mouth basis the Army devised a number of long-range programs in the hope that they would receive the support of Congress. As far back as 1927 a Ten-Year Ordnance Program had been adopted for the development and procurement of a limited number of items.[14] In September 1932, a Six-Year Rearma-

---

[8] (1) A compilation of official and public statements by War Department spokesmen on the inadequacy of Army appropriations and national defense measures between 1919 and 1941 may be found in Cater files, 1941 folder, General Reference Br OCMH. (2) A number of these statements appear in Truman Committee, *Hearings,* 1:364–68, Exhibit 36.
[9] Annual Report of the Chief of Staff, in Annual *Rpt of the SW, 1933,* p. 19.
[10] *Ibid.,* in Annual *Report of the Secretary of War to the President, 1934* (Washington: Government Printing Office, 1934), p. 39.
[11] *Ibid.,* in Annual *Report of the Secretary of War to the President, 1935* (Washington: Government Printing Office, 1935), p. 42.

[12] *Ibid.,* in Annual *Rpt of the SW, 1934,* p. 41.
[13] *Ibid.,* in annual reports of the Secretary of War, 1932–35, especially 1934, p. 42.
[14] Green, Thomson, and Roots, *The Ordnance Department: Planning Munitions for War,* pp. 46ff.

ment and Re-equipment Program, together with a corresponding Research and Development Program, was adopted by the Supply Division of the General Staff as a basic objective in the rehabilitation of the Army. The purpose of the six-year program was to develop and supply for the existing Army and National Guard the most urgent items of equipment; the period to be covered was 1936–41. Lack of funds prevented realization of these objectives, and, in any case, additional study of problems of mechanization and motorization indicated that the program was inadequate to meet any serious threat of war; it would be necessary to provide reserve stocks of equipment, requiring a year or more to produce in quantity, to be available for sudden expansion of the Army beyond its existing strength. Hence, it was deemed advisable to project the six-year program beyond the term originally contemplated.[15] Eventually a War Reserve Program was separately established with the goal of providing and maintaining stocks of critical, "long-term" items, which would be needed immediately to equip an expanding Army in the event of an emergency. In the late 1930's annual expenditures for this program averaged about $30,000,000.[16]

The circumstance initially arresting the deterioration of the Army's matériel condition was the availability of funds under New Deal measures to combat the depression and restore employment. In fiscal year 1934 a grant of $10 million from the Public Works Administration (PWA) was applied to the procurement of motor vehicles for the Army. By 30 June 1935 approximately $100 million had been allotted to the Military Establishment of the War Department from the PWA; of this amount $68 million went into construction projects (posts, camps, stations, depots, and the like)and the remainder into equipment, including $6 million for ammunition and $7.5 million for aircraft. By 1938 some $250 million of relief and emergency funds had been devoted to the rehabilitation of the Military Establishment.[17]

From 1935 to the end of the 1930's, the record reveals moderate but steady increases in appropriations and corresponding progress in the re-equipment of the Army. Apart from the greater liberality of the New Deal government, events in Europe as well as in the Far East exerted a real and increasing influence upon the course of U.S. rearmament. During this period an average of some $20 million annually was spent for equipment under the Rearmament and Re-equipment Program, $30 million for War Reserve, and $7 million for Research and Development.[18] The minimum motorization program for the peacetime Army, reported

---

[15] (1) Memo, ACofS G–4 for DCofS, 7 Sep 34, sub: Rearmament and Re-equipment Program, War Department. (2) Memo, ACofS G–3 for ACofS G–4, 27 Sep 34, same sub. (3) Memo, ACofS G–1 for ACofS G–4, 23 Oct 34, sub: Revision of Six-Year War Department Program, FY 1936 to 1941, Both Inclusive. All in G–4/29552–1. (4) Watson, *Prewar Plans,* p. 38.

[16] Frank, Requirements, p. 4.

[17] Annual Report of the Chief of Staff in Annual *Rpt of the SW, 1935,* pp. 53–54. For interesting sidelights on the Army and relief expenditures, see Robert E. Sherwood, *Roosevelt and Hopkins: An Intimate History* (New York: Harper & Brothers, 1948), pp. 76, 101. In its May 16, 1942 issue, the *Army and Navy Register* stated: "In the years 1935 to 1939 when regular appropriations for the armed forces were so meager, it was the WPA worker who saved many Army posts and Naval stations from literal obsolescence."

[18] (1) Background of the Army Supply Program [circa 1943], pp. 7–9 and Charts 4 and 5, OCMH. This little brochure was apparently written by Maj. Gen. Walter A. Wood, Jr., for lecture presentation. (2) Frank, Doc. 3.

WAR RESOURCES BOARD, *August 1939. Seated, left to right: Dr. Harold S. Moulton, Charles Edison, Assistant Secretary of the Navy; Edward R. Stettinius, and Louis Johnson, Assistant Secretary of War and Chairman of the War Resources Board. Standing: Cmdr. A. B. Anderson, Admiral Harold R. Stark, Dr. Karl Compton, John L. Pratt, Brig. Gen. George C. Marshall, Acting Army Chief of Staff; and Col. H. K. Rutherford.*

as 59-percent of the goal complete by the end of fiscal year 1936, had reached 79 percent by 1939. The 75-mm. field guns, left over from World War I, were gradually being modernized, both in mobility and in flexibility of fire, and the new 105-mm. howitzer for divisional artillery had been successfully developed. Stocks of the semiautomatic rifle had reached the point, with fiscal year 1939 appropriations, where "the initial equipment for all active units of the Regular Army and National Guard . . . [would] be available." [19] The Army had made similar progress in the light tank program and had recorded a modest beginning in the procurement of the medium tank.

Shortages in antiaircraft equipment, scout and combat cars, seacoast defense equipment, the 81-mm. mortar, the 37-mm. antitank gun, gas masks, radio equipment, and many other items had either been eliminated or substantially reduced. Measured by the later astronomical figures for the war years, the 1935–39 gains were paltry; but compared with the history of the preceding fifteen years they marked a substantial achievement and paved the way for the accelerated defense programs of 1940 and 1941.

The Munitions Program of 30 June 1940

Ever since Hitler's seizure of power in 1933, German rearmament and open

---

[19] Annual Report of the Chief of Staff, in Annual *Rpt of the SW, 1939*, p. 31.

threats against the peace had led to mounting unrest throughout the world. The last two years of the 1930's witnessed the transformation to actual invasion and open warfare. On 12 March 1938 Germany occupied Austria in a "bloodless invasion." Six more months brought the Munich pact and 12 March 1939, the invasion of the remainder of Czechoslovakia. Late in 1938, William C. Bullitt—U.S. ambassador to France—had returned from Europe with a dire message of warning to President Roosevelt. Mr. Bullitt forcefully described the fear which had spread throughout Europe and expressed his opinion of the inevitability of war. In particular, his description of the mighty German air force and the terror which it inspired made a profound impression on the President. The Bullitt report has been described as leading to the first "acute White House concern over the mounting powers of the Axis as a substantial threat to the security of the United States." [20] This concern led to a reappraisal of the state of American defenses, especially airpower, and to definite action to build them up.

From this time on, the nature of the Axis threat and the seriousness of America's state of unpreparedness became President Roosevelt's major concern. In view of the powerful isolationist and pacifist sentiment in the United States, he proceeded with caution. It nevertheless became known within the War Department that the President was anxious to secure an additional military appropriation from Congress in the near future, and G-4 went to work on estimates covering the more urgently needed items. On the basis of G-4's recommendations, the President went before Congress early in January 1939 with a request for a special

$110 million appropriation for the Army ground forces. This measure was passed by the House without change on 2 March, ten days before Germany overran Czechoslovakia, and was finally approved in May.[21] In the middle of the summer—9 August 1939—the President appointed the War Resources Board to review the existing Industrial Mobilization Plan, and three weeks later Germany invaded Poland. On 3 September England and France declared war on Germany and on 8 September 1939 the President proclaimed a state of limited national emergency.

The year 1940 opened in the peculiar atmosphere of what was known at the time as the "phony" war. Military planners in the United States—under no illusion as to the continuation of the impasse in Europe—regarded the letdown in operations as a fortunate gift of borrowed time. General George C. Marshall, testifying in February in support of the War Department budget for the coming fiscal year (1941), prophetically remarked: "If Europe blazes in the late spring or summer, we must put our house in order before the sparks reach the Western Hemisphere." [22]

Since 1936 General Staff plans for emergency mobilization of the Army had contemplated the immediate availability, on Mobilization Day, of an Initial Protective Force composed of the existing Army and the National Guard. A more inclusive force, proposed in the Protective Mobilization Plan, was to be available within ninety days after M Day by the induction of new recruits. In general, throughout the 1936–39

---

[20] Watson, *Prewar Plans,* pp. 131ff.

[21] 53 *Stat.* 642, 2 May 39, Second Supplemental Military Appropriation Act, FY 1940.

[22] Subcom. of the H. Com. on Appropriations, 76th Cong., 3d Sess., Hearings on H. R. 9209, *Military Establishment Appropriation Bill for 1941,* p. 3.

period, the PMP envisaged the availability of some 730,000 men in M plus 90 days, consisting of an IPF of 400,000 (165,000 Army and 235,000 National Guard) plus new recruitments of 330,000. Another 270,-000 men to be obtained shortly thereafter as "replacements" would bring the total to 1,000,000 men for whom equipment would have to be available in the vicinity of M Day. It was this hypothetical 1,000,000-man force which was the basis for the Army's equipment objectives during the late 1930's and on into 1940.[23]

At the time of General Marshall's testimony before the House committee, appropriations for 1940 and previous fiscal years had financed what was then termed "full equipment" for the existing forces of the Army and National Guard. The primary objective of the pending budget for fiscal year 1941 was therefore the provision of "critical items" for the PMP force of 1,000,-000 men—now stated as 750,000 for organized units and 250,000 individual replacements. Critical items were those difficult-to-procure items of equipment—ammunition, semiautomatic rifles, tanks, artillery, and so on—which would be needed immediately in an emergency but which would require from one to two years or longer to produce in adequate quantities. The early possession of such items was described by General Marshall as "like . . . gold in the vault against a financial crisis." [24] Included also in the War Depart-

ment fiscal year 1941 budget requests were the regular items normally covered by the annual appropriation, noticeably expanded in recognition of the existence of war in Europe.

Before the budget had been considered by the Senate, the apparent stalemate in Europe was broken with startling suddenness. On 9 April 1940 the German invasion of Norway began a rapid succession of events which in two short months saw the successful occupation of Norway, the capture of the Low Countries, the evacuation of Dunkerque, and the fall of France. The Axis threat to the Western Hemisphere and the rest of the world was now painfully obvious, and all previous estimates of U.S. military requirements were rendered obsolete. During this two-month period, the General Staff, the Under Secretary, and the various supply arms and services of the War Department were all engaged in constant review and revision of requirements estimates.[25] It was clear that any major defensive force would require vastly greater supplies and munitions than the PMP force only partly provided for in the pending budget. It soon became clear, also, that a major conversion and expansion of the nation's industry would be necessary if the supplies were to be produced in time.

---

[23] Watson, *Prewar Plans*, pp. 30, 128, 154. Throughout the 1930's both the Army and the National Guard were chronically below IPF strength, and the equipment objectives were not reached until after 1940.

[24] (1) Page 2 of hearings cited above, note 22. (2) Memo, ACofS G-4 for CofS, 15 Jan 40, sub: Remaining Shortages in Critical and Essential Items Required for the Present Existing Army and National Guard (After FY 1940), G-4/31349-1.

[25] For example, Memo, ACofS G-4 for CofS, 7 May 40, sub: Program for National Defense, submitting an over-all national defense program totaling $2,826 million beyond requests in the fiscal year 1941 budget. This program would provide critical equipment for a PMP strength of 1,166,000 men, temporary shelter, pay, rations, and maintenance of this force for one year, an air force of 5,806 planes, and miscellaneous facilities, spare parts, and so forth. The proposal was returned for further study, and on 6 June 1940, G-4 submitted an elaborate revision requiring $4.8 billion beyond the original fiscal year 1941 proposals of the War Department.   G-4/31349-1.

On 16 May 1940 the President addressed a special message to Congress, urging the development of aircraft productive capacity in the United States of fifty thousand planes per year and requesting immediate appropriations of $896 million for national defense. Of this amount, $546 million would go to the Army, $250 million to the Navy and Marine Corps, and $100 million to a special Presidential emergency fund. An additional $286 million in contract authorization was also requested. These requests were added to the regular military appropriation bill under consideration in the Senate, along with additions permitting Army expansion to the full peacetime strength of 280,000 specified in the National Defense Act of 1920. Under these influences, on 13 June 1940 a total Army appropriation of $1.5 billion in cash and $257 million in contract authorization was approved for the fiscal year 1941.[26]

Even before the passage of the regular appropriation act, successive German victories were compelling the consideration of additional measures to meet the situation. On 27 May 1940 the Chief of Staff requested a supplemental half-billion dollars for current production of tanks, antiaircraft guns, bombs, and three thousand planes. At the request of Col. James H. Burns, Executive for the Office of Assistant Secretary of War, $200 million was added for the creation of new productive facilities. Colonel Burns, who as the ranking officer in OASW was deeply involved in getting the industrial mobilization program under way, had been concerned for some time about the disparity in the length of time required to induct additional troops and the longer period required to provide them with critical equipment. The President approved these requests and placed them before Congress on 31 May. As a result, the First Supplemental National Defense Appropriation Act for Fiscal Year 1941 was approved and signed by the President on 26 June 1940.[27] This act provided $821 million in cash and $254 million in contract authorization and specifically permitted expansion of the Regular Army to a total of 375,000 enlisted men. Including the regular fiscal year 1941 appropriation, the War Department now had a total of some $3 billion to prepare for the emergency.

The important appropriation acts just described were not, however, sufficient to implement the President's 50,000-plane-capacity objective or to commit the economy to a long-range program of industrial mobilization. They represented essentially a short-run response to a series of events which had barely begun and whose culmination could only be a matter of speculation. What was needed in mid-1940 was a bold program which would look beyond the fiscal year and enable American industry to make the heavy capital commitments, plant expansion, and organizational changes essential to large-scale armament production. Such a program would state procurement objectives in large and round numbers, in contrast to the meticulous calculations used in previous years to defend to the penny each War Department budget request.

On 11 June 1940—a little more than a week after his appointment—William Knudsen, the NDAC commissioner for pro-

[26] (1) Public Law 611, 76th Cong., 3d Sess., Military Appropriation Act, 1941 (54 *Stat.* 350, 13 Jun 40). (2) For Presidential address to Congress on 16 May 1940, see *Vital Speeches,* VI (1939–40), 482–84.

[27] Public Law 667, 76th Cong., 3d Sess. (54 *Stat.* 599, 26 Jun 40). See also Biennial Report of the Chief of Staff of the U.S. Army to the Secretary of War, 1 July 1939 to 30 June 1941, p. 4.

LT. GEN. WILLIAM S. KNUDSEN,
NDAC Commissioner for Production, World War II.

duction, conferred with Assistant Secretary of War Johnson. Mr. Knudsen raised two basic questions, the answers to which he desired at the earliest possible moment: How much munitions productive capacity does this country need and how rapidly must it become available? [28] In reply to these questions, on 13 June 1940 Mr. Johnson presented the broad outlines of a program: (1) for the ground Army, productive capacity sufficient to meet the needs of an expanding Army of 1,000,000 men by 1 October 1941, 2,000,000 men by 1 January 1942, and 4,000,000 men by 1 April 1942; (2) for the aircraft program, annual productive capacity of 9,000, 18,000, and 36,000 planes, respectively, for the dates mentioned. The lat-

ter was in keeping with the 50,000-plane program called for by the President: 36,500 of these would go to the Army, 13,500 to the Navy. [29]

On 18 June Assistant Secretary Johnson outlined for Mr. Knudsen the probable cost of the program. On the basis of sample estimates, it would total more than $11 billion—over $6 billion for Ordnance, $3 billion for the Air Corps, and $2 billion for the remaining supply arms and services. This figure was considered too high by the President, and word was sent back to the War Department that cuts would have to be made. With these instructions in mind, G–4 supervised the preparation of an itemized and detailed program—more comprehensive than its earlier plan of 6 June [30]—which was completed on 20 June. This program known as the Munitions Program of 20 June 1940, amounted to some $7.3 billion. It contemplated equipping the Army with the critical items—over and above existing stocks and items provided in the fiscal year 1941 appropriations—necessary "for one year of a major national defense effort." This major effort assumed that the Army would be mobilized to a strength of 4 million men within fourteen months and would reach a strength of 2.6 million in theaters of operations at a corresponding period. The memorandum of transmittal noted that "it is of the utmost importance to realize that adequate production for such a force cannot be obtained in one year." [31]

The program of 20 June was transmitted to Mr. Knudsen and shortly thereafter received the approval of the President. As-

---

[28] Memo, Burns, Ex Asst to ASW, for ASW, 13 Jun 40, sub: National Policy on Munitions Productive Capacity, copy in G–4/31773.

[29] (1) *Ibid.* (2) Memo, Johnson for Knudsen, same date and file.

[30] See above, note 25.

[31] Confidential Memo (mimeographed), Johnson for Knudsen, 20 Jun 40, formally transmitting the Munitions Program of 20 June 1940, G–4/33473.

sistant Secretary Johnson subsequently summed up the situation for the Chief of Staff:

The main purpose is to put American industry to work in a big way and as expeditiously as possible to produce those important and essential machines of war, together with their accessories, ammunition, etc., that would require an extended period of time for their manufacture; and to fill in the gaps and deficiencies of present productive capacity by the creation of necessary additional capacity.

This program, approved by the Secretary of War, was submitted to the President by Mr. Knudsen and Mr. Stettinius of the Advisory Commission of National Defense. It was approved by the President. It should not be changed except by approval of this office and this office does not feel authorized to make changes except with the concurrence of Mr. Knudsen. *However, if you believe that changes should be made at this time, this office will gladly discuss them with Mr. Knudsen.*[32]

The 20 June program had been hurriedly put together and possessed a number of defects. G–4 was dissatisfied with certain features and appointed a committee to revise the plan within the terms of the basic directive. Also, for reasons of both urgency and practicality, it had become clear to Colonel Burns that specific procurement objectives should replace the creation of productive capacity for the first two stages of the ground forces' portion of the program. There were indications, moreover, that production bottlenecks would require a limitation upon the four-million-man program for critical items; it would therefore be preferable to set up the program as an objective to be accomplished as quickly as possible but without pinning it to particular completion dates.

Accordingly, a further meeting was held in the office of the Assistant Secretary of War. The result was the basic directive for what was to become known as the Munitions Program of 30 June 1940:

1. . . . it is desired that the Munitions Program of June 20, 1940 be revised as follows:
   a. Procure reserve stocks of all items of supplies needed to equip and maintain a ground force of 1,000,000 men on combat status.
   b. Procure all reserve stocks of the important long-time items of supplies needed to equip and maintain a ground force of 2,000,000 men on combat status.
   c. Create facilities which would permit a production sufficient to supply an army of 4,000,000 men on combat status.
   d. Procure 18,000 complete military airplanes (less the 2,181 planes for which funds have already been appropriated), together with necessary spare engines, spare parts, guns, ammunition, radio and other supplies and accessories pertaining thereto.
   e. Provide productive capacity available to the Army of 18,000 complete military airplanes per year, together with necessary engines and all other accessories and supplies pertaining thereto.
   f. Provide necessary storage for above.
2. Above to be ready for submission to the President by 9:00 a. m., July 1, 1940.[33]

With this mandate for revision and the latest troop basis supplied by the War Plans Division (WPD) of the General Staff, G–4 went into action to meet the forty-eight-hour deadline. It prepared standard forms to be filled in by each of the supply arms, listing items of equipment included in the existing PMP Critical Items Program; these would be needed in sufficient quantity for augmentation to a two-million-man force. A directive was sent to the various supply arms on 29 June, with instructions for computing

---

[32] Memo, Johnson for Marshall, 24 Jun 40, G–4/31773(2).

[33] Memo, Johnson, Actg SW, for CofS, 28 Jun 40, G–4/31773.

TABLE 17—MUNITIONS PROGRAM OF 30 JUNE 1940

[In Millions]

Item	Total	Deferred	Contract	Cash
Total	$5,897	$1,911	$2,072	$1,914
Essential Items for PMP	412	206	—	206
Critical items, 2 million men	2,286	700	900	686
Facilities for later expansion	717	317	100	300
18,000 airplanes	1,974	310	1,072	592
Airplane plant capacity	72	72	—	—
Storage and distribution	436	306	—	130

Source: Figures taken from Memo, Marshall for Johnson, 2 Jul 40, sub.: Program of Adequate Preparedness for the Army (written by Col. H. S. Aurand).

initial requirements, replacements, new items, estimated transportation costs, and funds required for warehouses, magazines, repair of arsenals, acquisition of land, and other needs. Indicating that time was of the essence, G–4 directed that the estimates be completed *in pencil* and the data returned at the earliest possible time, but *"in any event, not later than 4:00 P. M. this date."* [34]

On the next day, the final estimates were tabulated, and the program was henceforth known as the Munitions Program of 30 June 1940. At a preliminary conference with the President's advisers, it was suggested that requests for immediate appropriations be held to $4 billion; provisions in the bill for deferment of a portion of the costs for future financing by supplemental appropriations would permit the program to go ahead with a minimum of delay. Accordingly, the Chief of Staff submitted a recapitulation of the program as shown in Table 17, and on 3 July a meeting with the President took

place. The program was approved with negligible change, and in a series of supplemental appropriations throughout the fiscal year, Congress provided the necessary funds. [35]

The adoption of the Munitions Program of 30 June 1940 marked a major development in the preparedness policy of the United States. In the nineteen fiscal years 1922 through 1940, the United States had spent something less than $6.5 billion on War Department military activities. The 30 June 1940 program alone called for expenditures of $6 billion. Although this was little more than half the $11 billion program proposed by the War Department on 18 June, it was sufficient to get the rearmament program under way. Together with the $3 billion appropriated in the month prior to

[34] Memo, G–4 (no addressee), 29 Jun 40, sub: Instructions for Computation of Additional Critical Items Required for a Force of 2,000,000 Men, Tab A, G–4/31773.

[35] (1) A concise summary of the appropriations made to implement the Munitions Program is reproduced in Frank, Requirements, pp. 10–11. (2) The two principal appropriations for this purpose were the Second Supplemental National Defense Appropriation Act, FY 1941 (54 *Stat.* 872), approved 9 September 1940, covering some $3.9 billion, and the Fifth Supplemental National Defense Appropriation Act, FY 1941 (55 *Stat.* 123), approved 5 April 1941, covering nearly $1.6 billion.

the adoption of the program, the total Army commitment for the coming year was close to $9 billion. Contemporaneous Navy, Marine Corps, and other defense expenditures would amount to many more billions. Hitler might well have paused to read the signs of the times.

The Victory Program of 11 September 1941

The adoption of the Munitions Program of 30 June 1940, and its ratification in the form of appropriations by Congress, represented a major turning point in the rehabilitation of the U.S. Army. In spite of large elements of political isolationism, pacifism, and opposition to the administration, the U.S. Government had succeeded in launching a program of industrial mobilization and military procurement which would require from one to two years to bear significant fruit in the form of delivery of actual munitions. The passage of the Selective Service Act three months later indicated that the United States was ready, even in an election year, to match its mobilization of matériel with the mobilization of its manpower.

The 1940 program, great as it was in comparison with the Army's meager equipment objectives during the interwar period, was limited in concept. It was essentially defensive, designed primarily to repel a possible attack upon the Western Hemisphere. Although the size of the 1940 objective was sufficient to keep American industry, as well as the War Department, busy for many months to come, events throughout 1941 converged to force a reconsideration of U.S. military requirements. Observation of actual combat operations in Europe indicated the desirability of substantial changes in the organization and equipment of fighting

units of the Army. On 30 January 1941, a recomputation of supply requirements, based on revised tables of organization and allowances, indicated the need for an additional $600 million for essential items and $4 billion for critical items.[36] Moreover, British and French orders for munitions from firms in the United States, combined with the unprecedented demands of the Munitions Program, revealed an increasing number of material shortages and production bottlenecks. But this was merely the beginning of such difficulties. On 11 March 1941 the Lend-Lease Act was passed, appropriating some $7 billion for military and defense aid to nations at war with the Axis. It was evident to the U.S. military agencies that large sectors of their own procurement programs would be seriously jeopardized by this tremendous additional burden upon American industry and that a reconciliation of total requirements was essential. At the same time, Germany was consolidating its victory in Europe, and informed sources anticipated an early break with the Soviet Union. If Hitler were to conquer the Soviet Union, the outlook for the future of the entire Western Hemisphere would be grim. This prospect compelled the Army to survey all the probable alternatives and to formulate some conception of its requirements for an all-out war.

It was many months before the concept of hemisphere defense gave way to broader strategical foundation for U.S. Army requirements. The Army's G–4 had, in the meantime, developed a series of schedules to control procurement under the 1940 Munitions Program. These schedules, known as Expenditure Programs, served both as short-run statements of requirements and (after

---

[36] Frank, Requirements, p. 11.

appropriate adjustment) as approved programs of procurement. A separate Expenditure Program was developed for each appropriation act showing the quantity of each item to be procured under the specific appropriation and listing unfilled requirements needed to complete the Munitions Program under future appropriations. As the world situation continued to deteriorate in late 1940 and 1941, Army staff planners proposed successive increases in the PMP force and in procurement of both critical and essential items to meet the expansion. For each proposed expansion the supply arms and services were directed to prepare a tentative Expenditure Program, listing all the items required to meet the objectives stated in the directive. The accumulated statements of the several supply arms were reviewed, revised if necessary, and presented to Congress as the basis for a budget request. With the increasing liberality of Congress, appropriations were made substantially as requested, and G–4 would then approve the Expenditure Programs of the supply arms with only minor modifications. This procedure·for stating short-term budget requirements and approving expenditures continued long after the complete financing of the Munitions Program and was not discontinued until the summer of 1942 when the Army Supply Program (ASP) became the basis for budget requests and the sole procurement authority. All together eight Expenditure Programs were published from 12 August 1940 to 30 June 1942, authorizing procurement expenditures totaling nearly $34 billion.[37]

Meanwhile, numerous pressures for a complete statement of the demands upon the nation's productive capacity had been accumulating since early in 1941. On 18 February 1941 Mr. Knudsen had urged development of a unified American production program to meet all current and expected military and foreign requirements.[38] Throughout the spring of 1941 the Production Planning Board of the Office of Production Management called for the establishment of over-all production objectives based upon a general strategic plan.[39] The War Plans Division of the General Staff, pointing to the confusion resulting from numerous isolated proposals and demands upon American productive capacity, recommended the preparation of over-all estimates of munitions production required for national security. Accordingly, on 21 May 1941, the Chief of Staff—General Marshall—requested WPD to prepare "a more clear-cut strategic estimate" which would provide the basis for evaluating the many individual suggestions continually being made for increases in matériel. While WPD was at work on this difficult assignment, a request from the President provided both the authority and the national objectives upon which to base long-range strategic and procurement planning.[40]

The Presidential request, which led to the broad statement of strategy and requirements later known as the Victory Program, had its genesis in two memoranda prepared by Maj. Gen. James H. Burns who now, in addition to being the Executive in OASW, was assistant to Harry Hopkins on lend-lease matters. Convinced of the inadequacy of the existing industrial mobilization effort of the United States, General Burns urged both

---

[37] Approximately $20 billion of this amount was appropriated early in 1942. For further discussion of the Expenditure Programs, see Frank, Requirements, pp. 8–15, and supporting documents.

[38] CPA, *Industrial Mobilization for War,* p. 134.
[39] *Ibid.,* p. 136.
[40] Watson, *Prewar Plans,* p. 335.

Mr. Hopkins and the Secretary of War to work toward a raising of the sights. On 2 April 1941 he had prepared for Hopkins' signature a memorandum to the Secretaries of the War and Navy Departments urging the study and recommendation of an all-out program of munitions production. Hopkins, stating that it would exceed his authority to make such a request, dictated the substance of the Burns proposal in a new memorandum for the President's own signature.[41] During the same month General Burns prepared for Under Secretary Patterson's signature a similar memorandum to the Secretary of War, urging that a munitions program be undertaken sufficient "to achieve victory on the basis of appropriate assumptions as to probable enemies and friends and theaters of operation." Patterson not only signed the memorandum but obtained the approval of Secretary Stimson and had it forwarded to the Chief of Staff.[42]

These efforts bore no immediate fruit. But on 9 July 1941, two weeks after the German attack on the Soviet Union, President Roosevelt—in words obviously indebted to the earlier Burns memoranda—addressed identical letters to the Secretaries of the War and Navy Departments requesting the preparation of "over-all production requirements required to defeat our potential enemies." Stating that his request involved "the making of appropriate assumptions as to our probable friends and enemies and to conceivable theaters of operation," the President continued:

I wish you would explore the munitions and mechanical equipment of all types which in your opinion would be required to exceed by an appropriate amount that available to our potential enemies. From your report we should be able to establish a munitions objective indicating the industrial capacity which this nation will require.

I am not suggesting a detailed report but one that, while general in scope, would cover the most critical items in our defense and which could then be related by the OPM into practical realities of production facilities. It seems to me we need to know now our program in its entirety, even though at a later date it may be amended.

I believe that the confidential report which I am asking you to make to me would be of great assistance, not only in the efficient utilization of our productive facilities, but would afford an adequate opportunity for planning for the greatly increased speed of delivery which our defense program requires.[43]

Although the Presidential request was addressed to the problem of matériel requirements and more specifically to the "most critical items," it appeared to General Staff planners to require a comprehensive estimate of the size and composition of the Army needed "to defeat our potential enemies." Matériel requirements for the Army could not be computed *in vacuo;* they were always related to a given troop basis or mobilization plan indicating the total number of troops required by the plan and their detailed organization into armies, corps, divisions, and lesser organizational units. Each distinct type of unit within its own class (for example, infantry, armored, motorized, and other divisions) required different kinds and quantities of equipment according to established allowance tables. It was impossible, therefore, to compute matériel requirements in the absence of a relevant troop basis, which in turn would depend upon general strategic plans. The co-ordination of the troop basis with

---

[41] Ltr, Burns to Maj Gen Harry J. Malony, Chf of Military History, 13 Apr 49, OCMH 330.114.

[42] Memo, Patterson for Stimson, 18 Apr 41, JB 325, Ser. 692. The text of this important memorandum is reproduced in Watson, *Prewar Plans,* p. 332.

[43] Ltr, President to SW, 9 Jul 41, Frank, Doc. 14.

strategic plans was the responsibility chiefly of the War Plans Division of the General Staff.

Upon receipt of the Presidential directive, WPD immediately went to work to devise a comprehensive strategic plan and troop basis. The many assumptions and calculations which went into the plan have been recounted elsewhere in considerable detail.[44] Basically, the plan rested upon the calculated maximum number of troops available to the Army out of the nation's total population. With strategic assumptions that the major effort would be in Europe and that 1 July 1943 would be the date of full attainment of U.S. military strength, the planners estimated the number and types of organizational units required. Consideration was given also to the availability of shipping, the control of sea lanes, the neutralization of the Pacific area, and numerous other factors. On 23 August 1941, WPD forwarded the completed and highly secret troop basis to G–4.[45] It was then up to G–4 to determine the matériel requirements needed to support the Army organization detailed in the troop basis.

Three days later G–4 issued a directive to the Chief of the Air Corps and the supply services with basic instructions for the computation of requirements. The new requirements were to be those over and above all items already provided for by previous programs and were to be confined principally to critical items and motor vehicles. Some additional essential items were needed for the expanded PMP force. Quartermaster estimates were to be confined to critical

items of cloth and findings and motor vehicles.[46]

While the estimates of U.S. Army requirements were still in the process of formulation, the Secretary of War received another urgent request from the President. Hitler's attack on the Soviet Union on 22 June 1941 had added a potentially powerful ally to the anti-Axis alignment, but the Russians were desperately in need of munitions. Harry Hopkins, in his August visit with Marshal Joseph Stalin in Moscow, had received a preliminary indication of Soviet needs, and a more definitive conference had been arranged for 1 October. While this was pending, the President's new request, dated 30 August 1941, asked for a schedule of total U.S. production of important munitions and their recommended distribution among all friendly powers for the period ending 30 June 1942:

I desire that your Department, working in cooperation with the Navy Department, submit to me by September 10, 1941, your recommendation of distribution of expected United States production of munitions of war as between the United States, Great Britain, Russia and the other countries to be aided—by important items, quantity time schedules and approximate values for the period from the present time until June 30, 1942. I also desire your general conclusions as to the over-all production effort of important items needed for victory on the general assumption that the reservoir of munitions power available to the United States and her friends is sufficiently superior to that available to the Axis Powers to insure defeat of the latter.[47]

This meant that the new estimates would have to include not only U.S. requirements

[44] Watson, *Prewar Plans*, pp. 331–36.

[45] Memo, Actg ACofS WPD for ACofS G–4, 23 Aug 41, sub: Ultimate Requirements for the Army, Frank, Doc. 15.

[46] Memo, ACofS G–4 for Chfs of Services, 26 Aug 41, sub: Special Computation Relating to the Status of Equipment, Frank, Doc. 16.

[47] Ltr, President to SW, 30 Aug 41, WPD 4494–1.

for all its armed forces but the needs of Great Britain, the Soviet Union, China, and Latin America as well.

After desperate efforts to meet the President's deadline, the Army finally assembled its completed estimates. These requirements, together with an elaborate strategic estimate and statements of Navy and merchant shipping objectives, were published in a secret report by the Joint Board on 11 September 1941.[48] The total production requirements and their associated strategical foundation became known as the Victory Program, a title indicating the shift in purpose from mere hemisphere resistance to one of overcoming the potential enemy.

The term "Victory Program" possessed a variety of meanings both at the time of its appearance and in subsequent usage. Strictly construed, it referred to the ultimate requirements of munitions of all types, as estimated in the Joint Board report, necessary for the defeat of the Axis Powers. As an ultimate production goal, it thus included the Munitions Program of 30 June 1940 and all other past, current, and future procurement required to make up the ultimate Victory Program objective. The term was also loosely used to describe parts of the overall program, such as the Army or Navy component thereof, and frequently implied the strategic plan as well as the production requirements for victory. The successive re-

visions of the Army's troop basis continued to be known as the Victory Program Troop Basis long after the corresponding matériel requirement programs ceased to bear the same name.[49]

The ultimate production requirements specified in the report of the Joint Board carried only quantitative estimates of required matériel. Although estimated unit costs of Army equipment (except planes) were shown, the shortage of time and lack of reliable or complete cost data precluded any meaningful summary prior to the deadline set by the President. It was, nevertheless, evident that the total production requirements under the program would be staggering. Subsequent estimates indicated that the Victory Program would call for expenditures of nearly $150 billion and would require until spring of 1944 to complete.[50] U.S. Army ground forces under the proposed new troop basis totaled 216 divisions, 61 of which would be armored. Also planned were fifty-one separate motorized divisions and nearly half a million men for antiaircraft artillery units. Matériel requirements for all of these were exceptionally heavy as compared with regular infantry divisions. The Army's ground force requirements for additional critical items alone under the Victory Program called for

[48] JB 355, Ser. 707. Because of delays in reconciling Army and Navy estimates, the completed joint report was not delivered to the President until 25 September. (Watson, *Prewar Plans*, p. 351.) The seventeen-page report was buttressed by two appendixes. Appendix II, Army Requirements, was replete with maps, charts, tables, and statements covering not only production requirements but highly secret data such as detailed strategic assumptions and purposes, potential military objectives and targets, estimates of enemy strength, and the like.

[49] For additional treatment of the Victory Program, see Leighton and Coakley, *Global Logistics and Strategy, 1940–1943,* Ch. V.

[50] (1) Memo, Donald Nelson, Ex Dir SPAB, for SW, 11 Dec 41, cited in Memo, Brig Gen Brehon B. Somervell, ACofS G–4, for CofS, 16 Dec 41, sub: Victory Program, OCS 21145–42. (2) CPA, *Industrial Mobilization for War,* p. 140. (3) Civilian Production Administration, *Minutes of the Supply Priorities and Allocations Board, September 2, 1941, to January 15, 1942* (Washington: Government Printing Office, 1946) (hereafter cited as *SPAB Minutes*), mtg of 4 Nov 41, p. 24.

estimated expenditures of $29 billion.[51] The magnitude of the entire program had led General Marshall to conclude the 11 September 1941 Joint Board report in the following words: "The position of the Chief of Staff is that the maximum requirements of the Navy and Army, as related to tonnage and the probable conflicts in material, priority, and production facilities, should be surveyed by OPM and then if necessary readjusted by the Joint Board within the limits determined by OPM." [52] This was probably the first recorded statement in connection with the World War II production program which recognized the problem of over-all production "feasibility" and the broad administrative procedure for effecting the necessary cutbacks.

At the time of its formulation, the Victory Program was only a hypothetical plan, to be available in the event of full-scale participation of the United States in the war. It made no commitments, called for no immediate action, and was to be kept as a secret document within the War Department and other appropriate agencies. Nevertheless, a leading isolationist newspaper which had long been hostile to the administration was successful in obtaining a copy of the plan. In a widely syndicated news story this newspaper described the secret plan in great detail, quoting extensive passages verbatim and revealing the strategic plans of the United States in the event of war, the location of projected overseas bases, intelligence estimates of German strength, and similar matters. The account went on to indicate that the Victory Program represented "a war against the German people," rather than one to overthrow Hitler and the Nazi regime, and that the primary purpose of sending American forces outside the Western Hemisphere was "the preservation of the British empire." [53]

The attack upon Pearl Harbor three days later put an end to the political repercussions of this disclosure. But this incident, together with the multiplicity of problems involved in the Victory Program's compilation, reveals some of the difficulties faced by the Army during the defense period in determining "firm, long-range requirements" to be adopted as a positive production program. The lack of such requirements during the defense period has been cited repeatedly as a basic weakness of Army planning which complicated the tasks of NDAC and OPM in adopting appropriate policies in the fields of production, priorities, and other areas of economic mobilization. But it was impossible for the Army to come up with "dependable, long-range estimates," much less to make these the basis of an actual production program, in the absence either of adequate appropriations or of reliable assumptions as to future national policy, the course of world events, and the total military strategy to be adopted when and if the nation became involved in war. At the time of the fall of France, the Army submitted an $11 billion program and was given one of only $6 billion. In the delicate political milieu of 1940 and 1941 the only course which

[51] Tabulation, "Army Estimate of Production Requirements for the Victory Program—Critical Items Only," performed by Statistics Sec, World War II Div, OCMH, copy in OCMH.

[52] JB 355, Ser. 707, p. 17.

[53] Chicago *Tribune*, 4 Dec 41. The release of the article, which appeared three days before Pearl Harbor, was timed to "scoop" the new Chicago *Sun*—a competitor of the *Tribune*—on the day of its launching. For additional details, see Watson, *Prewar Plans*, pp. 359–60.

seemed open to the Army was to prosecute the Munitions Program as effectively as possible and to raise the sights as circumstances permitted and required. The Victory Program in the fall of 1941 was only a paper program but it provoked a storm of controversy which might have impaired the whole defense effort had it not been followed immediately by an actual attack upon the United States.

CHAPTER VII

Army Requirement Programs: Pearl Harbor to War's End

The President's Objectives and the War Munitions Program

The advent of Pearl Harbor converted the Victory Program from a planning document to a working basis for immediate expansion of Army procurement and subsequent requirements planning. Despite its heavy requirements, the Army's Victory Program had included only major items of equipment (critical items, motor vehicles, and the like). In response to a letter from Donald Nelson, requesting a statement of requirements by time periods, Assistant Secretary of War John J. McCloy pointed to the need for a restudy of the program in the light of recent events: ". . . it is now evident that the basic foundation on which the Victory Program was based should be re-analyzed prior to its commitment to a vast industrial effort".[1] Ten days later Secretary Stimson informed the President of the Army's procurement progress in the two and a half weeks since Pearl Harbor:

The Victory Program is now on its way to becoming a reality. The Office of Production Management and Supply Priorities and Allocations Board estimate that the total munitions production potential of the country for the year 1942 is approximately 40 billion dol-

lars. Of this 40 billion dollars, 27 billion dollars of munitions are already scheduled. . . . Of the margin available for new production in 1942, it is expected that approximately 6 billion dollars will be for ground army munitions, 3½ billion for aircraft and accessories, and the remainder for military construction, the Navy, Maritime Commission, and other purposes. . . . the War Department will continue with its re-analysis of the list of matériel originally submitted for the Victory Program to the end that its portion of that program will be on as firm a basis as it is possible to make it for an all-out industrial effort.[2]

Definite steps to obtain the desired revision followed shortly thereafter. On 29 December 1941 Brig. Gen. Brehon B. Somervell, the new G–4, issued a directive to the supply arms and the Air Forces calling for a recomputation of the Army's total requirements for equipment and ammunition through 30 June 1944. The new figures were to be based on three estimates of Army troop strength: Force A (4,150,000 men) to be mobilized by the end of 1942; Force B (8,890,000 men) required by the end of 1943; and a total force of 10,380,000 men to be available by 30 June 1944. All items of initial equipment, plus six months' com-

---

[1] Memo, McCloy for Nelson, Ex Dir SPAB, 16 Dec 41, sub: The Victory Program, Frank, Doc. 17.

[2] Memo, SW for President, 26 Dec 41, sub: Victory Program, Frank, Doc. 18.

bat supplies of equipment and ammunition, were to be covered in the new program.[3]

While the War Department was working on its program of total munitions requirements, high-level conferences on broad Allied strategy and the matériel requirements therefor were being held by President Roosevelt and Prime Minister Winston S. Churchill, along with the British Minister of Supply, Lord Beaverbrook. Influenced by Beaverbrook's observations Roosevelt independently announced, in his 6 January 1942 State-of-the-Union Message to Congress, his celebrated "Must" Program for the production of astronomical quantities of planes, tanks, merchant ships, and antiaircraft guns. The President was convinced that a dramatic, publicly announced program for selected crucial items would rally the American public behind the war production program and serve notice upon the entire world—allies, enemies, and neutral powers alike—that U.S. industrial capacity was so enormous there could be no doubt about the final outcome of the war. In announcing the program the President made clear that he was in earnest:

This production of ours in the United States must be raised above present levels, even though it will mean the dislocation of the lives and occupations of millions of our own people. We must raise our sights all along the production line. Let no man say it cannot be done. It must be done—and we have undertaken to do it.[4]

[3] Memo, Somervell, ACofS G–4, for CofAAF and Chfs of Services, 29 Dec 41, sub: Munitions Requirements for the Victory Program, Frank, Requirements, p. 24, and Doc. 19.

[4] *The Public Papers and Addresses of Franklin D. Roosevelt,* compiled by Samuel I. Rosenman, 1942 volume: *Humanity on the Defensive* (New York: Harper & Brothers, 1950), p. 32. For evidence of Lord Beaverbrook's influence in the de-

The President then announced the specific production goals which he had set for the nation:

Item	1942	1943
Planes	60,000	125,000
Tanks	45,000	75,000
Antiaircraft guns	20,000	35,000
Merchant ships (d. w. tons)	6,000,000	10,000,000

This dramatic announcement—made at a time when reports of fresh Allied losses were received almost daily—provided a degree of inspiration badly needed by the American public and allied nations. Nevertheless, it soon became evident that an attempt to realize the President's "must" objectives at all cost would severely hamper other segments of the war production program. Moreover, unless the selected items were accompanied by all the required complementary items, they could not be successfully utilized. The production of 185,000 planes without adequate landing fields, hangars, operating supplies, and maintenance facilities—to say nothing of trained personnel at all echelons—might well be a liability to the war program as a whole. The Army later attempted to raise its other requirements in keeping with the President's objectives, but the total added up to more than the nation was capable of producing. For several months, however, the President was adamant in his position that the goals should not be lowered and later permitted modification only when they were demonstrated as clearly unattainable, or on condition that any reductions would be compensated by increases elsewhere in the program. By the end of 1942, the modified objectives had become fairly well assimi-

termination of the President's "Must" Program, see Calendar of Hopkins Papers, Bk. V, Item 3, OCMH.

lated into the general production program and caused no great concern thereafter.[5]

In the meantime, after the announcement of the President's objectives on 6 January 1942, the War Department abandoned the Victory Program nomenclature for its new statement of requirements then under preparation:

The Victory Program has been replaced by the War Munitions Program. The document submitted to the Supply Priorities and Allocations Board containing quantities of various items for the Victory Program is now obsolete and has no further usefulness.[6]

The new estimates, captioned as the Overall Requirements for the War Munitions Program, were completed and distributed on 11 February 1942. The total dollar value of the new program was estimated at roughly $63 billion for the two-and-one-half-year period in question.[7]

Although a more accurate statement of Army requirements than the superseded Victory Program, the hastily computed War Munitions Program was defective in many respects. Its estimates had been made on the basis of total need, with generous allowances for combat maintenance, but without regard to stocks of equipment and ammunition on hand; to that extent it exceeded actual production requirements. On the other hand it failed to cover miscellaneous and expendable supplies, construction, Navy and lend-lease requirements to be filled by Army procurement, and other items. Moreover, its methodology of requirements computation was crude, omitting distribution requirements, zone of interior (ZI) replacement, and other refinements, as well as neglecting *in toto* the question of whether shipping facilities would be adequate to transport the Army and its equipment overseas at the rates contemplated by the several force augmentations. As a consequence of these inadequacies and in the light of developments which were taking place even before its completion, the Army's War Munitions Program was replaced, within two months of its publication.[8]

---

[5] It is interesting to note that two of the four items—merchant shipping and antiaircraft guns—were actually produced in greater quantities in 1942 and 1943 than initially called for by the President. Tank production was later deliberately cut back; total tank output for the war rested at 88,410, Whiting et al., Statistics, "Procurement," 9 Apr 52 draft, p. 37. Plane production fell behind in schedule but eventually exceeded the quantitative objectives of the President. Total U.S. plane production for the five-year period 1 July 1940 to 31 August 1945 ran to approximately 300,000, of which nearly 100,000 were produced in the single calendar year 1944 (actual figures 299,300 and 96,318, respectively). Civilian Production Administration, *Industrial Mobilization for War*, pp. 754, 962; CPA, *Wartime Production Achievements and the Reconversion Outlook*, p. 106. For further discussion of the President's objectives see (1) Leighton and Coakley, *Global Logistics and Strategy*, Ch. VIII; (2) CPA, *Industrial Mobilization for War*, pp. 299–92, 599ff.

[6] Memo, Maj Gen Richard C. Moore, DCofS, WPD, 7 Jan 42, sub: Former Victory Program, OCS 21145–51.

[7] (1) ASF Annual Rpt, 1943, p. 18. (2) CPA, *Industrial Mobilization for War*, p. 274.

[8] The War Munitions Program of 11 February 1942 has occasionally been referred to as "the first edition of the Army Supply Program." (Background of the Army Supply Program, p. 4.) Elsewhere it has been referred to as a "dry-run" edition of ASP. Donald F. Bradford, Methods of Forecasting War Requirements for Quartermaster Supplies (QMC Historical Study 14, May 1946) (hereafter cited as QMC Requirements), p. 34. It was, to be sure, a transitional computation of Army requirements leading to the first edition of ASP, but the directive upon which it was based (29 December 1941) appeared nearly a month before the Somervell memorandum of 25 January 1942 formally proposing the Army Supply Program. See also ASF Annual Rpt, 1943, p. 16.

The Army Supply Program

Background and Nature

Events Leading to Adoption of ASP— Observers of the Washington scene at the beginning of 1942 may well remember the peculiar atmosphere of urgency, confusion, frustration, and perpetual reorganization which characterized the early post-Pearl Harbor period. The word "defense" was summarily replaced by "war" in all agency names, programs, and activities; individuals and organizations alike, eager to contribute as directly as possible to the war effort, sought positions of indispensability in the prosecution of the war. All were looking for an objective and a mandate—a definite goal toward which to apply their energies and the authority to go ahead. For the home front, such objectives depended ultimately upon a firm and comprehensive statement of munitions requirements.

The U.S. Army in World War II was only one—albeit the major—claimant upon the nation's resources. The Army's strategic plans, which called for frequent re-examination and adaptation of its basic requirements, were a part of the larger strategic program approved by the allied powers at the highest level. The administrative machinery for formulating basic Allied strategy came into being gradually after Pearl Harbor.[9]

Briefly, top-level strategy of the United States and Great Britain was formulated by the Combined Chiefs of Staff (CCS), which reported directly to President Roosevelt and Prime Minister Churchill. The American members of CCS also constituted the U.S. Joint Chiefs of Staff (JCS), which was responsible for the development and co-ordination of basic strategic plans for the armed forces of the United States. The JCS consisted of the military heads of the Army, Army Air Forces, and Navy, together with the President's chief of staff.[10]

The Joint Chiefs of Staff, which gradually replaced the prewar Joint Board, originated early in 1942 and grew rapidly thereafter into a large and influential organization. Many joint staffs and committees were eventually created to support the work of JCS. Among these were the Joint Strategic Committee and the Joint Logistics Committee, whose activities in determining military priorities and adjusting total military requirements to production limitations brought them into the field of economic mobilization. Within the Army the Operations Division (OPD) replaced the War Plans Division of the General Staff and became the key staff agency which developed and co-ordinated broad strategic and logistical requirements into programs to be refined and executed by the procurement and distribution machinery of AAF and ASF.

The Army had procurement responsibility for equipment and supplies for a wide variety of non-Army users in addition to its own combat and supply arms and the AAF. Requirements for outside users, after broad screening by CCS and JCS, were assigned to the Army and in turn to its technical serv-

---

[9] The nature of this machinery, as well as the substantive decisions made thereby, is discussed in detail elsewhere. For example: (1) Cline, *The Operations Division;* (2) Maurice Matloff and Edwin M. Snell, *Strategic Planning for Coalition Warfare, 1941–1942* (Washington: 1953); (3) Leighton and Coakley, *Global Logistics and Strategy, 1940–1943;* all in UNITED STATES ARMY IN WORLD WAR II.

[10] Throughout most of World War II these were General Marshall (Army), General Henry H. Arnold (AAF), Admiral Ernest J. King (Navy), and Admiral William D. Leahy (Presidential chief of staff).

ices on the basis of normal procurement responsibility for the classes of items involved. The largest single category of additional procurement thus assigned consisted of the great array of lend-lease requirements for allied nations. Army procurement of lend-lease equipment and supplies amounted to many billions of dollars, in most cases involving items identical with those used by the U.S. Army and procured from the same sources under common contracts. Under the lend-lease machinery, munitions were assigned to all the allied powers, including the United States, from a common pool.[11]

A substantial portion of Navy (including Marine Corps and Coast Guard) requirements for certain classes of items was filled by Army procurement. Thus, 90 percent of all perishable foods and 85 percent of nonperishable foodstuffs for the Navy were purchased by the Army Quartermaster through the Chicago Quartermaster Depot. On the other hand, the Navy procured certain items for the Army, and in some cases joint procurement operations were conducted.[12] The Army also procured items for the Office of Strategic Services, the French forces in North Africa, and other non-Army users. In computing these requirements the Army acted only in a liaison and screening capacity; the agencies involved made their own estimates and periodically presented them for incorporation into the Army's statement of its total procurement requirements. By the end of 1941, the multiplicity of demands upon Army procurement made imperative the early development of a system for the orderly recording and programing of requirements; otherwise the Army's whole procurement program threatened to bog down in confusion.

During the last half of 1941, OPM and SPAB had been bringing increasing pressure to bear upon the procuring agencies for more definite statements of requirements and, above all, requirements spelled out in terms of time objectives. With excess industrial capacity rapidly disappearing the question of priority, or relative production urgency, became increasingly important. In a milieu in which everything could not be produced at once, the question of "when" to produce became co-ordinate with "what" to produce. Now, in the face of all-out war, the Army made renewed efforts to determine its needs by time periods, both for its own purposes and for those of the newly established War Production Board.

Within the Army, the most vigorous exponent of a fresh approach to the formulation of requirements was the new Assistant Chief of Staff, G–4, General Somervell. Known as a man of action from his early days as WPA administrator for the New York district and more recently as the reorganizer of the Army Quartermaster construction program, Somervell brought to G–4 an unusual combination of engineering knowledge, administrative ability, and drive. When he "took over" in G–4, his influence was felt from the start.[13]

---

[11] See discussion of policies of the Munitions Assignment Board in Leighton and Coakley, *Global Logisitcs and Strategy, 1940–1943*, Chapters X–XI.

[12] The cross procurement and joint procurement activities of the Army and Navy, as well as many other co-ordinating activities of the two services in the broad field of economic mobilization, are summarized in the so-called Draper-Strauss Report. (Rpt, Col William H. Draper, Jr., GSC, and Capt Lewis L. Strauss, USNR, Co-ordination of Procurement Between the War and Navy Departments (February 1945), 3 vols., ICAF Library.) A condensation of the Draper-Strauss findings is found in Millett, *Organization and Role of the ASF*, pp. 270–80.

[13] See Millett, *Organization and Role of the ASF*, Introduction.

G–4 had long been the duly constituted War Department agency for supervising the formulation of the Army's matériel requirements. With the advent of the Defense Aid Program and the growth of civilian production control agencies, as well as the expansion and addition of offices and agencies within the War Department, the total task of estimating military requirements had become widely scattered. Foreign military requirements, which of necessity cut into and shaped the formulation of the Army's own program, were handled by the independent Office of Lend-Lease Administration, with liaison groups in OASW as well as in G–4 and the various supply arms and services. The reconciliation of Army and Navy requirements, especially with respect to their impact upon raw materials and industrial facilities, was handled by the ANMB. The civilian mobilization control agencies— NDAC, OPM, SPAB, and now WPB—had been in continual contact with the Army, Navy, and Maritime Commission in an endeavor to determine the over-all objectives of war production.

Almost immediately after his arrival in G–4, General Somervell proposed the adoption by the War Department of a single, comprehensive Army Supply Program, to be set forth in a publication which would become the bible of the Army supply system. Responsibility for the consolidation and publication of all requirements (Army, Navy, lend-lease, and others) to be filled by Army procurement would be vested in a single agency of the War Department. This agency would be charged with the continual refinement and improvement of the program and with representing the War Department in relations with all outside agencies in matters of supply requirements.

GENERAL BREHON B. SOMERVELL, *Commanding General, Army Service Forces, throughout World War II. (Photograph taken in 1945.)*

Somervell believed that the appropriate agency for this task was an expanded G–4.

On 22 January 1942 he addressed a ten-page memorandum to the Deputy Chief of Staff, outlining with great vigor and in great detail the need for a consolidated Army Supply Program, the kind of organization required to administer it, problems to be faced, and methods of meeting them. The memorandum stressed such important matters as the development of a sound strategic base for requirements, keeping requirements within the realm of production feasibility, the need for a single set of requirements estimates based on a common set of assumptions, and the responsiveness of the pro-

ARMY AND NAVY MUNITIONS BOARD, 1941. *Seated, left to right: Brig. Gen. Charles Hines, Brig. Gen. H. K. Rutherford, Under Secretary of War Robert P. Patterson, Under Secretary of the Navy James Forrestal, and Capt. E. D. Almy, USN. Standing: Maj. G. K. Heiss, Col. H. S. Aurand, Cmdr. V. H. Wheeler, and Cmdr. L. B. Scott (ret.).*

gram to changes in the underlying economic and military situation. Somervell did not wait for a directive but concluded his memorandum with the words: "In order to make its Supply Program more complete and useful, the Supply Division, G–4, is proceeding at once with the following action . . . ." A full page followed listing intended activities on the part of G–4, all indicating the early launching of the Army Supply Program.[14]

Before the first complete edition of the

Army Supply Program could be published by G–4, the far-reaching reorganization of the War Department on 9 March 1942 had taken place. Instead of heading an expanded G–4, Somervell now found himself in command of the Army's entire machinery for procurement, economic mobilization, and supply—the Army Service Forces. Under the new regime, the development of the Army Supply Program was given top priority and there soon emerged a complex but systematic organization and procedure for determining and presenting the multifarious requirements upon Army procurement.

[14] Memo, Somervell, ACofS G–4, for Moore, DCofS, 22 Jan 42, sub: Army Supply Program, CG ASF, Chief of Staff, General Staff (1), 1941–42.

Character and Content of ASP—In its broadest sense, the Army Supply Program as developed by the Army Service Forces represented the entire framework of activity carried on by the War Department for equipping and supplying the U.S. Army and other recipients of matériel procured by the Army during World War II. In this sense, ASP was the integrated program of activity which included the formulation of the Army's matériel needs and the conversion of these requirements into programs, contracts, production schedules, procurement deliveries, and the distribution of finished supplies to troops in the field.

In its narrower and more specific sense, ASP was the periodically published document setting forth the long-range objectives of Army procurement in all important categories by calendar years for two and sometimes three years in advance. In this capacity, ASP became the Army's authoritative statement of requirements and its basic procurement directive. It was used as the basis for requesting Congressional appropriations, authorizing procurement expenditures, establishing production schedules, assigning priorities, determining raw material requirements, and allocating materials and other scarce resources. In short, the Army Supply Program became the foundation for the Army's entire procurement effort.

Inasmuch as ASP was a dynamic program attuned in varying degrees to constantly shifting circumstances and strategic needs, the types, quantities, and dollar value of supplies covered by the various sections changed from one edition to another. With the passage of time, ASP covered not only the Army's regular procurement and construction needs but Navy and lend-lease items, as well as special requirements for task forces, the Office of Strategic Services, the French forces in North Africa, and civil governments in occupied areas.

ASP was published in a number of sections. The first completed edition contained six sections, each appearing separately in 1942 at the indicated dates:

Section	Issued
I. Equipment–Ground	6 Apr
II. Equipment–Air	9 Apr
III. Miscellaneous and Expendable Supplies–Ground	17 Mar
IV. Miscellaneous and Expendable Supplies–Air	4 Jul
V. Construction	11 Apr
VI. International Aid–Miscellaneous	1 Sep

Section I, which covered ammunition as well as all important items of Army Ground Forces equipment—guns, tanks, motor vehicles, clothing, personal equipment, signal, medical, engineering items, and so on—was by far the most important. It normally accounted for some 80 percent of the total dollar value of the entire Army Supply Program. Along with basic equipment for the organized units of the ground forces, it included common items for the Air Forces, Navy, and allies under lend-lease. It was this section which was most affected by changes in the troop basis and which underwent the most frequent revision.

Section II covered items of equipment and munitions (except aircraft) peculiar to the Army Air Forces, regardless of procuring agency. Many of these were procured by the Army Air Forces directly; the greater share, consisting of important items such as ammunition, armament, and signal equipment, was procured by the several technical services under the ASF. Requirements for aircraft, as such, were omitted; these were entirely outside the Army Supply Program. Aircraft requirements were separately determined, in keeping with the

WEEKLY STAFF CONFERENCE, *Headquarters, Services of Supply, June 1942.*
Seated, left to right: A. R. Glancy, Brig. Gens. James E. Wharton, Henry S. Aurand,
Charles Hines, Charles D. Young, Maj. Gen. John P. Smith, Brig. Gen. Lucius D. Clay,
Robert P. Patterson, USW, Lt. Gen. Brehon B. Somervell, Commanding General, Army
Service Forces, Brig. Gens. Wilhelm D. Styer, LeRoy Lutes, Clarence R. Huebner, C. P.
Gross, Mr. James P. Mitchell, Cols. Frank A. Heileman, A. Robert Ginsburgh, and Albert J.
Browning. Standing: Cols. Clinton F. Robinson, Walter A. Wood, Jr., Robinson E. Duff,
Brig. Gen. A. H. Carter, Col. J. N. Dalton, and Capt. Harold K. Hastings.

President's objectives, and published as production schedules for engines, airframes,
and propellers. This was done by a joint
agency—the Aircraft Resources Control
Office (and predecessor agencies) at Dayton, Ohio—which handled all aircraft
scheduling and dealt directly with industry
and the War Production Board. The dollar
value of the Army aircraft program, though
less than total requirements for the Army

Service Forces, was far larger than that of
the air items in Section II of ASP, although
this section included air items for Navy and
lend-lease.

Sections III and IV—later incorporated
in Sections I and II as Part B of each—
covered expendable supplies (other than
ammunition) for the ground and air forces,
respectively, as well as all items of equipment (except motor vehicles) for zone of

interior posts, camps, stations, general hospitals, and other establishments. Also included in Miscellaneous and Expendable Supplies were thousands of minor items so numerous that they were frequently grouped together in classes and reported in dollar value rather than in quantitative terms. Among the more important expendable supplies were subsistence, fuel, and lubricants.

Section V (later designated as Section IV) comprehended all uncompleted War Department construction projects—proposed, authorized, and under way—essential to the execution of the Army's total war effort. Data included cost, source of funds, location, description, estimated completion dates, and eventually estimates of the total value of completed jobs as well as forecasts of annual maintenance, repair, and operating expenses for all completed War Department establishments. Data for highly secret construction projects, such as for the atomic bomb, were carried in a separate subsection with only limited distribution.

Section VI (International Aid, Miscellaneous)—later designated as Section III—did not appear until 1 September 1942, by which time Section I had already been twice revised. Its purpose was to concentrate in one section all minor items and expendable supplies required by the allied nations. Hence, all items of International Aid originally carried in Section III were transferred to Section VI upon its appearance. This procedure was particularly desirable because of the noncommon nature of many International Aid items and the difficulty of including them in the classification scheme used in Section III. Major items of equipment for lend-lease continued to be carried in Section I.

The procurement objectives stated in the Army Supply Program represented "required production" from U.S. sources rather than gross military requirements. Gross military requirements for given time periods were reduced by the exclusion of three categories in order to arrive at net required production: (1) supplies on hand; (2) overseas procurement; (3) production limitations.

The determination of "on-hand" figures was a laborious assignment never satisfactorily accomplished. Total supplies on hand consisted of quantities in the hands of troops, wherever located, as well as unissued stocks in depots, in transit, and at many hundreds of posts, camps, stations, and other installations. The acquisition of accurate, uniform, and timely inventories of unissued stocks of thousands of different items from all of the Army's scattered establishments and troop locations was a mountainous undertaking. Moreover, estimates of quantities in the hands of troops were at best a matter of rough judgment. For the first few editions of the ASP, a calculated over-all on-hand figure was used. This was a composite of available inventory figures for major issuing depots plus estimates of station supplies in the hands of troops. The last-named estimate was made by deducting calculated losses from previous issues; no attempt was made early in the war to burden field commanders with the taking and reporting of inventories. For the 1 August 1943 ASP, an attempt was made to gather inventory figures at posts, camps, and stations as well as at major issuing depots. This proved to be impractical, especially for several of the technical services, and by mid-1944 the use of inventories for requirements purposes was confined for all services to major issuing depots. At the same time the theoretical estimate of equipment in the hands of troops was abandoned. Except for known shortages, all troops were assumed to be fully equipped and supply "pipelines" filled. Thereafter requirements were largely determined by fluctuations in replacement needs and the distributional stock levels required to insure timely delivery.[15]

Overseas procurement, consisting primarily of subsistence items and miscellaneous supplies for troops based in the British Empire, was a part of the lend-lease program known as reverse lend-lease. It was given considerable encouragement by the agreement between the President and the British Prime Minister early in 1942 to make maximum use of the productive capacity of each allied country and to conserve shipping space wherever possible. By the fall of 1942 overseas procurement had reached sufficient volume to warrant the adjustment of planned procurement in the United States. Required production in the Army Supply Program was therefore reduced by the amount of anticipated overseas procurement under the War Department's General Purchasing Board.[16]

A major purpose of the Army Supply Program was to achieve a balanced program in keeping with production limitations as well as with military needs. Organizations and procedures for this purpose were difficult to develop but by the end of 1942 the task was fairly well in hand. Standard procedures were developed for the advance screening by ASF production personnel of preliminary estimates of requirements. Each of the technical services was required to develop "master production schedules," based upon actual contracts and deliveries thereunder, showing estimated monthly deliveries of each item of procurement in keeping with the annual production targets of ASP. A careful month-by-month comparison of production schedules with actual procurement deliveries revealed deficiencies in procurement, calling for appropriate action to overcome shortages of materials, facilities, manpower, or other contributory resources. Quite frequently, however, shortages of basic resources could not be overcome and constituted a definite limitation upon production. In this event, efforts were made, prior to the next edition of ASP, to adjust stated requirements to feasible levels. Major cutbacks for feasibility reasons were usually requested by the War Production Board after a careful exploration and discussion of the alternatives, and an appropriate notation was carried in the ASP to distinguish requirements thus modified from those representing true military needs.[17]

Those responsible for the determination of requirements realized from the beginning that the ASP would undergo continual revision to reflect changes in the troop basis, the improvement of military technology, the progress of the war, the refinement of esti-

---

[15] The problems associated with the use and abandonment of the over-all on-hand estimates are treated in greater detail in Frank, Requirements, pp. 44, 57–58, 71–74, 157, and documents cited therein.

[16] (1) Memo, Maj Gen Lucius D. Clay, ACofS for Materiel ASF, for Dirs Reqmts and International Divs ASF, 22 Feb 43, sub: Procedure for Securing and Disseminating Information Concerning Overseas Procurement to be Incorporated in the Army Supply Program, Frank, Doc. 59. (2) Memo, Brig Gen Walter A. Wood, Jr., Dir Reqmts Div ASF, for CofOrd et al., 22 Mar 43, sub: Adjustments in Section I of the Army Supply Program to Reflect Overseas Procurement, Frank, Doc. 57. (3) WD TM 38–210, Preparation and Administration of the Army Supply Program, 25 Jan 44, par. 131.13, Oversea Procurement. (4) Frank, Requirements, pp. 39–41.

[17] In the 1 August 1943 ASP, required production was reduced for more than 100 items in Section I because of production limitations. Ordnance suffered the most heavily with 83 items, or over 10 percent of all items listed, subject to such limitations.

mating techniques, and many other expected as well as unforeseen developments. Originally it was hoped that complete recomputations of the program could be limited to an annual basis, with interim changes only for individual items and categories as the need arose. Sweeping changes early in the program led to an announced policy of complete revisions once each quarter; by 1943, however, a planned schedule of semiannual recomputations, in February and August, had been adopted. Important interim changes in Section I were accomplished by the periodic publication of summary sheets reflecting such changes; these were distributed to all recipients of the Army Supply Program. Changes involving less than 10 percent of required production, or more in the case of readily procurable items, were made by the relevant technical service but not published until the next recomputation of the program.[18]

Each separate edition of ASP was the result of an intensive period of preparation and activity within the ASF. The recomputation cycle was launched with the issuance of a basic directive by Headquarters, ASF, to the technical services responsible for preparing the several segments of the program. The basic directive transmitted the latest revision of the troop basis, the methods of determining combat replacement and reserve levels, and so far as practicable all other specific policies and procedures affect-

ing the recomputation.[19] In addition to the specific directive governing the recomputation of individual editions, there was throughout the life of ASP a succession of memoranda and administrative orders constituting a cumulative statement of its general purpose, scope, policy, and procedures. These scattered instructions were replaced on 25 January 1944 by the issuance of War Department Technical Manual 38–210, entitled Preparation and Administration of the Army Supply Program.[20]

All together seven editions of the Army Supply Program were published from its inception to its formal replacement by the Supply Control System (SCS) in January 1945.[21] The early editions were relatively crude, showing cumulative instead of separate annual estimates and expressing required production in terms of physical quantities only. The lack of dollar-value totals was a considerable shortcoming, handicapping analysis and discussion of the program

---

[18] (1) Memo, Maj Gen James A. Ulio, TAG, for CG AGF et al., 12 May 42, sub: War Matériel Requirements, Frank, Doc. 36. (2) WD Memo W310–3–42, 26 Sep 42, Computation of Munitions Requirements, Frank, Doc. 37. (3) Memo, TAG for ACofS G–3 et al., 27 Feb 43, sub: Computation of Munitions Requirements, Frank, Doc. 82. (4) Memo, Wood for CofCWS et al., 5 Mar 43, sub: Changes in Section I of the Army Supply Program, Frank, Doc. 66.

[19] For copies of the basic directives underlying the seven major editions of Section I of ASP, see Frank, Docs. 23, 39, 47, 73, 83, 93, and 122.

[20] Publication of TM 38–210 was delayed for about five months because of differences between ASF and AAF over procedures relating to the Air Equipment Section of ASP. (Frank, Requirements, pp. 108–09.) This manual provides excellent insight into the procedures and problems involved in the complex task of determining Army requirements at the peak of the World War II procurement program. A copy of the manual is available as Frank, Doc. 106. The principal predecessor of TM 38–210 was SOS Admin Memo 38, 16 Sep 42, sub: Procedure of the Determination and Administration of the Army Supply Program. (Frank, Doc. 26.)

[21] The seven editions of ASP represented the original publication and major revisions of Section I; publication of other sections did not always appear on schedule with the corresponding edition of Section I. The successive editions of ASP were distinguished by dates, not by an edition number. The present discussion follows Frank, Requirements, which apparently treats the 29 May 1942 revision of Section I as a republication, rather than as a new edition.

TABLE 18—ARMY SUPPLY PROGRAM, SECTION I: ARMY GROUND FORCES REQUIREMENTS IN SUCCESSIVE EDITIONS OF ASP

[In Billions]

Date of Edition [a]	1942	1943	1944	1945
6 April 1942	$16.9	$31.6	—	—
1 September 1942	—	28.1	—	—
12 November 1942	—	22.2	—	—
1 February 1943	—	24.3	$26.8	—
1 August 1943	—	20.4	21.7	$19.6
1 February 1944	—	—	17.8	15.8
1 October 1944	—	—	18.3	17.3

[a] First three editions include Section III, later carried as Part B, Section I.

Source: ASP editions as indicated, except for first three. For first editions: WPB, Div of Statistics, tabulation of 8 Apr 42; second and third editions; Frank, Doc. 48.

TABLE 19—ARMY SUPPLY PROGRAM, SECTION I: REQUIRED PRODUCTION FOR CALENDAR YEARS 1943 AND 1944

[In Millions]

Technical Service	Year	Total of Parts A and B	Part A (Equipment–Ground)				Part B (Miscellaneous, Equipment and Supplies)
			Total	U.S. Army	U.S. Navy	International Aid	
Total	1943	$24,311.8	$19,278.7	$12,642.7	$1,110.2	$5,957.7	$5,033.1
	1944	26,757.8	21,077.0	15,284.1	1,020.4	4,580.0	5,680.8
Ordnance	1943	14,918.0	14,781.0	8,576.0	973.6	5,582.5	137.0
	1944	16,849.3	16,688.5	11,332.6	917.5	4,313.0	160.8
Signal Corps	1943	1,506.5	993.5	861.5	37.6	115.9	513.0
	1944	1,355.5	784.1	664.5	12.3	85.9	551.4
Corps of Engineers	1943	1,616.0	928.9	780.0	71.1	121.5	687.1
	1944	1,850.3	982.9	798.9	70.1	70.1	867.4
Chemical Warfare	1943	287.6	259.6	258.1	2.5	12.7	28.0
	1944	392.5	345.7	323.1	3.5	16.8	46.8
Medical Department	1943	473.2	301.6	249.6	2.6	49.8	171.6
	1944	378.6	245.2	204.1	3.2	38.0	133.4
Quartermaster Corps	1943	4,885.8	1,981.8	1,885.2	22.8	75.4	2,904.0
	1944	5,528.1	1,987.0	1,917.3	13.8	56.2	3,541.1
Transportation	1943	592.4	0	0	0	0	592.4
	1944	379.9	0	0	0	0	379.9
AAF (Miscellaneous Equipment)	1943	32.3	32.3	32.3	0	0	0
	1944	43.6	43.6	43.6	0	0	0

Source: Army Supply Program, Sec. I, 1 Feb 43.

until special tabulations could be made for the purpose. Since changes were often made in the interim, and since tabulations were made by different agencies, the resulting figures were often difficult to reconcile. This condition was rectified in the 1 February 1943 and subsequent editions, which contained dollar-value summaries and numerous improvements in form as well as substance.[22]

An indication of the magnitude of Army Ground Forces requirements, as well as the gradual reduction in the dollar value of these requirements under successive editions of ASP, is shown in Table 18. The largest share of the general reduction was represented by changes in the planned composition of the Army under which the number of heavily armored and motorized divisions was drastically cut.[23] Together with curtailment in the over-all size of the Army as planned at the beginning of 1942, reductions in unit costs, adjustments in the lend-lease program, and numerous other factors, this decision resulted in the paring of many billions of dollars from Army requirements as estimated at the beginning of 1942.[24]

TABLE 20—ARMY SUPPLY PROGRAM: COMPARATIVE MAGNITUDE OF SECTIONS I–IV IN MID-1943

[In Billions]

Section	1943	1944
I–Ground	$20.8	$22.0
II–Air	[a] 4.3	6.1
AAF Procurement	[a] 0.9	2.1
ASF Procurement:		
Ordnance	1.2	1.4
Signal	1.9	2.2
Chemical	0.3	0.4
III–Miscellaneous International Aid	1.0	0.5
IV–Construction [b]	2.8	

[a] AAF procurement covered for last 6 months only of 1943.

[b] Uncompleted projects to be put in place without specification of calendar year.

Source: Frank, Requirements, pp. 78–79.

A broad summary of Army requirements for Ground Forces matériel, classified by technical services, is furnished by Table 19. This table shows estimated requirements for the calendar years 1943 and 1944, as they stood on 1 February 1943. Especially to be noted are the heavy demands for Ordnance equipment and ammunition by allied nations under the lend-lease program. For 1943 these amounted to nearly two thirds of the Army's own requirements for such items.

The comparative magnitude of the several sections of ASP is suggested by Table 20, which contains partial figures from the program as it stood in the summer of 1943. At this time Section IV (Construction) car-

[22] During its heyday, Section I of the ASP was a handsomely bound volume, 9 x 13 inches, containing several hundred pages; the other sections were similar in format but with fewer pages. Each significant item of procurement was listed under the appropriate technical service. Data included the item entry, unit cost, stocks on hand, and net required production in physical quantities for each calendar year to supply the U.S. Army, Navy, and international aid. Total dollar-value figures were confined to summaries by procuring service and requiring agency.

[23] See below, page 156 and note 35.

[24] The Army's War Munitions Program of 11 February 1942, which included finished aircraft for the Army but omitted expendable supplies and other items, totaled some $62 billion in estimated expenditures for 1942 and 1943. See: (1) Statement of Brig Gen Lucius D. Clay before the War Production Board on 1 December 1942, in Civilian Pro-

duction Administration, *Minutes of the War Production Board, January 20, 1942 to October 9, 1945* (Washington: Government Printing Office, 1946) (hereafter cited as *WPB Minutes*), p. 166; (2) ASF Annual Rpt, 1943, p. 18.

ried $2.8 billion of uncompleted projects remaining to be put in place without specification of calendar year. Although the relative shares of the several sections of ASP fluctuated from one edition to another, Section I remained the overwhelmingly predominant portion of the Army Supply Program.

Major Developments Under ASP

The Feasibility Dispute—Despite the efforts of the ASF properly to control the Army's procurement program, there were numerous shortcomings—especially during the exploratory period of organization and planning to meet the numerous problems which descended upon the War Department immediately after Pearl Harbor. Foremost among the problems of 1942 was the determination of long-range Army requirements which, together with other essential programs, would be within the nation's capacity to produce. The controversy which developed between the Army and the War Production Board over this issue—later known as the Feasibility Dispute—was one of the most acrimonious of the war.

The Feasibility Dispute has been described in detail elsewhere,[25] but a brief recapitulation is necessary to indicate the Army's role in the controversy. Early in 1942 the War Production Board, particu-

larly its Planning Committee headed by Robert R. Nathan, became convinced that total military procurement objectives for 1942 and 1943, when added to the needs of the civilian and industrial economy, were greatly in excess of the nation's productive capacity. The problem was aggravated by the fact that proposed construction programs for both military and industrial facilities accounted for a substantial portion of the total war production program. In view of serious existing material shortages, it became clear that further diversion of materials to construction programs would result in still greater imbalance. Not only would new construction chew up vast quantities of materials needed for finished munitions; after their completion the new facilities themselves would be forced to remain idle or operate at a fraction of capacity for lack of raw materials.[26]

At various times in the spring and summer of 1942, WPB called the attention of the procuring agencies to the feasibility problem and some adjustments in programs were made. But the procuring agencies were preoccupied with placing contracts and expediting production; moreover, considerable research was needed to estimate the nation's production potential with any degree of accuracy. Finally, on 8 September 1942, Nathan transmitted to General Somervell an extended report on the feasibility problem prepared by Dr. Simon Kuznets, a WPB economist with an established reputation in the field of national income analysis.

---

[25] (1) John E. Brigante, *The Feasibility Dispute* (Washington: Committee on Public Administration Cases, 1950). (2) CPA, *Industrial Mobilization for War*, pp. 282–92. (3) Nelson, *Arsenal of Democracy*, pp. 376–81.

The general relationship between national productive capacity and military requirements is discussed in an informative article written during World War II by one of the leading generals in the Army Service Forces. See Maj. Gen. Lucius D. Clay, "The Army Supply Program," *Fortune*, XXVII, No. 2 (February 1943), 95ff.

[26] A number of Army facilities did in fact shut down after short periods of operation. But these shutdowns resulted from many causes, including curtailment of requirements and unanticipated increases in productivity as well as material shortages. Thomson and Mayo, The Ordnance Department: Procurement and Supply of Munitions. See also, Part Five, below.

The Kuznets analysis pointed to two major barriers to the attainment of existing production objectives: (1) inadequate capacity of the economy as a whole, measured by dollar-value estimates; (2) material shortages and defects in the scheduling of production all down the line. The report recommended a drastic curtailment of military procurement objectives and the establishment of a superboard—with full powers over the Army, Navy, Maritime Commission, and other agencies—to co-ordinate military strategy with production possibilities.[27]

The Kuznets report, together with a transmittal memorandum from Nathan elsewhere described as "somewhat peremptory in tone," came to Somervell's attention late on a Saturday afternoon. Somervell's reaction was immediate. He did not agree with the findings and referred to the proposal for a superboard on strategy as "an inchoate mass of words." He wrote out a reply to Nathan in longhand, concluding with the words: "I am not impressed with either the character or basis of the judgments expressed in the reports and recommend that they be carefully hidden from the eyes of thoughtful men."[28]

Needless to say, the Somervell memorandum provoked considerable discussion within WPB and a formal meeting of the War Production Board, on 6 October 1942, was devoted to a showdown on the issues. This meeting was attended by seventeen invitees, including Somervell and Nathan, in addition to the fourteen regular participants. Early in the meeting, Nathan reviewed the Kuznets feasibility study and urged the creation of "an administrative

mechanism to combine strategy and production."[29] Thereupon a general discussion of the feasibility problem ensued, in which the programs of the armed services came under considerable attack. Somervell conceded that the 1942 program would probably fall some 10-percent short of completion by the end of the year but indicated that the material-shortage problem was being relieved by a number of measures and that dollar figures could not be relied upon as a measure of national productive capacity. At this point, Leon Henderson, director of the Office of Price Administration (OPA) and ex officio member of the War Production Board, stated that dollar figures represented the "best common denominator of capacity." Then after a lull in the discussion in which it appeared that the meeting might end without a positive decision of the issues, Henderson is reported to have reflected on Nathan's $90 billion estimate of 1943 munitions capacity and to have stated in substance: "Maybe if we can't wage a war on 90 billions, we ought to get rid of our present Joint Chiefs, and find some who can." Henderson then "turned to Somervell and proceeded to make the most violent personal attack ever heard in a meeting of the War Production Board. . . . For a considerable period Henderson gave vent to every grievance he had accumulated throughout the first year of the war."[30]

The explosive 6 October meeting made it clear that early cutbacks in military requirements would have to be made. On the following day, Under Secretary Patterson addressed a memorandum to General Som-

---

[27] CPA, *Industrial Mobilization for War,* pp. 284–87.

[28] Brigante, *The Feasibility Dispute,* p. 83.

[29] CPA, *WPB Minutes,* 6 Oct 42, p. 140. Under Secretary Patterson regularly represented Secretary Stimson at WPB meetings. Both the Secretary of War and the Secretary of the Navy were members of the War Production Board.

[30] Brigante, *The Feasibility Dispute,* p. 95.

ervell conceding the correctness of WPB's basic position:

The WPB position, that production objectives ought not to be far in front of estimated maximum production, is believed to be sound as a general rule. Otherwise our scheduling of production cannot represent reality, and it is generally agreed that without realistic scheduling we will continue to suffer from maldistribution of materials, thus cutting down the actual output of finished weapons.[31]

Patterson went on to state that it would be up to the Joint Chiefs of Staff, acting within the framework of strategic considerations, to reduce the program to a limit set by WPB and that the bulk of the reduction would undoubtedly fall upon the Army and Navy; the aircraft and shipbuilding programs as well as those for expansion of raw material production probably would not be touched. Accordingly, at the next meeting of WPB, on 13 October 1942, Somervell and Patterson suggested that WPB inform the Joint Chiefs that their existing program, together with the President's objectives, was not capable of attainment. It would then be the JCS responsibility to redefine the program within the limits established by WPB.[32]

This was the solution actually adopted. It avoided the question of a superboard on strategy and production and spared WPB the necessity of again challenging the President's objectives, an unpleasant task which had been attempted with embarrassing results earlier in the year.[33] The Joint Chiefs went to work on the combined military program for 1943 and pared it down from $93 billion to $80 billion. Of the $13 billion reduction, $9 billion came from the Army

Supply Program alone.[34] This change, published in the 12 November 1942 edition, represented the greatest single reduction during the life of the Army Supply Program. To accomplish the reduction the Army revised its troop basis, decreasing its planned strength for 1943 and 1944 by some 300,000 men and effecting heavy reductions in armored, motorized, airborne, and infantry divisions, as well as in tank battalions, field artillery units, and tank destroyer battalions. Also, the Army at this time extended the practice of issuing only 50 percent of standard allowances of critical equipment to training units in the United States.[35]

The 12 November 1942 cutbacks in military requirements put an end to a controversial situation which had been growing in seriousness for nine months. There has since been some speculation as to why the resolution of the controversy was so long delayed.[36] The Army has frequently been charged with ignoring the existence of the feasibility problem early in 1942, and Somervell specifically with failure to understand the use of dollar-

---

[31] Memo, Patterson for Somervell, 7 Oct 42, CG ASF.

[32] CPA, *WPB Minutes,* 13 Oct 42, p. 144.

[33] CPA, *Industrial Mobilization for War,* pp. 281–82, 295.

[34] *Ibid.,* p. 289. Apart from the Army construction program, which was reduced by 31 percent, procurement for Army Ground Forces suffered the most drastic curtailment (21 percent). See Kent Roberts Greenfield, Robert R. Palmer, and Bell I. Wiley, *The Organization of Ground Combat Troops,* UNITED STATES ARMY IN WORLD WAR II (Washington: 1947), p. 215.

[35] Frank, Requirements, p. 35. The inadequate supplies of ammunition and equipment for training purposes throughout 1942 and early 1943 contributed to poor morale as well as impaired training in the Army Ground Forces. See Greenfield, Palmer, and Wiley, *Organization of Ground Combat Troops,* pp. 220–23. The changes in the structure of the Army at this time are summarized in Kent Roberts Greenfield, *The Historian and the Army* (New Brunswick: Rutgers University Press, 1954) pp. 60–85.

[36] For example, Brigante, *The Feasibility Dispute,* "Concluding Observations," pp. 107–15, wherein the author attributes responsibility for the delay to both the Army and WPB.

value estimates of national productive capacity. Neither of these offers adequate explanation. General Marshall, it will be recalled, had raised the feasibility question as early as September 1941, at the time of the submission of the Victory Program. Moreover, it was Marshall's suggestion at that time that any feasibility problem be resolved by a reformulation of the military program within limits established by OPM, the then existing civilian mobilization control agency.[37] Likewise, General Somervell—even before he became the head of the Army Service Forces—had clearly indicated his understanding that military programs would have to be kept within the limitations of productive capacity:

The supply program is primarily based on military need. It must, however, be conditioned by the practicalities of production and conflicts with Navy, Allied, and civilian needs. There is nothing to be gained and an actual danger in setting up requirements that are wholly impossible of attainment. This means that the Supply Division itself can only formulate a tentative program of requirements which must be reviewed from the procurement and allocation standpoint before it can be set up as a program for execution.[38]

The real issue, so far as Somervell was concerned, turned on questions of fact rather than principle. In the early post-Pearl Harbor period, he did not believe the data available were sufficiently accurate to afford a reliable measure of national productive capacity, especially in the field of munitions production. His distrust of dollar-value estimates was not a failure to understand the use of dollar figures in national income analysis but a direct inference from his knowledge of the state of procurement contract prices. In the spring of 1942 Somervell had testi-

fied at length before the Senate Appropriations Subcommittee on the impossibility of setting initial contract prices close to cost.[39] Initial contract prices, upon which the estimated dollar value of military procurement programs was based, would inevitably be greatly reduced as production got under way, and this reduction would reflect greater efficiency in the use of real resources with corresponding increases in physical productive capacity. In view of all the uncertainties in the spring and summer of 1942—the manifold problems of industrial conversion to war production, the constant flux in prices and costs, repeated changes in the composition of military requirements, and so on ad infinitum—Somervell considered it premature to rely on tentative national income estimates as the basis for a major reduction in the program, and he was optimistic in the matter of increased output and improved distribution of essential materials. Moreover, in common with President Roosevelt, Somervell believed in the efficacy of "incentive goals" as an important determinant of the nation's productive capacity. Finally, there is no doubt that both Somervell and Patterson—in their role as champions of the military program—customarily assigned a lower importance to civilian claims upon the nation's productive resources than they did to military requirements.

By the fall of 1942, however, the war economy had become sufficiently developed and stabilized to permit the satisfactory resolution of the Feasibility Dispute. The substantial completion of industrial conversion to war production, the corresponding development and stabilization of governmental war agencies, the steadily augmented and

---

[37] See above, page 138.
[38] Somervell memo cited above, note 14.

[39] See below, pages 352–53.

refined flow of statistical and other information, and the growing crisis in material shortages and the administration of material control systems all converged in late 1942 to force as well as to permit the necessary cutbacks in military programs. It is questionable whether intelligent and appropriate adjustments thereto could have been achieved much sooner in the absence of the necessary underlying conditions.

After coming to a head in October 1942, the controversy over feasibility rapidly subsided, and its resolution marked the widespread acceptance of one of the most significant lessons to be learned from the World War II industrial mobilization experience. This was the painful but unavoidable conclusion that even the U.S. economy, great as it was, could not undertake widely unattainable production objectives without slowing down production all along the line. The resolution of the Feasibility Dispute was soon followed by the successful adoption of the Controlled Materials Plan and collateral measures to ration the nation's industrial capacity for the achievement of balanced procurement objectives.

The War Department Procurement Review Board—A second major development during the life of the Army Supply Program occurred in connection with the review of War Department procurement activities during the summer and fall of 1943, when the war economy was approaching peak production. Early in the summer of 1943, the newly established top-level co-ordinating agency—the Office of War Mobilization (OWM)—requested each of the major procuring agencies to appoint a board of review to examine the composition of its requirement programs in terms of essentiality and balance and to make recommendations concerning the control and efficiency of procurement as a whole.[40] The War Department Procurement Review Board (WDPRB) was appointed as a result of this request. The Procurement Review Board studied the strategic plans of the Joint Chiefs of Staff, the background of the Army Supply Program, and the current status of requirements, procurement activities, and inventories of finished matériel. In the course of its activities, the board made two field trips and interviewed some seventy-three witnesses including War Department officials concerned with military requirements and procurement. The board's report of sixty-eight pages and associated material, submitted on 31 August 1943, furnishes excellent insight into the problems, achievements, and shortcomings of the Army's supply system at the peak of its World War II procurement program.[41]

In general, the board found that the Army's supply operations were successful: "No approved operation has been hampered by shortage. The quality of equipment has been good. All those connected with design, procurement, production, and distribution are to be commended on the

---

[40] The origin and history of OWM (later the Office of War Mobilization and Reconversion) are presented in Somers, *OWMR.* See pages 62–64 therein for background of the War Department Procurement Review Board.

[41] The complete report of the War Department Procurement Review Board—often called the McCoy Board for its chairman, Maj. Gen. Frank R. McCoy, USA (Ret.)—is Appendix B in the two-volume publication of the War Department entitled "Levels of Supply and Supply Procedure" (1 January 1944). This publication also includes the report of the Special Committee for Re-Study of Reserves (Richards Committee) (Appendix F); the McNarney Directive of 1 January 1944 (Appendix A); and detailed comments of War Department staff and command agencies on the recommendations of the two reports (Appendixes C and G).

results." [42] The board noted "a war cannot be run like an industry; the criterion is not low costs but victory. The enemy is resourceful: changes in strategy and equipment are constantly necessary—regardless of expense in money and materials—if the enemy is to be countered vigilantly, driven to the defensive, and finally overwhelmed." [43]

On the debit side, the board felt that the time had come for a much more adequate screening of requirements, especially for certain categories of supply. It found the Quartermaster Corps' ninety-day reserve supply of nonperishable food in the United States too high; the nation's food-raising capacity and a transportation system insuring quick movement, the board believed, would permit a substantial reduction in zone of interior reserves. The Army's methods of determining requirements for ammunition came in for particularly heavy criticism. The use of the "day of supply" concept, with arbitrary estimates of probable expenditures per gun, had resulted in the building up of huge reserves of ammunition:

Our stocks of small arms ammunition are now measured in billions of rounds. If we continue to produce on the basis of assumed figures which are widely variant from actual expenditures, our reserves of ammunition will soon be astronomical. They are now tremendous. The on-hand stock of small arms ammunition in this country amounts to some 2.5 billion rounds. In reserve in North Africa is an additional 1.4 billion rounds.

The Board is convinced that the War Department must take steps to bring production of ammunition and stocks of ammunition into the realm of reality. [44]

Extending its observations to the matter of reserve supplies in general, WDPRB

noted an increase in the value of major ASF items in storage from $2 billion to $4 billion during the period December 1942 to June 1943. Specific examples included stocks of gas masks (from 500,000 to 1,800,000) and demolition bombs (from 346,000 tons to 800,000 tons). Accordingly, the board recommended greater attention to inventory control and a thorough restudy of reserve levels. [45]

A further target of the board's criticism was the automatic supply of equipment to troops and organizations on the basis of established tables of allowances without distinction between different theaters and often without serious consideration of the actual usefulness of the equipment under specific circumstances. The report pointed out that complete organizational transport equipment was furnished to units on Pacific islands where roads still had to be hacked out of the jungle. Similarly, the board observed that 155-mm. howitzers, highly essential in ordinary terrain, might be entirely too cumbersome for the mountain roads of the Balkans. Complex radio equipment suitable for trained American troops was probably not practicable for Chinese troops supplied on a divisional basis by the U.S. Army. Furnishing full allowances of ground radio equipment to air squadrons in England appeared to be gratuitous since the British communications network could be used. [46]

The board also noted a repetition of the World War I tendency to overequip the individual American soldier:

In the last war the American soldier and many of his units were overequipped. As a result, the first engagement or extended march saw French villages and French roads

<hr>

[42] WDPRB Rpt, p. 61.
[43] Ibid., pp. 1–2.
[44] Ibid., p. 36. The "day of supply" concept is discussed at some length below; see pages 203 ff.

[45] WDPRB Rpt, pp. 46–52, 67.
[46] Ibid., pp. 48, 54.

HEAVILY BURDENED SOLDIERS DEBARKING *at Phosphate Pier, Casablanca.*

littered with discarded equipment. The Board senses that a similar situation exists in this war.

A visit to the New York Port of Embarkation provided visual evidence. It was a hot July evening and troops on a North River pier were pouring aboard a transport. As they went up the gangplank, bowed down with the weight of their equipment, they looked like pack mules. They carried their weapons, a full pack, a barracks bag, an overcoat, and an antigas suit. An additional barracks bag for each soldier already had been stowed in the ship's hold.[47]

These observations were pointed up with the statement that "the issue of equipment to individuals and units simply because the documentary tables call for it is sheer waste." [48]

Still another condition observed by the board was the failure to curtail construction and supply operations in obsolete theaters of operations:

No nation is rich enough or productive enough to supply and maintain battlefronts where there is no longer a battle.

---

[47] *Ibid.,* pp. 53–54. Lt. Gen. Lesley J. McNair testified before the board that the Casablanca landing indicated overequipment of troops. Elsewhere it has been noted that the amount of individual equipment in the North Africa invasion raised serious problems of "ships, space, loading and unloading, transportation, storage, deterioration of contents, theft, and failure of [duffel] bags

---

to catch up with fast moving combat units." Bradford, QMC Requirements, p. 73. As a result of this experience the War Department adopted The Soldier's Payload Plan, reducing the amount of equipment to be carried and providing for issue in the field of other needed items.

[48] WDPRB Rpt, p. 54.

The Caribbean area is a case in point. In the dark days of 1940 when it appeared possible that Germany might overrun Europe and Western Africa, when there was at least reasonable doubt as to the continued availability of the British fleet, we embarked on a program of bases in the Caribbean. When the tide of war turned in our favor, the need for these bases became less pressing. Nevertheless, construction of bases for large garrisons continued. Today we have in these areas "ghost" camps which cost more than $200,000,000 and which were laid out for garrisons that will probably never be there.

It appears evident that the difficulties encountered in the Caribbean will be repeated on a much larger scale in North Africa unless strong measures of control are taken forthwith to prevent such repetition.[49]

A similar illustration was the continuation of 1940 plans for modernization of U.S. harbor and seacoast defenses. Although it had been revised downward from time to time, the program still contemplated the completion of twenty-two 16-inch and eight 12-inch gun batteries in addition to fifty 6-inch gun batteries. In the light of current conditions, the board doubted the wisdom of the heavy gun program, particularly since it involved the manufacture and installation of mechanical and electrical components requiring the highest type of workmanship and shop facilities badly needed throughout the war production program. The board therefore recommended the re-examination and curtailment of the seacoast heavy gun program.[50]

Many of the recommendations of the Procurement Review Board had been put into effect by the time of its report.[51] A

major consequence of the report was the appointment by the Deputy Chief of Staff on 3 September 1943 of the Special Committee for the Re-Study of Reserves. This committee, known as the Richards Committee after the name of the chairman (Brig. Gen. George J. Richards), was charged with the responsibility for the re-survey of five specific areas of requirements determination: (1) the strategic reserve; (2) theater reserves; (3) stockpiles in the United States; (4) day of supply; (5) maintenance, distribution, and shipping loss factors.

Like the Procurement Review Board, the Richards Committee conducted intensive hearings and studies and submitted its report within a two-month period. While it warned that the heaviest fighting of the war still lay in the future, the committee also found the Army's current requirements estimates excessive and made numerous recommendations for their reduction. It also suggested the adoption of improved procedures in gathering pertinent data and in computing and screening requirements. The committee's fifty-seven specific recommendations were incorporated in whole or in part in a general implementing directive issued by the Deputy Chief of Staff on 1 January 1944. The McNarney Directive made a number of important changes in procedure as well as substance, transferring certain functions

---

[49] *Ibid.*, pp. 57–58.

[50] *Ibid.*, pp. 40–41, 66.

[51] In addition to thirteen formal recommendations made by the board, the investigation had re-vealed various other opportunities for the improvement of the procurement practices. On the other hand not all the official recommendations were considered desirable by the War Department. See WD, Levels of Supply and Supply Procedure, App. C, Comments of the War Department on the Recommendations and Related Conclusions Contained in the Report of the War Department Procurement Review Board, dated 31 August 1943.

from the Army Service Forces to the Supply Division of the General Staff.[52]

The general result of the reports of both the Procurement Review Board and the Richards Committee was a broad reduction in Army requirements together with increased attention to the improvement of the procedures for requirements determination. The reports had the effect of expediting the development of the Supply Control System, which gradually replaced the Army Supply Program in the last year and a half of the war.

The Supply Control System

By the end of 1943, procurement of initial equipment for the expanding Army was for the most part complete and stocks of munitions in many categories had reached comfortable or even excessive levels. After the report of the Richards Committee and the ensuing McNarney Directive, the ASF took steps to refine its methods of determining requirements and to bring into balance all stages of the procurement and distribution process. On 28 January 1944, Maj. Gen. Lucius D. Clay, Director of Materiel, indicated to all his staff divisions the need for many changes in procedure and announced that specific instructions would soon be issued.[53]

The new instructions issued on 7 March may be regarded as launching the Army's Supply Control System.[54] The basic purpose of the procedures established by the new system was to improve and co-ordinate four related activities: (1) requirements determination; (2) revision of procurement schedules; (3) distribution and issue of matériel; and (4) the disposal of surpluses. All items of procurement were to be divided into two control groups: Principal (P items) and Secondary (S items). P items were those which were important from a military or monetary standpoint and which fell into either or both of the following categories: (1) central control necessary because of production considerations (lengthy production "lead time" or controls over materials, components, manpower, facilities); (2) past issue experience inadequate for the computation of requirements (sporadic or special project issues). S items included all matériel not specifically listed as P items. Classification of items was made the responsibility of the technical service chiefs, who were directed to submit by 15 March 1944 lists of all items under their cognizance to be designated as P items. It was anticipated that many items in the P category would eventually shift into the S group as control procedures were perfected. Requirements for P items were to be carefully reviewed at least once quarterly and individually listed as long-range procurement objectives in the Army Supply Program. Requirements for S items were to be grouped in item or dollar categories deemed appropriate by the technical services for publication in ASP.

The new approach to requirements determination for all items was based on "sup-

---

[52] Memo, Lt Gen Joseph T. McNarney, DCofS, for CG AAF et al., 1 Jan 44, sub: Changes in Supply Procedure and Supply Levels. This document, hereafter cited as the McNarney Directive, is reproduced as Appendix A, in WD, Levels of Supply and Supply Procedure. The report of the Richards Committee, as shown above in note 41, is found in the same volume (Appendix F). Many of the actions required by the McNarney Directive had already been independently undertaken by appropriate echelons of the War Department as part of their regular responsibilities.

[53] Memo, Gen Clay, Dir of Materiel, for Dir Purchases Div et al., 28 Jan 44, Frank, Doc. 119.

[54] ASF Cir 67, 7 Mar 44.

ply and demand studies" to be conducted by the technical services. The total demand for each item was described as consisting of two elements: future issue requirements and total authorized stock levels. Future issue requirements were to be based wherever possible on recent issue experience. It was considered that this basis would be appropriate for most S items. The majority of P items, on the other hand, were not expected to possess stable rates of issue and requirements for these would have to be based on equipment tables and other data previously used in computing the Army Supply Program. In all cases, current and past issue data were to be accumulated and used in conjunction with other information in forecasting future needs. The total authorized stock level for a given item was defined as the quantitative sum of all stockage authorized to be physically held within the continental United States for depot distribution as reserves. Reserve levels were established at forty-five days of supply for the zone of interior and sixty days for theaters of operations distribution, plus certain special reserve categories.[55]

From the sum of estimated future issues and total authorized stock levels was to be deducted total stock on hand; the remainder indicated a "desired total receipts schedule." Against this schedule was to be matched total expected receipts from contracts in force, overseas procurement, reclamation schedules, and any other sources. The difference between desired and expected total receipts—that is, shortages or excesses—represented the "desired adjustment." Indicated shortages were to be overcome by augmenting procurement schedules; excesses were to be dealt with by curtailment

of procurement and, where appropriate, by disposal action. The new system focused attention upon supply and demand at depots in the United States through which the distribution of all Army supplies was actually or theoretically channeled. Morever, the system would force the co-ordination of all aspects of Army supply—requirements, procurement, distribution and issue, reclamation, stock control, and disposal of surpluses.[56]

The inauguration of the new system, soon to be known officially as the Supply Control System, required Herculean efforts. Major changes in organizations and procedures were necessary. In June 1944 the Requirements Division, formerly under the Director of Materiel, ASF, was merged with the Supply Control Division, formerly under the Director of Supply, ASF. The resulting new Requirements and Stock Control Division was placed in the Office of the Director of Plans and Operations. The rationale behind these changes was threefold: (1) Feasibility considerations were no longer a serious limitation upon general requirements, hence retention of the function of requirements determination by the office concerned with production matters—the Director of Materiel—was no longer required; (2) the great importance of inventories at this stage of the war called for the closest relationship between requirements determination and stock control; (3) this consolidated activity could best be directed from the highest planning echelon of ASF, where major plans originated for the pending shift from a two-front to a one-front war, with implications of drastic changes in requirements.[57]

---

[55] *Ibid.*, pp. 12–14.

[56] *Ibid.*, pp. 14–24.

[57] Millett, *Organization and Role of the ASF*, pp. 342, 355.

In order to carry out the purposes of the Supply Control System, planners devised an elaborate scheme of forms and records to permit the accumulation of up-to-date information on all elements and phases of the supply and demand situation. For P items the basic supply-control Long Form (WD AGO Form 0470) was developed. This form, which underwent a number of revisions, brought together on one page all important supply and demand information for the procurement item concerned, time phased by months for the three months preceding and following the date of estimate, and by quarters thereafter. For S items, stock record cards or supply-control short forms were maintained by each technical service. The general instructions governing the Supply Control System were published and revised in successive editions of ASF M–413, which superseded ASF Circular 67.[58]

The number of principal items under supply control coverage rose from 950 in August 1944 to nearly 1,900 by March 1945, when it accounted for approximately 80 percent of the total dollar value of ASF procurement. In December 1944 it was decided that all P items should be reviewed monthly and that the supply computations resulting therefrom would be published in the Monthly Progress Report, MPR–20

series. Thereafter the monthly progress reports took the place of the semiannual revisions of the Army Supply Program, and the 1 October 1944 edition of ASP (originally scheduled for 1 August 1944) was the last to be published. This final edition of the Army Supply Program contained requirements developed under SCS procedures and thus effected a transition to the new system.

Each monthly supply computation for the 1,900 principal items, initially performed by the technical services, was critically appraised in a "review meeting" attended by requirements, production, and distribution personnel from the technical services and ASF staff divisions. Representatives of the divisions were authorized to take final approval action for their respective agencies, and the computations as revised in review meetings became the official basis for publication in the monthly progress report. This procedure not only eliminated an enormous quantity of paper work but permitted a degree of staff co-ordination never before achieved. Furthermore, the 1,900 principal items published in MPF–20 represented a considerable reduction from the 4,500 items formerly listed individually in each semiannual recomputation of ASP.[59]

Secondary items under the Supply Control System numbered about 900,000 but constituted only 20 percent of the dollar value of ASF procurement. Spare parts accounted for the major share of secondaryitem procurement, and in March 1944 the Spare Parts Branch of the Requirements Division was established to co-ordinate various requirements, procurement, and distribution activities relating to spare parts. This branch did much to improve the flow of information as well as the formulation

---

[58] See ASF M–413, The Supply Control System, editions of 20 Jul 44, 22 Dec 44, and 10 Apr 45. Although the Supply Control System was the result of many developments, it owed much to the stock control system and supply and demand studies initiated by the Quartermaster Corps. The representations of the QMC led to a detailed study and report by Mr. Howard Bruce, who later succeeded General Clay as the Director of Materiel, ASF. The Bruce report was an important influence leading to the adoption of the Supply Control System. See: (1) Bradford, QMC Requirements, p. 51; (2) Risch, QMC Supply, I, 226–29.

[59] Frank, Requirements, pp. 159–63.

and execution of procurement policy in the field of its activity. In view of the large number and lower importance of S items, requirements thereof were at first reviewed only quarterly. In the spring of 1945, however, it was found that stocks and prescribed stock levels of secondary items amounted to some five billion dollars, or nearly a year's supply. Inasmuch as tactical plans for the remainder of the war indicated a substantial decrease in the rate of issue demand, a comprehensive survey of secondary items was ordered by the Commanding General, ASF.[60] The governing directive called for the suspension of procurement deliveries or the cancellation of contracts for items exceeding specified levels and ordered prompt redistribution and disposal action for all items reaching redistribution and disposal levels. Within four weeks the Office, Chief of Ordnance—Detroit, in response to the directive, completed the review of 216,303 secondary items, revealing stocks valued at $145,718,021 to be in excess of disposal levels. This so-called blitz review for all technical services covered more than 600,000 items and resulted in the cancellation of $491 million in procurement and the declaration of $334 million in property as excess.[61]

Continued attention to secondary items, highlighted by various directives, meetings, and visits of ASF personnel to stock control points, revealed that 6 percent of the more than 900,000 secondary items accounted for 80 percent of total annual procurement of these items. On 3 July 1945 an elaborate directive was issued calling for accurate monthly progress reports for secondary

items to be published as MPR–19, Secondary Items. The purpose of the directive was to bring increased pressure to bear upon the services in reducing procurement and effecting disposal actions, as well as to accumulate timely information. The first presentation of the supply position of secondary items on a monthly basis appeared in MPR–19, dated 30 June 1945. This publication, which covered some 833,000 secondary items, revealed that the value of the total stock on hand as of 30 June 1945 amounted to $3,194,000,000—a notable reduction from the estimate of $5 billion in the Somerville directive of 21 April 1945.[62]

The Supply Control System represented the final stage of the Army's organization and procedure for controlling procurement in World War II. Like the Army Supply Program, the Supply Control System was the focal point of all the Army's procurement and supply operations. But it was far more comprehensive and detailed than ASP. Instead of providing only annual production targets, revised twice a year, SCS contained monthly and quarterly details and was recomputed and republished each month. Instead of showing only requirements and stocks on hand at the beginning of each year, SCS showed the supply as well as the demand position of each item for each

[60] Memo, Gen Somervell, CG ASF for CofOrd, 21 Apr 45, sub: Excessive Stock on Hand in Secondary Items, Frank, Doc. 146.

[61] Frank, Requirements, p. 178.

[62] (1) Memo, Brig Gen Theodore M. Osborne, Dir Reqmts and Stock Control Div, for CofOrd et al., 9 May 45, sub: Supply Control–Progress Report for Secondary Items, and incl., Frank, Doc. 147. (2) Memo, Osborne for CofOrd et al., 5 Jun 45, same sub, Frank, Doc. 148. (3) Memo, Osborne for Somervell, 9 Jun 45, sub: Improved Reporting of Technical Services Supply Control for Secondary Items, ASF Reqmts and Stock Control Div 401.1. (4) Memo, Osborne for CofOrd et al., 3 Jul 45, sub: Instructions for the Preparation of Monthly Progress Report, Section 19, Secondary Items (Reports Control Symbol RLP–9), Frank, Doc. 149. (5) ASF, Monthly Progress Report, Section 19, 30 Jun 45. (6) Frank, Requirements, pp. 172–82.

time period involved. Also, SCS provided for all its users a wealth of detail formerly available only in the work sheets of the various offices responsible for compiling the Army Supply Program. The SCS Long Form for each principal item was a masterpiece of economy and arrangement for the presentation of comprehensive information on a single page. Divided into seven major areas,[63] as well as additional data sections, the Long Form contained individual spaces for nearly five hundred statistical entries. In addition to showing data for the detailed components of supply and demand for each time period, the Long Form contained an abundance of information such as the unit cost of the item, procurement lead time, supply classification, approved substitutes, replacement factors for each theater of operations, and special remarks.

The adoption of the Supply Control System was not without attendant disadvantages. Some of these were administrative in nature but others were substantive difficulties arising out of the basic character of the system itself. The task of preparing the elaborate assemblage of information and summaries once each month—especially in the developmental stages of the system—was a major ordeal for technical service personnel, requiring feverish efforts and long hours of overtime and leaving little opportunity for careful and considered review of the resulting estimates. More serious was the fact that marked, and sometimes violent, fluctuations in procurement schedules resulted from adjusting procurement to monthly changes in requirements estimates.

Early in 1945 the chief of the Procurement Division, Office of the Chief of Engineers, pointed up the consequences for Engineer procurement: "Production items cannot be handled on a 30-day 'stop and go' basis, primarily because of the lead time required and secondarily . . . because labor gets away from us never to return." [64] Fortunately, there were saving circumstances which minimized the consequences during the remainder of World War II. First, the overburdened technical services were slow in changing procurement schedules during the early months of SCS.[65] Secondly, as indicated in the following pages, by this stage of the war the trend of requirements for the great majority of all items was progressively downward, resulting for the most part in one-directional changes in procurement schedules.

The Supply Control System was developed in coincidence with the substantial increase in contract terminations during the final year of the war and greatly facilitated the making of termination decisions. Throughout 1943 it had been official policy under the Army Supply Program to keep to a minimum cutbacks in production and their resulting dislocations: "Because of the cost, difficulty and delay which result from changes in production schedules which have been agreed upon, and which are now serving as the bases for determining raw material allocations, the general policy established for the 1 August 1943 revision of Sec-

---

[63] These were I–Identification of the Item; II–The Past; III–The Present; IV–The Future; V–Stock Status; VI–Disposal; VII–Annual Data Comparisons. See WD AGO Form 0470 (Revision of 10 Apr 45), reproduced as Fig. 2, p. 8 of ASF M–413, The Supply Control System, 10 Apr 45.

[64] Memo, Chf Procurement Div for ACofEngrs for Military Supply, 29 Jan 45, sub: Terminations and Cutbacks, OCofEngrs Procurement Div. Ex Off file, Cancellations, Cutbacks, and Terminations, 1 Jan 45 through 31 Dec 45.

[65] Blanche D. Coll, Jean Keith, and Herbert H. Rosenthal, The Corps of Engineers: Troops and Equipment, a volume in preparation for the series UNITED STATES ARMY IN WORLD WAR II, Ch. XXII, MS, OCMH.

tion I of the Army Supply Program is to make no changes in required production for 1943 except where deemed absolutely necessary." [66] Peak production had been achieved by the end of 1943 only through heroic measures on the part of industry and government alike. With military requirements ultimately needed for the invasion of Europe still in doubt, the partial dismantling of the nation's productive machine so painfully created over a period of three years was considered to be an unnecessary and foolhardy proceeding. Hence, even though stocks of many items were accumulating beyond short-run needs, production cutbacks throughout 1943 were confined mainly to major items of imbalance, such as tanks, for which basic changes in organization and strategy had led to permanently reduced requirements. By mid–1944 the situation had materially altered. The new supply control procedures as well as independent studies indicated a fairly general overaccumulation of inventories and the consequent desirability of readjusting procurement schedules. The authorization of production in advance of scheduled requirements was prohibited except for special circumstances, and increasing numbers of contracts were terminated. [67] (See Table 60, page 696.)

Demobilization Requirements

During the last year of the war the necessity for demobilization planning placed heavy burdens upon requirements personnel while they were still in the throes of the change-over to the Supply Control System. Initial planning for demobilization had begun, however, many months before the adoption of the Supply Control System. On 7 October 1943, the Requirements Division, ASF, issued instructions to the chiefs of the technical services calling for the computation of a Special Army Supply Program for Demobilization Planning. These instructions established the basic concepts and procedures to be used in formulating requirements for the stages of demobilization following victory in Europe and the subsequent victory in the Pacific. The initial stage—the period of a one-front war following V–E Day—was described as Period I. The final stage of demobilization following the defeat of Japan was designated as Period II, although no computations for Period II, as such, were made in the several series of Army demobilization plans. For purposes of the initial "dry-run" or experimental computation, Period I was assumed to last for one year and Period II for six months. Hypothetical dates for V–E and V–J Days were assumed as 31 December 1943 and 1944, respectively. [68]

The resulting special computation of ASP for demobilization planning purposes was published on 1 December 1943. In general the methods of computing requirements for Period I were similar to those already in use in connection with the two-front war. Initial-issue, replacement, and distribution requirements were computed for the forces assumed to exist in the zone of interior and overseas at the end of Period

[66] Memo, Wood, Dir Reqmts Div ASF, for TQMG et al., 15 Jun 43, sub: Computation of Requirements Section I, Army Supply Program, 1 August 1943, Frank, Doc. 83.

[67] Authorization of advance production had also been restricted under ASP, but exceptions were more freely granted. Increased restrictions were adopted as early as January 1944. Memo, Brig Gen Hugh C. Minton, Dir Production Div ASF, for TQMG et al., 29 Jan 44, sub: 1944 Army Supply Program—Policies Affecting Production.

[68] Memo, Col Lee A. Denson, Actg Dir Reqmts Div ASF, for CofCWS et al., 7 Oct 43, sub: Special Army Supply Program for Demobilization Planning, and 5 incls, Frank, Doc. 150.

I. The basic differences from the regular ASP stemmed from problems relating to redeployment and demobilization. In the first special computation, it was assumed that the Army as a whole would shrink by 2,059,000 men (from 7,670,000 to 5,611,000) during Period I. This would reflect decreases from 5,465,000 to 2,246,000 men in the continental United States and possessions, and from 1,532,000 to 529,000 in the European-African area. Deployment to the Pacific-Asiatic area on the other hand would raise the strength in that area from 673,000 to 2,836,000. An even rate of demobilization of the 2,059,000 men was assumed during Period I, as well as an even rate of expansion to maximum strength in the Pacific-Asiatic area during the same period. These changes in troop strength introduced special considerations, since maintenance and severance allowances had to be provided for demobilized units and since large-scale redeployment to the Pacific area created novel requirements for transportation and special operational projects in addition to normal differences in the needs of separate theaters on opposite sides of the globe.

The second special computation of demobilization requirements appeared on 1 October 1944, the date of the final edition of the regular Army Supply Program. Period I for this computation was designated as the twelve months following 1 October 1944. The second special computation, like the first, was limited to Period I and was also merely a dry-run computation designed more to provide increased experience in demobilization planning than to arrive at anything like firm estimates of demobilization requirements. The directive ordering the second recomputation was far more detailed and realistic than its predecessor. In addition to

carrying special instructions tailored to the needs of individual technical services, it included plans for disposing of supplies in theaters, en route to theaters, at ports, en route to ports, and elsewhere. Also, it made more specific provision for establishing peacetime war reserves of equipment to be held in the United States for possible future mobilization needs. Since the new computation was based on a special Demobilization Planning Troop Basis, it reflected later developments in troop redeployment planning for the demobilization period.[69]

By the end of 1944 it was evident that the time was rapidly drawing near when firm demobilization requirements would have to be determined as the actual basis for procurement. Also, by this time the Supply Control System had been developed to the point where it was about to replace ASP completely; all future requirements would then have to be stated within the framework of SCS. On 8 January 1945 the Requirements and Stock Control Division called for a new computation of Period I requirements, this time to be performed under SCS procedures and published as a special edition of the Monthly Progress Report series. The ensuing publication reflected the elaborate accumulation of redeployment and demobilization plans which had been de-

[69] Memo, Denson, Chf Reqmts Div ASF, for CofCWS et al., 15 Apr 44, sub: Special Army Supply Program for Demobilization Planning, Section I, Period I, 15 July 1944, and 10 incls, Frank, Doc. 151. Publication of this estimate of demobilization requirements was, like the scheduled 1 August 1944 edition of ASP, delayed until 1 October 1944 because of difficulties in obtaining a satisfactory troop basis and the problems of merging supply control computations with the Army Supply Program.

veloped with increasing intensity since the summer of 1944.[70]

The 31 January 1945 computation of demobilization requirements assumed the cessation of hostilities in Europe on 30 June 1945 and a Period I duration of eighteen months thereafter. Computations were based on the War Department Troop Deployment and Supply Supplement of 1 December 1944. As before, even rates of demobilization and redeployment were assumed, but in the absence of direct redeployment data it was assumed that all troop redeployment from Europe to the Pacific would take place via continental United States. This meant that for requirements planning purposes all troops destined for the Pacific area would be completely reequipped within the United States. All theaters were classified as active or inactive, and stock levels, replacement rates, and other determinants of requirements were modified and applied in accordance with this revised theater status. Time-phased estimates were made of the percentage of recovery of all important initial equipment in each inactive theater. Recoverable equipment, including repaired equipment, was included as assets in computing net requirements, with an estimated time for transshipment to depots in the United States of forty-five days from date of availability at either staging areas.[71]

The computation of 31 January 1945, as set forth in MPR–20–X, represented a major achievement in bringing together the multiplicity of plans and assumptions for redeployment and demobilization and in producing estimates of Period I requirements which would more closely approximate actual procurement needs after V–E Day. During the ensuing weeks these estimates were intensively studied, and on 11 March 1945 the Director of Plans and Operations presented to the Commanding General, ASF, a formal report on the adequacy of Period I supply plans. The report recommended that MPR–20–X be continually revised on an up-to-the-minute basis so that it could immediately become the authorized procurement program upon the announcement of V–E Day. The report also recommended that procurement be authorized at once on the basis of MPR–20–X where requirements for the one-front war exceeded existing requirements for the two-front war as carried in the regular MPR–20. There were numerous items, either peculiar to the Pacific area or required in greater proportions as a result of the build-

---

[70] ASF, Monthly Progress Report, Section 20–X, 31 Jan 45. The "X" designation of specific monthly progress reports early in 1945 indicated their status as planning documents rather than approved programs. The full story of the development of demobilization planning in the final year of the war would fill many volumes. Among the principal planning documents prepared during this period were: (1) ASF Basic Plan for Period I (Redeployment, Readjustment, and Demobilization), 31 Oct 44, and revisions thereof; (2) Logistic Study for Projected Operations, ASF–P–SL–1, accompanying Memo for Chfs of Technical Services, 11 Dec 44, sub: Procurement Planning for Military Operations (3) Logistics Study for Projected Operations, ASF–P–SL–2, accompanying Memo for Chfs of Technical Services, 18 Dec 44, sub: Procurement Planning for Military Operations; (4) successive issues of War Department Troop Deployment and Supply Supplements thereto.

Additional references to sources may be found in: (1) Directive for the 31 January 1945 special computation, Memo, Maj Gen Walter A. Wood, Jr., Actg Dir of Plans and Opns ASF, for CofEngrs *et al.,* 8 Jan 45, sub: Supply Control Reports for Period I, and 2 incls, Frank, Doc. 152. (2) Frank, Requirements, Planning for Period I, pp. 183–207.

[71] Large movements of both troops and supplies were of course made directly from Europe to the Pacific. To the extent that such movements took place, the computed estimates of both supply and demand were overstated by amounts roughly canceling each other. See Frank, Requirements, p. 192.

up in the Pacific, for which requirements would increase with the change from a two-front to a one-front war. These included construction materials and equipment for building roads, airfields, railways, housing, and dock and storage facilities; material-handling equipment; tentage and tarpaulins; special packaging, crating and preserving materials, as well as new issues of clothing and supplies of health protection equipment, all made necessary by climatic conditions in the Pacific area. Distribution requirements resulting from the longer supply lines, nearly three times the length of those to Europe, were likewise generally increased. Transportation requirements would be heavier under the double strain of demobilization and large-scale redeployment to the Far East.

The recommendations submitted to General Somervell were tentatively approved by him, subject to his personal approval later of all items and dollar values representing absolute increases for the one-front war. The 31 January 1945 MPR–20–X revealed 544 items for which one-front requirements exceeded those for a continued two-front war. These were subject to careful screening and on 31 March 1945 General Somervell approved for increased procurement a limited list of eighty-nine items.[72]

Events in the spring of 1945 rapidly converged to bring to an end the Army's task of determining requirements for World War II. The spreading collapse of German resistance indicated that Allied victory in Europe was imminent. A new MPR–20–X to improve the statement of Period I requirements was ordered late in March and

was published as of 31 March 1945. In this issue no specific date was assumed for V–E Day, and Period I was defined as the nineteen months following V–E Day. The publication reflected revised instructions for establishing stock levels and computing replacement requirements. The equipment reserve for Period I (the successor to the strategic reserve briefly discussed in a later section) was blanketed into the War Department's planned war reserve for peacetime security. Greater attention was given to recoverable excesses of equipment in inactive theaters. Requirements for special operational projects in the Pacific were refined and time phased to provide for handling in theaters prior to operations. Numerous other considerations and refinements brought the 31 March issue of MPR–20–X into close conformity with actual procurement needs as they would materialize with the arrival of V–E Day.[73]

During the month of April 1945, various directives to the several technical services had the practical effect of adopting the 31 March 1945 MPR–20–X as the actual basis for procurement, and objectives based on the continuation of a two-front war were abandoned.[74] These directives reduced total procurement objectives for 1945 and 1946 by nearly eight billion dollars and "constituted a major adjustment of the industrial front to meet the new conditions of Period I." [75] Earlier, during the last week

[73] Memo and incls, Wood, Actg Dir of Plans and Opns ASF, for TQMG et al., 25 Mar 45, sub: Supply Control for Period I, MPR–20–X, 31 March 1945, and MPR–22–G–X, 30 April 1945, Frank, Doc. 155.

[74] The last issue of MPR–20 for the two-front war appeared on 28 February 1945. No issue of MPR–20 had appeared on 31 January, since all efforts were being applied to the first issue of MPR–20–X.

[75] Frank, Requirements, p. 202.

of March and the first two weeks of April, eighty-two uncompleted facility expansion projects, estimated to cost some $230 million and scheduled for full production after 1 September 1945, had been canceled. On 20 April 1945 additional instructions were issued to cancel virtually all facility expansions not required for Period I.[76]

Further important reductions in planned procurement were accomplished with the publication of MPR–20 of 30 April 1945. This was the first published program for the one-front war officially adopted as a basis for procurement, and the X designation was dropped. This issue reflected sharp reductions in the day of supply for ammunition, termination of production of the M4A3 tank, use of combined and generally lower replacement factors for the Pacific area, and the elimination of numerous requirements, including current unfilled demand for the European and Mediterranean theaters, initial equipment for French rearmament not supplied as of 30 April 1945, and reserves of arctic clothing and equipment. Other changes in addition to the foregoing resulted in cutbacks of combined 1945

and 1946 procurement objectives by nearly $5 billion.[77] The last few months of the war witnessed a steady reduction in the Army's computed requirements. (*Table 21*) The

TABLE 21—FINAL ESTIMATES OF ARMY PROCUREMENT REQUIREMENTS FOR WORLD WAR II

[In Billions]

Date of Estimate [a]	1945	1946
28 Feb 1945	$27.7	$22.7
31 Mar 1945	24.0	18.5
30 Apr 1945	21.6	16.2
31 May 1945	21.1	16.2
30 Jun 1945	19.7	14.8

[a] MPR–20 and MPR–20–X for indicated dates.

Source: ASF Monthly Progress Reports.

30 June 1945 estimates were the last to be made for World War II.[78] The arrival of V–J day in mid-August was the signal for the mass contract cancellations which brought the World War II procurement program to an end.

---

[76] *Ibid.,* p. 201.

[77] *Ibid.,* pp. 204–05.

[78] Frank, Requirements, p. 207.

CHAPTER VIII

The Methodology of
Army Requirements Determination

Some General Considerations

The Army's requirement programs in World War II were the end result of many millions of detailed calculations made by many thousands of individuals in the Army's complex organization in Washington, its numerous field establishments throughout the United States, and its far-flung network of organizations in overseas theaters. Each of these programs possessed its own basic assumptions and objectives, as formulated at high policy levels and spelled out in the directives and instructions which launched each individual program or recomputation. Indispensable to the development of all such programs was the underlying foundation of concepts, principles, and procedures which comprised the basic methodology of Army requirements determination.

With the heavy expansion of procurement during the defense period, the shortage of personnel experienced in applying the concepts and procedures of requirements determination was a serious handicap to the Army in computing, assembling, and presenting its requirement programs. Lack of knowledge in this area also handicapped the central mobilization control agencies in interpreting and screening military requirements. After Pearl Harbor the War Production Board had the task of appraising the validity of Army requirements as measured against the stated requirements of other claimants upon the nation's supply of resources. It soon became evident that the ability to make intelligent allocations of national productive capacity presupposed a dependable knowledge of the considerations which entered the determination all down the line for each claimant agency. This required a lengthy process of indoctrination—usually when time was lacking—in basic methodological matters before the rationale behind a given estimate of requirements could be comprehended, much less evaluated.[1]

As in virtually every other area of its activities, the Army at the beginning of the second world war had an extensive body of doctrine to govern the determination of requirements. Underlying all specific procedures was the twofold logistical principle that supply should be *adequate* and so far as possible *automatic:*

. . . combat troops should not have their attention diverted from their task of defeating

---

[1] As noted in the preceding chapter, the Army Air Forces, which gained substantial autonomy by the 9 March 1942 reorganization of the War Department, was responsible for computing its own requirements. AAF requirements for items other than aircraft were published in the Army Supply Program with only perfunctory screening by the ASF.

the enemy by anxiety concerning questions of supply. The impetus in the movement of supplies and replacements should be given by the rear, which so organizes its services that the normal routine requirements are replaced automatically and without the preliminary of requisitions. . . . Assurance of adequate supply necessitates provisions of the broadest character involving calculations . . . as to probable requirements incident to the development of operations and as to the time required for supplies to reach the troops. . . . Boldness in placing orders for equipment that will probably be required is essential.[2]

In application this principle meant that the determination of requirements would have to precede actual combat operations by from one to several years. Before such operations could take place, requirements estimates would have to be translated into appropriations, contracts, production schedules, procurement deliveries, and the distribution of matériel to the far corners of the earth.[3] Requirements determination was thus an act of *prediction,* whose fulfillment depended upon a complex array of unknown future events only partly under the control of those making the prediction. In view of this basic condition of uncertainty and the tremendous issues at stake, it was a fundamental principle of Army supply that all doubts were to be resolved in the direction of oversupply rather than undersupply. The worst kind of failure of a military supply system was conceived to be one which could be summed up in the words "too little and too late."

The most difficult phase of requirements

determination in World War II—from the standpoint of successful prediction—was the period in advance of the actual outbreak of war and up to the time when strategic plans had been crystallized, theaters of operations established, and rates of munitions consumption determined on the basis of current experience. It necessarily followed that, until long after Pearl Harbor, Army requirements rested upon broad considerations of the anticipated size and composition of the Army, generalizations regarding the character of its equipment needs, and a wide array of more or less arbitrary assumptions as to rates of equipment loss, ammunition expenditure, and other operational requirements. With the progress of the war, the concept of automatic supply based upon long-range estimates of future needs was substantially modified. Automatic supply gave way in large measure to supply on the basis of specific requisitions from theater commanders. This permitted procurement and issue of supplies more closely tailored to specific theater needs, as indicated by operational experience and changes in strategic plans.[4]

[4] (1) *Logistical History of NATOUSA–MTOUSA: 11 August 1942 to 30 November 1945,* compiled by Col. Creswell G. Blakeney (Naples, Italy: G. Montanino, 1946), especially pp. 53–54. (2) Leighton and Coakley, *Global Logistics and Strategy, 1940–1943,* especially Ch. XII, "The Army's System of Requirements and Controlled Distribution," and Ch. XIII, "The Support of Overseas Operations." Theater requisitions, except for normal replacement, were screened for essentiality under the current strategic plans. This work was done by the Operations Division of the General Staff, which translated the broad directives of the CCS and JCS into more specific terms for action by ASF. In this manner, theater projects were kept in conformity with the requirements of the strategic concept established by higher authority: Ltr, Col Vincent J. Esposito, professor of Military Art and Engineering, U.S. Military Academy, to Maj Gen Albert C. Smith, Chf of Military History, 15 Feb 55, OCMH.

[2] War Department Procurement Planning, par. 75.
[3] For purposes of mobilization planning, a basic principle of requirements determination was that war reserves must be adequate to equip and maintain troops until the rate of production could be brought up to the rate of consumption. This principle underlay the Munitions Program of 30 June 1940.

Broadly speaking, the Army's matériel requirements for World War II, as in other wars, fell into two classes—equipment and expendable supplies. Equipment items—such as clothing, rifles, tanks, trucks, and planes—were analogous to "capital" items in industry: they had a relatively long life and were normally "used up" only after repeated operations of the type for which they were designed. Expendable supplies, on the other hand, were comparable to "operating supplies" in industry and characteristically could be used only once. Expendables consisted of such items as subsistence, ammunition, various medical supplies, fuels, and lubricants.

This simple classification into equipment and expendables was the basis for the Army's broadest division of principles, terminology, and procedures in determining its requirements. Important logistical considerations demanded, however, a further classification which would recognize important differences in the character of demand for the various items of supply, and hence procurement. From this standpoint there were at least three major types of item: (1) items of regular or standard issue whose quantitive requirements depended primarily upon the size of the Army (subsistence, standard allowances of personal and organizational equipment); (2) expendable items whose demand fluctuated widely with variations in the intensity of combat (ammunition, aviation gasoline for fighters and bombers); (3) special equipment subject to urgent but often sporadic demands arising out of major strategic plans and operations and numerous special projects. Among the activities requiring special equipment were intensive overseas shipping operations, the creation or rehabilitation of port facilities, the clearing of sites for airfields, the building of trans-portation and communication systems in undeveloped areas, and a host of other construction projects at home and abroad. Equipment required for such operations included bulldozers, steamshovels, cranes, troop transports, tugboats, locomotives, rails, telephone poles, electric wire, lumber, concrete, and so on. Obviously, no clean-cut classification could be developed to reflect accurately all the various logistical considerations. The Army's approach to the problem was the use of five standard classes of supplies, some of which in turn were further subdivided. Two of these classes (II and IV) consisted primarily of equipment items; three of them (I, III, and V) represented expendable supplies.[5] This classification of procurement items according to the nature of demand for them was an important tool in the formulation of policies, such as the establishment of differential reserve levels, designed to insure adequacy of supply. Computed requirements were not, however, published in terms of this classification.

A third classification of procurement items was made, as already seen, on the basis of distinctions in their characteristics of supply, rather than of demand. In order to state requirements in terms of the diffi-

---

[5] The five classes of supplies were Class I, those consumed at approximately uniform daily rates under all conditions and issued automatically without requisitions (for example, rations); Class II, those for which allowances were fixed by tables of allowances and tables of basic allowances (clothing, weapons, and vehicles); Class III, fuels and lubricants (those for aviation were separately grouped as Class III (A)); Class IV, supplies for which allowances were not prescribed, or which required special measures of control and were not otherwise classified (aircraft (specially grouped as Class IV (E)), construction and fortification materials, and heavy machinery); Class V, ammunition, pyrotechnics, chemical warfare agents, and the like. WD TM 20–205, Dictionary of United States Army Terms, 18 Jan 44, pp. 271–72.

culty of procuremer.t, items were classified as "critical" or "essential." *Critical* items were those which required a long production period, generally a year or more. These were the items which required extensive conversion of industry, the development of new and difficult production skills, special machinery and equipment, and the solution of complex problems in research and development, material substitution, and other barriers to rapid production. In the critical category were ships, planes, tanks, guns, ammunition, surgical instruments, blood plasma, penicillin, and other items which as a whole or because of the inclusion of complex components were difficult and slow of production. *Essential* items were in many cases no less necessary to the Army than critical items, but they were obtainable on shorter notice, either through regular commercial channels or under special contracts involving relatively little industrial conversion. Essential items included a large number of Quartermaster items—numerous articles of clothing and personal equipment, food, soap, paper products, and miscellaneous housekeeping supplies—as well as larger items which American industry was well equipped to produce in large quantities on relatively short notice. The distinction between critical and essential items was most important during the defense period and the first year of the war. At this time the requirements for critical items were based on a planned force of approximately double the size of that for which essential items were stated.[6] The purpose of

stating requirements for critical items on an augmented basis was to make sure of their procurement and delivery—despite their lengthier production periods—in substantially the time needed to meet actual schedules of troop activation and deployment.

As indicated above, the point of departure in computing total Army requirements was the broad distinction between equipment and expendable items. Equipment requirements, as visualized throughout most of World War II, were composed of three principal elements—initial issue, replacement, and distribution. Requirements for expendables, on the other hand, were computed in terms of only two elements—consumption and distribution. The relative importance of the several elements, as well as the methods of their computation, changed substantially with the progress of the war.

Equipment Requirements

Initial Issue

"Initial issue" consisted of all types and quantities of equipment needed to outfit the expanding Army in its growth from barely 200,000 men at the beginning of 1940 to over 8,000,000 in 1945. It included standard allowances of post, camp, and station equipment in the United States as well as personal and unit equipment for organized components of the Army as these were activated and moved into overseas theaters of operations. In addition to standard allowances, initial issue also included exceptional issues to troops of all organizations,

---

[6] For example, the Munitions Program of 30 June 1940 called for the production of essential items for a force of 1,000,000 men and of critical items for 2,000,000 men. The Supplemental Estimates, FY 1942, provided for essential items for a force of 1,725,000 men, critical items for 3,000,000 men. By February 1943, the Army Supply Program stated requirements for both essential and critical items on the basis of the same troop strength, except that requirements for most critical items for training units in the United States during 1943 were reduced to 50 percent. Frank, *Requirements*, pp. 8–11, 54–55.

special allowances for task forces, and equipment for construction and other operational projects.

Most initial-issue requirements were determined by multiplying unit allowance figures by the number of units to be equipped. Unit allowance figures were obtained from official allowance tables published and kept current by the several using arms and technical services of the Army. The number of units to be equipped was obtained from the troop basis. Because of the apparent simplicity of multiplying known figures and summarizing the resultant totals, the determination of initial-issue requirements was commonly thought to be the easiest of the several stages in requirements determination. Actually, the process was unbelievably complicated, not only because of the multitude of items, sources of information, and other considerations involved, but because these were all subject to constant change. Moreover, the two basic determinants of Army requirements—the troop basis and unit allowances—were themselves mutually determining. A troop basis could not be developed without a preconceived pattern of unit allowances, and the composition of unit allowances in turn depended upon fundamental preconceptions as to the organization and structure of the Army as a whole.[7]

The Troop Basis—The troop basis was the most important variable in the determination of Army requirements. Prepared by the General Staff (G–3 in conjunction with OPD), the troop basis was the Army's official troop mobilization program, indicat-

ing the total number of armies, corps, divisions and miscellaneous supporting units—engineer, ordnance, chemical warfare, signal, cavalry, field artillery, and others—scheduled to be in existence at the end of each calendar year for two years, and sometimes longer, in the future. The heart of the troop basis was the number of Army divisions classified by types—infantry, armored, motorized, airborne, mountain, and the like. The troop basis indicated the number of enlisted men composing each type of unit and referred to the governing tables of organization for further details. A summary of the troop basis as it appeared at the end of 1942 is presented in Table 22.[8]

The troop basis was subject to change from time to time and any major change in it called for a recomputation of matériel requirements. Before Pearl Harbor the troop basis for procurement consisted of the several components of the Protective Mobilization Plan force, and matériel requirements to support the PMP were programed as funds became available. For broad purposes of industrial mobilization, the Munitions Program of 30 June 1940 established basic procurement objectives for forces of one million, two million, and four million men in terms respectively of essential items, critical items, and the creation of industrial capacity. As the Munitions Program got under way and the danger of war increased, the various PMP force requirements were successively raised to levels above those in the Munitions Program. Finally, in the fall

---

[7] Detailed illustrations of the mutually determining influence of organization and equipment for the Army may be found in: (1) Greenfield, Palmer, and Wiley, *Organization of Ground Combat Troops;* (2) Watson, *Prewar Plans,* especially Chapter VI.

[8] For a thorough discussion of the conceptual nature as well as the evolution of the War Department troop basis for World War II, see the following studies of Robert R. Palmer: (1) "Ground Forces in the Army, December 1941–April 1945: A Statistical Study."; and (2) "Mobilization of the Ground Army." Both in Greenfield, Palmer, and Wiley, *Organization of Ground Combat Troops.*

TABLE 22—VICTORY PROGRAM TROOP BASIS: SUMMARY OF 15 DECEMBER 1942 REVISION

Unit	Enlisted Strength per Unit	By 31 December 1943		By 31 December 1944	
		Number of Units	Total Enlisted Strength	Number of Units	Total Enlisted Strength
U.S. Army—Total [a]	—	—	7,500,000	—	9,000,000
AAF, Replacements, and Overhead—Total	(c)	(c)	3,085,304	(c)	3,386,491
Ground Units—Total	(c)	6,806	4,414,696	8,204	5,613,509
Headquarters	—	36	14,696	46	19,052
Field Armies	778	9	7,002	12	9,336
Corps	279	20	5,580	24	6,696
Armored Corps	302	7	2,114	10	3,020
Divisions	—	116	1,627,779	148	2,066,617
Airborne	7,970	10	79,700	14	111,580
Armored	13,796	26	358,696	35	482,860
Cavalry	11,476	2	22,952	2	22,952
Infantry	14,758	61	900,238	70	1,033,060
Motorized	16,085	13	209,105	17	273,445
Mountain	14,272	4	57,088	10	142,720
Supporting Units [b]	—	6,654	2,772,221	8,010	3,527,840
Armored (4)	Various	68	39,054	112	62,379
Cavalry (2)	"	22	36,040	26	42,272
Chemical (8)	"	220	57,338	260	68,002
Coast Artillery (21)	"	1,348	789,617	1,717	1,006,971
Engineers (23)	"	435	302,368	563	403,328
Field Artillery (16)	"	421	201,206	580	277,885
Infantry (4)	"	58	173,430	62	180,966
Medical (29)	"	1,089	287,631	1,453	392,160
Military Police (6)	"	347	119,706	428	136,060
Miscellaneous (9)	"	631	15,675	297	18,046
Ordnance (21)	"	995	205,336	1,167	240,462
Quartermaster (20)	"	469	232,242	591	279,635
Signal (21)	"	256	100,069	320	122,853
Tank Destroyer (4)	"	184	128,213	286	189,325
Transport. Corps (9)	"	111	84,296	148	107,496

[a] Includes AAF, as well as troops in training, replacements, etc., for ground forces.

[b] Figure in parentheses after each class indicates the number of distinctive *types* of unit in each class. Types of unit consisted of various kinds of specialized regiments, brigades, battalions, companies, or other groups.

[c] Not available.

Source: Adapted from Frank, Requirements, Docs. 72 and 75.

of 1941, the preparation of the Victory Program estimates marked the first statement of troop requirements considered to be necessary in order to win a full-scale war. As already indicated, at the time of its preparation the Victory Program was not adopted as an actual program of troop activation or matériel procurement. Shortly after Pearl Harbor, however, a troop basis was adopted which in size and composition was largely in keeping with the earlier Victory Program estimates.[9]

It was during 1942 that the great problems and controversies arose in connection with the establishment of a sound troop basis. Two major, interrelated questions predominated: What shall be the ultimate size of the Army? and What shall be its structural composition? The smashing successes of Hitler's armored divisions in Europe had indicated the need for a heavily armored and mechanized Army. Hence, the troop basis for the U.S. Army as conceived in 1941 and early 1942 was heavily weighted with armored and mechanized divisions, calling for a far greater physical and dollar volume of procurement than would an army of the same size composed chiefly of infantry and other more lightly equipped divisions. The total size of the Army, estimated to reach nearly 10.5 million men in 1944, likewise called for matériel requirements huge in comparison with the program eventually carried out.

A number of influences, including the Feasibility Dispute already discussed, emerged in the course of 1942 and thereafter to compel a reduction in the planned

size of the Army and even greater changes in its structure. A fundamental consideration was the lack of shipping capacity to move troops and supplies overseas; the mobilization of a huge Army, only to let it be frozen in the United States thousands of miles from combat areas, would be a wasteful undertaking.[10] The shortage of rubber, steel, and other materials, together with a re-examination of the strategic and tactical roles of armored, motorized, and other heavily mechanized divisions, led to successive reductions in these units. Increased emphasis on the importance of the air arm, the need for larger numbers of service troops, and growing indications of a manpower shortage dictated still further reductions in the size of the ground forces.

Early in 1942, the troop basis called for a total (by the end of 1944) of 213 divisions—including 88 infantry, 67 armored, and 34 motorized. By the end of 1942 these figures had shrunk to a total of 148 divisions, with 70 infantry, 35 armored, and 17 motorized. (*See Table 22.*) But this was barely half the reduction which was ultimately to take place. The final number of divisions activated by the U.S. Army in World War II was only 89—including 66 infantry and 16 armored; motorized divisions had been reconverted to standard infantry divisions and were discontinued as a separate type. Instead of attaining the early 1942 objective of 10.5 million men,

---

[9] This was the Troop Basis of 27 December 1941, upon which the War Munitions Program of 11 February 1942 was based. The term "Victory Program Troop Basis" continued to be used for the successive revisions of the troop basis until well into 1944. See above, page 137.

[10] Greenfield, Palmer, and Wiley, *Organization of Ground Combat Troops*, pp. 281–89.

The involved estimates and considerations entering into the availability of shipping to meet the Army's needs for movement of troops and matériel are described in the following: (1) Leighton and Coakley, *Global Logistics and Strategy, 1940–1943;* (2) Chester Wardlow, *The Transportation Corps: Responsibilities, Organization, and Operations,* UNITED STATES ARMY IN WORLD WAR II (Washington: 1951), Chapter V.

the actual peak strength reached by the Army in 1945 was 8,291,336.[11]

The troop basis was a fundamental determinant of requirements for replacement and distribution as well as for initial issue and applied to expendable supplies as well as to equipment. Since the troop basis was prepared for long-range planning purposes, it frequently differed both from the short-range troop activation schedules prepared by G–3 and from actual inductions and activations. Furthermore, the broad estimate of overseas shipment and deployment of troops to theaters of operations, as contemplated by the troop basis, was normally at variance with actual troop movements. This was inevitable in view of the many barriers to either the formulation or the perfect execution of complex plans for the mobilization, training, equipment, and transportation of millions of men for service in all parts of the world.

The disparity between different plans, as well as between plans and execution, occasionally reached sizable proportions and was a cause of frequent difficulty in determining and reconciling matériel requirements. In mid-1943, for example, the current revision of the Victory Program Troop Basis provided for 8.2 million men by the end of 1943, while the activation schedule of G–3 indicated activations not in excess of 7.6 million. The 15 August 1943 edition of ASP was computed on the larger basis, as directed by the Chief of Staff, to provide a strategic reserve of equipment to meet

contingencies and exploit favorable developments in combat operations.[12]

The strategic reserve was originally decided upon in November 1942 and was approved by the Chief of Staff and the President. The purpose of the reserve was to provide for the sudden activation of additional troops, either of the United States or of liberated forces in occupied countries, as circumstances and opportunities might require. The 1 February 1943 ASP contemplated a strategic reserve by the end of 1944 of approximately 20 percent of initial equipment needed to support the 7,500,000 U.S. troops then planned for activation. Since the strategic reserve omitted various categories of equipment and supplies, the computation of requirements to meet the reserve introduced many additional complexities into the task of requirements determination. The Richards Committee late in 1943 recommended the reduction of the planned strategic reserve by some 50 percent.

As a result of these recommendations and other developments, the Victory Program Troop Basis was revised and brought into line with troop activation schedules. A related development in the last year and a half of the war was the refinement of the troop basis to show expected troop deployment on a theater-by-theater basis. Only with such a breakdown was it possible to apply revised replacement and distribution factors which were also by this time developed on an individual theater basis.[13]

---

[11] (1) Watson, *Prewar Plans,* p. 344. (2) Figures for early 1942 taken from Frank, Doc. 30, showing troop basis data for the first edition of the Army Supply Program. (3) End-of-war figures for total divisional activations are found in Greenfield, Palmer, and Wiley, *Organization of Ground Combat Troops,* pp. 161, 189.

[12] Frank, Requirements, p. 67.
[13] For additional treatment of the strategic reserve, see: (1) Richards Committee Rpt, Pt. III, The Strategic Reserve, pp. 11–22; (2) WDPRB Rpt, Troop Basis, pp. 7–8; (3) Memo and 17 incls, Brig Gen Walter A. Wood, Jr., Dir Reqmts Div ASF, for TQMG *et al.,* 15 Jun 43, sub: Computa-

Unit Allowances—The second basic factor in the computation of requirements for initial issue consisted of unit allowances. Unit allowances were specified in allowance tables which at the beginning of the war were of two broad types: tables of allowances (T/A's), covering equipment issued at posts, camps, and stations, mostly in the zone of interior; and tables of basic allowances (T/BA's), covering equipment issued to organized units of the Army. In general, equipment issues authorized by T/A's were based on the functions and capacity of individual stations and remained at the installations concerned; such equipment included a multitude of camp and station furnishings, motor vehicles, and training equipment, in addition to personal clothing and other items required to administer the induction, training, and utilization of troops before their assignment to permanent, organized units of the Army. Equipment issued under T/BA's, on the other hand, became the property of organized units and moved with the individual divisions, regiments, and other units from station to station and ultimately into theaters of operations. T/BA's showed the full complement of allowances to *individuals* (clothing, blankets, personal equipment, and similar items per man) as well as allowances to *organizations* (number of vehicles, heavy weapons, signal items, and other units of

equipment per company, battalion, regiment, and so on).[14]

The task of formulating and keeping up to date the Army's numerous allowance tables was a formidable one. New items of equipment were constantly being developed and standardized, and old ones eliminated. Quantities of standard items were increased or reduced as wartime experience accumulated. A multiplicity of factors entered into decisions to change allowances and it was difficult to obtain relevant and accurate information; opinions were often conflicting and evidence fragmentary; the issues involved ran the gamut from the aesthetic qualities of the "Eisenhower jacket" to the role of basic weapons and equipment in modern warfare. The availability of raw materials and substitute items, the general procurement situation, and many other considerations besides purely military ones all played a part in the adoption of items for general issue purposes.[15]

As the war progressed the Army tightened its procedures for determining its allowances and for publishing and disseminating information on changes therein. Allowance tables were systematically reviewed in an attempt to reduce or eliminate items of equipment not strictly essential to the accomplishment of the mission of the organi-

tion of Requirements Section I, Army Supply Program, 1 August 1943, Frank, Doc. 83. This memorandum was the basic directive for the computation of the 1 August 1943 Army Supply Program.

For other references to the difficulties caused by the disparity between the troop basis and activation schedules, see: (1) Risch, *QMC Supply*, I, 213; (2) Bradford, QMC Requirements, pp. 40–41; (3) Lt Gen LeRoy Lutes, The Army Supply Program, 23 Sep 46, ICAF Lecture (L47–17), p. 5.

[14] The basic prewar regulations defining the purpose and scope of allowance tables and the procedures for their publication and revision are found in AR 310–60, Military Publications—Tables of Organization, Tables of Basic Allowances, and Tables of Allowances, 1 December 1936. This was superseded by the edition of 1 May 1941, bearing the same title.

[15] Greenfield, Palmer, and Wiley, *Organization of Ground Combat Troops*, pp. 265–68. For further information on the development, standardization, and allowance of equipment, see the various volumes on the technical services in the series UNITED STATES ARMY IN WORLD WAR II.

zation concerned.[16] Numerous scattered allowance tables, which before the war had been issued by each of the fourteen using and supply arms, were combined into fewer publications. On 1 October 1941, the Quartermaster Corps issued its consolidated T/BA 21, covering all Quartermaster clothing and individual equipment regardless of using arm or service. This led to the separation of personal from organizational equipment in official allowance tables. In October 1942, tables of equipment (T/E's) were introduced to cover all organizational equipment needed by units described in official tables of organization (T/O's). By August 1943 tables of equipment had been combined with tables of organization to become tables of organization and equipment (T/O&E's). Thereafter all allowances of personal clothing and equipment were published in tables of clothing and individual equipment.[17]

The computation of initial-issue requirements would have been far from simple even if a stable troop basis and unchanging allowance tables had prevailed throughout the war. Difficulties in adopting and using standard nomenclature and classification systems for the many tens of thousands of Army procurement items gave perennial trouble; standard allowance tables necessarily permitted discretionary issue of many items by troop commanders in the field; and production limitations dictated that the issue of both essential and critical items to troops in training be restricted to certain percentages of authorized allowances. Not only did the technical services have to make conjectures as to probable authorization of optional issues; they also were required to develop and apply probability factors as a basis for size tariffs and requirements based on variable allowances.[18]

Special Projects—Perhaps the most difficult task in computing initial-issue requirements fell to the Corps of Engineers and the Transportation Corps, both of which had to determine needs for complex and heavy items of equipment required for special operational projects. To the Transportation Corps fell the assignment of determining the considerable fleet of vessels and other transportation equipment which would be needed by the Army to carry out its mission. Army vessels in World War II included large and small transports, landing craft, lighters, ferries, tug boats, and motor launches.[19] Railway items procured by the Transportation Corps included locomotives, rolling stock, thousands of miles of track, and a wide assortment of related equipment. The Corps of Engineers was responsible for anticipating the Army's eventual needs for construction equipment and materials, port rehabilitation equipment, tractors, bulldozers, cranes, bridging equipment, aircraft landing mats, and many other major items of special equipment.

---

[16] (1) ASF Annual Rpt, 1943, pp. 15–16. (2) Greenfield, Palmer, and Wiley, *Organization of Ground Combat Troops*, pp. 217–20.

[17] (1) AR 310–60, editions of 12 Oct 42 and 28 Aug 43. (2) Risch, *QMC Supply,* I, 214. (3) A sample copy of T/O&E 6–67, covering Field Artillery Battery, 8-inch Howitzer, Motorized, Truck-Drawn, is shown in the 28 August 1943 edition of AR 310–60.

[18] Risch, *QMC Supply*, I, 215–16. (2) Bradford, QMC Requirements, pp. 73–74.

[19] For example, the Army's tug boat program in 1943 called for the procurement in 1943 and 1944 of 211 large tugs of 100 feet or more, as well as some 1,200 small tugs and motor-tow launches, to meet the unknown requirements of future operations in the islands of the Pacific, the rivers of Burma, the ports of Europe, and elsewhere throughout the world. (1) WDPRB Rpt, pp. 39–40. (2) Wardlow, *The Transportation Corps: Responsibilities, Organization, and Operations.*

Equipment for special projects could not be specified in regular allowance tables but was of vital importance to the ultimate success of the Army's basic mission. Moreover, it consisted largely of long-term, difficult-to-produce items whose requirements had to be determined at least eighteen months in advance of use. During the early stages of the war when Allied strategy was still in the process of formulation, the ASF was unable to obtain from either the General Staff or theater commanders anything like firm, long-range operational plans upon which to base special project requirements:

It just seemed impossible to get the Staff to understand the importance of *lead time* in production. This was . . . true of strategic and operational plans which affected in large measure the supply of equipment in addition to the basic troop equipment. Firm decisions on these plans were seldom made sufficiently far in advance to meet the required lead time for production. It was necessary for Army Service Forces to do its own strategic and operations planning in an attempt to out-guess the Joint and Combined Chiefs of Staff; otherwise we would not have been in a position to meet supply requirements of the operation finally decided upon.[20]

Many of the difficulties experienced by the ASF in determining special project requirements were removed as Allied strategy solidified and theater staffs accumulated field experience. In planning the Normandy invasion, for example, the European Theater of Operations (ETO) as early as August 1943 submitted requests for equipment and materials for the huge reconstruction project anticipated for the port of Cherbourg. Procurement directives to obtain the needed items were isued within the month—eight months before the actual invasion.[21]

The basic dilemma faced by Army planners in attempting to gauge special project requirements long in advance of actual need was simply the fundamental problem faced in the determination of all Army requirements involving a significant production period. This dilemma was aptly summed up by the War Department Procurement Review Board in 1943 after scrutinizing the validity of Army requirements in general:

Those charged with procurement are in an onerous and difficult position. If they hold up production on items which take a long time to produce, they may jeopardize an important military operation for want of material at the time it is needed. If they produce in advance of demand and the demand does not materialize, they may be charged with waste and unnecessary extravagance.[22]

Replacement

The Army's replacement requirements represented the quantities of equipment needed to offset losses after initial issue.[23] As soon as equipment was issued, it was subject to loss through depreciation, destruction, capture, abandonment, pilferage, and other causes. Actual loss rates varied widely both within and between theaters of operations because of differences in climate, ter-

---

[20] Gen Lutes, ICAF Lecture (L47–17). See also: (1) Leighton and Coakley, *Global Logistics and Strategy, 1940–1943*, Ch. XXVII; (2) Millett, *Organization and Role of the ASF*, Chs. III–VI.

[21] Logistics in World War II, pp. 58–59.
[22] WDPRB Rpt, pp. 39–40.
[23] The term "replacement" was not officially adopted by the War Department until 13 November 1943, with the issuance of WD Circular 297. Prior to this time the term "maintenance" had been used for this purpose, denoting requirements of additional equipment needed to "maintain" all forces in a state of full equipment in the face of operational losses. After the official change in terminology, "maintenance" was restricted to the concept of upkeep and repair. For simplicity the term "replacement" is used throughout the present discussion.

rain, intensity of combat, and other influences. They also varied within the zone of interior, depending upon whether equipment was intensively used in training activities or merely awaited overseas shipment. Because of the many uncertainties involved, even after combat experience was available, accurate prediction of replacement requirements was an ideal which could only partially be realized.

For most of World War II the Army determined its replacement requirements by the use of replacement "factors" which were multiplied by total initial issue to yield total replacement needs. Replacement factors were percentage figures indicating the estimated average *monthly* loss of each type of equipment from all causes.[24] A 5-percent factor indicated an average life expectancy of twenty months for the item involved. To keep a given force fully equipped for a full year, assuming an even loss-rate of 5 percent per month, would thus call for a replacement supply equal to 60 percent of initial-issue requirements.

Replacement factors were determined on the basis of a wide variety of considerations and were changed from time to time to reflect the latest dependable information. Until the middle of 1944, only two factors were specified for each type of equipment— one applicable to the zone of interior, and one (usually higher) for all theaters of operations collectively.

In using replacement factors, it was necessary to determine from the troop basis the anticipated average strength of overseas forces in each year in order properly to apply the theater of operations rates of replacement to total initial issues of equip-

ment which would be in use overseas. This consideration led to the adoption of techniques of computation which promoted considerable confusion and led to estimates of doubtful accuracy throughout a large part of the war. In order to standardize and simplify machine computations and associated procedures, it was desirable to relate the various segments of total requirements for each year to the single end-of-the-year strength figure as shown in the governing troop basis. Thus, in the first edition of the Army Supply Program (6 April 1942) the estimate of the average number of troops to be sustained overseas throughout the year was roughly 25 percent of the total end-of-period strength called for by the troop basis:

Item	1942	1943
Total end-of-year strength.	4,150,000	8,890,000
Average overseas strength.	1,000,000	2,250,000

For computational purposes, instead of directly prescribing a year's combat replacement requirements for the 1 million and 2.25 million men serving overseas for 1942 and 1943, the governing directive called for three months' (25 percent of one year) replacement requirements at theater of operations rates ·for the entire terminal strength, which was approximately four times as large as the anticipated average overseas force in each year. Although the actual number of months used for this purpose gradually shifted upward with the relative increase in overseas deployment, this method of computing overseas requirements, both for replacement and distribution (especially theater levels), was standard practice until 1944 when separate replacement factors and troop deployment figures were made available on a theater-by-theater basis. An analogous procedure was used for determining replacement re-

---

[24] Sinking losses and loss of personal equipment from separation of personnel from the Army were not included in replacement loss estimates.

quirements for troops in the zone of interior, employing the lower replacement factors appropriate to the ZI.[25]

Apart from errors resulting from the assumption that all theater forces were collectively composed of units reflecting the same composition as that of total forces contemplated by the troop basis, this method augmented the possibility of error common to all factor methods for determining requirements: a small change in a factor would result in a large change in total requirements when the factor was used as a multiplier against large magnitudes. Thus the number of months selected as the overseas multiplier became an independent and important factor itself, superimposed upon the underlying replacement factors which were themselves subject to error. Throughout 1942 and 1943 it was the practice to express this number of months in round-unit figures for computing replacement requirements; for computing stock-level requirements the multiplier was rounded to the nearest half month. Inasmuch as actual troop activations in 1942 and 1943 fell far below the end-of-year strength figures expressed in the troop basis (a difference of around 1.5 million men for 1943), it can be seen that the method of determining replacement and distributional requirements had a heavy upward bias. This result was aug-

mented by overestimates of average, as opposed to end-of-year figures, and even more by the lag in downward revision of replacement factors to reflect equipment loss rates that were lower than anticipated throughout the war.[26]

The specific rate of replacement called for by each of the Army's numerous and widely divergent, individual replacement factors was a matter of historical evolution. In the late 1930's the factors consisted largely of those inherited from World War I. Numerous changes in the types and uses of equipment, the quality of materials and construction, the destructiveness of enemy weapons, and other elements all combined to render the old factors obsolete. In December 1937 the General Staff ordered an annual revision of all replacement and distribution factors. At that time the Ordnance Department appointed a special board of officers, headed by Col. Clarence E. Partridge, to study the entire problem of replacement and distribution requirements. The resulting report (known as the Partridge Report) appeared on 13 June 1938 and made a substantial contribution to the theory of requirements determination.[27]

After the Partridge Report staff planners made efforts to obtain recent replacement data from German as well as British and French sources but the results were generally unsatisfactory. During this period the Army drew heavily upon the findings of development and testing personnel, recom-

---

[25] (1) Memo, Somervell, ACofS G–4, for CofAAF et al., 2 Mar 42, sub: Equipment Section of the Army Supply Program, Frank, Doc. 23. (2) Application of Maintenance Factors—Section I, Army Supply Program, Frank, Doc. 31. (3) Memo, Col Walter A. Wood, Jr., Dir Reqmts Div ASF, for CofCWS et al., 15 Jul 42, sub; Recomputation of Section I, Equipment, Ground Requirements for the Army Supply Program, Frank, Doc. 39. (4) Memo, Brig Gen Walter A. Wood, Jr., Dir Reqmts Div ASF, for TQMG et al., 15 Dec 42, sub: Computation of Requirements Section I, Army Supply Program, 15 January 1943, Frank, Doc. 73. (5) Wood memo cited above, note 13(3).

[26] Early in 1942, theater of operations replacement requirements for 1942 were based on an estimated *average* overseas force of 1,000,000 men. At the end of 1942 theater losses during the year (computed for the purpose of estimating stock and equipment in the hands of troops) were based on an average overseas troop strength of 0.4 million men. See page 3, par. 6*b*(2)(*c*) of Wood memo cited above, note 25(4).

[27] Frank, Requirements, pp. 114–15, and Doc. 107.

mendations of the using arms, and the experience of private industry with comparable items. Nevertheless, on the eve of Pearl Harbor many of the factors were admittedly artificial and could only be corrected in the future as information on current battle experience and other operations became available.[28]

With the March 1942 War Department reorganization, the function of supervising the determination of replacement factors formerly exercised by G–4 was transferred to the Allowance Branch of the Requirements Division, ASF. In September 1942 the Allowance Branch proposed the semiannual submission by theater commanders of reports on the adequacy of existing factors for both replacement and distribution in the light of current field experience. This proposal was rejected by the Control Division, ASF, on the ground that such reports would be too general and too infrequent to be of significant help under the rapidly changing conditions prevailing at this stage of the war. Moreover, throughout the early phases of the war, it was established policy to keep theater reporting and paper work to an absolute minimum.

Nevertheless, the pressure for improvement in the quality of replacement factors continued. As early as the summer of 1942 the Quartermaster Corps had questioned the basic methods for determining distribution requirements, and these were intimately related to the determination and use of re-

placement factors. But the greatest impetus to increased attention to replacement factors was the steadily rising proportion of total Army requirements represented by replacement needs as the war progressed. Replacement needs rose from around half of total requirements for 1942 to virtually 100 percent of all requirements for 1945. *(Chart 2)*

The shift from initial issue to replacement as the dominant element in Army requirements had important implications for the task of requirements determination. As already indicated, the basic method of determining replacement needs lent itself to astronomical variations in total requirements. An increase from 4 to 8 percent in the monthly replacement factor for an item with an initial issue of two per man for an eight-million-man Army would increase annual replacement requirements by 7,680,-000 units. In the early part of the war, substantial overestimates in replacement requirements for one million or two million men might easily be absorbed in the subsequent combat operations of a much larger force. Clearly, the need for accuracy in the determination of replacement requirements would attain urgent proportions as the war reached its maturity.[29]

On the other hand, if events proved that replacement factors had been set too low, major combat operations at the crucial stage of the war might be seriously jeopardized. To be sure, the Army provided reserve stocks for such contingencies but the time lag between requirements determination and procurement delivery of critical items as expressed in months was often

---

[28] As an indication of the state of pre-Pearl Harbor replacement factors, Frank cites the arbitrary factor of 10 percent for all Corps of Engineers equipment in theaters of operations and the flat rate of 1 percent for all such items in the zone of interior. Signal Corps replacement factors represented a combination of judgment and experience dating back to the days of the American Expeditionary Forces in World War I. Frank, Requirements, pp. 113–14.

[29] Economists will recognize in the variation of Army replacement requirements a specific illustration of the principle of "acceleration of derived demand." This concept is conventionally used in the analysis of fluctuations in the replacement demand for industrial capital goods.

CHART 2—APPROXIMATE RATIOS OF INITIAL AND REPLACEMENT REQUIREMENTS
TO TOTAL ARMY REQUIREMENTS, 1942–45 [a]

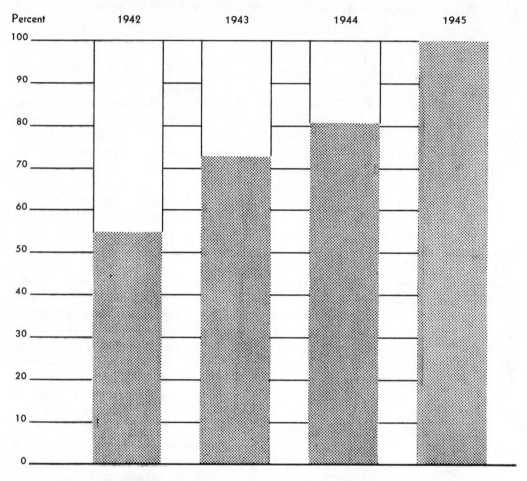

□ INITIAL REQUIREMENTS

▓ REPLACEMENT REQUIREMENTS

[a] Includes distribution attributable to replacement.

Source: ASF Manual, Determination and Use of Maintenance Factors and Distribution, July 1943, p. 32.

double the number of month's supply represented by combined stock levels. In any case, whether from the standpoint of avoiding wasteful procurement or insuring the adequacy of supply, it was necessary for the Army early in 1943 to undertake the most

careful refinement of its estimates of replacement needs for 1944 and 1945.

In view of all these considerations the Army began in 1943 an intensive program which eventually resulted in basic changes in its methodology of requirements determination. In February 1943 a separate Maintenance Factor Section was set up in the Program Branch of the Requirements Division, ASF. This section was charged with the establishment of basic methods and procedures to be followed by all the technical services in the determination and application of replacement and distribution factors. Almost immediately the new Maintenance Factor Section prepared for general use a memorandum stressing the importance of accurate replacement factors, defining numerous associated terms and concepts, and specifying procedures to be followed in gathering information from all sources for the purpose of bringing the factors up to date. Each technical service was directed to submit twice a year, in time for the semiannual revision of the Army Supply Program, a complete list of all current replacement and distribution factors under its cognizance.[30]

On 24 June 1943 theater commanders were directed to submit reports, at least quarterly, on all equipment losses and expenditures of ammunition and other important supplies in their respective theaters for the period in question. Commanders were requested to submit their estimates of the reliability of such data for the forecasting of future requirements. At the same time it was announced that specially trained officers would be sent to each theater to assist commanders in collecting the required data, to remain on temporary duty status until 1 October 1943. Thereafter it was expected that additional personnel regularly assigned to theaters would discharge this responsibility.[31]

In July 1943 a comprehensive manual—prepared by the Maintenance Factor Section—was issued by the War Department, expanding, revising, and consolidating all outstanding regulations and procedures for the determination and application of replacement and distribution factors.[32] By this time field teams representing each of the technical services were being organized and trained for the conduct of replacement factor surveys at posts, camps, stations, and depots in the zone of interior. As data on actual rates of replacement accumulated from both the ZI and theaters of operations throughout the remainder of 1943 and 1944, the Maintenance Factor Section made numerous changes—for the most part downward—in the individual factors for Army equipment. During the last six months of 1943, factor changes were made for 796 supply items. Of th⸱ 713 were downward revisions. Thus, the theater of operations factor for service shoes, which on 15 June 1943 had been lowered from 20.2 percent to 16.7 percent, was further reduced on 15 December 1943 to 14.2 percent. The theater of operations factor for tractors (Corps of Engineers equipment) was reduced on 30 August 1943 from 8 percent to 4 percent.[33]

Major refinements in the determination of replacement requirements took place in 1944. Since late in 1942 there had been

---

[30] TAG Memo S700–9–43, 20 Feb 43, sub: Determination of Distribution and Maintenance Factors.

[31] AG Ltr to CINC SWPA *et al.*, 24 Jun 43, sub: Determination of Maintenance Factors and Rates of Consumption and Expenditure, AG 400 (21 Jun 43 OB–S–SPOPP–M. This attempt to gather theater data was not altogether successful, largely because theater commanders did not give complete co-operation. ASF officers sent on this mission were, in many cases, assigned responsibilities in addition to, or in lieu of, those for which they were intended. Frank, Requirements, p. 121.

[32] WD ASF Reqmts Div, Manual for the Determination and Use of Maintenance Factors and Distribution, July 1943.

[33] Frank, Requirements, p. 122.

pressure from within the Requirements Division, ASF, as well as in certain of the technical services, to treat each theater of operations individually in the determination and use of replacement factors. Under the existing system, which used an over-all combat replacement factor for all theaters, the Army's total replacement requirements were subject to wide margins of error, especially in view of the deployment of increasing numbers of troops to areas differing widely in actual equipment loss rates. In June 1944, for example, data revealed that .30-caliber carbines were used up at the rate of only 0.4 percent per month in the North African Theater of Operations (NATO) but 9.3 percent in the South Pacific. Bayonets were replaced at the rate of 0.85 percent in NATO but 13.5 percent in the South Pacific Area. Trench knife replacements were twenty-five times as great in the South Pacific as in NATO, with a rate of 31.4 percent as compared to 1.26 percent.[34] For large items of equipment smaller differences between theaters would still exert an important influence on total requirements. Furthermore, as replacement factors were used more and more for the actual distribution of matériel to the various theaters, it was important from the supply as well as the procurement point of view to develop a more discriminating yardstick of individual theater needs. But the use of separate theater factors awaited the development of two prerequisites: information on individual theater loss rates, and a troop basis showing anticipated deployment by separate theaters.

In preparing for the determination of separate theater factors it was necessary greatly to increase the flow of information and experience data from the several individual theaters. The War Department Procurement Review Board in 1943 had noted the reluctance of theater commanders to become involved in paper work:

They share the impatience of the Duke of Wellington who said, in effect, "On with the campaign and an end to quill driving." But modern war does not parallel the campaigns of the past. . . . In the United States the whole industrial system has been realigned so that our productive effort may have its maximum effect on the field of battle. . . . Inventory control may have a vital effect on the outcome of the struggle, and overseas commanders should be conscious of the fact that it is not "quill driving," but an essential part of strategic planning.[35]

In accordance with the McNarney Directive of 1 January 1944, the commanding generals of the six major theaters were directed on 10 February 1944 to submit each month a comprehensive Report of Material Consumed for a long list of supply items classified by procuring technical service.[36] Data called for in the report included quantities of authorized allowances in the theater, losses, loss rates, and theater recommendations as to future replacement factors. Brief experience under this directive revealed that equipment actually in the hands of troops varied greatly from authorized allowances. This resulted in erroneous loss rates, since the rates were determined by relating issues to total allowances. On 14 May 1944 the instructions were amended to require all theaters to report actual quantities on hand with troops each month and to compute loss rates on this basis. This was a laborious assignment, especially since the reports eventually required a breakdown be-

[34] Ibid., p. 128.

[35] WDPRB Rpt, pp. 51–52.
[36] AG Ltr to CINC SWPA et al., 10 Feb 44, sub: Determination of Replacement Factors, Rates of Consumption, and Expenditure, 3 incls, AG 400 (5 Feb 44) OB–S–D–M.

tween active and inactive equipment within each theater.[37]

The first step in the use of separate theater factors was taken in July 1944 when all theaters were grouped into two major areas for factor purposes: the European area (including ETO and NATO) and the Pacific area (including the Central, South, and Southwest Pacific Areas and the China-Burma-India theater). Separate factors were established for the two major areas and requirements in the next edition of the Army Supply Program were computed on this basis.[38] By the end of 1944 the War Department was able for the first time to publish and apply separate factors for each of its six major theaters, in addition to the zone of interior. Theater commanders were notified of the change on 9 December 1944 and the new factors were published the following week.[39] In the meantime, the War Department troop basis had been refined to show troop deployment by individual theaters. Thereafter until the end of the war, replacement factors, as well as consumption factors for a number of expendable items, were maintained on an individual theater basis.

An indication of replacement factor magnitudes at specified dates may be found by reviewing figures for selected items of equipment for several technical services. (*Table 23.*) A portrayal of the life histories of the replacement factors covering each of the many thousands of individual items of Army equipment throughout World War II would make a fascinating story. Such a story would reveal the impact of many forces—changes in the strategy, intensity, and character of warfare, improvement or deterioration in the design, quality of materials, and construction of equipment items, the complexities and shortcomings of methods of requirements determination, and many other elements—all influencing the determination of the individual factors at various dates. One or two abbreviated examples will serve to illustrate the point. In mid-1944 the combat replacement factor for the M4 medium tank stood at 9 percent. Battle losses of 559 tanks in one month, after the Allied breakthrough of the Normandy hedgerows in July 1944, led to a change in the factor to 11 percent. In the autumn, increased German resistance resulted in more losses in excess of planned rates and the factor was increased to 14 percent. On 1 January 1945, after still more losses in the Ardennes, the factor was again increased, this time to 20 percent. During the same period the replacement factor for the 60-mm. mortar was doubled, rising from 15 to 30 percent per month; for the Browning automatic rifle the rate moved from 15 to 28 percent. Similarly, the combination of adverse weather conditions and sustained activity in the ETO in the winter of 1944–45 led to the widespread development of trench foot among U.S. troops. The daily change of socks ordered to alleviate this condition resulted in an increase in the replacement factor for the cushion-sole, wool sock from 11.1 to 25 percent, heavily affect-

---

[37] AG Ltr to CINC SWPA *et al.,* 14 May 44, sub: Determination of Replacement Factors, Rates of Consumption, and Expenditure, AG 400 (3 May 44) OB–S–D–M.

[38] AG Ltr to CINC SWPA *et al.,* 11 Jul 44, sub: Determination of Replacement Factors, Rates of Consumption and Expenditure, AG 400 (7 Jul 44) OB–S–D–M. The area factors were published in WD ASF Reqmts Div, Replacement Factors (Control Approval Symbol RME–8), revision of 15 Jun 44.

[39] (1) AG Ltr to CINC SWPA *et al.,* 9 Dec 44, sub: Determination of Replacement Factors, Rates of Consumption and Expenditure, AG 400 (28 Nov 44) OB–S–D–M. (2) WD ASF Reqmts Div, Replacement Factors (Control Approval Symbol RME–8), revision of 15 Dec 44.

TABLE 23—MONTHLY REPLACEMENT FACTORS FOR SELECTED ITEMS OF ARMY EQUIPMENT AT SPECIFIED DATES

Item	1942 [a]		15 Dec 43		15 Jun 44 [b]			15 Dec 44 [c]		
	Z/I	T/O	Z/I	T/O	Z/I	ETO Area	PAC Area	Z/I	ETO	SWP
Ordnance										
Howitzer, 105-mm., M2A1	([e])	3	0	3	0	4	4	0	4	3
Rifle, cal. .30 M1	([e])	5	0	5	0.5	2	2	0.5	5	3
Tank, Medium	([e])	7	0	7	0.5	9	9	0.5	14	10
Signal										
Radio, SCR–193	2	8	2	5	1	5.5	3	1	5	4
Radio, SCR–536	4	10	3	15	2	13	13	2	20	13
Wire, W–110	5	50	4	44	4	75	50	4	100	75
Corps of Engineers										
Grader, Road, Mtzd	1	10	1	4	2	8	8	2	8	8
Roller, Road, Sheepsfoot	([e])	([e])	0.5	3	0.5	3	3	2	8	8
Tractor, Crwl, Type	([e])	([e])	1	4	1	4	4	1	4	4
Chemical Warfare Service										
Flamethrower, Portable	5	10	2.8	16.6	2.8	12.6	16.7	2	8.3	8.3
Mask, Gas, Service	3	12	2.1	8.3	2.1	4.2	4.2	2	5	5
Mortar, Cml., 4.2″	1	3	0	12.5	0	10	12.5	0	7	8.3
Medical Department [d]										
Blanket, White	3.6	3.6	1.5	3	2	1	1	2	1.5	1.5
Kit, First Aid, 24-Unit	2	4	2.5	5	0.2	0.7	0.7	0.2	0.7	0.7
Sulfadiazine, USP, (Class 9)	([e])	([e])	([e])	([e])	20	220	220	30	220	220
Quartermaster Corps										
Breeches, Cotton, Khaki	8.3	25	5.6	11.1	([e])	([e])	([e])	([e])	([e])	([e])
Cot, Folding, Canvas	2.8	8.3	2.8	8.3	2.8	8.3	8.3	2.8	8.3	8.3
Outfit, Cooking, 20-Man	([e])	([e])	1.7	4.2	1.7	4.2	4.2	1.7	5.0	4.2
Shoe, Service	10	25	8.3	14.2	([e])	([e])	([e])	([e])	([e])	([e])

[a] Various dates.

[b] On 15 Jun 44, the overall T/O factor gave way to separate factors for ETO and Pacific Areas.

[c] On 15 Dec 44, factors were separately shown for 6 theaters, only two of which are shown herein.

[d] Expressed in rates per 1,000 men (except Kit, 1942 and 1943, and Blanket, 1943).

[e] Not shown in Source.

Source: ASF, Rqmts Div, "Replacement Factors" (Control Symbol RME–8) eds. of 15 Dec 43, 15 Jun 44, and 15 Dec 44. Earlier data from files of Requirements Division, ASF.

ing required production of this item for 1945.[40]

Many developments in the fields of requirements determination, procurement practice, and modern technology all converged in the course of the war to affect the significance of the Army's equipment

---

[40] This account is based on Frank, Requirements, pp. 129–30.

replacement factors. By 1943, in addition to their use in the computation of replacement requirements as such, replacement factors had also come to be used in determining certain elements of "distribution." The most important of these were various reserve or stock "levels" required to insure the availability of adequate supplies to troops at all times. Since these levels were expressed in terms of months or days of supply, it was necessary to have dependable rates of wastage per month or day to determine the quantities of equipment needed to establish any particular reserve level. As indicated in a later section, replacement factors gradually supplanted distribution factors in this computation. By the end of 1944 the Army's replacement factors served three official purposes:

(1) as fundamental bases in the computation of the over-all requirements for the Army Supply Program;
(2) as a unit of measure for the initial establishment of reserve levels in the zone of interior and theaters of operations;
(3) as a unit of measure in the supply of equipment and supplies to oversea theaters, bases, and commands.[41]

Spare Parts in Relation to Replacement—Of increasing importance as the war continued was the gradual shift from complete units of equipment to spare parts as the basis for estimating replacement demand.[42] It was standard practice from the beginning of the defense period for the Army to procure spare parts in varying proportions along with finished items of equipment. Spare parts for many items constituted a substantial portion of total Army procurement both in physical and dollar terms.[43] Some of the most complex and thorny problems in the administration of Army procurement and supply arose out of the spare parts program. The determination of requirements for spare parts was often more difficult than that for finished

items. The distribution of parts in proper proportions to Army installations throughout the world posed virtually insoluble problems. The establishment of a far-flung empire of maintenance and repair facilities equipped with tools and machinery and staffed with trained mechanics required the investment of billions of dollars and the employment and training of hundreds of thousands of military and civilian personnel. The build-up of the Army's repair facilities took a long period of time, thus forcing greater reliance, during the early stages of the war, upon complete replacement.

The Army's spare parts program, as part of the larger program of repair and maintenance, arose out of military necessity as well as the desire to maintain combatworthy forces at the least cost. Initial issues of complex items of equipment regularly included a complement of spare parts in order to permit emergency repairs under battle conditions, and additional quantities of parts were distributed to various repair echelons. In many instances the availability of spare parts was more important than complete replacement: the emergency repair in mid-ocean of an Army transport laden with troops and cargo was, for example, to be preferred to complete replacement. But in the year and a half after Pearl Harbor, in the general effort to attain high procurement objectives for complete end items, spare parts procurement was often subordinated. Parts originally earmarked for spare purposes were utilized in turning out additional quantities of end items. This practice, most notable in the case of aircraft procurement, became known as the "numbers racket" and was roundly criticized by the Richards Committee. As a result of the committee's recommendations, the McNarney Directive of 1 January 1944

---

[41] WD Cir 375, 15 Sep 44. This was modified by War Department Circular 123 of 24 April 1945.
[42] This development was visible as early as the spring of 1943. ASF Annual Rpt, 1943, p. 15.
[43] For example, the value of required production of automotive spare parts for the Army exceeded $1 billion for the calendar year 1944. ASF Annual Rpt, 1944, p. 105.

ordered both the AAF and the ASF to procure adequate spare parts even at the expense of reduction in the output of end items.[44]

The increased attention to repair and maintenance in the later stages of the war had the effect of reducing substantially the Army's procurement requirements for complete replacement. Reclaimed equipment returned to stock after previous replacement had the effect of increasing total assets to meet gross requirements, thus avoiding additional procurement. Lower-echelon repairs to in-service equipment accomplished a similar end by lowering replacement factors and hence replacement requirements. The general falling off of replacement rates for complete equipment was accompanied by the increased significance of spare parts replacement, making necessary a much more refined instrument of inventory and supply control. Such an instrument was made available in the spring of 1944 in the form of the Supply Control System, with its elaborate records of issue experience and monthly analysis of the supply and demand position of all important procurement items.

The development of the Supply Control System had important effects on the Army's methods of determining replacement requirements. After a study by the chiefs of the technical services in April 1944, planners concluded that accurate forecasts of requirements for numerous items could be made directly upon the basis of recent issue experience. Monthly redeterminations

of replacement rates would be made and substituted for formal replacement factors whose revision tended to lag behind the realities of recent issue experience, with generally inflationary effects upon total requirements. Consequently in June of 1944 the number of items to which War Department (G–4 approved) replacement factors were assigned was reduced from 4,300 to around 600.[45] At the same time concentrated attention to spare parts requirements led to a basic change in procurement policy. The practice for many items of equipment had been to order an estimated year's supply of replacement parts concurrently with the complete item. This resulted in unbalanced inventories. To remedy the situation, detailed information on issues of individual parts was obtained from the Supply Control System and from special teams sent to the European and Mediterranean theaters. Beginning in November 1944, spare parts procurement was based on actual issue experience and excess stocks were returned to manufacturers for completion of end items still under production. Basic allowances of spare parts for major ASF items were prepared, and by the end of 1944 more than 3,500 spare parts catalogs, covering 90 percent of all major items, had been published.[46]

The broad effect of the developments just described was not abandonment of formal replacement factors but confinement of their application to important tactical items of concern to the General Staff. Decisions as to the methods of computing replacement requirements for the much larger number

---

[44] (1) Richards Committee Rpt, p. 8, and Recommendation 10. (2) McNarney Directive, par. 10. It should be observed that *overprocurement* of spare parts for many items was likewise a serious problem throughout the war. Bad labeling and packaging with resultant loss of spare parts in storage resulted in exaggerating theater requisitions for spare parts.

[45] (1) Frank, Requirements, pp. 126–27. (2) WD Bull SB–38–4–WD, Replacement Factors, 11 Aug 45. G–4's authority over replacement factors had been reinstated by the McNarney Directive of 1 January 1944.

[46] ASF Annual Rpt, 1945, p. 181.

of less important items were largely decentralized to the several technical services.[47]

Distribution

Changing Concepts of Distribution—Initial-issue and replacement requirements, already discussed, would have been adequate for all the Army's equipment needs only on the assumption that these requirements had been predicted with perfect accuracy, that procurement to meet the requirements had been completed exactly as needed, and that the finished items had been miraculously and instantaneously transferred in proper proportions from factories in the United States to individual using troops throughout the world. Needless to say, any war waged under such an assumption would be lost almost before it began. The exigencies of warfare, the impossibility of perfect prediction of requirements in complete detail with respect to types, quantities, and time and place of eventual use, and the technical and economic aspects of production, transportation, and distribution all required that the process of procurement and supply be conceived and executed primarily on a bulk basis well in advance of actual need. These considerations made necessary the inclusion in Army requirements of the important element of distribution.

For World War II "distribution" referred to the additional quantities of matériel, over and above initial issue and replacement, required to "fill the pipelines" in the Army's world-wide system of supply. The basic purpose of allowances for distribution was to insure, without fail, the timely delivery of supplies from point of acceptance

from the procurement source to the point of ultimate issue. Often likened to their counterpart in a municipal water supply system, distributional requirements were theoretically large while the pipelines and reservoirs were being filled and extended, negligible when only minor leakages occurred after the system was filled, and negative when supply lines were curtailed or withdrawn. But the crude analogy was merely suggestive, since the military supply system comprehended many tens of thousands of different items instead of a single homogeneous commodity and involved numerous and constantly changing sources of supply, ultimate destinations, and techniques as well as channels of distribution. The Army's distribution system for World War II included not only matériel in transit via every available type of transportation throughout the world, but multitudinous inventories of equipment and supplies in post, camps, stations, warehouses, depots, and ports of embarkation in the United States and corresponding ports of debarkation, base depots, intermediate depots, advance depots, and ultimate supply dumps in forward areas.

In principle, the Army's distribution requirements as defined from time to time consisted of four elements:

1. stocks of matériel at various points of distribution;

2. matériel in transit;

3. distributional losses (ship sinkings and other in-transit losses); and

4. tariff of sizes for appropriate items.

Actually, there was considerable confusion throughout the war surrounding the entire concept of distribution. This confusion was reflected in numerous changes in the methods of computing distribution requirements, in the adoption of constantly changing and often inconsistent terminology, and in the

---

[47] WD Bull SB–38–4–WD, Replacement Factors, 11 Aug 45, Sec. I, 1*g*, Replacement Factors Developed by Technical Services.

unintelligible accounts which have subsequently appeared in connection with the entire subject.[48]

At the beginning of the World War II procurement program, little or no attempt was made to evaluate separately the several elements comprising distribution. In computing total distribution requirements for an item, a blanket distribution "factor" or percentage figure was applied to the sum of initial-issue and replacement needs. This factor varied from one technical service to another and frequently within a particular service for different classes or items of equipment. For the Corps of Engineers the distribution factor prior to Pearl Harbor was 10 percent for all items of equipment. For the Quartermaster Corps it was 25 percent for all nonsized items and 27 to 50 percent for most items subject to size tariffs. Distribution factors ranging all the way from 5 to 90 percent were used in computations of the Army Supply Program until mid-1943.[49]

Two basic assumptions underlay the use of distribution factors. The first was that distributional requirements were directly proportional to the total quantity of supplies needed to equip and maintain forces in the field. Therefore the application of a given percentage factor to the sum of initial issue and replacement was considered to yield the best available measure of distributional needs.[50] Distribution factors were, of course, subject to revision from time to time on the basis of experience; until the 1 August 1943 edition of the Army Supply Program which discontinued the use of distribution factors, directives for the recomputation of the program prescribed the use of "the latest approved distribution factors."

The second basic assumption was that after the distributional "pipelines" and "reservoirs" had once been "filled" no further quantities for distribution would be needed, except for specific types of leakage and loss which could thereafter be directly computed and provided for. Distribution was thus conceived primarily as a nonrecurring demand, under which maximum distribution allowances would remain "frozen" in supply pipelines until supply lines were eventually curtailed.[51] Accordingly, for any given period the distribution factor would be applied only to *increments* of total initial-

---

[48] For example, the terms "distribution" (a major element of total requirements) and "distribution factor" (a percentage figure used in determining "distribution") were often used interchangeably; elements of distribution were frequently defined as "replacement"; and the term "distribution" itself was repeatedly defined both as including and at the same time as not including overseas and other reserve levels. These inconsistencies even appear in the reports of the War Department Procurement Review Board and the Richards Committee, both of which made a special study of the subject. (1) WDPRB Rpt, especially pp. 18–22. (2) Richards Committee Rpt, p. 56.

[49] Frank, Requirements, p. 113. (2) Bradford, QMC Requirements, pp. 31–32. (3) Richards Committee Rpt, p. 56.
A distribution factor of 100 percent was used by the QMC for service shoes and several other items in computing requirements during the spring of 1942. QMC, Work Sheets—Mobilization and Training Program (Status of Equipment for Minimum Training and Mobilization Program During 1942, dated 21 Mar 42).

[50] This was the established doctrine at the beginning of the defense period. See: (1) Bradford, QMC Requirements, pp. 31–32; (2) Maj. Herbert A. Gardner, "Supply Requirements, Quartermaster Corps," *The Quartermaster Review*, XIX (March–April 1940), 59; (3) Maj. George A. Horkan, "The Quartermaster Problem—the Computation of Requirements," *ibid.*, 54–57.

[51] Individual items would, of course, continue to "flow" through the pipelines while total pipeline quantities remained frozen. Unfortunately, instances were reported throughout the war in which individual items, particularly of subsistence, remained in storage so long that substantial spoilage was experienced. See Richards Committee Rpt. pp. 73–74, recommending careful attention to rotation of stock.

issue and replacement requirements over the maximum for the previous period. This was accomplished without difficulty in the case of initial issue, which was by nature an incremental quantity for each period. But in applying the factor to replacement, which consisted largely of recurring needs from year to year, it was necessary in principle to isolate and use only increments to previous replacement maxima. In view of all the practical difficulties involved, no such accurate division of replacement requirements was made. For requirements through 1942, the distribution factor was apparently applied by the several technical services in accordance with their own interpretation of policy. But in the summer of 1942, and again at the beginning of 1943, the ASF Requirements Division directed that the distribution factor be applied only to initial issue and then only for requirements prior to 1944. Although this approach did not fully accord with the theory underlying the use of distribution factors, the limitation in question was prescribed at a time when every effort was being made to curtail requirements and with the assumption that various buffer elements in the total estimates would provide adequate reserves.[52]

By the fall of 1942, the use of the simple factor method for computing distribution requirements had been seriously challenged by the Quartermaster Corps. Requirements personnel in the Office of the Quartermaster General (OQMG) as early as July 1942 had pointed out that blanket distribution factors were both crude and inelastic. Instead of basing distribution requirements upon the specific elements entering into the distribution process, the factor method arbitrarily assumed that distribution bore a fixed or given ratio to total issue requirements (initial issue plus replacement). This assumption ignored completely the fact that even if total issue requirements remained fixed, distributional needs would vary widely with the expansion and contraction of supply lines throughout the world. OQMG personnel in 1942 feared that with supply lines steadily lengthening the existing distribution factors might prove to be grossly inadequate.[53]

The alternative proposed in the Quartermaster Corps was the so-called "carry-over method", which focused attention upon the principal element of distribution, that is, stocks (often referred to as reserves). The carry-over method contemplated the establishment of sufficient stocks, both in theaters of operations and in the zone of interior, to carry operating forces at all times until any probable interruptions in the supply function could be overcome. The quantitative carry-over of supplies to be held at various points of distribution would be prescribed in terms of stock or reserve levels, expressed as the number of months or days of supply deemed adequate by higher authority to meet the contingencies in question. A day of supply was defined as one thirtieth of one month of supply; one month of supply was determined by applying current monthly replacement factors to total initial issue for the forces concerned. With stock levels thus defined in terms of operational needs, separate computations could be made for "in-transit" requirements, sinking losses, and size tariffs. Total distribution requirements

---

[52] (1) Page 3 of Wood memo cited above, note 25 (3). (2) Page 4 of Wood memo cited above, note 25 (4).

[53] (1) Bradford, QMC Requirements, pp. 35–37, and memo cited therein, TQMG for CG SOS, 23 Jul 42, sub: Supplemental Computation of ASP. (2) Risch, QMC Supply, I, 218–21. (3) Frank, Requirements, pp. 115–17.

would then be functionally determined and would automatically possess the desired degree of flexibility.

The foregoing summary of the carry-over method is at once oversimplified and more inclusive than the original Quartermaster proposal. Many of the details and corollaries of the plan emerged only after repeated conferences and discussions. The ASF Requirements Division did not approve the plan at the time of its presentation; the entire process of requirements determination was in a state of flux and all of its elements required re-examination and clarification. Moreover, the Quartermaster proposals were accompanied by specific recommendations for stock levels which would have raised requirements at the very time when the Feasibility Dispute and other pressures were compelling reductions. But the basic merit of the plan was recognized, and its adoption by the Quartermaster Corps for the 1 February 1943 edition of ASP was approved. By the time of the 1 August 1943 recomputation, the plan had been adopted by the War Department for all technical services, and directives governing the computation of distribution requirements were amended accordingly.[54]

Stocks—The revised procedure for determining total distribution requirements called for careful attention to each of the elements of distribution. As the most important element, stocks (reserves) received the greatest attention and gave rise to the most difficult policy decisions and problems of control.[55] Stocks fell into a number of classes, including theater stocks, stocks reserved for theater needs at ports and filler depots in the United States, stocks at major distribution depots in the United States for zone of interior needs, and post, camp, and station stocks. Theater stock levels were prescribed by the General Staff and consisted of two components—a minimum level and an operating level. The minimum level was, so far as possible, to be maintained at all times to meet emergencies; the operating level represented working stocks over and above the minimum. Theater levels were determined in accordance with distance from the procurement source and other conditions. The 1 August 1943 Army Supply Program was designed to provide procurement adequate to establish and maintain minimum levels averaging 75 days of supply for all theaters, and operating levels of 45 days (operating stocks were considered to fluctuate in size from 0 to 90 days of supply, depending upon fluctuations in issues and ar-

---

[54] (1) TAG Memo S700–9–43, 20 Feb 43, sub: Determination of Distribution and Maintenance Factors. (2) WD ASF Reqmts Div, Manual for the Determination and Use of Maintenance Factors and Distribution, July 1943. The carry-over method was apparently first proposed by OQMG at a conference with ASF representatives on 13 July 1942. The proposal was reaffirmed in the 23 July 1942 memorandum of The Quartermaster General cited above, note 53(1). An alternative proposal was submitted by OQMG on 7 September 1942, followed by further conferences in which the basic principles of the carry-over method were approved. These were subsequently refined and integrated into the revised procedures for determining all the Army's distribution and replacement requirements. See Risch, *QMC Supply,* I, 218–21. The term

"carry-over" was never used by the War Department in its official terminology of requirements determination.

[55] The terms "stocks" and "reserves" were used more or less interchangeably throughout World War II, although reserves were sometimes thought of as minimum stock levels. Stock or reserve *levels* (often collectively referred to as "supply levels" or "levels of supply") were the quantitative *objectives* of stock control considered to be strategically essential or desirable. *Actual* stocks on hand at any time or place were usually different from and, as the war progressed, frequently in excess of, the prescribed levels. Richards Committee Rpt, especially Section IV, Theater Reserves, and Section V, Stock Levels in the United States.

rivals of matériel in transit). Total theater levels thus averaged 4 months of supply as measured by current replacement factors. At the same time theater of operations reserves to be maintained at ports and filler depots in the United States ranged from 50 days of supply for Ordnance up to 120 days for the Quartermaster Corps. Stock levels for troop requirements in the ZI consisted of 60 days of supply in distributing depots, plus an average of 60 days of supply at posts, camps, and station.[56]

The change-over from the use of blanket distribution factors to the expression of distribution requirements in terms of days or months of supply tended in practice to break down the distinction between distribution and replacement. Not only stock levels but in-transit and sinking-loss requirements were now expressed in terms of days or months of supply. Since replacement requirements were also expressed in terms of a number of months' supply applied to the entire terminal force in the troop basis for a given calendar year, it became standard procedure in the ASP to add the total number of days of supply required for distribution (likewise applicable to end-of-period strength figures) to the total for replacement and to lump the whole under the general heading of replacement (maintenance) requirements. Not only did this tend to confuse the record; policy makers at the time also apparently suffered considerable confusion over the distinction between replacement and distribution. Thus in the 1 February 1943 computation of ASP requirements, while the change-over to the new methodology was in transition, the technical services were ordered to continue the use of blanket dis-

tribution factors while at the same time making provision, under the heading of "maintenance," for 4½ months' theater stock levels for average overseas forces.[57] Although this double provision for distribution requirements was formally rectified by the abandonment of the use of distribution factors in the 1 August 1943 edition of ASP, the production requirements for 1943 were at this time frozen on the 1 February 1943 basis.[58]

Stock levels, regardless of type or location, were redetermined from time to time in accordance with the procurement as well as the strategic situation. The entire question of the state of Army stock levels was raised by the War Department Procurement Review Board in 1943 and shortly thereafter was carefully investigated by the Special Committee for the Re-study of Reserves (Richards Committee). The numerous findings and recommendations of the Richards Committee for the most part remain outside the scope of the present study. In general, prescribed levels as well as actual stocks both overseas and in the zone of interior were found to be too high. Substantial reductions and changes in procedures were ordered by the McNarney Directive of 1 January 1944.[59]

----

[56] Basis for the Determination of Maintenance and Distribution—1 August 1943 Revision, Section I, Army Supply Program, Frank, Doc. 84.

[57] (1) Page 4, pars. 7c and 7d of Wood memo cited above, note 25 (4). (2) Basis for the Determination of Maintenance, Army Supply Program Directive for Recomputation of January 15, 1943, Frank, Doc. 75.

[58] (1) Wood memo cited above, note 13 (3). (2) Frank, Doc. 84, cited above, note 56. (3) Richards Committee Rpt, pp. 56–57. The freezing of requirements for 1943 was done to avoid disruption of established production schedules. See above, pp. 166–7.

[59] The reductions were effected by the 1 February 1944 ASP. For stock levels before and after the reduction, see: (1) Comparison of Elements of Distribution for Classes II and IV Supplies, 1 August 1943 and 1 February 1944 Revisions of Section I, Army Supply Program, Frank, Doc. 95; (2) ASF Annual Rpt, 1944, pp. 102–03.

The actual procedures for computing procurement requirements needed to establish and maintain the prescribed stock levels were of labyrinthine complexity. For each edition of the Army Supply Program the governing directive laid down the broad stock-level objectives and the general estimating procedures to be followed. The great burden of obtaining the necessary detailed information and translating this information into requirements data in a form suitable for manipulation by automatic tabulating machinery fell to the technical services, working under the close supervision of the Requirements Division, ASF. A detailed understanding of the complexity of the problems surrounding this one element of distribution would provide for anyone a healthy insight into the magnitude of the task of determining Army requirements as a whole.[60]

In-Transit Allowances—Requirements to meet the elements of "in-transit distribution" were not separately calculated so long as the factor method of computing distribution requirements was used; the blanket factor was deemed adequate to cover all elements of distribution. With the adoption of the carry-over principle and the abolition of blanket distribution factors, it became necessary to compute separately the increments in each calendar year to the total quantity of matériel "frozen" in transit. This was accomplished by applying a complex formula which underwent change from time to time until no further additions to in-transit pipeline quantities were authorized. The procedure as revised in July 1943 called for the use of two weighted "in-transit times"—one for the zone of interior and one for theaters of operations collectively— as officially determined by the director of the Requirements Division, ASF, in consultation with the chief of the Transportation Corps and other technical service chiefs. In-transit time was the average period required in months or days for all types of equipment to be physically moved from points of acceptance at the procurement source to the zone of interior point of issue or the theater of operations port of debarkation. These two weighted periods were then applied to increments of initial and replacement issues destined respectively for the zone of interior and the theater of operations in the calendar year in question. In the 1 August 1943 ASP, which allowed an average of 45 days in-transit time to all theaters, theater of operations in-transit requirements for the year 1944 were defined as 45 days of supply to maintain the additional 3,186,000 troops to be sent overseas in that year; for the year 1945, the figure was 45 days of supply for 1,750,000 additional troops. At the same time, the approved zone of interior in-transit allowance was 15 days of supply at the lower ZI replacement rates and was applied to ZI troop requirements for the years in question.[61] By the end of 1943, transportation pipelines had generally been filled, and in accordance with the recommendations of the Richards Committee in-transit requirements were thereafter eliminated. This

---

[60] For additional treatment of the problems of Army stocks and stock levels in relation to requirements for World War II, see: (1) WD Levels of Supply and Supply Procedure; (2) Risch, *QMC Supply*, I, especially Chs. VI and X; (3) Bradford, QMC Requirements, *passim*; (4) ASF M–301, Army Service Forces Organization, 15 Aug 44; (5) documentary collection in support of Frank, Requirements.

[61] Basis for the Determination of Maintenance and Distribution—1 August 1943 Revision, Section I, Army Supply Program, pars. 1*d* and 1*g*; Tab C to Incl 1; and various tabs to Incls 2 and 3, Frank, Doc. 84.

change took effect with the 1 February 1944 edition of the Army Supply Program.[62]

Sinking Losses—The early editions of ASP made no specific provision for requirements to compensate for sinking losses, although actual losses were deducted from estimated quantities "on hand" in each revision of ASP. In the two 1943 editions of ASP a separate allowance equal to 2 percent of all theater of operations replacement requirements was included to cover sinking losses. This allowance conformed closely to rates of loss actually experienced. From 1 January 1942 to 1 October 1943, U.S. Army cargoes lost at sea totaled 1.74 percent of all cargoes shipped. After the peak loss of 6.72 percent for March 1943, sinking losses declined rapidly and amounted to only 0.39 percent for the six-month period, April through September 1943.[63] At the end of 1943, the Richards Committee, noting that the submarine menace had been fairly well overcome and that loss rates had fallen to less than a half of 1 percent, recommended the elimination of the sinking loss factor as a procurement requirement. This was approved in the McNarney Directive.[64]

Size Tariffs—The problems associated with "tariffs of sizes" were of particular importance in computing Quartermaster requirements, although other services were

faced with size problems.[65] During World War I the failure to predict the composition of total Army personnel by size groupings led to grave shortages in particular sizes of shoes and clothing. The nature of the problem is illustrated in the following statement of Senator James Wolcott Wadsworth, Jr., during the World War I Senate investigation of the War Department:

For instance, at Camp Custer it became necessary, in order that a detail of one regiment of infantry could go to target practice, to march half of the detail to the target range, as I understand it, with the available shoes that could be gotten together; that they then had to march back, change those shoes, and put them on the other half of the detail in order to send that half of the detail to the range, such was the scarcity of shoes that the men could wear, while at the same time thousands of pairs of shoes were there which no one could wear.[66]

In order to determine total requirements of shoes, it was not enough for the Quartermaster Corps to know in advance the total number of troops to be activated, the exact initial allowance of shoes per man, and normal replacement and distribution requirements. Provision also had to be made for wide differences in individual size requirements, and these could not be perfectly predicted.

The first approximation to a solution of this problem was the development of size tariffs, somewhat comparable to mortality tables for life insurance purposes. A size tar-

---

[62] Frank, Doc. 95, cited above, note 59 (1). For further definition of terms and procedures associated with computation of in-transit requirements, see WD ASF Reqmts Div, Manual for the Determination and Use of Maintenance Factors and Distribution, July 1943, pp. 16, 27–28.

[63] Richards Committee Rpt, p. 61.

[64] McNarney Directive, par. 54. For method of computing requirements to meet shipping losses in the 1 February 1943 ASP, see Basis for the Determination of Maintenance, Army Supply Program Directive for Recomputation of January 15, 1943, Tab D, Frank, Doc. 75.

[65] For example, Ordnance, as well as the Air Forces, had the task of supplying interchangeable fuzes and projectiles of different types which could be used in varying proportions in the expenditure of a given basic caliber of ammunition or type of bomb. The determination of spare parts requirements was also comparable in many respects to the task of computing size requirements.

[66] Senate Investigation of the War Department, 1918, p. 607, cited in Bradford, QMC Requirements, p. 19.

iff for a particular item indicated the probable number of units, based on past issue experience, required in each size to meet the issue requirements of a large number of troops (1,000-man, 10,000-man, and 100,-000-man bases were the most common). The process of constructing a dependable tariff of sizes ran into endless complications. The peacetime issue experience of the Army did not provide a satisfactory norm, and it was largely for this reason that the size tariffs of World War I had proved faulty. At the beginning of the procurement program for World War II, elaborate efforts were made to avoid a repetition of the earlier fiasco. Data were obtained from chain stores, mail order houses, and large retail establishments; the results were co-ordinated and distributed to field installations as guides in making requisitions and establishing inventories until the Army could accumulate adequate issue experience of its own. In November 1941 posts, camps, and stations were ordered to report weekly to the OQMG in Washington the sizes and measurements of each enlisted man. These reports were continued until September 1943 and provided much valuable information for the construction of size tariffs.[67]

Regional and other special conditions indicated that reliance could not be placed upon a single tariff of sizes for a particular item. For example, it was found that inductees from North Atlantic states were shorter and stockier than those at southern reception centers, and separate bases for stockage to meet initial issues had to be prepared. This did not apply to replacement centers since these were filled by men from all parts of the country. Also, the size

tariffs developed prior to 1942 were not appropriate to the new conditions which permitted the induction of youths of eighteen and nineteen years of age. Quartermaster studies in advance of the enabling legislation resulted in preparations to meet the needs of younger men of less weight and smaller stature.[68]

But the preparation of size tariffs was not by itself the solution of the problem of advance determination of size requirements. The crux of the matter was that no tariff—however representative it might be of the Army as a whole—could be relied upon to predict actual issues to small detachments and groups at widely different intervals in space and time. The smaller the group, the greater the probability of variations in size-distribution from that of the troop population as a whole. If a post quartermaster wished to be 100-percent certain of correctly fitting each of one thousand unknown recruits with a pair of shoes on a given day, he would have to have on hand one thousand pairs of shoes in every size.[69] Clearly, an attempt to provide complete certainty in meeting all size requirements at any particular time would result in the procurement and stocking of absurdly large quantities of matériel in the 5,500 to 6,000 different sizes found in Quartermaster shoes and clothing.

In resolving its size problems for both procurement and stock control purposes, the Quartermaster Corps engaged expert statisticians to apply the principles of probability theory to the mass of empirical data rapidly accumulating in the form of records of the issue experience of hundreds of Army in-

---

[67] Reports were forwarded on Individual Form 32. See Bradford, QMC Requirements, p. 83.

[68] *Ibid.*
[69] See Memo, Dir Military Planning Div OQMG for Deputy QMG for Supply Planning and Opns, 4 May 44, sub: Size Tariff Factors, cited in Bradford, QMC Requirements, p. 84.

stallations. A series of size-tariff factors was developed to show for each size of an item the percentage of excess stock needed—over and above the basic size-tariff allowance—to achieve a given degree of certainty in the adequacy of supply. Separate tables were prepared for various categories and types of clothing, such as regular, protective, arctic, jungle, mountain and winter warfare, parachute, and clothing for members of the Women's Army Corps. Size-tariff factors varied not only from size to size and item to item, but for larger and smaller groups of men. The probable number of men to be fitted at particular points of issue varied with the size of particular installations, as well as with the length of requirements periods. Thus when the annual requirements estimates under the Army Supply Program gave way to monthly estimates under the Supply Control System additional adjustments were necessary because of the relatively greater fluctuations from normalcy to be expected within the shorter periods. These adjustments were accomplished by the establishment of special "size levels." In mid-1944, when authorized stock levels for regional depots in the zone of interior were set generally at 70 days' supply in terms of anticipated issues, QMC size levels were 85 days for items requiring a size factor of less than 15 percent and 90 days for items with larger factors.[70]

Like all other facets of the task of determining Army requirements, size problems were far more complex than can adequately be portrayed in a brief treatment. Enough has been said to indicate that, thanks partly to the application of scientific analysis, American soldiers in World War II were

fitted much more adequately than their fathers in World War I.[71]

Requirements for Expendable Supplies

General

In principle, Army requirements for expendable supplies in World War II differed from equipment requirements in that they contained no counterpart of initial issue. Since expendables were procured for purposes of consumption rather than as permanent equipment, it was necessary to provide only for anticipated expenditures and for such stocks and other distributional requirements as were essential to insure the availability of supplies when and wherever needed.[72]

In practice the line of demarcation between equipment and many classes of expendables was not a clear one. Office supplies, for example, ranged from such clearcut expendable types as stationery, lead pencils, and paper clips through intermediate items (books, desk lamps, and drafting instruments) on up to large and highly durable items such as typewriters, furniture, and costly business machines. Supplies at posts, camps, stations, repair depots, and other installations ran the gamut from pure expendables such as soap, paper, chemicals, raw materials, numerous items of commercial

---

[70] Bradford, QMC Requirements, p. 45.

[71] For additional material, see: (1) Dr. Sidney Hoos, Some Size-Tariff Problems and Their Applications (30 June 1942); (2) Dr. Hoos, The Necessity for a Size Supply Level (20 September 1944); (3) Memo cited above, note 69. All cited in Bradford, QMC Requirements, pp. 82–85.

[72] There were, of course, initial requirements of expendables in the sense of mobilization requirements to meet a sudden outbreak of war and for subsequent Army expansion. But these were stocks awaiting issue and, as such, an element of distribution. WDPRB Rpt, p. 22.

TABLE 24—ARMY REQUIREMENTS FOR MAJOR EXPENDABLE ITEMS, 1 AUGUST 1943

[Dollars in Billions]

Year	Total ASP Section I	Major Expendable Items		Ordnance Ammunition	Subsistence	Petroleum Products
		Total				
		Value	Percent			
Total_____	$61.7	$20.0	32	$11.3	$7.3	$1.4
1943_____	20.4	4.8	24	2.5	2.0	0.3
1944_____	21.7	7.2	33	4.1	2.6	0.5
1945_____	19.6	8.0	41	4.7	2.7	0.6

Source: 1 August 1943 edition of Army Supply Program, Section I.

hardware, and spare and replacement parts to small hand tools, power machines, and heavy items of equipment. In the nature of the case there was substantial diversity both in the classification of items and in methods of determining their requirements.

The three most important expendable items required by the Army were ammunition, subsistence, and petroleum products. Each of these actually comprehended a whole class of items; collectively, they accounted for about a third of all ASF procurement for World War II.[73] In the three years 1943 through 1945 there was a strong upward trend in the ratio of expendables to total requirements. (Table 24) This was to be expected as subsistence requirements mounted to meet the needs of over eight

million men and as intensive combat operations followed the furnishing of the Army with its basic capital equipment.

Under the Army Supply Program, expendable items (except ammunition) for the ground forces, Navy, and lend-lease were carried in Section I–B Miscellaneous and Expendable Supplies. But this section also included many nonexpendable items not considered as important tactical equipment, and the same was true of the corresponding Section H–B, for Air Forces items. With the advent of the Supply Control System in 1944, all items were classed either as principal or secondary items without regard to their expendable or nonexpendable nature. For these and other reasons there are no available figures showing the ratio of requirements for expendables to total Army requirements for World War II. A rough estimate would place this figure in the range from one third to one half.[74]

[73] ASF procurement deliveries of ammunition, subsistence, and petroleum products in the calendar years 1942–45 amounted to approximately $26 billion or 38 percent of all deliveries of $69.2 billion for the period. This included subsistence and ammunition procured by ASF for Army Air Forces. The $26 billion consisted of Ordnance ammunition, $12.1 billion; CWS ammunition, $1.1 billion; subsistence, $11.4 billion; petroleum products (estimated), $1.4 billion. Whiting et al., Statistics, Procurement, pp. 15–18.

[74] See the various editions of ASP as well as note 73, above. This question, although of technical interest, is somewhat academic not only because of the indicated problems of classification but because of the generally expendable nature of all items in a global war.

As in the case of equipment items, Army requirements for expendables were based, so far as possible, on allowance tables and the troop basis. Instead of using replacement factors, which were appropriate to equipment, the Army used "consumption factors" or "the day of supply" to indicate estimated rates of expenditure. But there were many expendable items for which requirements could not be directly related to the troop basis, and for important items in this category special estimating techniques as well as special organizations within the Army were provided in order to obtain the greatest possible accuracy. The adoption of the Supply Control System marked an important advance in the methods of determining requirements for expendables since these lent themselves particularly to SCS procedures.[75]

Ammunition

Ammunition was of such fundamental importance to the functioning of the Army that every effort was made to insure the adequacy of supply, in terms of both sufficiency of procurement and timeliness of distribution. Apart from the question of its military significance, ammunition was of tremendous dollar importance in the total program of procurement. Its production,

storage, and distribution, moreover, called for a greater volume of plant and facilities expansion than any other single item. The policies and procedures relating to the determination of ammunition requirements were therefore under continual scrutiny, and the requirements were published in the equipment section of the Army Supply Program rather than with other expendable items. Since the major part of the war was fought with ammunition procured under the Army Supply Program, the present brief summary of the methods used in determining ammunition requirements is confined to the broad procedures used under ASP.

The basic unit of calculation in the determination of ammunition requirements was "the day of supply" for each caliber and type of ammunition. The day of supply represented the average number of rounds per weapon per day expected to be consumed on a theater-wide basis.[76] Like replacement factors for equipment, the day of supply for ammunition was established during the interwar period on the basis of World War I experience and was modified from time to time with new developments in weapons and fire power. Also, as in the case of replacement factors, until 1944 there was only one War Department day of supply (for each type of weapon) for all theaters collectively. No separate rates were shown

---

[75] Space limitations in the present discussion prevent further treatment of expendables except in the selected case of ammunition. For information and sources on the determination of subsistence requirements, see: (1) Risch, *QMC Supply*, I, 231–38; (2) WDPRB Rpt, pp. 33–35; (3) Richards Committee Rpt, pp. 68–74; (4) Computation of Subsistence Requirements for Section I of the Army Supply Program (2–1–43), Frank, Doc. 77; (5) The Methods of Computing Subsistence for the Army Supply Program, 1 August 1943, Frank, Doc. 89.

For petroleum requirements, see: (1) Risch, *QMC Supply*, I, 238–42; (2) Erna Risch, Fuels for Global Conflict (QMC Historical Study 9, 1952).

[76] The day of supply is not to be confused with the "unit of fire" (sometimes referred to erroneously as the "day of fire"). The day of supply in World War II was essentially a procurement concept, designed for the estimate of procurement requirements for the Army as a whole. The unit of fire was a tactical concept, designed to indicate the quantity of ammunition needed for combat purposes by forces at the divisional level. The unit of fire was typically greater than the day of supply. See: (1) WD FM 101–10, Staff Officers' Field Manual—Organization, Technical and Logistical Data, 21 Dec 44, par. 317; (2) Leighton and Coakley, *Global Logistics and Strategy*, 1940–1943, App. F.

for the zone of interior since, except for training purposes, ammunition was to be consumed only under combat conditions.

Total requirements for ammunition consisted of estimated expenditures plus distribution requirements. Estimated expenditures represented the sum of combat requirements plus training allowances in the zone of interior, which were separately calculated on the basis of the number of troops estimated to be in training in the United States during a given calendar year. A year's combat requirements for a given caliber were determined, in principle, by multiplying the day of supply by 365 and then by the total initial issue of weapons of that caliber in the entire theater of operations.[77] The sum of requirements for all calibers thus determined, plus special project allowances, represented total combat requirements for the Army as a whole.

Special methods were adopted by the Army Air Forces in estimating combat expenditures of bombs and aircraft ammunition to be provided by the Ordnance Department and the Chemical Warfare Service. During the life of the Army Supply Program combat requirements under these methods were based on the total number of combat planes scheduled for production, attrition rates for planes, the size and composition of bomb and ammunition loads, missions per month, and expenditure rates per mission.[78]

The methods for estimating distribution requirements for ammunition were basically the same as those for equipment and went through comparable stages of development. Reserve levels for ammunition were specifically established by the various directives for the recomputation of ASP; these differed in details from equipment levels. Requirements to bring stocks up to prescribed levels, in-transit requirements, and sinking losses were all converted into days of supply for the entire terminal force and were added to the figures for combat and training expenditures to determine total ammunition requirements.[79]

In its report late in the summer of 1943, the War Department Procurement Review Board pointed to the fact that the validity of Army requirements for ammunition turned largely upon the character of the day of supply and the manner of its application. Like other multipliers in the determination of requirements, day-of-supply

---

[77] The procedure actually used was similar to that for determining replacement requirements discussed above, pages 183–84. Instead of estimating directly the number of weapons in the theater for each year, the Requirements Division based its computations upon cumulative initial issues for the entire Army at the terminal strength for each year, as shown in the current troop basis. A year's combat requirements for a given caliber of ammunition thus became the product of three factors:

a. the day of supply

b. the number of initial-issue weapons for the total terminal force

c. the number of days of supply determined by

the formula: $\dfrac{\text{Average oversea force}}{\text{Total terminal force}} \times 365$

See Frank, Requirements p. 102, and Doc. 88.

[78] For example: (1) Ltr, Maj Gen Davenport Johnson, Dir of Military Reqmts, HQ AAF, to CG SOS, 8 Jan 43, sub: Basis for Computation of Procurement Requirements of Army Air Force for Army Air Force-Ordnance and Army Air Force-Chemical Warfare Service Equipment, Frank, Doc. 76; (2) revision of (1) above, dated 13 May 43, Frank, Doc. 90. For an appraisal of the results of these methods, see WDPRB Rpt, pp. 36–38.

[79] See: (1) Frank, Requirements, pp. 102–07; (2) Ammunition, a seven-page summary of procedures for determining 1943 ammunition requirements, Frank, Doc. 88; (3) Memo, Col Henry R. Westphalinger, Actg Dir Reqmts Div ASF, for CofOrd, 20 Dec 43, sub: Special Instructions for the Computation of Required Production for Ammunition for Section I, Part A of the Army Supply Program, 1 February 1944, and 3 incls, Frank, Doc. 101.

figures were initially established on the basis of arbitrary assumptions, and small errors would be multiplied to astronomical dimensions in total estimates: "They [factors] are based at best, in a war where new and untried automatic weapons are constantly appearing, on knowledgeful estimates and educated guesses. The present estimate of a day of supply for .30 calibre rifle ammunition is 5 rounds. If this factor were changed to 4.5 rounds or 5.5 rounds, it would make a difference of hundreds of millions of rounds in the Army Supply Program." [80]

As indicated earlier, the Procurement Review Board showed considerable concern over the mounting stocks of small arms and aircraft ammunition and recommended "a sober re-examination of the factors." [81] As a consequence, the Richards Committee shortly thereafter was specifically charged with the study of the role of the day of supply in estimating Army requirements. The Richards Committee made no objection to the basic method of computation but recommended greater efforts in obtaining current rates of consumption:

The Committee realizes that these factors with values as then known, were essential for this first computation. . . . All testimony indicates that the original values of some of these factors were much in error, as might normally be expected, and have had to be revised, generally downward. . . . The Committee believes that more positive action is indicated to secure factual data for correcting these factors to current conditions in order to better control production.[82]

Despite the Procurement Review Board's previous admonitions, the Richards Committee could find no basic fault with the status of ammunition stock levels in mid-1943:

Further consideration was given to 2,200,000,000 rounds on hand as of 1 July 1943, and the fact that current schedules provide for the production of 13,000,000,000 rounds in 1943 and 16,000,000,000 rounds in 1944.

Ammunition must be produced and enter the pipe line well in advance of its contemplated use. To avoid violent fluctuations in production, requirements must be based on an average consumption for the entire period of a war.

To date our campaigns have been on a minor scale. We have not yet encountered any large portion of either the German or Japanese Armies. Very few of our divisions have attained the average expenditure considered normal in battle. Stockages of ammunition have accumulated when battles were won with the expenditure of much less ammunition than anticipated. This condition is fortunate, and does not, of itself, imply incorrect factors, original over-supply or ultimate waste if collected, redistributed and expended.[83]

The committee went on to estimate the possible expenditures of thirty-eight divisions in active combat by the end of 1944 (half of the seventy-six divisions planned for overseas deployment). Using "unit of fire" figures and assuming seven days per month of heavy combat, the committee reasoned that a monthly rate of expenditure of 1.4 billion rounds was well within the realm of possibility. Existing stocks of 2.2 billion rounds would then amount to less than two months' supply. In its conclusions, the committee recommended that the day of supply be retained as a factor in determining ammunition requirements but that separate factors be established and kept up to date for individual theaters of operations.[84]

[80] WDPRB Rpt, p. 46.
[81] Ibid., p. 47. Also see above, page 159.
[82] Richards Committee Rpt, pp. 45–46.
[83] Ibid., pp. 49–50.
[84] Ibid., Recommendations 45, 46, 50.

On 10 June 1944 the War Department abandoned the single day of supply for all theaters and published separate days of supply for each of four major areas: the ETO, NATO, Asiatic and Pacific Theaters, and all other departments and bases including the zone of interior.[85] Although a troop basis showing deployment by theaters did not become available until 1 July 1944, the ASF, making use of recommendations of theater commanders, on 25 June 1944 published for the first time a computation of ammunition requirements based on individual theater needs. Thereafter, until the end of the war, increasingly detailed reports and recommendations from individual theaters were obtained and used for still further refinement of requirements estimates.[86]

Many influences went into the establishment and revision of day-of-supply figures. As in the case of replacement factors each day of supply had its own complex history and reflected the ebb and flow of combat activity, changes in the strategic and tactical situation, shifts in preferences for and uses of different weapons, developments in the technology of weapons and ammunition, and variations in the quality of estimating procedures. One or two illustrations will suffice to point up these influences. During the interwar period the day of supply for the old models of the .30-caliber rifle was two rounds. The newly developed Garand (M1, semiautomatic) was estimated to possess two-and-one-half times the rate of fire of the older models, and as early as 1938 the day of supply for this weapon was listed as five rounds. In the general revision of day-of-supply figures in December 1941, five rounds was made the day of supply for all .30-caliber ammunition on the assumption that the Garand would be used exclusively in combat. Later, in 1944, separate days of supply were once more shown for the older models since the Garand was not produced in sufficient quantities to fill all combat needs.[87]

Early in the war a high day of supply was in force for the .50-caliber machine gun, and enormous quantities of .50-caliber ammunition were procured. Attainment of Allied air superiority drastically curtailed the need for antiaircraft ammunition at the same time that sharp upward increases in requirements for heavy caliber ammunition were experienced. In general, the day of supply for small arms ammunition was gradually and steadily reduced as experience data became available. The opposite trend took place right up to the end of the war in the case of artillery ammunition, leading to the authorization of facility expansions some of which were not scheduled for completion until late in 1945.

A representative picture of the trends as well as the actual levels of the day of supply is shown by figures covering the principal weapons of the Army at specified dates. (*Table 25*) This abridged summary conveys but little of the complexities underlying the establishment, revision, and publication of day-of-supply figures. The complete picture would include the Army's entire catalog of weapons, numerous dates of revision, an array of percentage figures indicating for each caliber the composition of shell requirements for each day of supply (ball, tracer, armor-piercing, high explosive, white phosphorus, and so on), and by the end of

[85] AG Ltr, AG 471 (9 Jun 44) OB–S–D–M, 10 Jun 44, sub: Day of Supply for Ammunition, and incls.

[86] Frank, Requirements, pp. 104–07.

[87] Richards Committee Rpt, p. 47. Also see Table 25, opposite page.

TABLE 25—DAY OF SUPPLY OF AMMUNITION FOR THEATERS OF OPERATIONS
AT INDICATED DATES

[Rounds per Weapon per Day]

Weapon and Caliber	All Theaters				ETO [a]	
	30 November 1938	10 December 1941	1 February 1943	10 November 1943	10 June 1944	1 June 1945
Gun, Machine, cal. .30	150	150	150	100	70	45
Rifle, cal. .30, M1903, M1917	2	5	5	4	1.5	1.5
Rifle, cal. .30, M1	5	5	5	4	3	3
Gun, Machine, cal. .50, HB	90	90	90	50	25	9
Gun, Machine, cal. .50, AA	200	100	100	50	25	9
Mortar, 81-mm	5	5	5	5	12	18
Howitzer, 75-mm. Field, Pack	32	40	40	40	20	14.4
Howitzer, 105-mm. Field, SP	28	30	40	40	40	41
Gun, 4.5" Field	—	—	20	20	25	26
Gun, 155-mm. Field, M1	15	15	15	15	25	22.2
Howitzer, 155-mm. Field, M1	18	20	20	20	25	25
Howitzer, 8" Field	6	10	10	10	18	25
Gun, 8" Field	—	—	10	10	10	15
Howitzer, 240-mm. Field, M1	4	5	5	5	7	13

[a] Days of Supply were published for individual theaters after 1943; ETO rates selected as illustrative.

Source: TAG letters and inclosures, AG 471 series, for dates indicated.

the war numerous variations from theater to theater.

The broad subject of the Army's requirements for ammunition in World War II is a complex and controversial one, with ramifications extending throughout the whole process of procurement. At the outset of the war, shortages of ammunition—especially in the small arms category—assumed frightening proportions, and new productive facilities were hastily authorized and constructed to meet the combined demands of the Army, the Navy, and allied countries under the Defense Aid Program. Even before all of the facilities were completed, shortages of copper prevented most of them from operating at capacity. Fortunately, expenditure rates were low in the early stages of the war and production soon out-stripped current requirements. Unforeseen increases in efficiency raised actual output far in excess of the design capacity of most plants. This development, as well as independent factors such as the copper shortage and successive reductions in requirements, resulted in large excesses of plant capacity, partial rates of operation, and plant shutdowns long before the end of the war. It has been estimated that by the end of the war only one half of the twenty-one million tons of ammunition produced in the United States had been sent overseas and less than one fourth actually expended.[88] Some observers would see in this a substantial degree of confusion and waste. Others would see a combination of circumstances—most of them

[88] See Sherman, The Formulation of Military Requirements for Munitions and Raw Materials, p. 109.

unforeseen and many of them fortunate—
which made it unnecessary for the United
States to exhaust the reserves and the productive capacity it had provided in order to
achieve victory in a global war of uncertain
character and duration.[89]

Concluding Observations

The task of estimating military requirements for World War II was one of great
importance and great complexity. The
purely military aspects of the problem were
alone enough to stagger the imagination. If,
on 7 December 1941, the Army could have
instantaneously received for the asking any
desired quantity of each item of munitions
known to exist, the job of correctly stating
its needs would still have been stupendous.

Ideally, those responsible for the determination of requirements would first have
to know the exact size of the Army at all
dates until the end of the war; its subdivision
in terms of armies, corps, divisions, regiments, battalions, companies, and other
units; its composition in terms of infantry,
artillery, air, engineer, and other combat as
well as service arms; and the desired allowance of weapons, ammunition, personal
equipment, vehicles, rations, medical supplies, clothing, construction equipment, materials, spare parts, and other supplies for
each echelon of the Army organization.
They also would have to know precisely
when and where all these items were to be
delivered. This in turn would require a
knowledge of basic strategic plans, enemy
capabilities and probable intentions, related
plans of the Navy and allied nations, and

so on. After engaging in combat, meeting
enemy resistance, adjusting strategic and
tactical plans, and learning of the need for
new or altered weapons and equipment, the
Army would be faced with the continual
necessity for changing its requirements and
specifications to meet the new conditions.

The actual requirement problems faced
by the Army in World War II were far
greater and more complex than those reflected in the simplified situation presented
above. Munitions in any desired quantity,
place, and period of time could not be obtained by waving a magic wand. They had
to be designed, developed, produced, and
delivered by a complex process which engaged a major share of national resources.
Competing needs for resources, and especially for the ultimate resource—the nation's
manpower—imposed   serious   limitations
upon production feasibility. These limitations, as dramatically demonstrated in
World War II, forced a continuous reappraisal of the size, the structure, and operations of the Army as well as of its matériel requirements.

A review of the major phases of the evolution of Army requirement programs from
1920 to 1945 reveals a complete cycle.
World War I was followed by rapid disarmament and the nationwide scramble to
"return to normalcy." In an atmosphere
hostile to military preparedness and in the
absence of any urgent threat to national security, Army appropriations during the
1920's and early 1930's were pared to the
bone. The Army's size was kept below National Defense Act objectives, its wartime
abundance of equipment was used up or became obsolete, and its activities were confined to localized training and minimum
maintenance. The Army organization was
reduced to an incomplete skeleton, lacking

---

[89] For greater detail on the Army's ammunition
requirements and production program, see Thomson and Mayo, The Ordnance Department: Procurement and Supply of Munitions.

even the complementary units essential to a balanced structure at its existing depleted strength. Repeated protests by War Department Secretaries, Chiefs of Staff, and other spokesmen had little effect on the course of events. Under the circumstances, the Army relied upon advance planning and such research and development as it could finance to prepare itself for meeting wartime needs.

After 1935, in the face of growing unrest in Europe, modest increases in funds resulted in a gradual but significant rehabilitation of the Army. But not until the fall of France in June 1940, did the United States make an earnest effort to attain military preparedness. This great rearmament effort—known as the Munitions Program of 30 June 1940—was an across-the-board program of Army procurement designed to obtain as quickly as possible complete equipment for a force of over a million men and to create the industrial facilities for supplying difficult-to-procure items for a far larger force.

The Munitions Program of June 1940 was substantially less than the War Department had requested to meet the Axis threat. Still it was astronomical in magnitude when compared with previous levels of procurement, and the War Department was hard pressed to administer and control the program. The structure of the Army at every stage of anticipated expansion had to be carefully planned; tables of allowances and equipment for all Army units had to be revised and kept current with the adoption of new weapons and supplies; the new allowance tables had to be applied to the anticipated troop strength at successive stages of mobilization and deployment; construction and maintenance requirements for posts, camps, stations, arsenals, and a host of other military establishments had to be drawn up;

and finally all the various types and quantities of required matériel had to be consolidated and converted into dollars and cents in order to prepare the War Department budget, to devise orderly expenditure programs, and to place tens of thousands of contracts with industry.

Nevertheless, even before the Munitions Program was well under way, the continued deterioration of the world political situation dictated the progressive raising of procurement objectives. America's role as the arsenal of democracy, implemented by the adoption of the enormous lend-lease program in March 1941, and the increasing threat of actual involvement of the United States in a war with both Germany and Japan, compelled a thorough reappraisal of military requirements. Moreover, with the appearance of serious production difficulties and material shortages, the Office of Production Management began to press the military agencies for the development of firm, long-range estimates of requirements in order to enable industry to go forward with large-scale conversion and expansion activities essential to quantity production. The development of the Army's Victory Program in the fall of 1941, a paper program to be used in the event of war, was a step in this direction. With the advent of Pearl Harbor "the lid was off," and both the formulation of requirements and the placing of contracts were hurriedly consummated at high levels with the all-compelling objective of adequacy for meeting the crisis. Earlier estimates which seemed at the time of their adoption to be overstatements typically turned out to be understatements as the demands of mobilization and expansion continued to mount.

After Pearl Harbor and the announcement by the President of spectacular new production objectives for planes, tanks, guns, and merchant ships, the War Production Board found that military requirements for all the armed forces, plus the essential needs of the civilian economy, added up to more than the nation was capable of producing. Material shortages and production bottlenecks—culminating in the Feasibility Dispute—forced a reconsideration of all requirements estimates, and planned programs had to be brought within the scope of production possibility. At this stage of development, the task of computing Army requirements became increasingly complex. Not only did estimates for military end items require careful review and balancing, but all such items, when significant, had to be translated into their equivalent in scarce materials and other resources. Only with such information could the Army and the War Production Board make intelligent program adjustments and allocations of scarce materials. Thus, by the end of 1942 the criterion of *adequacy* in the determination of requirements was tempered by the need for *feasibility* and *balance* in the production and delivery of finished munitions.

By the end of 1943, war production in many categories had caught up with demand and the formulation of requirements reached a third stage of development. The findings of the War Department Procurement Review Board and the Richards Committee for the restudy of reserves called for a shift in emphasis from adequacy and feasibility to accuracy in the process of forecasting requirements. The initial equipping of the expanded wartime Army was nearing completion and substantial reserves of equipment were either in storage or scheduled for early delivery. The mounting supplies of war matériel would no longer automatically be absorbed by Army expansion, and the press-

ing needs of the civilian economy, many of them long deferred, demanded closer scrutiny of military requirements. It then became necessary to develop refined methods of reporting the issue, consumption, and inventories of military supplies in all theaters of operations as well as in military establishments throughout the United States. This refinement of procedures and estimates could be accomplished only after the firm establishment of theaters of operations, a step which for the first time made it possible to base requirements upon actual rates of consumption rather than upon hypothesis and conjecture. Replacement demand, rather than demand for expansion, became the new guide to Army procurement.

While the Army's Supply Control System for refining the determination of requirements was still in the process of development, the collapse of Germany in the visible future became reasonably assured and requirements determination entered a fourth stage—the planning of the shift from a two-front to a one-front war. This was a complex operation which entailed increases in numerous specific requirements in the face of a general reduction.

The final stage—planning for the tapering off of requirements and providing for widespread contract termination and reconversion associated with the end of the war— went on simultaneously with the third and fourth stages. Although the reconversion issue was highly controversial, particularly during the temporary resurgence of Germany in the Battle of the Bulge, the obvious desirability of an orderly transition from a war to a peacetime economy compelled substantial efforts on the part of reconversion specialists even as others continued to plan for war production.

Thus ran the cycle of military requirements—from an extended period of Army deterioration, through rapid mobilization and war, and back, for a time at least, to peacetime conditions. Both during and after World War II, there was a considerable lack of understanding of the problems involved in the determination of military requirements for technological warfare on a global basis. This situation existed in varying degrees in many sectors of the Army and complicated its task. But the misunderstanding was considerably greater and more widespread outside the Military Establishment, giving rise to unrealistic expectations and requests for "prompt" determination of "firm" and "accurate" statements of requirements which by their very nature could be only rough and changing approximations to eventual needs.

Perhaps the most common misunderstanding was the one reflected in numerous references to the Army's lack of firm strategic plans upon which to base its matériel requirements. Implicit if not explicit in these references was the assumption that strategy, of a kind not always specified, would provide the primary foundation for military requirements. Actually, the history of both the methods and the results of the Army's determination of requirements for World War II indicates that strategy played—and in the nature of the case could play—only a secondary role in the formulation of requirements. World War II was primarily a technological war, with the odds in favor of the side possessing the greatest abundance of technical and material resources. The victory of the United States and its allies represented a triumph of superior military power, consisting basically of a general and marked superiority of equipment and supplies in the hands of trained men. This superiority was the result of the adoption of a broad, across-the-board program of military requirements independent of the nation's commitment to any specific strategic plan.

The basic sequence of planning in World War II thus ran from requirements to strategy, not strategy to requirements. Once a preponderance of general military power had been established, strategy could be crystallized, and at this point the specific needs of strategy could be translated into additional specific requirements and special project needs. But because of the length of the average period of production, the adequate and timely supply of even these needs was in most cases possible only after they had already been anticipated and included in bold and imaginative requirement programs previously adopted.

The grounding of strategy in a general preponderance of military power was not unique to World War II. But it had profound significance for a nation which, except for its naval strength, had allowed itself over the years to become virtually disarmed. With the fall of France in 1940 the vulnerability of the Western Hemisphere suddenly became evident, and the attack on Pearl Harbor brought home the fact that America's survival depended upon the rapid attainment of superior military power.

This objective could not be gained by timidity. It required positive decisions, usually in the face of inadequate information and uncertainty as to the outcome but always on the side of boldness. Both in its Commander in Chief and in its military and civilian chiefs of supply, the U.S. Army in World War II was fortunate in having at the time of its greatest crisis the kind of bold leadership which was prerequisite to the attainment of decisive military power.

Such leadership would inevitably challenge feasibility limitations and, by establishing high production objectives, would raise the limits of feasibility itself.

Needless to say, the Army made numerous errors in forecasting its requirements for World War II, whether viewed from the standpoint of economic efficiency or of military necessity. But the goal, and to a considerable extent the very concept, of "precision" in the formulation of military requirements is a will-of-the-wisp. A victorious army is likely to be one which will end a war with surpluses of equipment and supplies:

There are a lot of people, sir, who would like to have us fire the last cartridge at the last Jap after we have eaten the last K ration and after we have dropped the last bomb in the last emplacement. We don't think we are going to be able to do that. Naturally, we are going to wind up with stocks . . .[90]

Conversely, an army whose supply situation is characterized by "too little and too late" is not likely to be victorious. In World War II the final result was a compromise between the exuberant demands of the individual procuring agencies and the more conservative estimates of those responsible for bringing all programs into balance within the limits of feasibility. Fortunately, the United States possessed both the resources and the opportunity to satisfy the unprecedented needs of its armed forces without seriously undermining the living standards of its civilian population.

[90] Testimony of Lt Gen Brehon B. Somervell, Truman Committee, *Hearings,* 26:12013.

PART FOUR

ARMY PURCHASING PROBLEMS
AND POLICIES

CHAPTER IX

Survey of Army Purchasing: 1940 to 1945

The procurement of Army matériel for World War II represented the greatest purchasing operation ever conducted by a single agency in the history of the American economy. The value of War Department procurement deliveries under supply contracts from 1 July 1940 to 31 August 1945 has been estimated at $117 billion, consisting of nearly $44 billion for the Army Air Forces and the remainder for claimants supplied by the ASF.[1] Yet even this figure, which would dwarf by comparison the operations of the nation's most gigantic corporation, fails to suggest the true magnitude of War Department purchasing activities in World War II. In order to obtain the needed deliveries of munitions and to train and house its troops, the War Department was obliged to contract, directly or indirectly, for many additional billions of dollars in industrial facilities, machinery and equipment, and Army installations throughout the world. The combined value of total war production for the Army, including its air forces, during this period has been estimated at approximately $180 billion.[2] Moreover, these figures

do not take into account the fact that the value of purchase contracts originally placed with industry in order to achieve these results was much higher: the canceled value of the Army's World War II contracts which were terminated prior to completion ran from $40 billion to $50 billion. (*See Table 60, page 696.*)

No amount of statistical presentation can fully reveal the complexities of the Army's wartime purchasing operations. The expansion of Army purchases to more than one hundred times their previous annual rate in peacetime suggests only the quantitative changes which took place as a result of the war. The most difficult aspects of wartime purchasing were those which involved qualitative departures from peacetime methods of buying and which required the development of an entire new philosophy of pricing and contract placement, as well as the formulation of countless other details of purchase policy. The following pages attempt to portray the background and nature of the problems faced by the Army in its wartime purchasing activities and the policies which were developed in an effort to provide their solution.

The Interwar Period

The revolution in Army purchasing activities and policies brought about by World War II can be understood only by contrast with peacetime procurement. Army pro-

---

[1] Whiting *et al.*, Statistics, "Procurement," 9 Apr 52 Draft, p. 14. These totals, computed from physical quantities delivered and unit costs of 1945, do not reflect final cost to the government; they do not, for example, take into consideration price changes or contract renegotiations. For other qualifications see source.

[2] Civilian Production Administration, The Production Statement (1 May 1947). See Table 2, p. 6, which is subject to qualifications similar to those in note 1, above.

curement in peacetime was practically synonymous with purchasing. The low volume of purchases in relation to the nation's industrial capacity made unnecessary any of the elaborate measures for the expansion of productive facilities, the allocation of raw materials and other supplies, and the expediting and control of production indispensable to procurement in time of war. For similar reasons, the purchasing function itself was largely confined to the awarding of contracts to low bidders under the rigid procedures prescribed for peacetime governmental procurement. Few of the complex problems of contract distribution, pricing, renegotiation, and related measures which came to be the essence of wartime purchasing activity and policy were experienced or more than dimly conceived during the placid period between the two world wars.

Total War Department appropriations in the nineteen fiscal years 1922 through 1940 amounted to some $6.4 billion, or an average of $339 million annually.[3] These appropriations provided for all War Department military activities—pay and subsistence of the Army, the support of the National Guard, the Organized Reserve, Citizens' Military Training Camps, and the Reserve Officers' Training Corps, the operation of arsenals and storage depots, War Department overhead, and many other activities in addition to the limited procurement programs of the regular supply arms and services. Peacetime purchasing was a routine function—small in magnitude, leisurely conducted, and relatively unencumbered by

issues calling for constant judgment and reformulation of policy.

As already implied, the essence of the Army's peacetime purchasing methods was the advertised demand for limited quantities of specific items, followed by the automatic award of a single contract to the lowest qualified bidder for each item. Under this procedure, prescribed by statute and rigidified by administrative order and court interpretation, no contract distribution problem existed. The question of which firms in the nation's economy were to receive contract awards was decided largely by the operation of the competitive, free-enterprise economic system. Likewise, pricing problems were for the most part nonexistent, and nothing approaching a price "policy" was required by the procuring agencies. Price, like the selection of the contractor, was the result of competition, and under competition it was presumed to be reasonably close to cost. Furthermore, under competition, cost itself would be held to a minimum, since it would reflect the expenses of the least-cost producer. The competitive bid system, in theory and to a large extent in practice, resulted in maximum efficiency of production, the conservation of government funds, and the absence of excessive profits to contractors—all without the conscious direction or concern of procurement personnel. It is hardly surprising, in view of the persistence of these idyllic conditions for nearly two decades, that contracting officers were ill-prepared to meet the Pandora's box of problems suddenly released in the summer of 1940 by the deluge of appropriations exceeding, within three short months, the total for the previous nineteen years.[4]

[3] War Department, Office of the Budget Officer, War Department and Total Government Appropriations and Expenditures—FY 1922 Through 1948 (3 April 1947), copy in OCMH. These figures do not include civil works projects conducted by the Army Engineers.

[4] War Department appropriations during the first quarter of fiscal year 1941 amounted to more than

The formal competitive bid system and all its associated procedures represented the accumulation of Congressional and administrative efforts over the years to insure maximum economy in governmental procurement. It provided safeguards against the inertia of public servants who were presumed to lack the stimulus of the profit motive and would probably fail to conduct their buying operations with the same aggressiveness as their counterparts in private industry. Also, it was designed to make extremely difficult if not impossible the collusion of public officers with individual firms and to keep to a minimum any possible corruption in the dispensing of public funds. Above all, it reflected the belief that the American economy was, on the whole, basically competitive and that prices obtained by the solicitation of competitive bids would, in fact, be close to cost and thus allow only a normal profit. That the competitive bid system had many shortcomings for military procurement, in both peace and war, has been indicated elsewhere.[5] Even its principal peacetime virtue—encouragement of and dependence upon widespread competition throughout the underlying economy—was to become a major handicap during the defense and war periods as the possibility and desirability of competition were drastically reduced.

Despite the relative simplicity of peacetime procurement, many specific difficulties arose in the administration of the prewar

system of competitive bidding. The preparation of "foolproof" invitations to bid, including the careful statement of specifications and contract terms, occasionally required the application of a complex admixture of legal and engineering principles. Arrangements for the public opening of bids at a specified time and place had to be made and scrupulously followed. The determination of the "responsibility" and hence the eligibility of each bidder required in many instances considerable industrial and engineering knowledge and investigation on the part of contracting officers. Questions as to the possible collusion of bidders and the noncompetitive status of particular firms or industries sometimes arose to plague procurement officials. For the most part, however, these difficulties did not become a major problem and except for large or unusual purchases, such as aircraft, could be handled on a routine basis.

Even in peacetime the practical necessity for numerous exceptions to the standard procedure arose, and over the years a number of exemptions were permitted by statute. Emergency procurement, which could not await the time-consuming process of advertising and related procedures, was exempt; purchases in amounts of less than five hundred dollars and contracts for various secret items of equipment were also exempt. Likewise, a number of types of purchase in circumstances where competition was inpracticable or nonexistent could be made by negotiation in the same manner as purchases by private firms. In this category were patented items, articles produced by a sole manufacturer, parts of apparatus already in use furnished by a single dealer, and items for which the price was fixed by governmental or other competent legal authority. In cases where advertising failed to elicit

---

$6.6 billion as contrasted with the $6.4 billion for the period 1922 through 1940. See W. B. Harris, A History of Army Purchasing, June 1940–June 1944 (5 September 1944), p. 1, OCMH.

[5] (1) John Perry Miller, *Pricing of Military Procurement* (New Haven: Yale University Press, 1949), especially Ch. III, "Peacetime Procurement Techniques Before 1939." (2) Holley, Buying Airpower.

TABLE 26—WAR DEPARTMENT PROCUREMENT: BY PURCHASING METHOD, 1937–1940

[Dollars in Millions]

Fiscal Year	Total	Invitations to Bid		Purchases by Other Agencies	QMC Purchase Notice Agreements	Open Market Purchases
		Amount	Percent			
1937	$434.1	$358.0	82.5	$18.7	$4.5	$52.9
1938	389.0	308.7	79.4	20.7	4.7	54.9
1939	457.1	375.5	82.2	24.4	4.4	52.8
1940	776.2	677.0	87.2	35.2	6.0	58.0

Source: ASF, History of Purchases Division, p. 27.

bids and further advertising was deemed useless, resort to open market purchases was permitted. But even for exempted items, administrative procedures were established requiring the informal solicitation of bids or other actions designed to insure economical procurement. Finally, for various reasons a number of items or item-classes were relieved by specific statutes from competitive bidding. Included in this category were advertising services, bunting, horses and mules, gages, jigs, dies, medical supplies, exceptional items of subsistence stores, and purchases from Indians. The purchase of aircraft, as well as aircraft parts and accessories, was subject to various procedures and exemptions which changed from statute to statute. Of all procurement problems faced by the War Department during the interwar period, aircraft purchase policy created the most difficulty. Frequent investigations and statutory changes by Congress complicated the task of obtaining the suitable development and production of aircraft.[6]

Many of the standard commercial items required by the War Department in peacetime were obtained by the Procurement Division of the Treasury, which conducted central buying on a large scale for federal agencies. The Procurement Division also served to co-ordinate the purchasing standards of all federal agencies by prescribing mandatory contract forms and procedures for the solicitation of bids and the making of awards. The War Department obtained most of its requirements of fuels and lubricants through the Navy, envelopes from the Post Office Department, paper and related items from the Government Printing Office, and a miscellaneous assortment of items from the Federal Prison Industries, Inc., and the Committee on Purchases of Blind-Made Products. In general, interdepartmental procurement in peacetime worked well, produced economies through large-scale purchases, and freed the War Department from much red tape which would have been associated with the advertising and placement of numerous small contracts.[7]

[6] (1) ASF, History of Purchases Division [circa 1945], pp. 1–28. The original of this manuscript is filed in OCMH under the title ASF, Production and Purchasing Division, Purchasing Policies and Practices. (2) Holley, Buying Airpower. (3) Miller, Pricing of Military Procurements, pp. 27–36. (4) Harry B. Yoshpe and Marion U. Massen, Procure-

ment Policies and Procedures in the Quartermaster Corps During World War II (QMC Historical Study 17, June 1947) (hereafter cited as QMC Procurement Policies), especially pp. 22–24.

[7] Yoshpe and Massen, QMC Procurement Policies, pp. 18ff.

Despite the numerous possible exceptions to the procedure, competitive bidding accounted for the overwhelming preponderance of War Department purchases in the interwar period. Purchases under this method amounted to well over 80 percent of the total during the four years immediately preceding the launching of the Munitions Program of 1940. (*Table 26*)

The Defense Period

The growing awareness of the United States of the dangers of Axis aggression prior to World War II can be measured roughly by increasing preparations in the field of military procurement. The invasion of Poland in September 1939 had little immediate effect upon the availability of procurement funds to the Army. Total War Department appropriations for fiscal year 1939 had been approximately $496 million, a figure not much above the average for the previous ten years. The 1940 appropriation was more than double this amount, and with an additional $100 million voted in February 1940, it totaled nearly $1.1 billion. But it was not until June 1940 that appropriations were made and related measures undertaken on a scale commensurate with the needs of a significant rearmament effort. Thus the term "defense period" has appropriately come to be used to denote the eighteen-month period from June 1940 to Pearl Harbor, during which the United States actively prepared for war. The defense period stands in contrast to the longer, twenty-seven-month "period of grace"—from the German invasion of Poland to the Japanese attack on Pearl Harbor—during the early part of which the intentions and capabilities of Axis aggression were more discernible than any defensive action on the part of the United States.

With the fall of France in June 1940, all doubts in the minds of the majority in Congress as to the reality of the national peril came to an end, and the rising determination of the United States to prepare its defenses was indicated by the steady stream of appropriations for rearmament. Before the month of June was out, Congress had provided $2¾ billion for War Department procurement. In August the Battle of Britain began and in the following month Congress made available an additional $4 billion. This was followed in October by a further $1.4 billion. The passage of the Lend-Lease Act in March 1941 brought another $4.8 billion to the War Department, making the total for fiscal year 1941 nearly $13.5 billion.

On 22 June 1941 Germany attacked the Soviet Union and eight days later the regular fiscal year 1942 War Department appropriation was made by Congress. This amounted to some $10.6 billion. After the announcement of the Atlantic Charter in August 1941, Congress added another $4¼ billion to War Department funds. Less than a month before Pearl Harbor, the "cash and carry" provisions of the Neutrality Act were repealed, and by Pearl Harbor another $7.4 billion had been granted to the War Department. Thus in the last six months of 1941 some $22 billion had been made available to the War Department over and above the $13.5 billion for the previous fiscal year. The eighteen-month total of nearly $36 billion was larger than the combined expenditures of the War and Navy Departments during World War I.[8]

---

[8] Figures for the defense period in above paragraphs taken from ASF, History of Purchases Division, pp. 29–31. Expenditures by the War and Navy Departments for World War I, as reported in annual reports of the U.S. Treasury, amounted to approximately $33 billion.

As in the case of all other areas of economic mobilization and procurement, the defense period brought about far-reaching changes in Army purchasing. To meet the avalanche of appropriations beginning in the summer of 1940, the Army's purchasing organization in Washington and throughout the entire United States was steadily expanded. District procurement offices were reactivated or newly established, and thousands of persons were recruited, trained, and put to work in the placement and administration of procurement contracts. New procedures and policies were developed, and most important of all, Congress provided a steady stream of new legislative enactments abolishing statutory barriers to rapid procurement and conferring upon the armed forces positive new powers indispensable to the enlistment of industry in the greatest industrial mobilization effort in the nation's history.

Among the first and most important legislative acts of the defense period was the National Defense Expediting Act of 2 July 1940.[9] This act authorized the Army to make all defense purchases under the new appropriations "with or without advertising," thus eliminating the legal compulsion to go through the time-consuming and often inappropriate procedure of formal advertising, waiting for suitable bids, and awarding a single contract to the lowest responsible bidder. Under the new legislation, the Army was free to make awards directly to allocated or other desired facilities, to broaden the procurement base by wide distribution of contracts under split awards to many producers of a single item, and to continue the advertising procedure on a modified basis as deemed essential or desirable.[10]

The defense expediting act outlawed the cost-plus-a-percentage-of-cost type of contract but gave specific sanction to the cost-plus-a-fixed-fee contract, subject to a maximum fee of 7 percent of estimated cost. This was a highly significant and timely provision. The straight CPPC contract of World War I proved expensive and wasteful; yet without some type of cost contract legally available, the Army in 1940 would have been unable to place many of its contracts for construction, research and development, and supplies. During the defense and war periods there were innumerable situations in which costs could not be estimated in advance with sufficient accuracy to warrant the adoption, by either the government or the contractor, of a fixed price at the time the contract was signed.

The National Defense Expediting Act permitted the government to make advance payments up to 30 percent of the contract price. This was a most important consideration underlying the decision of many producers to accept contracts and undertake cash outlays for conversion to war production; during peacetime the government had been prohibited from making any payments in advance of procurement deliveries, or equivalent performance, by the contractor.[11] Also, the act conferred upon the Secretary of War authority to construct and operate industrial plants, to be owned either wholly or partly by the government. This was the foundation upon which the War Department's vast assemblage of powder, ammu-

---

[9] 54 *Stat.* 712, 2 Jul. 40.

[10] The power to negotiate all contracts without

advertising was extended the following year by 55 *Stat.* 366, of 30 June 1941, and subsequently by the First War Powers Act.

[11] A similar provision for advance payments had been provided for World War I. See 40 *Stat.* 383, 6 Oct 17. For discussion of the administration of advance payments and other wartime provisions for the supply of working capital to contractors, see Chapter XXIX, pp. 674–78.

nition, chemical, atomic bomb, and other plants was to be built and operated during the next four years. Finally, the defense expediting act included provisions for licensing and prohibiting exports of machinery and critical materials, an important aid in conserving and making available these items during a period of grave scarcity.

Four days before the passage of the National Defense Expediting Act, Congress had provided the initial statutory basis for the granting of priority to all Army contracts and orders over civilian and foreign orders.[12] The 28 June 1940 act and the subsequent provisions for its execution were designed to facilitate both the placement and the administration of Army contracts; the authority to extend the priority power vertically to subcontractors and vendors was an important key to the completion of prime contracts on schedule. The 28 June 1940 act also suspended the provisions of the eight-hour law of 19 June 1912, which prohibited the employment of laborers or mechanics under government contracts or subcontracts for more than eight hours in any one day.[13]

On two successive days in October 1940, Congress enacted two statutes of far-reaching importance to Army procurement—the Second Revenue Act of 8 October and the Assignment of Claims Act of 9 October 1940. The revenue act contained the revolutionary "tax amortization" provision which exerted a profound stimulus upon

the expansion of privately financed production facilities during the defense and war periods. The tax amortization law converted high wartime tax rates from a liability into an asset so far as their effect on plant expansion was concerned. By permitting the complete charge-off, for tax purposes, of all approved new capital facilities within a period of five years or less, the act made it decidedly profitable for contractors to convert to war production and removed much of the sting of high wartime tax rates. The same act also suspended, for the duration of the emergency, the Vinson-Trammel profit-limitation act, which held aircraft manufacturers and shipbuilders to a flat profit rate of 8 and 12 percent, respectively.[14]

The Assignment of Claims Act was a major instrument in the mobilization of bank credit in support of war production. By permitting contractors to assign—to banks and other lending agencies—their claims to payment under government contracts, the act provided a high degree of security to lenders. Many of the financial aids to contractors developed in the course of World War II rested squarely upon the foundation of the Assignment of Claims Act.[15]

A number of other statutes enacted during the defense period deserve mention as facilitating the Army's purchasing activities. On 10 October 1940, the power to license and prohibit the export of critical items was augmented by the power to requisition such

---

[12] See 54 *Stat.* 676 (28 Jun 40), extended by 55 *Stat.* 236 (31 May 41), and later by the Second War Powers Act, 56 *Stat.* 177 (27 Mar 42). The priorities system is discussed in detail below in Part Six.

[13] On 9 September 1940 the suspension was qualified by a proviso requiring a payment of time-and-a-half for hours worked in excess of eight in one day. 54 *Stat.* 884.

[14] 54 *Stat.* 974ff., 8 Oct 40, especially Title III, beginning at 998. For further treatment of tax amortization matters and the suspension of the Vinson-Trammel act, see below, Part Five.

[15] 54 *Stat.* 1029, 9 Oct 40. For many years previously the assignment of claims under government contracts had been prohibited by law. See *Revised Statutes* 3477 and 3737.

items for military use.[16] The following year a
general requisitioning statute was enacted,
enabling the military services and other
agencies of the government to seize and fix
the compensation for any property, with
minor exceptions, considered necessary to
the national defense.[17] A related power, the
authority to place mandatory orders and to
commander industrial plants, was granted
by the Selective Service Act of 16 September 1940.[18] On 29 April 1941, Congress conferred upon the Secretaries of the War and
Navy Departments the power to waive the
terms, in both outstanding and new contracts, which required the filing of performance and payment bonds by contractors.[19]
These bonds had previously been required
of government contractors in order to
indemnify the government against non-
performance and to protect workers and
suppliers against nonpayment of charges
growing out of the prime contract. Such
bonds were practically unnecessary for contractors in an obviously strong financial position, and the costs of furnishing the bonds
merely increased the cost of the contract to
the government. In the case of other contractors, difficulties with surety companies
slowed down the placement and performance of contracts and threatened to undercut the purpose of Assignment of Claims
Act.[20]

The foregoing legislative enactments, together with the numerous revenue, appropriation, and other acts passed during the
defense period, laid the foundation for
American industrial mobilization and rearmament. Although basically the responsibility of the Congress, they were the products of the joint efforts of Congress, the
NDAC, and the procuring agencies. The
importance of an adequate legislative basis
for its entire procurement program was
never lost sight of by the Army. Throughout
the war legal and other experts in the War
Department devoted much of their time to
proposing and criticizing drafts of pending
legislation, testifying before appropriate
Congressional committees, and discussing
the issues with procurement personnel and
representatives of industry. Long before the
defense period the Legal Section, OASW,
had prepared lists of additional War Department powers which would have to be
authorized by Congress in order to meet the
necessities of emergency or wartime procurement. The prompt adoption of most of these
proposals at the outset of the defense period
helped make possible the substantial progress toward rearmament achieved prior to
Pearl Harbor.[21]

In utilizing its expanded legislative
powers the War Department undertook a
long succession of administrative changes
designed to streamline the cumbersome procedures of peacetime procurement and place

---

[16] 54 *Stat.* 1090. This authority was extended by
56 *Stat.* 467 (2 Jul 42) and 58 *Stat.* 624 (28
Jun 44).

[17] 55 *Stat.* 742 (16 Oct 41), subsequently extended by 56 *Stat.* 181 (27 Mar 42), 57 *Stat.* 271
(30 Jan 43), and 58 *Stat.* 624 (28 Jun 44).

[18] 54 *Stat.* 885, 16 Sep 40.

[19] (1) 55 *Stat.* 147, 29 Apr 41. (2) Public Law
800, 8 Oct 40, 76th Cong., 3d Sess.

[20] Surety companies, besieged with applications
for bonds early in the defense period, did not consider it worth while to issue bonds in amounts required by small contractors. Also, they claimed
status as financial institutions under the Assign-

ment of Claims Act and took prior assignments of
rights to the proceeds of the contracts. This was
greatly disturbing to banks, who feared involvement
in litigation with surety companies and were therefore reluctant to make defense loans necessary to
the execution of contracts. See Harry B. Yoshpe,
Production Control in the Quartermaster Corps,
1934–1944 (QMC Historical Study 8, December
1944), p. 59, for additional details.

[21] See legislative appendixes to the several editions
of the Industrial Mobilization Plans.

them on a basis adequate for the large-scale rearmament effort. On 12 June 1940, while the formulation of the Munitions Program was still under way, the Assistant Secretary of War alerted the supply arms and services to the greatly augmented procurement program and ordered all possible steps to be taken in anticipation of its adoption. Among the Assistant Secretary's recommendations were the advance issue of circular proposals, reduced time of advertising, prompt making of awards, splitting of awards, spreading work to subcontractors, simplifying and freezing specifications, eliminating pilot models where practicable, speeding up inspection, shortening delivery schedules under both new and existing contracts, rendering all possible assistance to manufacturers, and adoption of plans for the acquisition and training of additional personnel needed at all echelons.[22]

On 2 July 1940, the same day the enabling legislation was passed, OASW approved the use of CPFF contracts and authorized all supply arms and services to make use of the power to negotiate contracts without formal advertising wherever this would expedite the defense program.[23] In the summer of 1940 new contract forms and clauses were approved, signalizing the beginning of a movement that was to culminate in far-reaching changes in the powers of contracting officers and the adaptation

of contractual instruments to the manifold purposes of war. The steady revision and improvement of contract forms served to standardize, so far as desirable, contract terms and conditions for all technical services, to simplify purchase, shipping, and disbursing procedures, and to provide a flexible array of readily available "boiler plate" contract provisions embodying the fruits of the War Department's rapidly accumulating procurement experience.[24] Especially important during the defense and early war periods was the development and use of various types of preliminary contractual instrument—letters of intent, letter orders, letter contracts, and letter purchase orders—which enabled contractors to undertake work immediately on urgent items of procurement without waiting for a formal contract. Under these arrangements, each of which possessed considerable flexibility, contractors were authorized to acquire necessary machinery, equipment, materials, and other supplies and to proceed to manufacture the needed item of procurement in advance of agreement on specific contract terms such as price, quantities, detailed specifications, and similar matters. These were determined as rapidly as possible and the contractor was guaranteed reimbursement of all costs incurred prior to the adoption of a formal contract.[25]

Various administrative determinations during the defense and early war periods freed the supply arms and services from the compulsion to acquire supplies through

---

[22] Ltr, Johnson, ASW, to CofAC *et al.*, 12 Jun 40, sub: 1941 Procurement Program, copy in Special S. Com. To Study and Survey Problems of Small Business Enterprises, 77th Cong., 2d Sess., Hearings on S. Res. 298, *Problems of American Small Business*, 10:1301. These hearings, which extended from 15 December 1941 (76th Congress) through 18 December 1946 (79th Congress), will hereafter be cited as Senate, *Small Business Hearings.*
[23] Memo, Col John W. N. Schulz, Dir Current Procurement OASW, for CofAC *et al.*, 2 Jul 40, sub: Procurement Without Advertising, copy in Senate, *Small Business Hearings*, 10:1303.

[24] Standard contract terms were eventually codified, set forth, and kept current in War Department Procurement Regulations. PR 13, Forms of Contracts, contained a massive array of general contract forms to meet various types of purchase situation.
[25] (1) PR 13. (2) Yoshpe and Massen, QMC Procurement Policies, pp. 90ff. See also below, pages 247–48.

specified channels, such as the Procurement Division of the Treasury, the Federal Prison Industries, Inc., and the Committee on Purchases of Blind-Made Products.[26] Far more important in permitting timely and adequate procurement was a series of determinations made by the Under Secretary of War in 1941 and early 1942, relieving contracting officers from the prohibitions imposed by the "Buy-American Act" of 1933. This legislation, adopted at the bottom of the depression, forbade government purchase of materials or supplies from foreign countries except under highly restricted conditions. By March 1942 the Under Secretary had determined, in accordance with the applicable provision of the statute, that except for items of food and clothing further observance of the prohibitions would be contrary to the public interest. In the case of Canadian products, even food and clothing could be purchased by the U.S. Army as needed without regard to the problem of national origin.[27]

Numerous other changes in the Army's purchasing procedures and organization took place during the defense period. These included the relaxation of provisions governing liquidated damages for delayed deliveries, modification of performance, payment, and other bonding requirements upon contractors, and the establishment and refinement of procedures for administering advance and progress payments, guaranteed loans, and other financial aids to contractors. At the organizational level, large numbers of additional personnel from private industry were recruited, including specialists in many fields of purchasing, who brought new ideas and enthusiasm to the task of rationalizing the Army's buying methods and organization. In the field of subsistence purchasing, for instance, a nationwide network of market centers was soon established to permit rapid and efficient buying of meats, vegetables, and other food items in carload lots directly from sources of supply. This development and many others owed much to leading individuals in NDAC and the OPM, who possessed wide contacts throughout industry and carried a powerful mandate from the President as well as Congress to get the rearmament program under way as rapidly as possible.[28]

During the defense period, material shortages and the growth of the priorities system complicated the task of contracting officers and required the adoption of complex new procedures which tied together the functions of purchase, contract administration, and production control. As the procurement

---

[26] For further details, see Yoshpe and Massen, QMC Procurement Policies pp. 79–81.

[27] (1) OUSW Memos, 18 Apr and 24 Jul 41, sub: Determination Under Buy-American Act. (2) OUSW P&C Gen Dir 94, 27 Dec 41, sub: War Production Policy for Canada and U.S. (3) Hq SOS Gen Dir 30, 16 Mar 42, sub: Buy-American Act. (4) PR 5, Foreign Purchases.

[28] (1) Nelson, *Arsenal of Democracy,* pp. 99–104. (2) Testimony of Albert J. Browning, July 1941, Truman Committee, *Hearings,* 6:1623, 1630–32.

The elaborate and far-flung purchasing empire established by the Army to meet its needs for World War II had its foundations in the defense period. Some idea of the scope of this empire and the manner in which it came into being may be inferred from a study of certain subcomponents under the Quartermaster Corps. (1) Herbert R. Rifkind, Fresh Foods for the Armed Forces: The Quartermaster Market Center System, 1941–1948 (QMC Historical Study 20, 1951). (2) Marion U. Massen, Canned Vegetables: A Case History in Central Procurement at the Chicago Quartermaster Depot During World War II (CQMD Historical Study 3, 1943). (3) Marion U. Massen, Central Procurement of Dehydrated Vegetables for the Armed Forces (CQMD Historical Study 6, March 1945). (4) Marion U. Massen, Canned Meats Procurement for the Armed Forces During World War II (CQMD Historical Study 7, March 1946). (5) Risch, Fuels for Global Conflict, p. 147.

program accelerated and claimed a larger share of the nation's resources, many firms of all sizes found themselves cut off from sources of supply necessary to carry on their regular commercial business. At the same time the inevitable concentration of prime contracts in the hands of large corporations gave rise to complaints that the Army was discriminating against small business. To alleviate distress, minimize criticism, and broaden its procurement base, the Army established procedures to promote wider distribution of prime contracts and a greater degree of subcontracting by holders of prime contracts. The focal point of all these procedures and responsibilities was the contracting officer in each procurement office, for it was the contracting officer and his staff who were basically responsible for the administration as well as the placement of contracts. In turn, the contracts themselves represented the basic instruments for achieving the objectives of the entire procurement program.[29]

Despite the remarkable progress made by the Army in launching its heavy procurement program during the defense period, many unresolved problems remained or emerged on the eve of Pearl Harbor. Much confusion and duplication existed in the assignment of purchase responsibility for common items, not only among the supply arms of the Army but among the several

military procuring agencies. This allowed the competitive scramble for the available supply of many items to drive up prices, interfere with orderly production, and prevent equitable distribution. Moreover, interservice competition was not confined to end products. In the face of constantly rising requirements a shortage of productive facilities was inevitable. The facility allocation system was kept on a flexible basis and many firms were not covered by it. Hence, procuring agencies resorted to the hasty placement of long-term contracts— often in excess of balanced requirements— in order to "sew up" productive capacity for particular services.

Although the Army's purchasing organization had expanded considerably by the end of 1941, it was still far short of current needs, to say nothing of the expanded requirements of all-out wartime procurement. The problem of orienting personnel at all echelons to their new responsibilities was tremendous. There was a marked reluctance on the part of the several headquarters of the technical services to decentralize purchase responsibility; "directed" procurement from Washington headquarters often interfered with the negotiation and placement of contracts by district offices. Most pressing of all was the lack of an adequate philosophy and machinery for the pricing of military procurement in an economy in which the traditional mechanism of competitive pricing had largely disappeared or broken down. The absence of a well-developed pricing policy and the technical and organizational means for its implementation complicated the Army's use of its power to place contracts by direct negotiation and contributed to widespread overpricing and excessive profits, soon to be dramatically revealed.

---

[29] Contracting officers were the sole custodians of power to sign binding contracts for the War Department. They were appointed by the chief of each technical service or higher authority and included the technical service chiefs as well as other appointing officials. All contracting officers received their powers through a series of redelegations from the Secretary of War. (1) PR 107 (4–7–44) Authority with respect to procurement. (2) PR 204 (2–8–45) Contracting authority. (3) PR 302.3 (11–23–44) Contracting officer.

Pearl Harbor to V–J Day

The impact of Pearl Harbor upon Army purchasing activities transcended all developments in this field during the entire defense period. In less than a month, President Roosevelt had announced to the world the spectacular production objectives for planes, ships, tanks, and guns which set the pace for the entire war production effort. The Army had raised its over-all procurement program from the needs of a four-million-man Army, conceived primarily for defense, to the requirements of a ten-million-man Army dedicated to victory. Ten days after Pearl Harbor, Congress passed the First War Powers Act, which came to be regarded for the duration of the war as the Magna Charta of the procurement agencies as well as of the entire executive arm of the government. Title II of this act permitted the making or modification of any or all government contracts previously or thereafter entered into, as well as the making of advance, progress, and other payments related to such contracts, without regard to previously applicable provisions of law, so long as such action was deemed by the President to facilitate the prosecution of the war. The only significant strictures in Title II were the prohibition of the CPPC form of contract and the retention of existing statutory limits on profits.[30]

Under a sweeping redelegation of these powers [31] the Army in the first three months of 1942 placed nearly $15 billion in war contracts. So far as Congress was concerned "the lid was off," and throughout the entire war period the Army did not lack for money to carry out all its multifarious ac-

tivities. In two successive acts, on 31 January and 6 March 1942, Congress appropriated to the War Department new sums of $12.5 billion and $23.5 billion, respectively. Thus, in less than three months after Pearl Harbor, the War Department had received somewhat more in new appropriations than it had during the entire eighteen months of the defense period.

Large appropriations of money could not alone suffice to win the war. Appropriations had to be translated into finished munitions at the earliest possible date, and this in turn depended upon the rapid placement of contracts. Until after Pearl Harbor all contracts over $500,000 had to be reviewed and approved, both by the Under Secretary of War and the Office of Production Management, prior to actual placement. From the outset these contract "clearance" requirements had tended to slow down procurement and create interagency friction; as the number of contracts rapidly increased they became increasingly onerous. Ten days after Pearl Harbor the Under Secretary of War authorized the technical service chiefs to award all contracts, either for supplies or construction, up to $5 million without higher War Department approval and permitted redelegation of this authority under appropriate safeguards to the extent deemed necessary by the service chiefs. At this time contract review by the OPM was required for all contracts in excess of $1,000,000.[32] Shortly thereafter, following consultations with the procuring agencies, the newly established War Production Board discontinued its own separate contract review function and transferred its personnel concerned with that activity to the War and Navy Departments. Thus by 3 March 1942, interagency dupli-

---

[30] 55 *Stat.* 838, First War Powers Act, passed on 17 December and approved 18 December 1941.
[31] Executive Order 9001, 27 Dec 41.

[32] OUSW P&C Gen Dir 81, 17 Dec 41, sub: Decentralization of Procurement.

cation in contract clearance procedures and personnel was eliminated.[33]

Before the first quarter of 1942 had ended, it was evident that the War Department's existing organization and policies for procurement were grossly inadequate for coping with the flood of wartime contracts already in effect and certain to be placed in the visible future. The War Department reorganization of 9 March 1942, made under the authority of the First War Powers Act, was designed to bring order out of the chaotic conditions following Pearl Harbor. The procurement functions formerly divided between the Office of the Under Secretary of War and the General Staff were now concentrated under the Commanding General, Army Service Forces. Within ASF, the commanding general and his staff undertook to rationalize the entire procurement operation by the appropriate regrouping of functions and the creation of corresponding organizations and procedures to handle all functions, old and new, made necessary by the novel demands of modern industrial and economic warfare.

Under this reorganization the former Purchases and Contracts Branch, OUSW, became the Purchases Branch, Procurement and Distribution Division, ASF. Because of the scope and importance of the War Department's purchasing activities, many new functions were shortly acquired by the Purchases Branch, which soon attained division status in the Office of Procurement and Distribution (later Office of Materiel). Throughout the entire war period the Purchases Division was one of the most influential policy-making offices in the whole ASF organization. Although subject to supervision by the Director of Materiel and the

Commanding General, ASF, and ultimately by the Under Secretary of War, the Purchases Division was basically responsible for the formulation of all elements of War Department purchase policy affecting both the Army Air Forces and the technical services of ASF. It played a leading role in the development of principles for contract renegotiation when this was a pioneer endeavor on an uncharted sea; it sponsored and supervised the formulation of contract termination and settlement procedures, long before the establishment of the independent agency for this purpose—the Office of Contract Settlement. Above all, it carried the heavy burden of developing a basic philosophy of pricing—and the associated policies and instruments thereof—in a milieu in which the familiar process of competitive pricing had given way to a regime of administered price determination conducted by the procuring agencies themselves.

In addition to purely policy-making functions, the Purchases Division also discharged many supervisory and operating responsibilities. It was broadly responsible for the progress of the Army's procurement program in terms of the placement of contracts to meet scheduled requirements, the basic provision of important types of financial aid to contractors, and the removal of barriers to contract completion stemming from traditional contract terms and other long-established elements of purchase policy. The Purchases Division was concerned with the adequate organization of technical service headquarters as well as of the procurement districts, so that purchase policy could be efficiently implemented and controlled throughout the War Department. It aided these offices in obtaining key purchasing personnel and trained the Army's purchasing representatives for overseas procurement. It

---

[33] (1) WPB Gen Admin Order 12, 3 Mar 42. (2) CPA, *Industrial Mobilization for War*, p. 522.

instituted procedures and controls for local purchasing by field installations within the several service commands so that these installations could take advantage of large-scale purchasing by higher echelons and avoid encroachment upon local civilian needs.

On the Washington scene the Purchases Division represented the War Department to other governmental agencies, to Congress, and to industry. The director of the division was chairman of the WPB Procurement Policy Board, an interagency unit functioning under the auspices of the War Production Board for the formulation and control of broad wartime procurement and purchasing policies jointly affecting all procurement agencies. In its relations with Congress the staff of the Purchases Division prepared drafts of legislation, testified before appropriate Congressional committees, and interpreted the War Department's position on legislation affecting the purchase function. The division also had the general responsibility for the War Department's implementation of the various small business programs and policies established by Congress and the War Production Board. In its relations with industry the Purchases Division had numerous contacts with individual contractors, trade associations, and industrial leaders having membership on the War Department's Purchase Policy Advisory Committee. Throughout its life the Purchases Division, like other War Department offices and agencies, modified its organization and functions to meet the changing needs of the Army's fluid wartime procurement program.

Hardly had the War Department reorganization of 9 March 1942 been announced when the problem of overpricing and excessive profits in war contracts was thrust into the foreground of national atten-

tion. This development was the result of widely publicized hearings and findings of several Congressional investigating committees. The Army had already begun to explore ways and means of curbing these excesses; nevertheless, the Congressional hearings and the resulting renegotiation law compelled a concentrated and sustained attack upon the fundamental problem of the pricing of military procurement.

On 28 April 1942, the day of the passage of the first renegotiation law, the newly established Office of Price Administration issued its General Maximum Price Regulation, and in the following months OPA rose to a dominant position on the Washington scene. The thorny question of whether and to what extent military procurement would be subject to OPA price controls became a matter of major concern to the procuring agencies. The Army and Navy were properly fearful that the imposition of price ceilings or similar controls upon complex military end items such as aircraft, tanks, ships, and ordnance materiel would have grave consequences for the war effort. Most military end items were of novel and complicated design and had no previous price or production history. Any attempt to hold producers of such items to ceiling prices fixed in advance of production would inevitably cripple both the placement of contracts and the actual production of the items in question. Yet some means would have to be devised to keep the prices of war goods in line. With a steadily rising proportion of the nation's output going into military items, uncontrolled prices in this sector would add to general inflation, the dissipation of government funds, and the swelling of already excessive profits. Most dangerous of all, they would encourage the extravagant use of the nation's resources of materials and manpower, the ultimate limitations upon war production. The repeated prohibition, both in statutes and administrative regulations, of the wasteful CPPC form of contract would be reduced to a futile gesture if identical consequences were permitted to take place through uncontrolled prices and costs under either the fixed-price or CPFF form of contract. As events turned out, the procuring agencies were successful in obtaining the general exemption of military items from OPA price control. This arrangement was specifically contingent upon the development by the armed services of adequate means for controlling the prices of their own procurement, and it added substantially to the general pressure upon the services to develop a satisfactory pricing program.

Throughout the summer of 1942, the Purchases Division wrestled with the task of formulating an integrated body of sound pricing policies. Much intensive analysis of the issues was made by the War Department Price Adjustment Board in attempting to set forth the basic principles under which contracts would be renegotiated and excessive profits recovered from War Department contractors. By the late fall of 1942, sufficient knowledge had been accumulated to permit a broad synthesis of essential pricing and purchase policy. Hence, on 19 November 1942, as a result of a three-day conference of top-ranking purchasing officials at Tryon, North Carolina, a formal statement of War Department purchase policy was set forth. This pronouncement, which came to be known as the Tryon Statement, was the foundation of War Department pricing policy for the remainder of the war.[34]

The basic policy affirmation of the statement was that price and cost control should be achieved by careful negotiation of close prices early in the life of each contract. Only under initial close pricing, with periodic price revision to reflect the actual trend of costs, could sufficient downward pressure upon costs be achieved to stimulate maximum productive efficiency throughout the life of the contract and keep to a minimum the waste of real resources. This policy stressed the minimum use of the CPFF form of contract and the development on an intensive scale of cost-analysis procedures essential to sound pricing. Because of the dynamic and complex nature of wartime procurement, pricing policy and the organizations and procedures for its implementation underwent cumulative change and refinement until the end of the war.

Many other important purchasing problems of an administrative nature had to be resolved if vital military production was to be achieved in time to win the war. Foremost among the practical problems faced by the ASF immediately after Pearl Harbor was the decentralization of actual procurement responsibility and operations. Despite the desirability and necessity of adequate control over the Army's massive procurement program, the task of actual procurement was simply too great to be accomplished from the Washington headquarters of the seven technical services. The Army's wartime procurement organization had been planned for many years to rest upon the principle of decentralization as applied in World War I. But the district procurement offices had, on the whole, lain dormant during the interwar period and despite their reactivation during the defense period had not achieved by Pearl Harbor the degree of independence required to discharge their wartime responsibilities. This

---

[34] See below, page 277.

lack of independence was due partly to local inadequacies and partly to restrictions placed from above, chiefly at technical service headquarters in Washington. The service headquarters were understandably slow in permitting district offices to negotiate, unaided, important contracts many times the size of anything handled by the headquarters themselves during the long period of peacetime inactivity. In many cases the district offices lacked the personnel, the knowledge, and the general administrative facilities for adequately performing the tasks for which they would eventually have full responsibility. In other cases, however, district offices by the time of Pearl Harbor were far more familiar with available sources of supply and the productive capacity of potential contractors in their district than were the Washington headquarters. Not infrequently districts would receive special procurement directives from Washington, requiring the placement of a contract with a specific firm after the district had made ample surveys of facilities and conducted lengthy negotiations with another contractor considered more suitable for the procurement in question. Such interference by Washington headquarters was discouraging to local offices and deprived them of the degree of autonomy required to carry out their assigned functions.[35]

Effective decentralization of operational authority depended upon the development

of a uniform set of War Department procurement regulations and the adoption, so far as practicable, of uniform procedures throughout the several technical services and their many field procurement offices. The need for a comprehensive body of procurement regulations was painfully apparent at the time of the War Department reorganization in March 1942. For many years, regulations governing procurement had been scattered among a wide variety of sources—Army regulations, War Department circulars, OUSW circulars, and numerous special memoranda and documents issued for particular purposes by various echelons of the War Department. Nowhere was there a comprehensive bible of procurement to which contracting officers and others could have recourse in ascertaining War Department policy and practice. As a result, knowledge of the complexities of procurement—like the arcane rituals of ancient religions—became the property of an elite few who had carefully cultivated their lore over the years and had accumulated, filed, and cross-referenced their own collections of numerous scattered documents covering the subject. This confinement of a working knowledge of procurement policy in all its ramifications was an impossible barrier to decentralization of procurement operations, and immediately after the establishment of the ASF the Purchases Division went to work on a complete codification. Despite the magnitude of the task the first edition of the new Procurement Regulations was available by June 1942. All previous regulations, contained in the equivalent of some 1,500 pages, were rescinded and superseded by a single loose-leaf volume initially containing only one hundred pages. This edition was circulated among the technical services for criticism and suggestions, and on 1 Septem-

---

[35] (1) Col. Chester Mueller, *The New York Ordnance District in World War II* (New York: The New York Post Army Ordnance Association, 1947), p. 116. (2) ASF, History of Purchases Division, p. 82.

The subject of "directed" or "earmarked" procurement was intensively explored during the Senate hearings on small business problems. For informative testimony and statistics on this issue, see Senate, *Small Business Hearings,* 10: 1137–53, 1213–19; 11: 1432–77, 1484–94; 12: 1770–78.

ber 1942 an entirely new edition was published and widely disseminated. Thereafter, Procurement Regulations was revised once each month on the basis of interim circulars, and a system of distribution independent of The Adjutant General's Office placed revisions in the hands of users in a matter of hours after publication. Procurement Regulations eventually grew to many hundreds of pages but was well organized, clearly written, and carefully cross-indexed; with few exceptions the regulations could be easily understood and used by procurement personnel at all echelons.[36]

The consolidation of War Department procurement policies in the form of Procurement Regulations was a vital but not the only prerequisite to successful decentralization of the Army's purchasing operations. Despite the progress that had been made in expanding technical service headquarters and in reactivating procurement districts during the defense period, there had been no systematic, department-wide effort to control the pattern of mushrooming organizations or to simplify and standardize routine purchasing procedures.[37] As a result, the post-Pearl Harbor deluge of appropriations and contract authorizations found the services and the district offices still unprepared to handle the ensuing mass-purchasing operation on an efficient basis. Forms, documents, and procedures, as well as organizational structures, were far from adequately streamlined to permit the smooth and efficient dispatch of business on the scale of all-out war. Moreover, surveys instituted in 1942 by the Purchases Division, as well as by higher authority in the ASF, revealed widespread diversity in organization and methods, not only between the various technical services but among the numerous district offices of a given service. This diversity went far beyond the special requirements imposed by unique conditions peculiar to individual offices; it made impossible the application of uniform policies, reporting, and control procedures. The lack of structural similarity between different offices prevented the identification of common problems and posed a substantial barrier to effective intercommunication between different echelons in the total procurement organization.[38]

A few examples will suffice to indicate the kinds of diversity in operations and policy which hampered rapid contract placement and administration during the early war period. Certain procurement offices made wide use of their power to place contracts quickly by direct negotiation; others required a minimum of thirty days to solicit an inordinate number of potential contractors for a single item. One technical service, badly understaffed with experienced buyers but anxious to avoid any taint of venality, made a ruling that none of its personnel could deal with an entire *industry* if he had been associated with that industry during the previous five years. This virtually ruled out, *ab initio,* any possibility of obtaining qualified persons and went beyond the War Department's applicable regulation which confined the prohibition to par-

[36] By the end of 1944, Procurement Regulations comprised sixteen major sections with the following coverage: (1) General Instructions; (2) General Purchase Policies; (3) Contracts; (4) Bonds and Insurance; (5) Foreign Purchases; (6) Interbranch and Interdepartmental Purchases; (7) Disposition of Surplus and Unserviceable Property; (8) Federal, State, and Local Taxes; (9) Labor; (10) Plant Facilities Expansion; (11) Miscellaneous Purchase Instructions; (12) Renegotiation and Price Adjustment; (13) Forms of Contracts; (14) Requisitioning of Personal Property; (15) Termination of Contracts; (16) Priorities.

[37] ASF, History of Purchases Division, p. 79.

[38] *Ibid.,* pp. 87ff.

ticular firms with which the individual had formerly been associated. Some technical services decentralized their operations along geographical lines, while others had their district operations specialized along commodity lines. This basic organizational difference, apart from the relative merits of the two alternatives, made for especial difficulty in the matching of supervisory and control organizations at the staff level. Most services contracted almost exclusively for end items, but one service leaned heavily upon component buying; while this had certain advantages it multiplied the number of prime contracts and complicated the application of material controls, expediting and inspection procedures, property accounting burdens, and other operations. Undesirable duplication in the purchase of particular items, both within and between the several technical services, was discovered to exist in varying degree.[39]

As a result of continuing surveys sponsored by the Control Division, ASF, the Purchases Division devised a standard manual of procedures for all procuring offices. On 18 May 1943, a tentative manual M–603, Procurement District Operating Manual, was published. The need for greater detail and refinement, as well as for separate treatment of many problems peculiar to particular technical services, resulted in a thorough revision of the manual. Largely through the efforts of the ASF Control Division staff in consultation with the Purchases Division, a new and final version—ASF M–603, Pro-

curement Office Purchasing Procedures—was published in December 1944 and its provisions made mandatory. The purpose of the manual was to accomplish in the procedural field what Procurement Regulations had achieved in the policy field. The manual covered the entire contracting process—the receipt and processing of procurement directives, obtaining proposals, making awards, preparing and distributing contracts, preparing and distributing purchase action reports, the processing of contract modifications, supplemental agreements, and change orders, and countless other routine but essential activities of contracting officers. Although many of the prescribed operating procedures were already in effect the manual's publication marked an important step forward in simplifying and standardizing desirable procedures and in providing a sound basis for staff supervision and control.[40]

Throughout the defense period and the year-and-a-half after Pearl Harbor, the primary emphasis in the Army's procurement program had been the rapid placement and administration of contracts to insure the timely delivery of supplies to meet the needs of the expanding Army. During this period it was clear that the outcome of the entire war depended upon adequate procurement deliveries, and the Army was not disposed to sacrifice this major objective to the niceties of contract distribution, correct pricing, cost control, prevention of excessive profits, and so forth. By mid-1943 the initial needs of the Army—including its successful transship-

---

[39] These and many other purchasing difficulties were revealed in the Red Tape Report, submitted by a special committee appointed by General Clay in October 1942 to recommend improved purchasing procedures. (1) Maj Richard M. Leighton, History of Control Division, ASF, 1942–1945 (1946), pp. 166–67, MS, OCMH. (2) ASF, History of Purchases Division, pp. 80–82.

[40] Annual Report, Purchases Division, ASF, Fiscal Year 1944–45, accompanying Memo, Col Fred C. Foy, Dir Purchases Div ASF, for Dir of Materiel, 15 Jun 45, sub: Annual Report of ASF for Fiscal Year 1945, in files of Purchases Div ASF.

ment to theaters of operations—had been assured and the pattern of requirements was shifting to replacement and operational needs. By this time also, major achievements in the basic organization of the entire process of nationwide economic mobilization and procurement had been made, providing the indispensable foundation for refinements of detail. Accordingly, from mid-1943 to V–J Day, procurement policy was increasingly concentrated in two major areas: (1) improvement of basic policies and procedures already developed; (2) anticipating and preparing for the problems posed by the coming liquidation of the wartime procurement program.

In the first area, substantial progress was made both in the fields which have already been discussed and in numerous other aspects of purchase policy and procedure. In the field of pricing policy, the many new price revision and redetermination clauses for individual contracts were supplemented by a "company pricing" program designed to improve the over-all pricing policies of large firms holding many contracts, especially major subcontractors who could not ordinarily be reached by Army contracting officers. In the general area of price and cost analysis, new organizations, techniques, and programs were developed, eliminating much of the guess-work previously inevitable in the negotiation and placement of fixed-price contracts. A major program for converting outstanding CPFF contracts to fixed-price agreements was launched, and the number of CPFF contracts was greatly reduced by terminations, conversion, and restrictions upon new procurement. Liaison arrangements with WPB, the OPA, and other war agencies were perfected and the interagency frictions which characterized the earlier period were substantially reduced. Thus, in the field of OPA price control, War Department purchasing experts systematically reviewed many hundreds of price regulations, both old and new, to determine their effects upon Army procurement in the light of changing conditions. As a result of their recommendations, the OPA modified or withdrew objectionable terms of many of its regulations, thereby minimizing harmful effects upon procurement.

In response to the War Production Board's request, "mandatory flow-down" clauses were introduced in prime contracts to force the prompt placement of orders and subcontracts for contributory items. This insured the availability of many parts and components indispensable to war production and relieved suppliers with long production "lead time" from the necessity of speculating on future demand in a milieu of increasing contract termination. Also in response to representations by WPB, the Army imposed strict controls on local purchases by posts, camps, and stations in order to avoid impingement upon civilian needs for many commercial-type items undergoing extreme shortages. A revised agreement with the Smaller War Plants Corporation (SWPC) was reached, setting forth simplified and decentralized procedures designed to promote the widest possible distribution of Army contracts to small business. Increased efforts and patient negotiations by the Army's Procurement Assignment Board clarified and simplified the problems of procurement responsibility for thousands of items used by two or more technical services; assignment determinations—in addition to deciding purchase responsibility—also had to specify, in the case of each item, which service would be responsible for specifications, determination of requirements, provision of funds, and inspection.

In order to handle the increasing number of contract terminations throughout the last two years of the war, as well as to make ample provision for mass terminations upon the cessation of hostilities, the Purchases Division was faced with many problems. In addition to meeting problems of termination and settlement, the War Department had to revise its contract placement policy. To shorten its commitments as the end of the war approached, the ASF imposed increasing restrictions upon the letting of long-term contracts, quantities to be obtained, and the advance placement of contracts. Shorter term purchasing paralleled the shift in requirements planning from annual estimates under the Army Supply Program to monthly estimates under the Supply Control System. A monthly survey of outstanding preliminary contractual agreements was instituted and firm measures were taken to convert these into formal contracts; only by keeping letters of intent, letter purchase orders, and similar instruments to a minimum could the War Department protect itself against excessive termination charges and other complications resulting from the absence of standard termination articles in existing agreements. Extensive interchange of information between the Army and other government procuring agencies was provided in order to prevent termination of contracts which could be economically assumed by another agency in need of identical items. Similar measures were undertaken to prevent the placement of new contracts by one agency for items carried in surplus by another agency and hence likely to be disposed of. Purchase policy during the final year of the war also reflected shifts of emphasis in the field of price analysis growing out of the gradual liquidation of the war

program. With the reduction in pressure upon the nation's productive facilities, provisions for payment of overtime were less justifiable, greater competition could be expected, especially among subcontractors, and price revision articles could be used to take advantage of probable increases in efficiency. Likewise, with nongovernmental business absorbing a larger share of the efforts of contractors, the allocation of overhead costs to government contracts was subjected to closer scrutiny. Company pricing programs were used more and more to effect better pricing in individual contracts rather than to control a firm's over-all price and profit situation.[41]

From the foregoing it is evident that the Army's purchasing problems in World War II were of a magnitude and complexity to stagger the imagination. But no summary of broad policies and developments can do more than suggest the vast underlying structure of operations involving more than a million individual purchase transactions per year. Each of these transactions possessed its own interesting history and unique significance. Many of them were of simple, routine, or repetitive nature, involving only minor sums. Others, involving commitments running to nearly a billion dollars, would require many volumes to indicate their countless ramifications. No complete description will ever be made, since the written records—even if completely available—would reveal only a fraction of the total amount of planning, discussion, and effort which actually went into their execution.

---

[41] (1) *Ibid.* (2) Annual Report, Purchases Division, ASF, Fiscal Year 1943–44, in files of Purchases Div ASF.

CHAPTER X

Major Issues in Contract Placement

Military Responsibility for Procurement

A primary question in the field of contract placement was who should conduct the actual purchasing and contracting operations essential to military procurement. Consideration of this question, which arose early in World War II, illuminates a number of important aspects of the total task of economic mobilization.

Fundamental to the Army's entire scheme of organization and operation was the premise that it would have and retain direct responsibility and authority for the procurement of its own equipment and supplies. By the time of World War II, Army procurement was deeply rooted in history and law, going back to the early part of the nineteenth century. During the Revolutionary War, the Continental Congress had conducted or directed many of the procurement operations needed to fill the Army's crude and relatively small matériel requirements. In 1792 the U.S. Congress established the office of Purveyor of Public Supplies, whose procurement jurisdiction extended to arms and ammunition. The War of 1812—the first to be waged by the new republic—necessitated greater specialization of the military procurement responsibility. In March 1812 Congress created the position of Commissary General of Purchases under the Secretary of War and re-established the office of Quartermaster General which had existed during the Revolutionary period. In May 1812 the Ordnance Department was created, and by 1815 it had obtained permanent jurisdiction over the procurement of arms and ammunition. The overlapping procurement responsibilities of the Quartermaster General and the Commissary General were gradually clarified by the ascendancy of the Quartermaster General and the discontinuance, in 1842, of the office of the Commissary General of Purchases.[1] Meanwhile, the establishment of the Corps of Engineers and the Medical Department on a permanent basis in 1802 laid the foundation for eventual procurement responsibility in these branches of the Army. By the beginning of World War I, there were five Army branches or departments charged with procurement; by the end of the war the number had grown to eight.[2]

During the first year after America's entry into World War I, when confusion was rampant and the fruits of the nation's industrial mobilization were meager, considerable sentiment arose in favor of proposals to

[1] (1) Risch, *QMC Supply*, I, 3–5. (2) Green, Thomson, and Roots, *The Ordnance Department: Planning Munitions for War*, pp. 14ff. (3) *U.S. Statutes at Large*, II, 696–99, 816–18; III, 203; V, 513.

[2] (1) Francis B. Heitman, *Historical Register and Dictionary of the United States Army* (Washington: Government Printing Office, 1903), I, 41–43. (2) War Department, Engineer Procurement Manual, 1933 ed., p. 2, ICAF Library.

transfer military procurement out of the hands of the military departments into a civilian ministry of supply, or single department of munitions.[3] These proposals were rejected by President Wilson who decided instead to reconstitute the War Industries Board as the supreme co-ordinating agency, under a single powerful head. In his appointment of Bernard Baruch, Wilson specifically indicated that the procurement function was to be retained by the agencies established for that purpose:

The duties of the Chairman are:

----

(2) To let alone what is being successfully done and interfere as little as possible with the present normal processes of purchase and delivery in the several departments.[4]

The leading chronicler of the World War I industrial mobilization experience has summarized as follows the relationship of the War Industries Board to the purchasing function:

It should be said that, although it [the War Industries Board] was the exchange of the Government agencies involved in the prosecution of the war—the universal meeting-place of requirements, resources and facilities, maker of prices, moulder of contracts, accelerator and brake of industry—it was not a purchasing agency in the strict sense. Except for its own expenses it never spent a cent of Government money. It made agreements with the trades, but it did not sign contracts. Actual purchases, contracts, and all the details of business transactions were attended to by the proper agencies within the departments that were statutorily charged with purchasing functions. In a broad sense it was certainly a comptroller of purchases, but it did not make

them. This lack of actual purchasing power was sometimes a very serious handicap, but it was offset by a detachment from an infinitude of details and personal contacts that made for added power in dealing with the fundamentals of Government relations to the industry.[5]

The retention of the military procurement function by the military agencies was confirmed by the National Defense Act of 1920, and virtually all industrial mobilization planning during the following twenty years was predicated on this foundation.[6] In 1940 when Bernard Baruch was invited to give the newly established NDAC the benefit of his experience in World War I, he included as a major element of advice the warning to leave the actual contracting process in the hands of the military agencies.[7] No serious proposals were made during the defense period to disturb the basic pattern of procurement responsibility.

The attack on Pearl Harbor suddenly focused the country's attention upon the importance of war production as a major prerequisite of victory. Many of the nation's citizens who had given the matter no previous thought now assumed that no machinery or principles of procurement existed and that these would have to be established *de novo*. It was natural for such observers to suppose that the task of purchasing equipment and supplies was a matter for civilians and civilian agencies and that all the Army and Navy had to do in this area was to furnish a civilian production board with a statement of military requirements in the form of

---

[3] (1) Baruch, *American Industry in the War,* p. 23. (2) Clarkson, *Industrial America in the World War,* pp. 8, 69, 80.

[4] Ltr, Wilson to Baruch, 4 Mar 18, reproduced in Clarkson, *Industrial America in the World War,* pp. 49–50.

[5] Clarkson, *Industrial America in the World War,* p. 46.

[6] For a time in 1929 Brig. Gen. George Van Horn Moseley, who as Executive Officer of OASW had a prominent part in preparing the first industrial mobilization plan, believed that the Army should divest itself of procurement in time of war. He later concluded that this would be impracticable. See Maj. Eisenhower, AIC Lectures, 8: 20.

[7] Nelson, *Arsenal of Democracy,* pp. 90, 103, 199.

a "shopping list." The board would then do all the purchasing and attend to production matters, while the Army and Navy would devote full time to "fighting the war."

In addition to this simplified view, various pressures had accumulated by the time of Pearl Harbor to challenge the propriety of procurement by the armed services. By the beginning of 1942 the dislocations attending conversion of the nation's economy to war production were seriously felt in many communities. Emigration of labor from rural areas to centers of munitions production, together with the military draft of manpower, had denuded local communities of able-bodied farm workers, mechanics, unskilled labor and population in general. The plight of these "ghost towns" was matched by a contrasting set of conditions in overcrowded communities at the receiving end of "defense migration." These "boom towns" were unable to provide adequate housing, schools, utilities, and other community facilities. Small towns and substantial cities alike found their familiar atmosphere and customary conveniences destroyed by an invasion of construction workers, trailer communities, and hordes of free-spending war workers. Shortages of everything from seating space in schools, restaurants, and theaters, to parking space and staple grocery items soon developed to make life unpleasant for all concerned. Despite the evidence of widespread financial prosperity, many small businesses were obliged to shut down for lack of workers, managers, materials, parts, or general supplies.

The resulting chorus of complaints from all directions soon filled the newspapers and resounded in the chambers of Congressional investigating committees. As in the corresponding period of World War I, many critics of the existing order felt that the dislocations of the war effort were attributable to carelessness and indifference on the part of the military procuring agencies and that the hardships of war on the home front could be avoided or minimized by transferring the procurement function to civilian hands. The Tolan Committee of the House of Representatives quickly reached the conclusion that "poorly planned production" on the part of the War Department "has been the primary cause of the unplanned and unnecessary migration up to the present time." The committee recommended the centralization of all procurement in a single purchasing agency as the solution to the problem.[8]

In January 1942, some two months before the appearance of the Tolan Committee recommendations, Donald Nelson was engaged in drafting the Executive order which would define the powers of the War Production Board. The first great issue he had to resolve after becoming chairman of WPB was whether or not to remove the procurement function from the armed services and place it in the hands of a civilian organization. Nelson decided to leave this function with the military agencies, partly because of inherent advantages in the existing arrangement, and partly because of the irrecoverable loss of time required to create a new purchasing organization from scratch.[9] This decision was criticized as a sign of "weakness" on Nelson's part by many observers who were unfamiliar with the nature of military procurement but who believed

---

[8] H. Rpt. 1879, 77th Cong., 2d Sess., National Defense Migration, Third Interim Report of the Select Committee Investigating National Defense Migration, On the Need for a Single Procurement Agency To Effect All-Out Production and Achieve Full Use of Labor Supply, 9 Mar 42, pp. 1, 3–18, 83 ff.

[9] Nelson, *Arsenal of Democracy*, pp. 197–201.

on *a priori* grounds that all purchasing was necessarily a civilian function. Despite the fact that military procurement in peace and war had resided with the military agencies for more than a century and that it was firmly embedded in a mosaic of statutes, administrative regulations, court decisions, and organizational arrangements, critics of Nelson spoke as if he had suddenly turned over to the armed services a current and long-standing function of civilian agencies:

Everything that WPB attempted to do with respect to procurement was conditioned by the primary fact that Nelson had delegated the power of actual procurement to the Services.[10]

It is clear that Nelson could not "delegate" to the military agencies what they already possessed. On the other hand, he might have withdrawn the procurement function from them by so recommending to the President at the beginning of 1942. Nelson's decision against such a recommendation provided an easy target for criticism by many who viewed the administration of war production essentially as a contest of power between "civilians" and "the military," and who believed that the WPB chairman had needlessly "surrendered," "abdicated," "defaulted," or "frittered away" his powers to the military.[11]

The Nelson decision, followed by the War Department reorganization of 9 March 1942 and the WPB-War Department functional agreement of 12 March 1942, disposed of immediate proposals to transfer the responsibility for procurement.[12] But 1942, like the year after America's entry into World War I, was a year of feverish trial and error in harnessing the nation's resources for war production. By the end of 1942 the failure to reach stated production objectives, the development of strained relations between the Army and WPB, and increasing complaints of small business that it had been left out of the procurement program, all combined to raise anew basic questions of procurement policy and responsibility. There were complaints that the armed forces, and especially the Army, wanted to "take over" the entire economy.

On 16 December 1942 Under Secretary Patterson, alarmed by what he considered to be widespread misconceptions and by various proposals to remove military procurement from the military agencies, testified at length before the Truman Committee on the necessity of War and Navy Department retention of the procurement authority.[13] Two months later the War Department issued a printed brochure describing in considerable detail the reasons why it considered retention of the procurement au-

---

[10] CPA, *Industrial Mobilization for War,* p. 521.

[11] Nelson's alleged "default," or worse, in whatever decisions he made throughout World War II is the principal theme of Janeway, *The Struggle for Survival,* especially Chapter XI. But even a friendly observer regards Nelson's decision not to take over Army procurement as the starting point in "the progressive decline in the prestige and power of Donald Nelson." Bruce Catton, *The War Lords of Washington* (New York: Harcourt Brace and Company, 1948), pp. 115, 200 ff.

[12] The functional agreement, which broadly defined the respective activities of the War Production Board and the War Department, is reproduced in full in Millett, *Organization and Role of the ASF,* Appendix D.

[13] Truman Committee, *Hearings,* 16: 6675–95, especially 16: 6690–91. A week earlier, on the anniversary of Pearl Harbor, General Somervell had testified in similar vein before the Senate Small Business Committee. Senate, *Small Business Hearings,* 11: 1551–57. The most alarming proposal was a bill introduced into Congress for the combination of the existing functions of the procurement agencies with those of WPB into a new "super" economic mobilization agency. See Millett, *Organization and Role of the ASF,* pp. 284–85.

thority indispensable to military victory.[14] This publication set forth, in full, the grounds on which the War Department resisted all moves to divest it of procurement responsibility.

The crux of the War Department's position was that successful military operations were inseparable from successful military supply. Modern technology had raised the problem of adequate supply to a dominant place among the factors determining victory or defeat. Victory would go to the nation whose armed forces possessed superior mobility, destructive power, and stamina. These characteristics were largely determined by the quality and abundance of equipment and supplies in the hands of the troops. The task of obtaining adequate supply was a continuous and integral process from the determination of requirements, through the placing and administration of purchase contracts, all the way to the receipt, distribution, and servicing of finished munitions. To jeopardize this integrity and continuity by "ripping out" the purchasing function and placing it in the hands of another agency would be to court defeat.

In elaborating upon the integral nature of the procurement process, the War Department listed fifteen "major steps" in the flow of munitions: [15]

1. Strategical and tactical planning.

2. Development of requirements for all types of supplies and equipment, based on that planning.

3. Research to develop new and improved weapons and other matériel, including research to find available substitutes for scarce materials.

4. Design of items of supply and equipment, including the preparation of specifications and drawings.

5. Production and testing of pilot models.

6. Determination of facilities capable of producing military equipment, and construction of new facilities where necessary.

7. Placing of contracts.

8. Expediting and following up of production.

9. Inspection for quality.

10. Testing and proof firing.

11. Issuance of shipping orders to the manufacturers.

12. Transportation, both domestic and overseas.

13. Modification before distribution.

14. Distribution through bases and intermediate depots, subdepots, holding and reconsignment points, and ports of embarkation to troops either in the United States or overseas.

15. Maintenance of supplies and equipment, including procurement and distribution of spare parts and tools, salvage, and reclamation.

These steps occurred in rough chronological sequence for individual *units* of production, but all steps took place simultaneously for a given type of equipment as a whole. Thus, while some units of the medium tank were rolling off the production lines, others were being inspected at various stages of completion, some were undergoing modification before shipment overseas, and still others were being repaired, rehabilitated, or otherwise serviced in Army depots throughout the world, usually with the aid of spare parts and special tools supplied by the same manufacturer who built the tanks. At the same time new models were being developed and tested, designs and specifica-

---

[14] War Department, Military Responsibility for Equipping the Armed Forces (19 February 1943, 34 pp.), copy in OCMH.

[15] *Ibid.*, App. I, p. 13.

tions were frequently changing, and change orders were continually served upon and requested by contractors, both to improve the end product and to facilitate production. The search for substitute materials required constant communication between contractor and customer to ascertain the acceptability of all the many changes resulting from a given substitution. Inevitable revisions in military requirements and programs necessitated adjustments of production schedules, cancellation of some contracts, and revision of others—all on the basis of an intimate knowledge of the ability and performance records of various contractors, the state of production in the several plants, and so on.

These and many other elements in the complex process of military procurement were all related; actions could not be taken in one segment of the process without affecting other segments. In particular, all segments affected and were affected by actual details of the contractual process—selection of contractors, negotiation of terms, revision or termination of contracts, and countless aspects of contract administration and supervision, varying widely in nature from one type of procurement to another.

All proposals to lift procurement out of the logistical process and transfer it to a civilian agency would necessarily deprive the Army of its face-to-face relationship with producers of military equipment and supplies. This would mean, at best, delays, misunderstanding, and confusion in the transmittal—through a third party—of all specifications, orders, requests, proposals, and information between customer and producer. In practice, it would also inevitably mean the ever-increasing substitution of the judgment and decisions of the civilian procuring agency for that of the Army in such vital matters as delivery schedules, priorities, and the character and quality of military equipment and supplies.[16]

The War Department pointed out other disadvantages of a transfer of procurement authority: (1) scrapping the experience and knowledge of Army officers who had been seasoned and trained over a twenty-year period in procurement and economic mobilization, as well as in the design, development, production, and actual use of specific weapons and equipment; (2) the loss in morale to labor and management alike in destroying the direct relationship between the workingman and the fighting forces implicit in Army and Navy contracts with industry—Army and Navy E awards and attendant ceremonies had indicated the high morale value of this direct relationship; (3) military personnel could translate front-line observations and experience into the production of better weapons; (4) military personnel were likely to exhibit a greater sense of urgency and singleness of purpose in meeting procurement objectives in support of the military effort.

The War Department also dealt with major "misconceptions" or collateral criticisms of the armed forces often used in support of proposals to transfer the procurement authority. The first of these was the supposition that dislocations and inconveniences on the home front were the fault of the Army and Navy, or that such hardships could be avoided in any serious economic mobilization effort. In refuting this notion the statement on military responsibility pointed out that defense migration, curtailment of regular commercial business, failure of many small firms, and widespread shortages of materials and consumer goods were inevitable in any major war. Just as the mili-

---

[16] *Ibid.,* App. II, p. 17

tary draft of manpower necessarily caused dislocations and hardships in the lives of individuals so the draft of the nation's economic resources would cause unavoidable disturbances to the economic community. The War Department was concerned with minimizing these dislocations to the fullest possible degree consistent with its primary objective of winning the war; it had placed contracts outside of normal channels in order to avoid congested areas; it had made wide use of substitute materials, encouraged subcontracting, and achieved a wider distribution of prime contracts. But general shortages were inevitable and some businesses "simply cannot be used to make instruments of war. They must be taken care of by some other means than delaying our production of munitions." [17]

The other principal misconception was that the Army and Navy were seeking to "take over," "control," or "impose a military dictatorship upon" the national economy. The statement pointed out that the highest ranking officers of the War Department—the Secretary and the Under Secretary—were civilians operating under a civilian president; that the vast majority of officers, as well as enlisted men, in the wartime Army and Navy were recently inducted "civilians in uniform" with a confirmed civilian outlook; and that in any case regular Army and Navy officers fully subscribed to the American way of life under the Constitution and had no aspirations to dictatorship. The charge that "the military" aspire to dictatorship, the statement affirmed, "is uncharitable in peacetime, it is vicious in time of war." [18]

Finally, the War Department argued that the worst possible time for a transfer of such responsibility to a new and untried organization, which would have to be built up from scratch, was in the midst of a major war. The existing military procurement organizations had behind them two years of expanded, major, procurement operations under the leadership of seasoned procurement officers. Although much remained to be done, the War Department was proud of the accomplishments of its procurement organizations:

An army of over 5,000,000 men has been fully armed. Over 1,000,000 of them have been sent overseas fully equipped for combat duty, with the most modern and highly technical equipment known in history. They are presently conducting military operations in many theatres in all parts of the world. They are armed with varied and specialized equipment necessary to combat unprecedented conditions in the Arctic, in the tropics, on mountains, in swamps, deserts and jungles. A continuous flow of supplies is going to them daily. This would not have been possible with failure on the production lines. [19]

Many other illustrations were given of achievements on the war production front—achievements which did not "just happen" but rested solidly on the foundation of years of War Department planning. In view of all this, it would be disastrous to replace "one of the few phases of the war effort which has proceeded according to plan" with an "untried, unproven, experiment." [20]

After the publication of the War Department's statement in February 1943, proposals to transfer the procurement authority

[17] Ibid., p. 10. This quotation referred to a provision of the Small Business Act giving the WPB chairman authority to transfer the military contracting power to the Smaller War Plants Corporation. For further discussion, see below, Chapter XVIII.

[18] WD, Military Responsibility for Equipping the Armed Forces, App. V, p. 34.
[19] Ibid., App. III, p. 21.
[20] Ibid., App. I, p. 16.

gradually faded away. This development was the result not so much of the War Department's verbal representations as of achievements in the field of war production. Before the year was out, it became evident that the procurement program was highly successful in supplying both American troops and allied nations and that most of the associated problems were being resolved. In the face of the success of military procurement in meeting its basic objectives the question of procurement responsibility ceased to be a real issue.[21]

Development of the Negotiated Contract

Background and Early Use of Negotiation

The peacetime laws and regulations governing the letting of U.S. public contracts required that all such contracts, unless specifically exempt, be let to the lowest responsible bidder after an appropriate period of advertising and the observance of other prescribed formalities. These laws, together with an elaborate array of administrative regulations and judicial interpretations, were designed to insure procurement by the government at the lowest possible price and to give all potential bidders an equal opportunity to receive contracts.[22]

Both the machinery and the objectives of peacetime contract placement were unsuitable for emergency or wartime procurement. The period of time required to satisfy the various provisions of public contract law—preparation of invitations to bid, advertising for a sufficient period, allowance of a waiting period long enough for potential bidders to estimate and submit bids, and the numerous details attending the formal opening of bids, evaluation of bidders' qualifications, announcement of awards, and the like—ran into months and sometimes to more than a year.[23] All these procedures had to be completed before actual production could begin, and the delivery of the first completed items under the contract might still be a year or more away.

Apart from the question of time, compulsory award of contracts to low bidders would hinder the attainment of wartime procurement objectives in other ways. The lowest bidder—although technically qualified—might be much less suitable than many other firms for a particular contract: he might be less well equipped for rapid, large-scale production where quantity of output was a major consideration; his facilities might be much more urgently needed for the production of a different item soon to be contracted for; or he might be located in a labor-shortage area, in a "strategic" area vulnerable to enemy bombing attack, or far away from depot or port facilities. Conversely, for various reasons the most suitable producer for a given contract might not even submit a bid, even though potentially available.

Moreover, World War I had demonstrated that competitive bidding in time of

---

[21] Additional details and sources in this subject-area may be found in Millett, *Organization and Role of the ASF,* pp. 281–88.

[22] The basic statutes were Sections 3709 and 3710 of the *Revised Statutes,* dating back to the 1870's. Together with related material, they were prescribed and interpreted in Army Regulations (AR 5 series).

[23] For the Army Air Corps, whose emergency procurement program was perhaps the most urgent of all, the advertising period in peacetime had extended from 1 to 12 months, with an additional period of 1 to 3 months for the opening of bids, evaluation, and award. See S. A. Zimmerman, Procurement in the United States Air Force, 1938–1948 [circa 1950], pp. 70, 100–101, OCMH.

nationwide shortages was often either an empty formality or a farce. With competition in many lines all on the buying side of the market, solicitation of bids from overloaded suppliers would meet with little or no response. The few bids submitted were often so high as to indicate a complete lack of interest in additional contracts except at ridiculously inflated prices. As previously indicated, it was largely to avoid the consequences of such one-sided competition in a future emergency that procurement planning in the 1920's and 1930's included the allocation of the nation's productive establishments among the several procuring agencies. The compulsory award of contracts to the lowest responsible bidder without regard to other factors would run counter to the fundamental purposes and procedures of the facility allocation plans built up by the Army and Navy over the years.

For all these reasons a basic assumption and recommendation of Army procurement planning long before World War II was prompt suspension, at the beginning of an emergency, of the peacetime restrictions on contract placement. The suspension of these restrictions would give military procuring agencies the same freedom to negotiate contracts which private corporations had always possessed and which permitted them to conduct their purchasing operations with speed and flexibility. With freedom of negotiation the procuring agencies could place contracts with whatever firms, and under whatever procedures and terms, were necessary to assure the delivery of munitions in the quality, quantity, and time required to win the war.

Procurement planners were well aware that this freedom would not be an unmixed blessing. Like all significant freedoms it would entail grave responsibilities. Whatever the disadvantages of peacetime pro-

cedures, the automatic award of contracts to low bidders simultaneously disposed of the two most fundamental and difficult problems of contract placement—selection of contractors and pricing of procurement. In the absence of an automatic procedure, these matters would have to be determined in each instance by specific administrative decisions. Ideally, decisions of such importance and difficulty as those involved in the placing of major procurement contracts would be made only after lengthy investigation, study, and dispassionate analysis; in time of emergency, despite the best efforts of advance planning, they would have to be made in the face of inadequate information, great urgency, and political or other pressures.[24]

In formulating basic principles for the placement of contracts by negotiation, procurement planners were convinced of the desirability of utilizing competition in time of emergency or war so long as it was genuinely available. Even where the problem of contractor selection was clearly resolved by plant surveys and other features of facility allocation and procurement planning, the difficult problem of pricing would still remain. One important instrument in the pricing of negotiated contracts, as indicated in the Industrial Mobilization Plan, would be the application of cost analysis:

---

[24] In time of war political and similar pressures could be expected to decrease; at the same time the problem of urgency would be greatly increased. Shortly before the arrival of the emergency in 1940, the Army's Chief of Ordnance made the following remarks: "Should we undertake to get a removal of these legal restrictions in peacetime? Our conclusion is 'No.' . . . there are a great many disadvantages when you remove these restrictions. Politics come into play and all that sort of thing. . . . We can withstand political pressure in time of emergency that we can't withstand in time of peace." Gen Wesson, AIC Lectures, 16: 388.

(5) Prices will be determined by negotiation, controlled by the knowledge, obtained in peace time planning, of the items that make up costs and by all information that can be collected by the Government. A contractor refusing to take a contract at a fair price would be in a most unenviable position in war.[25]

But there were serious limitations upon the widespread use of cost analysis. The task of obtaining reliable cost information from thousands of contractors for a much larger number of individual contracts posed administrative as well as theoretical problems which were almost insurmountable. In the early stages of an emergency—with its inevitable confusion, shortages of trained cost accountants, and rapid changes in the trend of unit costs—effective price determination based solely on cost analysis for any large number of contracts would be impossible, and prices determined under such conditions would be highly unfavorable to the government.[26]

For these reasons the Army planned to make the widest possible use of competitive bidding consistent with the objectives of emergency procurement:

Where competition is possible within a procurement district, more satisfactory results will be secured by open bidding. This is true even among allocated facilities where requirements at the time do not exceed the production capacity for the item concerned. War conditions may change the method of securing competition and the number of producers available may be limited, but the policy of open bidding is sound and should be abandoned only when the necessity of the situation may so require.[27]

Emergency bidding procedures—assuming appropriate changes in regulations—would be of any required degree of informality; they could be limited to the most capable or desirable facilities whether allocated or not; and the procuring arms would be free to use or reject any or all bids, to make split awards, or to negotiate further if bids were unsatisfactory. By combining all the advantages of the facility allocation program with informal bidding among suppliers, the procuring agencies would approach a position of monopsony.[28]

In attempting to anticipate more specifically the areas in which competitive bidding might not be practicable in time of emergency, the planners identified two types of capacity shortage which would preclude effective competition: shortages of capacity for particular items and a general shortage for the economy as a whole. The former would exist at the outset of an emergency program in the case of complex, noncommercial, or military-type items not previously produced; for such items both the selection of contractors and contract pricing would have to be done by negotiation from the very beginning. On the other hand, a

---

[25] *IMP, 1933*, pp. 2–3.

[26] Because of administrative difficulties, it was proposed during the planning period to keep the number of the Army's adjusted-compensation contracts, which required extensive cost accounting, down to approximately one hundred. Capt Cheever, AIC Lectures, 12:344.

[27] OASW Planning Br Rpt, General Procurement Planning Conference, 1–2 December 1938, p. 43,

remarks of Maj Clarence C. Fenn, Legal Division. The use of competitive bidding to control and check contractors' cost estimates was urged in lectures to future procurement officers throughout the interwar period. For example: "What are the effective checks upon costs? . . . First, competitive bidding, if we can get it, is one of the most potent checks . . . do not underestimate the reliance that may be placed on competitive bidding when it generally exists." Prof. Thomas H. Sanders, Harvard School of Business Administration, Cost Accounting, 26 Oct 39, AIC Lectures, 16: 50 1/2.

[28] The term monopsony has become widely used in economics textbooks since World War II to denote a market situation consisting of a single buyer and a large number of competitive sellers. The monopsonist (single buyer) is able to exploit competition on the supply side of a market in a manner comparable to monopolistic exploitation of demand.

general shortage of capacity would not be reached for some time after the launching of an emergency program, depending on the size and tempo of the program. In any case, competitive bidding should continue to be used for each item of procurement as long as the existence of unused capacity provided genuine competition.[29]

Before any of these principles of contract placement could be put to the test, it was necessary to obtain clear authority allowing freedom of negotiation. The basic statute on government procurement, *Revised Statute* 3709, permitted direct purchases without advertising where immediate delivery was required by "the public exigency." But this provision had not been generally invoked for World War I until after war had been declared, and it was difficult to get agreement on what constituted an emergency sufficient to warrant administrative adoption in peacetime of a fundamental change of policy.[30] This difficulty had been dramatically indicated by the Foulois investigation concerning Army Air Corps procurement. As recently as 1934, a year after Hitler's rise to power in Germany, Maj. Gen. Benjamin D. Foulois—the Chief of the Army Air Corps—had been violently criticized for his aggressive use of the negotiated contract in attempting to build up the U.S. air arm. A committee of Congress reported that General Foulois had "willfully and deliberately violated existing law in the purchase of airplane and aircraft material" and recommended that he be relieved from his position as Chief of the Air Corps." Despite the fact that aircraft procurement by negotiation was authorized under a special statute and that the legality of the purchases in question was subsequently upheld by the Comptroller General, the investigating committee was able to report a number of months later that "we are informed that Major General Foulois has been stripped and shorn by the War Department of much of his power and authority." [31]

After the Foulois episode the purchase of aircraft in quantity under negotiated contracts was discontinued in favor of standardized competitive bidding procedures.[32] But by the summer of 1939, with war in Europe imminent, Assistant Secretary of War Louis Johnson felt that the time had come to greatly speed up procedures for aircraft procurement. On 10 July 1939, at a Washington conference of aircraft manufacturers and War Department officials, Mr. Johnson announced that a bill would shortly be introduced before the House authorizing "negotiation" as distinguished from existing procedures of contract placement.[33] No immediate action was taken by Congress; the outbreak of war in Europe in September was followed by the period of lethargy known as the "phony" war which lasted until the spring of 1940. But shortly after

---

[29] (1) Maj Minton, AIC Lectures, 14: 550, especially p. 600, remarks of Comdr Frank Dunham. (2) Maj Scott B. Ritchie, Planning Br OASW, The Allocation Division, 9 Dec 38, AIC Lectures, 15: 555. (3) Col MacMorland, AIC Lectures, 15: 589 1/2. (4) Col Hare, AIC Lectures, 17: 370–73. (5) Capt Cheever, AIC Lectures, 12: 336.

[30] Ltr of SW Newton D. Baker, 12 Apr 17 (WD GO 49, 1917), cited in Maj Ritchie, AIC Lectures, 15: 554 1/2.

[31] (1) *Congressional Record,* Vol. 79 (15 Jun 35), 9389. (2) The investigations were held by a subcommittee of the House Committee on Military Affairs. H. Rpt. 2060, 73d Cong., 2d Sess., 15 Jun 34. (3) This episode is recounted in some detail in Holley, Buying Airpower, Chapter VI.

[32] Col John W. N. Schulz, CE, Dir Current Procurement OASW, The Current Procurement Branch, OASW, 17 Feb 40, AIC Lectures, 16: 419 1/2.

[33] Zimmerman, Procurement in the United States Air Forces, 1938–1948, pp. 65–66.

the fall of France in June 1940, the desired provision was included as a major element of the National Defense Expediting Act, which authorized the Army to make all defense purchases "with or without advertising." [34]

The use of the negotiated contract for World War II proceeded substantially according to the pattern envisaged by procurement planning. The Army, immediately making wide use of its new powers, obligated the vast bulk of its procurement funds during the defense period under contracts classified as "negotiated." The great expansion of the aircraft industry, the construction of government-owned industrial facilities, the camp and cantonment construction program, and major supply contracts for guns, tanks, ammunition, and heavy equipment were undertaken almost exclusively on the legal foundations and informal administrative procedures of the negotiated contract. All of the Army's CPFF contracts and most of its large fixed-price contracts were of the negotiated variety.

The term "negotiation," as applied to the method of contract placement, was not used in the enabling statutes but came to be widely used in administrative discussions and regulations. It was defined early in 1943 in Army Procurement Regulations as "any method of contracting or purchasing, except the formal advertising and sealed bid procedure prescribed by Section 3709, Revised Statutes." [35] This definition did not preclude the use of advertising or competitive bidding where these were deemed desirable; it merely freed the agencies from the *compulsory* use of advertising, and the *compulsory* award of contracts to low bidders after ad-

vertising and bidding had been used. This freedom of procuring agencies to pick and choose among bidders after "informal" advertising was upheld by the Comptroller General early in the defense period: "The greater includes the lesser, and to the extent that such contracts may be negotiated without advertising, they may be made on the same conditions after advertising." [36]

Nevertheless, as anticipated in the planning period, there were many classes of procurement at the beginning of the emergency for which the discontinuance of public advertising and award to low bidders was neither desirable nor practicable. Since there was an abundance of idle capacity and vigorous competition at the beginning of the defense period, solicitation of bids from all potential suppliers promoted economy and fairness in the placement of contracts. Hence, in the procurement of most commercial and semicommercial items, the Army's supply arms and services continued to make use of existing channels of advertising and solicitation—although on a streamlined basis—as long as effective competition remained. The following remarks, made by an OASW official in the fall of 1940, reveal why the Quartermaster Corps did not abandon competitive bidding at that time:

Naturally with proper authority you can negotiate, you can just go to a firm and negotiate . . . but the Quartermaster Corps has been reluctant to do that because it hasn't been necessary. They have done a swell job of planning in that Corps and know where facilities are and what they want them to do and they want them to go under competitive bidding. It is more healthy.

The allocation system is based on plans for a major military effort. This is not a major military effort, except, you might say, in the

---

[34] 54 *Stat.* 712, 2 Jul 40. For additional legislation, see above, pages 220–22.

[35] PR 203.1 (2–8–45).

[36] B–12733, 9 Oct. 40, 20 Comp. Gen. 194.

Air Corps. Probably in some parts of the Ordnance Department . . . The Quartermaster Corps hasn't enough orders to place to interest facilities that it has allocated for its war load. It is really almost pathetic. That is why the Quartermaster Corps doesn't want to go to negotiated contracts.[37]

Available statistics indicate that in the first half of the defense period the bulk of the Army's procurement program, as measured by dollar value, was launched under contracts placed "without advertising." In his testimony before the Truman Committee in 1941, Under Secretary Patterson stated that, in the period 1 July 1940 to 1 March 1941, the War Department had placed contracts totaling an estimated $6,062 million. Of this total, approximately $4,447 million had been placed by "negotiation", and $1,615 million had been let to the lowest responsible bidder pursuant to advertising. Thus, in the first eight months of the defense period—when purchases soared to nearly ten times their value during the previous twelve months—74 percent of the value of War Department contracts had been placed by negotiation and only 26 percent by advertising. This contrasts with the record for the twelve months ending 30 June 1940, in which over 87 percent of the War Department's total purchases of $776 million had been made through advertising and invitations to bid. (*See Table 26, page 218.*)

On the other hand most small contracts—representing in number more than 99 percent of all contracts placed during the first eight months of the defense period— were the result of open competitive bidding. The figure of $1,615 million in awards to low bidders after advertising represented some 733,000 individual contracts; the value figure of $4,447 million for negotiated

contracts represented less than 6,000 individual contracts.[38]

These figures were possible because of the revolution in Army contract placement procedures which took place during this period. The formalities and restrictions which previously characterized public advertising were streamlined and relaxed until advertising became one of the instruments of contract placement by negotiation.[39] For negotiated contracts many steps taken under formal advertising were telescoped or discarded completely. Instead of resting upon the highly legalistic and passive type of solicitation characterized by peacetime circularization, posting of bulletins, and periodical advertising, contracting officers during the defense period aggressively solicited bids by telegram, telephone, and direct correspondence. For fairly sizable procurements, awards could even be made on the strength of information received over the telephone.[40] Moreover, with the development of letters of intent and other preliminary contractual instruments, contractors could be selected and committed to a project immediately; work could begin at once while company engineers and con-

---

[37] Col Hare, AIC Lectures, 17: 370, 373.

[38] Figures for the first eight months of the defense period, as cited by Under Secretary Patterson, are taken from Truman Committee, Hearings, 1: 29.

[39] Thus, as early as the fall of 1939, the peacetime advertising period of sixty days for the Medical Department was reduced to fifteen days. Memo, Lt Col Robert D. Harden for ASW, 26 Sep 39, SGO 400.12–1. Comparable streamlining of all steps in the procurement process was done by the several technical services to meet the requirements of large-scale rearmament.

Equally significant was the freedom to reject the low bidder after advertising, as indicated above, page 246.

[40] For example, in the case of the Quartermaster Corps, up to $5,000. At the end of 1941 this figure was raised to $50,000. Yoshpe and Massen, QMC Procurement Policies, pp. 61, 67.

tracting officers co-operated to develop additional specifications and contract terms.

The taking of informal bids and the use of price comparisons in making awards was standard procedure in the placement of contracts by negotiation. But in a more general sense the Army attempted to place all its negotiated contracts on a competitive basis, that is, on the basis of the ability of each contractor most effectively to supply the Army's procurement needs as represented by each contract. The significant change in the shift to negotiation was not abandonment of competition but the abandonment of one particular variable—lowness of formal bid price—among a complex of important variables as the governing determinant in the award of contracts. The following illustration, taken from the record of Medical Department procurement, indicates that the role of competition under the negotiated contract was significant, but that it was not confined to considerations of price:

. . . the Medical Department promptly utilized its new power to negotiate contracts. In August 1940, for example, a meeting was held in the New York depot, attended by representatives of surgical dressings manufacturers. Purchasing officers outlined the huge requirements of these items and emphasized the necessity of procuring them with all possible speed. Representatives were urged to submit bids promptly and were informed that contracts would be awarded on the basis of (1) delivery time, (2) price, and (3) production capacity of each firm. On the following day, when the meeting was resumed, the requirements in surgical dressings were allocated on a percentage basis to the firms represented. Within two weeks contracts had been drawn up and signed, and the mills began to produce the great quantities needed.[41]

[41] Capt Richard E. Yates, The Procurement and Distribution of Medical Supplies in the Zone of the Interior during World War II (31 May 1946), p. 32, copy in OCMH.

Despite its formal repudiation of low price as the controlling factor in the placement of contracts, negotiation became potentially the best guarantor of low prices as the defense program matured, shortages appeared, and competition declined in one sector of the economy after another. Long before Pearl Harbor the drying up of competition in specific lines was reflected by artificially high bids, the "step-laddering" of bid prices in successive proposals, and the reluctance or even refusal of firms to accept procurement contracts.[42] Under the flexible procedures of contract negotiation, with the powers of compulsory orders, requisitioning, and commandeering in the background, contracting officers could deal directly with specific firms in obtaining the placement of contracts at prices bearing a reasonable relationship to production costs. Nevertheless, neither negotiation nor any other method of contract placement could guarantee reasonable prices or successful procurement in the absence of effective control over the distribution of raw materials, the general price level, and other features of the economy as a whole.

Controversy Over Competitive Bidding

By the first quarter of 1942 the Army's retention of competitive bidding on even a partial and informal basis had come under criticism in testimony before the Tolan Committee of the House and the Truman Committee of the Senate. Procurement delays, the concentration of prime contracts among large firms, the difficulties faced by small business, the migration of labor to congested areas, and other undesirable aspects of the rearmament program mentioned in preced-

[42] Yoshpe, Production Control in the QMC, p. 60.

ing pages were attributed in varying degree to the reluctance or failure of contracting officers and their superiors to abandon completely the procedures of competitive bidding.[43] The publicity attending these statements, and their frequent repetition both during and after the war, went far toward establishing a standard version of events in this area of the history of World War II. According to this version, Army procurement officers were not alert to the necessity for speed during the defense period; competitive bidding should have been abandoned from the outset; failure to do so resulted from inertia, timidity, and other generally insufficient reasons; and finally, the Army was rescued from its self-imposed predicament by the joint impact of Pearl Harbor and pressure from civilian mobilization agencies. The following statements illustrate the viewpoint in question and indicate several distinct facets of the controversy over the Army's retention of competitive bidding:

The War and Navy Departments, accustomed to small-scale, meticulous, and slow purchasing procedures, had to be shocked into altering their practices to meet the necessities of larger-scale operation. . . . Legislation was required . . . to permit the negotiation of contracts. Congress granted the necessary authority in several acts, but it was not easy for contracting officers, mindful of a reckoning to come for inevitable errors of judgment, to shake off their habitual methods of slow and careful action.[44]

Against these suggestions [to begin purchasing on a really big scale, and others] the military put up surprising resistance. They were reluctant to give up the old system of competitive bidding, which protected each individual procurement officer against suspicion of unwise or improper purchases.[45]

Formal advertising and competitive bidding persisted, orders were placed without regard to the "allocation boundaries" worked out for the various services, and the whole system of M-Day procurement based on "Schedules of Production" signed by allocated facilities within the districts became overlaid with a conflicting pattern of current orders. . . . it was obvious that its [OASW's] insistence on the principle of competitive bidding and the tight controls and checks and balances imposed to prevent abuse of the negotiation process had sealed the fate of the allocation system from the start.

With the principle of contract negotiation with allocated facilities unable to supplant the existing practice of formal and informal advertising for bids, the basic structure of war planning fell apart.[46]

Turning promptly to the fulfillment of its mission, the WPB swept away the formal advertising method.[47]

[WPB Directive No. 2] afforded contracting officers the latitude which they needed to give proper consideration to the attainment of speed and quality of performance, the efficient use of materials, manpower and facilities, the distribution of orders among small war plants, and avoidance of tight labor areas, the maintenance of adequate labor standards, and innumerable other desirable objectives in contract placement.[48]

These statements all contain elements of truth or correct representations of conditions obtaining at certain times for particular items or areas in the field of Army

---

[43] (1) H. Rpt. 1879, 77th Cong., 2d Sess., 9 Mar 42, especially pp. 9, 17, 18B, 23, 26–27, 34–37, 50, 55, 90. (2) Truman Committee, *Hearings,* 6: 1584, 1589, 1595, 1607.

[44] U.S. Bureau of the Budget, *The United States at War,* p. 26.

[45] John Fischer, "The Army Takes Over," *Harper's Magazine,* Vol. 190 (May 1945), 484.

[46] AIC R56, Plans for Industrial Mobilization, 1920–1939, p. 76.

[47] Yoshpe and Massen, QMC Procurement Policies, p. 69. This refers to the issuance, on 3 March 1942, of WPB Directive No. 2 requiring the procuring agencies to place contracts by negotiation.

[48] ICAF, RP49, War Department Procurement Program in World War II (August 1946), pp. 11–12, ICAF Library.

procurement. But they fail to reveal a number of important factors essential to a balanced view of the competitive-bidding controversy as a whole. A brief examination of several such factors sheds additional light on the nature of the procurement process and the administrative as well as substantive difficulties faced by those responsible for launching and conducting the procurement program for World War II.

The retention of competitive bidding undoubtedly delayed the placement of individual contracts in particular instances. But considerable study would be required in each instance to determine the effects upon the procurement program as a whole. In many instances—especially for items of the type for which competitive bidding was retained—the simplest and most expenditious procedure for discovering qualified contractors was to use the channels of advertising and solicitation already in existence. Under the deluge of procurement directives which descended upon them during the defense period, procurement officers often found it far more practical to advertise in various ways and let potential suppliers seek out the procuring agency. If this failed, negotiations with particular firms could then be undertaken. In the meantime, while particular bid proposals were in the making, the procurement program as a whole went forward. Harassed and overburdened procurement staff had little opportunity to "sit back and wait"; they were fully occupied with the placement and administration of numerous other, often more important, contracts in all stages of development. Moreover, premature negotiations with particular sources, without sampling currently available capacity, could lead to the selection of less desirable contractors; this, in turn, could

more than nullify the advantages of prompt contract placement.[49]

Most criticisms of the Army's limited retention of competitive bidding originated in complaints by individual firms or communities which did not receive specific contracts or the volume of procurement contracts to which they thought they were entitled. Some of the critics recognized that small firms could not hope to produce as economically as large corporations and that competitive bidding automatically guaranteed the concentration of prime contracts among relatively few firms. As a result, considerable sentiment arose to authorize, and require, the procuring agencies to pay premium prices to small plants and to firms located in distressed areas. In the year after Pearl Harbor, legislation to this effect was passed. During the pre-Pearl Harbor period, however, War Department officials felt that it was both unwise and illegal to use the Army's procurement program for purposes other than equipping the nation's gravely undersupplied troops in time to meet a major crisis. Hence, OASW's original administrative order, instructing the supply arms and services on the use of the power of negotiation granted by the National Defense Ex-

---

[49] In July 1941 Mr. John D. Biggers, the OPM director of Production, testified that the procuring agencies had recently placed approximately $10 billion in defense contracts in a period of about thirty days. Truman Committee, *Hearings*, 6:1615. The tremendous pressure of deadlines and work loads upon inadequate procurement staffs during the defense period was seldom appreciated outside the offices concerned. During the final weeks of the fiscal year, when appropriations had to be spent or be lost to the procuring agency, the pressure to place contracts was enormous. Prospective contractors, well aware of this fact, often took full advantage of their bargaining position in the absence of competitive bidding. Fortunately, a contract renegotiation law was passed early in 1942 to provide a "backstop" against the pricing excesses of hasty negotiation.

pediting Act, stated specifically that this power was to be used only to expedite the national defense program.[50] This order was interpreted as preventing the payment of premium prices without a compensatory benefit in terms of quality of production or speed of delivery and as precluding the placement of contracts with particular firms merely in order to aid small business or distressed communities or at the sacrifice of speed or quality of procurement.[51] The only substantive limitation placed by the OASW directive upon the supply arms in their use of negotiation was the following eminently desirable provision:

In cases of procurement without advertising care will be exercised to obtain such degree of competition by informal inquiry as is practicable in the circumstances with a view to assuring economy and efficiency of procurement, consistent with the essential need of expediting and assuring the accomplishment of the defense program.[52]

Procedurally, the directive required submittal for clearance by OASW of all negotiated contracts in excess of $500,000 and the filing of a statement in the record for each negotiated contract "setting forth briefly the necessity for making procurement without advertising, comparative price and other

pertinent data, and a statement that the price is fair and reasonable."[53] The 2 July 1940 instructions had been anticipated by a lengthy letter on 12 June from the Assistant Secretary announcing a "greatly augmented and accelerated procurement program." This communication put all supply chiefs on notice that they were expected to take "the necessary steps for putting this program into operation without loss of time."[54]

Having thus emphasized the urgency of the defense program and having authorized the use of direct negotiation wherever necessary to the speedy accomplishment of this program, OASW issued no further general instructions on this aspect of contract placement until after Pearl Harbor. On 17 December 1941, Under Secretary Patterson exempted all contracts under $5,000,000 from clearance by OASW and "directed" the use of negotiation "in all cases where that method of procurement will expedite the accomplishment of the war effort."[55]

On the following day the First War Powers Act became law, removing all remaining statutory barriers to speedy procurement. Two and a half months later, in keeping with his decision to decentralize contract clearance to the procuring agencies, Donald Nelson issued War Production Board Directive No. 2. This directive ordered the use of negotiation and standardized for all procuring agencies the criteria for contract placement.[56] Like the earlier OASW instructions, the WPB directive still permitted the use of formal advertising where desirable and required contracting officers to ob-

---

[50] "The authority to purchase without advertising will be resorted to only in cases where this method of procurement is essential to expedite the accomplishment of the defense program." Memo, Col Schulz for CofAC et al., 2 Jul 40, sub: Procurement Without Advertising, par. 3a, copy in Senate, Small Business Hearings, 10: 1303.

[51] ". . . it is impossible to make an award to a firm solely because it needs business or it is in a locality which has not received substantial defense contracts." Memo, TQMG for USW, 22 Mar 41, cited in Harry B. Yoshpe, The Small Business Man and Quartermaster Contracts, 1940–1942 (QMC Historical Study 2, April 1943), p. 16.

[52] Par. 3b of Schulz memo cited above, note 50.

[53] Pars. 3f and 3g, Ibid.

[54] Ltr, Johnson, ASW, to CofAC et al., 12 Jun 40, sub: 1941 Procurement Program, copy in Senate, Small Business Hearings, 10: 1301.

[55] OUSW P&C Gen Dir 81, 17 Dec 41, sub: Decentralization of Procurement.

[56] See below, pages 263 ff.

tain informal bids whenever time permitted:

(a) Except as hereinafter provided, all such departments and agencies shall place all supply contracts relating to war procurement by negotiation;

Provided, That where consistent with the required speed of war procurement, notification of the proposed procurement shall be given to qualified possible contractors and quotations secured from them. The procedure provided by section 3709 of the Revised Statutes (41 U.S.C. sec. 5) shall be used only upon the specific authorization of the Director of Purchases of the War Production Board, or of such person or persons as he may designate.[57]

Whatever its implications for other procuring agencies, it is evident that paragraph (a) of WPB Directive No. 2 did not, in principle, change the War Department's previously issued instructions governing contract placement. The Under Secretary of War had already directed the use of negotion wherever it would serve the war effort; the WPB directive permitted departures from negotiation where negotiation would *not* serve the war effort. Both sets of instructions necessarily left the choice of methods in specific cases to individual contracting officers, subject to approval by higher authority. Since "negotiation," by definition, represented freedom of action for contracting officers, the positive phraseology of the WPB directive—making negotiation the "order of the day"—was unquestionably desirable under the new era symbolized by the passage of the First War Powers Act nearly three months before. Yet it may be doubted that a general directive upon contracting officers, calling for the exercise of previously granted freedom, represented a

genuine revolution in speeding contract placement by staffs already faced with heavy work loads, specific deadlines, and direct orders by superiors in the chain of command to discharge assignments with all possible speed.

In any event the real issues in the controversy over negotiation versus competitive bidding lay deeper than questions concerning the "inertia" of Army officers or their "reluctance" to use new methods. A review of these issues suggests that the complexities of military procurement—especially during the early and formative part of the World War II program—were such that frustrating delays and compromises in contract placement were inevitable despite the use of the best available methods.

Competitive Bidding and Item Standardization—Standardization of military items, and of the spare parts needed to maintain them, was a major consideration in appraising the relative merits of negotiation and competitive bidding. This is illustrated in the crucial area of automotive transportation, more specifically in the procurement of military trucks. Trucks were one of the most important items in the entire field of military procurement, since their availability and adequacy were directly or indirectly essential to all of the Army's logistical and strategic operations. It was in this area that World War I had yielded one of its most painful and significant object lessons and in which procurement planning carried some of its most fruitful possibilities.

The continual breakdowns in Army truck transportation in the theater of operations in World War I had demonstrated conclusively that it was not enough to produce thousands or millions of new vehicles for the Army. Effective truck operations depended upon satisfactory maintenance and repair,

---

[57] WPB Dir 2, 3 Mar 42, par. (a). The authority to allow Army purchases by formal advertising was later delegated to the director of the Purchases Division, ASF. See PR 240.2 (11–23–44).

a function vitally dependent upon simplification and standardization of parts. This in turn required the adoption of a standardized model for each weight category:

American troops in France used over 200 different makes, including some of French and British manufacture, other of Spanish and Italian design, and even a few captured German vehicles. As most parts were not interchangeable, this diversity of types created a spare parts and maintenance problem that was more than difficult—it was impossible. . . . There were some who felt that the only thing that saved motor transport from complete collapse was the Armistice that came on 11 November 1918.[58]

After World War I a long series of attempts by the Quartermaster General to obtain standardization of truck models was defeated by the requirement of competitive bidding. Under the collective weight of laws, regulations, decisions of the Comptroller General, and other pressures, the Quartermaster Corps was forbidden to issue detailed structural specifications for trucks—largely on the ground that trucks were commercial items and that standardization by the Army would eliminate competition. The consequences were inevitable:

Each time the Army announced its intention of buying new trucks, scores of manufacturers submitted bids. Nearly every time a different company was the low bidder and got the contract. As a result, the Army continued to add new makes and models to its heterogeneous collection of trucks left over from the World War.[59]

As one officer expressed it: "Vehicle types and models that fully meet military requirements are not practicable of production in quantity in time of war nor legally procurable in time of peace."[60] By 1936 the commanding officer of the Holabird Depot reported that the different vehicle models in the Army involved "nearly a million items of spare parts which neither the War Department nor any other authority can control."[61] In 1938 Assistant Secretary of War Johnson, addressing a convention in Chicago, branded the situation "absurd" and blamed the laws which required competitive bidding and "compelled the Army to accept the automotive vehicles of the lowest bidder."[62]

On the eve of the launching of the Munitions Program of 30 June 1940, Quartermaster General Edmund B. Gregory took steps to get out from under all the restrictions which had made standardized truck procurement impossible in peacetime. On 19 June he addressed to the Assistant Secretary of War an impressive memorandum, countersigned by the chiefs of four major using arms—Infantry, Field Artillery, Cavalry, and Coast Artillery Corps. In this memorandum he cited, with hearty approval, the following words of a representative of OASW concerning the emergency procurement of trucks: "In time of war we must be practical. We will take the best of our types available and immediately go into mass production."[63] General Gregory went on to state that five principal truck chassis types had been adopted by the Army as standard and that requirements for three

---

[58] Thomson and Mayo, The Ordnance Department: Procurement and Supply of Munitions, Motor Transport Vehicles—the Prewar Era, pp. 9–10.

[59] Ibid., p. 13.

[60] Col Brainerd Taylor, "Military Motor Transport," Army Ordnance, XVII, No. 99 (November–December 1936), 156.

[61] Vernon Carstenson, Motor Transport Under the Quartermaster General, 1903–1942 (1945), p. 59, Historical Sec. OQMG.

[62] Ibid., p. 69.

[63] Quoted from an address by Lt. Col. Edward E. MacMorland, OASW, before the Society of Automotive Engineers at White Sulphur Springs, West Virginia, 10 June 1940.

of these were most satisfactorily met by individual producers whose products had been thoroughly tested over a period of several years. The manufacturers in question—with whom The Quartermaster General (TQMG) wished to negotiate contracts immediately—were Dodge (1½-ton), General Motors (2½-ton), and Mack (6-ton). The Quartermaster General pointed to the grave responsibility involved in the procurement of trucks and the dangers of retaining competitive bidding in time of emergency. He foresaw a breakdown in field transport "due to difficulties of maintenance of varieties of vehicles" unless the desired degree of standardization could be achieved. The memorandum concluded:

This responsibility is now mine and I request the authority to proceed with negotiation of contracts, as indicated above, in order to take advantage of the lessons of motor vehicle maintenance learned from our World War experience. Legal authority for accomplishment will exist upon the enactment of H.R. 9850.[64]

OASW's response to this request was approval of the principle of standardization as well as the placement of contracts by negotiation, with two provisos:

The Assistant Secretary considers it necessary that quotations be obtained for comparative purposes and that no absolute action be taken as to standardization . . . which would give manufacturers a feeling of monopoly as applied to any particular type of truck.

Subject to the foregoing, negotiations may be entered into and recommendations as to award made to this office. In making such rec-

ommendations, full consideration may be given to the desirability of standardization and to additional costs and difficulties that would be entailed by non-standardization.[65]

Although the instructions of OASW called for only informal quotations, OQMG evidently found it simpler or otherwise desirable to obtain quotations through formal solicitation:

In view of the restrictions imposed by the Assistant Secretary of War, the following method will be used in procuring the five (5) types of vehicles in which the greatest degree of standardization is essential:

2½ ton

Regular invitation (accompanied by specifications) will be issued July 9, 1940. Bids to be opened July 25, 1940. This will be a price test, and in case the low bid is not satisfactory consideration will be given to negotiation. Pilot model will be required after award.[66]

Despite its formal appearance, the streamlined bidding procedure adopted by OQMG at this time for major vehicles allowed an average of only fifteen days between invitation and opening of bids and permitted rejection of the low bid without fear of successful challenge by the Comptroller General. This pragmatic and flexible use of competitive bidding enabled it to be properly classed as an instrument of negotiation.

The Quartermaster Corps continued to use advertising in the placement of vehicle contracts until February 1941, when OASW ordered its discontinuance:

On February 4, 1941 this office received instruction from the Under Secretary of War to suspend, until further notice, all public advertising for motor vehicle equipment for the

---

[64] Memo, Gen Gregory, TQMG, for ASW, 19 Jun 40, QM 451 T—M, Procurement FY 1941. TQMG's proposal was personally approved by General Marshall. See Memo, Brig Gen Richard C. Moore, ACofS G–4, for CofS, 3 Jul 40, sub: Procurement of Motor Vehicles by Negotiations (signed: "Approved. Geo. Marshall"). Both memos in OCMH.

[65] 1st Ind, Col Schulz, Dir Current Procurement OASW, 3 Jul 40, to Memo, TQMG for ASW, 19 Jun 40, copy in OHF.

[66] Memo, Brig Gen Richard H. Jordan, OQMG for TQMG, 6 Jul 40, sub: Motor Vehicle Procurement F. Y. 1941, OCMH.

defense program. Such procurement as has been accomplished since this suspension has been handled by securing informal quotations from manufacturers who have previously furnished satisfactory equipment of the various types involved.[67]

Whether and to what extent greater standardization of military vehicles could or should have been achieved is an open question. As compared with its predecessor, World War II witnessed great strides in standardization and reduction in the number of makes and models. Much of this was attributable to the elimination of a multiplicity of producing firms in the course of ordinary commercial competition, and to co-operative efforts toward standardization by the industry itself, during the interwar period when the automobile came of age. Offsetting these developments was the tremendous increase in the number and complexity of automotive items used to wage technological warfare in World War II, and the inevitable pressure for improved and special-purpose models as the war progressed. Under these influences the Army's task of repair and maintenance required the creation of an elaborate organization and complex procedures for the procurement, distribution, and storage of astronomical quantities and varieties of spare parts. As a result the spare part difficulties of the Army reached nightmare proportions and remained as one of the major unresolved logistical problems of World War II.[68] Yet it is doubtful that the limited retention of competitive bidding after 1 July 1940 played

more than a minor role in the creation of this problem.

Competitive Bidding and Manufacturer's Capacity—The view that the Army's partial retention of competitive bidding was not primarily the result of apathy or inertia, and that it was not itself a basic issue, is reinforced by a detailed study of the development and procurement of the jeep.[69] This study, made at the height of the procurement program in World War II, reveals some of the many pressures and conflicts of interest involved in the placement of contracts for a major, well-known, semi-commercial item. The jeep ($\frac{1}{4}$-ton truck) was developed by the American Bantam Company, a small firm which in the judgment of the Office of The Quartermaster General lacked the productive capacity to satisfy the Army's quantitative needs within the required period of time. Early in the defense period, OQMG opposed the desire of Infantry, Field Artillery, and other using arms to place a negotiated contract immediately with American Bantam to fill all the Army's current requirements. OQMG preferred to use competitive bidding in order to keep prices down and to open the field to Willys and Ford. Neither of these firms had shown great interest in producing $\frac{1}{4}$-ton trucks until American Bantam had pioneered a satisfactory model; nevertheless, The Quartermaster General felt that the facilities of Ford and Willys would be badly needed in the months to come. In the long and controversial history of jeep negotiations—during which the American Bantam Company lost out to its large competitors—the several automobile producers, the

---

[67] Memo, Gen Gregory, TQMG, for USW, 1 Apr 41, sub: Procurement Circular 43 WD 1940, OCMH.

[68] Thomson and Mayo, The Ordnance Department: Procurement and Supply of Munitions, Spare Parts.

[69] Herbert R. Rifkind, The Jeep—Its Development and Procurement Under the Quartermaster Corps, 1940–1942 (1943), Historical Sec OQMG.

Quartermaster Corps, the using arms, the Chief of Staff, the Secretary and Under Secretary of War, the NDAC, Congress, newspapers, and the public, all contributed to Army procurement policy. The significant observation for present purposes is the fact that although the jeep controversy, like a number of others, was aired within the framework of the controversy over the use of competitive bidding, the real concerns were the underlying substantive matters which affected the various parties involved.[70] For the Army the major issues were standardization, model improvement, and assurance of production and delivery in quantity. For the popular press and general public the chief concerns were the merits of large versus small business and the Army's seemingly inexplicable desire to award a contract to a large corporation, then under indictment for violation of the National Labor Relations Act, in preference to the small firm which, in co-operation with the Army, had created the item to be produced under the contract in question.[71]

In view of the foregoing as well as from other indications, it would appear that the controversy conventionally labeled as "competitive bidding versus negotiation" was really a complex array of separate issues. Each of these issues involved an element or criterion of contract placement policy of special importance to particular individuals or groups—usually those having a tangible stake in the outcome. So far as the present study is concerned no adequate evidence has come to light to indicate that the Office of the Under Secretary of War imposed any serious or undesirable restrictions upon the supply arms in their use of negotiation or that the supply arms were unduly slow in utilizing their newly received powers. After 1 July 1940, the real and controversial issues were not so much the procedures as the objectives and results of contract placement. These involved such questions as: Who will receive the many billions of dollars in military procurement contracts? How will the distribution of contracts affect the future of the American economy? Shall military procurement objectives prevail regardless of other considerations? What is the proper balance to be obtained among all the various objectives and what methods shall be used to achieve them?

---

[70] Truman Committee, *Hearings,* August 1941, Pt. 7, especially material under caption Competitive Bidding and Awarding of Contract for Army 'Jeep' Cars, at pp. 1971ff., 1980ff., and 2067ff., and Procedure Followed in Allocating Defense Contracts, at pp. 2059ff. and 2074ff.

[71] Further details in the jeep story may be found in: (1) Rifkind, The Jeep; (2) Truman Committee, *Hearings,* Pt. 7; (3) Thomson and Mayo, The

---

Ordnance Department: Procurement and Supply of Munitions, Spare Parts.

CHAPTER XI

General Policies in
Contract Placement and Clearance

Selection of Contractors

Army Selection Policies

Use of Allocated Facilities—The selection of Army contractors at the beginning of the emergency in 1940 was basically oriented by the facility allocation plans prepared during the interwar period. This was especially true for the Ordnance Department but applied in varying degree to the Air Corps and the other supply arms and services. The Quartermaster Corps and the Medical Department, whose procurement responsibility involved a large proportion of commercial-type items, were able to rely heavily upon public advertising to elicit current sources of supply when the emergency came. Yet even for these procuring arms the selection of contractors for most items was guided if not determined by the facility surveys and allocation plans of the previous decade.[1]

No comprehensive statistics are available to indicate precisely the extent to which contract placement in the defense period conformed to the facility allocation plans and accepted schedules of production of the preceding period. Nevertheless, the dominant influence of the prewar plans is evident both from such sample figures as are available and from statements by participants in the procurement program during the defense and war years:

In placing our orders with industry, we are following the "allocation system" whenever possible and practicable. The "education order" programs of 1939 and 1940 and the "production study" program of 1940 have been of great assistance. The net results of these programs will be a saving of funds from the 1940 appropriations, and, more important, a reduced time of delivery for a great many items.[2]

When the burden of the present defense program was placed on the Department, the supply services immediately started operating under the industrial mobilization plan. They promptly placed orders for munitions with plants previously allocated, using informal competition whenever possible.[3]

---

[1] "As it actually turned out, the low bidders were in most cases the plants that had in the past been allocated to do the job . . . . they had the courage to bid the lowest. There were millions of dollars in these first war orders and many manufacturers were afraid of the huge quantities involved. But the allocated plants were the ones that knew what was wanted and how to deal with the services courageously." Col Ray M. Hare, Survey and Allocation of Facilities, 29 Jan 46, ICAF Lecture (L46–16).

[2] Maj Gen Charles M. Wesson, CofOrd, The Current Procurement Situation in the Ordnance Department, 2 Oct 40, AIC Lectures, 17: 345 1/2.

[3] Testimony of USW Patterson, 15 Apr 41, Truman Committee, *Hearings,* 1: 30. Mr. Patterson's prepared statements cited in this and the following footnote contains a wealth of factual information on the launching of the War Department's emergency procurement program.

During the fiscal year 1941 to April 1 of this year, about $2,000,000,000 was appropriated for the use of the Ordnance Department for equipment and ammunition, and an additional $600,000,000 for new facilities. You may be interested to know that 98 percent by amount and 90 percent by number of Ordnance Department awards over $50,000 have been placed with companies which were allocated to the Ordnance Department under the industrial mobilization plan.[4]

A sample study made by the Army Industrial College in the spring of 1945 for all services except the Army Quartermaster Corps and Medical Department estimated that in four major industrial cities an average of 95 percent by value and 63 percent by number of war contracts through February 1943 were awarded to preselected facilities under the allocation plan.[5] Similarly, a Medical survey of contract placements in the calendar year 1940 revealed that, of 253 facilities receiving awards, 172 or 68 percent had previously been allocated to that agency.[6]

The allocation system—like the Industrial Mobilization Plan as a whole—was never invoked on a formal or mandatory basis. By the end of 1940 many orders on

the books of manufacturers conflicted with previously recorded interests and capacity credits as registered in the allocation plans. The conflict was especially evident in the case of allocated firms who had received British and French contracts, as well as "Army" facilities accepting orders placed by the Navy. In addition many adjustments and deviations from plan had been made by individual procuring arms within the War and Navy Departments. All these changes and the failure to place allocations on a mandatory basis at the outset of the emergency, led some observers to the erroneous conclusion that the allocation system had been scrapped in its entirety and the fruits of twenty years of planning "wasted."

Many factors entered into the decision of OASW and ANMB against formal invocation of the allocation system, and most of these had been anticipated in the planning period. Perhaps the chief consideration was the fact that compulsory application of the system had not been considered essential except in the event of a "maximum effort," and the Munitions Program of 30 June 1940 fell considerably short of such an effort.[7] As already indicated in the discussion of the development of the negotiated contract, the planners foresaw that in the face of varying degrees of idle plant capacity considerable flexibility would be required to determine which items and firms would best be handled by allocation and which by competitive bidding. It was recognized, moreover, that facility allocation plans could never be complete or accurate, however conscientious the procuring agencies might be. After mid-1940 many firms who previously had not felt

---

[4] *Ibid.,* 15 Jul 41, Truman Committee, *Hearings,* 6:1521.

[5] Memo, Clarence R. Niklason for Comdt AIC, 4, Apr 45, sub: Project XVII (24) AIC Plans–Use of the Industrialization Plan in World War II, abstract in OCMH. These figures, while consistent with other observations, were based on recorded facility interests (allocations) as of December 1941 and do not afford a direct indication of the use of previously allocated facilities during the defense period. The use of allocations data as of the end of 1941 reflected the assumption that Pearl Harbor, rather the launching of the Munitions Program, best represented the M Day of procurement planning.

[6] Yates, Procurement and Distribution of Medical Supplies in the Zone of the Interior During World War II, p. 30. Dollar figures for the awards in question would no doubt have revealed a higher concentration of procurement in allocated facilities.

---

[7] (1) Maj Ritchie, AIC Lectures, 15: 554½. (2) Col Hare, AIC Lectures, 17: 369, 373. (3) Col Hare, ICAF Lecture (L46–16), pp. 7–8.

it feasible or worth-while to participate in peacetime planning wished to share in the emergency program, and both the Army and Navy considered it desirable to place orders with such firms although they were outside the allocation system. Normally, these firms were surveyed as soon as possible and added to the list of allocated facilities, with the result that the list of recorded interests grew from around ten thousand at the beginning of the defense period to nearly thirteen thousand at the time of Pearl Harbor.[8] (*See Table 12, Page 58.*) At the same time many firms which had been found deficient were dropped from the list of allocated facilities. Business failures, the appearance of new firms, the development or adoption of new items of procurement, changes in quantitative requirements, the recognition of Navy claims upon certain facilities allocated by OASW, and other factors all required changes in facility allocation plans. Under the circumstances the several supply arms were permitted to make as much or as little use of their allocation plans as they found necessary to the accomplishment of their procurement mission.[9]

During this period of informal utilization, the allocation system was marked by vigorous efforts of all the supply arms and services to build up a complete and up-to-date inventory of available industrial facilities for each significant item of procurement. Conflicts of interest among the Army's supply arms and services were, as before, resolved

by OASW. Interdepartmental conflicts, as well as those occasioned by the procurement activities of foreign purchasing missions were resolved by various committees of the Army and Navy Munitions Board in conjunction with the Department of the Treasury. An important circumstance coinciding with the failure to place the facility allocation system in operation on a mandatory basis was the development of the priorities system in a manner not anticipated by the creators of the Industrial Mobilization Plan. This unexpected turn, recounted in detail at a later point, was a ruling of NDAC and OPM limiting the use of priorities to the placement, rather than the implementation, of prime contracts.[10] In this capacity the priorities system tended to assume the function originally contemplated for the facility allocation system.[11] Fortunately, by the beginning of the defense period a basic pattern of facility selection by the various procuring agencies had become well established under the allocation plans. Where shortages of existing capacity gave rise to potential interservice competition, there was a tendency for each procuring arm to negotiate with its own allocated firms for immediate expansion of productive capacity. This kept within bounds the scramble by procuring agencies for prime-contract facilities on the basis of unequally distributed priority currency. At the same time, in areas where excess productive capacity was available, the voluntary application of allocations provided needed flexibility and permitted the use of competitive bidding within the framework of negotiation.

---

[8] Yoshpe and Massen, QMC Procurement Policies, pp. 26–33.

[9] (1) Col Hare, AIC Lectures, 17: 369. (2) Page 30 of Yates MS cited above, Note 6. (3) Capt F. A. Daubin, USN, The Position of the Navy in Procurement Planning, in OASW Planning Br. Rpt, General Procurement Plannnig Conference, 1–2 December 1938, pp. 27–31.

[10] See below, Chapters XXII and XXIII.

[11] Yoshpe and Massen, QMC Procurement Policies, p. 35 and Note 60.

The allocation system had been designed to achieve two principal objectives—speeding up of conversion to war production and elimination of frantic competition among procuring agencies for identical facilities. In the opinion of Army officials most intimately concerned with the launching of the World War II procurement program, the system was successful in the attainment of the stated objectives:

The industrial mobilization plan has worked well in emergency. The 1917 spectacle of the Army and Navy crowding each other in the placing of orders and of the supply services of the Army getting into one another's way in the same plants has not been repeated. Months of valuable time have been saved. That, in the main, is the way contractors have been selected for the production of armament items.[12]

Nobody can deny that the industrial mobilization plan of the Ordnance Department, which I know something about, was carried out, because what Ray Hare has just told us was what I did in Chicago, where I examined personally twelve hundred plants from 1939 to 1940. When the order came in September 1940, I went to work with those plants that I knew, that were allocated to the Ordnance Department. So allocation does work.[13]

In view of the absence of compulsory allocation of facilities at the beginning of the defense period, a fundamental question naturally arises: What saved the World War II procurement program from the mad, competitive scramble for facilities which is reported to have all but wrecked the World War I program? Part of the answer, as already suggested, is to be found in two basic conditions which were not present for World War I. These were first, the eighteen long months between June 1940 and 7 December

1941, and second, the twenty years of prewar study, planning, and indoctrination in the field of procurement and economic mobilization. During the eighteen months of the defense period many mistakes, false starts, and conflicts were experienced and resolved which could not have been successfully hurdled in a much shorter period of time. In the twenty years of prewar planning, the various procuring arms and agencies had determined both a specific pattern of facility interests and the general principles for resolving conflicts of such interests. Like a system of ethics whose successful operation depends basically upon a knowledge of facts and consequences, the whole history of the allocation system during the interwar years provided the procuring agencies with essential knowledge and the will to co-operate. The self-restraint of the procuring agencies in World War II owed much to the enlightenment of the planning period. In a very real sense the allocation system succeeded without ever having been placed in formal operation:

Once the war purchasing program began, there was no effort to confine the procuring agencies to their allocated facilities or the plants to their previously accepted schedules of production although the various procuring agencies did respect each other's early plans. The allocation system had done its job. Actual contracts replaced the theoretical loads that had been placed to develop the capacity during the planning period.[14]

Other Factors in Contractor Selection— The most important requirement of Army contract placement policy throughout the defense and war periods was the ability of individual firms to produce munitions in the desired quality, quantity, and speed. But capacity to produce, in either the quantita-

[12] Testimony of USW Patterson, 15 Apr. 41, Truman Committee, *Hearings,* 1: 30.

[13] Statement of Brig Gen Donald Armstrong, Comdt AIC, 29 Jan 46, ICAF Lecture (L46–16), p. 9.

[14] Col Hare, ICAF Lecture (L46–16), p. 12.

tive or qualitative sense, was often an un-known and changing magnitude which, in advance of performance, could only be esti-mated and typically had to be developed and improved in the process of contract ad-ministration. Few if any manufacturing firms at the beginning of the defense period had the plant, equipment, and workers es-sential to the production and delivery of munitions called for by the war contracts which they ultimately received and fulfilled.

Under these circumstances, and after least price ceased to be a legal requirement of contract placement, many subsidiary factors played a part in the selection of con-tractors. With the launching of the Muni-tions Program, OASW foresaw that the sudden impact of large-scale procurement would be likely to create congestion of labor and serious overloading of such facilities as power and communications in particular areas. Supply arms and services were there-fore instructed to consider these problems, as well as the desirability of increasing na-tional productive capacity, in the placement of contracts.[15] By the spring of 1941, it had become apparent that performance ability on the part of individual contractors was becoming more and more dependent upon the availability of materials, parts, supplies, skilled labor, and other factors reflecting the status of the economy as a whole. As steadily rising requirements used up more and more available productive capacity, it was evident that large numbers of new and untried firms would have to be brought into the defense effort. Accordingly, the Army gave increasing attention to the splitting of awards among a number of producers,

avoiding dependence upon sole sources, and financing the creation of new facilities in all lines of production connected with the de-fense effort. By means of its authority to certify the expansion of industrial facilities under the tax amortization program, the Army played a major role in developing a broad and substantial foundation of produc-tive capacity widely dispersed throughout the national economy.[16]

By the fall of 1941, the rearmament pro-gram had brought about a number of unde-sirable consequences for the economy as a whole. These included "priorities unemploy-ment" (shutdowns resulting from material shortages) in numerous industries and com-munities, undesirable migration and con-centration of labor, shortages of housing, transportation, and other community facil-ities, and drastic shortages of machine tools and related equipment. From the stand-point of both national morale and efficient production, it was necessary to modify con-tract placement policies to relieve these con-ditions so far as possible. In a directive to the supply arms and services dated 5 September 1941, OASW established additional pro-cedures and policies to intensify the extent of subcontracting, to relieve distressed com-munities and industries, and to spread prime contracts more widely among small firms. In order to assist distressed industries and communities unable to obtain contracts on a competitive basis, price differentials up to 15-percent above low bid prices were au-thorized in the placement of prime contracts, and prime contractors could be reimbursed for similar differentials paid to subcontrac-tors. Subcontracting was further encouraged by giving preference in the award of prime contracts to firms who would make max-imum use of subcontracting. All bid pro-

---

[15] Memo, Col Schulz, Dir Current Procurement OASW, for CofAC *et al.,* 2 Jul 40, sub: Procure-ment Without Advertising, copy in Senate, *Small Business Hearings,* 10: 1303.

[16] See below, Chapter XX.

posals in excess of $50,000 had to carry a statement of the percentage of intended subcontracting and this statement became a part of the final contract. Requests upon supply arms by the Defense Contract Service of OPM to confine bids to particular regions in order to alleviate unemployment were to be granted unless departures from this policy were specifically approved. In order to insure the maximum use of existing machine tools, no new machine tool deliveries or priorities were to be given contractors, under either existing or new contracts, so long as qualified subcontracting facilities were available.[17]

Ten days after Pearl Harbor additional steps were taken to expedite selection of contractors and making of contract awards. Additional emphasis was placed upon the use of the negotiated contract, and supply arms and services were ordered to decentralize as rapidly as possible their machinery for contract placement. Contracts for new construction and machine tool installations were to be kept to an absolute minimum.[18] On 14 January 1942, OUSW issued a new directive stressing the importance of making the best utilization of each productive facility. To this end facilities capable of doing precision or other high-caliber work were to be reserved for such purposes; manufacture of simpler items and components was to be assigned, so far as possible, to secondary facilities and subcontractors. Contracting officers were reminded that increased prices could be paid for additional subcontracting needed to speed the defense program; they were also urged to provide for maximum subcontracting at the time of award, rather than to assume that this could be arranged after awards were made.[19]

Under the new urgency which confronted the nation after Pearl Harbor, direct negotiation of contracts without even the informal bidding of the defense period was used on a wide scale, and it became desirable for the central mobilization control agency to establish a uniform set of contract placement policies which would reflect the new conditions and govern all the procuring agencies. This was done in March 1942 by the War Production Board. As indicated in the following section, these policies underwent a number of modifications throughout the remainder of the war to reflect the changing posture of economic mobilization.[20]

Criteria Established by Central Control Agencies

At its first regular meeting on 21 June 1940, the National Defense Advisory Commission took steps to formulate a set of broad principles to be observed by the procuring agencies in the placement of defense contracts. Early in the meeting, Commissioner Hillman introduced a memorandum

---

[17] Memo, Brig Gen Harry K. Rutherford, Ex OASW, for Chfs of Supply Arms and Services, 5 Sep 41, sub: Distribution of Defense Orders, and 4 incls, copy in Senate, *Small Business Hearings*, 10: 1311.

[18] OUSW P&C Gen Dir 81, 17 Dec 41, sub: Decentralization of Procurement.

[19] OUSW P&C Gen Dir 8, 14 Jan 42, sub: Selection of Contractors for War Production.

[20] Special criteria in the selection of contractors for particular types or classes of procurement are discussed in the various histories of the technical services appearing in the series UNITED STATES ARMY IN WORLD WAR II. One of the most interesting and controversial areas of contractor selection was the field of construction, especially for Army camps and War Department-owned munitions plants. This subject is discussed in Jesse A. Remington and Lenore Fine, The Corps of Engineers: Military Construction in the United States, a volume in preparation for the series UNITED STATES ARMY IN WORLD WAR II, MS, OCMH.

setting forth the considerations which he believed important in placing negotiated contracts. In his statement, Hillman urged that contracts be so placed as to put existing idle equipment and labor to work, thereby avoiding the delay and expense of constructing new facilities. He also stressed the effective utilization and conservation of various labor skills, and the advantages to be realized from following the proposed policies.[21] At its next meeting the Advisory Commission adopted the Hillman memorandum, with minor changes, as a preliminary statement of commission policy to be used by the Coordinator of Purchases in developing purchase policy.[22]

On 28 August 1940 a three-man committee, under the chairmanship of Donald Nelson, was appointed to develop a comprehensive set of contract placement principles to be used both by the procuring agencies and by NDAC in exercising its clearance function. The policy statement prepared by this committee was formally adopted by the commission in its 6 September 1940 meeting and was released to the press. This statement set forth the following twelve criteria of contract placement:

1. speed of delivery;
2. quality of product;
3. price;
4. impact of defense program upon consumers;
5. adequate consideration of labor;
6. geographic dispersion of orders;
7. financial responsibility of suppliers;
8. avoidance of congestion of transportation facilities;
9. adequacy of power facilities;

10. preference to firms experienced under educational orders;
11. moral responsibility of suppliers;
12. use of negotiated contract whenever necessary to obtain above objectives.

The NDAC declaration contained a brief elaboration of each of these criteria and closed with a statement of labor policy to be observed in the placement of contracts. The labor statement emphasized the importance of conserving the humanitarian gains reflected by such legislation as the Walsh-Healey Act, the Fair Labor Standards Act, the National Labor Relations Act, and others.[23]

Although procurement policy was in a state of ferment throughout the remainder of the defense period, the Office of Production Management—successor to NDAC—made no formal changes in the contract placement principles adopted by the Advisory Commission.[24] But with the revolution wrought by Pearl Harbor many of the older criteria became obsolete. All of the government's functions and agencies for purchasing, contract clearance, and contract administration were reviewed and overhauled. The War Production Board's Directive No. 2 of 3 March 1942 not only required all procuring agencies to place their supply contracts by negotiation;[25] the directive also set forth the several criteria, in order of importance, to be observed in contract placement. At this time three criteria were stated, in the following order: (1) speed of delivery; (2) conserving of superior facilities for the more difficult items of production; (3) placement of contracts with firms needing the least amounts of addi-

---

[21] CPA, *NDAC Minutes*, mtg of 21 Jun 40, p. 2. The Hillman memorandum became NDAC Document No. 1.

[22] *Ibid.*, mtg of 28 Jun 40, p. 17.

[23] *Ibid.*, pp. 82–83.

[24] CPA, *Industrial Mobilization for War*, p. 142.

[25] See above, page 249.

tional machinery and equipment.[26] As indicated above, all these factors had been covered in previous War Department directives although, except for the first, no order of importance had been given.

Developments during the remainder of 1942 led to further modification of the general criteria for the selection of contractors. The Small Business Act, passed in the summer of 1942, required that special efforts be made in spreading war business among small firms. Also, with the induction of more and more men into the armed forces, serious labor shortages began to develop in many communities. Accordingly, on 10 October 1942, WPB Directive No. 2 was amended to give both labor-shortage and small-plant problems a place in the criteria of contract placement. At the same time, lowest price was added as a final criterion after all others had been met. The order of importance of the several factors was then as follows:

1. Speed of delivery.
2. Avoidance of new machinery requirements.
3. Avoidance of labor-shortage areas.
4. Conservation of special abilities.
5. Spreading production among as many firms as possible.
6. Lowest price.[27]

At this time the procedures for applying these criteria were in a rudimentary stage of development, especially in the case of the labor-shortage and small-plant problems. During the following year the War Manpower Commission drew up a careful classification of labor-shortage areas, indicating the relative degrees of labor shortage or surplus in various parts of the country. This classification was changed from time to time throughout the remainder of the war to reflect changes in underlying conditions, and procurement officers were required to place contracts accordingly. Specific details governing the placement of contracts according to labor-area classification were elaborated and stated in the Army's Procurement Regulations.[28]

Intensification of labor shortages and increasing awareness of the necessity for sound pricing led to a revaluation of the factors in contract placement in the fall of 1943. At this time WPB Directive No. 2 was again amended, reclassifying the priority of placement factors as follows:

1. Prompt delivery;
2. Manpower considerations;
3. Five other factors to be evaluated for individual contracts:
   a. Cost and efficiency of production:
   b. Small business concerns;
   c. Conservation of special abilities;
   d. Avoidance of creating new facilities;
   e. Saving of transportation.[29]

Under this amendment additional contract commitments in the critical west coast labor area were forbidden without prior approval of the War Production Board chairman or his designated representative. The inclusion of cost and efficiency of production reflected the realization that loose pricing encouraged the wasteful use of real resources, not merely of dollars and cents. Preference in the award of contracts was

---

[26] WPB Dir 2, 3 Mar 42. This directive was implemented within the War Department by Purchases Br SOS Gen Dir 34, 9 Apr 42, sub: Negotiated Purchases.

[27] WPB Dir 2, amended 10 Oct. 42.

[28] (1) PR 223.1–223.6 (2–8–45). (2) Byron Fairchild and Jonathan P. Grossman, The Army and Industrial Manpower, a volume in preparation for the series UNITED STATES ARMY IN WORLD WAR II, MS, OCMH.

[29] WPB Dir 2, amended 18 Sep 43.

therefore to be given to contractors who were willing to adopt close initial prices which would force a maximum of efficiency during the life of each contract. The emphasis under this criterion was not so much low procurement prices as efficiency in the use of manpower, materials, and other productive resources.

No formal changes in the September 1943 version of WPB Directive No. 2 were made for nearly a year and a half. There were, of course, many changes and refinements in the Army's application of the criteria of contract placement. Thus, in the case of labor-shortage areas, price premiums up to 15-percent above lowest bid prices could be made by contracting officers in order to encourage the placement of contracts outside the two most critical (Groups I and II) shortage areas. In the case of small business, the allowable premium ran to 15-percent above the average at which the purchase could be made from large firms. In both cases, the Purchases Division, ASF, could approve premiums up to 25 percent, and differentials above 25 percent could be authorized by the Commanding General, ASF.[30]

The establishment of production urgency committees in tight labor areas led to the modification on 10 February 1945 of the manpower criterion of WPB Directive No. 2. Under this amendment no new contracts or supplements, with certain specified exceptions, could be placed in Group I labor areas without the prior approval of the area Production Urgency Committee.[31]

The last major revision of WPB Directive No. 2 took place on 12 May 1945. After the collapse of Germany and the shift to a one-front war, policies had to be revised to retain and insure adequate war production while making provision for the reconversion of the national economy. In this revision the criteria of contractor selection were as follows:

1. Prompt delivery;
2. Manpower considerations;
3. Six other factors to be considered when relevant:
   a. Cost and efficiency;
   b. Release of multiple purpose plants;
   c. Avoidance of new facilities creation;
   d. Saving of transportation;
   e. Release of privately owned plants;
   f. Preference to small firms.[32]

The details of this amendment allowed wider discretion in the placement of contracts in manpower-shortage areas; thus renewal contracts could be placed in Group I (acute shortage) areas under various conditions so long as manpower ceilings for particular firms were not exceeded. The factors involving conservation of special abilities and spreading the work among a number of plants were eliminated. Release of privately owned plants from war production and retention of production in government-owned plants enabled private firms to get started in their individual tasks of reconversion. Also, preference in the placement of remaining war contracts was to be given to plants specializing in the type of work called for by the contract; multiple purpose plants capable of producing a variety of products were to be released for civilian work or other lines of war production. Finally, the May 1945 amendment pointed out that the factor of lower price (covered by 3a Cost and efficiency) would

---

[30] (1) ASF, History of Purchases Division, p. 100–101. (2) PR 223.8 (10–5–44).

[31] (1) WPB Dir 2, amended 10 Feb 45. (2) PR 223.2–223.6 (2–8–45).

[32] WPB Dir 2, amended 12 May 45.

grow in importance as manpower, transportation, and other shortages were overcome.

The foregoing summary indicates that the official policies governing placement of contracts were steadily modified to meet underlying changes in the war economy. Needless to say, there was often a divergence between announced policy and actual performance, and some policies were implemented more vigorously than others. For example, many who were actually engaged in the World War II procurement program felt that the Army's small war plants procedures were considerably more successful than those designed to prevent the placement of contracts in labor-shortage areas. Whereas the small plants program was represented by a specialized small war plants officer in each procurement office, the policing of manpower regulations was divided among the ASF Industrial Personnel, Purchases, and Production Divisions. More significantly, local production urgency committees, whose task it was to deny contracts to their particular areas, were composed predominantly of local personnel who found it extremely difficult to discharge this unpleasant function.[33]

Contract Clearance

External Clearance

From the beginning of the defense period until three months after Pearl Harbor, all important War Department contracts were subject to review and approval, prior to actual placement, by the National Defense Advisory Commission and its successor agencies. As early as 6 June 1940, when the basic functions of the newly established Advisory Commission were undergoing definition, President Roosevelt announced that all "important" contracts of the services would be cleared by the NDAC commissioner for defense, Mr. Knudsen.[34] Some two weeks later the NDAC's clearance authority was given a limited statutory basis in the First Supplemental National Defense Appropriations Act of 26 June 1940.[35] Within a short time the clearance requirement was administratively interpreted to cover all contracts in excess of $500,000, as well as all CPFF contracts and other important cases.[36]

The purpose of contract clearance was to insure that all major procurement contracts would be let in conformity with the various criteria of contract placement formulated by the central mobilization control agency. As already indicated, the initial criteria adopted by NDAC were more numerous and heterogeneous than those in the streamlined list adopted by the War Production Board after Pearl Harbor. Because of the number of issues raised by the NDAC list, the limited time available for clearance, and the fact that each NDAC commissioner had a potential interest in the terms of each contract, difficulties were inevitable. As a matter of administrative necessity the

---

[33] ASF, History of Purchases Division, pp. 110–12. For additional material, including other factors limiting the effectiveness of the urgency committees, see CPA, *Industrial Mobilization for War*, especially pp. 842–45, 854.

[34] CPA, *Industrial Mobilization for War*, p. 24.
[35] 54 *Stat.* 602–03. This applied only to expenditures of the War Department's Expediting Funds. In February 1941 the Attorney General ruled that so far as the appropriation statutes were concerned the NDAC's clearance functions were purely advisory. CPA, *Industrial Mobilization for War*, p. 25.
[36] (1) Memos, OASW for TQMG, 10 and 13 Jun 40, sub: Approval of Important Purchases by the Advisory Commission to Council of National Defense. (2) Memo, OASW for TQMG and CofOrd, 14 Oct 40. All cited in Yoshpe and Massen, QMC Procurement Policies, p. 64.

NDAC soon centered the clearance function in two individuals and their staffs—Mr. Knudsen, who cleared all major "hard goods" contracts (chiefly ordnance and aircraft), and Donald Nelson, who as Coordinator of Purchases was responsible for commercial-type items procured for the Army mainly by the Quartermaster Corps.

The requirement of contract clearance by the NDAC and its successors increasingly became a thorn in the side of the Army's supply arms and services, as well as the War Department as a whole. Since the clearance function could not be properly exercised without providing information to NDAC at numerous stages in the development of the Army's constantly changing and expanding procurement plans, the necessary procedures involved considerable duplication of effort and became excessively time consuming. Coming on top of the War Department's own screening procedures, as well as in a period when the procuring arms were understaffed and trying to make up for lost time, these requirements were certain to cause irritation. Moreover, the contract placement policies of the Advisory Commission differed in important respects from those of the actual procuring agencies. The primary concern of the Army and Navy—in accordance with their statutory mission—was the ability of prospective contractors to deliver, on schedule, finished munitions of adequate quantity and quality. The NDAC, on the other hand, also endeavored to control the defense program in such a way as to relieve unemployment of manpower and plant facilities in depressed areas, to conserve the gains of recent social legislation, to prevent profiteering in certain types of war contract, and to strengthen and balance the national economy for the long run.

Because of the great need for new manufacturing facilities for many kinds of munitions, one of the most important areas of the NDAC's clearance activities lay in the field of plant location approvals. Despite the haste with which most of these projects had to be pushed through, the NDAC made its influence felt, both in locating individual plants within a given area and in observing a policy of spreading new industrial facilities throughout the southern and western portions of the United States.[37]

One of the earliest issues in the area of contract clearance was the question of whether defense contracts should be placed with firms in violation of the National Labor Relations Act. This issue was brought to a head by protests of labor organizations against the award of contracts to the Ford Motor Company and two smaller firms then under indictment for labor law violations unrelated to the defense program. As a result of these protests, President Roosevelt sent a letter to the NDAC raising the question of clearance procedure in such cases. Shortly thereafter when the commission was reviewing the placement of an important aircraft engine contract, Commissioner Hillman indicated that the labor problem was more serious than the commission as a whole realized.[38] Nevertheless, since the Ford Motor Company was the only suitable facility readily available, the contract was awarded, although not without considerable irritation to all concerned.[39]

Another frequent issue in contract clearance was the question of whether prices in

[37] CPA, NDAC Minutes, pp. 34–35, 56, 147, and Index entry, Plant Sites, p. 176. See below, pages 447–50.

[38] CPA, NDAC Minutes, pp. 117, 122.

[39] (1) CPA, Industrial Mobilization for War, p. 59. (2) ASF, History of Purchases Division, p. 45. (3) Fairchild and Grossman, The Army and Industrial Manpower.

supply contracts included any element of
the cost of facilities for the items involved.[40]
The NDAC feared that contractors would
be reimbursed twice for the facility costs—
once in the price of the product, and separately through various special provisions.
Apart from the merits of this issue, it was
often impossible for Army contracting officers to state categorically that no charge
for facilities was included—either directly
or indirectly—in a proposed contract price.
Hence, applications for clearance accompanying contract proposals in many instances omitted any such statement. This
gave rise to considerable delay and controversy, especially in cases involving the tax
amortization feature.[41]

Soon after the establishment of OPM the
clearance of all Army and Navy contracts
was made the responsibility of the Purchases
Division, OPM, under the direction of
Donald Nelson.[42] Within the limits imposed by time, available personnel, and administrative feasibility, the War Department attempted to comply with the necessary procedures. In order to avoid, so far as
possible, the presentation of clearance requests at the last minute, the Army supply
arms and services were directed to submit
to OPM advance statements of requirements and proposed purchases in excess of
$50,000. The statements ordinarily indi-
cated the item, specifications, quantity,
estimated cost, proposed method of procurement, proposed dates for invitations of
bids or beginning of negotiations, delivery

schedules, and other pertinent information.[43] With such information, the director
of purchases for OPM could recommend,
in advance of actual negotiations, alternative purchase methods or sources of supply,
changes in specifications, or other modifications which he considered desirable. In
many cases, preliminary purchase plans
originated at depot or district offices remote
from Washington and these would have to
be sent to the technical service headquarters
and cleared with OPM and OUSW before
procurement directives could be sent to
the field.

When procurement plans reached the
stage of contract placement, the proposal
with an accompanying request for clearance was sent to the Contract Clearance Division, OPM. From there the proposal was
sent to the appropriate commodity branch
within OPM for review by commodity specialists. Price and cost data were checked by
the cost analysis section of the Contract
Clearance Branch, and the Contract Distribution Division of OPM was notified of
subcontracting possibilities. If new plant
construction was involved, the Plant Site
Board, OPM, was consulted.[44]

For a number of reasons the external
clearance of individual contracts was unsatisfactory to all concerned. From the
standpoint of OPM, there was rarely sufficient time for adequate scrutiny of all the
significant terms and implications of proposals undergoing review. With contract
placement policies still in a rudimentary
stage, it was difficult for OPM personnel to
know what tests to apply to proposals for
clearance purposes, and contracts could not

---

[40] CPA, *Industrial Mobilization for War,* p. 145.

[41] For discussion of this issue in greater detail, see
below, pages 469–71.

[42] Civilian Production Administration, *Minutes
of the Council of the Office of Production Management, December 21, 1940, to January 14, 1942*
(Washington: Government Printing Office, 1946)
(hereafter cited as *OPM Minutes*), mtg of 18 Feb
41, p. 7.

[43] (1) Yoshpe and Massen, QMC Procurement
Policies, p. 65. (2) CPA, *Industrial Mobilization
for War,* p. 144.

[44] Several other clearances were required for large
construction contracts. See below, page 315.

be held up pending the establishment of commonly accepted policy. Likewise, it was frequently impossible for the armed services to develop any realistic procurement proposals in advance of actual negotiations with specific firms. The result in many cases was the crystallization of an agreement between the procuring agency and the contractor by the time a clearance request could be developed and submitted to OPM. Thus OPM was often presented with a *fait accompli* which could not be economically disapproved. For their part, the procuring agencies chafed under the additional paper work and delays and felt that the clearance requirements involved unnecessary duplication of organizations and activity, with the necessity for the buyer to consult "the buyer's brother" at every stage in the negotiations Last minute changes were often necessary after formal clearance by OPM and these were sometimes made without OPM approval, to the understandable annoyance of that agency.[45] Under the circumstances the accomplishments of the external clearance procedure did not appear to warrant such delays, expense, and irritation.

As the defense period drew to a close, the increasing emphasis upon the speedy placement of contracts made necessary the streamlining of contract clearance procedure.[46] With the advent of Pearl Harbor it became evident that the existing cumbersome procedures could not be allowed to continue. On 13 December 1941 Under Secretary Patterson, observing that it normally took thirty days for a contract to be cleared in Washington by the service headquarters and the OPM, proposed that field officers of the Air Forces and the the Ord-

nance Department be permitted to award all new contracts up to $5,000,000 without the necessity of clearance in Washington. He further proposed that OPM representatives be physically stationed in various offices of the War Department to review the progress of procurement negotiations and emphasized that under such arrangements he expected contracts in excess of $5,000,000 to be cleared by OPM within forty-eight hours.[47]

For a brief time thereafter a compromise arrangement was adopted whereunder the OPM was to expedite its clearance procedures and confine its review to contracts in excess of $1,000,000.[48] This procedure was short-lived. Soon after the formation of the War Production Board, Donald Nelson reappraised the whole function of contract clearance and concluded that the only satisfactory solution under the new emergency conditions was to replace the existing duplicative machinery with an integrated procedure which would combine the contract placement and clearance functions in a single operation and agency. To this end he ordered the discontinuance of separate contract review by WPB, transferred key WPB purchase policy and contract clearance specialists to the armed services, and adopted measures to effect common standards of contract placement by all procuring agencies.[49]

---

[45] CPA, *Industrial Mobilization for War*, p. 145.
[46] CPA, *OPM Minutes*, p. 66.

[47] *Ibid.*, pp. 80–81.
[48] *Ibid.*, mtg of 19 Dec 41, p. 82.
[49] WPB contract clearance was discontinued on 3 March 1942 with the transfer of WPB personnel under WPB, General Administrative Order 12. CPA, *Industrial Mobilization for War*, p. 522. On the same day WPB Directive No. 2 established common criteria of contract placement for all procuring agencies. Further integration of procurement policy was indicated by the establishment of the Procurement Policy Committee, later to become the Procurement Policy Board, composed of representatives of the Army, Navy, WPB, and other key agencies.

Internal Clearance

The abandonment of the requirement of external contract review and clearance permitted the Army and Navy in the months after Pearl Harbor to move rapidly in the placement of contracts under the huge new appropriations provided by Congress, and to speed the conversion of industry to war production. At the same time it placed upon the procuring agencies responsibility for developing internal controls which would insure reasonable compliance with the requirements of sound contract placement policies. These policies were still in the formative stage early in 1942 and the subsequent experience of the Purchases Division, ASF, in reviewing all major contracts provided a fruitful basis for policy formation.

With the establishment of the Army Service Forces on 9 March 1942, a Contract Clearance Section was created within the Purchases Branch. This section superseded the separate Ordnance, Quartermaster, Signal Corps, and similar sections of the Purchases Branch, OUSW, which formerly discharged the clearance function for that office. The Contract Clearance Section (which later became a branch when Purchases was made a division) had the responsibility of screening all individual contracts in excess of $5 million submitted by each technical service.[50] During the early part of 1942, the clearance procedure was necessarily perfunctory as compared with later developments. Requests for clearance from distant offices usually were sent with a one-page covering memorandum from technical service headquarters stating the bare details

of the proposed transaction—name of manufacturer, item, quantity, unit price, total cost of supplies, delivery dates, and the like. Frequently the only material in support of the award consisted of reference to the governing Expenditure Program and the statement: "These prices are considered fair and reasonable." [51]

Gradually the procurement program passed from the emergency, "production-at-any-price" phase into a more orderly process supported by adequate organizations, procedures, and criteria for contract review. With the development of standard contract forms to meet various conditions of purchase and production, problems of ascertaining the desirability and legal sufficiency of individual contract clauses became less difficult, and more attention could be given to the fundamental problem of pricing in negotiated contracts. Also, the development of an adequate pricing philosophy made possible the refinement of procedures and information required in contract negotiation.

---

[50] Historical Report of Office of Asst Director for Pricing, Purchases Div, ASF, FY 1943, p. 10, file 319.1 Historical Reports, Purchases Div ASF.

[51] See copies of award approval requests in Office Chief of Ordnance, Legal Division, History of Ordnance Pricing Policy, Exhibit 18. History of Ordnance Pricing Policy is the short name used throughout the present volume to refer to a series of four historical summaries of Ordnance Department pricing policy prepared and maintained on file in the Legal Division, OCofOrd. The two most important of these are: (1) Memo, James F. Oates, Jr., Chf Purchase Policy Br, Legal Div OCofOrd, for Maj. Gen Levin H. Campbell, Jr., OCofOrd, 28, Jul 44, sub: Summary Report Respecting the Development of Ordnance Purchase Policy—January 1942–July 1944 (33pp.), with Exhibits 1–40; (2) Memo, Lt Col Earl Kribben, Chf Pricing Policy Br, Legal Div OCofOrd, for Maj Joseph P. McNamara, Historian Legal Div OCofOrd, 24 Apr 45, sub: History of Activities in Pricing Policy Branch—1 August 1944–1 April 1945 (26pp.), with Exhibits 41–87. Two shorter reports, with Exhibits 88–89, carry the history to 30 September 1945. Unless otherwise specified, references to page numbers refer to the original Oates report of 28 July 1944.

The contract clearance procedures established by the Purchases Division, ASF, eventually became a major instrument for improving and refining the pricing operations of the technical services and their district procurement offices. Instructions for preparing justifications of proposed prices and other terms of important awards were carried in Procurement Regulations and were elaborated in great detail by separate instructions from technical service headquarters. Requests for deviation from standard contract forms and clauses had to be supported by adequate justification. Information in support of proposed prices had to include a brief narrative history of the negotiations with the contractor, accompanied by data on comparative prices, components of price, and trends in both costs and prices. Cost breakdowns and comparisons of estimated costs with those already experienced by the contractor, as well as by other suppliers, were required along with much other information indicating that effective efforts had been made to obtain close prices.[52] Contracting officers, district award boards, and technical service headquarters became conscious of the fact that the review procedure would include a searching examination of all significant aspects of each important award and that the results would have an important bearing on the evaluation placed by Headquarters, ASF, upon the general contracting policies of each office concerned. By the beginning of 1944, the documentation requirements of major contract awards had grown to the proportions of a sizable research project.[53]

An indication of the possible ramifications of the Army's internal clearance procedure is found in the following remarks:

A contract of over $5,000,000 was presented to the Purchases Division several months ago for clearance. A careful study was made, resulting in strong indications of a lack of pricing controls which raised inferences of a lack of production control. With the concurrence of the service which submitted the contract and upon invitation of the contractor, one of our men spent considerable time in the contractor's plant looking into the problems which had been raised as a result of the analysis. Steps were taken to correct some of the conditions discovered. Recently another contract with the same contractor was placed with the same service, and I would like to call attention to the changes in prices on a number of important items. On one the old price was $763, the new $711; on another the old price was $123, the new $63; on another the old price was $88, the new $36; on another the old, $125, the new $97; on another the old, $161, the new $132; and on still another the old price was $151, while the new one was $135. In the presentation appeared the following statement: "Negotiations recently completed resulted in overall reduction of approximately $30,000,000." [54]

No reliable statistics are available to show the proportion which Army contracts subject to clearance bore to total Army procurement, but it was substantial. The dollar value of contracts cleared between 9 March and 30 June 1942 was reported to have exceeded $7.5 billion.[55] Preliminary estimates for the year ending 30 June 1943 cited the clearance of 1,052 contracts with a total commitment value of $35 billion, of which $19 billion represented AAF contracts and

---

[52] (1) PR 305.4 (11–23–44). (2) Ord Procurement Cir 207–44, 24 Jul 44.

[53] History of Ordnance Pricing Policy, Exhibit 18–A.

[54] Summary of Talk Made at Meeting of Chiefs of Technical Services, ASF, Held 1000, 18 January 1944, by Glen A. Lloyd, Asst Dir for Pricing, Purchases Div, Hq ASF, in History of Ordnance Pricing Policy, Exhibit 31, p. 21.

[55] ASF Annual Rpt, 1942, p. 21.

$11 billion, Ordnance.[56] For the year ending 30 June 1945, 770 contracts with an aggregate value of $16.6 billion were reported as having been cleared. In addition, by this time the Purchases Division had undertaken to develop measures looking to the review of a representative sample of contracts under $5 million from all major procurement offices.[57]

Contract Clearance and Program Control

The system of internal contract clearance developed by the ASF as an instrument of purchase policy worked well and appeared to be far more effective than any system of external clearance could have been. It confined the objectives of contract clearance to the improvement of the terms of individual contracts, with predominant emphasis upon sound pricing as a means of stimulating efficiency in the use of real resources. It made contract review and clearance an integral function of contract placement and the development of purchase policy. The decentralization of the clearance function to the actual procurement agencies united the authority to procure with the responsibility for procurement and permitted the refinement of purchase policy as rapidly as possible without sacrificing the basic procurement objective.

Nevertheless, both during and after the war, Donald Nelson was frequently criti-

cized for his decision to abandon the external clearance requirements inherited from NDAC and the OPM.[58] In appraising such criticisms it must be remembered that when the system of external controls was abandoned there existed neither the policies nor the machinery for effective contract clearance even within the procuring agencies, to say nothing of external agencies remote from the actual process of translating military requirements into deliveries of finished munitions. The various divisions, branches, and sections exercising clearance functions in the civilian mobilization control agencies had no clear or consistent conception of the purpose of contract clearance. Some regarded it as an instrument of price and profit control; others felt that it should control the distribution of contracts to geographical areas, to distressed communities, or small business; still others thought that it should be used as a device to implement desirable labor policy or promote a balanced postwar economy. In the welter of confusion over the many subsidiary objectives, and with the proliferation of clearance agencies and specific hurdles between submission and approval of award proposals, the main objective was subordinated. Delays to contract placement, already considerable, threatened to reach proportions big enough to defeat the wartime procurement program. Moreover, a fundamental precondition of successful large-scale procurement—the decentralization of the bulk of the task to the field—awaited the removal of external restraints and controls. For all these reasons the armed services felt that the removal of the objectionable controls was indispensable to the war effort, and Donald Nelson in his postwar account of the period

[56] History of Purchases Division, ASF, for Fiscal Year 1943, p. 5, accompanying Memo, Capt Joseph M. Howorth, Historian Purchases Div, for Dir Purchases Div, 30 Jul 43, sub: Historical Report for Fiscal Year 1943, file 319.1 Historical Reports, Purchases Div ASF.

[57] Annual Report, Purchases Division, ASF Fiscal Year 1944–45, p. 2, accompanying Memo, Col Foy, Dir Purchases Div ASF, for Dir of Materiel, 15 Jun 45, sub: Annual Report of ASF for Fiscal Year 1945 in files of Purchases Div ASF.

[58] CPA, *Industrial Mobilization for War*, pp. 521–25.

reaffirmed his conviction that his decision under the circumstances was correct.[59]

More recently, the abandonment of the War Production Board's contract clearance function in 1942 has been deplored as the surrender of WPB's power to achieve overall program control and to bring into balance the supply and effective demand for critical materials and other real resources. Discontinuance of the clearance function by WPB was held to be a surrender of civilian authority over military procurement, permitting the military procuring agencies early in 1942 to place contracts far in excess of the availability of real resources, with resulting imbalance and dislocation of the war production program. In this view the contract clearance function is conceived as the instrument for keeping total contract placements within the realm of production feasibility.[60]

As already indicated, the external, individual-contract review and clearance procedures in existence up to March 1942 were not designed to accomplish any kind of quantitative program control, and in the nature of the circumstances they could not have fulfilled this purpose. Adequate program control necessarily had to await the development of information, organizations, policies, and procedures which were virtually nonexistent early in 1942. In the dark days following Pearl Harbor the urgency of procurement was simply too great to await

the creation of an ideal blueprint for program control. In order to convert industry to full wartime production and get munitions into the hands of troops without delay, a bold program of contract placement was indispensable. To have adopted a timid policy at this time, despite the difficulties resulting from initial program imbalance, might well have been to lose the war. Only after the creation of the Controlled Materials Plan, or its equivalent, and the meshing of material allocations with contract placement and administration, such as was actually done after CMP was established, could effective program control have been obtained. A cardinal virtue of the Controlled Materials Plan, in contrast to procedures for contract clearance, was its decentralization to the procuring agencies of the task of placing and administering their individual contracts within the broad material allocations made by the War Production Board. After this procedure was firmly established, program balance in World War II was achieved with reasonable success and the external review of individual contracts was not an issue.[61]

Evolution of Wartime Pricing Policy

The outstanding feature of the pricing of military procurement in World War II was the replacement, on an unprecedented scale, of the traditional system of competitive or "automatic" price determination by a system of "administrative" price determination ultimately based upon elaborate techniques of cost and price analysis. This fundamental change in pricing methods had its beginnings in the defense period and by the end of 1943 constituted a major revolution in the nature of economic transactions for an im-

---

[59] Nelson, *Arsenal of Democracy*, pp. 198ff.

[60] David Novick, Melvin Anshen, and W. C. Truppner, *Wartime Production Controls* (New York City: Columbia University Press, 1949), pp. 382ff. "The placement of contracts is the force which sets the economic machine in motion . . . the power to review and therefore to control military procurement . . . was given away by the civilian group in a deliberate, conscious policy which could have been formulated only as a result of the failure to grasp the fundamental importance of the power." *Ibid.,* pp. 384, 386.

[61] See below, Part Six.

portant segment of the American industrial system. As a consequence of this change and because of the tremendous magnitude and scope of its purchasing activities in World War I, the Army was forced to come to grips with numerous problems and to take a leading role in the formulation of a basic philosophy of wartime pricing and its associated instruments of policy.

As already indicated, the Army's small peacetime purchasing activities in a milieu of competitive markets had required no such formal basis as a pricing "policy." The basic rule of contract placement in peacetime had been the purchase of government supplies at the lowest available price.[62]

For the bulk of Army procurement in the prewar period, the competitive bidding process had automatically and simultaneously resolved the two fundamental problems of contract placement—selection of contractors and determination of price. The launching of the great rearmament program in the summer of 1940 was the beginning of a series of developments which was to split these two functions of contract placement wide apart and create the necessity for a conscious pricing policy on the part of procuring agencies. With competitive bidding increasingly unable to perform its traditional functions and with its displacement by direct negotiation in more and more areas, the selection of contractors came to be governed by considerations other than price. But whatever the criteria of contractor selection,

the problem of determining appropriate prices remained.

The relative decline in "automatic" pricing for military procurement was only partly caused by the decline of competition as the rearmament program inexorably brought about full employment of the bulk of the nation's resources. A large and crucial segment of Army procurement consisted of projects of a type and scale for which competition was largely irrelevant and for which it could never furnish an appropriate pricing mechanism. In the forefront of these projects were the great aircraft, ammunition, tank, and other heavy equipment programs under individual contracts attaining the size, in some cases, of nearly a quarter of the national debt a dozen years previously. The novelty, magnitude, technological complexity, and urgency of these projects all combined to render competition—even at a time when a substantial percentage of the nation's resources was unemployed—inadequate for purposes either of contractor selection or the determination of appropriate contract prices.

The passage of time eventually revealed that from the standpoint of basic wartime pricing policy the Army was confronted with three broad categories of procurement: (1) complex projects or items of the type just described which were at no time susceptible of automatic, competitive pricing; (2) items for which automatic pricing—available and appropriate at the beginning of the defense program—gradually disappeared with the decline of effective competition; (3) items for which open, competitive capacity remained throughout the war.

During the defense period and for some time after Pearl Harbor, pricing for the first category of items went largely by default. For a large percentage of projects in

[62] See above, Chapter IX. "*Purchases, where made.* . . . all supplies for the use of the various departments and posts of the Army and of the branches of the Army service . . . shall be purchased where the same can be purchased the cheapest, quality and cost of transportation and the interests of the Government considered; . . . *Act June 30, 1902 (32 Stat. 514); 10 U.S.C. 1201; M. L., 1939, sec. 1928.*" AR 5–100, 7 Aug 40 par. 8.

this category, the problem of price determination was simply evaded by the adoption of CPFF contracts. For the remainder of this group—either because the pricing problem was less complicated or for other reasons—fixed prices were negotiated, albeit on the basis of estimates and procedures which later appeared crude.

For the second category, which included the numerical majority of its contracts, the Army continued to use competitive bidding until it became evident that effective competition had declined to the point where satisfactory prices were no longer obtainable on this basis. For some items this point was reached fairly early in the defense period; for others it was not reached until after Pearl Harbor. In any case, both for this category of procurement and the one just discussed, there was an inevitable lag between the appearance of the need for sound pricing principles and the actual development and application of such principles.

The third category, small in total dollar value as compared with the other two, consisted mainly of relatively simple items procured by Quartermaster, Engineer, Medical, and other services. For many such items sufficient available capacity among small business firms continued to exist throughout the war, a fact eloquently proclaimed by the existence and operation of the small war plants program after Pearl Harbor. In such circumstances competitive bidding could often be retained as a major instrument of price determination.[63]

Despite efforts of the prewar planners,

the ultimate ramifications of a comprehensive wartime pricing policy were scarcely envisaged by the Army or the other procuring agencies until some time after Pearl Harbor. The sense of overriding urgency, which increased throughout the defense period and reached its peak early in 1942, dictated the immediate placement of contracts and the launching of production "at any price." The tasks of converting industry to war production, of obtaining the necessary expansion of plant and equipment, and of devising a satisfactory system for distributing scarce materials to war suppliers, all took precedence over refinements of price. The inevitable result was the feverish placement of contracts at prices which later turned out to be far above actual costs of production. Negotiated prices were hurriedly approved on the basis of contractor estimates which included allowances for almost every conceivable contingency. But pricing in contracts placed through competitive bidding fared no better. By the end of 1941, effective competition for many classes of sellers had disappeared and prices in competitive-bid contracts were also based on generous estimates of cost. By the spring of 1942, there was substantial evidence of widespread overpricing in war contracts.

This general development was regarded in many circles as an unmixed evil. On the other hand, there were some who realized that overpricing in war contracts during the early stages of industrial mobilization might well represent the most desirable "policy" under the circumstances. It provided a powerful and undeniable stimulus toward rapid industrial conversion and all-out war production. At the same time it underwrote the government's determination to place rearmament above all other objectives and provided contractors with abundant finan-

---

[63] Thus, even where certain classes of procurement were earmarked for small firms, at premium prices if necessary, competitive bidding within the small-business area kept prices within reasonable limits and promoted efficiency in the use of resources. See below, Chapter XVIII, especially page 425.

cial means to execute their many responsibilities without delay. In this view there was little doubt that governmental largesse during the conversion period did much to break down the leisurely, conservative, dollar-conscious behavior of the American public, which during a decade of depression had chosen to waste its time and its resources in idleness rather than resort to the expenditure of dollars and cents.[64]

By the spring of 1942 circumstances had drastically changed. The nation was now at war and financial inducements to contractors were of secondary importance in completing the process of conversion to war production. The seriousness of the raw material problem in the face of tremendously expanded requirements, together with the rising tide of inflation, brought home to war production leaders the fact that the shortage of real resources was the ultimate limitation upon war production and that the nation was now faced with such a shortage. Overpricing in war contracts, which had so recently stimulated the full employment of idle resources and promoted speedy conversion to war production, was now threatening basic productive efficiency. War contractors, who had become the custodians of nearly half the nation's real resources, bore a heavy responsibility to use these resources

efficiently. But with excessive financial means at their disposal, individual contractors attempted to achieve their production objectives by means of excessive money outlays rather than by strict economies of real resources. The accumulation of excessive inventories of materials and supplies, the pirating and hoarding of labor, and the lavish and wasteful use of materials both in production and construction projects promoted the quick attainment of individual-contract objectives at the expense of the war program as a whole.

Those who were responsible for the war production effort realized that the improvement of direct controls was indispensable to the effective wartime allocation of the nation's resources. But in the spring of 1942 direct controls over labor and materials either were completely lacking or were in a rudimentary and chaotic stage of development. Conservation and substitution measures were only beginning to be effective. All these measures were faced with a slow, uncertain, and piecemeal development, whereas monetary inflation—proceeding basically from expenditures under war contracts—was a current and all-pervasive threat to efficiency. Whether operating under the CPFF form of contract or under loosely negotiated fixed-price contracts, war suppliers behaved in much the same manner. The wartime tax structure, with marginal excess profits tax rates of 90 percent, removed much of the power of the profit motive to reduce costs. Lavish expenditures by many fixed-price contractors cost them only ten cents on the dollar, for all practical purposes placing them in a cost-plus status.

It was within the framework of these conditions and subsequent developments in the spring and summer of 1942 that War Department purchasing officials undertook to

---

[64] Governmental expenditures during the depression of the 1930's were paltry by comparison with those in World War II. Nevertheless, by the time of Pearl Harbor they had come to symbolize the ultimate in large-scale governmental spending. For instance, the following comment of Senator Harry S. Truman upon General Somervell's aggressive prosecution of the Army's camp construction and procurement program: "I will say this for General Somervell, he will get the stuff, but it is going to be hell on the taxpayer. He has a WPA attitude on the expenditure of money." S. Com. on Military Affairs, 77th Cong., 2d Sess., Hearings on S. 2092, *Department of Defense Co-ordination and Control Bill*, 6 Mar 42, p. 7.

develop a basic pricing philosophy and began to forge the instruments of policy which would restore to the pricing function its erstwhile power to compel efficiency in the use of real resources. By the fall of 1942, after intensive efforts in the development of renegotiation policy, extended discussions with the Office of Price Administration, and much additional experience in the placement and administration of procurement contracts, key officials in the War Department were in a position to consolidate their ideas and experience in the form of a policy declaration which was to guide the Army's pricing activities for the remainder of the war. This declaration—subsequently known as the Tryon Statement—was the product of a three-day conference called by the director of the Purchases Division, ASF, and held at Tryon, North Carolina.[65]

The basic objective of War Department pricing policy, as expressed by the Tryon Statement, was the promotion of efficiency in the use of real resources—manpower, materials, and productive equipment. Instrumental to this objective was the basic principle of pricing policy—the attainment of

"close pricing" in all War Department purchase transactions. Close pricing meant the adoption, in advance of production, of prices close enough to costs to force contractors to produce efficiently if they were to avoid losses and make a profit. The statement recognized that under wartime conditions the attainment of this objective required the use of administrative controls not needed under normal competitive conditions. "Purchase control" over individual contract prices, rather than the use of general formulas and regulations (such as necessarily employed by the OPA), was considered to be the simplest and best method of price control.

The best instrument of purchase control, in the view of the Tryon Statement, was the employment of fixed-price contracts, "well negotiated on the basis of accurate cost experience and close estimates." The attainment of close prices in fixed-price contracts was to be achieved through two major avenues of approach. The first concerned the negotiation of initial contract prices. The attainment of close original prices required a careful analysis of estimated costs as submitted by contractors in cost breakdowns accompanying their bid proposals.[66] A major element in cost analysis was the segregation and classification of the contractor's risks under the proposed contract. All ordinary risks of management in organizing production and making deliveries were to be compensated by a normal element of profit included in the contract price. All other risks were to be transferred to the government and no cushions or specific elements to cover these risks were to be included in the price. The transfer of these risks was to be accom-

---

[65] Ten persons were listed as having composed the conference, which met from 30 October to 1 November, 1942: Col. Albert J. Browning, Director, Purchases Division; Dr. Maurice Karker, Chairman, War Department Price Adjustment Board; Dr. Melvin T. Copeland, School of Business Administration, Harvard University; Mr. William L. Marbury, Chief, Legal Branch, Purchases Division; Mr. Howard C. Petersen, OUSW; Mr. E. T. Gushee, Purchase Policy Section, Legal Branch, Ordnance Department; Col. C. E. Dyson, AAF; Maj. Burton E. Vaughn, Price Adjustment Branch, Purchases Division; Capt. Robert R. Bowie, Legal Branch, Purchases Division; Mr. Ernest Mahler, representing industry. Col. Browning, Dir Purchases Div ASF, Memorandum on Statement of Purchase Policies, 19 Nov 42, reproduced in Army Industrial College R57, Contract Pricing—Principal Developments (January 1946), p. 107, ICAF Library. This document also reproduces in full, at pp. 108–15, the Tryon Statement of Purchase Policies, 19 Nov 42.

[66] The term "bid proposal" included all contractor proposals or terms of offer in the negotiation of contracts, whether or not bidding was competitive.

plished wherever possible by specific contract clauses providing for government reimbursement of the contractor for cost increases sustained as a result of changes in wage rates, availability of materials, and other factors under the broad control of the government. Adverse changes in costs or the materialization of risks which were completely unforeseeable would be compensated by appropriate price increases or other relief under the First War Powers Act, which permitted the amendment of government contracts "without consideration" wherever necessary for the prosecution of the war. Adequate use was to be made of the War Department's compulsory pricing powers whenever a contractor was unwilling to adopt close prices.

The other basic approach to close pricing in fixed-price contracts was the advance provision for price adjustment, either periodically or otherwise, during the life of a contract. This was a most important provision and one which became of steadily increasing importance. In the light of the highly dynamic and fluid cost conditions of war production, almost all the War Department's important contracts could be considered as "long term." Any notion that it was possible to adopt a fixed and immutable price in each and every contract under the stated conditions was simply a contradiction of experience in the real world of wartime industrial economics. It was largely for this reason that the use of CPFF contracts was found necessary on so large a scale. On the other hand, completely unrestricted use of CPFF contracts would be tantamount to abdication of all efforts to achieve close pricing in advance of production. Unless the War Department were to abandon its efforts to establish contract prices as a means of continually exerting downward pressure

upon costs, it would have to discover a method of pricing which would provide this kind of pressure while still recognizing the dynamic nature of costs. The solution was found, both in principle and to a large extent in practice, in the form of progressive price adjustment under modified fixed-price contracts. These price adjustment features were an outgrowth of various types of "escalator" clauses providing for price increases on the basis of increases in wage and material costs.[67]

The Tryon Statement enunciated other War Department policies in the field of pricing. CPFF contracts were to be used only where there was no alternative. In the case of CPFF supply contracts, bonuses and penalty provisions were to be considered in order to stimulate cost reduction, and agreements were to be obtained for the conversion of these contracts to a fixed-price basis as soon as possible. Renegotiation was to be tied more closely to pricing by shifting the emphasis from recapture of past profits to repricing for future periods and by delegating the actual job of renegotiation to the services responsible for awarding contracts. Price and cost analysis methods were to be improved at the level of both prime contracts and subcontracts, and a broad program of research and education was to be undertaken in order to equip all concerned with the best possible tools of close pricing. This included the education of contractors as well as procurement agency personnel, and a high degree of policy co-ordination was to be obtained not only within the War Department, but interdepartmentally with the Navy and other procuring agencies.[68]

---

[67] The nature of these price adjustment provisions, and some of the problems on their administration, are discussed below in Chapter XIII.

[68] Statement of Purchase Policies cited above, note 65.

Thus by November 1942 the War Department had succeeded in formulating the broad pricing principles and the elements of a supporting program for the discharge of its pricing responsibilities in World War II. The Tryon recommendations became established War Department policy on 26 March 1943 with the publication of Revision 14 to Procurement Regulations. This revision announced the policies of the Tryon Statement and included new contract clauses which could be used by contracting officers to permit modifications in prices during the life of a contract.[69] Immediately thereafter, work was begun on a new pricing manual which would amplify War Department pricing policy and provide contracting officers with numerous suggestions and techniques for the attainment of close prices in the actual negotiation of contracts. As a result, ASFM–601, Pricing in War Contracts, was completed and published on 2 August 1943. This manual proved to be a useful and highly popular document, and by mid-1945 over ten thousand copies had been distributed.

The many subsequent elaborations and refinements of War Department pricing policy rested squarely on the foundations of the Tryon Statement. Nevertheless, many of the objectives of the statement proved difficult to attain. The conversion of CPFF contracts to fixed-price contracts on a substantial scale was delayed until the final year of the war. The hope that renegotiation could be shifted from an instrument of

profit recapture to one of forward pricing was far from realized, but the end in view was partially achieved by means of the company pricing program. The tools of price and cost analysis were greatly elaborated and refined, and substantial progress was made in drafting contract clauses which would achieve desirable results in the field of progressive price adjustment. The compulsory pricing powers of the War Department were seldom specifically invoked but exerted a substantial influence in obtaining contractor co-operation in a sound pricing program. The emphasis upon economy of real resources continued throughout the war, and progress was made in the troublesome task of distinguishing *earned* profits from those resulting merely from *overpricing*. Increasing use of exemption from renegotiation was allowed to encourage efficient contractors who were willing to adopt initial close prices. Basic to the entire pricing program was the proposition that contract prices and pricing policy should at all times serve to implement the war production program.[70]

---

[69] ASF, History of Purchases Division, p. 147.

[70] For other statements concerning War Department pricing policy in World War II, see: (1) ASF M–601, Pricing in War Contracts, 2 Aug 43; (2) ASF, History of Purchases Division, pp. 119–93; (3) History of Ordnance Pricing Policy and exhibits thereto; (4) Glen A. Lloyd, "Pricing in War Contracts," *Law and Contemporary Problems* (Duke University School of Law), X, No. 2 (Autumn 1943), 235–61; (5) Miller, *Pricing of Military Procurements;* (6) Yoshpe, Production Control in the QMC, Ch. VI; (7) AIC R57, Contract Pricing—Principal Developments; (8) Industrial College of the Armed Forces R58, Contract Pricing—Principal Developments (August 1946), ICAF Library.

CHAPTER XII

The Cost-Plus-A-Fixed-Fee Contract

Background and Nature

One of the most controversial features of procurement operations in World War II was the widely used cost-plus-a-fixed-fee form of contract.[1] Army commitments under all types of CPFF contract for that war exceeded $50 billion and amounted to nearly one third of all Army purchases. The nature and implications of the CPFF contract were widely misunderstood throughout the war, partly because of the complexities of the pricing problem and partly because of general ignorance of the many specific types of CPFF contract and the procedures set up for their administration and control. A review of the War Department's experience with CPFF contracts reveals the heart of the problem of contracting and pricing for wartime procurement and provides the foundation for an understanding of all wartime pricing methods, renegotiation activities, contract administration, and other facets of the total procurement problem.

The CPFF form of contract had been used in World War I but received far less publicity than the cost-plus-a-percentage-of-cost type of contract, which subsequently became the target of much investigation and criticism. World War I experience had re-

___

[1] CPFF contracts were often referred to simply as "fixed-fee" contracts.

vealed the extravagance and waste resulting from CPPC contracts, which rewarded producers in direct proportion to the money they spent in performing their contracts. Moreover, all cost-plus forms of contract came under heavy suspicion because they failed to provide a firm ceiling upon costs or expenditures. A fairly common sentiment in Congress and elsewhere on the eve of World War II might be summed up in the words: "Why not make the contractor quote a reasonable price and hold him to it?" Unfortunately, this prescription shed no light on how its laudable objectives were to be obtained, and neither the Congress, the War Department, nor any other authority was able to provide a formula which could. Accordingly, although the CPPC form of contract was outlawed from the beginning of the defense period, the CPFF contract was—upon recommendation by the War and Navy Departments—specifically authorized and permitted throughout the war.

There were many reasons why the Army in the defense and war periods could not have accomplished its procurement mission in the absence of various types of "cost" contract. The equipment and supplies required by the Army for World War II consisted mainly of items which were either completely new or required drastic changes in design and specifications in order to meet the standards and possibilities of modern technological warfare. This was true not only of such basic items of equipment as planes, tanks, guns, ammunition, radio, and radar, but applied throughout the whole range of Quartermaster, Medical, Engineer, Transportation, and other organizational and personal equipment. Hardly a single item—from uniforms and field rations on up to electronic equipment and the atomic bomb—was envisaged at the beginning of the defense period in anything like its "final" form at the end of World War II. In short, it was impossible for the Army at the beginning of its rearmament program to specify with any degree of stability what it wished to buy.

By the same token it was difficult if not impossible for contractors to determine future costs with any degree of accuracy. Even if final specifications had been known, contractors could not have forecast the prices of materials and labor for a period in the future certain to be faced with a generally rising price level, nor could they have been assured that these and other essential resources would be available in sufficient quantity to complete their contracts on schedule. Indeed, the advance assurance of adequate supplies of labor and materials at stable wage rates and prices would have been only a first step in permitting contractors to make reliable cost estimates. All the manifold tasks of converting to war production—expanding basic facilities, acquiring new machinery and equipment, training and allocating labor, organizing, co-ordinating, and refining production processes, discovering and contracting with hundreds of underlying suppliers and subcontractors, and so on—had to be accurately foreseen and the measures for their resolution anticipated before costs could be prophesied with any degree of reliability.

In view of these circumstances no reliable

businessman could contract to produce and deliver a novel item of equipment at a guaranteed or fixed price, unless the price were so high as to be almost certain to cover all the unpredictable and changing costs likely to arise under the contract. A slight margin of error under a fixed-price contract many times the size of a contractor's invested capital could easily force him into bankruptcy. On the other hand, the common assumption that the government's interests could be protected by the assignment of a fixed price to each of its purchase contracts simply reflected ignorance of the entire problem of economic mobilization and war procurement. Fixed prices too low to cover costs would cripple war production and defeat the whole procurement program. Prices which were too high would result in widespread waste, inefficiency, and unjust enrichment. Faced with the basic problem of getting production underway at the earliest possible moment, neither the Army nor its contractors could afford to take time out for protracted negotiation and debate over hypothetical future costs and "ideal" prices. Both necessity and common sense dictated the use of contracts which would provide a clear guarantee of the recovery of all costs, especially for such important and difficult items as planes, tanks, ammunition, and related materiel. At the same time, under the established policy and continuous pressure to minimize the use of cost-plus contracts, many contracts were hurriedly consummated at more or less arbitrary fixed prices, with adverse results which became evident during the hearings leading to the renegotiation act early in 1942.[2]

The essence of the CPFF contract was the agreement by the government to defray all

---

[2] See below, Chapter XV.

costs essential to the execution of the contract. Allowable items of cost were broadly defined by each contract, and important individual expenditures (for example, items in excess of $2,000) usually had to be approved in advance by the contracting officer. Many contracts, especially those of the Army Air Forces, carried specific reference to Treasury Decision 5000 for detailed interpretations of allowable costs. TD 5000 was originally promulgated by the Department of the Treasury as a collection of rules and principles for defining costs preliminary to the determination of excess profits under the Vinson-Trammel act as amended. In the absence of other comprehensive statements it came to be widely used by contractors and procuring agencies to define allowable costs for CPFF contracts.[3] Within this general framework the contracting officer's determination of allowable costs was final, as between the Army and its contractors, in the absence of the contractor's appeal within thirty days to the Secretary of War or an appeal board designated by him. All operations under CPFF contracts were subject to audit and possible disallowance of items claimed as costs, not only by War Department auditors but by the General Accounting Office (GAO) under the Comptroller General.

---

[3] This use of TD 5000 was criticized by the Comptroller General, who took the position that cost definitions for the purpose of defining excess profits were necessarily too liberal for determining cost reimbursement by the government. Largely because of contractor resistance, attempts to replace TD 5000 with more suitable cost interpretations long proved abortive. (1) ASF, History of Purchases Division, p. 269. (2) Ltr, Comptroller General Lindsay Warren to Hon. Robert R. Reynolds, Chmn Senate Com on Military Affairs, 27 Jan 44, in Subcom. of the S. Com. on Military Affairs, 78th Cong., 2d Sess., Hearings on S. 1268, S. 1280, and S. J. Res. 80, *Problems of Contract Termination* (hereafter cited as *Hearings on S. J. Res. 80*), pp. 661–63.

The fixed fee under CPFF contracts represented the contractor's compensation for undertaking and performing the contract. Except for the possible deduction of certain contingent items, consisting mainly of cost disallowances by the Comptroller General, it constituted a guaranteed clear profit on the contractor's operations under the contract. The fee was determined in advance of performance and was based on the scope of the contract and the nature of the contractor's responsibilities thereunder. In general, for any given class or type of CPFF contract, the magnitude of the contractor's contribution was measured by the estimated cost of the project at the time the contract was negotiated, and the fee was determined by the application of a standard or reasonable percentage figure to the estimated costs. This percentage figure varied from one class of contract to another and, in general, was reduced for all classes as the war progressed. In no case could the fee exceed the statutory maximum (10 percent of estimated cost for construction outside continental United States; 6 percent for most construction within the United States; 7 percent for all other CPFF contracts). Since it was fixed in advance of performance, the contractor's fee offered no positive inducement to lavish or wasteful expenditures as did the CPPC form of contract, which geared the contractor's profits directly to the amount of his expenditures in performing the contract. Under the CPFF form of contract actual costs for the completed contract might turn out to be substantially above or below the original estimates without affecting the fee. Significant changes in the scope of the contract at any time prior to completion did, however, call for appropriate increases or reductions in the fee.

Thus all major risks under CPFF contracts were transferred to the government, and the protection of the government's interest required careful control and auditing of costs as well as dependable estimating procedures to permit the advance determination of a reasonable fee. Advance cost estimates for CPFF contracts were subject to the same pitfalls as were faced in the prediction of costs under fixed-price contracts, but by eliminating the contractor's risks there was no necessity for the inclusion of large contingent items to protect the contractor's solvency against heavy, unforseen cost increases. If final costs turned out to be substantially less than the estimates, the government would benefit accordingly. This was not true of fixed-price contracts, which bound both parties to the price determined in advance on the basis of cost estimates.[4] In the case of CPFF contracts, the fee was the only element of cost rigidly determined in advance, and the fee was in all cases only a small percentage of the total.

Classes and Coverage of Army CPFF Contracts

With few exceptions the Army's CPFF contracts in World War II fell into four broad classes:

1. construction contracts;
2. experimental, research, and developmental contracts;
3. service and time-and-material contracts;
4. supply contracts for:
   (a) aircraft;
   (b) ordnance heavy equipment
   (c) ordnance ammunition.

A brief discussion of the nature and coverage of each of these will help to clarify a number of important issues in the Army's purchasing policies in World War II.[5]

Construction Contracts

The CPFF construction contract was widely used in the defense period and early war years to permit rapid expansion of the War Department's command and industrial facilities. Many factors—including the shortness of time for meeting deadlines, frequent changes in plans and specifications, unfavorable topographical features of available sites, and the shortage of contractors with suitable experience—all combined to make lump-sum contracts unsuitable for most large construction projects: a fixed price high enough to provide reasonable protection to the contractor was likely to be exorbitant from the standpoint of the government.[6]

The fees for CPFF construction contracts were based primarily upon a graduated schedule applicable to all projects in accordance with their estimated cost. Variations from the schedule were made in order to reflect the relative complexity of the project, the length of time required for construction, the degree of subcontracting contemplated, and other factors. Early in the defense period

---

[4] That is, prior to statutory contract renegotiation. It was precisely because of the absurd results of fixed prices in a milieu of widespread uncertainty that the renegotiation law was adopted. See below, Chapter XV.

[5] The following discussion refers primarily to formal contracts. Preliminary contractual instruments, such as letter orders, letter purchase orders, and letter contracts, were usually placed on a cost basis pending the formal adoption of either a CPFF or a fixed-price contract. In the interim, important preliminary instruments on a cost basis were often treated as CPFF contracts. Ltr, Brig Gen Hermon F. Safford, OCofOrd, to CG ASF, 22 Mar 45, sub: Cost-Plus-A-Fixed-Fee Contracts, file 161 CPFF, Purchases Div ASF.

[6] Fixed-price contracts for construction projects were referred to as lump-sum contracts. PR 304.1 (1–11–45).

TABLE 27—MAXIMUM FIXED FEES FOR
CPFF CONSTRUCTION PROJECTS WITH
CORRESPONDING PERCENTAGES OF ESTI-
MATED COST [a]

Estimated Cost of Project	Architect-Engineer Services		Construction Services	
	Fee	Per-cent	Fee	Per-cent
$100,000	$4,000	4.00	$6,000	6.00
$500,000	12,500	2.50	27,500	5.50
$1,000,000	20,000	2.00	47,500	4.75
$2,000,000	26,250	1.30	80,000	4.00
$5,000,000	45,000	0.90	156,000	3.12
$10,000,000	75,000	0.75	254,000	2.54
$50,000,000	300,000	0.60	800,000	1.60
$100,000,000	500,000	0.50	1,000,000	1.00

[a] Selected levels from complete list of 4 August 1941.

Source: Memo, Dir P & C Br, OUSW, 4 Aug 41 (Ex. 42 of ASF, History of Purchases Division).

all construction projects were divided into three broad classes for purposes of fee determination: (1) simple construction (camps, cantonments, general hospitals of temporary construction); (2) semicomplex projects (small arms and ammunition plants, storage depots); (3) complex projects (TNT, powder, complicated chemical processing plants). Projects in the first group were normally allowed the fees indicated in the base schedule; those in the second and third groups were allowed 110 and 120 percent, respectively, of the base-schedule fees.[7]

Because of criticism of the base schedule as a "minimum" schedule and on the basis of accumulating experience, the OUSW early in 1941 ordered a new "maximum" fee schedule, which shortly underwent sev-

---

[7] Testimony of Mr. Harry W. Loving, Chmn WD Contract Board, 25 Apr 41, in Truman Committee, Hearings, 1: 348–49.

eral revisions and refinements. (Table 27) In utilizing the maximum schedules, contracting officers were directed to arrive at fees in individual contracts by negotiation and to see that such fees were equitable, reasonable, and based on the contribution actually required of the contractor. Fees in excess of the maximum, if considered essential to national defense, could be authorized by the Under Secretary of War.[8]

Many of the conditions which prevented the adoption of fixed prices in construction contracts during the defense period also complicated the execution and administration of CPFF construction contracts. The urgency of deadlines, the shortages of qualified supervisory and control personnel in the organizations of both the War Department and contractors, the prevalence in statutes and regulations of outmoded, cumbersome, and inadequate accounting and other procedures, together with general disturbances to the economy as a whole, all added to the prevailing atmosphere of confusion. By the summer of 1941 the Truman Committee had received numerous reports of waste, inefficiency, and increased costs in the Army's construction program.[9]

Much of the reported inefficiency and increased cost was attributed to the use of the CPFF form of contract. In particular,

---

[8] See memorandum in Exhibit 42 to ASF, History of Purchases Division. Fees in excess of the prescribed maxima were confined generally to construction performed outside the territorial limits of the United States, where risks, performance difficulties, and the time required for execution warranted and required higher fees. Army Service Forces, Renegotiation Division, History of Renegotiation [circa 1951], Sec. IV, Pt. II, App. 2–A, Tab C, pp. 34–35, copy in OCMH. This history of the War Department Price Adjustment Board is hereafter cited as WDPAB History.

[9] S. Rpt. 480, Pt. 5, 77th Cong., 2d Sess., 15 Jan 42 (hereafter cited as Truman Committee, First Annual Rpt), pp. 232–74.

the Truman Committee felt that wasteful purchasing methods by contractors, excessive equipment-rental charges, and inefficient use of labor and materials were inevitable results of CPFF contracting.[10] Testimony and exhibits submitted by War Department representatives indicated that increases in the size and quality of construction projects, combined with faulty original cost estimates, accounted for the bulk of the alleged "cost" increases. Especially was this true for camp construction projects—the principal target of the early investigations—which were expanded and improved in countless ways between original conception and final completion. Among the camp improvement features were the addition of chapels, theaters, training facilities, utilities and buildings of many kinds, wider paved roads, greatly increased water supplies, individual rooms for noncommissioned officers, and many other facilities nonexistent in the camps of World War I, all reflecting the general increase in the American standard of living between the two wars. Because of the need for constant revision and expansion of plans, numerous supplements were added to most construction contracts, increasing their scope and estimated cost often to double the original calculations.[11]

In view of these factors the arbitrary classification of camp construction as "simple" was deplored by those who were intimately associated with the Army's construction program:

One of the misconceptions which unfortunately still exists, was the thought that the design and construction of camps was not difficult. Actually I found in many instances that camp construction involved problems more difficult than did that of munitions plants. . . . Contractors, experienced in directing construction of large buildings on a reasonably small piece of ground, with ample time for planning and good sources of competent labor, were utterly appalled by the much greater volume of work, widely spread out and the not too competent labor forces which were so hastily thrown together. When one considers that in general a camp had to be ready in 120 days from the time the decision was reached to build a camp, until the time that the first troops moved in in force one realizes the problems involved.[12]

Whatever the conditions leading to increased construction expenditures during the defense period, the original cost estimates—based on projects of smaller scope—had necessarily been hasty "guestimates" made in a different cost-price milieu from that prevailing at the time of project execution. The estimating procedures and cost factors used by the War Department, which came under criticism by the Truman Committee, tended to underestimate the costs of the program. When compared with completed or current project costs under rising prices, these unsatisfactory advance estimates gave a magnified impression of waste and inefficiency in the whole construction program. Apart from the presence of unpredictable factors, the inadequacy of the original estimates was attributable not so much to care-

---

[10] Ibid., pp. 248–61.

[11] See cost table in Truman Committee, Hearings, 1:373. Some idea of the monumental task of drafting a single construction contract may be inferred from an examination of the terms of the Army's contract for the construction of Fort Bragg at Fayetteville, North Carolina. The original contract of 1 September 1940, with several change orders and supplements, is reproduced as Exhibit 92, ibid., 6:1889–1912.

[12] Comments of Lt Gen Leslie R. Groves, accompanying Ltr, Groves to Gen Smith, Chf of Military History, 22 Jul 55, reviewing draft of History of Military Construction in the United States. This letter and review, hereafter cited as Groves Commentary, comprise 146 typed pages and are filed in OCMH. The remarks just quoted appear on pages 11–12. Also, on page 18: "I do not like the expression 'at simpler jobs.' None of the jobs listed, outside of airfields, were really 'simpler.'"

lessness or incompetency as to the sheer lack of time and personnel to do a thorough job.[13]

Nevertheless, there was sufficient evidence of waste and excessive expenditures under CPFF construction contracts to result in great pressure by the Truman Committee as well as others to abandon fixed-fee contracting in favor of fixed-price contracts for all new projects. In order to enlist the enthusiasm of contractors for the change-over, Congress exempted from renegotiation, for fiscal years ending after 30 June 1943, profits under fixed-price construction contracts negotiated under competitive bidding. The theory behind the exemption was that, with most of the construction program nearing completion, competition would insure contract prices close to reasonable cost and that exemption from renegotiation would then drive actual costs still lower. Competition for profitable construction contracts would thereafter force a progressive lowering of prices, and the ultimate savings to the government would be many times the increase in reward to contractors.

The exemption from renegotiation was effective in promoting the greater use of fixed-price contracts, but by 1944 the Truman Committee questioned the wisdom of the blanket exemption from renegotiation, especially in view of the practical limitations upon truly competitive bidding under wartime conditions.[14] Accumulating statistics revealed that profits under fixed-price contracts were many times the fees earned under CPFF contracts. For example, data covering twenty-three competitive-bid fixed-price construction contracts renegotiated by

the Army Corps of Engineers for fiscal years prior to 1 July 1943 revealed profits before renegotiation of $21 million out of total contract prices aggregating $139 million. This indicated a ratio of job profits to job costs of 18 percent before renegotiation—a ratio which was reduced to some 10 percent by recaptures of nearly $9 million in renegotiation.[15] Job profits before renegotiation for approximately six hundred competitive fixed-price construction contracts coming under the Navy Price Adjustment Board averaged 31 percent of job costs and in individual cases ran as high as 66 percent.[16]

On the other hand, contractors' profit (fees) under CPFF construction contracts averaged less than 2 percent of job costs. In April 1941 General Somervell testified that the ratio of construction fees to total construction costs actually experienced up to that time averaged only 1.7 percent, with architect-engineer fees for the same projects averaging 0.4 percent.[17] By January 1943 the average fee contained in Engineer construction contracts "had declined to 1.89 percent of the estimated cost, and this result seems to have been maintained thereafter." [18]

Perhaps the most comprehensive statistics on construction profit ratios were those supplied by renegotiation. Army Engineer Corps figures covering renegotiation of construction contracts for fiscal years 1942 through 1946 reveal the following comparisons: (1) while 1 out of every 5 fixed-price construction contracts was found to have earned excessive profits, this was true

---

[13] Groves Commentary, pp. 50–52, 135.

[14] S. Rpt. 10, Pt. 16, 78th Cong., 2d Sess., 4 Mar 44 (hereafter citied as Truman Committee, Third Annual Rpt), pp. 58–59.

[15] *Ibid.,* App. IX, p. 195.

[16] *Ibid.,* App. X, p. 196.

[17] Truman Committee, *Hearings,* 1:319. This result was partly attributable to the substantial excess of actual cost over the estimates upon which fees were based.

[18] ASF, History of Purchases Division, p. 260.

for only 1 out of every 100 CPFF contracts; (2) for contracts undergoing profit recapture, profit-cost ratios before and after recapture averaged 14.47 and 9.63 percent, respectively, for fixed-price contracts but only 2.15 and 1.80 percent, respectively, for CPFF contracts; (3) the average profit-cost ratio for fixed-price "clearance cases" was 5.65 percent; for CPFF clearances, 1.76 percent.[19]

The size of profit margins was not the major factor in weighing the comparative desirability of CPFF and fixed-price construction contracts. On the one hand, excessive or wasteful expenditures under CPFF contracts might increase total costs to the government by many times the amount of profits under fixed-price contracts. On the other hand, there was no guarantee that by adopting the lump-sum form of contract the government would actually receive—in the form of an economical price—the cost savings for which it was presumably paying in the form of higher contractor profits. Lt. Gen. Leslie R. Groves, in reviewing the Army's construction experience in World War II, was emphatic in his preference for the CPFF form of contract as the most economical for the government in a milieu of unstable prices, high taxes, and general economic uncertainty:

It is very interesting to note that on the big lump sum jobs entered into in 1941 that the contractors did not appear to be vitally interested in holding down wages. . . . their bids were extremely high. In the average case they were far above what the work would have cost under fixed fee. The reason for this was that to avoid the risk of financial disaster they had to provide for every possible contingency.[20]

There is no question in my mind but what these fixed price jobs were more expensive in many instances than would have been fixed fee work. Many disadvantages of the fixed price work are not easily apparent to those who were not responsible for performance. . . . The principal reason for excessive bids was the fact that in such a bid there was no limit to the losses a contractor might suffer. There was however a definite limit as to the profits he might make. . . . supposing the job cost him $20,000,000 and his profit was $1,800,000, by re-negotiation this would probably be reduced to $1,200,000, and his net profit after taxes would then be $108,000. . . . On the other hand, if his bid was not high enough he could easily be faced with a loss running as high as $3,000,000. . . . For this reason the average contractor included in his bid items for every possible contingency. These included too hot weather, too cold weather, rainy weather, dry weather, and everything else on a similar basis. It was an impossible situation and resulted in bids for as much as $34,000,000, where fair estimate where the tax situaion was not controlling would have been about $25,000,000. I found it impossible however to convince the proponents of lump sum bids as to the facts of life. They insisted on closing their eyes to this phase of the problem with the rather idiotic philosophy that anyone who earned enough to pay a 91% tax ought not to worry about his financial status.[21]

Fixed fee work is used by many very successful corporations. It has many advantages, including not only the ability to change plans but the securing of a higher quality of workmanship. Experience has shown that nothing is more costly to an owner than a contractor who is losing money. I do not like to see propaganda by the political opponents of fixed fee work being given a seal of approval.[22]

[19] WDPAB History, Sec. IV, Pt. II, App. 2–A, Tab C, pp. 52–53.
[20] Groves Commentary, p. 74.

[21] *Ibid.*, pp. 105–07.
[22] Ibid., p. 108. On the other hand, General Groves was highly in favor of the use of "fixed-unit-price" contracts for fairly standardized components (earth moving, concrete placing) of otherwise difficult construction projects. The remainder of such projects would be on a CPFF basis. Ibid., pp. 100, 105.

Whatever the merits of fixed-price contracts for the projects of known difficulty in a milieu of stable prices, it would be difficult to demonstrate their desirability under the conditions obtaining from 1940 to 1942. The larger and more difficult camp construction projects undertaken during this period and involving unforeseen drainage, utility, transportation, and other costs could not have awaited the careful negotiation of fixed prices. These projects had to be undertaken and completed without delay, and the same guarantee of cost-reimbursement which permitted wasteful expenditures also conferred the necessary power upon contractors, in a period long before material and manpower controls could be perfected, to pre-empt the resources necessary for timely completion of the projects.

Experimental, Research, and Developmental Contracts

Many contracts devoted to research, developmental, and experimental work were of the CPFF variety. Much specialized research, such as the exploration of alternative design possibilities and experimental work in connection with production processes, was carried on during the war under prime contracts for the production of various end items of equipment. But the conduct of basic research, the development of pilot models of new equipment, and numerous smaller projects were covered by separate contracts which recognized the explorative or trial-and-error nature of the bulk of the work. In order to be successful these projects could not be bound in advance to specific procedures or narrow budgetary limitations. On the other hand, by loosely defining the scope of research projects, contracting officers

could use the fixed-price form of contract while in effect retaining the CPFF principle: they could let a succession of fixed-price contracts until the desired results had been achieved. The Signal Corps was said to have placed all its research and development contracts for World War II on a fixed-price basis, and by the end of the war an increasing number of Ordnance research and development contracts were of the fixed-price variety.[23] In terms of dollar value, all CPFF contracts for research and development, even including the costs of the atomic bomb, probably did not exceed 10 percent of the Army's total CPFF expenditures.

Service and Time-and-Material Contracts

Of smaller magnitude were the service and time-and-material contracts used by the Army under particular circumstances and conditions. An important class of service contracts were those which launched and governed the Army Specialized Training Program (ASTP), administered by the Purchases Division, ASF, and conducted by colleges and universities throughout the United States. ASTP contracts covered all costs of operation and maintenance and included a fee for use of buildings and plant facilities; the fee was based on prewar book values or cost of buildings subject to a specified maximum per cubic foot for the best facilities used on a capacity basis. Except for costs of activation, all fees and costs were determined in advance at a specified rate

---

[23] (1) Memo, Col Joseph G. Bent, Jr., ICAF, for Dr. Kent Roberts Greenfield, Chf Historian, OCMH, 22 Mar 55, OCMH. (2) History of Ordnance Pricing Policy, supplement of 24 Apr 45, p. 19.

of payment per month during the period of training.[24]

Time-and-material contracts were another form of cost contract not strictly of the CPFF variety since they contained no fixed fee but provided reimbursement for materials at cost and direct labor at rates per hour which included profit and overhead. These were used where no practicable alternative existed and were in keeping with commercial practice. Typical illustrations included the repair of vessels and equipment, salvage operations, and minor service requirements at miscellaneous installations. This form of contract was approved by the Comptroller General as not in violation of the statutory prohibition of the CPPC form of contract.[25] Some service and repair contracts were, however, of the straight CPFF variety. Thus the only significant Quartermaster CPFF contract in effect in the spring of 1943 covered the sterilization and rebuilding of used shoes on a mass-production basis. Since the project was still on an experimental basis and the shoes varied so widely in condition, the setting of a fixed price was deemed impossible.[26]

Cost-Plus-A-Fixed-Fee Supply Contracts

By far the most important class of CPFF contracts used by the Army in World War II was the group of huge supply contracts under which a large portion of the Army's aircraft, heavy ordnance equipment, and ammunition were produced. CPFF supply contracts for sums over $10,000,000 accounted for nearly 30 percent of the value of all Army supply contracts placed throughout World War II. The greatest use of these contracts was made during the defense period and the six months following Pearl Harbor. (*Table 28*) But despite the increasing pressure against the employment of this type of purchasing, the CPFF contract continued to be used on an only slightly diminished scale until the last half of 1944, by which time the bulk of the Army's contract placements for World War II was over.

A fundamental feature of CPFF supply contracts, which set them apart from construction and other types of CPFF contract, was the nature of the fee. This had important implications in view of the repetitive type of operations involved under production contracts as opposed to construction and similar activities. The fixed fee in the case of supply contracts was something of a misnomer; it was not a lump-sum profit for the entire contract but was computed and stated as a guaranteed profit *per unit* of output. Unit fees were determined by the application of an accepted percentage figure—subject to the statutory maximum of 7 percent—to the estimated unit costs of the product. The total profit for the entire contract thus represented the multiplication of the unit fee by the total volume produced. With the production of astronomical quantities of output under assembly-line methods, especially in the field of small arms ammunition, small unit fees or variations therein resulted in extremely large total-profit figures. Inasmuch as unit fees were originally set at levels which were high in the light of even-

[24] ASF M–102, Training Unit Contract Instructions—ASTP and AAF College Training Program, 1 Dec 43.

[25] (1) B–38322, 8 Dec 43, 23 Comp. Gen. 410. (2) ASF, History of Purchases Division, p. 284.

[26] 2d Ind, Gen Clay, ACofS for Materiel ASF, for CofS ASF, 24 Apr 43, to Memo, Maj Gen Thomas J. Hayes, Actg CofOrd, for Hq ASF, 22 Apr 43, sub: Report of Steps Taken To Convert Ordnance CPFF Contracts to Fixed-Price Contracts, file 161 Fixed Fee, Purchases Div ASF.

TABLE 28—WAR DEPARTMENT SUPPLY CONTRACTS PLACED IN WORLD WAR II: RELATIVE USE OF FIXED PRICE AND CPFF SUPPLY CONTRACTS [a]

[Dollars in Millions]

Period	All Supply Contracts		Individual Supply Contracts Over $10,000,000			
			ALL		CPFF	
	Number	Value	Number	Value	Number	Value
Actual						
Total	92, 871	$114, 241	1, 490	$70, 526	471	$32, 890
Jun 1940–Dec 1941	11, 258	$14, 928	270	$10, 039	113	$5, 461
1942						
Jan–Jun	13, 200	23, 103	287	15, 854	99	8, 043
Jul–Dec	15, 336	18, 792	244	12, 169	72	5, 163
1943						
Jan–Jun	14, 546	17, 944	257	11, 774	69	4, 962
Jul–Dec	11, 613	12, 642	185	7, 572	52	3, 552
1944						
Jan–Jun	13, 209	16, 908	186	11, 026	46	4, 792
Jul–Dec	13, 709	9, 924	61	2, 092	30	917
Percentage						
Average	100	100	1.6	61.7	0.5	28.8
Jun 1940–Dec 1941	100	100	2.4	67.4	1.0	36.7
1942						
Jan–Jun	100	100	2.2	68.6	0.7	34.8
Jul–Dec	100	100	1.6	64.7	0.5	27.5
1943						
Jan–Jun	100	100	1.8	65.8	0.5	27.7
Jul–Dec	100	100	1.6	60.1	0.5	28.2
1944						
Jan–Jun	100	100	1.4	65.2	0.3	28.4
Jul–Dec	100	100	0.4	21.1	0.2	9.2

[a] Excludes contracts under $50,000 and contracts for subsistence, construction and facilities.

Source: Compiled from WPB, Bur of Program and Statistics, Mil Div, Cost-Plus Supply Contracts in the War Program of $10 Million and Over, Jun 40–Dec 44, 8 Mar 45.

TABLE 29—ARMY AIR FORCES AND ORDNANCE CPFF CONTRACTS: ADVANCE ESTIMATE OF COSTS IN INDIVIDUAL CONTRACTS OVER $10,000,000

[Dollars in millions]

Period	Air Forces		Ordnance	
	CPFF Contracts (Est. Cost)	Percent of all AAF Contracts Over $10,000,000	CPFF Contracts (Est. Cost)	Percent of all Ordnance Contracts Over $10,000,000
Total	$24,163.4	55.4	$8,709.2	40.2
1941				
Jun. 1940–Dec. 1941	$3,347.2	56.4	$2,113.7	63.3
1942				
Jan.–Jun	4,437.6	61.7	3,586.7	46.1
Jul.–Dec	4,010.4	50.4	1,152.4	39.5
1943				
Jan.–Jun	4,020.3	50.3	941.9	32.0
Jul.–Dec	2,929.0	65.3	623.2	27.4
1944				
Jan.–Jun	4,620.3	53.6	172.6	9.3
Jul.–Dec	798.6	54.2	118.8	22.6

Source: Compiled from War Production Board, Bureau of Program and Statistics, Military Division, "Cost-Plus Supply Contracts in the War Program of $10 Million and Over, June 1940–December 1944," 8 March 1945.

tual economies of large-scale production, profits usually soared as production got under way, indicating the need for successive reductions in unit fees. It was this high level of realized profits which led the War Department to conclude that all CPFF contracts, as well as fixed-price contracts, should be subject to renegotiation.[27]

Aircraft and Related Contracts—The greatest use of CPFF supply contracts, in both relative and absolute terms, was made by the Army Air Forces. In the four-and-one-half-year period from June 1940 to the end of 1944, the Air Forces placed nearly

$25 billion in CPFF supply contracts, accounting for over 55 percent of all its individual contracts in excess of $10 million. The total dollar value of Air Forces contracts in this category overshadowed the comparable Ordnance figure by a ratio of nearly 3 to 1.[28] (*Table 29*) CPFF supply contracts of the remaining Army technical services were negligible, amounting only to slightly more than $18 million.

[28] War Production Board statistics understate the volume of CPFF contracts originally placed by Ordnance. See below, Tables 32 and 33, pages 295 and 296. It is probable that the WPB figures represent estimates made subsequent to terminations or reconversion of a number of CPFF contracts to the fixed-price basis.

[27] See below, pages 367–368.

TABLE 30—UNIT COSTS AND FIXED FEES UNDER CPFF AIRCRAFT CONTRACTS FOR INDIVIDUAL CONTRACTS PLACED AT SPECIFIED DATES

Item and Company	Date	Quantity	Unit Cost (Incl. Fee)	Unit Fixed Fee	
				Percent	Amount
Airframes					
B-29–Co. "A"	9–16–41	240	a $711,505	6	$40,274
	1–31–42	500	a 631,527	5	30,073
	6–30–44	200	a 269,465	4	10,365
–Co. "B"	9–16–41	5	a 711,506	6	40,274
	6–30–44	300	a 276,609	4	10,639
B-17–Co. "A"	6–21–41	300	263,964	6	14,941
	1–30–42	2,650	192,767	5	9,179
	2–5–44	2,000	144,824	4	5,570
P-38–Co. "C"	6–20–42	1,800	82,418	5	3,925
	1–8–43	800	66,861	4	2,572
	6–30–44	1,700	67,589	3	2,000
P-47–Co. "D"	10–14–41	850	73,617	6	4,167
	6–30–42	2,000	63,535	5	3,025
	5–26–43	2,115	64,849	4	2,494
	6–30–44	1,800	52,630	3.9	1,976
C-54–Co. "E"	9–26–41	52	438,450	6	24,818
	7–31–42	45	377,933	5	17,997
	2–11–43	75	381,307	4	14,666
	2–11–44	150	259,067	4	9,965
Engines					
R-1820–Co. "F"	10–10–41	6,000	11,047	7	723
	4–11–42	12,420	9,723	6	551
	2–26–43	3,053	8,520	4	328
	4–20–44	9,876	6,760	4	260
R-2800–Co. "G"	11–5–40	1,037	26,284	5	1,252
	10–8–41	1,150	26,284	5	1,252
	2–21–42	2,479	25,725	5	1,225
	9–21–43	1,501	20,820	4	801
	3–18–44	8,461	15,860	4	610
Propellers					
Blade 6477–A–O	12–4–42	41,667	2,100	5	100
	2–16–43	3,070	2,080	4	80
–Co. "H"	11–22–43	7,480	1,250	4	48

a Excludes cost of assemblies furnished by government.

Source: Tab C of Memo, Maj Gen O. P. Echols, ACofAS, for Brig Gen A. J. Browning, Asst Dir for Mat, ASF, 15 Dec 44: Sub: Inspector General's Report on Fixed Fee.

A study of unit fees in the aircraft industry reveals that percentage profit margins were successively reduced as new contracts were placed. (*Table 30*) In general, fees in aircraft contracts let at the beginning of the emergency had amounted to 7 percent of estimated cost. This was reduced to 6 percent in the latter part of the defense period, 5 percent during 1942, and 4 percent in 1943 and thereafter. The great volume of awards during the defense period had converted aircraft contractors almost literally from pygmies into giants, and fees of even 5 percent on unfilled orders provided contractors with profits huge in proportion to their net worth.[29] The reduction in fees from previous levels to 5 percent met with relatively little opposition from contractors, but they stoutly resisted the Under Secretary of War's decision in September 1942, to limit fees to 4 percent. On 4 November 1942, the Under Secretary served notice on the Douglas Aircraft Corporation that unless it voluntarily accepted a 4-percent fee in its new contracts, the Army would issue mandatory orders under Section 9 of the Selective Training and Service Act. Thereafter all aircraft firms fell into line and no large contracts provided fees in excess of 4 percent. The 4-percent rate became fairly well standardized, operating both as a minimum and a maximum, so that differences in contractors' contributions could not be substantially compensated by rate adjustments. Important differences in the contributions of contractors were, however, recognized in at least three distinct ways: in the determination of excessive

profits under renegotiation; in basing contract fees on estimated costs minus the value of government-furnished materials; and in the greater percentage return upon investment automatically accruing to producers who turned out larger quantities in a given period of time. It was the Under Secretary's opinion near the end of the war that the adoption of the 4-percent rate had "benefited the government more than would have been the case if we had had a rule permitting a higher rate, and greater variation between different contracts."[30]

It should not be overlooked that nearly half of Army procurement from the aircraft industry was obtained through fixed-price contracts. Except for firms whose fixed-price business was relatively inconsequential by comparison, the profit levels under fixed-price contracts were about double those under CPFF contracts. (*Table 31*) For reasons already indicated in the discussion of CPFF construction contracts, no final conclusions as to the relative merits of the two forms of contract can be drawn from a comparison of profit margins.

Ordnance Equipment Contracts—The CPFF contracts of the Ordnance Department fell into two major classes. The first class consisted of contracts placed with private firms for production in private plants and covered heavy or difficult-to-produce items of equipment such as tanks, heavy gun carriages, machine guns, rifles, and miscellaneous metal components of ammunition. The total number of this group of contracts was never large, probably not exceeding sixty-five at any time, and declined steadily after the spring of 1943. The sums involved in individual contracts were, however, enor-

---

[29] By early 1944, Boeing, Bell, Lockheed, and Republic had multiplied their output over one hundred times since 1938, and the net worth of the four companies combined amounted to about 1 percent of their unfilled orders. ASF, History of Purchases Division, p. 260.

[30] *Ibid.*, p. 261. The 4-percent rate was adopted jointly by the Army and Navy in dealing with the entire aircraft industry.

TABLE 31—SALES AND PROFIT MARGINS UNDER CPFF AND FIXED-PRICE CONTRACTS: MAJOR AIRCRAFT FIRMS ASSIGNED TO AAF FOR RENEGOTIATION, 1943[a]

[Dollars In Thousands]

| Firm [b] | Net Renegotiable Sales | | Net Operating Profit [c] | | | |
| | | | Amount | | Percent of Sales | |
	CPFF	FP	CPFF	FP	CPFF	FP
Total	$3,313,972	$2,674,815	$170,504	$255,731	5.1	9.6
1		89,826		8,526	—	9.5
2	211,994	19,994	11,598	720	5.5	3.5
3	486,762	6,385	32,203	374	6.6	5.9
4	—	63,085	—	6,096	—	9.7
5	272,293	544,257	11,140	55,717	4.1	10.2
6	301,662	982,943	13,669	89,950	4.5	9.2
7	947,118	38,790	48,567	1,831	5.1	4.7
8	388,778	248,188	23,776	24,871	6.1	10.0
9	173,132	424,483	5,356	41,554	3.1	9.8
10	234,897	206,103	6,771	20,316	2.9	9.9
11	40,942	28,850	2,136	3,467	5.2	12.0
12	256,394	21,911	15,288	2,309	6.0	10.5

[a] Figures apply to renegotiable sales for fiscal year of each firm.
[b] Numbers are used in lieu of firm names.
[c] After state income taxes.

Source: Tab C of Memo, Gen Echols, for Gen Browning, 15 Dec 44, sub: Inspector General's Report on Fixed Fee.

mous. (*Table 32*) The larger contracts covered almost every conceivable type of industrial activity, including research and development, construction and conversion of buildings, provision of machinery and equipment, all activities associated with production, the furnishing of many millions of dollars' worth of spare parts, complicated packing and marking operations, and countless unspecified operations. The fees for these contracts were subject to the statutory maximum of 7 percent; in practice they ran between 5 percent and 6 percent of estimated cost.[31] A number of these contracts were

eventually terminated in various stages of completion; others were converted to fixed-price contracts after production got under way and operations could be reduced to a fairly well standardized and repetitive basis.[32]

Ordnance GOCO Contracts—The second class of Ordnance CPFF contracts covered the operation of the War Department's far-flung empire of government-owned contractor-operated (GOCO) industrial facilities. These were the huge chemical and manufacturing plants which provided the bulk of the ammunition used by the armed forces of the United States and its allies under lend-lease. Under these con-

[31] Amounts of individual fees were reported for five of the twenty-five major contracts listed in Table 32. In all five cases, the fee came within the range of 5.3 percent to 5.8 percent of estimated cost.

[32] Clay indorsement cited above, note 26.

TABLE 32—ORDNANCE CPFF HEAVY EQUIPMENT AND SUPPLY CONTRACTS: AS OF
15 APRIL 1943

Amount (Estimated Cost)	Firm	Principal Type of Matériel
$4, 775, 017, 893	Total	63 equipment and supply contracts
744, 000, 000	American Locomotive	Tanks, Medium
646, 602, 648	Pressed Steel Car	Tanks, Medium, M 4
558, 842, 260	Ford Motor	Gun Motor Carriages
483, 849, 721	Pullman-Standard Car	Tank, Medium, M 4
294, 914, 761	Baldwin Locomotive	Tank, Medium M 4
216, 598, 725	Lima Locomotive	Tank, Medium M 4
181, 383, 326	Firestone Tire & Rubber	Gun Carriage, 40-mm. AA
167, 106, 021	Ford Motor	Armored Cars
144, 484, 392	Pacific Car & Foundry	Tanks and spare parts
132, 278, 164	Ford Motor	Gun Director, M 5 and M 7
114, 243, 022	Ford Motor	Armored Cars
99, 325, 234	Ford Motor	Universal Carriers
93, 476, 894	Savage Arms	Browning .50 cal. Machine Gun
79, 977, 291	Remington Arms	Rifle, .30 cal. M1903 series
69, 528, 605	Bridgeport Brass	Cartridge Case items
49, 672, 128	Chase Brass & Copper	Ammunition components
49, 153, 481	American Brass	Brass ammunition cups .30 & .50 cal.
46, 853, 254	Baldwin Locomotive	Medium Tank, M 3
46, 047, 570	Edison Gen. Electric	.50 cal. AP cores
42, 152, 501	Massey Harris	Light Tanks, M 5
41, 711. 524	Buffalo Arms	Browning .50 cal. Machine Gun
34, 433, 165	Revere Copper & Brass	Brass ammunition cups, .30 & .50 cal.
34, 262, 920	Baldwin Locomotive	Heavy tanks
30, 402, 000	Savage Arms	Rifles, Lee-Enfield cal. .303
28, 791, 286	Blaw Knox	1,000-lb Bombs
344, 900, 000	Various	38 contracts under $25 millions

Source: Compiled from Ord Dept, Report on CPFF Contracts, 15 Apr 43.

tracts private operators, utilizing government-furnished materials and facilities, turned out the billions of rounds of small arms and artillery ammunition without which all other equipment and preparations for battle would be superfluous. Some idea of the magnitude of Ordnance operations under "management fee" contracts is conveyed by a view of cost estimates in individual operating contracts in excess of $100,000,000. (*Table 33*) The predomi-nance of small arms ammunition contracts in the Ordnance Department's management-fee arrangements resulted from concentration of production in large, integrated, government-owned establishments. Artillery ammunition metal components were supplied on a large scale by private firms under either CPFF or fixed-price contracts; propellant powder and high explosives were produced in separate government-owned plants; and the shell-loading and bag-load-

TABLE 33—ORDNANCE CPFF MANAGEMENT CONTRACTS: AS OF
31 MAY 1943

Estimated Cost (Excludes Cost of Facilities)	Ordnance Field Establishment	Prime Contractors	Principal Product
$5, 356, 726, 435	Total	All Companies	Various, under 74 management fee contracts reported 31 May 1943
485, 706, 563	St. Louis Ordnance Plant_____	U.S. Cartridge_____	Cal. .30 and .50 ammunition
354, 590, 928	Twin Cities Ordnance Plant__	Federal Cartridge_____	Cal. .30 and .50 ammunition
239, 898, 998	Radford Ordnance Works____	Hercules Powder_____	Smokeless powder
213, 292, 080	Lake City Ordnance Plant____	Remington Arms_____	Cal. .50 ammunition
193, 788, 235	Sunflower Ordnance Works___	Hercules Powder_____	Smokeless Powder
183, 055, 539	Utah Ordnance Plant_____	Remington Arms_____	Cal. .30 and .50 ammunition
181, 463, 123	Holston Ordnance Works_____	Tennessee-Eastman____	RDX
166, 101, 273	Denver Ordnance Plant_____	Remington Arms_____	Cal. .30 ammunition
162, 061, 339	Des Moines Ordnance Plant__	U.S. Rubber_____	Cal. .50 AP ball
155, 533, 500	Alabama Ordnance Works #1_	Du Pont_____	Smokeless powder; diphenylamine
155, 120, 468	Evansville Ordnance Plant___	Chrysler_____	Cal. .45 ammunition; cart. cases
150, 651, 660	Oklahoma Ordnance Works___	Du Pont_____	Smokeless powder
139, 168, 299	Milwaukee Ordnance Plant___	U.S. Rubber_____	Cal. .30 and .50 ammunition
131, 402, 510	Kankakee Ordnance Works___	Du Pont_____	TNT demolition blocks
126, 025, 000	Gopher Ordnance Works_____	Du Pont_____	Smokeless powder; diphenylamine
124, 701, 663	St. Louis Core Plant_____	McQuay-Norris_____	Cal. .30 and .50 AP cores
116, 506, 257	Alabama Ordnance Works #2__	Du Pont_____	Smokeless powder; diphenylamine
107, 729, 500	Alleghany Ordnance Plant____	Kelly-Springfield_____	Cal. .30 and .50 AP ball
107, 229, 500	Lowell Ordnance Plant_____	Remington Arms_____	Cal. .50 AP ball
1, 862, 700, 000	Other Ordnance Establishments	Various_____	55 contracts under $100,000,000

Source: Compiled from Ord Dept., Monthly Report of CPFF Contracts at Ordnance Exempt Stations, 31 May 43.

ing operations were, because of the great safety hazards associated with the production of artillery ammunition, completed in a number of widely dispersed government establishments.

As in the large aircraft CPFF contracts, the fees for operation of GOCO facilities were a specified amount per unit of output, determined in advance of production on the basis of estimated costs. In the case of small arms ammunition, initial contracts placed throughout 1942 generally used the same cost estimate and the same fees for all plants. As large-scale production got under way,

the trend of costs was generally downward and sufficient cost data were obtained to permit the downward negotiation of fees. In a number of cases, especially for .30-caliber ammunition, actual costs turned out to be generally in excess of estimates.[33] A comparison of costs and fees for the six prin-

[33] More prewar production experience was available for .30-caliber than for .50-caliber ammunition, and the Ordnance Department insisted on holding the .30-caliber estimates to relatively lower levels. Memo, Capt Gustav Seidler, AUS, for Maj Vaughan, 1 Mar 43, sub: CPFF Contracts in Small Arms Ammunition Procurement, file 161 Cost-Plus-A-Fixed-Fee, Renegotiation files ASF.

TABLE 34—COSTS AND FEES FOR SMALL ARMS AMMUNITION AT SIX ORDNANCE PLANTS AS OF 1 MARCH 1943: COST PER THOUSAND ROUNDS OF COMPLETE CARTRIDGES

Item and Plant	Caliber .30			Caliber .50		
	Ball	Tracer	Armor Piercing	Tracer	Armor Piercing	Incendiary
Cost Estimate						
All Plants (Average)	$38.46	$58.40	$67.28	$195.18	$210.51	$300.00
Actual Costs						
St. Louis	48.39	64.78	65.34	154.72	174.25	
Lake City	46.97	66.00	67.17	176.77	175.97	202.97
Denver	42.23	57.15	55.48	—	—	—
Utah	54.20	75.78	73.89	210.80	201.81	222.96
Twin Cities	48.56	67.79	66.57	174.73	183.81	198.91
Des Moines	51.50	67.55	69.17	147.67	182.74	176.23
Fee						
Amount						
Des Moines a	$2.00	$3.00	$3.60	$10.00	$11.00	$15.00
Other Five Plants	1.50	2.00	2.50	7.00	8.00	9.00
Percent of actual costs						
St. Louis	3.10	3.09	3.83	4.52	4.59	—
Lake City	3.19	3.03	3.72	3.96	4.55	4.43
Denver	3.55	3.50	4.51	—	—	—
Utah	2.77	2.64	3.38	3.32	3.96	4.04
Twin Cities	3.09	2.95	3.76	4.01	4.35	4.52
Des Moines	3.88	4.44	5.20	6.77	6.02	8.51

a Negotiations for downward revision were in process on 1 March 1943.

Source: Memo, Capt Seidler for Maj Vaughan, 1 Mar 43, sub: CPFF Contracts in Small Arms Ammunition Procurement.

cipal small arms ammunition plants as of 1 March 1943 indicates that interplant differentials were not, in general, large. (*Table 34*)

Fees for the production of powder and high explosives were, percentagewise, among the lowest for all contracting operations in World War II. (*Table 35*) The highest fees in this group were those allowed for the more novel, complex, and hazardous operations, running to 6.2 percent of actual costs in the case of smokeless powder. For shell-loading plants, which performed final operations on an assembly-line basis, fees averaged only 2.3 percent of total cost con-

sisting predominantly of the cost of components from other GOCO plants.[34]

Administrative Control of Fixed-Fee Contracts

The preceding pages have indicated the extent to which the CPFF contract was used by the Army in World War II, the classes of procurement involved, and representative

[34] The Ordnance Department furnished most of the know-how for the planning and operation of shell-loading plants. By contrast, the new ammonia plants of World War II, whose operations showed a 6.5-percent ratio of fees to costs, were operated under processes developed by contractors. Conversation, author with Dr. Robert O. Bengis, Industrial Div OCofOrd, 7 Feb 57.

TABLE 35—OPERATIONS UNDER CPFF CONTRACTS FOR HEAVY AMMUNITION: CUMULATIVE COSTS AND FEES TO 30 SEPTEMBER 1944

[Dollars in Thousands]

Class of Plant	Total Costs of Operation	Total Fees	
		Amount	Percent of Cost of Operation
Total___	$2,024,296	$81,880	4.0
Shell loading___	729,634	16,484	2.3
Bag loading___	81,928	2,492	3.0
Depots___	47,295	394	0.8
Smokeless powder___	596,645	36,929	6.2
RDX–TNT___	431,112	18,846	4.4
Ammonia___	47,861	3,128	6.5
Fiber container___	69,509	2,752	4.0
Ammonium nitrate___	20,312	855	4.2

Source: Price Liaison Section, Purchases Division ASF.

data on costs and fees. As part of the record it is desirable to summarize some of the administrative controls established, the protracted efforts to convert CPFF contracts to fixed-price contracts, and some general conclusions.

Administration of CPFF contracts improved substantially between the time the early construction contracts were let during the defense period and the last year or two of the war. Noteworthy improvements included the expansion and refinement of policies, procedures, and organizations for the advance estimating of costs, setting and revising fees, defining allowable elements of cost, and auditing contract operations. Numerous matters of policy and procedure involving the General Accounting Office were clarified, and, at a more basic level, organizations and procedures were developed for cost analysis and production control, resulting in substantial savings in material and manpower and increased efficiency of operations.

A fundamental requirement for CPFF contracts, which was nonexistent for fixed-price contracts, was the necessity for government audit and approval of all accrued costs under the contract. As far back as Pearl Harbor, it was evident that greater uniformity in defining allowable costs under CPFF contracts was needed throughout all the technical services and their field establishments. Existing regulations and practice were at once insufficient and overly elaborate to enable contracting and disbursing officers to make decisions on the allowability of many cost items. The novel conditions of war production gave rise to numerous problems and questions not covered by previous regulations. For example, what should be the policy concerning specific reimbursement by the government of such costs as employee bonuses, overtime and shift premiums, vacation pay, retirement programs, and various welfare activities? Should the fees of professional accountants and attorneys be included as operating costs, payable by the government, even when the services of such personnel were devoted to litigation against the government? What limitations should be placed upon advertising expenditures and what types of advertising should be considered as part of the company's normal operations? Should newspaper and radio advertising be placed on a par with conventional advertising in trade or technical journals? How about entertainment, charitable contributions, compensation and travel expenses of directors, the cost of plant newspapers, and the expenses of setting up an office with twenty-five people to administer payroll deductions for War Bond purchases? Who should defray the expenses of a truckload of Hollywood "cheesecake" imported to put on a War Bond drive or boost morale in the plant? [35] And what of ten thousand other more mundane questions— answered either unsatisfactorily or not at all by TD 5000—concerning the determination and allocation of overhead items of cost to specific contracts with firms holding dozens of contracts of many sizes in both the CPFF and fixed-price categories? Until definite answers to these questions were found, all cost reimbursement paid to contractors were purely conditional. The Comptroller General of the United States had the power to audit all CPFF contracts, to disallow specific cost items, and to "suspend" specific payments made by disbursing officers of procuring agencies. The procuring agencies were then required to recover all such payments by offsets or any other legal means.

At the same time that dependable answers to these questions in their many ramifications were lacking, the traditional peacetime method of detailed checking and auditing of government expenditures to the last penny before a contractor could be reimbursed put an impossible burden upon the War Department's struggling and often inadequate wartime fiscal and accounting organization. Rigid observance of detailed auditing requirements resulted in the expenditure of as much time and effort on small inconsequential items as on large and important ones. Contractors with relatively complete and efficient accounting systems were subject to the same procedures as those with inadequate and unsatisfactory systems. As a result of these conditions, contractors dealing with different technical services were subjected to different treatment for identical items, numerous disallowances were made by the Comptroller General, payments to contractors were slowed down, war production was hindered, and contracting and disbursing officers were obliged to look to the War Department for closer guidance. [36]

On 27 May 1942, two months after the War Department reorganization, the newly appointed director of the Fiscal Division, ASF, addressed an elaborate memorandum to all technical services, the AAF, all corps areas, and other major components of the War Department. This memorandum, which was countersigned by the Commanding General, ASF, and the Under Secretary of War, announced a new policy of selective and flexible audit procedures for work under CPFF contracts. The new procedures were designed to minimize routine checking,

---

[35] This is not a facetious or far-fetched illustration. Contracting officers, auditors, and the staff of the Comptroller General faced this issue and hundreds of similar specific problems in the course of the war.

[36] (1) ASF, History of Purchases Division, pp. 269–70. (2) Memo, Brig Gen Arthur H. Carter, Dir Fiscal Div SOS, for CofCWS et al., 27 May 42, sub: Administrative Audit of CPFF Contracts, reproduced in WD Manual for Administrative Audit of Cost-Plus-A-Fixed-Fee Supply Contracts, 14 Aug 42, Exhibit 44 in above cited history.

eliminate duplication of audit activities, and expedite payments to contractors. At the same time they were to improve and standardize cost allowance policies, insure adequate documentation of expenses, and provide more effective over-all accounting control. The basic philosophy underlying the new approach was the development within the contractor's own accounting organization of a system of internal controls, or checks and balances, which would automatically reveal irregularities and enable trained government auditors using selective audit techniques to protect the interests of the government. By August 1942 detailed regulations to achieve these purposes were embodied in two separately published manuals governing the auditing of CPFF contracts, one for supply contracts and the other for construction contracts.[37] Successive revisions of these manuals and the frequent publication of official cost interpretations, together with an augmented staff of trained accountants, steadily improved the auditing techniques of the War Department and adapted them to the exigencies of wartime cost control.[38]

At the end of 1943 the War Department employed approximately 6,400 auditors, many of them in minor grades, most of whom were devoted to the auditing of CPFF contracts. Considering also the greatly increased number of persons needed by contractors to meet the requirements of CPFF accounting, to say nothing of the associated expansion of the General Account-

ing Office, the costs of CPFF administration and the desire in many quarters to shift to fixed-price contracts can be easily understood.[39]

The refinement of auditing controls was an important element in protecting the government against improper charges and wasteful expenditures under CPFF contracts. But the War Department was equally concerned with the fostering of cost-reducing techniques in the basic processes of production. In this respect operations under important classes of the War Department's CPFF supply contracts were perhaps among the outstanding models of production and cost control in World War II.

The most closely knit and perhaps the most successful arrangement for the improvement of efficiency and the control of costs in a single munitions industry was the Ordnance Department's organization for the administration of its CPFF ammunition contracts. This arrangement was characterized by two developments—the establishment of specialized field co-ordinating agencies of the Ordnance Department, and the use of industry integration committees for the exchange of operational ideas and information.

In the summer of 1942, the Ordnance Department established two field control-agencies to govern its ammunition program— the Field Director of Ammunition Plants (FDAP) at St. Louis, and the Small Arms Ammunition (SAA) Suboffice at Philadelphia. The FDAP at St. Louis co-ordinated the activities of the artillery ammunition industry (calibers 20-mm. and higher) as well as the basic chemical components for all

---

[37] WD, Manual for Administrative Audit of Cost-Plus-A-Fixed-Fee Supply Contracts, 14 Aug 42 (later superseded by WD TM 14–1000 series) ; and WD CE Manual for Administrative Audit of CPFF Construction Contracts, 29 Aug 42.

[38] For additional information in this area, see the interim historical manuscript, History of Fiscal Services, 1940–1945 (3 May 1946), MS, OCMH.

[39] During World War II the General Accounting Office established 225 offices throughout the United States, each with a staff and contingent of field auditors, to expedite the audit of CPFF contracts. Hearing on S. J. Res 80, pp. 663, 694.

Ordnance ammunition, while the SAA Sub-office was responsible for smaller calibers.[40]

The original purpose of the establishment of the FDAP was to transfer the contract placement and administration activities of the Ordnance Department for this class of procurement out of Washington to a point in the field which would be closer to the operating plants. Of the total of seventy-three huge GOCO ammunition plants operating under Ordnance CPFF contracts, sixty-one were controlled by the FDAP at St. Louis. These consisted of several major categories—chemical, propellant powder, high explosive, and assembly (bag-, shell-, and bomb-loading) plants, as well as ammunition container plants. The FDAP became the "home office" for all these plants, co-ordinating their activities with those of the privately owned and operated industrial plants supplying metal components for the ammunition industry.[41]

Shortly after his appointment the first director of FDAP and his superiors in Washington decided to adopt standard procedures for the measurements and control of costs. The private operators of the GOCO plants, as previously indicated, received management fees established on a per-unit-of-output basis. These fees from the outset provided adequate incentive for rapid and high-quality production consistent with maximum safety requirements, but they exercised no positive inducement toward the reduction of costs. It was the belief of the FDAP that the regular publication and analysis of production costs on a plant-by-plant basis would stimulate competition among the various plants. With every plant manager as well as all employees anxious to make a good showing, the competitive spirit could be harnessed to pride and patriotism in lieu of the profit motive.[42] Also, with the accumulation of performance data the fees themselves, as well as renegotiation determinations, could be adjusted to reward low-cost operation. Accordingly, detailed reports of actual operations were required on a monthly basis for each plant, showing quantities of labor and materials consumed per unit of output for the various processes, trends in yields and rates of output, and dollar costs per unit. Analysis of these figures enabled the FDAP and the individual plants to detect the causes of weak spots as well as outstanding performance and to improve efficiency all along the line. The data were also invaluable for contracting officers and others in revising fees, in renegotiation proceedings, and for other purposes. Similar procedures were undertaken by the Small Arms Amunition Suboffice at Philadelphia for the twelve GOCO plants under its jurisdiction producing 90 percent of all small arms ammunition.[43]

---

[40] Small arms ammunition produced by Ordnance for both the United States and foreign nations included calibers .30, .303, 7.92-mm., 9-mm., .38, .45, .50, and .60. Thomson and Mayo, The Ordnance Department: Procurement and Supply of Munitions, Ch. 8, Small Arms Ammunition, p. 2. The heavy calibers included 20, 37, 40, 57, 60 (mortar), 75, 76, 81 (mortar), 90, 105, 120, 155, and 240 millimeters, as well as 3-inch and 8-inch calibers. The FDAP was also responsible for the production of bombs, mines, grenades, and other ammunition. Ibid., Ch. 7, Artillery Ammunition, p. 4.

[41] Rpt of Ord Dept, Administration of Cost-Plus-A-Fixed-Fee Contracts for Operation of Government-Owned Contractor-Operated Ammunition Plants (65 printed pages with maps and illustrations), 13 Oct 43, copy in OCMH.

[42] Thomson and Mayo, The Ordnance Department: Procurement and Supply of Munitions, Ch. 7, p. 42.

[43] (1) Seidler memo cited above, note 33. (2) ASF, History of Purchases Division, p. 277. (3) Rpt of Representative Albert J. Engel, Congressional Record, Vol. 90 (22 Jun 44), 6521.

Working in close co-operation with the FDAP and the SAA Suboffice were the appropriate industry integration committees established by the Ordnance Department to pool knowledge of production methods which would lead to increased output and reduced costs. Of a maximum of 131 committees in existence at one time, 75 were concerned with ammunition.[44] The efforts of the industry integration committees—combined with those of the ammunition field offices and the staff of both the Ordnance Department and the contractor at individual plants—resulted in an enviable record of cost reduction, increased output, and technical improvements in both end products and production processes. Thus, in World War I the price of TNT had ranged from 26 cents to 55 cents per pound; in World War II the cost of TNT produced in GOCO plants dropped from 29 cents to 7 cents per pound. In April 1941, 7.61 gallons of alcohol were required for each one hundred pounds of smokeless powder; by 1944 the figure had dropped to 1.9 gallons, saving an estimated 50 million gallons of alcohol for this one purpose alone. Numerous statistics in this area provide a substantial case for the efficiency of operations at the Army's ammunition plants under CPFF contracts.[45]

With all the various influences making for improvement of efficiency under the CPFF

ammunition contracts, it would be difficult to demonstrate that this form of contract was less satisfactory for its purposes than the fixed-price variety. On the strength of the record, the Ordnance Department was able to convince Headquarters, ASF, as well as the Under Secretary of War and Congress, that abandonment of the CPFF procedure in the ammunition procurement program would result in grave damage without compensating benefits. Unit costs of ammunition were highly sensitive to changes in volume, and unpredictable fluctuations in ammunition requirements right on up to the end of the war rendered the use of fixed prices unsatisfactory. Furthermore, because of the great safety hazards involved, it was desirable to eliminate profit-motivated pressures upon cost. Throughout all the efforts of the War Department to convert its CPFF contracts to a fixed-price basis, the Ordnance Department's GOCO contracts were exempted. Somewhat parallel administrative efforts were made for the control of operations under AAF CPFF contracts, but the size and complexity of aircraft procurement rendered impracticable the same degree of cost control.[46]

The Conversion of CPFF Contracts

Despite Congressional sanction of the CPFF form of contract at the beginning of the defense period, hostility toward this instrument remained throughout World War II. By the time of Pearl Harbor committees and individual members of Congress had received many reports of extravagant expenditures, pirating and hoarding of

---

[44] Lt. Gen. Levin H. Campbell, Jr., *The Industry-Ordnance Team* (Whittlesey House, New York: McGraw-Hill Book Company, Inc., 1946), p. 118. This book, whose author was the Army's Chief of Ordnance during World War II, is replete with practical information on the Ordnance task in all its ramifications. Committees were composed of Ordnance personnel and management representatives from each plant.

[45] Rpt of Representative Albert J. Engel, *Congressional Record*, Vol. 90 (22 Jun 44), 6519–25.

[46] For a brief summary of AAF administrative controls over CPFF contracts, see ASF, History of Purchases Division, p. 278.

labor, bidding up of the prices of materials and supplies, and the outright waste or destruction of scarce materials by CPFF contractors. Bills to prohibit or limit the use of CPFF contracts were regularly introduced in Congress both before and after Pearl Harbor, and the War Department was constantly on the defensive in explaining the necessity for CPFF contracting and the shortcomings of administration thereunder.

Operations under CPFF construction contracts came in for especially heavy criticism. A common complaint against fixed-fee construction contractors was their wasteful disposition of left overs at various stages of project completion. Thus, charges were made that many thousands of board feet of usable lumber were burned to avoid the trouble and expense of systematic collection and resale, that high-grade steel was plowed underground by bulldozers, and that expensive tools were sold at "give away" prices. Even more serious were complaints from workers, chambers of commerce, patriotic observers, and others of the damage to morale and the war production effort resulting from on-the-job idleness of thousands of workers with insufficient tasks to keep them occupied. Some of the most serious complaints emanated from critical labor-shortage areas in which excessive quantities of labor had been recruited under CPFF contracts at higher than prevailing wages and long in advance of actual need. These reports were not confined to the "tooling up" period early in the war but continued on into 1945. It began to be generally felt—especially in the case of the construction, shipbuilding, and aircraft industries—that only the pressure upon costs resulting from the existence of closely negotiated fixed prices could compel contractors to exercise minimum standards of efficiency. Even

loosely negotiated fixed prices, in the light of renegotiation and other factors, were thought to be preferable to a continuation of CPFF contracting.[47]

From the outset the War Department's directives and procurement instructions had stated the official policy of keeping the number of CPFF contracts to a minimum consistent with timely procurement.[48] On 1 July 1942 the WPB Purchases Policy Committee, on which the War Department had a leading position, proposed the transformation of CPFF to fixed-price contracts wherever possible.[49] On September 1942 the Under Secretary of War addressed a lengthy memorandum to the Army Air Forces stating the official policy of the War Department to discontinue the use of CPFF contracts for new procurement except where absolutely necessary and to take steps to convert existing CPFF contracts to the fixed-price variety whenever possible. Likewise, the Tryon Statement of War Department purchase policy, issued on 19 November 1942, called for the minimum use of CPFF contracts and their conversion to fixed-price agreements wherever feasible. Thereafter until the end of the war, the Army was engaged in an almost continuous effort to convert its out-

---

[47] In addition to the types referred to above, numerous examples of waste under CPFF contracts may be found in the hearings and reports of the Truman Committee, the House and Senate Military and Naval Affairs Committees, the appropriation committees, and others. See also *Hearings on S. J. Res. 80*. Many of these charges—notably the one concerning the burial of high-grade steel—collapsed upon investigation. Groves Commentary, pp. 110–11.

[48] These directives are so numerous as to preclude a detailed recital at this juncture. For important examples, see ASF, History of Purchases Division, pp. 234–58.

[49] Testimony of Donald Nelson, 2 Mar 44, in *Hearings on S. J. Res. 80*, p. 615.

standing CPFF contracts, with certain notable exceptions, to a fixed-price basis.[50]

Until the final year of the war the effort to convert CPFF contracts to a fixed-price basis was largely a failure. Although neither the AAF nor the Ordnance Department was eager to convert, the greatest barrier was the stubborn resistance of contractors. Faced with production problems of the first magnitude and still plagued with many of the identical pricing difficulties which made CPFF contracting necessary at the outset, the majority of aircraft and ordnance heavy equipment producers in 1943 and 1944 were unwilling to consider conversion. Few of them were willing to undergo the major financial and accounting operation required to effect the conversion process, and protracted negotiations with the General Accounting Office indicated that no conversion would be final until approved by the Comptroller General. Some contractors, moreover, felt that they had no legal or moral obligation to convert since they would not have accepted the original contract on a fixed-price basis. Still others believed it would be impossible to operate on a fixed-price basis.

The reluctance of contractors to convert is well illustrated by this verbal exchange between a leading aircraft engine producer (K) and the chief of the Production Division, Air Transport Service Command, at Wright Field (W):

K. Say, K. B. What's the matter with that contract of ours over there?

W. We have a directive from Under Secretary Patterson.

K. How would you like a directive from me now?

W. That's all right. We have lots of bosses.

K. Now, we have the plant going. It will be up to schedule this month. Why don't you turn it over to Wright and combine it with their Lockland operation and make it all one job. I will take Coppert and Newburgh out of there, and a few of our men and bring them back to Detroit. We've established the thing now. The job is of no interest to us.

W. I don't agree with you.

K. We don't seem to be able to get along satisfactorily with you fellows. . . . We can't write contracts that go through. We're not going to go through another mess of writing another contract. We have men all over the country. The labor situation is getting tough anyway. . . . There is no interest, no desire, on our part to undertake the job of writing the contract, or to shoulder the many changes that are involved.

W. What do you suggest that I tell them?

K. Tell them that we're not interested at all in continuing the operation of the Chicago plant under any other contract than what we have, and that we worked hard on that job and we'll have it up to full production this month, and if somebody can be enthused and interested in doing the job the other way, we will be perfectly willing to step out.[51]

The more important specific reasons underlying the opposition to conversion may be summarized as follows:

1. Many new contracts, such as for the B–29, still lacked sufficient cost experience

---

[50] The principal exceptions were research and development contracts (see above, page 288) and those covering Ordnance GOCO plants under the ammunition program. The latter were considered to be efficiently run under the special administrative procedures already described and to be subject to special considerations making fixed prices undesirable (see above, pages 294, 302). (1) Hayes memo cited above, note 26. (2) Rpt of Ord Dept, Administration of Cost-Plus-A-Fixed-Fee Contracts for Operation of Government-Owned Contractor-Operated Ammunition Plants.

[51] Excerpts from memorandum, Telephone Conversation between General [Kenneth B.] Wolfe and Mr. K. T. Keller, Chrysler Corporation, Detroit, Michigan, 14 March 1945, copy in OCMH. This concerned the proposed conversion, to a fixed-price basis of the contract covering the operation of the mammoth $175 million Chrysler aircraft motor plant at Chicago, Illinois. See first entry, Table 52, page 496.

upon which to base a mutually acceptable price.

2. Constant changes in specifications, under both old and new contracts for heavy and complex equipment, were necessary either for production reasons or to meet the needs of the using arms. Many of these changes would unsettle any fixed price as soon as it was established. Neither contractors nor procuring agencies had the time to debate the proper price adjustment called for by each change; this would be taken care of automatically under CPFF contracts.[52]

3. If conversions were prospective only (to cover the uncompleted portion of contracts), production shutdowns would be required in order to take inventories of all parts, supplies, materials, and goods in process. This would result in chaos and drastic curtailment of output.[53]

4. Retroactive conversions to the beginning of the contract required revisions of the contractor's accounting system, separate costing of government-furnished equipment, complete adjustments for fixed-fee sub-

contractors simultaneously working under numerous prime contracts, and other complications.[54]

5. It was feared by contractors and many officers of the War Department that all conversions would have to receive the approval of the Comptroller General. Recent rulings of the Comptroller General (B–34484 and B–34503) had indicated that he would require a full accounting of expenditures under the conversion and would overrule conversions where the fixed price was in excess of the amount payable under the original contract. Binding decisions between contractors and procurement agencies could not be made, and elaborate cost-accounting operations, the elimination of which was a basic reason for conversion, would continue thereafter.[55]

---

[52] Between two hundred and four hundred changes per month were reported to have been made on M4 and M4A1 tanks. For M5A1 tanks, the number of engineering changes was said to have been even greater. Incl 2 to Safford ltr cited above, note 5.

[53] Many contractors had not taken a physical inventory since the beginning of the war and, by 1944, individually held many millions of dollars worth of government-owned materials, parts, supplies, and subassemblies. In the spring of 1945 the Ford Motor Company indicated that the taking of a physical inventory for the conversion of one of its tank contracts would cause at least a three-week shutdown, with resulting loss of employees and objections from labor groups, as well as the shutdown of the Fisher (General Motors) and Chrysler plants which depended on Ford for tank engines. Ordnance Department Program—Conversion of CPFF Contracts, 18 Apr 45, attached to Memo Routing Slip, Col Harold Shepherd, OCofOrd, to Lt Col Frank S. Rowley, Chf Legal Br, Dir of Materiel ASF, 19 Apr 45, file 161 CPFF, Purchases Div ASF.

[54] In order for a fixed price to be adopted in a prime contract, it was necessary to obtain firm prices in important subcontracts, but this could not be done when the subcontractor was producing jointly for a number of primes under various contract conditions. The unraveling of the many practical and legal complexities involved might well run long after the end of the war. In March of 1945 it was estimated that under the most optimistic time schedule the conversion of Douglas Aircraft Company contracts could not be effected prior to 1 May 1946. Incl 2 to Memo, Maj Gen Oliver P. Echols, ACofAS Hq AAF, for USW, 2 Apr 45, sub: Conversion of CPFF Contracts to Fixed Price Basis, file 161 CPFF, Purchases Div ASF.

[55] Although the War Department officially took the position that conversions could be made without consulting the Comptroller General, failure to do so would leave contractors "holding the bag," since cost disallowances and suspensions by the comptroller still had to be reckoned with. For this reason some contractors insisted that their adoption of a conversion agreement would be made only with the written, advance approval of the Comptroller General. (1) Memo, Brig Gen Aaron E. Jones, OACofAS AAF, for Special Representative of USW, 12 Sep 44, Sub: Proposal of Lockheed Aircraft Corporation To Convert CPFF B–17 Contracts to Fixed Price. (2) Memo of Conf With the Under Secretary of War (unsigned), 28 Sep 44. (3) William C. Foster, Memo of Conf Held in Judge Pat-

By early 1944 only three aircraft contracts and eight ordnance CPFF equipment contracts of significant size had been converted.[56] At this time the whole conversion problem was highlighted by the introduction in Congress, by Senator Homer Ferguson, of Senate Joint Resolution 80 prohibiting the further use of CPFF contracts except when specifically authorized by the departmental secretary and calling for compulsory conversion of existing CPFF agreements within ninety days after the passage of the proposed legislation. Senator Ferguson introduced into the hearings on this resolution his own testimony and a report which cited flagrant examples of waste, inefficiency, contractor indifference, in-plant idleness of workers in critical labor areas, and other abuses under CPFF operations. During the extensive hearings, testimony was given by most of the war production leaders, including Donald Nelson and the Under Secretaries of the War and Navy Departments.[57]

As in previous hearings both before and during the war, the War and Navy Departments defended the necessity for CPFF contracting under various conditions and made strong representations that compulsory conversion, especially under a drastic time limitation, would play havoc with vitally needed war production.[58] As a result

the legislative proposal was abandoned, and the War Contracts Subcommittee of the Senate Committee on Military Affairs made the following statement:

We soon came to the conclusion that the form of contract is not the decisive factor in determining the efficiency or inefficiency with which manpower, materials, and machinery are put to use in war production. In fact, we have found many situations where highly effective operations were being conducted under cost-plus-fixed-fee contracts and where any other form of contract would have contributed to inefficiency.[59]

Although the threat of legislative compulsion to convert all CPFF contracts was once more removed, the net result of the hearings just described was increased pressure by the War Department for conversion by contractors in nonexempted categories. At the same time, rumors that the expiring renegotiation law would not be extended beyond 1944 led a number of aircraft contractors to look favorably upon conversion of certain of their contracts, some of them nearing completion, to a fixed-price basis. This about-face was looked upon with considerable skepticism in certain quarters of the War Department, where it was felt that conversion with probable higher profit margins would not be an unmixed blessing for the government.[60] Nevertheless, Under Secretary Patterson was firm in his view that in the long run conversion would be econom-

---

terson's Office, 28 Sep 44, sub: Conversion of CPFF Contracts to Fixed-Price Contracts and Continuation of Renegotiation During 1945. (4) Memo (unsigned), 6 Oct 44, sub: Discussion Relationships With the Comptroller General. All in file 161 CPFF, Purchases Div ASF.

[56] Testimony of Under Secretary Patterson, 7 Mar 44, in *Hearings on S. J. Res. 80*, p. 673.

[57] *Hearings on S. J. Res. 80*, pp. 591–764, covering the period 2–8 March 1944.

[58] The insuperable obstacles posed by the pending legislation are well described in: (1) Memo, Col Irving A. Duffy, OCofOrd, for Chf Legal Br, Dir of Materiel Hq ASF, 10 Jun 44, sub: Senate Military Affairs Committee Revision of S. J. Res.

80 Dated 15 May 1944; (2) Teletype, Carroll, Materiel Command Wright Field, to Chf Legal Br, Procurement Div ACofAS AAF, 6 Jun 44; (3) Memo (unsigned), 7 Jun 44, sub: Proposed Substitute for S. J. Res. 80. All under Tab C to Notes on the Settlement of Terminated Cost-Plus-A-Fixed-Fee Supply Contracts, 12 Oct 44, in file 161 CPFF, Purchases Div ASF.

[59] 78th Cong., 2d Sess., Year-End Report of the War Contracts Subcommittee to the Committee on Military Affairs Pursuant to S. Res. 198, 18 Dec 44, p. 1.

[60] Teletype cited above, note 58(2).

ical and in the public interest from other standpoints. He saw no difficulty in obtaining an extension of statutory renegotiation through 1945 and looked to renegotiation as a method of protecting the government against any major mistakes in pricing under conversion agreements.[61]

Despite persistent efforts throughout 1944 only a handful of conversions were effected. Early in 1945, however, a development occurred which undoubtedly helped to crystallize the Under Secretary of War's determination to insist upon the conversion of all CPFF contracts except those in the exempted classes. On 19 February 1945, there was officially transmitted to the Under Secretary a collection of reports and recommendations made by the War Department Inspector General following a special inspection in the summer of 1944 of contracts, operations, and earnings in a number of aircraft plants under War Department contracts. The Inspector General's findings were almost uniformly a recital of excessive fees and profits under CPFF contracts, resulting from substantial overestimates of costs at the time contracts were let. In addition, The Inspector General made frequent criticisms of waste and inefficiency, as well as of loose pricing in the case of fixed-price contracts. For almost every individual plant, The Inspector General recommended that fees be reduced or contracts converted to the fixed-price basis.

As one example, The Inspector General pointed to an initial contract calling for two thousand planes for a fee of $10.4 million, based on an estimated cost of $208.6 million. Despite heavy starting-load costs, the total cost of the planes turned out to be only $147 million. Nevertheless, a second lot of two thousand planes from the same plant

was contracted for at a fee of $7.2 million, representing a fee of 4 percent upon a calculated cost of $179.2 million. Since the heavy initial costs had already been paid for under the first contract, The Inspector General felt that the new arrangement was merely a device to allow excessive fees while specifying a nominal 4-percent profit rate. The Inspector General further noted that the fees at this plant (only one of several under the same operator) amounted to several times the outstanding capitalization ($6 million) of the entire firm.[62]

In the case of an aircraft engine manufacturer, The Inspector General noted that under the contract a fixed fee of 6 percent was allowed for the initial ten thousand engines, based on estimated costs of $25,315 per engine despite the fact that another firm was supplying a similar engine at the fixed price of $21,020. The Inspector General stated that the CPFF contractor in estimating his own costs had added over $4,000 per engine to the fixed price of his competitor for tooling costs, starting load, labor inefficiency, abnormal scrap, and similar items, resulting in additional fee costs to the government of $2.4 million under the contract. The Inspector General's further remarks in this case are typical of those in his report covering some twenty-one plants in the aircraft industry:

It is not believed a contractor should receive a fee based on inefficiency. The total fixed fee . . . to be paid the contractor is $29,301,-168.70. In this case the contractor assumes no risk except that some unrelated expendi-

---

[61] Foster memo cited above, note 55(3).

[62] IG, 29 July 1944, comment by The Inspector General in Special Inspection of the Administration of War Department Contracts . . . , Tab A, Incl 1 to Memo, Gen Echols, ACofAS Materiel and Services, Hq AAF, for Brig Gen Albert J. Browning, Asst Dir of Matériel ASF, 15 Dec 44, file 161 Cost-Plus-A-Fixed-Fee, Renegotiation files ASF.

ture made by him may not be allowable under the contract, as the contracting officer and/or the General Accounting Office may determine, which is on the whole a very small amount. In this case the Government has built the contractor a large expensive plant, has furnished him the machinery and equipment, and has advanced him funds with which to operate. He is now permitted to rehabilitate and to use some of his other plants to manufacture parts for the engine. He is reimbursed for salaries paid to all the executive officers and all other employees at this plant, and further he is reimbursed for a proportion of the overhead of the Detroit home office. Under the foregoing circumstances, it is believed that the present fixed fee is exorbitant and should be substantially reduced.[63]

By the time the official file was transmitted to Under Secretary Patterson, The Inspector General's report had been subjected to elaborate refutation and comment by the Air inspector and the director of Procurement, Air Technical Service Command, at Wright Field, the AAF Materiel Command in Washington, and the Under Secrechase policy.[64] Since The Inspector General had challenged the basic philosophy underlying the CPFF form of contract, indicating that established percentage fees ought to be applied to figures in the neighborhood of actual costs when these consistently fell below the advance estimates, a full-dress review was made of the nature and effects of CPFF contracting. The special representative of the Under Secretary pointed to the fact that The Inspector General's report

really called for a return to the outlawed CPPC form of contracting, that the reduction of actual costs below the advance estimates was precisely what the government hoped for in its CPFF contracts, and that the government had no more claim to a downward revision of the fee after contract completion than the contractor would for an upward revision if the circumstances were reversed.

Furthermore, the fees allowed by the AAF compared favorably with those of the Maritime Commission for shipbuilding and for the more complex production activities at Ordnance GOCO plants. The aeronautical industry was currently turning out 30 times the dollar value, as well as from 30 to 50 times the physical volume, of its production before the war but was only earning 15 times as much before taxes and 3 times as much after taxes. Renegotiation boards, with few exceptions, had found earnings in the aircraft industry reasonable, and the several reductions over the previous three years from 7 to 4 percent of estimated costs were thought to have carried fees as low as they could go without serious impairment of incentives. Finally, the special representative pointed to a basic difference between the American system for operating government-owned plants as contrasted with that of the British. The British engaged management on a fixed annual fee. The U.S. Government, on the other hand, in the case of both ordnance and aircraft plants provided fees on a per-unit-of-output basis. This rewarded management in proportion to its productivity, providing a powerful incentive to increased output:

In a discussion with British production officials within the last two weeks Brigadier General Albert J. Browning discussed the apparent greatly increased production in Government-owned plants in this country as

---

[63] IG, 2 August 1944, *ibid.*

[64] (1) Reply by Air inspector on each individual comment of TIG. (2) Memo, Brig Gen Orval R. Cook, Chf Procurement Div, Wright Field, for CG AAF, 11 Nov 44, sub: Inspector General's Report on Fixed Fees. (3) Memo, Gen Jones, Chf Procurement Div, ACofAS Materiel and Services, for Col Foy, Special Representative of USW, 15 Feb 45, sub: Army Air Forces CPFF Contracts Reply of The Inspector General. All in file 161 Cost-Plus-A-Fixed-Fee, Renegotiation files ASF.

compared with Government-owned plants in Great Britain. The British officials expressed amazement at the greater rates of production here. Since technical designs and equipment are roughly similar, the major difference appears to be in the manner of setting the compensation.[65]

In a separate memorandum the Under Secretary's representative stated his conclusion that the existing methods of setting fees were satisfactory and that The Inspector General had agreed that no further comments would be made on these points in future reports if the Under Secretary concurred in this conclusion.[66]

The basic impetus to conversion of CPFF contracts was not, however, a concern with excessive contractor earnings or the adequacy of incentives to output. Fundamentally, the objective was to obtain an across-the-board reduction in *costs,* expressed in terms both of dollars and real resources. The overwhelmingly preponderant element in total contract charges was not contractor fees or profits but costs. A small percentage reduction in costs would compensate many times for a much larger percentage increase in contractor earnings. The challenging problem facing the War Department was how to make cost expenditures painful to contractors without inhibiting their operations. This could not be achieved by an elaborate system of auditing and related controls as required in the case of CPFF contracts. Nor, as the hearings leading to the adoption of renegotiation in 1942 had so abundantly demonstrated, could it be accomplished merely by the adoption of generous figures in the simple fixed-price form of contract. Fixed prices based on artificially high advance estimates of cost, with no subsequent provision for cost re-examination, could be far more dangerous than fixed fees based on the same estimates. Ever since 1942 the War Department had been working on the seemingly insoluble riddle of how to establish, in advance of production, fixed prices which would be close to actual costs and at the same time encourage production efficiencies which would result in final costs far below the original estimates. By 1945 the Under Secretary believed that sufficient answers to this question had been found to warrant the discontinuance of the CPFF contract.[67]

Accordingly, on 8 March 1945 Patterson addressed a memorandum to the Commanding Generals, ASF and AAF, ordering the conversion, by the earliest possible date, of all War Department CPFF contracts not in exempted categories. The two commands were directed to submit, no later than 1 April 1945, a plan which listed each outstanding CPFF contract and the date when conversion was expected. The plan was to proceed on the assumption that contracts not so converted would be terminated and replaced by mandatory orders under the Selective Service Act and related legislation. Recently developed pricing articles in Procurement Regulations, as well as a new incentive-type contract introduced by the Navy, were available for establishing the new terms of the converted contracts.[68]

This decision marked the launching of a concerted drive at numerous echelons of the War Department to accomplish the huge task of conversion. Exploratory field trips

---

[65] Memo, Col Foy for USW, 19 Feb 45, sub: Fees on AAF CPFF Contracts, file 161 Cost-Plus-A-Fixed-Fee, Renegotiation files ASF.

[66] Memo, Col Foy, for USW, 19 Feb 45, sub: Recommendation as to Method of Setting Fees on Air Forces CPFF Contracts, file 161 Cost-Plus-A-Fixed-Fee, Renegotiation files ASF.

[67] See below, pages 330–32.
[68] Memo, USW Patterson for CG ASF and CG AAF, 8 Mar 45, file 161 CPFF, Purchases Div ASF.

were made by officers in the Purchases Division to apprise contractors of the decision and to hold preliminary discusions of the numerous problems involved. Leading CPFF contractors were called to Washington to attend a meeting in the Under Secretary's office, at which time they were informed that there was no turning back. A committee was established to draw up detailed procedures and devise means to circumvent the problem of physical inventories with their accompanying plant shutdowns. The Under Secretary and a delegation of high-ranking officials met with the Comptroller General and obtained his approval of the broad plans for conversion. Training classes were established in the field for negotiators, contract administrators, auditors, price analysts, lawyers, and others involved in the conversion program. The Army Air Forces and the Ordnance Department submitted comprehensive conversion plans in response to the 1 April deadline. These were found not to be sufficiently expeditious and revised schedules were called for, to be submitted not later than 1 June.

By mid-1945 the conversion program was making substantial progress and the outstanding value of CPFF commitments had been considerably reduced by terminations, completions, and conversions. With the advent of mass terminations signalized by V-J Day, the complexities of conversion were superseded by the complexities of contract settlement.[69]

---

[69] See below, Part Seven. Principal documents in support of the above paragraph include: (1) Memo, Harry E. Howell to Foster, 14 Mar 45, sub: Problem of Inventories in Converting CPFF Contracts; (2) Safford ltr and incls cited above, note 5; (3) Memo, Col Foy for Foster and Howell, 31 Mar 45; (4) Ltr, Gen Safford to CG ASF, 31 Mar. 45, sub: Plan for Converting CPFF Supply Contracts; (5) Echols memo (cited above, note 54) with incls, Plan for Conversion, with Exhibit A, and Copy of teletype, dated 3 Mar 45; (6) Ltr, William L. Marbury, Legal Asst to Dir of Materiel ASF, to Col D. C. Swatland, Materiel Command Wright Field, 4 Apr 45 (detailed summary of meeting of WD officials with the Comptroller General of the United States, 2 Apr 45) and attached outline of conversion plan; (7) Memo, Foster for CG AAF, 28 Apr 45, sub:ᵉ Conversion of CPFF Contracts to Fixed-Price Basis (eight pages of detailed procedures and problems). All in file 161 CPFF, Purchases Div ASF; (8) ASF, History of Purchases Division, pp. 254–58.

CHAPTER XIII

Pricing in Fixed-Price Contracts

The administration of its fixed-price contracts for World War II forced the Army to come to grips most completely with the basic issues of wartime pricing policy. As the nation moved rapidly through the defense period into a wartime economy, many of the functions of the traditional price system were supplanted to an unprecedented degree by direct controls. The allocation of basic industrial materials, to facilitate both the creation of industrial capacity and the production of finished munitions, was accomplished increasingly by administrative decisions and procedures stemming directly from the character of national war production objectives. The maintenance of the general price level for civilian-type products as well as for materials and supplies entering jointly into civilian and war goods was accomplished chiefly by controls set up and administered by the Office of Price Administration. The organization of production and the application and modification of technology within productive establishments were determined increasingly by criteria of engineering efficiency and feasibility, the necessities of conservation and substitution, the rapidity of invention resulting from the forced draft of scientific research and development, and other factors directing the use of real resources independently of considerations of price.

This independence of basic economic decisions from price considerations was, however, only partial, and it varied in degree from sector to sector of the total economy depending upon the necessity and practicability of alternative methods of control. After Pearl Harbor, when the supreme mandate upon the procuring agencies was the provision of adequate munitions in time to win the war, the role of price in placing most prime contracts was seemingly relegated to a minor position. But there was one pricing consideration so fundamental and all-pervasive for all military procurement that it was simply taken for granted. This was the requirement that prices in military contracts be adequate at all times to cover costs and permit the effective prosecution of the war production program. It was this requirement, rather than the "greed of munitions makers" or an unexplainable accumulation of one-directional errors, which resulted in the development of widespread overpricing in the year following America's entry into the war.

The CPFF contract may be regarded in this context as a device to outflank the formal problem of advance price determination while guaranteeing the coverage of all costs. Loosely negotiated fixed-price contracts achieved a substantially similar guarantee while at the same time observing the formality of advance agreement upon price. But neither the evasion nor the purely nominal discharge of the traditional requirement that contract prices be determined in advance could avoid the consequences of the failure to price correctly. Correct pricing required the minimization as well as the coverage of costs if economy of real resources and the proper control of profits, inflation, and the expenditure of public funds were to be achieved.

In order to attain these ends in the absence of competitive pressure upon costs, it became necessary for the procuring agencies to enter a field of operations completely foreign to traditional, peacetime procurement activities. This field was the examination and analysis of the costs of individual firms engaged in production under war contracts. Under normal business conditions the costs of a low-bid, fixed-price contractor were of no interest to the government and might even be said to constitute legitimate "trade secrets" properly confined to the management of the firm involved. In time of war, however, when the success of the procurement program and even the outcome of the war itself depended upon the most efficient utilization of all resources, the costs of each producing firm became a matter of concern to the nation as a whole. Accordingly, the Second War Powers Act, under Title XIII, gave the government the power to inspect and audit any books, records, documents, or physical evidence pertaining to war contracts, subcontracts, or orders in furtherance of war production.[1]

The use of this power, as well as the conduct of many other facets of the total procurement program, required a revolution in previously existing legal concepts, business practices, governmental procedures, and basic attitudes. The relationship between the government and its contractors

was gradually transformed from an "arm's length" relationship between two more or less equal parties in a business transaction into an undefined but intimate relationship —partly business, partly fiduciary, and partly unilateral—in which the financial, contractual, statutory, and other instruments and assumptions of economic activity were reshaped to meet the ultimate requirements of victory in war.

Under the new conditions, contracts ceased to be completely binding: fixed prices in contracts often became only tentative and provisional prices; excessive profits received by contractors were recoverable by the government; and potential losses resulting from many causes—including errors, poor judgment, and performance failures on the part of contractors—were averted by modification and amendment of contracts, with or without legal "consideration," whenever required by the exigencies of the war effort. These new conditions were bewildering and often disturbing to those with conventional attitudes, but in the main both business and government showed remarkable flexibility in adapting their behavior to practical necessity. In the absence of such adaptation the nation's heroic industrial accomplishments in World War II could not have been achieved.

The foregoing is not meant to suggest that the law of contracts was scrapped or that procurement activities in World War II proceeded in a legal vacuum. On the contrary, every effort was made to assure the legal sufficiency of all contracts at all times. The focal point of the legal revolution lay in the progressive modification of the law, first by Congress, next by the executive arm of the government culminating in opinions of the Attorney General, and eventually through ratification by the courts. The cardinal

---

[1] 56 *Stat.* 176, 27 Mar 42, Second War Powers Act.

principle underlying all these changes was the furtherance of the war effort.[2]

It was within this novel legal and institutional framework that the Army's basic policies and procedures in the pricing of war contracts were developed. Only in such a milieu of freedom of action and experimentation was it possible for the Army to forge and maintain the instruments of purchase policy which would be suitable for the complex, dynamic, and unprecedented needs of total economic mobilization.[3]

Price Analysis

The wide assortment of pricing techniques which eventually became known in the Army Service Forces as "price analysis" had its beginnings in the defense period. Many large contracts for aircraft, heavy ordnance, and other equipment were placed at this time on a fixed-price basis through negotiations with firms which were for all practical purposes "sole sources." In the absence of competitive-bid prices it was necessary to obtain cost estimates from each contractor in support of his price proposals. Because of the many uncertainties involved—including future prices and availability of labor and materials, the necessity for expansion of the contractor's plant, equipment, and organization, the lack of adequate accounting systems, and many other factors associated with conversion to war production—these cost estimates were often very crude. Nevertheless, because of the pressure to confine the use of CPFF contracts to cases where the problem of advance pricing was virtually hopeless, it was War Department policy to make maximum use of fixed-price contracts despite the unsatisfactory basis for many of the prices actually adopted.

In other areas of procurement, competition was initially available and contracts could be let to low bidders. As the rearmament program absorbed more and more of the nation's remaining productive capacity, it became necessary to make wide use of less efficient firms and to pay differential prices which would cover the increased costs of marginal firms. In negotiating prices under these conditions, informal bidding procedures provided data for price comparisons which could be used with varying degrees of effectiveness in persuading contractors to keep their prices in line. But with the disappearance of available capacity from more and more industries, each individual firm tended to become a monopoly or "sole source" for additional quantities and items of required procurement. Under these circumstances price comparisons would have to be supplemented by cost analysis on a wider and wider scale in order to insure reasonable prices and prevent the process of contract negotiation from degenerating into

---

[2] The classic example of the application of this doctrine was the opinion of the Attorney General (40 Op. Atty. Gen. 225, 29 August 1942), permitting the exercise and delegation of almost unlimited contracting powers by the Secretary of War under Executive Order 9001 of 27 December 1941. Executive Order 9001 was the detailed Presidential order delegating the sweeping powers the President had received under the First War Powers Act. These powers permitted the setting aside of the law of contracts wherever deemed essential to the war effort and in large measure resulted in the substitution of administrative law for previously existing statutory and common law. Under the Attorney General's opinion, redelegation of these powers without limit was permitted so long as this was essential to the prosecution of the war; otherwise they would amount merely to "dead powers."

[3] For a survey of numerous legal problems involved in procurement pricing in World War II, see David Fain and Richard F. Watt, "War Procurement—A New Pattern in Contracts," *Columbia Law Review*, Vol. 44, No. 2 (March 1944), 127–215.

a haggle over hypothetical claims with little foundation in reality.

These were the conditions existing shortly after Pearl Harbor when Congressional hearings gave wide publicity to the charge of profiteering in war contracts.[4] War Department procurement officials were well aware at this time of the necessity for closer pricing and that this would require more intensive use of cost analysis prior to the adoption of fixed prices in contracts. But they were also aware of what was not generally understood or appreciated by the public at large—the almost insurmountable difficulties associated with the task of developing the machinery and procedures for effective cost analysis on the scale required by the gigantic procurement program of World War II. For the larger part of 1942 the total procurement organization of the War Department was strained to the limit in determining requirements, translating requirements into contracts, developing new and improved weapons and equipment, refining specifications, searching out additional productive capacity, creating new capacity, participating in the development, launching, and operation of new material control systems, scheduling and expediting production, and discharging numerous other responsibilities. All these functions had to be performed while the Army was in the throes of the complete reorganization and expansion of its own far-flung establishment. Apart from the quantitative demands upon the time and energies of procurement personnel, the achievement of effective cost analysis depended upon the progress of the procurement program to reasonable maturity and stabilization, the development of established working procedures and rela-

tions with contractors, the creation or refinement by contractors of their own cost accounting systems, and the education of all concerned in the fundamentals of wartime pricing policy.

Instruments of Price Analysis

Notwithstanding these difficulties, considerable advance in developing the instruments of price analysis was made in 1942. A primary instrument was the contractor's proposal form, adopted or improved in 1942 by all the technical services. This form covered all important aspects of proposed contracts but was predominantly concerned with details of cost and price. It required the contractor's written statement of estimated costs in support of his proposal to undertake a given contract. With the refinement and standardization of proposal forms the required cost breakdowns became increasingly specific so that negotiators could more easily discover questionable inclusions in cost.[5]

A second instrument to facilitate price analysis was the negotiator's check list, which listed all significant considerations to be identified and weighed by negotiators in their evaluation of the propriety of proposed prices and other contract terms. The check list pointed to a wide variety of specific considerations under a dozen or more main headings such as item description, contract placement procedure used (formal competition, competitive negotiation, or sole-source negotiation), type of contract involved (fixed-price, modified fixed-price, or CPFF), comparisons of past prices and fac-

---

[4] See below, Chapter XV.

[5] By mid-1942 the Chicago Ordnance District had developed a standard eighteen-page proposal form for all important awards. History of Ordnance Pricing Policy, Exhibits 1, 13.

tors affecting their significance, basis for CPFF fees, individual categories of cost, effect of government-furnished tools and equipment upon price, effects of subcontracting upon pyramiding of taxes, profit, and so on, and the implications of proposed acquisitions of land, buildings, machine tools, and other equipment.[6]

A third instrument of price analysis developed in 1942 was the negotiation summary sheet, or its equivalent, used in procurement offices to provide a permanent record in each contract file of the significant considerations underlying each award. The details of the summary sheet varied from contract to contract since the basic purpose was to record important elements of the particular negotiation concerned. The summary sheets were invaluable both for providing important pricing information for use in future negotiations and for defending the terms of the contract should the occasion therefor arise.[7]

Still another tool of price analysis was available in the data prepared in support of contract clearance requests. Because contracts subject to the clearance requirement were larger and more important than others, negotiations were more complex and contracts had to be drawn with greater care. In order to provide adequate justification of contract terms reviewable by higher authority, clearance applications had to contain much more information on comparative prices, costs, and other factors than did the ordinary negotiation summary

sheets for smaller contracts. For all these reasons the detailed clearance applications provided a fertile source of information on many types of pricing situation.[8]

By 1943 the progress of the procurement program as a whole had reached the point where the War Department was able to devote a major effort to the task of war contract pricing in all its ramifications. In the spring of 1943, beginning with the definite adoption and publication in Procurement Regulations of the policies enunciated in the Tryon Statement, a thoroughgoing revision and consolidation of organizations, procedures, and instruments for improved pricing was undertaken. Within the Purchases Division, ASF, the office of Assistant Director for Pricing was created to concentrate under one head the supervision of all functions relating to price analysis, negotiation aids, contract clearance, renegotiation, price research, and liaison with the Office of Price Administration. Each technical service was made responsible for establishing at its headquarters level, one or more offices or agencies for the discharge of these functions, and every district or field procurement office was to install a price and cost analysis unit, staffed with competent personnel, to assume the many tasks required by the new close-pricing program. Elaborate liaison machinery was developed so that War Department pricing policy could be rapidly and efficiently transmitted and implemented throughout the Army's entire nationwide procurement organization. Close liaison permitted a two-way exchange of ideas and facilitated the prompt modification of procedures to reflect the realities faced by

[6] Price Negotiation Check List, accompanying Memo, Col Alfred B. Quinton, Jr., Asst to Chf Industrial Service OCofOrd, for Manufacturing Arsenals, Ord District Offices, and Operating Divs of Industrial Service, 22 Apr 42, sub: Contract Negotiations and Clearance of Awards, History of Ordnance Pricing Policy, Exhibit 2–A.

[7] See par. 2 of memo cited above, note 6.

[8] History of Ordnance Pricing Policy, Exhibit 18–A.

contracting officers in the front lines of procurement.[9]

One of the first steps taken under the new intensified pricing program consisted of measures to refine, simplify, and standardize the numerous contractor proposal forms in use by the technical services. By the end of 1943 twenty-one different proposal forms had been consolidated into two: War Department Procurement Form 1 (request for proposal), and Form 2 (contractor's proposal). As already noted, these forms were devised to elicit the cost and price data necessary for adequate analysis and negotiation of prices for all types of procurement. In order to minimize burdens upon industry, the forms were provided with "built-in" flexibility. They required individual contractors to supply only information pertinent to the particular negotiation and permitted a maximum of data to be filled in by the procuring agency. Even these revised forms underwent modification, and alternative forms were permitted for types of procurement peculiar to particular services.[10]

In addition to improving existing instruments of price analysis, the War Department undertook the development and refinement of many new sources of information. By the fall of 1943, the results of renegotiation for the first fiscal year under the program became available. The Purchases Division, ASF, maintained a central file of renegotiation data, including copies of all renegotiation agreements with forward pricing pro-

visions, for the use of all interested agencies.[11]

A special series of cost analysis reports for purposes of renegotiation was required of cost analysis sections in the technical services, and these reports were available to contracting officers for pricing purposes.[12] Some services, such as Ordnance, prepared a weekly digest of the basic terms of all significant purchase actions by the service's procurement offices throughout the country. The digest was circulated to all contracting officers as a guide to the latest contract prices and revisions thereof; additional data could be obtained by contracting officers upon request.[13]

Of more general significance was the index of contract price changes for all major categories of War Department procurement prepared by each of the technical services and published in consolidated form by the Purchases Division, ASF. The Army's price index series was initially undertaken in accordance with the Henderson-Patterson-Forrestal agreement to furnish OPA with information on the trend of prices for military procurement. It was generally recognized that statistics of price changes in the field of military goods, in the absence of information as to cost and profit margins, would hardly reveal the effectiveness of procurement pricing policy.[14] The Army's

[9] See PR 2, Sec. III, Contract Price Policies, Sec. IV, Negotiation of Contracts, and Sec. V, Price Supervision. An informative discussion of the operation of the price analysis program at technical service headquarters and depot levels is found in Yoshpe, Production Control in the QMC, Chapter VI.

[10] (1) ASF, History of Purchases Division, pp. 174–76. (2) History of Ordnance Pricing Policy, Exhibit 15.

[11] ASF, History of Purchases Division, p. 181.

[12] Memo and incls, Gen Browning, Dir Purchases Div ASF, for CG ASF et al., 14 Aug 43, sub: Cost Analysis Report for Renegotiation, ASF, History of Purchases Division, Exhibit 28.

[13] History of Ordnance Pricing Policy, Exhibits 22 and 22–A.

[14] This point was clearly and explicitly made in the very first issue as well as subsequent issues, of the Army's published price index series. ASF Purchases Div, Indexes of War Department Contract Price Changes, issue of 15 Jan 44, p. 1. For further discussion of this matter, see Thomas B. Worsley, Wartime Economic Stabilization and the Efficiency

price index was therefore used chiefly as an instrument of purchase policy in facilitating the discovery of prices which were out of line and which therefore required the prompt application of cost analysis and related procedures. The indexes were prepared with the technical assistance of the Bureau of Labor Statistics (BLS), which lent some of its key personnel to both the Army and the Navy for this purpose. [15]

The use of the foregoing instruments of price analysis, and of others which followed, was guided in considerable detail by the pricing principles described in the ASF manual, Pricing in War Contracts. This manual, which represented a distillation of the War Department's pricing experiences up to the time of its appearance, was a unique experiment in the diffusion of information and policy. The manual consisted of ideas and suggestions, rather than mandates and regulations which would tie the hands of procurement officers. It described the objectives of War Department pricing policy and the avenues to their attainment. Its fundamental theme was that sound pricing was essential to efficiency of pro-

duction and the success of the procurement program, and that prices which were either too high or too low would discourage productive efficiency. It recognized the necessity of fair and reasonable profits as an inducement to efficient performance as well as the legitimacy of such profits as a reward for achievement. Finally, it stressed the use of broad and informed business judgment rather than the application of detailed formulas in arriving at sound prices, at the same time cautioning that "judgment can be no better than the facts upon which it is based." Thus the Army's purchasing policy looked to the systematic accumulation of knowledge, in terms of both facts and principles, as the foundation for the whole pricing program.[16] As conceived under this program, price analysis embraced two basic procedures—price comparisons and cost analysis.[17]

Price Comparisons

Price comparisons involved the study and comparison of prices for the same or similar products in order to determine the extent to which particular prices or price proposals were out of line. If an item under consideration had been previously produced by the same company, the history of the company's past prices was reviewed. By the time the

of Government Procurement (Washington: National Security Resources Board, 1949), pp. 191–208.

[15] The first published Army-wide index appeared on 15 January 1944, and thereafter appeared as Section 1–D of the ASF Monthly Progress Report. See Memo, Gen Browning, Dir Purchases Div ASF, for USW, 15 Jan 44, sub: Indexes of War Department Contract Price Changes (accompanying ASF Purchases Div, Indexes of War Department Contract Price Changes, issue of 15 Jan 44).

For testimony as to the usefulness of the indexes, see: (1) Worsley, Wartime Economic Stabilization, p. 202; (2) Remarks of Lester Kellogg in Verbatim Official Report, Price Analysis Meeting, Ordnance Department, 2 and 3 August 1943, Cleveland, Ohio, copy in files of Purchases Div ASF, pp. 49–61. Mr. Kellogg was one of the experts assigned by the Bureau of Labor Statistics to the War Department to guide the construction of the Army price indexes.

[16] ASF M–601, Pricing in War Contracts, to Aug 43, pp. 1–4.

[17] The following summary of War Department techniques of price analysis is based primarily upon: (1) ASF M–601, Pricing in War Contracts, 2 Aug 43; (2) ASF, History of Purchases Division, Pricing, pp. 119–93; (3) History of Ordnance Pricing Policy; (4) PR 2, General Purchase Policies, especially Sec. V, Price Supervision; (5) Lloyd, "Pricing in War Contracts," pp. 235–61; (6) Verbatim Official Report, Price Analysis Meeting, Ordnance Department, 2 and 3 August 1943, Cleveland, Ohio; (7) Yoshpe, Production Control in the QMC, Ch. VI.

price analysis program had been launched, most items were procured from more than one source of supply; hence, it was usually possible to obtain a spread of past and current prices for all firms producing the item in question. The particular virtue of price comparisons lay in the fact that they provided immediate clues to irregularities in the price under consideration. Significant differences in comparative prices called for explanation, and this explanation could then be developed by an analysis of underlying costs, supplemented by other information.

In making price comparisons it was frequently of greater importance to study price *trends* than to compare existing prices. The analysis of comparative price trends could often lead to the detection of difficulties which could not be revealed by cost-analysis procedures applied to the accounts of the individual contractor. If the price trend was steadily downward for one or more producers of a particular item, the failure of the remaining producers to reduce prices indicated either the padding of costs or basic inefficiencies of production. Careful analysis of an individual contractor's cost accounts and costing procedures might reveal the padding of costs but could easily fail to indicate shortcomings in basic productive efficiency. Irregularities revealed by comparative price trends frequently led to engineering surveys which resulted in improved efficiency, actual cost reductions, and rectification of out-of-line prices. Moreover, the use of price trends did not require strict comparability of the procurement items involved. In a milieu of generally declining prices for a whole category of items, a presumption existed that the price of any item in the class should also decline. Hence, the test of competitive efficiency among producers was applied even when direct price

competition was not available as the basis for selection of contractors.

Use of price comparisons as an initial screening device to identify items which required further study was a corollary of the Army's price indexing work. Data gathered by the technical services in support of their price indexes existed in far greater detail than the data appearing in the series published for general distribution, which were of necessity confined to major items and classes of items.[18] Price indexes were not as revealing as indexes of trends in costs, but difficulties of preparing cost indexes on a wide scale were insurmountable. The use of price comparisons made it possible for the technical services to utilize their limited staffs of trained cost analysts for problem items and special cost studies.

The actual task of making specific price comparisons was far more complex than that implied by the simple term "price comparison." In order to determine in the first instance whether a given price was "really" higher than another, it was necessary to ascertain the comparability of the items involved. This required much time-consuming investigation and study to identify and evaluate differences in manufacturing tolerances, general specifications, packaging requirements, terms of shipment, quantities, delivery schedules, types of financing, facilities used, royalties, extent of subcontracting, and many other factors. For example, under some conditions a higher price might be justified under a delivery schedule extending over an eighteen-month period than for a contract calling for all deliveries within six months. This would be true where long-term

---

[18] The general indexes in the published series were based on individual-item indexes comprising some 50 percent of all War Department procurement. ASF, Monthly Progress Report, Section 1–D, Contract Price Changes, 31 Jan 45, p. 1.

commitments were undesirable because of rising costs, or for other reasons. In some cases a high proposal-price for a large quantity might indicate that a particular plant was not equipped to produce the required amount efficiently; in such cases the procurement officer might obtain lower prices by seeking out additional facilities and making split awards. Or again, two products with substantially similar general specifications might be differentiated on the basis of certain detailed tolerances; a required tolerance of one thousandth of an inch might increase component costs very heavily over a tolerance of one hundredth of an inch. The various elements entering into item comparability were known as price factors, and careful consideration of these was essential to an understanding of any specific purchase. In some cases preliminary analysis of price factors could obviate the need for a detailed cost study; in other cases it laid the necessary foundation for such a study.[19]

Cost Analysis

Cost analysis, the other main branch of price analysis, was designed to provide contracting officers with dependable information on the actual components or elements of which procurement prices were made up. Only with such information could contracting officers, in the absence of competitive pricing, apply a rigorous test to the propriety of any particular price. The findings of cost analysis not only supplied answers to questions raised by price comparisons, when these were available, but suggested many new questions to be raised in negotiating for new contracts or in revision of prices in existing contracts. The officially stated purposes of cost analysis were to evaluate price differentials attributable to variation in price factors among different producers of the same or similar items, to uncover hidden profits and unsegregated contingency charges, and to analyze profit elements in such a way as to permit the setting of prices and profits at levels which would maximize productive efficiency.[20]

The starting point in cost analysis was examination of the contractor's advance estimate of costs submitted with his basic contract proposal. The contractor's classification of costs and methods of exhibiting cost breakdowns were accepted and used wherever possible. Cost analysis was necessarily centered upon the major components of price. Meticulous accuracy was not attempted, both because of the lack of time and because of the inherent impossibility of accurate cost prediction. Attention was therefore focused upon items which were large, were easily overestimated, or afforded significant opportunities for padding. When preliminary analysis by a negotiator revealed the desirability of a more intensive cost investigation, or if technical accounting problems arose, the services of a cost analyst from the appropriate Cost Analysis Section or Fiscal Branch could be enlisted. In general, cost analysts were to be called in when the contractor could not explain his cost estimate, when his explanation of cost changes was inadequate, when he needed assistance in developing cost estimates, or when cost determinations were required for administering price adjustment articles.[21]

Four general approaches, or combinations thereof, were available in varying degree in applying cost analysis: (1) the contractor's cost figures could be tested for in-

---

[19] ASF M–601, Pricing in War Contracts, 2 Aug 43, pp. 7–13, and A–1 to A–15.

[20] Ibid., p. 19, Components of Price.
[21] Ibid, p. 21.

ternal consistency and for propriety of particular items without reference to experience under other war contracts; (2) the estimates could be compared with the contractor's own current and prior cost experience under specific contracts for similar items; (3) cost estimates for major categories could be compared with the distribution of costs under the contractor's recent operating statements; and (4) comparison could be made with the costs of other firms producing similar items. The degree to which any or all of these were used depended upon their relative availability, the financial amounts involved, and other factors.

Propriety and Consistency of Costs—The first approach was applicable to all cost estimates and, early in the procurement program when no comparative data were available, was often the only one at hand. Under this approach costs were scrutinized and tested for propriety along lines somewhat similar to tests for the general allowability of costs under CPFF contracts. Important raw material and parts prices, wage rates, freight rates, and other item costs were ascertained from reliable sources. Raw material requirements, scrap allowances, estimated labor requirements, and other important quantitative magnitudes were reviewed and cost extensions and tabulations checked for general accuracy. Both the actual allowances for and the allocations of indirect costs such as factory overhead, selling expense, and general and administrative expense were examined. When improprieties or discrepancies were revealed, they were challenged, and in the process of negotiation estimates were often scaled down and proposals revised. Many of the activities under this heading were of the kind dictated by

common sense and generally observed by private industry under comparable circumstances as essential to sound purchase practice.

Contractor's Prior Cost Experience—The second approach, comparison with the contractor's past costs experienced for the same or similar items, became available on a wide scale as the war production program went into high gear and repeat orders accounted for a substantial portion of all new procurement. Under these conditions it was possible to compare the new cost estimates with recent cost experience as well as with the original estimates underlying the previous contract. This permitted the ascertainment of cost trends and the deviation in realized costs from previous advance estimates. Cost trends were typically of greater significance in predicting future costs than average realized costs over the life of prior contracts. If new cost estimates were out of line with recently experienced costs, searching questions could be asked in the process of negotiation. It was not uncommon for contractors to submit new contract proposals calling for prices which were the same as, or even higher than, those in previous contracts, despite the fact that downward trends in costs had been experienced. The following unit-cost and price figures, taken from an actual case, illustrate some of the issues:

Item	Contractor's Proposal	Contractor's Past Costs	Contract Agreement
Material.........	$373	$364	$373
Labor...........	198	177	172
Factory Expense..	399	363	313
Total Mfg. Cost......	$970	$904	$858
General Expense..	15	15	15
Profit...........	63	49	56
Price.......	$1,048	$968	$929

In this case the contractor had submitted a proposal for a repeat order at a unit price of $1,048 with a cost breakdown as indicated in the first column. Upon request for cost data covering prior production, the company submitted the figures shown in the second column. Examination revealed that estimated future costs exceeded past costs by $9 per unit for materials, $21 for labor, and $36 for factory expense. Concentrating upon the latter two elements, the price analyst ascertained that the increase in estimated labor cost was due to the inclusion of an allowance for a possible increase in wage rates. Investigation revealed no reliable evidence of a pending increase. Moreover, past experience in developing labor efficiency indicated that future labor costs per unit would probably actually decline. Inquiry as to the contractor's costing methods revealed that factory expense was applied on the basis of direct labor dollars: for each dollar of increase in labor costs the company added another $1.71 in overhead charges. The $36 increase in factory expense had thus been based on the $21 labor cost contingency allowance. Further investigation revealed a probable increase in total volume of operations, so that factory expense per unit should actually decline. Under the circumstances, the contractor was asked to resubmit his bid. The negotiated final price, together with its breakdown, is indicated in the third column.[22]

Contractor's Operating Statements—A third approach in the application of cost analysis was the comparison of a contractor's proposal with past costs as revealed by his general operating statement rather than by cost allocations to specific contracts. One of the commonest experiences of procurement officers was the negotiation of contracts at apparently close prices only to discover later that realized costs turned out to be far less than the estimates. The usual reason for this was the drastic reduction of various indirect or overhead costs per unit as the contractor's general volume of business expanded. At the time each contract was placed, overhead costs were apportioned to the contract on the basis of past ratios. Even when the increase in volume under the new contract was taken into account, there was no guarantee of the future propriety of a given overhead allowance. Subsequent increases in civilian business, or additional war contracts later placed by other procuring agencies, tended to reduce costs for contracts already in existence. Nor did this process cease when firms reached "capacity" operations. Increases in efficiency with the accumulation of experience tended to release capacity for still further orders; by completing contracts ahead of schedule, the contractor could take on additional orders before the end of the year, thereby reducing overhead costs still further.

Notwithstanding this general tendency during the greater part of the war, contractors continued to use past ratios in preparing bid proposals and it was necessary for negotiators to obtain copies of contractors' most recent operating statements in order to evaluate the estimates. If a contractor's general business was comparable to the item under consideration, the ratios between various cost categories in the operating statement could be compared directly with those in the bid proposal. The following figures illustrate the kinds of comparison which often proved fruitful:

[22] *Ibid.,* pp. 23–25.

Item	Estimated Unit Cost in Proposal		Cost Breakdown in Operating Statement for 1942	
		Percent		Percent
Direct Material...	$1. 88	29	$836, 000	30
Direct Labor..	2. 25	35	1, 304, 000	47
Factory Expense...	1. 50	24	516, 000	19
Total Mfg. Cost..	$5. 63	88	$2, 656, 000	96
General Expense...	. 75	12	108, 000	4
Total Costs...	$6. 38	100	$2, 764, 000	100
Profit...	1. 12	18	1, 236, 000	45
Total Price or Sales..................................	$7. 50	118	$4, 000, 000	145

New Contract Data:
    Number of Items—280,000
    Value of Contract—$2,100,000
    Delivery Schedule—40,000 per month, 1 May to 30 November 1943
    1943 Estimated Sales, including this contract—$4,500,000

Analysis of the above figures reveals a number of differences between past and proposed cost ratios which called for explanation. The negotiator could show that the contractor proposed to load a total of $420,000 (for 280,000 units) in factory expense upon the new contract, despite the fact that in the previous year a total of $516,000 in factory expense sufficed for $4,000,000 worth of business. He could show that under the proposal the new contract would carry $210,000 in general expense, as against total general expense for 1942 of only $108,000. Since both these categories represented fixed costs and since the estimated volume for 1943 exceeded 1942 volume by a significant margin, fixed costs per dollar of output should decline. Moreover, the 45-percent profit realized in 1942 would cast serious doubts on the contractor's general pricing policy. Presentation of the issues in this light "often produced lower prices in a short time and without controversy." [23]

[23] *Ibid.*, p. 33. This kind of analysis and discussion represented the heart of contract negotiation

Costs of Other Contractors—The fourth major approach to cost analysis involved the comparison of costs of different producers making comparable items. This was the most complex and time-consuming approach of all and necessarily had to be used with skill. On the other hand, when successfully used it accomplished results beyond those of ordinary close-pricing techniques. By laying bare the specific reasons for greater or less efficiency, it stimulated the adoption of superior production methods by all firms engaged in the production of common items.

Intercompany cost comparisons were made either on the basis of cost data submitted in regular contract proposals or upon the basis of special cost studies during the course of actual production. In both cases great care had to be exercised to insure basic comparability of the figures involved. The

and took place throughout the entire war period. Even with constant refinement in the techniques and instruments of negotiation there was no substitute for hard work, a mastery of facts, and dedication on the part of individual negotiators.

cost-comparison technique did not assume that cost figures for different producers should necessarily be the same; rather, it insisted on adequate explanation of cost *differences*. Genuine cost differences proceeded from differences in item comparability [24] and differences in production methods. Nominal cost differences proceeded from differences in costing methods and accounting classifications. After all these differences had been ascertained, it was possible to distinguish between bonafide cost differentials which should be allowed in setting prices and unwarranted inclusion of contingency allowances and other forms of cost padding. From the standpoint of purchase policy, intercompany cost comparisons thus provided information for (1) a closer check upon the accuracy of the costs of each firm; (2) incentive pricing and the reward of superior productive efficiency; (3) selection of contractors for future orders.[25]

Special cost studies were undertaken for important items in order to stimulate cost control, to provide information for subsequent negotiations and price adjustment, and to test the general quality of price analysis activities. In the summer of 1943 the Purchases Division, ASF, requested each technical service to make and submit comprehensive price analysis studies for at least two important items. The most notable response to this request was the study made by Ordnance of the .50-caliber basic aircraft machine gun. The aircraft machine gun was one of the most important weapons used in World War II, and its procurement program over the war period ran to over half a billion dollars. In 1943 six producers, with

substantial differences in plant and equipment, production methods, wage rates, and other cost factors, were engaged in production of the aircraft gun. The first cost study, completed in September 1943, revealed a wide range of unit costs, with a 1 January 1943 range of prices running from $316 to $598 per unit including spare parts. Continued study and systematic efforts to narrow the range as well as to obtain a general reduction of costs succeeded in saving an estimated $25 million in the procurement of this item for fiscal year 1944.[26] In the fall of 1944 cumulative cost and price studies for four different dates revealed the following low and high contract prices in effect: [27]

Date	Low Price	High Price
1 January 1943	$316.48	$597.84
1 September 1943	283.92	397.49
15 May 1944	253.72	342.92
15 August 1944	225.00	339.99

At different times during this twenty-month period both the low-price and high-price positions were held by different firms.[28]

Even prior to the request of the Purchases Division, the Quartermaster Corps had un-

---

[24] Price factors as described above in the discussion of price comparisons, page 319.

[25] *Ibid.*, App. B–11.

[26] OCofOrd Industrial Div, Small Arms Br, Annual Report for FY 1944.

[27] Profit data available only for the 1 September date show a profit of $27.42 or 9.66 percent on the low price and $27.80 or 6.99 percent on the high price.

[28] OCofOrd Small Arms Br, Price Analysis of Browning Machine Gun, Caliber .50, M2, Aircraft, Basic, ASF, History of Purchases Division, Exhibit 29. The following observation was elsewhere made concerning the machine gun cost study: "The Small Arms Division, as revealed by this study, has successfully operated through the District Offices with the several contractors involved, with the result that the prices of the item have been continually reduced and the productive efficiency of the several contractors increased. It is understood that comparable studies will soon be completed covering all of the items procured by the Small Arms Division." History of Ordnance Pricing Policy, p. 19. See also, ASF, History of Purchases Division, p. 166.

dertaken a number of "yardstick" cost studies to be used in evaluating bid proposals and negotiating closer prices. Thus, on the basis of factory visits and studies of accounting and production methods, unit cost data of several producers of cotton cloth were obtained for each stage in the productive process. Data from these studies not only were useful in facilitating close pricing for the particular firms involved, but also permitted cost comparisons of integrated with nonintegrated producers. Since the initial yardstick studies of the Quartermaster Corps were undertaken before general pressure for closer pricing had developed, they were met with considerable resistance by contractors and others who felt that they interfered with production.[29]

Allowance for Profit—In addition to its concern with the analysis of costs as ordinarily defined, price analysis necessarily had to consider profit as an integral component of price. Under the competitive-bidding procedure of the prewar period, contracting officers had been unconcerned with the level of profits; whatever profit the low bidder could make under his contract was considered to be the appropriate reward of management. This view coincided with that of traditional economic theory, under which the services of the entrepreneur were considered as one of the basic factors of production. Competitively determined profits thus represented the normal cost of recruiting the services of the entrepreneur.

In wartime, competitive bidding for universally scarce resources—including the services of entrepreneurs—tended to convert ordinary profit-making into profiteering. For this reason among others, as already explained, negotiation was adopted as the basic procedure for contract placement, and it was the responsibility of negotiators to see that the contract price included an amount, over and above "other costs," representing a reasonable profit. If profit allowances in contract prices were too high, close pricing would be defeated, with resultant losses in efficiency; if they were too low, incentives to assume war contracts and ability to meet costs would be impaired. In determining the appropriate profit allowance many factors were considered, including the firm's own prewar profits history, comparative profits throughout the particular industry, and the various criteria for proper profits as developed in renegotiation.[30]

Because of the complexity of the nation's industrial economy no single profit rate could be established for all firms and all industries which could satisfy the requirements of equity, incentive, and other essential considerations. At least two generalizations may, however, be made concerning profit allowances in the Army's fixed-price contracts for World War II. First of all, the stated profit allowance used for pricing purposes was rarely equal to the final realized profit under a given contract. Realized profits were typically much higher, a fact abundantly demonstrated in renegotiation proceedings throughout World War II. High realized profits during the war were thus not the result of generous profit allowances in contracts; rather they were the result of failure to pare down advance cost estimates, that is, to price closely. Secondly, profits were a relatively small percentage of price. The really significant savings to the government depended upon reductions in *costs*, rather than profits. The true industrial "pa-

---

[29] (1) ASF M–601, Pricing in War Contracts, 2 Aug 43, pp. 28–29, and App. B–1. (2) Yoshpe, Production Control in the QMC, pp. 61–63.

[30] ASF M–601, Pricing in War Contracts, 2 Aug 43, pp. 35–37. See below, Chapter XVI.

triot" was therefore not the entrepreneur who emerged with the lowest profit, but the one who succeeded in producing at the lowest cost.[31]

Price Adjustment Under Contractual Articles

Escalator Clauses

Price adjustment under fixed-price contracts was first attempted in the form of price "escalation" based upon changes in wage rates and material costs occurring within the life of individual contracts. At the very beginning of the defense period, hastily drafted escalator clauses were incorporated in a number of the Army's major, long-term, supply contracts. Thus the Ordnance Department's tank contract placed with the Chrysler Corporation in August 1940 provided for a flat increase in the delivered price per tank for each one-cent increase in Chrysler's average hourly wage payments, and for each five-cent increase per one hundred pounds in specified raw material prices. Downward escalation was provided for decreases in the indicated costs, and provision was made to revise the formula in the event of specification changes.[32]

In September 1940 two types of escalator clause were approved by OASW for general use in Army contracts. The first of these permitted upward or downward price revisions in the event of changes in the contractor's wage scales resulting from the adoption of new legislation, regulations, or interpretations of law, or because of "any marked change in the economic situation over which the contractor has no control." Upward or downward price revision was also permitted if the actual cost of material and equipment purchased by the contractor within ninety days after placement of the contract rose or fell by more than 10 percent. Certified copies of the contractor's wage schedules and estimated material costs at the time of contract placement had to be filed with the War Department within thirty days thereafter. At the time of contract completion, actual wage and material costs were compared with the initial schedule to determine the amount, if any, of contract price adjustment to be made.[33] In operation this form of clause gave the contractor *carte blanche* to bid up labor and material prices to whatever level he found necessary for the prompt acquisition of resources. Because of the general, as well as the specific, inflationary effects of this clause, it was little used and soon abandoned.[34]

The second type of escalator clause approved at this time provided for price adjustments, not on the basis of changes in the contractor's own costs but upon broad price indexes unaffected by the contractor's own behavior. Price adjustments because of labor-cost changes were based upon changes in national average hourly earnings in durable goods manufacture, as compiled by the U.S. Bureau of Labor Statistics; in the case

---

[31] The various issues in connection with profits under war contracts are dealt with more extensively in the discussion of contract renegotiation in Chapter XVI, below.

[32] W–Ord–461. This contract and its provision for escalation were still alive in January 1945, having been perpetuated by some three hundred supplemental agreements. Only one adjustment, amounting to about $570,000, had been made under the escalator clause by this time. Army Service Forces, Purchases Division, Pricing Policies and Methods [circa 1945], p. 11, OCMH.

[33] Draft of escalator clause, approved 12 September 1940 by OASW, Exhibit 1 in History of the Escalator Clause (1 May 1945), by Leon Malman, Legal Div OCofOrd.

[34] *Ibid.,* p. 1.

of materials, the BLS monthly wholesale-price index for the appropriate group of commodities (for example, metals and metal products) was used. Thus if direct labor costs at the time of contract placement were estimated as 40 percent of the unit price of the product, a 5-percent increase in hourly wage rates for a given month over the base month would result in an increase of 2 percent in the product price for all units scheduled for delivery in the given month. Price adjustment for material-cost changes was made only once, based on increases in the wholesale-price index occurring early in the life of the contract.[35] The War Department reserved the right to substitute any other index for labor or material costs if in its judgment the specified indexes failed to reflect satisfactorily the increases or decreases in costs of material or labor under the contract. This provision permitted equitable price adjustment when the contractor's actual costs were considerably out of line with national averages, without providing the degree of cost-plus pricing offered by the first escalator clause.

With the increasing upward pressure on the nation's price structure during the defense period, the use of escalator clauses increased in popularity and many variants were in use by the supply arms and services. In the spring of 1941 the task of framing a standard escalator clause for the entire War Department was given to the committee then engaged in the development of a uniform War Department supply contract. This committee made an extensive study of the problem and after preparing numerous drafts succeeded by September 1941 in producing a form of clause which was approved by OUSW as mandatory whenever an escalator clause was used. As indicated by the

following résumé of the governing directive, the general principles applicable to the use of this clause clearly foreshadowed the philosophy underlying the later price adjustment articles:

1. The inclusion of an escalator clause should result in a lower contract price than if such a clause is not included. Before consenting to the use of the clause, the contracting officer should assure himself that all contingent elements in price to cover probable increased direct labor or material costs have been removed.

2. Escalator clauses should be used only in long-term contracts, generally involving a performance period in excess of 6 months.

3. The contract should be sufficiently large to justify the costs of administering the escalator clause; contracts for less than $100,000 generally will not warrant the adoption of escalation.[36]

The new uniform escalator clause was a clear but comprehensive statement, running to four, single-spaced, typewritten pages and covering numerous substantive and procedural aspects of price escalation. It consolidated the fruits of a year's experience with escalation under the expanding procurement program and represented a marked advance over its predecessors. It permitted either increases or decreases in the contract price, based on broad monthly indexes of price and wage movements as published by the Bureau of Labor Statistics. The use of broad indexes rather than the contractor's own costs served two purposes: it encouraged prudent purchasing on the part of contractors and protected them against demands for wage increases based on the ability of contractors to pass the increased costs on to the government. Both of these purposes were ancillary to the larger objective of preventing widespread

---

[35] *Ibid.*, Exhibit 2, draft dated 11 Sep 40.

[36] OUSW P&C Gen Dir 48, 17 Sep 41, sub: Price Adjustment Clause.

inflation throughout the economy. The uniform clause also limited price increases or decreases to the difference between estimated and actual costs, thus providing a powerful incentive for accurate initial cost estimates. High initial estimates reduced the amount of possible escalation; low estimates resulted in correspondingly low profits, since profit allowances for pricing purposes were based on initial estimates of cost.[37] Provision was made for special adjustments in the event of contract termination, important changes in production methods, or other unusual developments rendering the original estimates unsuitable as a basis for escalation. An amendment to the clause also permitted adjustments to take account of newly adopted payroll taxes as well as indirect labor and material costs.[38]

The uniform article did much to clarify and improve the standards of price escalation and was used in many large contracts. Nevertheless, there was increasing dissatisfaction with escalation under any formula, however devised. When applied to the contractor's own costs, the formula encouraged cost-plus operations; when applied to national averages it often unjustly rewarded or penalized the contractor when the averages had little relevance to his own cost conditions. Under the compromise formula in the uniform clause, price adjustments based on national averages were limited to changes in actual costs. This required the determination, after contract completion, of the contractor's actual direct labor and material costs and not only involved a postaudit by the War Department but opened the door to audit verification by the Comptroller General on much the same lines as required for CPFF contracts. This was fatal to prompt price adjustment and gave rise to red tape, delay, and three-way controversies over the propriety of numerous individual cost allocations and allowances. Because of the heavy administrative burden of applying escalator clauses, relatively few of them were actually invoked despite their presence in many contracts.[39]

After Pearl Harbor the growing evidence of widespread overpricing brought home the fact that escalation was only a partial approach to the problem of general price revision. Increases in wage rates and material prices were often more than offset by spreading of overhead under multiple contracts and by improvements in efficiency so that labor and material costs per unit of product were lower than before. It was clearly poor policy to provide price adjustment only for certain contingencies and not for others. If prices for Army procurement were to be fair and equitable and still provide adequate incentives to efficiency, all elements of cost and price would have to be considered. Under the pressure to improve its entire pricing procedure without delaying the placement of new contracts, the Army early in 1942 adopted the first of a series of price-adjustment articles which were to render the uniform escalator clause obsolete.[40]

---

[37] Ltr, Col H. R. Kutz, Legal Sec Fiscal Div OCofOrd, to All Contracting and Purchasing Officers of the Ord Dept, 19 Sep 41, sub: Price Adjustment Clause (Escalator Clause), par. 7, in Malman manuscript cited above, note 33.

[38] OUSW P&C Gen Dir 86, 17 Dec 41.

[39] See James F. Oates, Jr., Periodic Pricing and Price Adjustment (AIC Lecture, 10 April 1944), p. 7, reproduced as Exhibit 28 to History of Ordnance Pricing Policy.

[40] The uniform escalator clause was officially discontinued for new contracts on 26 March 1943 with the publication of Revision 14 to Procurement Regulations. In addition to administrative reasons the escalator clause was abandoned because of the greater stability of wages and material prices following the adoption of price controls and other stabilization measures. See PR 1232.1 (8–31–44). Subsequently escalation was permitted in specific

The Redetermination or Ceiling Article

The first of the new price-adjustment articles was the redetermination or "ceiling price" article adopted on 13 March 1942 and widely used thereafter.[41] This article was designed for use in contracts covering the production of items for which the contractor had no prior experience and could produce no reliable cost estimates. Under the article a tentative ceiling price, as well as an associated schedule of estimated costs, was established in the contract. The ceiling price, which typically included generous allowances for contingencies, was subject to downward redetermination on the basis of a formula after a specified percentage of total contract quantities had\ been completed. This percentage figure was divided into two parts: an initial "preliminary run," during which starting and development costs would be high, and a subsequent "test run," during which costs would presumably be normal and equivalent to those for the remainder of the contract. At the end of the test run the contractor submitted his actual costs of operation for the two runs, together with an estimate of the cost for the remainder of the contract, prorated on the basis of the test-run experience. If the new estimate of total contract cost was lower than the original estimate, the price would be reduced proportionately by an amendment to the contract. This had the effect of allowing the contractor the same profit percentage on the newly estimated costs as he was allowed on the original estimate.[42]

The redetermination article was highly popular but not conducive to close pricing. It was a convenient tool for hard-pressed contracting officers since it permitted rapid placement of contracts with little advance effort to obtain close prices on the theory that this would automatically be done later. Subsequent developments would almost certainly show price "reductions" which would "look good" for the record. From the standpoint of contractors, the redetermination article usually permitted a comfortably high ceiling price which would insure a profit even if efforts to achieve efficiency fell considerably short of the maximum. Under the original form of the clause, moreover, it was to the contractor's advantage to have high costs even for the test run: cost reductions prior to redetermination constituted a price reduction for the government, whereas cost reductions thereafter constituted profit for the contractor. Difficulties in administration constituted an even greater objection to the article's use. It frequently developed that the contractor's accounting system, despite an initial survey, was totally inadequate for the purpose, that he had taken no inventory or even a running inventory record, and that he could make no satisfactory segregation of costs applicable to the contract. In such cases it was necessary to abandon the use of the clause and seek a negotiated price by amendment to the contract under the First War Powers Act. In other cases administration of the clause was delayed until after contract

cases where government-fixed material prices—such as for rubber, gasoline, and lumber—were changed or other costs were measurably affected by governmental decisions. PR 351 (6–29–44).

[41] Purchases Br SOS Gen Dir 31, 13 Mar 42, sub: Use of Price Renegotiation Clause in Fixed Price Contracts. With the publication of Procurement Regulations the redetermination article became known as PR 341.1.

[42] For purposes of illustration, suppose that an original contract price of $12,000 had been established on the basis of estimated costs of $10,000 and a profit allowance of $2,000. If the test run indicated that total costs under the contract would fall by 20 percent to $8,000, then the price as redetermined would be $9,600, with a profit of $1,600.

completion, a failing which defeated the entire pricing operation and raised serious questions as to the legality of the contract on the ground that it had been converted to a cost-plus-a-percentage-of-cost basis.[43] Finally, the use of any pricing formula which relied upon the determination of "actual costs" inevitably led to detailed audits and myopic concentration upon past costs. This robbed the fixed-price contract of much of its *raison d'être* and substituted rigid formality for the flexibility essential to wartime contract negotiation:

> Since cost data was required to administer each of the early price adjustment articles (Redetermination and Price Revision) an accountant participated and in general contributed his judgment and his skill. He also colored the transaction by his background of training and experience, a background where disapproval exists unless and until facts are known in detail and exactly analyzed. This tendency to exactitude and precision tended to eliminate any vestige of negotiation and the parties drifted more and more to audits on the stream that ends only with the Comptroller General.[44]

Despite its shortcomings, the ceiling article was the most practicable form of price-adjustment article available during the period of heavy new procurement in 1942. It continued to be used in modified form throughout the war for new items for which only rough estimates of cost could be made in advance of production. In its revised form, the ceiling article was made more flexible by permitting other factors than test-run costs to be considered in the redetermination of price. Also, an important incentive feature was introduced by allowing the dollar profit contemplated under the original price to remain after redetermination.[45] Unfortunately, this feature rewarded the contractor equally whether his cost reduction was the result of efficiency or whether it represented merely the scaling down of a highly inflated initial cost estimate. As a result, the clause made it possible for contractors to retain profits which were much too high in relation to specific tasks performed.[46]

The Price-Revision Article

In order to overcome the disadvantages of the redetermination article, the Purchases Division attempted to popularize a companion article known as price revision, and often referred to as PR 341.2. The price-revision article was originally known as the renegotiation article, under which name it had been published on 13 March 1942 as an alternative to the redetermination article.[47] After the enactment of statutory renegotiation and the assignment of a specialized meaning to the term "renegotiation," the article was renamed and underwent a series of refinements as indicated in Procurement Regulations. In its developed form, PR 341.2 permitted either upward or downward revision of the entire price on the basis of negotiation rather than through applica-

---

[43] History of Ordnance Pricing Policy, p. 6. Contractors were required to maintain adequate accounting systems as a prerequisite to the use of price-adjustment articles. But in the early stages of the war, production considerations were relatively more important than bookkeeping, and it was often impossible for contracting officers to appraise, in advance, the adequacy of the accounting systems of all the firms under their procurement jurisdiction.

[44] *Ibid.* See the comparable problems of contract settlement by formula, as discussed below, pages 619–20.

[45] PR 341.1 (3–26–43).

[46] ASF, History of Purchases Division, p. 148.

[47] See below, page 353.

tion of a formula. The negotiations for revision were undertaken following a "trial run," covering not more than 40 percent nor less than 20 percent of total quantities under the contract. The costs experienced under the trial run were compared with the original cost estimates and were used as evidence of the contractor's efficiency. Negotiations could be flexible and permitted the award of higher profit margins for reduced costs. Failure to reach agreement resulted in retention of the original contract price. It was hoped that this article, by permitting upward as well as downward price revisions, would induce contractors to eliminate contingency allowances in price and accept closer initial prices.

Throughout 1942, however, contractors were still in the habit of dealing "at arm's length" with the government and were dubious of their prospects for a subsequent price increase in the event their actual cost experience proved unfavorable. Hence they preferred the safety of the ceiling article, and the price-revision article was relatively little used. This was true even after further refinements in the article were made in 1943 and 1944.[48] Also, contracting officers themselves were reluctant to use the price-revision article, especially at first. Many contracting officers reasoned that their procurement record would look better with a history of successive price reductions, such as would take place under the ceiling article, and they wished to avoid requests for price increases

and the consequent burden of negotiations under the revision article.[49]

The Development of Progressive Pricing

Developments in the latter part of 1942 laid the foundation for one of the most significant advances in both the theory and the practice of procurement pricing to be achieved in World War II. These developments included the increasing stabilization of the procurement program as a whole, some lessons learned from statutory renegotiation, and the crystallization of pricing policy in the Tryon Statement. By the fall of 1942, most contractors had overcome their initial production problems and had acquired considerable experience in producing items of military equipment. Many of them had accumulated a substantial body of cost information. More and more contracts now represented repeat orders or new orders for items similar to those already produced; in either case sufficient cost data could be made available early in the life of the contract to permit close pricing. The need for close pricing had already become abundantly evident in the War Department's experience with statutory renegotiation.[50] The fundamental lesson of renegotiation—to be hammered home repeatedly throughout the World War II procurement program—was that renegotiation could recapture excessive dollar profits but could never recapture the lost man-hours and materials associated with loose contract pricing. The crucial task of the contract-pricing process was the creation of effective downward pressure upon *costs* throughout the life of the contract. Only such pressure could induce or compel the contractor, in the absence of competition, to

---

[48] Oates, Periodic Pricing and Price Adjustment, p. 9. In order to avoid CPPC pricing, the instructions governing the use and modification of this article made the following statement: "[The article] will *never* be changed to obligate the Government to increase the price on the basis of costs or any other formula, or to do more than negotiate in good faith to revise the price." PR 1224.1 (4–28–44). This provision undoubtedly scared many contractors away from the use of the article.

[49] History of Ordnance Pricing Policy, pp. 5–6.
[50] See below, Chapters XV and XVI.

achieve maximum efficiency and continual improvement in his methods of total organization and production. Sound pricing thus meant not only pricing close to cost, but close pricing in *advance* of production.

Recognition of advance close pricing as the key to basic efficiency and cost control became the cornerstone of the Army's matured pricing philosophy in World War II. Directives, regulations, and statements of War Department procurement officials gave expression to this concept in many different ways. Thus:

. . . it is vitally necessary to obtain sound contract prices reasonably close to costs, since recapture of profits for past periods on renegotiation will not operate to control costs or inflationary tendencies.[51]
. . . you will never get a right price by a mere profit analysis. . . . The logical result of that is "waste all of the manpower you want, waste all the materials and machinery you want, do an inefficient manufacturing job and come out with a small profit and you are a patriot." There has been too much thinking of that kind . . .
The influence upon cost and efficiency in the plant by the price you fix is many times more important than the particular profit a contractor makes. The profit is a small element in total price, very often . . . The savings . . . don't come out of the profits, by and large; they come out of costs.[52]
. . . *prices should always be specifically agreed upon in advance of production* . . . . This alone is "pricing." It establishes a reward for efficiency and good management and a penalty for inefficiency.[53]

Unfortunately, a major difficulty loomed as a barrier to the determination of sound prices in advance of production for many of the Army's most important contracts. This was the long-term nature of almost any contract for large and complex items procured by Ordnance, the Air Forces, the Signal Corps, and other technical services.[54] Many of the Army's contracts ran to a year, a year-and-a-half, two years, or longer. Even with relatively stable and ascertainable costs as a basis for initial close pricing it was impossible to determine in advance that wage rates, material prices, availability of resources, and other factors would not change adversely to the contractor's interests long before the contract could be completed. But—assuming that external cost elements could be stabilized or separately dealt with— there was almost always a reasonable certainty that the contractor could, by hard work and efficiency under the pressure of close pricing, further reduce his unit costs of production. Under these circumstances an initial "close" price in a long-term contract would not long remain close to cost in the face of the very increases in efficiency which it had helped to bring about. Procurement officers were thus faced with a double paradox: sound prices, in order to achieve their purpose, had to remain close to cost; yet the whole purpose and effect of close pricing was to widen the gap between price and cost. Furthermore, a close price had to be ascertained in *advance* of production; but it was impossible to determine, in advance of production, what would constitute a close price by the time the contract was completed.

The resolution of this complex dilemma was accomplished by the abandonment of

---

[51] PR 231.1 (1–11–45).

[52] Remarks of Glen Lloyd, Asst Dir for Pricing, Purchases Div ASF, in Verbatim Official Report, Price Analysis Meeting, Ordnance Department, 2 and 3 August 1943, Cleveland, Ohio, p. 40.

[53] ASF M–609, Company Pricing, May 1945, p. 15.

[54] In addition to complex items requiring a lengthy production period, many simpler items were procured under long-term contracts because of the necessity—under the Controlled Materials Plan or for other reasons—for long-term, advance scheduling of materials, production, subcontracting, and deliveries.

the concept of a single correct or "ideal" price for each and every fixed-price contract, in favor of the adoption of the principle of progressive pricing at appropriate stages in the life of a contract. The Chicago Ordnance District had developed several experimental drafts of periodic repricing articles by the fall of 1942, and the principle of short-term pricing was incorporated as one of the elements of policy declared in the Tryon Statement. As a result, the War Department announced—on 2 January 1943— its pioneer contract clauses for the periodic adjustment of prices under long-term contracts.[55]

Early Periodic Pricing Articles—The basic features of progressive pricing were fairly simple. Unlike the earlier redetermination article, the periodic price-adjustment articles contemplated close pricing at the outset or very early in the life of the contract. Accordingly, their application was limited to cases where production costs were stable and fairly accurately known on the basis of past or current experience. For purposes of price adjustment, performance under the contract was divided into a number of specified periods, each running from three to six months. Because of the shortness of each period and in return for advantages under the contract, contingency allowances in price to cover external cost changes were to be substantially eliminated. Only contractors with satisfactory accounting systems, approved in advance, were eligible to use the articles. At the time of contract placement a firm estimate of costs was stated in the contract. Toward the end of each pricing period the contractor was required to submit a record of his experienced costs under the contract, and an adjusted price was then negotiated to cover production for the succeeding period. The adjusted price, which could be either higher or lower than the previous price, was to reflect the contractor's previous-period cost experience together with all other relevant factors. Negotiations were to be flexible and detailed audits avoided. Failure to reach agreement on a price adjustment left the previous price in effect, but unwarranted delays in negotiations or refusal on the part of a contractor to agree to a reasonable price adjustment subjected him to possible termination, compulsory orders, or other action. If the contractor succeeded, by skillful management, careful buying, or efficient production, in reducing costs for a particular period and if he made an appropriate reduction in price for the following period, he was to be allowed a higher margin of profit for the new period. Finally, in their fully developed role, the periodic articles contemplated the exemption of the entire contract, or appropriate portions thereof, from profit recapture under statutory renegotiation. This guaranteed in advance the retention of earned profits and protected the integrity of the incentive system under close pricing.

Two periodic price-adjustment articles were introduced at the beginning of 1943: Form I (PR 360.1) and Form II (PR 360.2). Form I was to be used for repeat orders or other contracts where costs were already known and close prices could be adopted at the time of contract placement. Under Form I, the contractor automatically received exemption from statutory renegotiation for the first period and could be exempted for succeeding periods at the contracting officer's discretion. Form II applied

---

[55] (1) WD SOS Memo S5–1043, 2 Jan 43, sub: Contract Clauses Providing for Periodic Adjustment of Price With Power of Exemption From Statutory Renegotiation. (2) Statement of Purchase Policies, 19 Nov 42, par. I, B, 5, in AIC R57, Contract Pricing—Principal Developments, pp. 108–15. (3) History of Ordnance Pricing Policy, p. 16.

to cases where costs were not immediately known but could be determined with reasonable accuracy by the end of the first period. At this time an adjusted first-period price was established along with a price adjustment to cover the succeeding period. Exemption from renegotiation for any period under Form II contracts lay at the discretion of the contracting officer. Throughout 1943 the use of the new articles was subject to specific approval by the Purchases Division, ASF.

Like the earlier price-revision article, which had also contemplated close pricing at the time of contract placement, the new periodic price-adjustment articles were resisted by both contractors and contracting officers. Contracting officers were fearful of the consequences of exempting contractors from statutory renegotiation as contemplated by the new price-adjustment articles. Some contracting officers felt that the appearance of higher-than-average profits after price adjustment was *ipso facto* proof of loose pricing. Others, although they understood the relationship between higher profits and increased efficiency, felt that they might have difficulty in convincing a later investigating committee of this relationship, or of the fact that their decision to exempt a particular contractor was not the result of collusion. Still others could not understand why it was necessary to take the trouble to achieve close pricing in the first place as long as the renegotiation law provided a "backstop" in the form of recapture of excessive profits. Finally, because of the novelty and implications of the authority to exempt from renegotiation, substantial restrictions on the use of this power were imposed by Headquarters, ASF: all contracts and amendments specifying the exemption had to have the prior approval of the Purchases Divi-

sion. This was an added deterrent to extensive use of the new powers. In addition to the difficulties concerning exemption from renegotiation, contracting officers tended to rely too heavily upon detailed cost accounting as the basis for price adjustment. This slowed down negotiations and discouraged wide use of the articles.[56]

For their part, contractors were slow to appreciate the advantages of the periodic articles. The greatest single barrier to contractor acceptance was the simple reluctance to forgo the comfortable protection of high initial prices which would provide a cushion against all possible contingencies.[57] Contractors in general reasoned that any excessive profits would be recaptured by the government in renegotiation; conversely, if losses were experienced it would be difficult to persuade contracting officers to make upward adjustments in price. Many felt that the amount of bookkeeping and the time required for periodic negotiations would seriously interfere with production. A discouragingly large number of contractors professed no interest in exemption from statutory renegotiation, as contemplated by the periodic articles, on the ground that the remainder of their war contracts were subject to renegotiation and they wished to maintain their automatic hedge against losses on an over-all basis. Normally, losses on particular contracts could be used to offset profits on others, thus minimizing renegotiation refunds. Losses on exempted contracts could not be so used, and—despite the possibility of retaining greater profits under

---

[56] (1) PR 1205 (1–11–45). (2) Remarks of Gen Browning, Dir Purchases Div ASF, in Verbatim Official Report, Price Analysis Meeting, Ordnance Department, 2 and 3 August 1943, Cleveland, Ohio, pp. 77–90. (3) History of Ordnance Pricing Policy, pp. 14–17.

[57] History of Ordnance Pricing Policy, p. 17.

exemption—a majority of contractors preferred to "play it safe." This reaction was not only a formidable obstacle to the use of the periodic articles but threatened to undercut the Army's whole close-pricing program. So long as this philosophy pervaded the thinking of contractors it would be impossible to adopt close pricing in individual contracts, and efficiency throughout the war production program would be substantially paralyzed by the insidious virus of cost-plus operations. Furthermore the possibility of setting off profits against losses gave rise to a significant amount of "unfair competition" by high-profit contractors who could afford to underbid other contractors not so situated under over-all renegotiation. For the foregoing and other reasons the periodic pricing articles and the power to exempt from renegotiation were relatively little used throughout 1943.[58]

Optional Periodic Pricing—Early in 1944, with indications that Congress might terminate the renegotiation law at the end of the year, the War Department redoubled its efforts to spread the gospel of close pricing. Great stress was laid upon the improvement of price analysis methods and a new "company pricing" program was launched.[59] Wider use of the periodic pricing articles was urged along with bolder use of the power to exempt closely priced contracts from statutory renegotiation. At the same time the increasing volume of terminations was leading to greater interest in close pricing on the part of contractors; as open capacity became available, competition for government contracts and repeat orders increased. This was accompanied by requests for the reinstatement of price-escalation clauses in contracts to cover wage and material cost increases which could no longer be offset by extra earnings from over-absorption of overhead costs under numerous contracts and capacity operations. The periodic pricing articles already in existence were unwieldy, since they called for price adjustment at stated intervals which did not coincide with underlying changes in costs.

To meet these conditions the Purchases Division, ASF, issued Revision 37 of the Procurement Regulations, effective 25 May 1944, making numerous changes. The most important innovation was the introduction of new optional periodic pricing articles—PR 360–A and PR 360–A.1. The distinctive feature of these articles was the fact that no price adjustment was required until a specific demand was served by either the contractor or the government. PR 360–A provided for prospective price adjustment only; PR 360–A.1 differed only by permitting retroactive price adjustment for the first period if the initial demand was made prior to delivery of 30 percent of the items. The optional feature freed all concerned from the administrative burden of periodic negotiations regardless of the underlying necessity therefor.[60] Specific limitations were imposed on the frequency of demands for price adjustment and informal cost reviews were adopted to protect the government's interests. To meet the special case of retroactive wage increases ordered by the War Labor Board, a special article (PR 360–B) was included. This permitted special adjustments not possible under articles providing only for forward price adjustments.

[58] (1) *Ibid.*, pp. 14–17. (2) Oates, Periodic Pricing and Price Adjustment, p. 13. (3) ASF, History of Purchases Division, pp. 180–82.

[59] See below, Chapter XIV.

[60] The term "periodic" continued to be officially used to describe all progressive pricing articles even after the optional feature eliminated the necessity for revision at stated periods. The terms are used interchangeably hereinafter.

TABLE 36—USE OF PERIODIC PRICING ARTICLES: BY ORDNANCE DEPARTMENT
1 APRIL 1943–1 OCTOBER 1944

[Dollars in millions]

Total contracts with 213 firms as of 30 September 1944	420
Type—awarded under periodic pricing articles:	
PR 360.1	147
OPI 3109	52
PR 360.2	133
PR 360–A	57
PR 360–A.1	18
PR 361.1	13
Status:	
In first contract period	279
In second and later periods	62
Completed or terminated	79
Value of total contracts	$2,370
Exempt from Renegotiation (33 contracts)	$236
Net savings by price adjustments	$81.1
Price reductions (146 items)	$83.0
Price increases (55 items)	$1.9

Source: History of Ordnance Pricing Policy, Exhibit 51, Ordnance Districts Periodic Price Adjustment Operation, 1 Apr 43–1 Oct 44, 30 Oct 44.

After the publication of the new optional articles, the principle of progressive price adjustment became accepted on a fairly wide scale. Contractors were apparently more willing to price closely in original contracts and to make successive reductions in subsequent negotiations. Not only did progressive pricing become increasingly popular in new contracts; many large contracts already in existence were individually amended to include one of the periodic articles. Demands for the reinstatement of general price-escalation clauses subsided although the special-purpose escalator clauses already mentioned continued to be used. The new articles were revised from time to time and still additional articles were developed before the war's end to meet new conditions. The technical service making the greatest use of the periodic articles was the Ordnance Department, which had taken a leading role in their development. On 30 October 1944 the Ordnance Department reported the results of eighteen months' experience with progressive pricing. (*Table 36.*)

As indicated by this report, nearly $2½ billion in Ordnance contracts were subject to progressive pricing by the fall of 1944. At that time the new optional articles were only about four months old and the original periodic articles (PR 360.1 and PR 360.2) predominated. The number of upward adjustments was slightly more than a third of the number of price reductions, but their dollar value was negligible. Although only a third of the contracts were beyond the first period, price adjustments had already resulted in estimated savings of some $80 million. Final savings under these contracts by the time of completion or termination were presumably several times this figure.[61]

---

[61] The author has been unable to discover detailed statistics for progressive pricing subsequent to those shown in Table 36.

The greatest use of the periodic articles was to come during the next few months. The greatly intensified expenditures of Ordnance equipment in the European Theater of Operations in the fall of 1944 and in the Battle of the Bulge in December created a crisis in Ordnance procurement which was to last until the spring of 1945. During this period the rapid expansion in Ordnance procurement operations resembled the hectic conditions in the months after Pearl Harbor. Sharp increases in the demand for heavy artillery, tanks, heavy transport vehicles, and the larger sizes of ammunition led to the placing of tremendous additional awards and the utilization of many new facilities without prior experience. This precipated a pricing problem, since many inexperienced and marginal operators were in no position to quote prices comparable to those of experienced producers. The value of the periodic articles in meeting this situation is indicated by the following remarks, included in a report made in April 1945:

In this connection, it should be observed that the use of the periodic pricing articles was of inestimable benefit to the Ordnance Department in securing fair and reasonable prices under these extraordinary conditions; the earlier campaigns for the more extensive employment of these articles bore fruit far beyond any previous estimates. At this writing, well in excess of $5,000,000,000 of Ordnance contracts, many of them with its most important contractors, are or have been covered by such articles. Price reductions secured have far exceeded price increases granted. The General Motors Corporation currently has over $1,000,000,000 of such contracts with Detroit Ordnance District alone.[62]

Other indications of the usefulness of price-adjustment articles appeared in a number of sources. The Signal Corps, in a study of savings from price reductions between April 1942 and November 1945 attributed savings amounting to $583 million to "price reductions made under price revision articles, negotiated forward price reductions and voluntary refunds."[63] Many illustrations of price reductions for specific items likewise gave testimony to the value of the periodic articles in conjunction with the Army's general program for close pricing. Thus:

Another example is that of a company manufacturing machine guns . . . In 1942 they had $50,000,000 in sales. After recapture they had profits of 20% plus on adjusted sales. The price before recapture could be calculated to be in the neighborhood of seven or eight hundred dollars a gun. After recapture it was four to five hundred dollars a gun.

We put in the Periodic Price Adjustment Article and the price for the last quarter of 1943 was $260 and the first quarter of 1944 was $253 a gun. The contract clause wasn't responsible for all of that, but it played its part.

The contractor felt no need to charge a high price to protect himself because he was currently protected by the fact that the price could be negotiated either up or down every three months, and he had the incentive through exemption to go after his costs, which he did in a big way.[64]

Exemption from statutory renegotiation, a feature of the above illustration, was never widely used by the War Department in World War II, either separately or in conjunction with progressive pricing. This was true even after the Purchases Division, ASF, delegated to the technical services the power

[62] History of Ordnance Pricing Policy, supplement of 24 Apr 45, p. 2.

[63] Memo, Lt Gen LeRoy Lutes, CG ASF, for USW, 27 May 46, sub: Continuation of Present Price Analysis Set-Up, Exhibit B.

[64] Oates, Periodic Pricing and Price Adjustment, p. 12. See also, ASF Annual Rpt, 1944, p. 117.

TABLE 37—INCENTIVE ARTICLE UNDER ARMY PROCUREMENT REGULATIONS

Negotiated Final Cost	Profit		Final Price to Government
	Amount	Percent	
$1,350,000	$0	0	$1,350,000 a
1,300,000	26,000	2.00	1,326,000
1,250,000	50,000	4.00	1,300,000
1,200,000 b	66,000	5.50	1,266,000 c
1,100,000	86,000	7.82	1,186,000
1,000,000	106,000	10.60	1,106,000
900,000	126,000	14.00	1,026,000
800,000	146,000	18.25	946,000

a Maximum (ceiling) price.
b War Department estimated cost, without contingencies.
c Target price.

Source: PR 378.4 (5–24–45).

to exempt, without higher approval and with authority for redelegation.[65]

The Incentive Article; Other Changes

Late in the spring of 1945 the various sections of Procurement Regulations concerned with price adjustment articles were completely revised and consolidated for more convenient and extensive use. At this time all the older articles were revised and renumbered, and several new articles made their appearance. Of most interest was a new "incentive article," which provided a sharing of cost savings between the government and the contractor.[66] The essence of

the incentive article was its provision, at the time of contract placement, of a range of prices—based on a corresponding range of estimated costs—above and below a "fair and reasonable price" known as the target price. A maximum or ceiling price was established, representing the lowest firm price acceptable to the contractor with the inclusion of all estimated contingencies. The target price represented the ceiling price stripped of all contingent allowances, and included only a "normal" rate of profit. The final contract price was established after contract completion on the basis of a review of the actual costs of performance, including realized contingencies. Such costs were known as "negotiated costs," indicating that they would be determined by reasonable accounting and other evidence as approved by the contracting officer, rather than by detailed audits subject to review by the Comptroller General. The lower the final cost, as negotiated after contract completion, the lower would be the final price to the government, but the contractor would receive a correspondingly higher profit. (Table 37)

[65] "The number of cases in which exemptions have been granted is relatively small." ASF, History of Purchases Division, p. 182. The reasons given were those already adduced above, pages 333–34. Also see above, Table 36, page 335.

[66] PR 378 (5–24–45). It should be observed that most of the earlier price adjustment articles were also "incentive" articles. The novelty of the new article was not that it introduced the incentive principle but rather that it spelled out the specific nature of the incentive in advance and in considerable detail.

The specific profit percentages and ranges of costs and prices were, of course, established by negotiation for each contract.[67]

The widespread revisions made in May 1945 represented the culmination of nearly five years of experimentation and experience with price-adjustment articles, beginning with the early escalator clauses used in the summer of 1940. Although some of the innovations came too late to be widely used in World War II, the accumulated heritage of experience with price adjustment was to bear abundant fruit in the extensive procurement operations of the Korean period and the longer period of the "Cold War." [68]

---

[67] PR 378.4 and 378.5 (5–24–45). By 30 June 1945 only one contract had been prepared by the War Department for use of the "incentive" clause. See ASF, History of Purchases Division, p. 156.

[68] During fiscal year 1952, contracts containing price-adjustment articles accounted for nearly three fourths of all contract placements by Army Ordnance, with CPFF contracts running a poor second and firm fixed-price contracts running to comparatively negligible figures. See Table II, accompanying Office Memo, Joseph C. Cruden, Asst Ord Comptroller—Pricing, ORDGC, for Chf Industrial Div, ORDIX, 27 Feb 53, copy in OCMH.

CHAPTER XIV

Multiple-Contract Pricing Review: The Company Pricing Program

Inadequacies of Individual Contract Pricing

In devising techniques for the negotiation of sound prices in its procurement contracts for World War II, the War Department quite logically placed primary emphasis upon its individual contracts. The development of price and cost analysis, the provisions of various contractual articles to facilitate close pricing, and even the formulation of broad pricing principles were basically geared to the negotiation and administration of particular contracts. By the fall of 1943, however, procurement officials realized that reliance upon attempts to obtain correct pricing in each individual contract was not sufficient to attain the fundamental objectives of War Department pricing policy. The shortcomings of the individual contract approach led to developments which culminated in the company pricing program adopted in 1944 and continued until the end of the war. This program was essentially a procedure for the review and correction of out-of-line prices and pricing practices of important war contractors, without waiting for the after-the-fact, profit-recapture technique of renegotiation.

A number of influences contributed to the development of company pricing. The most important of these was experience under the renegotiation law. The Renegotiation Act of 1942 had been adopted as an instrument both for recovering past excessive profits and developing sound forward prices which would prevent excessive profits in the future. As indicated hereafter, it was found totally impracticable to administer the renegotiation law on a contract-by-contract basis, and from the outset statutory renegotiation was applied to a company's total renegotiable sales for each past fiscal year.[1] This over-all approach to a company's war business revealed many defects in both the theory and practice of pricing on an individual contract basis. For a number of reasons, however, the renegotiation function became increasingly devoted to the recapture of past profits, and the majority of renegotiation agreements confined their treatment of current and future prices to the familiar "Boy Scout Pledge," under which the contractor promised generally to adopt a closer pricing policy in the future. Although the treatment of past profits under renegotiation created a favorable environment in which contracting officers could apply close pricing techniques in negotiating new contracts, it was clear that a major gap existed between renegotiation and forward pricing.[2]

A second influence leading to the company pricing movement was the discovery, both in renegotiation and from a wide array

[1] See below, pages 361–62.
[2] See below, pages 382 ff.

of independent sources, of the highly unsatisfactory status of prices in subcontracts. Roughly 50 percent of all Army procurement expenditures was transferred to subcontractors and suppliers, yet the War Department up to 1944 exercised relatively little control over subcontract prices. Under its fixed-price contracts the War Department was obliged to rely almost completely upon the integrity and ability of its prime contractors to insure payment of only reasonable subcontract prices. In the rapid tempo of wartime operations and under the compulsion of obtaining scarce, critical supplies and equipment, prime contractors often showed little resistance to high subcontract prices. Even under CPFF contracts, where the approval of Army contracting officers was specifically required for each purchase over $2,000 (or other specified figure), the opportunities for overcharging the government were numerous. Thus, one Ordnance subcontractor furnishing machine services and assemblies for CPFF producers of .50-caliber ammunition earned a profit of 67.83 percent on his 1942 renegotiable sales and was obliged to refund $1,634,000 in excessive profits. Another, supplying cartridge dies to Ordnance ammunition prime contractors, earned 56.25 percent and refunded more than $1,800,-000. Still another, supplying armor-plated body assemblies, earned 40.3 percent on a much larger volume and was required to refund approximately $10 million in excessive profits for his 1942 fiscal year.[3]

Notwithstanding the many examples of high profits received by first-tier subcontractors, Ordnance purchase policy officials noted that in general "the further down the subcontract line an individual war contractor is found, the higher the profits and the more excessive the price." [4] Profits of industries at the very base of the productive economy, that is, raw materials, could not be touched by renegotiation: agricultural interests, steel companies, the chemical industry, and others had succeeded in obtaining the statutory "raw material" exemption.[5] But renegotiation proceedings in industries above the raw material cutoff level had conclusively demonstrated the widespread existence of excessive profits among subcontractors and vendors. This was especially true for producers of standard commercial articles, many of which were subject to OPA price ceilings. Ceiling prices often tended to become minimum—as well as maximum—prices in an industry, and the more efficient producers were able to live quite handsomely under established ceilings. In many cases the tremendous expansion of output under conditions of declining unit costs enabled producers of standard commercial items to realize huge profits under prices which were little, if any, higher than prewar prices.[6] On the other hand, reports of the War Department Inspector General revealed substantial increases as well as unjustifiable differences in the prices paid by prime contractors and others for common parts and components such as spark plugs, generators, and bearings. Thus, while the Studebaker Corporation was able to purchase spark plugs for $.075, another War Department prime contractor was paying $.15; at the same time the govern-

---

[3] These are among cases cited in Memo, Oates, Chf Purchase Policy Br, Legal Div OCofOrd, for Gen Campbell, CofOrd, 13 Jan 44, sub: The Control of Subcontract Prices, History of Ordnance Pricing Policy, Exhibit 29.

[4] *Ibid.*, p. 4.

[5] See below, pages 376 ff.

[6] Producers of standard commercial articles tried valiantly to gain mandatory exemption from renegotiation but were not as persuasive as the advocates of the raw material exemption. See below, pages 377–78, and sources cited therein.

ment was buying spark plugs directly as spare parts at prices ranging from \$.24 to \$.65.[7]

The accumulating evidence of excessive prices and profits at all subcontractor levels indicated that the War Department's program for close pricing in individual prime contracts was in danger of substantial nullification. An excessive subcontract price—especially at several stages removed from the prime contract, normally resulted in a much greater increase in the ultimate prime contract price than the amount of the original excess. This was the result of costing and pricing practices throughout industry, which provided a significant mark-up on the cost of parts and materials with each successive transaction in the vertical journey from raw material to ultimate end product. When high mark-ups were applied at each stage to already inflated prices for underlying subcontractors, the cumulative effect was a substantial mushrooming of component costs in final end-product prices. Moreover, profit recaptures by the government through renegotiation and excess-profits taxation could never offset the increase in end-product prices resulting from pyramided costs.[8] Of greater importance, they could never recapture the lost man-hours and wasted materials resulting from the corrosion of efficiency inevitably associated with widespread loose pricing.

A common barrier to reduction of unit prices for standard commercial articles,

especially in subcontracts, was the unwillingness of producers to disturb their established price structure. Manufacturers of proprietary or standard items typically had developed over the years, at considerable advertising expense, conventional selling prices widely known and accepted by consumers. In many cases there were also long-established differentials to jobbers, distributors, and retailers whose services were indispensable to the marketing of the product. Manufacturers had found that frequent price fluctuations were highly unsettling, not only to the consumer market but to the entire structure of price differentials upon which their product distribution was based. Hence they had preferred, so far as possible, to maintain stable consumer prices and to absorb fluctuations in unit costs resulting from changes in material and labor costs, variations in overhead, and other influences, within the basic factory price. Although such manufacturers were most reluctant to reduce their product price to prime contractors or other purchasers—many of whom would continue to be customers after the war—they often proclaimed their willingness to surrender excessive profits through renegotiation refunds and excess-profits taxation and felt that this was all that should be required of them. But this procedure was not satisfactory to the War Department because of the pyramiding effect upon procurement costs and the waste of real resources already described.[9]

[7] Excerpt from Report of Inspector General on Tank-Automotive Center, dated 5 April 1943, cited in History of Ordnance Pricing Policy, Exhibit 29, p. 12.

[8] This was demonstrated in an ingenious tabulation incorporated in Ordnance Department, Legal Division, Purchase Policy Branch, Research and Inquiry Unit, Research Bulletin 6, The Importance of Close Pricing, History of Ordnance Pricing Policy, Exhibit 40.

[9] Joseph M. Dodge, Renegotiation Div, ASF, Controlling Profits from Prices on Standard Commercial Articles, 19 Jan 44, and accompanying tabulation, "Samples of Standard Product Companies" (profit margins before and after renegotiation for representative manufacturers of perishable tools, cotton and woolen textiles, bearings, and crystals), in History of Ordnance Pricing Policy, Exhibit 31, pp. 16–19; also in same history, Agenda for Regional Company Pricing Discussion, Exhibit 68, pp. 21–27.

For the above and many other reasons, War Department officials concerned with purchase policy concluded that it was necessary to supplement their efforts in the pricing of individual contracts with an over-all or "company" forward pricing program, administratively modeled along the lines of renegotiation, which would take up where renegotiation left off. First of all, a program was needed which could reach *any* war contractor, whether a prime contractor or remote subcontractor far beyond the reach of the War Department in its ordinary contractual relationships.[10] Also, apart from the question of accessibility of subcontractors, the over-all approach would overcome a number of other serious defects of individual contract pricing. The first of these was the frequent impossibility of adequate cost analysis based on cost statements submitted with bids or estimates in the process of individual contract negotiation. Time and again Army contracting officers had the experience of negotiating apparently close prices in each of a manufacturer's individual contracts — scrutinizing cost estimates, checking wage rates, material costs, and departmental, factory, and other overhead items, pruning all visible contingency allowances, and making awards at profit rates of perhaps 10 percent—only to discover later via renegotiation that profits actually realized ran to 20 percent, 30 percent, or even 50 percent. Manufacturers themselves often professed to be mystified by the results and to be anxious to co-operate in

rectifying the situation. Investigation soon revealed that padding of individual cost estimates, whether deliberate or otherwise, in many cases could not be detected by contracting officers without a general knowledge of all the contracts of the firms involved. In other cases, the close-pricing efforts of a given contracting officer were nullified by loose contracting practices of others, perhaps in different procuring agencies. Eventually those responsible for purchase policy realized that the costs which were common to two or more contracts formed a much larger proportion of total contract costs than was ordinarily understood. This was true not only of conventional overhead items, but of many items classified as direct costs.

The problem of correct allocation of costs to particular contracts was difficult enough at the time an individual contract was negotiated. The gravest difficulty of all, however, was the fact that *changes* in the manufacturer's over-all volume of business soon rendered obsolete the best cost estimates and allocations made at any particular time. This fact was of paramount importance in the case of large corporations with dozens or perhaps hundreds of contracts, both prime and sub, in various stages of completion, revision, termination, or renewal. To attempt to deal with this situation on a contract-by-contract basis would involve individual contracting officers in an endless maze of cost analysis without providing a satisfactory solution. On the other hand, a periodic review of a contractor's over-all business by a team of company pricing experts could control the general pricing practices of a contractor and correct as well as remove much of the detail ordinarily associated with individual contract negotiations.

---

[10] Renegotiation could reach all war contractors, whether prime or sub, except those exempted by statute. No such limitation existed for company pricing, which rested ultimately upon the pricing powers of departmental secretaries under Title VIII of the Revenue Act of 1943.

Adoption of the Company Pricing Program

Company pricing had its specific origins in the fall of 1943 when the Renegotiation and Purchases Divisions of ASF worked out a basis for joint action by procurement officers and renegotiation boards to deal with the pricing policies of a limited number of selected contractors.[11] At the same time, the Purchase Policy Branch of the Ordnance Department was at work on a positive program to improve advance pricing and obtain better control of prices in subcontracts. On 1 January 1944, ASF officials completed an elaborate draft of a Proposed Forward Pricing Program and circulated it among various echelons in the Ordnance Department. This proposal spelled out in considerable detail the objectives of the program, and the steps to be taken by Headquarters, ASF, the various renegotiation agencies, and all relevant offices of the Ordnance Department and other technical services. On 15 January the program was formally transmitted to General Clay, Director of Materiel, ASF.[12]

The resulting decision to inaugurate a company pricing program was fortified by Congressional hearings and discussions leading to the passage of the Renegotiation Act of 1943. Many observers, both in and out of Congress, had come to feel that con-tractors and procuring agencies had acquired sufficient experience to be able to achieve close prices in all future contracts, thereby making renegotiation unnecessary. As finally passed, on 25 February 1944, the new renegotiation law was slated to expire—in the absence of a six-month extension by the President—on 31 December 1944. At the same time, the procuring agencies were given the power, under Title VIII of the governing revenue act, to set mandatory fair prices on both prime contracts and subcontracts in cases where this objective could not be accomplished by voluntary negotiation.

On 18 January 1944, while this legislation was still pending, General Somervell called a meeting of chiefs of the technical services and ASF officials for a general review of War Department pricing policy, especially in view of the prospective expiration of renegotiation. At this meeting, Brig. Gen. Albert J. Browning announced plans for the intensification of War Department close-pricing endeavors along two lines: refinement of cost and price analysis in connection with individual contract negotiations, and the launching of forward pricing discussions on an over-all basis with contractors and subcontractors making excessive profits. Both programs would be fortified by a more liberal use of the power to exempt particular contracts from renegotiation in exchange for close prices and by the mandatory pricing power provided by Congress. The new approach to forward pricing was summed up by the Assistant Director for Pricing, Purchases Division, ASF, as consisting essentially of "a simple, integrated and effective business use of accounting, engineering, legal and statistical techniques without permitting any one [of

---

[11] Summary of Talk Made at Meeting of Chiefs of Technical Services, ASF, held 1000, 18 January 1944, by Glen Lloyd, Asst Dir for Pricing, Purchases Div, Hq ASF, in History of Ordnance Pricing Policy, Exhibit 31, p. 3.

[12] (1) Memo, Oates, for Col Duffy, Chf Legal Br OCofOrd, 4 Jan 44, sub: Forward Pricing Program, and incl, Proposed Forward Pricing Program—Submitted 1 January 1944 (32 pp. and 8 appendixes). (2) Memo, Col Duffy, ACofOrd, for Gen Clay, Dir of Materiel ASF, 15 Jan 44, sub: Forward Pricing Program. Both in History of Ordnance Pricing Policy, Exhibit 30.

these] to dominate beyond usefulness . . . on a business and production problem." [13]

Within the following two months, the procedures and objectives of company pricing were developed in considerable detail and on 29 March 1944 the program was launched on an experimental basis with a limited number of companies to be selected by each technical service.[14] On 5 July 1944 the program was made permanent and established on a broader basis.[15] With the decision to make the company pricing procedure permanent, the Army undertook

continuous efforts to create the necessary staff and organization, to educate contractors as well as procurement personnel, and to improve and refine the governing policies and procedures. Company pricing co-ordinators, responsible for the administration of the program, were appointed in the headquarters of each technical service and in each field procurement office having company pricing responsibilities. A steady stream of instructions and information concerning the program was distributed by each of the technical service headquarters, as well as by Headquarters, ASF, to appropriate offices throughout the country. Early in 1945 a series of seven regional meetings, sponsored by ASF, was held in order to consolidate experience under the program and further to educate workers in the field.[16]

During the same period War Department purchasing officials made numerous speeches before trade associations, meetings of contractors, and other business groups. News releases and articles by such officials on the nature of the company pricing program were published in newspapers, trade journals, and other media. These public relations activities were important not only for conveying information on policies and

---

[13] Summary of Talk Made at Meeting of Chiefs of Technical Services, ASF, Held 1000, 18 January 1944, by Glen Lloyd, Asst Dir for Pricing, Purchases Div, Hq ASF, in History of Ordnance Pricing Policy, Exhibit 31, p. 2. Other documents in this same exhibit recording the discussions at the 18 January meeting include: (1) Memo, Oates for Gen Campbell, 18 Jan 44, sub: Conference on Improved Pricing 18 January 1944; (2) Memo, Gen Somervell for Chfs of the Technical Services, 21 Jan 44, sub: War Department Contracting and Pricing Policy; (3) Summary of Talk Made at Meeting of Chiefs of Technical Services, ASF, Held 1000, 18 January 1944, by Gen Browning, Dir Purchases Div ASF; (4) Joseph M. Dodge, Dir Renegotiation Div ASF, Outline of Repricing Problems Created by the Eventual Elimination of Renegotiation, 19 Jan 44; (5) Dodge, Controlling Profits From Prices on Standard Commercial Articles, 19 Jan 44; (6) Memo, Gen Somervell for USW, 20 Jan 44, sub: War Department Policy for the Purchase of Supplies.

[14] Memo, Gen Clay, Dir of Materiel ASF, for CofOrd, 29 Mar 44, sub: Experimental Program for Review of Prices and Pricing Policies of Certain Selected Companies, and attached memorandum of procedures, War Department Experimental Program for Review of Company Pricing, 27 Mar 44 (21 pp. and appendix), History of Ordnance Pricing Policy, Exhibit 32.

[15] ASF Cir 207, 5 Jul 44, Pt. Three, Review of Company Prices and Price Policies. By this time the designation "company pricing" had become fairly well established in Army circles. In the Navy, which had launched a companion program in April 1944, the terms "forward pricing" and "price revision" continued to be used to describe the program. Connery, *The Navy and the Industrial Mobilization,* Ch. XII.

[16] The Ordnance Department was host to five regional meetings—Chicago, San Francisco, St. Louis, Boston, and Detroit. The Quartermaster Corps was host to the Philadelphia meeting, while arrangements for the New York meeting were handled by the Eastern Procurement District, Army Air Forces. The documents recording the discussions at these meetings provide unusual insight into the nature and practical operations of the company pricing program. See: (1) Regional Company Pricing Meeting, Philadelphia, Pennsylvania, 2–3 April 1945 (40 pp.), ASF, History of Purchases Division, Exhibit 38½; (2) Regional Company Pricing Discussion, Chicago, Illinois, 12–13 March 1945 (93 pp.), Exhibit 71; (3) Company Pricing Demonstration (35 pp.), accompanying A Typical Agendum for a Regional Meeting, Exhibit 68. Last two in History of Ordnance Pricing Policy.

procedures, but in overcoming the fears of many businessmen and their spokesmen that the new program would involve the widespread use of mandatory pricing powers or other undesirable features. Finally, through a series of ASF circulars, manuals, and changes in procurement regulations, all significant elements of the purposes and procedures of company pricing were elaborated in detail.[17]

Procedures and Results of Company Pricing

The basic procedures under the company pricing program involved the selection of contractors, preparation of data, negotiation, reaching agreement, and publication of the terms of agreements. The criteria for selection of contractors were high prices or costs, a record of excessive profits in renegotiation, or request by individual firms for special consideration of their pricing problems. Selections were made chiefly on the basis of renegotiation data, and priority was given to the more important cases. Responsibility for conducting negotiations fell to company pricing teams in the technical service having responsibility for renegotiation of the firm in question; assignments

were ordinarily made by the chief of the technical service but additional assignments could be made by the Purchases Division, ASF. Company pricing teams consisted basically of a procurement specialist, a renegotiator, and a price analyst, acting under a chairman; in appropriate cases additional representatives of other services or procuring agencies were included in the team.

Prior to negotiations the pricing team obtained all relevant data concerning the firm's activities from War Department and other sources. Copies of current contracts and their supporting cost breakdowns were obtained from procurement offices; renegotiation agreements, reports, financial spread sheets, and other data were available from price adjustment offices; price analysis sections could furnish comparative prices and costs, as well as occasional independent cost studies; fiscal sections provided audit reports and V–Loan reports; production scheduling sections furnished performance records and estimates of future volume.

The company pricing team analyzed the assembled data to ascertain the extent and causes of high prices, costs, and profits. Particularly scrutinized were allocations of common costs, prospective changes in manufacturing volume, subcontract prices, propriety of particular cost items, and differences in costs between the firm's civilian and war business. Having located so far as possible the weaknesses or objectionable features of a firm's cost and price policy, the team developed a specific plan looking to the correction of these defects. Basic agreement upon the plan by all government representatives was required in a final meeting before approaching the company. Also, complete co-ordination with other interested services and departments was sought in advance of negotiations. Co-ordination in-

---

[17] The original instructions on basic policies and procedures for the permanent company pricing program (ASF Circular 207, 5 July 1944) were superseded and amplified by ASF Circular 303, 13 September 1944, which in turn was superseded by ASF Circular 165, 8 May 1945. These basic policy and procedural instructions were eventually incorporated in Procurement Regulations (PR 3). On 30 October 1944, the Army issued its first manual on company pricing (ASF M–609). This manual was completely reissued, after a series of draft revisions, in May 1945. ASF M–609 was devoted to the art of negotiating successful company pricing agreements and contained a number of cases illustrating differences in contractors' cost conditions, price structure, profit situation, and other considerations calling for different types of agreement.

cluded (1) informing all interested contracting agencies that company pricing negotiations were being undertaken; (2) obtaining from each agency an agreement as to its participation or representation in the negotiations. Coordination made it possible to discuss all of a contractor's war business as a whole and to reach agreements which would be binding upon all interested agencies.

Company pricing negotiations could take place either in conjunction with statutory renegotiation (Class A procedure) or independently of renegotiation (Class B procedure), whichever was more convenient.[18] As in the case of renegotiation, an agenda for the meeting with company officials was carefully prepared and the successfulness of the negotiations depended in large part on the adequacy of total preparations. The meeting typically included an explanation of War Department price policies, the function of the company pricing program, a discussion of the issues brought out by the analysis of company data, a presentation by the company of its pricing problems, and the negotiation—so far as possible—of a proper pricing agreement.

Accumulated experience under the company pricing program revealed some half-dozen major problems or issues which most frequently arose in negotiations. These were (1) effects upon unit costs of future changes in volume of production; (2) discovery and elimination of contingent elements of cost; (3) determination and reduction of excessive subcontract prices; (4) determination of allowable profit margins

in estimating proper prices; (5) provision for specific adjustment of current prices, or cost elements entering future price negotiations; (6) voluntary retroactive refunds.[19]

Various types of agreement were developed to meet each of these problems. Thus, contractors were generally reluctant to enter into forward pricing agreements in the face of pending cutbacks in production schedules or in the general volume of war business. This reluctance was frequently overcome by an agreement upon short-term price reductions with a definite time limit, or reductions contingent upon the maintenance of a specified or graduated volume of sales. Many contingent items of cost, such as reserves for increases in cost of labor and materials resulting from OPA or War Labor Board decisions, were eliminated on the strength of inclusion of appropriate protective contract clauses in all of a company's relevant contracts.[20]

The problem of excessive subcontract prices was handled largely by direct War Department negotiations with a prime contractor's principal subcontractors. Wherever possible, specific price reductions were obtained from subcontractors, to be passed along to the prime. In the case of major components of end products, pricing teams endeavored to see that subcontract price reductions were passed along to the government and reflected in an appropriate reduction in the prime contract price. Where the number of subcontract price reductions was too voluminous to warrant corresponding reductions in the prime contract, the prime contractor would frequently agree to establish a "subcontract price reductions" account and to make a lump-sum refund to

---

[18] ASF M–609, Company Pricing, May 1945, pp. 4–8. Ordnance Department Class A agreements numbered about one fifth of Class B agreements. Ord Dept, Monthly Company Pricing Report—1945, 31 Mar 45, copy in History of Ordnance Pricing Policy, Exhibit 73.

[19] ASF M–609, Company Pricing, May 1945, par. 22, pp. 10–17.

[20] For example, PR 360–A (5–25–44).

the government at the end of a specified period. In these cases the contractor added his normal mark-up to the aggregate dollar value of subcontract price reductions in computing his lump-sum refund. In still other cases, a special discount arrangement for the benefit of the government was agreed to by manufacturers of standard articles. Each invoice covering sales to the government or to war suppliers carried a special stamped notation specifying the size and purpose of the discount. This device helped to protect the manufacturer's established price structure and served notice on customers that the reduction was to be passed on to the government. As a last resort, in the case of subcontractors whose long-established, competitive price structure would be seriously disturbed by price reductions or discounts, a rebate arrangement was permitted. Rebates to the government were made periodically to cover all renegotiable sales (war business) for the period.[21] Rebates were also used where a manufacturer's war business could not be identified as such at the time of sale. The War Department considered rebates as the least desirable form of price adjustment since they failed to eliminate pyramiding of costs upon an inflated base through successive echelons of contractors and suppliers.

In dealing with the question of profits and profit margins, the basic consideration was the avoidance of any disguised or undisguised cost-plus-a-percentage-of-cost arrangement. While all pricing arrangements had to allow a reasonable rate of profit upon legitimate costs, no arrangement was to permit any advance guarantee of profit or to result in basing profits upon actual uncontrolled costs. It was in this connection that

the War Department's basic pricing philosophy was recapitulated:

A positive statement of this principle is, *"prices should always be specifically agreed upon in advance of production."* These prices will normally include a reasonable, estimated profit—but realization of the profit will depend on the contractor's performance. If the contractor fails to perform as anticipated, he will sacrifice profit. Whether the technique of pricing is to set dollars-and-cents prices, or specific discounts from specific prices, or specific rates of rebate from specific prices, the prices should be firmly fixed in advance of production. This alone is "pricing." It establishes a reward for efficiency and good management and a penalty for inefficiency.[22]

The principle of advance pricing was applied in connection with the acceptance of voluntary retroactive refunds under company pricing agreements. Recapture of excessive profits already received was the exclusive province of renegotiation. But there was usually a lag of many months before renegotiation agreements were concluded for a particular fiscal year. In the meantime, excessive profits under loose forward prices would often accumulate. If a contractor wished to avoid a penalty in his next renegotiation for loose pricing throughout the current fiscal year, he was permitted to make a voluntary refund, retroactive to the beginning of the year, at the time of company pricing. In this manner he could restore himself to a current risk position, thereby forcing himself to live within the earnings provided by current prices. In the absence of such a refund an undue accumulation of profits prior to company pricing would remove much of the pressure to improve efficiency under a close-pricing agreement for the remainder of the year. On the other hand, retroactive refunds were

---

[21] For methods of determining renegotiable sales, see below, page 366.

[22] ASF M–609, Company Pricing, May 1945, p. 15.

recognized as a kind of rebate; like all rebates, they indicated the existence of pyramided costs at successive contractor echelons during the period covered by the rebate.

For reporting and other purposes, company pricing agreements were classified into one or more of five main types: (1) specific price changes; (2) discounts; (3) rebates; (4) understandings; (5) clearances. Specific price changes took many forms; they required the amendment of prime contracts as listed in the agreement or, in the case of subcontractors, reductions of price on standard or other articles as specified. In addition to effecting price reductions, company pricing agreements permitted price increases in appropriate cases where prices were too low for profitable operations. It was War Department policy to require, so far as possible, that each contract stand on its own feet. There was a notable tendency on the part of some contractors to underbid at break-even or loss levels in order to get additional business which would offset excessive prices and profits in other contracts. By thus diluting its over-all rate of profit realization, a firm could reduce profit recaptures under renegotiation and perpetuate excessive prices on important categories of its business. The requirement that each contract stand on its own feet was intended to discourage this practice.

Discounts and rebates have been briefly discussed above.[23] "Understandings" were agreements specifically correcting or improving various aspects of a company's pricing practices which had an important bearing upon future contract prices. Under this category were agreements to eliminate contingency provisions, revise accounting methods, refine cost-estimating procedures, and improve various purchasing practices.

Understandings often resulted in greater long-run savings than specific price reductions; they also simplified future contract negotiations for the contractor as well as for all procuring agencies.

A clearance, as the term implies, indicated that after review the contractor had demonstrated that his prices were fair and reasonable and that excessive profits were not being earned. Many firms selected for company pricing because of excessive profits in the previous fiscal year had subsequently experienced reductions in sales or other changes in circumstances, and by the time of the company pricing review their cost-price structure was considered to be satisfactory. Clearances were normally given for no more than ninety days and were subject to periodic review. Cases for which no company pricing action was necessary were considered administratively "canceled" and were not included as "clearances" in reports of company pricing agreements.

In order for the fruits of a company pricing agreement to be fully realized, it was necessary that knowledge of the terms of the agreement be disseminated to all procurement offices likely to be affected. This was a perplexing administrative problem and gave rise to many debates on the methods, form, and scope of the distribution of company pricing agreements. Some of the agreements on standard commercial articles potentially affected every procuring office in the country. Others, originally thought to apply only to Ordnance, or perhaps Air Forces offices, often turned out to be of interest to other services. In the case of complex agreements, certain portions of each would be of interest to one service and not to others, and most of them were originally not in a form to be quickly digested by busy contracting officials. In order to convey a

---

[23] See above, pages 346 ff.

maximum of pertinent information, ASF headquarters devised a standard reporting form, maintained central files of information, and permitted direct distribution of reports to interested agencies. It also published and gave wide distribution to a cumulative, alphabetical list of company pricing agreements currently in effect. The list, which was kept up to date by weekly supplements, indicated the name of the company, the procurement service and district making the agreement, the type of agreement, and the expiration date. With the aid of the list all procurement offices could immediately ascertain the existence of a company pricing agreement and could obtain copies thereof on short notice from the originating office. Although substantial improvement of reporting and dissemination procedures was made during the life of the program, the various issues were never resolved to the satisfaction of all concerned.[24]

Because of its late introduction into procurement operations in World War II, the company pricing program did not exert the influence which it otherwise might have. Furthermore, during at least the first half of the program its administration tended to lose sight of the basic purpose of cost *reduction* and to concentrate excessively upon *profit elimination:*

Judged in the light of its original concept as an aid to the pricing of individual contracts,

company pricing has not been a success since it was made permanent on 5 July 1944. Instead of concentrating on prices and improvements in companies' costing and estimating methods and practices, company pricing has tended to revert to that which predominated in 1942 and early in 1943, *viz.*, has the contractor been making, or will he make, excessive profits? . . . The prices and the practices which led to the excessive profits may or may not be considered; the important matter is that the Government gets back some money.[25]

As the main objectives of the program are the conservation of critical materials and manpower rather than the savings of money, per se, company pricing personnel must continually be reminded that emphasis must be placed upon elimination of cushions in price rather than on the contractor's profit margins, as only in this way can close prices which offer an incentive to lower costs be obtained.[26]

The complete revision of ASF M–609 in May 1945 did much to restore the desired emphasis.[27] By 30 June 1945, some 2,146 companies had been selected for company pricing review since the inception of the program, and 424 companies had concluded agreements with the War Department.[28] These agreements resulted in cost and price reductions in many thousands of war contracts and purchase transactions. In the nature of the case no statistics are available to show the savings—either in dollars or in real resources—accomplished by the agreements. That they were substantial is indicated by the following observation, made at the time the program was established on a permanent basis: "As a result of the com-

---

[24] (1) ASF M–609, Company Pricing, May 1945, Ch. 4. (2) ASF Cir 165, 8 May 45, p. 10. (3) Regional Company Pricing Discussion, Chicago, Illinois, 12–13 March 1945, History of Ordnance Pricing Policy, Exhibit 71, pp. 25–55. (4) Regional Company Pricing Meeting, Philadelphia, Pennsylvania, 2–3 April 1945, ASF, History of Purchases Division, Exhibit 38½, pp. 18–35, *passim*. (5) WD Hq ASF, Purchases Div, Company Pricing Agreements Currently in Effect, 31 Mar 45, copy in History of Ordnance Pricing Policy, Exhibit 72.

[25] ASF Purchases Div, Pricing Policies and Methods, p. 54.
[26] History of Ordnance Pricing Policy, supplement of 24 Apr 45, pp. 13–14.
[27] This undertaking was already in process at the time of the criticisms quoted above. See ASF Purchases Div, Pricing Policies and Methods, p. 55.
[28] ASF Annual Rpt, 1945, p. 213.

pany pricing program one large contractor holding over one billion dollars of war contracts modified his pricing policies, with a resulting reduction equivalent to 15 percent of the cost of his War Department contracts." [29]

The entire life of the program was less than eighteen months. On 4 September 1945, all negotiations looking to new com-

pany pricing agreements were ordered to cease immediately and existing agreements were not to be extended beyond the expiration of their current period.[30] By this time the contract settlement activities of the War Department were at flood tide and the valuable skills of company pricing teams were badly needed to cope with the complexities of negotiated settlements.

---

[29] ASF Annual Rpt, 1944, p. 118.

[30] ASF Cir 332, 4 Sep 45, Sec. VIII.

CHAPTER XV

Contract Renegotiation: Origins and Basic Procedures

The Background of Statutory Renegotiation

Statutory renegotiation of government contracts, introduced early in World War II, was the culmination of numerous efforts over a period of many years to enact legislation for the control of war profiteering. Such control had been notoriously ineffective for World War I, which was reputed to have created some twenty-three thousand new millionaires. From the armistice in 1918 to Pearl Harbor, sentiment against war profiteering was high, and approximately two hundred bills and resolutions were introduced in Congress to prevent or limit wartime profits.[1] These proposals ran the gamut from graduated excess profits taxes to plans for the outright "conscription" of capital and the complete confiscation of wartime profits. Few of these plans merited serious attention as practical measures but several were enacted into law. The Vinson-Trammel act of 1934 and the Merchant Marine Act of 1936 limited aircraft manufacturers and shipbuilders to a flat percentage rate of profit. In October 1940, at the beginning of the defense period, these partial measures were suspended and a steeply graduated ex-

cess profits tax was enacted. This legislation was the first to deal generally with the problem of profits arising out of World War II.[2]

By the fall of 1941 defense production had progressed to the point where unit costs for many contractors had fallen far below contract prices. In some cases it was clear that the original contract prices had been set much too high. But even when contract prices were originally close to cost, rapid improvements in organization, labor efficiency, and productive equipment effected substantial reductions in unit costs. Under the tremendously increased quantities called for by wartime contracts and supplements thereto, the spreading of overhead over larger volume caused fixed costs per unit to decline drastically.

The resulting high profit levels for many war contractors began to attract widespread attention. A series of investigations by the House Naval Affairs Committee, culminating in the celebrated Jack and Heintz case,[3] demonstrated that neither excess profits taxation nor the avoidance of the cost-plus form of contract could prevent profiteering

---

[1] H. Struve Hensel and Lt. Richard G. McClung, USNR, "Profit Limitation Controls Prior to the Present War," *Law and Contemporary Problems* (Duke University School of Law), X, No. 2 (Autumn 1943), 199.

[2] *Ibid.*, pp. 202–05. The excess profits tax, of course, had as a major purpose the raising of revenue to help finance defense expenditures.

[3] H. Com. on Naval Affairs, 77th Cong., 2d Sess., Hearings on H. Res. 162, *Investigation of the Naval Defense Program.* The Jack and Heintz case is covered by Part 1, 23 and 25 March, and 13 April 1942.

and wasteful expenditures by war contractors.

Jack and Heintz, Inc., an Ohio firm organized in 1940 and capitalized at $100,000, was under contract to the War and Navy Departments for the manufacture of aircraft starters. Between late 1940 and early 1942 the firm had received fixed-price contracts aggregating some $58 million. With the aid of a $3 million government loan for plant expansion and payments in advance of production running to several millions, Jack and Heintz had established by the end of 1941 a remarkable record for both production and profits. Attention became focused on the company because of lavish bonuses to executives and key employees, as well as widespread sharing of profits throughout the company.[4] Employees worked in twelve-hour shifts, receiving time-and-a-half for work in excess of eight hours, besides the usual double time for Sundays and holidays. Free lunches, vacations in Florida, monthly Saturday night banquets, and a variety of other employee services and benefits—including paid-up insurance policies and the distribution of Christmas baskets and watches costing over $39,000 for 1941—were some of the high lights of the employees' welfare program. A Navy audit indicated a unit cost of $272 for starters priced to the Navy at $600. At the same time the Army paid $750 for a model costing $292 to produce. Testimony revealed that the Navy Department had requested price reductions three times during the summer of 1941 but had been refused.[5]

The disclosures in the Jack and Heintz case, together with revelations of substantial profit-making elsewhere in the field of military procurement,[6] led to demands for immediate legislative action. The matter was quickly brought to a head by the Case amendment to the pending appropriation bill passed by the House on 28 March 1942. This provision called for a 6-percent profit maximum on all procurement covered by the appropriation bill.

Both the War and Navy Departments were opposed to any flat-rate profit limitation. Experience with thousands of contractors differing widely in capitalization, volume of war business, rate of turnover, complexity of production problems, and many other respects had convinced the departments of the inequity of any flat-rate provision. More important, they held that such a limitation would be useless for keeping costs low and would impair incentives in many instances to the point where both the placement and execution of contracts would be considerably slowed down. On the other hand, both departments recognized that excessive profits were a threat to procurement efficiency as well as to national morale and hoped for legislation which would eliminate these evils without giving rise to greater ones.

In presenting the War Department's position to the Senate Appropriations Subcommittee, General Somervell forcefully stated the difficulties of satisfactorily pricing military procurement in advance of actual production:

We are asking contractors to produce articles which have never been produced before.

---

[4] The payment of almost $40,000 in 1941 to the private secretary of Mr. Jack was perhaps the outstanding news item in the case.

[5] Hearings, 1:71–72, 143, cited above, note 3. Immediately after the investigation Jack and Heintz made drastic price reductions and agreed to renegotiate further in the event that its profits exceeded 6 percent of selling price.

[6] H. Rpt. 1634, 77th Cong., 2d Sess., 20 Jan 42. This report of the House Naval Affairs Committee contains over four hundred pages of information and statistics on the profits of individual firms.

We are asking other contractors to produce articles which they have never produced before. We are asking still other contractors, who have produced articles in small quantities, to produce them in vastly larger quantities. The result of all this is that neither the contractors nor the contracting officers can make an accurate forecast of the cost of performance.

Both parties know that there will be a period of adjustment during which costs will be high. Facilities must be converted, new facilities obtained, new personnel employed and trained to new methods, and new sources of supply developed. How long this adjustment period will last is a matter of uncertainty.

On the other hand, assuming that the contractor is able to master the problem and to get into production, a time will come when costs will suddenly drop. When this time will come, or how far the drop will extend, it is virtually impossible to foresee. Furthermore, even when costs appear to have reached a definite level, there is no assurance of stability. Changes in military strategy may cause changes in priority regulations which will effect the flow of supplies, with the result that costs will rise again. Changes in economic policy may result in increased costs of labor and materials.

The plain fact of the matter is that in many cases it is impossible to tell, until completion of the contract, whether the contractor suffers a heavy loss, or makes a large profit.[7]

General Somervell went on to describe measures recently adopted by the War Department to ascertain production costs, effect closer pricing, and recover excessive payments. These consisted of redetermination and renegotiation articles to be included in contracts where mutually satisfactory prices could not be initially determined.[8]

Under the renegotiation article, after a certain percentage of the items called for by the contract had been completed, the contractor's actual costs would become the basis for voluntary renegotiation and modification of the price. Such modification could be either upward or downward and provided for additional reimbursements or recovery by the government for items already delivered. It is thus clear that renegotiation, as originally developed by the War Department, was conceived as a technique of *pricing*. Congress, on the other hand, took it up eagerly as an instrument of *profit limitation*.

The Senate subcommittee was highly sympathetic to General Somervell's presentation and indicated a willingness to support an alternative to the Case flat-rate limitation. Chairman Kenneth McKellar requested that the War Department prepare a draft proposal of such an alternative. Two days later Somervell reappeared before the committee with a draft of a proposed joint resolution which would require contract renegotiation in cases where the appropriate department head found excessive profits. This draft, which was an amplification of the renegotiation article already mentioned, became the basis for the original renegotiation act. Changes made on the floor of the Senate and later in the joint conference made the bill substantially stronger than the War Department's hastily drafted proposal.[9]

---

[7] Subcom. of the S. Com. on Appropriations, 77th Cong., 2d Sess., Hearings on H. R. 6868, *Sixth Supplemental National Defense Appropriation Bill, 1942*, 31 Mar 42, p. 24.

[8] These articles are reproduced in their entirety in hearings cited above, note 7. They have been briefly discussed above, pages 329–30.

[9] The War Department draft may be found on pages 84–85 of the hearings cited above in note 7. The draft referred only to "renegotiation of the contract price," whereas the act also specifically provided for withholding payments or recovery of sums already paid. Moreover, the wording of the act gave the department head the power to make unilateral determinations. Under Secretary Patterson and his legal assistant, Mr. William L. Marbury, interpreted the War Department proposal as merely requiring the contractor to engage in renegotiation proceedings on a bargaining basis, with no power of unilateral determination. Mr. Patterson sub-

The resulting enactment—Section 403 of the Sixth Supplemental National Defense Appropriation Act—was approved on 28 April and became known as the Renegotiation Act of 1942.[10]

Basic Provisions of the Renegotiation Law

The 1942 Act and Amendments

The renegotiation act required the insertion of a renegotiation clause in all future prime contracts in excess of $100,000 made for Army, Navy, or Maritime procurement. The renegotiation clause provided for price reductions on future deliveries and refunds on past deliveries whenever profits under the contract were determined by the appropriate departmental secretary to be "excessive." [11] Likewise, prime contractors were required to insert a similar clause in their subcontracts exceeding $100,000. The authority of the secretary to renegotiate was not, however, confined to contracts in excess of $100,000 or to those containing a renegotiation clause. Subsection (c) of the act provided that any contract or subcontract was renegotiable where, in the opinion of the secretary, excessive profits were involved, regardless of whether such contracts contained a renegotiation clause. In determining the excessiveness of profits the departments were to disallow compensation of officers and employees in excessive amounts, as well as unduly large reserves and any other costs deemed to be unreasonable. The secretary of each department was clothed with the powers necessary for the implementation of the act, as well as with authority to delegate or redelegate such powers. The law was to remain in force until three years after the termination of the war. Also, it was retroactive to the extent that it covered contracts which had not been finally settled prior to the date of its enactment.

In the summer and early fall of 1942, pressures developed from a number of sources to amend the renegotiation act. During the hearings before the Senate Committee on Finance on the 1942 revenue bill, spokesmen for industry denounced renegotiation as unconstitutional, arbitrary, inequitable, unnecessary, provocative of confusion, and in general a detriment to rapid and efficient production.[12] The procuring agencies also desired amendments, largely of a clarifying nature, but they were reluctant to initiate any changes, fearing that the proposals would get out of hand and that the act would be emasculated or replaced by one of the ubiquitous flat-rate profit limitation proposals. Nevertheless, when it became evident that changes would be made they submitted their proposals and their representatives participated as witnesses in the

---

sequently conceded the wisdom of the stronger provisions of the act, (1) Testimony before Subcom. of the S. Com. on Finance, 77th Cong., 2d Sess., Hearings on Section 403 of Public Law 528, *Renegotiation of Contracts,* 29 and 30 Sep 42. (2) William L. Marbury and Robert R. Bowie, "Renegotiation and Procurement," *Law and Contemporary Problems* (Duke University School of Law), X, No. 2 (Autumn 1943), 223.

[10] Detailed documentation of the various steps in the adoption of the renegotiation act, as well as discussions of alternative proposals by the House Naval Affairs and Ways and Means Committees, may be found in WDPAB History, Sec. I, The First Act.

[11] The head of each government renegotiating agency was designated as a departmental secretary for the purposes of the act.

[12] S. Com. on Finance, 77th Cong., 2d Sess., Hearings on H.R. 7378, *Revenue Act of 1942,* 23 Jul to 14 Aug 42. A detailed summary of charges made by industry against renegotiation at this time, as well as the War Department's position and the step-by-step development of the October amendments, is found in WDPAB History, Sec. I, Pt. I.

hearings.[13] On 21 October the Revenue Act of 1942 was finally approved and Title VIII, Section 601, amended the renegotiation act in a number of respects, retroactive to 28 April 1942, the date of its original enactment.

The October amendments consisted of a number of substantive changes as well as clarifying statements supporting the policies already adopted by the War Department. Among the latter were a definition of the term "subcontract" to include subcontractors and vendors at any tier, and specific provision to permit either over-all or individual contract renegotiation, to make agreements final and conclusive for given periods, and to allow credit for excess profits taxes already paid by contractors. Likewise, the renegotiating departments were relieved of any implication— under the original provision calling for payment into the Treasury of recoveries under renegotiation—that price reductions on future deliveries were chargeable to their appropriations. Similarly, contractors and subcontractors were relieved of liability to the United States for excessive profits not actually received by them or for price reductions not passed along to the United States by intermediate contractors.[14]

The most important substantive changes were provisions for exemptions from renegotiation. Mandatory exemption was accorded to all firms with renegotiable sales of less than $100,000 for a fiscal year, as well as to all contracts and subcontracts "for the product of a mine, oil or gas well, or other mineral or natural deposit, or timber, which has not been processed, refined, or treated beyond the first form or state suitable for industrial use." Permissive exemptions, at the discretion of the departmental secretary, were allowable to contracts performed outside the United States, to the purchase of real property, perishable goods, and commodities priced by regulatory bodies, to agreements for personal services, leases, and licensing arrangements, and to agreements to be performed within thirty days. The principal purpose of the permissive exemptions was to reduce the administrative burden of handling thousands of cases for which profits either could be controlled at the source or for other reasons were not likely to be excessive.

The other major amendment at this time was the provision authorizing departmental secretaries to provide "that renegotiation shall apply only to a portion of the contract or a subcontract or shall not apply during a specified period or periods." This permitted the establishment after actual cost experience had been ascertained, of firm forward prices not subject to further renegotiation. This left the departments free to include incentive features in contracts looking to cost reductions, the benefits of which could be shared by efficient contractors.[15]

On 1 July 1943, Section 403 was further amended to bring under renegotiation the

---

[13] (1) S. Com. on Finance, 77th Cong., 2d Sess., Hearings on Section 403 of Public Law 528, *Renegotiation of Contracts,* 22 and 23 Sep 42. (2) Hearings cited above, note 9(1). Under Secretary Patterson's testimony of 29 September is a valuable summary of the purposes, philosophy, and general background of contract renegotiation. A substantially complete collection of Under Secretary Patterson's statements on renegotiation before various Congressional committees during the war years is available in ICAF R58, Contract Pricing—Principal Developments, App. C, pp. 173–317.

[14] Memo, Charles O. Pengra, Counsel for WDPAB, for the Board and Staff, 28 Oct 42, sub: Amendments to the Renegotiation Act, WDPAB History, Sec. I, Pt. I, App. Exhibit 4.

[15] Subsections (b), (c)(4), and (i)(2)(iii). See "Price Adjustment Under Contractual Articles," in Chapter XIII, above.

four wartime procurement subsidiaries of the Reconstruction Finance Corporation (RFC). The most prominent of these—the Defense Plant Corporation (DPC)—was active in constructing ordnance and aircraft plants for the War Department. DPC had entered numerous contracts for construction and equipment, as well as for machine tools under the "pool order" system. The War Department held that these were not subcontracts of the War Department but prime contracts of the Defense Plant Corporation, an agency not named in the renegotiation act. The Navy Department, on the other hand, took the position that the DPC was merely a financing medium for the plant expansion program of the armed forces and that the plant construction contracts were renegotiable. Counsel for DPC pointed out that the treatment of its contracts as subcontracts would probably result in subjecting them to audit by the General Accounting Office, a time-consuming feature that would have seriously impaired the serviceability of DPC-type financing. Shortly thereafter the Judge Advocate General of the War Department rendered an opinion that the DPC contracts were not renegotiable.[16] The War Department Price Adjustment Board, however, directed the technical services and the various price adjustment sections to submit information on profits under DPC contracts not included in renegotiation. As evidence of substantial profit making by DPC contractors continued to pile up, Under Secretary Patterson indicated in Congressional

hearings that the War Department would have no objection to extension of the statute to include the DPC.[17]

Two weeks after the "DPC amendment" Congress passed the so-called broker amendment, bringing all fees and commissions on war contracts in excess of $25,000 under the renegotiation law. Earlier proposals in Congress to outlaw the payment of contingent fees were shelved when various industries indicated that this would upset long-established buying and distributing arrangements. Likewise, after study, the Army and Navy found that their procurement of such items as food and textiles might be substantially impaired by the prohibition. Nevertheless, it was clear that excessive fees and commissions were being paid in connection with war contracts, and both the War and Navy Departments supported the bill which became law on 14 July 1943. Since most of the difficulties had involved Navy contracts, the administration of the amendment, with certain exceptions, was turned over to Sales and Service, Renegotiation Section, Navy Department.[18]

The Renegotiation Act of 1943

The major wartime change in the renegotiation law was made by the passage on

---

[16] Memo, Col Ernest M. Brannon, Chf Contracts Div JAGD, for JAG, 5 Feb 43, sub: Application of Section 403 of the Sixth Supplemental National Defense Appropriation Act, 1942, as Amended by Section 801 of the Revenue Act of 1942, to Contracts With DPC, approved by JAG, 5 Feb 43, in JAG files.

[17] Subcom. of the H. Com. on Appropriations, 78th Cong., 1st Sess., Hearings on H. R. 2996, *Military Establishment Appropriation Bill for 1944*, 26 May to 10 Jun 43.

[18] An illuminating discussion of the issues leading to the brokers amendment is found in W. John Kenney, "Coverage and Exemptions," section on "Brokers' and Representatives' Fees," *Law and Contemporary Problems* (Duke University School of Law), X, No. 2 (Autumn 1943), 268–71. This article, prepared by an official in the Office of the Under Secretary of the Navy, contains reference to numerous court decisions, legislative hearings, and other basic sources.

25 February 1944 of the Renegotiation Act of 1943. So called because was it part of the Revenue Act of 1943, this act was a complete revision of the former renegotiation act and applied to all war business for fiscal years ending after 30 June 1943. The principal changes effected by the act were (1) increase in the mandatory exemption from $100,000 to $500,000, of renegotiable sales for any fiscal year; (2) establishment of an interdepartmental board—the War Contracts P r i c e   A d j u s t m e n t   Board (WCPAB)—as the policy-making body and final administrative arbiter in renegotiation matters; (3) conferral of compulsory pricing powers upon the several procuring agencies; (4) specific provision for appeal of unilateral determinations to the U.S. Tax Court; (5) termination of renegotiation at the end of 1944, or six months later or earlier, at the discretion of the President. Other important changes included compulsory filing of financial data by contractors whose volume of business brought them within the scope of the act, clarification of the raw material exemptions, the addition of new exemptions, provision that cost allowances of the kind allowed by the Bureau of Internal Revenue for income tax purposes be allowed in renegotiation, and provision for renegotiation rebates in cases of shortening of the tax amortization period.[19] The factors to be used in evaluating the "excessiveness" of profits—largely a restatement of the principles already in use by price adjustment boards—were specifically listed in the act, with provision for the use of such other factors as the War Contracts Price Adjustment Board might deem necessary. Numerous other changes clarified the

administrative features and ratified the previous practices of the departments.[20]

The 1943 act was the product of protracted hearings before several Congressional committees in which business spokesmen as well as representatives of the renegotiation agencies testified at great length. The objections of business to renegotiation were as numerous as its spokesmen were vociferous, and for a time it appeared that the original act might be repealed entirely, or that crippling amendments would be made. But the representatives of the armed forces, and particularly Under Secretary of War Patterson, carefully and painstakingly went over all the issues, revealed the fallacies of many of the charges by business spokesmen, and stressed the necessity of retaining intact the renegotiation principle in the interests of economical procurement, the control of inflation, public morale, and the postwar reputation of business itself. Although the act which emerged was a compromise, it was for the most part satisfactory to the procuring agencies. The testimony at the hearings unquestionably did much to sell responsible business leaders and the community as a whole on the underlying soundness of the renegotiation principle. The 1943 act stood without significant amendment until the end of the war.[21]

---

[19] See below, pages 373–75.

[20] The Renegotiation Act of 1943 was enacted as Section 701(b) of the Revenue Act of 1943, Public Law 235, 25 Feb 44, 78th Cong., 2d Sess. Title VIII of the revenue act carries separate provisions for the mandatory repricing of war contracts.

[21] The life of the act was extended by the President (Presidential Proclamation 2631, dated 14 November 1944) to 30 June 1945, and by Congress (Public Law 104, 30 June 1945, 79th Congress, 1st Session) to 31 December 1945. A detailed record of the steps in the passage of the Renegotiation Act of 1943 is contained in WDPAB History, Sec. I, Pts. III and IV. The story of the many attempts to emasculate or repeal renegotiation during this period is a valuable case study in the

Organization for Renegotiation

The passage of the first renegotiation act soon after Pearl Harbor placed a substantial administrative burden on the three major procurement agencies, already struggling to keep abreast of their enormous purchasing and production problems. The burden of the War Department was especially heavy; not only did it have proportionately the largest share of renegotiation responsibilities but it was still in the throes of the major reorganization undertaken on 9 March 1942. Nevertheless, while the act was still awaiting the President's signature, the War and Navy Departments, the Maritime Commission, and the War Production Board issued a joint memorandum agreeing to the establishment of a price adjustment board within each of the three procuring agencies. WPB representation was to be provided on each of the three boards.[22]

The basic organizational structure adopted by the War Department for con-

tract renegotiation was the familiar decentralized, three-level hierarchy—a War Department Price Adjustment Board to conduct top-level administration and policy, separate price adjustment sections in the headquarters of each of the technical services at Washington, and local boards established by the technical services in their field offices throughout the United States. After September 1943 two superboards were imposed upon this structure for the purpose of co-ordinating all governmental renegotiation activities. The first such board—the Joint Price Adjustment Board—was established administratively under the delegated powers of the several departmental secretaries to co-ordinate the handling of all cases under the 1942 act. The joint board continued to function throughout the war with respect to renegotiable business for fiscal years ending prior to 1 July 1943. The second superboard—the War Contracts Price Adjustment Board—was, as already noted, established by Congress under the Renegotiation Act of 1943. The WCPAB supervised the renegotiation of all cases for corporate fiscal years ending after 30 June 1943.

The first War Department board was the Price Adjustment Board, Army Service Forces, appointed by General Somervell on 25 April 1942.[23] The mission of the board was "to advise and assist the Chief of the Purchases Branch [later division] . . . in securing adjustments and refunds in cases where it is thought that costs or profits of War Department contractors are or may be excessive." Placement of the board under the supervision of the chief of the Purchases

---

legislative process. The revised bill reported out by a majority of the Senate Committee on Finance would have granted extensive additional exemptions discriminating in favor of certain industries, even to the extent of refunding to them excessive profits already recovered. The preservation of renegotiation in a reasonably equitable and workable form owes much to the widely circulated minority report (S. Rpt. 627, Pt. 2, 78th Cong., 1st Sess., 6 Jan 44), prepared by Senators Walsh, Connally, La-Follette, and Lucas.

[22] Jt Memo, signed by Donald Nelson, Under Secretaries Patterson and Forrestal, and Chmn Land, 23 Apr 42, copy in WDPAB History, Sec. II, Pt. I, App. Exhibit A–4. This memorandum was partly a response to the pending renegotiation legislation and partly the result of the passage of the Second War Powers Act of 27 March 1942. Title XIII of this act authorized the President to order inspection of books of all war contractors, under penalty for refusal. The President delegated this power, which was intended to facilitate closer pricing, to the secretaries of the procuring agencies by Executive Order 9127 of 10 April 1942.

[23] Memo, Gen Somervell for Dirs of All Staff Divs SOS *et al.*, 25 Apr 42, sub: Price Adjustment Board, SOS, copy in WDPAB History, Sec. II, Pt. I, App. Exhibit A–5.

Division was clear indication that renegotiation was originally considered to be an instrument of pricing and purchase policy. By the end of June the implications of the statute as well as problems of internal organization were more clearly understood. The Price Adjustment Board, ASF, was then reconstituted as the War Department Price Adjustment Board and made responsible to the Under Secretary, instead of the chief of the Purchases Division ASF.[24] The Commanding Generals, ASF, and Materiel Command, AAF, were directed to establish price adjustment sections within their commands, under the direction of WDPAB. This was done on the third and eighth of July, respectively, by the ASF and Materiel Command; shortly thereafter, the technical services undertook to establish renegotiation field offices throughout the country, as needed.[25]

Functionally, the activities of the various War Department renegotiation units corresponded to their place in the organizational structure. Principals, policies, and procedures were developed by the War Department Price Adjustment Board. WDPAB not only developed broad principles but prescribed detailed procedures; it planned the general organizational framework, approved the establishment of field offices, set standards for renegotiation personnel, conducted training and indoctrination programs, arranged and conducted regional conferences, and represented the War Department in contracts with other governmental agencies and with Congress. A major task during the first year or two of its existence was the development and conduct of a broad program of public relations designed to educate contractors and the general community in the purposes of renegotiation and in the procedures required for its implementation. In addition, the board made all renegotiation assignments, first for the services within the War Department, later for all governmental agencies, reviewed all renegotiation agreements, and actually conducted the more important renegotiation cases. The board's chief administrative functions were carried on by four principal sections—executive, assignment, negotiation, and review—which persisted with certain changes until the summer of 1943.[26]

On 1 September 1943 the board and its administrative functions were absorbed by the newly established Renegotiation Division, ASF. This division was created primarily to speed up the processing and completion of agreements. Relatively few agreements had been reached by the beginning of

---

[24] Memo, USW for CG SOS and CG Materiel Command AAF, 30 Jun 42, sub: War Department Price Adjustment Board, copy in WDPAB History, Sec. II, Pt. I, App. Exhibit A–8. The Army Air Forces, established by the 9 March 1942 reorganization on a co-ordinate level with the Army Service Forces, was reluctant to "take orders" from General Somervell's ASF. The amenities were preserved by designating the chief of the Purchases Division, ASF, as the Special Representative of the Under Secretary of War when supervising Air Forces renegotiation activities. For this purpose separate stationery was used.

[25] (1) Memo, Col Howard A. Malin, Ex Admin Br, Hq SOS, for Dirs and Chfs, Staff Divs Hq SOS et al., 3 Jul 42, sub: Price Adjustment Sections, copy in WDPAB History, Sec. II, Pt. I, App. Exhibit A–9. (2) Memo, Brig Gen Bennett E. Meyers, CG Materiel Command AAF, for CG Materiel Center AAF, 8 Jul 42, sub: Contract Price Renegotiation, copy in WDPAB History, Sec. II, Pt. I, App. Exhibit A–10. (3) Teleg. CofOrd to All District Officers, 16 Jul 42, directing establishment of district price adjustment boards, reproduced in WDPAB History, Sec. IV, Pt. II, App. 2–A, Tab E, p. 1.

[26] (1) WDPAB History, Secs. II and III. (2) Transcript of Proceedings Regional Conference, WDPAB, on The Renegotiation of War Contracts at the Waldorf Astoria, New York City, 16 and 17 March 1944, in files of Purchases Div ASF.

1943, and by June of that year the backlog of unsettled cases, measured against current rates of progress, was alarmingly high. In order to centralize authority and expedite administrative decisions, the new director of the Renegotiation Division was made chairman of the War Department Price Adjustment Board and was vested with the full authority formerly belonging to the board as a whole. At this time the technical services ments had been reached by the Beginning of all 1942 cases by the end of 1943. Intensified efforts by all concerned, coupled with the new administrative machinery and the delegation of authority to the field to settle all cases under $5 million in renegotiable sales, resulted in substantial achievement of the objective.[27]

With the establishment of the renegotiation superboards, already indicated, the Renegotiation Division and WDPAB no longer determined top-level policy and principles. They continued, nevertheless, to review agreements reached by the technical services and field offices, to conduct "impasse" cases and other important renegotiations, to assign cases to all renegotiation agencies, and to refine and improve administrative procedures. An important work of the division was the publication of the War Department renegotiation manuals, which contained complete interpretations of the

law and procedural instructions for all War Department agencies.[28]

The price adjustment sections in the headquarters of the several technical services occupied an intermediate position between the War Department board and the field. They co-ordinated and supervised the activities of the renegotiation units under their jurisdiction, reviewed agreements reached by such units, and conducted the more important cases in their procurement areas. They were responsible for the progress of the field offices, transmitted current information and developments from the field to higher echelons, and—on the basis of their experience and special study—made recommendations in all renegotiation matters. The price adjustment sections assumed an important role in expediting the completion of cases when the Under Secretary—

---

[27] WDPAB History, Sec. II, Pt. II, p. 63. The slow progress in the completion of cases during a large part of 1943 was in part due to a marked tendency on the part of contractors to delay renegotiation in the hope of repeal or extensive "watering down" of the provisions of the statute. In an attempt to secure contractor compliance with the law the Under Secretaries of War and Navy issued a press release on 23 July 1943, stating that they would assume final jurisdiction and determination of cases in which there was unreasonable delay. This action to implement the law was criticized by opponents of renegotiation. *Ibid.*, p. 62.

[28] After the passage of the Renegotiation Act of 1943 there were two such manuals—Army Renegotiation Manual, Part I and Army Renegotiation Manual, Part II. Part I applied to fiscal years prior to 1 July 1943; Part II governed cases under the Renegotiation Act of 1943, for fiscal years after 30 June 1943. The first manual to be issued was the War Department Manual for Renegotiation, approved 15 August 1943, for internal use of the War Department. Distribution was withheld because of the pending establishment of the Joint Price Adjustment Board which was expected to issue its own manual covering general policy for all renegotiating agencies. The joint board, however, approved the use of the War Department manual until the appearance of its own regulation. The ensuing Joint Renegotiation Manual, which appeared simultaneously with the Army's Part I (27 January 1944), likewise covered cases for fiscal years ending prior to 1 July 1943. The official manual of WCPAB, originally issued 24 March 1944 to cover all cases under the 1943 act, was entitled Renegotiation Regulations and was published in the Federal Register. The Army's Part II did not appear until 19 May 1944. All of these were issued in loose-leaf form and were frequently revised. Copies of these, available in the Pentagon Army Library, are an excellent source of information on contract renegotiation in World War II.

in May 1943—delegated to them the authority for final settlement of all cases involving less than $10 million in renegotiable sales.[29]

The renegotiation field offices of the several technical services varied in number and location. Ordnance, following its long-established policy of decentralization, established a field office in each of its thirteen procurement districts. At the other extreme, the newly established Transportation Corps conducted all renegotiation activity from its Washington headquarters. In general, the services established field organizations as needed, consolidating or liquidating them as the peak load of activity was passed or as it became possible to make a more accurate appraisal of geographical needs. At one time or another there were authorized some forty-seven separate renegotiation field offices under the several technical services.[30]

The organization of the field offices varied, depending largely on whether they were independently established or integrated into a regular procurement district office. Usually there was a local board, which reviewed and passed upon all proposed agreements. The key operating personnel, regardless of organization, were the renegotiators and the financial analysts. Financial analysts had the task of collecting and examining financial statements and other records of

contractors. They made recommendations on such technical matters as methods of segregating renegotiable sales, allocation of costs and profits, disallowance of cost items, and so on, and assisted the renegotiator in meetings with company officials. The renegotiators were responsible for the conduct of proceedings with contractors and made original recommendations of the existence and amount of excessive profits.

The Renegotiation Process

Principal Features of Renegotiation

At the same time that it was involved in building an organization for renegotiation, the War Department was wrestling with basic problems of procedure and policy. The number, variety, and complexity of problems connected with the administration of renegotiation can barely be suggested by a brief treatment of the subject. In renegotiation, as in all areas of public administration, procedure and policy were inextricably related, and any separation of the two necessarily presents an artificial view. Furthermore, the whole concept of renegotiation was a pioneer endeavor in 1942 when the War Department began its explorations toward a desirable body of renegotiation doctrine. The issues involved were both extremely difficult and extremely delicate. In view of the almost unlimited authority of the departmental secretaries, business had genuine fears of renegotiation as a "100-percent surtax" on all earnings which the secretaries might choose to define as "excessive."

These fears must have been considerably allayed by the first official expression of the War Department's basic approach to renegotiation. This was a widely circulated memorandum from the special representa-

---

[29] As already implied, price adjustment sections of the technical services were authorized to redelegate to field offices final settlement authority for cases of less than $5 million. The extent to which this authority was exercised is indicated in the histories of the technical service price adjustment sections in WDPAB History, Sec. IV, Pt. II, App. 2–A.

[30] The actual count of established field offices was as follows: Air Forces 8, Chemical Warfare Service 0, Corps of Engineers 9, Medical Department 2, Ordnance 13, Quartermaster Corps 5, Signal Corps 2, and Transportation Corps 0, for a total of 39. Ltr, William H. Coulson, Deputy Chf. Renegotiation Affairs Br, OASA, to author, 10 Jun 52.

tive of the Under Secretary to the chairman of the War Department Price Adjustment Board, outlining basic principles and procedures.[31] The board was instructed to base its recommendations primarily on a study of a company's over-all profits from its war contracts for an entire year, rather than on an analysis of individual contracts. This approach enormously simplified administration and enabled contractors to offset profits on some contracts with losses on others.[32] Furthermore, the board was to reach agreements as quickly as possible and not attempt detailed audits of a company's books except in cases where it felt that information was inadequate, incorrect, or misleading. Because of the numerous uncertainties and government controls over war production, the board was not to attempt to recover "the last increment of possible excess profit," but to "take a practical and realistic view in arriving at an agreement." The attitude of renegotiators was to be firm but friendly, and renegotiation was to be conducted in a spirit of co-operation that would require a minimum of time and inconvenience for business executives. In the exercise of its statutory responsibilities, the board would make a positive contribution to the welfare of business by helping it reduce expenditures, increase efficiency, avoid the stigma of profiteering, and place itself in a sound competitive condition to meet the adjustments which would be required in postwar markets. This memorandum, as well as other statements of policy and procedure, was transmitted to all renegotiation offices when the program of actual operations began in the summer of 1942.[33]

The first task in the renegotiation process was the discovery of contractors likely to have excessive profits and therefore subject to renegotiation. This was no small problem for the War Department which had many thousands of subcontractors and vendors of whom it had no direct information. Numerous products and components ultimately ending in military procurement were sold and distributed through regular commercial channels and might pass through many tiers or stages before reaching a prime military contractor.

Various means were adopted for identifying renegotiable contractors. Procurement officers in the several technical services and in the field were requested to submit lists of manufacturers who appeared to

---

[31] Memo, Col Albert J. Browning, Special Representative of USW, for Maurice Karker, Chmn WDPAB, 8 Aug 42, sub: Policy, copy in WDPAB History, Sec. II, Pt. II, App. Exhibit 1.

[32] Contractors were properly entitled to offsets of profits by losses, but this would be difficult to accomplish on an individual contract basis. In addition to this advantage, over-all renegotiation had numerous administrative ones. It eliminated much duplicate treatment of many specific matters and minimized the baffling problems of allocation of fixed and other general costs common to many contracts. Firms could base their renegotiation reports largely upon their regular annual financial statements. They were allowed to use their regular fiscal year, which in most cases was identical with the calendar year.

[33] Other major statements of policy during the summer and fall of 1942 were: (1) WDPAB, Notes on Renegotiation, for Conf With Chfs of Supply Services and Materiel Command, AAF, 9 Jul 42. This 18-page document was prepared by Mr. Pengra, counsel for WDPAB. (2) WDPAB, Principles, Policies, and Procedures To Be Followed in Renegotiation, 10 Aug 42 (23 pp.). (3) *Ibid.*, revision of 20 Nov 42 (29 pp.). (4) Questions and Answers With Reference to Renegotiation of War Contracts (16 pp.), by Maurice Karker, Chmn WDPAB. (5) Minutes of Indoctrination Meetings, WDPAB, for meetings 1–5 (27 Aug–13 Nov 42). Transcripts of these minutes, together with Items (1)–(4), above, and much other early material on the development of renegotiation policy, are bound together in Renegotiation of Contracts, file 161, Purchases Div ASF.

have substantial amounts of war business. Information also came from the War Production Board and other governmental agencies, and occasionally from Congressional committees. Eventually, the Bureau of Internal Revenue made available copies of tax returns, and these became a major source of information. The Renegotiation Act of 1943 went far toward resolving the problem by requiring all firms with over $500,000 in war business to file special reports with the War Contracts Price Adjustment Board at the end of each year.

Closely related to the problem of identification was the question of which department and which subordinate service should conduct renegotiation with a firm having contracts with two or more agencies or services. Most of the firms involved had contracts with several services, and sound administration required that renegotiation of a particular contractor be conducted by a single service. In general, assignment was made to the agency and service having the largest share of a contractor's business, with representatives of other interested departments or services assisting if desired. This "predominant interest" basis of assignment was modified in cases where another agency conducted renegotiation for the majority of firms in the industry. The need for comparable treatment of competing firms made it desirable for a single service to handl all such firms. Ultimately a highly systematic assignment procedure was developed and its administration centralized in a single agency. Because it held the vast majority of all renegotiable contracts, the War Department undertook this task for all government departments, and all assignments were then made by the Assignments and Statistics Branch, Renegotiation Division, ASF, acting under a delegation of authority from the War Contracts Price Adjustment Board.[34]

The details of renegotiation procedure necessarily varied with the accumulation of experience, changes in the statute, and the special requirements of local and other offices.[35] In its developed form by the end of the war, renegotiation had incorporated many of the mechanics of federal income tax procedure. All contractors subject to renegotiation were required under the statute to file with the appropriate price adjustment board a return of their fiscal year's business within three months after the end of the year. The official form for this purpose— the Contractor's Information and Work Sheet for Renegotiation—was developed by the top-level price adjustment boards with the assistance of leading industrial and trade associations. The information and schedules called for by the work sheet gave a comprehensive picture of the contractor's business and included not only the necessary financial data but narrative descriptions of all considerations relevant to renegotiation. In addition to Exhibits 1 and 1a (special financial statements for renegotiation purposes), the following principal categories of information were required:

A. Annual Statements (certified copies of regular statements)

B. Ownership and Affiliations

C. Business of Contractor

---

[34] The complexities of assignment procedure are ably discussed in an address by Maj. Howard Dilks, Jr., Chief, Assignments and Statistics Branch, at the New York conference on 16 March 1944. This address is reproduced at pages 29–40 of the transcript cited above, in note 26(2).

[35] An authoritative, contemporary account of renegotiation procedure is found in Lt. Col. Paul B. Boyd, "Administrative Machinery and Procedures for Renegotiation," *Law and Contemporary Problems* (Duke University School of Law), X, No. 2 (Autumn 1943), 309–40.

D. Price Record
E. Government and Other Assistance
F. Plant Facilities
G. Income Account
H. Segregation (sales and costs)
J. Salaries (total compensation to each
     principal employee)
K. Reserves
L. CPFF Contracts
M. Terminated Contracts
N. Income Tax Data
O. Statement of actors (performance
     record)
P. Miscellaneous (royalties paid or re-
     ceived, revaluation of assets, types
     of escalator and redetermination
     clauses in contracts and action taken
     thereon and so on)

The mandatory filing of this information automatically furnished renegotiators with the bulk of information required and virtually eliminated the earlier problem of discovery and identification of renegotiable contractors. It not only saved many manhours of research and fact gathering by government analysts but it reduced the number of meetings with contractors and speeded the completion of cases.[36]

Before assignment of a case to the field, intensive screening and other preliminary work took place in the Renegotiation Division, ASF. The Assignments and Statistics Branch carefully reviewed contractor's renegotiation returns, transcripts of income tax returns, and other data to determine whether a case warranted assignment. If a contractor's renegotiable sales fell below the statutory minimum, if his margin of profit was clearly not excessive, if his total profit

was such that a recapture of less than $10,-000 was possible, or if other circumstances so indicated, the case was closed as "File–No Action." By confining actual assignments to cases where a reasonable possibility of excessive profits existed, thousands of manhours for both government and industry were saved and the work load kept to manageable proportions.[37]

After the screening process the Renegotiation Division assigned each case and forwarded the contractor's return to the appropriate renegotiation agency. The local office receiving the assignment formally notified the contractor of his assignment and arranged for an initial meeting—usually held at the offices of the local board.[38]

The renegotiation process consisted essentially of two steps: (1) determination of the amount of renegotiable profit actually earned by a contractor for the fiscal period under review; (2) determination of the extent to which such profit was deemed "excessive." The former was primarily the responsibility of the financial analyst assigned to the case. In preparing for the initial meeting, the analyst reviewed the contractor's report and made recommendations concerning segregation of renegotiable from nonrenegotiable sales, disallowance of excessive compensation and other unwarranted costs, and similar technical matters required by renegotiation policy. The renegotiator, in turn, reviewed the reports of the contractor and the financial analyst, studied available data for comparable firms, and attempted to

---

[36] Copies of the Contractor's Information and Work Sheet for Renegotiation (Budget Bureau No. 49–R173.3) and related forms may be found in WDPAB History, Sec. III, Pt. V, App. Exhibit 1.

[37] WDPAB History, Sec. III, Pt. I, App. Exhibit 3.

[38] Formal notification of a contractor constituted the official commencement of renegotiation proceedings for purposes of the statute of limitations. Subsection (c) (3) of the 1943 renegotiation act removed all liability for the return of excessive profits by a contractor if renegotiation proceedings were not begun within one year after his filing of his renegotiation return with the WCPAB.

familiarize himself with all important aspects of the contractor's operations.

At the initial meeting with the contractor—especially in case of the contractor's first experience with renegotiation—the purposes and philosophy of the renegotiation law were briefly explained, together with the major administrative principles and procedures. This was followed by a detailed review of cost disallowances and a discussion of the various elements in the contractor's performance record. When the substance of an agreement had been reached, the renegotiator prepared a formal agreement in writing, stating the amount of renegotiable sales involved, profits earned, and determination of excessive profits. The terms of settlement were set forth, including dates and amounts of refunds and (under the 1942 act) contract price adjustments on unfilled orders. The settlement agreement was then reviewed and signed by the authorized representatives of the renegotiating agency and the contractor.[39] In case of an impasse, the local board reported the matter to the War Department Price Adjustments Board. This board held *de novo* proceedings and then made a unilateral determination if it failed to secure a voluntary agreement.

For each agreement the renegotiator prepared for the record and for review by higher authority a detailed case history, describing the nature of the contractor's business, his production problems, and his performance record. All relevant financial data were included as well as the basis for all major decisions reached in the settlement or determination. This record, together with the written agreement, was forwarded to the governing technical service price adjustment section for review—and for approval if approval by higher authority was required. Cases involving renegotiable sales in excess of $10 million were reforwarded to the War Department Price Adjustment Board for review and approval. Finally, unilateral determination by the War Contracts Price Adjustment Board could be appealed to the U.S. Tax Court, which confined its review to issues disclosed by the record. Experience revealed that relatively few unilateral determinations were made and that of these only a few were appealed to the Tax Court.[40]

Once a renegotiation agreement had been approved by proper authority it was made final for the fiscal year covered, and no further review—except in case of fraud—was possible. This was qualified under the early operation of the 1942 act by the requirement of an end-of-year adjustment made in cases of agreements concluded before the end of the year. The 1942 act placed responsibility for repricing as well as profit recapture upon renegotiating agencies. Hence, it was desirable to conclude agreements without waiting for the end of the year, in order to take advantage of lower forward prices reached under the agreement. This end-of-year review and adjustment procedure proved to be time-consum-

---

[39] The authority to sign renegotiation agreements for the War Department rested on written delegations from the WDPAB. A specific resolution of the board of directors was usually required to authorize an officer of a private corporation to sign a renegotiation agreement.

[40] The War Department Price Adjustment Board issued a total of 944 unilateral determinations out of 75,818 assignments for the five years 1942–46. Of these, 698 unilateral orders under the Renegotiation Act of 1943 were subject to review by the War Contracts Price Adjustment Board. After review by WCPAB, 96 were cleared, canceled, or resulted in bilateral agreement. Of the remaining 602 unilateral determinations, only an unknown fraction were appealed to the U.S. Tax Court. WCPAB Final Report, Table IV, in WDPAB History, Sec. IV, Pt. III, App. 3–A.

ing and otherwise unsatisfactory and the procedure was abandoned. The Renegotiation Act of 1943, which separated the repricing from the recapture functions, removed any further occasion for early agreements and "post-mortem" adjustments.

An important element of renegotiation procedure was the provision for cancellation or clearance of assigned cases which indicated no excessive profits and therefore no necessity for refund. Cancellation was made in all cases where preliminary investigation by field offices indicated no significant possibility of excessive profits. Cancellations represented the largest single method of disposing of cases, accounting for over 37 percent of all those originally assigned during the five-year period of renegotiation, 1942–46. Clearance cases, as distinct from cancellations, were those which revealed no excessive profits after renegotiation meetings and after full investigation of performance and other factors. Clearances amounted to 25 percent of all assignments for the five-year period.[41]

Identification of Renegotiable Sales

Innumerable problems of policy constantly arose to call for changes or adjustments in renegotiation procedure. Two of these are discussed briefly to suggest the scope and complexity of the renegotiation process. The first of these concerns the segregation of a firm's renegotiable sales from its regular commercial business not subject to renegotiation. In the early days before clarifying amendments to the original act, this task was perhaps the most difficult in the entire administrative procedure of renegotiation. Prime contracts with military agencies posed no problem as they were readily iden-

tifiable and by definition constituted renegotiable sales. Likewise, subcontracts for parts and components peculiar to military end items were clearly renegotiable. But how should the War Department treat vendors supplying commercially standard materials, tools, and services to prime contractors or their subs, sometimes many tiers below the prime? Apart from questions concerning the legal renegotiability of purchase orders for standard items, there were complex problems of identification and allocation of sales. How was it possible to identify as war production a portion of the total sales of a producer of screws or nails to dozens of commercial distributors who might in turn, directly or indirectly contribute to the completion of a prime military contract?

The problem of legal renegotiability was resolved by the October 1942 amendments, which ratified the service's definition of the term "subcontract," and by administrative interpretations of the statute. The technical problem of proper segregation of renegotiable sales was handled—at least by the War Department—by accepting any reasonable basis used by the contractor for such segregation. The division between renegotiable and nonrenegotiable business was usually determined on the basis of spot-checks and sampling techniques applied to successive echelons in the chain of vendors and subcontractors. For various industries where the problem of segregation was troublesome, this method was frequently supplemented by identification of priority ratings or CMP allotment numbers and special studies by the War Production Board on national averages. The War Department took the position that no firm should be required to devote an unreasonable amount of research to the problem. By 1944, when a number of procedures and considerable data on segre-

---

[41] WDPAB History, Sec. IV, Pt. III, App. 3–A.

gation had been developed, the problem appears to have subsided to a level of secondary importance.[42]

Renegotiation of CPFF Contracts

A second important issue in renegotiation procedure was the treatment of CPFF contracts. At first, CPFF contracts were believed to be nonrenegotiable, on the ground that the profit (fixed fee) was controlled in advance and was covered by separate legislation limiting fees.[43] But it soon became clear that excessive profits were being earned by both primes and subcontractors under CPFF arrangements. This was particularly true of a class of contracts which called for a fixed fee per unit of output, as in the case of aircraft motor and frame production, various ammunition contracts, and others. Although these contracts were designed as CPFF, they were somewhat of a hybrid type, possessing both fixed-price and cost-plus elements. For purposes of risk elimination and cost recovery by contractors they were clearly cost-plus, since the government promised full reimbursement of all relevant costs. For purposes of profit determination they partook of the fixed-price type of contract inasmuch as profit per unit, determined in advance, was based on an estimated cost which included numerous contingencies of a kind which would disappear as volume production got under way. The CPFF *supply* contract thus had substantially different implications from the CPFF *construction* contract, which was not subject to highly repetitive operations and hence to the probability of highly increasing efficiency of production within the life of the contract. An oft-stated ideal of procurement policy was to convert all CPFF contracts to definite commitments—to fixed price or annual management fee for supply contracts, and to lump sum for construction contracts. Conversion of CPFF contracts was difficult, however, primarily because of strong contractor resistance to the change-over.[44]

By the end of 1942 the War Department had definitely decided that its CPFF contracts would be negotiated. Provision was made in all renegotiation proceedings for the segregation by a contractor of his fixed-price from his fixed-fee business. The fixed-fee business was separately renegotiated in accordance with criteria specially developed to meet the different problems obtaining for this type of contract. All construction contracts were assigned to the Corps of Engineers, which was from the beginning given authority to make final settlements. Other CPFF contracts were subject to standard assignment procedure but all proposed settlements thereof required review and approval by a special CPFF Committee of the War Department Price Adjustment Board. The board's CPFF Committee made a va-

---

[42] "About a year ago the question of segregation of sales and allocation of expenses was the number one trouble spot. But most offices have now mastered that difficult problem." Statement of Lt Col E. D. Scruggs, Chf Financial Review Sec. Renegotiation Div, 16 Mar 44, in transcript cited above in note 26 (2). Further data on the problem of segregation may be found in WDPAB History, Sec. IV, Pt. II, App. 2–A, Tab E. pp. 13–14.

[43] The First War Powers Act (Public Law 354, 18 Dec 41, 77th Congress, 1st Session) permitted the use of CPFF contracts subject to a maximum fee of 7 percent of estimated cost. On 16 May 1942, the Judge Advocate General submitted an opinion that CPFF contracts were nonrenegotiable. In addition to the reasons cited above, he stated that renegotiation of CPFF contracts might create a tendency on the part of contractors to allow their costs to rise. Memo, JAG for Chf Legal Div, Office Dir of Procurement and Distribution, SOS, 16 May 42, in JAG files.

[44] See above, Chapter XII. Also see ASF, History of Purchases Division, pp. 235–58.

riety of industry studies and obtained reliable data on efficiency standards in the ammunition, shell-loading, small arms, and aircraft industries, which accounted for the bulk of CPFF production contracts. Since the committee which made the studies also reviewed the renegotiation settlements, a high degree of co-ordination and application of information was achieved.[45]

In 1945, the WCPAB appointed a fact-finding committee to report on CPFF contract renegotiation. The committee reported a wide divergence in the nature and complexity of contractor operations in different industries, a divergence which rendered percentage profit-margins meaningless for interindustry comparisons. Likewise, there was wide diversity in the amount of value added by contractors in the different fields, making total cost or billing figures highly deceptive. The degree of supervision over subcontractors ranged from simple purchase operations at one extreme to extensive responsibility and control amounting to outright management at the other. In each case, all these factors had to be evaluated and appropriate adjustment made in determining excessive profits.[46]

In general, the percentage of profit (ratio of fixed fee to total allowable costs plus fixed fee) for CPFF contracts was substantially lower than profit margins on fixed price business.[47] This differential was mainly a re-

flection of the relatively low degree of risk associated with CPFF contracts. There was, however, always the risk that specific expenditures in the performance of a contract would be disallowed by the Comptroller General, who audited expenditures under all CPFF contracts. In such cases the contractor was not reimbursed for his expenditures but the disallowance was subtracted, for renegotiation purposes, from the fixed fee before determining its excessiveness. It was thus possible for the entire fee to be eaten up by disallowances. To protect the contractor from · relatively unprofitable CPFF contracts, WDPAB made appropriate allowances in renegotiating his fixed-price business. Although the renegotiation of CPFF contracts was highly important from an administrative point of view (some 30 to 40 percent of all War Department contracts over $10 million were of the CPFF variety), recaptures thereunder were small compared with those under fixed-price contracts. Total War Department recoveries from corporations (with minor exclusions), which accounted for 89 percent of all War Department recaptures under renegotiation, amounted to $6.6 billion. Of this amount only $54 million, or less than 1 percent, were recovered under CPFF contracts.[48]

Despite the efforts of government agencies to minimize the inconvenience and expense of renegotiation for contractors, the prep-

---

[45] Maj Robert W. Fort, Industry Studies, and Maj Gerson D. Lublin, Renegotiation of Cost-Plus-a-Fixed-Fee Contracts in WDPAB History Sec. III, Pt. VI, pp. 81–100, 113–14.

[46] WDPAB History, Sec. III, Pt. VI, pp. 84ff.

[47] Thus of 438 CPFF contracts assigned to the Corps of Engineers, only 5 were found to yield excessive profits. These profits, which represented 2.15 percent of aggregate contract costs before renegotiation, were reduced by recoveries to 1.80 percent. Profits on the 433 contracts found not to be excessive averaged 1.76 percent. These figures compare

with corresponding profit margins on lump-sum construction contracts of 14.47 percent before, and 9.63 percent after, renegotiation of 1187 contracts. On 4889 lump-sum contracts, profits averaging 5.65 percent were considered to be not excessive. WDPAB History, Sec. IV, Pt. II, App. 2–A, Tab C, pp. 52–53. Average profits on CPFF supply contracts for the War Department were 4.5 percent and 4.3 percent respectively, before and after renegotiation. WCPAB Final Report, Table III–C.

[48] (1) WCPAB Final Report, Tables III–A and III–C. (2) WDPAB History, Sec. IV, Pt. II, App. 2–A, Tab C, Exhibit C.

aration of the returns and the subsequent administrative burdens of renegotiation were unquestionably costly and time consuming for many firms. The larger corporations, with well-established accounting and record systems and large staffs of full-time legal and accounting personnel, felt the burden proportionately less than others. On the other hand, any concern subject to renegotiation—especially in view of the $500,-000 exemption and additional screening procedures—could hardly be considered as "small," and the money costs of administration were passed on to the government as allowable costs of operation.[49] In any case,

the combined outlays of both industry and government to support the administrative costs of renegotiation were only a small fraction of the excessive profits recaptured, to say nothing of increased industrial efficiency and other benefits of renegotiation.[50]

---

[49] Many firms took pride in the presentation of their performance record to the price adjustment boards and went far beyond "the call of duty" in assembling and submitting materials to supplement the formal report called for by the statute. The files of the War Department Price Adjustment Board are replete with brochures, folios, scrapbooks, documentary histories, and bound volumes telling the detailed story of the war production effort of hundreds of American corporations. Many of the volumes, handsomely printed and bound, with charts, tables, diagrams, photographs, and extended narrative description, provide extensive insight into the nature of twentieth century American industrial civilization.

[50] The final report of the War Contracts Price Adjustment Board (22 May 1951) indicates the total administrative cost of renegotiation to the government of nearly $41.5 million for the period 28 April 1942 to 30 June 1950. This cost, which consisted of $36 million in salaries and $5.5 million for rent, office supplies, travel, and so forth, does not include the time of procurement personnel, officials, and others who devoted much effort to renegotiation matters while officially serving in other capacities. No estimate of the comparable costs to industry has been made, but even if it were several times the cost to the government the total combined administrative costs would still be small as compared with the amount of excessive profits recovered.

CHAPTER XVI

Renegotiation: Principles and Policy

The broad principles of contract renegotiation as developed by the War Department fell into two categories: (1) principles used in determining—for purposes of renegotiation—the amount of profit earned by each contractor; (2) criteria for determining how much of this profit was "excessive" and therefore recoverable by the government. Since policies in both categories had a direct bearing upon the amount of profit ultimately retained by business, both were the subject of continuous and spirited controversy. The technicalities of renegotiation were so complex that the precise issues rarely received adequate treatment in the press or in public discussion generally.[1]

Definition and Measurement of Renegotiable Profits

In general, profit for purposes of renegotiation was determined in accordance with standard accounting practice as adapted by the Bureau of Internal Revenue for tax purposes. In a number of specific matters, however, differences between the basic purposes of renegotiation and those of taxation compelled a difference in treatment. The most controversial issues in defining renegotiable profits were treatment of income taxes, reserves for reconversion, tax amortization allowances, and various exemptions from renegotiation. The first three concerned, in principle, the task of distinguishing between cost and profit for purposes of renegotiation. The last was a problem of distinguishing between two classes of profit—profit which was subject to renegotiation and that which was not.

Income and Profit Taxes

Throughout the life of renegotiation, industry spokesmen urged that corporation income and profit taxes were part of the costs of doing business and that only profits remaining "after taxes" should be subject to renegotiation. It was their contention that after reduction by wartime taxes at unprecedented rates profits in most cases would clearly not be excessive and that, in any case, profits before taxes gave a grossly exaggerated view of true earnings available for retention or distribution to stockholders. Virtually every representative of industry who testified before Congressional committees on renegotiation strenuously urged the "after taxes" basis.[2]

---

[1] The reader interested in renegotiation principles omitted from this discussion, as well as in greater elaboration of the step-by-step development of all matters of renegotiation policy, may find much additional information in the various documents and sources cited in the previous chapter, especially those referred to above in notes 28 and 33, pages 360 and 362.

[2] The most extensive collection of the views of industry in this matter is found in the 1,100-page document *Renegotiation of War Contracts,* H. Com. on Ways and Means, 78th Cong., 1st Sess., Hearings on H. R. 2324, H. R. 2698, and H. R. 3015

The official position of the War Department from the beginning was that the original existence of abnormally high profits was attributable to overpricing, whether intentional or unintentional. Hence, it was the task of renegotiation to determine the level of profits which would have existed had prices throughout the life of contracts been reasonable. By eliminating excessive profits first, and then applying the statutory tax rates to the remainder, both the contractor and the government would be left in the position which would have existed had war products been correctly priced throughout the production period.[3]

Representatives of the War Department denied that income and excess profits taxes were part of the costs of production since any firm not receiving profits did not have to pay such taxes. In his testimony before the House Ways and Means Committee, Under Secretary Patterson pointed out that the proposal advocated by business would, in effect, require the procuring agencies to pay different prices to different contractors making an identical item because of their widely differing tax burdens.[4] This would amount to governmental assumption of a substantial portion of the contractor's rightful wartime tax responsibility and would be a nullification by an administrative agency of the tax policy declared by Congress. Also, it would defeat the basic anti-inflationary purposes of renegotiation by permitting lavish original expenditures costing contractors only ten cents on the dollar under the excess profits tax formula. Despite the repeated efforts of industry spokesmen to place rene-

gotiation on an "after taxes" basis, Congress corroborated the position of the War Department and the other government agencies by the Renegotiation Act of 1943.

The treatment of state income taxes was also a matter of considerable debate. Industry insisted that state taxes be deducted before consideration of renegotiation recoveries. One prominent manufacturer buttressed this argument with the claim that "millions of dollars of state corporation income taxes are being seized by renegotiation boards and given to the United States Treasury."[5] Again, the War Department's position was that the original excessive earnings should never have existed and that income taxes, whether federal or state, should be based on earnings properly determined as contemplated by the renegotiation statute. Otherwise, the federal government would be paying artificially increased state taxes in the form of exorbitant prices for military procurement. The policy of the War Department Price Adjustment Board did, however, take into consideration the amount of state income taxes paid by a contractor in determining the existence and amount of excessive profits. This policy was likewise reaffirmed in the Renegotiation Act of 1943.[6]

---

[5] Telg, John B. Hawley, President Northern Pump Company, Minneapolis, Minnesota, to All State Treasurers, 15 Sep 42, copy in OCMH.

[6] Some state treasurers suffered administrative embarrassment in connection with the refund of state corporation income taxes when income was reduced by renegotiation. There was also some discriminatory effect among states because of differing state laws on the permissibility of such refunds. It should be noted, however, that the over-all effect of federal expenditures upon state revenues was decidedly favorable. Corporations undergoing renegotiation were protected by the U.S. Treasury and War Department Price Adjustment Board policy from any loss due to state failure to make refunds. See W&MC, *Renegotiation of War Contracts,* testimony of Hon. Rollin Browne, President New York State

---

(hereafter cited as W&MC, *Renegotiation of War Contracts).*

[3] (1) *Ibid.,* pp. 41–43. (2) Truman Committee, 3d annual Rpt, pp. 60–61.

[4] Statement of USW Patterson, in W&MC, *Renegotiation of War Contracts,* especially pp. 816–17.

Reconversion Reserves

Perhaps the most controversial item in the early debates on renegotiation policy was industry's claim that reconversion reserves set aside out of profits during the war should be treated as part of the expenses of producing war goods. Charging such reserves to the cost of wartime procurement would have reduced the profit figure used for renegotiation purposes and therefore the amount of recovery through renegotiation. The position of industry, in brief, was that renegotiation made it impossible to build up financial reserves adequate to meet the costs and uncertainties of postwar readjustment.[7]

While sympathetic to the proposition that no industry should be penalized for having converted to war production, the War Department held that the problem of reconversion would have to be treated in its entirety by appropriate reconversion policies applied at the end of the war. The proposal to create reconversion reserves out of excessive profits would be grossly discriminatory between firms, would defeat the close-pricing policy of the procurement agencies, and in practice would have no direct relevance to bona fide reconversion needs. The War Department's position was well expressed in a letter by the chief of the Purchases Division, ASF:

The problem of the cost of post-war reconversion is one which concerns everyone. It must be recognized that the war will involve tremendous problems of post-war readjustment not only to firms engaged in fulfilling war contracts but also to most other economic groups. Firms now engaged in civilian business may face competition from products developed as a result of the war which will make their existing plant obsolete. Many economic groups such as the automobile dealers, the filling station operators, the owners of resort hotels and tourist camps are faced with a curtailment and in some instances a complete cessation of their normal business. Shall a government subsidy be provided in each case to reimburse owners of such businesses for losses incurred because of the war? The difficulty of computing accurately the extent of such losses and the dubious feasibility, from an economic point of view, of attempting to rehabilitate industries which may have become obsolescent because of advancing technology offer serious objections to any such proposal. Surely these same arguments apply to a firm which has been fortunate enough to continue profitable operations during the war by conversion to the production of war goods.

The proposal for a repeal of the statute plus a provision (in the Revenue Act) for a carry back of losses against excess profits taxes paid from 1940 to the end of the war for the five years after the close of hostilities would, in my judgment, lead to more inequities than it would alleviate. Corporations which made excessive profits could use Government money in the post-war period on marketing campaigns, development, research, etc. Firms could use the tax credit to develop products which they had not produced during the pre-war years. Certain of the munitions companies would find themselves in a position to start out in a new industry and develop a market with Government money. At the same time, those firms which patriotically attempted to eliminate excessive profits by reduced prices and voluntary refunds would find themselves in the post-war period without any comparable subsidy which might be employed to cover the cost of post-war conversion. That is to say, the availability of post-war credit and the size of that credit would depend upon the existence of excessive profits during the war years. This in effect, would amount to

Tax Commission, pp. 778–90, and Joseph J. O'Connel, Jr., Asst Gen Counsel, U.S. Treasury, pp. 1017–26.

[7] Like the question of taxes, the issues of reconversion reserves was, almost without exception, dealt with by every industry witness. Two interesting and opposing viewpoints, which throw considerable light on the question of the propriety of charging reconversion reserves to war production, were specially expressed by Congressmen Charles S. Dewey (Illinois) and Melvin J. Maas (Minnesota). *Ibid.,* pp. 180–84 and 999–1017.

rewarding those companies which earned excessive profits while penalizing those which recognized their responsibility to their country in the matter of excessive profits.[8]

Although industry spokesmen repeatedly proposed the outright repeal of renegotiation, or failing this, the deduction of reconversion reserves from profits, the War Department adhered to its basic position. Not only was this in harmony with the official position of the War Production Board; it was in keeping with the broad principle that reconversion costs and problems should be dealt with directly and uniformly by a nationwide program for demobilization and reconversion, rather than haphazardly and inequitably through the medium of wartime profiteering.[9]

Tax Amortization and Renegotiation Rebates

The proper treatment in renegotiation of allowances for "tax amortization" posed one of the most difficult and important problems of renegotiation policy. The tax amortization law, in effect, exempted from taxation the profits of contractors set aside during the war to pay for essential new capital facilities.[10] Underlying the amortization allowance was the premise that plant facilities created to produce munitions would be worthless after the war and accordingly should be paid for out of contractors' wartime earnings. This could not be done if such earnings were either taxed away or removed by renegotiation before the new facilities were completely paid for. Thus, on the surface it appeared that amortization deductions should be allowed as costs in computing profits subject to renegotiation just as they were in computing profits subject to taxation. This was the position taken by the War Department Price Adjustment Board in the summer of 1942.[11]

This stand was reinforced by the October 1942 amendments to the Renegotiation Act of 1942. Section (c) (3) of the amended act provided that the same deductions and exclusions allowed for tax purposes in the Internal Revenue Code should also be allowed in renegotiation. The logic of this position required full recognition in renegotiation of all amortization allowances for tax purposes, including accelerated amortization permitting 100-percent write-off in less than five years if war production should terminate before the expiration of the five-year period. Steps were taken to make this explicit in the renegotiation law and the Renegotiation Act of 1943 did so by providing for "renegotiation rebates."[12]

Meanwhile, during the development of renegotiation policy in the fall and winter of 1942–43, the Department of the Treasury

---

[8] Ltr, Col Browning to Mr. Paul W. Ellis, Div of Industrial Economics, The Conference Board, New York, New York, 24 Dec 42, OCMH.

[9] Even before the passage of the first renegotiation act, the chairman of the War Production Board had ruled that reconversion costs were not to be charged against war production. Ltr, Nelson to USW, 6 Mar 42, reproduced in WDPAB Instructions, PAB–7, 26 Jan 43. See also testimony of Col (later Brig Gen) Maurice Hirsch before the House of Representatives Select Committee on Small Business on 14 January 1945, in *Congressional Record*, Vol. 91, Pt. V (14 Jan 45), 6145–49.

[10] For a more detailed discussion of the nature and administration of tax amortization law, see below, Chapter XX.

[11] WDPAB History, Sec. I, Pt. III, p. 5.

[12] Section 403 (a) (4) (D) of Renegotiation Act of 1943, approved 25 February 1944. A renegotiation rebate was a repayment to the contractor of money previously collected from him as excessive profits but no longer considered excessive in view of the recomputation upward of the amortization deduction on the basis of a less-than-five year write-off. The provision for renegotiation rebates was made retroactive to the beginning of renegotiation.

had been strongly opposed to the unqualified allowance of amortization in renegotiation. Treasury spokesmen pointed to the original provision (Subsection (i)) in the tax amortization law which gave the government an interest in the residual value of amortized facilities if these should not, in fact, become worthless with the cessation of war production. This provision had turned out to be administratively unworkable and was repealed in February 1942 upon representations of the procuring agencies that they would protect the government's interest by the adoption of adequate, over-all pricing policies. For reasons already indicated, close pricing early in 1942 was an unrealizable ideal and, two months after the abandonment of Subsection (i), renegotiation was adopted for the specific purpose of counteracting the failure to price closely. In the view of the Department of the Treasury, renegotiation authorities had a special obligation in connection with tax amortization allowances—one which could not be discharged by the taxing authorities. This was the obligation not to treat amortization as an unconditional allowance in renegotiation but to modify it in accordance with a reasonable estimate of residual value.[13]

The chairman of the War Department Price Adjustment Board was opposed to any consideration of residual value on the ground that it would have an adverse effect on industry and was contrary to the intent of Congress. After a number of conferences the following statement was adopted in the spring of 1943 by the procuring agencies and the Treasury:

. . . amortization . . . will be deducted from such profits and not considered as representing excessive profits for purposes of renegotiation. In determining whether and the extent

to which profits remaining after deducting the amount of such amortization are excessive, consideration will be given to the extent that it appears that the contractor or subcontractor will have residual value in the amortized facilities so far as it may be reasonably ascertained.[14]

Although the chairman of WDPAB termed this statement a compromise, it represented abandonment of the Treasury position since it permitted the unqualified deduction of the full amortization allowance, regardless of residual value. The subsequent adoption of the statutory provision for renegotiation rebates confirmed this policy.[15]

The amount of residual value in a contractor's war-created facilities was not, of course, susceptible of precise measurement at any time and in many cases could not be even roughly determined until the war's end. Thus the real burden of reclaiming excessive profits obtained in the form of residual value of amortized facilities was left to renegotiation at the end of the war. Unfortunately, the end-of-the-war period provided far from ideal circumstances under which to compute residual value. The rapid demobilization of the armed services after V-J Day stripped the procuring agencies of many of their experienced renegotiators when they were most urgently needed. Wholesale termination of war contracts placed well-nigh insuperable burdens of termination and settlement upon available personnel. Removal

---

[13] WDPAB History, Sec. I, Pt. III, pp. 5–6.

[14] Jt Statement by the War, Navy, and Treasury Depts and the Maritime Comm, dated 31 Mar 43, cited in WDPAB History, Sec. I, Pt. III, p. 6.

[15] The chief of the Legal Branch, Purchases Division, ASF, pointed out that consideration of residual value *after* full allowance of amortization was not really a "concession to the Treasury" since this would normally be done by renegotiators as part of their general mandate. WDPAB History, pp. 7–8. citing Memo, Marbury for Amberg, (Special Asst to USW), 22 Jan 43, sub: Possible Amendment of Section 403 of Public Law 528, as amended.

of all wartime controls and rapid conversion to peacetime pursuits became the nation's first preoccupation and political watchword. Fears and predictions of mass unemployment militated against the determination of any but minimum residual value in war-created facilities.

As a result of all these factors, the Truman Committee concluded that the tax amortization feature was a major loophole in renegotiation and that "legal profiteering resulted from certificates of necessity." [16] The committee went on to state that this was especially true in the case of firms able to obtain renegotiation rebates under the provision for shortened amortization. The committee cited the case of twenty large oil companies whose excessive profits were computed at $65 million and who were obliged to refund only $6 million after receiving tax amortization credits in the sum of $59 million.[17] The rebate provision was also criticized by renegotiation authorities, in Truman Committee hearings and elsewhere, for its discriminatory results. Since rebates could be obtained only by contractors who had previously been required to refund excessive profits, the provision discriminated against contractors who had priced closely. Also, by placing a premium on the earning of excessive profits, the rebate provision tended to tear down the efforts of procuring agencies to obtain close original prices in new contracts.[18]

Although the rebate provision was a convenient and legitimate target for criticism, it was only partly responsible for the results indicated. Renegotiation rebates were justified, and indeed indispensable to the complete recovery by the contractor of his facility costs, if the facilities became worthless at the war's end. The basic source of discrimination under tax amortization was the application of the same rate of write-off to different types of facility having widely different degrees of economically useful value remaining at the end of the war.[19]

Exemptions From Renegotiation

Two classes of exemption were provided by the renegotiation law: mandatory exemptions required by the statute, and discretionary exemptions to be made by the departmental secretaries and later by the War Contracts Price Adjustment Board. Among the mandatory exemptions the two creating most controversy were the blanket exemption of all firms with less than $500,-000 in renegotiable sales and the so-called "raw material" exemption.

The raising of the blanket exemption to $500,000 by the Renegotiation Act of 1943 (formerly $100,000 under the October 1942 amendment) was done by Congress with the support of the War Department.[20] At the time of the hearings in September 1943, the renegotiating agencies were far behind in reaching settlements and genuine concern was felt over the possible failure of the en-

[16] S. Rpt. 440, Pt. 6, 80th Cong., 2d Sess., 28 Apr 48 (hereafter cited as Truman Committee, Final Rpt), p. 233.

[17] Ibid., p. 234.

[18] (1) Truman Committee, Hearings, 42:25552. (2) Norman C. Parkin, "Control of War Contract Profits," Harvard Business Review, XXVI (March 1948), 247.

[19] See below, Chapter XX.

[20] Testimony of Under Secretary Patterson, 20 Sep 43, W&MC, Renegotiation of War Contracts, p. 810. A year earlier, during the Senate hearings leading to the October 1942 amendments, Mr. Patterson had suggested a $250,000 floor. By 1943, when the administration of renegotiation seemed to have bogged down, even the Truman Committee recommended raising the floor to $500,000. S. Rpt. 10, Pt. 5, 78th Cong., 1st Sess., 30 Mar 43, Recommendation No. 3.

tire program. It was thought that exclusion of all cases under $500,000 would aid substantially in reducing the unsettled backlog without seriously impairing the program. By February 1944, however, when the increased exemption was finally adopted, the agencies had made substantial progress and could have handled the case load under the lower figure. From 1943 to the end of the war, all firms with less than a half million dollars in war business were untouched by renegotiation. Many of these firms realized annual profits of several times their net worth. In order to preserve their exemption, firms approaching $500,000 in war business in the course of the year tended to refuse additional war orders and in some cases the procuring agencies found it difficult to place contracts. Likewise, there was a tendency for firms to organize new companies so each could receive the full exemption. Although affiliated companies were treated as a unit for renegotiation purposes, it was sometimes difficult to identify such relationships. The chief defect of the $500,000 exemption, however, was its discriminatory effect, and considerable ill feeling resulted in various communities where exempted concerns were known to be making excessive profits.

In order to reduce the discrimination against firms exceeding the $500,000 figure, WCPAB adopted the policy of limiting recoveries to a figure which would keep adjusted sales after renegotiation above $500,000. Thus, a firm with renegotiable sales of $611,000 and profits of some $411,000 was required to refund only $111,000. This still left a profit of $300,000, or some 295 percent of the firm's net worth of $102,000. This administrative decision to give firms above the $500,000 floor a partial exemption was censored by the Tru-

man Committee after the war. The renegotiation agencies were in agreement by the end of the war that the exemption should be put back to the $100,000 figure in any future renegotiation law.[21]

The "raw material" exemption was added to the renegotiation law by Congress in the October 1942 amendments. No adequate explanation of the economic basis for the exemption appears in the hearings leading to its adoption.[22] Since it was not sponsored by the War Department or the other renegotiating agencies, the War Department's concern with the exemption was limited to the many administrative problems which arose. A parallel exemption for agricultural products in their raw or natural state was made mandatory by the Renegotiation Act of 1943. The administrative difficulties created by these exemptions centered on two considerations: (1) the determination of a specific list of commodities to which the exemptions applied; (2) the closely re-

---

[21] For illustrative case cited, see Truman Committee, *Hearings,* 42:25513–14. In explaining the administrative decision for partial exemption of contracts above the $500,000 floor, the Navy spokesman stated: "We tried to be fair and equitable. We did not think it would be fair and equitable if a man did $501,000 worth of business to take $100,000 away from him, and another man who may even have had a higher margin of profit but only did $499,000 worth of business, leave him scot free." *Ibid.,* 42:25544.

[22] See: (1) Subcom. of the S. Com. on Finance, 77th Cong., 2d Sess., Hearings on Section 403 of Public Law 528, *Renegotiation of Contracts,* 29 and 30 Sep 42; (2) S. Com. on Finance, 77th Cong., 2d Sess., Hearings on H. R. 7378, *Revenue Act of 1942,* 23 Jul to 14 Aug 42. The War Department was anxious to avoid the administrative problem of renegotiating suppliers of raw materials (WDPAB History, Sec. I, Pt. I, pp. 13–14), but the form of the exemption actually adopted probably gave rise to more administrative difficulties than would have existed in the absence of any special treatment. Yoshpe, Production Control in the QMC, p. 77, Complications Resulting From Revisions in Renegotiation Act.

lated problem of deciding for each commodity the stage in the production process at which the exemption ceased.

The task of formulating a "horizontal" list of exempted items was the easier of the two, although considerable research was necessary in many industries, such as chemicals, to decide how extensive the inclusions should be. The list as formulated became a part of the official regulations on procurement and renegotiation, and was used in preparing contract terms as well as in the renegotiation procedure.[23]

The problem of determining the "vertical" cutoff point of the exemption ran into greater difficulty and controversy. It was decided that aluminum and copper ingots were produced in advance of general distribution of these metals throughout industry and they were added to the exempted list. Because of differences in the organization and integration of the steel industry, the cutoff point in that industry was established below the ingot level, with only pig iron and lower levels exempted. There was some concern that even the inclusion of pig iron would be subject to criticism, in view of the high profitability of steel industry operations through the pig iron stage:

. . . in renegotiation we have occasion to give clearance to companies whose profits from, let us say, the forum of public opinion, might be considered excessive, but because of very effective well established lobbies in Washington, they secured raw material exemptions. For example, the steel companies and the lumber companies . . . have earned as high as 15 to 20 percent, and have received clearances in renegotiation.[24]

The pig iron exemption and the ingot exemptions for nonferrous metals were retained throughout the life of renegotiation. The Department of the Treasury originally took the strict position that the vertical cutoff point should extend no higher than the point where the special tax allowance for depletion ceased. The Treasury withdrew from this position in face of opposition by the War and Navy Departments and Maritime Commission, who pointed to the wording of the statute.[25] Later, on 15 July 1943, the Attorney General in a memorandum to the President indicated that the renegotiating agencies had exceeded their authority by including certain materials in the exempted list. The inclusion of aluminum ingots as a "raw" material was specifically questioned in view of the dispersal of aluminum to industry, at a lower level, in the form of bauxite. Nevertheless, the position of the renegotiating agencies was upheld on 16 November 1943 by the Joint Price Adjustment Board, with the implied approval of the White House and the Office of War Mobilization and Reconversion (OWMR).[26]

An additional administrative burden imposed by the raw material and agricultural exemptions was a further provision in the act to protect windfall profits resulting from increases in value of excessive inventories. The act provided for the exclusion from renegotiation of profits on inventories of exempted items held in excess of normal re-

---

[23] PR 1204.2 (6–7–44) and PR 1290.2 (8–31–44). PR 1290.2 contains a list of exempted raw materials and agricultural commodities.

[24] Regional Company Pricing Discussion, Chicago, Illinois, 12–13 March 1945, p. 85, remarks of Lt Esmond H. Coleman, in Exhibit 71 to History of

Ordnance Pricing Policy. In exempting steel industry profits through the pig iron stage, renegotiation officials determined the value of pig iron as the nearest basing-point price minus freight and handling charges from the point of production. WDPAB History, Sec. II, Pt. III, p. 3.

[25] WDPAB History, Sec. II, Pt. III, pp. 1–2.

[26] (1) Ibid., p. 5. (2) WDPAB Minutes, 11 Jul 43, Renegotiation of Contracts, file 161, Purchases Div ASF.

quirements for war production. A purchaser or user of exempted metals, for example, might realize a speculative profit on inventory holdings resulting from price increases allowed by the OPA. Despite the widespread material shortages and official regulations calling for elimination of excess inventories throughout the war, speculative profits on excess raw material and agricultural inventories were shielded from renegotiation. Not only did this apply to future renegotiations, but the act required—upon application by contractors within ninety days—a refund of such profits already recaptured from the beginning of renegotiation. The task of determining such refunds was a formidable one, involving virtually insoluble accounting problems and placing a substantial burden upon renegotiation personnel.[27]

In addition to the exemptions just described, the Renegotiation Act of 1943 made mandatory the exemption of contracts with other governmental agencies; contracts and subcontracts with religious, charitable, and educational organizations; construction contracts awarded as a result of competitive bidding; and subcontracts under exempted contracts.[28] The act also gave the War Contracts Price Adjustment Board discretionary authority to exempt individual contracts or certain classes of contracts. These included contracts to be performed outside the United States, contracts for standard commercial articles if competitive conditions protected the government from excessive prices, and others. All these exemptions gave rise to problems of administration, although some were little used.

It was generally conceded by the renegotiating agencies at the end of the war that few, if any, of the exemptions, whether mandatory or permissive, were economically or morally justified. The net result for practically all types was inequitable discrimination in favor of special groups as well as additional administrative effort in defining and applying the exemptions. The official History of Navy Department Renegotiation recommended—either directly or by implication—the restoration of the $100,000 floor, the elimination of the raw material, agricultural, and competitive-bid construction exemptions and all permissive exemptions, summing up the case as follows:

1. The Government should, on moral grounds, have been entitled to recover excessive profits on exempted contracts;

2. if a contract was exempt and excessive profits were not made, renegotiation would not have affected the contractor adversely;

3. if a contract was not exempt and less than reasonable profits were earned thereon, the contractor would have benefited through over-all renegotiation;

4. because of the additional administrative work involved in the consideration of contractors' requests for exemptions, it is doubtful if there was a sufficient reduction in the administrative burden during World War II to have justified permissive exemptions.[29]

The Determination of Excessive Profits

Development of Criteria Under the 1942 Act

The most urgent and delicate problem facing the War Department with the passage of the Renegotiation Act in April 1942

---

[27] Yoshpe, Production Control in the QMC, pp. 77–78.

[28] PR 1204 (6–7–44).

[29] Office of the Under Secretary of Navy, History of Navy Department Renegotiation, 3 vols. (1947), I, 251–52, JAG Library, Navy Dept. The Truman Committee, after postwar hearings with the principal renegotiation agencies, made recommendations closely paralleling those above. Truman Committee, Final Rpt, pp. 229ff.

was the establishment of criteria for the determination of the existence and amount of "excessive" profits. The only suggestion contained in the statute was the directive that "excessive" and "unreasonable" costs, reserves, and compensation to employees should be disallowed by departmental secretaries in renegotiation proceedings. While this injunction was useful in attacking the problem of excessive *costs,* it shed no light on what might be considered excessive *profits* after all appropriate costs had been charged to income.

Numerous meetings on the subject were held in the spring and summer of 1942 by members and staff of the ASF Price Adjustment Board and representatives of the Under Secretary of War.[30] The first concrete statement announcing the factors to be used in evaluating the excessiveness of profits was the Notes on Renegotiation, issued by the board on 9 July 1942. In this statement the board made clear a fundamental premise underlying renegotiation:

In the present emergency the existence of excessive profit is no indication that a company has taken undue advantage of the Government or that the contracting officers have failed to exercise their best judgment under all the circumstances where companies have been asked to produce war materials with which neither they nor others have had any previous experience.

As a vehicle which would conveniently express the relative magnitude of profits for all types of contract, the board adopted the term "profit margin." This was defined as the ratio of profit (before taxes) to sales or (for CPFF contracts) to adjusted costs. In determining a fair margin, consideration would be given to corresponding profits in

prewar years for the firm and the industry, with the understanding that under war conditions a company would not need as great a margin as under normal competitive conditions. Comparison would be made with the current margins of other firms in the industry operating under similar conditions. Downward adjustment would be made, on a graduated scale, for increasing volume of output. Upward adjustment would be made for a large ratio of labor to material costs, on the premise that, other things equal, a company doing most of the actual production to meet its contracts required and merited a greater profit margin than one which subcontracted most of its work.

Further upward or downward adjustments would be made on the basis of six performance factors: (1) quality of production; (2) rate of delivery and turnover; (3) inventive contribution; (4) co-operation with other manufacturers; (5) efficiency in use of raw materials; (6) efficiency in reducing costs. Additional adjustments would be made in a contractor's favor for assuming risks under fixed-price contracts, including risk of increase in cost of materials, possible wage increases, inexperience in new types of production, complexity of manufacturing technique, and delays from inability to obtain materials. Finally, in the case of contractors with substantial capital devoted to war production, the allowable profit tentatively determined would be checked against net worth to assure a fair return on investment. Net worth would be analyzed to determine to what extent it included accumulated profits from war business.

A basic element in the thinking of the War Department Price Adjustment Board was that its function was not to determine what profits *should* be, but what they ought *not* to be. While this might appear to be

---

[30] For the record of early discussions and policy developments of profit recovery criteria, see documents cited above in note 33, page 362.

merely a play upon words, it indicated that in the board's eyes no precise measure of the "proper" amount of profit was possible. Rather, it assumed that in any particular case there would be a twilight zone of uncertain size within which reasonable men might disagree but beyond which profits would clearly be regarded as excessive. Thus, early in its deliberations, the WDPAB established the position that no simple or final formula could be developed which could satisfactorily be applied to all of its heterogeneous thousands of contractors and subcontractors.[31]

Factors Listed in the 1943 Act

Throughout the remainder of 1942 and 1943 the conduct of actual renegotiation resulted in the refinement and addition of criteria for determining the excessiveness of profits. In response to the widespread feeling that the factors to be used in determining excessive profits should be expressly stated in the law, the criteria developed by the renegotiation agencies were incorporated into Section 403 (a) (4) of the Renegotiation Act of 1943:

In determining excessive profits there shall be taken into consideration the following factors:

(i) efficiency of contractor, with particular regard to attainment of quantity and quality of production, reduction of costs and economy in the use of materials, facilities, and manpower;

(ii) reasonableness of costs and profits, with particular regard to volume of production, normal pre-war earnings, and comparison of war and peacetime products;

(iii) amount and source of public and private capital employed and net worth;

(iv) extent of risk assumed, including the risk incident to reasonable pricing policies;

(v.) nature and extent of contribution to the war effort, including inventive and developmental contribution and cooperation with the Government and other contractors in supplying technical assistance;

(vi) character of business, including complexity of manufacturing technique, character and extent of subcontracting, and rate of turnover;

(vii) such other factors the consideration of which the public interest and fair and equitable dealing may require, which factors shall be published in the regulations in the Board from time to time as adopted.

Application of the Factors

The heart of the problem of renegotiation was not the selection of the proper factors but their actual application to particular cases. The task of evaluating a given contractor's performance in terms of each of the factors listed, of combining all the findings into an over-all judgment expressed in dollars, and of assuring comparable treatment of all firms in an industry and of one industry against another, was one which literally called for omniscience. The following brief discussion attempts to describe a few of the

---

[31] (1) WDPAB, Notes on Renegotiation, p. 16. (2) Price Adjustment Meeting in Cleveland, 18 November 1942, address of Mr. Karker, Chmn WDPAB, pp. 11–13, Tab 33. Both in Renegotiation of Contracts, file 161, Purchases Div ASF. Proposals to adopt a precise formula for profit recovery under renegotiation cropped up repeatedly throughout the war. Members of Congress as well as representatives of industry constantly deplored the vagueness of the statute and the wide latitude allowed administrators. Under Secretary Patterson testified that the best minds in the War Department had tried again and again to develop such a formula but could not do so. (1) W&MC, Renegotiation of War Contracts, pp. 826, 844, 850, 873, 882, 894. (2) Testimony of Brig Gen Maurice Hirsch, Chmn WCPAB, in Truman Committee, Hearings, 39:23258. The whole purpose of renegotiation was to avoid the rigidity and inequity of a simple formula, the prototype of which was the flat-rate percentage limitation on profits originally discarded in favor of renegotiation.

major problems arising and some of the principal policy conclusions reached by the War Department and the other renegotiating agencies.

Base-Period Comparisons—A relatively simple type of case for renegotiation was that of a competitive manufacturer whose war products were identical with his peacetime products (for example, chewing gum, standard electric motors). In such cases prewar earnings, with the 1936–39 period as a base, were a point of departure in measuring the excessiveness of wartime profits. In an early statement of policy, the Under Secretaries of War and Navy ruled that "in general the margin of profit which a company makes on its expanded war sales may be limited to one half or one third of the margin of profit on peacetime sales." [32] Thus a firm which had realized a $2 million profit on $10 million of sales in peacetime might be allowed in wartime $2 million profit on its first $10 million of renegotiable sales, $1 million on the second $10 million, and $⅔ million on the third $10 million. This would result in a wartime profit margin on sales of some 12 percent compared with the prewar margin of 20 percent on the lower volume. [33]

In actual practice, most contractors produced different products for war, had undergone substantial plant conversion, had unrepresentative base periods, or for other reasons were allowed substantially higher margins than they had experienced in the

base period. Thus, one official survey indicated that the wartime profit margin on sales *after renegotiation* was more than 30 percent higher than the base period margin for the largest firms and more than 130 percent higher for the smallest firms. (*Compare lines 3 and 11, Table 43, page 395.*) Probably the chief function of base-period analysis in renegotiation was its use as a floor below which wartime profits were not allowed to fall. [34]

Contractor's Efficiency and Quality of Production—Because of the inadequacy of dollar-value figures for measuring a contractors' contribution to war production, efforts were made to gauge contractor performance in terms of physical or engineering standards. Very early in renegotiation it became evident that there were no absolute standards of performance or efficiency. This was as true for engineering standards as it was for economic or administrative standards. Most war production consisted of new products produced with new equipment, new technology, and new or different materials. To complicate matters still further, neither the products nor the equipment, materials, and processes remained constant for very long. The only possible way of rating a contractor's performance was on a relative basis, comparing one contractor's performance with that of others engaged in similar production and making allowance for differences in individual circumstances. To accomplish this it was necessary to develop comparative tests for each of the various factors enumerated in the statute.

In most cases evaluation of the quality of the product was not a major problem in renegotiation. Established inspection requirements and procedures determined the basic acceptability to the Army of the contractor's

---

[32] Jt Statement of the Under Secretaries of War and Navy, 9 Feb 43, cited in WDPAB History, Sec. III, Pt. VI, p. 66.

[33] The allowance of a decreasing rate of profit on additional increments of sales above base-period averages was known as the incremental method. For its significance and other aspects of base-period analysis, see J. J. Lynch, Consideration To Be Given Base Period Results, paper read at Seminar on Renegotiation, Holabird, Maryland, April 1945, in WDPAB History, Sec. III, Pt. VI, pp. 66–72.

[34] *Ibid.*, p. 70.

output. The far more difficult problem was how to determine the relative importance of quality and quantity of production—for example, how much to penalize contractors for failure to meet delivery schedules in order to attain quality standards, or for failure to meet precise specifications in order that troops might receive needed equipment at the earliest possible date. Conversely, the tasks of rewarding superior performance were equally difficult. For some services, such as the Signal Corps, it was very difficult for renegotiators to know how to distinguish superior from ordinary performance in a milieu of complex and delicate manufacturing processes familiar only to highly trained engineering specialists. In the collection of recommendations submitted by the technical services for the improvement of renegotiation procedure, it was proposed that qualified engineers be assigned to renegotiation on a full-time basis.[35]

Value Added—An important development in renegotiation technique in the latter part of the war was increasing reliance on the "value added" concept. This technique was especially useful became of its wide applicability to all types of industry and product. Rather than looking to a contractor's gross billings or sales as an indication of his productive contribution, it confined attention to the net value of the processing actually done by the contractor. As defined by War Department renegotiators, "value added" meant "the amount of costs and expenses incurred by a contractor in the course of his renegotiable operations during a fiscal period, apart from the cost of subcontracting and material purchased."[36]

Companies with a high degree of integration, whose purchases of parts and materials were a small percentage of the value of their finished product, performed a greater service than nonintegrated firms whose ratio of material costs to final costs was high. Not only did the integrated firm typically perform a more extensive and complex productive task; it eliminated the several layers of profit normal to a series of subcontractor operations. The War Department thus allowed a greater retention of profits per dollar of sales for a large ratio of value added. In using the value-added technique, costs had to be carefully scrutinized to insure that increments in value did not consist of excessive costs. Even where higher costs were beyond the control of the contractor, such as high wages in a labor-shortage area, it was essential to make an adjustment to avoid rewarding a contractor with a greater amount of profit than his lower cost competitor.[37]

Contractor's Risks and Pricing Policy—The pricing aspects of renegotiation policy were developed in conjunction with procurement policy as a whole. War Department negotiators as well as contractors had to be trained and educated in the principles of sound pricing as soon as these had been discovered and formulated. As already shown, contractors tended to resist close

---

[35] *Ibid.,* Sec. IV, Pt. II, App. 2–A, Tab G, p. 11, and App. 2–B, Recommendation 17, Visits to Contractors' Plants.

[36] *Ibid.,* Sec. III, Pt. VI, p. 50.

[37] *Ibid.,* pp. 54–55. The Army's value-added technique was developed largely by Ordnance, which made numerous contributions to the theory and practice of renegotiation. A Research and Inquiry Unit for developing statistical data and techniques of renegotiation was established in the Purchase Policy Branch, Legal Division, OCofOrd. Results of analyses by this unit were published as Research Bulletins. The value-added approach was developed in Research Bulletins Nos. 1, 2, 3, and 7. Research Bulletin No. 7 consolidated the whole approach, and its recommendations were widely adopted throughout all renegotiation agencies. *Ibid.,* Sec. IV, Pt. II, App. 2–A, Tab E, p. 16.

TABLE 38—REWARD FOR FAIR PRICES: HYPOTHETICAL RENEGOTIATION OF THREE FIRMS WITH IDENTICAL COSTS[a]

Item	Company A	Company B	Company C
Sales	$150,000	$120,000	$100,000
Cost	90,000	90,000	90,000
Net Profit	$60,000	$30,000	$10,000
Renegotiation Recovery	54,000	21,000	0
Net After Recovery	$6,000	$9,000	$10,000
	Percent		
Profit-Sales Ratio:			
Before Recovery	40	25	10
After Recovery	4	7½	10
Profit-Adjusted Sales Ratio: After Recovery	6.25	9.09	10
Percent of Profit Recovered	90	70	0

[a] It is assumed that Companies A, B, and C produce the same number of identical items but sell them to the Government at different prices.

Source: Illustration reproduced from Page 48, Exhibit 30, History of Ordnance Pricing Policy.

pricing, both out of fear of loss and in hope of higher profits. At the time of contract negotiation they typically argued that the establishment of high initial prices was the only safe procedure for both parties: contractors would thereby receive the necessary protection, and renegotiation would subsequently return to the government any excessive profits. When the time for renegotiation came around they would often shift the argument: contractors were entitled to retain their high profits since these represented the appropriate reward for risk-bearing as well as for other contributions.

In attempting to overcome contractor resistance to close pricing, War Department renegotiators pointed to two basic aspects of the problem of financial risk in war production. The first of these concerned the effects of close pricing upon the contractor's own activities. A contractor who accepted an initial price close to cost demonstrated his willingness to accept in advance his responsibility to produce efficiently. If he was able by efficient methods to reduce costs, he would be allowed to retain a greater proportion of the resulting profit than if he had insisted on a high initial price to be followed by price reductions or retroactive refunds. Ideally, differential profit recoveries in accordance with the principle of close pricing would appear somewhat as in the accompanying illustration. (Table 38) In this case Company C would have assumed a real pricing risk; Companies B and A, little or none whatever. Contractors with a genuine pricing risk would exert greater pressure on their organizations to attain efficiency and reduce costs. Collectively, they would require lower governmental appropriations, create less need for high taxes and federal borrowing, and exert less inflationary pressure on the economy as a whole. In this respect renegotiation differed fundamentally from an excess profits tax, which encouraged lavish cost expenditures in the face of the inexorable recapture, without distinction as to merit, of excess profits from whatever source.[38]

A second aspect of the problem of risk was the degree to which this element, for contractors in general, changed between 1940 and the peak of the war effort. Early in the defense period the risks attending the assumption of a military procurement contract were in most respects far greater than they were after the nation had settled down to a full-fledged war. In 1940 and 1941 the expenses of conversion, the loss of regular peacetime business to competitors, the complete novelty of munitions production, and the great uncertainty over the future of the rearmament program were for many firms a tremendous hazard that could be voluntarily shouldered in peacetime only when covered by substantial inducements in the form of safe prices based on ample allowances for various contingencies. Such allowances might take the form of generous estimates of the costs of conversion, the quantity and cost of labor and equipment needed, and the amount and cost of raw materials required per unit of output. After Pearl Harbor not only was the whole peacetime psychology perforce thrown overboard, but the government provided substantial stability for many elements of cost previously

unpredictable. Wages and prices were brought under control, raw materials were channeled into war production, plant and equipment made available to war producers, government financing for both fixed and working capital was provided, and numerous other measures adopted—all calculated to eliminate or minimize the contractor's risks or transfer them to the government.

These fundamental changes were slow to receive understanding or recognition by contractors. Many of the practices and attitudes cultivated by industry during the uncertainties of the defense period tended to persist on into the war. While the impact of Pearl Harbor and of the Jack and Heintz revelations guaranteed the easy passage of the first renegotiation law early in 1942, during the next two years it was difficult both to keep the statute alive and to achieve the desired results in administration. Renegotiators were faced with a task impossible of adequate fulfillment from either a qualitative or a quantitative point of view. Not only did each case call for omniscience but the size of the total case load, in the face of inadequate time and facilities, made a satisfactory performance impossible. To this was added the separation between the renegotiation and pricing activities of the procuring agencies, coupled with perennial contractor resistance to both close original pricing and renegotiation. As a result, especially for the first year (fiscal year 1942), renegotiation not only left much to be desired in its influence on pricing but failed to effect profit recoveries in accordance with the criteria which had been developed. Sample statistics indicated that instead of providing a skillful excision of profits on the basis of merit, renegotiation was simply scaling down the profits of all contractors on a graduated basis. (*Table 39*) Those contractors

---

[38] Long before World War II, Bernard Baruch had conclusively demonstrated in a memorandum to the War Policies Commission the inevitable "cost-plus" pressures exerted by an excess profits tax. "The excess profits tax is not a substitute for price stabilization." See memo reproduced in Baruch, *American Industry in the War,* pp. 414–17.

TABLE 39—RATIO OF NET PROFITS TO SALES: BEFORE AND AFTER CONTRACTORS' 1942
RENEGOTIATION WITH BASE PERIOD COMPARISON

| 160 War Department Contractors [a] | Average Ratio of Net Profit to Sales | | |
| | For Contractors' 1942 Fiscal Year | | Percent for Base Period 1936–1939 |
	Percent Before Renegotiation	Percent After Renegotiation	
20 Contractors–Over 30% of sales	37.04	13.13	9.90
20 Contractors–25% to 30% of Sales	27.46	12.23	7.11
20 Contractors–20% to 25% of Sales	22.19	11.61	10.89
20 Contractors–15% to 20% of Sales	17.43	10.68	7.12
20 Contractors–12% to 15% of Sales	13.09	9.98	5.87
20 Contractors–10% to 12% of Sales	10.96	8.37	7.39
20 Contractors–8% to 10% of Sales	9.01	7.83	7.25
20 Contractors–Under 8% of Sales	5.56	5.02	5.04

[a] Classified by initial profit ratio–FY 1942 with twenty contractors selected at random from each percentage class.

Source: Contractors' 1942 Schedule A's, summarized on Page 47, Exhibit 30, History of Ordnance Pricing Policy.

who profited most before renegotiation were in general the ones who were left with the highest profits after renegotiation.

Because of the lengthy time lag between earnings and renegotiation, as well as the dispersion of contractors' fiscal years throughout the calendar year, these discouraging figures did not appear before the end of 1943. But already contractors had begun to "compare notes," and it became evident that the close-pricing efforts of the services were being jeopardized by the evident correlation between high initial and high retained profits. Increased awareness of this situation was a primary factor behind the intensified pricing activities of the ASF and the launching of the company pricing program early in 1944.[39]

As revealed by the statistical record, profit margins before renegotiation for War Department contractors fell substantially and

[39] (1) History of Ordnance Pricing Policy, Exhibits 29 through 32. (2) ASF, History of Purchases Division, Exhibit 34.

continuously after 1942. (See Table 42, page 392.) This indicated a notable improvement as the war progressed. Nevertheless, contractor resistance to close pricing persisted to the end of the war, and responsibilities of contracting officers, negotiators, and renegotiators were not easily discharged. One of the barriers to close pricing was the number of change orders issued by the procuring agencies. In spite of the merits of design stability for purposes of maximizing production, the Army could not be content with inferior planes, tanks, guns, and ammunition when the possibilities of improvement were obvious. Consequently, a common experience for many manufacturers was to get barely tooled up and ready for mass production only to be ordered to retool their production lines and retrain their employees to meet a change order. Such changes were costly and as often as not took place before the cost of the original setup had been amortized. Even where no change in design was involved a change order requiring additional quantities or accelerated delivery had much the same effect. The contractor would have to acquire additional equipment, revamp his production lines, obtain additional priority assistance, and so on, all adding to his cost for the year in question. After many such experiences contractors were reluctant to accept close initial prices, or to reduce their prices before completion of long production runs. The effects of change orders, like many other genuine obstacles to close pricing, had to be carefully considered in renegotiation determinations.[40]

Contractor's Net Worth—One of the most controversial elements in the statutory list of factors was the item of net worth. In postwar hearings on renegotiation, the price adjustment boards were criticized for inadequate attention to this element, and a number of examples were given of firms receiving an annual return after renegotiation of several times their net worth. It was intimated that the use of the ratio of profits to sales (instead of profits to net worth) as the vehicle for expressing profit margins tended to conceal the true rate of return and led to the retention of excessive profits.[41]

Actually, as representatives of the renegotiating agencies explained on frequent occasions, both the return on net worth and the return on sales were considered in each case as a matter of standard procedure. But these were just two of the many relevant considerations in renegotiation and were therefore not controlling. The ratio-to-sales margin had long been used by the business community for measuring the return on the volume of output, a more accurate reflection

of a firm's contribution than net worth. But just as gross sales gave a misleading picture of the contribution of firms with widely divergent ratios of value added, so did net worth present a distorted view of the true return upon invested capital. Firms with equivalent plant and equipment often had widely different ratios of equity to debt financing, and there were many types of ownership and creditor instruments—including common and preferred stocks, debentures, and bonds—shading imperceptibly into each other. Moreover, in precisely the area where the return on net worth showed the greatest extremes, that is, small business, the element of compensation in the form of salaries, bonuses, and similar payments was most significant in measuring the total return to the owners of the business.[42] (*Compare lines 13 and 19, Table 43, page 395.*)

The War Department Price Adjustment Board was well aware of the many problems associated with the treatment of net worth. Various methods were used to allocate each firm's total net worth between its renegotiable and nonrenegotiable business in order to reflect that portion of total net worth devoted to war business. Where specific items of plant, equipment, and working capital were devoted to war business, these were directly allocated to renegotiable sales. In most cases, however, renegotiable and exempt business were performed in the same plant and the allocation was made on the basis of renegotiable to total costs. Still other bases were used, such as ratios of value

---

[40] WDPAB History, Sec. III, Pt. VI, pp. 42–43.

[41] (1) Truman Committee, *Hearings,* 42:25506–18. (2) Truman Committee, Final Rpt, pp. 228–29; also, p. 234, Recommendation No. 4.

[42] For 150 companies with renegotiable sales under $500,000 for fiscal years ending between 1 January and 1 July 1943, the average ratio of executive compensation to net worth was 80.1 percent; for sales between $500,000 and $1 million, 45.9 percent; and for sales between $1 and $2 million, 22.4 percent. *Congressional Record,* Vol. 91, Pt. V (14 Jan 45), 6148, Table II.

added or charges for labor and burden, where the character of war and exempt business was dissimilar. Complications were added by the presence of government loans of working capital as well as government-furnished materials, machinery, and additions to plant. Excess working capital or investment assets, foreign plants, real estate, and other items not used in the manufacturing business subject to the allocation had to be deducted to provide a proper allocation base. Long-term debt advanced by owners or shareholders, especially in a closely held company, was treated as a portion of net worth when circumstances warranted. Long-term debt to outsiders, except in unusual instances, was considered as debt rather than net worth.[43]

Wherever comparisons among firms in a given industry showed wide differences in return to allocated net worth, careful scrutiny was given to all the relevant circumstances. In general, a 10-percent return on net worth before taxes was treated as a floor for purposes of profit recovery but no specific ceiling was recognized. A return of over 50 percent was considered questionable but allowable if justified by other factors.[44]

In considering the legitimacy of a given level of return upon allocated net worth, the price adjustment boards gave attention to the size and character of the business, and to peacetime patterns of capital turnover and return to net worth. A public utility concern with a low capital turnover might have a high profit-to-sales margin and a low return on net worth. A nationwide grocery chain, on the other hand, might typically exhibit a low profit-to-sales margin and a

high return on net worth. Small business, in peacetime as well as in war, exhibited a much wider range of percentage rates of return upon net worth than did industry as a whole.

The most exaggerated cases of high return to net worth during World War II involved firms whose renegotiable sales were less than $500,000 and were therefore exempt from renegotiation. Next came those with renegotiable sales slightly in excess of $500,000, who were not required to refund an amount greater than the figure which would reduce their adjusted sales to the $500,000 floor. (*See line 15, Table 43, page 395.*) [45] There is no doubt that small business fared relatively better in renegotiation than large business. On the other hand, because excessive-compensation disallowances and renegotiation recoveries fell more intimately on the owners of small rather than large businesses, many of the most vociferous complaints against renegotiation came from the small business sector.

Consideration of the net worth factor sheds light on the criticism, frequently made of renegotiation for World War II, that the spread or range of profit margins allowed after renegotiation was too narrow to reward efficiency adequately. This criticism is considerably weakened by the fact that the range of returns on net worth was several times the range of profit margins on renegotiable sales, the item subjected to criticism. Since it was the rate of return on net worth, rather than on sales, which provided

---

[43] Maj Clifford W. Michel, Return on Allocated Net Worth, paper read at Seminar on Renegotiation, Holabird, Maryland, April 1945, in WDPAB History, Sec. III, Pt. VI, pp. 73–80.

[44] *Ibid.*, pp. 77–78.

[45] The corresponding percentages for corporations classified in the same brackets by 1943 renegotiable sales volume were 89.8 percent, 72.9, 55.6, 46.7, 41.0, and 33.1 percent. *Congressional Record,* Vol. 91, Pt. V (14 Jan 45), 6148, Table II. The significance of these figures must be interpreted in the light of all the qualifications necessarily surrounding the definition and measurement of net worth.

the greatest contractor incentive, the validity of the criticism in question is considerably weakened.

The foregoing discussion of items considered in the determination of excessive profits indicates in general the magnitude and scope of renegotiation policy. It is not possible in a brief treatment to consider the many intangible items—the complexity of the contractor's business, his inventive and developmental contribution, the extent to which he supervised subcontractors and rendered them technical assistance, his cooperation with the government and other manufacturers in sharing trade secrets and forgoing royalties, and numerous other details—which were considered by renegotiation boards in making determinations. The complexities of even the simpler cases were such that final determinations could not be made with unimpeachable accuracy. For the more difficult cases the decisions could only be made on the basis of broad and informed judgment.

Renegotiation Statistics

The predominant role of the War Department in the field of contract renegotiation is revealed by the statistical record. An indication of the size of the administrative task is found in the total number of renegotion assignments and the manner of their disposition by major departments and by years from 1942 through 1946.[46] (*Table 40*) Of the grand total of 118,181 assignments for all five departments, the War Department received 715,818 or nearly 65 percent. This was virtually double the combined volume handled by the other four departments.

Each renegotiation assignment concerned a firm's war business for its own fiscal year. Thus most of the 20,416 assignments to the War Department for 1942 business were not made until 1943, and many were not settled until 1944 or later. The trend of assignments, reaching a peak for 1943, tended to parallel the general trend of procurement activity, but was modified by the effects of improved organization and screening procedure, gradually narrowing profit margins, and other factors.

In total number of assignments the Corps of Engineers led all War Department agencies, followed in turn by the Quartermaster Corps, Ordnance, and Air Forces. (*Table 41*) Within the technical services and the Air Forces, the distribution to various field offices throughout the country varied with the type of field organization, the volume of procurement done by the various districts, and so forth.

Of greater significance are the financial data on renegotiation. (*Table 42*) Out of total renegotiable sales of $223 billion, profits before renegotiation amounted to $28 billion, or 12.7 percent of sales. Recoveries of nearly $10 billion reduced this profit to about $18.5 billion, or 8.7 percent of adjusted sales.[47]

The gradual decline from 1942 to 1946 in profit margins before renegotiation indicates the broad effects of renegotiation and closer pricing. Average profit margins for all departments before renegotiation fell from 16.2 percent of sales in 1942 to 9.4 percent in 1946. Initial profit margins were thus, on an average, 72 percent higher at the beginning of the program than at the end. Measured simply by the level of per-

---

[46] Statistics for 1946 were included by the War Contracts Price Adjustment Board in its final report. They are reproduced herein as part of the total record of renegotiation for World War II.

[47] Renegotiable sales were reduced by the amount of profit recovered to reflect the value of such sales at proper prices.

TABLE 40—DISPOSITION OF RENEGOTIATION ASSIGNMENTS: 1942–1946

Contractors' Fiscal Year and Disposition of Assignments	All Departments	War Department	Navy [a] Department	RFC,[b] Maritime,[c] and Treasury
Total Assignments–All Years	118,181	75,818	24,067	18,296
Cancellations	58,046	32,908	12,112	13,026
Clearances	28,317	20,612	5,891	1,814
Bilateral Agreements	29,973	21,354	5,594	3,025
Unilateral Orders	1,845	944	470	431
Total Assignments–1942	32,252	20,416	6,514	5,322
Cancellations	12,330	5,536	2,683	4,111
Clearances	9,895	7,345	2,229	321
Bilateral Agreements	9,527	7,264	1,481	782
Unilateral Orders	500	271	121	108
Total Assignments–1943	37,207	23,240	7,859	7,108
Cancellations	19,451	10,786	4,215	4,450
Clearances	8,108	6,055	1,601	452
Bilateral Agreements	9,038	6,116	1,885	1,037
Unilateral Orders	610	283	158	169
Total Assignments–1944	25,979	16,832	5,703	3,444
Cancellations	12,193	7,069	3,019	2,105
Clearances	6,366	4,808	1,078	480
Bilateral Agreements	7,034	4,758	1,515	761
Unilateral Orders	386	197	91	98
Total Assignments–1945	18,025	11,784	3,469	2,772
Cancellations	10,124	6,508	1,802	1,814
Clearances	3,599	2,211	894	494
Bilateral Agreements	4,005	3,907	684	414
Unilateral Orders	297	158	89	50
Total Assignments–1946	4,718	3,546	522	650
Cancellations	3,948	3,009	393	546
Clearances	349	193	89	67
Bilateral Agreements	369	309	29	31
Unilateral Orders	52	35	11	6

[a] Includes Navy PAB and Navy Services and Sales Renegotiation Section.
[b] RFC subsidiaries named in Renegotiation Act of 1943.
[c] Includes Maritime Ship operations, formerly War Shipping Administration.
Source: Adapted from Table I–A, WCPAB, Final Report, 22 May 51.

centage profit margins and the rate of their reduction by 1946, the War Department record is somewhat poorer than the average. This is in part accounted for by the distortion in 1946 figures resulting from the effects of a few cases on the low total for the year.

Another way of viewing the progress of renegotiation from 1942 to 1946 is to compare the percentage of initial profit actually recaptured from year to year. For its 1942 war business, American industry was required to surrender through renegotiation

TABLE 41—WAR DEPARTMENT PRICE ADJUSTMENT BOARD ASSIGNMENTS: AS OF 6 FEBRUARY 1948

Army Service	Total		Years				
	Number	Percent	1942	1943	1944	1945	1946
Total	75,796	100.0	20,416	16,825	11,778	3,543	75,796
Air Forces	13,344	17.6	3,232	3,800	3,056	2,410	846
Chemical Warfare	1,440	1.9	290	390	385	310	65
Engineers	18,904	24.9	6,045	6,784	3,486	1,965	624
Ordnance	16,507	21.8	4,343	4,372	3,872	3,223	697
Power Procurement Officer	855	1.1	84	383	388	—	—
Quartermaster	18,109	23.9	4,646	5,746	4,138	2,591	988
Signal Corps	3,110	4.1	659	809	766	625	251
Surgeon General	1,552	2.1	428	456	382	269	17
Transportation	886	1.2	161	292	242	168	23
Army Price Adjustment Board	1,089	1.4	528	202	110	217	32

Source: WDPAB History V, Pt. II, App. 2A, Tab A, Exhibit VI-D.

an average of 48.5 percent of its initial profit. Because of more reasonable prices this percentage fell to 39 percent for 1943. For 1944 it fell to 27.3 percent, and for 1945 the total recovery was only 18.8 percent of initial profit. Over the same five-year period the average profit retention for all departments fell from 9.0 percent to 7.5 percent of adjusted sales. Renegotiation, together with related pricing techniques, had made substantial progress in effecting closer pricing by the end of the war.

An important area of analysis for which War Department statistics are lacking pertains to the spread or range of percentage profit margins after renegotiation. In the absence of such statistics, Chart 3, based on a large sample of Navy Department cases, may be taken as suggesting the situation prevailing for the War Department.[48] The chart reveals that nearly 60 percent of the 2,500 cases analyzed fell within the 10.0-percent to 12.9-percent bracket. This high concentration of cases around the average has given rise to the frequent charge that renegotiation failed to permit adequate rewards to the more efficient contractors.[49] As already indicated in the discussion of net worth, statistics of profit margins based on gross sales do not reveal either the full spread or the true significance of contractor earnings, either before or after renegotiation.

[48] Taken from History of Navy Department Renegotiation, Vol. III, Renegotiation Statistics. The author of this volume was Mr. Norman C. Parkin, who was active in renegotiation matters during and after World War II. In a conversation with the author, Mr. Parkin stated his opinion that the pattern of profit margins for the Army after renegotiation would closely approximate that of the Navy. Profit margins after renegotiation represent profits before taxes and thus do not indicate finally retained profits.

[49] See Miller, Pricing of Military Procurements, pages 181 ff., for a discussion of this issue and its implications. Profit margins for the 2,500 fixed-price cases cited above are notably higher than the over-all figures contained in Table 42. A substantial portion of the difference is attributable to the inclusion of CPFF contracts in Table 42.

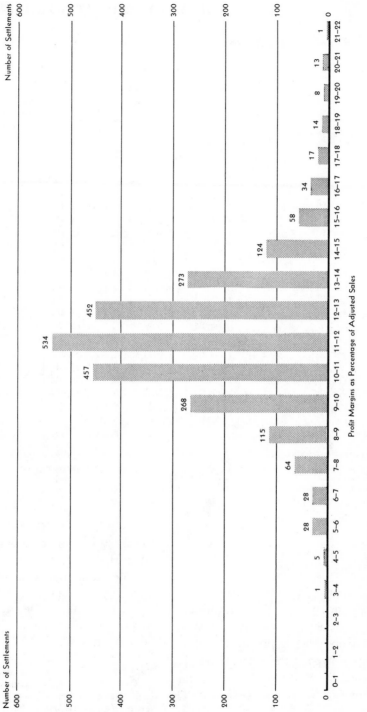

CHART 3—PROFIT MARGINS AFTER RENEGOTIATION (BEFORE TAXES):
NAVY DEPARTMENT FIXED-PRICE MANUFACTURING AND SHIPBUILDING
CONTRACTORS, 1942-45.

[2,492 Refund Cases Only]

Number of Settlements

Profit Margins as Percentage of Adjusted Sales

Source: History of Navy Department Renegotiation, Vol. III, Chart IV.

TABLE 42—RENEGOTIABLE SALES, PROFITS AND PROFIT MARGINS, AND AMOUNT RECOVERED [a]

[Dollars in Millions]

Contractor's Fiscal Year and Renegotiating Agency [b]	Before Renegotiation			After Renegotiation			Amount Recovered
	Net Renegotiable Sales	Basic Profit		Net Renegotiable Sales	Basic Profit		
		Amount	Percent of Sales		Amount	Percent of Sales	
Grand Total—All Years	$223,444	$28,351	12.7	$213,674	$18,581	8.7	$9,770
War Department	147,960	19,221	13.0	141,350	12,610	8.9	6,611
Navy Department	57,868	7,203	12.4	55,380	4,716	8.5	2,487
Total—1942	38,479	6,231	16.2	35,456	3,208	9.0	3,023
War Department	26,538	4,292	16.2	24,434	2,188	9.0	2,105
Navy Department	10,564	1,709	16.2	9,757	902	9.2	807
Total—1943	68,067	9,400	13.8	64,401	5,734	8.9	3,665
War Department	45,796	6,322	13.8	43,374	3,900	9.0	2,423
Navy Department	16,288	2,264	13.9	15,404	1,380	9.0	884
Total—1944	69,809	7,998	11.5	67,624	5,812	8.6	2,185
War Department	46,244	5,418	11.7	44,778	3,952	8.8	1,466
Navy Department	17,672	2,024	11.5	17,101	1,453	8.5	571
Total—1945	45,584	4,582	10.1	44,719	3,717	8.3	865
War Department	28,610	3,102	10.8	28,014	2,506	8.9	596
Navy Department	12,911	1,169	9.1	12,694	951	7.5	218
Total—1946	1,504	141	9.4	1,473	110	7.5	31
War Department	772	86	11.2	750	65	8.6	22
Navy Department	432	37	8.5	425	29	6.9	7

[a] Corporation Refund and Clearance Cases Only. Excluding brokers, agents, sales engineers, construction contractors, shipping contractors under charters, and contractors renegotiated on a completed contract basis. Data included represent cases accounting for approximately 89 percent of all recoveries.

[b] Totals include figures for smaller renegotiating agencies not specifically shown.

Source: Adapted from WCPAB Final Report Table III-A.

Concluding Observations

The military agencies, and in particular the War Department, exercised a dominant role in both the enactment and the administration of contract renegotiation for World War II. Army officials provided Congress with the prototype of the renegotiation law and assumed the major burden of assigning and processing renegotiation cases. The broad achievements and failures of renegotiation thus constitute a part of the Army's record of economic mobilization for World War II.[50]

The most obvious achievement of wartime renegotiation was the actual recapture of which War Department recoveries of excessive profits, totaling over $11 billion, amounted to nearly $7.5 billion. Much has

[50] The broad generalizations of this section do not purport to be a comprehensive evaluation of renegotiation. For additional observation and references, see: (1) Worsley, *Wartime Economic Stabilization,* Chs. 22 and 23; (2) Parkin, "Control of War Contract Profits," pp. 230–50.

been written about the implications of these figures, especially in the light of estimates that excess profits taxation in the absence of renegotiation would have recovered all but $3 billion to $4 billion of the $11 billion actually recaptured. One reaction has been that $3 billion to $4 billion—or even the entire $11 billion—was a relatively insignificant amount when compared with the $300 billion of total expenditures for military procurement for World War II, and that minor changes in excess profits tax legislation could have been substituted for the cumbersome and expensive process of renegotiation.

The War Department, the other procurement agencies, and the War Contracts Price Adjustment Board consistently rejected this interpretation on the ground that it overlooked both the major purpose and the practical results of renegotiation. The existence of the renegotiation statute was probably the most compelling single influence behind the close-pricing efforts of the procuring agencies. Both in its day-to-day administrative requirements and in its constant presence in the background, renegotiation was a perpetual reminder to contracting officers, to officials in charge of procurement policy, and to wartime contractors of the importance and necessity of close pricing. Although the War Department was able to show—over and above the $7.5 billion of actual recoveries—savings of some $4.5 billion on future deliveries under existing contracts as a result of renegotiation, the largest saving may easily have been the closer pricing of all new procurement under contracts made after the passage of the first renegotiation act in April 1942.[51]

---

[51] Ltr and Attachments, John R. Paull, Chmn WDPAB, to William P. Rogers, Com Counsel, 19 Sep 47, reproduced in Truman Committee, *Hearings*, 42:25887.

It is manifestly impossible to determine what the total dollar recapture under the excess profits tax would have been in the absence of renegotiation. Without the restraints upon price increases imposed both directly and indirectly by renegotiation, the dollar magnitude of total renegotiable sales and total profits before taxes would have been substantially higher—with the relative increase in profits outrunning the relative increase in prices and renegotiable sales. In a regime of rampant inflation and in the absence of renegotiation, total recapture via the excess profits tax might easily have been several times the number of dollars actually recaptured by renegotiation. But by the same token *un*recaptured profits would have grown as rapidly as recaptured profits, thus defeating the whole program of price and inflation control. The recapture of dollars representing substantial inflation in the prices of government procurement was simply a partial and belated recovery of additional government funds which should never have been spent. As pointed out repeatedly by Mr. Baruch as well as by the procuring agencies during the pre-World War II era, the innate cost-plus-features of the excess profits tax rendered it worthless as a means of controlling either prices or profits. In the absence of renegotiation or direct price controls, firms could have insured their retention of a high level of profits after taxes merely by pricing their output high enough to yield the desired net return.

The essential character of the renegotiation program was thus the opposite of that for an excess profits tax. The ultimate objective of renegotiation was to "write its own death warrant" by effecting progressive reductions in excessive profits *before*, rather than after, recapture. Measured by this test, renegotiation in World War II was remarkably successful. As indicated at an earlier point, the ratio of profits to sales before renegotiation for all agencies fell from 16.2 percent for 1942 to 9.4 percent for 1946.[52] If the original profits ratio of 16.2 percent had persisted throughout the war, initial profits on the more than $200 billion of renegotiable sales actually experienced from 1943 to 1946 would have been some $33 billion rather than $22 billion. But the cumulative inflationary pressure under looser pricing would have driven all dollar figures upward by unknown amounts.

The contribution of renegotiation to close pricing and inflation control cannot, of course, be accurately measured. By postwar standards the record of price and inflation control for World War II was outstanding. Much of the credit belongs to the OPA which resolutely controlled prices in the civilian goods and basic production sectors of the economy. But the OPA was obliged by administrative necessity no less than by the representations of the armed forces to rely upon the procuring agencies for control of the prices of war goods. The services, in turn, relied heavily on renegotiation in the absence of adequate knowledge of costs at the time contracts were let. It was largely the development of renegotiation procedures during the summer of 1942 which led to the Henderson-Patterson-Forrestal agreement exempting military goods from OPA ceiling-price control. It was also the recognition of the inadequacy of blanket price control as an instrument of profit control which led the services to recommend against mandatory exemption from renegotiation of standard commercial articles and similar products—an exemption proposed on the ground that these were subject to OPA controls.

[52] See above, page 388.

To the extent that it fostered close pricing and avoidance of inflation, renegotiation thereby promoted efficiency in the use of real resources, the ultimate wartime scarcity. Over and above efficiency resulting directly from closer pricing, the constant emphasis in renegotiation proceedings on productive contribution and efficiency undoubtedly added to the general wartime stimuli and pressures in this direction. Although renegotiation was often criticized as a positive deterrent to efficiency, no convincing evidence has been adduced. The alleged narrowness in profit differentials allowed to contractors of differing efficiency might well disappear of such margins were calculated on the basis of net worth rather than on total renegotiable sales. Moreover, each case must be reviewed on the basis of all the elements involved, in order to understand the results; no single statistical figure affords the basis for a meaningful comparison. In any event, contractor complaints during the actual course of their war production effort were directed not at the narrowness of the profit range (which was then unknown) but against renegotiation in principle as a deterrent to efficiency. Despite the impossibility of accurate appraisal of relative efficiency by renegotiators, it is probable that contractors were in no better position to make such an appraisal. The presumption is that renegotiators with a broad background of business and financial experience, with an abundance of information on numerous factors for all firms in an industry, and without a financial stake in the settlements, could make a more impartial and equitable appraisal.

In the eyes of Congress and the public at large, the chief purpose of renegotiation was to prevent a repetition of the debacle of World War I, which yielded widespread ex-

TABLE 43—EFFECT OF RENEGOTIATION ON CORPORATIONS GROUPED BY VOLUME OF SALES, 1936–1939: 3,178 REFUND CASES RENEGOTIATED BY ALL DEPARTMENTS FOR FISCAL YEAR 1943

[Average Dollar Amounts or Percentage per Case. Dollars in Thousands]

Item	Before (B) or After (A)		Grouping of Firms by Average Annual Sales, 1936–39					
	Taxes	Renego-tiation	Under $500	$500 to $999	$1,000 to $1,999	$2,000 to $4,999	$5,000 to $9,999	Over $10,000
Number of Refund Cases for 1943	—	—	1,203	702	524	435	170	144
Prewar Data (Average Annual Data Fiscal Year 1936–39)								
1. Sales	—	—	$255.5	$713.6	$1,427.8	$3,137.0	$6,933.0	$69,411.3
2. Profit on sales	B	—	$12.3	$49.0	$97.0	$238.2	$539.3	$6,042.1
3. Percent profit on sales	B	—	4.8%	6.9%	6.8%	7.6%	7.8%	8.7%
Wartime Data (Fiscal Year 1943)								
Sales:								
4. Renegotiable	—	B	$1,658	$2,393	$4,465	$7,304	$20,304	$103,677
5. Renegotiable	—	A	$1,448	$2,136	$3,929	$6,435	$18,257	$97,115
6. Total	—	A	$1,681	$2,846	$5,324	$9,896	$24,777	$177,423
Profit on sales:								
7. Renegotiable	B	B	$371	$486	$958	$1,587	$4,092	$17,837
8. Renegotiable	B	A	$161	$229	$422	$718	$2,045	$11,275
9. Total	B	A	$207	$361	$675	$1,330	$3,192	$20,539
Percent profit on sales:								
10. Renegotiable	B	B	22.4%	20.3%	21.5%	21.7%	20.2%	17.2%
11. Renegotiable	B	A	11.1%	10.7%	10.7%	11.2%	11.2%	11.6%
12. Total	B	A	12.3%	12.7%	12.7%	13.4%	12.9%	11.6%
13. Net worth	—	—	$203	$563	$1,229	$2,598	$7,051	$52,974
Percent earned on net worth:								
14. Renegotiable sales	B	B	182.8%	86.3%	77.9%	61.1%	58.0%	33.7%
15. Renegotiable sales	B	A	79.3%	40.7%	34.3%	27.6%	29.0%	21.3%
16. Total sales	B	A	102.0%	64.1%	54.9%	51.2%	45.3%	38.8%
17. Total sales	A	A	30.9%	20.1%	18.4%	16.6%	14.9%	14.8%
18. Nonrenegotiable sales	B	—	22.7%	23.4%	20.6%	23.6%	16.3%	17.5%
19. Compensation of principal executives	—	—	$57	$67	$84	$119	$185	$404
20. Percent of original profit finally retained	A	A	30.3%	31.3%	33.5%	32.4%	32.9%	38.2%
Comparative Data								
Percent increase, 1943 over 1936–39 annual average:								
21. Sales	—	A	557.9%	298.8%	272.9%	215.5%	257.4%	155.6%
22. Profit	B	A	1,582.9%	636.7%	595.9%	458.4%	491.9%	239.9%

Source: Adapted from Table I, *Congressional Record*, Vol. 91, Pt. V, p. 6148.

orbitant profits and resulted in a protracted era of resentment and controversy throughout the interwar period. Profiteering in World War I gave color to the naïve identification of war profits with the causes of war and facilitated the short-sighted policy of disarmament which left the United States woefully unprepared when the rest of the world was in flames. In terms of curbing unconscionable profits, renegotiation for World War II will undoubtedly be recorded as successful. Renegotiation recaptured one third of all initial profits on military production. In individual cases the percentage of recovery was much higher. In ten years of postwar discussion there have been no charges of general and unconscionable profiteering during World War II, and it is doubtful that such charges will hereafter arise.

On the other hand, it is patent that World War II was highly profitable for American industry despite the existence of both renegotiation and taxes. One study of the general order of the magnitude of profits finally retained indicates that profits retained after both renegotiation and taxes averaged some 15 percent of net worth for the largest firms and 30 percent for the smallest. (*Line 17, Table 43.*) When classified according to ac-

tual renegotiable sales in 1943, the final return on net worth after taxes ranged from 22.4 percent for the largest firms covered by the study to 48.9 percent for firms with sales between $100,000 and $500,000.[53] While there are some who would object to this general level of retained profits as too high, it would appear to have been appropriate to the restoration of a vigorous and dynamic industrial economy after a decade of depression and stagnation.

Perhaps the chief defect of renegotiation for World War II was the establishment, under the statute, of two classes of business—that which was subject to renegotiation and that which was not. The exemption of high profits on "nonwar" business at a time when the country was at war, and when high profits anywhere were primarily attributable to the war, was a poor way to reward all-out conversion to war production. As already indicated, the specific exemptions for selected industrial groups—whether mandatory or permissive—were unjustifiable. In the absence of the general exemption for nonwar business, it is doubtful that the numerous pressures for specific exemptions would have succeeded.

---

[53] *Congressional Record*, Vol. 91, Pt. V (14 Jan 45), 6148, Table II.

CHAPTER XVII

The Army and OPA Price Control

Background and Nature of OPA Price Control

Direct control over prices, as contemplated by the Industrial Mobilization Plan,[1] became the responsibility of the Office of Price Administration in World War II. As in the case of material controls, the development of the principles and machinery of price controls was a gradual process. Throughout 1940 and the early part of 1941, the NDAC Price Stabilization Division relied upon voluntary controls to keep prices of basic materials and commodities in line.[2] On 11 April 1941, in response to increasing upward pressure upon prices, the President ordered the creation of the Office of Price Administration and Civilian Supply.[3] During the remainder of 1941 a number of specific price controls were adopted, but these were confined principally to raw and semifabricated materials and exercised relatively little direct effect upon the placement of prime military contracts. The absence of specific legislation authorizing price controls and providing definite powers and methods of enforcement was a considerable

handicap throughout the defense period. Under these conditions, Army contracting officers were forbidden to purchase items containing materials bought at over-ceiling prices without the prior written approval of the Under Secretary of War.[4] Complete observance of this requirement would have placed insuperable burdens of detection and enforcement upon contracting officers, and it has been suggested that price ceilings were widely disregarded by contractors for military procurement during this period.[5]

With the advent of Pearl Harbor and the introduction of comprehensive price control legislation in Congress, the stage was set for controversy over application of formal price controls to military procurement.[6] On 19 December 1941 the Secretary of War and the Secretary of the Navy, after unsuccessfully appealing to the Senate Banking and Currency Committee, addressed a joint letter to the President requesting inclusion in the pending bill of a blanket exemption of

---

[1] See above, pages 93 and 229.

[2] (1) CPA, *Industrial Mobilization for War*, p. 33. (2) Worsley, *Wartime Economic Stabilization*, pp. 25–26.

[3] Executive Order 8734. OPACS became OPA in August 1941 with the transfer of Civilian Supply to the Office of Production Management. Leon Henderson, the NDAC commissioner for price stabilization, was the head of OPACS and of OPA until 1943.

[4] (1) OUSW Memo, 9 Jul 41, sub: Price Stabilization. (2) OQMG Cir Ltr 156, 16 Jul 41.

[5] Worsley, *Wartime Economic Stabilization*, p. 136, citing T. J. Kinsella, War Procurement and OPA (an unpublished manuscript in OPA Historical files).

[6] (1) H. Com. on Banking and Currency, 77th Cong., 1st Sess., Hearings on H. R. 5479, *Price Control Bill*, Pts. 1 and 2, August to October 1941. Under Secretary of War Patterson testified strongly in favor of vigorous price control legislation. 2:1519–52. (2) S. Com. on Banking and Currency, 77th Cong., 1st Sess., Hearings on H. R. 5990, *Emergency Price Control Act*, 9–17 December 1941.

all Army and Navy purchases from control by the Price Administrator. The Secretaries also requested the power specifically to exempt all materials, parts, and components ultimately entering into military items by certifying to OPA—either in advance or after sale—that such exemption was essential to the defense of the United States.[7] The reasons underlying this request have already been stated. They were, briefly, the impossibility of setting—in advance of production—appropriate price ceilings on novel, complex, military items having no previous price or production history, and the inevitable delays in contract placement and execution if producers of such items were squeezed between unpredictable costs and arbitrary price ceilings.

Although the President was sympathetic to the substantive arguments advanced by the Secretaries, he was not in favor of their proposal. On the following day he denied their request, stating his reasons:

It is absolutely imperative that final authority be vested in one person, and the Army and Navy must conform as well as everybody else. . . . The price Control Administrator . . . I am certain, will approve whatever exemptions are necessary. In the final analysis, if the Army and Navy are turned down by the Price Administrator, appeal always lies to the President.[8]

The Emergency Price Control Act passed on 30 January 1942 ratified all existing price schedules, gave the Price Administrator the power to issue maximum price regulations, and declared purchases above authorized

prices to be illegal.[9] No exemption was provided for war materials. The OUSW immediately advised the supply arms and services of the necessity for adherence to price schedules and requested reports of all instances in which the negotiation of contracts or the prosecution of war production was delayed by either the substance or the procedures of price control.[10]

The General Maximum Price Regulation

On 28 April 1942 the OPA issued its General Maximum Price Regulation freezing all prices, not specifically exempted or otherwise controlled, at the highest figure chaged by each individual seller during March 1942. In cases where individual manufacturers, wholesalers, or retailers had engaged in no transactions for a given item during March, the ceiling price was to be the highest price charged during that month by the most closely competitive seller of the same or similar items. Sections 9 and 10 of GMPR provided that commodities and services procured by the U.S. Government would be exempt to the extent later specified by individual price regulations. The effective date of the regulation was 11 May 1942 for manufacturers and wholesalers and 18 May 1942 for retailers.[11]

---

[7] Suggested addition of Section 208 to Emergency Price Control Act, reproduced in ASF, History of Purchases Division, p. 194.

[8] ASF, History of Purchases Division, p. 195. This episode is described in greater detail in Connery, *The Navy and the Industrial Mobilization,* pp. 227–29.

[9] 56 *Stat.* 23, 30 Jan 42.

[10] OUSW Memos, 31 Jan 42, sub: Price Control Information, and 13 Feb 42, sub: Exceptions to Maximum Prices.

[11] OPA GMPR Bull 1, 28 Apr. 42. The circumstances surrounding the issuance of GMPR are well summarized as follows: "In the spring of 1942 prices were rising steadily and neither the Treasury nor Congress were contemplating taxation or other fiscal controls on a scale that seemed sufficient to check the advance. Partly to gain time, partly as a tactical move to force action by the Treasury and Congress, and partly because it was the only available answer to an insistent demand for action, the

The difficulties of devising suitable exemptions to permit military procurement to proceed without delay soon became apparent. Eleven days after the issuance of GMPR, OPA announced postponement of its effective date to 1 July 1942 with respect to contracts of the War and Navy Departments.[12] During the "breathing spell" thus provided, the OPA and the services entered into intensive discussions in an attempt to ease the impact of the new regulation upon military procurement while protecting the basic purposes of price control.

Early in May, Headquarters, ASF, with the aid of the several technical services, prepared a long list of strictly military items, including subassemblies, components, and spare parts, for which it sought complete exemption from OPA price controls. In addition to specific items, the list proposed to exempt "all other equipment and supplies purchased by the military forces or any agencies thereof and for which there is no standard commercial counterpart."[13] The chief items remaining under price control would be Quartermaster items of commercial or closely similar design.

The Quartermaster General (TQMG) reacted violently to this proposal, which would provide relatively complete exemption for the other technical services while leaving his office saddled with all the substantive disadvantages and procedural red tape associated with price control. He was heartily in favor of general price controls and the stabilizing effects they would have upon the prices of military items as well as upon the economy as a whole. Accordingly, he opposed exemption of military items as a class and suggested a provision enabling the War Department, on its own authority, to negotiate specific prices above the maxima in cases where essential to prompt procurement. A blanket exemption, he thought, would be "something akin to burning down the forest to remove a few dead trees" and would subject War Department procurement officials to "the myriad forms of pressure that can and will be exercised once all restrictions are removed."[14]

Implicit in TQMG's response was the generally unsatisfactory position of Quartermaster items in the assignment of material priorities. If in addition to the disadvantages of lower material priorities the Quartermaster Corps would also be subject to discriminatory price controls, resources in general would shift even further to the production of noncontrolled items and procurement of Quartermaster items would be more difficult than ever. Nevertheless, sensing that his basic recommendations would not be acceptable, The Quartermaster General specified four major categories of items to be included in any general exemption of military items. These were vehicles, individual and organization equipment for troops,

General Maximum Price Regulation was issued." J. K. Galbraith, "The Disequilibrium System," *American Economic Review,* XXXVII (June 1947), 290. Dr. Galbraith, who was Deputy Administrator of OPA, indicated the consequences if prices under GMPR and other schedules had been maintained without change: "It meant that all kinds of accidental and often bizarre cost-price relationships would be perpetuated indefinitely." *Ibid.,* p. 295.

[12] OPA Supplementary Regulation 2 to GMPR, 9 May 42. This merely exempted *deliveries* prior to 1 July 1942. Since most contracts under negotiation during this period called for deliveries after this date, the chief virtue of the postponement was its indication that appropriate exemptions for war goods would be adopted in the interim.

[13] Memo, Hq SOS for Dale Maxwell, 7 May 42, sub: Price Regulation, and incl, cited in Yoshpe, Production Control in the QMC, p. 67.

[14] Memo, TQMG for Deputy Dir for Procurement and Distribution, Hq SOS, 13 May 42, cited in Yoshpe, Production Control in the QMC, p. 68.

special field equipment, and noncommercial-type subsistence supplies. In addition, TQMG insisted upon the necessity for War Department authority to negotiate individual prices above prescribed ceilings without prior OPA approval.[15]

This proposal of The Quartermaster General came too late for immediate adoption, since Headquarters, ASF, had already reached an agreement with OPA. On 13 May 1942, OPA issued its Supplementary Regulation 4, which exempted a long list of military items and their specialized components from GMPR. In general, OPA retained control of all basic materials and intermediate parts of a commercial nature, even when these entered into military end items. This was done to minimize pressure on price ceilings of goods entering civilian consumption, as well as to prevent undue diversion of production away from civilian channels. These consequences would almost certainly follow if military purchases of the same goods were generally permitted at prices above the ceiling for civilians. The supplemental regulation also exempted developmental and secret contracts as well as emergency purchases of less than one thousand dollars.[16]

Supplementary Regulation 4 provided exemptions only from the General Maximum Price Regulation. It left in effect all the existing price regulations covering individual items and classes of items and likewise left the way open for new specific regulations, which might include any or all military items previously exempted from GMPR. Since there were in effect, as of 1 April 1942, 112 OPA price schedules on items making up some 40 percent of the Bureau of Labor Statistics wholesale-price index, a substantial portion of military procurement was actually under price control.[17] The most heavily controlled sector of Army purchases was Quartermaster procurement, with its large array of commercial-type items. Many Quartermaster items were controlled by specific price schedules; but more important, virtually no quartermaster items were exempted from GMPR by the new supplementary regulation.

As a result of the sudden impact of GMPR, the Quartermaster procurement program was substantially slowed down. Ten days after his earlier memorandum eloquently pleading for retention of general price control over all War Department procurement, TQMG addressed a communication to the Commanding General, ASF, complaining of the paralysis of Quartermaster procurement and stating his inability to accomplish his mission "because of this General Maximum Price Regulation." [18] Under the existing regulations, QMC contracting officers could not compensate contractors for increased costs for overtime and multiple shift operations; hence their efforts to expedite delivery of badly needed items were often in vain. Nor could they make needed changes in design and specifications for many Quartermaster items, since such changes entailed increases in costs which could not legally be covered by price increases. Contractors endeavoring to live up to conservation and substitution measures promulgated by the War Production Board could not recoup their addi-

[15] Ibid.
[16] PR 1132.6.

[17] ASF, History of Purchases Division, p. 196. An OPA survey in the summer of 1942 revealed that "a surprisingly large number of war goods remained under GMPR despite exemptions." Worsley, Wartime Economic Stabilization, p. 144.
[18] Memo, TQMG for CG SOS, 23 May 42, sub: Unsatisfactory Current Status of Procurement, cited in Yoshpe, Production Control in the QMC, p. 68.

tional costs incurred in revamping production lines or purchasing higher priced substitute materials. The placement of many new or renewal contracts was delayed as contractors refused to accept March 1942 prices, which in many cases had reflected the availability of inventories or deliveries of materials and supplies under prior contracts negotiated with their own suppliers months before at low prices. Moreover, the procedural complexities required in order merely to observe the legally established price ceilings, to say nothing of processing appeals for relief, were alone a formidable barrier to rapid placement and execution of contracts.[19]

Many of these difficulties were soon overcome as OQMG and the Purchases Branch, ASF, negotiated with OPA to rectify the inevitable shortcomings of a necessarily arbitrary, pioneer measure hastily adopted to meet emergency conditions. A major improvement in the position of OQMG was obtained on 3 June 1942, with the issuance of Maximum Price Regulation (MPR) 157, covering a wide array of apparel and related articles for military purposes. This regulation allowed price increases to meet increased material prices and wage rates, as well as increased costs resulting from changes in specifications and shortened delivery schedules.[20] Six days later, the OPA granted complete exemptions from price control to ski troop equipment, field stoves and ranges, canteens, helmet liners, wire cutters, identification tags, metal insignia for enlisted men, paratroop knives, certain field rations, and related items.[21] Field jackets were exempted from GMPR on 27 May 1942. Highly important exemptions were obtained in a series of revisions of Supplementary Regulation 4, beginning on 1 July 1942. These included automobiles, trucks, trailers, and amphibians sold for military purposes, their spare parts and components, additional field rations, certain categories of canned meats, and specified dried and dehydrated fruits and vegetables sold to the armed forces. With the addition of these exemptions OQMG's request of 13 May 1942 was substantially fulfilled.[22]

In addition to relief for specific items, mostly in the area of Quartermaster procurement, the Army also soon obtained a number of important general modifications in OPA regulations. On 23 June 1942 the crippling limitation of the existing one thousand dollar maximum upon emergency purchases was removed from GMPR.[23] On 11 July 1942 contracting and finance officers of procuring agencies were relieved of all criminal and civil penalties imposed by the Emergency Price Control Act. This action freed contracting officers from the necessity of ascertaining that all prices in their procurement contracts conformed to OPA ceiling limitations; it did not, however, relieve sellers of their liability for failure to observe ceiling prices in war contracts.[24] Later in the year all sales and deliveries of commodities or services by the War Department

---

[19] Paralysis of QM Procurement Under Impact of GMPR, in Yoshpe, Production Control in the QMC, p. 68; also p. 71.

[20] Ibid., p. 69.

[21] Amendment 2 to Supplementary Regulation 4 to GMPR, 9 Jun 42.

[22] Yoshpe, Production Control in the QMC, p. 69.

[23] Amendment 5 to Supplementary Regulation 4 to GMPR, 23 Jun 42. Maximum Price Regulation 157 was similarly amended by its Amendment 3, 6 July 1942. Many other, but not all, MPR's eventually carried the same provision. PR 1132.5 (8–31–44).

[24] (1) OPA Supplementary Order 7, 11 Jul 42. (2) PR 1132.7 (8–31–44). Further details are recounted in Worsley, Wartime Economic Stabilization, pp. 141–42.

through its canteens, commissaries, post exchanges, and other sales stores were exempted from OPA price regulations.[25]

One of the most significant features of the entire structure of OPA price controls as related to military procurement was adopted on 3 June 1942, when a formal procedure was established to allow individual firms to seek relief from price ceilings affecting specific war contracts and subcontracts.[26] Under this arrangement contracts and subcontracts "essential to the war program" could be awarded at higher than ceiling prices provided the seller within five days filed an application for adjustment with the OPA. Originally, the regulation permitted payment, as well as negotiation, of the over-ceiling contract price, subject to possible refund by the seller if his appeal were denied by OPA. This was subsequently changed to permit payment only up to the ceiling price until a positive ruling was made by OPA granting the over-ceiling price. The role and experience of the War Department in this procedure will be discussed briefly at a later point.[27]

*Specific Price Regulations
Affecting Procurement*

The foregoing modifications and exemptions eased the impact upon military procurement of the burgeoning new price controls which came into being in the first half of 1942. But no sooner had major relief from GMPR been obtained than specific price regulations were drafted by OPA which proposed to retract major exemptions and threatened serious interference with procurement of military items. On 1 July 1942, OPA revised its machinery regulation (MPR 136), bringing a number of new items under control. The amended regulation, which became effective on 22 July 1942, imposed price controls on many important items procured by the armed forces, such as gasoline-, steam-, and diesel-engines, pumps and compressors, construction equipment, and even radio and radar equipment, as well as accessories and services necessary to the manufacture and maintenance of the items concerned. Inasmuch as an earlier version of MPR 136 had been issued without consulting them in advance, the Army and Navy were particularly sensitive on the subject.[28]

More serious than the machinery regulation were steps taken by OPA to place two of the Army's key combat items—aircraft and tanks—under price control. For some time the OPA had been concerned over the inflationary effects—upon wage rates, uncontrolled materials, and "wage goods" (consumer goods attracting heavy expenditures by wage earners)—of the tremendous expenditures of the aircraft industry operating largely under cost-plus-a-fixed-fee contracts. Accordingly, the OPA drafted a proposed aircraft regulation which would establish ceiling prices under a formula using wage rates, materials costs, and other factors in existence on 31 March 1942. Meetings

---

[25] OPA Supplementary Order 27, 14 Nov 42. The OPA retained the right to impose price controls on such sales whenever it deemed necessary. PR 1134.2 (2-8-45).

[26] OPA Procedural Regulation 6. PR 6 procedure—the name popularly given to the use of this regulation—was in addition to standard provisions of the Price Control Act for relief from ceilings. Standard provisions for relief included protests against regulations within sixty days after issuance, petitions for amendments or adjustments, and requests for OPA interpretation of regulations. Worsley, *Wartime Economic Stabilization,* p. 142.

[27] See below, pages 409–10.

[28] (1) Connery, *The Navy and the Industrial Mobilization,* p. 229. (2) Worsley, *Wartime Economic Stabilization,* p. 143. (3) ASF, History of Purchases Division, pp. 198–99.

were held with representatives of the aircraft industry to discuss the proposed schedules, and preliminary negotiations for a similar schedule were also made with the tank industry.[29]

General Exemption of Military Items From OPA Controls

These major moves to reverse the policy of exempting strictly military items from price control alarmed both the Army and Navy, to say nothing of the affected industries. The aircraft industry protested vigorously that it could not operate under the proposed schedule, especially under wage rates retroactively reduced to March 1942 levels.[30] In view of the urgency of the matter, the War and Navy Departments, acting jointly through their Under Secretaries, took prompt steps to obtain a binding decision that strictly military items would thenceforth be exempted, and kept exempt, from OPA price control.

On 23 July the Under Secretaries addressed a lengthy memorandum to Leon Henderson, the price administrator, requesting such a decision and stating in great detail the reasons therefor. The Under Secretaries emphasized the paramount importance of obtaining munitions on time, the special difficulties of military production (the creation of new facilities, acquiring and training labor, learning how to produce novel and complex equipment), and other considerations precluding the establishment of firm prices in advance of production. They indicated the crippling effects of both the substantive and procedural requirements of price controls under these conditions. The memorandum also indicated that the price of military items was only indirectly related to general inflation; the government alone purchased military items and their prices did not enter into the cost of living. Nor did the prices of military items determine the underlying raw material and commercial component prices; these were subject to price control by the OPA, to which control the War and Navy Departments subscribed even though they made many purchases of these and other civilian-type goods. The only contribution of the prices of military items to inflation was through the distribution of excessive wages and profits. High profits would be recouped through renegotiation and the excess profits tax; inflationary wages could only be satisfactorily prevented by adequate wage stabilization measures, which would have to be adopted in any case if price ceilings were to be maintained.

Finally, the memorandum indicated that the services were making steady and substantial progress in developing organizations, procedures, and policies for the sound pricing of military procurement. With the gradual stabilization of costs, the systematic acquisition of cost data by contracting agencies, and the development of new pricing techniques, the services would be able to perform a far more satisfactory job of pricing than could be accomplished by price ceilings of either the dollars-and-cents or formula variety. If OPA controls were to be imposed on war goods, the task of military procurement would be hopelessly divided, with the OPA supplanting the War and Navy Departments in actual negotiation of contracts.[31]

---

[29] Galbraith, "The Disequilibrium System," p. 299.

[30] Connery, The Navy and the Industrial Mobilization, p. 229.

[31] Memo, Patterson and Forrestal for Henderson, 23 Jul 42, sub: Maximum Price Regulation of Military Equipment. The full text of this important memorandum is reproduced in ASF, History of Purchases Division, pp. 199–206.

The effect of the Under Secretaries' memorandum, combined with other developments, led to OPA acceptance of the basic principle of exempting all specifically military items from maximum price controls. On 16 September 1942, Mr. Henderson replied at length, agreeing "to refrain, at this time, from further extension of maximum price control in the area of strictly military goods." Although he did not see eye to eye with the Under Secretaries on all their arguments, Mr. Henderson was not concerned with "who does the job of preventing inflation in the military goods area as long as it is done effectively." His agreement to the general exemption was conditioned upon adequate assurances from the War and Navy Departments that they would use all their powers to control both prices and profits as effectively as possible, and that they would furnish OPA with sufficient information on prices and procedures in the military-goods area to appraise the effectiveness of the services' pricing operations. At the same time, Henderson expressed assurance that the OPA would "expeditiously grant upward adjustments in maximum prices established for goods which remain under price control and which are purchased by the Services or by prime or subcontractors if such adjustments are necessary to cover costs and permit reasonable overall profits for the applicant concerned." [32]

For several weeks thereafter representatives of the OPA and of the services conferred on how to define the line of demarcation separating "strictly military goods" from all others. Mr. Henderson's letter of 16 September had referred to the exempted area as:

. . . commodities which are in such form that they will be used only for military purposes, except the sale made by the manufacturer who is the first to put the commodity in such form. Drawing the line above, as it were, rather than below the first emergence of the article in such form is necessary in order to avoid anomalous situations such as exemption of some rough castings while others, also destined for military use, remain under such control.

The services were concerned that this division, if literally adhered to, would mean OPA regulation of the prices of each finished military article. The OPA representatives made clear that such was not the intention:

By this statement we meant, in general, to cover only the first stage of processing, counting from the raw material up toward the finished product, where the article emerges in a form useful only for incorporation into a military item. Ordinarily, where the first stage *and* one or more subsequent stages of processing are performed by an integrated producer, the sale of his product at the second or later stage will be exempt. [33]

Agreement was reached on this basis, with the understanding that the details in particular cases would be determined later on their merits by mutual agreement. Having thus established the general line of demarcation, both the OPA and the services agreed that they would not seek to disturb existing regulations, whether above or below the line of demarcation, unless these gave rise to practical difficulties in either price control or procurement. The general

---

[32] Ltr, Henderson to Patterson, 16 Sep 42. This letter is reproduced in full in ASF, History of Purchases Division, pp. 207–12.

[33] Ltr, Donald H. Wallace, Dir Industrial Manufacturing Price Div OPA, to Maj Vaughan, Chf Price Administration [Adjustment] Br Hq SOS, 29 Oct 42, copy in History of Ordnance Pricing Policy, Exhibit 5.

agreement, embodied in several major documents including the correspondence already cited, became known as the Henderson-Patterson-Forrestal agreement, and was summarized and announced in a joint press release on 12 November 1942.[34]

This agreement between the OPA and the services remained intact for the remainder of the war. It has been estimated that approximately 35 percent by dollar value of Army purchases was left under OPA control from mid-1942 to V–J Day.[35] After the adoption of the Henderson-Patterson-Forrestal agreement the OPA made no major, formal criticism of the services' pricing policies for exempted goods, and the task of developing and applying such policies rested completely upon the services. This reflected the growing acceptance throughout the OPA of the Army-Navy view that maximum price controls for purely military items were unnecessary:

> For war goods, i.e., end products, capital goods, components or materials monopolized or largely monopolized by military employment, price control is, in principle, unnecessary. The monopsony of the procurement authority, especially when supplemented by actual or moral power to requisition, is an adequate substitute for price control.[36]

Also:

> During the course of that summer the Under Secretaries of War and Navy sought to have all war goods "without a civilian counterpart" excluded from price control. Partly because of this pressure and partly because wage stabilization came into being, the OPA abandoned the field. By present standards this was a happy withdrawal; it saved the agency from a complex and unrewarding task and one that in principle, was unnecessary.[37]

Procurement Problems Arising From Price Ceilings

Despite the exemption of some two thirds of Army procurement from OPA control, the Army's problems resulting from the application of price ceilings remained substantial. The majority of these problems centered upon Quartermaster items, especially food and apparel; but ceilings on lumber for Engineer construction projects, machinery and metals for Ordnance items, insecticides and other Medical Department purchases, as well as on general items such as packing and packaging, gave rise to continual difficulties and the necessity for relief.[38] A detailed study of the effects of price control upon Army procurement is outside the scope of the present volume; a few illustrations may serve, however, to indicate the seemingly endless complexities of price control which harassed the Army, the OPA, other governmental agencies, and contractors in the affected programs.

An Industry Case Study: Canned Meats

One of the most difficult areas of price control was that of meat and meat products.

---

[34] See documents in History of Ordnance Pricing Policy, Exhibit 5.

[35] ASF, History of Purchases Division, p. 215. Elsewhere it was stated that "approximately 62 percent of the value of all War Department contracts agreed on by the Under Secretary of War and the Price Administrator in September, 1942 continued to be exempt from OPA price control." ASF Annual Rpt, 1944, p. 119.

[36] Galbraith, "The Disequilibrium System," pp. 296–97. For definition of the term monopsony, see above, page 244, note 28.

[37] Ibid., p. 299. In a footnote on the same page Dr. Galbraith states: "I also had begun to doubt that control in this field had any close bearing on the problem of inflation. Mr. Henderson, although formally committed to the use of price controls in this area, had, I believe, more than passing sympathy for this view."

[38] Worsley, Wartime Economic Stabilization, Ch. 15.

The Army's experience with regulations covering canned meats indicates the practical difficulties in the way of establishing a balanced array of price ceilings for all vertical and lateral segments of a complex industry. The principal price controls affecting canned meats were the GMPR and various editions of three Maximum Price Regulations, all in effect by the middle of July 1942. The first of these (MPR 148), issued on 21 May 1942, covered a variety of pork products, including luncheon meat, sausage, ham, bacon, and pork and gravy. A second regulation (MPR 156), issued on 2 June 1942, covered nine canned items procured by the Army—including corned beef, meat and vegetables, and other items of beef and pork. The third specific regulation (MPR 169), effective 13 July 1942, covered beef carcasses and cuts suitable for canning.[39]

A major difficulty under these regulations was the so-called squeeze experienced by processors of canned meats whose own products were subject to price ceilings but who were faced with uncontrolled and rising prices of their raw materials. Under these circumstances meat canners refused to submit bids in response to Quartermaster solicitations. Thus in the spring of 1942 the Chicago Quartermaster Depot was faced with the responsibility of procuring for the various components of the armed forces some 10 million C rations and 15 million dozen units of other canned items covered by MPR 156. Of ten canners solicited all but one declined to bid, and after two months

less than a million of the C rations and 22 percent of the other items had been purchased. Potential contractors uniformly replied that the high cost of boneless beef precluded their supplying products at ceiling prices under MPR 156 without experiencing a substantial loss.[40]

Various proposals were made to break the bottleneck, including blanket allocations of meat to the armed forces, Army purchases of meat for canners, and arrangements for the Chicago Quartermaster Depot to act as a clearinghouse in reporting available meat supplies. None of these suggestions was adopted. Instead, the OPA on 24 July temporarily removed from ceiling-price control seven of the nine items covered by MPR 156.[41] These exemptions were to last only until the end of the year. Although the situation was temporarily eased, it was not long before contractors under long-term contracts had to ascertain what the future policy would be. The Chicago Quartermaster Depot was particularly anxious that ceilings not be re-established, on grounds that they would result in both higher prices and additional barriers to procurement:

. . . if new ceilings should be established at a rather low level we know that some of our biggest suppliers will automatically be eliminated, on the other hand, if a ceiling at a middle or high level should be established, there will be a tendency for all contractors who have been selling at prices below the ceiling to raise their bids and in the long run this will cost the Government money.[42]

This tendency of specific dollars-and-cents ceiling prices to curtail badly needed supplies, or to operate as highly profitable

---

[39] Massen, Canned Meats Procurement for the Armed Forces During World War II. This monograph supplied the material for the discussion in the following pages of Army experience under OPA meat price controls. Documents cited in notes 40 to 51, below, are quoted more extensively (at pages 181–95) in the study by Miss Massen.

[40] Memo, Brig Gen Joseph E. Barzynski, CQMD, for TQMG, 4 Jul 42.

[41] Amendment 1 to MPR 156, 24 Jul 42.

[42] Memo, Lt Col J. W. Fraser, CQMD, for Brig Gen Carl A. Hardigg, OQMG, 14 Nov 42.

"bulk-line" prices for an industry composed of many firms with widely differing unit costs, was a common barrier to efficient procurement.[43] The output of marginal and inefficient producers was needed to fulfill the Army's procurement program, but procurement officials preferred to negotiate differential prices close to the costs of individual producers rather than to pay a single price high enough to cover the costs of all producers. The following statement indicates the faith of procurement officers in their ability to avoid paying inflationary prices:

If the Office of Price Administration will leave it to our judgment we feel justified in assuring them that we will not pay inflationary prices for canned meats.[44]

A similar observation points to the inflationary possibilities of ceiling prices themselves:

. . . if any price ceilings were affixed they must recognize a spread of at least 8 to 10 percent between the relatively low cost of large efficient canners and the higher cost of either small or inefficient canners; and that the ceilings would tend to become the bid price in all cases, thus depriving the Army of its present ability to keep prices down through competition.[45]

Numerous discussions throughout the remainder of 1942 led finally to a "midnight hour" extension, on 31 December 1942, of the exemption until 1 April 1943. The same

cycle of events was repeated in the early months of 1943, and on 1 April 1943 the expiring exemption was indefinitely extended.[46]

The above-mentioned exemptions on finished beef products permitted contractors to bid up the price of beef suitable for canning purposes, and added to the increasing demand for basic price controls over livestock and intermediate products. Although carcasses and cuts of beef were subject to dollars-and-cents ceilings by the fall of 1942, slaughtering canners were not affected by controls at the carcass or cut level and "tended to bid low-grade cattle up to inordinately high prices, since they were exempt from price regulation on canned goods until January 1, 1943, and thus could pass the higher finished costs on to the Army." [47] At the same time, nonslaughtering canners found it virtually impossible to obtain meat supplies which would enable them to accept or fulfill Army contracts:

We have contacted all the packers here anywhere from one to three times per day to purchase boned canners and cutters for our contract and each day it tightens up more and more. The packers here are shying away from this type of meat, as they can not break even on the price they have to pay for cattle. With no ceiling on live cattle, they all shy away from the business . . . .[48]

Nor was the absence of balanced price controls throughout the meat industry to blame for all of the shortage. By February 1943 substantial black market operations were

---

[43] The term "bulk line" gained currency during the price administration activities of World War I. It referred to the establishment of a price high enough to cover the costs of firms producing the bulk of the output required from a given industry. Bulk-line prices inevitably yielded substantial profits for the more efficient firms while failing to cover the costs of marginal firms.

[44] Fraser memo cited above, note 42.

[45] Ltr, Gen Hardigg, OQMG, to OPA, (Attn: Dr. Phillip Wernette), 21 Nov 42.

[46] Massen, Canned Meats Procurement for the Armed Forces During World War II, pp. 182–86.

[47] Ibid., p. 191.

[48] Ltr, M. L. Sandler, Vernon Canning Company, Los Angeles, California, to CQMD (Attn: Mr. John E. Staren), 17 Feb 43.

diverting badly needed supplies from the Army and its sister services:

. . . after scouring the market for meat as far south as Baltimore, Md., and north to Cortland, N. Y., we are unable to find a slaughterer who is willing to sell us meat at established ceiling prices. Upon inquiring as to the reason for their refusal, the majority of the people contacted, told us that Black Market operators bid up the price of live stock to where the legitimate buyers cannot buy these cattle, slaughter, dress and bone them, and sell the meat at ceiling prices.[49]

On the same day a Texas canner reported that black market conditions in his part of the country had reached such proportions that his own purchases had been cut from one thousand live animals per day to less than one hundred: "The entire supply of livestock has been taken by the operators . . . we know are not operating within their Restriction Order or within the correct OPA structure." [50]

Difficulty was experienced, in the meantime, with canned items which had not been exempted. In the case of commercial-quality corned beef, a $32 price per dozen 6-pound cans had been set by OPA on the assumption that beef trimmings, selling at 14 to 15 cents per pound, would be used in preparing the finished product. Army specifications demanded a higher quality of meat, but the OPA nevertheless applied its regulation, based on the presumed use of inferior trimmings, to Army purchases.[51]

Fortunately, about this time an important ideological bottleneck was broken and high-grade South American beef, which had long been denied access to markets in the United States, was allowed to ease the general meat shortage.[52] In the case of pork products, ceilings were continuing to squeeze processors and to hinder Army procurement. One manufacturer of luncheon meat stated that even with the latest machinery and efficient production lines he could net only one-half cent per pound under the existing ceiling, a margin too small to make production worth while.[53]

The squeeze which took place under price ceilings occasionally resulted in absolute unprofitability; that is, prices were insufficient to cover costs. In most cases, however, there was no question of actual losses. Relief from price ceilings was generally sought because of the presence of an opportunity to earn a greater profit by producing items other than the ones under the ceilings in question.[54] Under these circumstances the use of the words "squeeze," "substantial losses," and similar terms was of doubtful

---

[49] Ltr, Mr. Albert Menner, Menner Packing Company, Newark, New Jersey, to Staren, CQMD, 4 Feb 43.

[50] Ltr, G. L. Childress, General Manager Houston Packing Company, to John J. Madigan, Chf Meat Br OPA, 4 Feb 43.

[51] This type of situation occasionally forced the Army to make liberal interpretations of its authority to award "developmental" contracts. These were exempt from price controls until costs could be ascertained as a basis for appropriate ceilings.

All such contracts were regularly reported to OPA, with relevant information, and OPA had the right to terminate the developmental period at any time. (1) Massen, Canned Meats Procurement for the Armed Forces During World War II, pp. 187–88. (2) PR 1132.4 (8–31–44). (3) Worsley, Wartime Economic Stabilization, p. 206, citing an OPA official who felt that the services "occasionally abused" their exemption privilege for developmental and secret contracts.

[52] Massen, Canned Meats Procurement for the Armed Forces During World War II, pp. 150–58, 183.

[53] Ibid., p. 184.

[54] The term "opportunity cost" is used in economics to describe the cost of surrendering a more desirable or profitable alternative. It is measured by the difference in return, or profit, between the most desirable alternative and the one actually selected.

propriety, particularly for a nation at war in which the "opportunity costs" facing soldiers in the front lines were also rather high. Nevertheless, the Army as well as the OPA was forced to reckon with the vitality of the profit motive, and perhaps the major part of the practical, day-to-day administrative activities under price control consisted of continual adjustments designed to equalize the returns from all legitimate operations. Only by minimizing the existence of undesirable opportunity costs could production, in so far as it was determined by price considerations, be kept in the channels most effective in promoting the war effort.[55]

Relief of Individual Contracts From Price Control

The foregoing discussion illustrates a few of the procurement problems associated with the establishment of ceiling prices for a given industry or product line. Also important in the Army's experience under OPA price control was the problem of obtaining relief from ceilings for particular contracts essential to the procurement program. This involved the submission to the OPA, by individual firms, of applications for approval of over-ceiling prices under Procedural Regulation 6. Under this procedure contracts would be negotiated and production undertaken at over-ceiling prices but final payment of the excess over the ceiling could not be made by the procuring agency unless and until approval was granted by OPA.

The two major issues under the PR–6 procedure were the criteria used by the OPA in allowing over-ceiling prices, and the procedural delays and complexities involved. The publicly announced standards established by OPA permitted price increases under PR 6 only if they were necessary to cover the costs of the item concerned, unless the firm's over-all earnings were less than its base-period (1936–39) average. In the latter case, a sufficient profit was allowable so that the seller could reasonably be expected to undertake production of the item in question. If the firm was currently earning between 100 and 115 percent of its base-period average, the allowable price under PR 6 could not exceed total unit costs. If earnings exceeded 115 percent of the base-period average, only manufacturing costs were allowed.[56]

Since the over-all profit position of the vast majority of firms was considerably in excess of 115 percent of the base-period average, the official PR–6 criteria offered no incentive to most contractors to undertake production of the items involved. The War Department's official position, in contrast to that of the OPA, was that each contract should offer an incentive for its own placement and execution, and that excessive over-all profits should and could be handled by renegotiation and other means. It was the general experience of the War Department that lack of a specific incentive was often a serious deterrent to procurement, "particularly when new facilities are

[55] Worsley, in reviewing the World War II experience, pointed to the administrative impossibility of achieving practical price equality in all areas. In view of this he recommended, for similar circumstances in the future, the fullest use of mandatory orders, requisitions, set-asides, and other allocations to force acceptance of reasonable profit allowances, regardless of higher profit opportunities elsewhere. *Wartime Economic Stabilization*, pp. 211, 215.

[56] OPA Field Price Instruction 5.

required or an unprofitable item must go back in production." [57]

Although the OPA officially never retreated from its position that a firm's overall profits should govern individual price decisions, many of its branches and field offices were actually making use of much more generous criteria. This divergence between precept and practice resulted in widespread lack of uniformity and was subject to much criticsm. Contractors were reluctant to accept orders and embark upon production if the most they could hope for was to break even on their new contract. The preparation of applications under PR 6 required the assembly of detailed cost information, statements of earnings during base-period years, and other time-consuming details. The OPA was often slow in reaching decisions—an inevitable result of the nature of the task and the perennial lack of a sufficient, trained staff to do the work. Moreover, many officials within OPA were extremely skeptical of the significance and accuracy of unit-cost data, and therefore of the validity of any judgments based thereon. The following statement by a high OPA accounting official highlights a problem which permeated all procurement pricing throughout the entire war:

No form calling for unit-cost information will produce particularly reliable results. This ought to be recognized by all those dealing with such matters. In general, unit-cost information derived by this method should be used, unchecked, only in the most trifling cases, where a *little* information can make no great difference. *There is a strong tendency, even among our most sophisticated economists and business specialists, to attach entirely too much weight to these computations.* They look impressive; they add up; but our experience in field checking them

in many branches is that they overstate actual costs 10 to 50 percent. This does not mean that those who submit them are dishonest; or even that their accounting records are bad. It means only that any statement of unit costs is subject to the exercise of large doses of judgment. Obviously the judgment will always be exercised in the direction of liberality. . . . in all cases of real importance a field examination should be made by a member of the accounting staff.[58]

The War Department's role in the PR-6 procedure for obtaining relief from ceiling prices was that of an interested party, since any government agency could appear as a party in the case of any application. The nature and principal details of the procedure were described in Army Procurement Regulations, and contracting officers could at the time of contract negotiation give preliminary advice to contractors on the merits of their case and the extent to which the War Department would support it. Applications involving contracts exceeding $5,000,000 had to be filed with the OPA in Washington, D. C.; for smaller contracts they could be filed with an OPA regional office.[59] At the policy level, the Purchases Division, ASF, attempted to prevail upon OPA to modify its general criteria in granting relief. Although the Army was not officially successful in PR-6 cases, it succeeded in obtaining more liberal criteria under similar procedures specially established under separate regulations.[60]

[57] ASF, History of Purchases Division, pp. 218–19.

[58] Memo, H. F. Taggart, Chf Accounting Div OPA, for Wernette, 3 May 43, sub: Revision of Form OPA–6PR1, cited in Worsley *Wartime Economic Stabilization*, p. 187.

[59] PR 1131.6 (8–31–44).

[60] Notably, in the case of important textile items which were "squeezed" as a result of the Bankhead amendment to the Emergency Price Control Act in 1944. (1) ASF, History of Purchases Division, pp. 215–17. (2) OPA Supplementary Order 107, 9 Mar 45.

Concluding Observations

Despite the many administrative and sub-stantive problems faced by the War Department as a result of OPA price controls, Army procurement officials were well aware of the importance of the price stabilization program—both to the economy as a whole and to the Army's own procurement program. The remarkable success of the United States in preventing widespread inflation throughout World War II—an achievement largely attributable to the tireless efforts and firm leadership of OPA—permitted the conduct of an orderly procurement program which would otherwise have been impossible. The effects upon Army procurement of OPA price control, as seen by those who participated in the World War II procurement program, have been summarized as follows:

Probably the most significant effects have been as a result of the stabilization of the general price level. The negotiating of firm prices, which in so many instances in World War I was impossible because of the instability of raw material costs, has in this war been possible as a result of the stabilization of the general price level.

In addition to the usual business advantages resulting from a stabilized level of prices, tremendous savings accrued to the benefit of the War Department in its vast procurement program, particularly at the lower level of the industrial processes where prices are beyond the control of the War Department.[61]

For its part the Army went to a great deal of effort to fulfill its basic agreement with OPA. As indicated in previous chapters, a major division of War Department procurement policy and activity was the close-pricing program for military goods. To keep

OPA informed of the results of these efforts, the Army developed a series of index numbers reflecting the trend of prices in all principal categories of Army procurement. These index numbers were prepared on a monthly basis for the period 1 January 1942 to mid-1945. (*Table 44*)

The items included in the Army's price indexes comprised some 50 percent of all War Department purchases and were broadly representative of all War Department procurement. In preparing the indexes all new contract prices as well as price revisions under existing contracts were utilized, with allowance for specification changes, packaging, freight, and other factors necessary to maintain comparability in the various time-segments of the series. Except for Army Air Forces contracts, no CPFF contracts were included in the indexes; likewise, items produced in GOCO plants were excluded. Price changes resulting from lump-sum refunds that could not be allocated to specific contracts were not included; hence, the index numbers do not reflect the full downward price movement. Appropriate weights were applied in combining index numbers of different items, item groups, and technical services.[62]

Except for Quartermaster procurement, which was heavily weighted with civilian and civilian-type goods, the Army's price indexes revealed a continuous decline in unit prices from 1942 to the end of the war. Although they could not, in the nature of the case, indicate that prices were uniformly held close to cost or that costs themselves had been adequately controlled, the indexes provided substantial evidence of a wholesome trend in the prices of military goods. This

[61] ASF, History of Purchases Division, pp. 219–20.

[62] Tables of monthly price changes in ASF, Monthly Progress Report, Section 1–D, Contract Price Changes, 30 Jun 45, pp. 7, 18.

TABLE 44—QUARTERLY INDEX OF CONTRACT PRICE CHANGES: 1942–1945 FOR WAR
DEPARTMENT AND COMPONENT AGENCIES

[October 1942 = 100]

End of Quarter	War Department	Army Air Forces	Army Service Forces	ASF Technical Services						
				Ordnance	Signal	Engineers	Chemical	Medical	Quartermaster	Transportation
1942										
1st	108.1	111.3	105.9	106.3	119.6	102.2	104.1	115.0	95.7	102.1
2d	104.6	106.8	103.0	104.3	101.5	101.8	103.3	110.9	98.1	101.7
3d	100.4	101.3	99.8	99.6	100.2	99.7	100.7	104.1	99.6	100.3
4th	98.4	97.2	99.2	99.0	96.2	100.1	99.6	98.3	101.7	99.9
1943										
1st	97.0	96.0	97.7	97.2	92.6	99.5	98.2	97.5	102.5	99.6
2d	94.8	94.1	95.4	94.3	86.8	99.1	96.6	96.3	103.6	98.9
3d	92.9	91.6	93.8	92.3	85.5	97.0	96.5	95.9	103.0	98.8
4th	91.1	89.0	92.6	90.6	83.9	95.5	95.8	95.4	104.0	99.1
1944										
1st	87.7	83.0	91.3	89.4	83.3	95.4	93.5	83.7	102.3	98.7
2d	84.5	79.0	88.9	86.3	79.7	94.3	90.9	77.9	102.1	98.3
3d	81.3	73.7	87.7	83.2	78.1	93.7	88.3	71.9	104.3	97.9
4th	80.5	72.9	87.0	81.9	76.3	94.3	86.7	67.7	105.0	97.5
1945										
1st	79.1	70.8	86.1	80.9	74.0	94.3	84.1	63.6	105.7	95.2
2d	75.7	64.3	86.1	80.2	72.5	94.5	80.9	58.9	108.5	93.8

Source: Tables of monthly price changes in ASF, Monthly Progress Report, Section 1–D, "Contract Price Changes, 30 Jun 45, pp. 7, 18.

conclusion is reinforced by comparison with the trend of prices for commercial and civilian-type goods, which showed moderate increases over the period in question.

The Office of Price Administration was skeptical of the significance of the Army's price series because of the inability of end-product price series to reveal the trend of costs and profits margins. But the task of obtaining throughout the war accurate and detailed cost estimates on an item-by-item basis, especially for the output of multi-product firms, was beyond the practical capacity of any agency. Indeed, the OPA itself measured its own success in holding the line against inflation by using Bureau of Labor Statistics price series subject to the same defects and in areas where profits on commercial business were even greater than those in war goods.[63]

---

[63] Worsley, *Wartime Economic Stabilization,* pp. 204–05.

CHAPTER XVIII

The Army and Small Business

One of the most difficult and controversial tasks in the whole field of economic mobilization for World War II was that of properly harnessing small business in the military procurement program. The Army's experience with small business from 1940 to the war's end went through three distinguishable phases. The first phase extended from the summer of 1940 to the summer of 1942, when the problem of small business emerged and received nationwide attention. The second phase, from the summer of 1942 to the end of 1943, was a period of transition during which legislation, organizations, and procedures were developed to provide a systematic solution of the small plants problem. The final phase, from early 1944 to the end of the war, witnessed the operation of the small war plants program in high gear and the successful attainment of its basic objectives.

Emergence of the Small Business Problem

Early Attitudes and Efforts of the War Department

In attempting to build a huge new Army from scratch, procurement officials proceeded with a basic purpose in mind. This was to obtain the desperately needed munitions in adequate quantity and quality with a minimum of delay. Under the circumstances the Army's purchasing policy was comparable to that of a rational individual or private corporation: it concentrated on its major objectives and responsibilities, placing its procurement contracts with those firms which, all factors considered, appeared to be most capable of providing satisfactory delivery.

In the early months of the defense period this policy received little or no criticism. Many small firms received defense contracts, many more became subcontractors, and all sectors of business prospered under the stimulus of the rearmament program following ten years of depression. By the spring of 1941, however, two developments began to appear. First, the growing shortage of materials made it difficult or impossible for an increasing number of firms to continue operations. The chief sufferers were small firms without defense contracts and hence without benefit of priority status. Secondly, accumulating statistics on contract placement revealed a high concentration of prime contracts among the largest corporations. In July 1941, OPM released statistics indicating that prime contracts of the Army and Navy with fifty-six companies accounted for three fourths of the dollar value of all prime contracts; six corporations held over $3 billion, or 31.3 percent of the total; and Bethlehem Steel alone had contracts of $927 million out of $9.8 billion.[1] This concentration, together

[1] CPA, *Industrial Mobilization for War,* p. 147. Later statistics showed that of more than $11 billion in prime defense contracts awarded in the

with the development of actual hardship in the case of many small firms and local communities, led to criticism of the Army's contract placement policies. These criticisms ran the gamut from inertia and neglect on the part of procurement officials to positive discrimination against small business under influence and pressures brought to bear by large corporations.[2]

There were many reasons why the bulk of Army orders during the defense and early war periods went to the larger firms. The principal and most compelling reason was the greater suitability and dependability of large firms for most production of the kind required by the Army. The predominant portion of the rearmament program, in terms of both dollar value and importance to the Army's fighting power, consisted of critical items of equipment—complex difficult-to-produce items requiring under the most favorable circumstances a lengthy period of production. The delivery of these items in time to meet the crisis—especially problematical in view of the eleventh-hour beginnings of the rearmament program—was dependent on the availability of large firms already equipped with abundant plant and machinery, specially skilled and trained workers, managerial know-how, financial stability, and established contacts with a wide array of suppliers. Many if not most of the urgently needed items of pro-

curement were still in the developmental stage, making it imperative that selected contractors have ample research and engineering staffs and smoothly functioning interdepartmental operations. In addition to the size and complexity of individual requirement items, the large quantities needed and the necessity for uniform specifications dictated the use of carefully controlled mass-production techniques most likely to be found in large-scale enterprises. In short, the very economic and technological advantages which had made American industry the envy of the rest of the world, and upon which the Allied Nations chiefly relied to win the war, were those most completely identified with big business.

This situation was summed up by Under Secretary of War Patterson early in 1941 at the opening session of the Truman Committee:

We had to take industrial America as we found it. For steel we went to the established steel mills. For automobiles we went to Detroit. So does the general public. Take airplanes: We place orders with concerns that can manufacture them, and contracts must be placed in line with the manufacturing facilities, existing and potential, of the particular company. The manufacturers are sharing a great amount of their work by subcontracting with other concerns. The Lockheed Co., for instance, has 350 subcontractors; the Boeing Co. has 325.

The situation in ordnance procurement is the same. Speed is of the essence, and speed made it necessary that orders be placed with concerns with whom preliminary arrangements for production of munitions had been made under the industrial mobilization plan in the years preceding the emergency. We needed medium tanks in large numbers, of uniform design, and we needed them quickly. We made contracts for them with Chrysler, Baldwin Locomotive, and American Locomotive. It would have been folly to have ignored the great productive facilities of these

---

last seven months of 1940, 60 percent went to 20 firms and 86.4 percent to 100 companies. *Ibid.,* p. 63.

[2] See: (1) Senate, *Small Business Hearings;* (2) Select H. Com. To Investigate the National Defense Program in Its Relation to Small Business, 77th Cong., 2d Sess., Hearings on H. Res. 294, *Study and Investigation of the National Defense Program in Its Relation to Small Business,* 1942: (3) Truman Committee, *Hearings,* especially Pt. 6; Yoshpe, The Small Business Man and Quartermaster Contracts, 1940–1942.

concerns and to have placed our business with companies that could not produce quickly.[3]

From the very beginning, the Under Secretary well knew that it would be impossible to avoid criticism in the handling of the military procurement program. But one criticism which he hoped never to face was that he had failed to provide the Army with the munitions it needed to achieve victory. This was emphasized by Leon Henderson in his testimony before the Truman Committee in the summer of 1941:

I sat with Secretary Patterson, incidentally, in the early days when there was a question of giving a contract on powder to somebody else, and I knew he gave earnest consideration to that matter, and he felt that if he made a mistake and there was a shortage of powder in this country he would be blamed, and he thought he ought to take the rap on picking a manufacturer known to be able to produce powder, and that he could handle that better than he could a shortage of powder.[4]

In addition to the issue of adequate productive capacity there were compelling administrative reasons for concentration of orders in large firms in launching the rearmament program. For any particular item the award of a few contracts with carefully selected firms minimized the rapidly multiplying tasks of contract placement and administration which stretched the capacities of overburdened and understaffed procurement officers to the limit. The problems of contractor selection, negotiation of prices and other terms, providing financial aid, obtaining priority assistance, issuing change orders, expediting production, auditing, making payments, and conducting continuous inspection of processes and products,

and all other aspects of contract administration which descended like locusts upon the procuring agencies as the national economy approached a wartime footing, would have been multiplied many times by splitting up large contracts into numerous smaller ones. Anyone familiar with the hectic atmosphere of procurement offices during this period could understand the reluctance of contracting officers further to complicate and slow down their work. This reluctance was increased by the fact that many small-business proposals were apparently unrelated to, and likely to frustrate, the attainment of fundamental procurement objectives.

Popular misunderstanding of the reasons for prime-contract concentration was paralleled by misunderstanding of the implications and effects thereof. The average layman was not aware that a substantial portion of total prime-contract expenditures would be transferred to small business under lucrative subcontracts and orders often executed under more attractive terms and conditions than direct government contracts. Nor did the layman stop to consider that the concentration of government contracts was merely an extension of the basic pattern voluntarily initiated by the American housewife, the general public, and the business community, including small business itself. It is interesting to note that the Army's distribution of prime contracts to small business during the period of rearmament was considerably more generous (approximately three fourths as against less than one half) than the redistribution—in the form of subcontracts—of war business by the business community itself. (*Table 45*) While these figures shed no light on dollar-value magnitudes, they suggest the vital and indispen-

---

[3] Truman Committee, *Hearings,* 16 Apr 41, 1:61–62.

[4] Ibid., 23 Jul 41, 6:1640.

TABLE 45—WAR DEPARTMENT PRIME CONTRACTS AND SUBCONTRACTS [a]

[Total Number in Effect at Specified Dates]

Date	Prime Contracts			Subcontracts		
	Total	To Small Business [b]		Total	To Small Business [b]	
		Actual	Percent		Actual	Percent
1 Jul 1941	23,458	16,918	72	141,804	74,809	53
1 Jan 1942	34,322	25,918	75	479,396	191,776	40
1 Jul 1942	76,291	54,567	72	671,315	284,560	42
1 Sep 1942	89,515	64,610	72	798,933	362,577	45

[a] Except Army Air Forces.

[b] Firms of 500 employees or less.

Source: Senate, Small Business Hearings, pp. 1177-91.

sable role played by large companies, not only as subcontractors in the war production program but as the most effective suppliers of major classes of goods and services.

Further indication of the extent to which prime-contract expenditures were transferred to small business is found in a sample study of subcontracting made by the ASF in the spring of 1943:

. . . analysis of 2,987 supply contracts awarded by the Army Service Forces during the period March 5 to April 15, representing a cross section of contracts placed during this period, disclosed that 25.2% of the dollar value of these primes was passed on to concerns with under 500 wage earners in the form of first-tier subcontracts.[5]

[5] Ltr, Maj Robert D. Holbrook, Actg Chf SWPB, Purchases Div ASF, to Mr. William Weinfeld, SWPC, 14 Aug 43, folder IV. (See supporting note in author's file, OCMH. It was impractical, especially under emergency and wartime pressures, to attempt to obtain more than sample statistics of dollar-value expenditures under subcontracts. For example, "To get the subcontractors on that basis we would have had to have prime contractors go through their files and pull out every order they had, and figure out how much was unshipped." Statement of Col Browning, Senate, Small Business Hearings, 10: 1181.

Obviously, first-tier subcontracts accounted for only part of re-expenditures under wartime procurement. Expenditures at lower echelons likewise benefited small business, and these low-echelon expenditures often took place long before government disbursements to prime contractors were completed.

Although the Army placed its procurement objectives and responsibilities above the goal of aid to small business as such, it took steps from the very beginning of the rearmament program to widen the distribution of contracts. From the Army's point of view these measures were designed primarily to broaden the production base and speed the mobilization program, but they had the effect of helping small business. Beginning with Assistant Secretary Louis Johnson's directive of 12 June 1940, which anticipated the launching of the Munitions Program, right on up to Pearl Harbor the War Department issued a steady stream of instructions and directives to the supply arms and services bringing pressure upon them to split awards among a large number of firms, obtain additional subcontracting, and bring new prime contractors into the program as rapidly as possible.[6]

Small Business Policies of NDAC and OPM

The NDAC recognized the desirability of bringing small business into the defense program as rapidly and fully as possible. Both Donald Nelson and Leon Henderson believed that this was necessary in order to help prepare the economy to shoulder the tremendous load of wartime production which would almost certainly be required in the future. At the same time, apart from

the objectives of rearmament, they felt it necessary to utilize the procurement program to relieve current hardship and to preserve a balanced economy for the post-war era.[7] On 25 October 1940 the NDAC created the Office of Small Business Activities, with Donald Nelson as director. Nelson worked closely with the Army, especially the Quartermaster Corps, and readily obtained important changes in purchasing methods which provided small firms with a larger share of business. These included the shift from purchasing f.o.b. Army depots to f.o.b. plant and limitation of the share of awards going to any one firm. Limitation of awards not only forced a wider distribution of contracts among firms of all sizes but also reduced the size of individual awards to quantities which could be handled by smaller firms.[8]

After the NDAC was supplanted by OPM, the Office of Small Business Activities was replaced by the Defense Contract Service, headed by Robert L. Mehornay, in the Production Division, OPM. The Defense Contract Service, organized in co-operation with the Federal Reserve System, established field offices throughout the country in thirty-six Federal Reserve district and branch banks. The function of these offices, which were staffed with businessmen, engineers, and lawyers, was to facilitate a greater degree of subcontracting as well as to guide qualified small firms to district procurement officers for possible prime contracts. On 17 February 1941, Un-

---

[6] For example: (1) Ltr, ASW Johnson to CofAC et al., 12 Jun 40, sub: 1941 Procurement Program; (2) Memo, Col Schulz, Dir Current Procurement OASW, for CofAC et al., 2 Jul 40, sub: Procurement Without Advertising; (3) Ltr, ASW Patterson, to Chfs of Supply Arms and Services, 20 Dec 40, sub: Use of Subcontractors in Defense Program; (4) Memo, USW Patterson, for Chfs of All Supply Arms and Services, 17 Feb 41, sub: Cooperation with Defense Contract Service in Facilitating Subcontracting; (5) Ltr, SW Stimson to CofOrd et al., 19 Feb 41, sub: Ordnance Production Under the National Defense Program; (6) Memo, USW Patterson for Chfs of Supply Arms and Services, 20 May 41, sub: Subcontracting of Prime Defense Orders; (7) Memo, USW Patterson for CofAC et al., 29 May 41; (8) Memo, USW Patterson for CofAC et al., 30 Jun 41, sub: Distribution of Defense Orders Among a Greater Number of Contractors; (9) Memo, Gen Rutherford, Ex OUSW for Chfs of Supply Arms and Services, 5 Sep 41, sub: Distribution of Defense Orders; (10) OUSW Office Order 11–B–1, 19 Aug 41, announcing creation of Army Contract Distribution Division, OUSW; (11) Memo, Rutherford for Chfs of Supply Arms and Services, 13 Sep 41, sub: Plans for Current Procurement; (12) Memo, Rutherford for Chfs of Supply Arms and Services, 26 Sep 41, sub: Clearance of Contracts Requiring Substantial New Construction or Extensive New Equipment; (13) Memo, Lt Col Frank W. Bullock, Purchases and Contracts Div, OUSW, for CofAC et al., 19 Nov 41, sub: Special Purchasing Procedure [for distressed communities and industries]. All of the above are reproduced in Senate, Small Business Hearings, 10:1301–34.

[7] Truman Committee, Hearings, 5 Jun 41, 5:1338, 1340–41; 23 Jul 41, 6:1634.
[8] For example, in the case of shoes, no one firm was permitted to bid on more than 15 percent of the entire award. Testimony of Donald Nelson in Truman Committee, Hearings, 5 Jun 41, 1336–37.

der Secretary Patterson addressed a lengthy memorandum to the chiefs of all the Army's supply arms describing in detail the contemplated organization and functions of the Defense Contract Service. While indicating that the determination of subcontractors was still the responsibility of prime contractors, Patterson urged "an intent and spirit of full cooperation with respect to the 'farming-out' program" and indicated that the program as outlined in his memorandum was "intended to be of real service in the prosecution of the defense program." [9]

Many commentators on procurement policies during the defense period did not appreciate that both legally and practically a prime contract had to allow contractors powers commensurate with their responsibilities. These powers necessarily included the authority to determine the extent to which subcontracting was practicable, as well as authority to determine the selection of particular subcontractors. After the nation was fully at war, and under the aegis of the First War Powers Act, procuring agencies could of course compel prime contractors to follow instructions. But even after Pearl Harbor the Army normally sought, and usually obtained, contractor action on the basis of persuasion and mutual discussion of the problems involved.

In August 1941, to combat the effects of growing material shortages and migration of labor, the War Department established the Army Contract Distribution Division, OUSW.[10] This office was given the responsibility for channeling defense orders for the relief of distressed industries and communities.[11] Two weeks later the President replaced OPM's Defense Contract Service with the Contract Distribution Division in the Production Division, OPM. Mr. Floyd B. Odlum, the head of the new division, was like his predecessor vitally interested in the welfare of small business and proceeded vigorously to expand the program. But as the emergency deepened no amount of redistribution of defense contracts could save all firms, and in the aftermath of Pearl Harbor thousands of additional small firms were forced to curtail or suspend operations. Many small firms ceased because of the departure of owners or key employees into the armed services or to positions in vitally needed defense production elsewhere. Others, such as automobile agencies, service stations, and hotel and tourist facilities in vulnerable areas, could find little or no place in the production of essential items. Still others could not be converted to defense production at all or before an indispensable period of exploration and adjustment. By the spring of 1942 both the House and Senate had established small business committees, conducted extensive hearings, and developed legislative proposals to deal firmly with the problem. The result was the Small Business Act of 11 June 1942.[12]

---

[9] Patterson memo, especially par. 10, cited above, note 6(4). The official history of the War Production Board states that in this memorandum "the War Department grudgingly recognized the existence of the Defense Contract Service" and compares it unfavorably with a Navy Department memorandum issued some ten days later which proclaimed "complete" (rather than "full") cooperation. CPA, *Industrial Mobilization for War,* p. 146.

[10] See above, pages 237, 261.

[11] OUSW Office Order 11–B–1, 19 Aug 41.

[12] 56 *Stat.* 351, often referred to as the Smaller War Plants Act. The small business committee of the Senate was established on 8 October 1940, that of the House on 4 December 1941.

The Small War Plants Program in Transition

*Slow Beginnings Under
the Small Business Act*

The passage of the Small Business Act marked the beginning of a new stage in the integration of small business into the wartime economy. The act required the chairman of the War Production Board, through a deputy to be appointed by him, "to mobilize aggressively the productive capacity of all small business concerns." It authorized the formation of pools of small firms exempt from the provisions of antitrust laws. It specifically recognized the likelihood of higher costs and prices in procurement from small business. It gave the WPB chairman wide powers to carry out the purposes of the act, including the authority to certify to procuring agencies the capacity and credit of individual small firms. Procurement officers were not compelled to let contracts to certified plants but were authorized to do so without the imposition of further requirements as to capacity or credit. The act also created a Smaller War Plants Corporation, with a capital stock of $150,000,000, to make loans or advances on whatever terms were deemed necessary to provide small firms with plant, equipment, materials, and working capital to be used for war or essential civilian purposes. It also empowered the Smaller War Plants Corporation to contract directly with procuring agencies to furnish these agencies with articles, equipment, supplies, and materials. Moreover, in a provision which was to raise considerable controversy, it required procuring agencies to place such prime contracts with the Smaller War Plants Corporation whenever the chairman of the War Production Board

certified that SWPC was competent to fill particular procurement requirements. The SWPC would then subcontract the work to small business concerns or others for actual performance.[13] The chairman of the board of SWPC was to be appointed by the chairman of the WPB and was therefore responsible to him.

Ten days after the passage of the Small Business Act the Army's Chief of Ordnance issued instructions to Ordnance district offices and operating branches, inclosing a digest of the act, putting all concerned on notice of their impending responsibilities, and indicating the firm intention of the Ordnance Department to co-operate fully with the purposes of the act.[14] Nevertheless, in the eyes of its sponsors, execution of the Small Business Act was slow. The official WPB order creating the Smaller War Plants Division, WPB, did not appear until 8 September 1942, some three months after the passage of the act.[15] In keeping with a WPB request, the Army did not set up its own organization and begin functioning until the WPB program had been laid out.[16] One week after the WPB order, the Director of Procurement, ASF, issued a directive to the technical services requesting the appointment of a small-business representative in each service headquarters and announcing the War Department policy of making every effort to award contracts, "both prime and sub," to small firms without waiting for certification by WPB or contract action by the Smaller War Plants Corporation. A detailed report from each service, indicating the con-

---

[13] 56 *Stat* 351, Sec. 4 (f) (5). (2) CPA, *Industrial Mobilization for War*, pp. 527–32.
[14] Ltr, Gen Campbell, CofOrd, 22 July 42, sub: Small Business Act, copy in Senate, *Small Business Hearings*, 10:1331.
[15] CPA, *Industrial Mobilization for War*, p. 529.
[16] Senate, *Small Business Hearings*, 10:1203.

tract actions achieved as a result of this directive, was requested by 15 October.[17] Two weeks after this directive, the creation of the Small War Plants Branch, Purchases Division, ASF was announced. This branch was to be responsible for general War Department policy and operations in the small war plants program.[18] Finally, on 30 October 1942, a basic procedure was established for screening Army requirements and allocating procurement to small plants recommended by the War Production Board.[19]

Meanwhile the respective chairmen of the Senate and House small business committees had become highly dissatisfied with the delays in the execution of the provisions of the Small Business Act. In a series of animated hearings before the Senate committee in October and December, the principal civilian and military officials in charge of the program were given a thorough grilling. The Army was criticized for creating large ammunition and other big plants throughout the country while many small businesses were failing; for "earmarking" at technical service headquarters, procurement for specific firms—thus limiting the ability of the district offices to spread work among small firms; and in general for the failure to accomplish "anything" under the small war plants program. England and Germany were held up as models in the utilization of small plants, the statement

being made of Germany that "there is not an idle plant in the whole country." [20]

It is interesting to note that while one Senate committee was citing England as a model in small plant utilization, another Senate committee was warning that "the United States should avoid the bitter experience of England, where 20,000 manufacturing plants were shut down almost overnight when a complete shift from what may be called a business-as-usual program to an all-out war effort was attempted." [21] In any case, Mr. Lou E. Holland, director of SWPC and head of the WPB Smaller War Plants Division, came in for especially heavy criticism by Representative Wright Patman, who had been invited to participate in the Senate hearings. When Mr. Holland testified that the Smaller War Plants Corporation thus far had not taken a single prime contract, or purchased any machinery for installation in small plants, Mr. Patman described the SWPC under Mr. Holland as "a complete flop" in discharging functions which were "the main reason for the passing of this law." [22] Despite the great difficulties and mitigating circumstances, Mr. Holland's days as director of SWPC were numbered, and shortly after the first of the year he joined his predecessors—Messrs. Mehornay and Odlum—as a former administrator of the small business program. He was succeeded by Col. (later Brig. Gen.) Robert Wood

---

[17] Ltr, Brig Gen W. H. Harrison, Dir of Procurement, SOS, to CofCWS *et al.*, 15 Sep 42, sub: Additional Work for Smaller War Plants, copy in Senate, *Small Business Hearings*, 10:1330.

[18] Memo, TAG for Chfs of Supply Services, 1 Oct 42, sub: Additional Work for Small War Plants, copy in Senate, *Small Business Hearings*, 10:1333.

[19] Memo, Gen Somervell, CG SOS, for Chfs of Supply Services, 30 Oct 42, sub: Procedure on Relationship With Smaller War Plants Division, War Production Board, folder VI.

[20] Senate, *Small Business Hearings*, 15 Oct 42, 10:1209, also 1204–20, *passim*.

[21] Truman Committee, First Annual Rpt, p. 198.

[22] Senate, *Small Business Hearings*, 15 Dec 42, 12:1658. At this time Mr. Patman felt that the taking of prime contracts by SWPC was indispensable to the program. Later, when he became aware of the difficulties and implications of such action, he abandoned this position. See below, page 428, note 39.

Johnson, who had recently been chief of the New York Ordnance District.[23]

The Formative Period of Army-SWPC Relations

The Congressional hearings and their attendant publicity brought heavy pressure upon the War Production Board, the War Department, and the other procurement agencies to intensify their efforts on behalf of small business. Between November 1942 and the end of 1943, a basic organization and procedure was developed for systematically channeling a maximum of prime contracts to small firms and for extending the degree of subcontracting under large prime contracts. It was during this period that the major substantive problems under the program were revealed and gradually overcome.

Within the War Department an Army "small war plants officer" was assigned to each procurement office in the field, as well as to each of the technical service headquarters. Similarly, the Smaller War Plants Corporation—which was soon made organizationally independent of the War Production Board—assigned its own procurement specialists to each technical service and to regional district offices.[24] The original machinery for channeling War Department procurement to small business was heavily concentrated in each technical service headquarters. SWPC procurement specialists in technical service headquarters reviewed each edition of the Army Supply Program to ascertain what items were suitable for production by small firms. An agreement was then reached with the technical service procurement staff as to the proportion of total procurement of each suitable item which would be allocated or allotted to SWPC. In some cases this allotment would be a specified percentage of the total procurement of each selected item; in other cases it was a specific quantity determined on the basis of all relevant considerations.[25] After receiving an allocation at technical service headquarters, the SWPC indicated the geographical distribution of its allotment and instructed its field representatives in each region to designate specific plants to be considered by local contracting officers in filling allocations. During the early stages of the program, however, a substantial portion of all designations was made at SWPC headquarters in Washington. Although SWPC allotments normally had to be filled by contracts to firms on the SWPC designated list, the selection of individual firms for actual award was made by the military procuring agencies.[26]

Many problems immediately arose in the administration of the program. The Small

---

[23] CPA, *Industrial Mobilization for War,* pp. 531–32. General Johnson, a Reserve officer, was chairman of the board of Johnson and Johnson. His experience with the small war plants program has been sketched in his thought-provoking little book, *"But, General Johnson—"* (Princeton: Princeton University Press, 1944). General Johnson resigned his position in the fall of 1943 because of ill health. He was succeeded early in 1944 by former Representative Maury Maverick.

[24] The Smaller War Plants Division, WPB, was transferred to SWPC on 18 March 1943. The SWPC chairman was, however, retained as the WPB deputy chairman for Smaller War Plants. CPA, *Industrial Mobilization for War,* p. 573.

[25] For example, in November 1942 the Quartermaster Corps decided to allot 10 per cent of all major procurement to the Smaller War Plants Division, WPB, which then designated specific firms for consideration by local contracting officers. Yoshpe and Massen, *QMC Procurement Policies,* p. 134.

[26] Memo and incl, Maj Alvin E. Hewitt, Chf SWPB Purchases Div ASF, for Dir of Materiel ASF, 16 Jun 43, sub: Review of War Department Policy Relating to Utilization of Small War Plants, folder I.

Business Act had deliberately omitted any definition of a "small" business, and the Army established its definition as any independent firm employing less than five hundred wage earners.[27] Army officials were well aware that in some cases large plants—such as power plants or other plants with highly mechanized or automatic equipment—might have less than five hundred employees. Conversely, in some industries plants with well over five hundred employees might be relatively small in relation to the leaders of the industry. The 1939 Census of Manufacturers had indicated that 98.9 percent of the total of 184,230 manufacturing establishments in the country employed less than five hundred workers. But 72.4 percent of the total, or 133,260 plants, had employed less than twenty workers. Only a tiny percentage of these smallest firms could reasonably be expected to be capable of handling prime contracts. The Army's definition was later ratified by SWPC, which added in its official definition an exception permitting the certification of a larger plant if it was one of the smaller plants in the industry or was doing a relatively small portion of the business of the industry.[28]

A basic problem faced by the Army as well as by the SWPC was the fundamental ambiguity of purpose in the Small Business Act. Although the act was nominally dedicated to the furtherance of war production through the mobilization of small business, its *raison d'être* was the preservation of American small business. The sponsors of the act deeply resented any implication that it was "a relief measure"; yet the constant references throughout the hearings to small business hardships and failures made it quite clear that the major purpose of the act was, in fact, the relief of small business. In view of this obvious reality as well as for reasons of administrative necessity, SWPC by the beginning of 1943 had decided to concentrate its initial efforts on plants which were in actual or prospective "distress." A "distressed" plant was defined as one whose current operations and unfilled orders for 1943 were less than two thirds of the plant's capacity. "Capacity" was defined as the plant's average level of operations for the five-year period ending in 1941, or the 1941 level if no history existed for the longer period. Under this definition a study revealed that, of 165,000 small plants in the country, only 3,500 were considered in actual distress.[29] Some small business advocates objected to the base-period definition of capacity as "limiting" the participation of small business in the war program to a previous level of operations. These spokesmen insisted that small business be given "a full meal" rather than "crumbs" and that *all* small business—not merely distressed firms—be taken into the war production program. The SWPC policy did not, of course, contemplate any limitation upon small business. It merely established a working priority designed to prevent "starvation" by some firms before attempting to provide a "full meal," with dessert, for all firms. Concerns operating at levels from two-thirds to full "capacity" were labeled "need work"; concerns operating at above this range but with still additional capacity were

---

[27] PR 225.4(b) (11–23–44).

[28] SWPC Field Ltr 57, 30 Jun 43. For statistical purposes the Army reported small plant contracts in two categories: plants with less than 100 employes, and plants with from 100 to 500 employees. For a discussion of the problems of definition and reasons why such a definition was omitted from the act, see Senate, *Small Business Hearings*, 11: 1605–07.

[29] Johnson, *"But, General Johnson —"*, p. 33.

labeled "open capacity." All these groups were designated for suitable procurement.[30]

Studies by the Army as well as by SWPC revealed that many small firms were already well occupied with war contracts, subcontracts, or essential civilian business. An intensive study and analysis of distressed manufacturing plants in the Greater New York area was conducted by the Small War Plants Branch, ASF, in the spring of 1943. This survey was undertaken to facilitate cooperation with SWPC in eliminating distress in the New York area, a project which had received considerable attention in the Senate hearings on small business. The study indicated that the actual degree of distress was much lower than generally assumed, including less than 2½ percent of all small industrial establishments in the area. It revealed many considerations which had an important bearing on the determination of actual distress. For example, backlogs of unfilled orders were highly inconclusive in determining distress since advance orders were not customary in many lines; production and shipment were largely conducted on an inventory basis. Also, many firms were operating at distress rates because of the loss of skilled labor rather than lack of potential orders. Moreover, profits were often maintained or even increased under distress rates of operation because of curtailment of overhead and other cost items; firms formerly furnishing both labor and materials now furnished only labor under profitable subcontracts.[31]

The small firms which fared well under the war program were generally the more aggressive, efficient, and well-organized firms, in lines of activity most suited to the needs of war production. Conversely, distressed plants were likely to be those least qualified to undertake military contracts. For this reason SWPC was in a difficult position. If it were to "certify" dubious or incompetent firms as capable of performing specific procurements, production failures would redound to the discredit of SWPC and jeopardize the small business program as well as actual procurement deliveries. Hence, the SWPC ordinarily preferred merely to "designate" firms which it thought capable and to leave final selections to the military procurement agencies with established organizations, procedures, and trained personnel for making facility surveys and evaluating all factors preliminary to the award of contracts. For its part, the Army—which was ultimately responsible for procurement deliveries—preferred to forestall the use of SWPC "certification" by providing a maximum of allocations to be filled by contracts to firms designated by SWPC.[32]

---

[30] SWPC Field Ltr 57, 30 Jun 43.

[31] See Memo, Maj Irving Salomon, Chf Special Problems Sec, SWPB Purchases Div ASF, for Maj Hewitt, Chf SWPB Purchases Div, 14 Jul 43, sub: Report on the Procedure, Results to Date, and Findings in the Special Project To Assist Smaller War Plants Corporation's List of So-called Distressed Plants in the New York Area, OCMH. A somewhat similar study was made of the role of small business in the Chicago procurement area. Ltr, Saloman to Hewitt, 15 Sep 43, folder IV.

[32] In May 1943 the SWPC Board of Directors resolved that all formal "certifications" under the Small Business Act could be made only upon express authorization by the board itself. At the same time the SWPC board defined "designation" as meaning that SWPC had investigated the facilities of the concerns designated and believed they were competent to perform the contracts for which they were designated. (1) Memo, C. W. Fowler, Ex Secy SWPC, for SWPC staff in Washington and field offices, procurement officers, and others concerned, 29 May 43, sub: Policy of SWPC Relating to Designations and Certifications; (2) Memo, Col Browning, Dir Purchases Div ASF, for CofCWS et al., 10 Jun 43, sub: Resolution Adopted by SWPC Board of Directors. Both in folder I.

During the first year of operations, SWPC designations proved to be widely unsatisfactory to Army contracting officers. Many specific examples were cited by Army procurement specialists of designees who were incompetent, too busy to bid, or otherwise not interested in the contract for which they had been designated. Frequently too many or too few designations were made for the size of the SWPC allotment. If too many designations were made, administrative burdens upon contracting officers were greatly increased; in some instances, moreover, firms informed that they had been designated "to receive contracts" could not be given contracts, became embittered, and complained to their Congressmen. If designations were insufficient, procurement officers often had to make last-minute efforts to locate suitable sources and were denied the opportunity to obtain adequate competitive comparisons. In numerous instances the major portion, or sometimes all, of SWPC designations for a particular procurement consisted of firms already on the Army's list of current sources; this meant that the allocation to SWPC was in effect gratuitous since the designated firms would have received consideration or actual contracts anyway. In some cases, rather than turn back an unfilled portion of their allocation to the procuring agency, SWPC procurement specialists would designate large corporations, firms in tight labor areas, or brokers who subcontracted the entire job— at a profit—to firms already producing for the Army. Contracting officers frequently complained that designees attempted to abuse the Small Business Act by insisting on premium prices not justified by actual costs and that firms were encouraged in this practice by SWPC personnel. In other cases, actual distress was created for existing Army

contractors, both in small and intermediate sizes, who could not be given repeat or continuation orders because of allotments to SWPC. District procurement offices found that relatively little effort was made by SWPC personnel to obtain subcontracts or essential civilian business for small firms, and that many SWPC designees for prime contracts were only suitable for subcontracting operations or nonmilitary business.[33]

Under the circumstances many designations were rejected by contracting officers in the early months of SWPC operations. While this tended to minimize procurement failures and contract delinquencies, it also created a certain amount of friction with SWPC officials and laid the Army open to charges that it was not "co-operating" with the program. Consequently, although relationships with SWPC personnel were on the whole harmonious, occasionally tempers flared and harsh words were spoken. An illustration is found in the handling of the Army's barge-building program in the spring of 1943, which serves to illuminate both the emotional cross-currents and the practical difficulties complicating military procurement in time of war.

Early in 1943 the Army Signal Corps had called the attention of Headquarters, ASF, to some unfortunate wording in an SWPC form for the notification of designated facilities. This form contained the words "it is hereby directed the following firms be considered as qualified SWPC–

---

[33] See data in folders I–VI. In order to eliminate undesirable practices, the Army's Small War Plants Branch in the summer of 1943 compiled a list of such practices, with representative examples under each heading, which had taken place at both the headquarters and field level of SWPC operations. Memo, Maj Holbrook, Chf SWPB Purchases Div ASF, for Col Foy, 22 Sep 43, sub: Examples of SWPC Activities, Incl 1: Field Activities, SWPC, and Incl 2: Hdqrs Activities, SWPC, folder IV.

WPB designees, and to receive the above procurement." This wording, as well as certain practices of SWPC personnel, implied that all designees would automatically receive contracts, and gave rise to high hopes and false expectations on the part of designated firms. On 2 April 1943, the chief of the Army's Small War Plants Branch wrote to SWPC headquarters requesting a change of wording in any manner which would overcome the difficulty. No answer was given to this letter, and the request was repeated on 17 June.[34]

In the meantime, during the month of May, the Army Transportation Corps made two large allotments to SWPC, consisting of 2,000 wooden barges and 350 steel barges. After the geographical allocation had been made to SWPC regional offices, numerous designations were made. It was, of course, standard procedure within the procurement offices concerned for designations to be made of more firms than would actually receive awards, since this was the only way in which a satisfactory identification, comparison, and evaluation of available facilities and bid proposals could be achieved.[35] Because of an apparent lack of restraint by

SWPC field personnel, most of the designees came to believe or were led to believe that they would automatically share in a "huge boat-building program." Many of those who failed to receive contracts became very much disgruntled and their complaints reverberated throughout the country. In the wooden barge program, one firm in Maryland submitted a bid of $5,183 per unit. The average price on contracts awarded was $3,675. When its bid was rejected this firm notified its Congressman who "brought pressure to bear upon the contracting officer." A Virginia firm which lost out to lower bidders equally in need of contracts carried its complaint to the Under Secretary of War; a rejected New York firm took the matter to Headquarters, ASF. From Florida to California the complaints of disappointed boatbuilders embarrassed the Transportation Corps.[36]

Since the Transportation Corps had prided itself on this relatively large effort to maximize small business opportunities, the resulting complications and ill-will came as something of a shock. No doubt this experience sheds some light on the contents of a letter only shortly thereafter to the Chief of the Transportation Corps by the chairman of SWPC:

My dear Sir:

On reflection, our conference of yesterday would seem to be rather unsatisfactory. First,

---

[34] Ltrs, Maj Hewitt, Chf SWPB Purchases Div ASF, to O. S. McPherson, SWPC, 2 Apr 43, 17 Jun 43, both in folder I.

[35] The availability of suitable facilities varied widely from one technical service to another. The QMC was often faced with far more designations than it could possibly use. The Medical Department reported one case of thirty-four SWPC designations for a small award that could be split at most into two contracts. On the other hand, the Signal Corps found it necessary to request that designations "will if possible, be at least twice the number needed for the allocated portion of the procurement." Memo, Maj Gen W. H. Harrison, Chf Procurement and Distribution Sec, OCSigO, for Dir Purchases Div ASF, 17 Nov 43, sub: Application of Signal Corps for Permission To Establish Special Smaller War Plant Procedure at Variance With Procurement Regulations, folder IV.

[36] Memo, Col Omar J. Ruch, Chf Procurement Div TC, for Dir Purchases Div ASF, 18 Jun 43, sub: Handling of Procurement Allocations by SWPC, folder I. In this memorandum Colonel Ruch paid high tribute to the SWPC procurement specialist assigned to the Transportation Corps in Washington: "The Liaison Specialist from SWPC to this division . . . handled the whole transaction with consummate skill; . . . It was due only to the skillful and untiring efforts of Mr. Mehen that the discontent and disappointment among small wood-working plants throughout the country was not more widespread."

you had not read the report by Mr. Ferris, and you spent some time disclosing your resentment to what you termed "interference by Government civilian agencies."

Let us make it clear that the Smaller War Plants Corporation is operating under a legal mandate from Congress, and it is my duty to carry out the will of Congress as expressed by the Smaller War Plants Act.

This country is not and will not be under the direction of a military junta. . . .

All of this leads me to re-affirm my position, which is that both the Smaller War Plants Corporation and the Transportation Corps could well afford to review our execution, as I feel confident a better job could be done.[37]

Many of the foregoing difficulties were more or less inevitable in the formative stages of the program and could be corrected with the accumulation of experience, the steady improvement of organizations, and the refinement of policy. But there was one feature of the Small Business Act which Army procurement officials considered above all others to be gratuitous and positively dangerous to the success of the procurement program. This was the provision for the SWPC to take prime contracts for military procurement following certification by the WPB chairman. To Army procurement officials this appeared as a device to set up a dual procurement agency and to take

the procurement function out of the hands of the War Department.

At the time of the passage of the Small Business Act, it appeared to some observers that the plight of small business was due to deliberate discrimination or neglect by the procurement agencies and that it could be cured by giving another agency the power to take over procurement in behalf of small business. Others, no doubt, believed that the threat or imminent possibility of such action would be sufficient to bring the established procurement agencies into line and to obtain a wider distribution of contracts through ordinary contractual procedures. In any case, the prime contract provision was included in the Small Business Act, and by the fall of 1942 members of Congress were urging upon SWPC the widespread use of this power. Donald Nelson, who firmly believed that the taking of prime contracts by SWPC should be done only in extreme cases and after thorough review, had made only a handful of certifications by mid-1943. Hence, a movement had developed to amend the act to give SWPC the power to take prime contracts directly on its own initiative. This move was stoutly resisted, not only by the procuring agencies, but by the WPB Procurement Policy Board, and the proposal was never adopted. Army procurement personnel believed that the adoption of such an expedient would open a whole Pandora's box of procurement troubles without helping the cause of small business.

In the eyes of the War Department, the placement of a prime contract with SWPC was of an undesirable species entirely different from contracts placed by the Army directly with its own suppliers. The ordinary prime contract gave the Army direct control over the selection of the actual manufacturers of its equipment. It permitted

[37] Ltr, Robert W. Johnson, Vice Chmn WPB and Chmn SWPC, to Maj Gen Charles P. Gross, CofTrans, 17 Aug 43, folder IV. General Johnson's attitude, as expressed in this letter, had in turn been influenced by a letter from General Somervell to Donald Nelson, criticizing a statement made by General Johnson at a recent press conference. In this letter General Somervell had stated: "It is, of course, extremely inadvisable for an officer in uniform to be reflecting views which are at variance with the expressed views of the War Department." Ltr, General Somervell, CG ASF, to Nelson, Chmn WPB, 14 Jun 43, folder I. See also, Johnson, *"But, General Johnson—"*, p. 47.

the Army to negotiate directly all the numerous terms of the contract—specifications, price, delivery schedules, packing, shipping, and storage requirements, royalty and patent provisions, and so on. It also permitted the immediate and continuous use of all the established and integrated machinery for contract administration and production control which had been developed at great effort over a period of three years. This included regular procedures for the making and liquidation of advance and progress payments, granting of priorities, allotment of controlled materials, adjustment of delivery schedules to changes in requirements and related portions of the procurement program, application of complex inspection procedures, direct issuance of shipping instructions, and many other features. Under wartime conditions the negotiation and signing of a contract was an indispensable but only a first step in the procurement process. The entire procurement process from the beginning to end required an intimate and continuous relationship between the actual suppliers of equipment and the agency responsible for delivery of finished munitions to troops in the field.

The placement of a prime contract with SWPC broke into this intimate relationship and turned over to another agency the task of selecting contractors, negotiating terms, and maintaining face-to-face relations with the actual fabricators of military equipment. Even if SWPC had acted only as a intermediary or interpreter of Army needs, the interposition of a third party—through which must be funneled all instructions, change orders, and continual communication with suppliers necessary under the high pressure and rapid tempo of wartime procurement—would create impossible frus-

tration and delay. But, in assuming prime contracts, the SWPC was not merely an interpreter of Army needs and policies; it was a policy-making intermediary with its own statutory responsibilities and objectives which frequently ran counter to those of the Army. Even when portions of the contract administration process—such as responsibility for inspection—remained with the Army, the basic integrity of the process would be destroyed: problems of jurisdiction would constantly arise and decisions made at early stages in the process would inevitably effect operations at later stages. All in all, officials responsible for military procurement felt that the prime contract provision of the Small Business Act was an unfortunate inclusion, and that its actual use should be discouraged whenever possible.[38]

As events turned out, the Army and the other procurement agencies were able to demonstrate that the exercise of the prime contract power by SWPC was unnecessary for accomplishing the basic purposes of the Small Business Act. By the end of 1943, the broad task of organizing the nation's economy for war production had been achieved. The expansion of productive facilities, the general conversion of industry, the successful operation of the Controlled Materials Plan, and the settlement of major inter-

---

[38] See: (1) Draft of War Department's Comment on Amendments to Public Law 603 Proposed by Senate Committee on Small Business (8 pp.); (2) Statement of Procurement Policy Board, WPB, on Smaller War Plants Corporation's Assumption of Prime Contracts (2 pp.); (3) Prime Contracts Between SWPC and the War Department, Tabs A through I. All accompanying Memo, Lt Col Robert D. Holbrook, Chf SWPB, for Col Foy, Asst Dir Purchases Div ASF, 19 Feb 44, sub: Amendments to Public Law 603 (Smaller War Plants Act) Under Consideration by the Senate Committee on Small Business, folder II.

agency controversies over organization and policy were now largely a matter of history. With munitions production at peak levels, and the programs for heavy and complex equipment well in hand, it was now possible for the Army to give the small business program a high priority. Improvements in the procedure for making allocations and designations facilitated the direct award of contracts to SWPC designees without the need for resort to the awkward and cumbersome device of SWPC prime contracts. By the end of 1943, even Representative Patman—who had earlier castigated Lou Holland for his failure to invoke SWPC's prime contract powers—was now out of sympathy with the use of that instrument.[39] As a result, the move to augment the prime contract power of SWPC was defeated and the actual use of the power was confined to a handful of relatively unimportant contracts. The new SWPC-War Department agreement of April 1944, establishing revised procedures, made no mention of SWPC prime contracts. By 1 April 1945, the SWPC had taken a total of only twelve prime contracts, amounting to some $32 million, and only half of these were for the War Department.[40]

---

[39] "Chairman Patman of the House Committee on Small Business, in a letter dated November 1, 1943 to the Chairman of the Smaller War Plants Corporation, stated that he saw little justification for Smaller War Plants Corporation insistence on taking a prime contract when an agency expressed a willingness to award business to one or more of a group of firms designated by Smaller War Plants Corporation as competent to do the work." Ltr, Brig Gen Albert J. Browning, Dir Purchases Div ASF, to Donald Nelson, Chmn WPB, 11 Dec 43, folder IV.

[40] History of Smaller War Plants Corporation (unpublished monograph, 1945), Pt. III, National Archives. Most of the prime contracts taken by SWPC in World War II are listed in SWPC, Fourteenth Report, p. 27, reproduced in S. Doc. 246, 78th Cong., 2d Sess., 2 Nov 44.

The actual experience of the War Department with some half-dozen prime contracts with SWPC was insufficient to determine the consequences of large-scale use of this instrument. Most of these were taken by SWPC in 1943 when it was under great pressure to make use of the prime contract power and was not fully prepared to do so. New procedures and contract terms had to be developed, suitable subcontractors located, and special arrangements made to obtain controlled materials. Apart from their general lack of sympathy for SWPC prime contracts, Army procurement officials felt that in at least half of the cases the particular procurements selected for the purpose were unfortunate. In one case the Army had already agreed to give the award to SWPC designees so that the exercise of the prime contract power was gratuitous so far as the cause of small business was concerned. In this case, specifications were incomplete and the Army wished to maintain its direct relationship with the contractor in order to supervise work on the project. In another case SWPC took the prime contract in order to pay a premium price to a large corporation whose bid was considered by the Army to be grossly excessive in terms both of cost analysis and comparative bid prices by all other firms, both large and small, involved in the bidding and award. In a third case SWPC spent three months, after certification by WPB, in an attempt to locate suitable subcontractors and obtain material allocations. SWPC finally placed a subcontract covering the entire procurement with a firm which had previously held an Army contract for the same item. On the other hand, while there were various delays in certification and contract placement, the record does not reveal any significant delays in procurement deliveries under SWPC prime contracts once the necessary subcontracts had been let.[41]

The Small War Plants Program in High Gear

By the beginning of 1944 the combined experience of SWPC and the Army, together with successive improvements in organization and procedures, had reached the point where definitive working arrangements could be established to govern the small war plants program for the duration of the war. Early in 1944 former Representative Maury Maverick, a vigorous exponent of small business, was appointed chairman and general manager of SWPC. Mr. Maverick immediately took steps to consolidate the fruits of eighteen months' experience into a written agreement between SWPC and the War Department. On 21 April 1944 such an agreement was signed jointly by Mr. Maverick and Under Secretary Patterson. In addition, during the following months subsidiary agreements with each of the technical services and the Army Air Forces were established, reflecting the variations in circumstances of the several services and the special procedures required in order to insure from each the greatest possible number of awards to small business consistent with the necessities of military procurement.[42]

[41] See above, note 38 (3).

[42] (1) Revised Working Relations Between War Department and SWPC, 21 Apr 44, reproduced as App. A to Twelfth Bimonthly Report of SWPC, in S. Doc. 223, 78th Cong., 2d Sess., 22 Jun 44. (2) Procedural Agreement Between the Air Technical Service Command, AAF, and the Smaller War Plants Corporation, 19 Oct 44 (superseding agreements of 9 Jun 44 and 25 Jul 44. (3) Ltr, Brig Gen Burton O. Lewis, ACofTrans ASF, to Mr. Jesse French, III, Chf Opns Bureau SWPC, 29 Jun 44

The procedural goals of the new agreements were to provide a maximum of decentralization, flexibility, and teamwork in the administration of the small war plants program. To attain these ends virtually all decisions as to selection of suitable items, size of allocations to SWPC, designation of individual firms, and award of contracts to small firms were made at contracting offices in the field. SWPC specialists and Army small war plants officers assigned to technical service headquarters confined their activities largely to policy matters and the general guidance of the program within the technical service concerned. Basic policy matters continued to be handled by the Small War Plants Branch in the Purchases Division, ASF, together with SWPC headquarters in Washington. Full opportunity was granted the SWPC specialist in the headquarters of each technical service to review the Army Supply Program and all procurement directives. When the SWPC specialist indicated an interest in further action by SWPC, this interest was noted on the procurement directive sent to the local contracting office. At each contracting office all procurement directives except for secret and confidential items, regardless of notations at higher echelons of probable SWPC interest, were jointly reviewed by the local SWPC specialist and the contracting officer. A joint decision was then reached as to:

1. Whether a particular procurement was suitable for manufacture by small concerns.

2. The minimum portions of suitable procurements which the contracting office would endeavor to place with SWPC designees.

(countersigned by Jesse French III). Last two in folder II.

3. The number of SWPC designations to be sought, their allocation by SWPC regions, and the deadline for submitting designations to the contracting office.

At least one set of drawings, specifications, and prints for each procurement was to be made available to the SWPC specialist, and as much additional descriptive information as required. In order to maximize the opportunities for small firms, the contracting officer was to make available to the SWPC specialist, for inclusion in the total list of SWPC designations, the name of all small plant sources known to the Army to be suitable for the procurement in question. The SWPC was required to include all such sources in its designations or furnish reasons for any .exclusions. Likewise, all SWPC designees were to be given an opportunity to bid or negotiate, except for exclusions satisfactorily explained by the contracting office. During negotiations the SWPC specialist was to provide the contracting office with all data obtained from the relevant SWPC regional offices concerning the small plants from which bids had been received; this information covered such matters as distress status of the firm in question and any other factors bearing on the suitability of the firm for the particular procurement involved. After negotiations had been completed or final bid prices received, but before choice of contract placement was made, the SWPC specialist was provided with abstracts of all bids and an opportunity to make representations in behalf of concerns designated by SWPC. The actual placement of awards was to be governed by the terms of WPB Directive No. 2, as amplified by War Department Procurement Regulations, stating in order of priority the several criteria of contract placement.[43] Subject to these general criteria, the contracting officer was to make every effort to fill, and if possible exceed, the percentage allotment for SWPC designees. Any disagreement between the SWPC specialist and the contracting officer was to be resolved by the chief of procurement for the contracting office concerned.[44]

The foregoing digest of procedures suggests, in part at least, the painstaking efforts eventually made to insure for small business a fair share of the military procurement program. Every Army contracting office was required to observe these procedures, and each office had its own small war plants officer, as well as its assigned SWPC specialist, to implement the program and represent the interests of small business. Under the various influences at work, the dollar value of Army contract awards to small business flourished beyond all expectations of the sponsors of the small business program.

Statistics of prime contract placement reveal the month-by-month progress of the War Department's small business program from the beginning of formal operating relationships with SWPC until the end of 1945. (*Table 46*) During the twelve-month period from June 1944 through May 1945, Army prime contract awards in excess of $10,000 each to firms with fewer than five hundred wage earners amounted to a total of over $6,546,000,000. This figure was the equivalent of a $65,000 prime contract during the course of the year to each of 100,000 firms. In order to suggest the full effect of Army procurement upon small business during the year in question, there must be added to this total an unknown

---

[43] See above, Chapter XI.
[44] PR 225.

TABLE 46—WAR DEPARTMENT PRIME CONTRACT AWARDS BY SIZE OF FIRM: MONTHLY PLACEMENT OF SUPPLY CONTRACTS IN EXCESS OF $10,000 EACH, NOVEMBER 1943–December 1943

| Period | All Contracts | | Contracts To Firms With Less Than 500 Wage Earners | | | |
| | Number of Contracts | Value in Millions | Number of Contracts | Value in Millions | Percent of All Contracts | |
					Number	Value
Total	576,133	$83,847	356,971	$15,027	62.0	17.9
Total—1942	65,382	$6,576	44,388	$922	67.9	14.0
Nov	38,246	$3,511	26,791	$576	70.0	16.4
Dec	27,136	3,065	17,597	346	64.8	11.3
Total—1943	241,531	$35,329	151,597	$4,448	62.8	12.6
Jan	28,141	$2,977	17,804	$327	63.3	11.0
Feb	25,049	1,643	14,749	349	58.9	21.3
Mar	23,377	2,762	15,387	337	65.8	12.2
Apr	22,132	3,118	14,040	463	63.4	14.8
May	22,660	2,088	15,069	384	66.5	18.4
Jun	27,296	3,171	17,605	419	64.5	13.2
Jul	20,606	4,884	12,638	333	61.3	6.8
Aug	19,483	4,083	12,651	308	64.9	7.6
Sep	14,506	2,651	8,702	396	60.0	14.9
Oct	13,436	3,502	7,914	419	58.9	12.0
Nov	12,798	2,964	7,735	421	60.4	14.2
Dec	12,047	1,486	7,303	292	60.6	19.7
Total—1944	163,114	$24,760	97,161	$4,951	59.6	20.0
Jan	12,702	$1,572	7,668	$292	60.4	18.6
Feb	12,081	2,499	7,116	261	58.9	10.5
Mar	13,762	1,826	8,336	345	60.6	18.9
Apr	14,472	2,328	8,980	418	62.1	18.0
May	16,066	1,785	9,679	421	60.2	23.6
Jun	14,985	3,151	8,849	585	59.1	18.5
Jul	12,028	2,349	7,142	396	59.4	16.9
Aug	15,643	1,843	9,437	437	60.3	23.7
Sep	12,765	1,690	7,275	435	57.0	25.8
Oct	12,735	1,882	7,535	415	59.1	22.0
Nov	12,963	1,837	7,542	429	58.2	23.4
Dec	12,912	1,998	7,602	517	58.9	25.9

TABLE 46—WAR DEPARTMENT PRIME CONTRACT AWARDS BY SIZE OF FIRM: MONTHLY PLACEMENT OF SUPPLY CONTRACTS IN EXCESS OF $10,000 EACH, NOVEMBER 1943– DECEMBER 1943—Continued

Period	All Contracts		Contracts To Firms With Less Than 500 Wage Earners			
	Number of Contracts	Value in Millions	Number of Contracts	Value in Millions	Percent of All Contracts	
					Number	Value
Total—1945_____	106, 106	$17, 182	63, 825	$4, 706	60. 2	27. 4
Jan_____	14, 778	$2, 893	8, 454	$702	57. 2	24. 3
Feb_____	13, 971	2, 548	8, 236	654	59. 0	25. 7
Mar_____	14, 780	2, 567	8, 688	702	58. 8	27. 4
Apr_____	14, 697	2, 504	8, 950	705	60. 9	28. 1
May_____	13, 675	2, 072	8, 442	571	61. 7	27. 6
Jun_____	11, 192	1, 500	6, 786	427	60. 7	28. 5
Jul_____	10, 250	1, 918	6, 227	421	60. 8	22. 0
Aug_____	5, 295	701	3, 180	282	60. 1	40. 2
Sep_____	12, 384	170	1, 505	103	63. 1	60. 4
Oct_____	2, 281	164	1, 501	77	65. 8	46. 9
Nov_____	1, 735	98	1, 138	35	65. 6	35. 7
Dec_____	1, 068	47	718	27	67. 2	57. 4

Source: (1) Smaller War Plants Corp., Bi-Monthly Rpts to Chairman, WPB.   (2) Small War Plants Branch, Purchases Div., ASF, Monthly Rpts to SWPC.

volume of subcontracts under the $21 billion in prime contracts to large firms during the same period, as well as prime contracts and purchase orders under $10,000 each to small suppliers.

Not only did the absolute value of Army awards to small business increase during the latter half of the war. The relative share of small business in total Army procurement also experienced a remarkable increase. For the calendar year 1943—the first full year for which statistics are available—small business received 12.6 percent of the total value of War Department prime contracts. For 1944 the figure rose to 20.0 percent; and for calendar 1945 it jumped to 27.4 percent, more than double the 1943 share.

Additional results of the Army's small business program are revealed by statistics of contract placement by separate categories of small business. These figures indicate that the relative share of Army procurement going to the smallest firms in the small business category (firms with less than 100 wage earners) increased from 3.5 percent for 1943 to 8.6 percent, or two and one-half times its earlier share, for 1945.[45] This was a greater rate of increase than that for small business as a whole, defined as including all firms with up to five hundred wage earners. Further statistics indicate that prime contracts placed with small business by the

[45] Small War Plants Br, Purchases Div ASF, Monthly Rpts to the Smaller War Plants Corporation.

TABLE 47—AWARD OF PRIME CONTRACTS BY SIZE OF FIRM: ANNUAL PLACEMENT OF SUPPLY CONTRACTS IN EXCESS OF $10,000 EACH, BY MAJOR WAR DEPARTMENT AGENCIES, 1943–1945.

Agency	Year	Value of Contracts (In Billions)			Percent		
		Size of Firm			Size of Firm		
		All Firms	500 or More Wage Earners	Under 500 Wage Earners	All Firms	500 or More Wage Earners	Under 500 Wage Earners
War Department—Total_____	1943	$35.3	$30.9	$4.4	100	87.4	12.6
	1944	24.8	19.8	5.0	100	80.0	20.0
	1945	17.2	12.5	4.7	100	72.6	27.4
Army Service Forces_____	1943	18.7	14.7	4.0	100	78.6	21.4
	1944	16.9	12.3	4.6	100	72.9	27.1
	1945	14.8	10.5	4.3	100	71.0	29.0
Army Air Forces_____	1943	16.6	16.2	0.4	100	97.6	2.4
	1944	7.9	7.5	0.4	100	95.0	5.0
	1945	2.4	2.0	0.4	100	83.1	16.9
Quartermaster Corps *_____	1943	3.2	1.6	1.6	100	51.0	49.0
	1944	4.5	2.3	2.2	100	51.0	49.0
	1945	4.5	2.2	2.3	100	48.0	52.0

* Quartermaster Corps figures for 1943 include prime contracts in excess of $1,000; for 1944 and 1945 include all awards in excess of $1,000 with exception of Management and Engineering, Service Utilities, and shelf stocks from retailers and distributors. Percentages rounded as in source.

Source: (1) Small War Plants Br, Purchases Div ASF, Monthly Rpts to SWPC. (2) Yoshpe and Massen, QMC Procurement Policies in World War II, p. 141.

Army Air Forces amounted to less than 10 percent of the value of such contracts placed by the ASF (Table 47). This was an inescapable consequence of the nature of AAF procurement, the bulk of which consisted of huge orders for aircraft and complex items of equipment in general not susceptible of production by small firms except on a subcontract basis. The Quartermaster Corps, on the other hand, because of the relatively simple and commercial nature of most of its procurement items, was able to deal directly with small firms on a wide scale. QMC awards to firms with less than five

hundred wage earners amounted to more than 50 percent by value of all Quartermaster contracts and accounted for nearly 45 percent of total War Department business with small firms.

On the basis of the record as indicated in the preceding pages it would appear that the Army made a reasonable and ultimately a successful effort to insure small business a fair share of war business. It is doubtful that the same results could have been achieved much sooner, given the country's initial state of unpreparedness and the Army's basic mission and responsibility toward the nation as a whole. On the other hand it is also doubtful that the same results would have been achieved either as soon, or at all, in the absence of the specific pressures and measures taken by the Congress of the United States. In any case, many firms which in 1940 were either nonexistent or small by any definition became large-scale enterprises by the end of the war and emerged to take an important and permanent place on the American industrial scene.

PART FIVE

EXPANSION OF FACILITIES FOR THE ARMY

CHAPTER XIX

General Aspects of Facilities Expansion

Prewar Planning and the Crisis of 1940

Historians of America's total military and logistic effort in World War II may well agree that the eighteen months of preparation before Pearl Harbor played a crucial if not a decisive part in the outcome of the war. During this period the Military Establishment of the United States was rehabilitated and the foundation laid for America's tremendous war production achievement. The greatest barrier to military preparedness at the time of the crisis of 1940 was the lack of capital facilities, and these required from several months to two years or even longer to create. To have delayed the construction of such facilities until the United States was actually involved in battle might have lost the war before it began.

The facilities problem faced by the War Department in the summer of 1940 was twofold. In order to expand, train, and support its ground and air armies, the War Department had to construct a countless number of receiving stations, camps, and cantonments, airfields, air bases, all their accessories, training and maneuvering areas, general storage and ammunition depots, staging and embarkation facilities, and a host of other establishments too numerous to mention. Facilities of this nature, designed for use in the actual maintenance and operation of the Army, rather than for purposes of procurement, were known as *command* facilities.

An equally important but vastly more complex problem facing the War Department was the development, in co-operation with industry and the central mobilization control agencies, of *industrial* facilities for producing munitions of war unprecedented in quantity and complexity. In the spring of 1940 the United States possessed a tremendous industrial potential: it had an abundance of raw materials, a large reserve of unemployed manpower, and the best assemblage of general industrial equipment and technical skills of any country in the world. Yet it lacked the specific equipment for turning out munitions of war.

The desperate and potentially tragic situation facing the United States in mid-1940 was understood by only a few. Speaking early in 1943, when the ultimate victory of the United States began to be safely predictable, Secretary of War Stimson disclosed our vulnerability at the beginning of the defense period: "We didn't have enough powder in the whole United States to last the men we now have overseas for anything like a day's fighting. And, what is worse, we didn't have powder plants or facilities to make it; they had all been destroyed after the last war." [1] The situation

---

[1] Henry L. Stimson, "America is Ready," *Army Ordnance Magazine*, XXIV, No. 137 (March–April 1943), 275.

in powder was duplicated throughout the whole category of munitions. There were not enough semiautomatic rifles in existence to equip even the skeleton Army of 1940, and existing facilities were capable of producing only two hundred per day; at this rate it would have taken more than fifty years to fill the requirements of World War II. As for major items, such as tanks, guns, and completed ammunition, specific plant capacity was virtually nonexistent. When viewed in the light of all the Army's other direct procurement requirements, and its manifold indirect requirements for raw and fabricated materials, commercial parts and supplies, components and subassemblies—to say nothing of Navy, Maritime, and other war requirements—these shortages of productive capacity indicated that nothing less than an industrial revolution would suffice to produce the needed output. The magnitude of the industrial revolution which was required, and which was actually to take place within the next three years, was only dimly perceived in the summer of 1940.

In the two decades after World War I, Army planning to meet wartime facility needs was an integral part of general mobilization planning. Requirements for both command and industrial facilities in time of emergency or war would be derived from the scale and phasing of troop mobilization, training, and deployment under the basic mobilization plans. The General Staff was responsible for determining the basic mobilization plan, and all Army agencies were responsible for computing their facility requirements under the basic plan. These requirements were screened and approved by OASW or the General Staff. New construction would be required to make up the difference between total facility requirements and the quantity of facilities already available.

The general plans and procedures for obtaining construction of new facilities of all types were announced and kept current by the Construction Division, Planning Branch, OASW, as part of the Industrial Mobilization Plan. In the late 1930's, OASW planning divided all War Department construction into three types: A, B, and C. Type A comprised all command construction, responsibility for which was divided between The Quartermaster General and corps area commanders throughout the United States. Corps area commanders were each required to establish a construction organization which would "make contact with capable contractors, negotiate contracts, inspect operations, and make payment for all construction required for mobilization of Corps Area Commands." The Construction Section, OQMG, would be similarly responsible for all remaining Type A, as well as for all Type B, construction.[2]

Type B, "supply arm and service construction," included all munitions plants which would, because of their specialized nature, have to be built and owned by the War Department. Among these were Ordnance and Chemical Warfare arsenals, powder plants, ammunition loading plants, facilities for producing heavy artillery, and the like. The detailed planning and sponsorship of these plants was the responsibility of the appropriate supply arm or service, subject to the approval of OASW. As in the case of command construction, these projects would be actually constructed by pri-

---

[2] War Construction Plan of the Construction Division, OASW, p. 7. A copy of this document, made 8 December 1937 by the Army Industrial College, is on file in the ICAF Library.

vate firms, under contract with the War Department. Construction would be supervised by OQMG and—depending on their type—the completed plants would be operated either by War Department officers and employees or by private managers as GOCO facilities.

Type C, "construction by an industrial facility," represented manufacturing plant and equipment to be constructed or installed by War Department prime contractors as needed for the completion of their regular supply contracts. Supply contracts would be of either the fixed-price or evaluated-fee variety, and contractors would make their own arrangements for facility expansion. Under fixed-price contracts the contractor would initially finance the necessary plant expansion but would be reimbursed over the life of a supply contract by the inclusion of plant amortization costs in the prices of the end products. In the event of early contract termination, the War Department would make equitable compensation to the contractor for any unamortized plant costs. As in ordinary business practice, facilities acquired under fixed-price contracts would be retained as the private property of the contractor. Evaluated-fee supply contracts required the War Department to defray the specific costs of all facilities essential to the completion of the contracts. These facilities would become government property and their construction was subject to governmental inspection, time keeping, and cost accounting procedure. Each supply arm or service would be responsible for the planning and supervision of its Type C facilities, which would be tied in with factory plans and accepted schedules of production under the allocated-facilities program envisaged by the Industrial Mobiliaztion Plan. Approval

of OASW was required for all projects costing over five thousand dollars.[3]

The procedures actually used during World War II to provide the necessary facility expansion departed substantially from the prewar plans. Nevertheless, these plans furnished the starting point for operations as well as the basis for analysis and policy formation by the National Defense Advisory Commission when it was created in 1940 to supervise the economic mobilization program. The evaluated-fee contract became the cost-plus-a-fixed-fee contract, legalized by statute on 2 July 1940. As already indicated, the CPFF feature was widely used in contracts for the construction of both command and industrial facilities.[4] It was also used in Defense Plant Corporation construction contracts in behalf of the War Department, as well as in supply contracts for governing the management of War department GOCO facilities. The biggest departure from the plans of the interwar period occurred in connection with private industrial expansion originally classified as Type C. The complexities attending the expansion of this class of facilities for World War II are recounted hereafter.[5]

The prewar plans for new construction were intended to cover all needed industrial expansion, whether in conformity with or in addition to existing facility allocation plans. In view of the impossibility of determining, for a unknown future war, the total eventual requirements for either command or industrial facilities, the War Department

---

[3] (1) OASW Planning Br Cir 3, 15 Oct 36 (draft copy), supplementing Cir 3, 28 Jan 35, sub: Emergency Construction. (2) War Construction Plan of the Construction Division, OASW, especially pp. 14–17.

[4] See above, Chapter XII.

[5] See below, Chapter XX.

adopted general plans for obtaining its needed facilities as rapidly as possible when specific goals could be formulated. These plans included the adoption and steady improvement of types and specifications for camps, cantonments, arsenals, proving grounds, munitions plants, and other facilities; the advance preparation of the construction industry to meet the problems of wartime construction; the establishment of commodity committees and plans for the procurement and conservation of construction materials in time of shortage; and studies and recommendations to meet many other facets of the wartime facilities problem.

As the War Department and the NDAC came to grips with the actual implementation of the plant expansion program in the summer of 1940 they were beset by many difficulties. The hypotheses and options of the planning period now had to be replaced by definite answers to specific questions. How much new plant capacity should be created? What products and what industries required such expansion? What firms should receive contracts to build plants and what firms should operate them? Where should the new plants be built? What contract terms would be adequate to stimulate defense construction and still protect the public interest? How could undersirable postwar effects upon the economy as well as postwar charges of graft and incompetence be avoided? What new legislation was needed to implement the program? How large a staff and what kind of organization would be needed in the War Department and other agencies to administer the program? Where could people with the necessary drive and know-how be found? Each of these questions and many more ramified into a thousand

subsidiary questions, each of which in turn required serious attention. Above all was the compelling necessity for speed. Hitler would not wait for these questions to be answered with precision and unimpeachable accuracy.

Many of the methods used by the government in solving these problems were unorthodox. Their conception and development required a combination of boldness and patient persistence on the part of those who planned and engineered the program. Numerous barriers of a political, economic, and legal nature had to be removed or surmounted at every stage in the undertaking. It was soon found that private capital was unable to finance the expansion on the scale and with the speed originally hoped and planned. The government thus had to assume financial responsibility as well as general leadership for the undertaking. The ultimate success of the program is attested by the tremendous volume of munitions production achieved by the end of 1943 and by the fact that war plant expansion in the three years ending with 1943 was equal to half the investment in manufacturing facilities during the preceding two decades.

As the defense program developed, four major classes of industrial expansion emerged, based upon the methods of financing used: (1) private financing with the aid of tax amortization; (2) government reimbursement of private capital outlays (the Emergency Plant Facilities (EPF) contract); (3) government ownership with private purchase option (Defense Plant Corporation financing); and (4) outright government ownership. The War Department performed a major role in the development and administration of each of these.

Land Acquisition by the War Department

In order to carry out its vast expansion of both command and industrial facilities, the War Department had to acquire unprecedented quantities of land. On 30 June 1940, total land holdings of the War Department amounted to 2,116,862 acres. By 1946 it had acquired nearly 44 million additional, for a total of 45,870,901 acres.[6] This aggregate of nearly 72,000 square miles was seven times the holdings of the Navy Department and greater than the combined areas of all six New England states. Most of the increase represented temporary acquisitions for the duration of the emergency—transfers by the President from the public domain and other federal agencies and leases from individuals and state and local governments. Nevertheless, outright purchases by the War Department amounted to 5,728,-876 acres, an area substantially larger than the state of Massachusetts. This land cost the War Department approximately $360,-000,000. In addition, annual rents paid for leased lands averaged some $50 million from the beginning of 1943 to the end of the war.[7]

Approximately 47 percent of the War Department's land holdings was devoted to military camps and stations, 25 percent to bombing and artillery ranges, 17 percent to ordnance plants and storage facilities, and the remainder to airfield, urban, and miscellaneous uses.[8] Army airfields typically required 160 acres for auxiliary landing fields and up to 2,500 or more acres for main fields containing facilities and personnel complements. Ordnance plants and storage areas usually ran from 5,000 to 20,000 acres; army camps and artillery ranges from 25,000 to 100,000 acres; and large maneuvering areas for both Ground and Air Forces far in excess of 100,000 acres.

The largest individual sites—running to more than 1,000,000 acres apiece—were acquired for aerial bombing and gunnery ranges. The Alamogordo (New Mexico) Army Air Base contained 1,262,000 acres; the Yuma (Arizona) AAF General Bombing Range, 1,603,000; and Wendover Field, Utah, 1,836,000 acres. The most gigantic of all—the Central Nevada AAF Bombing and Gunnery Range based at Tonopah, Nevada—embraced 3,313,000 acres, an area of over 5,000 square miles or more than four times the size of the state of Rhode Island. The three largest facilities of the Ground Forces were the Fort Bliss, New Mexico, antiaircraft firing range; Camp Irwin at Barstow, California; and the Desert Training Center, Indio, California. These contained 436,000, 639,000, and 781,000 acres, respectively.[9]

Although the probable difficulties of land acquisition played a part in the final selection of particular sites, they were usually not controlling, and the real work of acquisition began after sites had been determined.[10]

---

[6] U.S. Department of Agriculture, Bureau of Agricultural Economics, Acquisition and Use of Land for Military and War Production Purposes, World War II (War Records Monograph 5, August 1947), p. 5, Table 1. Much of the following discussion is based on this monograph, which in turn drew heavily from unpublished monographs of the War Department.

[7] Compiled from: (1) War Department, Quarterly Inventory of Owned, Sponsored, and Leased Facilities, 30 Jun 45; (2) Control Division, ASF, Statistical Review, World War II [1946], p. 88.

[8] U.S. Dept of Agriculture, Acquisition and Use of Land, pp. 4–5.

[9] WD, Quarterly Inventory of Owned, Sponsored, and Leased Facilities, 30 Jun 45.

[10] The problems involved in selecting sites for War Department facilities are discussed in detail elsewhere. See chapter on Site Selection in Remington and Fine, The Corps of Engineers: Military Construction in the United States.

At the beginning of the emergency the War Department contracted with private real estate brokers to make appraisals, conduct negotiations, obtain options, gain title clearance, and effect final settlement. This arrangement proved unsatisfactory and was subject to criticism in later investigations; the payment of normal commissions for transactions in which both buyer and seller had already been determined, the tendency of land prices to become inflated under what amounted to the discredited cost-plus-a-percentage-of-cost contracting procedure, and some of the methods used by brokers, all came under fire.[11]

Late in 1940, the War Department arranged to use the staffs of the Soil Conservation Service and the Forest Service on a reimbursable basis. This gave the War Department the benefit of a decentralized organization as well as experienced personnel. Finally, in May 1941, the War Department established its own Real Estate Branch in the Construction Division, OQMG, which later became the Construction Division, Corps of Engineers. Standard policies and procedures were adopted and disseminated by Washington headquarters: the actual process of acquisition was performed in the field in order to minimize duplication and waste of effort.[12]

The emergency acquisition of land was accompanied by hardship and confusion not ordinarily experienced in peacetime. Although the War Department utilized marginal cropland and wasteland wherever

feasible, much of its land requirements—especially for ordnance plants and airfields—was necessarily valuable farmland close to established towns and cities. Because of the urgency many areas had to be cleared and evacuated without delay. Owners, tenants, and temporary sharecroppers alike were suddenly required to vacate, often without prospect of a new location. The poorer individuals and families were frequently without sufficient funds to defray moving or storage expenses for themselves, their livestock and other belongings. Long established owners, elderly people, and others with unique property interests often suffered more from the loss of sentimental attachments and the frustrations of forced removal than from actual pecuniary damage. Farmers typically experienced the loss of a year's crop because of the inevitable time lag between notice of evacuation and final relocation. Since land for military establishments usually had to be acquired *en bloc*, retention by former occupants of particularly valuable or desirable tracts within the sites was impracticable.

The dislocations resulting from land acquisitions were not confined to individuals. Established communities were often dismembered, and occasionally entirely obliterated. Community facilities such as schools, roads, power lines, general utilities and even cemeteries were either lost or relocated. Not infrequently occupants of adjacent areas voluntarily chose to move rather than remain under the changed conditions. Local governmental taxing units—counties, townships, school districts, and the like—were faced with the disappearance of sizable portions of their tax base as buildings were moved or destroyed and title to the land transferred to the nontaxpaying federal government. This was particularly em-

---

[11] (1) H Com. on Military Affairs, 77 Cong., 1st Sess., *Hearings on Inquiry as to National Defense Construction*, April 1941. (2) Truman Committee, *Hearings*, 1:55ff.

[12] For greater detail, see Narrative Outline and Source Material for Historical Monograph of the War Department Real Estate Program [circa 1948] in Engineer Historical Div, OCofEngrs.

barrassing where local expenditures were not reduced by the evacuation, as in the case of outstanding bond issues and other fixed costs.[13]

Within the framework of its statutory powers the War Department developed a number of measures to reduce the hardships created by its land acquisition program. Unlike the Navy, whose land requirements were smaller and more highly specialized, the War Department attempted to obtain its privately purchased land by direct negotiation rather than by general condemnation proceedings. Wherever time permitted, extensive preparations and careful appraisals were made prior to negotiation. Appraisers' estimates were based on a composite of cost, capitalized income value, and comparative sale price of similar properties. In cases where negotiation failed to obtain

---

[13] An unpublished study by the Army Engineers gives an indication of the degree of loss in the tax base for counties, townships, and school districts resulting from War Department land acquisition. A survey of sixteen command facilities (forts and camps) indicated an average loss in assessed valuation of 1.0 percent for entire counties, 3.3 percent for townships, and 13.2 percent for school districts. The respective figures for the project causing the highest loss were 21.6 percent, 87.5 percent and 100 percent. For ordnance plants (fifteen projects) the average loss for townships and school districts was substantially higher:

	Percentage		
	Counties	Townships	School Districts
Average	0.6	10.2	18.6
Highest	17.6	69.8	100.0

It is apparent that individual townships, and especially school districts, experienced a crippling reduction in their sources of income. See study reproduced in U.S. Dept of Agriculture, Acquisition and Use of Land, p. 63, Table 8.

settlement or where immediate use of the land was necessary, the condemnation procedure was used and final settlement prices were decided by the courts.

The War Department avoided acquisition of private lands wherever possible, preferring to take advantage of public land made available by other federal agencies. Early in the program, at the request of land owners, it shifted from a policy of leasing to outright purchase of private land for camps and ordnance plants. Rental income ordinarily was too small to be of much help in relocation of displaced persons and the impracticality of postponing permanent relocation was soon realized as the emergency deepened. Tenant farmers were compensated for the loss of their lease-hold interest, which consisted for the most part of the loss of crops already seeded.

A feature of the land program which became of increasing importance by the end of the war was the War Department policy of outleasing land for agricultural purposes when such use did not interfere with military purposes. The chief source of such land use was the abundant acreage of top-grade farm land in the extended safety belts surrounding ordnance manufacturing and storage establishments. One such establishment—the Wabash River Ordnance Works in Vermillion County, Indiana—in 1945 succeeded in outleasing 16,009 of its total of 21,960 acres for rentals amounting to $97,589. During the previous year, when total acreage outleased was 14,506, the estimated crop production on this site was as follows: corn, 269,700 bushels; soybeans, 58,120 bushels; oats and wheat, 44,850 bushels; hay, 23 tons; grazing of 400 animal-units for six months. By 1946, nearly a million and a quarter acres in forty-two states were outleased by the War Department for agricultural and grazing purposes.[14]

The major burden of resolving the problems created by War Department land acquisitions fell to other agencies. Local governmental units, county agricultural agents, and, in urgent cases, the Red Cross did much to relieve the immediate problems of enforced migration. The Farm Security Administration and the Federal Public Housing Authority sponsored and financed emergency housing projects. Under the Lanham Act, the Federal Works Agency spent nearly $500 million in aid of local taxing units for schools, hospitals, water and sewers, recreation, and related community facilities. These expenditures in many instances afforded substantial compensation for loss of revenue to local tax units caused by War Department withdrawals of land.[15]

War Department Command Facilities

A brief review of the War Department's achievement in the provision of command facilities for the Army in World War II is essential to an understanding of the total task of economic mobilization. Command construction competed with the construction of industrial facilities—as well as with the procurement of finished munitions—for scarce materials, equipment, manpower, and managerial know-how. At all stages of their development—from planning through contract negotiation and administration to project completion—command installations presented numerous problems common to industrial facility expansion and end-item procurement. Army officials responsible for the development of command facilities were faced with a multiplicity of duties with respect to site selection and project approval, contract placement and clearance, land acquisition, priorities and other material controls, pricing and renegotiation, and ultimately demobilization and property disposition.

Some idea of the scope of the Army's far-flung empire of command installations in World War II may be inferred from the following partial list of establishments within the zone of interior alone: Army posts, camps, stations, forts, training and maneuvering areas, artillery and other ranges for for the Ground Forces; airfields, air bases and stations, bombing and gunnery ranges for the Army Air Forces; storage facilities—from remote ammunition depots to metropolitan warehouses—for all branches of the Army; repair and maintenance stations for all types of equipment; hospitals, convalescent and recreation centers; military police camps, Japanese relocation centers, prisoner of war camps; a network of harbor defenses and other installations throughout the entire country for defense against enemy attack; holding and reconsignment centers, ports of embarkation, staging areas, and related facilities to mount the tremendous overseas expeditions of troops and supplies; local induction centers, radio stations, laundries, market centers, special schools and offices (including the $78 million Pentagon building); and, not to be overlooked, research laboratories, proving grounds, testing centers, and supersecret installations symbolized most completely by the atomic bomb.

The command facilities most urgently needed by the War Department at the beginning of the mobilization period were camps and cantonments to accommodate the expanding Army. The increase in the authorized strength of the Army from

---

[14] *Ibid.,* pp. 81, 115.
[15] *Ibid,* p. 65.

THE PENTAGON, WASHINGTON, D. C.   *Picture taken in 1949.   Note complex network of roadways surrounding Pentagon.   Visible in upper portion of photograph is part of South Post area, Fort Myer, Virginia.*

174,000 to 375,000 during the fiscal year ending 30 June 1940 represented a major expansion in terms of the skeleton status of the Army for almost two previous decades. But this was miniscule when compared with the sudden upsurge made possible by the passage of the Selective Service Act on 16 September 1940. This legislation authorized the expansion of the Army to a total of 1,400,000, consisting of 630,000 selectees, 500,000 Regular Army, and 270,000 National Guard. Unfortunately, until the actual passage of the Selective Service Act, the Army did not possess either the funds or the authority for the wholesale camp construction program needed to accommo-

date the new recruits. Construction, which ideally should have been undertaken on a large scale throughout the summer, was delayed until bad weather contributed heavily to increased costs as well as soldier discomfort.[16]

At the beginning of the defense period the responsibility for constructing command facilities was lodged in the Construction Division of the Quartermaster Corps. The division's peacetime organization, designed largely for the maintenance and

---

[16] *Biennial Report of the Chief of Staff of the United States Army, 1 July 1939 to 30 June 1941, to the Secretary of War* (Washington 1941), pp. 1–8.

servicing of existing Army posts, was inadequate to the task suddenly thrust upon it.
By heroic efforts, coupled with rapid expansion and successive reorganizations, The
Quartermaster General's construction
agency had made an impressive record in
the creation of both command and industrial facilities by the end of 1941.[17]

The Army's construction organization
and activities were gradually transferred to
the Corps of Engineers. The Engineers had
long been responsible for overseas construction, as well as for river and harbor work
with the United States. In November 1940,
construction of Army air bases and other
Air Corps projects was transferred from
The Quartermaster General to the Chief of
Engineers. In December 1941 all remaining
construction activity was transferred to the
Engineers, freeing the Quartermaster Corps
for its numerous procurement and other ac-

tivities which had grown to unprecedented
magnitudes.[18]

The Army's Construction Division, under both The Quartermaster General and
the Chief of Engineers, had the responsibility for letting and supervising contracts
for private construction firms who performed the actual work. The contractual
arrangements for large projects typically
involved an architect-engineer contract and
a construction contract with separate firms.
The architect-engineer contract called for
the furnishing of all plans and engineering
drawings as well as for day-to-day supervision of the construction contractor to insure
that actual construction fulfilled the specifications. The construction contract was
either a fixed-price or CPFF agreement,
both of which permitted and relied upon
extensive subcontracting.[19]

The camps provided by the Army for
World War II were vastly superior to those
of World War I. Heating, plumbing, lighting, recreational, and other facilities were
more elaborate, more costly, and of more
enduring construction. The large size of
individual establishments, the great number of projects simultaneously under construction, and the pressure of urgent deadlines posed complex administrative problems, strained capacity to the limit, and
added heavily to costs. In rapid succession,
sites had to be selected, land condemned
and cleared, areas evacuated, access roads

---

[17] See observations of the Truman Committee in
S. Rpt. 480, Pt. 2, 77th Cong., 1st Sess., 14 Aug
41, Camp and Cantonment Investigation, p. 34.
Also War Department, OQMG, Construction Division, Report on the Activities of the Construction
Division, July 1, 1940 to November 1, 1941. The
accomplishments of the QMC Construction Division during this period owed much to the energy
and organizing genius of its chief, Colonel Somervell, who in less than a year and a half rose to the
position of Lieutenant General in command of the
Army Services Forces. Substantial insight into General Somervell's qualities as a leader is afforded
by the eight-page Plan of Organization of the Construction Division, OQMG, accompanying OQMG
Construction Div Ltr 361, 22 Jul 41. Part VII of
this document, The Functioning of an Organization, is a forceful exposition of the psychological
and spiritual elements essential to the successful
operation of any organization. For an informative
summary of the War Department's construction
problems and activities during the defense period,
see WD OQMG, Construction Div, Report on the
Activities of the Construction Division, July 1,
1940 to November, 1941. This document contains
nearly 300 pages of text, statistical tables, and
other material.

[18] (1) 54 Stat. 875, 9 Sep 40. (2) AG Memo for
CofEngrs, 20 Nov 40, sub: Air Field Construction. (3) 55 Stat. 787, 1 Dec 41. (4) Ltr, TAG
to TQMG, 3 Dec 41, sub: Transfer of Construction Activities from the QMC to CofEngrs, AG
600.12 (11–10–41) MO–D.

[19] See above, pages 283–88; also copy of the voluminous construction contract for Fort Bragg, at
Fayetteville, North Carolina, reproduced in Truman Committee, *Hearings*, 6: 1889–1912.

and spur tracks built, drainage and other utilities installed, and building construction expedited. The Army's problem was complicated by local shortages of established architect-engineers, construction firms, materials, and skilled labor. At every stage in the program numerous pressures were brought to bear to locate camps at sites favorable to special interests, to employ or purchase material from certain concerns, and to favor particular labor organizations. Intangible but important barriers of legislative and governmental administrative practice at local, state, and national levels had to be overcome.[20]

Total command construction for the Army in World War II, including overseas construction, exceeded in dollar value the construction of all War Department owned, sponsored, and leased industrial facilities.[21] As of 30 June 1945 the War Department had spent some $7.2 billion for command installations within the zone of interior. Estimated expenditures for overseas construction amounted to approximately $1.8 billion. Against this total of $9 billion, comparative expenditures for industrial facilities (War Department-owned plus War Department-sponsored DPC and EPF facilities) were only $8 billion, comprising $7 billion for complete establish-

ments and an additional $1 billion for government-furnished equipment to privately owned plants.[22] The achievements of the War Department in providing command facilities for the World War II effort are indicated in part by the statistical record (*Tables 48 and 49*).

Facility Clearance Procedures

The problem of central co-ordination and control over the expansion of facilities was one which seriously concerned the War Department as well as the central mobilization control agencies. The War Department's primary interest and responsibility was to insure the creation of sufficient facilities of both the command and industrial variety to enable it to fulfill its basic mission. The central mobilization control agencies, from the NDAC to the War Production Board, felt keenly their responsibility for controlling the expansion program in such a way as to satisfy a number of broad economic and social objectives. These objectives were in many respects similar to those underlying the criteria for clearance of regular procurement contracts. They included wide geographical dispersion of new facilities, avoidance of tight labor areas, prevention of duplication and overexpansion, and conservation of materials and other resources by limiting both the type and volume of expansions. The control procedures established to attain these objectives often conflicted with the requirements of rapid prosecution of the defense and war program,

---

[20] For a detailed treatment of Army construction in World War II, see the several volumes under preparation by the Corps of Engineers for the series UNITED STATES ARMY IN WORLD WAR II, especially Remington and Fine, The Corps of Engineers: Military Construction in the United States.

[21] War Department "sponsored" facilities as the term was applied in World War II, include EPF and DPC facilities but not private expansions under War Department-approved certificates of necessity.

[22] (1) WD, Quarterly Inventory of Owned, Sponsored, and Leased Facilities, 30 Jun 45. (2) Control Div, ASF, Statistical Review, World War II.

TABLE 48—WAR DEPARTMENT COMMAND FACILITIES: SUMMARY BY MAJOR TYPES

[Cost and Acres in Thousands]

Type	Number of Installations	Investment Cost (1 July 1940—30 September 1945)			Acres of Land		
		Total	Land	Construction	Total	Owned	Leased
Total	2,996	$7,295,558	$279,110	$7,016,448	29,103	24,368	4,735
Air Forces Tactical and Training	948	$2,008,211	$39,448	$1,968,763	18,170	15,500	2,670
Air Forces Storage	130	473,055	10,817	462,238	91	71	20
Air Forces Miscellaneous	437	510,341	11,449	498,892	1,438	569	869
Ground and Service Forces Training	231	2,262,580	110,325	2,152,255	8,136	7,287	849
Service Forces Storage	210	905,083	36,338	868,745	474	460	14
Ground and Service Forces Miscellaneous	259	214,846	16,736	198,110	552	320	232
Ports of Embarkation and Staging Areas	137	449,357	28,947	420,410	77	59	18
Prisoner of War Camps	166	100,186	884	99,302	80	29	51
Harbor Defenses	297	126,598	11,997	114,601	63	54	9
General Hospitals	67	244,531	11,399	233,132	20	17	3
National Cemeteries	114	770	770	0	2	2	0

Source: WD, Quarterly Inventory of Owned, Sponsored and Leased Facilities, 30 Sep 45.

thus giving rise to considerable controversy among all concerned.[23]

Because of the strictly military and often confidential nature of the War Department's command facilities, relatively little external control was exercised over their creation. The chief controls in this area were effected through material control systems and joint agreements to pare all types of construction to the bone.[24]

Industrial facility expansions, on the other hand, involved not only the broad social and economic considerations mentioned above, but intimately related questions of financing, competition among private firms, and the extent of control by military agen-

[23] For a more detailed study of facility clearance problems and procedures, especially from the standpoint of the central mobilization control agencies, see: (1) Reginald C. McGrane, The Facilities and Construction Program of the War Production Board and Predecessor Agencies, May 1940 to May 1945, (CPA, Historical Reports on War Administration, Special Study 19, 5 April 1946); (2) CPA Industrial Mobilization for War, pp. 77–81, 160–63, 385–409, 652–59; (3) Industrial College of the Armed Forces R83, Construction of New Facilities (January 1947), ICAF Library.

[24] (1) Jt Dir of the WPB and the War and Navy Depts on Wartime Construction, 20 May 42. (2) Dir, TAG to CG AAF, CGs All Depts and Corps Areas, Chfs of All Technical Services, and COs of Exempted Stations, 1 Jun 42, sub: Directive for War-Time Construction. McGrane, Facilities and Construction Program, discussion at pp. 82–83. For War Department internal procedures for programing and control of command construction, see historical monograph, Staff Supervision of the Construction Program (1946), prepared by Command Installation Branch Mobilization Division, ASF.

TABLE 49—WAR DEPARTMENT COMMAND FACILITIES: COST OF 50 LARGEST INSTALLATIONS
(1 JULY 1940–30 SEPTEMBER 1945)

Rank	Name and State	Cost	Rank	Name and State	Cost
1	Pentagon Building_____ Va_____	$78,078,747	26	Camp Claiborne_____ La_____	$37,347,356
2	Camp Hood_____ Tex____	75,964,727	27	Camp Breckinridge____ Ky____	36,598,300
3	Fort Bragg_____ N. C___	55,806,759	28	Camp Gruber_____ Okla___	36,516,099
4	Fort Dix_____ N. J____	54,492,709	29	Rome Army Airfield___ N. Y___	36,487,794
5	Fort Knox_____ Ky____	49,777,239	30	Camp Chaffee_____ Ark____	35,571,611
6	Fort Leonard Wood____ Mo____	49,548,046	31	Tinker Army Airfield___ Okla___	35,395,297
7	Wright Field_____ Ohio___	48,817,078	32	Camp Bowie_____ Tex____	35,311,726
8	Camp Campbell_____ Ky____	48,519,157	33	Camp Beale_____ Calif___	35,262,618
9	Aberdeen Proving Ground_____ Md____	46,268,923	34	Camp Davis_____ N. C___	35,121,515
10	Camp Shanks_____ N. Y___	45,527,425	35	Fort Devens_____ Mass__	34,630,190
11	Camp Polk_____ La_____	44,131,553	36	Letterkenny Ordnance Depot_____ Pa_____	34,200,436
12	Camp Crowder_____ Mo____	43,977,242	37	Robins Field_____ Ga____	33,667,975
13	Camp Atterbury_____ Ind____	42,761,402	38	Camp McCoy_____ Wis____	33,471,634
14	Camp Blanding_____ Fla____	42,526,095	39	San Francisco Port of Embarkation_____ Calif___	32,829,582
15	Camp Carson_____ Colo___	42,000,612	40	Camp Livingston_____ La_____	32,674,266
16	Susquehanna Ordnance Depot_____ Pa_____	41,920,312	41	Camp Gordon_____ Ga_____	32,224,098
17	Camp Lee_____ Va_____	41,387,736	42	Tooele Ordnance Depot_ Utah___	31,095,436
18	Camp Butner_____ N. C___	40,931,550	43	Fort Jackson_____ S. C___	31,077,753
19	Camp Pickett_____ Va_____	40,824,169	44	Camp Cooke_____ Calif___	30,696,246
20	Fort Benning_____ Ga____	40,312,170	45	Camp White_____ Oreg___	30,529,045
21	Camp Kilmer_____ N. J___	38,941,407	46	Fort George Meade____ Md____	30,511,688
22	Camp Edwards_____ Mass__	38,782,403	47	Camp Hale_____ Colo___	30,500,371
23	Kelly Field_____ Tex____	38,066,892	48	Navajo Ordnance Depot_ Ariz___	30,271,446
24	Red River Ordnance Depot_____ Tex____	37,830,070	49	Sioux Ordnance Depot__ Nebr___	30,210,337
25	Camp Shelby_____ Miss___	37,811,141	50	McClellan Field_____ Calif___	29,837,271

Source: WD Quarterly Inventory of Owned, Sponsored and Leased Facilities, 30 Sep 45.

cies over the development of the economy. For all these reasons, Congress in establishing the first War Department Expediting Funds for the creation of munitions plant capacity, had made their expenditure subject to the recommendations of the NDAC and the approval of the President.[25]

Pending the adoption of the Munitions Program of 30 June 1940, Assistant Secretary of War Johnson appointed a committee to prepare and submit a general program of industrial facilities expansion. On 24 June this committee submitted recommendations for the creation of new facilities aggregating nearly one and a half billion dollars:

Total_____	$1,383,050,000

Air Corps_____	415,000,000
Ordnance Department_____	949,915,000
Chemical Warfare Service_____	6,890,000
Quartermaster Corps_____	11,245,000

[25] 54 Stat. 602–03, 26 Jun 40.

These recommendations, based upon earlier War Department studies as well as current proposals of the relevant supply arms, indicated the types of plant to be constructed, without specifying locations.[26]

On the following day Mr. Johnson, by then the Acting Secretary of War, designated a six-man committee of officers—eventually known as the Site Location Board—to make recommendations for the general location of the plants to be constructed under the foregoing program. The Secretary stated a number of factors to be considered. These included the strategic grouping of related manufacturing facilities into self-sufficient areas (in order to minimize the effect of the loss of one or more areas), the prevention and avoidance of congested areas, and the availability of productive resources and transportation.[27] After submitting its initial general report, the new Site Location Board remained in existence as the War Department agency for the screening of major facility proposals of the various supply arms. Procedures were informal and the recommendations of the board had to receive the approval of the Assistant Secretary, the NDAC, and the President before specific projects could be undertaken.[28]

During the life of the NDAC, the War Department's new facility proposals were approved by the commission as a whole in regular meeting. The unwieldiness of the NDAC, composed of seven commissioners of co-ordinate authority but operating in separate fields, was nowhere more apparent than in the clearance of facility proposals. Projects which had been screened and approved by the staff of the commissioner for production would be presented for clearance at the full meeting of the commission, only to receive the objection that the commissioner for labor, or for transportation, or for consumer protection had an interest in the projects but had not previously seen the proposals. In view of the urgency, most of the objections were waived and eventually a procedure was established under which the co-ordinator for purchases was responsible for processing proposals through all interested commissioners.[29]

With the replacement of NDAC by OPM it became apparent that more systematic procedures for facility clearance were necessary. At an early meeting of the OPM council, Mr. Knudsen indicated that he was satisfied with the War Department's control over its Ordnance expansion projects, but there appeared to be some question over the control of Air Corps expansions. Together with recognition within OUSW of the need for tighter controls, this led to the establishment on 13 March 1941 of a new War Department Facilities Board.[30] This was

---

[26] (1) Memo, Col Harry K. Rutherford, Chmn, *et al.*, for ASW, 24 Jun 40, sub: Proposed War Department Program for Increasing Productive Capacity for Munitions. (2) Memo, Col James H. Burns, EX OASW, for ASW, 11 Jul 40, sub: Procedure on Munitions Plant Construction Program, the Awarding of Contracts and Supervision of Performance Thereunder, approved same date by ASW and distributed to supply arms, NDAC, *et al.*

[27] Ltr Orders, Louis Johnson, Actg SW, 25 Jun 40, in Office Chief of Ordnance, War Department Policy Concerning Sites for New Ordnance Depots (hereafter cited as OCofOrd, Policy re Sites), Exhibit 33.

[28] (1) Memo, Col Rutherford, Chmn, *et al.*, for ASW, 8 Jul 40, sub: Locations for Plants in War

Department Program for New Productive Capacity for Munitions. (2) Procedure in Selecting Contractors and Placing Contracts for Government Construction, in Brig Gen John W. N. Schulz, Dir of Purchases and Contracts, OUSW, 30 Jun 41, Report of the P&C Branch for FY 1941.

[29] CPA, *NDAC Minutes,* pp. 21, 22–23, 29, 34–35, 38–39, 55–56, and *passim.*

[30] (1) CPA, *OPM Minutes,* p. 2. (2) ICAF R83, Construction of New Facilities, p. 19.

followed by directives to all the supply arms specifying in detail new War Department procedures in the programing and clearing of all industrial facility projects. Under the new arrangements, each facility proposal submitted by a supply arm had to be supported by a detailed statement covering the nature, purpose, capacity, and location of the new project, its requirements for labor, the availability at the proposed site of adequate labor, power, transportation, water, fuel, housing, and other utilities, sources and amounts of principal raw materials, destination of principal products, the consideration of alternate locations, and other information. This information was to be used by the War Department Facilities Board in its deliberations and in its presentation of the project to OPM.[31]

On 17 March 1941 the OPM, successfully forestalling a movement in Congress to create a plant site board subject to rigid legislative requirements, established its own Plant Site Committee. On 6 May 1941 this body was formally designated the Plant Site Board and various clearance criteria were developed. The basic policy was one of broad geographical decentralization and full employment of available labor. This was supplemented by the principles of denying new facilities as long as existing capacity was available, and disapproving locations where the supply of labor, power, utilities, and housing was inadequate. Attempts were made to participate in the initial planning of War and Navy Department projects and

to co-ordinate the work of supply contract clearance with facility clearances.[32]

Despite the board's good intentions, its practical control over new facility projects was limited and confined principally to the veto power. The War and Navy Departments felt that their own internal screening procedures were adequate, that they were applying the same general standards as the board, and that the compelling need for getting the defense program under way precluded duplication of effort and lengthy negotiations after their own determinations had been made. For its part, the OPM board was reluctant to veto arrangements which had progressed too far to be economically abandoned, especially since the relative merits of alternative possibilities frequently could not be easily appraised or defended. Moreover, as a result of the proliferation of agencies which acquired an interest in and authority over facility expansions, the over-all process of formal clearance and approval was becoming unmanageable. For some projects initiated by the services approvals were necessary by OPM, the Defense Plant Corporation, the Lend-Lease Administration, the Bureau of the Budget, and the White House. To add to the paper work and delay, double clearance within the OPM was required—the Plant Site Board's conditional approval of the construction project, and separate approval by the Contract Distribution Division. It is small wonder that the initiating supply arms and services often lost patience with the procedure.[33]

---

[31] (1) Memo, USW Patterson, for CofOrd *et al.,* 5 Apr 41, sub: Revised Procedure on Munitions Plant Construction Program, the Awarding of Contracts and Supervision Thereunder. (2) Memo, Gen Rutherford, Chmn War Department Facilities Board, for Chfs of Supply Arms and Services and War Department Facilities Board, 23 Apr 41, same sub.

[32] (1) CPA, *OPM Minutes,* p. 10. (2) McGrane, Facilities and Construction Program, pp. 40–42.

[33] (1), Ltr, USW Patterson to William S. Knudsen, 15 Oct 41. (2) Memo, Gen Rutherford for Chfs of Supply Arms and Services and Members of the War Department Facilities Board, 17 Oct 41, sub: Clearance of War Department Projects by the

With the advent of Pearl Harbor these cumbersome arrangements were for the most part thrown overboard. On 10 December 1941 the President gave the Secretary of War a blanket approval obviating the need for White House clearance of facility expansions.[34] On 13 December, Under Secretary Patterson proposed to Mr. Knudsen that only facility projects and supply contracts involving more than $5,000,-000 be cleared either by his own office or by OPM, leaving all smaller projects to the discretion of the chiefs of the services. He further proposed that OPM representatives be stationed in the offices of War Department supply arms in Washington, at Wright Field, and in the various procurement districts, where they could be fully informed of all projects from their conception. Under these conditions Mr. Patterson would expect clearance of all projects by OPM within forty-eight hours.[35]

The Under Secretary's proposals were adopted in part by the OPM council in its meetings of 15 and 19 December 1941. It was agreed that OPM representatives would be stationed throughout the War Department as suggested and that facility projects and supply contracts under $1,000,000 would not require formal clearance by OPM. Awards over this amount, either for new construction or for end items of procurement, would be cleared by OPM's Director of Purchases. This avoided the duplication and delay resulting from the requirement of double clearance within OPM.[36] On 29 December 1941 the War Department Facilities Board was abolished, leaving the chiefs of the services responsible for projects under $1,000,000, and the Under Secretary's office for those over that amount.[37]

In the weeks after Pearl Harbor the nation's industry was deluged with new procurement contracts of almost every conceivable variety. As early as 7 January 1942, Mr. Knudsen, in one of OPM's last council meetings, noted that some fifty-five new munitions plants were being proposed and stressed the need for additional review procedures prior to the letting of contracts.[38] Three months after the establishment of the War Production Board the WPB Plant Site Board was created. This was an unwieldy body of fifteen members, only two of whom represented the armed forces, despite the fact that the vast majority of projects under consideration were those of the Army and Navy. It was the belief of the Army Representative that little was accomplished by this group.[39]

The expanded production goals of the services, combined with the mammoth Presidential Objectives established in January 1942, soon came under challenge on the ground of feasibility.[40] All previous criteria of facilities control—spreading of contracts to provide full employment,

---

Office of Production Management. These considerations are discussed in McGrane, Facilities and Construction Program, pp. 56–62.

[34] President Roosevelt to SW, 10 Dec 41.

[35] Ltr, USW Patterson to Knudsen, Dir Gen OPM, 13 Dec 41.

[36] CPA, *OPM Minutes,* pp. 80–82.

[37] Memo For Each Officer, 17 Jan 42, in Facilities files, USW, Facilities Procedure, June 1940–August 1942.

[38] CPA, *OPM Minutes,* p. 84.

[39] Memo, Col Hugh A. Murrill, Chf Facilities Resources Div for Lt Col Edgar Lewis, OUSW, 24 Aug 42. The WPB Plant Site Board was established on 16 April 1942 by WPB General Administrative Order 2–31. Except to note its abolishment in the fall of 1942, neither the official history of the War Production Board nor the special study by McGrane, makes mention of this body. (1) Facilities and Construction Program, p. 100. (2) CPA, *Industrial Mobilization for War,* p. 400.

[40] See Chapter VII, above.

avoidance of congested areas, the prevention of excessive postwar capacity, and others—were dwarfed by the new discovery that the total national production program was so great that available materials were inadequate to permit both the completion of planned facilities and the production of needed end items of procurement at the same time. Projected facilities of all kinds amounted to something like a third of the entire production program for 1942. The need for a systematic review of the entire war program became evident, and proposals for the drastic limitation of new authorizations or even the stoppage of projects already under way received increasing attention. In March 1942, Col. J. L. Phillips and Comdr. H. G. Sickel, the respective Army and Navy heads of the Priorities Division, ANMB, forcefully indicated to the ANMB Executive Committee, the probable consequences of a failure to curtail further expansion:

If we continue as at present, we shall have plants standing useless for lack of equipment or raw materials, or other things. Other plants will be turning scarce materials into items which cannot be used to oppose the enemy because of the lack of other things which should have been made instead. We shall have guns without gun sights, tanks without guns, planes without bomb sights, ships held up for lack of steel plates, planes which we cannot get to the field of battle because of lack of merchant bottoms.[41]

In a subsequent memorandum they recommended that machinery be established to provide firm estimates of material requirements for all procurement programs, centralized screening and programing of all new facility projects, and the review of projects already authorized to ascertain whether existing priority ratings were justified in terms of military necessity.[42]

At about the same time, WPB's Planning Committee under the chairmanship of Robert Nathan had completed a provisional study of the entire War Munitions Program and concluded that it was impossible of attainment. Among the recommendations of the committee was the drastic curtailment of construction objectives by nearly 50 percent.[43] The mutual concern of the ANMB Priorities Committee and the WPB Planning Committee over the imbalance in facilities planning led to the formation of an interdepartmental Committee on Industrial Facilities and Construction. The committee was composed of Nathan as chairman, and Colonel Phillips and Commander Sickel as the Army and Navy Representatives. The aims of the three-man committee were to develop and recommend measures for curtailing relatively unnecessary construction. After nearly a month the committee submitted its report. The general findings of the report were that materials were becoming increasingly scarce, there were many idle and unconverted facilities, new construction should be minimized to avoid postwar excess capacity, and consumption of scarce materials in existing construction programs could be substantially reduced by simplification of design and specifications.

The committee specifically recommended the creation of a full-time facility review board, with adequate powers and representation, to review and limit all facility programs. The existing WPB Plant Site

---

[41] Memo, Col J. L. Phillips and Comdr H. G. Sickel for Ex Com ANMB, 13 Mar 42.

[42] Memo, Phillips for Sickel, 26 Mar 42.

[43] Memo, WPB Planning Com and Statistics Div for Donald Nelson, 17 Mar 42 (Planning Committee Doc. 35), cited in McGrane, Facilities and Construction Program, p. 90.

Board would be replaced by the new board. Distribution of curtailments affecting the military services would be made through the Army and Navy Munitions Board. Throughout the committee's report ran the basic proposition that the diversion of scarce materials to further facilities expansion would deprive the nation's already expanded plant capacity of raw materials essential to the turning out of finished munitions.[44]

Despite the consensus among the three members of the committee, the War Department was not ready to surrender control of its facilities program and Colonel Phillips was directed to file a dissenting report. The minority report stated among other things that any moratorium on construction would delay the war effort, that the War Department was responsible to the President and Congress and therefore its decisions should not be reviewed by an outside agency, and that the War Department was capable of knowing how to conserve materials and objected to review of its designs and specifications.[45]

The War Department's unwillingness to come to grips with the feasibility issue is attributable to a number of factors. In the spring of 1942 both the War Department and the War Production Board were undergoing widespread organizational changes and improvements. Neither agency was certain of the ultimate scope of its authority over the myriad facets of economic mobilization and procurement. There was considerable mutual suspicion and the stated feasibility limitations were not accepted as reliable by the War Department. By mid-September, however, many of the issues were becoming clear to all concerned. With the refinement of the organization of the Army Service Forces, the acceptance of substantial cuts in the Army Supply Program, the agreement to adopt the Controlled Materials Plan, and the appointment of Ferdinand Eberstadt as Vice Chairman of the War Production Board, the stage was set for agreement on the basic procedures for facility clearance. On 21 September a preliminary agreement was reached by the War and Navy Departments, the Maritime Commission, and the War Production Board for the establishment of a Facility Clearance Board within the War Production Board. This arrangement was elaborated on 17 October by a formal WPB administrative order. The Facility Clearance Board was composed of two representatives each of the War and Navy Departments, one from the Maritime Commission, and two from the War Production Board. Final decisions of the board were vested in its chairman—Mr. Ferdinand Eberstadt, WPB's newly appointed Program Vice Chairman. The new board replaced the War Department's existing Special Committee on Facilities, ANMB's Facilities Clearance Committee, WPB's Plant Site Board and two other WPB committees.[46]

[44] (1) Ibid., pp. 91–92. (2) CPA, Industrial Mobilization for War, pp. 389–91.

[45] (1) McGrane, Facilities and Construction Program, p. 92. (2) Senate, Small Business Hearings, 11: 1520 ff. (3) An excellent summary of the general facilities problem in 1942 may be found in Statement of Fred Searls, Jr., Director, Facilities Bureau, WPB, ibid., 12: 1711–14.

[46] (1) Directive for Facility Clearance Board, signed 21 September 1942 by Patterson, Forrestal, Land, and Nelson, (2) Memo, Maj Gen Wilhelm D. Styer, CofS SOS, for ACofS for Materiel SOS, 21 Sep 42, sub: Facility Clearance Board, (3) WPB Gen Admin Order 2–61, 17 Oct 42.   The War De-

The purpose of the Facility Clearance Board was to provide a single comprehensive review and clearance of each industrial expansion project or program costing $500,000 or more, exclusive of machine tools and production equipment. The review was to cover necessity, location, method of construction, use of critical materials, manpower, and services. A subordinate body, the Facilities Clearance Committee, was to review all new projects from $100,000 to $500,000, as well as previously authorized projects regardless of size. Within the War Department, established organizations and procedures had been developed for originating, screening, and clearing new projects: Each technical service and the Materiel Command, AAF, had its own facility planning section which was required to present new proposals to the Facilities Branch, ASF. Although there were variations and changes in procedures, in general the Facilities Branch had the responsibility of presenting

War Department projects to the appropriate body within WPB.[47]

These new arrangements created for the first time an integrated procedure for the review and approval of all significant industrial expansion projects, regardless of origin. Authorization of projects was tied in with the allotment of materials under the Controlled Materials Plan, so that official clearance resulted in the grant of positive, as well as permissive, aid for all project undertakings. With successive reorganizations of the War Production Board and the creation of the WPB Facilities Bureau, the Facility Clearance Board and its subordinate committee gave way to successor organizations, although the general procedures remained much the same. By the end of 1943, with the virtual completion of the nation's facilities expansion program for World War II, the problem of facility clearance had subsided to relatively small proportions.

partment Special Committee on Facilities had been created on 8 May 1942 to deal with the WPB Plant Site Board. The ANMB Facilities Clearance Committee had been formally established on 21 February 1942, primarily for the purpose of allocating the capacity of existing plants among Army and Navy supply arms. Col Ray M. Hare, Chf, Facilities Div ANMB, Weekly Progress Report, 25 Feb 42.

[47] Col Joseph N. Dalton, Chf Admin Br, Hq SOS, to Chfs of Supply Services SOS, 17 Jun 42, sub: Responsibility for Planning New Facilities, Plant Expansion, and Conversion, SPAD 600.12 (6–16–42). For later procedures, see PR 10, Plant Facilities Expansions, Sec. III, Procedure for Obtaining Clearance and Approval of Industrial Facility Expansions.

CHAPTER XX

Private Industrial Expansion Under Tax Amortization

Background of the Amortization Law

Few if any Army contractors at the beginning of the defense period had the plant, equipment, and workers essential to the production and delivery of munitions called for by the war contracts ultimately received and fulfilled. By the spring of 1941, with the progressive expansion of Army, Navy, and Maritime requirements and the United States' assumption of the role of arsenal of democracy under the Lend-Lease Act, it was evident that the cumulative new requirements far exceeded the productive capacity envisaged in the peacetime facility allocation plans. Tremendous additions to the nation's total plant capacity, as well as greater utilization of existing plants, were found essential to the expanded procurement program.

Most of the additional productive capacity eventually developed by Army contractors was financed directly or indirectly by the War Department. The conversion and expansion of existing plants, the creation of new facilities—including machinery and equipment—and the augmentation and training of labor forces were accomplished with funds provided by the War Department, or by government lending agencies and the nation's banking system under War Department sponsorship. The bulk of these funds was made available to contractors under contract terms and collateral arrangements which covered all costs of production, including facility costs. All labor, management, and material costs were covered by lump-sum or unit prices in the case of fixed-price contracts, and by authorized costs and fees under cost-plus-a-fixed-fee contracts. Facility costs were covered either by special loans or grants or by estimated amortization allowances in contract prices for end items—depending on whether the facilities were government owned or under private ownership.

At the beginning of the defense period there were many reasons for attempting to obtain a maximum of the needed industrial expansion through private financing. In mid-1940 the Army did not have unlimited funds for investment in plant expansion. The War Department's newly acquired Expediting Funds were inadequate even to construct the specialized facilities needed for producing powder and ammunition. Much of the required new industrial plant and equipment would be of a general and heterogeneous nature similar to existing privately owned capacity, and in any case would have to be operated by private firms. Realism suggested that the best way to obtain the widespread expansion needed in all sectors of the economy was to enlist the initiative and know-how of private enterprise. This could be done with a minimum of government supervision by harnessing the profit motive within the general framework of the existing economic and industrial system.

Apart from reasoning devoted especially to achieving munitions production as quickly as possible there were secondary motives arguing for private investment in defense plants. Many individuals and groups felt that the Roosevelt administration was bent on "socializing" the nation's economy and that it would use the defense program to further this objective. Others, less concerned with such long-run implications, saw in government ownership of war plants a specific threat to their own profits, either in the operation or in the financing of various segments of the program. Also, if plants were generally built and operated by the government for the "duration," there would be complicated and controversial problems of plant disposition at the end of the emergency.[1]

[1] A revealing description of the political and economic atmosphere as it affected the expansion of emergency facilities at the beginning of the defense period is found in Ethan P. Allen, Policies Governing Private Financing of Emergency Facilities, May 1940 to June 1942 (CPA History Reports on War Administration, Special Study 12, 15 March 1946) (hereafter cited as CPA, Policies). The background, provisions, and philosophy of the tax amortization law are intimately discussed in David Ginsburg, The Tax Amortization Deduction, an address delivered before the Practicing Law Institute, New York, 24 March 1941. This was reproduced in mimeographed form (88 pp.) by the Office for Emergency Management and distributed as OEM Press Release, PM 252, 24 Mar 41. The War Department's role in the tax amortization program is well summarized in A Report to the Secretary of War on the Administration of Section 124 of the Internal Revenue Law Relating to the Issue of Necessity Certificates (15 February 1945, 20 pages including introduction). This report, signed by Under Secretary Patterson, was prepared by Col. George H. Foster, chief of the Tax Amortization Section during the greater part of its existence. It is hereafter cited as Foster Rpt.

Despite the widely expressed viewpoint that private capital should undertake the financing of plant expansion for national defense, private enterprise showed considerable reluctance to begin the task. Painful memories of a decade of depression could be summed up for many businessmen as a nightmare of excess capacity—plant and equipment built in the lush years of the 1920's only to stand idle at tremendous investment cost in the 1930's. No one knew how long the emergency would last or what percentage of new investment costs would be recouped during this period. Furthermore, in the face of abundant foreign and commercial orders not subject to statutory profit limitations, many firms were loath to undertake the construction of additional capacity in order to receive government contracts.

It was not, however, the prospect of inadequate earnings under government contracts or even of future excess capacity which furnished the greatest discouragement to business in undertaking the necessary expansion. The major deterrent was the existing structure of federal tax laws and regulations combined with the prospect of greatly increased rates of taxation. As early as June 1940, it was clear that Congress would soon enact an excess profits tax as well as increases in existing taxes on corporate incomes. These measures were needed to meet both the rising costs of rearmament and the pressure to take the profits out of war. Even further increases would be inevitable if the United States actually became involved in war.[2]

[2] As passed by the 8 October 1940 revenue act, federal corporate income taxes consisted of a 24-percent "normal" tax plus an excess profits tax with rates varying from 25-percent for the first $25,000 to 50-percent for excess profits beyond $500,000. These rates were increased after Pearl Harbor to the

Taxes on corporate net income, no matter how high, would not prevent capital expansion if all capital costs could be deducted in the computation of net income. It was at this point that a long-standing regulation of the Bureau of Internal Revenue became crucial to the facilities problem. This was the provision that annual capital costs beyond estimated physical depreciation could not be treated as deductible costs for tax purposes. In practice this meant that charges to business expense in any one year for the loss in useful value of buildings and machinery were limited roughly to 5 and 10 percent, respectively, of their original cost.[3]

The businessman was thus in an anomalous position. He was, in effect, asked by the procuring agencies of the government to incur heavy indebtedness for new plant and equipment, and was told by another arm of government that for tax purposes only a small fraction of his annual investment costs would be considered a legitimate cost of doing business with the procuring agencies. During the emergency he would be permitted neither to charge all of his emergency investment costs against income nor to accumulate out of earnings a sufficient surplus to absorb unamortized facility costs remaining when the emergency ended.

After the emergency was over, when the facilities might well be worthless, he would have the dubious privilege of continuing to deduct normal depreciation costs from meager or nonexistent earnings. To add to his discomfiture, tax rates in peacetime would almost certainly be reduced, thus further reducing the value of any postwar deduction for depreciation.

A still further complication stood in the way of expansion where it was most desperately needed—in the aircraft industry. By the terms of the Vinson-Trammel act, profits on government contracts for naval shipbuilding and for Army and Navy aircraft had been restricted to 10 and 12 percent, respectively, of contract price. On 28 June 1940, just when large-scale rearmament was about to be undertaken, these percentages were reduced to 8 percent.[4] While a true net profit figure of 8 percent might be more than ample in many cases, the big issue—as in the case of the excess profits tax—turned on the question "how shall profits be estimated?" If no more than ordinary depreciation could be deducted from gross income during the emergency, the true level of costs might be greatly underestimated, profits overestimated, and taxes increased. The consequence of thus defining business costs as taxable profits would have been even more severe for many contractors under the Vinson-Trammel 8-percent limitation than under the excess profits tax. This presented an impossible situation in an industry which had to be built virtually from the ground up in order to meet defense needs, and which after a short time was

point where the excess profits tax took as high as 90-percent of marginal corporate income.

[3] These were standard rates of depreciation allowable under Bureau of Internal Revenue regulations. A much larger percentage was allowed for small hand tools and other minor capital items. Under Section 23(e) of the Internal Revenue Code, "loss of useful value" resulting from adverse business conditions could be charged off when plant and equipment were permanently discarded. Since this could be done only for the year in which the loss was actually realized, the provision was worthless as a means of enabling facilities to pay for themselves when earnings were high.

[4] 54 *Stat.* 677, 28 Jun 40, Sec. 2. The original Vinson-Trammel act (48 *Stat.* 505, 27 Mar 34, Sec. 3) applied only to naval shipbuilding and aircraft. In 1939 Army aircraft were included for purposes of equalization (53 *Stat.* 560, 3 Apr 39, Sec. 14).

expected to shrink to a fraction of its size at the peak of the emergency.[5]

The solution to the problem thus appeared to lie in legislation specifically allowing defense contractors to write off their entire emergency capital costs during the period of the emergency. A similar provision had been used belatedly for World War I, and it was thought that the inadequacies of the earlier law could be avoided by the careful drafting of new legislation. In any case, the prime consideration was the commencement of plant construction without delay; the problem of unjust enrichment could be dealt with systematically at a later date.[6]

The first public statement preparing the way for tax amortization legislation was made by President Roosevelt in his Fireside Chat of 26 May 1940, in which he stated

that industry could not be expected to bear all the risks of the expansion program. Four days later the NDAC was established and immediately went to work on the problem. Shortly thereafter, the House Ways and Means Committee reported favorably upon the tax amortization deduction if buttressed by adequate excess profits tax legislation.[7] In his 10 July press conference, the President indicated that tax amortization, excess profits taxes, and suspension of profits limitation under the Vinson-Trammel act should all be considered simultaneously. Congressional hearings began as early as 9 August, but it was not until 8 October, over three months after the initial publicity attending the proposal, that the tax amortization feature—along with tax increases and suspension of the Vinson-Trammel act—was enacted into law.[8] How much effect this delay had in slowing down the defense program is uncertain, as considerable planning was required in any case before actual construction could begin. But once the proposal had received currency, contractors postponed the making of firm commitments until the actual passage of the desired legislation.

The amortization law permitted business firms, for purposes of computing income and excess profits taxes, to deduct from gross income 20 percent annually, for a period of five years, of the cost of all facilities created or acquired for national defense. This deduction was optional, and if elected, was to be in lieu of the normal deduction for de-

---

[5] Both the Army and Navy were steadfastly opposed to flat-rate profit limitations of any kind and sought the repeal or suspension of the Vinson-Trammel act regardless of the amortization problem. Apart from major inequities created by such legislation, the profit limitation made subcontracting practically impossible in the aviation industry. Also, the administration of the act consumed valuable time which could not be spared during the emergency. (1) Wesley Frank Craven and James Lea Cate, eds., *The Army Air Forces in World War II*, Vol. VI, *Men and Planes* (Chicago: The University of Chicago Press, 1955), pp. 306–08. (2) Holley, Buying Airpower.

[6] The Revenue Act of 1918, Sections 124(a)(9) and 234(2)(8) permitted a "reasonable" deduction from income to amortize the cost of war production facilities completed or acquired after 6 April 1917. Both the statute and the administrative provisions were loosely drawn, and the act was widely criticized. Final settlement with contractors was slow and litigation continued on into World War II. Investigation by the Couzens Committee of the Senate in 1926 revealed widespread abuses. The committee estimated that $210 million of a total of $597 million in amortization allowances was improper. E. Cary Brown and Gardner Patterson, "Accelerated Depreciation: A Neglected Chapter in War Taxation," *Quarterly Journal of Economics*, LVII (1943), 632–36, citing Sen Rpt. 27, 69th Cong., 1st Sess., Jan–Feb 1926.

[7] H. Com. on Ways and Means Rpt 2491, 76th Cong., 3d Sess., 10 Jun 40.

[8] 54 *Stat.* 974, 8 Oct 40, Second Revenue Act of 1940. The tax amortization features were contained in Title III (54 *Stat.* 998). The heart of the amortization provisions are found in Sec. 302, which added a new Section 124 to the Internal Revenue Code.

preciation and obsolescence. If the emergency were terminated or if individual facilities were declared by the War or Navy Department to be no longer necessary before the expiration of five years, complete amortization would be allowed over the shorter period. Each new facility receiving the amortization privilege had to be certified as necessary to national defense jointly by the NDAC and the War or Navy Department. The act also specified, in the controversial Section (i), that amortization was not allowable if the firm had been reimbursed by the government for more than normal depreciation of the facility, unless the government's interest in the facility were properly protected. Accordingly, specific certification of the fact of "nonreimbursement" (NR), or alternatively of "government protection" (GP), was required in addition to the basic certification of "necessity." This was likewise to be done jointly by the NDAC and the War or Navy Department. Only facilities constructed or acquired after 10 June 1940 (the date of the House report) were eligible.[9] Amortization was applicable only to that portion of a given facility considered to be necessary to defense needs, a provision susceptible of several interpretations and raising important questions of policy.[10]

Administration of the Tax Amortization Program

Organization and Procedures

The War Department took prompt action to discharge its responsibilities under the new law. On 15 September 1940 the Sec-

retary of War delegated all responsibility for tax amortization matters to the Assistant Secretary, whose office became that of Under Secretary three months later. In November a Tax Amortization Section was established in the Purchases and Contracts Branch OASW, new personnel with legal background were brought into the organization, and an initial set of instructions for administering the law was issued.[11] After the War Department reorganization of 9 March 1942, the Tax Amortization Section was successively attached to the Fiscal, Resources, Purchases, Production, and Readjustment Divisions of ASF. Throughout its existence, however, it was responsible to the Under Secretary and handled amortization matters for both the ASF and the AAF. In April 1941, the Under Secretary appointed an Advisory Board on Tax Amortization. The members of the board, drawn from prominent positions in civil life, were able to give competent and disinterested assistance in formulating policy as well as in processing the more difficult cases. The board's particular specialty was the handling of nonreimbursement and government protection cases. In January 1942 the law was amended, eliminating the need for NR and GP certification, and most of the board's functions ceased. Thereafter individual members were consulted from time to time, and a working committee of three members made regular trips to Washington in an advisory capacity.[12]

---

[9] The beginning date was later moved back to 1 January 1940 by House Joint Resolution 235 (77th Congress, 1st Session) of 30 October 1941.

[10] See below, pages 463–66.

[11] WD Procurement Cir 38, 9 Nov 40. The first chief of the Tax Amortization Section was Mr. Samuel Duryee, appointed in December 1940. He was succeeded in March 1941 by Lt. Col. (later Brig. Gen.) Edward S. Greenbaum who remained as acting chief until January 1942. Lt. Col. (later Col.) George H. Foster was chief from that time until the section ceased its functions in 1944. All three men had been attorneys with wide experience.

[12] Foster Rpt, p. 9.

ADVISORY BOARD ON TAX AMORTIZATION, *18 April 1941. Seated at desk, left to right: James Hall, Fred H. Hurdman, Under Secretary of War Patterson, James M. Landis, and Charles H. Murchison. Standing: Samuel S. Duryee, Dave H. Morris, Jr., George S. Olive, Bernard Knollenberg, James P. Baxter, and William L. Marbury.*

The basis for the War Department's grant of the amortization privilege was the filing of an application by a contractor, sub-contractor, or supplier of materials, products, or services ultimately contributing to national defense. Each applicant for a necessity certificate was required to file a standard application, within specified time limits, sworn as to truthfulness in all respects. An important part of the application was the standard "Appendix A," containing a complete listing of the required faciliites—land, buildings, machinery, equipment, and miscellaneous items—their estimated cost, and beginning dates of construction and operation. The applicant's statement of need for additional facilities had to be supported by data on his existing capacity, rate of output, number of shifts worked, and other matters, as well as similar prospective data after expansion. He was to furnish his estimate of industry-wide capacity and justify his own expansion if excess capacity existed elsewhere. Likewise, he had to show defense orders or inquiries for his product—from the procuring agencies, if a prime contractor, and from other defense suppliers if a subcontractor.

Upon receipt in the War Department each application was docketed and assigned for investigation to an examiner in the Tax Amortization Section. The examiner's report was the primary basis for certification or denial. To verify and supplement the information in the application the examiner in the Tax Amortization Section could draw upon the knowledge of industry specialists and consultants in the Resources Branch of the OUSW, the technical services, the NDAC or its successor agencies, and other offices of the government. Many of the proposals for plant expansion had been originally sponsored by local contracting officers in search of a source of supply; in such cases there was prima-facie evidence of need. The examiner's written report and recommendations were usually adopted and the certificate signed by the Under Secretary; in large cases or those involving new matters of policy the examiner's report was subject to review by the Advisory Board or key individuals in OUSW. In all cases—until this requirement was eliminated by statute—separate approval by the NDAC was required before the certificate could be accepted by the Collector of Internal Revenue.

On the basis of experience, the War Department Tax Amortization Section gradually built up a body of amortization "case law" which served as a guide to examiners in their handling of cases. At first transmitted in the form of individual memoranda, established precedents and principles were eventually codified into a Necessity Certificate Primer which was kept up to date for a time by supplements.[13] On 22 May 1942 the President approved a joint Army-Navy-WPB draft of regulations covering the more general policies and procedures to be observed. To the extent of

their coverage these regulations became the official policy guide and resulted in greater uniformity in the application of the law.[14] General War Department policies on tax amortization, as well as the details of eligibility and procedure in filing applications, were eventually made available to the technical services and field establishments as a part of Procurement Regulations.[15]

Criteria of Necessity

In determining whether a proposed new facility was entitled to a necessity certificate the Army developed two basic criteria of necessity: (1) essentiality of the product for which the facilities were required; and (2) shortage of capacity within the industry producing it. At first the bulk of the applications and approvals was fairly well confined to projects for the more important military end items and obvious components. Facilities for the supply and fabrication of basic materials in the production of planes, tanks, guns, and ammunition thus received first attention. Subsequently the shortages spread both vertically and horizontally throughout the entire economy until the Army found itself presented with applications more and more removed from its direct interests: ". . . for tanks, we needed steel; for steel we needed coke; for coke we needed coal; for coal we needed transportation. New facilities were needed to produce an enormous variety of items . . . ranging

---

[13] Necessity Certificate Primer, compiled by Professor Garrard Glen and Stanley Gewirtz (17 February 1942, 61 pages) (hereafter cited as Primer), bound copy in files of Tax Amortization Sec, Production Div ASF.

[14] Regulations Prescribed by the Secretary of War and the Secretary of the Navy, with the Approval of the President, Governing the Issuance of Necessity Certificates Under Section 124 (f) of the Internal Revenue Code (11 pp., legal size) (hereafter cited as Regulations), copy in files of Tax Amortization Sec, Production Div ASF.

[15] PR 10, Sec. IV, Amortization Deduction and Certificates of Necessity.

from alpha protein to fish oils, from igloos to synthetic rubber, from V-mail to yeast." [16]

"Shortage of capacity" was defined as either actual or prospective, and as relative to the industry as a whole rather than merely to the facilities of the individual applicant. Normally, the Army would deny certification for expansion if surplus capacity existed either in the plant of the applicant or elsewhere in the industry. Surplus capacity was deemed to exist where facilities were used for not more than one shift daily.[17] There were several exceptions to the industry-concept of shortage. Regional and local shortages were considered to justify individual plant expansion in an industry having surplus capacity elsewhere when (1) transportation costs were excessive; (2) available transport facilities were needed for other products; or (3) insuring of a regional supply was desirable. Expansion of an individual firm was authorized without reference to industry capacity when desirable in order to utilize special qualifications of individual manufacturers.[18] The issuance of certificates to meet prospective rather than existing shortages was based on logically anticipated consequences of known programs.[19]

Stemming from the two broad criteria of essentiality and shortage there were a number of subsidiary policies in the Army's issuance of necessity certificates. In general, certification of the following types of application was denied:

1. acquisition of second-hand facilities;

2. normal capital replacements;

3. luxury items and facilities only remotely related to the defense effort.

Each of these classes posed numerous problems, and numerous exceptions were required by offsetting factors. Denial of second-hand facilities rested upon the theory that only new construction constituted a net addition to capacity as a whole. But many applicants demonstrated that their purchase of facilities previously idle or engaged in nondefense production resulted in an actual addition to capacity in a defense industry. Moreover, land costs were specifically included in the statute as amortizable; the cost of land was an integral part of total facility costs and influenced expansion decisions in the same manner as building and equipment costs. By parallel reasoning, acquisition costs of existing facilities were considered amortizable, and certification for valid cases was granted.[20]

The policy of denying certification for normal replacement was intended to prevent improper exploitation of the amortization privilege. It was not the purpose of the law to grant substantial tax reductions to firms merely for doing what they normally would have done in the absence of the law—namely, replacing worn-out and obsolete equipment as such replacement came due. Furthermore, the granting of amortization for this purpose would stimulate replace-

---

[16] Foster Rpt, p. 1 of Introduction.

[17] Primer, pp. 36ff.

[18] Regulations, pp. 4–5.

[19] For example, storage facilities were authorized in advance of actual need. See following applications for necessity certificate: Updike Grain Corporation, WD–N–1413; Central Sugar Company, WD–N–2327; Valley Compress Company, WD–N–2065.

[20] Regulations, pp. 5–6, permitted certification of the acquisition of a going concern only if a substantial increase in defense production could be reasonably expected. Converted, as distinct from acquired, facilities were certifiable only to the extent of conversion expenditures. Intercompany transfers of locomotives, freight cars, ships, and barges were denied certification, as were transfers of facilities between firms with common ownership or ownership by related persons. Foster Rpt, p. 12. It should be noted that Section 124(f)(1) of the statute specifically included acquisitions as eligible when deemed essential.

ment far beyond normal levels, resulting in further tax reductions, inflation, and the consumption of additional scarce materials. In practice the Army found it impossible, in perhaps a majority of cases, to distinguish between "normal" replacement and replacement because of rapid deterioration under intensive wartime use or because of sudden "wartime obsolescence" characterized by the inability of existing equipment to meet wartime demands.[21]

Nevertheless, a number of applications were rejected on the ground that replacement rather than expansion of facilities was contemplated. An interesting case was the application of the Texas and New Orleans Railroad for certification of a new $1,400,-000 bridge over the Pecos River on the main line of the road near the Mexican border. Construction was approved by the War Production Board and began in the summer of 1943; application for a necessity certificate was filed in due time. The applicant contended that high wartime loads had resulted in considerable fatigue of the existing structure, which was approximately fifty years old. Repairs were needed with increasing frequency and the structure of the old bridge lent itself to easy sabotage (an Army guard had been maintained over the bridge from the beginning of the emergency). Failure of the old bridge would result in lengthy and time-consuming detours: traffic from San Antonio to El Paso would have to be rerouted via Fort Worth and Dallas, thence westward via another road. Investigation by the Tax Amortization Section disclosed that the old bridge was carried on the books of the railroad under the "retirement" system of accounting used by most railroads for road and structures. Under this system no annual depreciation was taken; the entire cost of the old bridge would be charged off in the year of retirement. The "retirement" system thus granted the railroad wide latitude to take lump-sum depreciation in years of high earnings. Certification of the new bridge would have enabled the road to charge off the full cost of both bridges within a period of five years or even less. Certification was denied on the ground that the age of the old bridge indicated that it was due for normal retirement.[22]

The issue of nonessentiality or luxury arose in two types of application: (1) Those covering facilities for the production of end items classifiable as nonessential; (2) those covering obviously essential facilities which included components classifiable as nonessential. Some items were ruled out as a class on the ground of nonessentiality; others were considered essential when devoted to certain uses but not to others; still others

---

[21] This observation is based on Memo, Lt Donald T. Rosenfeld for Col Greenbaum, 26 Aug 41, sub: Certification of Facilities Employed for Replacement Purposes, copy in OCMH. This memorandum systematically analyzed the replacement problem and concluded that clear-cut cases of simple replacement were largely confined to restorations after outright destruction, such as by sabotage, fire, explosion, or other unusual causes. All other classes of replacement typically involved increases in capacity by the adoption of equipment technologically superior to the equipment replaced. Thus the test of certification was thrown back upon the two basic criteria: Is the product of the facilities essential? Is there a shortage of capacity in the industry?

[22] Texas and New Orleans Railroad Company, WD–N–30552, especially Memo, Col Foster for USW, 14 Jul 44, sub: Application for Necessity Certificate, T&NO RR. See also similar denial in Yazoo and Mississippi Valley R. R., WD–N–27885. On the other hand, in Timken Roller Bearing Company, WD–N–1844, a new boiler plant was certified "due to the age and reduced usefulness of an old boiler plant," even though the old plant together with outside facilities was adequate to meet current needs. "It was felt that it is a better idea to certify new facilities and allow old ones to be used as standby in the case of an emergency." Primer, p. 48.

were considered—partly on principle and partly for administrative reasons—as too remotely connected with the defense effort to justify certification.

Among the denials on the ground of end-product nonessentiality were facilities for producing pies and soft drinks in the United States. Capital items, whether or not a component of essential facilities, were denied certification in the case of vending machines, electric signs, pool and ping-pong tables, and soda fountains. A flagpole, however, was certifiable. Air conditioning to provide ordinary comfort was denied but was approved when considered essential to precision work and other special purposes. Couches were ordinarily denied but approved for the use of female labor and for first aid purposes. City office buildings, retail facilities in general, and associated construction for community facilities were denied.[23]

A potentially complex issue which might have been a major administrative problem was the question of partial certification. Section 124 (f) (1) of the statute stated:

There shall be included [in the determination of amortizable cost] only so much of the amount . . . as is properly attributable to such construction . . . as the Advisory Commission to the Council of National Defense and either the Secretary of War and the Secretary of the Navy have certified . . . as necessary in the interest of national defense during the emergency period.

This was construed by the War Department to mean that facilities which were built for the express purpose of supplying nondefense as well as defense orders should receive only partial certification. Section 5 (e) of the standard application for a necessity certificate called for the applicant's "estimate of percentage of increase in pro-

ductive capacity which will be directly or indirectly absorbed in the Defense program." Most applications claimed 100-percent utilization for defense purposes and the War Department was not disposed to dispute reasonable claims. With few exceptions, such applications received 100-percent certification if the application as a whole was well supported. When the applicant showed a prospective division of output between defense and nondefense purpose, partial certification was granted; thus a 50-percent certification was made for facilities devoted half to defense purposes.[24]

With the approach of the end of the war and the transfer of the certification function to WPB, a new interpretation of partial certification arose. The War Production Board proposed the granting of certificates for only a fraction of the total cost of facilities—even when completely devoted to war purposes for the duration—on the ground that facilities then authorized would far outlast the war and would retain a high percentage of useful value for peacetime pur-

---

[23] (1) Foster Rpt, p. 11. (2) Primer, pp. 28–30.

[24] In The Davidson Transfer and Storage Company, WD–N–7026, a certificate was issued covering 65 percent of the facilities acquired, based upon applicant's estimate that 65 percent of its transportation activities were for defense. In White Cap Company, WD–N–3121, a 50-percent certificate was granted as a reasonable solution of a complex problem. The applicant acquired facilities to increase the output of metal closures for glass containers. Encouragement of glass packaging for foods was considered highly desirable to save scarce supplies of tin. On the other hand, the rubber gaskets required would consume equally scarce supplies of rubber. After consultation with WPB commodity specialists, a 50-percent certification was decided as "entirely arbitrary but not improper" in view of all the factors. Primer, p. 7. Foster Report, p. 17, cites a 30-percent certification of a building erected to produce 70-percent peacetime products and 30-percent war products. When the building was later devoted 100 percent to war production without extra costs, the owner's request for 100-percent certification was denied.

pose. This was particularly true of railroad equipment. WPB felt that a 35-percent certification would be a liberal allowance, adequate to induce the private construction of facilities still needed for the duration.[25]

Although the War Department had no objections to such a policy, particularly since its facility expansion program was largely completed, it felt that the WPB position challenged the basic philosophy of the statute. Inasmuch as the issue is central to an appraisal of both the wisdom of the statute and the War Department's role in its administration, the following statement by the chief of the Tax Amortization Division is pertinent:

Usefulness or non-usefulness of the facility after the war has not heretofore been considered as a proper factor to be considered in deciding whether a facility should be certified.

Inability to ascertain length of useful life was one of the primary considerations in the passage of the Act, and certainly neither the Act, our Regulations nor the practice from the first has required that consideration be given to this factor.

Of course, as the War Department decided that amortization was no longer essential to the War Department's activities, we should not complain of the restrictiveness of such a policy. However, adoption of such a policy by the War Production Board might later be used as the basis for a contention that the War Department had for three years indulged a wrong policy. It should be noted that this policy is not being written into the Regulations approved by the President, but is apparently being adopted solely as policy, based on the language of the Act.

I suggest that we advise the War Production Board that we do not agree that such a policy is required under the law and that if such a policy is to be followed . . . it be predicated upon the special circumstances surrounding

expansions at this time when the major requirements of the emergency can be met without additional facilities.[26]

The issue posed by the apparently conflicting positions was basically one of timing. The fundamental purpose of the tax amortization law, in the view of the War Department, was to obtain rapid expansion of facilities at a time when speed was of the essence and when practicable alternatives were not available. The intention of the act was to eliminate a major element of uncertainty over the ability of private industry to pay for the new facilities out of earnings. The guarantee of a five-year write-off of essential facilities for tax purposes, regardless of future considerations, was the instrument devised for the purpose. The War Department's application of this policy during the first three years of the program fulfilled the basic purpose of the law and obtained the necessary facilities in time to win the war. By the time of WPB administration the underlying situation had changed. To grant 100-percent write-off in the short period remaining would have amounted to the obvious grant of a wartime exemption for predominantly peacetime purposes. The War Department view was that if partial certification as undertaken by WPB could obtain additional facilities still required, well and good. If not, the alternative of government financing was preferable to 100-percent certification.[27]

---

[25] CPA, *Industrial Mobilization for War*, pp. 656–67.

[26] Excerpt from Memo, Col Foster to Brig Gen Edward S. Greenbaum, 15 Mar 44, sub: Tax Amortization.

[27] The War Department's interpretation of the general purpose and philosophy of the tax amortization law is lucidly expressed in the Foster Report. By mid-1943 the War Department tended to favor government financing (DPC or War Department-owned facilities) in cases where the probable losses on resale of plants would be less than Treasury losses on amortization within a period of two years or less.

Nonreimbursement and Government Protection

A major barrier to the successful use of the tax amortization feature during the first year and a half of its existence was the administration of the controversial Section (i) of the statute.[28] As indicated earlier, this section required the issuance, both by the NDAC and the War or Navy Department, of a certificate of "nonreimbursement" (NR) or alternatively "government protection" (GP) before the basic certificate of necessity could be honored by the Treasury.[29]

This requirement was introduced into the statute as a compromise measure to replace earlier proposals of an even more unsatisfactory nature in the original House bill. Many members of Congress, as well as individuals in the Department of the Treasury and the NDAC, were apprehensive that industry would "make a killing" out of the defense program. In particular they were fearful that, under various contractual arrangements with the procurement agencies, industry would be presented with a gift of new plant and equipment paid for by the government. This had happened to a considerable extent during World War I and officials in NDAC concerned with procurement policy were determined to prevent its recurrence.

Section (i) was designed not only to protect the financial interests of the government vis-à-vis those of industry but also to provide equality of treatment of contractors. Certain types of arrangement, such as the Emergency Plant Facilities contract, provided for the strict separation of the cost of plant facilities from the costs of end-item production by the same facilities. Under EPF, a separate contract was drawn to provide reimbursement of the contractor in full for his plant facility expenditures with the specification that the unit price of finished items of procurement would contain no element of the cost of the facilities. In this manner the government was assured against double reimbursement of the contractor for his facility costs.

Those who worked on the draft of the tax amortization law though they saw an analogous problem of double reimbursement in the allowance of accelerated amortization. Would not the inclusion of facility costs in a supply contract involving the use of tax-amortized facilities amount to double reimbursement of the contractor—once in the form of the tax amortization allowance, and again in the price of the finished product?[30] And, regardless of the double reimbursement theorem, was it not well understood that many tax-amortized facilities would in fact possess a substantial value at the end of the emergency? In order to attack both these problems, Section (i) was included in the amortization law. This section stipulated that facility costs in excess of normal depreciation must be excluded from unit prices in supply contracts in order for the contractor to receive an NR certificate and get the tax amortization benefit without further question. If the contractor could not obtain an NR certificate, he could receive the amortization allowance only by obtaining a GP certificate indicating satisfactory protection of the government's interest in the facilities acquired under the contracts in question. The precise measures

---

[28] Section (i), as it was generally called during World War II, was in reality subsection (i) of Section 124 of the statute.

[29] See above, p. 460.

[30] S. Rpt. 480, Pt. 2, 77th Cong., 2d Sess, 14 Aug 41, p. 41.

required of the contractor to satisfy the requirements of "government protection" were left to the NDAC and the War and Navy Departments.

As a part of its general purchasing policy the War Department adopted general measures to insure adequate protection of its facility interests. These measures were employed in all appropriate procurement contracts whether or not the satisfaction of the tax amortization statute was involved. They included all of the following, with specific omissions allowable, when appropriate, upon approval of the director of the Purchases Division, ASF: (1) maintenance of the facilities in good condition at contractor expense beyond the life of the existing supply contract for a period provided in the contract; (2) contractor retention of title to the facilities without encumbrance; (3) contractor not to alter the facilities without consent of the contracting officer; (4) contractor to give priority to government orders; (5) no further facility charges to the government in procurement contracts after full amortization of the original cost of the facilities; (6) release of contractor from all above obligations by payment to the government of a negotiated sum agreed upon as constituting fair and just return to the government for its prior payment for the facilities.[31]

It was evident to the procurement agencies from the outset that the implementation of Section (i) would present grave difficulties of administration. Under the law all government contracts and purchase orders for the products of tax-amortized facilities—even when placed long after the facilities had been completed and used for earlier supply contracts—would have to be subjected to the test of "nonreimbursement." In its endeavor to carry out the law, the Army was obliged to embark upon innumerable research projects covering thousands of supply contracts in order to ascertain the relationship of supply prices to facilities reimbursement. Some idea of the heavy work load imposed on contractors as well as on the Army is indicated by the following excerpt from a letter to an Army supplier:

The information desired should, in the case of each contract which may now be certified, state the number of units of each item to be supplied, the unit prices, and total contract price, prices at which the same or similar items were sold to the Government or to other purchasers prior, preferably to January 1, 1940, with a notation of discounts ordinarily applied, cost breakdowns of various items, comparisons with your catalogue or list prices which date back prior to the emergency, or any other evidence which would in your opinion indicate to the satisfaction of this office that the prices charged in your contracts with the Government do not include any return of cost greater than normal wear, tear, and exhaustion of emergency facilities.[32]

Even if every contractor had been in a position to submit convincing proof of "nonreimbursement," the paper work alone would have been a considerable barrier to the smooth administration of Section (i). But the task of determining statutory nonreimbursement in fixed-price contracts could not be disposed of simply by examining the contract price or even the wording of contracts. Even though the contractor and the contracting officer after elaborate negotiations had reached agreement on a contract of mutual advantage to the government and the contractor, and had excluded "excessive" facility costs from the contract,

---

[31] PR 1007.

[32] Ltr, Col Greenbaum, Actg Chf Tax Amortization Sec, to Joseph F. Taylor, Treasurer Bausch & Lomb, 24 Nov 41.

this fact could not be readily apparent to a third party. As envisaged by the NDAC, adequate proof of nonreimbursement required the submission by the contractor of detailed cost analaysis data. In the dark days after Dunkerque, the fall of France, and the attack on the Soviet Union, this appeared to the Army to be a waste of precious time and a gratuitous annoyance to contractors. Accurate prediction of costs was impossible in the fluid cost-price conditions of the defense period, especially for contractors with joint costs and those embarking on an entire new line of output. The crux of the matter was that the search for proof of nonreimbursement was the pursuit of a will-o'-the-wisp. Any representation of "normal" reimbursement of facility costs, whether by words or by figures, would be meaningless when appearing in conjunction with necessarily generous or flexible estimates for future material, labor, overhead, contingencies, and other cost items making up the contract price for the end item in question. Any advantage resulting from the exclusion of one type of cost labeled as "facility" cost could be canceled many times over by the padding or inaccurate prediction of other types of cost. Clearly, what was vaguely and unsuccessfully sought by Section (i) was some assurance of the achievement of sound pricing policies by the procurement agencies. But this was a task far beyond the scope of a tax amortization law and could not be accomplished by single-minded concentration upon the facilities aspects of supply contracts.

In view of all the difficulties, it is not surprising that the number of NR certificates issued by the Army fell far behind applications and below the number of basic necessity certificates issued. An even more serious bottleneck was clearance by the NDAC, which had to issue separate certifications based on its own investigations. In its desire to provide a thorough scrutiny of all the evidence, and handicapped by lack of first-hand knowledge and records, the NDAC delayed action and made frequent rejections, most of which were later cleared upon further review. Considerable friction developed between the Army and NDAC over the latter's insistence upon exhaustive and minute research into seemingly irrelevant issues. In one such case, in which the NDAC became concerned over the existence of monopoly profits acquired long before the defense period, a leading member of the Army's Advisory Board on Tax Amortization became more outspoken than usual:

Subordinate personnel of the Advisory Commission, however well-intentioned, have no justification for asking for data that may be of interest for entirely different purposes but that are unnecessary for a decent disposition of the case in hand . . . . It is true that investigation of the rate of profit may be desirable in order to promote better procurement policies or for other social purposes but . . . it seems wrong to harry applicants because examiners may have some purpose to serve other than the administration of Section 124 (i).[33]

By the summer of 1941, the volume of complaints voiced by contractors and echoed by newspapers reached major proportions. Contractors without NR certificates were left in grave doubt as to the validity of their basic necessity certificates and the plant expansion program was noticeably retarded. As a result of the mounting dissatisfaction, the NDAC was

---

[33] Memo, James M. Landis, Advisory Board on Tax Amortization, for Under Secretary Patterson, 15 Aug 41, sub: WD–NR–1138.

relieved of all its certifying authority on 30 October 1941 by a Congressional resolution. In the same legislation, Congress also attempted to ease the burden on the remaining certifying agencies by clarifying the requirements for NR certification.[34]

No amount of clarification could remove the basic defects of Section (i). The nominal exclusion of facility costs from supply prices without limitation of all other elements of price was a pointless proceeding. Moreover, if Section (i) had succeeded in its apparent purpose, it is doubtful that the amortization law as a whole could have achieved its avowed objective. This objective was to encourage facility expansion by enabling the contractor to retain earnings to meet his emergency capital costs. But tax relief, no matter how complete, was no guarantee of gross income sufficient to cover new capital costs. The only possible way for a contractor to defray capital costs out of earnings during the emergency was to receive prices in supply contracts sufficiently in excess of all other costs to return the entire capital investment within the emergency period. This not only would permit but also would compel reimbursement in excess of

normal rates of depreciation. In addition, the tax amortization benefit was required in order to prevent such reimbursement of capital from being labeled as income and taxed away at high wartime rates.

Nowhere in the debates and testimony over the repeal of Section (i) was there clear and explicit recognition of the double requirement of "excessive reimbursement" *and* accelerated tax amortization if the contractor's capital outlays were to be fully recovered by the end of the emergency period. The following note, however, appears in an unsigned memorandum, dated 9 January 1942, in War Department files: "If the Government does not pay for the facilities and the contractor is not 'reimbursed' under the contract or otherwise, how is he to pay for it? The facilities are presumably worthless to him at the end of 5 years." Yet when Senator Robert M. La Follette, Jr., who finally voted against repeal of Section (i), challenged the repeal proposal on the ground that double reimbursement was involved, War Department representatives failed to clarify the issue.[35]

On the other hand, complete reimbursement of the contractor plus the tax amortization benefit would be equitable both to the government and the contractor only on the assumption that the facilities became completely worthless at the end of the emergency. This was, of course, an unlikely probability for most facilities of the kind selected for private financing and ownership. Some plants would have a high residual value at the end of the war while others would be relatively worthless. The ratio of

---

[34] House Joint Resolution 235. An important feature of the resolution was elimination of NR certification of contracts of less than $15,000. It should be noted that NDAC was only a skeleton organization by the fall of 1941, having been superseded by OPM early in the year in all but the certification function. This factor was influential in the decision to eliminate NDAC's certification authority. See: (1) Arthur Krock, "The Stymie Over Amortization of Plants," in New York *Times,* 30 Apr 41, p. 2; (2) New York *Herald Tribune,* 9 Aug 41, "Policy on Plant Amortization Is Called Failure"; (3) *Wall Street Journal,* 5 Aug 41, p. 1, "Defense Plants—Provisions for Their Amortization May Be Liberalized Shortly."; (4) Washington *Times Herald,* 3 Aug 41, "Washington Daily Merry-Go-Round," by Drew Pearson and Robert S. Allen.

[35] (1) S. Com. on Finance, 77th Cong., 2d Sess., Hearings on H. J. Res. 257, *Nonreimbursement Certificates,* 22 Jan 42, pp. 9–10. (2) Unsigned memo, 9 Jan 42, in folder H. J. 257, Tax Amortization files, Purchases Div ASF.

residual value to original cost would not only exhibit wide variation from plant to plant and industry to industry, but for all plants would fluctuate from time to time. Many plants would be worth more five or ten years after the war than on the day the war ended. Clearly, the blanket treatment of all facilities of all contractors by a single yardstick would reward some contractors handsomely while conceivably failing to cover the costs of others. But the yardstick in question was not a matter of administrative selection; it was the statutory five-year period adopted as the basic foundation of the tax amortization law.

It was partly in order to achieve greater equity through individual contract provisions tailored to the circumstances of each supplier that the War Department, in company with the Navy, petitioned Congress to revoke Section (i). The chief concern, however, was to eliminate the enormous administrative burden of probing thousands of procurement contracts in order to ascertain something which in essence was not ascertainable, namely, that each contract viewed as a whole provided no more than "normal" reimbursement of the cost of facilities. By the end of 1941, two months after the termination of NDAC's certification activities, the War Department had issued only 278 NR certificates for 3,120 applications. Corresponding figures for GP certification were 30 certificates for 219 applications. On 5 February 1942 Congress repealed Section (i) *ab initio*. Thus Section (i), after causing many months of frustration, delay, and expense to all concerned, was deemed never to have been enacted, leaving only necessity certificates as the prerequisite to the tax amortization deduction.[36]

The repeal of Section (i) removed all doubt as to the contractor's receipt of the tax amortization benefit once he had received a necessity certificate. But it did not relieve the procuring agencies of their responsibility for protecting the government's legitimate interest in facilities. This task still remained in the hands of those charged with the development of procurement policy and the actual negotiation of individual contracts.[37]

Transfer of the Certification Function

With the repeal of the requirement for NR and GP certification, the implementation of the tax amortization program proceeded smoothly despite the flood of new applications after Pearl Harbor. By late 1943 the War Department's facilities program was practically complete; at the same time the scope of applications had grown successively wider, extending far into the area of the civilian economy. In an effort to get out from under the necessity for further excursions into the field of raw materials production, transportation, food production and processing, and the like, the Army on 25 June 1943 petitioned the newly established Office of War Mobilization for relief. As a result an Executive order was issued on 5 October 1943, limiting the scope of the program. Thereafter, certification was to be limited to facilities needed for military production for the Army and Navy. Approval of facilities for tax amortization would be disallowed unlesss application was made prior to construction. Government

---

[36] (1) H. J. Res. 257, 77th Cong., 2d Sess, approved 6 Feb 42. (2) Foster Rpt, p. 7.

[37] On this point, see testimony of Lt. Col. George H. Foster before House Ways and Means Committee, 2 January 1942, regarding House Joint Resolution 257, copyright in folder H. J. 257, Tax Amortization files, Purchases Div ASF. See also drafts of Patterson testimony before appropriate Senate and House committee, in folder H. J. 257.

financing was to be used wherever possible for additional facilities still needed.

This stiffened policy gave rise to many complaints as numerous applications were denied on the ground that they were nonessential to military needs. The railroads and the Office of Defense Transportation brought considerable pressure to bear upon the War Department for continued certification of railroad facilities. Largely because of such pressure the Army and Navy requested that their responsibility for further certification be terminated. This request was granted on 17 December 1943 and, except for cases on hand, all certification thereafter was done by WPB.[38]

By the summer of 1944, the remarkable progress of Allied operations in the European theater forced intensive consideration of the problem of contract termination and settlement. Under Section 124 (e) of the basic law, taxpayers were permitted to shorten the amortization period if the facilities ceased to be essential before the end of the full five-year period. This enabled contractors to compress their entire five-year amortization deduction into the shorter period. Shortening of the amortization period could be done only if the President issued a proclamation permitting such action or if the Secretary of War or Navy, under regulations, certified the nonnecessity of particular facilities. It was the view of the War Department that the issuance of nonnecessity certificates should be done by the procurement agencies themselves since these agencies bore the responsibility for contract settlement and the payment of termination claims. Under standard termination procedure, the procurement agencies would be obliged to pay contractors for loss

of useful value of emergency facilities not otherwise compensated.[39] If nonnecessity certificates could be issued at the time of settlement, termination claims could be reduced and settlement expedited. The War Department's position was overruled, however, on 30 September 1944, and the War Production Board was made the certifying authority for nonnecessity certificates.[40]

The Record of Plant Expansion Under Tax Amortization

In the three-year period from the passage of the tax amortization law to the transfer of certification authority to WPB, the War Department received a total of 31,047 applications for necessity certificates. On the basis of these, the department issued 26,775 certificates of necessity for all or a part of the facilities covered by the applications. The remaining 4,272 cases were denied, withdrawn, or otherwise disposed of.

The total dollar value of applications certified by the War Department came to $4,955,813,760.16. This represents some 70 percent of the value of all certifications issued throughout the war with Navy and WPB accounting for approximately 20 and 10 percent, respectively.[41] An indication of the wide array of industries affected by War Department certifications, and the relative importance of the tax amortization privilege to each, is found in a broad statistical summary (*Table 50*). This tabulation reveals

---

[38] (1) Executive Order 9406. (2) Foster Rpt, pp. 13–15.

[39] Memo, Foster, Chf Tax Amortization Br, for USW, 2 Aug 44, sub: Termination of Amortization Period for Emergency Facilities.

[40] Executive Order 9486. The general regulations governing the issuance of nonnecessity certificates were prescribed by the President in a companion order—Executive Order 9487, 30 September 1944.

[41] (1) Foster Rpt, p. 15. (2) The percentage breakdown appears in Army Industrial College R41, Financial Aids to Contractors (December 1945), Table 5, ICAF Library.

TABLE 50—WAR DEPARTMENT CERTIFICATIONS FOR TAX AMORTIZATION [a]
8 OCTOBER 1940–15 FEBRUARY 1945

Type of Product	Amount Certified	Percent
TOTAL CERTIFICATIONS	$4,612,836,000	100.00
Manufacturing: TOTAL	$3,032,014,000	65.74
Aircraft, Engines, Parts and Accessories	365,731,000	7.93
Ship Construction and Repair	12,234,000	0.27
Combat and Other Motorized Vehicles	100,547,000	2.18
Guns	95,846,000	2.08
Ammunition, Shell and Bombs	135,372,000	2.93
Explosives and Ammunition Loading	13,025,000	0.28
Iron and Steel:		
Basic	270,062,000	5.85
Fabricated	82,009,000	1.78
Nonferrous Metals and Their Products:		
Aluminum and Magnesium	306,462,000	6.65
Other	56,265,000	1.22
Machine Tools and Other Metal Working Equipment	158,603,000	3.44
Machinery and Electrical Equipment and Appliances	213,273,000	4.62
Chemicals:		
Synthetic Rubber	40,440,000	0.88
Other	288,405,000	6.25
Coal and Petroleum Products:		
Aviation Gasoline	437,727,000	9.49
Other	100,863,000	2.19
Food Processing	35,373,000	0.77
Miscellaneous	319,777,000	6.93
Mining and Industrial Service: TOTAL	$370,090,000	8.01
Mining	82,318,000	1.78
Gas, Light, Heat and Power:		
Electric Power Generation	123,837,000	2.68
Electric Power Transmission	109,032,000	2.36
Gas Manufacture and Transmission	48,499,000	1.05
Steam, Heat and Power	6,404,000	0.14
Transportation and Related Service: TOTAL	$1,171,382,000	25.40
Rail	1,066,868,000	23.13
Pipeline	17,654,000	0.39
Motor, Air, and Water	84,489,000	1.83
Terminal Facilities	2,371,000	0.05
Communication	6,419,000	0.14
Non-Industrial Service	32,931,000	0.71

[a] Omits certifications of less than $25,000 made after April 1943.

Source: Foster Rept., p. 16.

the railroad industry at the head of the list, with over a billion dollars in certifications, representing nearly a fourth of the entire War Department tax amortization program. Petroleum (aviation gasoline) and aircraft followed with $438 million and $366 million, respectively.

The tax amortization law and its administration will long be a subject of controversy. Early in the administration of the law the War and Navy Departments were charged with undue liberality, inadequate investigation of costs and necessity, and discrimination against small firms.[42] The War Department's position was that a bold program of plant expansion was essential, that current expansion efforts were unlikely to be adequate for total war, and that further elaborate investigation of costs and necessity would stifle the program without achieving any significantly desirable result. The unfavorable position of small business, to the extent that it existed, was not peculiar to the administration of tax amortization but was inherent in the larger problem of discovering the most effective role of small business in the industrial mobilization process.[43]

A careful appraisal of the War Department's administration of tax amortization for World War II would require a long and intensive period of research and analysis.

Viewed from the perspective of the present survey, it would appear that the department's handling of the certification function was as satisfactory as could be expected, given the urgency of the circumstances, the complexities of the task, and the objectives of the amortization statute. As pointed out by the Truman Committee, mistakes and inconsistencies occurred; yet in view of the desperate need, both before and after Pearl Harbor, for expansion of productive capacity in all sectors of the war economy, it is doubtful that many of the projects actually certified could be seriously criticized on the ground of lack of usefulness to the war effort. The early provisions of the law requiring elaborate investigation to determine "nonreimbursement" and "government protection" were administratively unworkable, and, in the light of subsequent developments, unnecessary in principle. The assorted instruments of careful contracting, continuous close pricing, and especially renegotiation, provided potentially adequate safeguards against unjust enrichment and needless dissipation of government funds. As already indicated, the application of these instruments was less than completely successful in preventing or recouping high profits realized through the use of the tax-amortization privilege.[44]

The more fundamental question of the basic wisdom of the amortization statute goes deep into the realm of social theory and philosophy. It is clear that the amortization law for World War II was abundantly successful in providing badly needed capacity for war production. It succeeded not only because it offered protection against losses but because it also made a frank appeal to the profit motive. The fram-

---

[42] Truman Committee, First Annual Rpt, pp. 39ff.

[43] For War Department reply to Truman Committee charges in 1942, see Memo, sub: Truman Committee Report on Tax Amortization, 19 Jan 42, in Truman Committee folder, Readjustment Div files, ASF. In evaluating charges of inadequate investigation of costs it should be noted that it was the responsibility of the Department of the Treasury, after project completion, to determine the actual cost of defense installations subject to the amortization deduction. Thus the War Department certified figure represented the *maximum* allowable cost.

[44] See above, pages 373–75.

ers of the amortization law were well advised in coupling its enactment with the passage of the excess profits tax and related increases in income taxation. The strongest practical feature of the rapid write-off privilege was the fact that, for purposes of facilities expansion, it converted high tax rates from a liability into an asset. The higher the rate of corporate income and excess profits taxes, the greater was the positive inducement to business to retain its earnings in the form of expanded plant and equipment. The strength of this inducement was multiplied by the advantages to be had at the end of the war in disposing of plants under capital gains and loss features of the income tax laws. The operation of the amortization feature thus shattered conventional beliefs that high tax rates would inevitably lead to the "drying up" of capital and the prevention of capital formation. By the adoption of appropriate administrative provisions in the tax laws, the effects of the rate component of taxation could be radically changed. With tax rates at their peak, the American economy in World War II exhibited the greatest capital expansion in its history—an expansion which went far toward guaranteeing the successful outcome of the war.

It would not be difficult to demonstrate that some firms and industries fared much better than others under the rapid write-off privilege. The favored firms were those whose newly created facilities possessed the greatest economically useful life after the war. The extent to which such economic longevity could be foreseen at the time of certification varied widely from firm to firm and from industry to industry, in much the same way as did the prediction of the life expectancy of individuals and units in various branches of the armed forces in World War II. What was not fully understood at the time of the launching of amortization was the extent to which governmental spending for years to come would invalidate many of the traditional assumptions underlying the operation of the private-enterprise economy.

CHAPTER XXI

Government Financed and Owned Industrial Facilities

The Emergency Plant Facilities Contract

In the summer and fall of 1940, when major segments of the defense program were temporarily stalled over the problem of facility expansion, the NDAC sought a method of reimbursing contractors for their emergency capital outlays which would guarantee, in advance of expenditure, the complete recovery of all capital costs. Such a guarantee was particularly needed in the aircraft industry, which had to be built virtually from the ground up in order to fill military requirements under the defense program. The large quantities of plant and equipment to be constructed during the emergency would in many respects be suitable for the peacetime production of commercial aircraft, but they were expected to be of little actual value at the end of the emergency because of shrunken markets. Moreover, in view of the uncertain volume of production to be undertaken or completed during the emergency, inclusion of plant costs in the unit price of the product afforded a far from dependable method of insuring complete cost reimbursement. Under these circumstances the stimulus of the tax amortization privilege would be insufficient to induce the necessary expansion; tax abatement alone would not guarantee the recovery, either during the emergency or

thereafter, of extensive capital costs. To meet this situation the NDAC developed a pioneer measure known as the Emergency Plant Facilities contract.

Briefly summarized, EPF was a method of financing which provided specific and complete reimbursement, over a period of five years, of facility costs incurred in the performance of supply contracts under the defense program. The usual EPF contract was awarded in conjunction with, or subsequent to, the award of a supply contract, and covered the construction or conversion of buildings, plus, if desired, the purchases and installation of machinery and equipment. The contractor made his own arrangements for expansion and provided initial financing—typically with funds borrowed from banks—and was to be reimbursed by the government in sixty equal monthly installments. In turn, facility costs were rigorously excluded from supply prices of all items produced from EPF establishments. Title to the new facilities was initially vested in the contractor but passed to the government when reimbursement was complete. Upon completion of the contract, the contractor had an option to retain the facilities by payment to the government of cost less depreciation or a lower negotiated price. If the contractor failed to exercise his option or if no agreement on terms could be reached, the facilities would revert to the government. In the case of "scrambled facilities" (government installations added to facilities already owned by contractors) the government was obliged to remove its property from the contractor's premises, restoring the latter to their previous condition. The government in any case pledged itself not to operate the facilities commercially and to give the contractor "first refusal" before sale to a third party.

The original proposals leading to the EPF type of contract were of a quite different nature from the final result. As early as 14 June 1940, Mr. Knudsen had proposed that such plants be financed by the Reconstruction Finance Corporation under its new lending powers.[1] Under the Knudsen plan, the RFC was to put up the entire capital for plant expansion and would also supply the necessary working capital. The facilities would be titled to the manufacturer, who would pay 3-percent interest on the loan covering the cost of the plant; working capital was to be supplied interest free. The plant and equipment were to be the sole security for the loan, which would be repaid out of earnings during the emergency. This would be guaranteed by loading the mortgage amortization payments into the unit price of each completed engine, or other product, on a prorata basis. Thus a $10,-000,000 plant built to turn out 10,000 aircraft engines would be paid for by including in the price of each engine an element of $1,000 representing capital costs. When the

RFC loan had been paid off, the plant and equipment would belong to the contractor.[2]

The adoption of this proposal would provide a powerful incentive to industry to create and operate additional facilities since contractors would have much to gain and nothing to lose. But the proposal fell through, chiefly because of Congressional and other objections to the treatment of the government's interest in the facilities, but also because of objections to the "exclusion of private capital" from the program.[3] Accordingly, the NDAC staff set about drafting a new type of facilities contract which would more adequately protect the government's interest and at the same time permit the American banking system to provide the funds.

The first draft of the EPF contract received in the War Department was dated

---

[1] (1) CPA, Policies, pp. 26–27. (2) Clifford J. Durr, *The Early History of Defense Plant Corporation* (Washington: Committee on Public Administration Cases, 1950) (hereafter cited as Durr, *History of DPC*), pp. 9ff.

[2] To avoid the necessity of paying a gift or income tax for the cost-free receipt of the facilities, the contractor would build the plant on government-owned land and would amortize the facilities over the life of the loan. This could be done under an established Bureau of Internal Revenue ruling that a building constructed on leased land may be amortized for tax purposes over the period of the lease. Under a purchase option to buy the land after the expiration of the lease, the contractor would then acquire clear title to both land and facilities. Durr, *History of DPC,* p. 13.

[3] Ginsburg, The Tax Amortization Problem, p. 12. For banker attitudes toward government financing, see Gerald T. White, "Financing Industrial Expansion for War: The Origin of the Defense Plant Corporation Leases," *The Journal of Economic History,* IX No. 2 (November 1949), 177–79. The attitude of certain members of Congress toward the early proposals is indicated by Clifford Durr, who was Assistant General Counsel for DPC in 1940: "About a week later Mr. Hotchkiss came by my office and stated that the deal approved on the 7th was all off. I asked him why, and he replied that some people on the 'Hill', meaning members of Congress, had heard about it and called Knudsen 'raising hell' about giving away plants paid for by the Government." Durr, *History of DPC,* p. 16.

2 August 1940.[4] This draft, in brief, provided that the contractor would construct the facilities with his own or borrowed funds and would be reimbursed over a period of five years in five equal installments. Thus the cost of the facilities would be separately established and reimbursed. No provision was made, however, for excluding the cost of facilities from the supply price of the product.

A prominent feature of this draft was the proposed basis for disposing of the facilities upon termination of the supply contract. This feature called for sale to the contractor at what was known as the fair value of the facilities. If the contractor desired to purchase the plant, he was to request an appraisal within thirty days after termination. Appraisal was to be made jointly by a representative of the contractor and a representative of the procuring agency. If they could not agree, a third appraiser would be appointed by the senior judge of the U.S. Circuit Court of Appeals of the circuit in which the facilities were located. The appraisers were directed to determine the fair value, which was defined as "the value which the Emergency Plant Facilities have to the Contractor without regard to their original cost and considering only the prospective earning power which they will add to the Contractor's plant under conditions then existing, making due allowance for the expense which the Contractor must incur if they are to be adapted to [his] normal peacetime activities." It was stipulated, however, that if the appraisers found a higher value in the open market, the facilities "may" be valued at such open market value. If the contractor was unwilling to buy the entire facilities at the appraised value, he could still "skim the cream" by purchasing any part of the facilities as individually appraised. All items not purchased were to be removed by the government, which agreed not to use the facilities in competition with the contractor except during war or national emergency.

This draft was subject to considerable criticism within the War Department.[5] But the NDAC was under great pressure from all sides to complete an acceptable form of the contract so that the defense program could get under way. Although a number of changes were made, others were obviously desirable when the NDAC announced the new contract to the press on 23 August. The wording of the press release was calculated to promote wide enthusiasm for the contract:

This plan represents striking progress in the evolution of Government procurement methods. It was prepared by the Commission and adopted after consultation with the War and Navy Departments and the Comptroller General. In substance, it offers what might be described as a bankable contract, one which will permit contractors to finance the expanded facilities through use of their own funds or the granting of credit from private sources.

Specifically, it has two purposes: First, to expedite signing of supplies contracts by assuring the contractor against loss on construction undertaken for military purposes; second, it safeguards the Government's interest in such facilities on termination or completion of the

---

[4] Memo, Lt Col Franklin T. Hammond, Jr., Legal Div OUSW, for USW, 12 Jan 44, sub: History of the Emergency Plant Facilities Contract (hereafter cited as Hammond History), and Exhibit 1, in USW 004.03.

[5] Memo, Col Hugh C. Smith (Ret.), Legal Sec Purchases and Contracts Br OUSW, for Col Schulz, 6 Aug 40, in Hammond History. Among many other criticisms Colonel Smith summarized the purchases option feature with the words: "These rules for appraisal seem to be all in the interest of the contractor."

contract. The Government's residual interest upon such termination is to be evaluated by the usual board of three appraisers, one appointed by the Government, one by the contractor and the third by the Senior Judge of the Circuit Court of Appeals of the Circuit wherein the facilities are located.[6]

Despite the declared acceptability of the newly announced contract, some officials within the NDAC, and elsewhere, were not convinced that the government's interest in the emergency facilities was being adequately protected. The issue was brought into the open by a memorandum of 4 September 1940, relating primarily to machinery and equipment, written by Mr. Henderson's legal assistant, David Ginsburg:

The essential fact, as I see it, is that the Government will pay for every cent of the cost of such facilities, and will assume every element of risk on the construction contract. Yet . . . we propose to *require* the Government to sell its interest in such facilities for whatever they may be worth to the contractor, or whatever they would bring on the market. What would such facilities bring on the market? Unquestionably, the answer is little or nothing, as World War experience plainly shows. Thus, although we have labored to sift the cost of the machinery and equipment out of the price of supplies and have at least illuminated the fact that the Government has an interest in the facilities financed through an increase in the cost of supplies, we propose to demand the sale of the Government's interest, so belatedly recognized, at a price set in the trough of a glutted market. To regard this as 'striking progress in the evolution of Government procurement' is to confuse form with substance. In my opinion, we would still be giving away plant and equipment.

. . . .

Of one thing, I am reasonably certain: that fairness to the contractor does not require, in addition to—

(1) a reasonable profit;

(2) a bankable contract; and

(3) assurance against risk of loss on new construction, a capital subsidy to the contractor in the form of free machinery and equipment. . . . Unless this formula is revised . . . our work will have been substantially fruitless.[7]

As a result of these and similar criticisms, the proposed appraisal feature was dropped and the cost-less-depreciation formula— previously mentioned—was adopted, with the alternative of negotiation for a lower price. The annual depreciation rates for the purchase option were stated in an appendix to each contract, and generally amounted to 5 percent for buildings, 12 percent for heavy machinery and equipment, and 50 percent for portable tools. Thus the contractor could be certain of purchasing the facilities at the end of the five-year period for 75 percent of building costs and 40 percent of cost for heavy machinery, with light tools thrown in.[8]

The effects of this change in policy were duly noted by the business community:

It is now obvious that this recapture figure—cost less depreciation—will run higher than it would have under the original plan

[6] NDAC Press Release, PR 80, 23 Aug 40, Hammond History, Exhibit 6.

[7] CPA, Policies, pp. 34–35.
[8] Considerable discussion and effort went into the establishment of the rates of depreciation. The NDAC Committee on Taxation and Finance on 30 November 1940 recommended rates substantially higher than those allowed by Treasury for income tax purposes. With some changes these were recommended to the War Department on 21 January 1941 and approved by the NDAC on 5 February. (1) *Ibid.*, p. 40. (2) Ltr, Donald Nelson, Dir of Purchases OPM, to ASW, 21 Jan 41, in USW files, General, Emergency Plant Facilities folder (hereafter cited as EPF folder). The War Department allowed higher than the recommended rates in early cases; eventually the rates were simplified and standardized for all types of facilities contract. Ltr, USW to Wayne Coy, Secy NDAC, 23 Aug 41, EPF folder, protesting denial of necessity certificate for EPF projects because of unexplained, excessive rates allowed by War Department.

to give the contractor a dominant option to buy the plant at its residual value as determined by arbitration. . . . This method was adopted to avoid the criticism that the government was giving the plants away. The Defense Commission is thinking not only about the popular outcry but also about the beefing by a contractor's competitors who don't get the benefit of the useful value left in a war plant.[9]

In addition to the revised basis for plant disposition, improved protection of the government's interest was sought by the provision of all EPF contracts that no part of the facility costs should be included in the supply price of the product. This provision would of course be subject to the same difficulties of administration which confronted procuring agencies in determining nonreimbursement under the tax-amortization program. In fact, developments soon required that all EPF contractors apply for, and secure, necessity certificates entitling them to the tax-amortization privilege. This resulted from a surprise ruling by the Treasury that reimbursement payments—by their nature a capital, not an income, transaction—were to be treated for tax purpose as gross income.[10] The same ruling, however, permitted the application of accelerated amortization to such facilities, thus "washing out" any income tax liability on the part of the contractor for reimbursement.[11] While EPF construction projects, by

virtue of their War or Navy Department sponsorship, were automatically granted necessity certificates, supply contracts for these facilities received the normal scrutiny before the issuance of nonreimbursement certificates.

The problem of making the EPF contract acceptable to bankers as a basis for construction loans ultimately led to contractual arrangements which played a significant part in the early obsolescence of this type of contract. Although the banks were outspoken in their antipathy toward government financing, they were unprepared to advance loans in the absence of elaborate arrangements for the guarantee of full repayment. The NDAC, working through the Federal Reserve System, had ascertained in September that the nation's banks were in a position to lend more than $3 billion for defense plant expansion.[12] Concurrently, the NDAC sponsored in Congress the Assignment of Claims Act, which became law on 9 October 1940.[13] This permitted contractors to assign to lending institutions their claims to reimbursement under government contracts, and each EPF contract contained a clause permitting such assignment. But the banks were not satisfied with a claim against the government to the full

---

[9] *Business Week*, No. 578 (September 28, 1940), 7.

[10] TD 5016, Sec. 19.126–6, effective 8 Oct 40. This ruling was doubly surprising in view of a confidential ruling two weeks earlier that reimbursement payments were not to be treated as income. See mimeographed copy of the Bureau of Internal Revenue ruling dated 25 Sep 40, Sec. 19.22 (a) 1, marked as Exhibit 8, Hammond History.

[11] This arrangement later turned out to be less than a perfect washing transaction. Reimbursement did not begin until the final cost certificate had been

approved, whereas tax amortization was subject to commencement as individual portions of the facilities were completed and placed in operation. Since large amounts were involved, this failure to match could result in substantial changes in tax liability. Unsigned copy of Memo, emanating from Audit and Accounting Section, 24 Sep 41, sub: Federal and State Income Taxes under EPF Contracts, in EPF folder.

[12] Ltr, Chester Morrill, Secy, to Donald Nelson, Chmn WPB, 11 Jan 44, in Exhibit 13, Hammond History. The "forty-eight hour test mobilization of bank credit" is described succinctly in NDAC Press Release, PR 126, 25 Sep 40.

[13] Public Law 811, effective 9 Oct 40, 76th Cong., 3d Sess.

value of the facilities. They were fearful that the emergency might suddenly end and that Congress would fail to make appropriations to the procuring agencies for complete discharge of their EPF obligations. Consequently, there was written into the EPF contract a provision that the entire unpaid balance of the cost of the facilities would become due to the contractor (and hence to the bank as assignee) in the absence of full appropriation and obligation of funds ninety days before the end of each fiscal year during the life of the contract.[14] In order to meet these terms, the War Department was obliged to hold perpetually idle out of its appropriations the full balance on all EPF facilities. The end result was a bad bargain for the War Department. It had to provide the funds for full financing, only to hold them idle as guaranty against the bank loans, while the banks collected $2\frac{1}{2}$–percent to 4–percent interest. To add to its discomfiture, the War Department was obliged to pay this interest, since interest charges were an authorized component of the final certified cost of the facilities; and this was at a time when funds were available from DPC for $1\frac{1}{2}$ percent.[15]

The numerous difficulties which arose in drafting the EPF contact were exceeded only by the problems which arose in its implementation. First of all were the delays in getting EPF arrangements under way. Before the contractor could safely sign a contract, he had to be sure that adequate financing would be forthcoming from the banks. But the banks were reluctant to make a commitment prior to the existence of a contract or at least a detailed "Appendix A"—the supporting schedule of land, buildings, machinery, and equipment which eventually documented all facilities contracts. Moreover, some of the contracts were so large that a single bank could not advance the necessary funds without exceeding the statutory limits to a single borrower. Conversely, some contractors feared banker control of their facilities when 100-percent financed by banks. Frequently banks would be unwilling to finance more than 50 percent of the cost of facilities in view of their high rate of depreciation and obsolescence; for many defense contractors 50-percent financing was no better than no financing. Thus, at a time when the contractor should have been ordering equipment and initiating construction, he was occupied in negotiating for credit.[16]

As these difficulties were resolved others took their place. Douglas Aircraft at Long Beach learned to its chagrin that the governor of California had vetoed the state tax-amortization bill. At the same time the

---

[14] See below, pages 483–84.

[15] Under the contract for the Ford Dearborn plant, the War Department paid 4-percent interest where bank funds were used, 2 percent for Ford's own funds. See draft of contract amendment in EPF folder. War Department interest payments under Air Corps EPF contracts to date of final cost certificates were estimated at $1,266,000. Interest on outstanding loans after final cost certification was paid by the War Department by the terms of supply contracts. After estimating that its total payments under such provisions would amount to $8½ million, the War Department arranged for immediate, complete reimbursement by amendment to all EPF contracts. (1) Memo, Maj Franklin T. Hammond, Jr., for USW, 30 Jun 42, sub: Interest Charges in Connection with Emergency Plant Facilities Contracts. (2) Ltr, Hammond to Lt Col Reginald C. Harmon, JAGD USAAF, Wright Field,

9 Jul 42, discussing reliance upon First War Powers Act to secure modification of EPF contracts. Both in EPF folder.

[16] An excellent summary of these and other difficulties associated with EPF is found in the testimony of Under Secretary Patterson before a meeting of members of the Senate and House Appropriations Committee. See memo of testimony in USW files, DPC (Gen.) No. 1.

state of California followed the U.S. Treasury in counting plant reimbursement as income, and Douglas was faced with an additional tax liability of $800,000. One observer, commented: "This ruling may well be the means of terminating the EPF form of contract not only in California, but in other states where a similar situation prevails." [17] The Douglas plant was thereafter taken over by the War Department as a government-owned facility.[18]

A perplexing matter under several EPF contracts was the problem of scrambled facilities. In the case of Glenn L. Martin, some $6 million in buildings were constructed on land belonging to the contractor. The War Department soon recognized that such an arrangement represented poor contracting since the obligation of the government to remove the buildings—if no agreement on price was reached at termination—reduced the government's bargaining position to nil. Accordingly, the War Department sought to take out a twenty-five-year lease on the land which was located in the heart of the Martin establishment. Martin was agreeable to the lease proposal, provided the government would not directly or indirectly use the leasehold to produce planes in competition with Martin. Although the War Department was quite willing so to restrict the lease, the Treasury Department felt that the Martin company would "derive income" from such restriction and would be subject to substantial income and excess profits taxes on such constructive income. Col. George H. Foster, head of the Army's Tax Amortization Unit, summed up this and similar negotiations

involving EPF contracts: "The result appears to be that an opportunity to place the Government in a more favorable position with regard to these buildings is being thwarted by Treasury. . . . We are simply in a horrible mess with these EPF contracts, and I think we should attack the issue, washing them out as bad rubbish." [19]

Another shortcoming of the EPF contract was its inadequacy for the financing of subcontractors and vendors, often in basic industries, producing ultimately for the War Department. The products of these firms were vitally essential to prime contractors producing planes, ordnance equipment, and other items. The plant facilities of such suppliers would retain a high percentage of their value for peacetime purposes and it was undesirable, in fairness to privately financed competitors, to provide full governmental reimbursement for their construction. Yet plant expansion for these was vital to the defense program. A modification of the EPF contract was made for such cases whereby the government would deduct, from its periodic reimbursement payment, an amount equivalent to depreciation rental as allowed for corresponding facilities under DPC lease agreements. But this meant that the bank which financed the contractor under an assignment of the claim to reimbursement would be covered only to the extent of the reduced claim, in some cases

---

[17] See memo cited above, note 11.

[18] (1) WD, Quarterly Inventory of Owned, Sponsored, and Leased Facilities, 30 Jun 45, p. 233. (2) Supplement to (1), 30 Sep 45, p. 1.

[19] Memo, Foster for Col Greenbaum, 26 Dec 42, sub: EPF Contracts, in USW files, General, Memos to Greenbaum folder. The unkind words for the EPF contract were numerous: "Although one or two of those who worked with the problem were inclined to take a mildly hopeful—or perhaps not entirely hopeless—view of the Emergency Plant Facilities Contract, others in the office considered it an abortion and justifiable only because nothing else was then available." Anderson, Introduction to the History of the Under Secretary of War's Office, Ch. V p. 162.

as low as 50 percent of total cost. This was a factor underlying the frequent inability of contractors to secure more than partial financing from banks.[20]

The first EPF contract entered by the War Department was consummated on 8 October 1940 with Boeing Aircraft for the construction of a B–29 airplane plant at Seattle, Washington. By April 1941, the Army Air Corps had entered a total of eleven EPF contracts, with a commitment value totaling some $133 million. By this time the superiority of the new DPC type of contract had been demonstrated and no further EPF contracts were entered by the Air Corps. Ordnance likewise found EPF of little use after the spring of 1941, entering only four such contracts after June of that year. Total Ordnance EPF contracts numbered twenty-seven, with a commitment value of some $56½ million. The only other branch of the Army to use EPF was the Quartermaster Corps, which entered three such contracts of an authorized value of a half million dollars; these were later taken over and administered by the Corps of Engineers.

Thus the War Department as a whole entered a total of forty-one EPF contracts, amounting to some $190 million. A number of these were later converted, for one reason or another, to straight War Department-owned facilities. As of 30 September 1945, the accumulated construction expenditures on all facilities then remaining in EPF status amounted to less than $110 million; of this figure, $75 million was represented by two plants—Ford at Dearborn,

Michigan, and Glenn L. Martin at Middle River, Maryland.[21]

The practical causes for the failure of EPF were—as already mentioned—higher interest rates, the absurdity of double provision of funds (once by the banks, again by War Department earmarked appropriations), the inadequacy of 50-percent financing for subcontractors and vendors, red tape and delays in getting projects started, controversy with the Treasury and state tax bodies, the complexities of scrambled facilities, and so on. Underlying these difficulties was the haphazard manner in which the EPF contract came into being. It was, first of all, a pioneer measure subject to all the vicissitudes of trial and error. It was conceived in an atmosphere of political uncertainty, confusion, and haste. Its initial sponsors, anxious to get the defense program under way, were too much inclined to neglect the government's interest, and considerable patchwork on the contract was necessary in order to redeem it. More patchwork was required to deal with tax problems and Treasury regulations, and still more to satisfy the banks. By the time the contract had reached final form it was hardly recognizable and perhaps even less understandable. The following *sentence*, appreciated most when read aloud, typifies the problems of both form and substance in the conception and administration of the EPF contract:

In the event that, on the date 90 days preceding the close of each of fiscal years which shall be wholly or in part included in the

---

[20] (1) Patterson testimony cited above, note 16. (2) Memo for Files, Warren S. Ege, 7 Apr 41, sub: Rental Arrangements under Defense Plant Corporation Lease Agreements and EPF Contracts, in USW files, DPC (Gen.) No. 1.

[21] Supplement cited above, note 18 (2), Previous figures on the number and value of EPF contracts by technical services are found in Memo, Maj S. K. Bradley, Chf Liaison Br, Purchases Div ASF, for Col Park Holland, 9 Sep 44, sub: Emergency Plant Facilities Contracts, in EPF folder.

period between the date of this contract and the date of full payment by the Government of the Government Reimbursement for Plant Costs hereunder, there shall not have been theretofore made available either by appropriation or contract authorization by the Congress and validly obligated by the Government to the performance of this contract funds, the appropriation and obligation of which will not lapse and which will not revert to the Treasury or be carried to the surplus fund prior to the close of the next succeeding fiscal year, in an amount sufficient to provide for the payment when due of the balance of Government Reimbursement for Plant Costs then remaining unpaid, or, if the acquisition and construction or installation shall not have been completed, the maximum amount of the Government Reimbursement for Plant Costs hereunder provided in Section 4 of Article II, this contract shall terminate and the amount of such balance shall on said date become due and shall, promptly after said date and before the close of the fiscal year then current, be paid by the Government to the Contractor out of the appropriations or contract authorizations originally or thereafter specified in connection with this contract.[22]

Defense Plant Corporation Facilities

Origins of DPC Financing

The EPF contract proved to be so cumbersome and otherwise unsatisfactory that it rapidly gave way to a superior type of arrangement. This new arrangement was found in the Defense Plant Corporation contract, which came to be used for the general expansion of such basic industries as aircraft, aluminum, magnesium, synthetic rubber, and steel. DPC financing also provided machinery and equipment for military contractors independently of building construction or expansion.[23]

Authority for the creation of the Defense Plant Corporation was provided by the 25 June 1940 amendment to the Reconstruction Finance Corporation act.[24] Under this amendment the RFC was authorized to create corporations with power "to purchase and lease land, to purchase, lease, build, and expand plants, and to purchase and produce equipment, supplies, and machinery for the manufacture of arms, ammunition, and implements of war." Facilities thus created by DPC could be leased to private firms for actual operation. While the amendment was still under consideration by Congress, RFC officials set about the task of devising satisfactory contractual arrangements. The terms would have to be sufficiently attractive to encourage private industry to utilize DPC financing and to operate defense plants

---

[22] Emergency Plant Facilities Contract (WF-12-26-40-500 (4)), Article II, Section 2. This provision, introduced for the benefit of the banks, turned out to be a boomerang, as banks and contractors alike found themselves with lucrative contracts subject to automatic cancellation as the end of the fiscal year approached. This feature was later amended in all EPF contracts to make cancellation optional with the contractor under the stated conditions. See: (1) copy of ltr, Chase National Bank to participants in Vultee Aircraft loan, 8 May 41; (2) Memo, USW for CofAC, 3 May 41, sub: Article II, Section 2, EPF Contracts, enclosing proposed amendment. Both in EPF folder.

[23] An informative treatment of the origin and early operation of DPC is to be found in White, "Financing Industrial Expansion for War," pp. 156–83. See also: (1) Hans A. Klagsbrunn, "Some Aspects of War Plant Financing," *American Economic Review*, (*Papers and Proceedings of the 55th Annual Meeting of the American Economic Association*), XXXIII (Supplement, March 1943), 119–27; (2) Durr, *History of DPC*, pp. *vii*, 43. All three of these authors were formally connected with DPC: Mr. White as historian, Mr. Durr as General Counsel, and Mr. Klagsbrunn as Executive Vice President.

[24] 54 *Stat.* 572, 25 Jun 40, Sec. 5. For background of the act, see U.S. Congress, Senate, Committee on Banking and Currency, *Hearings on S. 3938* (76th Cong., 3d Sess.).

thereunder. Also, arrangements for the disposition of the facilities at the end of the emergency would have to be provided in a manner which would at once be fair to the government, attractive to the prospective operator, and advantageous to the economy as a whole.

During the early stages of the development of the Defense Plant Corporation, considerable opposition to "government ownership" was expressed. Business was frankly concerned lest government-owned plants would continue to be operated in peacetime, in competition with private industry.[25] Also, the banks did not favor the use of government funds for the expansion of industry.[26] Within the RFC there was some reluctance to adopt a bold plan of financing: Mr. Jesse H. Jones—who held the purse strings of RFC—was known to be conservative and some of his subordinates feared that he

would not be willing to commit RFC funds to a venture which might result in substantial loss.[27] Even the War Department at first frowned upon DPC in preferring the better-known EPF-type contract.[28]

Despite the obstacles and opposition from various quarters, the Defense Plant Corporation was chartered on 22 August 1940. Discussion and negotiation with various firms, mostly in the aircraft industry, led to a clarification of the issues and the development of satisfactory arrangements for all concerned. On 3 September 1940, the first DPC contract was signed with the Packard Motor Car Company for the creation of an aircraft engine plant. As other firms reviewed the Packard arrangements, they quickly saw the advantages and by the spring of 1941 the DPC type of financing came generally to be preferred to EPF.

Basic Terms of DPC Contracts

The DPC form of contract was a gradual development and individual contracts varied with the type of facility concerned. The typical terms and procedures were as follows:[29] The Army (or other procuring

---

[25] Among the vigorous opponents of government ownership at the beginning of the defense period was Mr. William S. Knudsen, NDAC commissioner for production. (1) Durr, History of DPC, pp. 11, 12, 19, 21, 26. (2) White, "Financing Industrial Expansion for War," p. 180.

[26] (1) Durr, History of DPC, p. 23. (2) White, "Financing Industrial Expansion for War," pp. 177–79. White quotes the following from a speech in February 1941 by Mr. B. D. Houston, president of the American Bankers Association: "The American Bankers Association is well aware of the fact that the future independence of business may depend upon the extent to which bankers finance defense orders. If business is going to the government for the bulk of its credit now, it will be dependent on the government in the future." Although government financing came to be preferred by industry over private financing, it was not the policy of either DPC or the War Department to replace specific EPF contracts with DPC contracts in the absence of explicit consent of the banks concerned. Telg, Winthrop W. Aldrich, Chase National Bank, to Robert Patterson, and reply, 1 and 3 July 41, in USW files, DPC (Gen.) No. 1. Nevertheless a large proportion of Air Forces EPF contracts were converted to DPC financing at the specific request of the contractors.

[27] Durr, History of DPC, p. 8.

[28] Under Secretary Patterson's initial reaction to DPC was one of hostility. He had not been informed of the nature of the DPC contract and feared that DPC proposals would delay the expansion of facilities by upsetting the proposed EPF arrangements. At that time the EPF contract was being widely heralded by NDAC and the press as the key to rapid defense plant expansion. Mr. Patterson's hostility was short-lived. (1) Ibid., pp. 36–37. (2) Anderson, Introduction to the History of the Under Secretary of War's Office, Ch. V, pp. 168–69.

[29] DPC contracts were known as Plancors, from the name of the lending agency, and each contract was assigned a Plancor number. There were two general types: (1) Complete Plancors, each covering an entire industrial facility—land, buildings, and equipment; (2) "M&E Plancors," covering only machinery and equipment purchased by DPC

agency), in negotiating a supply contract with a private contractor, would determine the need for additional facilities. The contractor would prepare approximate specifications for the plant, including land and equipment, and the interested supply arm of the Army would act as the sponsoring agency. The DPC would then enter a contract with the private firm, agreeing to put up the money, as needed, for site acquisition and plant construction. The contractor (known as the lessee) would let contracts for the construction of the plant and the purchase of equipment. All contracts and equipment purchase orders of the lessee were subject to the approval of DPC, which maintained a supervising engineer at major construction sites. Title to the plant was vested in DPC, and upon completion the lessee would operate the plant in the production of defense supplies for the Army, Navy, or other defense supplier. The lessee typically paid a rental for the plant during the life of the contract. At the end of the emergency the operator-lessee had a ninety-day option to purchase the entire facility.[30]

Lessee's Purchase Option—Of primary importance in enlisting the interest of potential contractors in plant expansion in 1940 and 1941 were the terms under which the plants would be disposed of at the end of the emergency. While many contractors were fearful of the possibility of government ownership and operation after the war,

they were even more concerned that defense plants—with their up-to-date equipment and built-in know-how—might fall into the hands of competitors. It was thus desirable as a matter of both incentive and equity to give contractors an option to buy the plant at the termination of the contract. Moreover, the most advantageous location for new defense plants was frequently at the site of the defense contractor's existing plant, on land held by him for future expansion. This was desirable for reasons of both speed and economy; the contractor could supervise construction as well as management of the new plant with maximum convenience. An additional reason for the option privilege was the decision of DPC officials to keep new plant costs down; since the option price was tied to cost it was to the contractor's advantage to build well and efficiently.

Nevertheless, in the early negotiations at the beginning of the defense program, private industry did not appear to be greatly attracted by terms which would adequately protect the government's interest. Some of the early proposals leading up to both the EPF and DPC contracts would have resulted in the government practically giving away expensive plant and equipment to contractors who had built and operated them.[31] Although a number of such pro-

---

and rented to manufacturers for use in their own plants. While the first type is the primary concern of this discussion, many of the problems and procedures were common to both.

[30] An excellent summary of representative DPC lease arrangements is found in the four-page Memorandum for File, prepared by Sturgis Warner, 10 Jul 43, sub: Functions of the Defense Plant Corporation in Relation to the War Department Facilities Program (copy in OCMH).

[31] With a curious "dog-in-the-manger" attitude some contractors, in order to prevent plants from falling into the hands of competitors, were not satisfied with an option to buy. They wished to be given title virtually cost-free so that they could dispose of the plant as they saw fit. One aircraft manufacturer, when asked what he would do with such a plant at the end of the emergency if he found it excess to his needs, made the remark: "We will pull the roof off and let the rain come in." Durr, *History of DPC*, pp. 12–13. For additional discussion of some of the early proposals, see (1) White, "Financing Industrial Expansion for War," pp. 164–68; (2) Klagsbrunn, "Some Aspects of War Plant Financing," pp. 124–25.

posals had been tentatively approved, resistance by individuals in DPC and NDAC as well as by members of Congress resulted in a definite clarification of the government's interest and the adoption of measures to protect this interest. The firm option price to DPC lessees thus became cost less depreciation or cost less rental payments, whichever was higher.

In exercising his purchase option, the lessee was not permitted to "skim the cream" from the facilities by buying only strategic or especially desirable portions. The firm option price, at which the facilities would be sold to the lessee without further negotiation, was the higher of two figures: (1) cost, plus 4 percent interest, less rentals paid in; (2) cost less depreciation, subject to a minimum residual figure of 15 percent of cost. Depreciation rates were standard: 5 percent for buildings and similar installations; 12 percent for machinery and equipment; 25 percent for portable durable tools and automotive equipment. For "no-rental" facilities, described below, only the cost-less-depreciation formula was used. During the ninety-day period following termination of the contract, the lessee was free to negotiate with DPC and the sponsoring agency for a lower price. If the lessee failed to reach an agreement with DPC as to the price, he had "first refusal" rights for an additional ninety-day period. This meant that he had superior purchase rights over all outsiders at a price equal to the best offer. About a fourth of DPC projects did not include a purchase option, either because of lack of interest on the part of the contractor, or because the postwar distribution of the facilities involved broad issues of social policy.[32]

[32] White, "Financing Industrial Expansion for War," p. 182, especially note 92. Nonoption facilities included in the Geneva Steel Plant and aluminum, magnesium, synthetic rubber, and other

Rental Provisions—Rental arrangements for DPC facilities fell into three general categories:

(1) *No rental* ($1 per year—customarily referred to as "nominal" rental), used for noncompetitive, specialized facilities for direct suppliers to the government. Under this contract, no part of the facilities cost could be included in the supply price of the product. No-rental facilities in some cases were privately operated for a management fee similar to War Department-owned establishments.[33]

(2) *Depreciation rental*, a figure roughly equivalent to the actual deterioration of the plant during the life of the contract. This was designed for competitive-type facilities completely devoted to production for the government. The payments were calculated to place DPC lessees on a competitive basis with private contractors using their own equipment and thus obliged to recoup their plant depreciation costs in the supply price of their products. For purposes of administrative simplicity, the rental was usually expressed in terms of a percentage of net product sales calculated to yield the equivalent of the depreciation formula.[34]

plants. For a revealing treatment of these issues, see G. Herbert Stein, *The Disposal of the Aluminum Plants* (Washington: Committee on Public Administration Cases, 1948).

[33] The large aircraft plants (frames, engines, propellers, assembly) were no-rental facilities. In this class also were subcontractors for items ordinarily produced by no-rental primes in their own plant. See Ege Memo, cited above in note 20 (2). For summary description of various rental arrangements, see also Memo for File, F. H. Otto, 17 Oct 44, sub: DPC Lease Agreements . . ., in USW files, DPC (Gen.) No. 4.

[34] The depreciation rates for rental purposes were identical with those used in connection with the purchases option. Contracts calling for depreciation rental specified that there could be no facilities charges in supply contracts beyond rental payments. maintenance, taxes, and insurance.

(3) *Full rental,* a figure calculated to discharge full plant costs over a five-year period (the conventional expectation of the duration of the emergency). Full-rental leases contemplated the use of facilities for commercial as well as defense production.[35]

Facilities in the full-rental category included three subtypes: (1) so-called stepchildren—facilities not sponsored by any particular supply arm but in which the Army as a whole had the preponderant interest by virtue of the ultimate destination of the products; (2) basic industries—for example, aluminum and steel forgings, and other metal products—whose supply contracts were at least two steps away from the finished product purchased by the Army, and whose product prices were not subject to scrutiny; (3) plants producing both for defense and commercial purposes. In 1941 a number of expansions were authorized, especially by Ordnance, in order to provide capacity to meet anticipated requirements in excess of current needs. Such excess capacity could be used for commercial purposes without prejudice to the government's interest, especially in view of the full-rental provision.[36]

A further feature of DPC rentals was the frequent gearing of rental payments to plant costs by the application of a rough sliding scale. Thus, a manufacturer planning to build a $50 million plant might be charged a rental equivalent to 4 percent of plant cost, with the stipulation that the rate would go up to 8 percent if actual costs reached $100 million. Such an arrangement put pressure upon the contractor to keep his plant costs down. The majority of rental arrangements were, however, eventually placed on a percentage of sales basis. This eased the lessee's burden by co-ordinating rental payments with income. A sliding scale for this purpose was often adopted, calculated to produce the desired rate of cost amortization.[37]

War Department Take-Out Arrangements

In the evolution of the DPC contract and its accompanying arrangements, several steps are of particular interest with regard to the role of the War Department in the program. The first of these relates to the extent of War Department financial obligation under DPC contracts. Originally, the DPC staff had envisaged for all contracts a substantial rental payment to protect the solvency of its investment. The War Department, however, insisted upon rent-free arrangements for aircraft and similar large prime contractors engaged exclusively in turning out major items for national defense. The payment of rent would have forced up supply prices and dissipated War Department appropriations. Moreover, under prompting by NDAC—which was fearful of double payment to contractors for facilities costs—the War Department wanted a clear separation between the cost of facilities and the cost of completed munitions. In all cases where public funds were granted specifically to finance the expansion of facilities, steps were to be taken to insure

---

[35] Ege Memo, cited above in note 20 (2).

[36] (1) *Ibid.* (2) Memo, Franklin T. Hammond, Jr., Special Asst to USW, for USW, 18 Feb 42, in USW files, DPC (Gen.) No. 2.

[37] For example, in one particular contract involving a plant cost authorized at approximately $2.2 million, the DPC lease provided for annual rental payments of 4 percent of net sales in excess of $10 million. If procurement contracts were insufficient during the life of the DPC contract to yield any rental, the DPC would, in effect, retain complete equity in the plant.

that no part of facilities costs would be loaded into the unit price of the products.

The no-rental stand taken by the War Department put the DPC in an embarrassing position when it set out in 1940 to make funds available for plant expansion. In the absence of a substantial rental payment, the DPC would be left at the end of the contract with nothing to show for its investment except title to a plant which was both physically depreciated and potentially without a market for its products. This would have violated the basic principles of sound financing upon which the RFC had been organized. On the other hand, the War Department was hardly in a position to finance the entire plant expansion program. Until after Pearl Harbor, its special Expediting Funds for plant construction were limited; by the time appropriations were available in superabundance, the DPC had already assumed a significant and useful role in the defense program.

The solution was found in the so-called take-out letter. The take-out letter was a letter contract between the Army and DPC under which the Army agreed to reimburse DPC, out of current appropriations, for a substantial portion of the cost of the facilities. In the case of no-rental facilities the Army would typically pay DPC two fifths of the cost when the facilities were ready for operation. In addition, the Army agreed, upon termination of the lease, to request appropriations from Congress to reimburse DPC for any remaining unrecovered costs. Upon such reimbursement, title would pass in effect to the War Department; in any case, the DPC could not dispose of the facility without War Department approval.

In depreciation-rental contracts the Army also provided take-out arrangements except

that the cash payment was limited to 40 percent of cost less estimated rental returns over a five-year period. Thus for a $2 million plant renting for $150,000 per year, the Army would pay 40 percent of $1,250,000 or $500,000 in cash, covering any remaining DPC deficits by the contingent request upon Congress.

For full-rental contracts the Army provided no cash take-out since it was presumed that DPC would be adequately reimbursed over the life of the contract; the provision for contingency request upon Congress was made, however, to protect DPC against any possibility of less than full reimbursement.[38]

The take-out letter, originally proposed by the DPC, was drawn from two precedents: The EPF contract, which required the Army or Navy to earmark out of current appropriations 100 percent of plant costs; and the earlier loans of RFC to state and local governments for relief purposes. These loans had never been repaid and Congress eventually passed legislation permitting RFC to write them off. By agreeing to a partial cash take-out, the DPC was able to multiply the effectiveness of War Department funds while providing at the same time a substantial cushion to protect its own investment. If the contingency request upon Congress eventually became necessary, the onus would be upon the War Department rather than upon DPC. This arrangement

---

[38] In 1942 the provision for contingency request was dropped for full-rental projects except in those cases where the War Department wished to retain an interest in the facility after the emergency. Ege Memo, cited above in note 20(2). A concise summary of War Department take-out arrangements is furnished in Memo for File, Sturgis Warner, 3 Aug 44, sub: Calculation of War Department Firm Commitment on DPC Projects, in USW files, DPC (Gen.) No. 4.

was agreeable to Under Secretary Patterson, who obtained a careful opinion from the Judge Advocate General upholding its legality.[39]

As plant expansion got under way, various changes were made in the arrangements. The initial DPC proposal was a 60-percent take-out, but at War Department request this figure was shortly reduced to 40 percent.[40] In a number of important cases this was raised to 50 percent; in others it was as low as 16 percent.[41] In May 1945, the contingent request upon Congress was made applicable only in case of formal request by DPC, and then not before 1 July 1946.[42] By this date, as part of the national policy of readjustment and postwar reconversion, DPC had relieved the War Department of any obligation under the contingency feature.[43]

---

[39] (1) Memo, ASW for JAG, 29 Oct 40, and 1st Ind, JAG for ASW 12 Nov 40, file Contracts, JAG 161. (2) The take-out letter was first suggested by Mr. Hans Klagsbrunn, then assistant counsel and later executive vice president of DPC. Durr, *History of DPC,* pp. 39–40.

[40] Ltr, Jesse Jones, Federal Loan Administrator, to ASW, 12 Dec 40, in USW files, DPC (Gen.) No. 1.

[41] Memo for Record, Maj F. H. Otto, 8 Aug 45, sub: Facilities Expansions Recommended for DPC Financing November 1940 to February 1942, in USW files, DPC (Gen.) No. 5. The $175 million Chrysler plant in Chicago was covered by a 50 percent War Department take-out.

[42] Ltr, USW to DPC, 22 May 45, approved by Frank R. Roney, Vice President, DPC, in USW files, DPC (Gen.) No. 5.

[43] On 30 June 1945 Congress dissolved the Defense Plant Corporation and all other corporate subsidiaries of RFC, which took over all liabilities of its erstwhile subsidiaries. 59 *Stat.* 310, 30 Jun 45. Three years later Congress authorized the Secretary of the Treasury to cancel RFC notes in the amount of over $9.3 billion, representing unrecovered costs of national defense, war, and reconversion activities. 62 *Stat. 1187–88, 30 Jun 48.*

Operation and Administration

The implementation of the DPC contract, despite its relative flexibility, was beset with inevitable difficulties. A chronic problem was the treatment of "unrecoverable costs"—expenditures associated chiefly with alterations and conversions of existing plants to new uses. These expenditures might be essential to war production but would add little or nothing to the long-term value of the facility. They covered a multitude of purposes and took place throughout the life of the contract as well as at the time of original construction or conversion: also, particularly for M&E Plancors, they would often run to a substantial percentage of the total cost of the contracts. Typical items were the cost of transfer, storage, and installation of machinery, the provision and alteration of wiring and lighting fixtures, grading, cement work, raising of ceilings and roofs, and miscellaneous carpentry, electrical, and plumbing work. Such expenses were ordinarily provided for in direct government supply contracts; the difficulty lay primarily with subcontractors sponsored by the War Department and financed by DPC. The DPC was reluctant to make capital outlays for items of this nature, and the War Department felt that many of them should be absorbed by the contractor. If an overly liberal attitude were taken, it would result in a substantial windfall to manufacturers, enabling them to modernize their plant or otherwise profit at government expense; an overly stringent position would create inequities as well as impede production. Many negotiations were held between the War Department, the DPC, and private contractors but no fixed policy was ever reached. In some cases the DPC agreed to allow up to 10 percent of total cost for unrecoverables; in other cases the manufacturer would pay full rental or would charge such items to overhead; in still others the War Department would provide DPC with 100-percent cash take-out. The wide variety and constantly changing nature of unrecoverable costs required flexibility of policy on the part of all concerned.[44]

An important feature of DPC financing was the development of "rentra" agreements, under which machinery and equipment could be readily subleased and transferred from one plant to another with fluctuations in demand. Since all DPC equipment was government-owned and physically so identified, it could be moved across state lines without any of the barriers common to equipment covered by ordinary chattel mortgages in private financing. Each DPC lease contained a clause permitting the sublease of machinery to another supplier of the government upon written approval of DPC and the sponsoring military agency. This clause was designed primarily to permit the lessee to redistribute machinery to subcontractors in order to expedite production for his own defense contracts. Originally it had been proposed to provide the prime contractor with a pool of machine tools which he could assign, without government approval, to his various subcontractors as necessary in order to permit completion of the prime contract. It was felt, however, that this would place the subcontractors too completely in the power of the prime. Accordingly, the subleasing clause was devised as a compromise arrangement allowing the transfer of the prime contractor's regular machinery to his subs in specific instances, with proper government approval. Later

the clause permitted the Army and Navy generally to redistribute idle machinery to plants where it was most needed. Thus machinery and equipment under complete Plancors as well as under M&E Plancors were transferable from an original lessee or sublessee to any defense supplier. This feature was most important during the period of drastic tool shortages.[45]

Closely associated with rentra agreements was the development by the DPC of "equipment pool" orders, which began as early as 1940.[46] In order to assure itself—as well as all other qualified purchasers—of the availability of machinery and other equipment by the time its plants were ready, the DPC placed blanket orders for various types of machinery well in advance of knowledge of its ultimate requirements. This guaranteed the machine tool industry a steady volume of orders, enabling it to operate at capacity at a time when private industry was not in a position to provide a steady market. Under the pool system the equipment makers agreed to reduce the basic government pool

---

[44] Detailed memoranda and correspondence on the treatment of unrecoverables may be found in USW files, DPC (Gen.) Nos. 2 and 3.

[45] The operational details and problems associated with rentra agreements are too complex to be described here. The chief problems were twofold: (1) allocation of costs of dismantling, shipment, installation, and the like. (These were closely related to the problems of unrecoverable costs previously discussed.); (2) development of a sensitive, decentralized organization for detecting and disseminating information on the existence and nature of idle equipment. For a summary of War Department redistribution procedure at the height of the war production program, see: (1) WD Memo W5–44, 25 Jan 44, sub: Redistribution of Industrial Facilities Owned by Defense Plant Corporation Under War Department Sponsorship; (2) Memo and attachments, USW Patterson for CGs AAF and ASF, 26 Jan 44, sub: Transfer by "Rentra Lease" of Machinery Owned by Defense Plant Corporation—revised policy and procedures.

[46] See Klagsbrunn, "Some Aspects of War Plant Financing," pp. 126–27, for a concise description of the DPC equipment pool.

order by the amount of all subsequent firm orders for specific purposes, whether governmental or private. The administration of the pool system, like rentra agreements, involved many problems of organization, record keeping, and contract interpretation, but without this and the other devices the critical shortage of machine tools in the late defense and early war periods would have been far more serious.

Advantages of DPC Financing

The advantages of the DPC contract were numerous. Its flexibility and freedom from red tape permitted a maximum of speed. The project could be approved, plant sites acquired, and construction begun while many of the details of cost and specifications were still unknown. If subsequent additions were necessary or cost had been underestimated, an amendatory agreement could be made authorizing additional advances by DPC.[47] No protracted advance negotiations with private bankers were necessary and the contractor knew that full financing would be provided by DPC. The tax amortization problem, so burdensome under EPF because of the necessity for obtaining NR certificates with each and every supply contract, was completely outflanked by the

existence of government title to the facilities. Also, since the DPC was a corporation and not a government agency its expenditures were not subject to audit and disapproval by the Comptroller General, a well-known barrier to the bold expenditure of government funds necessary in time of emergency.[48]

From the Army's standpoint, there were a number of other considerations which made DPC financing attractive. The alternative in many cases would have been full financing out of the War Department's limited expediting funds. Under DPC a 40-percent take-out meant that a given appropriation could be spread two and a half times as far; under complete contingency arrangements, which ultimately represented nearly a fourth of the total, no Army funds were needed. Also, the Army had to pay only 1½-percent interest to DPC during its period of nonreimbursement as contrasted with 2½ to 4 percent under EPF contracts. Under the latter type of financing, the Army was placed in the anomalous position of having in effect to pay interest on its own earmarked appropriations; under DPC it could escape interest charges by cash payment at any time.[49]

---

[47] All DPC contracts contained a clause limiting total construction expenditures to a specified figure, based on current estimates. Few, if any, projects were completed within the original cost authorization, and leases had to be amended many times. For example, the contract for the Ford Willow Run project was amended seventeen times, raising the authorization from $47,620,171 (25 June 1941) to $96,487,067 (16 November 1943); the Chrysler Chicago engine plant authorization was increased in four amendments from $99,304,681 (16 April 1942) to $181,857,236 (5 September 1944). See USW files, DPC Plancor folders, alphabetical file. In all such cases the Army's take-out was increased proportionately.

[48] Under postwar legislation, government corporations have become subject to audit by the Comptroller General. 59 *Stat.* 597, 6 Dec 45, Government Corporation Control Act.

[49] The Army, rather than the contractor, paid interest on DPC loans for no-rental facilities since these belonged nominally to the War Department. By agreement with DPC the Army paid interest only on DPC advancements up to the amount of the take-out. Interest on the remainder of outstanding funds was treated in the same manner as the principal, that is, the remaining principal and interest thereon was payable only at the end of the emergency and only if Congress made appropriations therefor. Ltr, USW to DPC, 22 Apr 42, approved 24 Apr 42 by John W. Snyder, Executive Vice President, DPC, in USW files, DPC (Gen.) No. 2, also filed with individual Plancors. The

The DPC contract also provided substantial administrative economies and advantages for the Army. DPC had its own resident engineers at every construction site to pass upon all routine problems, thus freeing the Army's thinly spread and overworked Construction Division for the building of posts, camps, stations, arsenals, and other military projects. Moreover, the bulk of the legal and administrative burden in implementing the program was assumed by DPC at a time when qualified personnel in the OUSW and technical services were at a premium. Working relationships between DPC and War Department personnel were among the best in Washington.[50]

Another basic advantage associated with DPC as it eventually developed was the concentration in a single agency of a wide array of functions and responsibilities attending the national program of plant expansion. This feature had several distinct facets. First of all it simplified the problem of multiple military demand for common components and end products. Thus Army Ordnance, the Air Forces, and the Navy might each be interested in facilities capable of producing a given item. Traditionally each agency would sponsor its own separate facility expansion, with consequent duplication and inefficiency. DPC was often able to consolidate such requirements into one facility whose productive capacity would be allocated by

WPB with the assistance of ANMB and the several military agencies.

A second feature of centralized responsibility for facilities expansion was superior provision for the supply of "bits and pieces"—the countless variety of materials and components ultimately essential to military end items but produced by thousands of establishments many tiers below the level of military prime contractors and their immediate subs. The Army was vitally interested in the flow of such materials but to assume sponsorship of all these establishments would carry it far afield of its primary responsibilities. Especially in the later stages of the war, the DPC provided both financial and administrative support for thousands of smaller but indispensable plant expansions throughout the wartime economy.

Finally, it was unquestionably to the Army's advantage in dealing with contractors to have a buffer in the form of an agency with control over expenditures but without an immediate interest in procurement. Too often Army procurement officers were faced with the proposition, "Do you want this now or a year from now? If you want it now, it will have to be done this way." The desire to speed procurement, as well as to maintain harmonious relationships essential to smooth and expeditious day-to-day operations, made contracting officers vulnerable to such demands. The DPC, relatively aloof from such pressures and with the experience of dealing with thousands of contractors for all procuring agencies on plant construction matters common to them all, was often in a better bargaining position.[51]

1½-percent rate represented a concession by DPC in favor of government agencies; Mr. Jesse Jones originally insisted upon a 4-percent rate. See Ltr, Emil Schram, Chmn RFC, to ASW, 13 Dec 40, and related papers, in USW files, DPC (Gen.) No. 1. Under the letter agreement of 22 April 1942 the Army further reduced its interest payment by paying the full cash take-out at the time each lease was signed rather than at the time of completion of the facilities.

[50] Anderson, Introduction to the History of the Under Secretary of War's Office, Ch. V, p. 168.

[51] Some indication of the scope of DPC activities and the necessity for "driving a hard bargain" is found in Jesse H. Jones and Edward Angly, *Fifty Billion Dollars; Thirteen Years With the RFC, 1932–1945* (New York: The Macmillan Company, 1951), Chapter 22.

The Results of DPC Financing

Once the basic terms, take-out provisions, and administrative procedures for implementing the DPC program had been established, the execution of contracts sponsored by the War Department went forward rapidly. By 30 June 1941—the end of the first fiscal year of operations—101 agreements had been executed involving plant construction of a contractual value of $525 million. By the time of Pearl Harbor commitments had passed the billion dollar mark, and on 30 June 1942 the record stood at 648 agreements totaling slightly more than $2.5 billion.[52] Relatively few construction projects were initiated after mid-1942 but by the war's end the War Department had sponsored some 935 Plancors of all types with a commitment value in excess of $3 billion. A majority of the new Plancors after 1942 were of the M&E variety; nevertheless, the authorized value of complete Plancors rose steadily with successive amendments revising the permissible ceiling.[53]

The outlay of DPC funds for War Department facility construction, as estimated by the War Department for 30 September 1945, totaled nearly $3 billion (*Table 51*). Of this grand total, Air Forces facilities alone accounted for 82.6 percent, with Ordnance running a poor second at 13.9 percent. By type of expenditure, machinery and equipment accounted for 61 percent of the total, while buildings and related installations ran to 36 percent; land and miscellaneous costs together amounted to only 3 percent. A fourth of all expansions were financed on a purely contingent basis, that is, no War Department funds were required. Assuming a 40 percent average take-out for the remaining three fourths, the use of DPC funds in effect extended War Department facilities appropriations to more than three times their original size.

The extent to which DPC plant facilities were concentrated in large industrial establishments is shown in the fact that the largest twenty-six Plancors account for over half the cost of the entire War Department DPC program (*Table 52*). Although a few of these include one or more subsidiary plants, most of them represent large single establishments sponsored by the Army Air Forces. Two of these—the huge Chrysler engine plant at Chicago and the Basic Magnesium plant at Las Vegas—represent a fifth of the cost of all twenty-six. There was also a high degree of concentration of Defense Plant facilities in the northeastern part of the United States; twenty of the twenty-six facilities were located in the area north of the Ohio and east of the Mississippi Rivers.

---

[52] Fiscal year figures from Table, "Defense Plant Corporation Agreements Executed for Army," supplied by Aircraft and Equipment Division, Management Control Office, AAF, 4 Aug 42, in USW files, DPC (Gen.) No. 3. Also see: (1) OPM, Bureau of Research and Statistics, Government Financed Defense Industrial Facilities (2 December 1941); (2) AIC R41, Financial Aids to Contractors, Table 2, p. 17.

[53] See above, note 47. The reason for these increases varied widely from one Plancor to another but fell into two principal categories: (1) increases in unit costs of labor and materials, due to wage and price increases, overtime and multiple shift operations, use of substitute labor and materials, and so forth; (2) increases in the scope of the contracts, that is, in the authorized quantity of machinery, building installations, and services because of new developments or previous underestimates of need. Thus Amendment 4 to the Ford Willow Run lease allowed an additional $367,000 to permit construction of a new standby water main; the influx

---

of population into Ypsilanti and the creation of a new military installation adjacent to Willow Run severely taxed existing water resources, threatening a shutdown of the Willow Run plant in the event of emergency.

Table 51—Cost of DPC Plant Expansions Sponsored by War Department;[a]
1 July 1940–1 October 1945

[In Thousands]

Obligation and Sponsoring Arm	Total	Land	Construction	Equipment and Machinery	Other
War Department—Total	$2,862,620	$42,741	$1,028,469	$1,748,215	$43,195
Takeout—Total	2,182,272	26,802	734,928	1,402,641	17,901
AAF	1,845,429	21,380	615,543	1,199,325	9,181
CWS	1,292	13	852	428	—
CE	6,089	48	3,618	2,423	—
ORD	283,960	4,320	94,734	176,502	8,404
QMC	685	15	385	285	—
SC	44,660	1,025	19,733	23,586	316
ASF	157	1	63	92	—
Contingent Liability Only—Total	680,348	15,939	293,541	345,574	25,294
AAF	519,334	13,283	251,639	241,017	13,395
CE	2,563	42	536	1,973	12
ORD	116,018	1,472	29,540	75,088	9,918
QMC	313	22	115	176	—
SC	3,506	222	2,096	1,184	4
TC	994	123	622	249	—
ASF	37,620	775	8,993	25,887	1,965

[a] Complete plants or structural additions thereto only are included. For this reason, and because total authorizations exceeded actual expenditures, the figure of $2,862 million is somewhat less than total authorizations for War Department sponsored Plancors of all types.

Source: Compiled from WD Quarterly Inventory-Supplement, Special Rpt. of WD Owned, Sponsored and Leased Industrial Facilities, 30 Sep 45.

Less obvious than the statistical record of DPC plant expansion is the amount of intensive planning and effort which was brought to the program by those who were primarily responsible for its conception and execution. Within the War Department these were chiefly a handful of lawyers in the office of the Under Secretary and key personnel in the Army Air Forces in Washington and at Wright Field. The officers and staff of DPC worked with their opposites in the War Department as a team, probably more intimately and harmoniously than separate branches within most single organizations.

But behind the principal figures in the drama was an army of contractors, engineers, construction workers, government personnel, and others, all indispensable to the program. As for other segments of the nation's plant expansion program, DPC projects had to be cleared and expedited by the War Production Board and predecessor agencies, priority assistance obtained, administrative organizations established, records maintained, and countless other problems resolved. Above all, the program had to be geared and kept responsive to the changing needs of defense and war. Cut-

TABLE 52—MAJOR DPC FACILITIES SPONSORED BY WAR DEPARTMENT [a]

Rank	Company and Locations		Cost to U.S. Government
	Total Cost—26 Projects		$1,539,985,550
1	Chrysler (Dodge)	Chicago, Ill	173,647,431
2	Basic Magnesium	Las Vegas, Nev	132,695,356
3	General Motors (Chevrolet)	Buffalo, N. Y	120,055,095
4	General Motors (Buick)	Melrose Park, Ill	110,009,223
5	Ford Motor	Willow Run, Mich	86,595,661
6	Studebaker	South Bend, Ind	77,724,127
7	Wright Aeronautical	Lockland, Ohio	74,859,211
8	Wright Aeronautical	Woodridge, N. J	65,029,598
9	General Motors (Allison)	Speedway City, Ind	62,541,329
10	Ford Motor (Rouge)	Dearborn, Mich	59,800,671
11	Dow Magnesium	Velasco, Tex	56,514,718
12	Mathieson Alkali Works	Lake Charles, La	48,867,624
13	Dow Magnesium	Marysville, Mich	42,228,327
14	Continental Aviation	Detroit, Mich	41,971,682
15	General Motors (Fisher Body)	Flint, Mich	39,156,924
16	Packard Motor	Detroit, Mich	38,256,297
17	Curtiss-Wright	Cheektowago, N. Y	36,386,370
18	Sperry Gyroscope	North Hempstead, N. Y	36,380,123
19	Wright Aeronautical	Paterson, N. J	34,113,760
20	North American Aviation	Grand Prairie, Tex	32,604,623
21	Standard Steel Spring	Madison, Ill	30,231,525
22	Curtiss-Wright	Columbus, Ind	29,608,849
23	Thompson Aircraft Products	Euclid, Ohio	29,123,338
24	Higgins Aircraft	New Orleans, La	28,719,042
25	Boeing Airplane	Wichita, Kan	26,781,232
26	American Steel Foundries	E. Chicago, Ind	26,083,414

[a] Each project represents a complete plant or major addition to an existing establishment. Nos. 15, 21, and 26 sponsored by Ordnance; all others by Army Air Forces. Nos. 2, 11, 12 and 13 involved only a contingent liability of War Department; all others required cash-take-out.

Source: WD, Quarterly Inventory-Supplement Special Rpt of WD Owned, Sponsored and Leased Industrial Facilities, 30 Dec 45.

backs and cancellations had to be ruthlessly and quickly made, no less than expansions, conversions, and restorations. It was the flexibility and even informality of the DPC program which gave it the necessary speed and adaptability to successfully carry out the purposes for which it had been created.

War Department Owned Facilities

The largest and most important class of plants constructed for Army procurement

were those directly financed and owned by the War Department. This class accounted for 60 percent of the value of all War Department owned, sponsored, and leased industrial facilities by the end of the war.[54] In this group were the greatest single establishments in terms of both cost and size. The Sunflower Ordnance Plant at Lawrence, Kansas—the largest in value terms of all facilities built for the War Department in

[54] Quarterly Inventory-Owned Sponsored, and Leased Facilities, 30 Sep 45.

World War II—represented a capital investment of more than $180,000,000.

Industrial facilities owned by the War Department consisted chiefly of the large Ordnance plants designed to turn out the unprecedented quantities of ammunition and related products required for World War II. They also included plants built for the Chemical Warfare Service for similar purposes, as well as the big bomber assembly plants and related modification centers of the Army Air Forces. In addition, there were numerous smaller facilities—chiefly for Ordnance—comprising warehouses, machinery and tools furnished to private contractors, and land and buildings adjacent to and operated by established private firms. Financed from War Department Expediting Funds, supplemented by Defense Aid, Presidential Expediting Funds, and regular appropriations for supplies, War Department-owned facilities were built by private construction firms under CPFF contracts and operated by prime contractors for a management fee. Hence, they became familiarly known as GOCO plants. Their erection was supervised by the Construction Division of the Quartermaster Corps until 18 December 1941 when all War Department construction activity was turned over to the Corps of Engineers.[55]

There were two basic reasons for War Department ownership of certain types of facility. The most compelling was that the highly specialized nature of many plants left no alternative to War Department ownership. During peacetime there was no demand for tremendous quantities of powder, high explosives, ordnance chemicals, special shell forgings, loaded shell, bombs, and other ammunition. Machinery and equipment required to produce these were frequently so highly specialized as to be worthless for other purposes. Even buildings were of such specifications, layout, and location that private industry at the end of the emergency would be unwilling to acquire them except in unusual instances and at a fraction of their original cost. In the case of major aircraft assembly plants, any conceivable commercial demand would be too small to warrant the investment of private capital. The War Department was therefore faced with the necessity for outright ownership of the facilities if it hoped to get them built.[56]

A second important but somewhat less urgent reason for government ownership was the obvious desirability of avoiding a repetition of the post-World War I experience which saw the complete scrapping of munitions plants and the nation's utter lack of preparedness to fight a major war when Europe went down in defeat before Hitler. In a world still fraught with international tension and the threat of war, common sense dictated the retention and maintenance of the nation's important munitions producing establishments. Outright government ownership would furnish the best guarantee that specialized munitions capacity would actually be preserved in appropriate stand-by condition.[57]

General plans for the construction of new arsenals and ammunition plants for both

---

[55] See above, pages 484–85.

[56] Campbell, *The Industry-Ordnance Team,* especially Ch. 7.

[57] The War Department Site Location Board in July of 1940 recommended that new munitions plants be "of permanent construction" since they "will have to remain in reserve status for many years." Memo, Col Harry K. Rutherford (Chmn) *et al.* for ASW, 8 Jul 40, sub: Locations of Plants in War Department Program for New Productive Capacity for Munitions, Exhibit 34 in OCofOrd, Policy re Sites.

Ordnance and Chemical Warfare Service had been under way for a number of years before the crisis of 1940. During the inter-war period the art of munitions manufacture was barely kept alive in the United States by six manufacturing arsenals of the Ordnance Department and one of the Chemical Warfare Service.[58] The peak capacity of these arsenals, however, was less than 10 percent of total requirements for a major war. Moreover, they were all concentrated in the northeastern part of the United States. This made them strategically vulnerable to attack as well as to numerous other evils of narrow geographic concentration.[59]

Disturbed by this condition, G–4 in 1936 directed the Chief of Ordnance to appoint a board of officers to study the situation and recommend "an ideal set-up for Ordnance manufacturing and storage facilities in the United States." The board was directed to take into consideration five factors: strategic location, proximity to raw materials, proximity to probable theaters of operations, economy of operation, and climate.[60]

On 15 April 1937, the five-man board submitted its report. The board on its own initiative had added a number of additional criteria for desirable location—proximity to major industrial areas, labor, service industries, and over-all transportation considerations. The board concluded that all the existing facilities were poorly located from the strategic point of view. Without recommending the disestablishment of the existing arsenals, the board stated that from the standpoint of both peacetime economy and wartime security it was desirable to create two principal arsenals—an ammunition arsenal to be located somewhere in the Indianapolis–Cincinnati–Dayton area, and an armament arsenal at Rock Island, Illinois. The strategically safe area of the United States was defined as excluding the eastern seaboard east of the Appalachians and the western seaboard west of the Sierra Nevada–Cascade range.[61]

By the summer of 1940, the magnitude of the Munitions Program as well as changes in technology and other factors called for an expansion and revision of earlier plans. On 8 July 1940, the War Department Site Location Board submitted a report defining the strategic area within which plants might be located. This area was inclosed by a boundary line, approved with minor adjustments by General Marshal, some 200 to 250 miles within the national boundaries of the United States. Within the strategic area five internal areas were designated, each of which was to be roughly self-contained in terms of providing a balanced output of munitions. The specific locations of individual plants were to be selected by the supply branches concerned, in accordance with the general principles laid down by the board.[62]

For economic and other reasons, exceptions to these policy declarations were later

---

[58] The six Ordnance manufacturing establishments were the Frankford Arsenal, Philadelphia, Pennsylvania, Picatinny Arsenal, Dover, New Jersey, Rock Island Arsenal, Rock Island, Illinois, the Springfield Armory, Springfield, Massachusetts, the Watertown Arsenal, Watertown, Massachusetts, and the Watervliet Arsenal, Watervliet, New York. The chemical arsenal was located at Edgewood, Maryland near Baltimore.

[59] Maj Gen Charles M. Wesson, CofOrd, The Ordnance Department, 9 May 41, AIC Lectures, 19:53.

[60] Memo, Brig Gen George R. Spalding, ACofS G–4, for CofS, 8 Dec 36, sub: Location of Government Manufacturing Plants, G–4/28403–4.

[61] OCofOrd, Report of Board of Officers To Prepare Secret Plan Embodying an Ideal Set-up for Ordnance Manufacturing and Storage Facilities in the United States (15 April 1937, 37 pp.) Exhibit 20 in OCofOrd, Policy re Sites.

[62] See above, note 57.

made.[63] Under the pressure of time and successive increases in requirements, both the number and size of individual plants were increased over previous plans. Construction of new plants was frequently quicker and more economical than attempts to convert existing privately owned plants; in the case of some types of facility, such as those for the production of ammonia, no convertible plants existed. Moreover, the trend toward larger caliber guns and increased muzzle velocities made the hazards of ammunition loading, handling, and storage much greater. To provide an adequate safety factor the distance between loading lines in a single plant was increased from 400 to 1,800 feet. This required greater land areas per plant, and even the 4,500 to 6,000 acres recommended in 1940 gave way in practice to sites running from 10,000 to 20,000 acres. This increased the problems of land acquisition and the cost of plants, but the new plants turned out to be far more productive than indicated by their design capacities.[64]

By early 1941 the War Department's construction program, launched in the summer of 1940, was well along. A report on the status of the program as of 28 February 1941 indicates that contracts and other commitments had been made for 154 industrial projects totaling over a billion dollars in estimated cost. More than half this amount was devoted to Ordnance projects (*Table 53*), nearly a third to the Air Corps, and the remainder to Chemical Warfare, Engineer, and Quartermaster facilities. Most of the projected facilities were to be completed

and in operation sometime in 1941. A few, however, including certain of the big smokeless powder and ammonia plants, as well as plants for small arms and heavy artillery, were not to be in full operation until the summer or fall of 1942—two years after the program was launched. The projects under construction at the beginning of 1941 were the nucleus of the great Ordnance industrial expansion program which by the end of the war was to embrace 216 Ordnance-owned establishments costing in excess of $3½ billion.[65]

The passage on 11 March 1941 of the Lend-Lease Act, under which the United States was to supply munitions in unprecedented quantities to its allies in World War II, required a second wave of munitions plant construction. The third and last great wave of facilities expansion followed in the wake of Pearl Harbor. Of the several classes of plant expansion undertaken exclusively or predominantly for Army procurement in World War II, GOCO plants involved the greatest investment. By 30 September 1945, the cost of War Department-owned industrial facilities actually put in place exceeded $4.3 billion. This was 50 percent greater than the $2.9 billion invested in War Department-sponsored DPC facilities, and 40 times the $108 million invested in EPF facilities. Although it was somewhat less than the $4.6 billion in necessity certificates authorized by the War Department for private expansion under tax amortization, the latter covered a multitude of expansions throughout the general economy (such as for railroads) which often

---

[63] The Detroit Tank Arsenal, chemical plants in the Niagara Falls area, the Baytown Ordnance Works, and the San Jacinto Ordnance Depot near Houston, Texas, are examples of important installations located outside the strategic boundary. See ICAF R83, Construction of New Facilities, p. 8.

[64] *Ibid.*, pp. 5–6.

[65] Memo, Lt Col Theron D. Weaver for Dir Production Br OUSW, 5 Mar 41, sub: Summary of Construction Activities Under "Expediting Production" Funds, and incl, Summary of Construction Program for Manufacturing Facilities, Revised as of February 28, 1941.

TABLE 53—NUCLEUS OF ORDNANCE FACILITIES EXPANSION FOR WORLD WAR II:
ORDNANCE PROJECTS UNDER CONSTRUCTION AS OF 28 FEBRUARY 1941

Type of Project	Estimated Completion Date	Estimated Cost
Total		$593,174,821
Medium tanks (Detroit)	15 Aug 41	20,000,000
Garand rifles (Springfield Armory)	1 Apr 41	3,317,475
Smokeless powder (3 plants)	15 Mar 41–Aug 42	162,676,997
Bag manufacturing and loading (2 plants)	(a)	46,242,000
TNT, DNT, Tetryl (3 plants)	1 Jul 41–Nov 41	57,805,000
Bomb and shell loading (6 plants)	31 May–Dec 41	87,034,153
Small arms ammunition (2 plants)	Early 42	50,382,466
Ammonia and ammonia nitrate (2 plants)	Oct 41–Jun 42	37,300,000
Machine guns (equivalent for 5 private plants)	1 Dec 41	37,967,771
Armor plate (add. const. in private plant)	1 Apr 41	1,236,585
20 mm. aircraft guns (equipment)	1 May 41	3,000,000
155 mm. guns (equipment for private plant)	1 May 41–Jun 42	1,680,001
Shell forging and machining	Dec 41	6,064,996
Machine tools, gages, etc. (numerous projects)	(a)	30,796,317
Toluol (1 plant)	23 Oct 41	11,990,000
Proving ground	Jul 41	7,941,060
Arsenals and depots (additions to 21 locations)	Mid-41	27,750,000

a Not given in source document.

Source: Production Branch, OUSW, "Summary of Construction Program for Manufacturing Facilities, Revised as of 28 February 1941."

could not be specifically related to Army contracts.

Some idea of the magnitude of the War Department's industrial construction program, as well as of the size of individual establishments, may be had from a summary showing the total cost (land, buildings, equipment, and miscellaneous items) through 30 September 1945 of each of the fifty largest War Department-owned establishments (Table 54). In the case of those installations—such as arsenals—already in existence at the beginning of the defense period, the cost figure represents expenditures after 30 June 1940. The construction of many of these establishments was equivalent to the creation of a sizable new city—complete with streets and access roads, railroad lines, power plants, water and sewage

systems, extensive housing projects, and numerous other community facilities. Each of these establishments has its own unique and complex history, from its conception and early planning stages through initial construction activity, completion, wartime operation, and disposition at the end of the war.[66]

[66] Under the interim historical program ordered by President Roosevelt early in the war, virtually every establishment of the War Department prepared historical monographs describing its origin, growth, and wartime activities. Many of these are on file in the historical offices of the several technical services, and some with the Office of Military History. It would take a lifetime to read all of these carefully. The history of Chemical Warfare's Rocky Mountain Arsenal, for example, is composed of sixteen volumes of manuscript and documents aggregating more than a yard in thickness; yet it by no means tells the "whole story" of the Rocky Mountain Arsenal.

TABLE 54—INDUSTRIAL FACILITIES OWNED BY WAR DEPARTMENT: COST OF 50 LEADING ESTABLISHMENTS, 1 JULY 1940–30 SEPTEMBER 1945

Rank	Name and State		Cost	Rank	Name and State		Cost
1	Sunflower Ordnance Works	Kan	$182, 827, 798	25	Volunteer Ordnance Works	Tenn	$51, 921, 760
2	Badger Ordnance Works	Wis	127, 151, 487	26	Des Moines Ordnance Plant	Iowa	51, 861, 463
3	Gopher Ordnance Works	Minn	115, 119, 000	27	Plum Brook Ordnance Works	Ohio	50, 288, 966
4	Indiana Ordnance Works	Ind	113, 919, 357	28	Lone Star Ordnance Plant	Tex	48, 110, 631
5	St. Louis Ordnance Plant	Mo	111, 508, 832	29	Iowa Ordnance Plant	Iowa	48, 026, 086
6	Holston Ordnance Works	Tenn	107, 708, 667	30	Detroit Tank Arsenal	Mich	47, 973, 141
7	Aberdeen Proving Ground	Md	86, 469, 626	31	Springfield Armory	Mass	43, 849, 648
8	Radford Ordnance Works	Va	83, 264, 763	32	Wabash River Ordnance Works	Ind	42, 229, 925
9	Alabama Ordnance Works	Ala	78, 693, 706	33	Sangamon Ordnance Plant	Ill	41, 680, 280
10	Ravenna Ordnance Center	Ohio	77, 200, 138	34	Illinois Ordnance Plant	Ill	40, 924, 107
11	Twin Cities Ordnance Plant	Minn	76, 771, 144	35	Buckeye Ordnance Works	Ohio	39, 934, 827
12	Oklahoma Ordnance Works	Okla	71, 063, 582	36	Watervliet Arsenal	N. Y	39, 758, 053
13	Morgantown Ordnance Works	W. Va	69, 823, 614	37	Denver Ordnance Plant	Colo	39, 278, 711
14	Kankakee Ordnance Works	Ill	68, 134, 653	38	Picatinny Arsenal	N. J	35, 839, 103
15	Ford Motor Company	Mich	66, 797, 527	39	Pantex Ordnance Plant	Tex	34, 850, 269
16	Frankford Arsenal	Pa	64, 147, 783	40	Louisiana Ordnance Plant	La	33, 383, 886
17	Watertown Arsenal	Mass	60, 963, 757	41	Kansas Ordnance Plant	Kans	32, 770, 280
18	Rock Island Arsenal	Ill	60, 027, 760	42	Hoosier Ordnance Plant	Ind	32, 245, 612
19	Weldon Spg. Ordnance Works	Mo	59, 770, 084	43	W. Virginia Ordnance Works	W. Va	32, 054, 715
20	Lake City Ordnance Plant	Mo	57, 511, 516	44	Jayhawk Ordnance Works	Kans	29, 775, 763
21	Milan Ordnance Center	Tenn	55, 544, 567	45	Chickasaw Ordnance Depot	Tenn	29, 369, 213
22	Keystone Ordnance Works	Pa	53, 624, 194	46	Nebraska Ordnance Plant	Nebr	29, 248, 760
23	Elwood Ordnance Plant	Ill	53, 472, 418		Ozark Ordnance Works	Ark	29, 214, 637
24	Kingsbury Ordnance Plant	Ind	52, 026, 013	47	Arkansas Ordnance Plant	Ark	28, 483, 691
				48	Cactus Ordnance Works	Tex	27, 799, 378
				49	Bluebonnet Ordnance Plant	Tex	24, 943, 800
				50			

Source: WD Quarterly Inventory-Supplement, 30 Sep 45. Special Rpt. of WD Owned, Sponsored and Leased Industrial Facilities.

Manifestly it was impossible, especially in the hectic days of the defense period, to implement an undertaking as large as the War Department's construction program without an appreciable margin of error, waste, and other irregularities amounting in some cases to outright scandal. The Truman Committee, in its investigations of a number of specific projects, received numerous reports and allegations of extravagance, waste, padding of costs, kickbacks, "shakedowns" by union organizations, nepotism by both contractors and Army officers, and an assortment of other malpractices. Many of these charges were disproved by the War Department, and those which were valid were attributable for the most part to the lack of time to devise sound procedures, the shortage of experienced personnel, and the absence of adequate control organizations. Competition for labor, management, and materials, the novelty and magnitude of the tasks involved, the necessity for improvisation and overtime work, as well as for work under adverse weather conditions, all resulted in an increase in waste, mistakes, and dollar costs substantially above normal levels. The investigations of the Truman Committee, as well as information furnished by government auditors, private individuals, newspapers, and other sources, all assisted the War Department in reducing such irregularities to a minimum.[67]

[67] Truman Committee, *Hearings*, Pt. 1 (April 1941), Progress of the National Defense Program; Pt. 6 (July–August 1941), Army and Navy Rental of Equipment; Pt. 9 (November–December 1941), Wolf Creek Ordnance Plant; Pt. 20 (April–August 1943), Sunflower Ordnance Plant; also, for command construction problems of similar nature, Pt. 2 (April–May 1941), Camp Construction, Fort George Meade; Pt. 4 (May 1941), Construction of Camp Blanding; Pt. 7 (August–September 1941), Camp Construction. For typical findings of the committee, see Truman Committee, First Annual Rpt. For another viewpoint, forcefully expressed by one of the Army's leading construction engineers, see Groves Commentary (cited above, p. 285, n. 12), especially pp. 51–53, 61, 110–11. Greater detail in this whole area can be found in Remington and Fine, The Corps of Engineers: Military Construction in the United States.

PART SIX

PRODUCTION AND MATERIAL CONTROLS

CHAPTER XXII

Establishment of the Priorities System

Introduction

The expansion of productive facilities, as just described, was the most urgent problem faced by the Army at the beginning of the defense period. But long before the facilities problem had been resolved, it was overshadowed by a more fundamental problem—the task of organizing production throughout the economy to meet the requirements of a huge rearmament program, unprecedented in both urgency and magnitude. Very early in the program it became evident that the basic ingredient of production control was the channeling of productive activity at all levels of the economy into the output of the materials, parts, and finished products needed for the nation's defense. Although the measures adopted to achieve this result were often referred to as "material controls," they were also "production controls." Materials, like finished products, had to be produced, and most of them had to be produced within the United States. Moreover, under certain control systems—particularly the priorities system—the term "material" came to be all-embracing, including even end products.[1]

Scarcely had the Army's Munitions Program been launched in the summer of 1940 when the first material shortages made their appearance. Among the more noticeable early shortages were such items as cotton, flannel, and linen for uniforms, clothing and bedding; cotton duck and webbing needed for tentage, tarpaulins, and the numerous other canvas requirements of the armed forces; aluminum in various shapes and forms, indispensable to the tremendous aircraft program; and special alloy steels for armor plate and armor-piercing projectiles. Most of these items were semifinished materials and the immediate bottleneck to their production in adequate quantity was a shortage of equipment, such as textile looms and metal rolling capacity, rather than basic raw materials.

As contracts were placed in increasingly large numbers, the shortages spread both vertically and laterally throughout the industrial community. They soon included raw and crude materials at the base of the productive process; fabricated and semiprocessed items at intermediate stages; and complex parts and components (instruments, gages, motors, generators, compressors, and the like) required for the expansion of industrial capacity as well as for incorporation into military end products. A serious handicap to war production at all levels—whether in raw material, component, or end-product production—was the drastic short-

---

[1] OPM Priorities Regulation 1, 27 Aug 41, Sec. 944.1 (c); "'Material' means any commodity, equipment, accessories, parts, assemblies, or products of any kind." For the most part, however, the term "material" was used in World War II to indicate basic and intermediate supplies below the end-product level.

age of machine tools. The machine tool shortage was felt even before the United States began its own rearmament program, as a result of earlier British and French orders for American-produced aircraft and other war munitions. By the time of Pearl Harbor, when the United States settled down to the serious business of a nation at war, it was evident that America's military success depended upon the prior solution of the problem of feeding its vast industrial machine.

The eventual solution of the "materials" problem was achieved by the adoption of a complex array of control measures generally falling into three groups or categories: (1) controls designed to direct the flow of materials into their most important uses; (2) controls designed to prohibit or limit the consumption of materials in less important uses; (3) measures to increase the total supply of scarce materials. Controls in the first category began with the establishment of the priorities system in 1940, passed through various modifications including allocation systems and the Production Requirements Plan (PRP) in 1941–42, and culminated in the adoption of the Controlled Materials Plan in 1943. The second group of controls consisted of the various limitation, conservation, and substitution orders and programs which affected the majority of military end products as well as regular commercial items. The third category included intensified overseas purchase and importation, increased domestic production, and stockpiling. At the peak of the war, all these measures were the broad responsibility of the War Production Board, but many of them were initially sponsored and instituted by the Army. As the largest contracting agency

with the greatest variety of procurement problems, the Army played the largest role throughout the war in the actual use and operation of the several systems.

The classification of wartime material controls into the three broad types mentioned above is somewhat arbitrary since they overlapped and merged at many points. Moreover, they were not of equal importance. Of the three, controls in the first group were by far the most complete and all-pervasive. They affected intimately every significant producing firm in the entire economy and represented a degree of control over the operation of American industry never before attempted. Eventually, they required the detailed planning and scheduling of production programs of all procuring agencies and of the bulk of the nation's industrial output. Their application and refinement contributed heavily to the knowledge of production management on the part of business and industrial executives, as well as to the art of directing national economic activity into channels required by the national interest. In view of the importance which they assumed in the activities of the procuring agencies and in the process of industrial mobilization for World War II, they are accorded a predominant place in the present discussion.[2]

The systems developed to control the flow of materials in World War II were ultimately nationwide in scope and centrally administered by wartime superagencies. In addition to these external control systems, the complexities of wartime economic mobilization required the expansion or crea-

---

[2] Group 1 controls, as described above, form the subject matter of Chapters XXII through XXV of the present volume. A brief sketch of the Army's role in the adoption and administration of Group 2 and Group 3 controls is contained in Chapter XXVI.

tion, by each of the procuring agencies, of countless organizations and procedures for the internal management of their own immense programs. These new internal production-control arrangements consisted of the kind of administrative measures which any rational agency, in either private industry or government, would adopt under comparable circumstances to insure the success of its objectives. For the War Department they included: (1) The establishment, at all echelons, of comprehensive production schedules showing the projected delivery dates of all items of procurement in approved programs; (2) statistical, progress-reporting, and follow-up organizations to indicate the current status of all programs, to uncover or anticipate delays and delinquencies in the performance of contracts, and to reveal the character of the bottlenecks or other trouble spots responsible for delays; (3) trouble-shooting or expediting organizations to overcome delays, whatever their causes, and more specifically to assist contractors in obtaining equipment, materials, manpower, funds, engineering assistance, and other aids required to break production bottlenecks; (4) the development of new and expanded organizations, techniques, and regulations for the inspection and approval, at various stages of completion, of all items of military procurement.

Each of these activities was indispensable to the success of the program as a whole. The production expediting function, for example, was of such importance that Under Secretary Patterson once remarked that the War Department's top expeditor and trouble-shooter—Lt. Gen. William S. Knudsen—had been personally responsible for the accomplishment of 10 percent of the

Army's procurement program.[3] Inspection and its associated functions were of such magnitude and complexity that the War Department's inspection staff—including statisticians, mathematicians, physicists, chemists and other scientists—numbered over thirty thousand persons at the peak of the war effort. In all these activities, basic policy was formed by the Office of the Under Secretary of War and, after the War Department reorganization of 9 March 1942, by Headquarters, Army Service Forces under the broad supervision of OUSW. In either case, the great bulk of the Army's detailed production-control activities was executed by the several technical services and the Air Forces in their respective areas of procurement.[4]

Inauguration of the Priorities System

America's experience with industrial mobilization in World War I had indicated conclusively the need for direct governmen-

---

[3] Millett, *Army Service Forces*, p. 31. After OPM's replacement by the WPB, former OPM Director General Knudsen became Lieutenant General, in charge of production, in the Office of the Under Secretary of War.

[4] Limitations of time and space have precluded detailed discussion of these aspects of wartime procurement in the present volume. Further information may be obtained from the several histories of the technical services in the series UNITED STATES ARMY IN WORLD WAR II. An excellent treatment of this whole area with abundant documentation of primary source material, is to be found in the following pioneer monographs prepared by Dr. Harry B. Yoshpe for the Army Quartermaster Historical Studies: (1) Production Control in the QMC; (2) Labor Problems in Quartermaster Procurement, 1939–1944; (3) [with Marion U. Massen] QMC Procurement Policies. An additional study by Dr. Yoshpe in this field is Army Industrial College R44, Organization for Production Control in World War II—A Study of the Follow-up and Expediting Function of the War Department, 1939–1945 (February 1946), ICAF Library.

tal controls over the distribution of materials to insure effective war production.[5] Material control devices used in World War I included preference-rating certificates, industry-wide preference orders, allotments among industries, conservation regulations, and other measures. These controls, however, were rudimentary in both scope and intensity as compared with those eventually developed in World War II. Following the usage of World War I, the term "priority" was widely used throughout the planning period to describe the general nature and purpose of all systems of direct controls for channeling scarce materials to their most important wartime uses.

As indicated early in the present study, the Industrial Mobilization Plan contemplated the use of automatic "priority classification ratings" as the simplest and most advantageous method of material control at the beginning of an emergency.[6] Although studies had been initiated during the planning period to develop the details of a wartime priority system, these had never been completed. As a result, only the broad outlines of a priority system were available upon the arrival of the emergency in 1940.[7]

The adoption of the Munitions Program of June 1940 signaled the need for prompt development of specific and detailed priority plans which could be applied as soon as shortages appeared. This presented the Army with a threefold problem of priority.

First of all, the Army's vast procurement program had to be arranged into a kind of master schedule, showing the order of urgency of the various military end products called for by the program. This was the responsibility of the General Staff, operating chiefly through its Supply Division (G–4), and the various supply arms and services. Secondly, agreement had to be reached with the Navy—the other principal claimant upon the national economy in war—as to which portions of the respective Army and Navy programs were to be deemed of equivalent importance and therefore to receive an equivalent priority status. This was the task of the Joint Board (later the Joint Chiefs of Staff) which represented the ranking prewar body for making joint strategic decisions of the armed forces. Finally, the Army had to see that adequate priority measures were adopted by industry to insure the production of military goods on time and in the proper sequence. Under the terms of the National Defense Act of 1920, and ensuing organizational arrangements, this was primarily the responsibility of the Assistant Secretary of War in conjunction with the Army and Navy Munitions Board.

The first step in the establishment of the priorities system for World War II was taken by the Assistant Secretaries of War and Navy on 17 June 1940, with the creation of the Priorities Committee, ANMB. This was in keeping with the Industrial Mobilization Plan, which contemplated that the ANMB would guide the economic mobilization effort in an emergency until the establishment of a civilian-directed central mobilization-control agency. The committee was directed to organize a simple and effective system, based on strategic plans of the two services, whereby priorities could

---

[5] (1) Baruch, *American Industry in the War;* (2) Clarkson, *Industrial America in the World War;* (3) Maj Frank W. Gano, A Study of Priorities (App. 5 to AIC Course 40, 1938–39, 182 pp., appendixes, and bibliography), ICAF Library.

[6] See above, page 89.

[7] A priorities annex to IMP was apparently proposed but never completed. See Tentative Draft—Priorities Annex, 10 May 39, AIC, copy in ANMB, Navy Section, Correspondence and Reports, 1922–42, 1941 folder, National Archives.

be placed upon production orders to industry. The system was to include "priorities on materials, machine tools, etc., required for such production." The committee was also to act as a liaison agency with any "Priorities Commissioner" who might be appointed in the NDAC "to handle the subject on a national basis." [8]

While the ANMB committee was at work on this assignment, legislation sponsored by the War and Navy Departments was passed by Congress to provide the legal basis for requiring industry to give priority treatment to Army and Navy Orders. Section 2 (a) of the National Defense Expediting Act, approved on 28 June, contained the following provision: ". . . deliveries under all orders placed pursuant to the authority of this section and all other Naval contracts or orders and all Army contracts or orders shall, in the discretion of the President, take priority over all deliveries for private account or for export." [9]

In the meantime G–4 had determined the general strategical priority for items in the Army's Munitions Program. The G–4 proposal, concurred in by the War Plans Division of the General Staff, established three broad classes—a, b, and c—representing respectively complete aircraft and accessories, antiaircraft matériel, and other material. Items in classes b and c were ranked

internally in order of importance, thus facilitating a future subdivision of these classes if this should become necessary.[10] These recommendations were integrated into a broad program of production and facilities expansion by the Planning Branch, OASW. The Navy had been at work on its corresponding program, and on 5 August the Joint Board and the two Assistant Secretaries approved the official version for both the Army and the Navy. This became the first ANMB priorities directive. Its formal announcement on 12 August 1940, together with detailed instructions for its application, marked the birth of the World War II priorities system.[11]

The first ANMB priorities directive was a classification of military procurement objectives into ten degrees of urgency with corresponding priority ratings ranging from A–1 to A–10; a top rating of AA was reserved for emergencies. The following summary indicates the specific portions of the Army program allotted to each rating scale:[12]

---

[8] Memo, ASW Johnson and ASN Lewis Compton, 17 Jun 40, sub: Establishment of Priorities Committee, ANMB. The two Assistant Secretaries were ex officio cochairmen of ANMB.

[9] 54 *Stat.* 676, 28 Jun 40. This power was extended by the Selective Service Act of 1940 (54 *Stat.* 885, 16 September 1940 which gave the President authority to commandeer plants for defense production, and the act of 31 May 1941 (55 *Stat.* 236), specifically extending the priority power to civilian supplies, foreign purchases, and subcontracts. The powers under the May 1941 act were retained by the President until their delegation to OPM on 28 August 1941 by Executive Order 8875.

[10] Memo and incls, Lt Col Henry S. Aurand for Gen Moore, DCofS, 26 Jun 40, sub: Priority of Production for Items of Equipment.

[11] Ltr, Robert Patterson and Lewis Compton To All Supply Arms and Services of the Army and Bureaus and Offices of the Navy Department, 12 Aug 40, sub: Priorities, with 5 incls: (1) ANMB Priorities Instructions; (2) Preference Ratings on Contracts; (3) Contractors' Extension of Preference Ratings; (4) Memo; Establishment of Priorities Committee, ANMB; (5) Dir Priorities Committee 5 Aug 40 (Joint Board 355; Serial 656, 7–25–40). The Navy program had been previously laid down in Memo, Adm Harold R. Stark, CNO, for Bureaus and Offices, Navy Dept, 9 Jul 40, sub: Priorities in Material Procurement, Op–23,–1, JJ 40/L 8–3 (400612), Ser. 107023.

[12] (1) ANMB Priorities Dir, 5 Aug 40; (2) Memo, Gen Rutherford, Dir Planning Br OASW, to Priorities Com ANMB, 4 Oct 40, sub: Material in A–1 Priority. Throughout the defense and war periods the term "priorities directive" referred to the authoritative document establishing the several

A–1   Complete equipment for authorized Regular Army (375,000 men) and National Guard (235,000 men).

Attainment of first aircraft objective—12,835 planes by 1 October 1941, including production facilities and operating bases for same.

A–2   Critical and essential items for PMP (1,200,000 men), including one year's maintenance, and construction required for authorized selective service training.

A–3   Seacoast and overseas defenses (including antiaircraft, aircraft warning, and other equipment).

A–4   Attainment of second aircraft objective—18,000 planes by 1 April 1942, including production facilities and operating bases for same.

A–5   Critical items of equipment and construction for 2,000,000-man Army.

A–6   Essential items for same.

A–7   Expansion and construction of facilities (government or private) for 18,000 annual plane production and for production of critical equipment for maintenance of 2,000,000-man Army.

A–8   Passive defense for Army installations.

A–9   Facilities expansion to provide for Army augmentation beyond 2,000,000 men.

A–10   Educational orders and additional reserves of critical and essential items.

The application of priorities was to be accomplished by means of a "preference-rating" certificate bearing the rating established in the priorities directive for the military end item concerned. At the request of the NDAC, the new priorities system was to be applied to industry on a voluntary basis until such time as the President found it necessary to use his mandatory powers re-

cently acquired under the National Defense Expediting Act.[13]

Also at the request of NDAC, priorities were to be confined to "critical items" only, and the ANMB's covering letter of 12 August indicated that lists of critical items would shortly be furnished to contracting officers. The "Critical List" was to consist of noncommercial items, that is, military end products and components designed to military specifications. Since ratings were to be used only to expedite military programs, no rating scale was specified at this time for civilian products, although B, C, D, and lower classes were mentioned for possible future use. All military production was thus to be "superimposed" on the civilian economy. This meant, in effect, that no direct curtailment of civilian production was currently contemplated.[14]

During the weeks after the announcement of 12 August 1940 the ANMB, the OASW, and the supply arms and services were busily engaged in launching the new system. First of all, under continued pressure by NDAC, the ANMB was obliged to issue for the use of contracting officers a list of items for which preference ratings were authorized. The Navy promptly issued its Critical List on 14 August, but it was more than two months later before the Army, under the prodding of NDAC, had compiled a list which it deemed even temporarily satisfactory. The

---

priority rating classes. "Priorities instructions" and other documents contained rules and regulations for the implementation of the directive.

[13] Although the gentler sounding term "preference rating" was more appropriate than "priority" to a voluntary, peacetime system, it was retained after the system was placed on a mandatory basis. The terms were used synonymously, although strictly speaking the broader term "priority" referred to the general principle of granting precedence to more urgent items, whether by means of ratings, allocations, rationing, or other devices. The "preference rating" was thus a specific instrument of priority policy.

[14] NDAC Press Release, PR 69, 12 Aug 40.

Army and Navy items were then combined in the first official joint list, issued 23 October 1940.[15] The Critical List subsequently became a source of much difficulty and controversy.[16]

A second prerequisite to the assignment of preference-rated orders to industry was the protection of contractors from the operation of the "liquidated damages" clause. This provision, which was a standard feature of most contracts of the federal government, imposed financial penalties upon contractors for failure to complete their contracts on schedule. Unless this provision were waived, contractors would be unwilling to defer existing or future low-rated government orders in favor of higher ones. To meet this problem, the President requested all government agencies to refrain from acting under the liquidated damages clause in all cases of delay resulting from the application of preference ratings. The War Department implemented this by the issuance of a procurement circular and appropriate changes in Army Regulations.[17]

In theory, the application of preference ratings was simple. Each military prime contract or purchase order for an item on the Critical List would be assigned the priority rating called for by the ANMB directive if in the opinion of the contracting officer preferential treatment was necessary for completion of the contract on schedule. Actually conveyed in the form of a certificate signed and "authenticated" by the contracting officer, the preference rating required that the contractor schedule his operations, including the disposition of his inventory, to insure completion and delivery of the preferred item on time. This was required at the expense of other contracts—Army, Navy, private, or export—bearing no preference rating or a lower rating. Lower or nonrated contracts were to be disturbed only if necessary, and then only to the extent necessary. Contracts bearing equal preference ratings were to be completed in order of delivery dates specified in the contracts. The initial effect of a preference rating was thus the placing of a preferred claim upon the plant capacity and inventory of the prime contractor or other direct supplier of military procurement.

Of greater significance, especially as material shortages began to appear, was the authority given to prime contractors, subcontractors, and vendors under various conditions to "extend" their ratings to immediate subcontracts and purchase orders for tools, materials, and other supplies. Extension of a rating was accomplished on a simple form announcing the priority status of the order and requiring of the subcontractor the same type of preferential treatment which was required for the prime contract.

---

[15] (1) List of Items for Which Preference Ratings Are Authorized, October 23, 1940, with covering ltr, Col Charles Hines, Ex Secy ANMB To All Supply Arms and Services of the War Department and Bureaus and Offices of the Navy Department, 23 Oct 40, sub: Priorities—Items for Which Preference Ratings are Authorized. (2) Ltrs, Donald Nelson to Col Rutherford, 15 and 26 Aug 40, and Rutherford to Nelson, 28 Aug 40 regarding issuance of Critical List.

[16] See below, pages 528–37.

[17] (1) Ltr, Roosevelt to SW and SN, 8 Oct 40. This action was apparently prompted by the ANMB, whose 10 July draft of priorities instructions (par. 4) raised the issue. (2) A procurement circular of the War Department requiring action similar to that requested by the President had been drafted on 4 October. Memo, Gen Rutherford, Dir Planning Br, for Capt Almy [USN], 5 Oct 40, and incl. (3) WD Procurement Circular 36, 23 October 1940, announced changes in AR 5–140 and AR 5–200 authorizing the general omission of liquidated damages clauses in future contracts and instructing contracting officers to grant extensions of time of performance in appropriate cases.

In order to prevent the use of rating extensions to obtain larger quantities of scarce supplies than were needed, the purchaser was obliged to subscribe to the statement that the item was essential to completion of the prime contract, and that the specified quantities were no greater and the delivery date no earlier than necessary for the contract. Until 1942 this statement had to be approved and countersigned by the contracting officer or local inspector of the Army or Navy. A subcontractor or vendor receiving a rated order was to inform his customer immediately if the requested delivery date could not be met, with reasons therefor. In such cases, the supply arm or service concerned would attempt to resolve the problem by locating another subcontractor, rescheduling, or other measures. If necessary, the matter would be taken to the ANMB, which could grant a "higher than routine" rating, or adopt other measures to expedite production.[18]

Contracting officers, responsible for the completion of urgent programs or schedule, immediately made wide use of their new priority powers and soon found it necessary to use preference ratings wherever these were authorized. Only one month after the announcement of the new system, Assistant Secretary Patterson foresaw its probable breakdown if it were not applied with restraint and protected by intelligent scheduling and other measures:

Effective scheduling of manufacturing operations by the Supply Arms and Services will be required to meet the above objectives and to avoid unnecessary conflicts in the administration of the priorities system already established. It is obvious that it is not only unnecessary but may be harmful to the defense program as a whole, to initiate and expedite production of all items or of all components of an item simultaneously. Under the priority system, all components will bear the same priority rating as the complete item and this rating will be the same as that of many other items. Unless some method of differentiating between these priorities is established, the priorities system will break down because of congestion in one or more categories.

The proper scheduling of *delivery dates* necessary for the completion of key components of an item and of the major items is the only method for obtaining orderly and efficient progress in the War Department Program. Proper scheduling will keep out of the market those who are not in immediate need of materials, tools, equipment, etc. Priority is designed to give orders so deferred the preferential treatment needed when their turn comes under the scheduling system.[19]

Mr. Patterson's prediction was borne out within a month. On 30 September, OASW received word that 97 percent of the two thousand machine tools on order from Warner and Swasey carried an A–1 priority: "It does not require any elucidation to convey the idea that Warner and Swasey are completely confused. . . . It is therefore imperative that something be done this week to break A–1 into at least four subdivisions." [20] By the end of October congestion in the A–1 category—particularly for the machine tool industry—was so great that subcontractors besieged with orders bearing A–1 extensions were at a loss as to how to proceed. As the pressure increased, Army and Navy representatives agreed that an extensive subdivision of the A–1 classification was necessary; the original classification was not only vague and wide in scope but was composed of items of widely varying urgency. On 27 November the ANMB is-

---

[18] Memo, Donald Nelson, Coordinator of National Defense Purchases, for the President, 15 Oct. 40.

[19] Ltr, ASW Patterson to CofAC, 19 Sep 40, sub: Priorities and Scheduling. Identical letters were sent to all the Army's supply arms.

[20] Memo, Lt Col A. B. Johnson for Gen Rutherford, Dir Planning Br OASW, 30 Sep 40.

sued a new directive, dividing the A–1 class into ten subgroups: A–1–a to A–1–j.[21] The A–1–a class was confined to supplies and facilities for selected manufacturers of machine tools and gages; military end items received ratings from A–1–b to A–1–j. This elevation of critical production equipment to the head of the list was recognition of the inadequacy of priorities for end items in the absence of the availability of all necessary contributory items.

By the end of 1940 the priorities system was rapidly becoming a familiar part of the American industrial scene, and the War Department had established internal agencies at various levels for planning and conducting the operation of the system. These included priorities units in both the Planning and Production Branches, OASW, in the offices of the chiefs of supply arms and services, and in field offices of the various services. The first priorities unit, created 10 July 1940, was the Priorities Division, Planning Branch, OASW. The officers in this division composed the Army half of the Priorities Committee, ANMB; the division thus functioned principally as the "home base" for the Army officers attached to ANMB. In the Production Branch, OASW, the Priorities Section (later Division) established on 25 October 1940, became the principal War Department co-ordinating agency for priority matters. It supervised the supply arms and services in the execution of priority policy, adjusted priority conflicts between two or more Army establishments, maintained liaison with other government priority agencies, and assisted the ANMB and higher echelons in determining policy and operating procedures. It became the nucleus of the War Department's top priority agency in the Resources Division (later Production Division), ASF, after the departmental reorganization on 9 March 1942.[22]

Evolution of Civilian Priority-Control Agencies

The leadership of the ANMB in establishing the priorities system at the beginning of the emergency had long been contemplated by the Industrial Mobilization Plan. But IMP recognized the broad desirability as well as the political necessity of vesting central control over the priorities system in a civilian superagency responsible for the over-all control of the national economy in time of war. This type of control was desirable both from an administrative and a political point of view. As the industrial

---

[21] [Memo] Hines, Secy ANMB, to SW and SN, 4 Dec 40, sub: Priorities, Changes in, with incl, ANMB Directive, Priorities Committee, 27 Nov 40, It should be recorded that the need to subdivide the A–1 category had been anticipated at the outset; See Incl (2) to Patterson and Compton ltr of 12 Aug 40, cited above, note 11 (2).

[22] Annual Report of the Production Branch, OUSW, for FY Ending 30 June 1941. A rich heritage of information on the early operation and development of the priorities system is found in the file of Weekly Progress Reports, Priorities Section, Production Division, OUSW (file 319.1 Production Div ASF) prepared by Maj. (later Col.) Elmer E. Barnes, CE, who was chief of the section from its inception until after the War Department reorganization of March 1942. The reports are hereafter cited as Barnes, Weekly Progress Rpt, with date. For additional detail on War Department organization for handling priorities, see: (1) OASW Planning Br Office Order 37, 10 Jul 40, establishing Priorities Division; (2) Mohler, Administrative Log of the Production Division, Headquarters, ASF, and Its Antecedent Agencies, 1939–45; (3) Industrial College of the Armed Forces R60, Priorities and Allocations: A Study of the Flow of Matériel to War Suppliers (September 1946) ICAF, Library. ANMB Priorities Com Cir 1, 9 Dec 40, sub: Description of the Preference Rating System, gives an informative summary of the status and operation of the priorities system at the end of 1940.

mobilization process absorbed more and more of the nation's productive resources the problem of management alone would reach formidable proportions, requiring the assistance of large numbers of industrial experts and administrators. More important, from the standpoint of national policy it was desirable that decisions directly and pervasively affecting the entire economy be made by a body with broad civilian representation. This view was consistently held by the Army.[23]

The Advisory Commission

As it became apparent that the Advisory Commission to the Council of National Defense had been given the top-level co-ordinating role cast for the War Resources Administration in the Industrial Mobilization Plan, the ANMB deferred to the commission in matters of broad policy. In the summer of 1940, the NDAC had used its influence, principally in a negative or restraining manner, in modifying the ANMB's blueprint for priorities. But it was not until the end of the year that the NDAC was ready to enter the field of actual priorities administration and to consolidate its power as the senior policy determining agency in the field. By this time—after four months of operation under the operating control of ANMB and the services—it was clear that priorities were causing dislocations in the civilian economy.[24]

The NDAC wished to retain control of priority decisions affecting not only civilian end products but all commercial and industrial materials and supplies entering into production of both military and civilian end items. Hence, it did not want the President's priority powers granted by Congress the previous June to be delegated directly to the military services.

On 4 September 1940 a report was circulated in a regular NDAC meeting that the Army and Navy were seeking an amendment to the selective service bill which would give them separate authority to establish priorities.[25] To counter this move the commission gave Donald Nelson, Co-ordinator of National Defense Purchases, the task of drafting a proposal to the President to delegate his priority powers to a board to be established within the NDAC. This body would determine broad priority policy and would be headed by an administrator to recommend as well as carry out policy. The proposal was submitted to the President on 15 October and on 21 October the President approved the proposal and authorized the NDAC Priorities Board to replace the system on a mandatory basis. The order provided for the promulgation of rules and regulations to be approved by the President, and on 15 December, after numerous conferences with the ANMB and the services,

---

[23] (1) Memo, Gen Rutherford for ASW, 23 Oct 40, sub: Executive Order Establishing a Priorities Board in the Advisory Commission; (2) Memo, Rutherford for Donald Nelson, Administrator of Priorities, 12 Nov 40; (3) Memo, Rutherford for USW, 13 Jan 41, sub: Organization for Priority; (4) IMP, 1939, p. 6.

[24] A major incident late in 1940 was the demand of the Secretaries of War and Navy that the aircraft industry devote all its resources to the pro-

duction of military aircraft, except for maintenance and replacement of civilian aircraft. The NDAC appointed a special Committee on Aircraft Priorities and on the basis of the committee's reports made a compromise adjustment. CPA, *NDAC Minutes* and Minutes of the NDAC Priorities Board, November, 1940 through January 1941.

[25] CPA, NDAC Minutes, 4 Sep 40. This was the power to commandeer plants, if necessary. It was included in the Selective Service Act both because it was recommended in the Industrial Mobilization Plan and because of popular demand to provide for the "conscription of capital" to balance the power to draft men for military service.

the official rules and regulations of the Board were issued.[26]

Under the new NDAC regulations the ANMB and the services retained control over the determination and administration of military priorities. Contracting officers, under ANMB regulations, were to continue to assign and extend preference ratings; higher-than-routine ratings and similar adjustments were to be made by the ANMB. The NDAC Priorities Board, however, reserved to itself the authority to assign or extend ratings to materials not on the Critical List, and the list could not be amended without the board's approval. On the other hand, major policy changes were to be determined by the board "after due consultation" with the procurement agencies and the ANMB. Consultation was insured by the appointment of ANMB representatives as advisers to the Board.

The Office of Production Management

The NDAC Priorities Board, as such, was short-lived. On 7 January 1941 the President created the Office of Production Management and delegated all of his priority powers to this Agency.[27] A new OPM Priorities Board replaced its NDAC predecessor and a new Priorities Division, headed by Edward R. Stettinius, Jr., supplanted the organization of the NDAC administrator. Mr. Stettinius and his assistants immediately conferred with Army and Navy officers in an effort to provide a proper divi-

sion of effort and authority between the OPM and the services.

The negotiations which followed were complicated by a proposal by Secretary of the Navy Frank Knox to abolish the priority functions of the ANMB. Mr. Knox's view was that "the continued existence of two Priorities Boards, on in the OPM and the other in the Army and Navy Munitions Board, is an unnecessary waste of effort and time." He further felt that the concentration of all priority activities in an independent agency "would eliminate one of the frequent causes of friction between the two departments.[28] This proposal was in part the outgrowth of earlier efforts of the Navy to obtain from Donald Nelson, shortly after he became the NDAC Priorities administrator, a more favorable position for Navy procurement than accorded by the 5 August 1940 directive of the Joint Board. Mr. Nelson and his associates had refused to involve the NDAC in decisions on relative priorities among military items, clearly a function of the military agencies.[29]

Under Secretary Patterson and his Planning Branch chief, Brig. Gen. Harry K. Rutherford, were firmly opposed to the shelving of ANMB's priority functions. General Rutherford pointed out that ANMB had handled perhaps 90 percent of

---

[26] (1) Executive Order 8572, 21 Oct 40. (2) Executive Order 8612, 15 Dec 40.

[27] Executive Order 8629, 7 Jan 41. NDAC personnel and policies were largely taken over by OPM. For greater detail on the OPM priorities organization and its early problems, see CPA, *Industrial Mobilization for War*, pp. 171–77.

[28] Ltr, Knox to Stimson, 9 Jan 41.

[29] (1) CPA, *Industrial Mobilization for War*, p. 67. (2) NDAC, Priorities Board, Mins, 5 Dec 40. (3) Memo, Knox for Nelson, 12 Nov 40. Mr. Knox proposed to place the defense program into four priority classes: AA–1, to cover Navy needs for the existing fleet; AA–2, Navy needs for the new fleet; A–1, further items for the new fleet and equipment for the existing Army and National Guard; A–2, equipment for the new Army. Mr. Stimson, to whom Mr. Knox had handed his proposal at the 12 November Cabinet meeting, replied that the proposal was properly one for the consideration of the Joint Board. Memo, SW Stimson for the SN, 13 Nov 40, copy in OCMH.

the problems arising in the actual administration of priorities and that no other agency was equipped to do so; that most of ANMB's work involved screening, policing, and other operations in the application of military priorities requiring intimate knowledge of military programs; and that in the absence of the ANMB type of organization a host of minor problems internal to the military services would be congested at the top of the priority control system, seriously interfering with the policy-making function.[30]

As a result, the Knox proposal was withdrawn but OPM adhered to the position that its Priorities Division should retain the sole authority to issue or extend preference ratings for "industrial" materials and supplies, even when these were vital to subcontracts for high-rated items of military procurement under prime contracts of the War and Navy Departments. Operations on this basis proceeded for about a month, but OPM was unable to handle the flood of priority applications from industry:

. . . it proved impossible for Stettinius to recruit and train a staff large enough . . . With no field organization, OPM was compelled to rely on the procurement officers of the Services, and even in Washington the volume of paper work proved too much for the personnel available.[31]

By the middle of March 1941, a comprehensive agreement between OPM and ANMB had been perfected and a revised priority system, retaining the significant features of its predecessor under NDAC, but

groomed for mandatory compliance by industry, was ready for launching. On 15 March the ANMB sent a detailed set of new priority instructions to all supply arms of the Army and bureaus of the Navy. Together with these instructions were the latest revision of the Critical List and a complete sample set of the new printed OPA preference-rating forms. These forms, listed below, were soon to become well known to industry and procuring agencies alike for their essentiality to daily operations and for the large volume of paper work which they entailed: [32]

Form Number	Purpose	Number of Copies per Application
PD-1	Material user's application for rating	5
PD-1-A	Supplier statement re application for rating	6
PD-2	Rating certificate—Domestic Civilian contracts	6
PD-3	Rating certificate—Army and Navy contracts	7
PD-4	Rating certificate—Other U.S. Gov't contracts	7
PD-5	Rating certificate—Foreign Gov't contracts	10

Under the new arrangements all preference ratings were to be issued over the name of Mr. Stettinius, the director of Priorities. The actual issuing authority, however, was divided between OPM and the military procuring agencies. Contracting officers in the field were supplied in advance with OPA serially numbered and machine-signed PD-3 preference rating certificates. These officers would continue to assign and authorize

---

[30] (1) Memo, USW Patterson for SW, 14 Jan 41; (2) Memo, Gen Rutherford for USW Patterson, 13 Jan 41, sub: Organization for Priority; (3) Memo, Rutherford for Stettinius, Dir Priorities Div OPM, 18 Jan 41, sub: Continuance, With Certain Modifications, of Priorities Procedure in Current Use by War and Navy Departments.

[31] CPA, Industrial Mobilization for War, p. 173.

[32] Complete copies of ANMB Priorities Instructions, the revised Critical List, and OPA Priorities Division forms of this date may be found in Exhibit 5, Vol. II, in Priorities and Control of Materials in the Ordnance Department, 1940–45 (hereafter cited as Ordnance Priority Docs.) copy in OCMH. The sixteen-page Priorities Instructions issued by ANMB at this time provides an excellent description of the priorities system as it existed in 1941.

extension of original ratings for military contracts in accordance with the ANMB priorities directive and instructions. Higher-than-routine ratings, as before, were to be assigned by ANMB on appeal by contracting officers through the chiefs of their supply arms or services. The emergency AA rating and all ratings for items not on the Critical List were to be assigned by OPM. Likewise, all additions to the Critical List required OPM's approval. The application of priorities to services—such as power, labor, and transportation—was specifically prohibited, and these remained outside the scope of the priorities system throughout its existence.

Thus, within little more than two months after its creation, the OPM had consolidated the authority gained by NDAC over priorities policy and had commenced operations in a field which was certain to expand enormously within the coming months. With the benefit of legislation and additional delegations of power from the President, OPM issued a series of orders throughout 1941 which gradually transformed the priorities system from a voluntary basis to one requiring mandatory observance by industry.[33]

The Supply Priorities and Allocations Board

The next development in organization for central priority control was the establishment by the President, on 28 August 1941, of the Supply Priorities and Allocations Board. The creation of SPAB was made necessary by broad conflicts of policy in materials allocation. Challenging OPM's authority were the newly created Office of Price Administration and Civilian Supply,

under Leon Henderson, and the Lend-Lease Administration under Harry Hopkins; both were concerned with obtaining enough materials for their respective programs. In order to resolve conflicting claims effectively, SPAB was composed of widely representative interests and was made the highest policy determining body on all priority matters.[34] Its decisions were executed by OPM, the ANMB, and other operating agencies, whose basic organization and operating responsibilities were left largely unchanged. The OPM Priorities Board was, however, abolished with the establishment of SPAB. Although it was soon replaced by the War Production Board and left little imprint upon the internal functioning of the priorities system, SPAB resorted to direct allocation of scarce materials on an increasing scale. This was tacit recognition of the inadequacy of the priorities system and helped to pave the way for its replacement by more effective control systems.[35]

The War Production Board

On 17 January 1942 the War Production Board was created as the supreme industrial mobilization control agency, replacing both OPM and SPAB. General responsibility within the WPB for priority matters was vested in James S. Knowlson, the director of Industry Operations. Mr. Knowlson, as did his predecessor Mr. Stettinius a year earlier, shortly reached a working agreement with ANMB on priority policy and procedures. On 18 February the

---

[33] CPA, *Industrial Mobilization for War*, pp. 92, 179–80.

[34] Executive Order 8875, 28 Aug 41. SPAB's membership consisted of Knudsen, Hillman, Stimson, Knox, Henderson, Hopkins, and Henry A. Wallace. Vice President Wallace was chairman and Donald Nelson the executive director.

[35] (1) CPA, *Industrial Mobilization for War*, pp. 109–14. (2) CPA, *SPAB Minutes*.

ANMB issued a new and elaborate set of priorities instructions, running to some thirty-two pages and bearing the signed approval of Mr. Knowlson.[36] With the adoption of these regulations the priorities system and the overhead arrangements for its administration may be said to have reached substantial maturity.

The establishment of the War Production Board did not immediately alter the basic role of the ANMB in administering the priorities system for the military and related agencies. During 1942, however, a number of developments combined to strip the ANMB of most of its functions in this field. With the creation of the Army Service Forces under General Somervell, Army personnel in ANMB were gradually withdrawn into the new supply organization. Direction of the technical services and the conduct of relationships with the War Production Board were centered more and more in the various divisions of ASF, which was organized to administer all War Department procurement activities. With the departure of Ferdinand Eberstadt from ANMB in September, the announcement of the Controlled Materials Plan, and the increasing concentration of authority within WPB for all production control measures, it was evident that the role of the ANMB in priorities matters would thereafter be confined chiefly to the issuance of the military priorities directives and similar matters requiring the close co-operation of the Army and Navy.

During the summer of 1942, when the pattern of Army-WPB relationships was

just emerging, mutual suspicion and considerable friction arose between the two agencies. Donald Nelson, the WPB chief, was under criticism for having "surrendered" control over priorities, as well as other matters, to the armed forces. Partly to counter this criticism, and partly to curb what was felt to be an important source of priorities inflation, Nelson announced on 22 August that he had withdrawn, effective 7 September 1942, the authority of military contracting officers to assign preference ratings:

The fundamental weakness in the present administration of priority ratings by the Army and Navy contracting officers is that it is an attempt to administer a control system, which must often restrict parts of the program for the benefit of the whole, through field officers whose primary function is expediting the particular parts of the program entrusted to them. Accordingly, the War Production Board will immediately undertake supervision over the functions now exercised by contracting and procurement officers of the armed services with relation to the issuance of priority orders and certificates.[37]

Thenceforth, contracting officers would "propose" military ratings to WPB field officers, who would decide upon the actual rating to be issued. This process was to be expedited by the placement within WPB district offices of liaison personnel from the military agencies in the field.

Alarmed by the shortness of the notice, the prospect of substantial delays to procurement, and the breaking of an important link in the military contracting and procurement process, the Army and Navy submitted a counterproposal to Nelson, which he ac-

[36] ANMB Priorities Instructions, 18 Feb 42. This document is invaluable for affording a definition of terms, procedures, and problems associated with the priorities system at the peak of its existence. A similar view of the system in its final form, especially from the standpoint of the Army, may be found in PR 16, Priorities.

[37] Ltr, Nelson to Patterson, Forrestal, and Eberstadt, 22 Aug 42, in Ordnance Priority Docs., Exhibit 21.

cepted.[38] This was the assignment of WPB review analysts to military procurement offices in the field where proposed ratings could be approved or rejected at the source. Under this arrangement the contracting officer could immediately assign the rating approved by the review analyst. He could then, if he wished, appeal the rating to a WPB-ANMB Priority Appeals Committee in Washington.

The new arrangement went into effect on 10 September 1942. Although subject to shortcomings in practice, it worked harmoniously and gave substantial impetus to the growing practice of joint utilization of personnel. Thereafter an increasing number of officers from the War and Navy Departments were placed within various operating, staff, and committee organizations of WPB. This expedited decision making, gave broader representation to the composition of WPB, and materially improved interagency relationships. Under the circumstances, there was less need for ANMB activity on its earlier scale.[39]

---

[38] (1) Ltr, Patterson, Samuel M. Robinson, and Eberstadt to Nelson, 27 Aug 42. (2) WPB Priorities Dir 2, 10 Sep 42, sub: Military Rating Procedure. (3) Brig Gen Theron D. Weaver, Dir Resources Div SOS, For All Supply Services SOS, 4 Sep 42, sub: Signing of PD–3A Priority Certificates by War Production Board Representatives.

[39] (1) Millett, *Organization and Role of the ASF,* Ch. XVI. (2) ICAF R60, Priorities and Allocations, pp. 12–14. (3) CPA, *Industrial Mobilization for War,* p. 301. The following comment, made at the end of October 1942, reveals certain aspects of field operations at the time: "Under Priorities Directive No. 2 there appears to be a very cooperative relationship between Army and Navy and WPB offices. Most certificates are being taken to the WPB offices for approval as the majority of Army and Navy offices do not have sufficient flow to warrant a half or full time WPB Review Analyst in the Services' offices. Despite explanation and because of the fact that neither the Services nor the WPB have the Directive, the new approval is regarded by all parties as 'eye wash.' " Observations From Field

Changes in the Basic Rating Structure

Priority Directives in the Defense Period

A fundamental problem throughout the life of the priorities system was the determination of a basic rating structure which would truly reflect the strategic needs of the armed forces. As originally conceived, this task was simply one of indicating the order or precedence in delivery to be accorded the various items of completed equipment called for by the military procurement program. This was clearly a military—not a civilian—responsibility, to be performed on the basis of a joint agreement between the Army and Navy, or ultimate determination by the Commander in Chief. As already indicated, the task was actually accomplished by means of a priorities directive setting forth a number of preference-rating classes and the items or programs assigned to each. The determining authority was originally the Joint Board, later the Joint Chiefs of Staff; the directive itself was published and distributed by the Army and Navy Munitions Board.

Unfortunately, the simple concept of the establishment of a fixed and dependable scale of "military priorities," to be implemented by the proper harnessing of the nation's industrial economy, did not adequately reflect the realities of either military strategic planning or industrial organization and operation. So complex were the needs of the armed forces that is was impossible for the services, with painfully inadequate staffs and pressed by cruel deadlines, to construct a blueprint of a "perfect"

Education Meetings Concerning Priorities Representatives, par. 4, in Ordnance Priority Docs., Exhibit 24.

military procurement program to fit even a fixed set of strategic assumptions. To add to the difficulty, a satisfactory strategical foundation upon which to base a scale of military priorities never became available. With the dynamics of global warfare constantly calling for changes in strategic plans, with rates of equipment loss and ammunition expenditure changing from day to day and varying from one theater to another, with research and development making large segments of planned procurement obsolete, and with inevitable changes in the availability of raw materials and other productive resources, a stable preference-rating structure was inconceivable. Merely from the standpoint of the necessity for periodic redetermination of military requirements, the basic preference-rating structure would be subject to constant revision.

All this was foreseen but dimly when the priority system was launched in the summer of 1940. Equally difficult to foresee was the extent to which the military preference-rating structure would be upset by the need to provide nonmilitary ratings to support the general industrial and civilian economy. The Army had long realized that the assignment of priorities to military end items, without corresponding priorities over plant, machinery, equipment, and materials to produce such items, would be a futile gesture. Hence the original ANMB blueprint for a priorities system had proposed the automatic and unlimited extension of military priorities throughout the industrial system as a means of insuring the availability of all items contributory to preference-rated military end products. This arrangement would have confined the basic rating structure to a system of purely military priorities, with "industrial" priorities taking a derivative rather than a co-ordinate status. Such a system could only endure so long as military requirements could be "superimposed" upon the nation's economy without creating fundamental dislocations or running into over-all feasibility limitations. When these developments occurred, it would be necessary to intersperse the military rating scale with ratings for other essential needs.

Paradoxically, the ANMB proposal for unlimited vertical extension of priorities was emasculated at the beginning of the program when it would have been most feasible only to be adopted soon after Pearl Harbor when material shortages were reaching their peak. In any case, with the growth of lend-lease, basic economic, and civilian requirements and the spread of shortages throughout the economy in 1941 and 1942, the stage was set for deep-seated disagreement. Much of the controversy and acrimony surrounding the priorities system, especially in late 1941 and throughout 1942, was generated in debates over the relative position in the total rating structure of non-military items.

As a result of the many factors involved, some half-dozen or more basic priorities directives were issued by ANMB throughout the life of the system, and most of these were subject to numerous amendments before giving way to a successor. Three types of change were made by the various revisions: (1) new rating classes were established; (2) new items or programs were included in existing classes; (3) the position of old items in the rating scale was changed. In addition, with the refinement of requirements estimates and additional experience under the system, a more fundamental type of change—the placing of quantitative limitations upon various programs within the several rating classes was introduced.

Even the original priorities directive of 5 August 1940, was far from a simon-pure rating scale for military end items.[40] Classes A–1, A–4, A–7, and A–9 were either partly or completely devoted to industrial facilities—whether government-owned or private—for the production of military end items, and similar provision for industrial facilities was included in the Navy section. The first revision, known as the Priorities Directive of 27 November 1940,[41] created the subdivisions of the A–1 class, and, as already indicated, had as a major purpose the placing of critical machine tools and gages as sole occupants of the new A–1–a class at the head of the list. Here again was an indication that military end items could not be quickly obtained merely by giving them a high position in the rating structure. Contributory items essential to military production were needed *prior* to the completion of end items and might well require a higher priority status.

By the summer of 1941—with the passage of the Lend-Lease Act, the separate issuance of industrial and civilian ratings by OPM, and the generally increasing momentum of military programs—ratings below the A–1 class had become increasingly less effective. On 20 August 1941, the ANMB, under the direction of the Joint Board and with the approval of Mr. Stettinius, issued a completely new priorities directive. Navy, Air Forces, and Maritime requirements were in general placed at the top of the rating structure. At the same time all military procurement was lifted out of the A–2 to A–10 classes and placed in A–1; military items not specifically placed in higher classifications were blanketed into A–1–j.[42]

The August 1941 Priorities Directive represented, in one respect, an advance in technique over its predecessor of the year before. It introduced, although on a limited scale, specific quantitative restrictions upon the amounts of procurement accorded various ratings. Quantity limitations had become necessary for two reasons—first, to combat the general "priorities inflation" which threatened to wreck the entire system, and second, to give effect to the principle long known to economics as "marginal utility." The original priorities directive had been for all practical purposes "open ended"; the vague description and status of programs in each rating class permitted virtually unlimited procurement in each class. This meant that the grand total of priority claims issuable for all classes could far exceed the capacity of the nation's facilities, materials, and other contributory items to honor the claims. But even more damaging, the absence of quantity limitations gave each rating class an absolute and unlimited priority over all lower classes, no matter how essential the lower-rated items might be to a balanced program. If the total claims of high-rated classes exceeded total available supplies of essential materials, *none* of the lower-rated classes could be produced until *all* of the more favored classes were complete. The system thus violated the elementary principle of economics that the importance of any item or class of items is a *relative*—not an absolute—magnitude and diminishes per unit as the number of available units increases. In terms of the Army's procurement needs, it meant that 10,000 aircraft engines without any frames, or vice versa, or 10,000 of both without any

---

[40] See above, pages 509–10.

[41] This was not a complete replacement of the 5 August directive, since it did not, except by removal of certain programs, affect classes A–2 through A–10.

[42] ANMB Priorities Directive, 20 Aug 41.

aircraft guns or ammunition, would be use-less. A *balanced* program, using an equiva-lent amount of materials, might produce 5,000 completely armed and equipped planes. By the same token, planes without pilots, pilots without clothes, and an Air Force without well-equipped ground forces could not win the war.

In the August 1941 directive, the con-struction program for Navy and Maritime vessels, instead of being lumped into one rating category, was distributed into three. Vessel completions scheduled for 1941 were classified as A–1–a, 1942 as A–1–b, and 1943 as A–1–c. In this way, ship construc-tion not scheduled for delivery until 1943 could not, for example, pre-empt materials needed by the Army for the defense of the Panama Canal (rated A–1–b) although this in turn was considered less vital than sched-uled 1941 ship completions. In the same manner, production of .303-caliber rifles up to 2,000 per day was given an A–1–d rating; quantities in excess of 2,000 per day were rated A–1–f. Replacement of Navy aircraft under A–1–b was limited to 1,000; the same rating for new naval aircraft con-struction, other than 4-engine bombers, was limited to 2,473 units.

Despite these and similar quantitative ratings, the August 1941 directive was still predominantly "open ended" and priorities inflation continued with increasing severity. By the end of 1941, it was becoming evident to many observers that the priorities system was an inadequate instrument for control-ling the distribution of the nation's mate-rials. Yet until a new system could be de-vised and put into operation, the old one had to be used. Even though it meant further inflation of a depreciated system, a new "shot in the arm" was required for urgent military programs.

Major Developments After Pearl Harbor

Pearl Harbor brought in its wake pres-sures from many directions for a thorough revision of the existing priorities directive. On 6 January 1942, the President an-nounced to Congress and the world his new "Must" program for obtaining astronomical quantities of certain crucial weapons of war—planes, tanks, machine guns, mer-chant shipping. In mid-February the Com-bined Chiefs of Staff, established on 26 January as a result of the Anglo-American discussions in December, proposed the laying of a broad strategic base for priorities in the production of critical munitions. The War Production Board, faced with the problem of dovetailing industrial and civilian priorities with those for munitions, was insistent upon the early realignment of military ratings to accord wth both the latest strategic objectives and the availa-bility of resources.[43]

The next most specific impetus to a re-vision of the existing military rating struc-ture came from the Army and Navy Muni-tions Board. On 21 February, Under Secre-taries Patterson and Forrestal requested the Joint Chiefs of Staff—which functioned as successor to the Joint Board and as the American Section of CCS—to take prompt action "with a view to the immediate is-suance to the Army and Navy Munitions

---

[43] (1) Min (S), CCS 5th mtg, 17 Feb 42, Item 3. (2) CPA, *Industrial Mobilization for War*, p. 294. The preference-rating levels assigned to industrial and civilian items at the time of Pearl Harbor are concisely shown on pages 8–9 of *Report on the Office of Production Management to the United States Senate in Compliance With Senate Resolu-tion 195, Relating to Policy, Methods, Plans, and Programs for the Allocation or Distribution of Materials* (Washington: Government Printing Office, 1942).

TABLE 55—ESTIMATED MILITARY PROCUREMENT EXPENDITURES IN 1942 AND PERCENTAGE
DISTRIBUTION BY RATING CLASS, 26 FEBRUARY 1942

Expenditures and Rating	Total	Army	Navy	Maritime
Estimated Expenditures in Millions of Dollars	a $55,993	$41,011	b $11,624	$1,919
Percent Distribution by Rating Class	100	100	100	100
A-1-a	56	c 50	77	56
A-1-b	12	12	10	42
A-1-c	8	11	3	0
A-1-d	5	6	3	0
A-1-e	2	2	3	0
A-1-f	2	3	0	0
A-1-g	4	4	0	0
A-1-h	1	1	1	0
A-1-i	9	11	2	2
A-1-j	1	0	1	0

a Total includes small amounts for "Navy Defense Aid" and "Treasury Procured Lend-Lease."
b Excludes $29 millions of Navy expenditures authorized to carry "AA" ratings.
c Air Corps comprised the bulk of Army A-1-a ratings.

Source: Memo, ANMB (sgd Hines) to CCS (American Section), "Resume of Priorities Situation and Request for Revised Directive," 26 Feb 42, JB 335, Ser. 745, and CCS 400.17 (2–20–42), Section 1, both cited in Lt Col S. E. Otto, 1942—Priorities in Production for 1942 and 1943 (March 1950), MS, Historical Section JCS, p. 6.

Board of a revised basic directive, reclassifying the relative importance and amounts of the various major items in the military program in accordance with present military objectives." [44]

The basis for ANMB's request was the congestion of the top priority categories resulting from numerous, piecemeal changes in the directive since its issuance in August 1941. This imbalance, especially conspicuous following the new appropriations and all-out program after Pearl Harbor, was a major threat to the successful equipping of the armed forces. Evidence of the degree of congestion in the upper rating classes was provided in a supplementary memorandum. (*Table 55*) It is apparent from these figures that, apart from any other shortcomings, the priorities system was failing to achieve its avowed objective of "purposeful discrimination," and that a drastic revision in the basic structure was necessary.

The task of drawing up a satisfactory priorities directive early in 1942 was fraught with well-nigh insuperable obstacles and has been described in detail elsewhere. [45] The Joint Chiefs passed the assignment to their Planning Staff, which in turn delegated the spade-work to another JCS staff agency, the

[44] (1) Memo, ANMB (signed Patterson and Forrestal) for CCS (American Section), 21 Feb 42, sub: Resumé of Priorities Situation and Request for Revised Directive, 26 Feb 42, JB 335 ser 745, and CCS 400.17 (2–20–42), Sec 1, both cited in Lt Col S. E. Otto, 1942, Priorities in Production for 1942 and 1943 (March 1950), MS Historical Sec JCS, p. 4. This request was made at the suggestion of Ferdinand Eberstadt, whose appointment as chairman of the ANMB was confirmed by President Roosevelt on the same day.

[45] (1) Otto, 1942, Priorities in Production for 1942 and 1943. (2) Leighton and Coakley, *Global Logistics and Strategy, 1940–1943*, Ch. VIII. (3) CPA, *Industrial Mobilization for War*, pp. 293–305.

Joint Strategic Committee. Despite its name, this committee did not have responsibility for formulating basic U.S. strategy, and no fundamental plans or blueprint of projected military operations had been made available. These were only gradually coming into being with successive Allied conversations at the highest level. Thus the committee, in trying to base priorities upon strategy, found itself working in a strategic vacuum. At the same time, with admonitions from WPB that the program must be kept within the limits of feasibility, the committee soon found itself not once, but many times traversing the complete circle of gearing strategy to production and production to strategy. Mindful of the need for a "balanced program"—a useful concept but one which in 1942 was rapidly becoming a verbal cliché—the committee soon found itself "a focal point where all the various views on priorities within the services were drawn together in an effort to reconcile them in an acceptable manner." [46] A "balanced program," in the eyes of each contending claimant for high priority ratings, tended to be the one which placed its own claims at the head of the list and balanced the remainder of the program around its own as the independent variable. Both the Navy and the Air Forces were adamant that their major programs properly belonged at the head of the list. Industrial and civilian priorities, as well as those for the less privileged military supply arms and services, would have to fall into line as best they could. At the center of the problem was the "Must" program demanded by the Commander in Chief, which was not to be challenged on the ground of either feasibility or balance: "Let no man say it cannot be done. It must

be done—and we have undertaken to do it." [47]

On 10 April 1942 the JCS sent its recommendations, based on the intensive labors of the Joint Strategic Committee and the Joint Planning Staff, to the President for approval. The President concurred in the recommendations, which made provision for the "Must" program, and ordered that they be translated into an ANMB directive. At the same time he sent a memorandum to Donald Nelson, reiterating the necessity for successful accomplishment of the "Must" program and stating that the necessary priorities and allocations for facilities to achieve the revised military program "should receive the concurrent approval of the Army and Navy Munitions Board." [48]

On 20 May the ANMB sent a draft of its proposed new priorities directive to the WPB. The purpose of the directive was to lift the military program for 1942 well out in front of all other production objectives. To do this it placed the 1942 program (and materials needed in 1942 for the 1943 program) into four new "superrating" classes: AA–1 through AA–4. A rating of AAA was reserved for emergencies. Roughly 50 percent of the 1942 program (including 50 percent of the President's Objectives) was carried in specific quantitative terms in Class AA–1. A general note at the end of the

---

[46] Otto, 1942—Priorities in Production for 1942 and 1943, p. 7.

[47] Presidential Address to Congress on the State of the Union, 6 Jan 42. As indicated previously, the President's "Must" program was, in principle, accomplished, although internal readjustments and specific cutbacks were found desirable. See above, pages 141–42.

[48] (1) Memo, President for Mr. Nelson, 1 May 42, incl to Memo, President for JCS, 1 May 42, sub: Recommendations to Joint Chiefs of Staff for Priority of Production of War Munitions, and CCS 400.17 (2–20–42), Sec. 1, both cited in Otto, 1942, Priorities in Production for 1942 and 1943, p. 20. (2) CPA, *Industrial Mobilization for War*, pp. 281, 295.

directive made the following statement: "No additional ratings may be issued in the foregoing categories, nor will any allocations of materials be made, which are prejudicial to production of the end items or facilities covered thereby, without the concurrence of the Army and Navy Munitions Board."

Reactions in the War Production Board to the draft directive were immediate and spirited. In view of the fact that the military programs covered by the new superratings would absorb most of the nation's basic resources, it was apparent that projects vital to the maintenance of the industrial and civilian economy would have to be accorded comparable priority if they were to be achieved. But if the necessary industrial and civilian ratings could not be issued without the concurrence of ANMB, the military services would have a veto power over an area clearly belonging—under both the Executive order establishing WPB and the prewar Industrial Mobilization Plans drawn by the services themselves—to the civilian superagency in charge of the nation's wartime economy. For this reason, as well as others, the WPB Planning Committee recommended nonapproval of the directive.[49]

To the Planning Committee, as well as others in the War Production Board, the ANMB draft directive indicated an effort by the armed forces "to take over" the operation of the nation's economy. To the military services, on the other hand, it represented their legitimate concern—in the dark days after Pearl Harbor—that only items which were truly essential be given a coordinate position with top military programs. In order to protect the new military rating scale against indiscriminate dilution by allocations and ratings ordered at all

echelons in WPB, the ANMB wanted a specific opportunity to review any additional superrating proposals before they went into operation. The associated "veto power" would merely balance the power otherwise available to WPB to cancel the effect of the military ratings with new ratings of its own.[50]

Despite the doubts of many on his staff, Donald Nelson had faith in the possibility of reaching satisfactory agreement with the services in the day-to-day operation of the proposed directive. He therefore decided to accept it after it had been amended by ANMB to include certain materials for the 1943 program and revised ratings for the Maritime Commission's shipbuilding program. In a discussion with the President, he obtained Mr. Roosevelt's approval of the basic principle that essential civilian items later be included in the higher rating scale. On 12 June 1942, the new priorities directive was officially issued by ANMB, with the new ratings to take effect on 1 July. The official directive still contained the requirement of ANMB concurrence in the assignment of additional ratings within the new series, but Nelson did not consider this binding. He instructed his subordinates that projects indispensable to the maintenance of the industrial and civilian economy were to receive the necessary rating. ANMB was to be consulted and its concurrence solicited, but its nonconcurrence was not to stand in the way "if the responsible official determines that the national economy can only be maintained in that way." The necessary implementing order was to be issued

---

[49] CPA, *Industrial Mobilization for War*, pp. 296–99.

[50] For a discussion of this episode in relation to the general question of Army-WPB friction at this time, see: (1) Millett, *Organization and Role of the ASF*, Ch. XIV; (2) Otto, 1942, Priorities in Production for 1942 and 1943, Secs. I and II; (3) CPA, *Industrial Mobilization for War*, pp. 293–305.

and the ANMB or the armed services could appeal, if they chose, to the WPB chairman.[51]

This conflict over rating authority was liquidated by the end of September by a series of events. In the middle of August, Joseph L. Weiner—head of WPB's Office of Civilian Supply—obtained from ANMB Chairman Eberstadt approval of the creation of a new AA–2–x rating band, midway between AA–2 and AA–3 in the military program, to provide supplies and services for urgent foreign and domestic industrial programs. On 20 September 1942, Eberstadt left the ANMB to become vice chairman of WPB. This move, together with the impending adoption of the Controlled Materials Plan sponsored by Eberstadt, left the ANMB with a minor role. On 23 September, in response to a query by JCS, the ANMB noted that the controversy over concurrences had been "satisfactorily adjusted." [52]

Two other noteworthy amendments to the new rating structure were made shortly after the issuance of the 12 June 1942 Priorities Directive. The first involved the transfer of all aircraft programs into the AA–1 bracket. Previously, in February 1942, the entire aircraft program had been placed by WPB into A–1–a, then the highest rating class. The 12 June directive of ANMB split

the program four ways: the bulk of the program was specifically covered into classes AA–1 through AA–3; nonrerated items were left in A–1–a. The aircraft industry, solidly backed by the Army Air Forces, the Navy Bureau of Aeronautics, and the WPB director of Aircraft Production, vigorously protested this cleavage into four segments, stating that it would destroy any possibility of meeting existing aircraft production schedules. Aircraft spokesmen pointed first to the wholesale confusion and administrative burden which would attend any effort to rerate each and every one of the hundreds of thousands of prime contracts, subcontracts, and purchase orders then outstanding. This procedure alone (which would be unnecessary if all oustanding aircraft ratings in A–1–a could be rerated AA–1 by a blanket order) would, it was charged, threaten production delays of two to three months. More important was the permanent damage which would result from the effect of split ratings upon actual production schedules: ". . . because of the complexity of the aircraft production system involving the nicely balanced flow of thousands of parts and components—all with varying lead times and most of them common to two or more types of airplanes— the application of split-ratings would cut directly across existing schedules, destroying flexible control and any certainty that these schedules could be met." [53] As a result of these representations, and after full discussion by the Under Secretaries and the Assistant Secretaries for Air of the Army and Navy, the ANMB on 4 August moved all portions of the aircraft program into AA–1. Thereafter, in order to remove at least part of the resulting disadvantage to other high-

---

[51] (1) Memo, Nelson for William L. Batt, James S. Knowlson, Leon Henderson, Joseph L. Weiner, and C. H. Matthiesen, Jr., 19 Jun 42, sub: Effect of the Rerated Military Program on Work of the War Production Board, and CCS 400.17 (2–20–42), Sec 1, both cited in Otto, 1942—Priorities in Production for 1942 and 1943, p. 34.

[52] (1) Memo, ANMB (signed Weaver and Keleher) for JCS, 19 Sep 42, sub: WPB-ANMB Conflict With Respect to Concurrences, and CCS 400.17 (2–20–42), Sec 1, both cited in Otto, 1942—Priorities in Production for 1942 and 1943, p. 26.

[53] Otto, 1942—Priorities in Production for 1942 and 1943, p. 28.

rated items in the military program, all AA–2 ratings were given equal status with AA–1.[54]

The other change, the creation of the AA–5 rating class, was made on 25 September 1942 by Eberstadt in his capacity as chairman of the WPB Requirements Committee. This classification was created to permit effective allocations, under the new Production Requirements Plan, of metals not provided for under military programs in the top four superrating bands. Since PRP had been made mandatory on 1 July 1942 for most of American industry some such step was essential if PRP was to function.[55]

The basic problems faced and the procedures developed in adopting and implementing the Priorities Directive of 12 June 1942 represented a marked advance in the establishment of military priorities and their general relation to industrial and civilian ratings. Controversy over the relative position of important programs, whether military or civilian, reached its peak in late 1942 with a succession of conflicts among the synthetic rubber, aviation gasoline, landing craft, destroyer escort, Maritime, and similar programs. The major conflicts were gradually ironed out with the resolution of the well-known Feasibility Dispute in October and November, the scaling down of the

general military program, the adoption of the Controlled Materials Plan, and numerous specific compromises. On 30 April 1943, a new priorities directive was issued to replace an interim directive for the 1943 program. The existing scale of superratings was retained, and these remained for the duration of the war although the specific coverage of the ratings was repeatedly changed.

Despite its diminished role in the day-to-day administration of priorities after the fall of 1942, the ANMB continued for the next year to issue the basic military priorities directive. The final one in the series was apparently that of 8 October 1943, covering military programs through 1944. By mid-1944 the major war production goals had been achieved and controversy had shifted to problems of reconversion.

In preparation for V-J Day and the transition to a peacetime economy, WPB instituted a simplified rating system. After 1 July 1945, all military procurement of an urgent nature was assigned an MM rating. Effective 30 September, all outstanding AA ratings were canceled, leaving only MM ratings for military procurement and CC ratings for spot civilian purchases. The CC ratings were nonextendible for any purpose. The MM ratings were extendible for operating supplies but not for capital items such as machine tools and equipment. The AAA rating was retained for emergency use in breaking bottlenecks wherever needed.[56]

---

[54] (1) *Ibid.*, p. 29. (2) WPB Amendment 4 to Priorities Regulation 1, Sec. 944.5 (b).

[55] CPA, *Industrial Mobilization for War*, p. 300.

[56] *Ibid.*, pp. 946–49.

CHAPTER XXIII

Priorities: Problems in Application and Operation

The Critical List and Preference-Rating Extensions

Perhaps the most controversial feature of the priorities system from its inception in the summer of 1940 until well after Pearl Harbor was the role of the so-called Critical List. This feature exerted a profound influence upon the development of the priorities system. It created considerable friction between the armed services and the early priority-control agencies, and was an important factor in the later insistence of the services upon the adoption of a vertical system of material controls. A consideration of the various issues surrounding the development and application of the Critical List goes to the heart of the problem of organizing production controls in a complex industrial economy.[1]

The exact origin of the Critical List is shrouded in considerable mystery. In order to trace its beginnings it is necessary to go back to the eight-week period between 17 June 1940—when the ANMB Priorities Committee was appointed—and 12 August when the new priorities system was announced. Under its 17 June mandate from the Assistant Secretaries, the Priorities Committee had proceeded on the assumption

that the purpose of a priorties system was to insure, so far as possible, the production and delivery of procurement items in order of their strategic importance or urgency. This meant that an item assigned a given priority rating must have a superior claim, as against lower rated items, upon a manufacturer's facilities and upon all contributory materials or services—from whatever source—needed by the manufacturer and his suppliers to produce the completed item. All this had been contemplated by priority proposals under industrial mobilization planning in the interwar period.

Accordingly, the committee's first draft of the proposed new system (10 July 1940) provided that priority ratings assigned to prime contracts could be automatically "extended" to successive subcontracts or orders all down the contractual chain, thus requiring preferred treatment of all items contributory to the prime contract: "This priority rating, if necessary, may be automatically extended to materials, services, machine tools, related production machinery, equipment, and supplies essential to production and the scheduled completion of these contracts."[2] To implement this purpose the

[1] See above, pages 510–11, for earlier discussion of the Critical List.

[2] Draft of Ltr, Johnson, ASW, and Lewis Compton, ASN, To All Supply Arms and Services of the Army and Bureaus of the Navy, 10 Jul 40 sub: Priorities, with 3 incls: (1) Draft Rules and Regulations, Priorities Committee, ANMB, 10 Jul 40

committee's proposed "priority certificate" for prime contracts contained the following provision: "This rating will be placed conspicuously on all subcontracts issued by you *or any of your subcontractors* [italics in original], and on all orders for materials, services, machine tools, or other items contributory to this contract, *or its subcontracts* [italics added]." This provision for automatic extension of preference ratings to all subcontractor levels was fundamental to the Army's conception of the meaning and purpose of priority. It recognized the probable futility of assigning a high priority to military end items without a corresponding priority to obtain delivery of essential supplies to contractors at all levels in the vertical chain of production. But this conception of the operation of a priorities system was not effectively used until after the system was slated for replacement. The barrier to its use was the establishment of the Critical List, and the list's subsequent, unanticipated transformation in function.

On 23 July 1940 a meeting of procurement officers, held under the auspices of the ANMB Priorities Committee, was called in order to give the military supply arms and services an opportunity to help shape the details of the new system. Several important decisions were made at this meeting, including one to limit the assignment of priorities to critical items:

The question was raised—should all contracts carry a priority number? After some discussion, it was decided that it would probably be better to limit the field to critical items only. Commander Sickel stated that he would

have a list prepared in the Navy Department to correspond with the Army's critical items.

It was felt that there might possibly be items not now listed as critical for which it would be desirable to obtain priority. Provision will be made to include such items in the Class A priority list when recommended by chiefs of services.[3]

This decision, which was apparently independent of any representations made by the NDAC, was evidently an agreement to concentrate the priority power upon items of military equipment long referred to in Army planning circles as critical items. These were primarily Section I items in the procurement planning list—difficult-to-procure items such as planes, tanks, guns, and ammunition—for which extensive facilities would have to be built and whose production in quantity could not be achieved for at least one year, perhaps two. It was primarily to obtain these items in quantities adequate for an expanded Army of the future that the Munitions Program of June 1940 was launched. And it was the impact of this huge program which created the need for a system of priority.

The 23 July decision to establish a list of critical items was thus a decision to establish some kind of priorities directive to provide selectivity in the assignment of original preference ratings to military prime contracts. With the appearance of the first ANMB priorities directive the following month, there was no need, in principle, for a separate critical list. In so far as the directive needed amplification (since it was only a skeletonized outline of broad programs), this could be done by detailed amendments or supplements to the directive. Neverthe-

---

(6 pp.); (2) ANMB Draft of Priority Certificate for Army and Navy Contracts, 10 Jul 40; (3) ANMB Draft of Purchaser's Certificate of Priority, 10 Jul 40 (all in mimeographed form). A complete set of the 10 July 1940 draft instructions may be found in the ICAF Library.

[3] Memo, Lt Col A. B. Johnson, Priorities Com, for File, 24 Jul 40, Box 29, ANMB, Navy Sec. Correspondence Rpts, 1922–42, Priorities Regulations folder, National Archives.

530   THE ARMY AND ECONOMIC MOBILIZATION

less, under pressure brought to bear by the NDAC, the Critical List was published as a separate document. Ironically, this instrument—whose original purpose was to insure the early completion of important prime contracts—soon had the effect of limiting the power to execute many of these same contracts.

A closely related decision was reached by the procurement officers on 23 July:

The next question was—should we allow any echelon below the prime contractor to use Purchaser's Certificate of Priority? The consensus of the meeting was that the privilege of passing priorities to lower echelons should be limited to prime contractors only, and that subcontractors or suppliers would not have the privilege of passing on the priority rating. It was brought out that there would be cases, undoubtedly, when it would be necessary to grant priority to purchases made by subcontractors or suppliers, but that they should be provided for by applications to the Priorities Committee from the representatives of the contracting officer through his chief of branch or bureau.[4]

This limitation was a control device to prevent the abuse of the extension privilege; it did not prevent the procuring agencies, working through the ANMB, from issuing ratings essential to the completion of subcontracts or orders at any level. Moreover, the ANMB could relax this rule at any time; alternative procedures and controls at the field level could be established if later developments required.[5]

Meanwhile, the NDAC had already begun to exert some influence in the field of priorities. On 6 July the ANMB sent an advance copy of its 10 July draft plan to NDAC's deputy commissioner for production. His response indicated the commission's reaction at this stage: "The plan, as outlined, seems to be simple and complete and we have no suggestions or criticisms to offer with regard to it. However, we feel that the plan should not be put into operation until circumstances have developed a clear need for it. Making the plan effective is bound to be a shock to industry and to the public at large." [6]

Shortly thereafter, NDAC's priority responsibilities were centered in Donald Nelson and his staff. On 27 June, Nelson had been appointed Coordinator of National Defense Purchases, with the responsibility among other matters for investigating and passing upon the granting of priorities to national defense orders. By mid-July Nelson was already negotiating with the services on an informal basis.[7] The earliest written indication of his attitude is found in a letter of 3 August 1940: "I have looked through the memorandum on ANMB proposed priorities procedure and would like to discuss it with you before this is made public to your procurement agencies. . . . I think there are several things about this system which will cause a great deal of difficulty and would not like to see it put into effect until after it has been discussed with the commission." [8]

The nature of Mr. Nelson's objections to the ANMB plan can only be inferred from collateral evidence. The essence of the mat-

---

[4] *Ibid.*

[5] This limitation was, in fact, removed effective 9 December 1940. Thereafter any rating which could be extended by a prime contractor could be successively re-extended as far as necessary. Memo, ANMB (signed Charles Hines) for SW and SN, 4 Dec 40, sub: Additional Priorities Instructions.

[6] Memo, John Biggers for Col Hines, ANMB, 11 Jul 40, in file 141 Priorities System, 1940–April 1941, National Archives. Also see Memo, Hines, Secy ANMB, for Biggers, 6 Jul 40, sub: Priorities.

[7] CPA, *Industrial Mobilization for War*, p. 64.

[8] Ltr, Nelson to Col Rutherford, Dir Planning Br OASW, 3 Aug 40, in file 141.32 Priorities—Procedures, ANMB, 1940–41, National Archives.

ter is that the NDAC was not ready in the summer of 1940 to sanction the extensive application of priorities to standard commercial items, materials, or civilian-type products. Under the influence of British and French purchases, American industry was experiencing greater prosperity than it had at any time during the previous decade and was in no mood for controls which would interfere with its regular commercial business. The NDAC feared that the sudden impact of priorities upon industry would lead to "scare buying," speculation, and hoarding of materials with consequent widespread price rises. Also, it was undoubtedly concerned with the political repercussions of any appearance of "all-out" industrial mobilization for war in an atmosphere heavily charged with isolationism, especially in an election year confronted with the third-term issue. Moreover, even in the summer of 1940 the NDAC felt the need for firm retention of civilian control over the industrial mobilization process.[9]

As a result of this concern, the NDAC prevailed upon the ANMB and the services to confine the assignment of original preference ratings to contracts for military-type end items and important fabricated components of a noncommercial type. This was agreeable to the services since they had no desire at this time to assign priorities to all of their procurement contracts covering

everything from subsistence to post exchange items and office supplies. The new priorities instructions issued on 12 August were drawn up accordingly, and the procuring arms were informed that lists of critical items would be made available to them.[10]

After considerable prodding by Nelson throughout the summer, the ANMB finally issued its first official Critical List on 23 October 1940. By this time, however, circumstances had materially changed. Two days earlier the President had created the NDAC Priorities Board delegating to it his priority powers conferred by statute on 28 June.[11] The NDAC now insisted that the Critical List be used not only to limit the assignment of original ratings for *prime* contracts, but also to limit the *extension* of preference ratings. Thenceforth, preference ratings could not be used even by prime contractors (to say nothing of lower tier contractors) to acquire materials and supplies to fulfill their high priority contracts unless the needed materials were specifically mentioned in the Critical List. But (except for a provision favoring the aircraft industry) the list had been deliberately drawn to exclude materials and supplies of a general nature and the NDAC forbade the addition of any items to the list without its prior consent.[12]

---

[9] (1) CPA, *Industrial Mobilization for War,* p. 64. (2) Remarks of A. C. C. Hill, Jr., 27 Jul 45, Before Policy Analysis Staff, in file 020.1, WPB Histories, National Archives. (3) Memo, Maj Barnes, Priorities Sec Production Br OASW, for Col Young, 7 Jan 41, sub: Defense of Procurement Activities Under the Various 1941 Appropriations. (4) CPA, *NDAC Minutes,* 4 Sep 40, p. 80; 21 Jun 40, pp. 4–5; 2 Aug 40, p. 50; 9 Aug 40, p. 57; 28 Aug 40, p. 77; 11 Oct 40, pp. 99–100. (5) Novick, Anshen, and Truppner, *Wartime Production Controls,* pp. 43–44.

[10] ANMB Priorities Instructions, 12 Aug 40, par. 2.

[11] Executive Order 8572, 21 October 1940.

[12] For special treatment accorded the aircraft industry, see below, pages 534–35. The establishment of the Critical List did not prevent the granting of blanket ratings by ANMB for complete construction projects (both command and industrial facilities), which were specifically rated in the priorities directive. (1) Memo, ANMB To All Supply Arms and Services of the WD and Bureaus and Offices of the Navy Dept, 23 Oct 40, sub: Priorities—Items for Which Preference Ratings Are Authorized, par. 4. (2) ANMB Additional Priorities Instructions, 4 Dec 40, par. 1(e).

"The Lord giveth and the Lord taketh away." The Critical List had now been transformed into a device which granted priority to critical items and then automatically withdrew that priority the moment it was applied. To be of any practicable value a priorities system would have to insure preferential treatment in the delivery of materials and supplies going into high-priority end products. Although there were occasions on which the Army and Navy had to apply their priority powers to obtain acceptance of military orders by prime contractors, the real problem faced by the services during the defense period was the implementation of their contracts after they had been placed. This had also been true during World War I:

The first certificates of priority were issued at the end of September of 1917, and during the following 14 months the Board and Committee dealt with over 211,000 applications for them. . . . The object of these certificates was not to direct producers to complete certain orders ahead of other orders, but rather to permit them to secure the materials, equipment, and transportation which would enable them to produce goods according to contracts or agreed estimates of scheduled output. A large proportion of the certificates were issued by systems of automatic ratings.[13]

By delaying the extension of preference ratings to materials and supplies essential to the completion of military contracts, the NDAC facilitated the very process of "scare buying by nonmilitary users" which the

Critical List restriction was allegedly designed to prevent.[14]

The practical effect of the Critical List under the new ruling was to outlaw the extension of preference ratings (with the exceptions noted) until such time as the NDAC and its successors could be prevailed upon to add—in peacemeal fashion—specific materials, parts, and supplies of a "commercial nature." This converted the direct, automatic system of priorities planned by the services into a cumbersome, roundabout arrangement which was to bog down in a welter of negotiation and controversy for the next year and a half. By attempting to insulate the civilian economy from the inevitable impact of a huge procurement program, it helped to delay for many months a true relization of the magnitude of impending material shortages and the necessity for a tight system of material controls.

Although the implications and effects of the Critical List restriction were later painfully obvious, they were not so apparent in

---

[13] Memorandum on Priorities in the World War, Col Leonard P. Ayres, 12 Nov 40, attached to copy of Memo, Gen Rutherford for Nelson, 12 Nov 40, in file 206 Priorities to 10 Mar 41, Priorities Sec Production Div ASF. A handwritten notation on Col Ayres' memorandum states that portions of it were read to the NDAC Priorities Board on 12 November 1940.

[14] Quoted phrase from Novick, Anshen, and Truppner, *Wartime Production Controls*, p. 43. The following statement is the only indication found in War Department records, after diligent search, of the rationale underlying the NDAC's imposition of the Critical List: "The views of the Advisory Commission, Council of National Defense, were emphatic that commercial items should be omitted until circumstances proved the necessity for their inclusion. The commission reasoned that if preference ratings were assigned generally to commercial items, price rises were inevitable." Barnes Memo cited above, note 9(3). It should be noted that, in the absence of price controls, price rises were inevitable by virtue of the tremendous increase in demand resulting from the rearmament program. This increase in demand could not be concealed or exorcised merely by the absence of priorities. The failure to apply priorities meant that materials would tend to go to the highest bidder rather than to urgent military production as such, thus providing an additional incentive to price increases.

the hectic days of the early defense period when quick decisions had to be made by officials new to the field of economic mobilization and without adequate staffs or the time to reach studied conclusions. Perhaps the most remarkable aspect of the Critical List controversy is the fact that there was no dispute at the time of the list's adoption and transformation in function.[15] The first vigorous objections to the new rule were made by representatives of the supply arms and services before the ANMB Priorities Committee on 13 December 1940.[16]

Interservice Discrimination; Abolition of the Critical List

Whether for lack of understanding of its real implications or for other reasons, the services had been remarkably docile in their acceptance of the Critical List limitation on rating extensions. But almost immediately after its imposition, procurement personnel in the Army began to feel its effects. It then became apparent that it made little sense for the Army to possess overriding priorities for strategic military end items only to have its procurement objectives thwarted by its inability to extend the priority power to materials and components. These were frequently available at the preference-rating level assigned to the end item for which they were required; without the extension of this rating, however, irreplaceable materials would go to lower-rated projects or to non-rated orders of regular customers eager to

build up their inventories. Many suppliers, desirous of giving preference to orders under military contracts, remarked that all they wished was official recognition on their orders of the importance of the prime contract to show to their regular customers. Such demonstration would serve as protection against ill will and possible legal liability under prior contracts.[17]

To be sure, after 15 March 1941, contractors could apply directly to the OPM on PD–1 applications for individual rating certificates, but the required paper work and inevitable delays discouraged such action.[18] OPM had neither the organization nor the specific knowledge of particular military contracts to process such applications effectively. Likewise, the ANMB could apply to OPM for additions to the Critical List when it was obvious that the items in question were no longer available in the open market. At best this was time-consuming and at worst resulted in no relief:

These twenty items are the accumulation of about four months in operation of the system, as compared with the original list of about two hundred items. Our efforts to have the list extended in the meantime have been unsuccessful. The inability of our procurement officers to obtain ratings on these items is interfering with production.[19]

Moreover, relief provided by piecemeal additions to the Critical List would cover only limited areas of the general problem and would appear as belated recognition of a need which—under the original ANMB plan—would have been automatically supplied at the outset. Procurement officials of the Army felt that the Critical List limitation

---

[15] A careful search of War Department and ANMB records has given no indication that the Army or Navy objected, even mildly, to the adoption of the rule limiting the extension of ratings to items on the list.

[16] Memo, Maj Barnes for Gen Rutherford, 13 Dec 40, sub: Debatable Point in Established Priorities Procedure, copy in Barnes, Weekly Progress Rpt.

[17] Memo, Maj Barnes for Gen Rutherford, 9 Jan 41, sub: Priorities—Defect in Procedure.

[18] See above, page 516.

[19] Memo, Gen Rutherford for Gen Moore, DCofS, 29 Jan 41, sub: Automatic Priorities.

was a negation of the whole concept of priority and that it slowed down the process of rearmament without making any contribution to the solution of the materials problem.

As a matter of note, the priorities system from its inception until well into 1942 discriminated heavily against the regular supply arms of the Army in favor of the Air Corps and Navy. This discrimination operated in three ways: (1) the Air Corps and Navy enjoyed substantially higher ratings for the bulk of their programs; (2) the imposition of the Critical List reflected additional discrimination; (3) producers for the Air Corps in early 1941 were granted automatic blanket ratings for the procurement of scarce materials and components.

The succession of priorities directives from August 1940 to June 1942 gave top priorities to the building and equipping of aircraft and naval vessels and installations. In the directive of 27 November 1940, which gave A–1–a only to machine tool builders, the A–1–b category was devoted primarily to the Navy, while A–1–c was split jointly by Navy and the Air Corps. These two services got the lion's share of all ratings down to A–1–g, which also included combat vehicles and antitank guns and ammunition for the Army. The majority of Ordnance items were carried in A–1–h and A–1–i, while the Quartermaster Corps dropped to A–1–i and A–1–j. In general, this disparity persisted until mid-1942.

The assignment of high preference ratings to the Air Corps and Navy was, of course, the decision of the Joint Board and was thus taken to represent the official concept of the relative strategic importance of the various items in the total military program. Nevertheless, it was not the intention of the Joint Board thereby to prevent Ordnance, Quartermaster, Signal Corps, and other supply arms from procuring equipment and supplies essential to a balanced military machine:

In determining priorities supply arms and services were not called upon for representation as the quantities and times of their requirement were already known to the General Staff. Priorities have never been broken down nor classified by supply arms and services. The original breakdown made by the General Staff was by items; the breakdowns subsequently made by the Joint Board and the Army and Navy Munitions Board have all been by military objectives. Quartermaster items in these objectives have the same priority as Ordnance items, Signal items, or any other Army items.[20]

Yet practical discrimination was the unfortunate by-product of an open-ended priorities system which continually deferred lower rated items as long as the influx of new higher-rated items absorbed all available productive capacity. As previously noted, this condition was finally recognized and substantially improved by the new quantitative rating structure produced by the Joint Chiefs of Staff in June 1942.

A second discriminatory effect was produced by the operation of the Critical List. This resulted partly from the composition of the list and partly from the more liberal interpretation placed upon it by the Air Corps and Navy, whose aggressive methods of implementing their programs were sometimes considered "high-handed" by personnel in the older supply arms of the Regular Army. Thus in the original and apparently tentative Navy list of 14 August 1940, both

---

[20] Memo, Gen Moore, DCofS, for ASW, 13 Dec 40, sub: Statement Concerning Priorities Contained in Report of TQMG to the ASW, Dated December 11, 1940, G–4/32103. This memorandum was written in response to the complaint of The Quartermaster General concerning the unsatisfactory position of QMC items in the November 1940 subdivisions of the A–1 class. Ltr, TQMG to ASW, 11 Dec 40, file 319.1 A–S–PR–L (SBA–20).

aircraft and ships were listed with the sweeping definition "all types, complete." In the 23 October list—the first one to have joint approval and wide application—the definition of aircraft was broadened to read "all types, complete, or components, accessories, materials, parts—including lighter than air." Protected by this all-embracing provision, the Air Corps had little to lose by the prohibition of rating extensions to items not on the list, and its relative position was improved by the denial of the extension privilege to others. The Navy for a time achieved a similar result by a ruling of Rear Adm. Samuel M. Robinson, chief of the Bureau of Ships and subsequently chief of the Navy's Office of Procurement and Material, abolishing the Critical List and permitting the application of priorities to all basic materials required for the manufacture of naval end items. In the meantime, procurement policy officials in OASW and the older supply arms of the Army pressed for relief from the Critical List by more conventional methods:

The Navy has issued new instructions which abolish the critical list and permit application of priorities to all basic material needed in manufacture of the military items required. This is the procedure which our office has been arguing for, for months. The same principles were recommended formally on January 18 in a memorandum, prepared here and signed by General Rutherford, to Mr. Stettinius. The O.P.M., however, rejected the principle, maintaining that special authority for priority must be granted by the O.P.M. where the item is commercial unless that item has already been reviewed by the O.P.M. and added to the critical list. It is understood that Admiral Robinson has taken a firm stand on this matter and has stated that he will not change the instructions already sent out—that he will carry the matter to the President if necessary. . . . One thing is clear, the War Department and the Navy Department must follow the

same procedure on a principle as important as this one.[21]

In addition to the double advantage of higher ratings and the automatic extension privilege, the Air Corps early in 1941 became the beneficiary of a third priority measure giving it a preferred position in the general procurement program. This was the assignment by OPM of blanket preference ratings to producers of military airframes, engines, and propellers.[22] Blanket ratings, officially promulgated under "general preference orders," enabled specified contractors to use a single rating on all their purchases of scarce materials enumerated in the order. Blanket ratings typically provided a rating level well out in front of competing demands and included all major materials and components likely to cause procurement difficulty. In addition, they carried the enormous administrative convenience of not requiring recourse to contracting officers, the ANMB, or the OPM for countersignature or clearance. It is small wonder then, that the relatively underprivileged members of the Army's supply arm and services complained loudly and bitterly of their plight during the period when the priorities system was the chief instrument for obtaining deliveries of materials, components, and finished items.[23]

---

[21] Barnes, Weekly Progress Rpt, 5 Mar 41; also, *ibid.,* 26 Mar 41: "It is increasingly difficult to counsel our own Services to follow the prescribed procedure in the face of Navy violations."

[22] E. R. Stettinius, Jr., Summary of Priority Action Taken by OPM During First Half of 1941, in OPM Press Release, PM 553, 3 Jul 41. An illuminating discussion of the nature and effects of blanket ratings is found in Novick, Anshen, and Truppner, *Wartime Production Controls,* Ch. IV. See also, ANMB Priorities Instructions, 15 Mar 41, par. 25, Blanket or Company Ratings.

[23] (1) Memo, Gen Wesson, CofOrd, for USW, 12 Mar 41, sub: Probable Failure of the Ordnance Program. (2) Memo, Wesson for USW, 2 Jun 41, sub:

The mounting tension over the role of the Critical List resulted in a succession of modifications by OPM until the final abolition of the list on 2 February 1942. The first major revision, on 15 March 1941, was the addition of the following general rule:

1. *Parts and Accessories:* The items that appear on this list shall be deemed to include all fabricated parts and accessories necessary for the completion, maintenance or mechanical operation thereof, which are designed to meet military qualifications, and as designed are not commercially useful for civilian purposes.

The restrictiveness, as well as the ambiguity, of the phrase excluding "commercially useful" items led to its withdrawal the following month.[24] Also in the 15 March edition of the Critical List a number of basic materials were introduced—chiefly metals for high-speed alloy steels, aluminum and magnesium, chemicals, cotton linters (essential to the manufacture of high explosives), and synthetic rubber. On 1 May 1941, most standard metals were added, including ferro-alloys, iron and steel products, and lead. The 1 June 1941 list broadened the field to include a number of commercial-type end products—photographic, sound, and X-ray equipment, office machines, blankets, mattresses, various types of cloth, articles of clothing, and others. Thus by mid-1941 the Critical List had lost all semblance

of homogeneity and, although its restrictive effects had been considerably relaxed, it posed a major complication in the day-to-day administration of the priorities system.[25]

By the fall of 1941, OPM was ready to agree to the removal of critical list restrictions on extension of preference ratings to materials so long as these were "physically incorporated" into the end products. At the same time the OPM proposed that Army and Navy officials be prohibited from assigning ratings to any materials not to be physically incorporated in rated end products. This limitation was not at all acceptable to the armed services. In a joint letter to the OPM, Under Secretaries Patterson and Forrestal, speaking for the ANMB, pointed out that such a provision would prevent the Army and Navy from assigning or extending ratings to materials and productive equipment entering into the construction of plant and facilities vital to the production of strategic munitions. It would also prevent the Army from extending a rating on high explosives to the procurement of alcohol, for example, large amounts of which were consumed in explosives production without being physically incorporated into the end product.[26]

The ensuing discussions, colored by the new urgency inspired by Pearl Harbor, led to the complete abolition of the Critical List and to new priority procedures for handling construction projects, individual pieces of

Necessary Measures To Prevent Failure of the Ordnance Production Program. (3) Memo, Maj Barnes, Chf Priorities Sec, Production Br OASW, for Gen Rutherford, 9 Jan 41, sub: Priorities—Defect in Procedure. (4) Memo, Gen Rutherford, ANMB, for Gen Moore, DCofS, 29 Jan 41, sub: Automatic Priorities. (5) Memo, Gen Gregory, TQMG, to USW, 16 Aug 41, sub: Revision of Priorities System. (6) Memo, Gregory to Priorities Div ANMB, 20 Mar 42, sub: Priorities Affecting Quartermaster Procurement.

[24] Barnes, Weekly Progress Rpts, 23 and 30 Apr 41.

[25] Personnel using the Critical List testified that by early 1942 it "had expanded to resemble an encyclopedia." Col William H. Hutchinson, Priorities and the Preference Rating System, 15 Feb 46, ICAF Lecture (L46–31).

[26] Ltr, ANMB to Nelson, Dir of Priorities OPM, 26 Nov 41, sub: Amendment of Priorities Division Administrative Order No. 1. Throughout the Critical List controversy the ANMB had retained authority to assign ratings to construction projects for command and service-owned industrial facilities.

productive equipment, and maintenance, repair, and operating supplies. A prominent feature of the new procedure was the elimination of certificates and military countersignatures on all preference-rating extensions. Thereafter, an indorsement on the purchase order was all that was required for such extensions. The new procedure, combined with the abolition of the Critical List, saved many thousands of man-hours on the part of both contractors and military personnel.[27]

Other Problems in the Operation of Priorities

Extent of Preference Accorded Higher Ratings

As defense orders spread throughout the economy in the fall of 1940, manufacturers' production schedules became more and more congested. The change from a voluntary to a mandatory system in 1941, first for military and later for essential civilian orders, removed much of the pressure upon suppliers by their regular customers to ignore ratings and make deliveries under nonrated commercial orders.[28] But with defense orders competing more and more with each

other, the simple directive to give preferred scheduling to higher ratings left unanswered many questions essential to sound decisions by contractors. Should a manufacturer, upon receipt of a higher rated order, cease production immediately on items halfway through the productive process? If he did, much time in organizing and setting up production lines would be lost and overall defense production would suffer. Moreover, if such displacement were made mandatory what guarantee of completion would the new order have if it were displaced in midprocess by a still higher rating? In the case of orders for identical items could a new, higher-rated order pre-empt units already completed but still undelivered? And if so, would customers under lower-ratings have to see their orders processed from the very beginning after each pre-emption?

All these issues were vital to military procurement, and contracting officers were deluged by questions from industry. The Army took steps to clarify the regulations and to prevent the "piracy" of completed units or the repeated displacement of lower-rated orders. Through written regulations and in repeated discussion and conferences, it emphasized to its contracting officers and to industry that interruption to previous orders should be made *only* to the extent necessary to meet the actual required delivery of the supplanting order and that schedule delivery dates would have to meet the test of military urgency.[29] Since the Army had a greater proportion of lower-rated contracts than its sis-

---

[27] See below, pages 546 ff. The effective date of the abolition of the Critical List was 2 February 1942. OPM, Priorities Div, Amendment to Div Admin Order 1, 12 Jan 42. The complete new rules governing the priorities system at this time are found in ANMB Priorities Instructions, 18 February 1942.

[28] For example, machine tool builders were under heavy pressure by the automobile industry to furnish tools to them in disregard of priorities. A number of the larger builders had assured the ANMB Machine Tools Committee earlier in the year that they could handle the system on a voluntary basis. By the end of 1940, they requested that priorities be made mandatory in order to relieve them of the ill will and possible legal complications of refusing delivery to preferred or other customers under contract. ICAF R60, Priorities and Allocations, p. 16.

[29] This was a basic requirement of the priorities system from its inception. (1) ANMB Priorities Instructions, 12 Aug 40, Par. 5 (b). (2) ANMB Additional Priorities Instructions, 4 Dec 40, Par. 1 (c). (3) ANMB Priorities Instructions, 18 Feb 42, Par. 15 (a) (ii). Despite constant exhortation and supervision, it was never possible to prevent greater use of ratings than was necessary to meet authorized schedules.

ter service, it took the lead within ANMB in proposing for these some measure of protection. It objected to the practice of indiscriminately serving new orders on producers already booked to capacity, and urged that supplanting orders be accompanied by a certificate of the procuring official that all other practicable sources of supply had first been explored and rejected for adequate reasons.[30] Navy representatives within the ANMB gave their approval but the Navy Department, which enjoyed a generally higher priority status than the Army, refused to ratify the agreement.[31] After repeated efforts the Army finally obtained a compromise agreement which was incorporated into the official regulations:

. . . material on hand that has not been completed to fill a specific order rated A–10 or higher may not be diverted and delivered under a subsequently accepted but higher rated contract. Likewise, material in the course of production on a contract or order rated A–10 or higher and scheduled for completion within 15 days after acceptance of a higher rated contract or order may not be diverted to the latter contract. It is to be noted, however, that these provisions are not effective if the subsequently placed contract or order bears an AA rating.[32]

This regulation, together with subsequent amendments, was only partially successful in preventing repeated delays to lower-rated orders. Although it afforded protection against the more flagrant kinds of piracy, it

could not deal with the fundamental shortcoming of the priorities system—the inability of rating scales alone to achieve balanced production in the face of widespread shortages of materials and productive capacity. A few weeks after the adoption of the AA series of rating scales in mid-1942, it was found that mill capacity in major industries could accommodate only the top rating; thus it was impossible in the fall of 1942 for steel fabricators to accept any orders bearing less than AA–2 (by this time elevated to equivalence with AA–1); all others tended to be perpetually deferred.[33]

Equally difficult in determining the proper degree of preference was the problem posed by "split ratings." Split ratings occurred under two typical conditions. The first was the necessity faced by subcontractors to "basket" a large number of rating extensions received by them on many separate orders. In placing their own orders for materials or parts, subcontractors and vendors would have to show on the face of each order the quantity of each item which they were authorized to purchase at each rating level. An order might thus be split three ways: 40 percent AA–2, 30 percent AA–4, 30 percent A–1–a. If the supplier adhered strictly to the regulations, he might be able to produce only that portion of the total order which was covered by the highest rating. In many cases this would have meant the dismantling of a production line just as it had reached peak efficiency. It is understandable that many suppliers in these circumstances chose to "throw the book away"

[30] (1) First Ind, Col Thomas J. Hayes, Dir Production Br OUSW, for Priorities Com ANMB, 29 Jul 41, to Memo, Gen Lewis, Asst Chf Production Div, Industrial Service Ord Dept, for Dir Production Br OUSW, 25 Jul 41, sub: Priorities. (2) Ind, Hayes to Memo for Priorities Com ANMB, 5 Aug 41.
[31] Barnes, Weekly Progress Rpts, 7, 21, and 28 Oct 41.
[32] ANMB Priorities Instructions, 18 Feb 42, p. 29, Sequence of Deliveries. For later rulings, see: (1) PR 1670 (10–15–43); (2) WPB Priorities Regulation 1, Pt. 944.7 and amendments.

[33] Ltr, Gen Safford, ACofOrd, to Gen Weaver and ANMB, 5 Oct 42, sub: Priority Ratings for 1943 Program, and 14 incls, in Ordnance Priority Docs., Exhibit 26. General Safford pointed to the probable stoppage, within ten days, of production of tank components at the Chrysler plant unless these could receive an AA–1 rating.

and complete the entire order at little additional cost in resources. The same situation existed when split ratings resulted from quantity limitations in the priorities directive. In the case of large prime contractors, close adherence to the directive was both necessary and desirable because of the large quantities of materials involved. In the case of small subcontractors for minor parts or components far down the line, it was often a matter of common sense to complete an entire order in one production run.

A particularly difficult aspect of the split rating problem was the administration of the "item by item" ruling adopted by the War Production Board when shortages were at their peak. Because of the heterogeneous array of parts and materials going into many complex components, quantity limitations on many ratings had to be expressed in terms of dollar value. In the re-extension of such ratings, it was supposed that manufacturers would distribute the total allowed dollar value over the various parts and materials in the proportion in which each entered into the rated product. But more often than not, manufacturers' inventories were "long" on readily available materials and "short" on generally scarce items. The inevitable result was that contractors used a disproportionately large amount of the total allowed dollar value for purchasing scarce items for inventory. This accentuated the very shortages which controlled preference ratings were designed to minimize. The WPB therefore ruled that rating extensions should be confined to amounts which could be justified on an "item by item" basis. This provision was more honored in the breach than in the observance, and the technical difficulties of accounting and enforcement were so great that the provision was reluctantly abandoned. Fortunately, by the time of its formal aban-

donment, the general problem of material shortages had passed the crisis.[34]

Throughout the life of the priorities system, problems of this type plagued contractors, contracting officers, and the War Production Board. Because of the many opportunities for abuse of discretion, regulations had to be tightly drawn. On the other hand, good judgment and even patriotism, intelligently construed, sometimes required unauthorized departures from the rules in order to win the war.[35]

Higher-Than-Routine Ratings

An integral part of priorities procedure under the ANMB was the authorization of spot ratings higher than allowed by the current priorities directive. Such "higher-than-routine" or "out-of-line" ratings were frequently required in order to break specific bottlenecks threatening the completion on schedule of major items or even entire programs. This up-rating could not, as was frequently supposed, be performed by contracting officers. It could only be done by the

---

[34] (1) Draft Memo, Gen Weaver, Deputy Dir Resources and Production Div ASF, for Chfs of Technical Services, 5 Apr 43, sub: Use of Split Preference Ratings by Army Contractors During the Second Quarter 1943, and incl, WPB Ltr CMPL–122, 16 Mar 43. (2) Memo, Lt Col William H. Hutchinson, Chf Priorities Br, Production Div ASF, for Chf Office of Liaison and Co-ordination, ODM ASF, 6 Nov 43, sub: Proposed Basic Rating Structure for First Quarter 1944, par. 8.

[35] OPM Priorities Division, *Priorities and Defense* (Washington: April 1941), "Questions and Answers," p. 16: "Q. Should a manufacturer upset his production schedule for goods in process in order to comply with a preference rating suddenly imposed on an order? A. Preference ratings should be complied with. A problem of this kind, however, calls for the exercise of sound judgment and skill in scheduling. In cases of special difficulty, the matter should be brought to the attention of the military service involved or the Priorities Division, whichever assigned the rating."

ANMB (later the WPB) after application by contracting officers through the chiefs of their supply arms. By mid-1941 applications for special consideration had become so numerous that a large staff of officers in the ANMB was devoted to their review and disposition.[36]

Priorities personnel in the Army and Navy were aware, early in the life of the system, that widespread use of higher-than-routine ratings could easily whittle away the basic priorities directive to the point where the entire procurement program would be thrown out of balance. On the other hand, considerable flexibility was needed in translating strategic priorities for end items into industrial priorities for components, parts, and materials. Although it was only implicit and imperfectly understood, the basic theory underlying the priorities system was a presumption—the presumption that the assignment of equal ratings to two different end items would result in the production of both items on schedule. But with delivery schedules and (even more significant) production periods varying widely for equally rated items this presumption was open to serious question. The matter was further complicated by the fact that the length of the production period for different components of the *same* end item, frequently contracted or subcontracted to different producers, showed extreme variations.

It was on this ground that the existing philosophy underlying the whole priorities

system was challenged by an Ordnance officer in the War Department.[37] In a study submitted to OUSW, Maj. William F. Sadtler pointed to the 37-mm. antitank gun as a typical example of the weakness of the system. The gun consisted of five principal components—the tube, the mechanism, the carriage, the sighting system, and the control set. The tube, the carriage, and the mechanism each required distinct production techniques, although they all fell into the broad category of metal working. The sighting equipment required elements produced only by the optical industry as well as precision work ordinarily available only from instrument makers. An analysis of delivery schedules and actual performance revealed that the chief bottleneck was the production of mechanisms and that these were being seriously held up because of a higher-priority rating properly assigned to a similar aircraft gun. While deliveries of the completed antitank gun were held to the least common denominator (the delivery of mechanisms), completion of the other components was creating a storage problem as well as absorbing the use of facilities, manpower, and materials at a more rapid rate than required for actual end-product utilization. Although only a minor disadvantage in the case of the 37-mm. gun, these considerations could and did become of major importance for heavy items of equipment ordered in large quantities, such as tanks. Major Sadtler's proposal was to replace the existing system of strategic or end-item priorities with one of production or "process" priorities. This would require the initial assignment of different preference ratings for different components, based upon

---

[36] The ANMB Priorities Committee had approximately a hundred officers devoting full time to screening applications. Each division of the committee was headed jointly by an Army and a Navy officer. Concurrence of both was necessary before any out-of-line rating could be authorized. This prevented mutual encroachment by the Army and Navy upon each other's programs. Col Hutchinson, ICAF Lecture (L46–31), p. 3.

[37] The Fallacies of the Present Priority System, unsigned and undated photostatic copy in OCMH files, bearing AGO–CRB file 400.174 Priorities, Preference Ratings (6). Associated material identifies the officer as Major Sadtler, Ordnance Dept.

the estimated length of the manufacturing period of each.[38]

This proposal, although sympathetically received, was rejected by OUSW. The reasoning behind the rejection, as well as substantial insight into the nature and operation of the priorities system, is provided by the following quoted material:

The Priorities Directive announces the relative precedence of programs from a strategic viewpoint. This means that if all programs cannot be completed within the desired time objective, precedence is given to those in the higher positions. This strategic alignment then becomes the order of preference in manufacture until such time as industrial factors are encountered which throw a particular program out of phase as to deliveries of its related items. When this occurs it is the principle of operations . . . to apply priority adjustments to the specific item or component which is thrown out of balance. The procedure . . . consists of reporting the circumstances by the Chief of Branch to the Priorities Committee, ANMB, presenting all facts relative to the industrial delay, the established delivery schedules, the preference rating required to overcome the particular manufacturing delay, and the prospective interference which would be caused to higher rated items under manufacture in the same plant if the recommended priority adjustment is approved.

It should always be recognized that the solution of unbalanced deliveries does not necessarily lie in adjusting existing priorities. In many, if not in most, instances the fault lies in failure to recognize the longer time of manufacture for a particular item and the consequent neglect in placing this item under manufacture at an earlier time, or neglect in developing additional productive capacity for its manufacture.

It is not practical to predict accurately the manufacturing time differentials for all components or for all programs in advance. To attempt to do so would require assumptions regarding such variable and unpredictable factors as management difficulties, labor trou-

bles, and production engineering problems. Any one of these factors could work to upset basic assumptions upon which time-priorities might have been based. We therefore would be faced with the necessity of priority adjustments in either case. Since such adjustments would be required whether strategic interests or component timing was used as the governing principle underlying the established priority precedence, it would seem better to anchor the system to strategic principles as is now done.[39]

It is thus clear that under the priorities system there was no systematic procedure for the treatment of what eventually came to be known as "lead time." This factor was later given an appropriate place in determining material requirements and allotments on a time basis under the Controlled Materials Plan. But CMP was confined to three basic materials—steel, copper, and aluminum— and was geared to carefully scheduled end-product programs. The priorities system, on the other hand, covered at its peak the whole gamut of materials, part, and components entering into unknown and constantly shifting programs. Under the circumstances, the advance incorporation of lead-time factors into priority decisions was a practical if not a conceptual impossibility. The only visible means for dealing with the problem at that stage in the evolution of material controls was a continuous flow of "after the fact" priority adjustments in the form of higher-than-routine ratings.

As to be expected, therefore, the large volume of adjustments constantly required gave color to charges of irresponsible inflation of priorities by rerating officers. The term "leapfrogging" was aptly used to describe the migration of items into higher rating

---

[38] Ibid., p. 4 and Exhibit B.

[39] Portions of Comments by Lt. Col. E. E. Barnes on Study Prepared by Maj. W. F. Sadtler, Ordnance Department, entitled the Fallacies of the Present Priority System, 14 Dec 41.

classes in order to obtain precedence over competing items which had obtained earlier precedence by the same process, or which represented new, higher-rated programs not in existence at the time the previous rating had been assigned.

Whatever the factors explaining specific rerating decisions, the actual number of out-of-line ratings authorized was small in proportion to those requested. Screening officials at each echelon in the p r o c e s s complained constantly of the number of inadequately supported requests for priority assistance or requests which were unnecessary or irrelevant in view of alternative solutions. Thus in February 1942 an officer in the Production Branch of OUSW observed that for a majority of requests "no good reason" was given for a higher rating and that "in 90 percent of the cases the matter had been adjusted without recourse to priorities." [40] In April 1942 the Ordnance Department deplored the indiscriminate resort to requests for up-rating as a cure-all for production difficulties:

From the experience of priorities personnel in the Ordnance Department it seems reasonable to estimate that not more than one out of every six requests for higher priority ratings are actually deserving of such action. Frequently a higher priority rating would not solve the problem. In some cases the item for which priority assistance is requested might actually have to be stored when completed since other components of the military item are lagging in production. In other cases, to grant higher priority ratings on specific material orders would seriously delay a project of greater importance.[41]

Some indication of the efforts made by the Army to keep to a minimum the issuance of out-of-line ratings may be inferred from the steady stream of instructions sent to the various supply arms and services, and by them to establishments in the field. Governing instructions in increasing detail were in evidence from the original announcement of the priorities system on 12 August 1940 until the end of the war.[42] As early as mid-1941 the basic policy had been announced of issuing higher-than-routine ratings only as a last resort, and then to limit their issuance to cases where relatively small quantities of material or equipment were needed to complete a large contract.[43] Applicants not only had to pass this "low input—high output" test, but also to show exhaustion of alternatives. In the 16 August 1941 instructions, the alternatives included:

1. Early placement of orders by anticipation of requirements;
2. Simplification of design;

---

[40] Lt Col L. M. Johnson, Procurement Br OUSW, 26 Feb 42, commenting on Memo, Lt Col Gaillard for Brig Gen Thomas J. Hayes, 23 Feb 42.

[41] Commentary on Production Requirements Plan, p. 6, one of 2 incls to Memo, Lt Col Robert A. Kohloss, Jr., Priorities Sec Production Br, Industrial Service Div OCofOrd, for Brig Gen Charles Hines,

ANMB, 30 Apr 42, sub: Production Requirements Plan, in Ordnance Priority Docs., Exhibit 18.

[42] For example: (1) ANMB Priorities Instructions, 12 Aug 40, par. 13; (2) Ibid., 15 Mar 41, par. 16; (3) Ibid., 18 Feb 42, par. 6; (4) Memo, Gen Hines, Ex Secy ANMB, For Supply Arms and Services, War Department, and Bureaus and Agencies, Navy Department, 17 Jun 41, sub: Requests for Higher-Than-Routine Ratings; (5) Memo, Col Hayes, Dir Production Br OUSW, for Chfs of All Supply Arms and Services, 16 Aug 41, sub: Priorities—Requests for Higher-Than-Routine Preference Ratings; (6) [Memo] ANMB (signed Hines and Keleher) To All Supply Arms and Services of the Army and Bureaus and Offices of the Navy Department, 10 Feb 42, sub: Requests for Higher-Than-Routine Preference Ratings; (7) [Memo] Gen Safford, OCofOrd, To All Ordnance Industrial Division Establishments, 23 Apr 43, sub: Applications for Higher-Than-Routine Preference Ratings; (8) same for same, 6 Mar 44, same sub, and Exhibits A and B; (9) PR 16, Priorities, Sec. XIII, Special Rating Procedures and Scheduling Assistance; (10) ICAF R60, Priorities and Allocations, pp. 23–28, and additional sources cited.

[43] Hines memo cited above, note 42 (4).

3. Specification of use of standard items and materials;

4. Examination of all possibilities of substitution;

5. Efforts to obtain material or equipment from other sources under the present preference rating;

6. Efforts to increase production by discussing with the contractor the possibilities of: using extra shifts; subcontracting; revision of production technique; renting or purchasing suitable second-hand equipment which may have been previously disposed of by the contractor through sale to other contractors or through transfer to nondefense jobs.[44]

With the removal of all Controlled Materials from the orbit of the priorities system and the evolution of the war production program as a whole, the organization and procedures for handling special rating requests were streamlined. A new Special Rating Division, WPB, was established, consisting of Army and Navy representatives as well as WPB personnel. All requests for higher-than-routine ratings were thenceforth made on a new form—WPB Form SR–1—which could be filled out only by the procuring agencies, not by private contractors. Run-of-the-mill requests could be processed and disposed of at lower echelons, but all applications for emergency (AAA) ratings had to be approved by the Special Rating Division.

The AAA rating, established in mid-1942 to succeed the old AA emergency rating, represented the ultimate in higher-than-routine ratings.[45] As just mentioned it could be is-

sued only by the Special Rating Division, WPB, and was typically limited to small dollar-value quantities of materials or components which could break strategic bottlenecks without seriously interfering with major programs. Special procedures and thorough investigations were required for all such applications and notification of the decision was made to contractors by telegram. The policy of refusing to assign the AAA rating to entire projects or programs was studiously observed throughout its history and kept the rating from depreciating in value. (*Table 56*) The following summary of the dollar value of AAA approvals for all purposes indicates the circumspection with which the rating was used; in a period when national war production ran well over $75 billion annually, AAA ratings applied to less than one tenth of 1 percent of the total. By the end of the war approximately 60,000 AAA ratings had been approved, covering material to the value of $156 million.[46] Thus the smashing of bottlenecks by AAA ratings in the last three years of the war was accomplished by an average rating value of only $2,600.

Compliance Problems and Procedures

Fundamental to the success of the priorities system was adequate compliance on the part of both industry and the procuring agencies. The priorities system was, in effect, an additional currency system superimposed upon the regular monetary economy. Debasement of preference-rating currency, either by excessive authorizations at the source or by "counterfeiting" and exaggera-

---

[44] Hayes memo cited above, note 42 (5).

[45] The AAA rating superseded AA at the time of the JCS directive of 12 June 1942. Although AAA was the highest priority *rating*, a still more powerful instrument of priority was available in the form of the WPB "production directive." This was a direct order from WPB to divert completed or nearly completed items from some other order, or to schedule production ahead of other orders, regardless of preference rating. Memo, Gen Weaver, Deputy Dir Resources and Production Div SOS, for Chfs of Tech-

nical Services, 28 Jan 43, sub: Program Determination No. 266—Precedence of AAA.

[46] Undated memo prepared by Lt Col Casey in Jun 45, copy in OCMH.

TABLE 56—NUMBER AND VALUE OF AAA RATINGS APPROVED BY WPB SPECIAL RATING DIVISION AS OF 3 FEBRUARY 1945

Period	Number of Cases	Value
Total	49,353	$135,854,030
Value of material delivered on AAA ratings	—	129,467,921
Net Value of undelivered material as of 3 Feb 45	—	6,386,109
1942 (1 Aug. thru 31 Dec.)	5,837	42,937,726
1943 (1 Jan. thru 31 Dec.)	22,589	56,167,889
1944 (1 Jan. thru 31 Dec.)	18,916	33,848,396
1945 (1 Jan. thru 3 Feb.)	2,011	2,900,019

Source: Daily Report, 3 Feb 45, Special Rating Division, WPB.

tion of claims by individual purchasers, would create runaway inflation and wreck the system. Excessive authorization at the source was ultimately checked by quantity limitations in the priorities directive. The task of controlling the use of priority claims by purchasers was a major object of compliance measures, established initially by ANMB and the services.

In addition to controlling the volume of preference-rating currency outstanding, government officials had to insure that properly issued priority claims would actually control the behavior of suppliers. If suppliers or producers of scarce items failed to give proper precedence to priority orders, large-scale "black market" operations would result and the basic purposes of the system would be defeated. This aspect of compliance was of great importance to the military procuring agencies. But unless specific complaints of violations affecting military procurement were forthcoming to the ANMB, it took no action. The general enforcement of priority regulations upon industry was left to civilian mobilization agencies.

The immediate task of the ANMB in obtaining compliance was to see that preference-rating certificates and extensions, authenticated or countersigned by military personnel, did not authorize the use of higher ratings or the purchase of greater quantities of material than were required in order to fulfill the relevant contracts. This meant that the assignment of proper *delivery dates* in preference-rating instruments, as well as ratings and quantities, was an essential ingredient in compliance. In order to check these factors, the ANMB on 4 December 1940 issued instructions to all supply arms of the Army and Navy requiring contracting officers to send to the ANMB Priorities Commitee two copies of every preference-rating certificate issued for prime contracts. Likewise, countersigning or approving officers were required to forward two copies of all rating extension certificates.[47]

---

[47] ANMB Additional Priorities Instructions, 4 Dec 40. When the new OPM preference-rating forms were introduced on 15 March 1941, the ANMB received one copy (the quadruplicate) of all PD-3 rating and extension certificates; another copy (the

As copies of preference-rating instruments began to flow into ANMB in large numbers, it became apparent that a systematic reviewing procedure was essential. It was not until 29 April 1941, however, that an organized system for even minimum review went into effect. Under new procedures established at this time, reviewing officers in ANMB were to record, upon check sheets devised for the purpose, all defects found in rating certificates. In the case of minor defects, chiefs of supply services would receive copies of check sheets pertaining to their contracts and would take steps to educate offending personnel and prevent a repetition of such errors. Major defects subjected the rating certificate to possible revocation and were separately recorded. Copies of major-defect check sheets were sent to the Production Branch, OUSW, for indorsement to the appropriate chief of service, notifying the service of revocation unless adequate justification were forthcoming by return indorsement. Unfortunately, because of inadequate facilities for checking, the only defect classified as "major" was an erroneous rating (violation of the priorities directive or Critical List). Quantity and delivery date violations were listed as "minor." [48]

During the first three weeks of this procedure, 45,980 certificates (including extensions) were reviewed. Of these, 55 percent pertained to Air Corps contracts, 20 percent to Navy, and the remainder to Army and other government agencies. Of the Army and the Air Corps certificates, a total of 398 were found to have major de-

fects. It is interesting to note that 360 of these, or over 90 percent, pertained to the Air Corps alone.[49]

At first the notices of major defects in rating assignments and extensions did not result in revocation of ratings. But during the week of 11 June 1941, 470 revocations were ordered by the Under Secretary of War. All but six of these were Air Corps ratings, the majority covering extensions to three aircraft subcontractors. Investigation revealed that most of the improperly rated extensions derived from a single improperly rated prime contract. Others resulted from prime contracts covering several items with different ratings; Air Corps countersigning officers had approved extensions based on the highest rating. To prevent future difficulty a representative of OUSW spent several days at Wright Field, where a new system of review procedure was installed.[50]

With the spread of material shortages and the increasing number of priority actions, it became evident that the ANMB review procedure would have to be drastically overhauled. By mid-August 1941 the ANMB was being deluged with from twenty thousand to twenty-five thousand certificates weekly. Review operations were from two to three weeks behind schedule. ANMB had

septuplicate) went to the relevant Army supply arm or service or Navy bureau.

[48] Lt B. W. Covington, Priorities Sec Production Br OUSW, Progress Report on Reviewing of Preference Rating Certificates, attached to Barnes, Weekly Progress Rpt, 21 May 41.

[49] *Ibid.* Government agencies using priorities included Coast Guard, Coast and Geodetic Survey, and others performing small amounts of defense procurement and obtaining ratings through the ANMB Priorities Committee. Toward the end of May it was reported that "The Air Corps continues to be the greatest abuser of the rating system." Barnes, Weekly Progress Rpt, 28 May 41.

[50] Barnes, Weekly Progress Rpts, 11 and 25 Jun and 30 Jul 41. Under the new arrangement Wright Field prepared a master list of all contracts awarded prior to 1 July 1941, listing all items and correct preference ratings. These were distributed to Air Corps procurement districts for guidance in assigning ratings. Ratings for all subsequently awarded contracts were cleared through ANMB and forwarded in weekly lists to the districts.

neither the personnel, the office space, or even the filing cabinets essential to the task: "Three or four hundred thousand [certificates already reviewed] are piled up on the floor of the Facilities Division." Review was perfunctory for most certificates and nonexistent for many. Because of the absence of serial numbers on certificates, coupled with inadequate filing systems, it was not possible to survey all rating extensions associated with a given prime contract. Thus no check could be made of quantitative padding of orders or of improper advancement of delivery dates.[51]

The result of this crisis was the decentralization of the bulk of review operations to the various supply services. Effective 1 November 1941 all supply arms and services were directed to establish a priorities compliance section in the office of the chief. Thereafter, all rating extension certificates were to be examined by service compliance sections for correctness of ratings, quantities, and delivery dates. Errors in these crucial factors were to result in revocation. Prime contract rating assignments (which were only a small fraction of the number of rating *extensions*) would continue to be reviewed by the ANMB although the services also were urged to review this class of certificates and take independent corrective action. Compliance sections in the services were to maintain adequate records and provide progressive training and education of all personnel engaged in priority matters. A monthly inspection of each compliance section would be made, for purpose of co-ordi-

nation and control, by the priorities staff in the Production Branch OUSW.[52]

This decentralization of routine compliance operations, freeing ANMB from an impossible administrative burden, occurred none too soon. At the time of its announcement, copies of preference rating certificates were flowing into ANMB at the rate of seventy thousand per week.[53] After a few weeks of operation it was evident that the new procedure was successful, and it was even suggested that with the problem well in hand a system of spot checking would be adequate for the purpose. By this time, however, the OPM—also plagued with mountains of undigestible paper work in connection with all its PD certificates—was undertaking drastic simplification of priorities procedures. The first step—elimination of the use of rating certificates for extensions involving less than $500 in materials—was expected to yield a 60-percent reduction in the volume of certificates reviewed by compliance sections.[54]

With the advent of Pearl Harbor, the creation of the War Production Board, and the substantial revision of the priorities system effective 15 March 1942, all rating extensions regardless of amount, were accomplished by the purchaser's indorsement on

---

[51] Memo, Lt Col Elmer E. Barnes for Lt Col J. L. Phillips, Priorities Com ANMB, 6 Aug 41, sub: Observations on Present Procedure for Reviewing Preference Rating Certificates and Recommendations for Corrections of Defects, incl 2 to Barnes, Weekly Progress Rpt, 13 Aug 41.

[52] Memo, Brig Gen Thomas J. Hayes, Dir Production Br OUSW, for Chfs of Supply Arms and Services, 13 Oct 41, sub: Establishment of a Priority Compliance Section in the Offices of the Chiefs of Supply Arms and Services.

[53] Barnes, Weekly Progress Rpt, 14 Oct 41.

[54] *Ibid.*, 9 and 23 Dec 41. The effective date of the $500 exemption for all but machine tools and similar items was apparently some time in December 1941. OPM Priorities Div Supplement 6 to Admin Order 1, cited in Gen Lewis, Asst Chf Production Div, Industrial Service OCofOrd, to CGS All Ord Dept Mfg Arsenals and All Ord Procurement Districts, 23 Dec 41, sub: Preference Rating Extensions, in Ordnance Priority Docs., Exhibit 11.

each purchase order. No approval by contracting or inspection officers was required, but the purchaser in certifying his order represented that his purchase complied with WPB regulations governing quantities, ratings, and delivery dates for preference-rating extensions.

The indorsement was required to show the name of the contracting agency and prime contractor, prime contract number, original preference-rating and certificate number, and the name of the cognizant field officer in charge of compliance under the prime contract. This information (the minimum for satisfactory review) was transmitted down the chain of suppliers by means of successive purchase orders, and purchasers were required to send copies of each certified purchase order to the indicated compliance officer.[55]

Under the new simplified procedures, the priority compliance sections in the Army's technical service headquarters were transformed into supervisory agencies, and compliance operations were transferred to the field. Local contracting, procurement, and inspection officials previously responsible for authenticating PD–3A certificates were now required to review all priority actions under prime contracts in their jurisdiction and take the necessary corrective action. All certified purchase orders were to be checked for validity of ratings, quantities, delivery dates, and other relevant items. Incorrect purchase orders were to be revoked unless corrective action was taken by purchasers promptly after notification. In the event of revocation, suppliers were requested to return the original purchase order to the com-

pliance officer and to suspend production and delivery. Recalcitrant purchasers or suppliers were cited to the ANMB, which would, in co-operation with the War Production Board, institute corrective action including possible criminal prosecution.[56]

Thus from early 1942 on, military procurement personnel assigned preference ratings only to prime contracts. Rating extensions for materials, parts, and supplies were automatically applied by contractors, without countersignature and subject only to "after the fact" review and compliance measure.[57] Thereafter, the largest part of the priorities system was in effect operated under an "honor system," with American industry chiefly responsible for its success. As new systems of production and material control partially supplanted the priorities system, further relaxations were made. Purchase order indorsements were simplified to the point where satisfactory review was no longer possible and copies were no longer required to be sent to compliance officers. There is evidence that this relaxation resulted in increased violation of regulations.[58]

---

[55] ANMB Priorities Instructions, 18 Feb 42, par. 14, Extension of PD–3A.

[56] ANMB Priorities Instructions, 18 Feb 42, par. 16, Responsibility and Authority of Army and Navy Contracting, Procurement, and Inspecting Field Offices. Memo, Gen Hayes, Dir Production Br OUSW, for CofOrd, 24 Feb 42, sub: Administration of Priorities Compliance Activities Under Revised ANMB Priorities Instructions Dated February 18, 1942, in Ordnance Priority Docs., Exhibit 14.

[57] This applied to supply contracts generally. Special procedures governed ratings and extensions for construction contracts, machinery and equipment, and maintenance, repair, and operating supplies. ANMB Priorities Instructions, 18 Feb 42, pars. 9, 10, and 11.

[58] Memo, Maj John S. Swaim, Ord Dept, for Chf Priorities Div, Production Br, ASF, 5 Oct 43, sub: Comments on Present Status of Priorities Compliance, in Ordnance Priority Docs., Exhibit 36.

In any case by 1943, responsibility for compliance had gravitated almost completely out of the custody of the military services into the orbit of the War Production Board. As the character of violations became more subtle, their detection required increasing resort to detailed examination of a firm's records and correspondence. This was especially true as the impetus to violation became more and more an upward pressure from underlying suppliers rather than a downward pressure from purchasers initially armed with inflated preference ratings. Perhaps the greatest problem in late 1942 and 1943 was the perennial insistence of suppliers, during negotiations preliminary to placement and acceptance of orders, that prospective purchasers obtain and extend a higher rating than that originally tendered. Suppliers would insist that they were "booked to capacity" with higher ratings even when this was not the case, and purchasers hesitated—because of the delay as well as for other reasons—to request official inspection of the supplier's books. Suppliers in turn felt the same pressure from their own underlying suppliers, all of whom wished to receive high ratings in order to build up their inventories or take care of other customers. The inevitable result was widespread application by purchasers for higher-than-routine ratings, the unwarranted advancement of delivery dates, and other irregularities.[59]

---

[59] (1) *Ibid.* (2) Report of Special Committee on Preference Rating and Allied Controls, Program Adjustment Committee, WPB, 24 Oct 43, Report No. 10 by Program Adjustment Subcommittee on Compliance, Copy in OCMH. The Army representative on this subcommittee was Col. William H. Hutchinson, chief of the Priorities Branch, Production Division, ASF.

Throughout the life of the priorities system it was apparent that most compliance problems resulted from the novelty and complexity of the regulations, their frequent internal inconsistency or seeming lack of relevance to the job at hand, the task of educating and disseminating information to all concerned, and the very nature of production under wartime conditions. It was difficult to expect industry to comply with regulations which often were not known by contracting officers and field representatives of civilian agencies. These in turn were continually hampered by inadequate staff and facilities, personnel turnover, and the incessant pressure to reach quick decisions and turn out work at top speed. During the early days when huge organizations, such as the major aircraft plants, were building facilities, tooling up, and laying in materials and supplies to complete their contracts, dependable contract objectives and production schedules were nonexistent. A prime CPFF contract with an initial ceiling value of $20 million might be raised by a stream of amendments to ten times its original figure. Neither the contractor nor the military countersigning officer could tell what the production objective would be or even the quantity of materials required to achieve a given objective. The countersigning officer might be a Reserve officer suddenly recalled to active duty from a banking firm, an automobile dealership, or a college faculty to find himself confronted with the task of approving scores of complex purchase orders and rating extensions daily. Even an officer thoroughly trained in industrial engineering would have to become familiar with thousands of technical details, input-output ratios, and other information difficult or impossible to obtain, in order to do a technically correct job of validation.[60]

It is not surprising, therefore, that the War Production Board announced in the spring of 1943 that out of 75,000 investigations of priority compliance, only 247 suspensions were issued, 59 criminal prosecutions instituted, and only 1 prison sentence imposed.[61] Nor is it surprising, on the other hand, that "it has been told that one manufacturer built a million dollar factory with a preference rating he had received on a $500 order." [62]

[60] "Some officers did nothing but countersign all day long. Naturally it was impossible, under these circumstances, to do any real checking of delivery dates or quantities ordered." Hutchinson, ICAF Lecture (L46–31), p. 3.

[61] New York *Times,* 20 Mar 43, p. 21.

[62] Hutchinson, *op. cit.,* p. 5.

CHAPTER XXIV

Material Controls in Transition

Allocations and Scheduling

The priorities system in its developed form was an attempt to control the flow of scarce materials by starting at the top of the productive process, namely, at the end-product level. Preference ratings assigned to end products, when extended vertically down to producers of basic materials, were expected to direct the flow of these materials. But no sooner had the priorities system been adopted and placed in extensive operation than collateral control measures were introduced which eventually came into serious conflict with priorities. These measures, instead of beginning at the end-product level, involved the application of direct controls at the source of supply.

It was the policy of NDAC, continued by OPM, to forbid the extension of military preference ratings to basic industrial and commercial materials until the central control agency could adopt measures designed to minimize dislocations of the civilian economy. In accordance with this policy, the addition of an important basic material to the Critical List was typically delayed until it could be accompanied by the issuance of an M order (material order) which placed the material under "industry-wide-control." The implications of such control were concisely stated by the OPM shortly after placing aluminum under industry-wide control:

Putting aluminum on the critical list meant that the Army and Navy Munitions Board and agents of the services could issue preference ratings against it. But, since the metal was also put under industry-wide control, this meant that the allocations made by the Priorities Division [OPM] would take precedence over individual certificates in case of conflict.[1]

Thus the introduction of allocations provided OPM with an effective tool enabling it to retain final control over the distribution of scarce materials.

The aluminum order (General Preference Order M–1, issued 21 March 1941) was the first of a long series of M orders, most of which were revised many times with the gradual tightening of controls until their ultimate relaxation at the end of the war. The M–1 order on aluminum supposedly "brought all aluminum deliveries under allocation."[2] Actually this phrase—which was similar to those often used to describe the techniques of most of the early M orders—

---

[1] OPM Priorities Division, *Priorities and Defense*, p. 10. On 31 May 1941, by 55 *Stat.* 236, the President was expressly given the power to apply priorities and allocations to any orders or contracts, civilian or military, at all contractor levels. This removed all doubts as to the legality of priority action to meet indirect military and general industrial requirements. OPM's General Counsel, John Lord O'Brian, had previously indicated that these powers were implied in the act of 28 June 1940. CPA, *Industrial Mobilization for War*, p. 175; for opposite view, see p. 192; for accounts of problems, see pp. 90, 96, 102–5, and 110.

[2] CPA, *Industrial Mobilization for War*, p. 179.

was something of a misnomer. The aluminum order required mandatory observance of preference ratings, except when otherwise directed by OPM, and limited deliveries of aluminum for nondefense uses to various percentages (from 80 percent down to 10 percent) of the amount used in 1940 for the same purpose.[3] This curtailment of nondefense consumption did not, however, provide a system of "complete allocation" in any meaningful sense. It left producers free to select their nondefense customers as long as total shipments in each end-use category did not exceed the allowable percentage. Moreover, initial allocation procedures varied widely from one material branch of OPM to another, were loosely applied, and were intended only to supplement, not to replace the established priorities system.

By the spring of 1941, the American economy was experiencing the greatest wave of prosperity since 1929. Material suppliers everywhere—faced with the cumulative demands of British and French military orders, the huge rearmament program of the United States, and the consequent rise in civilian consumption expenditures—found themselves unable to handle the flood of orders. At the same time, sharp increases in speculative demand—in direct competition with military orders—were felt in all sectors of the economy. Particularly noteworthy was the rush of consumer durable-goods industries to lay up heavy inventories in anticipation of impending decisions to place positive restrictions on non-defense consumption of scarce materials.

The War and Navy Departments, as well as an important segment of OPM, had been pressing for some time for the curtailment of nondefense industries.[4] On 3 May 1941 a voluntary curtailment, negotiated by OPM Director General Knudsen, was accepted by the automobile industry to become effective 1 August 1941. After this agreement had been reached, steel companies made "extraordinary efforts . . . to ship the greatest possible tonnage of steel to the automobile companies before July 31, 1941."[5] With similar demands from producers of electric refrigerators, washing machines, and other consumer hard goods, to say nothing of requirements for plant and equipment, steel mills were booked far beyond capacity. Not only did many essential civilian industries (for example, containers) lose out in the scramble for steel and other metal products; even military contractors armed with high preference ratings found their steel deliveries badly delayed and in some cases were unable even to place their orders.[6]

A brief sketch of the development of controls over the supply of steel up to the fall of 1941, as viewed from the Office of the Assistant Secretary (later the Under Secretary) of War, is of interest in outlining the origins of allocation systems in World War II. From almost the very beginning of the defense period, the Army and Navy had recommended that the steel industry adopt a system of allocations such as proposed by the Steel Plan developed by the Army and the ANMB during the interwar period. Estimates of War Department steel requirements for a major rearmament effort had been turned over to the NDAC on 13 June 1940. On 24 September 1940, with steel consumption rising at an extremely rapid

---

[3] *Ibid.*

[4] As early as October 1940, the War Department had urged that commercial production of aircraft be halted to permit the production of military planes. See note 24, Chapter XXII, above.

[5] CPA, *Industrial Mobilization for War,* p. 193.

[6] *Ibid.*

rate, the War Department again recommended that the Steel Plan be placed into effect. No specific reply was given to this proposal but on 5 November 1940 a memorandum from NDAC to the Assistant Secretary of War stated that available information "indicates we are on the safe side for full steel production." On 24 January 1941, in the face of increasing difficulty in obtaining structural shapes for constructing Army facilities, the OPM Steel Priority Committee stated that there was no shortage of steel for civilian or defense purposes. At the same time the committee refused a member's request for issuance of a public statement against inventory increases. At the 31 January meeting of the committee, specific cases of unsatisfactory steel deliveries were presented; but attempts by the Army and Navy to have structural shapes placed on the priorities Critical List met with no success.

As steel shortages spread from shapes to alloys and plates, representatives of the Army and Navy repeatedly requested the addition of these items to the Critical List, but without result. On 12 February 1941 the Under Secretary of War—in a letter to the chief of OPM's Iron and Steel Branch—once more called attention to the Steel Plan, explained its nature in detail, and stressed the necessity for co-ordinating civilian with defense requirements. But both the steel industry and OPM's Steel Priority Committee continued to resist efforts to place steel under mandatory controls, stating that capacity was adequate or would shortly be improved, and that in any case priorities "should be avoided as long as possible."

At the 14 March 1941 meeting of the Steel Priority Committee, shortages of nickel steel as well as of tungsten were discussed but no action was taken to place them under mandatory control. On the following day the Army and Navy Munitions Board issued a new Critical List, adding special-treatment steels and bullet-core steel to the list of items to which preference ratings could be applied. At the next weekly meeting of the Steel Priority Committee this body passed a formal resolution condemning the action of ANMB in adding certain steels to the Critical List.

Meanwhile, steel deliveries in an increasing number of categories were falling further and further behind defense needs. On 28 May 1941 a list of two hundred delayed deliveries of steel, whose nonavailability was holding up aircraft and other vital production, was furnished OPM, together with a request that mandatory priorities be immediately instituted on alloy steel. OPM replied a few days later that priorities were not required and that the new general preference order on steel would take care of the situation. But this order,[7] in the view of the services, was only a "complicated system of expediting" whose effect was "barely noticeable." Steel in abnormal quantities was still flowing to the automobile industry, and on 3 June 1941 OASW requested that OPM take immediate steps to regulate the flow of tonnages into nondefense industries.

The first major improvement in the steel situation, in the Army's view, was announced on 1 August 1941 when pig iron was placed under mandatory allocation, effective 1 September 1941, by order M–17. But a companion order, M–21 of 9 August 1941, placing all steel products under mandatory priorities, was not similarly successful—apparently because steel shortages had passed the stage where they could be rectified by priorities. Accordingly, on 27

---

[7] General Steel Preference Delivery Order, 29 May 41.

August 1941 the Under Secretaries of the War and Navy Departments—acting as the Army and Navy Munitions Board—again recommended to OPM Director General Knudsen the adoption of a system of steel allocations such as contemplated by the Steel Plan. Two months later OASW was still preparing forceful memorandums attempting to convince OPM that the time had passed when simple priorities could be effective in channeling steel supplies to their most urgent uses.[8]

The realization in the late spring and summer of 1941 that grave material shortages, as in the case of steel, were no longer merely "potential or "impending" but had actually arrived, was a bitter pill for OPM to swallow in the face of its earlier reassurances in this area. But it was also a disconcerting fact to the military procuring agencies. The latter, having fought for months with only indifferent success to have priorities extended to basic materials, now found their preference-rating currency sadly depreciated. Ironically, the depreciation was at this stage only in part attributable to the cause almost universally ascribed— the prodigality of military contracting officers in issuing and extending preference ratings. The basic difficulty was the critical lack of productive capacity throughout all segments of the economy for meeting at short notice the huge requirements of a major rearmament program. Moreover, with commercial demand for materials skyrocketing, and with priorities only partially

and belatedly applied to them, it was inevitable that powerful groups in private industry would be favored and that both rated and nonrated defense orders for materials would suffer.

By the fall of 1941 the overriding defect of the priorities system was becoming painfully apparent: it failed to provide a positive guarantee of delivery to any item; it could only offer a relative urgency standing, unrelated to conditions of supply and subject to momentary change with changes in other variables in the total supply-and-demand equation. Preference ratings thus came to be widely and aptly referred to as "hunting licenses." What was needed was some method of grasping material supplies at their source and of making specific allotments to important uses—allotments which once made could be relied upon. Without this element of certainty in the availability of essential materials, production and delivery schedules were meaningless and war production was in jeopardy.

Whatever the effects of the repeated suggestions of the Army and Navy, it seemed to an increasing number of observers in the fall of 1941 that a system of allocations, controlling material deliveries at the source of supply, was the logical successor to the priorities system. As early as September Donald Nelson had indicated this belief in his testimony in hearings on the price control bill.[9]

By the end of 1941 OPM's material branches had become well established and in an effort to cope with the serious shortages now evident were making extensive

---

[8] The preceding paragraphs are based primarily upon Memo, Steel Distribution by Allocations for National Defense, 29 Oct 41, in National Archives Record Group 225, file 470.1/203.2–9.1. This twelve-page memorandum was apparently prepared in OASW for the Army and Navy Munitions Board as the basis for a request that OPM immediately place all steel products under an allocation system.

[9] (1) Memo, Lt Col Joseph W. Battley, Chf Liaison Div OUSW, for Director Planning Br, 10 Oct 41, sub: Priorities and Allocations. (2) H. Com on Banking and Currency, 77th Cong., 1st Sess., Hearings on H. R. 5479, *Price Control Bill*, 1941.

use of their powers of allocation. A regular procedure of many of the branches was to require submission, for their advance approval, of the proposed monthly mill delivery schedules of all important producers in the industry. Prior to each month's allocation of mill capacity, the applications of prospective material users were scrutinized to determine the importance of their requests, their inventory position, and other data. Producers' mill schedules were then rearranged by the OPM branches in accordance with their judgment and latest information on relative urgencies, and the mills were instructed to make shipments accordingly. This channeling by OPM of all shipments of individual producers to their various customers represented the allocation process as developed by the spring of 1942. Under this procedure shipments could be tailored to the inventory position of recipients, thus reducing inventory hoarding. Since no shipments could be made which were not specifically approved, the flow of materials to nonessential uses could be prevented. Moreover, a positive guarantee of delivery could be made to all material users whose needs were considered sufficiently urgent to warrant inclusion in approved delivery schedules since these schedules were limited to actual mill capacity. These features of the allocation procedure represented a distinct advance over the priorities system and were later incorporated into the Controlled Materials Plan. The scheduling technique was also to become the foundation of General Scheduling Order M–293 and the later Component Scheduling Plan (CSP).[10]

Unfortunately, the allocation procedures used in late 1941 and early 1942 had several grave defects. First of all, the decisions of the several material branches were unco-ordinated. A producer of Army tanks might receive a sufficient allocation of steel but fail to receive a sufficient quantity of copper. This meant not only that he could not meet his tank delivery schedule, but that he would possess more steel than he could actually use. Secondly, the material branches, either individually or collectively, were hardly the best authority on the relative importance of requests for the materials which they were dispensing. To the extent that their allocations differed from established preference-rating patterns, they tended to vitiate basic decisions of the Joint Board as to the relative urgency of military items and programs. Allocations reflected the varying degrees of pressure brought to bear by the multiplicity of competing interests, including not only the different branches of the Army and Navy but all other defense claimants and a wide array of nondefense users as well. Thus, for the final quarter of 1941, when it was generally believed that 100 percent of all copper shipments were rated A–10 or higher, a preliminary survey disclosed that 20 percent of all shipments were unrated and that only 45 percent had gone to A–1–j or higher ratings.[11] There was grave danger that arbi-

[10] See below, pages 597–99. The detailed allocation procedures of the various branches may be inferred from a study of the various M orders. See also, *Report on the Office of Production Management to the United States Senate in Compliance With Senate Resolution 195, Relating to Policy, Methods, Plans, and Programs for the Allocation or Distribution of Materials.* A valuable analysis of the philosophy and procedures of the various allocation systems may be found in Novick, Anshen, and Truppner, *Wartime Production Controls,* especially pp. 37–38, 48, 65–67.

[11] Barnes, Weekly Progress Rpt, 17 Mar 42, citing Census Bureau tabulation of OPM metal questionnaires (PD–275). This result undoubtedly reflected lack of compliance on the part of industry as well as laxity in the making of allocations.

trary and un-co-ordinated allocations by the several OPM material branches would degenerate into complete planlessness.

A third difficulty confronting allocation proposals in the peacetime atmosphere of 1941 was the absence of price ceilings. Faced with unstable and generally rising prices, contractors felt compelled to take material deliveries in large quantities which might not be needed for many weeks or months. This was especially the case under fixed-price contracts extending over fairly long periods:

We believe that contractors feel that they are compelled to resort to this practice in order to avoid financial loss, even bankruptcy in some instances. Under these circumstances, a contractor probably would feel that he could conscientiously sign an affidavit that he had "not taken delivery in larger quantities or at an earlier time than needed for his contract." No matter how much affidavits are worded, their interpretation would be subject to the individual contractor and . . . the net result would be that the water would not be squeezed out of the orders. . . . We feel strongly that this problem must be definitely solved before any allocation plan, which is based on the contractor's statements of "needed" quantities, can be successful.[12]

The coming of Pearl Harbor put an end to vacillation over the question of price controls and the political feasibility of adopting a tight system of material controls. But it did not, of itself, furnish the technical and administrative know-how or the organizations necessary to design and implement such a system, which perforce had to be far more complex than any body of industrial controls ever before attempted. It was nevertheless evident by the beginning of

1942 that neither the "end-product" approach of the priorities system, nor simple allocations at the source of supply, could separately provide the desired solution. The priorities system failed to budget material claims within the available supply. Allocations at the source could not satisfactorily evaluate competing needs. Somehow a marriage of the two systems would have to be effected. The Production Requirements Plan (PRP), presently to be described, brought about such a marriage. Unfortunately—to press the figure of speech still further—this turned out to be a "shotgun wedding" and lacked certain fundamental prerequisites of an abiding relationship.

The Production Requirements Plan

The mandatory application of the controversial Production Requirements Plan in mid–1942 ushered in a significant stage in the development of material control systems for World War II.[13] PRP—as the plan was universally called—had its origin in the Defense Supplies Rating Plan (DSRP) instituted by OPM in May 1941.[14] DSRP was a device to overcome the special difficulties faced by manufacturers and vendors of standard "shelf" items used either directly or indirectly in defense production. These items ran the gamut from commercial hard-

[12] Memo, Gen Hines, Ex Secy ANMB, for Blackwell Smith, 28 Aug 41, sub: Comments on Your Proposed Basic Priorities Procedure Dated 25 Aug 41, Incl 2 to Barnes, Weekly Progress Rpt, 3 Sep 41.

[13] Detailed description of PRP, as well as considerable background and evaluated material on the plan, is found in Novick, Anshen, and Truppner, Wartime Production Controls, Chs. V and VI. These chapters draw heavily from the widely circulated WPB mimeographed memorandum, David Novick for Knowlson, August 1942, sub: Description of the Production Requirements Plan and Its Operation. A cogent analysis of PRP, together with the steps leading to its adoption and ultimate demise, is available in CPA, Industrial Mobilization for War, Pt. II, Ch. 12.

[14] (1) OPM Press Release, PM 402, 19 May 41. (2) Defense Supplies Rating Order P–6.

ware—nails, screws, nuts and bolts, hinges, locks, ordinary hand tools, and similar items—to fairly complex products such as electric motors, pumps, compressors, and other important components of modern mechanical equipment. The Army made direct purchases of substantial quantities of such items, but its chief concern was their availability on short notice, to contractors and subcontractors turning out military equipment.

By the spring of 1941 inventories of many standard commercial items had been depleted and producers experienced difficulty in obtaining materials for their manufacture and replacement. The use of individual preference ratings for this purpose was cumbersome and inadequate. Extensions of ratings on military prime contracts trickled slowly down the chain of subcontractors and were frequently prohibited by rules governing the extension privilege. In any case, manufacturers of standard items would have to accumulate from numerous purchasers a sufficient number of individual extensions for each preference-rating class to permit material purchases in economical quantities. Moreover, this accumulation of claims and the subsequent manufacturing process took place *after* instead of in advance of inventory depletion of finished items. Where rating extensions under military contracts were not available, materials for replacement could be obtained only by filing numerous PD–1 applications with the OPM in Washington. This procedure, especially during the growing pains of OPM's organization, was costly and fraught with repeated delays.[15]

Under DSRP a manufacturer could elect to apply to OPM in advance for a preference rating to cover an entire quarter's supply of scarce materials, components, and re-

lated supplies. His application (OPM Form PD–25) recorded his dollar volume of both defense and nondefense work, consumption and inventory status of materials for the past quarter, and estimated material requirements for the current and succeeding quarters. OPM would review the application and assign an A–10 rating to cover specific quantities of all approved materials, including parts and assemblies, needed for defense purposes. This rating was to be used in place of all individual ratings and extensions and could itself be re-extended by suppliers on the strength of a copy of the original rating order. Thus by submitting one application per quarter the manufacturer could hope to be assured in advance of a sufficient quantity of materials to cover his entire quarter's needs.[16]

By November 1941 some five thousand firms were operating voluntarily under DSRP and similar plans developed for health supplies and for maintenance and operating supplies. Priorities inflation had by then rendered the A–10 rating of relatively little value for scarce metals and the several quarterly plans were merged into the more elaborate Production Requirements Plan.[17] Introduced at this time on a voluntary basis, PRB provided for the quarterly issue of preference ratings (in some cases allocations) to cover the purchase of some two hundred materials, specified on OPM Materials List No. 1. Ratings assigned under PRP were limited to specific quantities or dollar value of materials but ranged from A–1 through A–9—a substantial improvement over the flat A–10 rating under DSRP. Nevertheless, many manufacturers working on high-rated military con-

---

[15] See above, page 516.

[16] Novick, Anshen, and Truppner, *Wartime Production Controls,* pp. 77–81.

[17] Preference Rating Order P–90, 3 Dec 41.

tracts enjoyed a superior rating under the existing priorities system and elected to remain outside PRP. Others refused to come under the plan because it entailed much paper work each quarter and was advantageous only for firms distributing their products to large numbers of purchasers.

Pearl Harbor and the establishment of the War Production Board made it evident to the military services as well as to WPB that the problem of materials distribution had reached a crisis. Two steps would have to be taken with a minimum of delay: (1) the development of satisfactory estimates of material requirements; (2) the replacement of existing material control schemes with a system which would guarantee that claims to scarce materials would be honored once these claims had been validated. This required that allotments to claimants be limited to total available supplies.

Those responsible for the development of PRP saw in it the answer to both these problems. Why not generalize PRP on a mandatory basis for all industry? With universal coverage, WPB could tabulate total material requests from all industry for a quarter in advance or perhaps longer. With this information and knowledge of available supplies from its various material branches, WPB could make quantitative allocations of materials to all industry on a plant by plants basis. Total allocations would be kept within available supplies, thus achieving what the priorities system had failed to do.

On the day after Pearl Harbor, Donald Nelson suggested to the ANMB that all Army and Navy contractors be brought within PRP under ANMB supervision. The ANMB was unwilling to apply the plan to fabricated materials, finished parts, and subassemblies, so the matter was temporarily dropped.[18] Throughout the early months of 1942, WPB continued to broach the subject and the services studied the various versions of the proposal. Within the Army the Quartermaster Corps was the only service reacting favorably. This was due largely to the fact that QMC procured many standard commercial items from large numbers of small firms for which the PRP procedure was especially suited. Also, because of its generally low ratings, the QMC had fared poorly under the priorities system and welcomed any prospect of an improvement in status.[19]

Within the Army, the most complete analysis of the PRP proposal was submitted by the Ordnance Department. In a closely reasoned critique, Ordnance held: That PRP was gravely defective as a means of determining quantitative material requirements; that it would seriously disturb the rating pattern established by the priorities directive (which would have to be the starting point in any allocation procedure); that it failed to provide the information essential to effective centralized allocations; that its "horizontal" procedure was too inflexible to permit vital interim adjustments;[20] that it would make production

---

[18] Ltr, Nelson to Gen Hines, Secy ANMB, 8 Dec 41, and reply thereto, cited in Notes on the Production Requirements Plan, [prepared by Col John D. Millett] p. 2.

[19] (1) Notes on the Production Requirements Plan, pp. 3, 6. (2) Yoshpe, Production Control in the QMC, pp. 37–39.

[20] The term "horizontal" was used in World War II to describe a materials control system which involved direct dealings between the central control agency of the government and each individual producing firm. Each firm would thus submit its requirements directly to the control agency and this agency would transmit allotments directly to each firm. A "vertical" system, on the other hand, channeled requirements estimates and material allotments vertically through the procuring agencies and the contractual chain associated with each prime

scheduling and contract administration by the services well-nigh impossible; and that it was defective in other respects. While conceding the procedural advantages for certain types of material-using firms, the Ordnance Department concluded that these were far outweighed by the basic defects of the plan.[21]

The Ordnance Department view was shared by Ferdinand Eberstadt, the chairman of ANMB, whose survey of the problem had convinced him of the superiority of a vertical system of allocation. In various exchanges with WPB, Eberstadt and the services made clear their opposition to PRP and the reasons therefor; they nevertheless offered full co-operation when WPB finally announced its decision to adopt the plan on a mandatory basis.[22]

Despite the objections of the services and many of his own staff, Nelson finally decided in favor of PRP. With the passage of each month in early 1942 the priorities system had fallen into increasing disrepute. Also, in the spring of 1942, Nelson was under considerable criticism and pressure because of WPB's considered estimate that the 1942 production target, including the President's

"Must" Program, could not be fulfilled. Drastic action was necessary and the proponents of a revised mandatory PRP, with a specific proposal to offer, gained headway. On 13 May 1942, Nelson advised the Under Secretaries of the War and Navy Departments that he had tentatively decided to make PRP effective 1 July 1942 on a nationwide, mandatory basis. The plan was announced to the press on 30 May, and on 10 June the implementing order (Priorities Regulation No. 11) was issued—barely three weeks before the plan was to take effect.[23]

The new version of PRP provided for quarterly allocation of scarce metals to all industrial users under the plan. The metal list included all important shapes and forms of steel, copper, and aluminum as well as some two dozen other metals and alloys. Certain classes of user, including the construction, transport, public utilities, and mining industries, as well as firms using less than $5,000 of metals per quarter, were exempt. Each metal-consuming firm under the plan was required to submit to WPB its comprehensive application, on Form PD–25–A, by the middle of each quarter preceding the quarter for which the metals were required. Form PD–25–A served both as a statement of total metal requirements and as an application for a corresponding allocation by WPB. Information covered by the completed form included the previous quarter's shipments of the firm's products, classified into prescribed industry or product groupings and applicable preference-rating classes. Also recorded for the previous quarter was the consumption and

---

contract. A more picturesque nomenclature labeled all ratings or allotments under the vertical procedure as "horse" ratings; those under the horizontal method were referred to as "cow" ratings. Col Hutchinson, ICAF Lecture (L46–31), p. 5.

[21] Ordnance Priority Docs., Exhibit 18, Comments on the Production Requirement Plan. This seven-page single-spaced copy carries no signature or date but was apparently written at the end of April 1942.

[22] (1) Notes on the Production Requirements Plan, pp. 3–8. (2) ASF Annual Rpt, 1942, p. 20. (3) Memo, Eberstadt for Batt, WPB, 21 Mar 42, sub: Suggested Organization of Commodity Committees and Procedure for Commodity Allocation. (4) Memo, Eberstadt for Knowlson, Vice Chmn WPB, 9 Aug 42. (5) Ltr, Eberstadt to Ernest Kanzler, 12 Sep 42, cited in CPA, *Industrial Mobilization for War,* pp. 481, 483.

[23] For an indication of the opposition within WPB to the adoption of PRP, and the pressures which led Nelson to decide in its favor, see CPA, *Industrial Mobilization for War,* pp. 457–63.

end-of-quarter inventory status, of each listed metal. For the advance quarter, estimated metal requirements as well as estimated shipments of finished products (similarly classified by product groups and rating classes) were to be listed.

Thus the War Production Board would receive in the middle of the third quarter each applicant's record of second-quarter production and related metals consumption together with his estimated production and metals requirements for the fourth quarter. By summarizing all applications, the WPB Requirements Committee would have the estimated total requirements of each metal for all industry.[24] Corresponding estimates of supply would be furnished by the WPB material divisions. It would then be the task of the Requirements Committee to allocate the available supply of each metal among the various metal-using industries. For this purpose some 230 metal-using industry groups had been set up. The group allocations made by the Requirements Committee would be transmitted to the various WPB industry and materials branches. These would in turn decide upon the amounts to be allocated to individual plants in each industry group, staying within the total allocation for each group and taking account of each firm's inventory position. Firms would be notified of their allocation in sufficient time to permit them to place their orders for the quarter with their suppliers.

Although the term "allocation" was generally used in connection with the distribution of metals under PRP, the system was actually a hybrid combination of allocations and preference ratings. The individual di-

rection of all shipments of all materials covered by PRP was manifestly an administrative impossibility. The larger part of the task of materials distribution to metal-using firms was accomplished by making quantitative purchase authorizations supported by preference ratings (usually not more than three different grades for a single purchaser). Total authorizations were kept within total available supply but most individual purchasers were obliged to locate their own suppliers. Direct allocation was used to cover the more urgent cases or where otherwise considered feasible and desirable. Preference ratings continued, of course, to be used for all materials outside the coverage of PRP.[25]

To meet its obligations and needs under PRP, the War Department—operating through Headquarters, ASF, and the ANMB—undertook numerous changes in internal organization and procedures. It also recruited and assigned sufficient staff to provide adequate representation and collaboration with WPB. On 14 August 1942 the Priorities Branch of the Resources Division, ASF, was redesignated the Priorities and Allocation Branch and made responsible for the supervision of Army operations under PRP. As early as 1 June, the ANMB had created an Allocations Steering Committee to collaborate with WPB in the establishment and operation of the plan. Among the efforts of this committee was the issuance of the series PRP Procedural Instructions for the use of military staff members concerned with the details of administration.[26]

---

[24] Except for small firms and exempted industries. These would receive their requirements under existing or special procedures out of a "kitty" reserved for the purpose.

[25] (1) CPA, *Industrial Mobilization for War,* pp. 464–65. (2) Comments cited above, note 21.

[26] (1) Resources Div Office Order 25, 14 Aug 42. (2) Notes on the Production Requirement Plan, p. 7. (3) Yoshpe, Production Control in the QMC, p. 39. (4) ICAF R60, Priorities and Allocations, pp. 48–50.

The most important function of Army personnel in the administration of PRP was membership in the numerous WPB committees at various echelons concerned with the actual making of allocation decisions. The composition and status of these committees was in a constant state of flux as WPB sought to gear its own organization to the novel and unpredictable administrative requirements imposed by the sudden adoption of PRP. In making its allocation decision, WPB needed the advice and assistance of the military procuring agencies. These in turn had a vital interest in seeing that both the industry groups and individual firms producing important military equipment actually received sufficient metal supplies for the purpose. For the third quarter of 1942 the WPB Requirements Committee subdivided its broad task of allocation among numerous product group subcommittees upon which ANMB was represented. At the processing level for specific allocations to individual plants, the ANMB was also represented by analysts who reviewed the proposed allocations made by WPB analysts. The Army representatives for ANMB were drawn from the Production Division, ASF. With the gradual curtailment of ANMB operations, the ASF provided direct representation to WPB, headed at the operational level by the Army PRP officer. At the broad policy level, the Army was represented by Maj. Gen. Clay, the Army member of the WPB Requirements Committee.

Operations under PRP for the third quarter of 1942 represented a series of improvisations which differed radically from both the announced plan and its later developed form. The time between the plan's announcement and the effective date of operations was simply too short to permit either industry or the relevant governmental agencies to develop the necessary organizations, procedures, training programs, and actual performance required to implement the plan. Additional complicating factors were the appearance of the new Priorities Directive of 12 June 1942, requiring the rerating of tens of thousands of contracts and purchase orders to conform to the new AA rating series, and the introduction of Priorities Regulation No. 10. This regulation imposed upon industry the Allocation Classification System, which required all manufacturing firms to place a set of end-use symbols upon each purchase order or contract outstanding or issued after 1 July 1942. The purpose of the system, which partly duplicated the function of preference-rating symbols, was to enable WPB and others to identify the end use and therefore the relative importance to the war effort of each purchase. The physical burden and the complex problems of interpretation thus placed upon industry were so great that the completion date of this operation was delayed beyond the time when it could be of any use in making even fourth-quarter allocations. Disillusionment with the end-use classification scheme resulted in its revocation on 5 November 1942.[27]

Many other shortcomings of PRP appeared during its first trial period, so that its full operation was postponed until the fourth quarter of 1942. The administrative and procedural difficulties were considerably reduced in the fourth and subsequent quarters. But the bitter third-quarter experience, combined with increased pressure from the services as well as numerous elements within WPB for a vertical system of material controls, indicated clearly that PRP's days were numbered. On 2 November 1942 the Controlled Materials Program was announced,

---

[27] CPA, *Industrial Mobilization for War*, p. 470.

with provision for retaining PRP on a diminishing scale until the full transition to the new system could be effected.[28]

The question of whether PRP actually "failed" or whether it had not been given a fair chance was the subject of debate long after its demise. Considerable criticism has been directed at the services, especially the Army, for their "implacable" and "stubborn" hostility toward the plan. This criticism was frequently accompanied by the charge that the Army and Navy wished to "take over" and "run" the wartime economy.[29] Apart from the fact that the Army and Navy supplied vigorous co-operation in the plan's administration, these criticisms are wide of the mark. The objections of the services to PRP rested in a rational analysis of its fundamental weaknesses—defects which, as noted above, had been foreseen by the Army's Ordnance Department and appeared to be of such nature as to preclude any possibility of the plan's success in meeting the basic problems at hand.

[28] The overwhelming difficulties confronting the initial quarter's atempt to operate under PRP, and some of the bizarre results, are excellently portrayed in CPA, *Industrial Mobilization for War,* pp. 465–72.

[29] For example, "The unremitting opposition of the military was rooted in two considerations. The first was a belief that the control of war production was a military and not a civilian function, one to be exercised by the Army and Navy and not by the War Production Board." Novick, Anshen, and Truppner, *Wartime Production Controls,* p. 133. Also, ". . . the idea of military control of the economy in time of war was firmly held and vigorously advocated by officials of the War and Navy Departments and the military chiefs. . . . Military leaders . . . never abandoned the sincere conviction that they could run things better and more expeditiously than could the civilians. This approach was involved, for example, in the transition from the Production Requirements Plan to the Controlled Materials Plan." U.S. Bureau of the Budget, *The United States at War,* pp. 280–81.

The overriding defect of PRP, in the eyes of the Army as well as others, was its "horizontal" approach to the control and distribution of all materials.[30] This approach, for the great bulk of military procurement, had certain inherent weaknesses which crippled the control procedure at every important stage of its planning and execution. The first and most obvious weakness of the horizontal approach was its failure to go directly to the task of estimating material requirements. Instead of beginning with carefully balanced production programs drawn by the claimant agencies responsible for defining the major objectives of the war effort, PRP relied upon the statements of thousands of individual manufacturers each interested in obtaining what he considered a satisfactory share of materials. Not only were total requirements likely to be overstated. Because they were based upon the projection of past input-output ratios for production in large part different from that in future quarters, the stated requirements did not reflect the specific needs of the future period for which materials were requested. Moreover, the thousands of requests from separate manufacturers bore no readily identifiable relationship to each other or to common end-product programs. Hence it was impossible to determine the material requirements essential to the execution of any given program or segment thereof or even for the completion of specific, individual end products. In the absence of this information, it was impossible to make allocations which could be expected to achieve the purposes in view.[31]

This defect was magnified and became painfully apparent when it was necessary to

[30] See note 20, above.
[31] This point is well developed in CPA, *Industrial Mobilization for War,* p. 469.

make allocations substantially less than estimated requirements. Faced with the necessity of making allotments equal to only 80 percent of stated requirements, WPB had no satisfactory method of making selective cutbacks of less important programs. This situation was particularly evident in the fourth quarter of 1942 when the Requirements Committee was forced to make across-the-board cuts for all industry groups. Such a makeshift technique was bound to result in anomalies. It did not mean a simple 20-percent reduction in all programs, unsatisfactory as that might have been. Because of the impossibility of insuring that all subcontractors under an important prime contract would receive balanced allocations, it was impossible to guarantee any desired percentage of completion for any given program.[32]

The second fundamental defect of the horizontal method was its emasculation of the power of the procuring agencies to control their own programs and make intelligent adjustments in logistical plans, production schedules, contracts, and all related matters. Under a vertical control system, material allotments by WPB would be given directly

to the Army, Navy, and other claimant agencies, to be subdivided by them to the best advantage among their various programs. Material shortages, indicated by an allotment less than requested by claimant agencies, called for prompt adjustments in the production schedules of hundreds of prime contractors. For example, a shortage of copper for the Army would require a rebalancing of programs among the various technical services. Within a single service alone, such as Army Ordnance, this might require the curtailment of production by certain copper-using contractors under the ammunition program while leaving other schedules fixed. At the same time it might call for an increase in the schedules of firms equipped to use steel. Decisions of this kind could be made only by Army administrators familiar with the technical and strategic needs of the Army and having an intimate knowledge of Ordnance contracts, production schedules, the capabilities and performance records of various contractors, and a variety of other considerations.

As already indicated the horizontal method of allocation, typified by PRP, called for direct allocations by the War Production Board to each firm in the economy. It thus removed from the procuring agencies effective control over the internal management of their own programs and transferred this control to another agency technically unqualified and basically not responsible for the task. It imposed an insuperable administrative burden upon the central control agency, making it responsible for detailed decisions vitally affecting the individual contracts and programs of the Army, Air Forces, Navy, Maritime Commission, Petroleum Administrator, Rubber Director, and all the other claimant agencies responsible for carrying out their respective

---

[32] For the fourth quarter of 1942, the Program Adjustment Committee, a subsidiary of WPB's Requirements Committee, recommended allocations to military programs in the following ratio to stated requirements: Carbon steel 80 percent; alloy steel, 87½ percent; stainless steel, 80 percent; copper for aircraft and radio, 87½ percent; copper for other military items, 82 percent. These recommendations received the concurrence of the Army and Navy, in view of the lack of any alternative and were approved with few exceptions by the Requirements Committee. But because of the unsatisfactory effects upon particular programs, the services insisted on the right to make adjustments by means of material-division allocations at the mill level. These allocations, of course, ran counter to PRP procedure and hindered the full operation of the plan. Notes on the Production Requirements Plan, pp. 10–12.

segments of the war effort. Some idea of the nature of this administrative burden may be inferred from the mechanics required to accomplish interim allocations needed for the sudden expansion of a single program, such as amphibious craft for the Army. Instead of the transfer of a single steel allotment by WPB to the Army, to be passed down to users via the prime contractor, the War Production Board under the horizontal procedure would have to undertake simultaneous negotiations with dozens and perhaps hundreds of subcontractors at all echelons in an attempt to determine their additional steel requirements and make the necessary additional allocations.

In the face of these shortcomings of the horizontal procedure, the services felt that they would be derelict in their basic responsibilities to acquiesce in the permanent retention of PRP. That PRP was unsuited to the needs of the services is evident from the history of its origin and the circumstances of its adoption on a mandatory basis. It came into being as an exception to the basically vertical procedure of the priorities system in order to accommodate the special needs of firms for which the horizontal approach to materials distribution was more appropriate. It was made general and imposed upon all industry at a time of major crisis when no well-developed alternative was available and when any action promising an improvement was better than none. Nevertheless, the efforts of the Army and Navy to retain control over the internal management of their own programs exposed them to the charge of attempting to "take over the economy."

While PRP did not provide the "solution" to the materials distribution problem, it cannot be recorded as a "failure." It was the first systematic attempt to balance total

material requirements against available supplies. It brought new understanding of the necessity for the careful programing of national requirements and many collateral actions without which any control system was foredoomed to failure. Its horizontal methodology was a superior technique for insuring the flow of materials to an important segment of the wartime economy, a fact which was recognized in the B-product procedure of the Controlled Materials Plan.[33] Furthermore, it made a vital contribution in recording and controlling the inventory position of material users. By bringing into balance manufacturer's inventories of scarce materials, PRP laid a solid foundation for the successful operation of the Controlled Materials Plan which followed.[34]

Finally, the PRP experience provided a rich lesson in the administration of a war economy. This lesson was the full appreciation—on the part of the Army, Navy, War Production Board, and all others concerned—of the indispensability of adequate preparation in launching a nationwide program intimately affecting all parts of the economy. Such preparation would of necessity require careful and meticulous planning, the provision of adequate staff and facilities at all levels, and the intensive training of personnel in all operating agencies of government and private industry—all far enough in advance of the effective date of operation to insure a smooth transition to the new system. The administrative success of the Controlled Materials Plan, and the

---

[33] See below, pages 591 ff.

[34] Ltr, Novick to Gen Smith Chf of Military History 15 Feb 55 in OCMH files. It is Mr. Novick's view that the failure to deal with the inventory problem during the Korean crisis resulted in less satisfactory operations under CMP in 1951–53 than in World War II.

later contract termination and settlement program, owed a heavy debt to the experience acquired under PRP.

Special Procedures for Machine Tools

An important contribution to the basic philosophy of material control was made by developments in the distribution of machine tools. Machine tools were the first and most important class of items in short supply at the beginning of the defense period, and remained so until well into the war. The first extensive application of priorities was made to machine tools with the result already described—the establishment on 27 November 1940 of the new A–1–a category devoted to tool priority. The necessity of top priority for machine tools lay not only in their basic essentiality to major production programs such as aircraft, ordnance, and shipbuilding; machine tools were necessary for their own reproduction.[35]

By the beginning of 1941, it was evident that the priorities system alone could not provide adequate control over the production and distribution of machine tools. Some method was needed for refining the degree of preference within each rating category, especially at the top of the scale where the congestion of orders was greatest. Various proposals led to the adoption on 7 July 1941 of a "master preference list," compiled by

ANMB and circulated to machine tool builders by OPM.[36] This list gave a numerical urgency standing within each rating band to a total of 676 military prime contracts considered of top importance and requiring machine tools for their completion. Machine tool orders would first be filled for contractors having the A–1–a rating in the sequence of their standing on the master preference list. Then all A–1–a orders without urgency standings would be filled in accordance with existing priority regulations. The same procedure would be followed down the line for each preference-rating class. Unfortunately, this did not result in balanced distribution since the urgency standings, like the preference-rating classes, were "open ended" and permitted contractors high on the list to order more tools than they needed and to specify delivery earlier than actually required. The inevitable result was the hoarding and inefficient use of tools by some contractors while others saw their important production programs delayed for lack of similar tools. The situation was later vividly described by an official of the machine tool industry:

The Machine Tool Industry very early in the war effort made a survey of 50 of the highest-ranking contracts on the Preference List. We found there just what you will find in any war effort. . . . We had new machines pouring into a plant that for six months would have no sewer. We had machines pouring into a plant where the foundations had still to be put into the ground and where at least two months would be required before the

---

[35] The machine tool industry was its own greatest customer before the war. A concise description of the nature and mobilization problems of the machine tool industry, including bibliography, may be found in Industrial College of the Armed Forces SR49–26, The Machine Tool Industry (15 April 1949), ICAF Library. See also ICAF R60, Priorities and Allocations, Continued Difficulties in the Application of Priorities to Machine Tools, pp. 18–22, and sources cited therein.

[36] Supplemental Order 1 to OPM General Preference Order E–1, 7 Jul 41. The original E–1 order (26 March 1941) had assigned an A–10 rating to all defense orders not otherwise rated. It also provided that delivery dates for equally rated orders could be decided by agreement between producers and consumers.

machines could be brought in out of the weather and put under cover.[37]

Quantity limitations were finally imposed, effective 15 January 1942, with the issuance of OPM General Preference Order E–1–a and a revised master preference list. The new list specified the number of machine tools which could be purchased under each urgency number; the urgency standing lapsed when tool orders up to the prescribed number had been accepted by builders.[38]

The new master preference list was a marked improvement over its predecessor, but it was obsolete even before it could be issued. The tremendous increase in procurement contracts after Pearl Harbor resulted in a new flood of high-rated machine tool orders which had to be fitted into the list. Experience with the previous revision, which had required four months to consummate, indicated that existing procedures were entirely too cumbersome. Each of the supply services of both the Army and Navy had to be consulted for any material change since all were likely to be affected, and final clearance was required by OPM. Moreover, it was now evident that distribution controls alone could not resolve the basic shortage of capacity in the machine tool industry.

Under the leadership of Ferdinand Eberstadt of the ANMB, the problems of increased production and improved distribution were attacked simultaneously. With the aid of government financing of plant expansion and the development of the "pool order" system, machine tool output was raised in 1942 to six times its prewar peak. On 30 April 1942 the new General Preference Order E–1–b introduced a system of machine-tool allocations. Under this order 75 percent of the industry's capacity was allocated to military (including Maritime) needs; the remainder went to civilian and foreign orders. The ANMB subdivided the military allocation among the various services on the basis of their relative quantitative requirements as represented by orders already on the books of manufacturers. This was done for each class of tools, so that Army Ordnance, for example, would receive 10 percent of the total capacity available for the production of 14-inch engine lathes if its orders for that type represented 10 percent of the total of all similar orders upon the industry. This 10 percent, in turn, would have to be spread among the various producing firms handling that type of equipment so that no one service could pre-empt the best facilities available.[39]

The beneficial effect of the new system of allocations was noticed almost immediately. With each contracting agency held to a fixed percentage of capacity, a premium was placed on the most efficient use of that capacity. Overordering and undue advance in delivery rates was held in check as interservice competition at the local procurement level was eliminated. Furthermore, with each service assured of scheduling control over its own share of capacity, adjustments could be made quickly and as needed to

[37] Tell Berna, The Machine Tool Industry in World War II, 26 Mar 46, ICAF Lecture (L46–60). Mr. Berna was general manager of the National Machine Tool Builders Association. An indication of the congestion in the top rating classes and the relative position of orders lower in the scale is found in the number of urgency standings in the several classes under the original master preference list: A–1–a, 195; A–1–b, 297; A–1–c, 92; A–1–d, 59; A–1–e, 5; A–1–f, 7; A–1–g, 21. Incl to Barnes, Weekly Progress Rpt, 9 Sep 41.

[38] (1) OPM General Preference Order E–1–a, 12 Jan 42. (2) Barnes, Weekly Progress Rpt, 13 Jan 42 and attachment.

[39] Capt Elmer R. Henning, USN, Machine Tools in World War II, 28 Feb 46, ICAF Lecture (L46–41).

supply low-rated programs when the requirements of balance dictated a change in status.

Although the system of allocations under E–1–b was still vulnerable to pressures for preference, its basic principle was sound and represented a major contribution to the rationale of materials distribution. This principle—the rationing of the total available supply among the several claimant agencies, to be further subdivided according to the same principle—became the foundation for the Controlled Materials Plan. Before the year was out, CMP was adopted as the central control device for the nation's war production program.[40]

[40] The following is a representative view of the effectiveness of E–1–b: "No device is perfect, but no means of bringing order out of chaos was found during the course of World War II which worked as well as this one. In any future emergency we should place our initial reliance on a similar procedure and only modify it if demanded by the situation as a whole. I have an idea that little modification will be found possible or desirable." Ralph Flanders, The Machine Tool Industry in World War II, 26 Mar 46, ICAF Lecture (L46–60). Mr. Flanders, formerly president of the Jones and Lamson Machine Tool Company, was later president of the Federal Reserve Bank of Boston. Subsequently he became United States Senator from Vermont.

CHAPTER XXV

The Controlled Materials Plan

The Adoption of the Controlled Materials Plan

The Controlled Materials Plan, officially announced to the public on 2 November 1942, has been generally acclaimed as the instrument which finally resolved the complex problem of material and production controls for the American economy in World War II. In both its original form and in its subsequent numerous modifications and refinements, CMP was the product of the combined thinking and experience of many individuals and many agencies. Yet despite its varied background, the plan owed perhaps as much to the Army as to any other single agency for its conception, its development, and its ultimately successful operation.

As already indicated in earlier sections, by mid-1942 the success of America's war production program, and with it the prospects of ultimate victory for the United Nations, appeared to rest upon the discovery of a satisfactory system for the distribution of basic industrial materials. The summer and early fall of 1942 were unquestionably the lowest point of the war in terms of morale on the war production front. Production was rising but fell far short of the goals established by the President and the armed forces. The War Production Board, the military services, and the other wartime agencies were still in the throes of expansion and successive reorganization. American industry was undergoing the last of a series of major efforts to convert to war production, with all the confusion attending its adaptation to a regime of complex and uncertain governmental control measures. The American public—harried by the simultaneous pressures and uncertainties of the heavy draft of its manpower for military service, large-scale migration of defense workers and their families to centers of war production, and acute shortages of housing and other consumer goods and services—looked to Washington for guidance out of the confusion.

In such an atmosphere, both military and civilian leaders responsible for war production chafed under the inadequacy of existing instruments for discharging their heavy responsibilities. Jurisdictional disputes and interagency friction were inevitable as rival solutions to common problems were urged. Basic requirements of essential national policy and procedure were often obscured by interagency suspicion and the labeling of proposals and programs as "military" or "civilian." At the very time when the problem of selecting a definitive material control system reached its crisis, the major wartime agencies were engaged in a number of heated and widely publicized controversies. These included the aforementioned Feasibility Dispute over the capacity of the economy to support military programs; the relative priority of basic production and facility expansion programs; the final authority to schedule production; and the scope of operations to be assigned to the respective agencies at all echelons.

The announcement of the Controlled Materials Plan to a large degree put an end to this mood of doubt, dissension, and frustration. The boldness of the plan, the challenge of putting it into effective operation, and the knowledge of its irrevocability all captured the imagination. For it was generally understood in Washington that with the adoption of CMP "the chips were down." Just as D Day was later to represent the supreme Allied effort on the military front, so the launching of CMP represented the supreme effort on the war production front. In view of the tremendous stakes, failure was unthinkable; but nothing less than the commitment of the entire economy to the principles of CMP would suffice to make it effective. Thus the Controlled Materials Plan, apart from its intrinsic importance, became a rallying point around which the various agencies and war production leaders gathered to submerge their differences and address themselves to the common task which lay ahead. Although important disagreements over major aspects of the plan appeared in the course of its development, these were virtually all resolved by the time of the plan's full operation and were never strong enough to destroy the fundamental unity of purpose which had been achieved.

The conceptual basis of the Controlled Materials Plan had been indicated as early as 1938 by Army planners in the Commodities Division, OASW.[1] Probably because of the influence of the prewar plans, the Army was the earliest advocate of a tight system of material controls in areas where priorities were inadequate. In August 1941,

Quartermaster General Gregory outlined and strongly advocated a system which in principle was indistinguishable from the later Controlled Materials Plan:

A system of allocating all critical and strategic materials should be set up and administered by some agency with full knowledge of both defense and non-defense requirements and present and prospective supplies thereof. The War Department should be required to compute its requirements covering critical and strategic materials for a given period and submit the same to the above agency. This agency will, in turn, make an allocation of available materials to the War Department. . . . The determination of the allotment to be made to each supply arm and service would be made by a War Department board or committee, and would be based upon the relative importance of the requirements of the respective arms and services. Even though a supply arm or service should not receive an allotment equal to its total requirements under this system, it would be able to plan for substitutes or defer procurement until such materials were available.[2]

But the Quartermaster proposal was a voice crying in the wilderness. As long as the more powerful claimants were able to operate under the priorities system, proposals for a sweeping reform lack sufficient urgency to force the issue. Nearly a year later, after PRP had been made mandatory, an officer in the Resources Division, ASF, criticized the conceptual failure of PRP to tie material distribution to programed requirements and suggested a system substantially equivalent to CMP:

It is suggested that the only possible basis of allocating critical materials and securing intelligent adjustment of programs to quantities so allocated, in the case of military, naval, and facilities construction requirements, is to make such allocations at the level of the re-

---

[1] See above, pages 92–93.

[2] Memo, Gen Gregory, TQMG, for USW 16 Aug 41, sub: Revision of Priorities System, file QM161–PC–Proc. (Priorities).

quirement programs themselves; and to impose on the originators of these requirement programs the responsibility for adjusting their programs to such allocations, when they are reduced below original program requirements.[3]

By the end of the summer of 1942, suggestions and proposals for the "ideal" materials distribution system had become so numerous as to suggest the existence of a nationwide essay contest. Army Ordnance had long advocated its own warrant plan, Navy had a similar plan, General Motors and the steel industry each had plans, and many individuals and trade associations presented their ideas ranging from fragmentary suggestions to elaborate and complex proposals.[4] Within the War Production Board there were wide divergencies of opinion as to the most suitable system, with varying emphasis on horizontal versus vertical allocation. The most important WPB plan was that developed by Ernest Kanzler, the deputy chairman on Program Progress. The Kanzler plan helped to crystallize WPB opinion in favor of a vertical system.[5]

The prime mover behind the adoption of the Controlled Materials Plan was not, how-ever, initially a representative of industry or the War Production Board, but the new chairman of the Army Navy Munitions Board—Ferdinand Eberstadt. Eberstadt had been active in breaking the machine tools bottleneck and was impressed with the possibility of extending the principles of the E–1–b procedure to important basic materials.[6] Familiar with the problems of the Army and Navy, he was convinced of the necessity for a vertical system of materials distribution. The specific incident which set in motion the chain of events culminating in the adoption of CMP was a memorandum sent by Eberstadt on 9 August 1942 to James Knowlson, WPB's director of Industry Operations. Following a brief summary of the evolution of material and production controls up to that time, Eberstadt stated:

It is submitted that with the Country substantially on an all-out war basis, the principles of Order E–1–b can now be extended to other fields of important but scarce materials, with beneficial results.

To fit the foregoing proposal into existing organizations, it is contemplated that the Requirements Committee [WPB] would allocate broad bands of the various materials in question to the military, basic economic, and foreign uses for a period, say of 3 months in advance. A.N.M.B. could then allot to the various Military Services, Aircraft, Ordnance, Ships, etc., their respective proportionate amounts of these materials and they in turn would schedule them to the best interests of their respective programs. This type of allocation, it is presumed, would be confined to those materials with respect to which a real scarcity exists.

After setting forth various possible ramifications of the proposal, including provision for horizontal allocation in appropriate cases, the memorandum concluded:

The above system has the merit of confining decisions at the highest levels to broad ques-

---

[3] Memo, Maj Maurice R. Scharff, Power Unit Facilities Sec, for Ex Priorities Br, Resources Div SOS, 27 Jun 42, sub: Production Requirements Plan and the Control of Critical Material.

[4] CPA, Industrial Mobilization for War, pp. 484–85.

[5] Ibid., p. 482. The Kanzler plan was itself similar to earlier plans: "Mr. Ernest Kanzler's proposed scheduling plan . . . is in essence identical to that presented by the Ordnance Department and the Allocations Steering Committee to the Army and Navy Munitions Board and the War Production Board some months ago, and is the Ordnance scheduling plan with the methods for handling policy distribution added." Memo, Lt Col James Boyd Office for Liaison and Co-ordination SOS for ACofS for Materiel, 16 Sep 42, sub: Scheduling Plan, and incl, Analysis of Scheduling and Material Control Program as Outlined by Mr. Ernest Kanzler.

[6] See above, pages 564 ff.

tions and decentralizing the detail . . . . This plan recognizes and fits into the present broad lines of organization. The basic distribution of materials between the military, basic economic, Lease-Lend, and other export would be made by the War Production Board . . . but the actual scheduling and directing of materials, particularly in the military field, would be taken over by those who are responsible for procurement and production, which can not be carried out without control of the flow of materials in accordance with their schedules.[7]

Knowlson turned the Eberstadt memorandum over to Robert Nathan, chairman of WPB's Planning Committee. Nathan immediately recognized its significance and enthusiastically sent a direct reply to Eberstadt: "I find your memorandum extremely interesting and provocative. Without question, many of the proposals you suggest are extremely important and we should move in that direction as quickly as possible." Nathan then went on to state three prerequisites to the satisfactory operation of such a plan: (1) balancing of the over-all production program within the available supply of critical materials; (2) proper scheduling of end items and components in the balanced program; (3) adoption of a tight system of disbursing materials to meet the schedules.[8]

Eberstadt's energy and administrative ability had been noticed by WPB leaders as early as July, at which time he was tendered an appointment within the War Production Board. After his 9 August memorandum, he was again approached, this time with the offer of an appointment carrying the broad responsibility for putting into effect such a plan as he had advocated.[9] As a result,

Eberstadt left the ANMB on 20 September 1942 to become vice chairman of the War Production Board in charge of Program Control. In the interim he had effectively prepared the military services for the assumption of heavy responsibility in the new undertaking and was able to assure the War Production Board of their wholehearted cooperation.[10]

WPB's confidence in Eberstadt was justified. Immediately upon his appointment, he set about the creation of a Committee on Materials Control Plan with broad representation from WPB and the services. Beginning with its first meeting on 30 September, this committee and its principal subcommittee—working behind locked doors in a series of meetings and conferences rarely equaled in intensity of purpose—hammered out the plan which was to organize and integrate the nation's economy for the duration of the war. The formal announcement of the Controlled Materials Plan on 2 November 1942 followed Eberstadt's appointment of WPB by only six weeks.[11]

Basic Features of CMP

The Controlled Materials Plan was a system of rationing applied to the three most important industrial materials—steel, copper, and aluminum—about which the

---

[7] Memo, Eberstadt, Chmn ANMB, for Knowlson, 9 Aug 42, sub: Priorities.

[8] Memo, Nathan, Chmn Planning Com WPB, for Eberstadt, Chmn ANMB, 27 Aug 42.

[9] CPA, *Industrial Mobilization for War,* p. 260.

[10] Ltr, Eberstadt, Chmn ANMB, to Kanzler, Dir Gen for Opns WPB, 12 Sep 42.

[11] Further details on the initial formulation of CMP are found in: (1) CPA, *Industrial Mobilization for War,* Pt. III, Ch. 12, *passim,* especially pp. 485–86; (2) U.S. Bureau of the Budget, *The United States at War,* pp. 304–07. For a general description of the nature and operation of CMP, see Novick, Anshen, and Truppner, *Wartime Production Controls,* Ch. VIII. Additional details pertaining to the Army's experience under CMP may be found in ICAF R60, Priorities and Allocations, The Controlled Materials Plan, pp. 53–97.

whole war production program turned. It departed substantially from the methodology of its two major predecessors, the priorities system and the Production Requirements Plan. In contrast to the priorities system, which was an open-ended, currency-type system, CMP limited its material allotments to available supplies and imposed a closed system of accounting and auditing which made impossible the inflation of claims to scarce materials. Since no allotments were issued for materials beyond the aggregate capacity of suppliers, each recipient of an allotment was assured of receiving his allotted materials on schedule. By contrast with PRP, CMP was a vertical control system enabling it to accomplish certain indispensable objectives which were administratively impossible under a horizontal plan. These objectives may be summed up in the term "program control," and their attainment flowed from three outstanding aspects of CMP: (1) Its estimates of material requirements were, so far as possible, derived from approved production programs specifically geared to the war effort; (2) it assured the completion of important end products by providing supplies of controlled materials to all subcontractors associated with a given prime contract; (3) it decentralized detailed operations to the agencies responsible for conceiving and administering the several production programs.

CMP was constantly modified and refined both before and after it went into full effect, but the basic features essential to an understanding of Army operation under CMP may be briefly described. The plan's operational cycle began with the quarterly determination of requirements for controlled materials by a number of claimant agencies under general rules laid down by the WPB.

The claimant agencies were of two kinds—procuring and nonprocuring; collectively, they represented all users of controlled materials throughout the economy.[12] Material requirements of the procuring agencies were to be based upon their established or tentative production schedules for all procurement programs. The mechanics of requirements determination involved the use of unit bills of material supplied by prime consumers (prime contractors) to their respective contracting agencies. The unit bill of materials covered the material requirements, per unit of finished product, of all secondary consumers (subcontractors and suppliers at any level) as well as of the prime consumer. The quantity of each controlled material shown in the unit bill was multiplied by the number of units of the end product required to be delivered in each month in accordance with the governing production schedule. An appropriate "lead time"—the number of months between the required date of shipment of the controlled material by the supplier and the completion of the finished end product—was shown in the bill of materials. The claimant agency, in tabulating its material requirements, would apply the lead time to each production schedule in order to show correctly the month in which the controlled materials were actually required. Nonprocuring claimant agencies, such as WPB's Office of Ci-

[12] At the time of CMP's adoption the seven claimant agencies were: War Department, Navy Department, Maritime Commission, Aircraft Scheduling Unit (agent for Army Air Forces and Navy Bureau of Aeronautics), Office of Lend-Lease Administration, Board of Economic Warfare, and Office of Civilian Supply, WPB. On 8 January 1943 six additional claimant agencies were announced: National Housing Agency, Office of the Rubber Director, Office of Defense Transportation, Petroleum Administration for War, War Food Administration, and WPB Facilities Bureau. CPA, *Industrial Mobilization for War*, p. 668.

vilian Supply, made less use of bills of materials; their estimates were based chiefly on applications from manufacturers, past experience under PRP, general forecasts of consumption needs, and whatever additional specific information could be obtained.

All claimant agencies were obliged to present their statement of requirements to WPB a full quarter in advance. The WPB Requirements Committee, which had the task of making bulk allotments of each controlled material to each claimant agency, was a representative body upon which all claimant agencies had membership. The Requirements Committee, working through a large staff and various subcommittees, would obtain from the appropriate material division in WPB the latest estimate of the supply of each controlled material for the quarter in question. After a careful scrutiny of affected programs, and discussion of the relevant strategic, logistical, production, and other factors, available supplies were then allocated, in the form of a "program determination," among the various claimant agencies. This distribution of bulk allotments to the several claimant agencies was made two months before the beginning of the affected quarter.

The next step in the process, the distribution of allotments to prime consumers by the claimant agencies, was to be completed within the following month. Within each claimant agency, programs and schedules would have to be adjusted or curtailed in order to permit the agency to live within its allotment. The agency was assisted in this process by a review of each prime consumer's quarterly application for controlled materials, filed with the claimant agency on CMP Form 4–A. This application reflected the consumer's inventory position and other factors, and often called for smaller quantities of controlled materials than indicated by the bill-of-materials calculation.

After its allotment decisions had been made, the claimant agency transmitted to all its prime consumers their revised and approved production schedules together with their allotments of each controlled material to support the schedules. Prime consumers were instructed to immediately pass on to each of their secondary consumers a subsidiary production schedule related to the prime contractor's own schedule together with an allotment of materials sufficient to implement the schedule. The process was repeated by all subcontractors under a given prime contract.

Each allotment transmitted to a prime consumer carried an individual number, which was to be repeated on all subsequent reallotments down the contractual chain and used by all concerned in placing their orders with controlled material suppliers. All firms were instructed to place their orders with mills as far as possible in advance of the opening date of the allotment quarter so that mill schedules could be arranged in time to permit maximum production. Except in the case of special "designated allotments," firms were free to select their own suppliers of controlled materials. Controlled materials producers were permitted to accept only orders bearing allotment numbers and were required to schedule them in order of receipt. Orders beyond their capacity, except for specified allowances to permit flexibility, were to be rejected.[13] Rejected orders would be redirected by contractors to unfilled productive capacity still remaining in the system until all allotments were used and capacity filled.

---

[13] WPB, Controlled Materials Plan (2 November 1942), Restriction on Shipments by Producers of Controlled Materials, p. 12.

It was the supposition and hope of CMP that its control of the flow of steel, copper, and aluminum would—by resolving the nation's most fundamental material shortages—provide the basic direction of the war production program within the pattern set by balanced requirements.[14] All other scarce materials would continue to be distributed by preference ratings or other established procedures. A prime consumer under CMP—such as a manufacturer of Army trucks—would automatically receive an appropriate preference rating along with his authorized production schedule and allotment of controlled materials. This rating, which was extendible to quantities required to meet the authorized schedule, would enable both prime and secondary consumers to obtain essential noncontrolled materials. Because of the great importance of meeting CMP schedules, special efforts were made to insure adequate supplies of all contributory items. Military contracts not under CMP schedules, such as makers of military clothing, obtained their preference ratings through the regular PD–3–A procedure.

An important exception to the basic vertical procedure of CMP was the horizontal allotment of controlled materials by the War

Production Board for the production of so-called B products. These were specifically listed items of the type for which vertical allocation was supposedly too cumbersome and for which PRP was originally designed. The composition of the B list immediately became an object of heated controversy with consequences described in a subsequent section.[15] Other special procedures included the handling of small orders, maintenance, repair, and operating supplies, and distribution of controlled materials through warehouses.

The abortive experience of the hasty introduction of PRP was fresh in the minds of all concerned. Hence, the launching of CMP was carefully planned to allow time for building necessary organizations, education and training of employees, and refinement of procedures. Although CMP was officially announced on 2 November 1942, it was not to go into full operation until the third quarter of 1943. For the second quarter of 1943 CMP was to be used as completely as possible under the circumstances, but PRP was to remain in effect to ease the transition. Thus, all firms in the economy could place advance orders for second-quarter requirements of controlled materials up to a substantial percentage of their first quarter PRP allocation; duplicate allotments subsequently received under CMP were to be canceled. Various other devices were employed to facilitate the shift to CMP as smooth as possible.[16]

Army Preparations for Launching CMP

The adoption of the Controlled Materials Plan placed an unprecedented burden of

---

[14] Actually, the supply and distribution of a single material—carbon steel—became the focal point of operations under CMP: "The chief problems raised were on the total quantities of controlled materials to be allotted and the distribution of the over-all quantity of carbon steel among claimant agencies. The adjustment of total requests for other controlled materials to the supply available for allotment was not a difficult task once carbon steel was brought into balance since it involved chiefly the balancing of other materials to carbon steel allotments." Memo, Charles E. Kohlhepp, Dir Program Bureau, for Julius A. Krug, Program Vice Chmn 24 Sep 43, sub: Fourth Quarter Allocations Under Controlled Materials Plan. Carbon steel requirements and production accounted for all but a minor fraction of the output of the steel industry.

[15] See below, pages 591 ff.

[16] WPB, Controlled Materials Plan (2 November 1942), Transition, pp. 16–17.

planning, organization, training, and related preparations upon the Army. As the largest and most diversified of all the claimant agencies the Army was confronted with the greatest number and variety of procurement programs, contracts, contractor relationships, and controlled material requirements. Also, as the leading sponsor of a vertical system of material controls, the Army bore a heavy moral responsibility for the successful operation of the new system.

Although CMP was widely advertised as not "taking effect" until the second quarter of 1943 (and then only to the extent practicable), the actual operating responsibilities of the claimant agencies began immediately. In order to permit second-quarter deliveries of controlled materials under CMP, the whole process of the determination and distribution of allotments would have to be completed during the first quarter. The greatest task of all—the determination of eighteen-months' advance requirements for controlled materials—was scheduled for completion by 1 January 1943. To meet this deadline in a matter of weeks the Army's technical services and ASF staff divisions had to conduct actual operating tasks while simultaneously building new organizations, recruiting and training personnel, interpreting, refining, and modifying the deluge of WPB regulations, and conducting discussions and debates on major matters of policy which affected the basic concept of CMP.

With the adoption of CMP, it became apparent that responsibility for the supervision and effective operation of the plan within the Army should be concentrated within a single staff division in Headquarters, ASF. The logical place for such responsibility was in the organization of the Assistant Chief of

Staff for Materiel (later Director of Materiel), who had general responsibility within the ASF for all Army procurement activities. Accordingly, the Production Division, ASF, was designated as the War Department claimant agency under CMP and was given the task of devising procedures, training programs, organizational changes, and general Army-wide policy in all CMP matters.[17]

Within the Production Division, ASF, the key planning and regulatory unit was the CMP control Branch. This branch was the focal point within the Army for the flow of information, the development of basic organizational and training needs, the establishment of new procedures, and the discussion and resolution of major operating problems pertaining to CMP. The chief of the CMP Control Branch played several important roles. As the Army controlled materials officer (ACMO), he handled the bulk of conference and liaison activity with the War Production Board on matters of CMP operation and procedure and was an alternate Army representative on the WPB Controlled Materials Board. Within the ASF he was chairman of the CMP Control Committee, composed of representatives of the various branches of the Production Division, as well as of the Office of the Director of Materiel. The CMP Control Committee served to keep all appropriate ASF staff agencies abreast of CMP matters and to in-

[17] The Production Division was originally established on 20 July 42 by SOS General Order 24. On 29 December 1942, by SOS Circular 96, it was merged with the Resources Division in order to bring production and material controls under common direction. The Resources and Production Division was redesignated simply as the Production Division on 17 May 1943 (Production Div Office Order 38, 17 May 43, and ASF Cir 32, 18 May 43).

sure proper co-ordination of activities within Headquarters, ASF.[18]

To provide adequate organization and uniformity of operations at the technical service level, a number of steps were taken. As early as 16 October 1942, while CMP was still in the draft stage, the director of the Production Division had requested each of the technical services to appoint a responsible full-time officer or civilian to head up work under the new system. These officials were also to participate in the review and modification of the emerging draft plan.[19] Three months later, a general directive was sent to the services requiring each of them to establish a central planning section which would be responsible for the supervision of all CMP operations within the service. A primary responsibility of the central planning section was the preparation and maintenance of master procurement and production schedules upon which CMP requirements and allotments would be based.[20] Shortly thereafter, the technical service representatives appointed under the 16 October directive were designated as CMP control officers, and their duties were spelled out in some detail. These officers, who typically held key positions in the central planning branches, functioned at the technical service level much as did the Army controlled materials officer at the Army-wide level; broadly stated, their task was to make CMP work effectively within their

respective services.[21] All technical service control officers were ex officio members of the CMP Control Officers Committee, which met monthly under the sponsorship of the Production Division, ASF. This committee was the chief instrument for co-ordinating the CMP activities of the several services and for providing necessary changes in regulations or other solutions to technical service problems.[22]

An important contribution to the rationalization of Army organization and procedures for launching the Controlled Materials Plan was the series of management surveys conducted by the Control Division, ASF, during the first three months of the program. Reports based on these surveys covered all aspects of the program in both the ASF headquarters organization and within the several technical services. Because of the cogency of the reports and the prestige of the Control Division, a number of significant improvements were made.[23]

Inasmuch as the ramifications of CMP spread throughout the Army's entire massive procurement organization, thousands

---

[18] (1) Resources and Production Div Office Memo 5, 4 Mar. 43. (2) CMP Control Committee, Minutes.

[19] Memo, S. E. Skinner, Dir Production Div SOS, for Chfs of Technical Services, 16 Oct 42, sub: Allocations of Material.

[20] Memo, Gen Ulio, TAG, to Chfs of Supply Services, 16 Dec 42, sub: Organization of Central Planning Sections and Preparation of Schedules.

[21] Memo, Gen Minton, Dir Resources and Production Div, for Chfs of Services et al., 10 Feb 43, sub: Functions of CMP Control Officers.

[22] Undated memorandum in files of Production Division, ASF, sub: History of CMP Control Branch.

[23] The Control Division was a part of General Somervell's office and its recommendations received immediate and careful consideration. The principal recommendations under the CMP surveys were the improvement of the training program, the provision of additional competent personnel, and the rearrangement of functions in numerous instances. (1) Control Division, Hq ASF, Controlled Materials Plan Functions and Organization in the Resources and Production Division (25 January 1943). (2) Memo, Gen Minton, Dir, Resources and Production Div, for ACofS for Materiel, 22 Mar 43, sub: Control Division Survey of CMP. (3) Maj Leighton, History of Control Division, ASF, pp. 13–14. (4) ICAF R60. Priorities and Allocations, pp. 61 ff.

of new employees had to be added and the activities of others modified. An integral ingredient in the plan to launch CMP was the systematic training of individuals in all agencies. The War Production Board initiated CMP training with an intensive three-day course for some five hundred key employees within WPB and the claimant agencies. The course consisted of a series of lectures and written materials on the plan as a whole and its major special aspects. It included question and answer sessions as well as a lengthy CMP "problem" to be worked out overnight between sessions. A number of brief written examinations were given in order to judge the effectiveness of the course.[24]

The training program ultimately adopted by the Army was designed not only to prepare its own representatives for their appointed tasks but to provide Army contractors with an intimate, effective, and enthusiastic knowledge of CMP. Without the thorough understanding and whole-hearted co-operation of contractors, CMP could easily go the way of PRP. The Army's first training efforts under CMP centered in the use of training films developed by the Civilian Personnel Division. Partly because of the general nature of the films and partly because of the manner in which they were used, this approach was deemed to be inadequate.[25]

On 10 April 1943 the chief of the CMP Control Branch proposed an intensive program of training in CMP field operations. Training was to be given to Army personnel at various echelons, to be followed by the systematic interview and training of all important Army contractors. The program was formally launched on 22 April with a target date for completion of 31 July 1943. The substance of the program was built around a detailed three-day Field Operations Course, which was carefully laid out in an instructor's textbook of some 120 pages. The textbook was prepared in the latter part of April 1943 and thus had the benefit of six months of intensive discussion and substantial experience under CMP. It covered all significant operating features of CMP including preparation of bills of materials, various classifications and treatment of B products, preparation of manufacturers' applications for controlled materials, relationship of CMP to production scheduling, control of inventories, special procedures for maintenance, repair, and operating supplies, construction and facilities, warehouse and small orders, placement of orders with metal mills, all stages of the allotment process and the general effect of CMP upon production control and purchasing. Question and answer sessions, outside reading assign-

---

[24] Memo, C. L. Bowman, Chf Training and Information Sec, CMP Control Br, for Skinner, Dir Production Scheduling, 12 Jan 43, sub: Comparison of WPB and SOS Courses on CMP.

[25] (1) Memo, Col John S. Cooke, ACMO, for Chmn CMP Bd WPB, 13 Dec 42, sub: War Department Progress on CMP. (2) Memo, Cooke for Dir Resources and Production Div SOS, 21 Jan 43, sub: CMP Training. (3) Memo, Skinner Dir of Production Scheduling, for Gen Minton, 23 Jan 43. (4) Memo, Cooke for Dir of Production Scheduling ASF, 30 Apr 43; sub: CMP

Training. A major difficulty in the early CMP training efforts of the Army was the division of responsibility between the Civilian Personnel Division, ASF, which had general cognizance of training methods and programs within the Army, and the Resources and Production Division, which was responsible for the implementation of CMP. The personnel division was handicapped by lack of detailed knowledge of CMP, and the Resources and Production Division wished to take over all CMP training activities and integrate them with the actual administration of the plan. This was the procedure later adopted in the development of the field operations training program.

ments, and written examinations were among the features of the course.[26]

Under the directive establishing the program, each technical service was required to designate for training an appropriate number of representatives who would in turn be required to interview and train contractors in the field. Each service was required to submit a list of its prime contractors, alphabetically by states, to the CMP Control Branch. All duplicate names were submitted to a co-ordinating committee of CMP control officers, who designated a single service to train each contractor. Officers in the CMP Control Branch trained technical service representatives and then accompanied them to district offices to launch the field training program. When this was well under way, further training and administration of the program was left largely to the technical service CMP control officer and his assistants. After enough field service employees had been trained, the service CMP control officer would take them in groups of twos and threes to visit contractors for experience in interviewing and training key workers in each plant. These meetings were "down-to-earth" sessions on the contractor's own problems, designed both to assist the contractor to meet all CMP requirements with a minimum of difficulty and to develop information on operating problems which would assist policy makers in making desirable adjustments in the plan.[27]

The Army's Field Operations Training Program proved to be eminently successful. In approximately three months some 3,600 Army officers or employees and 8,287 War Department contractors were trained under the program. The results of the basic program were briefly summarized by the Army controlled materials officer:

. . . these reports show that the training program has fulfilled a real need, was enthusiastically received by contractors, has provided uniformly trained personnel, has reduced paper-work through proper understanding and application of CMP principles, and has facilitated completion of Army contracts on schedule. In addition, CMP training has resulted in a more efficient use of the limited quantity of steel, copper, and aluminum allotted to the War Department by the War Production Board.[28]

An important contribution to the successful launching and operation of the Controlled Materials Plan within the Army was the systematic dissemination of information to all concerned with the functioning of the plan. This was accomplished not only by the prompt distribution of available WPB regulations, orders, bulletins, and pamphlets but by the issuance of ASF and technical service directives, circulars, memoranda, and other media. Early in 1943 it was decided to combine all CMP information and procedural instructions into a comprehensive manual which would be kept up to date and would serve as a single

---

[26] (1) Memo, Col Cooke, Chf CMP Control Br, for Dir Resources and Production Div ASF, 10 May 43; sub: Field Operations Course. (2) Army Field Operations Course and Training Manual for CMP.

[27] (1) Col Cooke for Dir Resources and Production Div ASF, 10 Apr 43, sub: Program for Personal Contacts by Services with Contractors. (2) Memo, Gen Minton, Dir Resources and Production Div, for Chfs of Services *et al.*, 22 Apr 43,

sub: CMP Program for Personal Contacts by Services with Contractors.

[28] Memo, Col Cooke for Asst Dir of Production, Production Div ASF, 14 Sep 43, sub: CMP Training for Army Personnel and Contractors. Exhibit 1 of this memorandum shows the number of trainees for each technical service. The Corps of Engineers led all the services with 1,854 service personnel and 3,802 contractor trainees. Ordnance was second with 245 service personnel and 1,773 contractors.

authoritative source of information.[29] The constant succession of changes in CMP details and the necessity for the firm establishment of organizations and procedures delayed publication until 30 September 1943. At this time ASF M–602, Controlled Materials Plan Operation, was published and widely distributed. Consisting of some 250 pages of carefully organized instructions and descriptive material, supplemented by numerous charts and diagrams, the manual covered all aspects of the Army's responsibilities under CMP. It was planned to keep the manual current by issuing revised paragraphs to be distributed to all holders. This was eventually found to be impractical and on 18 March 1944 the method of formal revision was abandoned and the manual remained only as an overall guide and reference work. Thereafter all operating personnel were to be guided by current instructions from the Production Division, ASF.[30]

A further effort to insure the successful launching of CMP was represented by the "trial run" of CMP for mechanical time fuzes produced by ordnance contractors for the Army and Navy. This test operation was conducted mainly in January and early February 1943 in conjunction with the War Production Board and covered requirements and allotments of controlled materials for six prime consumers and thirty-eight secondary consumers for four months, March through June 1943. The experiment was given a "green light" by all concerned in order to gather experience in advance of the general second-quarter CMP run. Despite the fact that the experiment was on a highly simplified basis (for example, no B products were involved), it revealed many of the operating problems which were later to appear on a large scale. These included numerous types of error in filing CMP–4–A applications for materials; problems attending changes in schedules and specifications; the difficulties of maintaining balanced inventories and the relationship of parts to materials inventories; and the necessity of extending contracts and schedules beyond the required "lead time" for materials. The trial run resulted in a wider dissemination of instructions to contractors and alerted CMP operating personnel to difficulties previously unanticipated.[31]

The Determination of Requirements for Basic Materials

The task of determining in detail the quantities of basic materials entering into military end items was completely foreign to the Army's peacetime procurement operations. Military procurement in the period between the World Wars was so small relative to the economy as a whole that it had no appreciable effect upon material supplies. Contractors were responsible for completing projects on schedule and placed their orders for materials accordingly.

---

[29] Preparation of the manual was ordered by the Chief of Staff, ASF, on 1 March 1943. (1) Memo, Cooke for Dir Resources and Production Div ASF, 21 Apr 43, sub: Status of CMP Operations Manual. (2) Memo, Cooke for Chf Materials Br, Resources and Production Div, 17 May 43, sub: CMP Operations Manual. (3) Memo, Cooke ExO Production Div ASF, 1 Jun 43, sub: Simplification and Standardization of Procedures and Practices–CMP Operations Manual.

[30] Changes No. 1 to ASF M–602, 18 Mar 44. For additional reasons underlying the discontinuance of revisions, see Memo, Gen Clay, Dir of Materiel, for CofS ASF, 11 Dec 43, sub: Army Service Forces Manual M–602. The manual is a permanent source of information on the complex responsibilities of the Army under CMP.

[31] Memo, Cooke for Chfs of Services et al., 3 Feb 43, sub: CMP Trial Run—Mechanical Time Fuzes.

During most of the interwar period, supplies of raw materials in relation to demand were abundant—so much so that governments as well as private interests in various parts of the world resorted to schemes for the curtailment of output and the artificial support of prices. Under these circumstances, there was no occasion for concern over the quantity of materials entering into either individual items or procurement programs as a whole.

Procurement planning officers were nonetheless well aware that a war emergency would completely upset the peacetime balance of supply and demand. Not only would material control systems be found necessary in time of war but their administration would soon require definite knowledge of the quantities of important materials essential to the completion of military programs. Accordingly, early in the interwar period the Commodities Division was established in the Planning Branch, OASW, for the purpose of estimating the Army's wartime needs of important materials and of taking steps to insure the adequacy of wartime supply.[32]

The Commodities Division and its associated commodity committees in the interwar years never possessed the resources or manpower to make detailed estimates of Army material requirements for all stages of an emergency. Furthermore, the expenditure in peacetime—on a scale comparable to that eventually attained in World War II—of efforts to determine indirect material requirements would have been a preposterous undertaking. Contemporary estimates of end-product requirements for a future war, in terms of either types or quantities of equipment, were too incomplete and unstable to permit more than rough approximations of required quantities of material ingredients.

As a result, it was only after the Munitions Program was well under way that the necessity and possibility of intensive study of Army material requirements arose. As shortages of particular materials appeared or were considered likely, requests for statements of material requirements began to be made. The resulting estimates were necessarily crude since bills of materials for items of military equipment were almost nonexistent, procurement programs were continually undergoing revision, and no systematic procedures or organizations had been created to make the necessary computations.

After Pearl Harbor and the emergence of material shortages as the major bottleneck to war production, it was apparent that the task of estimating material requirements would have to be realistically approached. This meant the hiring and placement of many hundreds of additional employees throughout the Army establishment, the identification of thousands of material ingredients of finished items of military equipment, the development of standard nomenclature and code numbers, the acquisition of batteries of complicated tabulating machines with experienced operators, and extensive correspondence with Army contractors to acquire unit bills of materials for items of military procurement. The refinement and use of the necessary procedures was a laborious and often uninspiring task.[33]

An important step in laying the foundation for accurate statements of material requirements was the development of the ANMB Red Book, which established de-

---

[32] See above, pages 86 ff.

[33] A concise statement of the Army's problems in computing material requirements made during the formative period of CMP is the four-page Memo S5–32–43, Gen Ulio, TAG, 9 Feb 43: General Policy—Material Requirements.

tailed classifications and coding for a wide variety of materials. The Red Book went through a number of editions and contained specifications and descriptions of hundreds of items within the major material classes— basic agricultural and forest products, iron and steel and ferro-alloys in numerous shapes and forms, nonferrous metals, chemicals, fabrics, fuels, and lubricants.[34] By the latter part of 1942, the Red Book was issued jointly by the Army, Navy, Maritime Commission, and the War Production Board, and its classification had become widely accepted as the basis for the analysis and expression of material requirements. It continued to be used after the adoption of CMP, not only for noncontrolled materials, but for basic bill-of-materials analysis of controlled materials. Since the Red Book classification was more detailed than CMP codes, data from bills prepared on the Red Book basis could usually be transformed without additional information into requirements figures for the purpose of CMP.[35]

The first effort to provide the foundation for a comprehensive determination of the Army's indirect requirements for materials was made many months before the formulation of the Controlled Materials Plan. On 9 January 1942, the Under Secretary of War directed each Army supply service to obtain bills of materials for all items of procurement.[36] The accumulation and refinement of bills of materials for the many thousands of Army procurement items was a slow and tedious process, complicated by lack of time and personnel on the part of contractors as well as the technical services. Moreover, contractors themselves often had only rough knowledge of the gross stock weight of materials required to turn out finished items never before produced.[37]

Early in September 1942, the Combined Production and Resources Board ordered a general survey of military requirements for materials for the eighteen-month period ending 31 December 1943. This survey, which was actually supervised by the War Production Board, required the Army to make within approximately one month its first comprehensive study of its indirect requirements for steel, copper, aluminum, and rubber. Known within the Army as Basic Industrial Materials (BIM) Job 0012, the

---

[34] The following exotic samples taken verbatim from the October 1942 edition of the Red Book give some indication of its detailed coverage: Mica, block, muscovite; Mica, block, phlogopite; Barathea, 18 oz., O.D.; Wigan, black; Coir fiber; Istle, tula; Istle, juamave; Istle, pita; Istle, palma; Loofa sponges; Pyrethrum flowers; Chloroacetophenone; Dichloradifluoromethane; Resin, synthetic, polymethacrylates (one of twenty listed classes of synthetic resins); Uranium, "a heavy, rare, radioactive element used in pigments for glassware and porcelain, and as an alloying element in some steel."

[35] The Red Book classification was well received by industry. "In our opinion, this classification of materials was definitely a great step forward in accounting for critical and strategic material requirements and consumption, and should be made a part of every production material analysis system in use today." Origin and Development of Material Analysis, prepared by T. R. Murphy, Accounting Dept Ford Motor Company, incl to Ltr, Murphy to Control Div SOS, 4 Sep 42.

[36] (1) Memo, USW for All Supply Services, 9 Jan 42, sub: Computation of Basic Industrial Material Requirements, cited in par. 1 of Memo, Hq SOS for the Services of Supply, 30 Sep 42, sub: Bills of Materials. During most of 1941, the services had been directed to base their requirements estimates for specific materials upon bills of materials. (2) Memo, Col Clifford V. Morgan, Chf Commodities Br, Resources Div, for Dir Resources Div SOS, 28 Aug 42, sub: Bills of Materials.

[37] " . . . it was shown that the quantity of aluminum per plane varied as much as 2,000 pounds, depending upon whether the bill of materials came from the manufacturers, the Army Air Forces, the War Production Board, or Alcoa." Memo cited 36 (2) above.

survey called for a degree of intensive activity and co-ordination of effort never before undertaken for the purpose. Thousands of bills of materials had to be hurriedly acquired or revised, procurement and production schedules prepared or revised, IBM equipment and operators obtained, and numerous conferences, directives, and memorandums employed to define procedures, convey instructions, and make necessary adjustments in the program.[38]

The experience obtained from BIM Job 0012 was of tremendous importance in indicating the nature of the task which would be a quarterly responsibility under the Controlled Materials Plan. A formal study and report of the results obtained under the survey led to detailed recommendations for improving the various steps and stages in the production of material requirements estimates. A statistical tabulation revealed that approximately 17,000 items of procurement had been analyzed, requiring nearly a million individual punch cards in order to compute the requirements for the four materials involved. The technical services alone expended some 18,500 man-hours in preparing the data and another 19,000 man-hours in actual machine calculations. The combined effort within the technical services thus ran to nearly 19 man-years of effort in terms of the peacetime 40-hour week.[39]

The adoption of the Controlled Materials Plan revolutionized both the philosophy and the procedures of material requirements determination. Instead of relying upon estimates of material requirements gathered previously, partially, haphazardly, or incidentally to other purposes, CMP instituted a built-in set of procedures which insured the determination of requirements: (1) on the basis of specific, identifiable, end-product programs; (2) in the precise material categories and for the exact time periods covered by the allotment process. Under CMP each claimant agency was obliged to present once each quarter its total requirements for each controlled material classification.[40] Under the original plan, requirements estimates were to cover the eighteen-month advance period (beginning with the base quarter) and were to be shown separately by months for the first twelve months, with a lump sum for the terminal six months. After experience under the plan was obtained, it was found satisfactory to state only quarterly figures for a year in advance.

The Army's presentation was divided into three broad groups and also into a number of major programs. The three basic groups were production; construction; and maintenance, repair, and operating supplies for Army-owned establishments. Production requirements were classified into some thirty-four major programs. This classification enabled the WPB Requirements Committee, as well as the Army, to adjust allotments on the basis of program or end-product importance. In addition to submitting its require-

---

[38] (1) Memo, Gen Ulio, TAG, for Chfs of Supply Services, 24 Sep 42, sub: Computation of estimates of raw and basic industrial material requirements. (2) Memo, Ulio for Chfs of Supply Services, 3 Oct 42, same sub, with 2 incls.

[39] Memo, John D. Witten, Chf Statistician SOS, for Brig Gen W. H. Harrison, Production Div SOS, 3 Nov 42, sub: Analysis of Computation of Material Requirements, BIM Job 0012, and Recommendations. Because of the shortage of qualified operators, it was necessary in some instances to work an individual as much as seventy-two consecutive hours without relief.

[40] CMP operations initially covered 39 controlled-material classifications composed of separate basic shapes or forms as follows: carbon steel, 13; alloy steel, 12; copper, 6; aluminum, 8. Steel requirements were expressed in short tons, others in thousands of pounds.

ments thus summarized, the Army was also required to submit to WPB at least one complete set of detailed tabulations which would show program subdivisions to any desired degree.[41]

A complicating factor in the statement of requirements under CMP was the necessity for showing separately requirements for "A" and "B" products. "A" products were those for which the Army would receive and make material allotments directly to its contractors. "B" products were those for which contractors would receive material allotments directly from the War Production Board. The Army did not state its *material* requirements for B products; it merely stated the number of units or the dollar value of the B products which it required in each time period. The computation of controlled materials entering into such products would be made by the War Production Board. The Army would be granted a blanket allotment of materials for its total B-product needs, and this allotment would be charged off as the WPB alloted materials to producers of Army B products.

In order to keep CMP responsive to changing needs it was soon found desirable to make continuous changes in the specific coverage and form of requirements estimates. Accordingly, each quarter's requirements were based on a specific WPB directive which announced the classification of materials and programs, the time period to be covered, the designation of the appropriate B-product list, and similar matters. In general, these changes resulted in substantial simplification of CMP over its lifetime.[42]

The complexity of the Army's task in determining its material requirements can only be suggested in the present survey. The first basic step, the development of adequate bills of materials, ran into endless complications. Bills of materials were of several types. A *detail* bill carried a separate analysis of the material content of each part or group of parts for a complete end product. For large and complex items like planes and tanks a detail bill might run to many hundreds of pages. A *summary* bill merely listed the total content of each material in the complete end product. A *complete*, as distinguished from a *partial*, bill covered all materials, not merely controlled materials under CMP. For many iems of Army procurement there were numerous models with variations in design and material content ranging from slight to major differences. Frequently a *prototype* bill could be used for all models within certain limits of variation. Similar to the prototype bill was the *modal* bill, representing a weighted average of the material consumption experienced by different contractors producing the same item.[43]

---

[41] The original breakdown contained some eighty Army programs. Memo, Eberstadt for USW, 16 Dec 42, sub: Presentation of Army Requirements under CMP.

[42] ASF M–602, Controlled Materials Plan Operation, 30 Sep 43, Pt. III, Requirements.

[43] (1) WPB, CMP Instructions on Bills of Materials, 15 May 43. (2) WPB, CMP Div, Papers Presented at the Special Three-Day CMP Courses of Instruction for Key Personnel, January–February 1943, Bills of Materials, version of 10 Feb 43. (3) Memo and incls, Hq SOS for the Supply Services, 30 Sep 42, sub: Bills of Materials. (4) Memo, Gen Ulio, TAG, for Chfs of Supply Services, 29 Nov 42, sub: Bills of Materials for Controlled Materials Plan. (5) Memorandum for All the Supply Services, 6 Mar 43, sub: Bills of Materials Under the Controlled Materials Plan. (6) Preparation of Modal Bill of Materials for the Scheduled Item, Step 0–2.6 in Procedure for Preparing Tabulating Decks of Unit Weights, App. A to Report on Standard Procedures for Preparing Controlled Material Requirements in the Supply Services, issued by Requirements Branch, Resources and Production Div, ASF, 15 Apr 43.

For all bills of materials there were a number of technical and administrative problems. Responsibility for the preparation of bills was placed on the prime contractor. This was a considerable burden especially where the number of subcontractors supplying parts, components, and subassemblies ran into large numbers. The Army therefore attempted to confine its requests for bills of materials and revisions thereof to items for which total material requirements were significant. On the other hand, the Army was obliged to make a systematic check of bills for accuracy and completeness. Comparisons were made with previous bills of the same contractor or of other contractors, and individual bills were scrutinized for internal consistency and accuracy of computations, as well as for errors in the light of known specifications, manufacturing processes, and so on. The basic item of importance in all bills was the gross or rough stock weight of material required to yield the specified material content in the finished product. Because of the inevitable losses in processing, as well as losses due to rejects, testing, and spoilage, actual material requirements greatly exceeded the net material content in finished items.[44]

For many items of procurement, bills of materials could not be obtained for lack of time or were otherwise impractical. In such cases material requirements were based on engineering estimates, dollar-value ratios, statistics of past consumption, or other methods. Engineering estimates were customarily used for construction projects as well as for nonrepetitive production items. The statis-

tical approach was most appropriate to civilian-type items in the electrical and other industries turning out a miscellaneous variety of products.[45]

Perhaps the most complex single element affecting the preparation of bills of materials, the computation of material requirements, and the determination of material allotments under CMP was the factor of lead time. Lead time was the nexus which linked bills of materials to master production schedules in the calculation of material requirements by time periods.[46] The Army's production schedules called for delivery of finished items of procurement at certain dates. The manufacturing process which incorporated raw materials into the finished item often required many months. Hence, actual material requirements antedated end-item delivery dates by time periods varying with each material for each product.

As in the case of many other aspects of requirements computation it soon became evident in the determination of lead time that absolute accuracy was not only impossible but not essential. After much study and analysis of the problem, the Requirements Branch of the Production Division, ASF, prepared and disseminated a comprehensive statement of Army doctrine on the subject of lead time. Elaborating upon the War Production Board's official definition, the governing memorandum discussed in detail the nature and implications of lead time, the considerations entering into the

---

[44] Handling Bills of Materials, Statement B, 11 Feb 43, in Forms and Procedures for Operation of CMP in the Signal Corps, prepared by L. W. Greenwood and J. L. Huck, Consultants, issued by Resources Br, Materiel Div, OCSigO, 1 May 43.

[45] WPB paper, Bills of Materials, 10 Feb 43, cited above, note 43 (2).

[46] The War Production Board's official definition of lead time was "the time interval expressed in months between the required delivery of materials from the plant of the supplier of the listed materials and final acceptance or delivery of the procurement item." Memo, and incls, Maj John A. Sargent, Chf Reqmts Br Resources and Production Div ASF, for TQMG et al., 7 Apr 43, sub: Lead Time, p. 2.

choice between average and detailed lead time, and the treatment of inventory, transportation, inspection, and other factors at all contractor levels affecting lead time.[47]

For purposes of presenting requirements estimates, Army and WPB officials decided to use a weighted average lead time for all controlled materials entering a given end item. Exceptions were permitted in the case of large items, such as ship construction, involving an array of lead times varying tremendously in length and complicated by irregular production schedules. Although the determination of an appropriate average lead time was a complex process, often performed on electrical computing machines, once the determination was made it was a relatively simple matter to incorporate the lead factor into further mechanical calculating operations. Lead time was always expressed in units of months, with an arbitrary minimum of one month.

Two basic sets of data entered into the calculation of material requirements—data from bills of materials, and data from master production schedules. Bills of materials specified the unit weights of required materials for specific end items; production schedules specified the quantities and time periods for the required delivery of end items. After all bills of materials had been received and checked for accuracy, they passed through a standard processing operation. This included coding and editing in various ways in order to facilitate the manual punching of basic tabulating decks of IBM cards. A similar lengthy process attended the preparation of data from master production schedules. This included the establishment of firm production schedules, ultimately based on the Army Supply Pro-

gram, and the detailed coding and editing of the schedules to permit the incorporation of all relevant data—end items, programs, time periods adjusted for lead time, and other information—into the basic tabulating deck.

The heart of the process of material requirements computation was accomplished on mammoth electric accounting machines, together with punch cards and various automatic sorting, collating, calculating, and tabulating devices. Without these unbelievably complex and versatile machines and their experienced operators, the task of requirements determination would have been virtually impossible. Within the Army a standard procedure was developed, providing in detail for every step of the process. For each technical service the standard operation required no less than seventeen complete decks of punch cards. Beginning with manually punched cards and progressing through various stages of electrical punching, machine operators converted the raw data from individual, detail bills of materials up through various summary stages, and then collated these data with master production schedules to present finally a mechanically calculated and recorded summary of total material requirements by material classes for time periods and by programs. In accomplishing this task, whole batteries of IBM machines would be in operation twenty-four hours per day behind locked doors in order to meet the final deadline.[48]

_____

[47] Ibid.

[48] Some idea of the complexity of an IBM run of Army controlled material requirements may be inferred from a scrutiny of the following documents: (1) Interim Report on the Joint Project by Central Planning Sec, Production Service Br, Industrial Div, OCofOrd, and Reqmts Br, Resources and Production Div, Hq ASF, With Respect to Material Requirements and Certain Related Subjects, 12 Mar 43; (2) Report on Standard Pro-

The accumulated statements of requirements of the various technical services were turned over to the Requirements Branch, Production Division, ASF, for consolidation into the over-all Army statement to be submitted to WPB. The detailed statement of total Army requirements submitted each quarter was sufficiently voluminous to fill several books of standard format. Although the Army's task of estimating material requirements each quarter was nominally finished when it submitted the estimates to WPB, it was in fact only the beginning of a lengthy process. This process included the defense of estimated requirements before the various WPB offices involved in the allotment process. Also, for the first few CMP runs, it included collaboration with WPB in detailed postallotment audits of requirements to provide a check on the Army's methodology, accuracy, and general performance.[49]

The Allotment of Controlled Materials

The basic division of the nation's supply of controlled materials was made by the Requirements Committee of the War Production Board. This division took the form of allotments to the various claimant agencies representing the total demand for materials. Although the military procuring

agencies were from the outset directly represented on the Requirements Committee, the final decision—in case of dispute over the share of materials given to each agency—rested ultimately with the civilian chairman of the War Production Board.

Shortly after CMP had been firmly established on an operating basis, WPB's new Program vice chairman, Julius A. Krug, took steps to affirm WPB's policy-making role in the allotment of materials to claimant agencies. Mr. Krug was aware, on the one hand, that the bulk allotment of each controlled material to each claimant agency, without any control over suballotments by the agencies, could lead to substantial abuse. On the other hand, by this time WPB had acknowledged the wisdom of allowing each agency legitimate discretion in the internal management of its own programs. The resolution of the problem was made in a carefully worded memorandum to all claimant agencies:

Thus far, an over-all allotment of controlled materials has been made to each Claimant Agency for subdivision among specific programs at its discretion. The Requirements Committee has not assumed, and in my judgment, should not assume the responsibility of the Claimant for the areas within its jurisdiction. At the same time, the Requirements Committee . . . has the right and the obligation to assure itself that materials allotted to a Claimant are not diverted to objectives that at the time of original authorization would not have received the same degree of preference over competing objectives.

Existing procedures are inadequate to preserve the principle of trusteeship of the Claimant in the use of materials allotted to it at the expense of the claims of other Agencies.[50]

cedures for Preparing Controlled Material Requirements in the Supply Services, issued by Reqmts Br, Resources and Production Div ASF, 15 Apr 43; (3) Signal Corps study cited above, note 44.

[49] See: (1) elaborate volume of documents transmitted with Memo, Lt Col John A. Sargent, Chf Reqmts Br, for Asst Dir Production Div ASF, 14 Jul 43, sub: Audit of Controlled Materials Requirements—4th Quarter, 1943 (Machine Job 22); (2) binder of statements by technical services transmitted with Memo, Maj John C. Swartley for Chf Production Service Br, Production Div ASF, 23 Oct 43, sub: Screening of Controlled Material Requirements, Job 25.

[50] Memo, Krug, Program Vice Chmn WPB, To All Claimant Agencies, 13 Jul 43, sub: Procedure for Allotment of Controlled Materials to Programs.

Under the new procedure announced by the Program vice chairman, a program determination by the Requirements Committee would be accompanied, when considered desirable, by a tentative subdivision of the aggregate allotment among broad general programs of a claimant. If the claimant's subsequent allotments to specific programs did not conform with the basis on which the aggregate allotments had been made, the Program vice chairman reserved the right to question the agency, to present the matter to the Requirements Committee for its consideration, and to take such further action as in his judgment seemed appropriate.[51] This precautionary measure apparently served its purpose.[52]

The detailed process of making controlled material allotments was considerably simplified by early amendments to CMP, often made at the request of the claimant agencies. One of these provided that steel allotments would be made in fewer material categories than those in which requirements were expressed. Accordingly, one over-all allotment was made to each claimant for all thirteen classifications of carbon steel, and one for the twelve forms of alloy steel. This was done on the theory that with an over-all balance between supply and allotments for the major categories, only minor adjustments would be necessary to prevent substantial overordering of particular shapes or forms. These adjustments could be made partly by curtailing programs drawing heavily on shapes in tight supply. For some forms, such as steel plate,

where stated requirements were great in proportion to known capacity, specific quotas for the several agencies could be established and implemented by mill directives. As a result of the policy of minimizing the kinds of allotment, there were only sixteen allotment categories as compared to the total of fifty-six used in the statement of requirements. In view of the tremendous amount of bookkeeping at all levels of the allotment process, this simplification prevented the system from collapsing under a burden of paper work.[53]

A second simplification was the making of all allotments on a quarterly instead of a monthly basis as originally planned. In order to prevent the congestion of delivery orders upon mills for any given month under the new procedure, the War Production Board issued an order restricting consumers to the use of approximately one third of their quarterly allotment in any one month within the quarter. This restriction would have resulted in considerable hardship to many Army contractors with small quarterly allotments because of the difficulty of placing small orders and receiving separate small shipments one third the size of the quarterly figure. Perhaps of greater importance, many contractors had ascending, declining, or sporadic production schedules calling for concentrated activity within a particular month. The Army therefore requested and obtained permission to authorize monthly delivery of any

---

[51] Ibid.

[52] The author has found no indication in War Department files of WPB objections to the Army's subdivision of controlled materials, and the War Production Board's official history makes no mention of any unwarranted diversion of controlled materials by claimant agencies.

[53] WPB, Rpt of Chmn, 9 Oct 45, pp. 50–51. Early in 1944, after the crisis in materials had passed, the Army and Navy proposed a reduction in the number of all allotment and requirements categories under CMP to four—carbon steel, alloy steel, copper, and aluminum. Memo, Gen Clay, Dir of Matériel, for the Program Vice Chmn WPB, 23 Feb 44, sub: Procedural Simplification of the Controlled Materials Plan. Although this drastic proposal was rejected, some reduction was made in the number of copper and aluminum classes.

portion of a consumer's quarterly allotment with the understanding that total deliveries in any one month for all Army contractors collectively would not exceed one third of the Army's total quarterly allotment from WPB. This authority was in turn delegated to each of the technical services with a comparable stipulation. In this manner internal flexibility was provided without destroying the over-all control necessary to preserve the system.[54]

From its inception, CMP had recognized the necessity for firm advance allotments beyond the current quarter in order to permit dependable planning for important long-term contracts. Firm advance allotments of controlled materials permitted reliance upon production schedules and justified the long-term commitment of other resources to such programs. Also, under this procedure, claimant agencies and contractors were relieved of the immense burden of having each quarter to reallot and reorder materials to cover the same schedules. In the original plan, claimant agencies were allowed to make forward allotments for future quarters up to specified percentages of the firm allotment made by the WPB Requirements Committee for the base quarter. These percentages were 80, 60, and 40, respectively, for the first, second, and subsequent quarters following the base quarter. The Army found these percentages, especially for quarters immediately following the base quarter, too low to accomplish the underlying purpose of the advance allotment procedure. This was true because

controlled material orders in accordance with WPB regulations had to be placed with mills anywhere from 30 to 120 days in advance of the month of delivery, depending upon the shape or form concerned. Accordingly, for the third quarter of 1943, WPB granted authority to the Army (and one or two other claimant agencies) to make advance allotments in the three succeeding quarters up to 100 percent of its third quarter allotment. For the fourth quarter, WPB reduced this percentage to 90, 80, and 60 percent on the ground that the 100-percent basis was too risky and that claimant agencies should be treated more uniformly.[55] These percentages remained (with some variations among the several material classes) for several quarters until the easing of material shortages in the face of program cutbacks made possible allotments substantially equal to requirements.

Before the latter part of 1943, it was the practice of WPB to cancel advance allotments and substitute the new total allotment as this was authorized for each current quarter. Beginning with the fourth quarter of 1943, WPB accounting was placed on a "net allotment" basis. This meant that only plus or minus adjustments would be made to the advance allotments previously authorized, thus reducing the volume of paper work for all concerned.[56]

[54] (1) Memo, Col Cooke, ACMO, for the Dir Controlled Materials Div WPB, 6 Feb 43, sub: Suggested Change in Procedure in Authorizing Deliveries. (2) Memo, Gen Minton, Dir, Resources and Production Div, for TQMG et al., 17 Feb 43, sub: Limitations on Quarterly Grants of Allotment for Class A Products Under the Controlled Materials Plan.

[55] (1) WPB, Controlled Materials Plan (2 November 1942), p. 7. (2) Memo, Col Cooke for Dir Program Bureau WPB, 8 Mar 43, sub: Advance Allotments. (3) Memo, Gen Minton for CofEngrs, 20 Mar 43, sub: Advance Allotments. (4) WPB Program Determination 331, 4 May 43. (5) Gen Clay, Dir of Materiel ASF, for Chmn, Requirements Com WPB, 10 Aug 43, sub: Advance Allotments. (6) Memo, Kohlhepp, Dir Prog Bureau, for Krug, Program Vice Chmn WPB, 24 Sep 43, sub: Fourth Quarter Allocations Under Controlled Material Plan.

[56] WPB, Controller's Report on the Operation of the Controlled Materials Plan for the Fourth Quarter, 1943, December 1943, p. 74.

The basic process of receiving and passing down allotments each quarter represented an intense period of activity for all concerned. Since controlled material orders could not be honored without an allotment number, it was important that contractors at all levels receive their allotments as quickly as possible. As soon as the Army received its allotment from WPB, the Production Division, ASF, through its Program Control and Requirements Branches, determined the share going to each supply service. If shortages were involved, two general "rules of thumb," or some compromise between them, were applied. If the requirements of a single service represented as much as 90 percent of the total, that service absorbed the entire shortage and the remaining services received allotments equal to the stated requirements. If the Army's total requirements were fairly well divided among the various services, all of them shared the deficit on a proportionate basis.[57]

Each supply service, upon receiving its own allotment, made its distribution among its prime consumers. This step was facilitated by the practice of making tentative determinations in advance so that only minor adjustments would be necessary at the time of actual allotment. Such "earmarkings" were based upon each prime contractor's carefully screened CMP–4–A application for the quarter in question together with the latest revision of his production schedule. In the event that a service received an allotment short of its stated requirements, it would request its principal

contractors to ascertain inventory and other considerations, involving both prime and secondary consumers, which might permit an allotment lower than originally requested without disturbing production schedules.[58]

After all possible internal adjustment had been made, each service drew up a balance of its unused allotments and shortages. Unused allotments were returned to the Production Division, ASF, and requests for additional allotments were made for those material categories in which urgent needs remained. To meet such needs the Production Division would then redistribute any returned allotments; if none were available and specific needs warranted, the division would actively seek additional returns. After no further adjustments internal to the Army could be made, the Production Division would return surplus allotments to WPB and request additional allotments to cover remaining shortages in other material categories. During the first two quarters of CMP, WPB made supplemental allotments to meet shortages wherever it could. Thereafter it adopted the policy of making a single firm allotment per quarter, and subsequent adjustments were made by transfers between agencies. Trading of allotments–particularly among the military procuring agencies—gave desired flexibility to the program and was approved by WPB as long as all such transfers were duly recorded.[59]

---

[57] (1) Determination of Allotments to Supply Service and Subsequent Adjustments, 6 Apr 43 (unsigned draft of procedure), in files of Production Div ASF. (2) ASF M–602, Controlled Materials Plan Operation, 30 Sep 43, Pt. IV, Sec. 404 Allotment Functions of Headquarters, ASF.

[58] (1) Memo, Gen Minton, Dir Resources and Production Div, for CofEngrs et al., 13 May 43, sub: Allotment of Controlled Materials for Third Quarter. (2) ASF M–602, Controlled Materials Plan Operation, Pt. IV, Sec. 402, Allotting Procedure in the Technical Services. (3) Ordnance Operations Under Controlled Materials Plan, (1943). (3) ICAF R60, Priorities and Allocations, pp. 82–89, Accounting Control and Disbursement of Allotments.

[59] (1) Memo, Gen Minton, Director, Resources and Production Div, for Dir Requirements Div SOS, 13 Mar 43, sub: Effects of Changes in Au-

Although the basic distribution of allotments took place once each quarter, constant minor adjustments made the allotment process a continuous affair. Thus, the Army developed standard procedures for reclaiming unused and excessive allotments from contractors faced with changes in or failure to meet production schedules or with other special circumstances. By stretching its allotments as far as possible, the Army was able to avoid any significant curtailment of production schedules for reasons of controlled material shortage throughout the life of CMP.[60]

An illustration of the speed with which allotments could be made to contractors is indicated by a report describing the second quarter 1943 distribution by the Supply Division, Office of the Chief of Engineers. This office received its allotments from the Production Division at 10:00 A.M., Saturday, 6 February 1943. All twelve engineering districts were immediately notified by telephone to standby for their allotments to be made later in the day. In the Washington office, OCofEngrs, allotments were distributed to programs and subprograms and then further divided into allotments by district. The allotments of each material by subprogram and by district were telephoned to the districts between 6:00 and 8:00 P.M. the same day. On Sunday, 7 February, the districts completed previously prepared letter grants of allotment for each prime consumer. These grants were distributed by mail or special messenger on the same day. In cases where this notification would not reach prime consumers by Monday, 8 February, advance notification was made by telephone. All prime consumers were urged to cover their mill orders immediately with letter certification bearing the allotment number assigned by the Army. Many of these certifications reached the mill level on Tuesday, 9 February 1943.[61]

Each allotment to a prime consumer was covered by a specific allotment number which afforded a complete identification of the sources and nature of an allotment. Thus, W–2345–678–3Q43 indicated an Army (War Department) allotment to its program 2345 covering its production schedule 678 for the particular contractor in the third quarter of 1943. In passing along this allotment to secondary consumers the prime contractor and his various subcontractors used an abbreviated allotment number—in this case W–2–3Q3—indicating only the claimant agency, the first digit of the full program number, and the quarter. Although this simplification made it more difficult to trace back allotment authority at lower contractor levels, the simplification was necessary to avoid a prohibitive amount of recording and filing for contractors at all echelons.[62]

All claimant agencies and all contractors were required to keep and preserve for at least two years all records of allotments received and distributed. Such records were subject to inspection by WPB. Persons willfully issuing suballotments in excess of total amounts authorized to them were subject to a fine up to $10,000, or imprisonment, or both.[63]

Early in the operation of CMP it was discovered that from 10 to 15 percent of

thorized Procurement on the Allocations of Controlled Materials. (2) WPB, Controller's Report on the Operation of the Controlled Materials Plan for the Second Quarter, 1943, pp. 38–40.

[60] This was, of course, also due to other factors. See below, page 590.

[61] Incl B to SOS CMP Cir 10, 3 Mar 43.

[62] WPB, Controller's Report on the Operation of the Controlled Materials Plan for the Third Quarter, 1943, September 1943, p. 70.

[63] WPB CMP Regulation 1, par. aa.

each quarter's allotments remained unused. This "wasting" of allotments was commonly referred to as "attrition" and was the result of a number of factors. Army and WPB studies of attrition indicated four major classes of influence at work: (1) overstatement of requirements; (2) reductions in actual operating requirements for controlled materials; (3) allotment "hoarding" at all echelons; (4) the use of alternate sources of controlled material supplies.

Overstatement of requirements resulted from erroneous bills of materials, failure adequately to consider inventories, and the tendency at all echelons to pad requirements in anticipation of shortages. Reductions in actual operating requirements stemmed from a variety of considerations— failure to meet production schedules (referred to as "slippage" and caused by shortages of resources other than materials, technical difficulties, "Acts of God," and the like, reduction in production schedules because of contract changes or cancellation, and changes in specifications permitting conservation of controlled materials. Allotment "hoarding" was both voluntary and involuntary. Inevitable delays in passing down allotments through the vertical chain of contractors resulted in the cumulative waste of allotments. Contractors at all levels also deliberately reserved portions of their allotments to meet unexpected demands. Finally, small amounts of controlled materials were obtainable, without specific charge to allotments, from warehouses and through similar small order procedures.[64]

The original version of CMP had anticipated the need for keeping material mills booked to capacity and had authorized claimant agencies to make allotments up to 105 percent of their own allotments received from WPB. Also, controlled material mills were authorized to accept orders bearing allotment numbers up to 105 percent of expected production in any month. As the significance of the attrition factor became evident, the Requirements Committee, WPB, made its total quarterly allotments in excess of estimated supply. Thus for the fourth quarter of 1943, carbon steel allotments were 110 percent of estimated supply, the figure for alloy steel was 111 percent, and allotments for copper products ranged from 100 to 109 percent of estimated supply.[65] The technique of overallotment, both at the WPB and the claimant agency level, combined with the provision for overordering at the mill level, served to compensate for the waste of allotments and prevented losses of production which would otherwise have occurred. In the early quarters of CMP, unforeseen slippages in the steel expansion and production program were fortunately offset by substantial underestimates of attrition, thus resulting in a balance between steel supply and allotment orders actually presented to mills. In time, improved accuracy in estimating both supply and attrition enabled the War Production Board to make allotments close to the quantity needed to keep capacity output and the use of allotments in balance.[66]

[64] (1) Memo, Maj. John A. Sargent, Chf Reqmts Br, Resources and Production Div, for Col Frank R. Denton, 4 Jun 43, and attached study, Wasting of Allotments, dated 22 May 43. (2) Memo, Col Denton, Asst Dir for Production ASF, for Program Vice Chmn WPB, 1 Nov 43, sub: Army Attrition— Third Quarter, 1943. (3) WPB, Controller's Report on the Operation of the Controlled Materials

Plan for the Third Quarter, 1943, September 1943, pp. 10–11, 59–64. (4) ICAF R60, Priorities and Allocations, pp. 87–89.

[65] Memo, Kohlhepp, Dir Program Bureau WPB, for Krug, Program Vice Chmn WPB, 24 Sep 43, sub: Fourth Quarter Allocations under Controlled Materials Plan, p. 5.

[66] CPA, *War Production Achievements and the Reconversion Outlook*, p. 50.

The B-Product Controversy

A fundamental problem in formulating and launching the Controlled Materials Plan was the determination of the extent to which a horizontal allocation procedure would be used under the plan. Eberstadt's original proposal for a vertical system had explicitly stated that such a system could provide for horizontal allocation where this was most suitable.[67] The initial version of CMP accordingly provided for horizontal allocation of materials for the production of items to be known as B products. A specific list of B products was to be published and all items not included therein would automatically be classified as A products. The A products would be subject to the standard vertical procedure under which claimant agencies would submit their material requirements to WPB and receive allotments for vertical subdivision among their contractors. In the case of B products, claimant agencies would obtain quarterly dollar or quantity estimates of their contractors' requirements of B products as such. These would be consolidated and submitted to WPB, which would total up all requirements of B products, convert these into controlled-material equivalents, and make material allotments direct to B-product producers in accordance with decisions of the WPB Requirements Committee.[68]

Two closely related problems immediately emerged in connection with the B list: (1) What general principles would be used in selecting items to be listed as B products? (2) How could the B list be "frozen" and all B products clearly defined? The latter consideration was an all-important prac-

tical one, inasmuch as A products were themselves defined as all products not on the specific B list. Unless all manufacturers, claimant agencies, and the War Production Board could quickly and uniformly identify any manufactured product as either A or B, the determination of material requirements and all other CMP operations would be at sea. This possibility was a real threat to the success of the plan during the first few months after its adoption.[69]

The first question raised fundamental issues of policy: the larger the B list, the smaller the role of vertical allocation. A large B list would, in effect, constitute a substantial repudiation of the basic principle of CMP, and with it the possibility of close control of the flow of materials in accordance with the urgency of end-product requirements. It soon became apparent that the battle which the services had so recently fought to obtain a vertical system of material controls was now to be fought all over again, although on a smaller scale, in the B-product controversy.

The Army's first misgivings concerning the B list appeared even before CMP was formally adopted. On 21 October 1942, the Corps of Engineers submitted preliminary comments on the CMP draft plan which had been released the day before. Noting the inconsistency of items suggested for the B list, the Engineers remarked:

In connection with the handling of "Class B" items the Corps of Engineers is in a peculiar position since many of its items will be in

---

[67] Eberstadt Memo, cited above, note 7.

[68] WPB, Controlled Materials Plan (2 November 1942).

[69] (1) Ltr, Skinner, Dir Production Div SOS, to Eberstadt, 5 Dec 42. (2) Memo, Skinner, Dir of Production Scheduling SOS, for Dir CMP Div WPB, 26 Jan 43, sub: Suggested Simplification of CMP Procedure. (3) Unsigned Memo for File, 28 Jan 43, sub: Simplification of Operation Under CMP. (4) Memo, Gen Minton, Dir Resources and Production Div ASF, for Br Chfs, 11 May 43, sub: Class B Products for the Third Quarter 1943.

this class. The Corps of Engineers is unwilling to jeopardize its procurement program by allowing other agencies to make decisions which may affect drastically the ability of this office to fulfill its obligations. For example, this office will allocate material for the production of trailers for the portable air compressor program on a given schedule. Another agency will be allocating material for the compressors, possibly on another schedule.[70]

As the nature of the B-product list began to emerge in greater detail in succeeding drafts of CMP, the objections of the Engineers became more pronounced:

The entire question of the handling of Class B products is extremely unsatisfactory [italics in original]. The list of Class B products has apparently been prepared without an underlying philosophy as to the selection of items to be included in the list. It was the understanding of this office that the Class B list was prepared in order to permit simplification of procedures and yet the present draft of the plan contemplates as much work by the Claimant Agencies on Class B items as on Class A items. Unless the procedure involved in handling Class B items is clarified and unless the Class B list is prepared on a more rational basis, the plan cannot be considered satisfactory to the Corps of Engineers.[71]

The official version of CMP announced on 2 November 1942 contained only a provisional and highly general list of B products, with the statement that a definitive product classification would be issued promptly. The classes of items included in the provisional list consisted of general industrial machinery, (for example, compressors, pumps, condensers, heat exchangers, power boilers), civilian-type end items (agricultural machinery and equipment,

consumers' durable goods, and so on), and fabricated components and intermediate products (bearings, nuts, bolts, screws, switchgear, electrical accessories, and similar items).[72]

During the remainder of November and December the composition of the B list was the subject of almost daily conferences and memorandums among the various interested groups. These included not only personnel of the War Production Board and the several claimant agencies, but representatives of trade associations and industry groups, many of whom had strong convictions on the manner in which their allotments should be handled.[73] Much of the discussion between claimant agencies and WPB was held in the WPB Engineering Board of Review, which had the basic responsibility for drawing up the B list. Finally, at the end of December, WPB issued its Official CMP Class B-Product List, containing hundreds of items and item classes defined as B products.[74]

The publication of the official list threw the B-product controversy wide open. When the Army reviewed the new list, it found to its surprise and chagrin that large segments of its direct procurement programs fell into the B-product category. This meant that material allocations vital to the pro-

---

[70] Memo, Brig Gen Raymond F. Fowler, Chf Supply Div OCofEngrs, for Dir of Production, Hq SOS, 21 Oct 42, sub: Comments on Controlled Materials Plan.

[71] Memo, Gen Fowler for Dir of Production SOS, 28 Oct 42, sub: Comments on Revised Draft of Controlled Materials Plan.

[72] WPB, Controlled Materials Plan (2 November 1942), pp. 43–44.

[73] Many firms feared the amount of paper work under vertical allocation and were anxious to be treated as B-product producers. The initial version of CMP permitted firms to apply for the type of procedure they preferred. This provision was characterized by the official WPB history as a veritable Pandora's box. CPA, *Industrial Mobilization for War*, p. 665.

[74] WPB, Official CMP Class B Product List, 21 Dec 42. An intermediate version of the B list had appeared on 14 November. WPB, Controlled Materials Plan—General Instruction on Bills of Materials, 14 Nov 42, pp. 10–21.

duction of crucial items of equipment were removed from Army jurisdiction and turned over to the Office of Civilian Supply and various material divisions of the War Production Board. All items which qualified as civilian-type end items appeared on the B list, even though these items were produced in Army owned and operated establishments or by private firms whose entire output was under Army contract. The B list included bulldozers, steamshovels, cranes, and other construction and materials-handling equipment used all over the world by Army Engineers in clearing jungles, building airfields, loading and unloading military equipment, and numerous other activities. Removal of these important items from the A-product classification meant not only a corresponding loss of Army control over the internal management of its own programs. It also signified the substitution of horizontal for vertical allocation, with a corresponding diminution of responsibility on the part of allotment recipients to devote scarce materials to any particular end-product program.[75]

But the 21 December B-product list went even further. It included a long list of military aircraft equipment and components (for example, torpedo directors, hoist assemblies, guns, magazines, and other armament). Some of these items had apparently

been added in contravention of agreements reached in earlier discussions:

. . . it is understood that there was an agreement at the . . . meeting of the Engineering Board of Review that Guns and Magazines . . . should be treated as Class A products . . . . This office strongly protests the procedure by which substantive changes, such as the aircraft list, can be made "official" without any review by regularly constituted Boards having Services of Supply [ASF] representation.

Furthermore, it is disturbing to see such items as engines and tractors added to a B list which is already too large. It has been the assumption of this office that major component or end item programs would not be considered for Class B treatment unless there were specific reasons for so doing. In the case of engines and tractors, the only reasons which have been brought to the attention of this office are such that almost any other major component or end item program could be shifted on the same basis. Such an attitude, if extended, could easily result in a complete breakdown of the Controlled Materials Plan.[76]

An additional factor in the B-product controversy was WPB's ruling that claimant agencies were prohibited from obtaining bills of materials for B products. Requests for B-product bills were confined to WPB's own staff to reduce the tremendous burden of work imposed on industry in the launching of CMP. But the effect of the prohibition was to prevent claimant agencies from making an accurate determination of A-product requirements for controlled materials. Existing bills of materials for A products typically included substantial material requirements for B-product components entering into finished A products. The only way the Army could compute its controlled material requirements for A products for

---

[75] The granting of material allotments to individual B-product producers was transferred early in 1943 from the Office of Civilian Supply to WPB's industry divisions concerned with the various classes of end product. CPA, *Industrial Mobilization for War*, p. 492. Although this was regarded as an improvement by the Army (which had representatives in the various industry divisions), it was the firm position of the Army that the distribution of allotments to all its contractors under scheduled procurement programs should be performed by the technical services responsible for administering these programs.

[76] Memo, Col Cooke, ACMO, for Dir Controlled Materials Div WPB, 2 Jan 43, sub: Official CMP Class B Products List, 21 Dec 42.

the first CMP period was to compute total material requirements and then deduct the estimated quantity of materials entering into B products and components. But this could not be done without bills of materials for B products, and the Army was obliged for the second and third quarters of 1943 to rely on obsolescent bills of materials and other information already in its files. Moreover, the same problem arose every time a product was transferred from the B to the A list, or vice versa.[77]

Army procurement officials now viewed the B list as a kind of Trojan horse which threatened to wreck the entire Controlled Materials Plan. This view was not confined to the Army and the other military procuring agencies but was shared by an important element within the War Production Board itself:

The "B" List was not published until late in December, making it utterly impossible for the Claimant Agencies to calculate their requirements in accordance with the instructions to Claimant Agencies. Furthermore, the "B" List is altogether too long, complicated and confusing. This made it almost impossible to obtain Bills of Materials or Requirements for these products and will make the task of issuing allotments unnecessarily involved and difficult. I cannot refrain from registering my disgust at the whole philosophy that permitted this to happen.[78]

Along with the simplification of paper work in the "A" chain in the second quarter, I view

it as essential that the products now on the "B" List be reincorporated into the vertical system to the greatest possible extent, beginning in the third quarter. This is necessary to restore the vertical integration between flow of materials into components and end-products, and flow of components into end-products, which is the basic purpose of CMP.[79]

Throughout the first half of 1943, the Army made a series of proposals looking to the reduction in size of the B list and elimination of the restriction against obtaining bills of materials.[80] On 26 March the Army controlled materials officer submitted a drastic proposal to abolish the B list and to simplify the basic allotment process. The heart of the new proposal was the elimination of allotments to all consumers of controlled materials below the prime contractor level. Claimant agencies would continue to receive allotments and agency programs would, as before, be tailored to conform to allotments received. Each prime contractor would receive a token allotment of controlled materials to cover his authorized production schedule and that of his subcontractors. Each subcontractor would be given a production schedule based on the availability of controlled materials but he would be free to order materials, without a

---

[77] (1) Memo, Col Cooke for Mr. Harold Boeschenstein, Dir CMP Div WPB, 1 Dec 42, sub: Procedure for Estimating Program Requirements Under Controlled Materials Plan. (2) Memo, Cooke for Dir Resources and Production Div ASF, 21 Apr 43, sub: Elimination of Organizational Duplications, Overlappings, and Conflicts. (3) ASF Annual Rpt. 1943, Ch. V, Procurement Problems, p. 71.

[78] Memo, H. O. King, Chmn Copper Reqmts Com, for Eberstadt, Program Vice Chmn WPB, 29 Jan 43, sub: Recommendations for Distribution of Copper Under the Controlled Materials Plan for 2d Quarter 1943.

[79] Memo, Lincoln Gordon, CMP Div WPB, for Boeschenstein, Dir CMP Div WPB, 19 Jan 43, sub: CMP—Simplification of Paper Work and Curtailment of B-Product List.

[80] (1) Memo, Col Cooke, ACMO, for Boeschenstein, 6 Jan 43, sub: Classification of Engines under CMP. (2) Memo, Skinner, Dir Production Scheduling SOS, for Vice Chmn WPB, 28 Jan 43, sub: Product Classification Under CMP (The B List Problem). (3) Memo, Col Cooke for Dir CMP Div WPB, 9 Feb 43, sub: Proposed "B" List Policy for Third Quarter. (4) Memo, Cooke for Dir CMP Div WPB, 15 Feb 43, same sub, and incl, Proposed "B" List for Third Quarter. (5) Memo, Cooke for Dir CMP Div WPB, 4 Mar 43, sub: Proposed Principles Governing Classification of Products.

specific allotment, in amounts required to fulfill his authorized schedule.[81]

On the same day that this proposal was submitted to the War Production Board, the chief of the Requirements Branch, Production Division, ASF, submitted a detailed criticism of the proposal to the Army controlled materials officer. This critique, which was widely circulated within the Production Division, pointed to the serious loss of control over the flow of materials which would result if the plan were adopted:

During the last two months, a great many collateral benefits have been noted as a direct result of the provisions in the C.M.P. which provide for a definite balance of schedules within an allotment of material and definite records to confirm the fact that such a readjustment was made. *A close observation of the operations of the Supply Services in this connection indicates that the token allotment recommended in the proposed simplification would not insure . . . that actual procurement would be carefully scheduled and actually related to material allotments* [italics in original].[82]

On 21 April 1943, the proposal was rejected by Mr. Julius A. Krug, the Program Vice Chairman, WPB. Krug characterized the the proposal as equivalent to the unlimited extension of priorities, which "does not provide for any basis for checking orders for critical materials so certified against bona

fide requirements." [83] By this time, however, sentiment within the Army for the proposal had cooled considerably.

The accumulated pressure from within as well as outside WPB for a resolution of the B-product problem led to a series of modifications of the existing arrangements. On 15 May 1943, WPB announced a new B-product list together with a list of Class A Civilian Type End Products. The latter was a list of important items formerly on the B list, such as equipment used by Army Engineers, for which claimant agencies could elect to make allotments on a vertical basis. Other changes included the elimination of military aircraft items as well as a number of clarifications which simplified the interpretation and application of the B list.[84]

The really significant change, which effectively disposed of the B-product controversy as a major issue, came about on 23 June 1943. On this date the Production Executive Committee, WPB, voted to approve a short list of "excluded B components" and, effective with the first quarter of 1944, to permit claimant agencies to treat all other items as A products if such items were required to meet regularly scheduled procurement programs. At the same time, claimant agencies were given authority to obtain complete bills of materials for all items in their procurement programs except for the excluded B components. The practical effect of this disposition of the B-product problem was to abolish the B list for the procurement agencies (except for the twenty-two excluded B components) but to retain it for all other purposes. WPB still had control

---

[81] (1) CPA, *Industrial Mobilization for War,* p. 676. n. 41. (2) Memo, Col Cooke, Chf CMP Control, Br, for Dir Resources and Production Div ASF, 20 Mar 43, sub: Proposed Simplification and Enforcement of the Controlled Materials Plan, and Attachment A (mimeographed): Summary of Proposed Simplification of the Controlled Materials Plan, and Simplification of the Controlled Materials Plan.

[82] Memo, Maj Sargent, Chf Reqmts Br, for Chf CMP Control Br, Resources and Production Div ASF, 26 Mar 43, sub: Comments on Proposal To Alter CMP.

[83] Ltr, Krug, Program Vice Chmn WPB, to Gen Clay, ACofS ASF, 21 Apr 43. See also CPA *Industrial Mobilization for War,* pp. 675–78, for a discussion of this episode.

[84] WPB, Official CMP Class B Product List and Class A Civilian Type End Product List, 15 May 43.

over the broad area of the detailed determination of requirements and allotments for the maintenance of civilian supply and the basic industrial economy.[85] The

Controlled Materials Plan was thus effectively restored to a vertical basis of operation where that type of operation was most essential—in the execution of military procurement geared specifically to military requirements.

---

[85] (1) Ltr and attachment, Krug, Program Vice Chmn WPB, to Gen Clay, 12 Jun 43. (2) Memo, Clay for Program Vice Chmn WPB, 16 Jun 43, sub: Proposed Revision of CMP Procedure for Class "B" Products. (3) CPA, *Industrial Mobolization for War*, p. 679. The list of excluded B components, as well as the detailed procedure under the new arrangement, is contained in the atachment to the Krug letter of 12 June 1943.

CHAPTER XXVI

Other Measures for Control and Conservation of Materials

Miscellaneous Controls

The Controlled Materials Plan rapidly achieved its basic purposes and remained throughout the war as the instrument for channeling the supplies of steel, copper, and aluminum into their most important uses. No other materials were brought directly under CMP although a number of them become so critical that the priorities system proved inadequate for their effective distribution. Special allocation systems were therefore devised for tires, lumber, cotton textiles, woolen and knit goods, pulp and paper, and chemicals. These systems drew heavily from the experience of CMP but were tailored to suit the nature of the material and the organization of the industry concerned. Their common feature was the budgeting of available supplies in accordance with the urgency of need as indicated by careful estimates of requirements. As in the case of priorities and CMP, the administration of these controls on behalf of the War Department was supervised by the Production Division, ASF, with the details of operation falling upon the various technical services. Each of these systems presented its own problems and peculiarities, but as in the case of controlled materials the improved methods of distribution combined with expanded production and curtailment of procurement objectives gradually eased the shortages.[1]

Component Scheduling

An important sector of production for World War II was represented by complex intermediate parts essential to the completion of end items of procurement. These intermediate units—commonly referred to as components—represented a wide array of items including motors, generators, compressors, heat exchangers, electrical measuring instruments, engine accessories, antifriction bearings, and others. By the end of 1942, serious shortages in these categories were interfering with facility expansion programs and the production of major items of munitions. Among the procurement programs affected were AAF aircraft, Navy destroyer escorts, and ship construction by the Maritime Commission and by the Army Transportation Corps. Facility completion programs jeopardized by component shortages included those for synthetic rubber and aviation gasoline as well as in varying degree the six hundred scheduled construction proj-

---

[1] (1) ICAF R60, Priorities and Allocations, pp. 97–98. (2) CPA, *Wartime Production Achievements and the Reconversion Outlook*, pp. 73–98, *passim.* (3) CPA, *Industrial Mobilization for War*, pp. 826–34; Novick, Anshen, and Truppner, *Wartime Production Controls*, Chs. X–XIX.

ects of the Army and corresponding projects of the other procuring agencies.[2]

In December 1942, a committee headed by Maj. Gen. Lucius Clay submitted proposals for dealing with thirty-four important components required in common by various claimants.[3] After intensive study of the problem under WPB auspices, a priority rating of AA–1 for all thirty-four components was authorized by Ferdinand Eberstadt.[4] This proved to be only a temporary expedient and, on 26 February 1943, WPB issued its first General Scheduling Order (M–293). This order initially covered thirty-six classes of components handled by eleven of WPB's industry divisions and divided all listed components into three degrees of critical importance with corresponding degrees of control. An unlabeled class—the least critical—was subject only to periodical status reports by manufacturers. The next group—known as X components—was subject to "order-board" inspection and revision by WPB; component manufacturers' schedules, once screened and approved by WPB, were "frozen" against all interference and had to be followed. The Y group—consisting of seven types of highly critical components—could not be purchased or ordered without prior specific approval of WPB, which placed approved orders under frozen schedules with the manufacturer deemed most appropriate.

These efforts to control component delivery schedules were, in the view of the military procuring agencies as well as others, inadequately related to end-product programs.[5] As in the case of control over producers' mill schedules for basic industrial materials,[6] separate decisions by the several WPB industry divisions failed to provide a balanced and properly timed flow of components and parts at all contractor levels into predetermined end-product programs on the basis of relative importance. The chief, as well as highly important, result of scheduling under the original order M–293 was the "dehydration" of order boards by screening out all duplicate orders, prematurely placed orders, and others deemed to be not important enough to be included in a particular delivery schedule.[7]

To achieve a greater degree of program control in scheduling components, M–293 went through several modifications designed to approximate the vertical programing and allotment procedure typified by CMP. As early as June 1943, the Component Scheduling Plan was superimposed on M–293 for certain key components, programs, and claimant agencies. This plan attempted to obtain from claimant agencies a statement of their requirements for control components up to twenty-four months in advance. The capacity of component manufacturers was allocated by WPB against the stated requirements and firm schedules were prescribed. Unfortunately, the burden of paper work and the fact that CSP was applied to manufacturers on a voluntary basis resulted

[2] (1) CPA, *Industrial Mobilization for War,* pp. 683–84, 692. (2) Construction Scheduling Section, Historical Report, 12 Jun 43, incl to Memo, Lt Col F. W. Crandall, Production Div ASF, for Dir Control Div ASF, 6 Jul 43, sub: Annual Historical Report of the Production Division and Its Branches.

[3] CPA, *Industrial Mobilization for War,* p. 683.

[4] WPB Program Determination 270, 22 Jan 43.

[5] CPA, *Industrial Mobilization for War,* p. 692.

[6] See above, page 554.

[7] Findings of the Subcommittee on Scheduling Practice in Relation to Preference Ratings, 13 Oct 43, App. A to Report No. 10 of Special Committee on Preference Ratings and Allied Controls, transmitted with Memo, L. Gordon (Chmn) *et al.,* for Kohlhepp, Chmn Program Adjustment Com WPB, 24 Oct 43, sub: Report of Special Committee on Preference Ratings and Allied Controls.

in its attaining only indifferent success. In order to tighten up the program in the fall of 1943 the so-called Z component procedure was added to M-293. This covered sixteen control components and eight subcomponents and made CSP mandatory at the discretion of certain claimant agencies. In general, the objectives of Z component procedure were to identify orders at all contractor levels with end-product programs, to mesh the delivery dates of all intermediate products with end-product schedules, and to decentralize much of the paper work to the field.[8]

The foregoing attempts at component scheduling met with considerable opposition from industry because of the paper work involved and a fairly widespread feeling that they were of dubious value. In 1944 the Z procedure was dropped and the X procedure was modified to reduce paper work, especially by confining the procedures to major firms representing the bulk of a given industry. By this time the peak demand had passed and the general refinement of war production schedules and procedures under both private and governmental direction had added substantially to productivity. Thus World War II ended without the achievement of, or the compelling necessity for, more than fragmentary scheduling control techniques at the level of complex components.[9]

Export Controls

An important group of material controls initiated at the beginnig of the defense period

aimed at preventing the exportation from the United States of scarce materials, tools, and equipment. In the fall of 1939 after the outbreak of war in Europe, losses of crude rubber and tin by re-export to Europe had become large enough to alarm the ANMB. With the increased foreign demand for American machine tools, scrap iron, ferro-manganese, and other strategic and critical materials sought for industrial use or stockpiling by the U.S. Government, it became apparent that unrestricted foreign purchases posed a serious treat to American defense objectives. Exhortation and "moral embargoes" failed adequately to curb these losses and on 2 July 1940 the President was authorized to prohibit or curtail the exportation of critical materials.[10]

Under the new legislation an export licensing system was established, to be administered by the administrator of Export Control. The administrator and his staff relied heavily upon the Army and Navy Munitions Board in reviewing export applications and in reaching decisions as to which items were essential to the defense needs of the United States.[11] For various reasons, owners of materials denied export licenses were sometimes

---

[8] The shipbuilding program of the Army Transportation Corps was a principal "guinea pig" in the application of the Z procedure. CPA, *Industrial Mobilization for War*, pp. 692–93.

[9] (1) *Ibid.*, pp. 834–35. (2) CPA, *Wartime Production Achievements and the Reconversion Outlook*, p. 15. (3) Novick, Anshen, and Truppner, *Wartime Production Controls*, pp. 284–86.

[10] 54 *Stat.* 712, 2 Jul 40. See also, Jt Releases of the War and Navy Depts, 11 Oct 39, Statement by the Army and Navy Munitions Board on Strategic and Critical Raw Materials; and 19 Jan 40, Statement by Army and Navy Munitions Board on Exports of Essential Raw Materials.

[11] Brig Gen R. L. Maxwell, Administrator of Export Control, Export Control, 31 May 41, AIC Lectures, 19:101ff. By mid-1941, the Office of Export Control under General Maxwell had some 425 personnel, including approximately 100 Army and Navy officers and some 50 to 60 "top grade" Civil Service personnel. *Ibid.*, p. 104 therein. The Office of Export Control and its successor agencies were the counterpart of the War Trade Administration proposed in the Industrial Mobilization Plan for the control of foreign trade in time of emergency and war.

unwilling or unable to sell to domestic purchasers. It was soon found that positive measures were needed to direct the flow of materials frozen under export embargoes into actual defense uses within the United States. In response to this need, Congress on 10 October 1940 conferred upon the President the authority to requisition material which had been denied export.[12] Under the new procedures, the War and Navy Departments, acting through ANMB, were empowered to determine the need for requisitioning specific items and to sell or otherwise dispose of them. Actual requisitioning was performed by the administrator of Export Control in behalf of the department concerned. The formal requisition process consisted of seizure of the property, followed by hearings under the administrator to determine "the fair and just value." The administrator then made specific recommendations to the President on the terms of compensation. The President's determination, which typically followed the recommendations, could be accepted or rejected by the owner. If accepted, the owner was immediately paid the value in full as determined. If rejected, the owner received 50 percent of the determined value and was presumably free to take his case to the courts.[13]

In actual practice, requisitioning was employed only as a last resort. In most instances, with the requisitioning power in the background, the War and Navy Departments were able to procure the items in question on the basis of negotiation. Shortly before Pearl Harbor, the requisitioning power

was extended by statute to include virtually all kinds of property within the United States, not merely that which had been denied export license. At this time the broad supervision of requisitioning was placed under OPM and its successor agencies.[14]

Government-Furnished Materials

A positive program for insuring an adequate supply of scarce materials and equipment to Army contractors was developed in the form of Government Furnished Materials (GFM) and Government Furnished Equipment (GFE). Introduced as a temporary expedient in World War I, the device of having the government furnish materials was found to have certain advantages.[15] With its far-flung purchasing facilities and statutory powers the War Department could obtain scarce supplies far more easily than could small private contractors. With the advance guarantee of GFM a larger number of contractors was encouraged to bid, and contracts were more widely diffused among small business. Also, contractors were less inclined to slow down production and hoard labor and other resources because of material shortages. By purchas-

---

[12] 54 *Stat.* 1090, 10 Oct 40. This act was implemented by Executive Order 8567, 15 Oct 40.

[13] All War Department requisitions under the 1940 act were apparently settled without litigation. ASF, History of the Purchases Division, p. 373.

[14] (1) *Ibid.,* pp. 361 ff. (2) Harry B. Yoshpe, The Flow of Materials to War Suppliers, circa 1946 (preliminary draft, copy in OCMH, hereafter cited as Yoshpe, Flow of Materials), p. 101. The Office of Export Control, under an administrator, was the first of the economic warfare agencies of the United States, and was succeeded in turn by the Economic Defense Board, the Board of Economic Warfare, and the Foreign Economic Administration.

[15] The War Department in World War I found it necessary to supply its aircraft contractors with certain grades of lumber and textile products in order to meet aircraft specifications. AAF, Historical Section, History of the Bureau of Aircraft Construction, 1919. During the interwar period the Quartermaster Corps supplied clothing contractors with cloth and garment findings. Yoshpe, Production Control in the QMC, p. 22.

ing for a number of its contractors at one time, the Army could eliminate competitive bidding for numerous small lots and thereby effect purchasing economies. Moreover, inspection was simplified and the Army could obtain greater uniformity and higher quality of both materials and finished items of procurement.[16]

With the growth of material and equipment shortages as well as for other reasons, the utilization of GFM and GFE in World War II spread to all of the Army's technical services.[17] In the case of GFE (machine tools and industrial equipment), various kinds of equipment were furnished to contractors, chiefly for Ordnance procurement, under the terms of supply and facility contracts and in conformity with the regulations and procedures for property accountability and cost allocation referred to in an earlier chapter.[18] The GFM procedure, in its simplest and strictest sense, was used primarily by the Army Quartermaster Corps for the purchase of more or less standardized raw materials to be furnished to a variety of contractors producing the same item. The term "GFM" was sometimes used, however, to include contracting by the Army for complex parts, components, and subassemblies to be delivered to specific prime contractors such as aircraft final assembly plants and the huge Ordnance ammunition and shell-loading plants. The GFM procedure, construed in this sense, was widespread throughout Army procurement during World War II. In general, the use of GFM was limited to a relatively few bottleneck situations, where the particular urgency and other specific

factors justified the government's assumption of activities which were normally the responsibility of contractors in private industry.[19]

Broadly speaking, government-furnished materials were supplied under one or the other of two alternative methods: (1) the price discount method, under which the price of the end product to the Army was reduced by the value of freely furnished GFM; (2) outright sale of GFM at a fixed price with no reduction in end-product prices. Intermediate arrangements permitted the sale of GFM at reduced or fixed prices reflected in adjusted end-product prices. Because of the complexities of War Department property accountability regulations, outright sale of GFM was in many instances to be preferred. On the other hand, the loss of control involved in outright sale restricted the use of this method to special types of situations.[20]

Increasing use of GFM and GFE forced widespread changes in the antiquated peacetime property accountability regulations of the War Department. Originally designed to cover the issue of personal and field equipment to troops, the regulations provided for the personal financial liability of accountable officers and frequently prohibited the transfer of property and equipment. The same regulations which made an officer financially liable for the loss of his side-arms or binoculars were at first technically applicable to a contracting officer responsible for vast quantities of supplies and equipment in the possession of contractors or in warehouses remote from his personal supervision. Adequate revision and codification of the regulations governing property accountability were slow in coming and existing rules

[16] Yoshpe, Flow of Materials, pp. 76, 79–80.
[17] Ibid., p. 77.
[18] See above, Chapter XXI, esp. sections on DPC and War Department-owned facilities.

[19] Yoshpe, Flow of Materials, p. 79.
[20] Ibid., pp. 76–78, and sources cited therein.

had to be widely ignored to meet the new urgency. As instances of contractor misappropriation or mishandling of GFM came to light, responsible officials sought a thorough and systematic revision of the regulations. A major revision was initiated on 16 February 1943 by issuance of the War Department Industrial Accounting Manual. This accomplished many reforms, including abolition of time-consuming surveys and reports of losses by military personnel completely unfamiliar with the complexities of the contracts a n d circumstances under which GFM was advanced and used. Sound business practices were substituted for obsolete procedures, and the details of accountability and financial responsibility were made largely a matter of contract terms and administration. Under these conditions, officers accountable for industrial property were made subject to appropriate discipline in lieu of a hypothetical financial liability which was meaningless in view of the pecuniary magnitudes involved. Numerous other changes and revisions before the end of the war served to bring the War Department's accountability regulations into line with the realities of modern procurement practice.[21]

Importation and Stockpiling

During the twenty years of interwar planning the Army and Navy were engaged in the study and recommendation of measures concerning what might have become a major instrument for anticipating and forestalling shortages of basic raw materials vital to the defense of the nation. This was a program for importing and stockpiling, during the favorable conditions of peacetime, strategic materials which were available exclusively or predominantly only from abroad. The experience of World War I had dramatically indicated the unwisdom of delaying the importation of strategic materials until the country was in the stage of large-scale mobilization or actual participation in war. In 1917 and 1918, at the very time when foreign sources of supply were largely cut off, demand for manganese, chrome, vanadium, mercury, tin, and other strategic materials rose to unprecedented levels. The consequent shortages sent prices skyrocketing: ferro-manganese went from $37.50 per ton to $400.00; ferro-vanadium from $2.20 per pound to $5.50; tungsten from $7.50 per unit to $80; tin from 38 cents per pound to $1.10; mercury $38.85 to $125 per flask.[22]

In its extremity the United States in World War I found its ore-bearing ships sunk as they attempted to run the gauntlet of German submarine warfare; scarce and costly shipping facilities, not to mention manpower, were transferred from other badly needed uses to the importation of scarce materials, often to end up at the bottom of the ocean; naval vessels were diverted from other urgent duties to the convoy of strategic materials. In addition to shipping difficulties, foreign sources were often preempted by the preclusive buying of the enemy or made unavailable through lack of internal transportation and production facilities. Thus the United States was obliged to ship coal to Brazil to enable railroad locomotives to bring manganese ore from the interior to the seaboard. At one time consideration was given to the use of airplanes to fly vanadium ore concentrates from the

[21] For further details, see: (1) ASF, History of Purchases Division, pp. 550–52, and sources cited therein; (2) Control Division ASF, Control of Government Furnished Material (draft of proposed ASF manual, 15 August 1945).

[22] Baruch, *American Industry in the War*, pp. 149–64.

interior of Peru to the seacoast.[23] Experiences of this kind later prompted the following observation by a prominent spokesman for the steel industry:

As a matter of national defense in time of need, it seems to me there should be a prohibition on the use of domestic supplies of manganese in peacetime, and preservation of the limited amounts that we have. The Manganese Producers' Association however, would not agree with me on that.[24]

As early as 1921 the War and Navy Departments undertook continued studies looking to the establishment of a program for stockpiling strategic materials. In 1933 the National Resources Board recommended the stockpiling of "deficiency" minerals. After further studies, Congress included the sum of $3½ million for stockpiling purposes in the 1938 Naval Appropriations Act. Additional amounts of $500,000 for the same purpose were authorized in each of the two following years. These funds were used for Navy purchases of manganese, chrome, tin, tungsten, optical glass, and manila fiber.[25]

On 7 June 1939, after recommendations of the ANMB and other agencies, Congress passed the Strategic War Materials Act, which permitted the ANMB to determine the quantities and qualities of materials to be purchased and retained in a military stockpile. Actual appropriations for the purpose were left to future acts of Congress, and until the spring of 1940 totaled only $10 million against earlier ANMB recommendations of between $202 and $690 million. The act itself was hedged with "Buy-American"

limitations. These limitations not only subordinated the Strategic War Materials Act to the Buy-American Act of 1933, but included a special provision allowing domestic producers up to a year to develop and produce, without giving bond for delivery, the needed materials in preference to spot purchases from foreign sources.[26]

Tied down by these restrictions, limited by meager appropriations, and for various other reasons, the ANMB was unable to go forward with a vigorous program and made its actual purchase recommendations cautiously. Moreover by 1940—after a year of war in Europe and with the adoption of the United States own large-scale Munitions Program—the very same difficulties of skyrocketing demand, shortages of ocean shipping, and failures of supply at the source which plagued the United States in World War I had reappeared to cripple preparations for World War II. The Strategic War Materials Act was too inadequate and had come too late to do more than partially realize the objectives of a realistic stockpiling program.[27] All these factors thus combined to nullify interwar planning for a successful importing and stockpiling program.

In order to meet the needs of an across-the-board program of industrial mobilization, Congress on 25 June 1940 passed new legislation providing for large-scale purchases of a wide variety of strategic and critical materials from all available sources.[28] This legislation authorized the establishment

[23] *Ibid.*, pp. 150–51.

[24] Dr. Walter S. Tower, Ex Secy American Iron and Steel Institute, Problems and Trends in the Iron and Steel Industry, 29 Oct 35, AIC Lectures, 12:122½.

[25] ANMB, Report to Congress on Strategic Materials, reproduced in S. Doc. 5, 79th Cong., 1st Sess., 29 Jan 45, p. 5.

[26] (1) 53 Stat. 811, 7 Jun 39, Sec. 5. (2) 47 Stat. 1250, 3 Mar 33, Buy-American Act.

[27] (1) Industrial College of the Armed Forces R78, Stockpiling Activities of the War Department and Other Agencies, 1939–46 (November 1946), ICAF Library. (2) Yoshpe, Flow of Materials, pp. 83–85. (3) Supply Priorities and Allocation Board Report 25. The Stockpiling Program, 7 Oct 41. (4) Truman Committee, Hearings, 42:25675.

[28] 54 *Stat.* 572, 25 Jun 40.

of the Metals Reserve Corporation, a sub-sidiary of RFC, which was given ample funds and adequate powers to obtain ma-terials both for current industrial use and stockpiling purposes. Because of these cir-cumstances, the ANMB stockpiling program under the 1939 act was frozen by agreement at $70 million (the level of total appropri-ations by mid-1940) and was confined to materials indispensable to munitions pro-duction and meeting exacting specifica-tions.[29] The broad objectives to be carried out the Metals Reserve Corporation were determined by NDAC and its successors, OPM and WPB, in consultation with the War and Navy Departments and other agencies of the government. By 1 November 1944, Metals Reserve had purchased some $1.7 billion of strategic and critical materi-als, representing a quantity of 19 million tons, 11.6 million of which were imported from abroad.[30] Although the proportions of purchases going into stockpiles varied widely from commodity to commodity, by far the greater proportion of the program as a whole went into current wartime industrial con-sumption.

With actual stockpiling operations in World War II conducted almost entirely by civilian agencies, the War and Navy Depart-ments once more set about the study and formulation of long range stockpiling ob-jectives. Included in these efforts were the preparation of suitable postwar legislation as well as opposition to various inadequate "stock pile" bills introduced in Congress largely for the benefit of the American min-ing industry.[31] On 2 January 1945, in re-sponse to a requirement in the Surplus Prop-erty Act of 1944, the ANMB submitted to Congress a report and recommendations on postwar stockpile objectives and policy.[32] Attached to the report was a confidential list of the recommended maximum and mini-mum stockpile goals for a long list of stra-tegic and critical materials. In its policy recommendations, the ANMB pointed to the substantial depletion of U.S. mineral re-sources during World War II and the in-creased necessity for relaxing the various Buy-American restrictions of previous legis-lation.

Early in 1946, with the experience of two world wars fresh in mind, Congress under-took to enact new stockpile legislation. The result was the Stockpiling Act of 1946, which replaced its predecessor of 1939.[33] Despite the recommendations of ANMB and despite references in the policy state-ment of the act to the necessity for conserv-ing the deficient resources of the United States, the act retained verbatim the Buy-American restrictions of the prewar legisla-tion. President Harry S. Truman reluctantly signed the act, pointing to the increased costs, the further depletion of America's in-adequate underground reserves, the jeop-ardizing of national security, and the dam-aging effects upon U.S. foreign economic policy—all resulting from the inclusion of the restrictive features.[34]

Conservation of Materials

An important segment of the total pro-gram for increasing the flow of scarce ma-terials to their most important uses was the

[29] ICAF R78, Stockpiling, p. 5.

[30] Charles B. Henderson, Chmn RFC and Presi-dent Metals Reserve Corporation, Report on Activi-ties of Metals Reserve Corporation From 28 June 1940 to 1 November 1944 (mimeographed), p. 35, cited in ICAF R78, Stockpiling, p. 17.

[31] ICAF R78 Stockpiling, p. 9.
[32] Rpt cited above, note 25.
[33] 60 *Stat.* 596, 23 Jul 46.
[34] ICAF R78, Stockpiling, p. 21.

development of direct measures for reducing the consumption of materials in less important uses. The curtailment of relatively nonessential uses of materials for the economy as a whole was the broad responsibility of the War Production Board and its predecessors. Such curtailment was accomplished in general by the various L (limitation) and M (material) orders issued by WPB. These orders contained a wide variety of restrictions, including the reduction or prohibition of the manufacture of specified end products, or the limitation or prohibition of the use of scarce materials for various products and purposes. The terms of L and M orders, especially before Pearl Harbor, usually exempted the military services in whole or in part. Later, with the growing seriousness of material shortages, these exemptions were substantially reduced or eliminated. In practice, the major responsibility for initiating and applying conservation measures to military procurement rested with the services themselves. Not only were the services active in promoting their own conservation measures; frequently these became the prototype or model for similar measures which were extended to the entire economy.[35]

Within the Army, the term "conservation" came to embrace a number of activities all designed to reduce the consumption or waste of scarce materials. These included substitution of more abundant materials, simplification and standardization of procurement end items, improvement of manufacturing processes, more efficient methods of distribution, improved utilization and maintenance of end items, and various reclamation and salvage measures. In addition to these conservation efforts, the Army undertook periodic reviews of its procurement requirements in order to minimize materials consumption when this could be done without jeopardizing military objectives.[36]

Systematic measures for conserving scarce materials were formally adopted by the War Department on 11 June 1941, soon after the material shortage problem had attained prominence and threatened to remain for an indefinite period. At this time the Under Secretary announced the necessity for a comprehensive program of conservation and directed the supply arms to appoint qualified persons to co-ordinate the relevant activities within each service.[37] Two days later a Conservation Section was established within the Commodities Division, OUSW. The function of this office was to direct attention, as needed, to materials requiring conservation measures; to receive and summarize reports from the supply arms; to transmit information on the results of conservation activity to OPM and other interested bodies; and to act in co-operation with OPM, the ANMB, the supply arms and services, and other branches and divisions in OUSW in carrying out conservation measures.[38] Thereafter the Army's organization and procedures for conservation underwent numerous changes.

Throughout the defense and war periods, the Army collaborated with numerous outside agencies in carrying out the program.

---

[35] For a more extensive treatment of the Army's conservation activities in World War II, see: (1) Industrial College of the Armed Service Forces R87, Conservation Within the Army Service Forces During World War II (March 1947), ICAF Library; (2) ASF annual rpts, 1942–45; (3) Yoshpe, Production Control in the QMC, pp. 27–36. See also the volumes of the individual technical services in the series UNITED STATES ARMY IN WORLD WAR II.

[36] ICAF R83, Conservation, p. 2.
[37] Memo, USW Patterson for Chfs of Supply Arms and Services, 11 Jun 41, sub: Conservation of Certain Basic and Semi-finished Materials.
[38] Memo, Gen Hines, Dir Planning Br OUSW, 13 Jun 41, sub: Conservation of Materials.

Among these were the many interested subdivisions of the War Production Board and its predecessor agencies, the Navy Department, Maritime Commission, Petroleum Administration for War, Office of Defense Transportation, Lend-Lease Administration, War Food Administration, National Housing Agency, and the Procurement Division of the Treasury. Continuous liaison was maintained, either by Conservation representatives or through the Research and Development Division, ASF, with scientific and engineering groups such as the National Academy of Science, the American Standards Association, the American Society for Testing Materials, the Society of Automotive Engineers, the National Inventors Council, and the Federal Specifications Board. Likewise, the Army was represented on numerous standing committees organized to deal with specific segments of the nationwide conservation program. Included in these were such diverse groups as the Combined Conservation Committee of the Combined Production and Resources Board, the U.S. Conservation Coordinating Committee, the Iron and Steel Scrap Dealers Industry Advisory Committee, and committees for the die casting industry and waste materials dealers.[39]

The achievements of the War Department's conservation program can be briefly indicated through examples of the major categories of activity in the program. In the realm of substitution heroic efforts were made to change specifications, manufacturing processes, tooling and equipment, and other factors to permit the replacement of scarce materials by those in relatively greater supply. Thus, after extensive experimentation by research laboratories and and contractors, the Army succeeded in developing

steel cartridge casings in place of those made of copper and brass. This was expected to save 600,000,000 pounds of copper by the end of 1943 for artillery cartridge cases alone.[40] Savings of zinc in substituting steel for brass cartridge cases were estimated for the same period at 260,000,000 pounds. The conversion of motor vehicle cargo bodies from steel to wood was expected to save 75,000 tons of steel in 1942 and 350,000 tons in 1943. When all available aluminum was needed for aircraft manufacture, the savings of this metal were calculated at 1.4 million pounds by eliminating aluminum in radio sets; 85 million from Army Quartermaster supplies; 17 million from the substitution of steel or secondary aluminum in fuze production; 35 million from substitution of plastics in another type of fuze; 9 million by replacement of aluminum with steel in searchlights; and so on.[41] The substitution of enamelware for nickel in medical utensils saved 113,000 pounds of that metal in the first six months of 1943. Another 2½ million pounds were to be saved by the end of 1943 from Quartermaster items, and 45 million pounds through substitution in armor plate and armor-piercing shot.[42]

Small items as well as large were scrutinized for possibilities of substitution, since these individually in large volume, and collectively for all the Army's needs, consumed tremendous quantities of materials. Thus the Army "made do" with plastic instead of metal bugles, plastic buttons, plastic insignia, plastic raincoats, plastic identification discs, and other plastic items, ad infinitum. Not infrequently substitute materials adopted under the compulsion of necessity turned out to be superior in many ways to

---

[39] ICAF R87, Conservation, passim.

[40] ASF, Annual Rpt, 1943, p. 77.
[41] (1) ASF Annual Rpt, 1942, p. 23. (2) Ibid., 1943 p. 77.
[42] Ibid. 1943, p. 77.

the ones replaced. Glass gages used to replace steel gages in Ordnance plants were corrosion free, resisted abrasion better, lasted longer, and did not expand so readily from transmitted body heat as steel ones.[43]

Throughout the war, utilization of substitutes was a complex and dynamic program. At any particular time, numerous substitutes for a single material were likely to be found in use depending on the nature of the end item. Thus reclaimed and synthetic rubber were substituted for natural rubber in tires, steel for rubber in tank tracks, and plastic for rubber in raincoats. Also, in some cases "reverse substitution" became desirable as the production of scarce materials soared to unprecedented heights following completion of new facilities. By early 1944, the supply of aluminum and magnesium had grown to such a point that new uses of these metals were actually encouraged.[44]

Cutting across all segments of the War Department's conservation program was the task of revising specifications for military end items. As already indicated, revised specifications were necessary to permit the use of substitute materials. The systematic review of specifications also permitted important material savings by simplification and standardization of end items. In many cases this could be accomplished without sacrifice of performance characteristics; in other cases the loss in performance was unimportant or less important than material savings. Thus the reduction in tread depth and tread radii in rubber tires for Army combat vehicles saved substantial amounts of rubber; the resulting loss in tire mileage was considered not significant in view of combat conditions in overseas theaters.[45]

A corollary of design simplification was the reduction in the number of permitted types or models of procurements items. To insure that simplified designs would serve their purpose it was necessary for the Army to "standardize" designs, eliminating all specifications except those approved on the simplified basis. By mid-1942, when material shortages had reached their peak, 1,200 Army specifications had been revised or approved in accordance with conservation requirements, and 425 had been canceled altogether. By the same time, in collaboration with the National Bureau of Standards, the Army had adopted 17 Simplified Practice Recommendations and 12 Commercial Standards issued by the bureau. Sample achievements of the Army in carrying out its standardization program were the reduction of 44 specifications for chests and tool boxes to 1; 87 models of small gasoline engines to 47; 63 models of engine-driven generators to 14; 21 trailer-chassis models to 15; 170 color standards to 72; 26 types of waterproof ignition oil to 1.[46] In order further to reduce the total number of outstanding procurement specifications, the Army in late 1942 undertook a long-range program of collaboration with the Navy in the formulation of Joint Army-Navy Specifications (JANS). By early 1945 some 155 JANS had been formally adopted. The official adoption on a modest scale in World War II of consolidated specifications for the Army and Navy marked the beginning of a program with profound possibilities for the improvement of future procurement practices of the armed services.[47]

In the important area of construction, enormous savings were accomplished by the

---

[43] *Ibid.*, 1943, p. 77.
[44] ASF Annual Rpt, 1944, p. 144.
[45] *Ibid.*, 1943, pp. 71–72.

[46] (1) *Ibid.*, 1942, p. 19. (2) *Ibid.*, 1943, p. 77.
[47] Rpt, Col Draper and Capt Strauss, Co-ordination of Procurement Between the War and Navy Departments, I, 34–35; II, 85–115.

flat prohibition, subject to individual appeals, of the use of numerous scarce materials. This policy was announced in ANMB Priorities Instructions of 18 February 1942. To carry out the policy the ANMB on 1 April 1942 issued the first edition of the List of Prohibited Items for Construction Work. The list, which was amended from time to time and widely circulated throughout the Army and elsewhere, was an important instrument in the application of the Directive for Wartime Construction, approved on 20 May 1942 by the Army and Navy Secretaries and the chairman of the War Production Board.[48] The list was used not only by the Army and Navy but also by the War Production Board and the Defense Plant Corporation in screening and "stripping" applications for approval of construction projects. The prohibitions in question forced the development and use of substitute materials on a wide scale, thus serving the same purpose as design simplification and other such techniques in eliminating need for critical materials.[49]

Improved manufacturing p r o c e s s e s brought substantial savings of scarce materials as well as other benefits. These were conceived largely by civilian employees in the production establishments of government and private contractors. Originating in engineering departments as well as on the production line, these improvements were often adopted as a result of employees' suggestion systems sponsored or encouraged by the War Department and the War Production Board. Although frequently motivated by the need for materials conservation, the improvements typically had beneficial results far wider in scope. Many millions of man- and machine-hours, as well as materials, were saved, and—often of even greater importance—delivery of badly needed munitions and equipment for the Army was speeded. For example, a new method of producing adapter boosters for Army Ordnance made use of built-up stampings instead of machining from bar stock. This saved 1,800,000 machine hours in addition to 23,000,000 pounds of steel.[50] Illustrations of this type could be multiplied by the thousands through an examination of the wartime suggestion system files in both government and private establishments.

Improvements in distribution included a countless variety of techniques and procedures for locating and making available to producers idle or unused materials and equipment, expediting shipment of materials and end products, revising methods of packing and packaging to reduce breakage and wastage, and so on. In collaboration with the War Production Board the Army prepared and circularized lists of idle equipment and materials to war contractors, and engaged in many activities for the redistribution of all types of property in furtherance of the war effort.[51] Major revolutions in transportation and shipping procedures were effected by the War Department independently or in collaboration with other agencies. For example, Army construction and supply contracts normally provided for payment for materials based on "railroad weights." This meant the weight as recorded on railroad track-scales, a facility not readily or universally available during peak operations. In order to eliminate frequent backhauling and delays incident to railroad weighing, the War Department in 1942 en-

---

[48] See above, pages 447–48.

[49] For additional detail, see ICAF R87, Conservation, Ch. VII, Conservation in Construction, pp. 66–7, 76.

[50] ASF Annual Rpt, 1942, p. 23.

[51] (1) PR 7, Disposition of Property. (2) ASF Annual Rpt, 1943, Redistribution and Salvage, pp. 79–80.

tered agreements with certain carriers to accept shippers' weights as administered by territorial weighing bureaus. Eventually the specification of "railroad weights" was forbidden in contracts for all supplies and materials, including coal.[52]

Very large savings were effected by the development of protective packaging for the prevention of rust, corrosion, and other damage to finished items of equipment. It was estimated that improved packaging reduced damage to overseas shipments by 50 percent. In addition to measures for the protection of finished items containing scarce materials, new packing techniques by mid-1943 had effected savings in shipping space equivalent to requirements for 10 percent of total Army overseas shipments. During the first half of 1943 the redesign of shipping boxes was said to have saved 75,000 tons of shipping space, equal to the capacity of eight Liberty ships. This development was at a time when the shortage of steel was a matter of grave concern and steel requirements for ship construction was a major item of controversy.[53]

As a part of its conservation program as well as in furtherance of other objectives, the Army trained its personnel both in and out of uniform in the proper handling, use, and preservation of equipment and supplies of all kinds. This ran the gamut from the care of rifles to the conservation of food, and from the operation of huge pieces of industrial equipment to the maintenance of typewriters. Elaborate repair and maintenance organizations were established

throughout the zone of the interior and in overseas theaters, and rigid requirements were established for the periodical inspection, maintenance, overhaul, and rebuilding of equipment. The magnitude of these operations is suggested by partial statistics available for the latter part of the war. The Army's "fifth echelon" repair shops (operating under the technical services for the rebuilding of unserviceable equipment) returned to service approximately $2 billion of unserviceable material and equipment in the twenty-month period 1 January 1944 through 31 August 1945. In the last twelve months of the same period, Army "fourth echelon" maintenance (replacement of unserviceable parts and assemblies, primarily under service command jurisdiction) restored approximately $4 billion in material. During this time the Army employed, on an average, 48,200 and 24,500 persons respectively in its fourth and fifth echelon maintenance establishments.[54]

A still further effort by the Army to conserve scarce materials was reflected in its diverse salvage operations. Closely related to redistribution and maintenance, and functioning as an integral part of the War Production Board's nationwide salvage program, Army salvage operations grew from negligible beginnings in the defense period to the equivalent of an important industry by the end of the war. During the extensive scrap drives of 1942 the Army streamlined its contracting methods for the sale of scrap and obsolete and surplus equipment, and ordered its establishments to ferret out all possible supplies of such material. Obsolete guns, mortars, vehicles, and other matériel

[52] PR 1182 (8–31–44). (2) WD Cir 284, 25 Aug 42.

[53] ASF Annual Rpt, 1943, pp. 77–78. Changes in packing and packaging were also made to reduce the consumption of scarce packing materials and to permit the substitution of other materials for this purpose. Risch, QMC Supply, I, pp. 202–06.

[54] (1) Control Div ASF, Statistical Review, World War II, pp. 9–10. (2) ASF Annual Rpt, 1944, Ch. 16, Maintenance Service, pp. 273–80. (3) Ibid., 1945, pp. 254–58.

at Army posts were turned in for scrap. Kitchen waste at posts, camps and stations was salvaged and sold under standardized procedures. Crate-fastening methods were revised in order to permit the maximum salvage of lumber. With the growth in overseas shipments and operations, an increasing volume of salvage was recovered from overseas theaters. Thousands of tons of fired cartridge cases, the tracks of tanks and half-trucks, lumber, and wide varieties of scrapped equipment were recovered. Long before V-E Day the return from overseas of all types of property—scrap, repairable, and surplus equipment—had reached mountainous proportions. The salvage centers earlier established in eastern and coastal service commands for the segregation of salvage, gave way in September 1944 to ASF Classification Depots created to serve each major port of embarkation. These depots separated all returned property into appropriate classes under the three main categories of "serviceable," "repairable," and "salvage". After V-E Day the classification depots at eastern seaboards were abolished after overseas theaters were able to handle their own classification and repair operation.[55]

It is evident that the conservation activities of the Army, together with those in other sectors of the nation's economy, were an indispensable ingredient in the solution of material shortage problems in World War II. No amount of rational apportionment of scarce materials—through priorities, CMP, and other allocation devices— would insure the adequacy of supply in the absence of direct measures, such as described above, to prevent major leakages and loss.

[55] (1) ASF Annual Rpts, 1942, p. 21; 1943, pp. 79–80; 1944, pp. 130, 144; 1945, pp. 245–46. (2) PR 7, Disposition of Property.

PART SEVEN

CONTRACT TERMINATION AND SETTLEMENT

CHAPTER XXVII

Contract Termination: Background and Preparations

Nature and Implications of Contract Termination

During World War II the Army canceled thousands of its procurement contracts because of reductions in estimated requirements, obsolescence of particular items, more important demands upon a contractor's facilities, and for other reasons.[1] Beginning with a mere handful of cancellations prior to Pearl Harbor, terminations began to assume importance in 1942. In the summer of 1943, when procurement deliveries attained peak rates, there was a rapid increase in cancellations, and by the fall of 1944—with the approach of victory in Europe—the problem of widespread terminations had become a major concern of the War Department. Toward the end of 1944 the sudden increase in requirements associated with the Battle of the Bulge caused a substantial decline in the number of terminations. But shortly thereafter, from the collapse of German resistance in the spring of 1945 until V-J Day, contract termination and its associated problems became the number one item of business for all the procurement agencies as well as for the entire business community. Before V-J Day arrived, the War Department had canceled 59,000 of its ultimately terminated 135,000 World War II prime contracts. On V-J Day alone 48,000 contracts were terminated, and during the following year the War Department continued to be actively engaged in liquidating its tremendous war procurement program.[2]

Contract termination and its associated procedures represented the core of the process of Army materiel demobilization. This process may be summed up as the resolution of three broad groups of problems: (1) problems connected with the decision to terminate contracts; (2) problems dealing with the settlement of terminated contracts; (3) problems involving the disposition of war

---

[1] The termination of a war contract (not to be confused with contract completion) involves the cancellation of all remaining work under the contract at some stage prior to completion.

[2] Two valuable studies of contract termination in World War II are: (1) Office of Contract Settlement, A History of War Contract Terminations and Settlements (July 1947), 84 pp. including 19 pages of bibliography (hereafter cited as OCS, History). This was prepared by Reynold Bennett, later of the Legal Office, OCofOrd. (2) "War Contract Termination," Law and Contemporary Problems, X, No. 3 (Winter 1944), 427–560, and No. 4 (Spring 1944), 561–696. This study was published by the Duke University School of Law and consists of a dozen articles on the subject written by actual participants in the termination problem at the time of the drafting and passage of the Contract Settlement Act. The principal article in the series is the richly documented "Policies and Procedures for the Termination of War Contracts," pp. 449–517, by Leon Malman, then chief of the Legal Unit, Contract Termination Section, OCofOrd.

matériel. A brief consideration of each of these affords some indication of the nature and complexity of the issues concerned.

The decision to terminate a particular contract during World War II was the end result of many prior decisions. First of all were decisions concerning military requirements. Changes in military strategy, the progress of the war, the development of new and improved items of procurement, the accumulation of adequate reserves, and many other considerations dictated cutbacks in the procurement of particular items or of broad classes of matériel. After a decision to effect cutbacks, many complex questions had to be decided. Should the contracts of the least efficient producers be terminated completely and all remaining production be concentrated in the most efficient plants? Or should all contracts be proportionately reduced by partial termination? Should the Army base its cutback decisions only on its own direct interests such as economy of procurement, quality of output, security considerations, maintenance of reserve capacity, and the like? Or should it adjust its termination policy to reflect the existence of labor shortage and unemployment areas, problems of transportation and crosshauling, the needs of small business, the demands of regional and local groups, civilian consumption requirements, reconversion issues, and other matters of broad postward policy? A moment's consideration will indicate that all the diverse and controversial issues which entered into the formation of contract placement policy earlier in the war inevitably entered into cutback and termination policy. Thus the whole area of contract termination was aptly described during the latter half of World War II as "procurement in reverse," signifying that the majority of problems encountered during the expansion of procurement would have their counterparts during the contraction of the procurement process.

The second broad group of problems concerned the terms and procedures for the settlement of terminated contracts. What should the Army pay to a producer of tanks whose $300 million contract was canceled after only a third of the items had been completed and whose plant was bulging with special machinery, materials, parts, subassemblies, and tanks in various stages of completion? Should the tank producer, for the loss of his bargain, be allowed in addition to all his costs the total profit orginally contemplated when the contract was let? This would be his right under common law in the absence of an agreement to the contrary. But could the government in good conscience pay out hundreds of millions in profits for work not done while American soldiers were giving their lives for $50 per month? What legal basis, if any, did the government have for paying a less amount, and how should such lower amount be determined? How should the tank producer compensate his four hundred immediate subcontractors for the termination of their contracts following the termination of the prime? Should he be allowed to negotiate whatever settlement he could with his subs and pass the charges on to the government? And what about the thousands of sub-subcontractors, extending all the way down the chain of production, whose contracts in turn must be wholly or partially terminated and settled? The consequences of the termination of just one large prime contract by the War Department could produce ramifications whose unraveling might well run into years of auditing, negotiation, correspondence, and debate without producing a final settlement. It is small wonder that the War Department, with over a hundred thousand outstanding prime contracts in the middle of 1943, became gravely concerned over the prospect of mass terminations at the end of the war.

But the problem of defining the precise terms for the settlement of war contracts was subordinate to an even larger consideration—the task of insuring the transition of the American economy from wartime to peacetime operation with the utmost dispatch and smoothness. The vast majority of war producers operated primarily on borrowed capital, often many times the amount of their peacetime capitalization. A sudden cancellation of contracts would find them with both their fixed and working capital tied up in war plant, equipment, and inventories of raw materials and goods in process. With their operating income closed off, they could not maintain their swollen payrolls unless adequate interim financing and prompt settlement were forthcoming. The alternative to such measures would be mass unemployment which might well wreck the reconversion effort and precipitate a prolonged depression. The resulting economic chaos and loss in national income might well be of far graver damage to the economy and to the government itself than any probable losses incurred through overpayment in rapid contract settlement or nonrepayment of generous termination loans. It was this general background which made prompt settlement and adequate financial assistance the keynote of contract termination policy for World War II.

The third broad group of problems comprising the process of contract termination dealt with the difficult and delicate tasks involved in the disposition of war matériel. At the time of contract termination a contractor's plant would typically be stocked with wartime equipment, machinery, raw materials, purchased parts, and partially fabricated goods in all stages of production. Most of this would have relatively little peacetime value and its prompt removal was prerequisite to a rearrangement of the plant and the resumption of peacetime production. But in the absence of alternative arrangements, this wartime inventory would belong to the government upon settlement of the contract. Prompt plant clearance would thus depend upon prompt decisions on the part of military contracting officers overburdened with the task of liquidating mass terminations at the end of the war. Upon the contracting officer and his staff would fall the principal burden of making specific decisions in response to specific questions concerning the disposition of each and every item of inventory. Should a given item be scrapped, salvaged, retained by the government for possible future use, sold to the contractor, or placed on the open market? And for each item of equipment, machinery, raw material, purchased part, or partially fabricated product, what was a fair value upon which to base any or all of these decisions? What about the major problems of nationwide economic policy involved in the disposition of surplus materials of all kinds, whether in the hands of contractors, in government depots, arsenals, and warehouses in the United States, or overseas? To what extent should the government be interested in the financial returns from property disposals and to what extent in other—often mutually conflicting—objectives such as quick sale and disposal, prevention of profiteering by speculators and middlemen, and preservation of future markets for established producers?

Finally, what of the broad issues in the sale and subsequent operation of billions of dollars' worth of complete industrial establishments created for World War II? Should the government be willing to sell virtually new plant and equipment for as little as thirty cents on the dollar in order to speed reconversion, and to allay the fears of those who saw in government ownership a threat to established institutions? Or should it hold on indefinitely to its multi-billion-dollar industrial empire in order to recoup a maximum of costs and prevent private interests from making a "killing." What steps should the government take to insure that plant disposal would not further augment the concentration of industrial ownership and power?

All these problems and many more were of such magnitude and importance that only Congress could properly establish the basic policies governing their final resolution. Yet Congress would have to rely heavily on the procuring and mobilization-control agencies for the information and recommendations essential to the establishment of basic policy. Fortunately for the national economy, these agencies were better prepared to advise Congress and to discharge the tasks of contract administration than had been the case at the conclusion of World War I.

Evolution of Contract Settlement Policy

The Liquidation of
World War I Contracts

The armistice of 11 November 1918 found the United States ill prepared to meet the problems of economic demobilization. America's entry into World War I a year and a half earlier had found the nation similarly unprepared for mobilization, and the bulk of supplies for U.S. troops abroad was actually furnished by its allies. By the end of the war, the United States had barely completed the tooling-up stage of mobilization

and many of its contracts had been let within a month or two of the armistice. As a consequence responsible officials had devoted little thought to termination problems and to the development of the necessary organizations and procedures. Perhaps most significant of all, they saw little relation between the liquidation of war contracts and the problems of postwar adjustment. Contract termination and its associated problems were thus regarded largely as a matter of governmental housekeeping and budgeting.[3]

After the armistice, the complexities of the termination problem were soon revealed as the War Department and other agencies proceeded to cancel or suspend their procurement contracts. Only a portion of the contracts provided for termination at the government's convenience and there was little uniformity in the termination clauses. Some contracts, let under the terms of appropriation acts which specified the termination privilege, were deemed to contain the clause by implication. Many others were

---

[3] The present brief sketch merely presents a few of the highlights of the World War I contract termination problem. For additional information, see the following selections and sources cited therein: (1) I. J. Gromfine and J. Donald Edwards, "Termination After World War I," *Law and Contemporary Problems* (Duke University School of Law), X, No. 4 (Spring 1944), 563–93; (2) Stuart Portner and Victor Gondos, Jr., Preliminary Checklist of the Records of the War Department Claims Board, 1918–22 (February 1943, 105 pp.), National Archives PC 43–22; (3) Problems of Contract Termination, Letter and Supplementary Material From the Secretary of Labor to the Subcommittee on War Contract Termination of the Committee on Military Affairs, U.S. Senate, November 20, 1943, 78th Cong., 1st Sess., Subcommittee Report (Committee Print), 1944 (148 pp.) (hereafter cited as Labor Dept, Problems of Contract Termination); (4) J. Harry La Brum, "Termination of War Contracts for the Government's Convenience," *Temple University Law Quarterly*, XVIII, No. 1 (December 1943), 1–60; (5) OCS History, App. B, Bibliography and Legislation–World War I, pp. 66–69.

covered by no termination provision whatever; it was thus necessary for the War Department to "suspend" such contracts and negotiate supplemental agreements to settle the contractors' claims. If negotiation failed, the contracts were held to have been breached and settlement was left to litigation. To add to the difficulties, a substantial volume of procurement had been obtained under oral or other informal arrangements later declared to lack a valid governmental commitment. Special legislation was required to validate such commitments and furnish a basis for settlement.[4]

The War Department in November 1918 thus found itself with doubtful authority to terminate many of its contracts; without organizational machinery to process contractors' claims; without established criteria for effecting settlement; and, as subsequent events painfully demonstrated, without authority to effect a binding settlement. Of the thirty thousand termination claims presented by contractors for World War I, over three thousand were appealed to the Court of Claims alone. These appeals "averaged three and one half years for final settlement; many represent masterpieces of dragged-out litigation." [5]

As if the problems of legislation, administration, and litigation growing out of World War I terminations were not enough to discourage all concerned there was added—three and a half years after the end of the war—a fourth category: investigation. A preliminary inquiry by a Congressional committee led Congress in May 1922 to appropriate $500,000 to be spent by the Attorney General for the investigation and punishment of war frauds. On 20 July 1922, a War Transactions Section in the Department of Justice was created for this purpose. The activities of this group have been succinctly described in the following words:

For almost four years this unit busied itself with a wholesale reexamination of war contract settlements. In February of 1923, when the inquisition movement reached its climax, it joined forces with the War Department in the form of a Joint Board of Survey. The group was established to examine literally *all* war transactions in the War Department which had not hitherto been audited or reported to the War Transactions Section.[6]

Failing to find more than a handful of cases of outright fraud, the War Transactions Section concentrated its efforts chiefly on the recovery of money paid out in what it considered overgenerous settlements or in other cases where recovery was technically possible. These efforts were facilitated by previous rulings of the Supreme Court that the government was not bound by mistakes of its officers, even in the absence of fraud. At the end of its four years of activity, the section had recovered about $13 million against its own expenditures of $2½ million. During the same period, only 37 fraud indictments had been returned with 2 convictions and 2 pleas of guilty.[7]

Available statistics indicate that total War Department contract commitments for

---

[4] This was accomplished by the Dent Act (40 *Stat.* 1272), approved 2 March 1919. In the meantime, by virtue of a decision of the Comptroller of the Treasury, the Secretary of War "was powerless to make any payments for uncompleted items on any of the contracts which fell short of the formal requirements of the Law." La Brum "Termination of War Contracts," p. 12. This caused substantial hardship to many contractors who found their working capital tied up in materials and partly finished goods. More than 7,000 claims were subsequently filed under the Dent Act.

[5] Gromfine and Edwards, "Termination After World War I," p. 586. The Bethlehem Steel case was not finally settled until after Pearl Harbor.

[6] *Ibid.*, p. 588.

[7] Final Report of the War Transactions Section (30 June 1926), cited in *ibid.*

World War I amounted to $22 billion. By
the time of the armistice $14.5 billion in de-
liveries had been made, leaving some 30,000
uncompleted contracts with a face value of
$7.5 billion. Of these, approximately $1½
billion were approved for completion, leaving $6 billion to be canceled. In the 25-day
period following the armistice cancellation
plans were delayed, a circumstance which
helped to ease the impact. During this
period, $2 billion in additional procurement
deliveries were made. At the time of abrupt
cancellation early in December, the uncompleted portion of canceled contracts
totaled about $4 billion. Against this
amount, claims of around $700 million were
filed and were subsequently settled for $530
million.[8]

Although there was some difference of
opinion by the outbreak of World War II as
to the efficiency and equity with which
World War I terminations had been settled,
the predominant recollection was one of
widespread unpreparedness, confusion, delay, litigation, and even inequity.[9] This general impression early in World War II was
a strong factor in the determination on the
part of the various war agencies and of interested members of Congress to plan for termination well in advance and thereby to

avoid a repetition of the "failure" of World
War I.[10]

Development of the
Negotiated Settlement

Contract termination played little or no
part in the peacetime procurement activities
of the War Department. Under the limited
budgets of the interwar period, purchases
were carefully planned and made only for
necessary supplies. Hence, there was little
occasion for cutting off work prior to full
contract completion. Nevertheless, to provide for sudden changes in specifications and
requirements for complex items such as aircraft, OASW in 1927 promulgated for optional use a termination article for "technical material and supplies." This provision
was little used and made no contribution to
the drafting of a wartime termination article to be employed on a large scale.[11]

In contrast to the situation in current procurement, the preparation of an adequate
termination article was a major concern of
procurement planners responsible for devel-

---

[8] (1) Labor Dept, Problems of Contract Termination, p. 61. (2) La Brum, "Termination of War
Contracts," p. 4.

[9] Gromfine and Edwards, "Termination After
World War I," *passim.* A common rumor widely circulated early in World War II was that contractors
in World War I had received "only 14 cents on the
dollar" for their terminated contracts, the implication being that they were out of pocket for the bulk
of their expenditures. Actually they received in the
neighborhood of 75 percent of their claims, which
in many cases were heavily padded. The 14-percent
figure referred to the ratio of total payments to the
commitment value of the uncompleted portion of
terminated contracts, a completely meaningless
figure for judging the equity of settlements.

[10] Attorney General Francis Biddle, testifying in
1943 before a Senate Military Affairs subcommittee,
indicated that World War I settlements were well
handled. *Hearings on S. J. Res. 80,* 9 Nov 43, 5:344.
See also La Brum, "Termination of War Contracts,"
pp. 17–18 and references. A favorable estimate of
the speed and equity of World War I settlements
is made by Mr. Mark A. Brown, Vice President,
Harris Trust and Savings Bank and member of
the War Department Purchase Policy Advisory
Committee, in Leverett S. Lyon, *et al., Your Business and Postwar Readjustment* (Chicago: The
University of Chicago Press, 1944), pp. 45–47. Mr.
Brown pointed out that only 995 claims out of
27,000 terminations remained unsettled by 1 July
1920. Further, in the celebrated Bethlehem case
settled finally in 1942, the contractor had long since
been compensated for his costs and fixed fee; the
only unsettled issue was a disputed incentive payment to the contractor.

[11] (1) AR 5–140. (2) ASF, History of Purchases
Division, p. 287 and Exhibit 46.

oping wartime contracting policy.[12] During the 1920's and 1930's the draftsmen of war contract forms included termination provisions in their proposals.[13] In September 1939, OASW announced six approved contract forms to take care of most procurement situations and each of these contained a termination clause.[14] But the use of these forms was not mandatory and the various supply arms and services tended either to use their own termination articles or to omit termination provisions entirely from fixed price contracts. The uniform CPFF supply contract promulgated by OASW in August 1940 contained a standard termination article providing for government assumption of all of the contractor's obligations.[15] But for most of the defense period—during which procurement activity expanded tremendously—there was no standard termination article in use in War Department fixed-price contracts.

This deficiency was rectified in October 1941 when Under Secretary Patterson made mandatory the inclusion of a termination article in all standard fixed-price contracts.[16] The article provided for termination at the convenience of the government and settlement in accordance with a formula. The formula required payment of the contract price for all completed items; for the uncompleted portion of the contract the contractor

was to be paid all costs plus a profit allowance for work actually done. The profit allowance was to be made at the same percentage rate that would have been realized on the entire contract. This became the standard War Department termination article and was later embodied in the first issue of Procurement Regulations on 1 July 1942.[17]

Up until the spring of 1942 terminations, heretofore merely incidents in the expanded procurement program, were handled largely by contracting officers in the field as part of their responsibility for contract administration. With America's entry into war on 7 December 1941, the nation's attention was focused on the task of obtaining maximum production and there was properly no great concern with the problem of mass terminations at the end of the war—perhaps five, perhaps ten, years hence. But a development in April 1942 forcibly brought to the attention of the War Department the fact that large terminations in increasing number would soon become a major wartime problem and that failure to handle them satisfactorily might well play havoc with wartime procurement. At this time the Ordance Department found it necessary to cancel $7,-000,000 in contracts for a certain item before actual production had begun.[18] The plant and facilities involved were badly needed by a different contractor for the production of another critical war item. In attempting to arrange prompt settlement and

---

[12] See above, pages 70 ff.

[13] ASF, History of Purchases Division, p. 288.

[14] Short forms for simple or small purchases merely provided for equitable settlement by "the Chief of the Branch concerned." Long forms provided for settlement by formula similar to that in the 1927 article for technical material. ASF, History of Purchases Division, p. 288.

[15] Ibid. Termination of CPFF contracts did not, however, pose the pricing difficulties encountered in fixed-price terminations.

[16] This was a feature of War Department Supply Contract No. 1, announced on 13 October 1941.

[17] PR 324.

[18] The account of the Ordnance Department's difficulties in the settlement of this termination and its role in the development of the negotiated type of settlement is presented by Lt. Col. Harold Shepherd, "Settlement of Ordnance Contracts," Army Ordnance Association Report (Army Ordnance Association, Washington, D. C.), Vol. 2 (August 9, 1943). See also, Malman, "Policies and Procedures for the Termination of War Contracts," pp. 462–63.

clear the plant the Ordnance Department ran into serious difficulties. The wording of the formula settlement in the recently adopted termination article required the contracting officer to certify that all costs reimbursed in settlement were actually incurred by the contractor. Few contracting officers, faced with personal liability for overpayment, would be willing to make such a broad certification without the protection of a detailed audit even though the over-all terms of the settlement were clearly favorable to the government. Moreover, the Comptroller General took the position that, if a contract contained a formula for settlement, the formula would have to be adhered to unless it could be shown that an alternative settlement was more advantageous to the government, in which case the General Accounting Office would require satisfactory demonstration that the costs of performance allowed the contractor were actually incurred by him. This defeated the major purpose of an alternative method of settlement, since proof of a more advantageous alternative would first require an audit under the formula.[19]

The Comptroller General had always possessed the authority to audit all expenditures under cost-plus-a-fixed-fee contracts and to disallow questionable items. Contractors had no reason to complain, on principle, of CPFF audits since the government under CPFF contracts was required to reimburse contractors for expenditures rather than for procurement deliveries. But under a fixed-price contract the contractor merely agreed to deliver a specified product for a specified sum. His costs were tra-

ditionally his own business and he kept his books accordingly. Under the novel and urgent conditions of all-out conversion and production for war, he had neither the time nor the occasion for meticulous documentation of each transaction and operation, and his books were typically not devised to facilitate detailed audit procedures. The worst fears of the Ordnance Department in this connection were confirmed when a preliminary survey of the $7 million Ordnance cancellation disclosed it would take nine months for a staff of fifteen auditors working full time to make a 100-percent audit that would rigorously satisfy the formula and stand up to General Accounting Office review.[20]

Realizing that its termination problems had just begun and that it would be physically impossible to carry on a procurement program and at the same time effect settlements according to a detailed formula, the Ordnance Department, through its Legal Branch and in consultation with OUSW and the Purchases Division, ASF, undertook the creation of a plan which would protect the government's interest, permit prompt and final settlement, and still satisfy all the legal requirements. Out of these efforts there emerged the plan for a *negotiated* settlement between the government and the contractor. Such a settlement would represent a merger and compromise of all claims and counterclaims under the contract and

---

[19] The Comptroller General's position was formalized in his opinion B–28750, 1 October 1942, similar to a ruling of his predecessor, the Comptroller of the Treasury, in connection with World War I contracts. 25 Comp. Dec. 398, 25 Nov 18.

[20] Shepherd, "Settlement of Ordnance Contracts," p. 4. Malman cites another case, involving some 3,300 claims through the third tier of subcontractors for which an estimated 13,440 man-days would be required to complete a detailed audit. This was the equivalent of 50 men working 11 months. Selective audit procedures considered adequate to protect the government's interest in a negotiated settlement for this case would require only five men working four months. Malman, "Policies and Procedures for the Termination of War Contracts," p. 462, n. 64.

would become, in the form of an amendment, a part of the contract itself. This procedure was founded in well-established principles of common law and appeared to be permissible for the procuring agencies even without the benefit of the First War Powers Act and related Executive orders.[21] A negotiated settlement would have the virtue of both speed and finality, since it would be no more subject to General Accounting Office review than an original contract price fixed by the contracting parties.

Provision for a negotiated settlement of all War Department terminations was approved by the Under Secretary and in November 1942 was officially incorporated in Procurement Regulations. The standard termination article set forth in the regulations was modified to call for settlement by payment to the contractor of "such sum as the Contracting Officer and the Contractor may agree by Supplemental Agreement is reasonably necessary to compensate the Contractor for his costs, expenditures, liabilities, commitments and work in respect to the uncompleted portion of the contract." [22] If the contractor and contracting officer failed to agree within ninety days after termination, or a longer agreed period, the contracting officer was directed to make settlement in accordance with the formula previously available. The new regulations urged maximum use of the principle of negotiation by all War Department agencies and a direc-

tive by the Under Secretary made it clear that all outstanding War Department contracts could be amended by agreement with the contractor, *even after termination,* to provide for settlement by negotiation.[23]

Background and Passage of the Contract Settlement Act

The adoption of the negotiated settlement by the War Department marked a major step forward in its handling of termination problems. But it was only a first step and numerous additional problems were presented as the war progressed toward its conclusion. The acceptance of the principle of negotiation was, by itself, an inadequate guide to contracting officers in devising actual terms of a satisfactory settlement. The formula adopted in 1941 offered general guidance but needed much elaboration to cover important problems of even relatively simple settlements. Moreover, the desirability of allowing the services to negotiate binding settlements was soon severely challenged, and it eventually became clear that extensive new legislation would be needed to resolve the issue and to make firm provision for many other elements of termination policy.

As early as the spring of 1942 the War Production Board became interested in contract termination policy. At that time the Procurement Policy Branch, WPB, appointed a subcommittee including representatives of the procuring agencies to work on the development of a uniform termination article and regulations for all agencies. The meetings of the subcommittee served to advance the thinking of all concerned but

---

[21] In addition to the fact that contract settlement by negotiation had long been sanctioned in common law, it was held by both the Attorney General and the War Department Judge Advocate General to be specifically authorized for government war contracts by the First War Powers Act (18 December 1941) and Executive Order 9001 (27 December 1941). (1) 40 Op. Atty. Gen. 225, 29 Aug 42. (2) Opinion of the Judge Advocate General (SPJGC 164) dated 18 Dec 1942.

[22] PR 324.1 (c).

[23] Memo, USW for CG ASF, 8 May 43, reproduced in Shepherd, "Settlement of Ordnance Contracts," p. 3.

led to no definitive agreement and the committee was disbanded after a year of labor.[24] All members had agreed on the desirability of settlement by negotiation and the provision of adequate interim financing to contractors. But the War Production Board representatives felt that over-all control of termination settlements should be lodged in a civilian agency, a matter that the services were not yet willing to concede in view of the intimate relationship between current terminations and wartime procurement. The chief stumbling block to agreement, however, appeared to be differences between the Army and Navy on the length of the termination article and the basis for calculating the contractor's profit in settlement of cases under the formula after failure of negotiations. The Navy wished to include a definition of termination costs specifically or by reference in each contract whereas the Army preferred to leave this matter to a joint regulation. For settlements under the formula the Navy held fast to a flat 6-percent profit rate for work actually done on the uncompleted portion of the contract, while the Army preferred a flexible arrangement permitting the rate of profit contemplated for the contract as a whole at the time of placement.[25]

The Army's opposition to the flat-rate profit allowance rested on both equitable and practical grounds. A 6-percent guarantee would provide a windfall to inefficient producers currently operating at a loss or at much less than 6 percent; it would penalize efficient producers currently earning

much more than 6 percent and would discourage the amendment of profitable contracts to include the new termination article; it would make no distinction between profits on unprocessed raw materials and parts on the one hand, and extensively processed materials on the other, thus penalizing the contractor who had done substantial processing and rewarding the accumulation of idle raw material inventories; finally, it would tend to be used by contracting officers as a norm for establishing the rate of profit on negotiated settlements.[26]

In the meantime, the War Department was faced with an increasing number of terminations which called for definite policy decisions. Contracting officers and technical service headquarters were embarrassed by the degree of latitude arising from lack of specific regulations. The technical services began to develop their own organizations, forms, procedures, and policies which tended to diverge not only from service to service but sometimes within a single service. Industry complained of the duplication of effort involved when two or more procuring agencies or services made separate audits of a firm's books in connection with the termination of numerous individual contracts. Contractors were slow in presenting termination claims, partly for lack of established procedures, party out of reluctance to consummate settlements which might later be reopened, and partly because of inertia or preoccupation with production under other war contracts.[27]

---

[24] (1) CPA, *Industrial Mobilization for War*, p. 655. (2) OCS History, p. 8. (3) WPB, Procurement Policy Board, Doc. 115, 14 Sep 43, and attached longer version of proposed WPB termination regulation for fixed-price supply contracts, dated 21 Sep 43.

[25] ASF, History of Purchases Division, pp. 293–96.

[26] Memo, Maj Gen Arthur H. Carter, Fiscal Dir, for Dir of Materiel ASF, 18 Nov 43, sub: Proposed Army-Navy Joint Termination Article.

[27] (1) War Department, Bureau of Public Relations, Press Branch, Release, 28 Sep 43, Report on Contract Termination, delivered by Gen Browning, Dir Purchases Div ASF, at WD Conf of Industry, Labor, and Newspaper Leaders, 28 Sep 43, Wash-

The first step in bringing a degree of order into the picture was the publication of War Department TM–320, the Termination Accounting Manual for Fixed-Price Supply Contracts, often referred to as TAM.[28] Although issued by the Office of Fiscal Director primarily as an accounting aid, TAM was a fairly comprehensive guide to both contractors and contracting officers in matters of substance as well as procedure in the settlement of terminated contracts. Shortly thereafter, on 14 August 1943, a new termination section (PR 15) was added to Procurement Regulations, setting forth termination and settlement procedure in detail and supplanting in general the previous provisions of PR 324 contained in the basic section on contracts (PR 3).

A major development at this time was the establishment on 22 June 1943 of the Contract Termination Branch, Purchases Division, ASF.[29] The creation of this branch was designed to provide top-level policy formation and staff supervision of all termination activities of the War Department. As in the case of renogotiation, the director of the Purchases Division was made Special Representative of the Under Secretary of War when dealing with the Air Forces. The Contract Termination Branch immediately set about the task of obtaining more rapid settlement of outstanding terminations and of providing a regular flow of adequate statistics on all phases of contract termination. It was soon revealed that as of 21 June, the day before the establishment of the branch, a total of 3,778 terminations had been directed by the War Department since Pearl Harbor. Of these, 1,952 cases had been settled. Of the remaining unsettled cases at least 493 were more than 6 months old and an additional 411 cases (378 of them Air Forces) were of uncertain duration. In terms of dollar value, total War Department cancellations by the time of the establishment of the Contract Termination Board had exceeded the figure for the entire World War I termination experience.[30]

The summer and fall of 1943 witnessed a marked increase in the number of terminations and in public and Congressional interest in the problem. Congress' formal attention to termination problems was first attracted by a legislative proposal of the War Department aimed at clarifying its authority to provide financial assistance to contractors and subcontractors pending final settlement of their terminated contracts. The resulting hearings in the House Military Affairs Committee proved of much interest to certain members of the Senate and soon several bills had been introduced in both houses. As the discussion and hearings proceeded, all aspects of the termination, settlement, and property disposal problem began to receive wide consideration.

On 18 October 1943, Comptroller General Lindsay Warren in his testimony before the House Military Affairs Committee threw a bombshell into the proceedings. He attacked the War Department's proposal for interim financing (the wording of which

---

ington, D.C. (2) S. Rpt. 12, Pt. 4, 78th Cong., 1st Sess., July 1943 (Committee Print). (3) Memo, Asst Dir Purchases Div for Dir of Materiel, 30 Aug 43, sub: Contract Termination. (4) Memo, Maj F. C. McCoard for Col Bryan Houston, Special Representative of USW, 17 Sep 43, sub: Contract Termination.

[28] This Manual was revised and republished as War Department TM 14–1005 on 1 June 1944.

[29] Memo, USW for CG AAF and CG ASF, 22 Jun 43, sub: Staff Work on Current Contract Terminations.

[30] (1) ASF, History of Purchases Division, p. 298. (2) Report on Contract Termination by Col Bryan Houston [circa October 1943].

was very broad) as "an arrogant snapping of fingers in the face of the Congress" and proposed that "the War Department should be peremptorily stopped in what it is now proceeding to foist on the Congress and the Nation." [31] He agreed that the War Department had the legal power to negotiate settlements of fixed-price contracts but warned that unless this power were transferred by statute to the Comptroller General the looseness of the War Department's Procurement Regulations and the "proven inefficiency" of contracting officers would result in the dissipation of untold millions of taxpayers' money. In support of his charges he cited 270 examples, taken from CPFF settlements, of alleged illegal or unauthorized payments to contractors which had been approved by contracting officers and subsequently suspended by the General Accounting Office.[32]

The unfavorable publicity resulting from the Comptroller General's charges and the specter of General Accounting Office power to reject all termination settlements provoked Under Secretary Patterson's immediate return to the hearings. Although he had previously given a careful and detailed account of the magnitude of the problem facing the War Department, and of the department's expanding organization and procedures for safeguarding the government's interest in termination settlements,[33] he now re-emphasized these and proceeded step by step to refute the charges which had been

made. He pointed out that perhaps 90 percent of the 270 suspensions by the General Accounting Office either had been subsequently allowed by GAO after investigation or had originally been called to the attention of the GAO as the result of regular War Department auditing procedures. He further indicated that over a recent four-month period the General Accounting Office had made no exceptions to 99.95 percent of all War Department vouchers. Disallowances by the General Accounting Office, moreover, totaled less than 10 cents per $1,000 of expenditures under War Department contracts. Summing up he stated:

I think that the record before you plainly shows the careful and conscientious job being done by the War Department and its officers. The microscopic percentage of the questioned transactions, the debatable nature of many of them, and the fact that most of them were first questioned within the War Department itself established this. In handling this enormous number of transactions [30,000,000 procurement vouchers since 1940], under the pressure of time imposed by the war, any organization will inevitably make errors and mistakes of judgment. The War Department has, of course, made such mistakes in the past, including some of the cases cited by the Comptroller General, and we will make similar mistakes in the future. But we must insist that the record of our officers is remarkably good and demonstrates that they are conscientious, hardworking, and capable.[34]

The controversy over whether the Comptroller General or the procuring agencies should have final settlement authority, together with other elements of termination policy, was thoroughly aired in the closing months of 1943 and in early 1944 before various committees of both houses. These included the committees concerned with military and naval affairs, appropriations,

---

[31] H. Com. on Military Affairs, 78th Cong., 1st Sess., Hearings on H. R. 3022, *Authorizing the Secretary of War To Use Funds for Adjustment of Contracts,* June and October 1942, 2:189–90.

[32] These cases, with a brief comment on each, were incorporated into the record. *Ibid.,* 2:194–218.

[33] *Ibid.,* 2:144–82. Under Secretary Patterson's original testimony, as reproduced in these pages, constitutes a valuable statement and analysis of the whole termination problem.

[34] *Ibid.,* 2:260.

the judiciary, and small business, as well as several special committees—the Senate Committee Investigating the National Defense Program (Truman Committee) and the newly established committees of both houses on Post-War Economic Policy and Planning; of the latter, the most important was the Senate committee headed by Senator Walter F. George. It was evident that, by the end of the legislative year, Congress would lay down a comprehensive statute which would define in considerable detail the elements of contract settlement policy and establish a top-level civilian agency to supervise the law's administration.

Several developments in the latter part of 1943 were of significance both for dealing with current termination problems and for providing Congress with guidance for its legislative effort. On 20 November 1943, the Under Secretary ordered the establishment of the Readjustment Division, ASF, with general responsibility for all War Department problems of matériel demobilization.[35] The Readjustment Division functioned as a control organization within the War Department—supervising the actual settlement operations of the technical services, initiating and clarifying matters of policy, conducting extensive training and public relations activities, and representing the War Department to other governmental agencies in matters under its jurisdiction. It func-

tioned through five branches—Contract Settlement, Property Disposal, Control (statistical and analytical), Training, and Information. The Readjustment Division upon its establishment took over the activities of the former Contract Termination Branch, Purchases Division. Beneath the Readjustment Division as the War Department's top-level organization were termination units in technical service headquarters and in district procurement offices, the latter being generally responsible under local contracting officers for actual settlement negotiations.

While the War Department was thus perfecting its organization for termination, progress was also made in the development of a uniform termination article. Late in the summer of 1943 the Under Secretaries of War and Navy decided to submit the disagreements of the two services to arbitration. Assistant Secretary of War McCloy, whose duties did not include procurement, served as arbitrator. His decision was that the Navy's cost definition and profit formula should be adopted but that the War Department's termination article should serve as the basis for a new uniform article.[36] Before the agreement could be fully implemented, developments external to the services broadened the area of discussion and resulted in reconsideration of the whole termination problem.

On 12 November 1943, under the supervision of the Office of War Mobilization (later the Office of War Mobilization and Reconversion), the six major procurement agencies (the War, Navy, and Treasury Departments, the Maritime Commission, the RFC subsidiaries, and the Foreign Economic Administration) established the Joint

---

[35] WD Admin Memo S–102, 20 Nov 43. Also see History of the Readjustment Division, ASF [circa 1946] (hereafter cited as ASF, Readjustment History), copy in OCMH, for a broad description of organization and functions of the division. This study consists of Vol. I (text, 194 pp.), Vol. II (13 appendixes), and Vol. III (supplement, 56 pp.); unless otherwise indicated, all citations herein refer to Vol. I. The Readjustment History was written by Reynold Bennett, then a first lieutenant in the Transportation Corps and later author of the OCS History.

[36] ASF, History of Purchases Division, pp. 303–04.

Contract Termination Board (JCTB). This organization, whose chairman was Mr. John M. Hancock of OWM, was charged with the development of a uniform termination article and a uniform program for handling terminations by all the agencies. Working through a number of subcommittees, the board carefully explored all aspects of the problem. Its first major contribution was the drafting of a uniform termination article for fixed-price contracts—based on the recent Army-Navy agreement—and an associated statement of principles of cost determination. On 8 January 1944, the Office of War Mobilization made mandatory the use of this article in all new war contracts, with certain exceptions in behalf of administrative simplicity. JCTB was also making extensive studies of such matters as the development of a uniform CPFF termination article, the desirability of including a termination article in subcontracts, the possibility of companywide settlements and direct governmental settlement of subcontractors' claims, administrative safeguards against fraud, review and appeals procedure, and the issuance of cost interpretations and manuals of instruction.[37]

An outstanding development, which did much to influence Congressional thinking and shape the legislation which followed, was the submission on 15 February 1944 of the widely heralded Baruch-Hancock Report on War and Post-War Adjustment Policies.[38] This report—sponsored by the Office of War Mobilization—contained broad recommendations on all aspects of the demobilization problem, but much of it was focused on contract settlement procedures. The report was unequivocal that settlements would have to be "fair, fast, and final"; otherwise the reconversion effort would bog down in a welter of wholesale unemployment. The chief ingredients of the report's recommended policy for contract settlement were the negotiation of final settlements by the procuring agencies, generous and immediate interim financing for contractors, and a vigorous sixty-day plant clearance policy. The following passage of the report is typical of its content and style:

Any course, such as that proposed recently by the Comptroller General, would quibble the Nation into a panic.

The Comptroller's suggestions, as we understand it, was that he review every settlement before payment and that no payment be final until approved by him. Pending this audit, the Comptroller proposed that advances and loans be made; but the amounts would be entirely inadequate to keep business and jobs going. If such an audit before payment were decreed, no war contractor would know where he stood, prime contractors would be unable to pay subcontractors, banks would be reluctant to make adequate loans, billions in working capital would be frozen. The delays in settlement could force many concerns into bankruptcy. It would mean unemployment by audit.

The essential thing to remember about these contract settlements is that they be fair—fair both to the Government and to the contractor. What is fair can be determined just as well in a matter of weeks as in years.[39]

During the final months of 1943 the War Contracts Subcommittee of the Senate Committee on Military Affairs had been working on a contract termination bill. The subcommittee chairman, Senator James E. Murray,

---

[37] The activities of JCTB are described at length in Bernard M. Baruch and John M. Hancock, *Report on War and Post-War Adjustment Policies* (15 February 1944) (hereafter cited as Baruch-Hancock Rpt).

[38] *Ibid.,* p. 53. The Uniform Termination Article developed by JCTB is reproduced in full at pages 83–86 of the report; the widely used Statement of Principles for Determination of Costs is found at pages 87–89.

[39] *Ibid.,* p. 8.

was also chairman of the Senate Small Business Committee and had been actively following the termination problems of small business for nearly a year. Senator Murray collaborated closely with the Senate Committee on Post-War Economic Policy and Planning, and on 11 February 1944—four days before the submittal of the Baruch-Hancock report—S. 1718 was introduced jointly by Senators Murray and George. Early in May, after considerable discussion and revision in committee, the bill was passed by the Senate and referred to the House Judiciary Committee, which reported the bill favorably with an amendment. At the same time, a rival bill had been reported by the House Military Affairs Committee which would have placed the Comptroller General in charge of termination settlements. A third bill, presented by the House Naval Affairs Committee, offered still another proposal. The House Rules Committee recommended the Murray-George bill, which was also favored by Baruch and Hancock. This was soon passed by both houses and became the Contract Settlement Act of 1944, later described by Senator Murray as "one of the most carefully considered pieces of legislation ever to have been enacted by the Congress." [40]

The Contract Settlement Act was a 25-page document setting forth the broad objectives of the act and providing comprehen-

sive policies governing its implementation. It created the Office of Contract Settlement (OCS), to be headed by a director and advised by the Contract Settlement Advisory Board, composed of representatives of the principal procuring agencies, the War Production Board, the Smaller War Plans Corporation, and the Attorney General. The director was ordered to prescribe policies, procedures, and standards under the act and was empowered to require their observance by all concerned. He was directed to submit quarterly reports to Congress, summarizing the progress of terminations, termination settlements, interim financing, and other developments that would enable Congress to evaluate the administration of the act and the need for additional legislation. [41]

The act emphasized the necessity for speed, equity, and finality in the settlement of terminated contracts. The negotiated settlement, to be effected by the contracting agencies, was made the kingpin of contract settlement procedure. As a basis for negotiation the act permitted the use of "actual, standard, average, or estimated costs," or "any other equitable basis" deemed appropriate by the contracting agencies. It specified numerous types of cost to be included or excluded from settlement, without prejudice to other types not mentioned in the act. Negotiated settlements would be final, and the termination functions of the General Accounting Office were limited to review, after final settlement, to determine

---

[40] (1) 58 *Stat.* 651, approved 1 Jul 44. (2) Senator James E. Murray, "Contract Settlement Act of 1944," p. 683. Senator Murray's article provides a valuable condensed history and summary of the Contract Settlement Act. (3) Allen W. Maddren, "Administrative and Judicial Machinery," pp. 659–82. Last two in *Law and Contemporary Problems* (Duke University School of Law), X, No. 4 (Spring 1944). (4) Bertram M. Gross, "The Role of Congress in Contract Termination," *Ibid.*, X, No. 3 (Winter 1944), 540–58. (5) OCS History, Ch. V, pp. 14–20.

[41] After the passage of the act the staff and committees of JCTB were absorbed by OCS. The JCTB itself became the Contract Settlement Advisory Board. In response to the act, nine quarterly reports were eventually submitted to Congress by the director. These reports (hereafter cited as OCS Rpt, number, and date) constitute a valuable source of information on contract termination and settlement problems as they arose.

whether actual payments to the contractor were in accordance with the settlement and whether the settlement had been induced by fraud. Cases of suspected fraud were to be reported to the Department of Justice for investigation and collection, and special provisions were made for the punishment of fraud. The Comptroller General was given permission to investigate the settlements of each agency for the purpose of reporting to Congress whether settlement procedures were efficient and adequate to protect the interests of the government.

In order to ease the impact of terminations, the act specified that notice should be given as far in advance of termination as possible. Interest was to be paid on all amounts due to a contractor, at the rate of $2\frac{1}{2}$ percent per annum, for the period from 30 days after termination to date of final payment. Within 30 days after application, contractors and subcontractors were to be provided with interim financing, consisting of advance and partial payments on the contract or of termination loans guaranteed by the government. A policy of rapid plant clearance was adopted, requiring the government to remove all termination inventory from the contractor's premises within 60 days after submission of the contractor's inventory statement. If the government failed to remove the inventory within the 60-day period, the contractor was authorized to store it at government expense.

Many other provisions of the act—including settlement by government determination in the event of failure of negotiation (with procedures for contractor appeals), the validation of informal and defective contracts or commitments such as provided by the Dent Act of 1919, and the personal non-liability of government officers for settlement payments not involving their own fraud—

were additional testimony to the thoroughness with which the drafters considered their legislation. An important feature of the act was the latitude and flexibility allowed in actual administration when such flexibility was essential to a practical and common-sense approach. Most of the actual procedures of settlement had their basis either specifically or by implication in the wording of the act.

War Department Preparations for Mass Termination

The preparations of the War Department, the other governmental agencies, and the many tens of thousands of the nation's war contractors for handling mass terminations at the end of the war represent perhaps the greatest co-ordinated and detailed planning effort in the nation's history. The success of the Controlled Materials Plan—due largely to its careful and detailed planning—was fresh in the minds of those who were responsible for demobilization planning. All were determined that the nation's reconversion effort should not fail through lack of advance thinking and preparation.

With the passage of the Contract Settlement Act the War Department's termination planning activities went into high gear. These activities comprehended four broad categories: (1) the progressive elaboration and refinement of termination regulations to meet the various problems raised by actual termination experience; (2) the creation of termination organizations in both government and industry; (3) the education and training of contractors and government employees in termination problems and procedures; (4) the reaching of specific pretermination agreements with as many contractors as possible in order to minimize the work load and the number of decisions which would have to be made at the peak of termination activity.

The chief contribution in the first category was the publication, effective 1 November 1944, of the Joint Termination Regulation (JTR), which soon became the bible of contract termination matters. JTR represented the combined efforts of the Army and Navy to spell out in complete detail all aspects of termination law and procedure. Consisting of nine major sections and several hundred pages, it contained statements of policy, definitions of terms, facsimiles of official forms, and detailed regulations and procedures binding upon all contracting officers in the termination and settlement of contracts. It superseded the Army's PR 15 and the Contract Termination directives of the Navy, and carried as an appendix the joint Termination Accounting Manual, which superseded the Army's TM 14-1005.[42] Although it was not binding upon agencies other than the Army and Navy, it was used by other agencies as a guide in making settlements. It was also a principal reliance of prime contractors, who found in it information on how to proceed in obtaining interim financing, preparing settlement proposals, settling subcontractor claims, disposing of inventory, and in resolving many other problems. The distribution of JTR was so widespread that a special Joint Army-Navy Distribution Center was established in New York City.[43]

JTR was kept up to date by a stream of amendments. These were so numerous during the first few months that a complete revision of JTR was issued on 20 April 1945. This revision contained a reproduction of the Contract Settlement Act and all regulations of the Office of Contract Settlement, as well as other material. Revision No. 2, effective 20 June 1945, was a partial revision of some two hundred pages.

The War Department, as the principal contracting agency, played a major part in shaping policy and procedure as enunciated by the Director of Contract Settlement. Since the Office of Contract Settlement was a policy making and co-ordinating office, it drew the subject matter of its decisions and regulations from the operating agencies. Representatives of these, in turn, composed the larger part of the Contract Settlement Advisory Board, upon whom the director relied heavily in reaching policy decisions. Relations between the War Department and the Office of Contract Settlement were harmonious and characterized by a minimum of red tape; problems at the operating level flowed up to the OCS and back down again in the form of decisions which were promptly incorporated into JTR for general application.[44]

---

[42] See above, page 623.

[43] Eventually known as the Readjustment Distribution Center, 90 Church Street, New York City, New York. This office also handled the distribution of informational and training materials prepared for contractors by the Army and Navy. Copies of JTR may be found in OCMH or the Pentagon Army Library. JTR was the work of an Army-Navy committee guided largely by Col. William H. Draper, Jr., chief of the Contract Termination Branch,

Readjustment Division, ASF, and Capt. Lewis L. Strauss, USNR. Their work together on termination problems common to the two services convinced Colonel Draper and Captain Strauss of the advantages of closer co-ordination of Army and Navy procurement activities and led to the widely circulated Draper-Strauss Report in February 1945, Co-ordination of Procurement Between the War and Navy Departments.

[44] The director of OCS characteristically gave immediate attention to the problems of the operating agencies. For example, on 6 September 1944, General Clay wrote the director pointing to difficulties arising out of existing regulations in instituting pretermination agreements. On the following day the director replied: "I have your letter of September 6 dealing with predetermination of costs and prices

The story of organizational growing pains, of the difficulties of mobilizing some 30,000 War Department termination employees by V–J Day, or of the problems of retaining qualified officers and civilians during the general exodus back into private industry at a time when the War Department's contract settlement activities were at their peak, would be too long for inclusion here.[45] Likewise, only a hint can be given of the magnitude of the task faced by business firms, individually and collectively, in developing their termination organizations. The War Department from the beginning urged upon contractors the importance of a well-developed termination organization with adequate office space, facilities, and authority. Large corporations often established a complete termination department, staffed with experts in many fields and co-ordinate in authority with other major operating departments. Complex realignments of the duties of the "old line" departments—such

as purchasing, production, and accounting—became necessary. Many firms developed their own extensive termination manuals, spelling out detailed procedures and responsibilities.[46] Exceptions and variations were necessary in the case of different units in multi-plant organizations. Small firms often had to conduct their termination activities with part-time personnel or by "robbing" the regular staffs of production and accounting personnel to meet particular crises.[47]

The area of greatest activity in preparing for the deluge of mass terminations was probably that of public relations and training. It was all-important to the success of the program that the industrial community and the nation as a whole be educated in the full implications of the problem. The tasks imposed by the total termination and settlement process were novel and onerous. In the absence of a general atmosphere of urgency—fully appreciated by business, workers, and the entire community—contractors would be dilatory in preparing and submitting termination claims, financial institutions would be slow

---

as a method simplying and speeding up the settlement of terminated contracts; and I hereby exempt from Directive Order 2, of the Office of War Mobilization, dated February 24, 1944, the arrangements in the textile, clothing, and related fields recommended by you." Ltr, Robert H. Hinckley, Dir OCS, to Gen Clay, Dir of Materiel ASF, 7 Sep 44. Again on 6 October 1944, Under Secretary Patterson wrote a lengthy letter to the director pointing out the widespread unwillingness of CPFF contractors to conclude settlement agreements because of the danger of vitiation of the agreement through post-audit and disallowance by the General Accounting Office. The very same day the director wrote the President for relief. Five days later the President referred the matter to the Attorney General, who on 31 October confirmed final settlement authority for CPFF contracts in the contracting agencies. 40 Op. Atty. Gen. 328, 31 Oct 44. Copies of above cited letters and opinion of Attorney General in Purchases Div file 161 Contract Termination.

[45] The general character of the War Department's organization for termination has already been described. See above, pages 622–25. For greater detail, see ASF, Readjustment History, pp. 8–17.

[46] A number of contractor-issued manuals are on file with the records of the Readjustment Division, ASF. [In Departmental Records Branch, AGO, Alexandria, Virginia.] The Allis-Chalmers Manufacturing Corporation's manual Termination Procedure, issue of 20 November 1944, contains 11 sections of 136 pages in addition to numerous forms.

[47] For example, the following remarks of a small contractor, quoted in Memo, Gen Browning, Asst Dir of Mat, for CofEngrs, 22 Aug 44, sub: Termination Personnel: "We are terribly short-handed, and are having considerable trouble in keeping pace with delivery schedules, but I was compelled to take two men from the Welding Department for 2½ days while we counted carefully, under the surveillance of these civilians, all the Work in Process, Purchased Parts, channels, etc. . . . Manpower, at least with the small war plants, is at a premium. For the past ten days, I have spent most of my time at the warehouse, with little time for more important things."

in granting termination loans, plant clearance would bog down, and the whole reconversion effort would be jeopardized. Dissemination of information was not enough; the War Department and the other contracting agencies found it necessary to resort to exhortation on a nationwide scale.[48]

In implementing its program the War Department utilized all available public relations media. Its officials issued a multitude of press releases, held numerous press conferences, gave talks over the radio, made speeches before trade associations and civic groups, and spread the gospel of termination throughout the country. Newspapers, magazines, trade papers, and business and professional journals co-operated in various ways—by sending qualified reporters and representatives to speeches and conferences, by allotting ample space to termination news, and by carrying editorials and special feature articles, often prepared by War Department staff writers, on the latest developments and issues. The widespread publicity given the program did much to enlist the co-operation and even enthusiasm of contractors in meeting the termination and settlement problem.

More directly related to the practical execution of the program was the task of imparting systematic information on settlement procedures. As part of its technique for educating contractors on a nationwide scale,

the War Department individually or in collaboration with the Navy prepared and distributed millions of pieces of termination literature—ranging from the complex and detailed JTR and its revisions to brochures, booklets, pamphlets, and training materials and posters—all calculated to inform and educate termination officials in both industry and government. The Baruch-Hancock report had recommended issuance of a booklet of instructions to contractors. The Readjustment Division immediately set about the drafting of the first Contractor's Guide.[49] By early summer in 1944, 300,000 copies of this clearly and attractively presented booklet had been distributed. A year later a new joint Army-Navy edition of the guide was printed and 300,000 additional copies distributed. In November 1944 the deputy director of the Readjustment Division drew up a Pretermination Flyer, a four-page circular summarizing problems of plant clearance. Some 300,000 copies of this were distributed, either through contracting officers in the field or through the Joint Army-Navy Distribution Center. In order to utilize the far-flung contacts and machinery of trade associations throughout the country, the Readjustment Division, in co-operation with the Navy, brought forth the monthly Production Adjustment Bulletin. The bulletin was primarily a feeder for trade association periodicals and carried digests of changes in JTR, notices of training programs for contractors in various centers, statistics, news items, and termination cases of interest. In these and numerous other publications, the War Department made free use of diagrams, cartoons, color charts, and other expository devices designed to

---

[48] War Department termination personnel often found it difficult to understand the delay of contractors in filing claim for amounts due them. Baruch-Hancock Rpt. p. 13: "It its reported to us that in the past an average of 4 months has been required to get contractors to submit claims. Only a part of this slowness can be laid to preoccupation with the war or to inadequacies of Government policy. Contractors will have only themselves to blame if they do not get set to handle the problems of termination."

[49] Readjustment Division, Contractor Guide (WD Pamphlet 34–2, 1 June 1944).

simplify, clarify, and emphasize its message.[50]

In order to prepare industrial and other groups to fulfill their specific roles in the termination process, the War Department organized a wide array of training programs. These represented different areas of specialization and degrees of intensity and included the following: (1) conferences; (2) small contractor training; (3) university courses; (4) special centralized schools; (5) on-the-job training.

Conferences were arranged both in Washington and the field to meet the needs of the groups concerned and to deal with specific problems. Thus early in 1944, the Readjustment Division held a two-day regional staff conference in Washington for leaders of industry in the six New England states. The conference was presided over by General Somervell and attended by representatives of the technical services. It represented one of the earlier attempts to acquaint industrial leaders with the current thinking of the War Department on termination and surplus disposal problems. Conferences were likewise held in Washington and the field for formulating policy and training contractors in problems of salvage. Regional conferences for termination training personnel were held by the Readjustment Division in Philadelphia, Atlanta, and Chicago. The Army Air Forces conducted two contractor conferences on the west coast in July 1944.

In general the conference technique was utilized to stimulate the thinking and obtain the enthusiastic support of key officials in both industry and government circles.[51]

The education of subcontractors was a vital element in the War Department's pretermination planning and training program. Unless the claims of subcontractors were promptly presented and settled at all stages in the contractual chain it would have been impossible for prime contractors to present their final claims to the government. While many of the nation's largest manufacturing concerns were largely engaged in subcontract work, it was still true that the smaller firms constituted the vast majority of War Department subcontractors. Not only were the smaller firms likely to have meager staffs and facilities for handling termination matters; they were also the farthest removed from direct contact with the War Department.

To meet the problem of subcontractor training the War Department developed several approaches. One of the most important was the utilization of the facilities of the Smaller War Plants Corporation. The SWPC had 14 regional offices and 100 district offices throughout the country, and these were used to disseminate information to the 35,000 war contractors which it represented. In the year ending with the spring of 1945, SWPC sponsored some 125 meetings attended by approximately 10,000 individuals representing 5,000 firms. At these meetings small business was made aware of its role in the demobilization program and the necessity for adequate preparation.[52] By the spring of 1945 the War Department had developed, in conjunction with the Navy, the highly successful Four-Hour Basic

---

[50] Material in this paragraph is elaborated in ASF, Readjustment History, pp. 88ff. The following discussion of War Department termination training activities likewise relies largely on this monograph. Other sources supporting the discussion are: (1) History of Fiscal Services, 1940–1945, Chs. XXIII, Army Finance School, XLV, Contract Termination, and LXVI, Fiscal Training; (2) Memorandum on Contract Termination Training and Organization (unsigned), 12 Sep 44, in file 161 Contract Termination, Control Div ASF.

[51] ASF, Readjustment History, pp. 99–102.
[52] Ibid., 98–99.

Course, more familiarly known as the ABC Course, in termination procedures. Primarily concerned with the filing of claims and the filling out of the required settlement proposal forms, this course provided down-to-earth information and was well received by contractors throughout the country. The ABC Course, which was conducted by trained representatives of the War and Navy Departments, reached an estimated 30,000 individuals representing over 20,000 separate firms in 283 different cities and towns. All together, some 900 class meetings were held.[53]

Despite these efforts of the Army and Navy the training of subcontractors and small prime contractors would have been substantially less successful had it not been supplemented by the effective work of trade associations, chambers of commerce, manufacturers' organizations, the Automotive Council for War Production, the Committee for Economic Development, other nonprofit organizations, and even individual major contractors. These organizations sponsored or conducted numerous termination courses and training activities which reached many thousands of smaller contractors who for one reason or another were unable to attend the government-sponsored courses.

Somewhat similar in purpose and effect were the short termination courses offered by universities in various parts of the country. Early in 1944 the University of Pennsyl-

vania, in co-operation with Army and Navy procurement offices in the Philadelphia area, began offering three-day contract termination courses for both prime contractors and subcontractors as well as others interested in termination matters. Some 2,500 contractor personnel, representing about 1,200 firms, were trained at this institution. Other universities provided similar offerings.[54] The Readjustment Division actively co-operated with nongovernmental training organizations by furnishing information, materials, recommendations, and other assistance.

The most concentrated and highly developed type of termination training was made available by the War Department through the medium of centralized schools, established to train government specialists in termination matters. In June 1944, the Army Industrial College in Washington, D. C., was reactivated and began training officers to act as members of settlement teams. The standard course varied from three to four weeks in duration. Beginning in July 1944, the AIC also instituted a two-month termination course for Army Air Forces officers. By 1 September 1945, over 3,700 students were graduated from readjustment courses by the college.

All together some half-dozen major centralized termination training schools were conducted by the War Department. The Fiscal Director's School, established at Duke University in October 1943 (moving in 1944 to Fort Benjamin Harrison, Indiana) graduated 3,300 students—officers, enlisted men, and civilians—from courses in fiscal and auditing aspects of termination. The Judge Advocate General's School at Ann

[53] The effectiveness of the Four-Hour ABC Course led to the introduction in June 1945 of the Four-Hour "XYZ" Accounting Course. This course featured organized discussion of termination accounting problems by war contractors and government representatives. Such problems were often the heart of settlement difficulties. By V-J Day, 60 of these meetings had been held in 25 cities and were attended by 2,500 contractor employees representing 1,636 firms. *Ibid.,* p. 109.

[54] A partial list of participating universities includes Boston University, New York University, University of California, University of Michigan, University of Indiana, Western Reserve, and Xavier University. *Ibid.,* p. 108.

Arbor, Michigan, in addition to its other responsibilities, trained 500 officers in the legal aspects of contract termination. The Army Air Forces Termination Officers' Training School at Vandalia, Ohio, trained nearly 800 officers and civilians in Air Forces termination and procurement matters. Over 1,200 Air Forces auditing personnel received termination accounting education at the Budget and Fiscal office, Wright Field, Dayton, Ohio. The Harvard University Graduate School of Business Administration, which had for many years conducted special courses in procurement matters for Army officers, trained 329 AAF officers in a course equivalent to the one given Air Forces officers by the Army Industrial College. A unique combination of formal instruction and on-the-job training was provided Signal Corps officers and enlisted men at the Signal Corps Contract Termination School, Fort Monmouth, New Jersey. The course consisted of three weeks' training in the school and one week on-the-job training in the Monmouth Signal Corps Procurement District. Because of the unusually complex nature of Signal Corps procurement and termination problems, students were carefully selected and limited to personnel with considerable experience in the settlement of actual termination cases. Further to fa-

cilitate Signal Corps contract settlements, the Fort Monmouth school conducted a ten-day course for contractors, who remained in residence at the school from 8 to 18 November 1944. A total of 402 military personnel and 13 civilians were enrolled in the course for Signal Corps personnel, and 51 Signal Corps contractors took the contractor-training course.[55]

Much of the success of the Army's contract settlement program for World War II is attributable to the extensive preparations and training which went into the program. The training sessions and materials provided contracting organizations as well as governmental agencies with knowledge and information essential to the discharge of the contract settlement process. Moreover, by bringing contractors and the government into close association in the study of illustrative problems where no immediate interests were at stake, they promoted a deeper understanding and more rational appraisal of the issues involved. The development of the contract settlement procedures discussed in the following chapter owed much to the close association and collaboration of all parties to procurement contracts.

---

[55] Ibid, pp. 104–08. See also other sources cited above, note 50.

CHAPTER XXVIII

Termination and Settlement Procedure

General Settlement Procedure

Contract termination and settlement procedure, reduced to bare essentials, consisted of three steps: (1) the serving of a termination notice by the contracting agency; (2) presentation by the contractor of his settlement proposal (generally referred to as the contractor's "claim"); (3) the negotiation of the settlement agreement. Each of these steps had many possible ramifications, and for large settlements approval by higher authority was required before final agreement could be reached.

The standard settlement procedure was known as the vertical settlement system. It was so described because all termination claims under a given prime contract were passed in successive stages up the contractual chain into the hands of the prime contractor. Each subcontractor's claim would thus be reviewed by his immediate customer who in turn would incorporate all his subcontract termination costs into his own claim. The prime contractor, standing at the top of the contractual chain, would then present to the government the total accumulated termination charges under the entire contract. In this manner the contracting agency negotiating the settlement would deal directly only with the prime contractor instead of with perhaps a thousand or more contracting firms at all stages of production under the contract. This procedure followed the pattern of relationships established in the basic contracting and subcontracting process, under which the government had privity of contract and direct face-to-face relationships only with the prime. But just as the processes of wartime procurement required deviation from the traditional contracting procedures, so did the urgency and complexities of the contract settlement process call for departures from the standard settlement procedure.[1]

The decision to terminate a contract was made, as already indicated, only after a careful review of various considerations, many of which were unconnected with the circumstances of the individual contractor.[2] In anticipation of termination, government representatives held preliminary discussions with the contractor whenever feasible in order to reach tentative agreement on as many issues as possible.[3] These included such matters as "stop-work" points, the classification, valuation, and disposition of contractor's inventory, allocation of common inventory and overhead costs, termination and settlement of subcontractors' claims, and so on. In many cases, "pretermination planning" for important prime contracts resulted, as pointed out later, in written pretermination agreements which bound the

---

[1] The nature of these departures will be examined in a subsequent section. See below, pages 643 ff.

[2] See above, pages 614–16. Also JTR, Sec. II, Pt. 3, Distribution of Cutbacks.

[3] JTR 242; JTR, Sec. II, Pt. 2, Advance Preparations for Termination Settlements.

government and the contractor to specific procedures and terms to be used in the final settlement. In other cases informal agreements were reached; although not binding, these usually disposed of many troublesome issues in advance of termination, thus expediting final settlement when the pressure of time was greatest.

The actual notice of termination was a letter (or telegram followed by letter) to the prime contractor, identifying the terminated contract, stating the date on which work—in whole or in part—should cease, and any other necessary instructions. The War Department also sent copies of termination notices to assignees, guarantors, and sureties of the prime contractor to enable them to protect their interests.[4] Upon receipt of the termination notice, the contractor was obligated to stop all further work immediately or by a specified date. In special cases where safety, the clearing of machinery, or other common-sense considerations dictated a continuance of work, the contractor could so proceed but had to notify the contracting officer immediately and obtain written approval. He was also required to terminate immediately all his relevant subcontracts and to see that subcontractors in turn terminated their subcontracts, and so on down the contractual chain. No contractor at any tier was entitled to reimbursement for work done, either by himself or his subcontractors, after the official stop-work date.[5]

The second step—the presentation of the settlement proposal—was the responsibility of the contractor. This step centered in the use of official settlement proposal forms, first developed by the War Department and later revised and made standard by the Office of Contract Settlement. The importance of these forms in organizing and directing the termination activities of all contractors, in simplifying and standardizing their settlement proposals, and in resolving many individual problems cannot be overemphasized. As in the case of the income tax, these consisted of a basic form supplemented by schedules and separate forms calling for all necessary supporting information. A "short form," OCS Form 1a, was used for expeditious settlement of claims amounting, after deduction of disposal credits, to less than $1,000. Form 1, for presenting claims on the so-called inventory basis, was the generally used "long form." [6] A copy of Form 1, containing illustrative figures, is reproduced on pp. 638–39.

In support of the contractor's Form–1 claim were detailed inventory schedules on Forms 2a through 2d, which classified all inventory items into specified groups— metals, raw materials, purchased parts, finished components, finished product, and miscellaneous. Work in process was listed separately because of the special disposal problems relating thereto (most partially completed items had only scrap or salvage value). Each item of inventory had to be listed and carefully described according to regulations. Appropriate columns opposite

---

[4] JTR 245 (3).

[5] JTR 251.1; JTR 251.3 The drafting of an appropriate termination notice demanded great care in order to anticipate all issues arising out of its service. Standard forms of telegraphic notices as well as of letter notices for the various types of contract were provided in the regulations. JTR 243; JTR 941; JTR 942. The War Department was able to prepare and serve some 48,000 notices of termination within a day or so of V-J Day only as a result of careful organization and planning and

around-the-clock efforts on the part of Army termination personnel.

[6] OCS Form 1b was used for settlement proposals submitted on the "total-cost" basis. This basis of settlement was relatively little used. Copies of OSC settlement proposal forms are reproduced in JTR, Sec. IX, Statutes, Orders, and Forms.

each item called for such information as quantity, condition, unit of measure, unit and total cost, and contractor's offer (if he desired to retain the item) or proceeds of sale (if sale by the contractor had been authorized and consummated). The inventory schedules served a double purpose: they were the heart of the contractor's claim for settlement, and they were an important instrument in the difficult problem of property disposal. From the inventory schedules the contractor built up lists and catalogs of government property available for redistribution and disposal. The very nature of the process of taking inventory and filling out the schedules placed pressure upon the contractor to reach decisions and make specific efforts toward inventory disposition.

A "schedule of accounting information" (Form 3) was a part of each long-form settlement proposal and supplemented Forms 1 and 2. This was a signed statement by the contractor concerning the accounting methods used in preparing the settlement proposal. It called for the name of the firm's public acountants, if any, the name of any governmental agency previously reviewing the firm's books in connection with a settlement, method of determining inventory quantities and prices, method of allocating common inventory items, and many other items designed to facilitate analysis of the proposal as well as to discourage any irregularity on the part of the contractor. On the back of Form 3 was a tabulation of all indirect factory expense for the plant or department in which the contract was performed, with the amount and basis for allocation to the terminated contract.

The bulk of the typical contractor's claim consisted of his actual outlays on materials, parts, labor, and other expenses required to build up and process his inventory. In return for reimbursing the contractor for all such items, the government would, of course, receive title to the entire heterogeneous inventory thus accumulated. To the sum of all the contractor's costs on the uncompleted portion of the contract was added the estimated allowable profits on such costs, together with specific expenses of settlement (cost of taking inventory, salaries of termination employees, and the like). Further additions were subcontractors' termination claims paid by the prime, and a charge at the regular contract price for completed items undelivered at the termination date.[7]

From the total charges thus computed were deducted disposal credits accruing to the government from contractor retention or sale of any portion of the inventory, and all payments previously made by the government on the uncompleted portion of the contract. These consisted of advance, partial, or progress payments which often amounted, because of the government's liberal policy of advance financing, to the greater share of the contractor's gross termination charges. The remaining net charge to the government was in effect a final due bill under the contract, satisfactory settlement of which would discharge all obligations of both parties under the contract.[8]

The preparation of the contractor's settlement proposal was the end result of an intensive period of activity by the prime contractor, all relevant subcontractors, and the contracting officer's staff. It was the

---

[7] Contractor reimbursement for settlement of subcontractor termination claims for work in process was limited to actual settlement costs. Amounts paid or payable for pretermination deliveries by subcontractors were, however, considered as part of the contractor's own costs upon which he was allowed his contractual rate of profit. JTR 541.3.

[8] That is, all obligations except items specifically reserved in the settlement agreement and interest on the payment as finally determined.

Form Approved.
Budget Bureau No. 17-R001.

[Read Instructions for Use of Standard Contract Settlement Proposal Forms]

SETTLEMENT PROPOSAL

For Use by Prime Contractor or Subcontractor Under Terminated Fixed-Price War Supply Contract

This proposal applies to (check one):

☒ A prime contract with the Government, or

☐ Subcontract or purchase order No(s). _____

with _____
(Name of contractor who sent Notice of Termination)

_____
(Address)

If moneys payable under the contract have been assigned, give name and address of assignee **None** _____

Is Form 3 (Schedule of Accounting Information) attached? If not, explain _____ Yes ☒ No ☐

Young Manufacturing Company
(Company)

1234 South East Street
(Street address)

Dayton 12, Ohio
(City)   (State)

Govt. Agency **Army Signal Corps**
Govt. Prime Contract No. **W-001-sc-100**
Contractor's Reference No. **YB411**
Effective date of termination **October 4, 1944**

This is proposal No. **1** under this termination and is deemed to be
☐ interim, or ☒ final. (Check one.)

Status of Contract or Order AT EFFECTIVE DATE OF TERMINATION

Products covered by terminated contract or purchase order		Finished		Unfinished or not commenced		Total covered by contract or order
		Previously shipped and invoiced	On hand			
			Payment to be received through invoicing	Included in this proposal	To be completed (Partial termination only)	Not to be completed	
SC 322 M instruments	Quan.	1,240	200			960	2,400
	$	1,364,000	220,000			1,056,000	2,640,000
	Quan.						
	$						
	Quan.						
	$						

PROPOSED SETTLEMENT

No.	Item	Use Columns 2 and 3 only where previous proposal has been filed (See Instructions)		Total proposed to date	Leave blank
	(1)	Total previously proposed (2)	Increase or (decrease) by this proposal (3)	(4)	(5)
1.	Metals (from Form 2a)			28,425	
2.	Raw materials (other than metals) (from Form 2b)			21,503	
3.	Purchased parts (from Form 2b)			25,309	
4.	Finished components (from Form 2b) (See Sch. A)			19,399	
5.	Miscellaneous (from Form 2b)				
6.	Work in process (from Form 2c) (See Sch. A)			179,115	
7.	Dies, jigs, fixtures and special tools (Form 2d)			17,630	
8.	Other costs (from Schedule B)			1,080	
9.	General and administrative expenses (from Sch.C)			8,774	
10.	TOTAL (Items 1 to 9, inclusive)			301,235	
11.	Profit (explain in Schedule D)			15,062	
12.	Settlement expenses (from Schedule E)			2,763	
13.	TOTAL (Items 10 to 12 inclusive)			319,060	
14.	Settlements with subcontractors (from Schedule F)			7,297	
15.	Acceptable finished product (from Form 2b)				
16.	Allowance for interest. To be determined at time of final settlement				
17.	TOTAL (Items 13 to 16, inclusive)			326,357	
18.	Disposal credits (from Schedule G)			61,567	
19.	Partial, advance, or progress payments (less Sch. H)			200,000	
20.	TOTAL CREDITS (Items 18 and 19)			261,567	
21.	NET SETTLEMENT (Item 17 less Item 20)			64,790	

CERTIFICATE

The undersigned, individually and as an authorized representative of the contractor, certifies that he has examined this Settlement Proposal and that, to the best of his knowledge and belief: (1) AS TO CONTRACTOR'S OWN CHARGES—The Proposed Settlement (exclusive of charges set forth in Item 14) and supporting schedules and explanations have been prepared from the books of account and records of the contractor in accordance with recognized commercial accounting practices; they include only those charges allocable to the terminated portion of this contract; they have been prepared with knowledge that they will, or may, be used directly or indirectly as the basis of settlement of a claim or claims against the United States or an agency thereof; and the charges as stated are fair and reasonable. (2) AS TO SUBCONTRACTORS' CHARGES—(a) The contractor has examined, or caused to be examined, to an extent it considers adequate in the circumstances, the claims of its immediate subcontractors (exclusive of claims filed against such immediate subcontractors by their subcontractors); (b) the settlements on account of immediate subcontractors' own charges are fair and reasonable, said charges are allocable to the terminated portion of this contract and said settlements were negotiated in good faith and are not more favorable to its immediate subcontractors than those which the contractor would make if reimbursement by the Government were not involved; (e) the contractor has received from all its immediate subcontractors appropriate certificates with respect to their claims, which certificates, if the claims are for more than $1,000, are substantially in the form of this certificate; and (d) the contractor has no knowledge leading it to doubt (i) the reasonableness of the settlements with more remote subcontractors or (ii) that the charges for them are allocable to this contract. Upon receipt by the contractor of amounts covering settlements with its immediate subcontractors, the contractor will pay or credit them promptly with the amounts so received, to the extent that it has not previously done so. The term subcontractor as used above includes suppliers.

The undersigned certifies that to the best of his knowledge and belief the statements with respect to accounting matters made in the above Certificate are true.

J. Gillean
(Supervisory accounting official)

Controller
(Title)

Young Manufacturing Company
(Name of contractor)

By _Henry Myers_
(Authorized official)

President   **November 20, 1944**
(Title)   (Date)

When the space provided for any information is insufficient, attach separate supporting schedules.

SCHEDULE A	ANALYSIS OF INVENTORY COST			

Furnish the following information (unless not reasonably available) in respect of inventories of finished components and work in process included in this proposal:

	Total Direct Labor	Total Direct Materials	Total Indirect Expense	TOTAL
Finished Components	8,024	3,387	7,988	19,399
Work in Process	67,805	43,810	67,500	179,115

SCHEDULE B	OTHER COSTS		(ITEM 8)

Item Loss on facilities	Explanation	Amount	Leave Blank

1 Cincinnati 12" x 36" cylindrical grinder, Type KK   10,200
Sold to Walter Cory Co. as authorized by contracting officer   7,500

Loss applicable to this contract   2,700

Loss applicable to terminated portion of contract $\frac{960}{2,400}$ x 2,700   1,080

This machine was purchased specifically for and is usable only on this contract. Title was tendered to the Government and sale was directed by the contracting officer.

SCHEDULE C	GENERAL AND ADMINISTRATIVE EXPENSES		(ITEM 9)

Detail of expenses 6 mos.to Sept.30,1944	Method of allocation	Amount	Leave Blank

Officers' salaries	78,375	Total manufacturing cost	
Office salaries	182,077	incurred six months ended	
Social security taxes	9,107	Sept. 30, 1944 10,357,218	
Traveling expenses	18,954	Per cent of general and	
Telephone & telegraph	7,835	administrative expense to	
Professional services	24,303	mfg. cost incurred 3.44%	
Dues and subscriptions	4,412	Total items no. 1 through no.	
Stationery and postage	7,118	8 of summary 292,461	
Taxes	10,432	3% of 292,461 - item no. 9	
Miscellaneous	13,675	of summary 8,774	
Total	356,288	Operations under contract were begun Aug. 3, 1943. Inventory included in this proposal was produced within the last five months.	

SCHEDULE D	PROFIT		(ITEM 11)

Explanation:		Amount	Leave Blank
Total - item 10 of summary		301,235	
5% thereof - item no. 11 of summary		15,062	

Profit rate contemplated in bid proposal   5%

Ed. No. Note: If profit is otherwise computed under the authority of General Regulation 7 of the Office of Contract Settlement, an appropriate explanation will be given.

SCHEDULE E	SETTLEMENT EXPENSES		(ITEM 12)

Item	Explanation	Amount	Leave Blank
Crating lumber		432	
Packing materials		57	
Cost of taking inventory		1,742	
Charges for clerical help from termination unit		532	
Total item no. 12 of summary		2,763	

SCHEDULE F	SETTLEMENTS WITH IMMEDIATE SUBCONTRACTORS AND SUPPLIERS		(ITEM 14)

Name and address of Subcontractor	Brief description of product canceled	Amount of Settlement	Leave Blank
Electronic Research Co.	Dynamotors 6V; 1p Type D400		
1939 Factory St.,Buffalo, N.Y.	(paid Nov. 10, 1944)	5,222	
National Wire Inc.	Wire, bare phosphor bronze #12 YB		
1443 W. St., Pittsburgh,Pa.	(paid Oct.25,1944)	50	
Sump Pump Co.,	Circuit breakers 2 Volt Type,104D		
2000 Hill St.,Jackson,Mich	(unpaid)	2,025	
Total item no. 14 of summary		7,297	

SCHEDULE G	DISPOSAL OR OTHER CREDITS		(ITEM 18)

Description		Amount	Leave Blank
Total from column 8 - Form 2a		19,370	
" " " " - " 2b (Raw Materials)		17,350	
" " " " - " 2b (Purchased Parts)		13,675	
" " " " - " 2b (Finished Components)		1,027	
" " " " - " 2c		10,145	
Total item no. 18 of summary		61,567	

(If practicable, show separately amount of disposal credits applicable to acceptable finished product included in Item 15)

SCHEDULE H	PARTIAL, ADVANCE OR PROGRESS PAYMENTS		(ITEM 19)

Date	Explanation	Amount	Leave Blank
October 30, 1944	Partial payment	100,000	
November 15, 1944	" "	100,000	
Total - item no. 19 of summary		200,000	

When the space provided for any information is insufficient, attach separate supporting schedules.

prime contractor's responsibility not only to prepare his settlement proposal as such, but to develop a concrete program for disposing of termination inventory held by himself and by the various tiers of subcontractors. This was a task requiring the joint efforts of all concerned. Often a substantial portion of the termination inventory could be used by the contractor for remaining contracts with other procurement arms or agencies, a matter best known to the contractor himself. The same situation applied to subcontractors and it was to the advantage of the government no less than of contractors to minimize packing, reshipment, and other expenses of material redistribution. On the other hand, many contractors were unfamiliar with the problems of marketing scrap and salvaged materials and needed expert assistance.

In addition to meeting the many problems associated with inventory—counting, recording, classification, segregation, retention, sale, or removal and storage on behalf of the government—contractors were required to obtain and settle their subcontract claims as expeditiously as possible so that the cost of all claims under a terminated contract could be passed up the line and incorporated in the claim of the prime with a minimum of delay. To accomplish this, contracting officers were instructed by termination regulations to develop, at the initial posttermination conference with the prime contractor, a time schedule calling for completion of the various steps in the settlement process by certain dates. Thus the prime contractor's inventory schedules were, if possible, to be submitted within thirty days of termination, with partial inventories submitted earlier. Similarly, a time was to be set for any application by the prime or subcontractors for interim financing, for subcon-

tractor inventory schedules and settlement proposals, and for any partial proposals of the prime covering a portion of his own charges. The final settlement proposal of the prime contractor, except for the complicated cases, was to be submitted wherever possible not later than sixty days from the termination date. The suggested deadline for review of the proposal by procuring agencies and negotiation of the final settlement was ninety days after the termination date.[9]

In view of the many important decisions which had to be made prior to the submission of the contractor's settlement proposal, and in order to expedite the whole process, contracting officers and their staffs were enjoined by regulation not to delay action until after proposals were submitted. They were required in all important settlements to work with the contractor continuously in disposing of termination inventory, in making and approving subcontract settlements, and in preparing the contractor's settlement proposal.[10] In actual practice, therefore, the settlement process was a joint effort at every stage rather than a series of separate steps respectively by the contractor or contracting agency.

The third and final step in the general settlement process was normally the responsibility of the contracting officer and his staff. This consisted of a careful review of the contractor's claim by specialists, followed by negotiation with the contractor and conclusion of a mutually satisfactory settlement agreement. The minimum review accorded all settlement proposals for Army contracts was the so-called office review, which involved a careful scrutiny of all aspects of the claim by members of the contracting officer's

---

[9] JTR 255, Time schedule for settlement.
[10] JTR 711.3.

staff. This review not only tested the proposal itself for internal consistency, legality, and reasonableness, but brought to bear other information on the contractor's history, operations, financial structure, and general characteristics. Such information was available from the files pertaining to the letting and administration of the terminated contract as well as from other contracts let by the procuring agency. If the contracting officer was not satisfied with the adequacy and reliability of the data in the settlement proposal, he could request additional information from the contractor or request members of his staff to visit the contractor's plant and examine plant records or other evidence to the extent necessary When any such additional examination was made the reviewers were required to submit written reports and recommendations to the contracting officer.[11]

Actual settlement negotiations with the contractor were conducted by a team of specialists operating under the direction of the contracting officer. The team consisted of legal, accounting, engineering, and property disposal personnel whose services were co-ordinated by the negotiator in charge.[12] Since the contracting officer could not personally participate in most negotiations, he was represented by a negotiator appointed to head up the team. Each specialist was qualified to protect the government's interest in his particular area. Thus Army engineering and inspection personnel assigned to a team frequently had intimate knowledge of

the state of the contractor's inventory—its quantity, quality, value, allocability to the terminated contract, and other relevant matters. War Department accountants, familiar with official termination accounting procedures and with the accounting practices of contractors in general, could detect internal inconsistencies in the settlement proposal or inconsistencies of the proposal with the books of the contractor. Property disposal experts could facilitate difficult decisions with respect to the scrapping, sale, contractor retention, or other disposition of materials. The essence of the negotiated type of settlement, conducted by a team of experts, was its flexibility in permitting common-sense adjustments and compromises which would protect the government's interest in the over-all settlement while avoiding a stalemate in negotiations over minor technicalities.[13]

Arrival at a final agreement was typically the culmination of a series of discussions and partial agreements on a step-by-step basis. The final agreement was drawn up as a supplement to the basic contract. Its general form and content were prescribed in current official termination regulations, which reflected the accumulated experience of all the procurement agencies. In addition to containing the basic settlement terms, the final agreement carried special reservations of varying nature. Thus, in addition to the normal statement of disposal credits, offsets for

---

[11] JTR 724.1.

[12] The composition of the team varied with the size and complexity of the settlement. JTR 711.2, Settlement team. Some teams might have as many as fifty people. See Memorandum on Contract Termination Training and Organization (unsigned), 12 Sep 44, in file 161 Contract Termination, Control Div ASF.

[13] The fact that War Department negotiated settlements were conducted by a team of experts rather than by a single individual was strongly emphasized by Under Secretary Patterson in his testimony before Congress prior to the passage of the Contract Settlement Act. Such teamwork minimized the possibility of either error or fraud, an important consideration in the debate with the Comptroller General over final settlement authority. Malman, "Policies and Procedures of the Termination of War Contracts," p. 507.

advance payments, and other specific counterclaims of the government against the terminated prime contract, the agreement reserved the government's right of subsequent over-all renegotiation, and its rights under various royalty, patent, facility, and other provisions. Similar reservations were made to protect the continuation of those normal rights of the contractor which were outside the contemplation of the settlement as such.[14]

The contracting officer had sole authority to execute all settlement agreements. For large settlements, however, he was by regulation forbidden to exercise this authority in the absence of certain review and approval procedures. The principal requirement was review by the local Settlement Review Board. This board had to review prior to execution all fixed-price settlements involving a payment of more than $25,000 and all fixed-fee adjustments under CPFF contracts with a terminated value in excess of $50,000. In addition, the chief of the relevant technical service could require board review of any particular settlement before execution. Also, the contracting officer could at his own discretion submit to the board for its advice any proposed settlement or specific problem thereunder.[15]

The review board had to give prompt consideration to all matters submitted to it and to report its recommendations to the contracting officer in writing. Failure to act within thirty days automatically constituted board approval. Board disapproval of any settlement precluded its execution by the contracting officer unless it was subsequently approved by the head of the office in which the board was established.

In addition to local board review, all War Department settlements exceeding $500,000 required approval by such higher authority as the chief of the relevant technical service prescribed. The chief of each service could also prescribe a figure lower than $500,000 for this mandatory review procedure if he deemed it desirable.

In the event that a negotiated settlement for all or any part of a termination claim could not be reached, or if the contractor were dilatory in negotiation, the contracting officer was authorized to make a determination of the disputed amounts due. Determinations were based on the formula prescribed in the termination article of the contract or, in the absence of such formula, upon an equivalent formula in JTR. Because of the inflexibility and greater amount of work involved, this type of settlement was unattractive to both contractors and procuring agencies and was relatively little used.[16]

Appeal from determinations could be made in several ways. Under the standard Disputes Article of War Department contracts, appeal from the contracting officer's decision could be made within thirty days to the War Department Board of Contract Appeals. This board granted a full hearing and afforded the contractor an opportunity to present evidence in support of his claim. The board's decision was final within the War Department. Appeal from its decision, or directly from the decision of the contracting officer, could be taken to the Appeals Board of the Office of Contract Settlement. Procedure of the OCS Appeals Board was similar to that of the War Department board. Even a decision of the OCS board did not exhaust the contractor's remedy.

---

[14] JTR, Sec. VII, Pt. 4, Settlement Agreements.

[15] Settlement review boards consisted of three or more responsible officers or civilians of the War or Navy Departments and were established, so far as possible, in each office empowered to negotiate final settlements. JTR 581.

[16] OCS History, p. 62.

He could still take his case to the U.S. Court of Claims or to a U.S. District Court. Both courts could likewise receive cases which by-passed both the War Department and OCS appeals boards. An indication of the relatively small number of termination appeals is found in the record of the OCS Appeals Board, which as late as 31 March 1947 had received on appeal less than one tenth of one percent of all settlements. The number of cases taken to the courts was undoubtedly even smaller.[17]

Special Settlement Procedures

While the general procedure for contract settlement was being developed, continual search was made for special methods of handling difficult problems and for additional optional procedures which would expedite the settlement process on any reasonable and equitable basis. The more important of these special procedures were developed mainly by the War Department and contributed substantially to the success of contract settlement operations for World War II.

No-Cost Settlements

A major factor in the ability of the contracting agencies to handle their enormous workload of termination claims was the popularization of the "no-cost" type of settlement. As implied by its name, the no-cost settlement was a waiver by the contractor of any claim against the government resulting from the termination of his contract. In return for the waiver the contractor had the right to retain and dispose of his

termination inventory as he saw fit. Moreover, he was freed from the onerous task of taking inventory and preparing and filing inventory schedules. He had no settlement proposal to prepare and participated in no time-consuming negotiations. Hence, he was free to devote his time and energy to production under other war contracts or to meeting his problems of reconversion.[18]

Against these obvious advantages the contractor had to weigh the value of his termination claim. Several types of situation indicated the clear advantage of a no-cost settlement. First were the thousands of small claims which were not worth the bother of formal settlement procedures. Next were cases where the contractor's inventory was worth more to him than the value of his termination claim. Such cases usually involved inventories of scarce or difficult-to-acquire materials, parts, and perhaps even partially processed materials, which the contractor could immediately use on other contracts, sell advantageously on the open market, or reserve for his subsequent use. Finally, a consideration facing many contractors was the avoidance of taxes and renegotiation payments which might well absorb the entire profit realized on a termination claim. If a firm had already earned excessive profits, the receipt of further profits for the same renegotiable year would merely involve an additional and unnecessary double exchange of funds.

Until the end of 1943, procuring agencies as well as contractors were concentrating on all-out production for war. Termination of a particular contract frequently meant that the contractor merely shifted his efforts to the production of similar items under other contracts, using the same materials, equip-

---

[17] *Ibid.* Also see Chapter XII of the OCS history for a concise but informative discussion of the principal decisions of the OCS Appeals Board and the issues resolved thereunder.

[18] ASF, Readjustment History, pp. 43–46.

ment, and labor. Since the termination resulted in little additional expense, the contractor more often than not would simply sign a "no claim" agreement and proceed under his new contract. By the end of 1943, 80.5 percent of all War Department termination settlements, representing 63.6 percent of the value of settled canceled commitments, had been closed "without claim." [19] Early in 1944, as replacement contracts became more difficult to obtain, the ratio of "no cost" to total settlements began to drop. During the first six months of 1944, no-cost settlements represented 64.3 percent in number and 45 percent by value of all settlements. By the end of 1946, when the task of contract settlement for World War II was nearly over, no-cost settlements by the War Department for both fixed-price and CPFF contracts represented 53.8 percent by number but only 14.8 percent by value of cumulative canceled commitments. [20]

Because of the importance of the no-cost type of settlement in speeding and simplifying the whole termination program, the War Department took steps to encourage its widest use. One of these steps was made possible by a ruling from the Bureau of Internal Revenue that the execution of a no-cost settlement would not affect the contractor's right to deduct for tax purposes all costs under the terminated contract which were otherwise allowable under existing regulations. Prior to this ruling, which was sought by the War Department as well as by industry, there had been increasing reluctance on the part of contractors to execute no-cost

settlements. [21] This ruling clarified the right of contractors to possible tax benefits resulting from inventory losses. Under the ruling, contractors could deduct inventory losses realized in the year of termination from taxable income for that year. If the loss were realized in a subsequent year, the contractor might likewise realize a tax saving through loss-carryback provisions or by the utilization of otherwise unused excess profits credits. The prospect of inventory losses and revaluations at the time of mass terminations was a major factor for many firms in electing settlement procedures and planning their readjustment policy. As soon as the ruling was issued, the War Department had it widely distributed with instructions that contracting officers point out its possible advantages to contractors before the end of the year. [22]

Of even greater complexity than the associated tax problems were the possible effects of no-cost settlements upon renegotiation. A principal advantage of the no-cost settlement was its administrative simplicity combined with the possibility of reduced tax payments and reduced payments in renegotiation. Renegotiators, however, were faced with the problem of ascertaining the validity of inventory losses claimed in renegotiation. A careful identification of inventory items upon which loss was claimed

---

[19] ASF, Monthly Progress Report, Section 14–A, Contract Terminations, 30 Apr 44, pp. 1, 8–9.

[20] (1) *Ibid.*, 31 Dec 45, pp. 34–35, 52–53. (2) WD, Progress Report, Section 5–A, 31 Dec 46, pp. 11–14.

[21] Joseph D. Nunan, Commissioner, 1944–22–11883, Mimeograph 5766, to Collectors *et al.*, 1 Nov 44, regarding Sec. 29.42–1. The bureau ruled that no amount would be included in income as a result of the termination.

[22] Memo, CG ASF for Chfs of All Technical Services, 3 Nov 44, sub: No-Cost Settlements. The memorandum concluded ". . . it is suggested that the ruling and any information . . . be sent to your procuring officers by wire, and this matter be given very high priority in view of the inherent possibilities of largely eliminating the present termination backlog."

would require detailed audit procedures largely nullifying the administrative benefits of no-cost settlements. Moreover, the substantive effects of allowing inventory losses in renegotiation might discriminate in favor of contractors with excessive profits and militate against closer pricing. These issues were part of the general problem of the proper relationship to be established between termination and renegotiation, the ramifications of which cannot be explored in a general study. After a survey of the problem, it was decided that the benefits of the no-cost settlement to the government and to contractors generally outweighed the disadvantages and inequities. Contractors were assured that they would be fairly treated in renegotiation and their reluctance to enter no-cost settlement in consideration of renegotiation matters was largely dispelled.[23]

The nearly 72,000 no-cost settlements effected by the War Department, representing almost $7 billion in canceled contract commitments, were a major contribution to the entire readjustment program. Although the value of contracts settled by the War Department on a no-cost basis was half again as great as that of all other contracting agencies combined, the department's use of the no-cost procedure was relatively the lowest for all agencies. A comparative study, based on settlements effected through 30 September 1946, indicates that each of the other agencies had a higher percentage of no-cost settlements in terms of both number and value. (*See Table 63, page 699.*)

Pretermination Planning and Agreements

In the broadest sense, pretermination planning by the War Department comprehended all its advance efforts connected with the termination and settlement problem. As already described, these included the War Department's complex training program, the early efforts to develop a standard contractual termination article, the establishment of internal organizations to deal with termination and reconversion, the perfection of administrative policy and procedures, the obtaining of suitable legislation from Congress, and the sum total of its pretermination relations with contractors and others designed to facilitate the liquidation of war contracts.

By the summer of 1944 the term "pretermination planning" began to take on a narrower and more specific meaning. As early as 1943, it had become evident that the circumstances facing a large prime contractor at termination would require tens of thousands of decisions before a settlement proposal could be made. These decisions—pertaining to the scrapping, retention, sale, or storage of hundreds or thousands of items of raw materials, components, and partly finished products, the allocability of inventory and overhead costs to terminated contracts, the basis for settlement of subcontractor claims, and many other issues in termination—were novel both as to substance and procedure. The Army's experience with a few large terminations in 1942

---

[23] (1) Memo, W. James MacIntosh, General Counsel for WDPAB, 2 Aug 44, sub: Waiver of Termination Claims—Effect on Statutory Renegotiation. (2) Memo, W. E. Harrington, Deputy Dir Renegotiation Div, for CG ASF, 12 May 45, sub: Advice to the Members of the National Association of Manufacturers' Subcommittee Studying Cost Accounting Procedures as to Method of Handling Termination Claims, Control Div file 161. (3) Jacob K. Lasser, *How to Speed up Settlement of Your Terminated War Contract* (New York: McGraw-Hill Book Company, Inc., 1945), pp. 158–59. (4) Research Institute of America, Contract Termination Guide for Contractors and Subcontractors (June 1944), How to Relate Termination to Renegotiation, pp. 67–73.

which remained unsettled throughout 1943 and well into 1944 indicated that, no matter how elaborate the education, training, and general preparation of contractors might be, an important element was lacking. Some method was required whereby much of the actual work of settlement could be achieved *prior* to termination. This was found to be essential for at least two major reasons: (1) to reduce the posttermination workload to manageable proportions; (2) to prevent the incurrence by the government of substantial unnecessary costs.[24]

The first of these considerations was uppermost in the minds of the larger contractors whose complex, day-to-day operations at the center of a network of hundreds of subcontractors foreshadowed the magnitude of the termination problem. Outstanding for its advance planning to meet the challenge of termination was the Studebaker Corporation. The director of Studebaker's termination activities, Mr. Courtney Johnson, did much to develop and apply the possibilities of the pretermination agreement and to sell the idea to industrial leaders throughout the country. Starting with a few specific decisions pertaining to the disposition of bulky inventory items to be made after termination, planning at Studebaker gradually spread to include all items of inventory for

a particular contract, then to the basis for allocating factory overhead, administrative expense, profit percentages, and posttermination items of expense. To put its decisions to the acid test of acceptability by the contracting officer, Studebaker assumed a hypothetical termination of its current contract for the M29 cargo carrier (the weasel) and prepared a complete termination claim for submission as a dry run to the Chicago Ordnance District. The purpose of the experiment was not to secure acceptance of the dollar amounts proposed in the claim, but to obtain agreement on the methods of computation, inventory items to be scrapped, retained, or tranferred to the government, and similar matters. After intensive study of the proposal by the Chicago Ordnance District, the Office of the Chief of Ordnance, and the Readjustment Division, ASF, a revised pretermination agreement was completed and incorporated into the basic contract on 24 November 1944.[25]

Although not the first pretermination agreement to be concluded,[26] the Stude-

---

[24] An important case which brought increased attention to the desirability of greater pretermination planning was the Army's tank contract with the International Harvester Company. This contract was canceled early in 1943 and required sixteen months for settlement. The termination represented a canceled commitment of some $217,000,000, involved 2,400 subcontractors, and gave rise to claims in the neighborhood of $25,000,000. At the time of its settlement in July 1944, it was the largest termination settlement processed by the War Department. (1) Memo, Gen Somervell for CofOrd, 25 Jul 44, sub: International Harvester Settlement, file 161 Contract Termination, Control Div ASF. (2) ASF, Readjustment History, p. 128.

[25] The general background of Studebaker's pretermination planning activities is excellently depicted in An Address by Mr. Courtney Johnson of the Studebaker Corporation on Thursday, 7 December 1944 (19-page mimeographed reproduction by the Army Industrial College of address given for the AIC War Readjustment Course). See also Studebaker pretermination material accompanying following letters: (1) Courtney Johnson, Asst to Chmn of the Board, Studebaker Corporation, to Gen Browning, Asst Dir of Materiel ASF, 12 Sept 44, sub: Predetermination of Property Disposal and Other Factors in Anticipation of Contract Termination; (2) Johnson to Maj C. T. Everett, Head Contract Termination Sec, Tank-Automotive Br, Chicago Ord District, 9 Feb 45; (3) Johnson to Col Curtis G. Pratt, Readjustment Div ASF, 3 May 45; (4) Johnson to Chetwood-Aiken Company, Philadelphia, Pennsylvania, 23 May 45. All in file 204.5 Readjustment Div ASF.

[26] "The first formal pretermination settlement agreement was consummated on 26 October 1944 by the Quartermaster Corps with Botany Worsted Mills." ASF, Readjustment History, p. 92.

baker case was of major significance in demonstrating the capacity of a large corporation, with current procurement deliveries of $40 million per month and over 400 first-tier subcontractors, to reach binding decisions on policies and procedures well in advance of termination. Studebaker immediately went to work on its other major contracts and also did much pioneer work in developing model pretermination agreements between prime contractors and their subs. Numerous copies of its agreements were distributed throughout the country to aid other contractors in solving their termination problems.[27]

Even before Studebaker submitted the experimental claim for the weasel, the Army had decided to generalize the benefits of the company's planning experience. On 8 August 1944, General Somervell announced to the chiefs of the technical services the institution of a selective pretermination planning program.[28] Two days later, the details of the plan were forwarded by the director of the Readjustment Division. A total of 183 of the War Department's leading contractors were apportioned among the technical services. Each service, operating through its field offices, was to collaborate with these assigned contractors in developing a written termination plan. Such plans would represent informal agreements resolving in advance of termination as many issues as possible. While not binding on either contractors or the government, the plans were expected to be implemented in the absence of major changes in the underlying situation. Included in the instructions was a letter from the Studebaker Corporation indicating the kind of planning required. A formal report of its progress was requested from each technical service by 1 October 1944.[29]

In the meantime, the Readjustment Division had also been developing the pretermination planning idea along somewhat different lines. On 19 June 1944, Lt. Col. C. M. Gilmour of the Termination Branch, Readjustment Division, proposed the actual predetermination of contract termination charges in the form of a binding agreement as a means of keeping settlement charges borne by the government to a minimum.[30] Colonel Gilmour pointed out that existing methods of computing termination charges were a thinly disguised cost-plus-a-percentage-of-cost method of payment. Although the First War Powers Act had explicitly outlawed CPPC contracts, the existing formula upon which the negotiated termination rested allowed the contractor all his costs plus 2 percent profit on unprocessed materials and 8 percent on work in process. This furnished a positive inducement for all contractors to build up their inventories to a maximum in anticipation of termination, thereby saddling the government with the additional inventory costs as well as profit allowances upon unnecessary inventory. Existing inventory limitations under CMP and other WPB regulations applied only to a fraction of all materials. Likewise, current termination regulations provided for full compensation for all allocable inventory, subject only to the restriction that the inventory could not exceed the needs of the entire contract. Colonel Gilmour proposed that pretermination agreements could be made which would determine reasonable in-

---

[27] See documents cited above, note 25.

[28] Memo, Gen Somervell for TQMG, 8 Aug 44, sub: Termination Planning, Purchases Div file 161 Contract Termination, 1 Sep 44–31 Oct 44.

[29] Memo, Col David N. Hauseman, Dir Readjustment Div, for CofTrans, 10 Aug 44, sub: Fixed Contract Termination Charges, Purchases Div file 161 Contract Termination, 1 Sep 44–31 Oct 44.

[30] Memo, Col Gilmour for Col Draper, 19 Jun 44, sub: Fixed Contract Termination Charges.

ventory and other charges allowable upon termination for various brackets or stages of contract completion. The settlement charge would be based upon a specified working inventory level and other considerations, and would be expressed either as a graduated lump sum, varying with the stage of contract completion, or as an amount per unit permitting a simple "count and multiply" procedure upon termination. This would at once eliminate most of the workload at termination, discourage the wastage of materials, and keep termination charges to a minimum.

The possibilities of Colonel Gilmour's suggestion were immediately recognized and brought to the attention of General Browning.[31] On 22 July in a lengthy memorandum, General Browning authorized the technical services to make predetermination agreements with contractors, either in new contracts or by amendment to existing ones. The general philosophy underlying the plan of a fixed termination charge was described together with various advantages of the plan. Two days later, he sent more elaborate instructions pointing to the experimental nature of the predetermination program and encouraging the services to exercise ingenuity in fitting the plan to the circumstances of each contract. All agreements thus

reached would be subject to approval by the Readjustment Division.[32]

Shortly thereafter the Office of Contract Settlement, in response to the War Department's request, conferred its blessing upon the program:

Any department or agency of the Government may embody in any contract a special agreement to pay the contractor, as fair compensation for the termination of the contract, amounts specified in the contract or to be readily computed according to specific methods, standards or bases appropriate to the particular contract and set out therein, in lieu of any other compensation therefor, whenever the department or agency determines (1) that the available data permits [sic] a reasonable forecast, consistent with sound commercial standards, of the factors involved in determining what will be fair compensation for termination in the case or class of cases and (2) that such agreement will substantially facilitate settlements, plant clearance, reconversion from war to civilian production or the efficient use of materials, manpower and facilities or will otherwise promote the objectives of the Contract Settlement Act of 1944.[33]

---

[31] Mr. Glen Lloyd, who had worked closely with General Browning on the Army's company pricing program, was instrumental in selling the idea to General Browning. Mr. Lloyd saw a close similarity between forward pricing and the advance determination of termination charges. He therefore recommended that negotiation of advance settlements be tied in with the company pricing program of the Purchases Division, ASF. Memo, Lloyd for Gen Browning, 25 Aug 44, sub: Administration of Program for the Predetermination of Termination Questions and Claims, Purchases Div file 161 Contract Termination, 1 Sep 43 through July 1944.

[32] (1) Memo, Gen Browning ,Assist Dir of Materiel, for Chfs of the Technical Services, 22 Jul 44, sub: Negotiation of Fixed Termination Charges. (2) Memo, Browning for Chfs of Technical Services, 24 July 44, inclosing unsigned, five-page, mimeographed Memo, 22 Jul 44, sub: Experimental Program for Simplying Termination Procedures and Predetermining Termination Allowances. (3) Memo, Gen Clay, Dir of Materiel, for Asst Dir of Materiel and Dirs Production, Purchasing, and Readjustment Divs, 4 Sep 44, sub: Predetermined Termination Settlements and Advance Arrangements as to Elements of Termination Settlements, in Purchases Div file 161 Contract Termination, 1 Sep 44–31 Oct 44.

[33] OCS Regulation 3, 27 Sep 44, amending OWMR Dir Order 2. See also: Ltr, Gen Browning to Mr. Arnold Stifel, 22 Sep 44, Purchases Div file 161 Contract Termination, 1 Sep 44–31 Oct 44: "Today the Director of Contract Settlement approved our plan of predetermined settlements, and the regulations will be issued in the next few days."

A number of predetermination agreements were soon reached, especially with smaller contractors whose termination problems were relatively simple. It was soon recognized that the objectives of this program were intimately related to those of the pretermination planning program involving the 183 leading contractors. Although the latter began with the idea of reaching only tentative agreements, the experience of Studebaker and other firms indicated that binding agreements could be reached and would provide the most certainty for all concerned. Accordingly, both plans were merged into a general Pretermination Planning Program, the purpose of which was to conclude as many written pretermination agreements as possible—binding agreements where feasible, and informal agreements on issues requiring greater flexibility because of the uncertainties of future prices and market conditions.

By 31 August 1945, the War Department had consummated 1,637 formal pretermination agreements with contractors, in addition to 1,570 informal agreements.[34] These 3,200 arrangements in advance of termination, some of which involved individual firms holding a half-billion dollars in war contracts, were a major factor in the ultimate success of the War Department's contract settlement operations. The agreements varied considerably in scope, some providing a complete basis for settlement, others covering only certain areas. Collectively, they covered a wide variety of subject matter, the principal items of which were as follows:

1. Disposition of specific items or classes of inventory.

   a. Retention by contractor.

   b. Transfer to the Government.

   c. Scrapping.

2. Definition of agreed stop-work points.

3. Rates and methods of computing general and administrative expense, overhead, or other indirect expense.

4. Treatment of engineering and tooling costs and other nonrecurring starting-load expenses.

5. Allowance for special facilties.

6. Determination of rates or amounts of profit.

Of these several problem areas, a brief discussion of stop-work points will illuminate a termination problem that had general economic implications.

With the passage of the War Mobilization and Reconversion Act of 1944, it became definite national policy not to continue production of war matériel in excess of military needs in order to ease the process of national readjustment at the end of the war.[35] Hence it was the established policy of the procuring agencies to order immediate cessation of work with the serving of a termination notice. Exceptions allowed by the Office of War Mobilization and Reconversion included considerations of safety, clearance of machinery, and bringing work in process to a useful or marketable stage where the additional costs would be more than compensated by the additional value to the government. The last-named exception was at first officially discouraged by the War Department on the ground that it placed contracting officers in the position of making highly speculative decisions. It was feared that the authorization of additional production at a time when the market was glutted by sur-

---

[34] ASF, Readjustment History, p. 95.

[35] This policy was expressed in Section 202 of the act, which permitted certain exceptions under the direction of OWMR.

pluses would result in the dissipation of War Department funds for the prospect of uncertain gains, which in any case would be recouped by the surplus disposal agencies rather than by the War Department.[36]

The need for a more definitive and enlightened stop-work policy was demonstrated by a number of War Department terminations in the fall of 1944. These terminations required the abrupt cessation of work and much of the related termination inventories had to be disposed of as scrap. Later, with the increase in requirements accompanying the Battle of the Bulge, some of these contracts were renewed and manufacturers had to start production runs anew. It was then painfully obvious that a policy which would have permitted production under terminated contracts to be carried to reasonable stop-work stages would have prevented substantial losses.[37] In its pretermination agreements drawn up during 1945, the War Department gave careful consideration to the entire problem; as a result detailed definitions of stop-work stages, especially for the textile and similar industries, were incorporated in such agreements.

The stop-work stages were carefully designed by experts, largely from the War Production Board and industry, to permit production after termination continued long enough to bring work in process to the first economical stopping point. Not only was this a desirable procedure from the standpoint of nationwide conservation of materials and parts; it also placed the War Department in a better bargaining position with contractors in determining the retention or sale price of termination inventory. In spite of earlier misgivings, by bringing work in process to a marketable stage the War Department did not have to accept individual contractors' retention offers at scrap prices.[38] Likewise, the incorporation of stop-work points in pretermination agreements enabled contractors to plan with greater certainty their readjustment programs and especially facilitated the clearance of plant and machinery.

The complexity and significance of the Army's pretermination agreements are barely suggested in the foregoing brief discussion. Many of the agreements were based on extended conferences with representatives of an entire industry, such as steel, textiles, clothing, and leather. As in the case of most economic mobilization issues, representatives of WPB, OWMR, OCS, and other superagencies and procuring agencies participated in the program. Nevertheless, the Army was the leader in developing and utilizing the pretermination agreement as an effective instrument of early contract settlement. With the arrival of V–J Day the Pretermination Planning Program came to an end, and in the face of mass contract ter-

---

[36] (1) Memo, Gen Clay, Dir of Materiel ASF, for TQMG, 4 Jul 44, sub: Contract Termination Policy To Be Followed on V-Day, Control Div file 161 Contract Termination; (2) Ltr, USW Patterson to Hancock, Chmn JCTB, 15 Jul 44. (3) Memo, Col Draper, Chf Contract Settlement Br, Readjustment Div, for Gen Clay, 15 Sep 44, sub: Cut-Off Point. (4) Memo, Brig Gen David N. Hauseman, Dir Readjustment Div, for Dir of Materiel, undated, sub: Stop-Work Policy, copy in OCMH.

[37] (1) Hauseman Memo, cited above, note 36(4). (2) Memo, Col Draper, Asst Dir for Contract Settlement, for Gen Hauseman, 1 Jan 45, recommending a plan for completion of important items more than 50-percent finished.

[38] General Hauseman (see references above, note 36) cited the example of Army shoes having a cost of $3.50 and negligible scrap value at the point of termination. By spending another 50 cents to bring the shoes to completion, the Army could sell the shoes for $2.00 to UNRRA or the civilian market thus reducing the net termination cost from $3.50 to $2.00.

minations the full fruits of the program began at this time to be realized.[39]

The Consolidated Termination Program

With the sharp rise in terminations beginning in the summer of 1943, many of the operating and procedural problems associated with widespread termination began to appear. An important group of problems arose from the fact that the typical manufacturing firm was working on not one war contract, but many, representing orders from several supply arms of one or more procuring agencies. Some of these orders might be prime contracts; others would be subcontracts, varying widely in the number of tiers or stages removed from the prime contract. Many of the largest manufacturing firms in the country, such as the Aluminum Company of America (ALCOA), the General Electric Corporation, and the large steel companies, actually did a greater volume of business on subcontracts than on direct orders placed with them by the procuring agencies.

Under the standard vertical settlement procedure each terminated contract was separately processed, audited, negotiated, and settled. This meant that a large contractor holding hundreds of subcontracts in addition to a number of prime contracts was faced with a steady procession of auditors, inspectors, and other representatives of Ordnance, Signal Corps, Engineers, Quartermaster, and so on, to say nothing of the various Navy bureaus and higher level contractors who had the task of approving for payment the claims of their underlying subcontractors. Much of the work was sheer duplication, involving the auditing of overhead and other accounts common to many contracts. Each set of auditors had to be newly indoctrinated in the nature of the firm's books and business operations. The system was annoying to contractors and expensive to the Government.

The first step to rectify the situation was taken on 18 October 1943 with the decision by the Army to appoint a permanent Field Accounting Representative (FAR) to each of four large corporations.[40] All auditing and accounting activity required by the War Department to settle the company's terminated contracts, whether prime or sub, was consolidated in the Field Accounting Representative. The FAR was thus responsible for the accounting review—as required by Procurement Regulations and the Termination Accounting Manual—of all the company's settlement proposals regardless of the technical service concerned. He made the physical inventory check on which the proposal was based. He examined the settlement proposals of the company's subcon-

---

[39] The following commentary made shortly after V–J Day is illustrative. "Because of pretermination settlement agreements, the Botany Worsted Mills were able to resume full production on civilian fabrics after a two-day holiday following the announcement by the President of the surrender of Japan, at which time notices of termination of the company's war contracts were received. The management is enthusiastically satisfied with the results of the agreements and expressed the opinion that the manner in which their pretermination settlement agreements have been handled and the principles and regulations on which they are based could not be improved upon." Memo, Maj T. F. Parks, Pretermination Br, Readjustment Div, for the Asst Dir for Contract Settlement, 7 Sep 45, sub: Report of Travel.

[40] Gen Ulio, TAG, to CG AAF and Chfs of Technical Services, 18 Oct 43, sub: Accounting review of termination settlements of contracts with companies holding many War Department, prime and subcontracts, SPX–167 (18 Oct 43) SPPDL–MB–A. The four corporations were Alcoa and Bendix, assigned to the Air Forces, and General Motors and Allis-Chalmers, assigned to Ordnance.

tractors, as well as the company's own proposals forwarded in turn to its customers. He was authorized to discuss his findings with the company, and was required to submit them to the contracting officer having jurisdiction over the prime contract. Contracting officers, in effecting settlement, were authorized to rely upon the audits and reports of the FAR. The FAR was instructed to keep appropriate records, to co-operate closely with renegotiators, and to co-ordinate his work with any War Department administrative CPFF audit conducted at the project. The directive announcing the new procedure indicated that it would be expanded as soon as justified by the results.[41]

It soon became evident that efficient accounting review was not enough to guarantee the prompt settlement of contracts. Many of the most difficult problems revolved about the pricing and disposition of termination inventory and other physical property. Accordingly, on 28 January 1944, disposal advisory officers were placed in the four companies together with the FAR. The basic responsibility of the disposal advisory officer was to make recommendations to the contracting officer concerning the disposition of property and to assist contractors in their disposal efforts. This relieved the FAR of many of his inventory problems and freed contracting officers from the necessity of an independent investigation of the numerous issues in property disposal.[42]

The results of the four-company experiment were favorable and on 24 February 1944 the program was expanded to a total of 29 companies assigned to the various

services as follows: Army Air Forces, 8; Ordnance, 13; Quartermaster Corps, 1; Signal Corps, 3; Transportation Corps, 1; Corps of Engineers, 3. The next logical step was to include the Navy in the program thus eliminating the major remaining source of duplication. This was done initially on 18 March 1944. By the time of the issuance of the Joint Termination Regulation in November, the program had acquired its permanent name—the Consolidated Termination Program.[43]

Companies desiring to come under the program made written application and were selected on the basis of the following qualifications: (1) large number of war contracts; (2) large volume of termination claims; (3) demonstrated ability to process termination claims efficiently; (4) probability of more expeditious settlement after assignment. The number of companies under the program grew slowly as procedures were being developed throughout the summer and fall of 1944. As of 20 November 1944, there were 31 participants. This grew to 63 in June 1945, and later to "nearly one hundred." [44]

By the end of 1945, when the peak of terminations had passed, the War Department recognized that the program would be discontinued for each assigned company as soon as the workload had been reduced to

---

[41] *Ibid.*, par. 2.

[42] Memo, Col Hauseman, Dir Readjustment Div, for CG AAF and Chfs of Technical Services, 28 Jan 44, sub: Advisory Officers to Expedite Disposal of Property on Termination in Companies Holding Many War Department Prime and Sub-Contracts.

[43] (1) Memo and 3 incls., Hauseman for CG AAF and Chfs of Technical Services, 24 Feb 44, sub: Contract Termination Field Accounting Representatives and Disposal Advisory Officers. (2) Jt Dir, 18 Mar 44, published as Sec. V, ASF Cir 80, cited in ASF Cir 166, 1 Jun 44. (3) JTR, Sec. VIII, Pt. 2, Consolidated Termination Program for Selected Contractors.

[44] (1) JTR 829. (2) JTR (Revision No. 2, 20 Jun 45), pp. 3505–07. (3) OCS History, p. 31. Of the sixty-three participating firms in June 1945, six were assigned to the Navy and nineteen were subsidiaries of other participating corporations assigned to the Army.

the point where it could be handled by the normal vertical settlement procedure. Hence, the general rule was adopted that all claims arising out of terminations made after 31 December 1945 and all claims submitted after 31 March 1946 would be excluded from the program and processed under standard procedures. Exceptions could be made by the Readjustment Division. Nevertheless, the various projects were rapidly liquidated and little, if any, activity under the program continued beyond 30 June 1946.[45]

The significance of the Consolidated Termination Program was much greater than the number of participating companies would indicate, inasmuch as it was confined to very large concerns having a high dollar volume of war contracts. Not only were settlements of the contracts of the participating companies expedited; settlement and payment of all other related contracts, in both higher and lower contractor echelons, were also facilitated. Moreover, as indicated in the following section, the Consolidated Termination Program provided the groundwork for the establishment of the company-wide settlement program.

Company-Wide Settlements

Even before the introduction of the Consolidated Termination Program, there had been extended discussion in termination planning circles of a basic alternative to the standard vertical settlement procedure. As early as April 1943, Mr. Clarence L. Collens, chairman of the Contract Termination Committee, National Electrical Manufacturers Association, had proposed an over-all

company settlement plan.[46] Subsequently, other representatives of industry, the armed services, Congress, and the Joint Contract Termination Board all explored the possibility of direct settlement procedures between the government and individual contractors at all levels in the contractual chain.[47]

The desire for direct settlement stemmed from a number of shortcomings of the vertical settlement procedure. Under the ver-

---

[45] ASF, Readjustment History, Vol. III (Supplement), pp. 16–19.

[46] AIC Special Course in Contract Termination, 3–13 Jan 44, Committee Report on Problem 8, Overall Company Settlements, p. 1, ICAF Library. Mr. Collens, who was president of the Reliance Electric and Engineering Company, testified at length on his proposal before the Senate Military Affairs subcommittee. *Hearings on S. J. Res. 80,* Pt. 1. The substance of Mr. Collens' plan is contained in his Memorandum on Procedure for Merged or Over-All Claims Under War Contract Terminations Rendered Direct to the Government by the Claimant, 26 Nov 43, in source cited in note 47.

[47] The initial responsibility for developing a company-wide settlement plan fell to the JCTB Subcommittee on Overall Settlements. After the passage of the Contract Settlement Act of 1944 the policy-making role fell to the Director of Contract Settlement. In either case, the principal labors fell to Army and Navy personnel in subcommittee and departmental staffs. See the following documents in Bibliography on Company-Wide or Merged Claim Settlements, issued by the Navy, 18 Jan 44, copy in Readjustment Div file 161: (1) Memo, Comdr H. F. Linder for Capt L. L. Strauss, 4 Dec 43, sub: Outline of Policy and Procedure for Contract Termination and Property Disposal; (2) Proposed Statement of Policy on Termination Procedure, Navy draft, 17 Jan 44, PM601/ALW:adc; (3) AIC Com Rpt on Problem No. 8 (cited above, note 46); (4) Excerpt from Memo, USN Forrestal for Senator Murray, 11 Jan 44, sub: Company Settlements; (5) Memo prepared by WD, n.d., sub: Tentative Plan for Over-All Company or Group Termination Settlements, Combined With Renegotiation Settlements Where Possible; (6) Memo, Lt (jg) A. L. Wadsworth for Lt Col F. Workum, 21 Dec 43, sub: Suggestions for Redraft of Overall Company Settlement Plan; (7) Collens' memo cited above, note 46; (8) Memo, Wadsworth to Comdr Linder, 18 Jan 44, sub: Industrial Concentration of War Production.

tical system the original notice of termination would have to filter down from the prime contractor to all subcontractor levels before steps would be taken at the lower levels to discontinue work. In the meantime, unnecessary production and additional costs to the government would continue to pile up. When it came to the task of settlement, each war contractor faced the task of accumulating the claims of all lower echelon subcontractors before he could present a complete claim of his own. By the time the accumulated claims reached the prime contractor many weeks would often elapse. More time would elapse before the prime contractor's claim was approved and payment made. Since intermediate contractors were reluctant and frequently unable to settle with their subcontractors until they themselves had received payment for their subcontract costs, many subcontractors down the line were left "holding the bag" until the lengthy process was completed. If any intermediate contractors should become insolvent during the process, lower tier subcontractors might find themselves permanently unable to recover their costs.

Apart from these considerations, the vertical settlement system contemplated the separate processing and settlement of each individual terminated contract. With some 250,000 prime contract terminations in the offing for all procuring agencies, the prospective workload for processing all claims on an individual contract basis was appalling. It was estimated that the number of first-tier subcontract claims would run to 800,000, and lower tier claims to many millions.[48] A single large subcontractor might be faced with the task of preparing claims on several thousand terminated contracts and purchase orders within a few short months. Each of these claims would require separate compilation, presentation, auditing, and approval. Likewise, the termination inventory for each would have to be separately priced, segregated, and stored or otherwise disposed of. These property disposal decisions—far below the prime contractor but ultimately subject to the approval of the contracting officer—were crucial to prompt reconversion but susceptible of great delay under orthodox vertical procedure. If some means could be found of merging all claims of a single firm over a period of time into one consolidated claim against the government, a tremendous amount of duplicate processing, auditing, inventory treatment, and other activities could be eliminated. Furthermore, all subcontractors beneath a direct settlement would find the processing time for their own settlements substantially reduced.

Impelled by these reasons, planners devoted much intensive research and investigation late in 1943 and throughout 1944 to development of a satisfactory plan for company-wide settlements.[49] Investigation revealed that the obstacles to such a plan were formidable. The problem of properly identifying lower tier purchase orders and subcontracts as associated with a particular terminated prime contract appeared in many cases to be impossible of solution in the absence of the very process of vertical communication which the company-wide plan sought to avoid. Then, too, if the government were to assume the obligation for direct settlement of subcontracts, higher echelon contractors would have to be released from all liability and procedures would have to be developed to protect the government from

---

[48] *Hearings on S.J. Res. 80,* 1:14.

[49] See above, note 47.

double payment. Negotiation and settlement under a company-wide system would have to be conducted by a single contracting agency for many unfamiliar contracts which had been placed and administered by other procuring agencies and districts in all parts of the country. Large numbers of government auditors and others composing settlement teams would have to be recruited, trained, and placed in residence at plants coming under the system. New legislation and administrative regulations, with cross-delegation of powers among procuring agencies, would have to be devised and approved. Many other problems of a novel and complex nature were faced by the planners.

The more enthusiastic advocates of company-wide settlement proposed that it be used on a wide scale throughout the economy, regardless of the size of individual plants. Others proposed an intermediate course, suggesting limitation of the scheme to the 3,000 plants representing 90 percent of the subject matter of termination claims. The Baruch-Hancock report pointed to the inherent difficulties of the plan but nevertheless recommended that contracting agencies "launch immediately a vigorous experiment, fully exploring its possibilities." The Contract Settlement Act of 1944, following the Baruch recommendations, authorized the use of the company-wide system on such basis as the Director of Contract Settlement found desirable.[50]

In May 1944, the Army began its first experiment in company-wide settlement with the selection of the Allis-Chalmers Manufacturing Corporation and the Bendix Avia-

tion Corporation. Both firms were participating in the Consolidated Termination Program, a fact which provided a substantial basis for operations under company-wide settlement. In October, some four to five months after the program was initiated, General Clay reported its progress to the Director of Contract Settlement. He found that at this stage it required excessive personnel and excessive time in developing information on internal procedures of the corporations, that it posed grave difficulties in property disposal and identification of subcontracts, and that it tended toward excessive accounting review. Nevertheless, he recommended the continuance of the program: "Our tentative conclusion is that this type of settlement will work, but because of the difficulties outlined in the preceding paragraphs it will probably be of use only for limited application." [51]

On 29 May 1945, after a year of experimentation by the Army, the Office of Contract settlement defined in broad terms the program and policies for company-wide settlement. On the same date ASF set forth in detail the procedure to be followed under the program. These procedures were refined and published on 20 June 1945.[52]

The basic features of the standard companywide settlement plan were a compromise between the extremes of completely merged-claim settlement and settlement on a contract-by-contract basis. Those com-

---

[50] (1) AIC, Special Course in Contract Termination, pp. 4ff., Selection of war producers to be included. (2) Page 3 of Linder memo cited above, note 47(1). (3) Baruch-Hancock Rpt, p. 52. (4) Contract Settlement Act of 1944, Sec. 7(c).

[51] Ltr, Gen Clay to Hon. Robert H. Hinckley, Dir OCS, 12 Oct 44, Readjustment Div file 161 Direct Settlement, Nov–Dec 44. General Clay stated that the Chicago Ordnance District had assigned sixteen people to the Allis-Chalmers Corporation, and the Midcentral Procurement District, AAF, had assigned thirty-four to the Bendix Corporation.

[52] (1) OCS, Regulation No. 16, 29 May 45. (2) ASF Circular 192, 29 May 45. (3) JTR (Revision No. 2, 20 Jun 45), Sec. VIII, Direct Settlement of War Contracts on a Companywide Basis.

panies desiring to use the procedure applied to the appropriate Army service or Navy bureau and were selected on the basis of a number of qualifications similar to those for the Consolidated Termination Program. Selected contractors were assigned to the appropriate service or bureau, which was represented by a "designated officer" located at or near the contractor's termination headquarters. The assigned contractor entered a master agreement pledging himself to the company-wide procedure and agreeing not to assert claims in any other manner unless authorized.[53]

Within fifteen days after receiving each termination notice, the assigned contractor filed an abstract of the notice with the designated officer, who in turn notified the applicable prime contracting officer. If the latter wished to exclude the termination claim from the company-wide procedure because of the complex nature of the claim, adverse effect upon war production, or other reason he so advised the designated officer who would then exclude it along with any other exclusions deemed advisable.[54] If his claim was accepted, the assigned contractor then prepared and submitted to the designated officer a settlement proposal for each claim, using the standard procedure for prime contract settlement claims.[55] The designated officer, with the aid of his specially trained, on-the-spot settlement team for property disposal, review, auditing, and negotiation, was in a position to reach an agreement with maximum expedition. In contrast to normal settlement procedures, a settlement agreement under the company-wide system could cover any number of termination claims. Moreover, property disposal decisions covering large quantities of inventory pertaining jointly to many claims could be made as a unit, often in advance of the contractor's submittal of termination claims.[56] The designated officer had substantial latitude in adapting procedures to the needs of his particular situation.

Some idea of the scope of activities under a single company-wide settlement organization may be had from a review of salient features of the operation at the Aluminum Company of America. A survey by the Readjustment Division early in 1944 had disclosed that Alcoa was supplying the armed forces, directly or indirectly, with approximately $70 million in war matériel per month. Only 5 percent of this was done under prime contracts, the remaining 95 percent being supplied under subcontracts with 2,000 customers at numerous levels in the contractual chain. It was estimated that 55 percent of Alcoa's output went ultimately to the Army Air Forces, 30 percent to Navy aircraft, and the remainder to Army Ordnance and Quartermaster. To carry on its war production, Alcoa operated 2 mines, 4 ore plants, 12 reduction plants, and 20 fabricating plants.[57]

Alcoa was assigned to the AAF under both the Consolidated Termination Program and the company-wide settlement

---

[53] JTR 854, Master agreement for companywide settlement.

[54] Out of approximately the first 1,000 cases at Alcoa, only 3 were excluded from company-wide settlement. One of these was excluded at the request of the Navy contracting officer, and the other two by the designated officer. Ltr, Maj Robert L. Fisher, AAF Plant Representative, to Lt Col Robert H. Andrews, Chf Jt Settlement Br, Readjustment Div, 31 Jul 45, in Readjustment Div file 161/JS/Aluminum Co. of America, 1 Jan 44 to 31 Jul 45 (hereafter cited as Readjustment Div, Alcoa file).

[55] JTR 855, Procedure.

[56] JTR 855.9, Disposal of property.

[57] Readjustment Div, Report on Contract Termination Procedures, Aluminum Company of America, Pittsburgh, Pennsylvania, 10 Apr 44, in Readjustment Div, Alcoa file.

plan. Shortly before V-J Day it was estimated that Alcoa would soon present between 35,000 and 50,000 termination claims. In the opinion of the designated officer, it would take anywhere from one to three years to settle these claims under existing company-wide settlement procedures. With Alcoa's termination expenses, reimbursable by the government, running to $35,000 per month, continued operation under existing procedures might cost the Government over $1,000,000 for this item alone. Adding the expenses of maintaining a large AAF designated office and settlement team, and the even greater economic and social costs of delayed reconversion, it was apparent that substantial streamlining of the whole procedure was essential.[58]

A major stumbling block to prompt approval of subcontract claims under the direct settlement method was the JTR requirement that evidence of allocability of subcontracts to terminated prime war contracts be furnished in the form of detailed certificates of allocability from higher level contractors.[59] Fulfillment of this requirement in a large percentage of cases had broken down because of the volume of paper work, the difficulty of quantitative allocation of each item of each purchase order at every step in the contractual chain, and for other reasons. To overcome this difficulty, alternative procedures were devised. First of all, Alcoa agreed to cease work on all production

deemed to be war business upon receipt of general notification by the War Department instead of waiting for the receipt of individual termination notices. Then, from its total termination claims it agreed to a standard percentage deduction to compensate for excessive "quantitative allocation." The percentage deduction was based upon the analysis of a representative number of carefully investigated test cases. A similar deduction was made to avoid breaching the legal requirement that the sum of termination settlements under any prime contract not exceed the contract price. The adoption of these procedures, which would not have been allowable without the flexibility and discretion permitted by the negotiated settlement, saved the settlement procedure from bogging down completely in a mass of red tape.[60]

A second major problem was the separate processing of thousands of individual termination charges. The standard company-wide settlement procedure contemplated the merging of claims as far as possible. Because of Alcoa's complex sales organization, with numerous offices throughout the country each receiving notices of complete or partial termination, it was at first thought necessary to prepare a separate claim for each item of each purchase order. This procedure was workable for a fairly large volume of terminations but could not be expected to withstand the deluge of V-J Day terminations. Accordingly, a plant-by-plant procedure was devised under which each of Alcoa's fabricating plants would present one com-

---

[58] (1) Ltr, Maj Fisher, AAF Plant Representative, to Col Andrews, Readjustment Div, 20 Aug 45; (2) Office of the AAF Representative at Aluminum Company of America, Proposal for Settling V-J Day Claims of Aluminum Company of America, 22 Aug 45; (3) Proposal for Settlement of V-J Day Claims of Aluminum Company of America, 30 Aug 45. All in Readjustment Div, Alcoa file.

[59] JTR 855.8.

[60] (1) Ltr, Roy A. Hunt, President, Aluminum Company of America, to Maj Fisher, AAF Plant Representative, 14 Sep 45; (2) AAF Plant Representative, "Report to the Settlement Board," undated copy, in folder Proposed Plant-by-Plant Plan for Aluminum Company of America. Both in Readjustment Div, Alcoa file.

bined claim covering the termination charges on all terminated war orders being performed at that particular plant. Supporting each partial claim would be a documented summary of all material and direct labor charges. To such charges would be applied over-all percentages for factory burden, corporate general and administrative expenses, profits, and so on, thus eliminating similar calculations for each and every item of individual purchase orders.[61] As in the case of allocability and other problems, the successful resolution of the problem of processing individual claims could be effected only by the adoption of a commonsense, businesslike approach in lieu of a microscopic audit procedure hypothetically calculated to achieve 100-percent accuracy on an item by item basis.

By the end of March 1946 the company-wide settlement program at Alcoa had been completed. The terminated value of contracts handled under the program exceeded $135,000,000.[62] In accordance with the prearranged plan, Alcoa ceased work on all war orders on the day following the announcement of the Japanese surrender. If it had waited until individual termination notices had trickled down to it through prime and intermediate contractors, it would have put into processing an estimated additional 50,000,000 pounds of aluminum.[63] As it was, Alcoa had on hand on V-J Day some 300,000,000 pounds of aluminum in various stages of fabrication for the fulfillment of war contracts. The chief barrier to expeditious settlement was not the processing of claims, as such, but

delays in decisions by the RFC and other agencies in the disposition of termination inventory.[64] Some of these delays no doubt reflected uncertainty concerning the government's over-all postwar policy in the matter of concentration of ownership in the aluminum industry. In any case, in view of the innumerable problems existing in late 1945, the liquidation of the company-wide settlement program at Alcoa by the end of the first quarter of 1946 was a notable achievement.

At the peak of the program there were only thirty-one company-wide settlement teams assigned by all agencies, bearing out General Clay's earlier prediction of its limited applicability. But far from indicating the failure of the program this limitation was perhaps responsible for its success. The basic philosophy underlying this view is best expressed in the following words, written at a time when the program was still in the planning stage: "There is a key to the contract settlement problem. It lies in awareness of the amazing extent of the concentration of war production and war contracts in a relative handful of firms. . . ."[65] By the end of 1946, when the program was drawing to a close, the 31 company-wide teams—dealing with less than one tenth of

---

[61] Ibid.

[62] Ltr, Malcolm A. White, Chf Readjustment Br, to Roy A. Hunt, President, Aluminum Company of America, 2 Apr 46, Readjustment Div, Alcoa file.

[63] Hunt ltr cited above, note 60 (1).

[64] (1) Ibid. (2) Ltr, Fisher to Andrews, 29 Aug 45. (3) Ltr, Robert A. Hurley, Actg Chmn Surplus Property Bd, to Gen Hauseman, Dir Readjustment Div, 11 Sep 45. (4) Memo, Lt Col V. H. Knoop, Fixed Price Settlement Br, Readjustment Div, for Asst Dir for Contract Settlement, Readjustment Div, 20 Sep 45, sub: Visit to Aluminum Company of America. (5) Ltr, Col Fisher, Resident Readjustment Officer, to A. A. Throckmorton, Chf Nonferrous Metals Section, Office of Surplus Property RFC, 13 Nov 45. (6) Ltr, Fisher to F. W. Huston, Chf Warehousing Div Office of Surplus Property RFC, 28 Nov 45. (7) Ltr, Fisher to Col Andrews, Chf Fixed Price Settlement Div ASF, 30 Nov 45. All in Readjustment Div, Alcoa file.

[65] Linder memo cited above, note 47(1).

one per cent of all war contractors—had accounted for the settlement of over 67,000 claims, involving some 15 percent of the total dollar amount of all termination claims.[66]

Other Subcontract Settlement Procedures

A primary concern of Congress and others engaged in drafting the Contract Settlement Act was the plight in prospect for tens of thousands of smaller subcontractors at the time of mass terminations. As already indicated, many observers felt that the vertical settlement system was too slow and cumbersome to insure prompt payment to lower tier contractors and that widespread losses and insolvency would result. These fears were cogently expressed by a contemporary participant in termination planning:

The present system of settling with subcontractors may well be compared to the old-fashioned bucket brigade method of putting out a fire. . . . In many cases there are five or ten hands through which a subcontractor's claim must go before it can reach a contracting agency. . . . Each time the bucket is passed, another set of accountants is usually called in to make a new examination before allowing it to go up the line. . . . In many cases the man in Hartford or Philadelphia may be completely uninterested in worrying about the Peoria claim anyway or, if he gets paid on it, in passing the money down the line to Peoria. Furthermore, after Germany is beaten, and especially after the defeat of Japan, many little men in the bucket brigade—and some big ones also—will close up shop. Their subcontractors will then have no place to go. They will be termination orphans in the post-war storm.[67]

The Consolidated Termination Program and the company-wide settlement plan represented partial solutions. Both helped to speed up payment of subcontractors, whether above or below the firms assigned under these programs. In the case of company-wide settlement, a handful of giant subcontractors received direct settlement and payment of their claims by the government. But under both programs only subcontractors in the same chain as the assigned firms were helped directly although all contractors benefited from the speeding up of settlements in general. Nevertheless, the problem of assuring and expediting individual payments to the vast majority of subcontractors still remained.

The subcontract settlement problem was complicated by the fact that the government ultimately bore all subcontract charges while having no direct liability to subcontractors. Under peacetime conditions, the government would simply place its prime contract with the lowest bidder. Other things equal, the lowest bidder under a prime contract was the one who had obtained the most favorable subcontract terms. In any case, the government was assured of procurement deliveries at least cost, and the payment of subcontract claims was a private transaction between the parties, subject to established principles of the law of contracts.

Under wartime procurement, however, true competition no longer existed and there was abundant opportunity for contractors all down the line to pad their cost estimates which were the basis for the negotiated price of a military end item. Hence, the government was obliged, in self-protection, to develop and apply the various pric-

---

[66] OCS History, p. 33.

[67] Gross, "The Role of Congress in Contract Termination", pp. 544–45. Mr. Gross was staff director of War Contracts Subcommittee, Senate Committee on Military Affairs. See also John S. Carter, "Problems Arising Out of the Subcontractor Relationship," *Law and Contemporary Problems* (Duke University School of Law), X, No. 3 (Winter 1944), 518–28.

ing techniques already described to insure reasonable treatment in fixed-price contracts. But a reasonable contract price for completed end items was no guarantee that the government would not be heavily overcharged in termination claims for work performed on the terminated portion of canceled contracts. Again, in self-protection the government reserved the right to refuse reimbursement to prime contractors for their subcontract termination costs if such costs were unreasonable. The only way the government could insure the reasonableness of subcontract claims was to insist that such claims receive adequate review before payment. Unfortunately, such a requirement—if interpreted to mean individual review by government personnel—would spell the complete breakdown of the readjustment program at the time of mass terminations following V-J Day. Neither the procuring agencies nor any other offices of government had the staff to provide review of each and every subcontract claim arising under terminated prime contracts. The only practicable solution to the problem was to make higher-echelon contractors responsible for review of subcontracts, placing upon them the authority and responsibility for satisfactory settlement of their own subcontractors' claims. This could be accomplished by the adoption of definite subcontract settlement regulations, supplemented by training programs and a system of spot checks to insure compliance.

The early War Department regulations in this area stressed the importance of contractor responsibility in the examination of subcontract claims and held the contractor to the standard of scrutiny that a businessman would employ in the conduct of his own affairs. The regulations required an office review as a minimum and called attention to a number of specific matters to be checked for each claim. Further review was to be made if the contractor judged it necessary. This could involve requests upon subcontractors for additional information, a visit by members of the contractor's accounting staff to the subcontractor's plant, or even an audit of the subcontractor's books by qualified accountants of the reviewing contractor.[68] War Department Procurement Regulations required the reviewing contractor to subscribe to a notarized certificate that he had provided an examination of the claim which he deemed adequate and that in his opinion the dollar amount of the claim was fair and reasonable, proposed in good faith, and not more favorable to the supplier than the undersigned would make in the absence of reimbursement by the government.[69] When the succession of subcontractor claims and their accompanying certifications reached the contracting officer, the latter was empowered to require such additional examination as he deemed necessary to protect the interests of the government. Thus the whole system of subcontract review rested largely on the discretion of the contracting officer. This wide discretionary latitude permitted substantial variation in reviewing standards from one procuring office to another. On the one hand, this could lead to laxity in protecting the interests of the government; on the other, no subcontractor at any level could be certain that a settlement made in good faith would not be overturned when it reached the contracting officer.

With the accumulation of experience, the War Department endeavored to tighten up

---

[68] (1) WD TM 14–320, pars. 2401–07, 3701–06. (2) WD TM 14–1005, pars. 38–44, 102–08.

[69] PR 15–440. The certification procedure was continued throughout the termination program: JTR 632(3); JTR 642.3(c); JTR 987.1.

its subcontract review procedures and improve the workability of the system. An analysis revealed that over 90 percent of all subcontractor claims amounted individually to less than $10,000.[70] Early in 1944 the department revised its regulations to provide separate settlement procedures for three classes of subcontractor claims: (1) mandatory review prior to settlement by contracting officers of all claims in excess of $10,000; (2) blanket authority to all war contractors to review and settle all claims of less than $1,000; (3) granting of special delegations of authority to reliable contractors to settle all claims of less than $10,000. Procedures (2) and (3) were revokable if abused and, in order to insure performance, War Department accountants under the contracting officer made selective checks of various classes of settlement. In the absence of fraud, a settlement made under delegated authority was binding on all concerned, and could not be reviewed, either by higher tier contractors or by the government.[71] The adoption of standard procedures for delegating final settlement authority to contractors did much to clarify responsibility and to expedite binding settlements at all contractor levels. By 31 August 1945, the War Department had made 4,762 delegations of authority of type (3).[72]

An important aim in developing subcontract settlement procedures was to get subcontractors to relinquish their common law rights to anticipated profits under terminated contracts. There was no substantial reason, at a time when the government was devising measures for the protection of subcontractors, for the latter to demand a more favorable basis of settlement than that accorded prime contractors.

A significant step in eliminating subcontractor claims for full anticipated profits was the announcement by OWM, on 29 May 1944, of the approved subcontract termination article promulgated by the Joint Contract Termination Board.[73] This article—which could be voluntarily included in subcontracts, either originally or by amendment—provided for "fair compensation" of subcontractors on a basis equivalent to that in the Uniform Termination Article for prime contracts. Whether or not a subcontract contained the approved article, it was the policy of the government to favor a settlement made in accordance therewith. Since the contracting officer could refuse reimbursement of the prime excessive subcontract costs, either the prime or another intervening contractor would shoulder the burden of any excess payment. Higher level contractors were therefore reluctant to settle any lower tier claims which departed substantially from the approved basis. This was a heavy deterrent to unreasonable demands by subcontractors since a prolonged delay in payment might mean insolvency.[74]

---

[70] ASF, Readjustment History, p. 47.

[71] JTR 642.5, Recognition of authorized settlements. The original provisions for delegated authority were made by PR 15–325.2, May 1944.

[72] (1) ASF, Readjustment History, p. 48. (2) JTR, Sec. VI, Pt. 3, Review of Subcontract Settlement Proposals by War Contractors, and Pt. 4, Review of Subcontract Settlements by Government Personnel.

[73] OWM Dir Order 6, 29 May 44, and attached statement of policy by JCTB.

[74] Termination claims of subcontractors unwilling to settle on a fair basis could be excluded from the negotiated settlement of the prime contract and left to subsequent determination. JTR 613.1. As of 30 September 1946, the AAF reported 4,476 unassumed subcontractor exclusions involving $230 millions in canceled commitment value. At the same time, Army Ordnance reported 62 unassumed exclusions of $1.5 millions in canceled commitments. WD, Progress Report, Section 5–A, 30 Sep 46. These figures represent complicated, controversial, and contingent liabilities and do not necessarily

The procedures thus far described were designed to expedite subcontract settlements and still protect the interests of the government. Another important class of procedures had as a primary purpose the protection of subcontractors against default by their customers. Included in these were supervision of payments to prime contractors for subcontractors; duplicate payment where higher tier contractors failed to pass down the original payments; and direct settlement of subcontract claims of firms not included in company-wide settlements.

The first of these procedures was used in cases of actual or imminent insolvency, bankruptcy, receivership, or corporate reorganization on the part of a war contractor. Upon the complaint of subcontractors in such situations, the contracting officer was required to supervise all payments to the war contractor on account of the termination claims of his subcontractors. Such payments could either be made directly to the subcontractor by the contracting agency or they could be placed in a controlled partial payment account disbursable by the prime contractor only with the countersignature of the contracting officer. In either case, detailed regulations carefully protected the rights of all concerned.[75]

The making of duplicate payments permitted—as a matter of equity and good conscience—the payment of fair compensation to a war contractor who had been deprived of payment and had no reasonable chance of securing payment even though payment had already been included in the settlement with another war contractor. All such payments to War Department sub-

contractors required the approval of the Readjustment Division, ASF.[76]

Direct settlement of subcontracts—other than under the company-wide settlement plan—was used only on a limited basis to facilitate particular settlements which could not be accomplished equitably or expeditiously by the higher tier contractor.[77] In such cases the War Department had to have the written approval of the head of the local procurement district or other office, and each settlement was limited to a stated maximum figure. In general, prime contract settlement procedures were used in direct settlement of subcontracts. In all cases, the subcontractor was required, as a condition of direct settlement, to release his customer from liability or to assign his claim to the government. The choice between these two was made by the contracting officer at the time of settlement. Assignment of the claim was obtained when the government had a continuing interest which would be protected thereby.[78]

The vast majority of subcontract claims settled or approved directly by the War Department were at the first tier level. Many of these were subcontracts under prime CPFF contracts, which frequently called for government assumption of all subcontractor claims. Others were difficult claims under prime fixed-price contracts, originally excluded from settlement of the prime in order to eliminate delay. Still others were settlements under the company-wide settlement plan, or under the provisions of JTR permitting direct settlement in individual cases for a variety of reasons. By 30 June 1947, the total number of first tier subcon-

---

imply unreasonableness on the part of subcontractors. Unassumed exclusions were either later assumed for direct settlement by the government or were settled through normal procedure.
[75] JTR 367; JTR 651; JTR 667; JTR 954.

[76] JTR 652.3. Duplicate payments were authorized by Section 7(f) of the Contract Settlement Act.
[77] JTR 662.4(2).
[78] JTR 663.3.

tracts settled or specifically approved by the War Department ran to nearly 460,000, over three times the number of War Department prime contract settlements for World War II.[79]

The Settlement of CPFF Contracts

Special procedures for settling CPFF contracts were necessary because of the traditional authority of the General Accounting Office—headed by the Comptroller General—to audit and disallow payments under contracts calling for Government reimbursement of contractors' costs. CPFF contractors were kept currently paid for their expenses (as well as a pro rata share of their fixed fee) by local disbursing officers after careful review of cost vouchers, contract terms, and other data. The additional review by the GAO, whether done in the field or in Washington, inevitably took time and it was usually several months before either the procuring agency or contractor knew whether a given item would be approved or rejected. Even approval after audit was not conclusive, inasmuch as the GAO had the power (prior to the Contract Settlement Act) to re-examine a contractor's accounts at any time.[80]

Under these conditions, CPFF contractors at the time of termination found themselves dealing with a government that wore two hats. The government (War Department) would make a "final" agreement with the contractor, binding him to a termination settlement necessarily based, in part, on payments already made at the time of termination. Later, the government (Comptroller General) could disallow payments previously made and compel the government (War Department) to withhold any further payments due the contractor under *any* contract. In the rare event that these withholdings were inadequate to cover disallowances, numerous other instruments were available for collection.

For this reason contractors from the outset were extremely reluctant to enter final settlement agreements under CPFF contracts. At the end of 1943, of the 220 prime contracts which had been terminated by the War Department, not one involving a termination claim had been settled.[81] During the next six months the situation was but slightly improved; only four CPFF termination claims were settled within the period. By the end of the summer of 1944, the settlement of some $6 billion in terminated CPFF contracts (largely for Army aircraft) was hanging fire pending a clarification of the final settlement authority of the contracting agencies.[82]

The Contract Settlement Act, which gave the procuring agencies unequivocal authority to negotiate final settlements, did not exempt CPFF contracts from its terms. But since the Act did not at the same time remove the responsibility of the GAO for auditing CPFF contracts prior to termina-

---

[79] Report of the Under Secretary of War to the Secretary of War, 1 July 1945 to 30 June 1947, p. 19.

[80] There was apparently no statute of limitations and it was doubted that the General Accounting Office could legally waive its right to future examination. Ltr, USW Patterson to Robert Hinckley, Dir OCS, 6 Oct 44, in file 161 Contract Termination, 1 Sep 44–31 Oct 44, Purchases Div ASF.

[81] ASF, Monthly Progress Report, Section 14–A, Contract Terminations, 30 Jun 44, p. 32. It should be noted that the typical CPFF prime contract was many times larger and more complex than the average fixed-price contract, and was expected to require a longer settlement period. Also, as of 31 December 1943, of the 220 terminated CPFF contracts, 79 had been settled on a no-cost basis.

[82] OCS Rpt, No 1, Oct 44, pp. 18–19.

tion a number of troublesome problems arose. Did the power of the services to make final settlement apply only to items in the terminated portion of a contract? Or did it apply to any item of dispute under the entire contract? If the former were true, no binding settlement of the contract as a whole could be made by the procuring agencies. If the latter were true, these agencies could, in the process of settlement, override the carefully considered decision of the Comptroller General in matters over which he had long had final administrative authority.

The resistance of contractors finally forced action to break the log-jam. On 6 October 1944, Under Secretary Patterson wrote the Director of Contract Settlement that a decision would soon have to be reached. CPFF contractors were not only refusing to enter settlement agreements. In many cases, they also declined to assume any responsibility for disposal of termination inventory or for settling subcontractors' claims if they could not at the same time reach a binding agreement with the government on all items of cost whether incurred before or after termination. In taking this position, contractors were within their legal rights.[83] Furthermore, they had little or nothing to lose since a settlement would yield only a relatively small additional payment in comparison with the potential value of rights relinquished on the completed portion of the contracts. The Under Secretary therefore urged that final settlement authority for

all items in terminated CPFF contracts be confirmed in the contracting agencies.[84]

On 31 October, the Attorney General in a lengthy opinion found the authority of the contracting agencies under the Contract Settlement Act to include all claims under a terminated contract, including those arising under any portion of a CPFF contract performed prior to termination. This opinion rested on the wording of Section 3(h) of the act, a sentence which had been drafted with considerable perspicuity and foresight: "The term 'termination claim' means any claim or demand by a war contractor for fair compensation for the termination of any war contract and any other claim under a terminated war contract, which regulations prescribed under this Act authorize to be asserted and settled in connection with any termination settlement." Since the basic purpose of the Act was to expedite the fair settlement of contracts, and since settlement could not be expeditiously accomplished on a piecemeal basis, the Attorney General concluded that the Director of Contract Settlement had the authority to issue regulations adequate to the purpose.[85]

In order to implement the Attorney General's decision the several agencies involved held conferences to determine procedures. The contracting agencies unanimously agreed that every effort be made to answer satisfactorily any informal inquiries or exceptions raised by the GAO in connection with the completed portion of the contract. The new procedures adopted at this time provided that within the 60-day period following termination the contracting officer was to submit to the General Accounting

---

[83] The contracting agencies could, of course, make a unilateral determination, but this would likewise be inconclusive and subject to expensive and prolonged litigation in the courts. Most CPFF contracts bound the government to assume and pay the claims of subcontractors after termination. Also, the government was required by the Contract Settlement Act to remove termination inventory, title to which technically passed to the government prior to termination.

[84] See USW ltr. cited above, note 80. Mr. Hinckley promptly requested an opinion from the Attorney General; see above, pages 629–30, note 44.

[85] 40 Op. Atty. Gen. 328, 31 Oct. 44.

Office answers to all outstanding GAO inquiries and exceptions.[86] At the end of the 60-day period ("audit status date") the GAO was to advise the contracting officer of any uncleared matters still remaining in connection with the contract. A further 30-day period beyond the audit status date was allowed to facilitate final clearance with the GAO. Thereafter, the contracting officer was free to proceed with final settlement of all items except formal disagreements with the GAO still outstanding. Only the highest procuring authority in the contracting agency was permitted, under the regulations, to effect an agreement in conflict with the position of the General Accounting Office.[87] The resolution of the CPFF controversy thus gave the government the full benefits of the extensive organization and experience of the General Accounting Office without permitting undue delays in final settlement. The importance of rapid settlement of CPFF contracts may be inferred from the fact that such contracts accounted for 28 percent of the value of all War Department terminations and 24 percent of the value of terminations by all other agencies. (*See Table 61, page 697.*)

Even in the absence of interagency conflicts, CPFF settlements were necessarily complicated and time-consuming. The Joint Contract Termination Board had completed its uniform termination article for CPFF contracts in April 1944, and with the issuance of JTR in November a tentative set of procedures was adopted.[88] These were perfected in April 1945, after resolution of the controversy with the GAO. The special CPFF settlement procedures covered all cost and cost-plus-a-fixed-fee contracts; reimbursable cost portions of fixed-price contracts; and letter orders, letter contracts, letters of intent, and letter purchase orders providing for current reimbursement of allowable costs. All regular provisions of JTR applied to CPFF settlements except where specifically inapplicable or in conflict with the special CPFF regulations.[89]

The complexities of CPFF termination and settlement problems cannot be adequately portrayed in a necessarily brief treatment of the subject. A few figures concerning the Army's tank contract with the Baldwin Locomotive Works may, however, give some indication. On 27 October 1941, Baldwin contracted to produce a number of medium tanks at an estimated cost of $22 million and a fixed-fee of $1,540,000. By 14 May 1943, a succession of supplements had raised procurement called for by the contract to an estimated $296 million with a fixed fee of over $14 million. Termination reduced actual procurement deliveries under the contract to $92 million. Of the $204 million terminated, over $24 million was represented by termination inventory at the Baldwin works alone. Many millions more in inventory was held by 400 subcontractors throughout the country. During the life of the contract, more than 125,000 purchase orders and changes were issued by Baldwin. To administer the contract, the Ordnance Department had a staff of between 400 and 500 persons continuously stationed at the Baldwin works, approving action, auditing, inspecting, and checking. The contractor, in his termination claim, estimated that at

---

[86] JTR, Sec. V, Pt. 6, Basis for Settlement of Cost-Plus-A-Fixed-Fee Contracts, 20 April 1945.

[87] For example, the Under Secretary of the War Department or the Secretary of the Navy. JTR 563.6(2).

[88] Ltr, Col R. A. Cutter, Chmn Subcom on Contract Clauses, to Hancock, Chmn JCTB (final draft), 29 Apr 44, and incls, in Readjustment file, Jt Contract Term Bd.

[89] JTR, Sec. V, Pt. 6, Basis for Settlement of Cost-Plus-A-Fixed-Fee Contracts.

the time of termination all but approximately $4 million in costs had been previ-
ously reimbursed. As a result of negotiation
this was reduced to slightly more than $3.5
million.[90]

The elaborate array of contract settlement
procedures for World War II reflected the
magnitude of the war production program

and the underlying complexity of American
industry in the middle of the 20th century.
The development and application of these
procedures made possible the rapid and efficient discharge of one of the greatest administrative tasks in the nation's history. The
character of this achievement is more fully
revealed by the following review of the
terms of settlement, the financing of contractors, the rate at which settlements were
made, and the results of the program as a
whole.

---

[90] Negotiator's report of proposed settlement, Termination of Contract W–670–ORD–1814 with the
Baldwin Locomotive Works, 13 Dec 44, Readjustment Div, file Baldwin Locomotive Works.

CHAPTER XXIX

Contract Settlement in Operation

The Terms of Settlement

The central purpose of the entire system of contract settlement was the payment of fair compensation to war contractors for work done on their terminated contracts. Promptness of payment was an essential ingredient but the heart of the settlement problem was the task of defining and applying principles of settlement which would be fair both to the contractor and to the ultimate purchaser—the general public. Most of the difficulties were associated with the settlement of fixed-price contracts; as already indicated, reimbursement for terminated CPFF contracts presented no great theoretical problems inasmuch as reimbursable costs were defined in each contract and elaborated in special manuals and regulations devoted to the purpose.[1]

Very early in the settlement program, the procuring agencies recognized that fair compensation in the case of terminated fixed-price contracts consisted of the following elements: (1) the full contract price for all items completed under the contract prior to termination; (2) all costs allocable to the terminated portion of the contract; (3) a reasonable profit on work undertaken or performed as represented by the costs in (2); (4) posttermination expenses, including the

costs of the contractor's termination organization and expenses of storing and protecting government property. The sum of all costs in categories (1), (2), and (3) was not to exceed the total price specified in the procurement contract.[2]

The complexity of the Army's task of determining the kinds and amounts of contractor reimbursement under each of these categories for more than 100,000 contracts varying widely in purpose and scope cannot be adequately described. The chief problems centered around category (2), and to a smaller extent (3).

To illustrate the initial difficulties, suppose a firm with a number of war contracts had agreed in a contract undergoing settlement to deliver 10,000 jeeps at a fixed price of $1,000 each. Suppose also that at the date of termination, 6,424 jeeps had been completed and would be paid for, under standard termination provisions, at their full contract price. Two broad problems of cost allocation would immediately arise in con-

---

[1] See Chapter XII, above. It was, however, necessary to develop a CPFF termination article to provide for posttermination expenses and other considerations. See above, page 663, note 81.

[2] These four categories of reimbursement were contained in the standard termination article adopted by the War Department in October 1942, and were continued under the Contract Settlement Act throughout the program. See Malman article in *"War Contract Termination,"* cited above, page 613, note 2(2), App. C, "Article . . . Termination for the Convenience of the Government." See also, PR 15–443, 14 Aug 43. The exclusion of posttermination expenses from the limitation on total reimbursement did not appear in the 1943 regulations, but was later recognized as a valid exclusion. JTR 534.2.

nection with the settlement: (1) how much of the contractor's general costs used for all his productive activities—costs of plant, facilities, equipment, managerial and administrative organization, common inventory and the like—could be considered as attributable to production under the jeep contract? and (2) how much of the expenses allocable to the jeep contract were properly attributable to the *terminated* portion thereof?

To answer the first question properly the Army would have to decide, for example, to what extent advertising and entertainment expenses, officers' salaries and bonuses, employees' pension costs and separation pay, research and development expenditures, sales commissions, travel expense, and so on ad infinitum, were proper expenses of war production, and then determine the proportion thereof allocable to the particular contract in question. To answer the second question the Army would have to decide, among other things, how to distribute between the completed and uncompleted portions of the jeep contract such irregular costs as high starting load, special engineering, design, layout, planning, and other preparatory expenses. The greater the cost which could be allocated to the terminated portion, the greater would be the amount paid in settlement of the contractor's termination claim, over and above amounts paid for completed deliveries.

The present brief review of the terms of contract settlement can do no more than provide a sampling of the standards used in cost and profit determination. The evolution of the principles of fair compensation for termination claims has been touched upon in the preceding two chapters and is elsewhere described in greater detail.[3] At

[3] OCS History, Ch. VI, pp. 21–28.

the beginning of 1944, the principal authoritative document was the "Statement of Principles for Determination of Costs upon Termination of Government Fixed-Price Supply Contracts" issued by the JCTB.[4] These principles were largely incorporated in or ratified by the Contract Settlement Act, which gave the Director of OCS the authority to issue further clarification and changes. This was done principally under OCS Regulation No. 7, which stated in considerable detail the philosophy and principles of fair compensation, and Regulation No. 14, which introduced a series of OCS interpretive rulings known as "Termination Cost Memorandums" (TCM's).[5] All together sixteen memorandums were issued under the following headings:

1. Recognized Commercial Accounting Practices.
2. General, Administrative, and Distribution Expense.
3. Common Items.
4. Partners' and Sole Proprietors' Salaries.
5. Application of the Limitation of Subparagraph 1(i) of the Statement of Cost Principles.
6. Materials Acquired Prior to Date of Contract.
7. Initial Costs.
8. Rejects.
9. Loss on Facilities.
10. Engineering and Development, Special Tooling, and Preparatory expenses.

[4] See above, page 626, note 38.
[5] The complete texts of these documents may be found in the following sources: OCS Regulation 7 in OCS First Rpt, October 1944, pp. 76–81; OCS Regulation 14 and TCM's 1–9, in OCS Third Rpt, April 1945, pp. 25–38; TCM's 10–16, in OCS Fifth Rpt, October 1945, pp. 26–36. The amended "Statement of Principles" is found in OCS First Rpt, pp. 70–72.

11. Settlement Expenses, Costs of Protection, and Disposition of Property.
12. Depreciation.
13. Advertising Expense.
14. General Experimental and Research Expense.
15. Cash Discounts on Purchases.
16. Severance Pay.

The interpretations and rulings in the Cost Memorandums were promptly incorporated in the Joint Termination Regulation and used by the Army and Navy in making settlement.

In answering the broad questions of cost allocation noted above, the Contract Settlement Act and related regulations laid down the principle that the accounting system used by the contractor would be relied upon in settlement if it reflected the costs reasonably necessary for the performance of the contract and was consistent with recognized commercial accounting practice. The governing regulations pointed out that costs includible in fixed-price settlements were generally broader in scope than those ordinarily contemplated in factory cost accounting and recognized by the government under CPFF contracts. Greater liberality was accorded the treatment of costs under fixed-price contracts because of the greater risks assumed under such contracts, the absence of cost definitions in the contract, and the presumption that the contractor's obligation to deliver at a fixed-price entailed the authority to make the necessary decisions involving production costs. Cost and accounting data were to be regarded as guides to the ascertainment of fair compensation rather than as rigid measures thereof, and contracting agencies were advised against the expenditure of greater time and effort than the advantages of absolute accuracy warranted in obtaining and interpreting cost data.[6]

General expenses, not directly related to production, such as salaries of officers and clerical employees, general office expenses, dues and memberships, professional fees, financial expenses, and general selling and distribution expenses—except items prohibited by the Statement of Cost Principles—were considered allowable costs of war production with the appropriate portion thereof allocable to terminated contracts. Any basis of allocation was permitted so long as it was reasonable in the light of the circumstances of the particular case and consistent with the general principles laid down. Special treatment was indicated for cases where the ratio of raw material costs to processing costs was out of line, for unusual degrees of subcontractor supervision, for distribution and service contracts, and other special situations.[7]

Allowance was permitted for salaries of proprietors and partners in unincorporated firms to the extent that such individuals devoted their time to the contracts in question. The amount of the salaries was to be reasonable taking into account the nature and extent of the services rendered, the general level of compensation for persons similarly situated elsewhere, the amounts paid prior to the receipt of government contracts, and the increase in the volume of business due to war contracts. Thus, even if such individuals did not explicitly charge their firm for their

---

[6] OCS Regulation 7 and TCM No. 1, 22 Feb 45 Sec. 6(b) of the Contract Settlement Act contained the following wording: "To the extent that such methods and standards require accounting, they shall be adapted, so far as practicable, to the accounting system used by war contractors, if consistent with recognized commercial accounting practices."

[7] OCS, TCM No. 2, 22 Feb 45.

services, the firm was assured of compensation therefor to the extent applicable in termination.[8]

Initial or "starting load" costs, resulting from the difficulties of getting production satisfactorily under way in the early stages of the contract, could be separated from normal production costs and properly allocated between the completed and terminated portions of the contract. The basis for allocation was ordinarily the ratio of pre-termination deliveries to total contract requirements, but some other basis—such as machine or labor hours—could be used where more equitable results would be obtained. High starting load costs reflected the costs of training labor for new tasks, excessive spoilage and defective work resulting from inexperienced labor, idle time associated with changeovers to new methods, and so forth. Similar treatment was given to engineering, developmental, and other preparatory costs, although these planning-type costs were kept distinct from "initial costs" of the operating type.[9]

An important consideration for a majority of fixed-price contractors was proper compensation for special facilities which they had purchased in order to perform their contracts. At the time of termination they would have recouped only a portion of the cost of the facilities through reimbursement for actual deliveries. Hence, provision was necessary for defraying any loss sustained by the contractor on special facilities as a result of termination. To qualify as such, proof was necessary that special facilities had been specifically required for the discharge of war contracts and that they were not economically usable by the contractor in his other business. The loss was calculated by allocating the total cost of the facilities among the various war contracts involved, and between the completed and terminated portions thereof, usually on the basis of completed deliveries made and required under the contracts. No allowance for depreciation was made, and the proceeds from the final disposition of the facilities were credited to the government as disposal credits in the termination claim. The net loss determined under this procedure thus automatically accounted—in theory, at least—for all the special facility costs whether resulting from depreciation, obsolesence or loss in useful value due to economic conditions. The practical application of these provisions necessarily gave rise to serious problems calling for the careful ascertainment of facts and the exercise of sound judgment. The really difficult decisions under this heading fell to the contracting or disposal officer who approved the retention or sale value of the equipment.[10]

A somewhat less complicated isue, but one which involved potentially heavy governmental expenditures as a result of mass terminations, was whether and to what extent the government should reimburse contractors for severance pay granted to employees laid off because of contract termination. Contractors would certainly not be averse to granting substantial amounts of severance pay to their employees if they could be assured in advance of reimburse-

---

[8] OCS, TCM No. 4, 22 Feb 45. Salaries of corporate officers were normally explicit and allocable on the same basis as other general expenses.

[9] OCS, TCM No. 7, 22 Feb 45.

[10] OCS, TCM No. 9, 5 Apr 45. Apart from termination regulations, the "facilities clause" in procurement contracts carried provisions for protecting the government's interest in special facilities. Nevertheless, the government was obliged to assume the loss on special facilities as part of the costs of war production, and the amount of the loss depended on the sale or retention value of the facilities covered in the settlement.

ment by the government. To prevent the termination provisions from conferring wholesale and indiscriminate bonuses upon war workers, the OCS—some ten days after V-J Day—announced its severance pay regulation. This provided that severance pay was an allowable cost of war production provided the contractor was required to make such payments (1) by statute, (2) by written agreement, or (3) by the operation of an established policy constituting an implicit agreement. No amount could be included for severance pay where payment was contingent upon recovery from the Government. Within the framework of these restrictions, severance pay was allocable to terminated contracts according to the circumstances of each contractor and the established principles of termination cost allocation.[11]

Allowable advertising expense for settlement purposes included both the cost of maintaining an advertising department in the contractor's organization and the expenses of exploiting outside media such as newspapers, magazines, billboards, radio, and paid endorsements. Amounts of advertising expense nominal in relation to a contractors' other expenses were includible in general expenses and allocated on the same basis. Large amounts were considered individually on their own merits, chiefly in terms of consistency with the contractors' prewar program. The average dollar amount of advertising expenditures during the base period 1935–39 was the maximum chargeable jointly to government contracts and the contractor's other business during the period of operation of the terminated war contracts. Moreover, advertising expense was first chargeable to the contractor's remaining commercial business up to the

prewar percentage of such charges. Thereafter, charges were allocable against war contracts up to a rate not in excess of the prewar percentage against sales. Thus if the contractor's commercial business was maintained throughout the war at prewar levels, no advertising expense was to be charged against his government contracts. Newly organized firms without a prewar base were granted amounts determined on the basis of individual circumstances.[12]

In the absence of any special limitation on reimbursable advertising, experimental, and similar general expenses, it would have been possible for contractors in advance of termination to have created substantial postwar assets in the guise of current expenditures for war production. Although this result was inevitable in any large mobilization program, the Statement of Cost Principles attempted to curb excesses by limiting reimbursement for such expenditures. Subparagraph 1 (i) of the statement limited the aggregate allowance for experimental and research expense, engineering and development and special tooling, loss on facilities, special leases, and advertising. These items were known as "costs subject to limitation" and could not be compensated collectively in excess of the amount which would have been available for them out of the contract price after all other costs were met, had the contract been completed instead of terminated. Since "all other costs" did not include profit, the limitation applied only when it appeared at the time of termination that the contract would have been completed at a loss. As a result of termination the contractor could be "bailed out" of an unprofitable contract; but he could not also get the benefit of free advertising, research, special fa-

---

[11] OCS, TCM No. 16, 24 Aug 45.

[12] OCS, TCM No. 13, 26 Jul 45.

cilities and the like, beyond the stated limitation.[13]

The allowance of profit on terminated contracts was confined to profit on work actually performed and did not include the common-law element of anticipated profit for the entire contract. Profit on the completed portion of the contract was presumed to have been included in the price paid for any items completed prior to termination. Profit on the terminated portion was paid in final settlement and was based on actual performance in connection with the terminated portion. Any reasonable procedure was permitted for arriving at a fair profit although three methods were suggested in the regulations:

1. The amount agreed upon or consented to at the time the contract was negotiated. This was the amount either explicitly stated in the contract or used in negotiating the contract price.

2. The amount which would have been earned had the contract been completed. This was to provide a general basis where alternative methods were not available. It was, however, altogether too hypothetical and too complicated to afford a satisfactory basis, and was not generally used.

3. The amount which the contractor agreed to accept in the event of termination. This figure could be expressed either in a termination article in the original contract, or in a pretermination agreement.[14]

Where the total profit contemplated at the time of original negotiation was used as the basis for settlement, the amount allo-

cable to the terminated portion was to represent the ratio of work performed on the terminated portion to the total work contemplated by the contract. The regulations recognized the difficulties in arriving at such a ratio, cautioning against the use of any single criterion and suggesting numerous considerations which might enter into such calculations.[15]

A special problem in the case of many contracts was the effect of price adjustment articles upon profit determination. These articles, included in contracts where a firm fixed price could not be determined at the time of negotiation, called for the use of a tentative price which would be redetermined or "adjusted" upon the occurrence of a specified event such as completion of a certain percentage of the contract.[16] The termination of such contracts prior to the required adjustments raised the question of whether the profit allowance, as well as payment for completed articles, based on the terms of the original contract would be too high or too low. In general, JTR provided that if termination occurred after the event calling for price adjustment, the adjustment negotiations or computations should be completed and their effects incorporated in the settlement. If termination was made prior to the event, neither party had a right to a revision of the contract price of completed articles delivered prior to termination; but, in the settlement, weight would be given to the fact that the contract contained a price adjustment article.[17]

In order to determine whether actual settlements were being made fairly, the Office of Contract Settlement sponsored several independent field surveys. All to-

---

[13] OCS, TCM No. 5, 22 Feb 45. In view of the numerous difficulties in determining what costs "would have been" had the contract been completed, it is probable that this limitation was broadly interpreted.

[14] JTR 533.1.

[15] JTR 533.2, especially JTR 533.2 (2).

[16] See above, pp. 325–38.

[17] JTR 535.1.

gether four intensive surveys, conducted by staff members of leading public accounting agencies, were made during the period from December 1944 to June 1946. The reports were, in general, favorable and indicated that actual settlement payments by the Government were appreciably lower than the maximum permissible under the terms of the Contract Settlement Act.

The first survey, conducted from 29 November to 31 December 1944, covered 573 completed settlements in 36 procurement offices of the various contracting agencies throughout the country. Total claims of $91.6 million had been settled for $81.5 million, or 89 percent of claims. In 133 cases no profit was claimed or allowed. For 366 cases permitting statistical tabulation, allowed profits averaged 5.3 percent of the contractors' own costs. This figure, however, had little significance since many allowable costs, such as various items of overhead, settlement expenses, and so on, had not been claimed. Contractors' apparent indifference to the full possibilities of termination claims reflected a high level of earnings in the face of renegotiation and excess profits taxation. Since the survey covered cases involving between 15 and 20 percent of the dollar value of all fixed-price settlements to the end of 1944, it provided a representative sample of settlement operations prior to the application of the Joint Termination Regulation.[18]

The second survey covered 425 settlements made between 1 December 1944 and 30 April 1945. Total claims of $163.2 million for these cases were settled for $147.5 million, or slightly more than 90 percent of claims. In 360 cases, profit was allowed; profit averaged 5.9 percent on contractors' own costs for the 292 cases susceptible of statistical analysis. The second survey indicated substantial progress by procurement offices in discharging their settlement responsibilities.[19]

The third survey, made during the third quarter of 1945, was directed to an analysis and improvement of the contracting agencies' organizations and procedures for meeting mass terminations. Hence, it was not designed to evaluate the equity of actual settlements.[20] The fourth survey, made in June 1946, was prompted by statistical evidence that an increasing number of large settlements were made substantially on the basis of the contractors' claims. It was feared that this indicated a growing laxity on the part of contracting agencies in screening out and disallowing improper elements of reimbursement. Accordingly 83 large fixed-price settlements negotiated at 17 procurement offices of the War and Navy Departments were analyzed. The findings revealed that the rough equivalence of claims and settlements was the inevitable and desirable result of improved termination procedures. Contractors were in general submitting controversial questions to the contracting agencies for decision before preparing their settlement proposals. This eliminated in advance the major areas of disagreement. In other cases, revised claims had been submitted after agreement was reached on controversial items in the original proposal.[21]

The cumulative evidence of the four independent surveys furnished substantial indication that the interests of the government were being adequately protected while con-

---

[18] OCS Second Rpt, January 1945, pp. 7–9. As of 31 December 1944, the gross settlement value (before disposal credits) of completed fixed-price settlements for all contracting agencies was $522 million. *Ibid.*, p. 49.

[19] OCS Fourth Rpt, July 1945, pp. 8–9.
[20] OCS Fifth Rpt, October 1945, pp. 17–18.
[21] OCS Eighth Rpt, July 1946, pp. 21–22.

tractors were being dealt with fairly and with reasonable speed in settlement.

Financing of Contractors

A major concern of war contractors before the passage of the Contract Settlement Act was the fear of serious financial embarrassment or even insolvency as the result of sudden, widespread termination of their contracts. Under the most sanguine estimates of rapid settlement, contractors could not expect to be able to present their claims and receive payment before several months had elapsed from the date of termination. Many considered the problem of obtaining adequate cash to support their payrolls and other expenditures in the interim to be the major hazard in the whole readjustment process. This was especially true for subcontractors. Subcontractors were faced with the prospect of a longer settlement period, were more likely to be financially overextended than primes, and did not have the "gilt-edge" security of direct liability of the government.

The War Department's role in termination financing was essentially an extension of its activities in supplying contractors with working capital for production purposes. These activities were indispensable to wartime procurement long before their adaptation to the final liquidation of the war effort. The three principal mechanisms for providing contractors with working capital throughout World War II were advance payments, guaranteed loans, and partial payments.[22]

[22] The furnishing of fixed capital to Army contractors is discussed above in PART FIVE, EXPANSION OF FACILITIES FOR THE ARMY. In the interest of simplicity, discussion of the War Department's role in supplying contractors with working capital has been deferred until the present chapter.

Advance Payments

As already indicated, the National Defense Expediting Act of 2 July 1940 authorized the making of advance payments to war contractors up to 30 percent of the contract price.[23] Although the wording of this statutory provision was virtually identical to that of its World War I predecessor, the administration of advance payments in World War II was apparently more liberal and efficient. During World War I, advance payments were treated much like ordinary bank loans, and contractors were obliged to put up acceptable security to guarantee performance of the contract and hence repayment of the advance. As a result of negotiations over the question of security, the War Department in World War I acquired a heterogeneous collection of collateral instruments ranging from bonds, stocks, plant mortgages, and life insurance, to mortages on contractors' own homes.[24]

Partly as a result of the philosophy laid down by Assistant Secretary of War Johnson at the beginning of the defense period and partly as a result of experience thereafter, advance payments in World War II were treated as independent advances in the

[23] See above, page 220. An *advance* payment was distinguished from partial and progress payments by the fact that it was made in advance of performance or cost incurrence by the contractor. A *partial* payment, in one sense, was payment for "partial delivery," that is, delivery of completed items representing a portion of the total number of items called for by the contract (PR 303.6). The term "partial payment" was also used by the Army in World War II to include progress payments. *Progress* payments, used extensively by the Navy and Maritime Commission but less so by the Army in World War II, were payments after incurrence of costs but prior to delivery (PR 303.6, 330, and 331).

[24] Address of Colonel J. C. Mechem, Office of Fiscal Director, ASF, in AIC Seminar, War Department Financial Aids to Industrial Production, 15 November 1945, pp. 16–17.

performance of specific contracts, guaranteed solely by the contract itself and the terms of its administration.[25] Under these terms advance payments, upon authorization, were paid into a special bank account to be used by the contractor solely for the purposes of the contract. The government retained a first lien on funds in the account as well as on inventory purchased therewith. The degree of control over disbursements from the account depended on the size, reputation, and financial responsibility of the contractor. In some cases only advance approval, once each month, of the contractor's budget was required; in other cases the contracting officer's countersignature was necessary for each withdrawal. Liquidation of advances was usually accomplished by proportional deductions from payments for delivery of completed items rather than by a simple repayment of the advance. Thus, if a contractor was given a 30-percent advance, he would receive only 70 percent of the contract price in payment for all deliveries until contract completion; the remaining 30 percent would be credited to him as repayment of advances. Moreover, as additional security in guarantee of contract completion and repayment of advances, he had to place in the special account all but perhaps a tenth of the 70-percent payments against deliveries. Under these arrangements the contractor, at any stage of contract completion, would retain for his uncontrolled use what was in effect a reasonable profit for actual deliveries.[26]

Like most types of financial aid to contractors, whether private or governmental in nature, advance payments were at first made cautiously and timidly. In accordance with the War Department policy of encouraging a maximum of financing from private sources, contractors during the defense period were required to show need, as well as nonavailability of private credit at fair rates of interest, in order to obtain advance payments. All advances had to be authorized by the Assistant Secretary of War. Throughout the defense period no interest was charged on advances, on the theory that the War Department was not a lending agency and Congress had not intended that interest be charged.[27]

After Pearl Harbor the great increase in the demand for credit by old and new contractors of all sizes, together with the difficulties of getting private lending institutions to streamline their loan agreements and lending procedures, led to a much more liberal advance payment policy on the part of the War Department. With the passage of the First War Powers Act shortly after Pearl Harbor, advance payments could be made up to 100 percent of the total contract price. The Under Secretary of War delegated to technical service chiefs, with power of redelegation, authority to determine advances up to 50 percent of the contract price on all contracts under $5,000,000. Applicants no longer had to show nonavailability of private credit, and all steps in the administration of advance payments were streamlined. Furthermore, the liberalized advance payment policy was to be made known to prospective contractors so that "no bidder would be 'handicapped or preju-

---

[25] During the early part of the defense period, performance bonds were required of contractors in general and these provided security for repayment of advances. In unusual cases, "advance payment" bonds were required to guarantee performance of contractual provisions covering advance payments only. See PR 321.4 and 406.4.

[26] Ibid., p. 17. See also PR 321 in its entirety, and PR's 347, 348, 348A and 348B.

[27] (1) Yoshpe, Production Control in the QMC, p. 56. (2) Page 18 of Mechem Address, cited above in note 24.

diced' in the award of contracts because of his need for an advance payment," and contracting officers were required to report all cases of refusal to grant advance payments.[28] However, upon the complaint of commercial banks and at the insistence of the Navy, the War Department modified its no-interest policy. Except under special circumstances, all advances under new contracts entered on or after 8 June 1942 carried interest charges of 2½ percent upon unliquidated balances.[29] The cumulative amount of War Department advance payments grew rapidly after Pearl Harbor, rising from some two thirds of a billion dollars at the end of 1941 to $3⅓ billion at the end of 1942 and $5 billion by the end of 1943.

In 1943 and 1944, the regulations governing the authorization and use of advance payments were adapted to meet the needs of termination financing. Under the new rules amounts on deposit in advance payment accounts at the time of termination could be used at the discretion of the contracting officer to make payments chargeable to terminated contracts. Amounts previously authorized but not made available could be added to such accounts. Additional authorizations, although officially discouraged in favor of partial payments under the new procedures, could be made after termination by the contracting officer. As before, total advance payments under any particular contract could not exceed total charges under the contract.[30]

Although the standard advance payment procedures exhibited a certain measure of

rigidity and "red tape", pooled accounts used by the larger contractors permitted considerable administrative flexibility. These accounts often covered a number of contracts in various stages of completion and termination. Inasmuch as advance payments could ordinarily be made available immediately, they were the most rapid means of mobilizing working capital for prime contractors. Subcontractors were not eligible to receive direct advances from the government, but prime contractors were authorized and in many instances urged to make readvances to subcontractors. Nevertheless, for various reasons readvances rarely got below the first tier, and in general were an unsatisfactory means of financing subcontractors.[31] A more successful arrangement was the use of advance payments by prime contractors to make partial payments to subcontractors in the settlement of terminated contracts.[32]

By the end of World War II, the cumulative amount of advance payments authorized by the War Department was approximately $13 billion. This represented authorizations to more than 1,500 contractors operating under some 4,000 contracts. Of this amount more than $7 billion was actually advanced or paid over to contractors. In view of the character of advance payments as revolving funds, the maximum amount outstanding at any one time was much less, amounting only to some $2 billion. (*Chart 4*) The vast bulk of total advances was made for the purpose of financing production, but an indeterminant

[28] Yoshpe, Production Control in the QMC, p. 57.

[29] (1) AIC R41, Financial Aids to Contractors, pp. 39–40. (2) PR 321.12 Interest, and 321.13, Exceptions to Interest Requirements.

[30] JTR, Sec. III, Pt. 3, Use of Advance Payments for Interim Financing.

[31] Page 18 of Mechem Address, cited above in note 24.

[32] See below, pages 683–86. Also PR's 349 and 349A.

CHART 4—WAR DEPARTMENT ADVANCE PAYMENTS: ADVANCES, RECOUPMENTS, AND BALANCE OUTSTANDING

[End-of-Quarter Status]
30 June 1941–30 September 1945

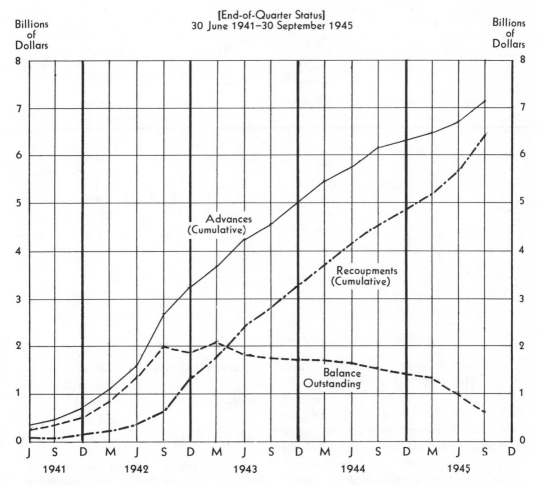

Source: AIC, Department of Research, WD Financial Aids to Industrial Production, 15 Nov 45, p. 18½.

amount—perhaps as much as $1 billion— was attributable directly to termination requirements.[33] The Army Air Forces made wide use of advance payments for termination financing, obtaining an estimated 90 percent of its financing by this device.[34]

The relative use of advance payments within the War Department varied widely

---

[33] The increase in cumulative total advance payments of around a third of a billion dollars in September and October 1945 may safely be ascribed to termination financing, and termination needs during the preceding two years might well have accounted for an additional two thirds of a billion.

[34] ASF, Readjustment History, p. 77. This statement undoubtedly referred only to working capital for prime contractors; fixed-capital requirements in the aircraft industry were enormous and working capital for subcontractors was supplied largely by guaranteed loans.

TABLE 57—WAR DEPARTMENT ADVANCE PAYMENTS, STATUS AS OF 31 AUGUST 1945

[Dollars in Millions]

Agency or Service	Advance Payment Deposits		
	Cumulative Total		Balance Outstanding
	Amount	Percent	
War Department	$6,934.9	100.00	$873.5
Army Air Forces	3,766.3	54.3	627.5
Army Service Forces	3,168.6	45.7	246.0
Ordnance	2,466.9	35.6	213.6
Engineers	312.5	4.5	6.4
Signal	251.1	3.6	12.8
Transportation	68.8	1.0	2.1
Chemical	37.6	0.5	7.0
Quartermaster	27.3	0.4	2.5
Medical	0.6	(a)	0.1
Overseas Theaters	2.8	(a)	0.9
Special Services	1.0	(a)	0.6

a Less than five hundredths of one percent.

Source: AIC R41, Financial Aids to Contractors, Tables 6 and 7.

from one procuring arm to another (*Table 57*). It is apparent that the Army Air Forces and the Ordnance Department accounted for the lion's share of advances, while the Quartermaster Corps made far less use of this form of financing than suggested by the relative size of its procurement program.

The War Department's advance payment program was remarkably successful, not only in providing financial resources for the war effort and its liquidation, but in recouping outstanding funds. Losses on advance payments amounted to only $1.5 million or about one fortieth of 1 percent of all advances made. Interest payments received by the War Department on advance payments amounted to $30 million or about twenty times the losses of principal. This record of recoupment of principal and ratio of earnings to losses was notably better than the War Department's experience with guaranteed loans.[35]

Guaranteed Loans

A second major source of working capital for war contractors was the government-guaranteed loan. This instrument was adopted early in 1942, primarily for the purpose of meeting the urgent problem of subcontractor financing. After Pearl Harbor the pressure upon procuring agencies and prime contractors to increase the amount of subcontracting had become very great. As a result, many thousands of small firms who

[35] Report of the Under Secretary of War to the Secretary of War, 1 July 1945 to 30 June 1947, p. 21.

were unable to finance themselves were brought into the field of war production.

Since these firms were not prime contractors, they were ineligible to receive direct advance payments. Then, too, most prime contractors were unwilling—in view of their ultimate liability—to assume responsibility for subadvances to subcontractors, especially to those below the first tier. Regular commercial banks were prevented by tradition and in some instances by specific regulations from making bold and rapid advances to firms untried in the field of war production. The Smaller War Plants Corporation, with its special funds, powers, and responsibility for supplying the needs of small firms, had not yet been established. Under all these limitations a number of small producers of important items found themselves with insufficient funds to continue operations. This situation was dramatized by the testimony of an Army Air Forces colonel early in 1942 that "the entire aircraft program" was being held up for lack of a critical ingredient produced by a small subcontractor who had been unable to obtain adequate financing.[36]

To meet this problem the President, acting under the recently adopted First War Powers Act, authorized the major procuring agencies (Army, Navy, and Maritime Commission) to make or participate in direct loans and to guarantee loans made by financing institutions to contractors, subcontractors, or others whose work was considered "necessary, appropriate or convenient to the prosecution of the war."[37] With these broad new powers and the immense appropriations made to them in the first three months of 1942, the procuring agencies might have become—in addition to their

other functions—huge lending agencies comparable to the Reconstruction Finance Corporation. Instead, the Under Secretary of War and other officials responsible for economic mobilization preferred, so far as possible, to make use of the established institutional machinery and idle lending capacity of the nation's commercial banking system, operating under the direction of the Federal Reserve System. The War Department had already supported new legislation broadening the powers of the Federal Reserve System, and intensive negotiations with Federal Reserve authorities soon resulted in the establishment of the wartime system of guaranteed loans.[38]

The new guaranteed loans, initially known as V–Loans, were obtained by contractors from their own banks and were guaranteed both as to principal and interest by the contracting agency holding a preponderant portion of the borrower's war contracts. The amount of the loan and the rate of interest were determined by negotiation between the borrower and the lending bank subject to a maximum interest rate of 5 percent. As soon as the bank and the bor-

---

[36] AIC, War Department Financial Aids to Industrial Production, p. 18.

[37] Executive Order 9112, 26 Mar 42.

[38] The guaranteed loan system for war production followed the precedent established in the 1930's by the federal government in the field of housing. Nevertheless, the pathway to launching of the new system was by no means smooth, as indicated by the following: "We got off to a rather difficult start on the guaranteed loan program. It was a new idea. The banks were timorous about it to start with, although I would like to say that by and large they have done a fine job. The bank's lawyers were worried about it and frightened. Some of them thought the guarantee was no good. A lot of people thought the President did not have the power to issue the Executive Order and, as a result of that, the original guarantee was a very complicated thing. I am sorry it was so, but we could not control it. We had to get the banks in and in order to get them in we had to satisfy their lawyers and the lawyers had a perfect field day on it." Page 20 of Mechem Address, cited above in note 24.

rower agreed upon the amount and terms
of the loan, the bank applied to the Federal
Reserve bank of its district for a guarantee.
The War Department maintained a Liaison
Officer—appointed by the Office of Fiscal
Director, ASF—in each Federal Reserve
bank for consultation on applications for
War Department guarantee. The Liaison
Officer reviewed the recommendations of
the Federal Reserve bank, consulted the
contracting officers involved, determined the
borrower's eligibility, and approved or rejected the application. As the program developed the Federal Reserve banks received
increasing delegations of authority from the
War Department, and took over many of
the duties of Liaison Officers.[39] Thus, except
for specified types of cases, including all
loans in excess of $100,000, the Federal
Reserve bank was authorized to execute the
guarantee on behalf of the War Department.

The guarantee supplied by the War Department was an agreement to purchase,
within ten days after demand, a specified
percentage of the loan from the financing
institution. Actual purchases were made by
the Federal Reserve bank as fiscal agent of
the War Department. In return for the guarantee the lending bank paid to the War
Department a graduated "guarantee fee"
equal to a specified percentage of the interest
payable by the borrower on the guaranteed
portion of the loan. For V–Loans this fee
ran from 10 percent, when the guaranteed
percentage of the loan was 60 percent or
less, up to a range of 30 to 50 percent for
guarantees in excess of 90 percent.[40]

An important feature of the V–Loan was
the right of the prospective borrower, in return for payment of a fee, to negotiate a loan

commitment from his bank in advance of
actual need with the option of drawing on
the commitment only to the extent desired.
A loan commitment, supported by a War
Department guarantee, constituted a line of
credit against which a contractor could draw
at any time without having to pay interest
on large unused balances. The total amount
of guarantees therefore greatly exceeded the
amount of loans outstanding at any particular time. On the other hand, since repeated borrowings and repayments could be
made within the limits of established commitments, cumulative disbursements under
the program eventually exceeded total
guarantee authorizations.

Although the guaranteed loan program
was begun mainly to help small subcontractors, its advantages soon resulted in its use by
firms in all categories. Whereas advance
payments generally required segregation of
a contractor's accounts on a contract-by-
contract basis, a single V–Loan could be
made to cover all a firm's contracts whether
prime or sub. The V–Loan was therefore
especially recommended for three important
classes of contractor: (1) firms holding contracts with a number of different procuring
arms or agencies; (2) firms performing simultaneously as both prime contractors and
subcontractors on government orders; (3)
firms holding a large number of contracts
and purchase orders.[41]

The suitability of the V–Loan to the needs
of large corporations is indicated by the fact
that the largest single industrial loan commitment in the nation's history was made
under the War Department's guaranteed
loan program. This was the "King Kong"
credit of one billion dollars established in
October 1942 to finance the contracts of

[39] Pages 19–21 of Mechem Address, cited above
in note 24. (2) PR 319 through 320.8.

[40] AIC R41, Financial Aids to Contractors, p. 52.

[41] PR 319.1.

the General Motors Corporation. Some 475 banking institutions participated in this credit, which was arranged by the Federal Reserve Bank of New York. It was soon ascertained that the aggregate capital and surplus of all the banks in the United States at that time was in the neighborhood of only $5.75 billion. Under the general rule limiting loans to a single borrower to 10 percent of a lending bank's capital and surplus, the combined capacity of all commercial banks in the United States available for lending to General Motors at this time was only some $575 million. Shortly thereafter the billion-dollar loan commitment was reduced to $500 million.[42]

The adaptation of the guaranteed loan system to the needs of termination financing took place in a series of developments beginning with the original V–Loan agreement of 1942. At that time no general plans for termination financing existed. In order to make the guaranteed loan program more acceptable to contractors as well as to banks, a special clause was introduced into the standard V–Loan agreement. This clause provided for suspension of maturity and assumption of interest payments by the guarantor upon termination of any of the governing contracts in the ratio of terminated to current contracts.[43] While this provision would cushion the shock of termination, it still did not permit new borrowings

against terminated contracts; moreover, it later proved embarrassing to the War Department after improved methods of termination had been adopted.[44] In 1943 the VT–Loan was developed to cover the financing of both current and terminated war contracts. The 1944 V–Loan Guarantee was a simplified form eliminating the distinction between V– and VT–Loans. While designed primarily to finance production, it could, at the discretion of the lending agency, provide new funds after termination.[45]

The final stage in the evolution of the guaranteed loan was the T–Loan, specifically designed on recommendation of the Baruch-Hancock report to afford a maximum of assistance to contractors undergoing termination. The T–Loan was administered in the same manner as its predecessors, but its application was confined to terminated contracts and its terms were somewhat more liberal. The maximum interest rate was 4½ percent and the War Department's guarantee fee was reduced by as much as 50 percent.[46] Loan commitments could be negotiated before termination, to be drawn upon thereafter only as

---

[42] (1) AIC R41, Financial Aids to Contractors, p. 55. (2) Page 21 of Mechem Address, cited above in note 24. (3) ASF Annual Rpt, 1943, p. 197.

[43] JTR 322. This ratio could easily be determined by the lender since war contracts were typically assigned to lending institutions under terms providing that all government payments under the contract be made directly to assignees. Assignees were notified of terminations at the same time as contractors. The guaranteed loan program rested heavily upon the permissive foundations of the Assignment of Claims Act of 1940.

---

[44] Page 20 of Mechem Address, cited above in note 24.

[45] JTR 323.4.

[46] It is of interest to compare the scale of War Department guarantee fees for V–Loans with that for T–Loans:

Guaranteed Percentage	War Department Guarantee Fee (Percent of interest on guaranteed portion)	
	V–Loans	T–Loans
60 or less	10	10
65	12½	10
70	15	10
75	17½	10
80	20	10
85	22½	15
90	25–30	20
95	30–50	30
Over 95	30–50	50

(1) AIC R41, Financial Aids to Contractors, p. 52. (2) OCS, Termination Financing for War Contractors, pp. 21–24.

needed; the commitment fee was not to exceed one fourth of 1 percent per annum on the unused balance of the total commitment except where the bank elected to charge a flat fee not to exceed $50. Although T–Loans were available only after termination, commitments provided advance insurance against the freezing of working capital by sudden contract cancellation. Borrowers were required to reduce T–Loans as rapidly as they received payments or credits in settlement of terminated contracts, and final maturity of the loans was to be no later than 30 days after final contract settlement.[47]

Contractor borrowing under T–Loans fell far short of expectations at the time of the program's announcement. By 30 June 1946, only 842 applications for commitments totaling $391 million had been made for all contracting agencies. Furthermore, contractors found little need to draw against their commitments; total T–Loans outstanding at any one time reached a peak of only $30 million in December 1945 and thereafter steadily declined.[48]

Aside from the effective partial payment system for terminated contracts, presently to be described, the principal reason for the small volume of T–Loans is to be found in the high degree of financial liquidity provided for war contractors throughout the period of the war as a whole. Much of this liquidity is attributable to a variety of causes unrelated to the pretermination stages of the guaranteed loan program. In its entirety the

guaranteed loan program provided 6,333 War Department contractors with over $8 billion in authorized guarantees.[49] As in the case of advance payments, guaranteed loans represented a kind of revolving fund: while cumulative disbursements to War Department contractors exceeded $9 billion by the end of October 1945, the average amount of guaranteed loans outstanding was only about $1⅓ billion during the peak of the program from mid-1943 to mid-1945. Uncollectible guaranteed loans amounted to less than one twentieth of 1 percent of total borrowings. Income from guarantee fees approximated $25 millions, which was reduced by losses amounting to $3.8 million.[50]

Even more than in the case of advance payments the preponderance of guaranteed loans went to contractors and subcontractors for the Army Air Forces. Out of a total of approximately $7.9 billion in War Department guaranteed loan authorizations made by 31 August 1945, the Air Forces accounted for nearly $5.1 billion as against only $2.8 billion for the Army Service Forces. This heavy use of borrowed working capital in relation to the size of the aircraft procurement program reflected the tremendous expansion of all segments of the aircraft industry in order to meet the needs of World War II. Of the ASF total of $2.8 billion in guaranteed loans, Ordnance contractors took an estimated $1.6 billion, the Signal Corps $0.7 billion, and all other tech-

---

[47] See OCS, *Termination Financing for War Contractors,* for a complete copy of the standard T–Loan agreement (pp. 25–31), the standard T–Loan Guarantee Agreement (pp. 21–24), the loan formula (p. 32), and other information concerning T–Loans. See also JTR 325, Procedure for T–Loan guarantee, and JTR 326, Factors to be considered by guarantor.

[48] OCS Eighth Rpt, July 1946, p. 12.

[49] Page 19 of Mechem Address, cited above in note 24.

[50] Report of the Under Secretary of War to the Secretary of War, 1 July 1945 to 30 June 1947, p. 16. This report shows combined earnings of $25.5 million for War Department guarantee fees and interest receipts on direct loans. The War Department's direct lending program was relatively insignificant, totaling only $62.8 million for World War II. See AIC R41, Financial Aids to Contractors, p. 45.

nical servics together somewhat less than $0.5 billions.[51]

Partial Payments

The basic philosophy of the Baruch-Hancock Report and the ensuing Contract Settlement Act was that the liquidation of the war effort should be "fair, fast, and final." In keeping with this philosophy, major emphasis in the field of termination financing was placed upon a procedure which would recognize the right of contractors to immediate reimbursement of costs already incurred in the performance of terminated contracts. Such reimbursement would make borrowing unnecessary; it would be directly related to the contractor's eventual termination claim and would constitute a part of the settlement process itself. Termination financing of this type was made available in the last year of the war by a fundamental revision of existing partial payment systems of the several procuring agencies.

On 8 September 1944, the Office of Contract Settlement established a uniform partial payment system for all procuring agencies. The new system was an outgrowth of partial payment provisions in the old War Department standard termination article, revised Army Procurement Regulations, and the Uniform Termination Article promulgated by the Joint Contract Termination Board.[52] Under the new procedures, adequate interim financing was to be made in the form of partial payments to be granted within 30 days after application. Three types of payment were authorized: (1) immediate partial payments, based on contractors' estimates; (2) cost-supported partial payments; (3) controlled partial payments into special accounts.

Immediate partial payments were designed to afford financial assistance to contractors without waiting for a cost investigation. As soon as a contracting agency received an application from a war contractor, whether prime or sub, it was required to grant a partial payment up to 90 percent of the contractor's own costs. Within the 90-percent over-all maximum, the contractor was to receive not less than 75 percent of the contract price of completed articles not delivered plus 75 percent of the estimated cost of raw materials, purchased parts, supplies, direct labor and overhead allocable to the terminated portion of the contract (except for the cost of special facilities and other items likely to be controversial). Lower payments were to be made only upon the contractor's request or in cases where the contracting agency had reason to believe that the application was not made in good faith, was excessive in amount, or that the interests of the government required denial or payment of a lower amount.[53]

Cost-supported partial payments, which required the submission of substantial ac-

---

[51] The subdivision of the War Department total into the several components above was made by the Army Industrial College using actual ratios found by the Fiscal Director, ASF, for 30 December 1944. See AIC R41, Financial Aids to Contractors, p. 54.

[52] Before the passage of the Contract Settlement Act, contracting officers had been personally liable for overpayments in the settlement of terminated contracts. In self-protection, contracting officers demanded detailed audits before making substantial partial payments. The inevitable delays involved in obtaining audits defeated the use of such payments for interim financing. The Contract Settlement Act relieved contracting officers of all personal liability in the absence of their own fraud. The essentials of the new partial payment system were incorporated in a revision of PR 15, under the broad authority of the Contract Settlement Act, even before the issuance of OCS Regulation No. 2. ASF, Readjustment History, pp. 79 ff.

[53] (1) OCS Regulation 2, par. 3. (2) JTR 352.

counting data (usually in the form of an actual termination claim), could be substantially greater. In this case the maximum was the total amount estimated by the contracting officer to be due the contractor by reason of termination. This included 100 percent of the contract price of undelivered completed articles; 90 percent of the cost of raw materials, purchased parts, supplies, direct labor, and allocable manufacturing overhead; a reasonable percentage of other allowable costs under the contract; and such additional amounts deemed by the contracting agency to provide the contractor with adequate interim financing. Contractors who had previously received one or more partial payments could obtain additional amounts, up to the maximum allowable, under the cost-supported procedure.[54]

Controlled partial payments were authorized to be made to war contractors deemed to be insolvent or in imminent danger of insolvency. The solvency test was applicable both to contractors making application and to contractors forwarding applications from lower tier contractors since the latter had to be protected from nonreceipt of payments transmitted down the contractual chain. Controlled partial payments were initially deposited in special bank accounts and were released as particular items of cost or payments to subcontractors were approved by the contracting officer. Specific regulations for handling controlled accounts were developed by the individual contracting agencies.[55]

Regardless of type, all partial payments were subject to diminution by the amount of any unliquidated balances of advance and partial payments previously made under the contract, and by the amount of all credits arising out of contractor retention or sale of property whose costs of production were included in the application.[56] Also, all partial payments were to be made in such a manner as not to impair any valid assignment of a claim under the contract without the consent of the parties.[57] In order to discourage excessive estimates in connection with partial payment applications, a penalty of 6 percent was to be charged the contractor on any excess of his estimate over the amount determined in final settlement to be due him.[58] In addition, if he received partial payments in excess of the amount finally due, he was required to pay interest on the excess at the rate of 6 percent per annum until the government was repaid. The Director of Contract Settlement could suspend or modify the penalty for overstatement of claims, but not for overpayment. If a contractor attempted to avoid these penalties by failing to file an actual termination claim, the contracting agency could resort to the standard provision of all partial payment agreements which permitted the government, under stated conditions, to demand immediate repayment of all partial payments or any portion thereof.[59]

Subcontractors' applications for partial payment were normally filed with their customers. If the customer possessed delegated authority to make final settlement with his subcontractors he could grant a partial payment, from his own funds or funds allotted

[54] (1) OCS Regulation 2, par. 4. (2) JTR 353.
[55] (1) OCS Regulation 2, par. 5. (2) JTR 356; JTR 954.
[56] JTR 344.
[57] JTR 345.
[58] JTR 316.
[59] (1) JTR 316. (2) OCS, Form 4, Application for Partial Payment, Sec. IV, Agreement of Applicant, par. (3). The director of Contract Settlement delegated authority to the contracting agencies to suspend or modify the overstatement penalty. As a result the penalty was rarely applied unless the overstatement was judged to be willful.

to him for the purpose, without the specific approval of the contracting officer. In the absence of delegated authority the subcontractor's application was transmitted up the chain to the contracting agency. Each intervening contractor above the applicant, including the prime, was required to subscribe to the application, stating that he had no reason to doubt the propriety of the amount requested and recommending that the payment be made. At the same time, he agreed to credit or reimburse promptly his immediate subcontractor with any amount received for the benefit of the applicant. Contractors unwilling to subscribe to these statements were required to give written explanation of their position.

The vertical procedure was considered essential both to establish allocability of subcontracts to particular prime contracts and to insure proper treatment of offsets held by higher tier contractors against those in lower echelons. Throughout the war many contractors rendered financial assistance to their subs by means of loans, advance payments, and other arrangements. The resulting claims against subcontractors were normally liquidated by credits for deliveries under the contract. The government had no knowledge of such offsetting claims against subcontractors and relied on the vertical processing of applications and payments to permit their proper discharge.

Exceptions to the vertical partial payment procedures were to be made when there was evidence of unwarranted delay under normal procedures, or where direct settlement arrangements with subcontractors were in effect. Also, as indicated, exceptions were made in cases of delegated settlement authority or of insolvency.

A further development to speed partial payments to subcontractors was the establishment of special funds in possession of responsible war contractors out of which subcontractors could be granted partial or final payments without specific approval by the contracting officer. Selection of funded contractors was limited to those already given delegated authority to make final settlement of subcontract claims not in excess of $10,000. Funds were obtainable either in the form of special partial payments earmarked for the benefit of subcontractors, or in the form of direct loans by the contracting agency. Under either procedure the contractor desiring the fund made application by letter to the contracting officer requesting a specified amount of money and furnishing pertinent information. Approval of the application was followed by the signing of an agreement on administrative details and the transmittal of the funds. The loan procedure required more rigorous qualifications for approval but was more flexible in its administration. Both procedures were available to either prime contractors or subcontractors; in the case of subcontractors the short-circuiting of the normal vertical procedure was often substantial and eliminated many steps in the processing of applications and the reverse flow of money payments.[60]

Of the several methods of interim financing created by the Contract Settlement Act, partial payments were by far the most widely used. By 31 December 1945, when over 95 percent of its World War II contracts had been terminated, the War Department had made approximately $1.5 billion in partial payments. As of that date $722 million in partial payments under fixed-price contracts was still outstanding; an additional $48 million was also outstanding to subcon-

[60] (1) JTR 364 (Revision No. 2, 20 Jun 45), Funds for the benefit of subcontractors. (2) OCS Fourth Rpt, July 1945, pp. 21–22.

tractors under CPFF contracts. Of the $722 million for fixed-price contracts, $368 million had been made under cost-supported procedures against termination claims of $887 million. The remaining $354 million was paid in advance of claim. Assuming that War Department partial payments made after 31 December 1945 rose proportionately with those of all agencies, they totaled some $2.3 billion by the end of the program.[61] This would approximate 50 percent of the $4.4 billion eventually paid by the War Department in final settlement of all its war contracts.

It is apparent that the objectives of the Contract Settlement Act in the area of termination financing were abundantly realized. By providing virtually 100-percent liquidity of contractor investment in termination inventory, the Act stimulated the availability of private credit, with or without government guarantee, on favorable terms. Loans under previous borrowing arrangements including V–Loans of all types were freely renewed or extended in an atmosphere of general liquidity. Moreover, by the end of the war many contractors were in a strong financial position and were able to supply the bulk of their own working capital needs.

Termination financing was but the final phase of the larger task of supplying contractors with the financial means for the

execution of their production responsibilities throughout the war. As in the case of fixed capital for the expansion of facilities, the provision of adequate working capital required drastic departures from conventional standards and procedures long observed in private banking operations. These changes were at first resisted or adopted only reluctantly by the banking community, but after Pearl Harbor all barriers were broken down as the full implications of the nation's war production assignment began to be revealed. The vigorous action of the government in providing advance payments and other direct financial aids to contractors set the pattern for the bold program of war finance which removed, for the first time in many years, all monetary limitations upon the full utilization of the nation's economic resources.

The Disposition of Contractor Inventory

An inevitable accompaniment of contract termination was the problem of what to do with leftover materials, parts, tools, and machinery acquired or produced by the contractor for the purpose of fulfilling his contract. Such leftovers had to be promptly disposed of for several reasons: to clear contractors' plants for work on other war contracts and to permit reconversion at the end of the war; to rechannel scarce, critical materials into current production where they were most needed; to permit final settlement of terminated contracts; and to avoid transfer to the government of unneeded matériel which would be costly and burdensome to store and dispose of at a later date.

Under the terms of procurement contracts the government received title to termination inventory not sold or retained by contractors. The War Department, of

---

[61] Figures as of 31 December 1945 taken from ASF, Monthly Progress Report, Section 14–A, Contract Terminations, 31 Dec 45, Partial Payments, pp. 26–28. Partial payment statistics were not regularly reported in Monthly Progress Reports or their successor, War Department, Progress Reports. The rough estimate of $2.3 billion for the War Department at the end of the program was determined by applying the proportions existing at the end of 1945 to totals for all agencies as of 30 June 46, after which there was relatively little new termination financing. OCS History, p. 46; OCS Eighth Rpt, July 1946, p. 12.

course, reserved the right in all cases to claim any termination inventory desired by it for production or supply purposes, as well as secret, confidential, and restricted material whose release was deemed contrary to national security. With these exceptions, the policy of the department was to release a maximum of contractor inventory to the private industrial economy.[62]

Standard contract provisions required that whenever inventory was sold or retained by the contractor the sale or retention price (which was credited to the government in settlement) had to be approved by the contracting officer. Unfortunately, many items—especially goods in process—had no substantial resale value and had to be disposed of as scrap. This led to a number of complications when unneeded contractor inventory began to appear on a large scale with the upsurge of Army contract terminations in mid-1943. Contracting officers, new to the complexities of property disposition and fearful of unfavorable publicity, criticism, or worse, were reluctant to authorize sale prices below cost. The inevitable result was the slowing down of termination settlements, the clogging of industrial facilities with left-over materials, and unnecessary shortages elsewhere in the war economy.

On 30 June 1943, Under Secretary Patterson took steps to correct the situation. On that date he issued instructions that all War Department contracting officers be directed to adopt a bold policy of property disposition, stating that such officers would be supported in the exercise of their honest judgment. The instructions fully recognized all the difficulties, stating in part:

Frequently this material must be sold at a substantial amount below its cost. In many instances, work in process must and should be sold as scrap for scrap prices. It is inevitable that losses will take place. Rarely will delay in disposing of such property help the war effort or result in any substantial savings to the Government. Under present circumstances, no materials should be hoarded merely in the vague hope that at some future date the property may have a future use or a greater value.

The same policy must be applied to obsolete or unneeded machinery and equipment. Where it has no suitable use in production it should be disposed of promptly so that the scarce and critical materials out of which it is made can be used in the manufacture of new and vitally needed instruments of production.[63]

Procurement Regulation 15—the Army's new termination regulation issued on 14 August 1943—incorporated the Under Secretary's letter verbatim and contained procedures for its implementation. No limitation, other than the exercise of honest judgment, was placed on contracting officers' authority to approve sale or retention prices. In deciding whether a price was fair or reasonable, the contracting officer was to consider the nature of the property, general market conditions and prices, the location

[62] JTR 411; JTR 441. The term "contractor inventory," as used in the Surplus Property Act of 1944, was a broader concept than "termination inventory" as defined in the Contract Settlement Act. "Termination inventory" consisted of leftover materials, small tools, and parts which would have been incorporated in, or used up in production of, finished items. "Contractor inventory" included termination inventory and also machinery covered by special contract clauses, government furnished material, and other items. Inasmuch as the principles governing the disposition of contractor and termination inventory were substantially the same for purposes of the present discussion they are here used interchangeably. See ASF, Readjustment History, p. 135, and JTR 400.2.

[63] Memo, USW Patterson for CG AAF and CG ASF, 30 Jun 43, sub: Disposition of Contractor-Owned Property on Termination of Contracts for the Convenience of the Government, reproduced in PR 15–350.2.

of the property, the utility to the Government of the property if title were taken, storage and transportation costs, and the necessity for prompt disposition as a step in the settlement of the termination claim.[64]

In order to facilitate disposition, contracting officers were to grant as much discretionary power to prime contractors as practicable. Under the terms of the War Department's standard termination article for prime contracts, contractors agreed to use their best efforts to sell their termination inventory in the manner, to the extent, at the time, and at the price or prices directed or authorized by the contracting officer. Since time was of the essence in selling to advantage it was desirable to eliminate so far as possible the need for advance approval of each transaction by the contracting officer. Accordingly, contracting officers were authorized to grant advance permission to contractors to dispose of various classes of property at stated discounts from cost, and this authority could be extended by prime contractors to their subs. The discount levels were fixed by the contracting officer and frequent periodic reports by contractors of sales under this authorization were required.[65] Sales at scrap prices required that the property be identified as scrap and that the purchaser provide a warranty not to resell except as scrap in accordance with OPA and WPB regulations. To assist the contracting officer in doubtful cases the several technical services were required to make available to him, on request, appraisal personnel who would render assistance with a minimum of formality and paper work.[66]

The channels for disposition of termination inventory varied with the trade practices of the industry, the nature and relative scarcity of the material, and the contractor's own situation. Standard parts and materials were the easiest items to dispose of since they had a wide variety of uses. If the contractor had no foreseeable need for them, they could be sold in the open market or returned to the supplier with the government defraying expenses of packing, transportation, and related costs. Strategic and critical materials were redistributed in accordance with applicable WPB regulations and the needs of other contractors. Work in process was to be realistically valued and scrapped whenever necessary. Both contractors and contracting officers were urged to use their imagination, ingenuity, courage, and aggressiveness in disposing of property. Telephone calls were to be preferred to letters; informal, flexible procedures were to replace formality.[67]

Despite the general urgency and the pressures from above, contracting officers throughout 1943 and 1944 found it difficult to move termination inventory with sufficient speed to keep pace with new terminations. Repeated admonitions were made by the Under Secretary, the Commanding General, ASF, and later the Surplus War Property Administrator.[68] On the other hand, a number of "atrocity" stories concerning Army destruction of supposedly useful property or sales at seemingly "give away" prices

[64] PR 15–358, Sale price.

[65] PR 15–359, Grants of discretionary power to prime contractor.

[66] PR 15–360, Ascertainment of value.

[67] PR 15–361. Channels of disposition.

[68] (1) Memo of USW Patterson dated 28 Dec 43, cited in ASF, Readjustment History, p. 138; (2) Memo, CG ASF for Chfs of Technical Services, 4 Mar 44, sub: Property Disposition in Contract Termination, quoted in Ord Procurement Cir 65–44, 8 Mar 44; (3) SWPA, Statement of Policies to be Followed by Government Agencies in the Sale of Contract Termination Inventories, 21 Apr 44.

had appeared in newspapers and Congressional hearings. Contracting officers found themselves squeezed between the upper millstone of pressure to get the work done and the lower millstone of public criticism for doing their work. By the end of 1944, with the specter of mass terminations looming on the horizon, it was becoming increasingly clear that conservatism, born of tradition and nurtured by fear of criticism, might defeat the whole reconversion program.

Two difficult classes of decision faced contracting officers in the disposition of termination inventory: (1) decisions to accept prices substantially below cost in order to move the property; (2) decisions to scrap costly work which had no immediately foreseeable use. As indicated later, the question of price policy was a perennial issue, and the governing regulations were changed many times to satisfy changing pressures and conditions. The other delicate issue, the question of when to scrap costly assemblies or work in process, is perhaps best illuminated by the following:

Consider a part in our aviation engine. An aviation engine is made up of parts that are beautifully finished. For instance, pistons; they are great big aluminum pistons. You could put one right up on the mantlepiece. They look like they are made of platinum and set with diamonds, and they cost about like that too. Now, let's say that the contract is terminated and there were 10,000 of those pistons on hand. Let's say at the same time that that engine is not going to be built again in the foreseeable future, and let's say furthermore that they don't need any additional lifetime spare parts, which is actually the case with pistons . . . .

Let's suppose that there are 10,000 left over. They are packed in cotton, in special cartons and handled like eggs. If you have a fingernail scratch on one it is ruined. You say to the contracting officer, "We recommend them to be scrapped." He says, "All right,

throw them out in the scrap pile. Let the rain and snow fall on them—put them under the hammer and smash them up." I am glad I am not a contracting officer. That is the kind of decision that has to be made.

What is the alternative? You pack them, you box them, you crate them, you ship them and you put them in a warehouse, and you watch them for five years . . . and then you scrap them.

That is the other solution of the problem, and that's the solution I don't believe the country can stand . . . . I think it is fair to say that if the Government takes over a hundred dollars worth of material and goes through all this preparation for storage . . . packing, crating, shipping, renting a warehouse, putting a watchman on the job—and then after a length of time, perhaps a year, they sell the material for $100, only about $50 would be realized. The expense eats up the remainder. It would be a short length of time before it would have no value at all even if you sold it at the original price. You have used up the original value in trying to take care of it.[69]

While these issues were being debated among contractors and the procuring agencies, steps were being taken to formulate a broad, consistent attack upon all aspects of the federal surplus property problem as part of the larger task of reconversion. A major factor in shaping public opinion and national policy in this whole area was the Baruch-Hancock report of 15 February 1944. Beginning with a sixty-day plant clearance policy for termination inventories, the report presented recommendations on all major aspects of the surplus property problem. It indicated the need for prompt, effective, orderly handling of termination inventories and other government surpluses in order to expedite war production, combat

---

[69] Excerpt from An Address by Mr. Courtney Johnson of the Studebaker Corporation on Thursday, 7 Dec 44, War Readjustment Course, AIC, pp. 11–12.

inflation, speed the resumption of civilian employment, reduce the national debt, and lower postwar taxes. It stressed the need for immediate action in order to take full advantage of the excellent disposal conditions in the remaining months of the war, and pointed to the shortage of civilian-type goods and materials as well as those for war production. These shortages provided a superior market which could absorb the bulk of government surpluses pending the reestablishment of peacetime levels of production. Among the basic principles of disposal recommended in the report were selling "as in a goldfish bowl" with records always open to public inspection; selling as much and as early as possible without disrupting normal trade; scrapping what must be scrapped, but no deliberate destruction of *useful* property; use of regular channels of trade, so far as possible, in disposing of particular properties; no sales or rentals to speculators and promoters; equal access to surpluses for all businesses; fair market values with proceeds of all sales going to reduce the national debt. The report recommended the creation of a Surplus Property administrator within the Office of War Mobilization to establish basic policy and co-ordinate the activities of the disposal agencies. The War Department and the other procuring agencies would be represented on a Surplus Property Policy Board chaired by the administrator.[70]

Four days after the publication of the Baruch-Hancock report the President established the Surplus War Property Administration (SWPA) in the Office of War Mobilization.[71] SWPA was headed by an administrator, who was assisted in policy determination by an Advisory Board, composed of representatives of some fourteen government agencies, including the War Department. SWPA was a policy-making agency; actual sales of surplus property—except for termination inventories, small lots, and other exceptions—were made by the five disposal agencies, who received for disposal the surpluses declared by the procuring and other property owning agencies. SWPA promptly set about two major tasks—the making of interim regulations to establish policy and co-ordinate the disposal activities of the various agencies, and the drafting of permanent surplus property legislation.[72]

The largest segment of the government's long-run disposal problem consisted of the

---

[70] Baruch-Hancock Rpt, Pt. IV, Addendum 2, Surplus Property, pp. 56–68. The report proposed that actual sales be made by four disposal agencies: (1) Treasury, Procurement Division, for consumer goods other than food; (2) RFC (preferably a new corporation within RFC) for all capital and producers' goods; (3) Maritime Commission, for ships and maritime properties; (4) Food Administrator, for all food. This recommendation was shortly adopted by the Executive order establishing the Surplus War Property Administration with the addi-

tion of a fifth disposal agency, the Foreign Economic Administration, for all overseas surpluses.

[71] Executive Order 9425, 19 Feb 44.

[72] The Surplus Property Act of 1944, approved 3 October 1944, was based largely on SWPA recommendations. It created a three-man Surplus Property Board (SPB) to replace SWPA. On 1 October 1945, as a result of an amendment to the Act, the Surplus Property Administration (SPA) headed by a single Administrator replaced SPB. On 1 February 1946 SPA gave way to the War Assets Corporation (WAC), which in turn was taken over on 25 March 1946 by the War Assets Administration (WAA). WAA persisted until the surplus disposal job was practically completed. In 1948 its remaining duties were assumed by the General Services Administration (GSA). Meanwhile, overseas disposal had passed progressively from the Foreign Economic Administration to the Army-Navy Liquidation Commission, and then to the Department of State (Foreign Liquidation Commissioner). See SPA, Quarterly Progress Report—Fourth Quarter 1945, pp. 11–12, 48; WAA Quarterly Progress Report—First Quarter 1946, pp. 6–7.

eventual surpluses of finished items already in the hands of the procuring agencies. In mid-1944, however, these surpluses had not yet developed and the disposition of contractor inventory was the most pressing surplus property problem. On 21 April 1944 SWPA issued its Statement of Policies to be followed by Government Agencies in the Sale of Contract Termination Inventory.[73] The statement urged a bold policy of inventory disposition, stressing the importance of scrapping unusable work in process and selling to contractors who would put materials immediately into other war production or essential civilian work; at the same time it proposed safeguards against unduly low prices.

Under ensuing regulations SWPA limited the authority of contracting officers to approve retention or sale prices. For any portion of inventory under termination claims of less than $10,000 the contracting officer could approve the price only if it were "the best price obtainable." This was defined as the best price offered after reasonable efforts to test the market, with due allowance for the location and other circumstances of the particular material.[74] Inventory associated with termination claims of more than $10,000 was classified into four groups: (1) scrap; (2) crude or simple raw materials; (3) used production equipment; (4) other materials.

Scrap could be sold or retained at the going market price without offering it to the general public under competitive bidding. If the market price could not be realized, the material could be sold only under competitive bidding, the government reserving the right to reject all bids at a price deemed to be inadequate. To prevent unwarranted classifications as scrap, material sold as scrap in the absence of competitive bidding could only be used or resold for scrap purposes, and the purchaser was required to sign a warranty to this effect. Release of the warranty could later be obtained by payment to the government of the difference between the scrap price originally paid to the government and the current value of the material for non-scrap uses.[75]

Raw materials could be sold only at the going market price, except that quantities at any one location, if less than minimum commercial quantities, could be retained or sold to any buyer at the best price obtainable. Used production equipment, including machine tools and listed categories of industrial products, were subject to SWPA Regulation No. 3, which authorized sale prices at standard percentages of cost, depending upon the length of time the equipment had been used. The percentages declined with each month of use, running from 90 percent for less than 1 month down to 50 percent for 36 months or more in the case of retentions. For sales to others, the corresponding percentage was 5 percent less, in order to compensate for removal costs and prevent undue favoritism to existing holders of equipment under war contracts.[76]

All other materials could be retained or sold only at the best obtainable price in excess of 75 percent of cost, or at a lower price

---

[73] The statement was drawn up by an interdepartmental committee of SWPA, composed of representatives of the War, Navy, Treasury, and Justice Departments, the RFC, and the Bureau of the Budget. Shortly thereafter, on 2 May 1944, JCTB delegated to SWPA all its authority on price policy applicable to termination inventories. OCS History, p. 39.

[74] JTR 432.3; JTR 433.

[75] JTR 434.

[76] JTR 435.1 (Revision No. 1, 20 Apr 45), Crude or simple raw materials, and JTR 435.2 (Revision No. 1, 20 Apr 45), Used production equipment.

if equivalent to that currently charged by normal sources of supply. Exceptions were made for "nominal quantities" under $2,500 (best price obtainable) and in cases where the material could not be sold in a reasonable length of time at the minimum price indicated above. In such cases the material could be sold on a negotiated basis to domestic "buyer-users" at the best price obtainable, under a warranty not to resell at a profit. If negotiation failed to yield a sale within a reasonable period, the item could be sold on competitive bids to the highest bidder. Civilian-consumer type items could not be thus sold since these were to be turned over to regular disposal agencies for sale.[77]

The adoption of the 75-percent-of-cost floor under retention or sale prices for termination inventory was done over the objections of the War Department, which took the position that this would unduly delay disposition and plant clearance. This position was borne out by events and with the approach of V–J Day and mass terminations, the regulations were modified to reduce or eliminate the floor while tightening up the procedures in other respects. Under the revision, contractors were permitted to retain for their own use any property at prices which were fair and reasonable and not less than the proceeds that could reasonably be expected if the property were offered for sale. No minimum price was stated, but appropriate review procedures were required of the owning agencies and the contractor was required to state in writing his intention not to resell at a profit. All scrap sales under termination claims in excess of $10,000 had to be made under competitive bidding, subject to contracting

agency approval of the price. Serviceable property for similar size claims had to be advertised locally seven days in advance and the price was subject to a minimum of 50 percent of cost. The "nominal quantity" figure was reduced from $2,500 to $300 and other changes were made.[78]

The numerous provisions and changes in price policy suggested by the foregoing are testimony to the complex nature of the disposal problem faced by the War Department and the other procuring agencies. Each of the provisions and each of the changes was made on the basis of experience, tempered by the changing circumstances of the nation's economy but subject always to the inexorable pressure of urgency. As the principal procuring agency, the War Department was faced with the greatest volume of unneeded termination inventory and the greatest array of disposal problems. This fact gives rise to some basic questions of appraisal: How did the War Department—and thus the taxpaying public—fare in the disposition of its termination inventory costing many hundreds of millions of dollars to produce? What was the total volume of termination inventory generated by World War II contract cancellations and what percentage of cost was recovered as a result of sales? Although no precise answers can be given to these questions, available statistics reveal the essence of the story.

From 1 June 1944 through 31 August 1945, War Department contractor inventory available for disposition totaled approximately $710 million in cost value. Of this amount, some $353 million had been retained or sold for the government by contractors, $226 million was transferred to government ownership, and $131 million

---

[77] JTR 435.3 (Revision No. 1, 20 Apr 45), Other materials.

[78] ASF, Readjustment History, pp. 144–45.

TABLE 58—WAR DEPARTMENT CONTRACTOR INVENTORY DISPOSALS: 1 SEPTEMBER 1945–
31 DECEMBER 1946

[Dollars in Millions]

Disposal Class	Cost	Proceeds	Percent of Cost
Total Disposal Credits	$2148.9	$310.4	14.4
For Contractors' Own Use	353.5	138.7	39.3
Small Lot and Inventory Sales	49.0	11.8	24.1
Unserviceable Property—Competitive Bid	1045.1	31.5	3.0
Unserviceable Property—Negotiated Sales	466.9	18.9	4.1
Serviceable Property—User Buyer	91.6	35.8	39.0
Serviceable Property—Other	142.8	73.7	51.6

Source: WD, Progress Report, Section 4–G, 31 Dec 46, p. 34.

was in process of disposition.[79] At this time a new statistical reporting system was inaugurated and subsequent figures were based on dispositions after 1 September 1945. From this date through 31 December 1946 when some 98 percent of all World War II terminated contracts had been settled, an additional $4 billion in contractor inventory was disposed of. War Department dispositions accounted for $3 billion, the remaining $1 billion being declared surplus to disposal agencies. Of the $3 billion of War Department dispositions, $2.3 billion was retained or sold by contractors, the remainder being redistributed for use by the War Department and other government agencies for donations and for salvage.[80]

An analysis of disposal credits for War Department contractor inventory other than

plant equipment for the period subsequent to 1 September 1945 reveals the relative return to the government for the several classes of sale. (*Table 58*) Since these figures cover more than two thirds of War Department dispositions for the period, a 15 percent return on its contractor inventory may be inferred as typical for the War Department. As indicated above, the return for scrapped items ran from 3 to 4 percent. Although these figures are of interest, they do not in themselves shed much light on the wisdom of disposal price policy. The important consideration was the readjustment of the nation's economy. Low disposal prices, apart from reflecting market conditions in a surplus market, were a means of accomplishing rapid reconversion from war to peace. To the extent that these prices were lower than the value ultimately realized by purchasers, the government presumably received revenue via subsequent income tax collections and lower refunds under loss-carryback and excess profits credit provisions.

The War Department record in the matter of plant clearance is also of interest. The

[79] ASF, Monthly Progress Report, Section 14–B, 30 Jun 44, p. 8 and 31 Aug 45, p. 28. Of the total figure of $710 million, some $65 to 70 million was on hand 1 June 1944. The systematic recording of War Department termination inventory statistics began with the month of June 1944. *Ibid.*, issue of 30 Jun 44, p. 8.

[80] WD, Progress Report, Section 4–G, 31 Dec 46, p. 34.

TABLE 59—PLANT CLEARANCES EFFECTED BY THE WAR DEPARTMENT 1 SEPTEMBER 1945–
31 DECEMBER 1946

Clearance Period	All Clearances		Inventory, Materials		Plant Equipment	
	Number	Percent	Number	Percent	Number	Percent
Clearances—Total_____	105,193	100	95,665	100	9,528	100
40 days or less_____	62,626	59	57,668	60	4,958	52
41 to 60 days_____	30,409	29	27,416	29	2,993	32
Over 60 days–within waiver_____	6,875	7	6,106	6	769	8
Over 60 days–beyond waiver_____	5,283	5	4,475	5	808	8

Source: WD, Progress Rpt, Section 4–G, 31 Dec 46, p. 32.

60-day plant clearance requirement of the Contract Settlement Act could be waived in individual cases by agreement between the contractor and the contracting officer. During the hectic period of mass terminations following V-J Day it was impossible for the War Department in all cases to effect clearance within the required time. In order to effect prompt clearance and storage arrangements the War Department acquired many millions of square feet of storage space at strategic points throughout the country. It also made numerous arrangements to store inventory on contractor's premises, paying them a suitable storage fee. From 1 September 1945 through 31 December 1946, the War Department received 105,295 plant clearance requests. At the end of the period, only 102 remained uncompleted. The disposition by time periods is also of interest. *(Table 59)* In only 5 percent of all cases did the War Department fail to complete plant clearance within the time specified by the Contract Settlement Act or agreements thereunder. Nearly 60 percent of all cases were completed in 40 days or less, well within the 60-day target. Thus, with a few exceptions, the objective of prompt plant clearance—so important to

rapid reconversion—was accomplished. A major factor behind its achievement was the rigorous requirement of the statute which established a specific goal well in advance of mass terminations and permitted exceptions only with the consent of the affected contractors.

Statistics of Contract Termination

Like the record of most large-scale mobilization activities carried on under the stress of war, contract termination and settlement statistics fall short of 100-percent accuracy or completeness. No systematic record of terminations was kept in the War Department prior to the establishment of the Contract Termination Branch in the Purchases Division, ASF, in June 1943. Early reports, which attempted belatedly to account for all terminations occurring "after Pearl Harbor," were inaccurate and constantly subject to revision. Changes in the needs of the program from time to time made difficult the maintenance of continuity and comparability. CPFF termination statistics were the last to be developed and the first to be curtailed after termination activity subsided. The basic statistics shown herein were compiled from a number of sources and are believed to represent the best available data.[81] (*Tables 60, 61, 62, and 63*)

Table 60 summarizes the broad record of the War Department's experience in contract termination and settlement for World War II. This table shows the progress of terminations and settlements from the practical inception of the termination program in mid-1943 to its virtual completion. For the entire period the War Department terminated over 135,000 prime contracts. Nearly half (59,000) of these were terminated prior to V-J Day. By the end of September 1945—the first full calendar month after V-J Day—95 percent of all World War II terminations had been effected. Corresponding settlement figures indicate that 47,000 settlements had been accomplished by V-J Day and over 63,000 by the end of September. By the end of 1945 over 80 percent of all World War II contracts eventually terminated by the War Department had been settled, and a year later only a handful remained for disposition.

The dollar figures shown in Table 60 reveal additional aspects of the termination and settlement record. Total canceled commitments of the War Department exceeded $46 billion—more than ten times the $4 billion of World War I cancellations. Against

this amount, actual settlement payments were under $4.5 billion or less than 10 percent of canceled commitments. This contrasts favorably with the 14-percent figure for World War I, which thus may be said to have cost the government 40 percent more than World War II in the settlement of each dollar of canceled commitment. This substantial improvement was attributable in part to the better planning and more fortunate circumstances, already described, associated with the World War II termination problem.

Further study of Table 60 indicates that terminations were settled more rapidly in numbers than in dollar value. This was partly the natural consequence of the greater difficulty and delay connected with large and complicated settlements. It was also the result of a definite effort by the War Department to settle quickly the maximum number of contracts when confronted with mass terminations. This yielded the widest distribution of settlement payments throughout the economy in a short period of time and rapidly narrowed administrative responsibility to a relatively small number of cases. Under this policy the War Department settled nearly 65,000 contracts in the last six months of 1945.

Table 61 gives a broad comparison of the termination activity of the War Department with that of the other contracting agencies. The War Department's $46 billion in canceled commitments represents 70 percent of the total for all contracting agencies. By number of individual terminations, its share of the total was only 42 percent. This smaller percentage reflects the large number of small-contract cancellations made by subsidiaries of the Reconstruction Finance Corporation—the Defense Plant Corporation, Metals Reserve, Defense Supplies, and so

---

[81] Sources for Table 60 data are as follows for the indicated dates: (1) 31 Dec 42: ASF, History of Purchases Division, p. 304; (2) 21 Jun 43 through 30 Sep 43: monthly and special reports (all typescript) of Contract Termination Branch, Purchasing Division, ASF (copies in OCMH); (3) 31 Dec 43 through 31 Mar 46: data transcribed or computed from ASF, Monthly Progress Report, Section 14–A; (4) 30 Jun 46 through 31 Dec 46: WD, Progress Reports, Section 5–A; (5) 31 Mar 47: OCS History, App. A, p. 65; (6) 30 Jun 47: Report of the Under Secretary of War to the Secretary of War, 1 Jul 45 to 30 Jun 47, p. 19; (7) 31 Dec 51: GSA, *War Contract Terminations and Settlements, Thirtieth Report, Jan 52.*

TABLE 60—WAR DEPARTMENT CONTRACT TERMINATIONS AND SETTLEMENTS
CUMULATIVE PROGRESS AT SPECIFIED DATES

End of Quarter or Specified Date	Number of Contracts			Canceled Commitment Value (In Millions)		Cash Payments[a] to Contractors (In Millions)
	Terminated	Settled	Pending	Terminated	Settled	
1942						
December 31_____	1,900	([b])	([b])	$1,868	([b])	([b])
1943						
June 21_____	3,778	1,836	1,942	([b])	([b])	([b])
June 30_____	5,785	3,497	2,288	([b])	([b])	([b])
July 31_____	7,325	5,097	2,228	4,336	1,655	([b])
August 31_____	8,520	6,191	2,329	5,756	1,975	([b])
September 30_____	10,569	7,379	3,190	6,499	2,206	([b])
December 31_____	15,666	11,485	4,181	9,806	3,047	63
1944						
1st Quarter_____	21,718	15,917	5,801	12,981	4,334	102
2d Quarter_____	26,255	20,978	5,277	14,155	6,156	175
3d Quarter_____	29,788	25,713	4,075	16,949	8,579	287
4th Quarter_____	34,071	30,967	3,104	18,847	11,707	414
1945						
1st Quarter_____	38,280	35,427	2,853	19,416	14,108	522
2d Quarter_____	53,271	42,766	10,505	28,121	16,966	635
3d Quarter_____	128,362	63,323	65,039	43,376	19,045	891
4th Quarter_____	130,408	107,428	22,980	45,034	22,734	1,253
1946						
1st Quarter_____	132,726	125,982	6,744	45,175	30,555	2,488
2d Quarter_____	133,326	130,872	2,454	46,040	41,203	3,873
3d Quarter_____	133,504	132,781	723	46,127	43,617	4,170
4th Quarter_____	133,851	133,457	394	46,305	44,951	4,298
1947						
1st Quarter_____	134,337	133,973	364	46,421	45,572	4,369
2d Quarter_____	134,701	134,354	347	46,400	45,800	([b])
1951						
4th Quarter_____	135,517	135,478	39	46,698	46,668	([b])

[a] After disposal credits.
[b] Precise data not available.

Source: ASF Monthly Progress Rpt., Sec. 14-A, and supplementary data. See above, p. 695, note 81.

TABLE 61—WAR CONTRACT TERMINATIONS AND VALUE OF CANCELED COMMITMENT BY AGENCY AND TYPE OF CONTRACT THROUGH 31 MARCH 1947

[Dollars in Thousands]

Item	Total	War	Navy	Maritime	RFC	Treasury
ALL CONTRACTS						
Number of Terminations_____	321, 068	134, 340	63, 673	10, 335	109, 789	2, 931
Total Commitment Value ᵃ_____	$65, 748, 000	$46, 422, 000	$16, 472, 000	$939, 000	$1, 728, 000	$187, 000
Average Commitment Value____	$205	$346	$259	$91	$2	$64
FIXED PRICE CONTRACTS						
Number of Terminations_____	319, 663	133, 499	63, 335	10, 325	109, 574	2, 930
Total Commitment Value ᵃ_____	$48, 254, 000	$33, 479, 000	$12, 496, 000	$599, 000	$1, 494, 000	$186, 000
Average Commitment Value____	$151	$251	$198	$58	$1	$64
CPFF CONTRACTS						
Number of Terminations_____	1, 405	841	388	10	215	1
Total Commitment Value ᵃ_____	$17, 494, 000	$12, 944, 000	$3, 975, 000	$341, 000	$234, 000	(ᵇ)
Average Commitment Value____	$12, 451	$15, 391	$11, 763	$34, 057	$1, 088	$327

ᵃ Total commitment value figures rounded.
ᵇ Less than $500 thousand.
Source: Adapted from OCS, History, p. 65.

forth. The canceled commitment value of these small RFC contracts averaged only $1,600 compared with the $346,000 average for the War Department—the highest for all agencies.

Table 61 also reveals the high average canceled commitment value of CPFF terminations. For all agencies, CPFF contract cancellations were less than half of 1 percent in number. Yet this small number accounted for over 25 percent of the value of total terminated commitments. The War Department's $13 billion in CPFF cancellations accounted for nearly 75 percent of the total; its average commitment cancellation per contract was, however, overtowered by the $34-million average for the ten high Maritime cancellations.

Tables 62 and 63, in addition to showing the relative use of no-cost settlements already discussed,[82] reveal other significant relationships.

Table 62 shows the number and value of settled terminations for each of the War Department technical services through 31 December 1946. Army Ordnance alone effected over 35,000 terminations or more than 25 percent of the War Department total. In terms of canceled commitment value for both fixed-price and CPFF contracts, the Air Forces headed the list with over $21 billion—nearly half the War Department total. Together, Ordnance and the Air Forces accounted for five sixths of all

[82] See above, pages 643–45.

TABLE 62—WAR DEPARTMENT CONTRACT SETTLEMENTS: BY TECHNICAL SERVICE, TYPE OF
CONTRACT, AND TYPE OF SETTLEMENT

[Cumulative: 7 Dec 41—31 Dec 46]

Agency and Type of Contract	Number of Settlements			Canceled Commitment Value (In Millions)		
	Total	No-Cost	Claim	Total	No-Cost	Claim
ALL CONTRACTS						
War Department:						
Actual	133,457	71,681	61,776	$44,950	$6,654	$38,296
Percent	100.0	53.8	46.2	100.0	14.8	85.2
FIXED-PRICE CONTRACTS						
War Department—Total	132,654	71,279	61,375	$33,130	$6,056	27,074
Army Air Forces	17,485	8,518	8,967	12,622	1,930	10,692
Ordnance	35,026	19,112	15,914	13,248	2,632	10,616
Signal	23,817	11,551	12,266	2,813	508	2,305
Engineers	25,499	16,301	9,198	11,770	352	1,418
Chemical	3,830	1,872	1,958	625	137	488
Medical	5,051	3,459	1,592	120	56	64
Quartermaster	18,206	8,026	10,180	1,360	331	1,029
Transportation	3,740	2,440	1,300	572	110	462
CPFF CONTRACTS						
War Department—Total	803	402	401	$11,820	$598	$11,222
Army Air Forces	548	329	219	8,712	478	8,234
Ordnance	184	51	133	3,026	102	2,924
Engineers	71	22	49	82	18	64

Source: WD, Progress Rpt, Section 5–A, 31 Dec 46.

War Department cancellations by number and over 99 percent of CPFF canceled commitments.

Concluding Observations

The foregoing account of the contract settlement activities of the War Department portrays the salient features of the problem, the policies and procedures adopted for its resolution, and the statistical record of the results achieved. The account would be incomplete, however, without a broad summary of the general results of the program, especially in the light of subsequent criticisms of the World War II contract settlement process.

In terms of its broad objectives the contract settlement program was eminently successful. A task of overwhelming proportions, with potentially grave consequences for the nation's postwar reconstruction, was

TABLE 63—COMPARATIVE USE OF NO-COST SETTLEMENTS: BY PRINCIPAL
CONTRACTING AGENCIES

[Fixed-Price Contracts through 30 September 1946]

Agency	Number of Settlements			Canceled Commitment Value (In Millions)		
	All Settlements	No-Cost Settlements		All Settlements	No-Cost Settlement	
		Number	Percent		Value	Percent
War	131, 998	71, 003	53. 8	$32, 674	$6, 051	18. 5
Navy	60, 328	39, 309	65. 2	10, 597	3, 082	29. 1
Maritime	9, 326	7, 436	79. 7	392	131	33. 4
RFC	106, 244	97, 702	92. 2	981	669	68. 2
Treasury	2, 671	1, 974	73. 9	151	99	65. 6

Source: OCS Ninth Rpt, Oct 46.

achieved with a degree of rapidity and smoothness which appeared highly improbable to many sober observers in 1943 and 1944. The program was boldly conceived and boldly executed. At the same time, it was the beneficiary of far more detailed and meticulous planning than perhaps any other operation of similar magnitude in the nation's history. It represented the combined and integrated efforts of all the procuring and appropriate control agencies. Narrow jurisdictional lines were dissolved as procuring and control agencies jointly formulated policy, and as procuring agencies frequently conducted actual operations in each other's behalf. Thus the history of War Department contract settlement operations—greatest in magnitude and variety for all the agencies— is largely the history of settlement activities for the nation as a whole.

The keystone of the whole program was the negotiated settlement, effected by the procuring agencies, and made final except for cases of fraud. The process of settlement by negotiation was not the substitution of personal caprice and bargaining for established principles of fair compensation.

Rather, it was the use of carefuly defined rules of settlement which could be applied with intelligent flexibility, thus preventing the crippling of common sense and simple equity by hair-splitting, bureaucratic technicality. Under the governing regulations, anticipated profits under terminated contracts were relinquished by contractors and subcontractors generally. On the other hand, terms of settlement provided a liberal definition of costs and profits for work actually performed. Such liberality was in keeping both with the needs of nationwide economic readjustment and the premises of equitable government. The principle of finality of settlement by the procuring agencies was an integral part of settlement by negotiation. To have made all settlement agreements subject to later approval by another agency would have relegated the original negotiations to the status of pantomime. A "settlement" without finality would have been a contradiction in terms; by the same token it would have perpetuated long into the postwar period the very task which had to be accomplished as a precedent to peacetime economic activity.

To state that the major administrative and substantive foundations of the contract settlement program were properly conceived, and that the program as a whole was "successful," is neither to imply perfection nor to overlook the fact that an indeterminate amount of waste and fraud were present. The Comptroller General of the United States, in his postaudit of contract settlements, discovered a number of cases of contractor fraud as well as instances of collusion by officers or employees of the procuring agencies. Unfortunately, the official reports of the incumbent Comptroller General tended to exaggerate the amount and nature of various kinds of overpayment and went out of their way to create an impression of wholesale fraud and scandal in the conduct of the contract settlement program.[83] The burden of these reports was not the obvious need for swift and adequate punishment of the parties to fraudulent transactions, but the alleged unwisdom of Congress in failing to require the Comptroller General's approval of all settlements before they became final.

The sixth and final report, made in 1950, summarizes the results of General Accounting Office review of World War II contract settlements. As of 30 April 1950, the GAO had examined 9,239 settlements covering 26,566 terminated contracts or roughly one twelfth of the total for all agencies. The Comptroller General concluded that improper payments of some $20.9 million in

549 settlements had been "induced by fraud," and these were so certified to the Department of Justice. In addition to the fraud allegations the final report cited nonfraudulent overpayments of nearly $4.3 million in connection with 684 settlements. The Comptroller General thus pointed to a total loss to the government of some $25 million with the implication of many more millions in unknown losses on settlements not reviewed.[84] All of the reports were couched in supercharged language condemning the Contract Settlement Act, settlement personnel in the procuring agencies, and the alleged waste, extravagance, and fraud experienced under the program.[85]

A sober analysis of the Comptroller General's charges indicates that his general position with respect to the operation of the Contract Settlement Act was untenable. Many of his cases upon examination had no substantial merit; perhaps a majority had been discovered by the Army auditors prior to GAO review; the meritorious cases discovered solely by the GAO staff amounted in dollars to only a small fraction of 1 percent of all World War II contract settlement

---

[83] The Comptroller General made a total of six reports to Congress on the operation of the Contract Settlement Act of 1944 as required by Section 16 thereof. These reports were dated 27 August 1945, 26 July 1946, 10 July 1947 (printed as S. Doc. No. 75, 80th Cong., 1st Sess.), 24 February 1948 (S. Doc. No. 121, 80th Cong., 2d Sess.), 1 August 1949 (S. Doc. No. 108, 81st Cong., 1st Sess.), and 19 May 1950.

[84] 1950 report, pp. 6–7, 9–10.

[85] For example, from the 1950 report: "careless, inept, or overgenerous contracting officers" (p. 2); "overwhelming proof of the vast and unnecessary damage where . . . representatives of the contracting agencies were authorized to audit themselves and to pump out of the Treasury such amounts as they approved" (p. 8); "The foregoing summarization . . . throws light but partially on the full damage wrought by the Contract Settlement Act of 1944" (p. 9); "This unbridled waste and extravagance was revealed only as an incident. . . ." (p. 9); "the tragic consequences when the Congress releases the reins that control the public purse" (p. 12); "The sad story of operations under the Contract Settlement Act of 1944. . . ." (p. 12). But the comptroller was not without a sense of humor: "One firm presented three termination claims which were so outlandish in amount that they were even rejected by the contracting agency." 1947 report, p. 7.

payments.[86] In large part, the postwar findings of the Comptroller General were comparable in nature to his 270 cases introduced into the 1943 hearings and refuted at the time by Under Secretary Patterson—cases turning largely on the differences between the cautious, legalistic approach appropriate to a peacetime government accounting agency and the pragmatic philosophy of wartime procuring agencies who authorized any cost reasonably necessary to the effective prosecution of the war.[87]

Available statistics indicate that the percentage of the fraud allegations subsequently upheld in court was small. As of 31 December 1948, out of 220 cases sent to the Department of Justice, 167 had been dismissed for insufficient evidence to warrant criminal proceedings and 99 similarly rejected for purposes of civil proceedings. Of the remainder, 10 criminal and 23 civil proceedings had been started, with the rest still under investigation.[88] While the lack of successful fraud actions does not prove absence of fraud, it casts some doubt on the extreme interpretations made by the Comptroller General.

The exact amount of fraud and "overpayment" involved in World War II contract settlements will never be known. In the nature of the case, there can be neither a universally acceptable definition nor an accurate measure of these magnitudes. That there was considerably more than there ought to have been is certain. That there was much more than to be expected, considering the vast scope, complexity, and urgency of the program is not so certain. But it is doubtful that under the most liberal estimates the combined losses from fraud and unwarranted overpayment in World War II settlements amounted to as much as half a day's national income. Many times this amount might easily have been lost if the contract settlement program had faltered, despite the presence of other conditions favorable to the smooth reconversion of the nation's economy.

---

[86] Even if the entire $25 million had been established as unwarranted overpayment, the total loss would have amounted to less than one half of 1 percent of the total settlement payments of $6.5 billion for all agencies.

[87] For reference to cases cited in 1943, see above, page 624.

[88] Legislative Brief on the Armed Services Contract Settlement and Property Disposition Act of 1949, p. 31. This study, prepared by the Air Force 9–6691, AF), is on file in the ICAF Library.

PART EIGHT

EPILOGUE

CHAPTER XXX

The Summing Up

Historical Recapitulation

Prewar Planning and the Launching of Rearmament

For a period of twenty years, under the statutory responsibilities conferred in 1920 upon the Assistant Secretary of War, the Army bore the principal burden of insuring the nation's industrial preparedness to meet a war emergency. Within the limitations imposed by lack of funds, insufficient personnel, public indifference or hostility, and the inherent obstacles to planning for so uncertain and difficult an enterprise, the Army's prewar plans were realistic and thorough. First to be undertaken was the development of specific procurement plans, which resulted in basic specifications for military items, balanced estimates of initial requirements, and the earmarking of specific industrial capacity to permit the immediate launching of a rearmament program. At the beginning of the defense period the procurement plans were revised, expanded, and put to work. When the emergency arrived, the availability of these plans and the knowledge gained in their preparation made possible the rapid placement of contracts without the degree of floundering, delay, and confusion apparent at the beginning of World War I.

Also contributing to victory in World War II were the Army's general procurement plans and the complex array of studies in the field of nationwide industrial mobilization.

General procurement planning reviewed the whole field of procurement law, devised the form and principles of wartime contracting, and prepared new legislation to remove the crippling barriers of peacetime law and to create additional powers essential to emergency procurement. Industrial mobilization planning produced studies and recommendations for the apportionment of basic industrial capacity and for the application of wartime controls in many fields: prices, materials, labor, foreign trade, transportation, and other categories. The several versions of the Industrial Mobilization Plan also contained important organizational proposals, not only for existing and new governmental agencies essential to wartime functions, but for harnessing and integrating the nation's basic industries into a unified war effort. The War Production Board, the Office of Price Administration, the Board of Economic Warfare, and many other World War II organizations and agencies bore remarkable resemblance to prototypes suggested in the Industrial Mobilization Plan.

At the time of the crisis brought on by the fall of France, President Roosevelt decided against the formal adoption of the Industrial Mobilization Plan. In view of the precarious political situation in 1940, the President was unwilling to relinquish personal control over the rearmament effort. The state of the nation's economy, moreover, made the complete adoption of the IMP unnecessary in some respects and undesirable in others. In the face of idle plant capacity and unemployed manpower still remaining after ten years of depression, and because the Munitions Program of 1940 was only half the size of the "maximum effort" contemplated by the IMP, compulsory allocation of facilities was considered unnecessary. Under the conditions of 1940, prompt utilization of available capacity was more important than allocation.

The eighteen-month "defense period" between mid-1940 and 7 December 1941 thus became the "transition period" contemplated by the Industrial Mobilization Plan. Many of the actions taken and policies adopted during this period were in general accordance with the provisions of IMP; others were not. No amount of planning could have been "complete," nor could the planners have guaranteed that their program, however meritorious, would be adhered to by those selected to lead the nation in time of emergency. But the basic purpose of the Industrial Mobilization Plan—the analysis of the problems of mobilizing the nation's economic resources and the preparation of comprehensive recommendations and plans to be used at various stages of the emergency—was fulfilled. Despite the fact that it was never formally adopted, the Industrial Mobilization Plan, together with all its associated planning activities throughout the interwar period, made a vital contribution to the nation's preparedness and eventual victory in World War II.

Determination of Requirements

Two basic objectives underlay the determination of Army requirements for World War II: winning the war and saving American lives. There is little doubt that America's outpouring of war matériel,

rather than an allied preponderance of manpower, was the dominant factor in winning the war. Moreover, the same superiority in the quality and abundance of weapons, supplies, and services that turned the tide of war also reduced the loss of American lives to a fraction of the losses sustained by the Axis powers. Not only were total casualties for the entire war much less but in individual actions the hand-to-hand combat loss rates among American soldiers were usually the lowest of the combatant nations. By substituting prodigality of matériel for prodigality of manpower the United States demonstrated that its oft-criticized "materialism" was an instrument for enhancing the effectiveness, the comfort, and the survival of its fighting forces as well as its citizens on the home front.

A major factor in the nation's success in equipping its armed forces was the boldness of the procurement programs established by the military agencies. The procurement goals of World War II were high in both qualitative and quantitative terms, requiring for their fulfillment the best efforts of the nation's scientists, industrial management, and manpower. At the beginning of the defense period the War Department proposed a program of rearmament double the size of the Munitions Program actually adopted. But the country was not yet ready to undertake so large a program, or indeed to prosecute the one in hand with full vigor. It therefore became necessary throughout the defense period to make successive additions to the initial program as the gravity of the crisis increased and as the United States assumed the role of "Arsenal of Democracy." Finally, under the greatly expanded programs after Pearl Harbor—centering around the President's spectacular objectives for the production of ships, planes, tanks and guns—total requirements exceeded the nation's physical productive capacity. In the face of this development, boldness in the determination of requirements had to be tempered by feasibility and balance. In the fall of 1942 the War Production Board ordered major cutbacks in military programs and, under the decision of the Joint Chiefs of Staff, the bulk of the cutbacks came from the Army's ground forces program.

Despite the high level of military requirements throughout the war, the economic needs of the civilian population were adequately filled. Many segments of the civilian population found their living conditions and standards substantially improved as a result of wartime prosperity and full employment. In any case, as compared with civilian populations in both allied and enemy countries, the American public found itself relatively unscathed by the total requirements and consequences of the war.

Purchasing Policy

The basic objective of Army purchasing policy was "to get the goods," that is, to obtain on schedule the delivery of munitions needed to win the war. To this end the Army created a vast purchasing organization whose offices and agencies were to be found in every state of the union. Relying basically upon decentralized operations under central staff direction, the Army's procurement activities penetrated and vitally affected all areas and departments of the national economy.

Primary emphasis in the procurement program was placed on the selection of competent contractors and on the support of these contractors in the discharge of their responsibilities. Procurement contracts went first to facilities designated in prewar plans or to other firms with established reputations and demonstrated capacity for production. This policy reinforced existing tendencies in the economy for business to gravitate to large corporations. After the major problems of converting the economy to a wartime footing had been resolved and basic requirements filled, contract distribution was increasingly influenced by nonmilitary considerations and a larger share of war business was given to small firms.

Army pricing practices, like the selection of contractors, also reflected the military objective (getting the goods) first and other considerations later. This resulted in generous prices for military items, a development which had much in its favor during the defense period and early post-Pearl Harbor era. In the face of the urgent need for munitions and the impossibility of accurate advance pricing, contracting officers felt obliged to devote their efforts to launching and expediting production rather than to "haggling over price." After a decade of economic stagnation and business failures, generous prices provided the greatest single stimulus to rapid production, relieved contractors of their perennial fear of insolvency, and furnished them with abundant means for discharging their new and difficult responsibilities. On the other hand, once full employment and conversion of the nation's resources to war production had been attained, overpricing became increasingly dangerous to economic efficiency, and corrective measures had to be devised. The formulation and administration of a sound pricing policy, adequately differentiated and responsive to a multiplicity of changing circumstances, was an unbelievably difficult and never-ending assignment.

The difficulties of wartime pricing resulted in the adoption, early in 1942, of statutory contract renegotiation. Pioneered by the War Department, and enacted into law by Congress to prevent war profiteering, renegotiation was one of the major innovations of World War II in the field of economic mobilization. It was the initial hope of Congress as well as of the War Department that renegotiation would bring about "close pricing" and thus "write its own death warrant." But close pricing, in terms of the standards of prices and profits of the prewar decade, was not achieved in World War II. The task was too great, the time too short, pricing staffs and cost accounting systems too inadequate, the resistance of contractors too heavy, and the sustained will for the job lacking on the part of most procurement officers. The goal of uniformly close pricing by all agencies for all contractors was gradually recognized as a will-o'-the-wisp, and renegotiation was retained throughout the war as an essential backstop to recapture excessive profits inevitably accruing despite even the best efforts of pricing personnel. The task of renegotiation thus developed into the process of deciding whether and to what extent each contractor, on the basis of his over-all performance record, was entitled to retain profits which might otherwise be considered "excessive." This task called for omniscience but could not be avoided. With all the pressures and difficulties involved, it is not surprising that contractors as a whole were treated generously in renegotiation.

In spite of evident shortcomings in the execution of purchase policy, the efforts of the procuring agencies to implement a system of close pricing, combined with renegotiation and high rates of taxation, did succeed in keeping retained profits generally within the range of propriety. World War II

was not followed by revelations and condemnations of wartime profiteering comparable to those which took place after World War I. Meanwhile, the primary objective of Army purchase policy—the filling of procurement requirements in time to win the war—was abundantly realized.

Expansion of Facilities

Most of the numerous camps, cantonments, training establishments, and other "command facilities" required for the operation of the Army in World War II had to be built from scratch after mid-1940. This was also true of the special processing plants needed to turn out the great quantities of powder, high explosives, small arms and artillery ammunition, poison gas, and other munitions supplied by the Army's Ordnance Department and Chemical Warfare Service. After World War I all the government-owned powder plants had been destroyed, and only a handful of government arsenals—operating in peacetime on starvation budgets—remained to keep alive the art of ammunition making.

In addition to command facilities and highly specialized ammunition plants, the Army and its sister procuring agencies in 1940 required an across-the-board expansion of general productive capacity throughout the economic system. During the depression of the 1930's much of the nation's industrial plant and equipment had been allowed to atrophy. The failure of the American economy to grow at normal rates over a period of ten years meant that many of the scientific, engineering, and technical developments of the 1930's lay dormant. Under the circumstances, much of the unused plant capacity available at the beginning of the defense period was obsolescent. With the great expansion of industrial activity following the adoption of the Munitions Program of 1940, productive capacity in all sectors of the economy rapidly became inadequate.

The War Department's facility expansion program was as virile as its procurement program as a whole. Both in the establishment of facility requirements and in the methods of facility financing, the Army used bold estimates and vigorous, open-handed administration. Instead of using cramped, inefficient, and obsolete facilities merely because of their availability, the Army ordered for its major programs the construction of vast new enterprises designed in accordance with the latest engineering developments and equipped with the finest machinery obtainable. Under such sponsorship and with the efforts of the Advisory Commission, the Defense Plant Corporation, and other agencies, the creation of industrial capacity in the United States during three short years was as great as it had been for the preceding decade and a half.

By mid-1942 it had become evident that in the face of general shortages of materials the Army's facility expansion program was overambitious and would have to be cut back. In particular, plant capacity for small arms ammunition soon proved to be excessive, and some plants were shut down or reduced to part-time operation. It is possible that the post-Pearl Harbor waves of facility expansion in this field could have been foreseen as excessive at the time of their adoption. On the other hand, the emergence of excess capacity might be regarded as a result of the favorable progress of the war. Low rates of expenditure in the European Theater, and the unforeseen capitulation of Japan at least a year ahead of schedule, made unnecessary the consumption of the last available round of ammunition or the use of the final increment of plant capacity hurriedly created in the eleventh hour of the nation's need.

In many respects the most significant area of facility expansion was the general addition to the nation's industrial capacity under "tax amortization." Some 80 percent of the World War II tax amortization program was represented by War Department certifications, most of which had been made by mid-1942. This program proved to be highly effective in breaking down the resistance of private industry to capital expansion early in the defense period. In addition to its effectiveness in stimulating aircraft production and industries contributory thereto, the Army's tax amortization program provided badly needed capacity for the production of materials, parts, supplies, machinery, and equipment essential to general war production and the maintenance of the industrial economy.

As long as additional privately-owned capacity appeared to be essential to the military procurement program, the Army was liberal in its certification policy. After mid-1943 the military agencies were no longer greatly concerned with general industrial expansion and the certification function passed to the War Production Board. During this period the evident approach of the end of the war called for a tightening of certification policy and the War Production Board adopted the practice of partial certification, commonly on a 35-percent-of-cost basis. But there was no conceivable formula—especially in the earlier stages of the war—which could accurately anticipate the amount of economically useful life that would remain in facilities at the war's end. It was precisely for this reason that Congress, in the face of the urgent necessity for stimulating capital expansion, had adopted the bold concept of 100 percent write-off of emergency facilities within a five year period.

The liberal use of this provision by the Army and Navy during the defense period and early in 1942 undoubtedly conferred high profits upon contractors—profits which in many instances were not finally realized by individuals until the end of the era of plant disposals, property sales, corporate mergers, and refinancing long after the war was over. But as in the case of purchase policy, the primary objective of the facility expansion program was achieved. The United States and her allies attained the matériel superiority necessary to overwhelm the enemy. Moreover, the same productive facilities which were created to win the war constituted the cream of the nation's postwar heritage of plant capacity available for future emergencies and for supplying the large and expanding requirements of peace.

Production and Material Controls

America's industrial mobilization experience in World War I had convinced Army planners that the ordinary price system was an inadequate instrument for the allocation of the nation's resources in time of war. Accordingly, the Industrial Mobilization Plan contemplated that in an emergency a system of direct controls would be superimposed upon the regular price system to insure the most effective distribution of productive capacity and scarce materials. At the same time, price controls would be applied to prevent inflation, distortion of the price structure, unjust enrichment, and other evils.

This general scheme was eventually adopted to govern the apportionment of a large share of the nation's productive resources in World War II. Price controls of the ceiling variety and rationing of consumer goods were administered by the Office of Price Administration. Because of their typical lack of a price and production history, military goods were exempted from OPA controls and left to special pricing procedures administered by the procuring agencies in the course of the contracting process. After Pearl Harbor—with the tightening of material control systems, the development of a regime of price ceilings, and the great expansion of procurement programs without regard to price considerations—the pricing process became primarily a device to insure that the money costs of production under each contract would be covered. The function of resource allocation was in large part shifted from the price system to direct administrative decisions governing the placement of contracts and supported by wartime material control systems.

The technical problems involved in developing material control systems adequate to the needs of World War II posed perhaps the greatest challenge faced by economic mobilizers during the war. Three general types of system for the distribution of scarce materials were ultimately utilized—priorities, allocations and budgeting—reflecting three different approaches to the control problem. The priorities system was the earliest, simplest, and most widely used of the three. Devised and administered by the Army and Navy Munitions Board at the beginning of the defense period, priorities were a kind of additional currency superimposed upon the nation's existing monetary system; by the end of the defense period they had become an important factor in allocating the nation's basic resources.

With the great increase in programed requirements after America's entry into the war the burden carried by the priorities system became too great for the system to handle. Inflation of priority ratings reached the point where only orders with top ratings had any assurance of delivery, and lower ratings became worthless. In the critical months after Pearl Harbor the problem of adequately controlling the flow of materials to individual firms throughout the economy appeared to be so complex as to defy solution. Finally, after a period of intensive debate and experimentation with various allocation schemes, the War Production Board and the procuring agencies adopted the Controlled Materials Plan—a tight system of material controls of the budget variety envisaged in the Army's prewar plans.

The announcement of the Controlled Materials Plan in November 1942 committed the nation to its most difficult and heroic undertaking in the World War II economic mobilization program. The application and refinement of the new system, together with related developments, succeeded by late 1943 in bringing a high degree of order into the entire field of war production. The budgeting principle used in the Controlled Materials Plan was later successfully extended to lumber, tires, and other materials not covered by CMP as shortages of these items reached critical proportions. Nevertheless, the priorities system—because of its simplicity and general applicability—was revised and retained throughout the war to direct the flow of the numerous materials, parts, and supplies not governed by more specific controls.

The Army was directly or indirectly involved in many other activities concerned with the availability of materials to meet the needs of war. The peacetime efforts of the Army and Navy to import and stockpile strategic and critical materials had been largely thwarted by inadequate budgets and the crippling limitations of "Buy-American" legislation. After the fall of France, responsibility for stockpiling as well as for augmenting domestic production was given to new government agencies with large budgets and adequate powers. Under the guidance of NDAC and its successors, domestic production of aluminum and magnesium— to mention two outstanding examples— soared to unprecedented heights and became more than adequate for the tremendous aircraft programs of the Army, Navy, and Lend Lease. Likewise, imports of strategic and critical materials after Pearl Harbor, although obtained at the cost of many lives and many ships, eventually rose to unanticipated levels. At the same time, around-the-clock efforts of the Army's technical services and their contractors resulted in thousands of material-saving changes in specifications and production processes. The ultimate solution of the materials problem was thus achieved by a combination of measures—controlled distribution, augmented supplies, and drastic conservation programs—supplemented by production scheduling orders and other controls essential to the balanced progress of war production.

Contract Termination and Settlement

Long before the end of World War II the attention of the military procuring agencies was forcibly directed to the necessity of preparing an adequate legislative and administrative framework for the orderly liquidation of the nation's war production program. As early as the spring of 1942 the cancellation of several large projects by Army Ordnance revealed the complexity of the contract settlement problem, and demonstrated the impossibility of prompt and satisfactory settlement of terminated contracts under existing laws and administrative regulations.

By mid-1943 the cumulative dollar value of War Department contract cancellations for World War II—made necessary by changing military requirements, shortages of materials, and other circumstances—exceeded the department's total for its entire World War I experience. With over a hundred thousand prime contracts still in effect at this time, the War Department became gravely concerned at the prospect of mass terminations and administrative chaos if the war should suddenly end. In addition to current pressures to make adequate preparations for the task of nationwide economic demobilization, government administrators were plagued with recollections of serious failure in this area in World War I, as well as with widespread fears and predictions of postwar depression and unemployment.

All these influences led to a concerted program of planning, legislation, and administrative preparations on the part of Congress, government agencies, and the entire industrial and business community. The central theme and purpose of the program was rapid demobilization and reconversion of the nation's economy to the pursuits of peace.

The substantive problems of economic demobilization fell into three broad areas: contract termination, contract settlement, and disposal of government property. Termination decisions resulted primarily from reductions in military requirements with the approach of victory and the accumulation of excess stocks of war matériel. Nevertheless, both the timing and the distribution of cutbacks were influenced by labor shortages and surpluses, civilian requirements, differences in contractor efficiency, and many other nonmilitary considerations. All these factors had their counterparts in the build-up of the war production program—a circumstance which led wartime observers to label the whole contract termination and settlement process as "procurement in reverse."

The second and third areas—contract settlement and property disposal—were to a large extent mutually dependent; together they constituted the heart of the task of economic demobilization. The basic responsibility of contract settlement was prompt reimbursement of contractors for their expenditures of money and effort on contracts up to the point of termination. Discharge of this responsibility required the development of a body of complex regulations based on broad principles of fair settlement, together with elaborate organizations and procedures for carrying out the policies thus evolved. The keystone of the whole program was the negotiated settlement, under which the procuring agencies were given authority to make binding settlements without reference to the Comptroller General. This carried over into contract settlement, for both fixed-price and cost-plus-a-fixed-fee contracts, the same degree of contractual authority and freedom of bargaining which the procuring agencies had been given at the beginning of the war to permit the effective placement of original contracts.

The negotiated settlement, stoutly resisted by the Comptroller General, was authorized by Congress in the Contract Settlement Act of 1944. This legislation owed much to a special report prepared by Bernard Baruch and John M. Hancock under the auspices of the Office of War Mobilization and Reconversion. The Baruch-Hancock report insisted that settlements be "fair, fast, and final," that sixty days was in general a sufficient period in which to effect settlement, and that in the interim contractors be made liquid by adequate termination financing. Throughout the report ran the basic theme that full employment and national prosperity in the postwar era were the primary objectives of reconversion policy, and that these objectives were consistent with standards of fairness both to contractors and to the government.

The liquidation of the nation's war production program was carried out with the same kind of boldness which characterized the wartime build-up. Rigorous deadlines were established for various stages of the process, and contracting officers were forced to make promptly decisions that might otherwise have been postponed indefinitely. Under generous settlement payments and provisions for termination financing, the nation's economy was placed in a highly liquid financial position, facilitating the reconverson process with a minimum of dislocation and unemployment. Surplus war matériel was sold for what the traffic would bear, unfinished items of procurement were typically sold for scrap, and contractors' plants were rapidly cleared. While the pressures for prompt reconversion in many cases resulted in settlements seemingly unfavorable to the government, a realistic appraisal of reconversion losses could charge them partly to the inevitable costs of war and partly to the price of a vigorous postwar economy.

Concluding Observations

This volume has attempted to recount and summarize the basic role of the U.S. Army in planning and participating in the war production activities of the United States in World War II. Both as the statutory industrial mobilization planning authority during the interwar period, and as the principal wartime procuring agency, the Army and its air arm played a crucial part in the direction and execution of the nation's war production program. But it must be evident to the reader of this record, as well as to all who lived and served on the home front in World War II, that the war production achievements of the United States reflected a truly national effort, representing the combined contributions of all its citizens. Without the unremitting efforts and wholehearted co-operation of the nation's industrial workers and management no amount of planning or direction could have produced the munitions and supplies which made allied victory possible. Nor could the Army have successfully conducted and administered the program for which it was responsible without the central direction of the nation's war production effort by the President and the civilian agencies appointed to discharge this task. Finally, none of these achievements would have been possible unless the program had been sponsored and underwritten by the Congress of the United States, which provided the authority, the funds, and the ultimate responsibility for the execution of the war effort.

In appraising the Army's record in the field of economic mobilization—and a fortiori that of the nation as a whole—it is necessary to keep in view the economic consequences of the war as well as the success of wartime policies in achieving victory. The condition of the national economy in the postwar era was a direct outgrowth of the policies and activities pursued by the procuring agencies and the government as a whole throughout the war period. It is not too much to say that the over-all merits of the program of economic mobilization for

World War II cannot be fruitfully discussed without reference to its impact upon the postwar period.

The United States was plunged into World War II by the crippling attack, without warning, of a powerful aggressor. The war aims of the United States were the defeat of its enemies and the suppression of international aggression. Yet the unanticipated by-products of the war were of scarcely less significance than the realization of the nation's war aims. Instead of experiencing postwar depression and the widely predicted unemployment of eight million men, this country after World War II found its economy stronger than ever. As a result of the war the nation brought an end to more than a decade of depression, raised both its real and its money income to unprecedented heights, and embarked on an era of capital expansion which dwarfed all previous records. While playing a major role in combat operations throughout the world, the United States ushered in a new industrial, technological, and scientific revolution, and at the same time gave a majority of its citizens a better standard of living than they had before the war.

The war program tore down the barriers to occupational and geographical mobility of labor, put millions of people back to work, rehabilitated their atrophied and forgotten skills, and trained old and new workers in new skills, new processes, new techniques, and new administrative methods. While achieving peak utilization of its manpower for the first time in many years, the nation found it unnecessary to sacrifice any significant gain of its recent social legislation, much less to "regiment" its civilian workers. The great contribution of American labor in World War II was made possible by a permanent addition to the total labor supply—in its qualitative as well as its quantitative dimension—resulting directly from the war program.

Also for the first time in more than a decade the nation made full use of the technical know-how, organizing ability, and driving energy of its business executives and leaders. The role of the businessman, half-forgotten and discredited during ten years of economic stagnation, was abundantly restored as the basic problem faced by American industry ceased to be that of finding "something to do" and became a proliferation of interesting problems under the heading "how to do it." The tasks of converting and expanding facilities, of recruiting, training, and utilizing manpower, of discovering and developing new materials, new sources of supply, new processes of production, and even the new end products of war production itself, provided businessmen with the greatest challenge and opportunity of their generation. The response to this challenge was the application of rational and scientific methods to the solution of industrial problems on a scale never before attained. Intensified research and development, job analysis, engineering planning, quality control, cost accounting and analysis, and improved techiques of personnel and industrial relations became the heritage as well as the instruments of World War II. The new knowledge and experience acquired during the war by business executives and managers at all echelons of industry constituted an important and permanent addition to the nation's economic resources for peacetime production.

The role of science and technology in World War II is well known, yet the all-pervasive and permanent effects of the war upon them, and in turn upon mankind as a whole are but dimly understood. Like the temporarily eclipsed businessman, scientists and engineers during the 1930's found their services of doubtful market value. The war brought insatiable demands for the fruits of both pure and applied science as military procurement programs were designed to exploit the maximum possibilities of technological warfare. Physicists, chemists, and mathematicians were soon in short supply, just as were engineers and technicians in all fields and at all levels of practical and theoretical training. The result of this forced draft of science and technology was a scientific revolution—a revolution which embraced the biological as well as the physical sciences. Although the most spectacular results were achieved in the physical sciences, the development and large-scale production of penicillin, the sulfa drugs, blood plasma, and countless other medical items, as well as major advances in surgery and postoperative therapy, were among the many contributions of the war.

Paradoxically, the desirable social and economic consequences of the war resulted to a large extent from the extravagant scale on which the war was waged. Combined war production requirements, centering in the programs of the armed forces, were quantitatively so great and qualitatively so all-embracing that they not only harnessed but taxed to the limit the economic potential of the entire nation. The same material shortages which were the country's despair in the dark days of 1942 became avenues to material abundance as they led to drastic measures which introduced a new era of plentiful aluminum, magnesium, plastics, and special alloys, as well as augmented supplies of oil, steel, rubber, and other war-developed and expanded resources. Likewise, in the face of the diversion of 12 million men into the armed forces, the pressure upon the nation's ultimate productive resource—its manpower—forced a constant outpouring of invention and improvements in manufacturing organizations, processes, procedures, machinery, equipment, and other facilities—all resulting in long-run increases in national productivity. In thus bringing to full fruition the nation's productive power, the huge requirements of war created the great aggregations of equipment, skills, and scientific and technical knowledge which constituted America's postwar economic inheritance.

The boldness of the production objectives for World War II was matched by the boldness of the administrative and fiscal methods used in their achievement. The task of rapidly shifting the nation's productive resources from peacetime pursuits to the difficult and unfamiliar tasks of war required imagination of the highest order and a willingness to use vigorous and unorthodox measures. The government in World War II imposed a greater number and variety of restrictions upon conventional freedoms than ever before; but it also shook off a multiplicity of peacetime restrictions upon freedom of action—not only with respect to its own operations but for those of private industry as well. It gave its procurement agencies unlimited spending powers and virtually complete freedom of action in the placing, administration, and settlement of contracts. On the other hand, it freed private enterprise from the operation of the antitrust laws, permitted industry to charge off the full costs of new investment in five years or less, and supplied it with the material and financial means of fulfilling its contractual obligations.

In short, the government entered into an intimate partnership with industry and labor—a partnership in which private enterprise for the first time in many years was given the opportunity to realize its full potential. In this partnership, industry found a new kind of freedom—the freedom to operate at full capacity in the knowledge that all costs would be recovered and a fair profit obtained. Despite the regime of wartime controls, the central characteristic of free enterprise—freedom of basic operations under the stimulus of the profit motive—was maintained. Although the government as the major customer of industry specified the objectives of most industrial operations, private industry made and carried out the vast bulk of the decisions on the production front which won the war. At the same time American labor found in this partnership the opportunity for full employment, generous earnings, development of its skills, and a great expansion in the size and strength of the permanent organizations representing its long-range interests.

As a result of its spectacular performance in World War II, together with the industrial and financial revolution which made this performance possible, America's system of private enterprise was revitalized and made stronger than it had been for many years. American industry had again demonstrated that it could turn out a greater abundance and variety of goods and services with more efficiency and speed than had yet been done by any other economic system. A major factor in this achievement—the *sine qua non* of a successfully functioning free enterprise economy—was adequate monetary demand for the products of industry. This monetary demand was furnished by the tremendous expenditures of the armed forces—expenditures in large part made possible by the great increase in the nation's money supply resulting from the bold program of deficit financing authorized by Congress and administered by the Treasury Department and the Federal Reserve System. The expanded supply of money persisted beyond the end of the war and made possible in the postwar era a level of monetary demand adequate to permit full employment and capacity operations for the nation's greatly expanded economy. These results were, to be sure, reinforced by a resumption of military expenditures during the period of Korea and the "Cold War." The general benefits resulting from full employment and high productivity in the decade after the war greatly outweighed the disadvantages and inequities of the degree of inflation experienced during the same period.

The mistakes, shortcomings, and failures in the planning and execution of the nation's war production program—on the part of the Army as of all other agencies—were many and varied. Victory in World War II, on the home front as in the fields of battle, did not come easily or without its portion of error, waste, and tragedy. Nor were the permanent effects of the war on the nation's economy all desirable. But the broad pattern of the war production effort, in its methods as well as its results, was unquestionably one of success. To many observers in mid-passage the wartime program appeared to be constantly taking the wrong course. Yet, like the progress of a skillfully directed sailing vessel which in crossing the ocean must constantly tack before changing winds, the course of the war program when seen in large perspective was surprisingly direct.

No single account can adequately describe, or even list, all the factors which led to the success of the nation's program of economic mobilization in World War II. One indispensable element, among all others, should be re-emphasized. This was the unparalleled degree of national unity and will to victory brought about by the Japanese attack on Pearl Harbor. Without such unity of purpose at the time when it was most desperately needed, it would have been impossible to administer a program whose success depended on the co-operation and support of the whole people. Unity of this kind in a large nation composed of widely different groups and interests is not often or easily attained. Ironically, it was presented to the United States, as a free gift, by this nation's enemies on the morning of Sunday, 7 December 1941.

The knowledge gained from the experience of World War II has permanent significance and validity. But every war in the history of mankind has involved its own unique set of political, military, economic, technological, and other conditions and objectives. The lessons learned from the study of one particular war will poorly serve the planners and administrators appointed to prepare for future crises if these lessons consist merely of actual solutions to particular problems existing in the past; in World War II the United States was favored by a combination of circumstances which may never recur.

For perhaps the last time in its history the nation's ocean barriers furnished a generous measure of protection from serious damage or invasion by a hostile power. Also, in a war in which the survival of free democratic institutions was at stake, this nation's efforts were preceded by those of other nations engaged in a common cause. The heroic resistance of these allies provided this country with an indispensable period of eighteen months of borrowed time—a period considered by industrial mobilization planners

between the wars to be the minimum essential to adequate rearmament. Finally, in undertaking its vast rearmament program in mid-1940, the United States started from a condition of widespread unemployment of men, machines, and productive resources in general. Great as were the shocks and dislocations accompanying the transition from peace to a war economy—a transition not fully completed until long after Pearl Harbor—they were relatively small by comparison with those which would necessarily arise in the absence of huge surpluses of idle resources.

For these and other reasons, World War II may well turn out to be the last war of the "classical" type envisaged by the industrial mobilization planners of the interwar period. In preparation for such a war a relatively unarmed, nonaggressor nation placed its principal reliance on the ponderous mechanism of industrial mobilization during a period of presumed safety from attack. Wars of this type are obsolete in an era of international hostility and nuclear technology in which a hostile power could create, without warning, an atomic holocaust in the nation's midst. In such an era, when weakness is an open invitation to aggression and all-out war is the short, certain pathway to international destruction and chaos, many of the successful prescriptions and advantageous consequences associated with World War II have lost their relevance. Industrial mobilization planning can no longer be regarded as an adequate substitute for military power in being. Nor in the atomic age can victory in war be considered an acceptable alternative to the prevention of war.

Bibliographical Note and Guide to Footnotes

The Army and Economic Mobilization was written on the basis of a wide variety of source materials located chiefly in various offices and agencies of the Department of Defense in and around Washington, D. C. The principal sources of information were governmental records, especially those of the War Department—the senior predecessor of the Department of Defense. Nongovernmental records—books, periodicals, and other publications—also supplied valuable insights and information.

The records of the United States Government in the mid-20th century have become so voluminous and heterogeneous in character that the methods and tasks of the historian working in this area have undergone a substantial revolution. The graduate historiographer at the beginning of the century was a kind of Sherlock Holmes—a trained sleuth skilled in the art of extracting a maximum of reliable information from a paucity of sources. Today, in the complex field of governmental operations and policy, the age of scarcity is past, and the historian is faced with a bewildering superabundance of documentary materials which must somehow be surveyed, abstracted, studied, comprehended, evaluated, and appropriately synthesized into a readable summary—all within a period considerably shorter than a single lifetime.

In this milieu the historian of government policy and administration is interested first and foremost in documents containing the highest yield of significance per page. Such documents are typically the general reports and summaries, the major directives and manuals, the books of regulations, codes, and statutes which reveal the basic tasks, methods, and accomplishments of those responsible for forming and executing governmental policy. Documents of this type, devised during the course of actual operations in order to appraise, influence, and control the general trend of events in the relevant areas, are primary sources *par excellence*. As indicated in footnote citations herein, the present volume relies heavily upon such sources.

A second important class of primary documents consists of those which collectively reveal in detail the multitudinous pressures, problems, and other reasons for the formulation and development of specific policies. These documents are the countless individual memoranda, letters, telegrams, notes, clippings, abstracts, forms, diaries, logs, studies, exhibits, tabulations, ad hoc reports, and other materials found in the operating files of the numerous offices and agencies involved during the time period in question. These primary sources are of a lower order of generality than those described in the preceding paragraph, but they are indispensable to a genuine understanding of the origins, nature, and consequences of the general policies and procedures under review. Inevitably, only a minute fraction of these materials can be perused by a single investigator.

Under these circumstances it is fortunate for students of America's World War II experience that an official governmental historical program was firmly established by the President at the beginning of the late war. This program forced the preparation of historical reports and summaries by every significant unit in each of the several war agencies of the Federal government. These reports and summaries are still to be found in the remaining records of many governmental units. In addition to other uses they served as the basis for the more general historical monographs of the wartime agencies and their principal divisions, written at the end of the war or shortly thereafter.

As a result of the interim historical program, later historians have inherited a wealth of secondary sources of information prepared by those who were typically participants in or close observers of the events about which they were writing. These secondary sources quickly convey to the student the basic events, problems, and atmosphere of the war period. Of perhaps even greater significance, the interim monographs are frequently accompanied by elaborate documentary appendixes containing copies of the specific memoranda, directives, reports, and other primary documents actually used to direct and control the war effort. These documentary collections, in the eyes of interested historians, are among the most valuable fruits of the entire program.

The principal monographs used in support of the present volume, together with their important documentary appendixes, may now be found in the General Reference Branch, Office of the Chief of Military History, Department of the Army, Washington, D. C. These include the histories of the major Army Service Forces divisions—Requirements, Purchases, Renegotiation, Readjustment, and Control—as well as the Quartermaster Historical Series, the History of Ordnance Pricing Policy, and other monographic studies. The General Reference Branch, OCMH, also has in its collection of materials many of the principal wartime manuals, regulations, studies, reports, and

other major primary sources initially described above.

Most of the detailed records examined in support of the present study were found in the Army's Departmental Records Branch (DRB), Adjutant General's Office (now known as the Military Records Branch, Region 3, General Services Administration), Alexandria, Virginia. As the principal repository of Army and War Department files, DRB contains both types of primary source materials described above, as well as many of the lower-echelon historical reports and summaries prepared during and shortly after World War II. The holdings of DRB are described in detail in *Federal Records of World War II*, Vol. II, Military Agencies, prepared by the General Services Administration, Archives and Records Service, The National Archives (Washington, 1951), and are further amplified in the bibliographical appendix (pp. 743–50) of *Global Logistics and Strategy*, a companion to the present volume in the War Department subseries of THE UNITED STATES ARMY IN WORLD WAR II. The two principal collections within DRB used in support of the present volume are those of the Army Service Forces and the Office of the Under Secretary of War. Each of these collections is in general subdivided into the holdings of the component offices and divisions as they existed at the end of the war.

The third major source of information for the present volume was the unique collection of materials on economic mobilization available in the library of the Industrial College of the Armed Forces. Most useful were the materials for the prewar period—especially the bound copies of the contemporary lectures presented to successive classes of students. The college library also contains many other primary source materials, as well as a comprehensive collection of published and unpublished secondary sources.

Two other repositories of information and source materials should also be mentioned: the National Archives, which frequently served as a dependable source of last resort for prewar Army materials as well as wartime materials from non-Army sources; and the Army Library in the Pentagon whose general and legislative reference services were a convenient source of information to the author on numerous occasions.

Copies of most individual documents cited in footnotes have been assembled in the author's collection in the files of OCMH maintained for possible future reference. When such copies could not be obtained, reference has been made to the location of the source by file number. In many cases, copies of individual documents are available as numbered exhibits of the historical monographs referred to above and are specifically cited in footnotes.

List of Abbreviations

AAF	Army Air Forces
ACMO	Army Controlled Materials Officer
ACofAS	Assistant Chief of Air Staff
ACofEngrs	Assistant Chief of Engineers
ACofS	Assistant Chief of Staff
ACofTrans	Assistant Chief of Transportation
Actg	Acting
Adm	Admiral
Admin	Administrative
AEC	Army Extension Course
AFL	American Federation of Labor
AG	Adjutant General
AGF	Army Ground Forces
AGO	Adjutant General's Office
AIC	Army Industrial College
ANMB	Army and Navy Munitions Board
AP	Armor Piercing
App.	Appendix
AR	Army Regulation
ASF	Army Service Forces
ASN	Assistant Secretary of the Navy
ASP	Army Supply Program
ASTP	Army Specialized Training Program
ASW	Assistant Secretary of War
Attn	Attention
AUS	Army of the United States
Bd	Board
BIM	Basic Industrial Materials
Bk.	Book
BLS	Bureau of Labor Statistics
Br	Branch
Bull	Bulletin
CCS	Combined Chiefs of Staff
CE	Corps of Engineers
CG	Commanding General
Ch.	Chapter
Chf	Chief
Chmn	Chairman
CINC	Commander in Chief

CIO	Congress of Industrial Organizations
Cir	Circular
Civ	Civilian
CMP	Controlled Materials Plan
CNO	Chief of Naval Operations
CO	Commanding Officer
CofAAF	Chief of Army Air Forces
CofAC	Chief of Air Corps
CofCWS	Chief of Chemical Warfare Service
CofEngrs	Chief of Engineers
CofOrd	Chief of Ordnance
CofS	Chief of Staff
CofTrans	Chief of Transportation
Com	Committee
Comdr	Commander
Comdt	Commandant
Comm	Commission
Conf	Conference
Cong	Congress
CPA	Civilian Production Administration
CPFF	Cost-Plus-a-Fixed-Fee
CPPC	Cost-Plus-a-Percentage-of-Cost
CQMD	Chicago Quartermaster Depot
DCofS	Deputy Chief of Staff
Dept	Department
Dir	Director; Directive
Div	Division
Doc	Document
DPC	Defense Plant Corporation
DSRP	Defense Supplies Rating Plan
d. w.	Deadweight
Ed	Edition; editor
EPF	Emergency Plant Facilities
ETO	European Theater of Operations
Ex	Executive
Ex Asst	Executive Assistant
ExO	Executive Officer
FAR	Field Accounting Representative
FDAP	Field Director of Ammunition Plants
Fig	Figure
FM	Field Manual
FY	Fiscal Year
G–1	Personnel
G–2	Intelligence

G–3	Organization and Training Division
G–4	Supply
GAO	General Accounting Office
Gen	General
GFE	Government Furnished Equipment
GFM	Government Furnished Materials
GMPR	General Maximum Price Regulation
GO	General Order
GOCO	Government-Owned Contractor-Operated
GP	Government Protection
GP	Group
GPO	Government Printing Office
GSA	General Services Administration
GSC	General Staff Corps
Hon.	Honorable
H	House of Representatives
Hq	Headquarters
H. R.	House of Representatives
ICAF	Industrial College of the Armed Forces
IG	Inspector General
IMP	Industrial Mobilization Plan
Incl	Inclosure
Ind	Indorsement
IPD	Industrial Personnel Division
IPF	Initial Protective Force
JAG	Judge Advocate General
JAGD	Judge Advocate General's Department
JB	Joint Board
JCS	Joint Chiefs of Staff
JCTB	Joint Contract Termination Board
JANS	Joint Army-Navy Specifications
J. Res.	Joint Resolution
Jt	Joint
JTR	Joint Termination Regulation
Ltr	Letter
M Day	Mobilization Day
Memo	Memorandum
M&E Plancors	Machinery and Equipment Plancors
Mil	Military
Min	Minutes
MPR	Maximum Price Regulation; Monthly Progress Report
MRO	Maintenance, Repair, and Operating Supplies
MS	Manuscript

Mtg	Meeting
NA	National Archives
NATO	North African Theater of Operations
n. d.	No date
NDAC	Advisory Commission to the Council of National Defense
NPAB	Navy Price Adjustment Board
NR	Nonreimbursement
OACofAS	Office of the Assistant Chief of Air Staff
OASA	Office of the Assistant Secretary of Army
OASW	Office of the Assistant Secretary of War
OCMH	Office Chief of Military History
OCofEngrs	Office Chief of Engineers
OCofOrd	Office of the Chief of Ordnance
OCS	Office of Contract Settlement
OCSigO	Office of the Chief Signal Officer
OEM	Office for Emergency Management
OHF	Ordnance Historical File
OO	Ordnance Office
Op	Opinion
OPA	Office of Price Administration
OPACS	Office of Price Administration and Civilian Supply
OPM	Office of Production Management
Opns	Operations
OQMG	Office of the Quartermaster Corps
Ord	Ordnance
OUSW	Office of the Under Secretary of War
OWM	Office of War Mobilization
OWMR	Office of War Mobilization and Reconversion
ORDGC	Office Chief of Ordnance, Comptroller's Office
ORDIX	Office Chief of Ordnance, Executive Office of the Industrial Division
PR	Press Release; Price Regulation; Procurement Regulation; Procedural Regulation
Par.	Paragraph
P & C	Purchases and Contracts
PD	Priorities Division
Plancors	DPC Contracts
PMP	Protective Mobilization Plan
PRP	Production Requirements Plan
Pt.	Part
PWA	Public Works Administration
QMC	Quartermaster Corps
Rcd	Record

RDX	Research Development Explosive Cyclonite
Reqmt	Requirement
RFC	Reconstruction Finance Corporation
Res	Resolution
Ret.	Retired
RP	Research Project
Rpt	Report
S	Senate
SAA	Small Arms Ammunition
SCS	Supply Control System
Sec	Section
Secy	Secretary
Ser	Serial
Serv	Service
Sess	Session
SGO	Surgeon General's Office
SN	Secretary of the Navy
SOS	Services of Supply
SPA	Surplus Property Administration
SPAB	Supply Priorities and Allocations Board
SPB	Surplus Property Board
Stat.	*Statute*
SW	Secretary of War
SWPA	Surplus War Property Administration
SWPB	Small War Plants Branch, Purchases Division, ASF
SWPD	Smaller War Plants Division (SWPD), WPB
T/A	Table of Allowances
TAG	The Adjutant General
TAM	Termination Accounting Manual
T/BA	Tables of Basic Allowances
TC	Transportation Corps
TCM	OCS Termination Cost Memorandums
TD	Treasury Decision
T/E	Table of Equipment
Telg	Telegram
TM	Technical Manual
Tng	Training
TNT	Trinitrotoluene
T/O	Table of Organization
T/O & E	Table of Organization and Equipment
TQMG	The Quartermaster General
USA	U.S. Army
USA (Ret.)	U.S. Army (Retired)
USN	U.S. Navy

USNR	U.S. Naval Reserves
USW	Under Secretary of War
Vol.	Volume
WAA	War Assets Administration
WAC	War Assets Corporation
WCPAB	War Contracts Price Adjustment Board
WD	War Department
WDPAB	War Department Price Adjustment Board
WDGS	War Department General Staff
WDPRB	War Department Procurement Review Board
WPA	Works Progress Administration
WPB	War Production Board
WRA	War Resources Administration
WRB	War Resources Board
ZI	Zone of Interior

UNITED STATES ARMY IN WORLD WAR II

The following volumes have been published or are in press:

The War Department
Chief of Staff: Prewar Plans and Preparations
Washington Command Post: The Operations Division
Strategic Planning for Coalition Warfare: 1941–1942
Strategic Planning for Coalition Warfare: 1943–1944
Global Logistics and Strategy: 1940–1943
Global Logistics and Strategy: 1943–1945
The Army and Economic Mobilization
The Army and Industrial Manpower

The Army Ground Forces
The Organization of Ground Combat Troops
The Procurement and Training of Ground Combat Troops

The Army Service Forces
The Organization and Role of the Army Service Forces

The Western Hemisphere
The Framework of Hemisphere Defense
Guarding the United States and Its Outposts

The War in the Pacific
The Fall of the Philippines
Guadalcanal: The First Offensive
Victory in Papua
CARTWHEEL: The Reduction of Rabaul
Seizure of the Gilberts and Marshalls
Campaign in the Marianas
The Approach to the Philippines
Leyte: The Return to the Philippines
Triumph in the Philippines
Okinawa: The Last Battle
Strategy and Command: The First Two Years

The Mediterranean Theater of Operations
Northwest Africa: Seizing the Initiative in the West
Sicily and the Surrender of Italy
Salerno to Cassino
Cassino to the Alps

The European Theater of Operations
Cross-Channel Attack
Breakout and Pursuit
The Lorraine Campaign
The Siegfried Line Campaign
The Ardennes: Battle of the Bulge
The Last Offensive

Index